United States of America
Each State's Electoral Votes for the Presidency

ME 4

VT 3

NY 33

NH 4

MA 12

MN 10

CT 8

RI 4

WI 11

MI 18

PA 23

NJ 15

IA 7

IL 22

IN 12

OH 21

DE 3

MD 10

WV 5

VA 13

DC 3

MO 11

KY 8

NC 14

TN 11

SC 8

AR 6

MS 7

AL 9

GA 13

LA 9

FL 25

the new american democracy

Morris P. Fiorina

Paul E. Peterson

Harvard University

Allyn and Bacon
Boston
London
Toronto
Sydney
Tokyo
Singapore

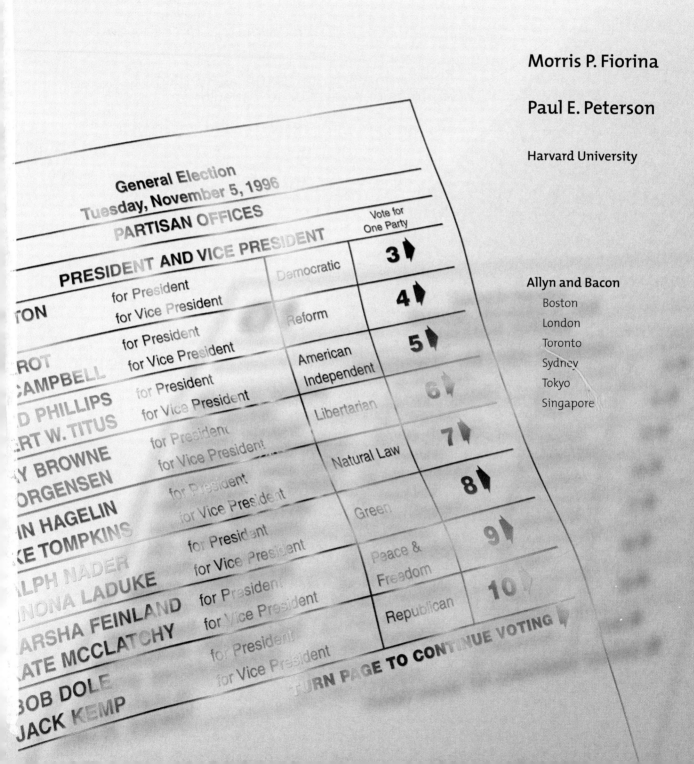

dedication

TO GEORGE COLE, JOHN KESSEL, WAYNE MERRICK,
AND OTHER MEMBERS OF THE ALLEGHENY COLLEGE
POLITICAL SCIENCE DEPARTMENT, CIRCA 1966

AS WELL AS TO HARDING C. NOBLITT, CONCORDIA COLLEGE

ALL OF WHOM INTRODUCED THE AUTHORS TO THE
WONDERS OF AMERICAN GOVERNMENT

IN APPRECIATION FOR THEIR TEACHING EXCELLENCE

Vice President, Editor in Chief:
Paul A. Smith

Senior Development Editor:
Sue Gleason

Development Editor:
Jan Fitter

Editorial Assistant:
Kathy Rubino

Vice President, Director of Marketing:
Jeff Lasser

Production Coordinator:
Marjorie Payne, Marbern House

Editorial Production Service:
Thomas Dorsaneo

Text Design, Illustration, & Page Layout:
Seventeenth Street Studios

Photo Research:
Sarah Evertson, Image Quest

Permissions Research:
The Permissions Group

Manufacturing Buyer:
Megan Cochran

Copyright © 1998 by Allyn and Bacon
A Viacom Company
160 Gould Street
Needham Heights, MA 02194

Internet: www.abacon.com
America Online: keyword: College Online

Library of Congress Cataloging-in-Publication Data

Fiorina, Morris P.
      The new American democracy / by Morris P.
Fiorina and Paul E. Peterson.
          p.   cm.
      Includes bibliographical references and index.
      ISBN 0-02-337770-4
      1. Democracy—United States. 2. United States—Politics and government.
   I. Peterson Paul E. II. Title.
JK1726.F56 1998   97-34742
320.473—dc21   CIP

Printed in the United States of America

10 9 8 7 6 5 4 3 2 1   02 01 00 99 98 97

Photo Credits:
Photo credits are found on page 792, which should be considered extensions of the
copyright page.

about the authors

MORRIS P. FIORINA

Morris P. Fiorina is Frank Thompson Professor of Government at Harvard University. After receiving an undergraduate degree from Allegheny College in Meadville, Pennsylvania, he earned a doctorate from the University of Rochester in 1972. He then taught for a decade at the California Institute of Technology before moving to Harvard in 1982. He has been a visiting professor at the Graduate School of Business at Stanford.

Fiorina has written widely on American government and politics, with special emphasis on representation and elections. He has published numerous articles, and five books: *Representatives, Roll Calls, and Constituencies*; *Congress—Keystone of the Washington Establishment*; *Retrospective Voting in American National Elections*; *The Personal Vote: Constituency Service and Electoral Independence* (coauthored with Bruce Cain and John Ferejohn); and *Divided Government*. He has served on the editorial boards of a dozen journals in the fields of political science, economics, law, and public policy, and from 1986 to 1990 he served as chairman of the Board of Overseers of the American National Election Studies.

In his leisure time, Fiorina favors physical activities, including hiking, fishing, and sports. Although his own athletic career never amounted to much, he has been a successful youth baseball coach for fifteen years. Among his most cherished honors is a plaque given by happy parents on the occasion of an undefeated Babe Ruth season.

PAUL E. PETERSON

Paul E. Peterson is the Henry Lee Shattuck Professor of Government and Director of the Center for American Political Studies at Harvard University. He received his B.A. from Concordia College in Moorhead, Minnesota, and his Ph.D. from the University of Chicago.

Peterson is the author of numerous books and articles on federalism, urban politics, race relations, and public policy, including studies of education, welfare, and fiscal and foreign policy. He received the Woodrow Wilson Award from the American Political Science Association for his book *City Limits* (Chicago, 1981). In 1996 his book *The Price of Federalism* (Brookings, 1995) was given the Aaron Wildavsky Award for the best book on public policy. He is a member of the American Academy of Arts and Sciences.

It is not only when writing a textbook that Peterson makes every effort to be as accurate as possible. On the tennis courts, he always makes correct line calls and has seldom been heard to hit a wrong note when tickling the ivories.

brief contents

detailed contents

The Foundations of the New American Democracy

chapter 1

chapter 2

The Ingredients of
the New American Democracy

Government in the New American Democracy

IV Elections and Public Policy

contents of boxes

at the state & local level contents

At the State & Local Level Boxes

preface for students

THIS TEXT GROWS out of a decade of teaching the introductory course at our university. As we listened to each other's lectures each year, we noticed that our course was evolving into one whose underlying theme was both more specific than and different from the themes that could be found in contemporary American government textbooks: elections and their repercussions became the primary connecting thread that tied together our lectures and discussions. In part, this emphasis reflected our own backgrounds and interests. Fiorina has devoted his professional career to the study of elections—both narrowly, in the sense of why people vote the way they do, and more broadly, in the sense of how elections affect politicians, political institutions, and the policies they produce. Peterson began his career with a focus on citizen participation in the War on Poverty and later studied the way the federal system constrained the options of local elected officials. In recent years, he has examined the ways elections shape the policy response to budget deficits, welfare needs, race relations, educational issues, and the changing foreign policy environment. But it was not just our own research interests that brought election issues to the fore. Both of us attempt to keep our lectures connected to present-day government and politics, and as a reflection of a changing reality, we found our lectures increasingly infused with the connections between elections and the work of government.

We have learned from our own students that you are keenly aware of the way elections affect the decisions and strategies of political leaders, as well as a great many other things that happen in government. As a result, we have written a new kind of American government textbook, one that gives a central place to elections and their consequences.

LEVEL AND TONE OF THIS TEXTBOOK

It is common today to criticize the preparation and motivation of American undergraduate students: the belief that students are less well prepared for college work and less motivated to undertake it than in the "good old days" is widespread. This viewpoint has led some instructors to oversimplify their courses and the readings they assign. This, in turn, has led some publishers to urge textbook writers to oversimplify their books to make them more suitable for this contemporary world.

Our view is that you may be different from students of a generation ago, but that does not necessarily mean that you are any less capable. Some think students are less proficient in skills such as writing. Perhaps so, but you also have skills that were nonexistent years ago (we bet that more of you surf the Internet today than do your professors!). As for motivation, that is something not purely your responsibility. It is our responsibility as teachers to make the material as stimulating to your interests and as relevant to your lives as possible. Our premise in this book is that undergraduate students are fully capable of understanding arguments that are logically developed and clearly expressed. For this reason, this book emphasizes meaning and significance by placing essential factual material in a larger thematic context—that of elections.

Some remarks on the tone of the book are also in order. Some individuals in American higher education would protect students from intellectual discomfort. The consequences of such beliefs include well-intentioned efforts to place some subjects and arguments outside the boundaries of class discussion. We do not agree with this approach. Our view is that politics is fundamentally about conflict. People have conflicting interests and, even more seriously, conflicting values. Politics is the nonviolent resolution of such conflicts. People can settle their disagreements and rise above their dislikes through political deliberation, or they can pick up weapons, as so many have over the course of human history.

We believe that you need to learn to engage in such political deliberation. Within the bounds of civil discourse, you should be challenged, even at times provoked. Education proceeds by having to defend one's viewpoints and by learning to understand and challenge those of others. Thus, in the chapters that follow, we consider arguments that some of you may find uncomfortable. And on occasion we will offer a conclusion that is at odds with conventional thinking. In the realm of education, a better, clearer understanding supersedes all other values.

SPECIFIC FEATURES

This book has several specific features, many related to our elections theme, to which we call your attention:

- Each chapter draws you into the subject matter with an **opening vignette** on a high-interest issue or incident. Examples include a comparison of differing media and public responses to Vietnam-War-era events (Chapter 9—The Media); President Clinton's stand on gays in the military (Chapter 13—The Presidency: Powers and Practice); and the Clarence Thomas hearings (Chapter 15—The Courts). A bridge paragraph follows each vignette, linking the vignette with a preview of the topics to be covered in the chapter.

- To illustrate the book's focus on electoral forces, each chapter includes a box entitled **Election Connection**, describing the relationship between elections and institutions or policies, often by describing how a particular election shaped a feature of American government. For instance, Chapter 4's describes California's Proposition 187; Chapter 9's details the media's role in the election of 1960; and Chapter 10's reports on the campaign finance scandals of 1996 and 1997.

- Each chapter also contains a special box that compares some feature of American government with a similar feature in other countries. This **International Comparison** will give you a better understanding of the strengths and limitations of American democracy by letting you think about real alternatives, not just unattainable ideals. Chapter 1's looks at the timing of elections in other democracies; Chapter 2's looks at the making of a constitution in Russia; Chapter 5's investigates polling in other countries; Chapter 10's explains why campaign financing isn't such a big issue in other countries; and Chapter 16's explores how the legal system in France might deal with the paparazzi implicated in Princess Diana's death.

- You are given an opportunity to exercise your own critical thinking by considering a **Democratic Dilemma** in each chapter. Will policy changes or institutional reforms actually achieve the goals their proponents claim? This special box presents arguments pro and con, challenging you to reflect on the issues. Chapter 10's looks at the lot of vice presidents; Chapter 12's presents a debate between the delegate and trustee viewpoints; and Chapter 16's quotes two students' viewpoints on free speech on campus.

- State and local politics and government are a huge—and growing—part of American public life, but many books on American government relegate discussions of state and local politics into a single, separate chapter. This text integrates discussions of state and local politics and government into the mainstream of the text. In many locations throughout the text—at headings as well as Election Connections, Democratic Dilemmas, and other boxes—you will find special **At the State and Local Level** annotations to highlight this coverage.

- Beyond these special features, each chapter is sprinkled with **general-interest boxes**, including an excerpt from the 1912 play that coined the phrase "melting pot" (Chapter 4); information about the "motor voter" law (Chapter 6); a profile of top Washington lobbyists (Chapter 7); a day in the life of a Tammany Hall politico (Chapter 8); an example of muckraker writing (Chapter 9); a discussion of the Telecommunications Act of 1996 (Chapter 12); a Machiavellian interpretation of Lincoln (Chapter 13); and an actual edit of a piece of legislation (Chapter 14).

- Because we are emphasizing what is new in American democracy, we provide the most up-to-date information and examples possible, including the following:

  Full description and analysis of the 1996 elections.

  Discussion of the campaign finance scandal unearthed in 1996 and 1997.

  Analysis of 1996 welfare reform efforts.

  Erosion of power of Speaker of the House of Representatives Newt Gingrich in 1996–1997.

  Analysis of the 1997 balanced-budget agreement.

  President Clinton's initial use of the item veto in August 1997.

  1997 Supreme Court decision giving more power to state governments.

  1997 Senate fight over Clinton's nomination of Massachusetts Governor William Weld as ambassador to Mexico.

  1997 Supreme Court decisions affecting the Whitewater scandal.

  1997 Supreme Court decision affecting separation of church and state.

  1997 trial and conviction of Oklahoma City bomber Timothy McVeigh.

  French paparazzi are implicated in Princess Diana's death.

- In addition, each chapter includes full **marginal definitions** for key terms that are boldfaced in the text and included in the end-of-book Glossary.

- At the end of each chapter are a **Chapter Summary**, **Key Terms** (alphabetized, with page references), and annotated **Suggested Readings**.

SUPPLEMENTS FOR STUDENTS

Supplementary materials are available from Allyn and Bacon to support your learning.

STUDY GUIDE TO THE NEW AMERICAN DEMOCRACY

A study guide, prepared by Larry Elowitz of Georgia College, is available that includes chapter synopses, learning objectives, study tips, research ideas, Internet sources, and fill-in, matching, multiple-choice, and short essay questions with answers.

PRACTICE TESTS

A set of free Practice Tests allows you to simulate the test-taking experience with 20 real multiple-choice test items per chapter.

TEN THINGS EVERY AMERICAN GOVERNMENT STUDENT SHOULD READ

Most instructors believe that there are many primary documents or seminal essays in the field of political science that their students should read. However, many published readers are either too costly or too comprehensive for the time available during the term for ancillary reading. In response to this need, Allyn and Bacon compiled a lengthy list of documents, essays, and book chapters frequently assigned in American government classes. They distributed this list as a "ballot" to teachers across the country and asked them to "vote" for the reading selections they would most like to have their students read along with their textbook. Based on a tally of the "votes," Allyn and Bacon is providing a free anthology of the "top ten" selections that instructors "elected" for use in class.

CD-ROM

A set of interactive learning modules is available for students to purchase in CD-ROM form. Combining text, graphics, still photographs, and video, the CD-ROM contains study modules on Congress, the presidency, and the judiciary, as well as an extensive archive collection of historical and current resources.

WEBSITE

The World Wide Web site for this textbook, at http://www.abacon.com/fiorina, offers a wealth of activities and links to other sites relevant to American government.

ALLYN AND BACON QUICK GUIDE TO THE INTERNET FOR POLITICAL SCIENCE

A special handbook to the Internet in general and to political science resources in particular.

to our colleagues

ALTHOUGH THE TEXT CHAPTERS that follow speak directly to students in ordinary and engaging language, in this preface we would like to set forth, in more professional terms, with supporting observations by several of our profession's most thoughtful scholars, the reasons we found it necessary to write this text.

A generation ago, Robert Dahl, one of the leading political scientists of the century, published a textbook entitled *Pluralist Democracy in the United States.*[1] Dahl was the acknowledged leader of the pluralist school of American political science, which viewed American politics as a collection of distinct arenas in which leaders of well-established interest groups bargained over the substance of public policies, with public officials involved both as brokers and as thoughtful representatives of broader societal interests. Political institutions were viewed as regularized bargaining arenas in which leaders were constrained by more-or-less clear rules. *Groups. bargaining, leaders,* and *representation* were the operative terms for understanding American politics.

American politics has changed a good deal since Dahl wrote. Indeed, Dahl himself recently noted a number of these changes:

> *Without intending to do so, over the past thirty years or so Americans have created a new political order. Although it retains a seamless continuity with the order it has displaced, in its present form it constitutes something so new that journalists, commentators, scholars, and ordinary citizens are still struggling to understand it.*[2]

Dahl argues that this new political order is more fragmented than the old one, and more plebiscitary. The proliferation of interest groups combined with the deterioration of party organizations has strengthened divisive forces and weakened unifying ones. Such political developments, along with social and technological changes, have left public officials more exposed to popular pressures than in the past. As a consequence, Dahl contends, representation and deliberation have suffered. He worries that these changes might create "a pseudo democratic facade on a process manipulated by political leaders to achieve their own agendas."[3] Gabriel Almond, another leading political scientist of Dahl's generation, weighs in with similar sentiments:

> *Television and radio have largely preempted the print media and the primary opinion leaders. . . . Domestic and international events are brought into the living room with powerful visual and emotional impact—a telepopulism that constrains and distorts public policy. The deliberative processes of politics are diluted and heated by this populism, and by "instant" public opinion polls based on telephone samples.*[4]

Although we do not agree with every particular of these indictments, we recognize that they serve to emphasize that something *has* happened to American government since the time when an earlier generation of scholars characterized it as a pluralist democracy. For good or ill, it has become something closer to a popular democracy. In the pages that follow we describe the forces that have brought about these changes as well as their impact on contemporary politics, institutions, and policies.

As we considered the range of introductory texts available for the American government course, we discovered that available books, however worthy, did not match our views. In the first place, many gave less emphasis than we would like to topics that are essential parts of contemporary American politics—elections, most obviously, but also closely related topics such as public opinion, political participation, and the media. Second, in many texts the role of prime mover is implicitly assigned to the courts, whereas we see judicial activity as itself a response to changing electoral contexts. Third, contemporary textbooks typically separate the study of elections from other major headings: constitutional fundamentals, bureaucratic politics, the courts, and the formation of public policies. As James Stimson comments :

> In our texts public opinion is a chapter or two. The various branches of government are usually a chapter each. And the connection between what the public wants and what the government does is on the page fold between them. Public opinion is conceptualized as a set of measures and processes that do not speak to government. Governing institutions are studied in a manner which doesn't deny public opinion influence, but doesn't permit its active study. When citizens of Washington, D.C., could not vote the analogy was complete; all opinion was outside the beltway, all government was inside.[5]

This book breaks down the artificial and unfortunate separation identified by Stimson. Rather than just discussing public opinion in one self-contained chapter, political participation in a second, and elections in a third, then moving on to a succession of institutional and policy chapters, we give public opinion and electioneering their due in individual chapters devoted to those topics. We also trace their effects on many other political and institutional processes, culminating in discussions of why American public policies have the shape they do. Thus, although this book contains chapters bearing the familiar titles, the chapters are linked by an extended discussion of the pervasiveness of electoral influences in the new American democracy.

To say that public opinion, political campaigns, and elections are of great import is to offer neither a celebrationist nor a critical interpretation of American politics. The shift to a more popular democracy is to be praised for its notable accomplishments. However it also gives rise to many concerns, such as the opening it allows for special interests that provide campaign workers and financing, as well as the limits it places on the opportunities for reflective consideration of the long-range consequences of policy choices. But such concerns do not necessarily force one to rush to a critical judgment either. The shift toward a more popular democracy did not happen overnight, nor is it altogether contrary to the country's constitutional origins. It takes a braver critic than either of us to contend that American government is unable to survive more direct encounters with the public.

Nor should our emphasis on elections to suggest a focus on anything so narrow as what happens on election day or on the campaigns that precede it. When we say that elections play an important role, we are thinking not only of their direct effects but also of the ways in which they affect the thinking of interest groups, parties, and public officials, both elected and appointed. It is not so much elections themselves as their anticipation that provides so much of the motive power in contemporary political life in the United States.

Our colleagues will be understandably skeptical of any attempt to squeeze the study of American government into any single thematic frame—even one defined as broadly as is our understanding and interpretation of electoral influence. The subject matter of American government is voluminous, and a balanced introductory course must touch on its many aspects. We certainly do not believe that elections explain all that needs to be known about all aspects of American government and politics. Our general approach is to examine the incentives that are at work in American politics. Many of these incentives are created by the Constitution, and it is of the utmost importance to understand how the Constitution still shapes contemporary politics. Also, if electoral incentives are often a major force, they are not the only one. Some leaders risk their reputations with the public for the good of the country. Some act out of ideological commitments, regardless of their electoral consequences. Some realize that foreign policies must take into account the interests of nations throughout the world. Where these and other nonelectoral factors are important, we recognize that fact and proceed accordingly. The result is a book that is more focused than most American government texts, but not one that forces the whole subject into a single theme.

We do not believe this book could have been written even as recently as a generation ago. For, although elections have always been central to American politics, we believe, like Dahl, that American politics has become significantly more plebiscitary in the late twentieth century. The contributing factors are widely recognized. Transformations in the process of nominating and electing candidates have produced an individualistic politics in which each candidate forms his or her own organization rather than relying on a common party organization. Transformations in communications technology—survey research, phone, fax and the Internet—have made it possible for politicians to learn the political impacts of their decisions almost instantaneously. Transformations in the media have generated a seemingly insatiable demand for news material—a demand often satisfied by stories about political conflict. In this context, interest groups have mushroomed, polls and primaries have proliferated, and the electoral calendar has fragmented, so that governors often are not elected at the same time as presidents, and mayors often are not elected at the same time as either. As various commentators have observed, the United States seems to be characterized by a more-or-less continuous campaign: somewhere, almost all of the time, public officials' electoral fates are on the line. Older concepts used to characterize pluralist politics—groups, bargaining, leaders, and representation—are still important, but a full and accurate account of American politics today must also include careful consideration of the roles played by the media, polls, and campaigns and elections.

APPROACH AND ORGANIZATION

This book cuts across the old categories that characterize existing American government texts: historical development, political "inputs," institutions, and policy "outputs." Although we discuss all these aspects of American politics, we approach them in a more integrated manner. Following are a few illustrations of our approach:

- Contemporary practices are compared and contrasted with those existing in earlier periods, making the historical material more relevant to today's readers.

- Chapters on so-called political inputs focus on the roles of individuals, groups, parties, and the media in electoral politics.

- Analyses of Congress, the presidency, the bureaucracy, and the judiciary do not just describe the main institutions of government; they also show how elections shape the behavior of officeholders within these institutions.

- Civil liberties and civil rights are treated not simply as the result of judicial decisions but also as the product of electoral forces. The placement of these chapters in the policy section of the book, instead of at the beginning as part of the historical foundations of American government, highlights the extent to which basic constitutional rights are themselves shaped by public opinion and electoral outcomes.

- Discussions of public policies do not just list policy problems or classify types of policies, but show how elections in particular and politics in general shape the way policies are addressed and adopted.

Finally, the book offers a critical but fair picture of American government and politics. Any objective observer must recognize that American government and politics have numerous shortcomings. We point out many of them and explain why they exist. But throughout the text we show that, judged against realistic standards, American politics and government are not nearly as blameworthy as the evening news and tabloid shows often suggest.

SUPPLEMENTS FOR INSTRUCTORS

Supplementary materials are available from Allyn and Bacon to enhance instructors' teaching.

INSTRUCTOR'S MANUAL

The Instructor's Manual, prepared by Danny M. Adkison of Oklahoma State University, is intended as the ideal resource for new instructors—especially teaching assistants who may be teaching American government for the first time. It includes chapter overviews, detailed lecture outlines, key terms, Ideas for Lecture or Discussion, which may be used as the basis for entire lectures, and lists of transparencies.

TEST BANK

The Test Bank, prepared by Sue Davis of Grand Valley State University, provides more than 2,500 multiple-choice, true/false, and essay questions. A Computerized Test Bank in IBM (DOS and Windows) and Macintosh formats is also available.

TRANSPARENCIES

A set of 50 crucial illustrations from the textbook is available, in full-color acetate format, to enhance lecture presentations.

VIDEO LIBRARY

Those who adopt the text can choose from a wide range of videos on every major course topic. Consult your Allyn and Bacon representative for details.

ACKNOWLEDGMENTS

We want to thank the many people who helped us with the preparation of this book. Our deepest gratitude goes to the many undergraduate students whose expectations forced us to refine our thinking about American government over the past ten years. We also thank numerous cohorts of teaching fellows for their perceptive questions, comments, and criticisms. We are also especially grateful to Bruce Nichols, who first argued the need with us for a new-century approach to the introductory text on American government. The Center for Advanced Study in the Behavioral and Social Sciences provided generous support for Paul E. Peterson's work on the text during his academic year there.

Harding Noblitt of Concordia College read the entire manuscript in search of errors of fact and interpretation, saving the authors much embarrassment. In addition, portions were read by Danny Adkison, Sue Davis, Richard Fenno, Gary Jacobson, Barry Rabe, and Chris Stamm, whose comments helped with fact checking. We especially appreciate John Ferejohn and the undergraduate students at Stanford University who took his course in the fall of 1996 for testing an early draft of the entire manuscript, and Jay Greene and his students at the University of Texas at Austin who used page proofs in the fall of 1997. Larry Carlton supplied important factual material. Research assistance was provided by Ted Brader, Jay Girotto, Donald Lee, Jerome Maddox, Kenneth Sheve, Sean Theriault, and Robert Van Houeling—as well as William Howell who, in addition to making many other contributions, helped write the regulatory policy section in Chapter 18. Rebecca Contreras, Alison Kommer, and Sarah Peterson provided staff assistance.

In the course of writing this book, we benefited from the advice of many instructors across the country. We deeply thank all the following, but we are especially grateful for the expert advice of Stephen Ansolabehere, Richard Fenno, John Ferejohn, Bonnie Honig, William Mayer, and Diana Owen.

Joseph A. Aistrup
Fort Hays State University

Peri E. Arnold
University of Notre Dame

Bruce Berg
Fordham University

Stephen A. Borrelli
University of Alabama

Jeffrey Cohen
University of Kansas

W. Douglas Costain
University of Colorado, Boulder

Claude Dufour
University of Illinois, Chicago

Evelyn C. Fink
University of Nebraska

Richard Fox
Albuquerque TV-I Community College

James Gimpel
University of Maryland

Kenneth L. Grasso
Southwest Texas State University

Roger W. Green
University of North Dakota

Edmund Herod
Houston Community College

Christopher Howard
College of William & Mary

Jon Hurwitz
University of Pittsburgh

Joseph Ignagni
University of Texas, Arlington

Michael Johnston
Colgate University

William R. Keech
University of North Carolina

Kenneth D. Kennedy
  College of San Mateo

Fred A. Kramer
  University of Massa-
  chusetts, Amherst

Silvo Lenart
  Purdue University

Brad Lockerbie
  University of Georgia

Laurel Mayer
  Sinclair Community
  College

David Mayhew
  Yale University

Leonard Meizlish
  Mott Community
  College

Richard Murray
  University of Houston

Charles Noble
  California State
  University, Long
  Beach

Colleen O'Connor
  San Diego Mesa
  College

Rex C. Peebles
  Austin Community
  College

Richard Pious
  Barnard College

David Robinson
  University of Houston
  —Downtown

Francis E. Rourke
  Johns Hopkins
  University

Daniel M. Shea
  University of Akron

James R. Simmons
  University of
  Wisconsin, Oshkosh

Dennis Simon
  Southern Methodist
  University

Paul Sracic
  Youngstown State
  University

Eric Uslander
  University of
  Maryland

Shirley Anne Warshaw
  Gettysburg College

William Weissert
  University of Michi-
  gan

Christine Williams
  Bentley College

Martin Wiseman
  Mississippi State
  University

Thomas Yantek
  Kent State University

We are indebted to editors Robert Miller, Steve Hull, Joe Terry, and Paul Smith for their unfailing enthusiasm for the project throughout its lengthy development. We are grateful to Jan Fitter for keen editorial assistance, and we owe a tremendous debt to Sue Gleason, a publishing house version of a general contractor, whom we privately refer to as "the boss."

We also want to express our appreciation for the many other essential Allyn and Bacon contributions, including those of Sandi Kirshner, Tom Dorsaneo, Marjorie Payne, Judy Fiske, Jeff Lasser, Lou Kennedy, Sarah Evertson, and Leila Scott. Last, but certainly not least, we wish to thank the sales representatives who have brought this text to political scientists across the country. Despite all this assistance, however, errors undoubtedly remain, for which we must accept the blame. We invite you, the reader, to share with us by letter or by email (CAPS@Eudora.Harvard.edu) any that you identify.

M.P.F.
P.E.P.

the new american democracy

BILL CLINTON   for Vice President
AL GORE   for President
ROSS PEROT   for Vice President
JAMES CAMPBELL   for President
HOWARD PHILLIPS   for Vice President
HERBERT W. TITUS   for President
HARRY BROWNE   for Vice President
JO JORGENSEN   for President
JOHN HAGELIN   for Vice President
MIKE TOMPKINS   for President
RALPH NADER   for Vice President
WINONA LADUKE   for President
MARSHA FEINLAND   for Vice President
KATE McCLATCHY   for President
BOB DOLE   for Vice President
JACK KEMP

the new american democracy

N THE NIGHT OF November 3, 1992, at 10:30 P.M. eastern time, the networks declared that Bill Clinton had picked the Republican "lock" on the presidency. Before Clinton, Republicans had won five of six races for the nation's highest office, three of them by landslides. How did

Clinton succeed where his predecessors had failed? Clinton was a "new" Democrat—a group that in the mid-1980s began to argue that the party's traditional positions no longer were electorally viable. Polls indicated that many people resented taxes and had grown skeptical of government programs; moreover, the party seemed to have lost touch with "middle America." The new Democrats set out to reposition the party closer to the mainstream of American politics.

Seizing the opening created by a slow economy, Clinton addressed the hopes and fears of working Americans. But of his main campaign issues, the only one designed to appeal to old Democrats was his promise to provide universal health care coverage. New Democrat Clinton promised a tax cut, a pledge usually made by Republicans. He kept his distance from the civil rights leader Jesse Jackson, and he criticized black singer Sister Souljah for expressing racial hostility in the lyrics of her songs. Clinton appealed to middle-American values by praying in public, attending church on Sundays, using biblical phrases in his public appeals, emphasizing the importance of individual responsibility, and vowing to "end welfare as we know it," a phrase that would have sounded natural coming from the mouth of Republican President Ronald Reagan.

Americans have never been enthusiastic about welfare: Although they recognize the need to help the unfortunate, giving money to able-bodied people clashes with the traditional values of hard work and individual responsibility.[1] Criticism of the welfare system grew during the 1970s and 1980s, as the percentage of babies born to unmarried women soared, as two-worker families asked why they should support nonworking mothers, and as conservative intellectuals charged that welfare had created a "culture of poverty."[2] In truth, welfare expenditures are relatively small, and accounts of welfare abuses often were exaggerated. Moreover, public opinion was somewhat biased by media distortions of the degree to which able-bodied people and racial minorities receive welfare.[3] But critics of the welfare system were gaining the upper hand in the debate, and by the early 1990s Americans were receptive to calls for radical reform.

During the campaign, Clinton promised to get people off the welfare rolls and into jobs within two years of receiving benefits. Following the election, however, welfare reform disappeared into the files of the Oval Office, as the president emphasized more traditional Democratic policies.[4] His economic plan called for tax increases, and he threw the full weight of his presidency behind a major overhaul of the health care system. Meanwhile, controversies over such "hot button" issues as allowing gays in the military, handgun control, and an assault weapons ban mobilized political opponents. The administration struggled through its first two years and, with falling approval ratings, entered the 1994 election season in a vulnerable position. Republicans charged that new Democrat Clinton was just an old Democrat in disguise: he favored gays and opposed guns; he raised taxes and proposed a massive government intervention in health care; and he had broken his campaign promise by doing absolutely nothing about welfare. Apparently on the strength of such attacks, Republicans swept to victory, capturing control of Congress for the first time in forty years.

Welfare reform was high on the Republican agenda, and in December 1995 the Republican Congress challenged the president to approve a Republican bill to "end welfare as we know it." Clinton twice vetoed the bill, arguing that its provisions went too far.[5] In the summer of 1996, the now-vulnerable Republicans, desperate to maintain control of Congress, passed a somewhat weaker version of the welfare reform bill and sent it to Clinton for his signature.

The bill was denounced by many Democrats. New York Senator Daniel P. Moynihan, the party's leading expert on social policy, pronounced that in turning welfare over to the states, the bill reversed sixty years of federal policy. Critics warned that the states would not fund programs adequately, and that the training, jobs, and day care required to move welfare recipients into the workforce simply did not exist. Moynihan bitterly charged that the legislation was based on the belief that "the behavior of certain adults can be changed by making the lives of their children as wretched as possible." [6] Clinton stood in a commanding position in his bid for reelection, and many supporters felt that he could easily afford to veto the bill once again.

Republicans disagreed. They believed that they had put Clinton on the horns of a dilemma. Speaker Newt Gingrich commented that Clinton would accept the bill "because he can't avoid it and get reelected. That is the only reason." [7]

Despite Clinton's comfortable lead in the polls, his principal campaign adviser, Dick Morris, agreed with the Republicans. He urged the president to sign the bill, to remove any possibility that welfare would flare up as a campaign issue. To the dismay of many prominent Democrats, Clinton agreed with Morris that the political risks of rejecting the bill were too great. He signed the bill, promising to seek changes in the next Congress. Clinton's sense of the risk of not signing was shared by others in his party. Of the 16 Democratic Senators who stood for reelection in 1996, only Paul Wellstone of Minnesota voted against the bill.

his story of welfare reform is typical of policy making in democracies in general, and modern American democracy in particular. Ambitious politicians advance proposals that are carefully crafted to help get them elected. Their proposals are shaped by polls indicating the state of public opinion. Yet, politics is dynamic because, although public opinion is rooted in stable, underlying values, opinion on current issues also responds to social change, political debate, and the way the media portray social problems. When elected officials deliver on popular promises to the public, they take issues away from potential challengers. When they fail to deliver on such promises, they are attacked by opponents who claim to better represent the people. Ambitious politicians, electoral pressures, public opinion, the media—these are key elements of modern American democracy.

The elections of the 1990s underlie many of the most important developments in American government on the eve of the millennium. Indeed, the central theme of this book is that elections are the key to understanding contemporary American democracy. Not only are elections more important in the United States than in other democracies, but they are more important today than in most earlier periods of our history. This reality provides the thread that ties together the many facts and findings contained in the chapters that follow.

Elections are so widespread and continuous in the United States that unusual locations are often pressed into service as polling places. This grocery store in rural Texas gives a busy parent the opportunity to cast her vote in a local election.

Two points deserve emphasis from the outset. First, our conception of elections is broad. We are referring not just to what happens on election day, nor even just to what goes on during the official campaign. Rather, when we write about elections we include the anticipation of and the preparation for future elections. Looking ahead to the next election affects what presidents propose, what they sign, and what they veto; what Congress passes and what it kills; whom groups support and whom they oppose; whom and what the media cover, and whom and what they ignore. Just as the winner of an Olympic event may have been determined on the training fields two years earlier, so the outcomes of elections may be determined by the actions of candidates, groups, contributors, the media, and other political actors far in advance of the campaigns.

A second important clarification is that when we write about the importance of elections we are not making simplistic claims that the "people" rule. Quite the contrary, elections are not always free and open expressions of popular sentiments. Elections often give more power to some groups than to others. Sometimes they allow special interests to block actions desired by the majority. On other occasions, they may leave leaders deadlocked, because competing pressures cannot be resolved. Whether elections are truly open and representative and whether they are mechanisms for achieving good government varies with time and place.

Of course, to say that elections are a key ingredient in American democracy, even the key ingredient, is not to deny that there are other important elements as well. Elections are part of a large, complex political system. They are closely bound up with the historical evolution of American government, the political behavior of American citizens, the workings of the country's basic institutions, and the nature of the policies that the process produces. All these topics are covered in the chapters that follow.

Because Americans take elections so much for granted, we begin by calling attention to the sheer magnitude of electioneering in America.

Elections and Government in America

Unbelievable as it may seem, more than half a million people in the United States are elected officials, about one for every 500 Americans. If all elected officials were put in one place, they would exceed the population of Cleveland.[8]

Most Americans are unaware of the ubiquity of elections in their country, but the United States has more elections that select more officials for public offices than any other country on earth. *National elections,* in which voters choose the officials of the federal government, receive the most attention. These important elections, held every two years, determine the identity of the president, vice president, 100 senators and 435 members of the House of Representatives.

But national elections are only the tip of the iceberg, and it is a mistake to ignore the hundreds of thousands of elections that occur at other levels. State and local politics and government are a huge—and growing—part of American public life. Most books on American government segregate discussions of state and local politics into a chapter or two often placed at the end of the book. In contrast, this book integrates discussions of state and local politics and government into the main text. These discussions are highlighted with the heading "At the State and Local Level" first seen below.

BELOW THE TIP OF THE ICEBERG

Elections are among the most important factors that connect state, local and national politics. While national elections get the lion's share of media attention, a larger number of voting opportunities occur in *state elections,* where voters select officeholders in the fifty states. In every state, voters elect the governor and the state legislature as well as various other officials, such as the lieutenant governor, the treasurer, the state's attorney, the auditor, and perhaps state railroad and public utility commissioners.

The number of elections expands further when one considers *local elections,* which determine officials for all governments below the level of the state. Voters in cities elect mayors and city councils. Voters in the more than 3,000 counties elect sheriffs, county treasurers, and county boards. Voters choose the members of 90 percent of the nation's 16,000 school boards, as well as numerous officials responsible for the governance of towns, villages, and special districts.

Even the judicial system—often thought to be insulated from political pressure—is permeated by elections. In thirty-seven states, at least some judges are elected. Altogether, Americans elect more than 1,000 state judges and about 15,000 county, municipal, and other local judges and officers of the court.[9] Moreover, in recent years judges have been increasingly subject to **recall elections**, in which dissatisfied citizens attempt to remove incumbent officials from office during their terms.

Although half a million elected officials sounds like a large number, there are far more elections than there are elected officials. First of all, most officials must win two elections before they can take office. In the **primary election**, each party chooses a nominee who then squares off against the other parties' nominees in the **general election** to see who wins the office. In *nonpartisan elections,* where candidates do not run as the nominees of parties, primaries are sometimes used to narrow the field of candidates. Access to the primary ballot is open to any potential candidate with the supporters and money to gather the required number of signatures and pay the filing fees. In one election year, humorist Will Rogers commented that, "Everybody was running that could get some cards printed. It was a great year for the printers."[10]

Second, to this extensive list of elections that choose office-holders, we must add all those in which the people directly decide on public issues. In twenty-seven states plus the District of Columbia, citizens vote on issues by voting on initiatives, referenda, or both. An **initiative** is a proposed law or amendment to a state constitution placed on the ballot by a citizen petition. A **referendum** is a law or state constitutional amendment proposed by a legislature or city council that goes into effect only if approved by a specified majority of voters. In initiatives and referenda, citizens directly decide budgets, taxes, laws, and amendments to state constitutions.[11] Some states, such as California, frequently have more initiatives on the ballot than elected offices to be filled.

Americans have become accustomed to the great frequency and variety of elections. But observers from other countries are struck by the seemingly constant presence of Americans at the polling booth. A noted British analyst, Anthony King, has argued that "American exceptionalism"—the distinctive shape of American government and politics when seen from an international perspective—arises not from our individualistic political culture, nor from the fragmented nature of our

■ **recall election**
Attempt to remove an official from office before the completion of the term.

■ **primary election**
Preliminary election that narrows the number of candidates by determining who will be the nominees in the general election.

■ **general election**
Final election that selects the officeholder.

■ **initiative**
Proposed laws or state constitutional amendments placed on the ballot by citizen petition.

■ **referendum**
A law or state constitutional amendment proposed by a legislature or city council that does not go into effect unless the required majority of voters approve it.

ELECTIONS IN AMERICA

Americans vote far more often than the citizens of other democracies. Professor L. Sandy Maisel has compiled the following list of election days in various American towns and cities.*

There are so many elections and so many elected officials in so many jurisdictions in the United States that it is difficult to compile accurate data on the subject. For example, we had heard that residents of Houston, Texas, voted for more elected officials than Americans in any other jurisdiction.

How many? A call to the County Clerk's office was met with a "we have no idea" response. Conversations with University of Houston professors elicited the estimate that a resident of Houston was represented by 126 elected officials, judges included, at all levels of government.† We challenge our

readers to find jurisdictions in which citizens can vote for even more officials! Contact us at www.abacon.com/fiorina.

* L. Sandy Maisel, *Parties and Elections in America*, 2nd ed. (New York: McGraw-Hill, 1993): 2-3.

† Professor Richard Murray, as reported by Professor Jay Greene, personal communication, April 10, 1997.

Boca Raton, Florida
Odd year
　March: Municipal election
　September: Initiative
Even year
　March: Presidential primary, municipal election
　September: Federal, state, and county primaries

San Diego, California
Odd year
　September: Primary for municipal, county, and some school district elections
　November: Municipal, some county, and some school district

elections (initiative and referenda)
Even year
　June: Primary for presidential, some state, some municipal, some county and some school district elections
　November: Presidential, some state, some municipal, some county, and some school district elections‡

Whitefish Bay, Wisconsin
Odd year
　February: Nonpartisan primary for judicial offices; party primaries for

municipal and county offices
　April: Nonpartisan judicial election; municipal and county elections; constitutional amendments
　July: Approval of school budget
Even year
　Nonpartisan primary for judicial offices; primary for municipal and county offices
　April: Nonbinding Democratic and Republican primary for presidential delegates; nonpartisan judicial election; partisan

municipal and county election; referenda on constitutional questions
　April: Democratic caucuses §
　July: Approval of school budget
　September: Primary for federal, state, and county offices
　November: General election for federal, state, and county officials

‡ County and school district terms are staggered; some elections are held each year.
§ Democratic party had a nonbinding primary and later binding caucuses to send delegates to the national convention.

institutions, as many have argued, but from the multitude and frequency of our elections (see the first *International Comparison*, on page 10, a special feature that will appear throughout this book):

> Americans take the existence of their elections industry for granted. Some like it; some dislike it; most are simply bored by it. But they are all conscious of it, in the same way that they are conscious of Mobil, McDonald's, Larry King Live, Oprah Winfrey, the Dallas Cowboys, the Ford Motor Company, and all the other symbols and institutions that go to make up the rich tapestry of American life. In a meaningful sense, America is about the holding of elections.[12]

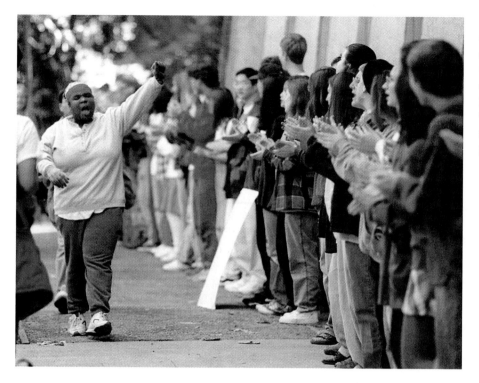

More than 400 University of California, Santa Cruz students shut down the Student Services Building in protest of the passage of Proposition 209 in the November 1996 state election. The proposition banned student affirmative action programs based on race or gender.

⭐ AT THE STATE & LOCAL LEVEL

AMERICANS VOTE DIRECTLY

Affirmative Action, 1996

California voters considered a ballot initiative to end state and local affirmative action programs. Citizens in five other states attempted to place similar propositions on their ballots.

Term Limits, 1994

Eight states had referenda on whether to impose term limits on their members of Congress.

Campaign Finance Reform, 1994

Six states had referenda concerning campaign finance reform.

Anti-Gay Rights, 1994

Two states—Idaho and Oregon—had anti-gay rights initiatives on their ballots.

Crime, 1994

Five states had ballot measures to ensure the rights of crime victims.

Taxes, 1994

Three states—Missouri, Montana, and Oregon—had referenda on whether to require voter approval of some new taxes.

Gambling, 1994

Ten states had referenda on whether to legalize, expand, or restrict gambling.

Smoking, 1994

California's voters rejected an initiative that would have weakened the state's antismoking laws.

SOURCES: Rebecca Boyd, "84 Years of Initiatives in California," *The Sacramento Bee*, August 4, 1996, A11. Dana Priest, "Ballot Names May Yield to Ballot Measures," *The Washington Post*, November 2, 1994, A9. Kathryn Wexler, "Women's Groups Take on California Initiative; Nationwide Support Bolsters Effort to Preserve Affirmative Action Programs," *The Washington Post*, March 3, 1996, A3.

In contrast to Americans, many of whom can vote more than a dozen times for scores of candidates and issues in any given four-year period, citizens of other democracies vote for fewer offices and vote less frequently. Consider Great Britain, which elected John Major Prime Minister in 1992 and replaced him five years later. In each of these elections Britons voted for only one person—a candidate for parliament. Between these two elections, Britons voted on only two other occasions, for only two offices—their local councillor and their representative to the European Community.

Between Bill Clinton's two election victories, the French voted four times: for Parliament in 1993, for president in April and May of 1994 (they have a two-round system), and for local mayors in 1995. Similarly, between 1992 and 1996 the Japanese voted five times, twice each for the upper and lower houses of the Diet (their parliament), and once for local officials.

Even to our North American neighbors the United States looks peculiar. In Mexico a presidential election is held every six years. Congressional elections are held every three years. Some states hold state and municipal elections at the same time as congressional elections, while others hold them at a different time. But at most a Mexican citizen votes four times in a four-year period: in presidential, congressional, state, and municipal elections.

In Canada, too, provincial and municipal elections may or may not be coordinated with national elections. If the elections are not coordinated, a Canadian would vote at most three times (national, provincial, municipal) in a four-year period, except for an occasional referendum, such as Quebec's vote on secession in 1995. Canadian officials are well aware of the contrast between the two systems. Prime Minister Jean Chrétien recently commented that "In your system, you guys campaign for 24 hours [a day] every [day for] two years. You know, politics is one thing, but we have to run a government."*

* David Shribman, "In Canada, the Lean Season," *The Boston Globe*, May 23, 1997, A3.

GOVERNMENT AND POLITICS

Ironically, despite the fact that Americans choose hundreds of thousands of their public officials in elections, and despite the fact that they can make specific policy decisions through initiatives and referenda, many Americans are frustrated by their governments. According to polls, Americans no longer have the same degree of trust in government they once had (see Figure 1.1). Citizens believe that government costs too much, delivers too little, and wastes their tax dollars. Citizens think politics is needlessly contentious and often corrupt. Many are unenthusiastic about major party presidential candidates like Bill Clinton and Robert Dole in 1996, and yearn for new leaders like former General Colin Powell. Many are suspicious about the established TV networks and major newspapers, and turn to alternative information providers such as talk-show host Rush Limbaugh. Many are

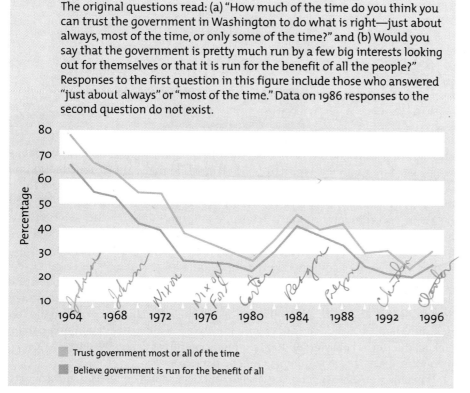

The original questions read: (a) "How much of the time do you think you can trust the government in Washington to do what is right—just about always, most of the time, or only some of the time?" and (b) Would you say that the government is pretty much run by a few big interests looking out for themselves or that it is run for the benefit of all the people?" Responses to the first question in this figure include those who answered "just about always" or "most of the time." Data on 1986 responses to the second question do not exist.

Trust government most or all of the time

Believe government is run for the benefit of all

frustrated with existing political processes, and support radical reforms such as constitutional amendments to balance the budget and limit the number of terms elected officials may serve.[13]

To some extent, suspicion of government is healthy. By their very nature, governments threaten human liberty. The great German sociologist, Max Weber, wrote that **government** is that institution in society which has a "monopoly of the legitimate use of physical force." [14] Government is the only institution that legally can take people's property (by taxing them), imprison them (by arresting and convicting them), and even kill them (by executing them). As George Washington put it a century before Weber: "Government is not reason, it is not eloquence—it is force." [15]

government
The institution in society which has a "monopoly of the legitimate use of physical force".

Because government has the ability to make people do things they may not want to do, people have good reasons to distrust and fear it. Those who participate in politics generally do so because they want to see the powers of government used for some particular purpose. At times the purposes are high-minded, as when Abraham Lincoln asked soldiers to fight to end slavery and save the Union. At times the purposes are less honorable, as when Richard Nixon tried to use the Internal Revenue Service to punish political critics. And most of the time purposes are mixed. The country's current president, Bill Clinton, offers a good example. No one would deny that he entered politics partly in order to satisfy his personal ambitions.[16] But only a few of his most bitter enemies would deny that he also is trying to create a better country for future generations. By the same token, Robert Dole, Clinton's opponent in the 1996

When campaigning for president, Jimmy Carter professed: "All I want is . . . to have a nation with a government that is as good . . . as are the American people."

presidential campaign, was both a savvy politician and a man of high ideals. Some critics saw him as a mean-spirited politician, while many supporters thought he deserved the Medal of Honor that President Clinton awarded him some weeks after the 1996 election.

Since governmental power is fearsome and the motives of those who use it mixed, citizens understandably are suspicious of it. Why then do we have governments at all? In fact, if former President Jimmy Carter had been correct, government would be unnecessary. When campaigning for president, Carter professed: "All I want is . . . to have a nation with a government that is as good and honest and decent and competent and compassionate and as filled with love as are the American people."[17] These are generous sentiments, but with all due respect to the former president, government is necessary precisely because such qualities are often lacking in human behavior. As another former president, James Madison, wrote, "If men were angels, no government would be necessary."[18]

If people were always good and honest and decent and competent and compassionate and filled with love, there would be little need for government. Governments are designed less for the times when people agree than for the times when they disagree. The real world is not "Barney's World," where "I love you, you love me, we're a happy family." Quite the contrary: No matter who you are, what you believe, what you want, or how you behave, the unfortunate fact of life is that some of your fellow citizens dislike you for exactly that reason. People can settle their disagreements and rise above their dislikes through peaceful political means, or they can take up weapons and kill each other, as Americans did in the Civil War and so many peoples of the world have done before and since.

The great English political theorist, Thomas Hobbes, made the most basic case for government and politics. A world without government, he said, would be nothing less than "a war of all against all." Life would be "nasty, brutish and short."[19] Government is not a perfect solution to human conflict, and citizens *should* be suspicious of its powers. But government is the best solution for human conflicts that human beings have yet contrived, and civilized life is unimaginable without it.

Types of Government

Author Samuel Johnson once commented that "I would not give half a guinea to live under one form of government than another. It is of no moment to the happiness of an individual."[20] Johnson was wrong. Lives can be terribly damaged or greatly improved, depending on the type of government under which they live. Twenty-three centuries ago Aristotle classified governments into three basic types: government by one person, government by the few, and government by the many. Although others have proposed more complex classifications, Aristotle's simple scheme remains a useful point of departure.

GOVERNMENT BY ONE PERSON

Government in which a single person has ultimate power comes in several varieties. Emperors, pharaohs, kings, tsars, and other monarchs ruled by right of heredity or religious designation, dictators and other despots, by support of the army or the police. The quality of government by a single ruler depends upon who is in charge. The ruler can put the welfare of the people first, last, or anywhere in between. But placing the coercive power of government in the hands of one person requires unlimited trust in that person, and no one is so deserving: "Power tends to corrupt and absolute power corrupts absolutely." In the twentieth century alone, millions of people were put to death by rulers who gained near-absolute power: Germany's Hitler, the Soviet Union's Stalin, China's Mao, and Cambodia's Pol Pot.

GOVERNMENT BY THE FEW

Government by the few is generally known as an **aristocracy**, if leaders are eligible by birth, or an **oligarchy**, if leadership is determined by wealth, military power, or membership in a political party. In the past many countries were ruled by aristocracies, but in the modern world birthright no longer seems a sufficient justification for ruling over others. Oligarchies can still be found, however. The most important example exists in China, where a small group of Communist party leaders has remained in power since 1946. Oligarchies have some advantages over dictatorships—to a limited extent, members of the oligarchy can check and balance each other. But here, too, power tends to corrupt, as the few take advantage of their position to acquire wealth at the expense of the rest of society.

GOVERNMENT BY THE MANY

Government in which power is shared by all citizens is called a **democracy**. The word derives from the Greek word *demos*, which means "people." In its purest form, **direct democracy**, all citizens participate directly in the making of government decisions. In Aristotle's time, direct democracy was practical because citizenship was limited to free adult men with property, who in many Greek cities numbered no more than a few thousand. Something close to a direct democracy still exists in a few New England towns where governmental decisions are made at town meetings. But even there, all citizens do not have equal influence: Most people do not show up for the meetings, some speakers are more persuasive, and some decisions cannot wait for the next meeting.[21]

Clearly, direct democracy in large countries such as the United States is not practical. Even with the modern wonders of e-mail, fax machines, and other forms of electronic communication, each citizen cannot participate directly in every governmental decision. People would have to be continuously attending meetings in order to decide all the questions that must be resolved. No time would be left for anything else.

Cambodian leader Pol Pot. Although it is nearly two decades since he was in power, Pol Pot's presence can still be felt. For example, the country is still suffering from an absence of skilled doctors and nurses to replace those liquidated in a purge Pol Pot ordered.

■ **aristocracy**
Government by a few leaders made eligible by birthright.
■ **oligarchy**
Government by a few who gain office by means of wealth, military power, or membership in a single political party.
■ **democracy**
System in which governmental power is widely shared among the citizens, usually through free and open elections.
■ **direct democracy**
Type of democracy in which ordinary people are the government, making all the laws themselves.

TWO MODELS OF DEMOCRACY

The Popular Model	The Responsible Model
Elections express the popular will	Elections grant popular consent
Elections determine policies	Elections determine leaders
Citizens vote prospectively	Citizens vote retrospectively
Direct democracy is preferred, when practical	Representative democracy always is preferred
Popular participation is necessary for effective democracy	Clear accountability of leaders is necessary for effective democracy
Democratic politics should advance the civic education of citizens	Democratic politics should produce effective governance

representative democracy
An indirect form of democracy in which the people choose representatives who determine what government does.

Because direct democracy is usually impractical, government by the many generally is **representative democracy**, an *indirect* form of democracy in which citizens choose representatives who in turn determine what government does. While the people rule only indirectly in representative democracy, so long as there are free and open elections it is fair to say that the government is democratic. Opponents of democracy clearly recognize the key importance of free elections. As dictator Joseph Stalin once observed to a colleague, "The disadvantage of free elections is that you can never be sure who is going to win them."[22]

Although they agree on the need for free elections, political theorists disagree about other factors necessary for the workings of an effective representative democracy.[23] Most of the arguments can be summarized by distinguishing between two general types or models of representative democracy, a popular model and a responsible model.

popular model of democracy
Type of representative democracy in which ordinary people participate actively and closely constrain the actions of public officials.

In the **popular model of democracy**, citizens play an active role in government decisions. In its purest form, popular democracy strives to be as close to a direct democracy as a representative democracy can be. Elections are viewed as opportunities for the popular will to express itself. They provide *popular mandates*, that is, instructions from the voters for public officials to adopt specific policies. In order for elections to work this way, citizens must be well-informed about public issues and vote in ways consistent with their opinions on these issues. And people vote prospectively: They look to the future as they vote. As a result, each election becomes an opportunity to decide on specific public policies.

Those who favor the popular model say that democracy is more than a mechanical process for producing outcomes; it is also an educational forum in which individuals become better citizens by participating in democratic deliberation. Through participation the public can achieve consensus and formulate better policies. Thus, popular democracy is expected to produce both better citizens and better policies. The process of participation transforms "private into public," "conflict into cooperation," "bondage into citizens."[24]

responsible model of democracy
A type of representative democracy in which public officials have considerable freedom of action but are held accountable by the people for the decisions they make.

Critics say that popular democracies are inefficient systems in which everyone can talk but no one can act. These critics favor a **responsible model of democracy**, in which citizens play a more passive role. Citizens choose public officials but do not tell them what to do. Elected officials are given the responsibility to govern and are held responsible to the people for the decisions they make. In this model, elections are occasions at which citizens grant or deny *popular consent* rather than grant popular mandates. In order for elections to work this way, citizens need not be well-informed. They vote retrospectively, looking more to the past than the future. They decide whether incumbents have done a good or a bad job. If the voters approve, they reelect incumbents; if voters disapprove, they vote in a new group of leaders.

Critics of responsible democracy say that it is hardly democracy at all.[25] In fact, critics sometimes refer to the responsible model as "elitist democracy," because in responsible democracies, elites—those who hold office, manage the parties, and lead the interest groups—dominate the political process. Those who favor the responsible model do not deny that it gives ordinary citizens a modest role relative to elites (whom they prefer to call leaders), but they claim that widespread popular participation in government is unnecessary, or even harmful, since ordinary people are often badly informed. Defenders of the responsible model believe that, as long as the public can occasionally give a general evaluation, a responsible democracy will usually produce better government than one produced by a popular democracy, because public officials are better informed than citizens as a whole.

POPULAR AND RESPONSIBLE DEMOCRACY IN THE UNITED STATES

In the real world, of course, pure types do not exist; every real-world democracy has both popular and responsible elements. Yet democracies differ in the degree to which they tend toward one or another direction. Britain, for example, is a good example of the responsible model. Members of Parliament are chosen by the people, but in the normal five-year period between elections, the governing party has considerable capacity to undertake independent action—sometimes extending to fairly radical actions like nationalizing and denationalizing industries.

The United States has always been a more popular democracy than its European counterparts. When the French scholar, Alexis de Tocqueville, visited the United States during the 1830s, he was astounded by the extent of popular participation. "It must be seen to be believed," he exclaimed to his fellow French citizens. "No sooner do you set foot on American ground than you are stunned by a kind of tumult... Almost the only pleasure an American knows is to take part in the government and discuss its measures."[26]

The principles of popular democracy were from its earliest days an integral part of American politics. "Where annual elections end, there slavery begins," said the second president, John Adams, arguing that citizens must have frequent opportunities to instruct and judge their representatives.[27] The third president, Thomas Jefferson, wanted to "divide the country into wards." As one scholar has pointed out Jefferson thought that in these "small autonomous constituencies [little republics, he called them] free men could control their own political destinies."[28]

The framers believed that words on paper—which they called "parchment barriers"—were no guarantee of good government. Words alone would not prevent majorities from suppressing the rights of minorities. The framers thought the rights of individuals could be best protected by "buttressing" the "parchment barriers" in the Constitution with something firmer, namely by a system of checks and balances, which divided power among different representatives chosen in different elections. Each national office was assigned a separate **constituency**, a set of people entitled to vote for the holder of that office, and officeholders would be chosen by these different constituencies at different times. Thus, senators were to be chosen by state legislatures for six-year terms; presidents and vice presidents were to be

constituency
Those legally entitled to vote for a public official.

chosen by electors (themselves chosen in a manner specified by the state legislature) for four-year terms; and members of the House of Representatives were to be elected directly by the voters for two-year terms. Consequently, each public official was answerable to separate constituencies at different times.

In this way, the framers constructed a responsible democracy, even while allowing for many popular elements. With power divided among many elected officials, each with a specific constituency, leaders have the interest and capacity to resist both popular passions and attempts by potential tyrants to seize power. According to Madison, "Ambition must be made to counteract ambition. The interest of the man must be connected with the constitutional rights of the place."[30] Two hundred years of non-tyrannical government confirm the validity of his vision.

Elections: Key to the New American Democracy

Many of the original features of the Constitution remain intact, but American politics has evolved in the direction of greater popular participation. Ever larger proportions of the population have gained full rights of citizenship, the connection between representatives and the public has become increasingly direct, national institutions are now less insulated from popular influence than previously, and the number and frequency of elections, coupled with the more extensive campaigning that accompanies them, have increased. These trends have accelerated dramatically in recent decades—to the extent that we believe it is no exaggeration to title this book *The New American Democracy*.

THE PERMANENT CAMPAIGN

The new American democracy is marked by the presence of what has been called the **permanent campaign**, a situation in which the next election campaign begins as soon as the last one has ended—or even earlier.[31] Only six months after Bill Clinton was reelected president, the campaigns for 1998 and 2000 already were under way. In early 1997, the president was apparently delegating much of the responsibility for formulating domestic policy to Vice President Al Gore, who was expected to defend the administration's policies in the elections of 2000. But Richard Gephardt, the Democratic majority leader in the House of Representatives, also has intense presidential ambitions; he began distancing himself from the Clinton-Gore administration in anticipation of running against Gore in the presidential primaries in 2000.[32] On the other side, Steve Forbes, a wealthy Republican presidential candidate who ran surprisingly well in some 1996 primaries, was already out on the "rubber chicken" circuit (addressing small groups at dinner meetings), building grassroots support for the next presidential campaign. And all of this was three and a half years before the next presidential election!

At least five factors have contributed to the permanent campaign: the separation of election days, the decay of party organizations, the spread of primary elections, developments in mass communications, and the proliferation of polling.

Together these factors have moved American democracy in a significantly more popular direction.

★ **AT THE STATE & LOCAL LEVEL**

SEPARATION OF ELECTIONS

In principle, all public officials could be elected on the same day and serve, say, the same five-year term of office. All who wished could stand for reelection simultaneously. Such an arrangement—one gigantic election day every five years—would greatly reduce the time taken up by campaigning and voting.

A century ago, most officials were elected on the same day. Usually, citizens could cast votes simultaneously for president, senator, representative, governor, mayor, state representative and state senator, city council, and so forth. In a few states one still can vote for most offices on the same day, but the trend in the past half-century has been to separate election days.[33] Most Americans now turn out to vote for president at one general election, for governor at another, and for mayor at still another. Primary elections, as well as those for local offices, are held earlier in the election year. Initiatives and referenda may be held on still other occasions. As a result, Americans are repeatedly called to the polls. For example, a conscientious citizen in California would have had to go to the polls on eight separate occasions in 1995–1996. And as election dates have proliferated, electioneering has become a continuous feature of American politics. There is very little "quiet time" during which no campaigns are in progress.

DECAY OF PARTY ORGANIZATIONS

Elections are not meaningful unless voters have a genuine choice among candidates. In most democracies, political parties provide the choices. Many Americans

Candidates begin campaigning far in advance of the actual presidential election. Al Gore (left) was rumored never to miss an opportunity to campaign for the 2000 Democratic nomination. As early as Bill Clinton's 1997 inauguration, yet looking ahead to the 2000 presidential election, Steve Forbes mailed to select individuals a necktie (right) repeating his proud admission that he is nothing more than a "capitalist tool."

The political terms *left wing* and *right wing* had their origin in the seating arrangement of the postrevolutionary French Assembly, where conservatives occupied the "right" side and liberals, the "left" side.

have little good to say about parties, but most political scientists regard parties as essential to the workings of a representative democracy. Parties organize elections in ways that make it easier for voters to choose; and they concentrate political power so that governments can govern. Since just before the Civil War, the two major parties in the United States have been the Republican and Democratic parties.

Although clear differences between Republicans and Democrats cannot always be detected, the two parties give voters a choice by espousing different political philosophies. The Republican party leans in a more conservative direction; its activists and leaders generally favor less government, lower taxes, less regulation of business activity, empowering state and local governments, and traditional family values. The Democratic party leans in a more liberal direction; its activists and leaders usually favor a strong federal government, more extensive social programs, more regulation, and toleration of alternative lifestyles. Conservatives sometimes are called the "right" or the "right wing," while liberals are called the "left" or the "left wing."

Because the philosophies of the two parties generally differ, the voter is given a meaningful choice. And because party positions on issues shift only gradually, they provide continuity to political life, making it easier for voters to make choices on election day.

A century ago many of the Republican and Democratic party organizations were called "machines," because they were strong, disciplined organizations that could mobilize large numbers of voters on election day. But civil service reforms and social changes killed off the machines. As a consequence, today's politicians cannot depend on party organizations whose workers can deliver pretty much the same vote for all the candidates of the party. Instead, elected officials must construct their own organizations and develop personal constituencies to achieve election and reelection.[34] And such personalized support is less reliable than the partisan support shared by numerous candidates in earlier eras.[35] Thus, incumbents today must invest more of their time and resources in preparing for their reelection fights: Their fates rest in their own hands.

★ AT THE STATE & LOCAL LEVEL

SPREAD OF PRIMARIES

In most countries, candidates for office are selected by a small number of political party leaders. A hundred years ago this was the standard procedure in the United States as well. Candidates were picked in "smoke-filled rooms" by party "bosses." To eliminate the corruption that often accompanied such deal-making, reformers secured the passage of laws giving voters the right to select party nominees by means of primary elections.

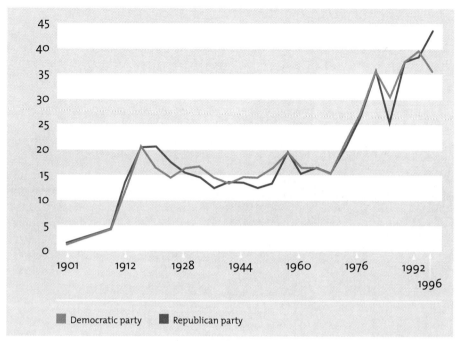

FIGURE 1.2

Growth in the Number of Presidential Primaries

SOURCE: *Congressional Quarterly's Guide to the Presidency*, ed. Michael Nelson (Washington, D.C: CQ Press, 1985); America Votes 20: *A Handbook of Contemporary American Election Statistics*, ed. by Richard M. Scammon and Aline V. McGilluray (Washington, D.C.: CQ Press, 1993); Rhodes Cook, "Primaries," *Congressional Quarterly*, Jan. 13, 1996, pp. 98–99.

Although they came into use about a century ago, primaries did not become a significant part of the selection of presidential candidates until after World War II (see Figure 1.2). The first presidential candidate who owed his nomination in any substantial measure to winning primaries was Dwight D. Eisenhower, elected in 1952. And as late as 1968, Hubert Humphrey, the Democratic nominee, did not enter a single primary.

Today, primaries are a pervasive part of the political process and make a substantial contribution to the permanent campaign. Because primaries are held in advance of the general election, they shorten the interval between one election and the next. As previously stated, behind-the-scenes planning for the presidential election of 2000 began in early 1997. The public phase of the campaign will be under way in mid-1999, six months before the primaries begin in the spring of the year 2000, and only two and a half years into Clinton's second term. Nor is the permanent campaign limited to the campaign for the White House. Some members of the House of Representatives face primaries more than six months before their two-year terms end. For example, on April 9, 1996, Representative Greg Laughlin (R.-TX) was defeated in a primary, scarcely fifteen months after he had taken the oath of office.

MASS COMMUNICATIONS

Technological advances in communications also have helped to make campaigns continuous. Rather than relying on party organizations, today's candidates make every effort to get their names in the papers and their pictures on television. Moreover, today's interactive mass communications provide citizens with opportunities to talk back to politicians as well as to be talked to. Long-distance telephone rates are so cheap that many people are willing to call or receive calls from any-

President Bill Clinton denied any relationship with Gennifer Flowers but was remarkably open in defending his private life in the midst of the media "feeding frenzy" surrounding his alleged affairs.

where in the United States. Dozens of cable television channels enable candidates to communicate with small, well-defined audiences. C-SPAN provides continuous coverage of debates in the Senate and the House of Representatives as well as other political events, giving people outside Washington a chance to observe public officials directly. Radio talk shows have increased in popularity. And conversation on the Internet, often error-ridden and conspiratorial, is a fast-growing mode of political communication.

Today's media have obliterated the distance that once separated elected officials from the voting public. Virtually every move a prominent politician makes is now evaluated for its political motivations and implications. Even the distinction between public and private life has eroded. The financial and medical histories of elected officials are considered public knowledge. Reporters ask candidates almost any question imaginable, no matter how irrelevant, tasteless, or unrelated to politics and government. For example, when Gennifer Flowers claimed to have had an affair with Bill Clinton, the media went into a "feeding frenzy." [36]

PROLIFERATION OF POLLING

Finally, the shift toward a more popular democracy owes much to the advent of polling. It is a statistical fact that one can obtain a reasonable indication of the state of public opinion by interviewing about 1,000 citizens. If used carefully, polls can provide politicians with a fairly good idea of the current public thinking about an issue.

Of course, leaders have always been concerned about public opinion. In the closing days of the Constitutional Convention in 1787, George Washington proposed a major change in the representational scheme for the House of Representatives so that the new Constitution would stand a better chance of being ratified by the states. Abraham Lincoln waited for a military victory to issue the Emancipation Proclamation, abolishing slavery, so that a happy public would be especially inclined to support it. Politicians are traditionally portrayed as having their "ear to the ground" and their "finger to the wind." But until the introduction of modern polling, beliefs about the state of public opinion were only guesses. Modern polling techniques are much more precise, and provide everyone the same information.

Polling has become a major industry, because politicians hunger for information about the state of the public mind. So eager are they to know the views of voters that in the words of some critics "Polls give some politicians, weaker ones, more information than is good for them, particularly if they can't resist the temptation to follow the 51 percent of their district who seemed to be against the Bill of Rights between Tuesday and Thursday of last week." [37]

It is not just the politicians who want to know about the state of public opinion; the media have become increasingly focused on it as well. The media have made public opinion a much more important part of their coverage both by sponsoring polls and by incessant reporting of their results (see Figures 1.3 and 1.4).

Polling contributes to the permanent campaign by making electoral implications visible from the beginning. When a new issue arises, politicians no longer wonder about the state of public opinion. They find out within days, sometimes hours. Does the public support President Bush's recommendation that the country go to war to defend Kuwait against Iraqi aggression? Two-thirds of the country does, the polls reported; the country went to war. Does the public support U.S. involvement in the Bosnian-Serbian conflict in former Yugoslavia? The country is split, the polls reported; the Clinton administration dragged its feet for two years before committing American troops. Obviously, the polls were not the only factor in either case, and in general it is certainly desirable that leaders know the public

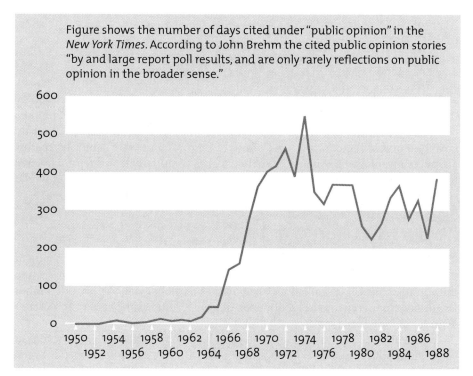

Figure shows the number of days cited under "public opinion" in the *New York Times*. According to John Brehm the cited public opinion stories "by and large report poll results, and are only rarely reflections on public opinion in the broader sense."

FIGURE 1.3

Today's Media Love to Report on Polls

SOURCE: John Brehm, *The Phantom Respondents* (Ann Arbor, MI: University of Michigan Press, 1993): 4.

FIGURE 1.4

Today's Media Love to Conduct
their Own Polls

SOURCE: Data taken from Everett
Carll Ladd and John Benson, "The
Growth of News Polls in American
Politics," in *Media Polls in American Politics*, edited by Thomas E.
Mann and Gary R. Orren (Washington, DC: Brookings, 1992), p. 23.

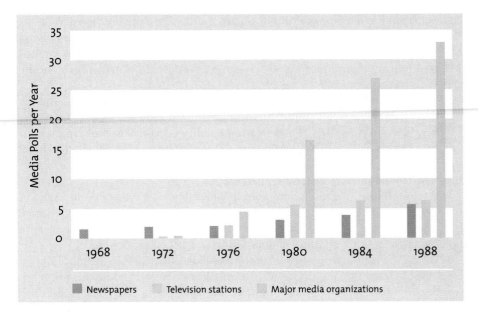

mind. But as British Prime Minister Winston Churchill observed in the darkest days of World War II, "Nothing is more dangerous in wartime than to live in the temperamental atmosphere of a Gallup Poll, always feeling one's pulse and taking one's temperature."[38] Some observers would agree with such a judgment even in peacetime.

Minorities and Elections

To say that American democracy is moving in a popular direction is *not* to say that a majority of the people govern. Elections by themselves do not guarantee a condition of political equality in which each citizen has equal influence on the government. On the contrary, special-interest groups and other minority interests are often advantaged by such electoral factors as voter participation, primary elections, and the need for campaign resources—both financial and volunteer worker support.

VOTER PARTICIPATION

In most U.S. elections, most people do *not* vote. The biggest turnout occurs in presidential elections. But even in the 1996 presidential election, only 49 percent of the adult population cast a ballot. Turnout rates in other elections are much lower. In the 1994 congressional election, for example, voter turnout was 35 percent. Turnout in local elections drops off even further.[39]

While an individual vote may not count for much, collectively, the vote is an important political resource. Groups of people who vote at higher rates have more influence. For example, older people vote more frequently than the young or the

Despite the frequency of local and national elections, the majority of Americans do *not* turn out to vote —thereby advantaging the committed citizens who do.

poor.[40] Not surprisingly, programs for the elderly are much better funded than programs that serve the young and the needy. Turnout is not the only explanation, of course, but elected officials naturally will tend to pay greater heed to the demands of frequent voters than to those of nonvoters.

PRIMARIES

Voter turnout in primary elections is even lower than in general elections. The Republican presidential campaign in 1996 was hotly contested: Robert Dole, the eventual Republican nominee, was challenged by seven other major candidates. Yet the total number of people who voted in all the primaries of *both* major political parties was only 22.3 million, less than one-eighth of the adult population.[41]

Those who vote in primaries are usually more involved and more committed than citizens who don't vote; often they take more extreme positions on the issues. Republican primary voters tend to be more conservative than the typical American, and Democratic primary voters tend to be more liberal. To win primary elections, political candidates are tempted to appeal to the more extreme elements of their parties. As a result, differences between the candidates become exaggerated, leading Americans who take middle-of-the-road positions to become disenchanted with both sides.

CAMPAIGN FINANCE

While the results of some campaigns are forgone conclusions, most campaigns need to be financed. From providing relatively cheap materials such as campaign stickers and buttons to funding air travel and, above all, TV advertising, campaigns require money. Moreover, campaigns today increasingly rely on hired help rather than the party workers of earlier eras. As a result, almost the first job of the candidate is to figure out a strategy for raising money.

About a quarter of the adult population has ever given to a campaign, and a much smaller percentage regularly gives substantial amounts. A good deal of fund-raising is done by small groups, who typically have special political interests they seek to promote. For example, some executives of high-tech industries located in California's "Silicon Valley" were particularly interested in defeating an initiative on the California ballot in 1996 that would have subjected their industry to additional litigation. The group withheld donations to President Clinton's campaign until he announced his opposition to the initiative. Also, both the Democratic and Republican Committees were forced to refund numerous contributions from illegal foreign sources. And, in the aftermath of the 1996 campaign, the U.S. Senate launched a wide-ranging examination of campaign finance abuses that were suspected by many to involve unethical or illegal influence-peddling by both parties. In the eyes of some cynics, the congressional hearings seemed to demonstrate that Americans have the best government that money can buy.

On the other hand, interest group influence is not necessarily pernicious. Many political scientists think interest groups are essential to the workings of a representative democracy.[42] For one thing, they keep elected leaders informed about the diversity of social needs and desires that need to be accommodated. But elected officials naturally will be tempted to listen more closely to groups that make large campaign contributions. In consequence, groups that represent wealthy interests may be advantaged in American electoral democracy.

CAMPAIGN WORKERS

Volunteer work can substitute for paid labor. People can stuff envelopes, knock on doors, make phone calls, stage campaign rallies that will impress the news media, and drive voters to the polls. To get volunteers, candidates may appeal to **single-issue voters**, people who care so deeply about some particular issue that a candidate's position on this one issue determines their vote. For example, many members of the National Rifle Association are prepared to work against any candidate who supports gun control. As a result, it has been difficult to pass laws regulating the sale of guns, despite support for the idea among a majority of voters. Pro-life and pro-choice activists are other contemporary examples of single-issue voters. Many incumbents naturally will give greater weight to the intense views of single-issue voters, from whom they recruit campaign workers.

In sum, those committed enough to donate time or money or labor to campaigns may have extra influence. As one reporter comments:

> The fiction of one vote for one person still is maintained politely in high school classes in civil government; but men and women who touch practical politics, if only obliquely, know that men and women now may have as many votes in government as they have interests for which they are willing to sacrifice time and thought and money.[43]

All in all, free elections are not guarantees that majorities rule; they are only opportunities for majorities to rule.

single-issue voter
Voter who cares so deeply about some particular issue that a candidate's position on this one issue determines his or her vote.

Campaign workers illustrate the observation that "men and women now may have as many votes in government as they have interests for which they are willing to sacrifice time and thought and money."

Majorities and Elections

Although single-issue voters and other kinds of special interests at times may wield unusual influence, such groups lose much of their clout when a clear majority of the voters take a strong interest in a subject. In 1994 Congress approved a ban on assault weapons—despite the opposition of the National Rifle Association— once it became clear that most Americans opposed their unrestricted availability. And consistent with the moderate views of the American people, the Democratic Congress from 1990–94 did not pass the "Freedom of Choice Act," nor did the Republican Congress of 1995 adopt an amendment to outlaw abortion.

Moreover, majorities remain powerful even when the public is uninformed about or unaware of an issue. Elected officials realize that the media spotlight might suddenly illuminate what seems to be a dark corner. Most of the time incumbents think twice before taking actions in back rooms if those actions cannot be defended once the doors are opened.[44]

Moreover, if elected officials take positions not supported by a majority of their constituents, those positions may become campaign issues. Even if politicians try to keep their actions hidden, they cannot count on succeeding. Challengers pore over the incumbent's record, searching for unpopular votes cast, positions taken, or statements made. If the opposition finds one vote or statement that seems at all questionable, the matter almost certainly will become an issue. As discussed previously, Bill Clinton signed an historic welfare reform bill about which he had serious doubts, because he knew a veto would have made welfare reform a major campaign issue.

Of course, elected officials can sometimes take unpopular positions and still survive, because most voters are not single-issue voters. But elected officials cannot routinely take positions contrary to those of their constituents and expect to escape the wrath of the electorate indefinitely. Since leaders are never sure which potential issue will explode, they tend to be cautious in handling all of them. The power of

Serious presidential candidates are unlikely to take a position contrary to that held by a large majority of voters. Thus, on some issues, the positions of the Democratic and Republican candidates are similar. For example, as the following table shows, in 1996 President Clinton and Republican candidate Robert Dole both took majority positions on a series of issues where a clear majority of the public fell on one side of the issue. In contrast, Clinton and Dole took distinct positions on several issues where the public was divided more or less evenly.

Issue	Public Opinion	Clinton's Position	Dole's Position
Clear Majority			
Reduce budget deficit	82%	Yes	Yes
Cut taxes	74%	Yes	Yes
Limit welfare payments	70%	Yes	Yes
People need social security	88%	Yes	Yes
Give priority to environmental factors	62%	Yes	Yes
Divided Public			
Cut capital gains tax	51%	No	Yes
Increase defense spending	42%	No	Yes
Constitutional amendment allowing prayer in school	52%	No	Yes

SOURCES: The Gallup Poll Monthly, January 1995, 3; April, 1995, 19; Survey by the Gallup Organization for the Employee Benefit Research Institute, January/February 1994.

minorities is thus limited by the potential threat that the majority will become activated. Ordinarily, majorities exercise their influence less by articulating their views than through the calculations of public officials who anticipate public opinion long before it asserts itself. (See the first *Election Connection*, a special feature that appears regularly in this book.)

Reform?

The United States pays a price for the pervasiveness of its elections. Continuous electioneering creates a governmental system that is unattractive in many respects. Scandals—real and trumped-up—are common; inefficiency and stalemate are widespread; important policy problems fester; and effective actions are delayed or compromised away.[45]

Doonesbury   BY GARRY TRUDEAU

Many people understandably are frustrated by American government, but reform proposals should be viewed cautiously. Often reforms call for further movement toward popular democracy—more opportunities for constituencies to influence government such as more elections (primaries, initiatives and referenda, recalls), more opportunities to exert popular pressure (open public meetings, electronic town halls), or more power for elected officials (oversight of independent boards and commissions). Americans apparently believe, with John Dewey, that "The cure for the ailments of democracy is more democracy." [46]

Such reforms ignore the fact that political leaders already anticipate upcoming elections. Indeed, some commentators argue that popular influence on government may be part of the problem, not the solution.[47] Each public official answers to a somewhat different constituency. This would not be of any great importance if all constituencies were similar, in which case they would demand much the same thing from their political representatives. But America is a diverse country, and the constituencies of elected officials reflect that diversity. People have conflicting interests, and even more importantly, conflicting values. Even if hundreds of officials were personally in agreement—which is unlikely—their views of government programs and policies often would conflict because they have an electoral incentive to represent the views of the constituencies that elect them.

An incentive is anything someone values: Usually, we think of money or some material object. Businesses offer commissions as an incentive to their salespersons. Professional athletes' contracts contain performance incentives, such as bonuses for making the all-star team. When it comes to politics, however, of primary importance is the **electoral incentive**: the desire to be elected and reelected.

To say that an important political incentive is electoral does not mean that election is an end in itself, although it is for some. A pollster who advised the president during his first term in office told one of his colleagues that "Clinton tacks to the right when the wind is blowing right. Then he tacks to the left when it is blowing left . . . But he always knows his ultimate destination." When asked what that destination was, the pollster replied, "Back to the White House for another four years." [48]

Virtually every elected official is subjected to such cynical allegations, even though none of them, Clinton included, is as guilty as charged. The simple fact is that, even for officials who genuinely want nothing more than to serve their fellow citizens, election is a prerequisite. Unless elected, politicians are just ordinary citizens. For this reason alone, electoral incentives are an important—sometimes the most important—motivation for their behavior.

Governmental decisions require agreement among many different public officials representing distinct constituencies. It is impossible for decisions to be reached

■ **electoral incentive**
Desire to obtain or remain in an elected office.

Is Constitutional Reform Necessary?

One of the most important tensions in democratic political thought is that between responsiveness and efficiency. Because people disagree, a government that is highly responsive to the wishes of individual citizens is unlikely to solve problems quickly and efficiently. Alternatively, an efficient government is likely to run roughshod over the preferences of some citizens. Where to strike the balance is a perennial question. Some commentators think that in the contemporary United States the balance has swung too far in the direction of responsiveness. Governmental processes are open, and citizens have every oppor-tunity to make their wishes known. As a result, critics complain, govern-ment is slow and unable to deal effectively with the problems.

At the national level, a public interest group, The Committee on the Con-stitutional System, has proposed a series of con-stitutional amendments designed to ensure that elections produce one-party control of govern-ment, so that divided party control does not slow down the processes of government. Among other things, voters would not be allowed to vote for candidates of opposing parties, and terms of office would be coordinated, so that members of the House of Representatives would be elected for four years at the same time as the president, and senators would also be elected at the same time, either every four or every eight years. Following is an excerpt from a discus-sion of these constitu-tional reform proposals. What do you think? Is the Constitution out of date? Are reforms like these necessary?

Paul E. Peterson:
Most people say the Constitution is one of the most marvelous docu-ments for governing a nation ever prepared. You favor reforming one of its central components, the part that calls for the sep-aration of powers between the legislative and the executive

without resolving differences generated by these constituencies. Unlike chief execu-tives in the business world, presidents cannot fire members of Congress, governors cannot remove members of their state legislatures, and mayors cannot dismiss mem-bers of their city councils. Political leaders must either persuade their opponents or bargain for their support. In democratic politics the resolution of conflicts proceeds by negotiation, bargaining, and compromise.

With different constituencies, the electoral incentives of individual officials hin-der their ability to work together. Thus, some have argued that reforms that shift American politics in a still more popular direction may worsen problems rather than improve them. (See the first *Democratic Dilemma*, a special feature that appears regularly in this book.)

If reforms are to be effective, they must take into account political leaders' incentives. All too often reformers not only forget that premise but act on its oppo-site, substituting good intentions and rosy scenarios for realistic analyses. Informed appraisals of reform require the kind of realistic, incentive-based institutional analy-sis that the framers of the Constitution provided us. It is this kind of analysis that is provided in the chapters that follow.

branches. Why is there a need for this reform?

Lloyd N. Cutler:

Constant stalemate between the executive and legislative branches has left the government unable to take decisive action on any number of problems, of which the budget deficit may be the most severe example. The problem requires corrective measures that extend to some provisions of the Constitution.

If there were a four-year House term and all legislators had the same time horizon as the president of at least four years, then voters would think more in party terms than they do today.

Peterson:

Some people have said the division of power actually has some valuable aspects to it. When there is executive mismanagement or abuse of power, then we have got the legislative branch to act as a check. How is the kind of change that you are talking about likely to affect this system of checks and balances?

James L. Sundquist:

If you think that it is less dangerous to have an indecisive, ineffective government, one that can't act and make mistakes, then you would be in favor of the present system.

Cutler:

The real issue is whether you can govern this country in a complex era by a national town meeting in which 535 legislators and an elected president all make up their own minds, don't stick together, form different coalitions on every single issue, and essentially conduct themselves as if each is the button pushed by a national, state, or district opinion poll.

SOURCE: "Restoring Effective Government: A Conversation on Constitutional Reform with Lloyd N. Cutler, James L. Sundquist, and Paul E. Peterson, *Brookings Review* (Fall 1987: 18–23. To improve readability of excerpt, discussion has been rearranged and ellipses have been deleted.

The Benefits of an Electoral Democracy: A Pretty Good Government

As noted earlier, an irony of the new American democracy is that, while citizens have more opportunities than ever before to influence their government, Americans have been growing increasingly unhappy with it. In our view, a significant part of the sour national mood is difficult to justify on the basis of objective conditions. While there is no denying that serious problems and unresolved conflicts exist, there is more that is right with the United States than political commentary often suggests. Too often, political commentary uses unrealistic standards of evaluation.

An old maxim—frequently quoted by President Clinton—states that "the best is the enemy of the good." Any policy or institution will fall short when judged against some abstract standard of perfection. Perfection does not exist in the real world, but the wish for perfection in government and politics often makes people unhappy with their government and their leaders. Sometimes this is good, sometimes it is not. It causes the greatest harm when people abandon the "pretty good" for something worse. As the great American jurist, Learned Hand, once commented, "even though counting heads is not an ideal way to govern, it is at least better than breaking them."[49]

If American politics and government are so blameworthy, why are the governments of so many new democracies adopting institutions similar to those found in the United States? And why, throughout history and continuing today, have so many people left family and country behind to start anew in the United States?

Across the entire sweep of human history, most governments were controlled by one or a few. Many were tyrannical. A government that did not murder and steal from its subjects was about as good a government as people could hope for. And, unfortunately, tyrannical governments are not just a matter of ancient history. In recent years Americans have watched in horror as civil war or genocide has engulfed Cambodia, Iraq, Azerbaijan, Bosnia, Rwanda, Burundi, Chechnya, Albania, and Zaire. Official tyranny and worse remains a contemporary reality.

To be sure, Americans should not set too low a standard for their political life: No one would seriously argue that Americans should be satisfied just because their country has not dissolved into warring factions, as in Bosnia. But Americans should think seriously about the question of appropriate standards for evaluating their political system. Critics selectively cite statistics showing that the United States is worse than Germany in this respect, worse than Japan in that respect, worse than Sweden in some other respect, and so on. But can one conclude with confidence that any other government of a large country works better? We think the answer is no. This judgment should not discourage us from continuing to strive for a better government, but it should remind us that we are striving for levels of achievement never before reached by real governments responsible for large populations. Only when comparing the United States with other countries do we see that American democracy, for all its faults, has extraordinary capacities as well. Once the problems that America faces are placed in comparative perspective, it may turn out that the government created under the United States Constitution not only has a demonstrated resilience that has stood the test of time but also an impact on its citizens today in ways that compares favorably with the effects of the governments of most other countries.

Defenders of democracy often cite Winston Churchill's remark that, "democracy is the worst form of government except all those other forms that have been tried."[50] Churchill's observation applies with special force to the new American democracy, which carries this form of government toward its popular extreme. Citizens in the United States enjoy many things that citizens in other lands only dream of. Not only can American citizens vote more often, but Americans can also speak their minds more freely, find out more readily what their government is doing, and encounter a government less likely to discriminate against them on the basis of race, religion, gender, social status, sexual preference, or anything else.

Citizens of the United States have had a government that has a better record than any other government at protecting them against foreign aggression while usually avoiding unwise involvement in foreign conflicts. On average, citizens of the United States are wealthier than citizens of any other comparably large country. They are better housed, better fed, and better clothed. When compared with most other countries, they enjoy better communications, a superior national transportation system, better medical services, and safer work environments. Their physical environment is more protected against degradation. Even the annual fiscal deficits and the public debt that are such a current political concern compare favorably to the deficits and debts of most other industrial countries.

The United States is not the best at everything, of course. Economic inequality and poverty rates are higher in the United States than in countries with comparable living standards. More homeless people are visible on our city streets than in other industrial countries, a sign that the safety net has gaping holes, although it may also be a sign that poor people in the United States move about more freely than the poor of other nations.[51] More people are murdered and more are imprisoned in the United States than in almost any other industrial country. Just why the United States does poorly at some things and well at others will receive consideration in the pages that follow.

There is much that can be learned by looking at what other countries do well. The Europeans and the Japanese have more efficient public administrators. The Norwegians and Swedes have more effective welfare systems. Police officers in Britain and Japan do not carry guns, except under special circumstances. The Canadians have universal medical care at significantly lower cost than in the United States. The subway systems of Paris, Munich, and Tokyo are cleaner and more efficient than the subways of New York, Boston, and San Francisco. In the 1980s, the South Koreans and the Taiwanese enjoyed economic growth rates five or more times higher than the United States.

But while there is much to be learned from other countries, comparative analyses suggest that not much would be gained by substituting the institutions of any other country for the ones that the United States now has. Such comparisons reveal that the United States, for all its problems, has as good a government as exists anywhere, and a better one than most. Despite the dissatisfaction of many Americans with their government, they would be hard-pressed to find a superior alternative.

Chapter Summary

The new American democracy is more open to popular influence than ever before. It is characterized by a permanent campaign punctuated by numerous elections. Changing technologies have contributed to this situation, especially developments in mass communications and public opinion polling. Institutional changes have also contributed, especially the weakening of political parties and the proliferation of primary elections. Procedural changes, such as the disaggregation of the electoral calendar, also have contributed. In the midst of a permanent campaign, electoral considerations are never far from the minds of elected officials, who are more numerous today than ever before.

When balancing the costs and benefits of this movement toward a more popular democracy, it is not easy to decide which way the balance tips. When elections and electioneering become pervasive, it changes the way in which government does business: It is more difficult to plan for the long run, and it seems harder to find acceptable compromises. Yet the advantages of more widespread participation are clear as well. The needs of once excluded groups are now given at least partial consideration. The concerns of voters cannot be easily ignored. Problems are quickly converted into public issues. Altogether, American political institutions are still the envy of the world.

The theme outlined in this introductory chapter is elaborated throughout the remainder of the book. Of course, there is more to American government than elections and electioneering. In the ensuing chapters we follow the electoral theme of this chapter through the broad range of institutions and processes that make up American government, culminating in the policies that government produces. In the remainder of Part I we discuss the Constitution, the system of federalism, and the underlying cultural predispositions that provide the foundations for the country's political life. In Part II we discuss the voters, groups, parties, and news media that provide the material for government action. In Part III we turn to the central political institutions, Congress, the presidency, the bureaucracy, and the courts. Finally, in Part IV we discuss a broad range of public policies, including civil liberties, civil rights, domestic policy, economic policy, and foreign policy.

Key Terms

aristocracy, pg. 13

constituency, pg. 15

democracy, pg. 13

direct democracy, pg. 13

electoral incentive, pg. 27

general election, pg. 7

government, pg. 11

initiative, pg. 7

oligarchy, pg. 13

permanent campaign, pg. 16

popular model of democracy , pg. 14

primary election, pg. 7

recall election, pg. 7

referendum, pg. 7

representative democracy, pg. 14

responsible model of democracy, pg. 14

single-issue voter, pg. 24

Suggested Readings

Blumenthal, Sidney. 1982. *The Permanent Campaign.* New York: Simon & Schuster. Describes the electioneering side of the new American democracy.

Chubb, John, and Paul Peterson, eds. 1989. *Can the Government Govern?* Washington, DC: Brookings. Collection of essays on problems of governing a democracy that is moving in the popular direction.

Cronin, Thomas. 1989. *Direct Democracy: The Politics of Initiative, Referendum, and Recall.* Cambridge, MA: Harvard. The most up-to-date study of direct democracy in the United States. Takes a generally positive view.

Dahl, Robert. 1961. *Who Governs?* New Haven: Yale University Press. Though a specific study of New Haven, Connecticut, the book shows more generally how elections shape power and influence.

Downs, Anthony. 1957. *An Economic Theory of Democracy.* New York: Harper. Seminal theoretical discussion of how elections shape the activities of voters, candidates, parties, and interest groups.

Key, V. O. Jr. 1964. *Politics, Parties and Pressure Groups.* 5th ed. New York: Thomas Crowell. Dated but still definitive text on parties and interest groups.

King, Anthony. 1996. *Running Scared: Why Politicians Spend More Time Campaigning Than Governing.* New York: Free Press. Provocative study by a British political scientist who shows how elections shape contemporary American politics.

Lowi, Theodore. 1969. *The End of Liberalism.* New York: Norton. Classic study of the way in which groups have gained power over government.

Mansbridge, Jane. 1980. *Beyond Adversary Democracy.* New York: Basic Books. Compares alternative understandings of democracy.

Marone, James A. 1990. *The Democratic Wish.* New York: Basic Books. Brilliant historical analysis that shows how Americans have long tried to cure the ills of democracy by extending citizen participation.

Schattschneider, E. E. 1960. *The Semi-sovereign People.* New York: Holt, Rinehart & Winston. Classic analysis that explains why elections do not ensure equal political influence.

Stanley, Harold, and Richard Niemi. 1995. *Vital Statistics on American Politics.* 5th ed., Washington, DC: CQ Press, 1995. Indispensable source of facts and figures about American government and politics.

Tocqueville, Alexis de. 1945. *Democracy in America,* Vol. I and II, Philips Bradley, ed. New York: Alfred Knopf. Nineteenth-century French observer's insightful interpretation of the democratic experiment in the United States.

2

establishing a constitutional democracy

HOUGH REVERED TODAY,
the United States Constitution,
when presented to the voters for
their approval in 1787, was not
immediately popular everywhere.
When asked to give the State of
Virginia's assent to the Constitution, elected delegates to the
state's ratifying convention heard

35

an intense, powerful debate among some of the country's greatest political figures. Cried Patrick Henry, the eminent, if erratic, American patriot, "Before the meeting of the late Federal Convention at Philadelphia [where the Constitution was written] . . . a general peace, and a universal tranquility prevailed in this country;—but since that [meeting people have become] exceedingly uneasy and disquieted." Escalating the rhetoric, Henry shouted: "I conceive the republic to be in extreme danger. . . . Here is a revolution as radical as that which separated us from Great Britain. . . . Our rights and privileges are endangered, and the sovereignty of the States [are] relinquished. . . . The rights of conscience, trial by jury, liberty of the press. . . all pretensions to human rights and privileges are rendered insecure, if not lost."[1]

When fellow Virginian James Madison heard these words, he privately questioned Henry's motives. Madison was the one person who, more than any other, had designed the Constitution, and he was extremely concerned that Henry's opposition could doom its ratification. Writing to a friend, he suggested that Henry was opposing the Constitution so that he could create a separate southern nation: "I have for some time considered him as driving at a Southern Confederacy."[2]

Publicly, Madison replied to those criticizing the Constitution by arguing that the proposed government, far from endangering the people's freedom, would protect them from a tyranny imposed by a particular group or faction. "Among the numerous advantages promised by a well-constructed Union, none deserves to be more accurately developed than its tendency to break and control the violence of faction." Majority faction was especially dangerous, Madison said, because the majority could easily suppress minority dissent. The Constitution, he said, would prevent majority factions by dividing power between the state and national governments. It further divided national power among Congress, the president, and the judiciary, making it extremely difficult for any faction to oppress the rest. Madison thought that, in fighting factions, the very size of the country was a "most palpable advantage." He persuasively claimed: "The influence of factious leaders may kindle a flame within their particular states, but will be unable to spread a general conflagration through the other states." Swayed by the arguments of Madison and his allies, the delegates to the Virginia convention rejected Henry's argument and ratified the Constitution.[3]

n this chapter we shall show that, in order to win public acceptance, the Constitution was designed to appeal to those who were asked to ratify it. The chapter will also discuss the way in which the Constitution built upon the country's previous experience as British colonies, how the document expressed and consolidated the ideals expressed during the Revolutionary War, and how it applied well-known British political theories to American circumstances. Because the Constitution succeeded in these respects, it was ratified by delegates to state conventions by voters in what essentially was the country's first national election.

The First National Election

The very foundation of the U.S. government, then, is the product of an election in each of the thirteen original states. The nation's basic governing document, the **Constitution**, was drafted in the summer of 1787 at a convention held in Philadelphia. The Constitution took effect only after it had been approved at state ratifying conventions in nine of the original thirteen states.

Voters in 1787 were receptive to political reform. In the four years since the end of the Revolutionary War, the country had suffered an emotional letdown. Many blamed the **Articles of Confederation**, the United States's first basic governing document (1781–1789) and forerunner to the Constitution. Yet ratification of the Constitution was hardly inevitable. Victory was achieved only because the **Federalists**, those who wrote and campaigned on behalf of the ratification of the Constitution, provided strong leadership, mobilized voters, sidestepped obstacles, and crafted powerful arguments in favor of ratification.

The Federalists offered an anxious public not only a new constitution but the return of its revolutionary leader, General George Washington. Washington chaired the Constitutional Convention and was expected to become the first president. Other prominent Revolutionary War figures also attended the convention. Benjamin Franklin, the diplomat who had secured France as an ally and now 81, served as the quiet-spoken senior citizen. James Madison, a key member of the Continental Congress, provided intellectual leadership. Alexander Hamilton, a hero at Yorktown, emerged as a rising star during the New York ratification campaign.

The **Anti-Federalists**, those who opposed ratification of the Constitution, lacked a national leader. The one man who could have galvanized the opposition, Thomas Jefferson, author of the Declaration of Independence, was now serving in Paris as Minister to France. He expressed doubts about the absence of a Bill of Rights but otherwise remained aloof from the debate.

The Anti-Federalists thought the Constitution could be voted down in any one of the thirteen state legislatures. However, they were taken by surprise. The convention delegates, instead of following the old rules, made up a new one. They wrote into the new Constitution a provision saying that it would take effect as soon as nine states agreed. They also provided for ratification not by state legislatures but by elected delegates at ratifying conventions.

With energy and organization on their side, the Federalists won the first rounds easily. Conventions in four of the smaller states—Delaware, New Jersey, Georgia, and Connecticut—ratified the document by an overwhelming vote within four months of its signing in September 1787.[4] With Ben Franklin's prestige and a few strong-arm tactics, Pennsylvania also quickly approved. Massachusetts signed on as well, after getting Federalists to promise to add a Bill of Rights. By the end of 1788, Federalists had persuaded eleven of the thirteen states to ratify the Constitution, and George Washington was elected president in February 1789 (see Election Connection). North Carolina ratified later that year. Rhode Island, the smallest state, finally gave its grudging approval on May 29, 1790 (see Table 2.1).

At the time the Constitution was adopted, the United States was not a modern democracy. For example, only male property owners could vote in the election of delegates to the ratifying convention. Yet the provisions in the Constitution had to win the approval of a cross-section of these voters. Those who wrote the Constitu-

Constitution
Basic governing document for the United States.

Articles of Confederation
The United States' first basic governing document (1781–1789) and forerunner to the Constitution.

Federalists
Those who wrote and campaigned on behalf of the ratification of the Constitution.

Anti-Federalists
Those who opposed ratification of the Constitution.

George Washington Is Elected as First President

George Washington, appearing concerned but regal, at his inauguration as first president of the United States.

The first presidential election was extremely dull. No issues arose and no campaign allegations were made; the vote was unanimous. Yet the votes cast by the Electoral College on February 4, 1789, may have been as important as any ever cast. The election of George Washington as the nation's first president got the country off to a good start.

Unanimity was certainly an advantage, because the election process itself created many questions. In only five states did the voters choose the electors. Electors in two states—Rhode Island and North Carolina—did not vote because the states had yet to ratify the Constitution. The New York legislature, still opposed to the Constitution, refused to pick any electors. In New Jersey the electors were designated by the governor and his council. In four other states the electors were chosen by the legislature.

Yet virtually everyone was pleased with the new president. Though a great war hero, he had always deferred to the Continental Congress. As a former member of the Virginia colonial legislature, he did not disdain politics. Because he was both a speculator in western lands as well as a slave owner (known for his generous treatment of those who worked for him), he was acceptable to both northern and southern states.

SOURCE: Stanley Elkins and Eric McKitrick, *The Age of Federalism* (Oxford University Press, 1993); Thomas A. Lewis, *For King and Country: The Maturing of George Washington, 1748–1760* (New York: HarperCollins, 1993).

tion had to be sensitive to regional differences, immediate governmental needs, and inherited political traditions. And the country's political traditions, rooted in colonial practice but transformed by the revolutionary war experience, were especially significant.

TABLE 2.1

Voting of Delegates at Constitutional Ratifying Conventions.
Article VII provided that "The Ratification of the Conventions of nine States, shall be sufficient for the Establishment of this Constitution."

States (in order of ratifying)	Date	Yes	No
Delaware	Dec. 7, 1787	30	0
Pennsylvania	Dec. 11, 1787	46	23
New Jersey	Dec. 18, 1787	38	0
Georgia	Jan. 2, 1788	26	0
Connecticut	Jan. 9, 1788	128	40
Massachusetts	Feb. 6, 1788	187	168
Maryland	Apr. 26, 1788	63	11
South Carolina	May 23, 1788	149	73
New Hampshire	June 21, 1788	57	47
Virginia	June 25, 1788	89	79
New York	July 26, 1788	30	27
North Carolina	Nov. 21, 1789	194	77
Rhode Island	May 29, 1790	34	32

SOURCE: Lauren Bahr and Bernard Johnston, ed., *Collier's Encyclopedia* (New York: P. F. Collier, 1992), Vol. 7, p. 239.

The Colonial Experience with Democracy

Though the United States would become the world's first large, stable democracy, no sign of democracy is to be found in the first British plans for government in America. (See Figure 2.1 for dates of important steps toward democratization.) At the time Queen Elizabeth encouraged Sir Walter Raleigh to explore America in 1584, British rulers claimed to govern by **divine right**, a doctrine stating that God selects the sovereign for the people. Queen Elizabeth delegated her authority over the Colony of Virginia to Raleigh. But just a few years after the first permanent settlement in Jamestown, Virginia, a representative assembly was formed. Relations between the settlers and the company that owned Raleigh's charter grew so strained that the king withdrew the charter. Virginia became a **royal colony**, one governed by the king's representative upon the assembly's advice.

A small group of religious dissenters, now remembered as the Pilgrims, intended to sail to Virginia in 1620. When their ship, the *Mayflower*, was blown off course and arrived in what is now Provincetown, Massachusetts, the Pilgrims reached American shores without a clear governmental framework. The Pilgrims, rejecting the divine right of kings, believed that individuals were to decide for

divine right
Doctrine that says God selects the sovereign for the people.

royal colony
Colony governed by the king's representative upon the advice of an elected assembly. See proprietary colony.

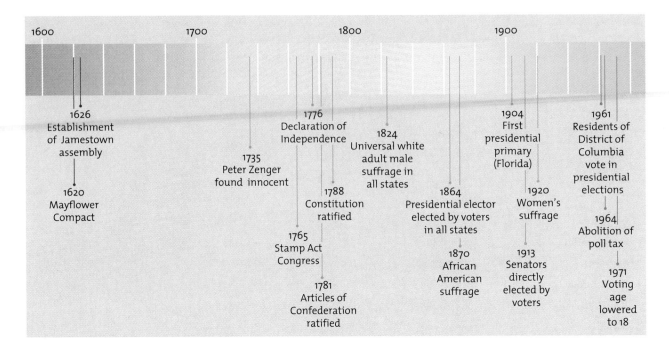

FIGURE 2.1

Key Points in the Democratization of the United States

Timeline entries:

1626 Establishment of Jamestown assembly

1620 Mayflower Compact

1735 Peter Zenger found innocent

1765 Stamp Act Congress

1781 Articles of Confederation ratified

1776 Declaration of Independence

1788 Constitution ratified

1824 Universal white adult male suffrage in all states

1864 Presidential elector elected by voters in all states

1870 African American suffrage

1904 First presidential primary (Florida)

1920 Women's suffrage

1913 Senators directly elected by voters

1961 Residents of District of Columbia vote in presidential elections

1964 Abolition of poll tax

1971 Voting age lowered to 18

■ **Mayflower Compact**
First document in colonial America in which the people gave their expressed consent to be governed.

■ **proprietary colony**
Colony governed either by a prominent English noble or by a company. See royal colony.

■ **colonial assembly**
Lower legislative chamber elected by male property owners in a colony.

■ **colonial council**
Upper legislative chamber appointed by British officials, upon the recommendation of the governor.

themselves on both religious and political matters. Their first political decision is still revered as the very beginning of the democratic experiment in America. Before leaving the ship the Pilgrims signed the **Mayflower Compact**, the first document in colonial America in which the people gave their expressed consent to be governed. The Pilgrims promised to "covenant and combine ourselves together into a civil Body Politick, for our better Ordering and Preservation." The principle that government was by the people's consent was thus established from the very beginning of colonial settlement.[5]

GOVERNANCE OF THE COLONIES

As European settlement on the American continent grew apace, so did issues of politics and governance. Many colonies were initially organized as **proprietary colonies**, governed either by a prominent English noble or by a company. Settlements organized by companies, such as the Jamestown colony, were founded almost exclusively for economic gain, including the search for gold. But several of the most successful colonies were, like the Pilgrims' settlement in Massachusetts, or the Maryland colony established for Catholics by Lord Baltimore, founded as places for the practice of religious beliefs. The more economically motivated of the proprietary colonies often ran into political difficulties and were eventually reorganized as royal colonies. On the eve of the Revolution, nine of the thirteen had become royal colonies.

In both proprietary and royal colonies, power was divided between the governor and a two-chamber legislature. The **colonial assembly** was the lower legislative chamber elected by male property owners in the colony. The **colonial council** was the upper legislative chamber appointed by British officials, upon the recommendation of the governor. Governors were appointed by either the proprietor or the king.

Governors could veto any legislation passed by the legislature, but usually, instead of vetoing legislation, they maintained support in the assembly by means of their

patronage power—the power to hand out jobs and benefits. Governors appointed as sheriffs, judges, justices of the peace, militia officers, magistrates, and clerks those whom they could count on for support. In Massachusetts, for example, 71 percent of the members of the 1763 assembly were simultaneously justices of the peace, giving "the Governors vast Influence."[6]

Though the governors' patronage influenced colonial assemblies, the assemblies had the power to levy taxes, and they used this authority to achieve broader influence, often obtaining financial control of the salaries of the governor and his appointed officials.[7] Meanwhile, the colonial councils lost position and prestige, gradually becoming little more than advisory bodies.

patronage
Appointing individuals to public office in exchange for their political support. Widely practiced in the eighteenth and nineteenth centuries and continues to present day.

VOTING QUALIFICATIONS

If the assemblies were gaining control over colonial affairs, this did not mean they were democratic in the modern sense of the word. From the very beginning, women, slaves, and indentured servants were excluded from the voting rolls. Even male white voters usually had to meet certain property qualifications: In Virginia they had to own 25 acres and a house. In Maryland and Pennsylvania, voters needed to be worth 50 acres or 40 pounds. By 1750, these qualifications disenfranchised as much as one-quarter to one-half of the male population (see table 2.2).[8]

In sum, the foundations for the American democratic experiment were established during the colonial era. Although suffrage was restricted to male property owners, elections made a difference. Elected colonial assemblies acquired the power to tax and spend. Further, colonial leaders developed the skills necessary to bargain with one another and build public support for common objectives. For example, Thomas Jefferson won both public respect and election to the Virginia assembly after persuading the farmers of his community to work together and clear the Rivanna River, making it navigable for their common benefit.[9]

TABLE 2.2

Voting Qualifications by Colony at the Time of the Revolution

Colony	Qualifications
Massachusetts	Male, 21, freeholder
New Hampshire	Male, 21, except paupers
Rhode Island	Male, 21, free of the company
Connecticut	Male, 21, freeholder, civil in conversation
New York	Male, 21, freeholder or renter, 6 months residence
New Jersey	Male, 21, freeholder, 1 year residence
Pennsylvania	Male, 21, taxpayer, 2 year residence
Virginia	Male, 21, freeholder
Maryland	Male, 21, freeholder, 1 year residence
North Carolina	Male, 21, freeholder, 1 year residence
South Carolina	Male, white, 21, taxpayer, freeholder, 2 year residence
Georgia	Male, 21, taxpayer, 6 months residence.

SOURCE: Robert J. Dinkin, *Voting in Revolutionary America: A Study of Elections in the Original Thirteen States, 1776–1789* (Westport, CT: Greenwood Press, 1982); Robert J. Dinkin, *Voting in Provincial America: A Study of Elections in the Thirteen Colonies, 1689–1776* (Westport, CT: Greenwood Press, 1977).

Spread of Democratic Ideals During the Revolutionary War

The democratic practices that began during the colonial period were reinforced by the struggle for independence.[10] Democracy suddenly had to be defended against the power of the king. The revolutionary struggle began with opposition to a tax, quickly swelled into a question of rights and representation, and finally led to a Declaration of Independence cast in language that would shape American politics for decades to come.

TAXATION WITHOUT REPRESENTATION

Though the road to independence would lead to the articulation of democratic ideals, it began as a tax revolt. The British government thought it quite reasonable to ask the colonial people to help pay for the cost of military protection from attacks by both French and Spanish troops and by indigenous tribes. To help pay for quartering British troops in America, the British government announced in 1765 that it was about to impose a **stamp tax**, which required that people purchase a small stamp to be affixed to pamphlets, playing cards, dice, newspapers, and marriage licenses and other legal documents. To the British, the stamp tax seemed perfectly reasonable, and it was smaller than the one they themselves paid. But to the colonists, who had never before paid a direct tax, it was an outrageous imposition by King George III on a free people.

Colonial leaders opposed what they said was **taxation without representation**, the levying of taxes by a government in which the people are not represented by their own elected officials. To organize their protest, nine colonies sent delegates to a **Stamp Act Congress**, which became the first political organization that brought together leaders from throughout the colonies.

The Stamp Act Congress gave the clearest expression to the American demand for representative government. One of its resolutions boldly proclaimed "that the only Representatives of the People of these Colonies are Persons chosen therein by themselves, and that no Taxes . . . can be Constitutionally imposed on them, but by their respective Legislature."[11] This insistence on "Rights and Liberties" was ignored in Britain, but in Boston a group of citizens calling themselves the "Sons of Liberty" hung in effigy the city's proposed tax collector. They then looted his home and that of the lieutenant governor for good measure. As violence spread throughout the colonies, tax collectors resigned their positions, others refused to take their places, and colonial assemblies banned the importation of English goods, making homespun clothes fashionable. Patrick Henry, one of the more rambunctious members of the Virginia assembly, shouted, "Caesar had his Brutus; Charles the First his Cromwell; and George the Third ['Treason!' cried the speaker of the assembly]— *may profit by their example. If this be treason, make the most of it.*" In the face of a tax revolt inspired by such rhetoric, the Stamp Act became quite unenforceable, and within a year Parliament repealed the legislation.[12]

The British ignored the American demands for representation. They also unwisely replaced the stamp tax with a tax on tea, arousing passions even further. Colonists were urged on by antitax groups and such leaders as John Hancock and Samuel Adams, who began calling themselves **Patriots**, a political group defending

stamp tax
Passed by Parliament in 1765, it required people in the colonies to purchase a small stamp to be affixed to legal and other documents.

taxation without representation
Levying of taxes by a government in which the people are not represented by their own elected officials.

Stamp Act Congress
A meeting in 1765 of delegates from nine colonies to oppose the Stamp Act; the first political organization that brought leaders from several colonies together for a common purpose.

Patriots
Political group defending colonial American liberties against British infringements.

American liberties against British infringements. In 1773 many Patriots organized the Boston Tea Party, a nighttime frolic in which they dumped shiploads of tea into the city's harbor. Outraged at such law-breaking, Parliament punished the Bostonians by shutting down democratic institutions in the Massachusetts colony. It withdrew the colony's charter, closed its General Assembly, banned town meetings, blockaded the Boston harbor, and strengthened the armed garrison stationed in the city.

THE CONTINENTAL CONGRESSES

The Patriots responded by calling, in 1774, the **First Continental Congress**, the first quasi-governmental institution that spoke for nearly all the colonies. Attended by delegates from twelve of the colonies, the Continental Congress issued a statement of rights and called for a boycott of British goods, a measure the Patriots hoped would weaken the British economy.

To put down the incipient insurrection, British soldiers marched out of Boston harbor on April 19, 1775, in search of weapons hidden in the nearby countryside. Warned by Paul Revere that the British redcoats were coming, six hundred Patriots fired shots at Concord that Ralph Waldo Emerson would later claim were "heard round the world." Certainly, word of the shots spread throughout the colonies, even to the Virginia assembly, where Patrick Henry cried, "Give me liberty, or give me death." Delegates from thirteen colonies went to Philadelphia to participate in the **Second Continental Congress**, the political authority that, beginning in 1775, directed the struggle for independence. On July 4, 1776, the Continental Congress proclaimed a **Declaration of Independence**, the document asserting the political independence of the United States of America from Great Britain. For seven long years the Patriots struggled against British soldiers to defend their declaration of independence. The **Tories**, who opposed independence, lost their property and were imprisoned or chased from the colonies—some 80 thousand fleeing to London, Nova Scotia, or the West Indies. In 1783 the British recognized American independence in the Treaty of Paris.

One of the infamous revenue stamps that fired colonists' opposition to the tax imposed on the American people by the Stamp Act of 1765. This particular two-pence stamp appeared on an almanac.

Theory of Rights and Representation

The democratic experiment had officially begun, with the new nation committing to government by the people. Americans transformed colonial practice into a political doctrine stating that government leaders, if they are to be obeyed, must be chosen in elections.

THE DECLARATION OF INDEPENDENCE

No single document better expresses the democratic spirit that animates American politics than the Declaration of Independence. Written mainly by Thomas Jefferson, the document both denounced King George III and expressed the country's commitment to certain democratic truths. The Declaration asserts that God gave people the "right to life, liberty and the pursuit of happiness." To preserve those rights, the people form a government. But the people's consent is given on the condition that the ruler safeguard certain inalienable rights. If a king violates these rights, the people may and should form a new government.

■ **First Continental Congress**
The first quasi-governmental institution that spoke for nearly all the colonies (1774).

■ **Second Continental Congress**
Political authority that directed the struggle for independence beginning in 1775.

■ **Declaration of Independence**
Document signed in 1776 declaring the United States to be a country independent of Great Britain.

■ **Tories**
Those who opposed independence from Great Britain.

We hold these truths to be self-evident that all men are created equal, that they are endowed by their Creator with certain unalienable Rights, that among these are Life, Liberty and the pursuit of Happiness. That to secure these rights, Governments are instituted among Men, deriving their just powers from the consent of the governed, That whenever any Form of government becomes destructive of these ends, it is the Right of the people to alter or to abolish it, and to institute new Government, laying its foundation on such principles and organizing its powers in such form as to them shall seem most likely to effect their Safety and Happiness. . . .

When a long train of abuses and usurpations, pursuing invariably the same Object evinces a design to reduce them under absolute Despotism, it is their right, it is their duty, to throw off such Government, and to provide new Guards for their future security. . . ."

SOURCE: Declaration of Independence.

AMERICAN POLITICAL THINKING

The Declaration of Independence "epitomizes and summarizes" a train of political thought that originated in England.[13] By the time of the revolution, the notion that kings had a divine right to rule had already been discarded by serious political thinkers. In its place, three principles had already been established in British political theory, (1) government is by the consent of the governed; (2) power should be divided among separate institutions; (3) citizen rights must be protected. Each theoretical development would shape the writing of the Constitution.

CONSENT OF THE GOVERNED   As early as 1651, Thomas Hobbes, England's greatest political theorist, said that kings governed not by divine right but by the consent of the governed. People form a government, because without a government they live in a state of nature in which there is a "war of all against all." Without a government, everyone must become a criminal simply to avoid being a victim. Life becomes "nasty, brutish and short." Hobbes argued that only a sovereign king having absolute power can prevent the war of all against all. If power is divided among more than one person, conflict among them becomes inevitable.[14]

SEPARATED POWER   Hobbes was ruthlessly coherent. Accept his premise that individuals are selfish and shortsighted, and his conclusion that the people readily consent to be ruled by an absolute sovereign seems almost inevitable. But the English, more pragmatic than consistent, shunned Hobbes's ruthless defense of absolute kingly power in favor of a softer argument for mixed government as set forth forty years later by John Locke. Though Locke said Hobbes was correct in saying government must have the consent of the people, Locke did not think it had to be unified in the hands of a king.[15] Instead, he argued that governmental power took three different forms, each requiring a different institution: legislative, executive, and judicial. A country's constitution should create a **separation of powers**, a system of government in which different institutions exercise the various components of governmental power. Locke thought each institution should be under the control of a different element of society, as follows:

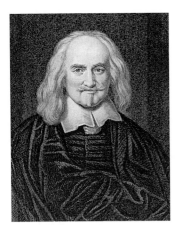

Thomas Hobbes (1588–1679) held that humans are by nature warlike and selfish. His treatise Leviathan held that the only way to maintain human society was for individuals to consent to rule by a single, all-powerful leader or government.

■ **separation of powers**
A system of government in which different institutions exercise different components of governmental power.

1. *Legislative power*, the making of law, to be exercised by two chambers of the legislature, the upper controlled by the aristocracy and the lower beholden to the people.

2. *Executive power*, the enforcement of law, to be exercised by the king.

3. *Judicial power*, the application of law to particular situations, exercised by independent judges chosen by the upper chamber.

Great political theorists often come to conclusions that differ but little from existing governmental practice. So it was with John Locke, who set forth a theory that closely resembled English government. England had a legislature or parliament consisting of two chambers—the House of Lords (representing the aristocracy) and the House of Commons (representing the people). Executive power was exercised by the king. The House of Lords appointed the judges.

Cynics have said that the English discovered Locke's wisdom before he set it down on paper. More accurately, Locke's genius consisted of making theoretical sense of English practice, giving the English a way of reflecting upon and defending a constitutional arrangement that had evolved haphazardly over many centuries.

A MORE PARTICIPATORY DEMOCRACY Not long after Locke wrote, British practice changed. Power, instead of being separated among the three branches, was concentrated in a small group of ministers drawn from parliament but appointed by the king. The system was held together more by patronage and corruption than by a balance of power among separated institutions.[16]

This patronage-based system provoked intense opposition from a group known as **Whigs**, who developed a countertheory of citizen rights and representation. The most important political thinker among the Whigs was James Harrington. In place of parliamentary control over a great nation, Harrington favored small republics that would protect individual freedoms. In place of patronage and connections, he preferred virtuous citizens elected to public offices for short periods of time. In place of an aristocracy of birth, he recommended a natural aristocracy in which ordinary citizens would choose leaders from the most noble among them.[17]

Although Harrington and other Whigs advanced a more participatory doctrine of rights and representation than previous theories, they did not embrace political participation by all citizens. Prevailing thought was that only male property owners had the necessary virtues to be good citizens of the republic.

Whig criticism of the British government made sense to many American colonials. The rough equality of colonial America stood in sharp contrast to the court intrigues in London. The rising colonial leaders thought of themselves as a natural aristocracy distinct from the inherited nobility in Britain. The more Parliament imposed taxes and interfered in colonial affairs, the more apparent became English corruption. The more the English government insisted on the ultimate sovereignty of the king, the more obvious it became to Americans that taxation without representation was illegitimate.

The Whig theory of rights and representation was explicated forcefully in *Common Sense*, written by Thomas Paine.[18] The book, read by 20 percent of the American population in the months before the Declaration of Independence, declared kingship to be "the most bare-faced falsity ever imposed on mankind." Instead of contributing to peace, as Hobbes had said, a hereditary monarchy "makes against it." Peaceful government is better achieved by representatives "who . . . have the same concerns at stake" as the people. If elections were frequent, representatives would establish a "common interest with every part of the community."

■ **Whigs**
Political opposition in eighteenth-century England that developed a theory of rights and representation.

Government after Independence

The Patriots in America made these participatory ideals their own during the seven years they fought for American independence from England. During the Revolutionary War, the colonies, now calling themselves "states," constructed governments of their own. For the most part, the thirteen new states pretty much kept their colonial institutions "with Parliament and the King left out."[19] But the pace of democratization picked up. Eight of the thirteen states eased the property qualifications for voters, and five lowered them for candidates for the lower house of the state legislature.[20] The percentage of state legislators who had great wealth declined, giving new political opportunities to those from more modest backgrounds (see Figure 2.2). Governors were elected annually in ten states, and the number of terms they could serve was limited in six states.[21]

Some felt the Whig theory of the rights of man should apply to women. John Adams's wife, Abigail, in a letter to her husband, who would become the nation's second president, proposed giving women their rights and liberties as well: "In the new code of laws . . . I desire you would remember the ladies, and be more generous and favorable to them than your ancestors. . . . If . . . attention is not paid to the ladies we are determined to foment a rebellion, and will not hold ourselves bound by any laws in which we have no voice, or representation." But many of those who espoused Whig theory were unwilling to come to terms with all of its implications. Even Abigail Adams's husband, John, argued against making any changes in voting qualifications: If changes are made, "there will be no end of it," John Adams said. "Women will demand a vote; lads from twelve to twenty-one will think their rights not enough attended to; and every man, who has not a farthing, will demand an equal voice."[22]

FIGURE 2.2

Those Who Were Wealthy in State Legislatures During the Revolution

SOURCE: Calculated from Willi Paul Adams, *The First American Constitutions: Republican Ideology and the Making of the State Constitutions in the Revolutionary Era* (Chapel Hill: University of North Carolina Press, 1980), pp. 295–311.

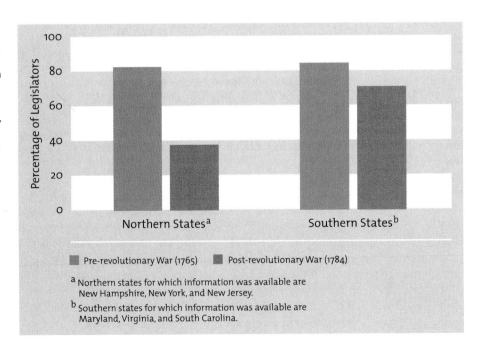

Pre-revolutionary War (1765)   Post-revolutionary War (1784)

a Northern states for which information was available are New Hampshire, New York, and New Jersey.

b Southern states for which information was available are Maryland, Virginia, and South Carolina.

The Articles of Confederation (1781–1789)

The new country needed, above all, a sense of national unity. In one of its more inspired decisions, the Second Continental Congress helped bring the nation together by appointing George Washington, a Virginia plantation owner, as commander of a continental army—even though most soldiers initially came from northern colonies. But while the Continental Congress was prompt to take the needed military steps, reaching constitutional decisions took much longer. The idea of creating a national government was so foreign to the colonial experience that it took the Continental Congress nearly five years after declaring independence to write and win ratification for the country's first constitution, the Articles of Confederation. (In the meantime, the Continental Congress did its best to govern by means of its own cumbersome procedures.)

The Articles of Confederation, proposed in 1775, finally ratified in 1781—eight years before the Constitution. Those eight years were marked by governmental instability.

PROVISIONS OF THE ARTICLES

The very name of the Articles of Confederation, ratified in 1781, suggests its extremely limited character. In the Articles own words, they amounted to little more than a "firm league of friendship" in which "each state retains its sovereignty, freedom and independence." Moreover, during the Confederation, Congress had limited powers. Although it could declare war, it could raise an army only by requesting states to muster their forces. Congress could not tax citizens directly; instead, it had to rely on voluntary contributions from the states. Congress could coin money, but it could not prevent states from also doing so. As a result, the country was flooded with many different currencies. Congress could negotiate tariffs with other countries, but so could the states. Most significantly, Congress could not regulate commerce among the states. Instead, states imposed trade barriers on one another. New York, for example, taxed New Jersey cabbage and Connecticut firewood.[23]

Scuffles broke out around the western Massachusetts country-side during the time of Shays' Rebellion (17), when impoverished farmers and revolutionary war veterans pressured the state court to suspend foreclosure on their property. The fact that Congress could not put down such rebellions reflected on the weakness of U.S. government under the Articles.

■ **Shays' Rebellion**
Uprising in western Massachusetts in 1786 led by revolutionary war captain Daniel Shays.

Members of Congress were elected annually by state legislatures. Each state, no matter how large or small, was equally represented. On all important issues, a super-majority of nine states had to agree before action could be taken.

The Articles of Confederation did not create a system of divided powers along lines Locke had envisioned. Its executive power, such as it was, consisted of a Committee of the States, to which each state appointed one delegate. This Committee could not decide any important issues, and nine of the thirteen delegates had to agree before the Committee could take any action at all. Most judicial functions were left to the states. Disputes between states were settled by ad hoc committees of judges.

GOVERNMENT UNDER THE ARTICLES

The unsatisfactory quality of the Articles became evident almost immediately. Virginia delegate James Madison came to see the need for a new constitution when he found it impossible, as a member of Congress, to keep states from issuing their own money. Trade among the states was impeded by constant quarrels over the relative worth of the coins of New York, Pennsylvania and Virginia.

Shays' Rebellion, an uprising in western Massachusetts in 1786 led by revolutionary war captain Daniel Shays, was especially disruptive. A group of impoverished, back-country farmers, unable to pay their taxes or mortgages, tried to intimidate the courts into forgiving their debts. Many prominent leaders felt that state governments were too weak to quell these kind of public uprisings. Most embarrassing, a group of ex-soldiers from the continental army descended upon Congress to obtain their rightful back pay. Members of the Congress appealed to the State of Pennsylvania for help, but when none was forthcoming they fled to Princeton College.

Though domestic unrest raised serious questions about political stability, threats from foreign countries were even more disturbing. The British disputed the boundary between its Canadian colonies and the United States. Also, the British navy dragooned U.S. seamen into service, claiming that anyone who spoke English must be British. The Spanish, in possession of Florida and the lands west of the Mississippi, claimed large segments of what is today Mississippi and Alabama (see Figure 2.3). Even France, a revolutionary ally, blocked U.S. trade with its islands in the West Indies and demanded repayment of money advanced during the revolution. Resolution of these disputes was complicated by the fact that Congress could not prevent states from engaging in their own negotiations with foreign countries.

The Constitutional Convention

None felt the deficiencies in the Articles more keenly than George Washington and James Madison. An avid speculator in land west of the Appalachian mountains, Washington was frustrated by the inability of the states to work together to build canals and roads that would help develop the country's interior. Madison despaired of Congress's inability to raise money.

Madison and other reformers met to discuss needed constitutional reforms in 1786 at what became known as the **Annapolis Convention**, but inasmuch as they

■ **Annapolis Convention**
1786 meeting to discuss constitutional reform.

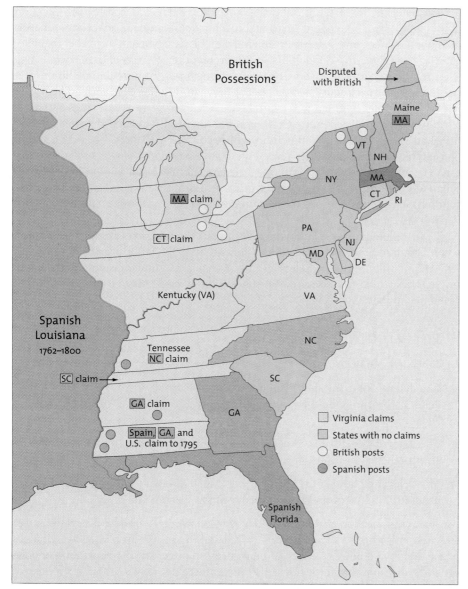

FIGURE 2.3

North America at the Time of the Writing of the Constitution.

SOURCE: Wesley, Edgar B., *Our United States: Its History in Maps.* (Chicago: Denoyer-Geppert Co., 1965), p.37.

represented only five states, they were unable to propose major constitutional changes. However, later that year, in the aftermath of Shays' Rebellion, Madison persuaded Congress to ask each state legislature to elect delegates to a convention in Philadelphia to consider possible amendments to the Articles of Confederation. Every state legislature but Rhode Island's agreed to do so.

For the most part, states sent political leaders who favored major constitutional change; most of those opposed to changing the Articles stayed away. Patrick Henry, when asked to be a delegate, refused, saying he "smelt a rat." True, ten delegates left before the Constitution was completed, and another three refused to sign the document, but the great majority of those in Philadelphia agreed that the national government needed to be strengthened.

The delegates to the Constitutional Convention did not constitute a cross-section of the population. The people who met in Philadelphia were bankers, merchants, plantation owners, and speculators in land west of the Appalachians.[24] Yet the delegates had not gone to Philadelphia just to protect the interests of their social class. They felt the country as a whole needed a stronger government that could provide political stability, effectively mediate conflicts among the states, and defend the nation from foreign influence.[25]

Nor were the delegates any single-minded caucus. Chosen by state legislatures, they had strong political connections within their home states. Coming from all parts of the United States, they represented different regions with conflicting interests. Two cleavages were paramount. Delegates from big states often found themselves disagreeing with delegates from small states. And delegates from the southern slave states opposed those from northern states, whose economies did not depend on slavery.

These differences were submerged during the opening weeks of the convention, when a spirit of unity and reform filled the Philadelphia hall. But as the four-month convention progressed, the delegates pulled back from some of the more far-reaching reforms and searched for compromises that would produce a document that could be ratified.[26]

THE VIRGINIA PLAN

Three general decisions were made at the very beginning of the convention.

■ The delegates agreed to hold their discussions behind closed doors. They knew that if debates were held in public, disagreements could be exploited by Anti-Federalists.

■ The delegates decided not to amend the Articles of Confederation but to write an entirely new constitution.

■ Virginia Plan
Constitutional proposal
supported by convention
delegates from large states.

■ The delegates chose as the basis for their initial discussions the **Virginia Plan**, the constitutional proposal supported by delegates from large states.

The Virginia Plan had been prepared by Madison (with Washington's active involvement) prior to the gathering in Philadelphia. It proposed massive changes in the design and powers of the national government, creating a separation of powers along the lines that John Locke had recommended. To win popular support for the new constitution, the Virginia Plan called for ratification by state convention delegates "expressly chosen by the people."[27]

Instead of a single Congress, Madison proposed two chambers. The lower chamber—the future House of Representatives—would be elected by the voters. The upper chamber—the future Senate—would be elected by state legislatures.

The Virginia Plan changed representation in Congress dramatically from the pattern existing under the Articles of Confederation. Instead of giving each state one vote, the number of representatives and senators depended on the size of a state's population. In short, under this plan, Virginia, Pennsylvania, and other more populous states had much more power than under the Articles.

The Virginia Plan also gave the national government vast powers far beyond those exercised by the old Congress. The new Congress could legislate on all matters that affect "the harmony of the United States" and could negate "all laws passed by the several states."[28] It could also use force to ensure that states fulfilled their duties.

According to the Virginia Plan, the weak executive power under the Articles was to be replaced by a president to be chosen by the legislature. The Supreme Court would have the authority to resolve disputes among individuals from different states, something that could not be done under the Articles of Confederation. The Virginia Plan received strong support from two of the most populous states—Virginia and Pennsylvania—as well as from states that expected to grow rapidly in population in the next few years—North Carolina, South Carolina, and Georgia.

THE NEW JERSEY PLAN

Delegates from smaller states, especially New Jersey and Delaware, became increasingly uneasy about the Virginia Plan, not so much because it gave too much power to the national government, but because they were afraid it would be dominated by the bigger states. Two weeks or so into the convention, these states offered an alternative design prepared by William Patterson that became known as the **New Jersey Plan**, the small-state proposal for constitutional reform.

The New Jersey Plan also separated powers into three branches, but instead of creating a House and Senate, it kept a one-chamber Congress in which each state had one vote. It also envisioned a more limited national government. Unlike the Virginia Plan, it did not grant Congress general legislative power. Instead it gave Congress specific powers, including the power to levy taxes on imported goods, the power to compel states to pay their share of taxes, and the power to regulate "trade & commerce with foreign nations" and among the states. The judicial branch, under the New Jersey Plan, could hear only specific types of cases, such as those involving treaties or foreigners.[29]

Despite these limitations, the New Jersey Plan still strengthened the national government well beyond what existed under the Articles. The supporters of the New Jersey Plan were not so much opposed to a stronger government as afraid that the big states would control it. As one delegate observed at the time, "Give New Jersey an equal vote, and she will dismiss her scruples, and concur in a National system."[30]

THE CONNECTICUT COMPROMISE

The convention nearly collapsed when a majority of the delegates rejected the New Jersey Plan. Delegates from the small states thought about leaving Philadelphia, killing all hope of successful ratification. The large states flirted with the idea of forming their own union, then using economic pressure to force small states to join. To calm the unsettled waters, Franklin proposed beginning each session with prayer, though the idea was rejected on the grounds that money to pay a chaplain was unavailable.

To cool the debate, issues were turned over to a committee controlled by moderates. The committee reported back a split-the-difference compromise offered by delegates from the middle-sized state of Connecticut. Proposing a Congress along the lines it is known today, the **Connecticut Compromise** created a House proportionate to population and a Senate in which each state was represented equally. Small states were placated by their strong representation in the Senate. The big states were mollified by the requirement that representation in the House of Representatives be proportionate to a state's size.

■ **New Jersey Plan**
Small-state proposal for constitutional reform.

■ **Connecticut Compromise**
Constitutional convention proposal that created a House proportionate to population and a Senate in which each state was represented equally.

THE CONNECTICUT COMPROMISE

The Connecticut Compromise was necessary in order for the Constitution to win ratification in both big and small states. The Compromise created a House of Representatives that represented states according to their population and a Senate in which each state had two senators.

States Ordered by Population	House of Representatives	Senate
Virginia	10	2
Massachusetts	8	2
Pennsylvania	8	2
Maryland	6	2
New York	6	2
Connecticut	5	2
South Carolina	5	2
New Jersey	4	2
North Carolina	4	2
Georgia	3	2
New Hampshire	3	2
Rhode Island	1	2
Delaware	1	2

SOURCE: Congressional Quarterly, *Guide to U.S. Elections*, 3rd ed. (Washington, DC: Congressional Quarterly, 1994), p. 359.

A Government of Separated Powers

Once the delegates accepted the Connecticut Compromise, they found it relatively easy to broker other differences between the Virginia and New Jersey Plans. Following the Virginia Plan they created a government with three branches, legislative, executive, and judicial, dividing powers among them. But consistent with the New Jersey Plan they limited the powers of all three branches.

CONGRESS

As called for in the New Jersey Plan, the convention delegates gave Congress a number of specific powers, including the powers to tax, coin money, regulate commerce, declare war and maintain an army (see Table 2.3). But to meet the concerns of the proponents of the Virginia Plan, they included the **necessary and proper clause**, which says that Congress has the power to do whatever is necessary to carry out its other powers. What is necessary and proper? Some thought it meant only what was absolutely essential. Other delegates thought it meant anything convenient and useful. The phrasing was ambiguous enough that all delegates could interpret the language to their own liking.

The delegates were also influenced by the Whig theory on rights and representation that had proved so powerful during the Revolutionary War. Following Whig theory, the Constitution said that members of the House of Representatives were to be chosen by the voters and to be subject to reelection every two years. Still, the democracy that was created was more of a responsible than a popular type (see Chapter 1). It departed from the Whig theory by not establishing a limit on the number of terms that could be served. The delegates modified Whig theory even further when it came to the Senate. They were to be elected not by voters but by state legislatures, and they were given a six-year term of office.

■ **necessary and proper clause**
Says Congress has the power to do whatever is necessary and proper to carry out its other powers.

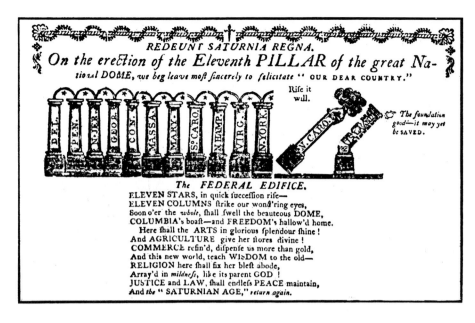

REDEUNT SATURNIA REGNA.

On the erection of the Eleventh PILLAR of the great Na-tional DOME, we beg leave most sincerely to felicitate " OUR DEAR COUNTRY."

Rise it will.

The foundation good—it may yet be SAVED.

The FEDERAL EDIFICE.

ELEVEN STARS, in quick succession rise—
ELEVEN COLUMNS strike our wond'ring eyes,
Soon o'er the *whole*, shall swell the beauteous DOME,
COLUMBIA's boast—and FREEDOM's hallow'd home.
Here shall the ARTS in glorious splendour shine !
And AGRICULTURE give her stores divine !
COMMERCE refin'd, dispense us more than gold,
And this new world, teach WISDOM to the old—
RELIGION here shall fix her blest abode,
Array'd in *mildness*, like its parent GOD !
JUSTICE and LAW, shall endless PEACE maintain,
And *the* " SATURNIAN AGE," *return again.*

At the time of this cartoon's publication, only eleven states had ratified the Constitution. The cartoonist eagerly awaited North Carolina ("Rise it will.") and Rhode Island ("The foundation good—it may yet be saved.") joining the new Union.

The delegates settled on a delicate political solution to the question of voter qualifications. They said states could establish their own eligibility requirements, except that anyone eligible to vote for the lower chamber of the state legislature must also be allowed to vote in elections for the House of Representatives. By wording the Constitution in this way, the delegates avoided changing state voting requirements but still guaranteed the vote to all those already eligible. This open-ended language also permitted the gradual, state-by-state extension of the right to vote to many excluded from the electorate in 1787.

TABLE 2.3

Constitutional Powers of Congress, Constitutional Limits on States

Congress Has the Power to:	States Have No Power to:
Declare War	Wage War unless attacked
Raise and support armies	
Lay and collect taxes and tariffs	Levy tariffs
Ratify treaties	Make treaties
Borrow money	
Regulate commerce among the states	
Coin money	Coin money
Establish post offices	
Issue patents and copyrights	

The Constitution also gives Congress the more general power . . .

"To make all Laws which shall be necessary and proper for carrying into Execution the foregoing Powers, and all other Powers vested by this Constitution in the [national] government."

SOURCE: U.S. Constitution, Article I. See Appendix, pp. 683–687.

THE EXECUTIVE

Some analysts have claimed that many convention delegates secretly harbored a desire to create an executive who had powers comparable to a British king.[31] But except for Alexander Hamilton, who actually made a proposal along these lines, the delegates were too practical to treat such an idea seriously. They knew that voters would reject out of hand a Constitution that threatened the return of anyone comparable to King George.

Instead, the Constitution keeps presidential power under tight congressional control (see Table 2.4). Presidents are made commander-in-chief of the armed forces, but only Congress can declare war. Presidents can call Congress into session and speak to Congress, but they cannot dismiss Congress nor prevent it from meeting. Presidents are given the power to veto congressional legislation, but Congress can pass it over their veto with a two-thirds vote.

■ **advice and consent**
Support for a presidential action by a designated number of senators.

Other presidential powers can be exercised only with senatorial **advice and consent**, support for a presidential action by a designated number of senators. For example, the president can sign treaties with foreign countries, but treaties can take effect only if two-thirds of the Senate gives its consent. Also, the president can appoint both judges and executive branch officers, but appointees have to be confirmed by a majority of the Senate.

The impeachment clause makes clear the president's ultimate dependence on political support from Congress. The House of Representatives can impeach the president for "high crimes and misdemeanors." If impeached, the president is tried in the Senate. If convicted by a two-thirds vote, the president is removed from office. Though no president has ever been convicted, Andrew Johnson avoided it by only one vote and Richard Nixon chose to resign in the face of almost certain impeachment and conviction.

THE ELECTORAL COLLEGE

Despite the fact that they gave presidents only limited powers, delegates to the Constitutional Convention found it extremely difficult to agree on a method of selection. Once again, the battle was between the big and small states. If the president were chosen by popular vote, big states would prevail because most people

TABLE 2.4

Congressional Checks on Presidential Powers

Presidential Powers	Congressional Checks
Make treaties	Two-thirds of Senate must ratify
Appoint judges and executive officers	Senate must confirm
May convene Congress	Congress must meet each year
Commander in chief	Congress declares war
Veto legislation	Two-thirds override by both chambers
Execute laws	Enact laws
Inform Congress	No check
Receive foreign ambassadors	No check
Pardon criminals	No check

SOURCE: U.S. Constitution, Articles I, II. See Appendix, pp. 687-689.

The Electoral College Compromise

Delegates to the convention found it difficult to agree on the best way of selecting the president of the United States. Big states wanted presidents chosen by a popular vote or by the House of Representatives. Small states wanted the president chosen by the Senate or by some process that would give each state the same vote. To win ratification by voters in both big and small states, some kind of compromise was needed.

The compromise they reached was a two-stage procedure sufficiently complicated that both sides could claim victory. But the procedure can result in the election of minority presidents.

Election Procedure:

First Stage:
Voters in each state choose as many electors as they have representatives and senators; president picked by majority of electors; if no candidate has majority, three top vote-getters go to second stage.

Gives Advantage to:
Big states

Second Stage:
Members of House of Representatives voted by state delegation; each delegation has one vote; must choose from top three candidates; winner must receive majority.

Gives Advantage to:
Small states

Problems:
Second-stage presidents may not have received the most popular votes and they may be picked as the result of bargaining, leading to charges that the president was corruptly chosen. Elections of Presidents Thomas Jefferson and John Quincy Adams, both selected at second stage, were marked by extreme conflict.

Even presidents selected by the Electoral College may have fewer popular votes than another candidate. Presidents Hayes and Harrison did not have a popular majority. President John Kennedy had only 100 thousand more votes than Richard Nixon but won the Electoral College by an overwhelming majority.

SOURCES: U.S. Constitution, Article II, sec 1.
See Appendix, pp. 687–688. Arthur M. Schlesinger, Jr., ed., *History of American Presidential Elections, 1789–1968*, Vol. 2 (New York: McGraw-Hill, 1971).

lived in big states. If the choice was made by the House of Representatives, big states would once again dominate. If the choice resided in the Senate, the small states would have extra clout.

The delegates finally agreed on a compromise that created the **Electoral College**, those chosen to cast a direct vote for president by a process determined by each state. The Electoral College was part of a two-stage procedure so complicated no one knew which side had won (see Election Connection). The first stage involves the selection of the Electoral College. Each state chooses the same number of electors as it has senators and representatives in Congress. (In addition, as a result of the passage of the Twenty-Third Amendment, the District of Columbia casts three votes.) If a candidate receives a **majority** (50 percent plus one) of the electoral vote, that person is elected president. For example, Bill Clinton in 1996 received 379 out of 538 electoral votes, a clear majority, reelecting him president for a second term. But if no candidate receives a majority in the Electoral College, the action moves to the House of Representatives. If for example the vote of the Electoral College had

Electoral College
Those chosen to cast a direct vote for president by a process determined by each state.

majority
50 percent plus one.

Should the Electoral College Be Reformed?

The Electoral College Is a Disaster Waiting to Happen

The Electoral College system tends to magnify tremendously the relative voting power of residents of the larger states—a thousand voters in Scranton, Pennsylvania, are far more important strategically than a similar number of voters in Wilmington, Delaware. This inequity also places a premium on the support of key political leaders in large electoral vote states. . . .

If no candidate receives an absolute majority of the electoral vote, the House of Representatives chooses the president from among the top three candidates. Is such an Electoral College deadlock likely to occur in terms of contemporary politics? And would the consequences likely be disastrous? A simple answer to both questions is yes.

It has been shown that, in 1960, a switch of fewer than 9,000 popular votes from Kennedy to Nixon in Illinois and Missouri would have prevented either man from receiving an Electoral College majority. The House of Representatives procedure, which would have followed, is an awkward relic of the compromises of the writing of the Constitution.

Under the present system, there is no assurance that the winner of the popular vote will win the election. If 9,245 votes had shifted to Ford in Ohio and Hawaii [in 1976], Ford would have been elected president with 270 electoral votes, despite Carter's 51 percent of the popular vote and margin of 1.7 million votes.

—Lawrence D. Longley, Professor, Lawrence University

The Electoral College: A Paradigm of American Democracy

The Electoral College is a paradigm of the American democracy because it is based on popular votes aggregated state by state: thus it is both democratic and federal. This outcome is fitting because our Constitution created a democratic federal republic. We are not, never have been, and were not intended to be, a simple democracy because a simply democracy is a form of tyranny—a majority tyranny. The founders fully understood majority tyranny, and they devoted their every effort to prevent it.

A runner-up president is possible, but it is very improbable. The real issue is the fact that the Electoral College system favors certain kinds of coalitions and harms others. But no electoral system is neutral; every system favors certain groups.

—Judith A. Best, Professor State University of New York at Cortland

SOURCE: Excerpted without ellipses from "A Parley: The Electoral College: A Paradigm of American Democracy," *This Constitution* (Fall 1986), no. 12, pp. 19–25.

been split three ways among Bill Clinton, Robert Dole, and Ross Perot, and none had received more than 50 percent of the electoral vote, then the election would have been decided in the House of Representatives. The last time this happened was in 1824.

The Constitution does not require that the members of the Electoral College be chosen by the voters. Instead, the manner of selecting electors was left up to the states. Constitutional silence on this key matter was not an accident. Some delegates thought the president should be elected by the people; others felt this could lead to tyranny. The convention compromised the question, as it did so many, by leaving the issue up to the states. Not until 1864 did the last state, South Carolina, give voters the power to vote directly for its electors (though by the 1820s electors were chosen by the voters in the great majority of states).[32]

Some think the Electoral College compromise has proven to be less of a success than the Connecticut Compromise. For example, in three elections, 1824, 1876, and 1888, the person winning the most popular votes was not selected president. Some scholars favor eliminating the Electoral College altogether, on the theory that the person receiving the most popular votes should win the election. Others think that the Electoral College, for all its faults, helps to maintain the two-party system and provides representation for both the states and the people (see Democratic Dilemma).

THE JUDICIAL COMPROMISE

Most convention delegates thought the country needed a Supreme Court to adjudicate conflicts among the states. They also found it fairly easy to agree that justices should be nominated for life-time positions by the president and confirmed by a majority of the Senate.

The delegates differed over whether the Supreme Court needed lower federal courts to assist them. Advocates of the Virginia Plan thought lower federal courts were needed because state courts "cannot be trusted with the administration of the National Laws."[33] Advocates of the New Jersey Plan said the state courts were sufficient. They also thought "the people will not bear such innovations."[34] The delegates compromised the issue by leaving it to Congress to decide whether lower federal courts were needed. The first Congress created a system of lower courts, whose essentials have remained intact to this day. The Court system is described in Chapter 15.

The delegates also seem to have disagreed on whether or not the Supreme Court should be given the power of **judicial review**, court authority to declare laws null and void on the grounds that they are unconstitutional. Although Madison's account of the debate over judicial review is sketchy, many delegates, it seems, favored judicial review as a check on the power of state legislatures. Yet when two delegates opposed judicial review, there is no record of anyone rising to its defense. Though scholars have puzzled over the lack of debate at the convention on an issue that would loom large in later years, the lack of debate is probably best explained by political expediency. Judicial review had provoked controversy in North Carolina and Rhode Island, and convention delegates avoided an issue that might endanger ratification.

Instead of calling for judicial review, convention delegates inserted into the Constitution an ambiguous phrase that has become known as the **supremacy clause**, which says the Constitution is the supreme law of the land, to which all judges are bound. To some, this phrase simply told state judges to be mindful of the Constitution when interpreting state laws. To others, it gave the Supreme Court the power to declare both state and federal laws unconstitutional. The issue would not be settled for another 20 years, when the Supreme Court interpreted the supremacy clause as giving the Court the power of judicial review over both federal and state laws.

> **judicial review**
> Court authority to declare laws null and void on the grounds that they are unconstitutional.

> **supremacy clause**
> Says the Constitution is the supreme law of the land, to which all judges are bound.

COMPROMISING ON THE SLAVE ISSUE

The delegates never seriously contemplated eliminating slavery under the Constitution, though one delegate said it was their moral duty to do so. The delegates knew that southern states would not ratify the Constitution if they abolished slavery. The debate over the slave question took other forms. Northerners wanted to end the international slave trade. Most southerners argued that the slave trade, however despicable, was necessary to fuel economic growth in the unsettled parts of the South. The two sides compromised by agreeing not to abolish the slave trade for another 20 years, and abiding by this provision, Congress waited until 1808 before taking that step.

Northern delegates did not want to count slaves when figuring state representation in the House of Representatives. Southerners thought they should be counted. The two sides came up with the expedient, if disreputable, **three-fifths compromise**, which counted slaves as "three-fifths" of a person. The clause identified slaves not by name but as "other persons." Failing to talk about slavery in explicit terms was yet another way of reaching compromise. Not until after the Civil War did the Fourteenth Amendment repeal the three-fifths clause.

North and South also split over tariffs. Northerners wanted to give Congress the right to impose tariffs on imports; southerners were afraid this would be used to protect northern manufacturing at southern expense. In exchange for the three-fifths compromise, southerners agreed to let Congress impose tariffs on foreign goods.

■ **three-fifths compromise**
When calculating representation in the House of Representatives, it counted slaves as three-fifths of a person; repealed by the Fourteenth Amendment.

The Bill of Rights

The delegates to the Constitutional Convention made one mistake so serious it nearly ruined their chances of securing ratification: They failed to include within the Constitution clauses that clearly protected the liberties of the people. It is not easy to see how the delegates to the Philadelphia Convention, who in other respects showed excellent political judgment, could have made such a serious political miscalculation. Ever since the Revolutionary War, the Whig concept of rights and representation had become part and parcel of American constitutional thinking. A month before Jefferson wrote the Declaration of Independence, with its ringing endorsement of the "right to life, liberty and the pursuit of happiness," the Virginia assembly had passed a Bill of Rights protecting free speech, the right of the propertied to vote, the right to a trial by jury, the right not to be compelled to testify against oneself, and other civil liberties.[35] Similar provisions were approved by statute or incorporated into the first constitutions adopted by most of the other states. Yet when Charles Pinckney offered a motion to guarantee freedom of the press at the Constitutional Convention, a majority voted the motion down—on the grounds that regulation of speech and press was a state responsibility.[36]

The convention majority may have been technically correct, but they failed to appreciate how powerfully the demand for the protection of civil liberties would resonate with the voters. The Constitution, to win popular acceptance, needed to express explicitly the Whig theory of rights and representation that the country had taken to heart during the Revolutionary war. When it failed to do so, Thomas Jefferson wrote from Paris that he thought a Bill of Rights needed to be added.

Eventually, the Federalists recognized their mistake. To win ratification in Massachusetts, Virginia, and New York, they promised to enact a **Bill of Rights** as a series of amendments to the Constitution that would guarantee civil liberties. Two states, North Carolina and Rhode Island, wanted to make sure the Federalists made good on their promise. Though they probably would have ratified the Constitution at some point simply to avoid becoming isolated states, they withheld their approval until after the first Congress fulfilled the Federalist promise to add a Bill of Rights.

■ **Bill of Rights**
The first ten amendments to the Constitution that protect individual and state rights.

James Madison (1751–1836)—along with Alexander Hamilton and John Jay, one of the original Federalists. Madison served as a representative in Congress from 1789 through 1797, as Thomas Jefferson's secretary of state from 1801 through 1808, and as fourth president of the United States from 1809 through 1817.

The Bill of Rights has played such a central role in the country's constitutional development that all of Chapter 16, on civil liberties, is devoted to its explication.

The Anti-Federalist–Federalist Debate

Although the absence of a Bill of Rights gave Anti-Federalists powerful ammunition for their assault on the Constitution during the ratification campaign, their critique of the document was more broadly based. Drawing on the Whig theory of rights and representation, they attacked the Constitution for laying the groundwork for a national tyranny. They said the shift in power from the states to the national government took power from the people. The number of representatives in Congress was too small to include a cross-section of citizens from all parts of the United States. Presidents could become virtual kings, because they could be reelected again and again for the rest of their lives. The reelection of senators and representatives would create a political aristocracy.[37]

To answer these Anti-Federalist arguments, three Federalists, Alexander Hamilton, James Madison, and John Jay, wrote a series of newspaper essays, now known as the *Federalist Papers*, which are generally regarded as the finest essays on American political theory ever written.[38] The authors argued that tyranny could come either from without or within the country. The external danger came from European countries, who were eager to divide the new nation into several parts so that each could be controlled. The Constitution would help prevent this division by creating a stronger national government that could defend the country.

Threats to liberty could also come from groups and factions within the country seeking to impose their will on others. The greatest threat to liberty came from a majority faction, because it could so easily impose its will on minorities. The authors of the *Federalist Papers* said the Constitution would prevent majority tyranny by creating a system of **checks and balances**, a division of governmental power into several branches by the Constitution, giving each branch the power to block the actions of the others. Power was split between the states and a national government. At the national level, power was separated among three branches, legislative, executive, and judicial. The legislative branch was further divided into two chambers, a Senate and

Federalist Papers
Essays written in support of the Constitution's ratification that have become a classic argument for the American constitutional system.

checks and balances
Division of power into several branches by the Constitution, giving each branch the power to block the actions of the others.

a House of Representatives. Each was elected in a different way, making it more difficult for any momentary majority to seize total power.

In retrospect, the Federalists seem to have had the better argument. The Federalists had a plan for the future; the Anti-Federalists had nothing to offer but the unsatisfactory status quo. When the Anti-Federalists claimed that the Constitution stripped the people of their rights and liberties, they relied on the not very convincing argument that the governments of large nations would trample the liberties of the people. The writers of the *Federalist Papers* analyzed the situation more accurately; by creating a system of checks and balances that divided power into different branches and different levels, and grounding each level in elections, the ambition of one politician would check that of others.

Amendments to the Constitution

The delegates to the Constitutional Convention, realizing the document they were writing was not perfect and that unforeseen circumstances could arise, discussed ways in which the Constitution might be amended. Small states wanted unanimous consent of state legislatures. Big states felt that a unanimity rule would lead to stagnation and protracted conflict. Southern states were afraid that if amendments could be easily made slavery would be endangered.

To obtain agreement, a complicated formula was put together that allowed amendment by any one of four different procedures (see Figure 2.4). The simplest, and the most frequently used, way to amend the Constitution requires a two-thirds vote in both Houses of Congress and then ratification by three-quarters of the state legislatures. Twenty-six of the twenty-seven amendments to the Constitution have been enacted by this procedure. On one occasion, the amendment that repealed prohibition, the state legislatures were bypassed in favor of state ratifying conventions attended by delegates chosen by the voters (the same procedure used to ratify the Constitution itself).

An amendment may also be proposed by a call for a national convention by two-thirds of the state legislatures. Although no amendment proposal has ever succeeded via this method, this approach is now being tried by those favoring term limits for members of Congress. Term-limits sponsors have chosen this procedure because they do not think two-thirds of Congress will ever vote to impose term limits on

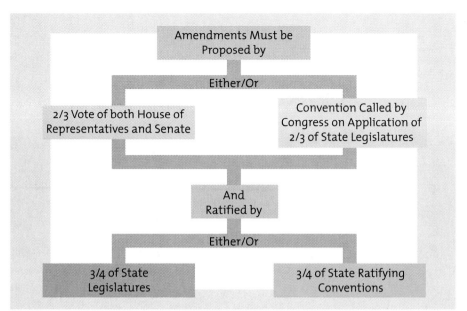

FIGURE 2.4

Amending the Constitution:
A Two-Stage Process

SOURCE: U.S. Constitution,
Article V. See Appendix, p. 690.

themselves. To get around this block, they are asking two-thirds of state legislatures to call a national convention. So far the effort has not achieved much success.

Amending the Constitution requires such overwhelming majorities that only seventeen amendments have been enacted since the ratification of the Bill of Rights, less than one amendment every twelve years. Thousands of amendments have been proposed over the decades, but almost all fail to win approval. The hurdles a proposed amendment must jump are so high that even popular amendments that have the endorsement of both political parties are not approved. For example, many people thought that the Equal Rights Amendment, which said that men and women had equal rights, would win approval in the 1970s. The amendment received overwhelming support in both Houses of Congress in 1971-72 and was quickly ratified by thirty-four states. But when the proposed amendment became intertwined with abortion and other disputed issues, it failed to win ratification by the final three state legislatures necessary to provide the required three-quarters approval.[39]

The one kind of amendment that seems capable of jumping the several high hurdles needed to achieve adoption is one that extends democratic practices. Despite the complicated procedures that are in place, thirteen amendments since the Bill of Rights have tightened the electoral connection well beyond what was originally envisioned by the Constitution—by either broadening the electorate, extending civil liberties, or making more direct the connections between leaders and voters. Five amendments specifically extended the suffrage to citizens previously excluded from voting—African Americans, women, people over the age of eighteen, residents of the District of Columbia, and those unwilling or unable to pay a poll tax. Eight other amendments also have corrected procedural deficiencies thought to be inconsistent with democratic practice (see Election Connection).

Originally, the Constitution was ratified by a small electorate of white male property owners. Amendments to this Constitution have broadened and extended popular participation, both enhancing and complicating the practice of American government. The Constitution laid the foundation, but the edifice erected on its pillars has proved more adaptable than even the delegates to the convention could have imagined.

Amendment	Year Ratified	Provision
12	1804	Distinguishes electoral vote for president and vice vice president.
13	1865	Abolishes slavery.
14	1868	Guarantees citizens the right of due process and equal protection before state law. Removes three-fifths compromise.
15	1870	Extends suffrage to African Americans.
17	1913	Direct election of senators.
19	1920	Extends suffrage to women.
20	1933	Shortens time between election and day Congress and president assume office.
22	1951	Two-term limit on presidents.
23	1961	Extends presidential suffrage to residents of District of Columbia.
24	1964	Abolishes tax on voting.
25	1967	Determines procedures for filling the Office of the Vice President if it becomes vacant.
26	1971	Extends suffrage to 18-year olds.
27	1992	Postpones congressional pay raises until next election.

SOURCE: U.S. Constitution, Amendments as listed. See Appendix, pp. 691–698.

The Constitution: An Assessment

The debate over the Constitution did not end with its ratification in 1788. The influential historian, Charles Beard, wrote in 1913 that the Constitution represented a victory for the propertied classes against the masses of the people.[40] According to Beard, wealthy people wrote the document and only people with property were allowed to vote in the ratification campaign. But modern-day historians Bernard Bailyn and Gordon Wood see it as the ultimate product of the republican ideal of citizen rights and representation that motivated the revolutionary patriots.[41] In their view, the Whig ideals that spurred the war of independence were given practical expression in the Constitution.

A STEP BACKWARD

Both sides to this debate probably overstate their case. The adoption of the Constitution consolidated changes in citizen participation and representation that had already taken place in many states. The adoption of the Constitution did not extend the right to vote, but neither did it further restrict it. The Constitution divided powers that had been lodged in a single representative body under the Articles of Confederation, but each of the new entities—House, Senate, Congress, courts—was ultimately grounded in the people. Senators were elected by the legislatures of each state, but the members of each state legislature were chosen in popular elections. Presidents were chosen by electors, but the electors were chosen according to state rules, which since the 1830s have generally called for direct elections by the voters.

The judges were appointed for life, but they were selected by the president and confirmed by the Senate. If the U.S. government under the Constitution was at best a more responsible democracy in 1789, a more popular democracy evolved within the framework it set forth, though it took a Civil War to incorporate all races into the democratic process.

There remains much in the Constitution to criticize. The powers of the Supreme Court are poorly defined. The Electoral College, though praised by some for representing both states and people, is thought by others to be a funny contraption that has more than once failed to work well. Many issues are papered over with vague, ambiguous wording.

Certain clauses in the Constitution are especially disturbing to the modern eye. Written by 55 prosperous gentlemen, the document falls far short of expressing contemporary democratic ideals. The Constitution explicitly permitted the slave trade to continue until 1808, despite the fact that many delegates thought it heinous. Nothing was done to extend voting rights to women, indentured servants, slaves, youth, or those without property. Until the Bill of Rights was added, nothing was said about basic freedoms of speech, religion, and trial by jury, which are now taken for granted.

But one cannot judge eighteenth-century decisions by twenty-first century principles. Most flaws were written into the Constitution not to frustrate voters but to achieve ratification. Slave issues were compromised because it was the only way to get the support of voters in both northern and southern states. The Constitution says nothing about the right to vote, because every state had its own voting rules. Had the Constitution proposed changing them, the states would have seen the provisions as violations of their sovereignty. The procedures for electing the president were designed to reduce conflicts between large and small states. The one big mistake the convention could most certainly have avoided—neglecting to include a bill of rights—was corrected by the first Congress.

If one wants to censure the Constitution for its undemocratic features, one must first criticize the limits on suffrage imposed by state voting laws inherited from the colonial period. Historians estimate that only 20 percent of the electorate and 5 percent of the adult population voted.[42] The country was no longer ruled by King George III, but it was hardly a full-fledged democracy. The Constitution was written to win the support of the white, male, property-owning population. That it could do so—and still leave open the possibility for greater democratization in the centuries to come—is to the honor, not the discredit, of those meeting in Philadelphia.

ACHIEVEMENTS

Though it is easy to disparage the Constitutional Convention for what it failed to achieve, the delegates wrote a document that contributed to the solution of two of the most immediate and pressing problems facing the United States. First, it created a unified nation capable of defending American sovereignty from the machinations of foreign powers. True, the United States would fight an unsuccessful war against Britain in 1812. But the Constitution kept the country from splitting into pieces at a time when Britain, France, and Spain, fighting among themselves, were all looking for a piece of the action in the New World. Instead of falling prey to European ambitions, the United States profited from these wars by seizing the opportunity to make the Louisiana Purchase, in 1803, which doubled the size of the country. The new lands were eventually incorporated into the Union as new member states.

Second, the new Constitution facilitated the country's economic development by outlawing state currencies and eliminating state tariffs. As a result, trade among states flourished, and the United States grew into an economic powerhouse faster than any had expected.

In addition to solving these immediate problems, the Constitution created a framework that facilitated an ever-more popular democratic experiment. In contrast to Thomas Hobbes, who said that a country could avoid chaos only by lodging power in a sovereign king, those who wrote the Constitution subscribed to a countertheory of checks and balances. If a constitution separates powers into many parts and each part represents a different set of interests, then liberty can be protected by giving minorities the opportunity to protect themselves from tyrannical majorities. The many compromises at the Constitutional Convention produced this kind of power separation that checked and balanced competing interests. The interests of big states, small states, northerners, southerners, commercial entrepreneurs, farmers, property owners, and debtors were all woven into the constitutional fabric.

In the two centuries that followed, the main lines of cleavage have changed. People no longer worry much about conflicts between big and small states or differences between commerce and agriculture. The country today has quite different ethnic, gender, cultural, income, and generational differences to resolve. But the Constitution still gives each of the many different groups and interests the opportunities to voice its concern.

The very ambiguities embedded in the Constitution have also been a plus. Written as compromises among conflicting interests, such vague phrases as "necessary and proper" and "Supreme Law of the Land" have had the elasticity necessary to accommodate powerful social and political forces the founders could not have anticipated. Over the centuries the Supreme Court has interpreted ambiguous constitutional phrases in ways that have allowed the Constitution to remain a living document. In subsequent chapters we shall discuss ways in which the compromises of 1787 have been redefined and given new meaning in response to changing political circumstances.

The Constitution's extraordinary adaptability over a prolonged period of time constitutes no small accomplishment. Although the United States is often thought of as a relatively new country, its governing arrangements have remained intact for much longer than those in most other countries. Of all the great industrial democracies, only the British system comes close to enjoying basic governing arrangements that date back as far as those of the United States. And even the democratic features of British government are newer than those of the United States. Not until 1867 did most British men get the right to vote.

Most other countries have much newer constitutions. The latest Russian constitution was adopted in 1993 (see International Comparison). The current Spanish constitution was promulgated in 1978, the French constitution dates back only to 1958, the Danish to 1953, and the German, Italian, and Japanese constitutions to the late 1940s.

THE STAIN OF SLAVERY

Despite everything positive that can be said for the Constitution, the stain of slavery remains indelible. The Constitution validated the slave trade and stated that slaves could be counted as three-fifths of a person. The Constitution also explicitly required free states to return escaped slaves to the place from which they had fled.

Dividing and checking concentrations of power prevented the tyranny of the majority. But it also prevented a majority from undoing the tyranny of slavery. By denying the national government the capacity to bring slavery peacefully to an end, separation of powers helped perpetuate the slave system at a time when the practice

With the disintegration of the Soviet Union in 1988, the new Russian Republic needed a constitution. In 1993 voters ratified one, creating a government not unlike that of the United States: three branches, including a president, a judiciary, and a national assembly that had only one chamber. A federal system divided power between national and local governments. The Constitution includes a Bill of Rights.

Despite the similarity between the Russian and the U.S. Constitutions, legal and political differences remain:

Legal Differences

1. The Russian president can issue emergency decrees without legislative approval. Some wonder whether a future president will use this power to transform the country back into a dictatorship.

2. Local governments in Russia depend almost entirely on the national government for financial resources, and many of their leaders are appointed by the president, making local governments less independent than state governments in the United States.

Differences in political circumstances

1. The U.S. Constitution was written by revolutionary leaders who had won the country's independence. The Russian constitution was written after the Soviet Union had lost the Cold War.

2. George Washington was a military hero. The first Russian president, Boris Yeltsin, was a dissident political leader. Though initially popular, he did not command the same trust and respect from all groups and factions that Washington enjoyed.

3. The first U.S. Congress was controlled by the Federalists, strong supporters of the new Constitution. Opponents of Yeltsin won a majority in the legislature.

4. The Bill of Rights was ignored when a local government, Chechnya, declared independence and a bitter war ensued.

SOURCES: Antti Korkeakivi, "The Reach of Rights in the New Russian Constitution," *Cardozo Journal of International and Comparative Law*, Vol. 3 (Summer 1995), pp. 229–50; Amy J. Weisman, "Separation of Powers in Post-Communist Government: A Constitutional Case Study of the Russian Federation," *American University Journal of International Law and Policy*, Vol. 10 (Summer 1995), 1365–98.

A relatively youthful constitution has been put into effect in the new Russian Republic. Russia is still finding its way after the disintegration of the Soviet Union in 1988—vividly symbolized by the removal of statues of communist leaders throughout Soviet bloc nations. Here, a demolition worker shields the eyes of a statue of Lenin, during efforts by city authorities to remove the state from its place of honor in Bucharest, Romania.

was disappearing throughout the rest of the world. Perhaps it is too much to ask of any constitution that it provide the tools for resolving what had become an intractable problem. Perhaps it was, as Abraham Lincoln once said, only providential that "every drop of blood drawn with the lash shall be paid by another drawn with the sword."[43] It is not easy to think how one could have designed a constitution that could have both freed slaves and won ratification by the voters of 1788.

Chapter Summary

The Constitution was written to rectify difficulties the country experienced under the Articles of Confederation. The national government could not raise its own army, levy its own taxes, or regulate commerce among the states. Many leaders felt the country too weak to fend off potential threats from Britain, Spain, and France.

To rectify these defects in the Articles, delegates met in Philadelphia in 1787 to write a new constitution. Congress was given additional authority, an independent executive branch was formed, and the framework for a national judicial system was put together. Though drafted in secret, the Constitution had to win voter approval in a ratification campaign. To win voter support, the Constitution built on the experiences of the colonial period. The

basic design of the new government, including plans for a Congress, a president, and a Supreme Court, was consistent with John Locke's famous theory of mixed government and familiar to voters living in states that had legislatures, governors, and state courts.

To win ratification, the Constitution had to reach many compromises. Congress was given not a general power but a set of specific powers, along with the capacity to do anything "necessary and proper" to carry out these specific powers. Differences of opinion between delegates from big and small states were compromised by creating a Senate that gave equal representation to all states and a House of Representatives that represented states in proportion to their population. Presidents were selected via a com-

plicated two-stage system, which included a cumbersome Electoral College arrangement. The Supreme Court was neither given nor denied the power of judicial review. Differences between the North and South were compromised by preserving the slave trade for 20 years and counting slaves as three-fifths of a person.

The convention delegates erred in not including a Bill of Rights in the Constitution. But during the ratification campaign, Anti-Federalists insisted upon, and the Federalists finally agreed to, ten amendments to the Constitution that became known as the Bill of Rights. Though the procedures for amending the Constitution are complicated, 17 amendments have been approved since the Bill of Rights, 13 of which shifted American democracy in a participatory direction.

Key Terms

advice and consent, p. 54

Annapolis Convention, p. 48

Anti-Federalists, p. 37

Articles of Confederation, p. 37

Bill of Rights, p. 58

checks and balances, p. 59

colonial assembly, p. 40

colonial council, p. 40

Connecticut Compromise, p. 51

Constitution, p. 37

Declaration of Independence, p. 43

divine right, p. 39

Electoral College, p. 55

Federalist Papers, p. 59

Federalists, p. 37

First Continental Congress, p. 43

judicial review, p. 57

majority, p. 55

Mayflower Compact, p. 40

necessary and proper clause, p. 52

Suggested Readings

Adams, Willi Paul. *The First American Constitutions: Republican Ideology and the Making of the State Constitutions in the Revolutionary Era.* Chapel Hill: University of North Carolina Press, 1980. Reveals that much of what seems original in the Constitution was already in place in many states.

Bailyn, Bernard. *The Origins of American Politics.* New York: Alfred Knopf, 1968. Identifies the sources of the American Revolution in colonial thought and practice.

Beard, Charles A. *An Economic Interpretation of the Constitution of the United States.* New York: Free Press, 1913. Interprets the writing of the Constitution as an effort by the wealthy to protect their property rights.

Commager, Henry Steele, ed. *Documents of American History.* 6th ed. New York: Appleton-Century-Crofts, 1958. Collection of key primary documents in American history.

Elkins, Stanley, and Eric McKitrick. *The Age of Federalism.* New York: Oxford University Press, 1993. Authoritative account of political life during the first decade after the adoption of the Constitution.

The Federalist Papers. New York: New American Library, 1961. Powerful defense of the proposed Constitution by Alexander Hamilton, James Madison, and John Jay under the pseudonym, Publius.

Hartz, Louis. *The Liberal Tradition in America.* New York: Harcourt, Brace, 1955. A difficult but rewarding book that describes the distinctive quality of the American political tradition.

Morgan, Edmund S., and Helen M. Morgan. *The Stamp Act Crisis: Prologue to Revolution.* Chapel Hill: University of North Carolina Press, 1953. Readable account of key events leading to the revolution.

Roche, John P. "The Founding Fathers: A Reform Caucus in Action." *American Political Science Review* 55 (Dec 1961): 799–816. Identifies the election connection at the Constitutional Convention.

Storing, Herbert J., ed. *The Anti-Federalist.* Chicago: University of Chicago Press, 1986. Selection of Anti-Federalist writings.

Tuchman, Barbara W. *The First Salute: A View of the American Revolution.* New York: Ballantine, 1988. Shows how the struggle for power among European countries affected the outcome of the revolutionary war.

Wood, Gordon S. *The Radicalism of the American Revolution* New York: Alfred Knopf, 1992. Portrays the unleashing of a democratic ideology during the struggle for independence.

TURN PAGE

3

federal, state and local government

N 1990 CONGRESS passed the Gun-Free School Zones Act, making it a federal crime to carry a lethal weapon on the grounds of a public school. Responding to a series of highly publicized crimes on public school grounds, Congress enacted the law even though gun-toting in school was already outlawed in most states. Some critics said Congress had reacted impulsively to public clamor to "do something" to stop a wave of highly publicized incidents of school violence. They said that Congress had violated principles of federalism by passing laws on matters they saw as strictly state and local problems. Supporters of the new legislation replied that the congressional power to regulate commerce gave it the right to control the presence of weapons in public places.

Shortly after passage of the Gun-Free School Zones Act, Alphonso Lopez, an ordinary teenager with neither a criminal record nor known as a school trouble-maker, foolishly took a .38 calibre handgun to school. Instead of leaving the matter to local officials, a U.S. district attorney, acting on a complaint filed by a federal agency, prosecuted the youth under the new federal law. When Lopez was convicted and given a six-month term in a federal prison, he appealed his conviction on the grounds that the Gun-Free School Zones Act violated Texas sovereignty. The Supreme Court agreed. Instead of landing in jail, Lopez joined the marines.

Chief Justice William Rehnquist, speaking for a five-member majority of the Supreme Court (all appointed by Republican presidents), said "that Congress may [not] use a relatively trivial impact on commerce as an excuse for broad general resolution of state and private activities." The remaining four justices dissented on the grounds that "guns in schools significantly undermine the quality of education in our nation's classrooms" and that "education . . . has long been inextricably intertwined with the nation's economy."[1]

he *Lopez* decision raises many questions. What is meant by federalism? Why did the court say that the State of Texas and all other states are sovereign? How is power divided among the national, state, and local governments? In this chapter we define federalism, discuss the contemporary debate over federalism, describe the way in which the system of federalism has evolved, discuss the rise of cooperative federalism in recent decades, review the debate over federal grant programs, and describe the organization and modern-day responsibilities of state and local governments. Throughout the book, we shall highlight our discussions of the way in which state and local governments operate in specific institutional and policy domains. As we shall see, both elections and Supreme Court interpretations of the Constitution have helped shape the American federal system.

The Federalism Debate:
It's New but It's Old

Federalism divides fundamental governmental authority between at least two different levels. In the United States, the fundamental units are the national government and the state governments, each with the power to act independently of the other. To be a federal government in a democratic system each fundamental level of government must have 1) its own set of elected officials, 2) its own capacity to raise revenues by means of taxation, 3) independent authority to pass laws regulating the lives of its citizens, and 4) the power to define its boundaries.

Local governments are not fundamental units in the U.S. federal system. According to a long-standing legal doctrine known as **Dillon's rule** (after the Iowa state judge, John Dillon), local governments are, in legal terms, mere creatures of the state. A state legislature can, at any time, alter the boundaries of any local government, expand or narrow its power, or completely abolish it altogether.

As a principle of government, federalism has had a dubious history. The great fighter for Brazilian independence, Simon Bolivar, once observed: "Among the popular and representative systems of government, I do not approve of the federal system: It is too perfect; and it requires virtues and political talents much superior to our own."[2] Federalism remains on the margins of political respectability even today. The vast majority of countries in the world have a **unitary** form of government, in which all authority is held by a single, national government. In these unitary systems, local governments are simply administrative outposts of the national government. In Britain, for example, Parliament has the power to abolish all local governments, a power it has often used to redesign the country's county and municipal governments.

- **federalism**
  Division of fundamental governmental authority between at least two different levels of government.

- **Dillon's rule**
  Legal doctrine that local governments are mere creatures of the state.

- **unitary government**
  System under which all authority is held by a single, national government.

"FEDERAL" HAS MANY, NOT ALWAYS CONSISTENT, MEANINGS

Federalism: A type of government in which power is divided between two or more levels of government.

Federal government: The national government in Washington, D. C.

Federal system: The national (federal), state, and local governments in the United States.

Federal grants: Grants from the federal government to state and local governments.

Federalists: Those who supported the ratification of the Constitution.

Federalist Papers: Essays defending the Constitution written by Alexander Hamilton, James Madison, and John Jay during ratification campaign.

Federalist party: One of the first two major political parties, which included most but not all those who supported ratification of the Constitution. The second president, John Adams, was a Federalist. The party disappeared after 1815. Alexander Hamilton remained a Federalist, but James Madison became a Democratic–Republican.

Government	Year	Main Reason for Federalism	Main Problem Today
European Community	1992	Enhance economic growth	Achieve economic integration but protect national identities
German	1949	Protect liberty; prevent Nazism	Incorporate eastern Germany
Russian	1993	Protect ethnic minorities	Prevent rise of dictatorship
South African	1996	Protect white minority	Maintain interracial agreement on Constitution
Chinese	Has not happened	Protect Taiwan in Unified China	Only an idea

Although most countries have unitary forms of government, federalism has long been thought ideally suited to U.S. conditions. Federalism was an essential part of the Constitution, because the document could not have been ratified had the identity of the existing states not been retained. Federalism also facilitated the admission of new states to the union, helped government respond to ethnic and cultural diversity, and facilitated the nation's extraordinary economic development. As early as the 1830s, the keen French observer of American politics, Alexis de Tocqueville, noted, "One can hardly imagine how much [the] division of sovereignty contributes to the well-being of each of the states that compose the Union. In these small communities . . . all public authority [is] turned toward internal improvements. . . . The ambition of power yields to the less refined and less dangerous desire for well-being."[3] Federalism has even enjoyed a small gain in popularity worldwide, especially in places undergoing major political change (see International Comparison).

THE CONTEMPORARY DEBATE

Long before federalism had gained any semblance of international respectability, Americans had reached an almost universal consensus on its worth. But the exact distribution of powers between the national and the state governments has been a subject of great debate that refuses to go away. Indeed, the two political parties disagree more about its meaning today than they have for over fifty years.

Today's partisan debate goes well beyond the pluses and minuses of specific government programs: Each political party tends to have a distinctive conception of the best way to organize American government. Although differences between the parties are not always sharp and clear, many Republicans think the sphere of the national government should be limited. Much that is now funded by the national government should be devolved to state and local governments. These Republicans reason that state and local governments are closer to the people, more in touch with their needs, and less likely to waste taxpayer dollars. Alternatively, many Democrats think that such problems as environmental pollution, providing educational opportunity, and care for the sick and the poor are too big and sprawl too widely to be resolved at state and local levels. However, some Democrats, including President Clinton, favor devolution of some federal programs.

In the early 1990s, the debate focused on the issue of **unfunded mandates**, the imposition of federal regulations on state and local governments without appropri-

unfunded mandates
Federal regulations that impose burdens on state and local governments without appropriating enough money to cover costs.

ating enough money to cover their cost. On October 27, 1993, a number of state and local officials held "National Unfunded Mandates Day." In a rally held on the steps of the City Hall in Columbus, Ohio, they called for a halt to additional rules and regulations imposed on state and local governments unless the national government paid for the cost. Complaining that cities were suffering "spending without representation," Columbus Mayor Gregory LaShutka said cities would have to spend $54 billion on ten major federal mandates over the next five years.[4]

At the time the rally was held, countless mandates had reached the statute books.[5] For example, state and local governments had to ensure equal access to public facilities by disabled persons but were given little money to cover construction costs. Clean-air legislation asked state and local governments to reduce air pollution but skimped on the funding necessary to do the job.[6] Medicaid required expanded services for low-income recipients, but, for many states, the law funded only half the cost of the program.[7]

Members of Congress have strong incentives to impose mandates on state and local governments but to leave them unfunded. When a mandate is imposed, members of Congress get the credit for helping constituents. When it is left unfunded, Congress avoids the taxpayers' wrath.

Despite the long-standing popularity of unfunded mandates on Capitol Hill, the 1994 election brought them to an end, at least for the time being. Republican candidates campaigned in favor of governmental **devolution**, the return of governmental responsibilities to state and local governments. When Republicans won a majority in Congress, they passed a statute banning any new law that was not adequately funded and reduced the size and scope of many federal programs.

> ■ **devolution**
> Return of governmental responsibilities to state and local governments.

FEDERALISM AND THE RATIFICATION OF THE CONSTITUTION

CONSTITUTION, TENTH AMENDMENT: *"The powers not delegated to the United States by the Constitution, nor prohibited by it to the States, are reserved to the States."*

This contemporary debate resembles a much older one that divided Federalists and the Anti-Federalists at the time the Constitution was being ratified. The Federalists (some say they should have been called Nationalists) took a position in favor of a strong national government. They felt that national strength was needed to overcome the rivalries among the states. The Anti-Federalists [some say they should have been called Federalists] wanted to keep the national government as limited as possible, fearing that a powerful national government could trample the liberties of the people.

The Constitution itself represents a compromise between these competing views. To appease those who wanted a weak national government, the Constitution denied Congress a general legislative power, instead giving it only specific, delegated powers, such as the powers to levy taxes and regulate interstate commerce. It also gave states independent authority, such as the responsibility for appointing officers in the militia. In addition, it guaranteed existing state boundaries, saying that no state can be stripped of its territory or divided into parts without its consent. The Anti-Federalists also won as part of the Bill of Rights the Tenth Amendment, which reserved to the states all power not delegated to the federal government.

To satisfy the Federalists, the Constitution gave Congress, in addition to its delegated powers, the authority to undertake all activities "necessary and proper" to

DIVIDING A STATE

States are clearly sovereign in at least one respect: Their boundaries cannot be altered under the Constitution without the consent of both the state and the federal government, except that Congress conceded to Texas at the time of its admission to the Union the right to divide itself into five states. Though Texans have never seemed much interested in this option, Massachusetts (and Congress) in 1819 did agree to let Maine become a separate state. Many such changes in state boundaries have since been proposed. Some have said that California should be divided into northern and southern halves. Others have proposed separating New York City from the rest of the state. Some north Floridians have wanted a separation between themselves and the state's panhandle. But only one state, Virginia, has ever lost a portion of its territory against its will. When Civil War broke out in 1861, the counties in western Virginia formed their own government, which they called West Virginia. Despite the dubious constitutional standing of this rump government, Congress passed and Abraham Lincoln signed a law recognizing the new state.

supremacy clause
Constitutional provision that says the laws of the national government "shall be the supreme Law of the Land."

carry out its enumerated powers. It also enacted a **supremacy clause** stating that national laws "shall be the supreme Law of the Land . . . any Thing in the . . . Laws of any State to the Contrary notwithstanding," a statement that comes close to saying (yet does not quite say) that only the national government is truly sovereign.

The Evolution of Federal Theory

Since the Constitution compromised many of the differences between Federalists and Anti-Federalists, the issues raised at the time of the ratification campaign have never disappeared from American politics. Instead, the shape of American federalism has fluctuated over the decades (see Figure 3.1). Both Supreme Court decisions and the outcome of key elections have defined and redefined the nature of American federalism.

judicial review
The authority of courts to determine whether laws are unconstitutional.

Supreme Court decisions have had a fundamental impact, because the Supreme Court has the power of **judicial review**, the power to declare both federal and state laws unconstitutional (see Chapter 15). When the Supreme Court declares a law of Congress unconstitutional, as it did in the Lopez case, it not only limits federal power but often expands the arena in which states are considered sovereign. The Supreme Court may also declare state laws unconstitutional, a power necessary for preserving national unity.

Elections have been no less important for defining American federalism. Quite apart from the indirect effect that elections have on the makeup of the Supreme Court, they can have direct and immediate effects on the federal system. As the unfunded mandates law reveals, changes in the control of Congress can have broad repercussions. In the pages that follow we shall see how key national elections have often altered the shape of federalism.

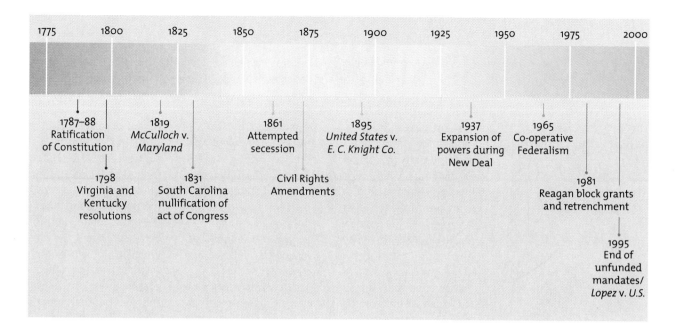

FIGURE 3.1

Major Events Shaping American Federalism

DUAL SOVEREIGNTY

Much of the legal debate over federalism, both historical and contemporary, turns on the doctrine of **dual sovereignty**, which says both the national and state governments are sovereign in their own sphere. As a legal and political doctrine, dual sovereignty is an American invention that challenges Thomas Hobbes's powerful argument stating there could be only one sovereign (see Chapter 2). If sovereignty is divided, Hobbes said, the competing sovereigns will inevitably come into conflict with one another, driving the country into a state of war of all against all.

The *Federalist Papers* defended dual sovereignty by turning Hobbes's argument on its head. While Hobbes said that anything less than a single sovereign would lead to a war of all against all, the writers of the *Federalist Papers* argued that the best way of preserving liberty was through the division of power. If power is concentrated in any one place, it can be used to crush individual liberty. Even in a democracy there can be the tyranny of the majority—the worst kind of tyranny because it is so stifling, complete, and seemingly legitimate. By dividing power between the national and state governments, the possibility that any single majority will be able to control all centers of governmental power is lessened.

dual sovereignty
A theory of federalism saying that both levels of government are sovereign within their own sphere.

DOCTRINE OF NULLIFICATION

Dual sovereign theory was an entrenched part of constitutional understanding during the first decades following the adoption of the Constitution. Some thought state sovereignty so complete they propounded the doctrine of **nullification**, a principle affirming that state legislatures can nullify acts of Congress if they threaten state or individual liberties. The doctrine was first enunciated in 1798 in response to the passage of the Alien and Sedition Acts, which outlawed criticism of government officials (see Election Connection). A Federalist-controlled Congress enacted the legislation to suppress the growing power of the Democratic–Republican Party, led by Thomas Jefferson. Invoking the doctrine of nullification, outraged Jeffersonians

nullification
A doctrine developed by John Calhoun saying that states have the authority to declare acts of Congress unconstitutional.

Federalism and the Election of 1800

Federalism helped American democracy survive in the year 1800 its first major test, the peaceful transition of power from one political party to another. By dividing power between national and state governments, federalism helped the country survive a crisis. The party that lost the election did not use the army to stay in power, because they knew the Virginia militia could frustrate any military attempt to prevent the other party from coming to power. At the same time, the losers, though badly defeated in national politics, could take some comfort in the fact that they still remained in control of some state governments.

Thomas Jefferson, founder of the Democratic–Republican party, waged an all-out campaign to defeat President John Adams, a Federalist. So bitter was the feud between the two parties that Congressman Matthew Lyon, a Democratic–Republican, spit in the face of a Federalist member on the floor of Congress. To silence the opposition, Congress, controlled by the Federalists, passed the Alien and Sedition Acts, making it illegal to "write, print, utter, or publish … any false, scandalous and malicious writing … against … the Congress of the United States, or the President."* Newspaper editors supporting the Democratic–Republicans were quickly indicted, and ten were convicted. Matthew Lyon was sentenced to a four-month jail term for claiming that President Adams had an "unbounded thirst for ridiculous pomp, foolish adulation, and selfish avarice."†

Despite the Alien and Sedition Acts, Thomas Jefferson and his vice presidential nominee, Aaron Burr, won most of the electoral vote. But, amazingly, when the votes were counted, Jefferson gained only a tie, a bizarre result created by weaknesses in the original design of the Electoral College (since corrected by the Twelfth Amendment).

Under the Constitution, as originally written, each college member casts two votes for president, without indicating which vote was for the president and which for the vice president. The person receiving the most votes was named president; the runner-up became vice president.

All the Democratic–Republicans electors voted for both Jefferson and Burr. Though they clearly intended Jefferson to be the president and Burr to be vice president, the vote ended in a tie. Since neither had a majority, the president was chosen by the House of Representatives, elected two years earlier. Federalists, well represented in the old House, voted for Burr. For thirty-four ballots Jefferson was unable to obtain a majority. The Jeffersonians contemplated calling out the Virginia state militia. Eventually, one Federalist abstained, giving Jefferson the presidency. The crisis ended.

* Henry Steele Commanger, *Documents of American History*, 6th ed. (New York: Appleton-Century-Crofts, 1949).

† Thomas A. Bailey, *The American Pageant: A History of the Republic*. (Boston: D. C. Heath, 1956), 177.

SOURCE: Stanley Elkins and Eric McKitrick, *The Age of Federalism* (New York: Oxford: 1993).

in Virginia and Kentucky passed state resolutions voiding the laws. Their defense of the right of free speech was praiseworthy, yet by using the doctrine of nullification to defend free speech Virginia and Kentucky laid down a legal doctrine that would eventually tear the country apart.

At first, the doctrine of nullification had no serious consequences. On the contrary, it was firmly rejected in **McCulloch v. Maryland**, a sweeping Supreme Court decision handed down in 1819 that is among the most important the Court has ever made.[8] The issue involved the Bank of the United States, an entity thought by commercial interests to be vital to economic prosperity but one hated by many farmers and debtors. Responding to popular opinion, the State of Maryland levied a tax on the bank. McCulloch, an officer of the Maryland branch of the bank, had refused to pay the tax. Deciding in favor of McCulloch, Chief Justice John Marshall said that Maryland could not tax a federal bank, because the "power to tax involves the power to destroy."[9] If a state government could tax a federal agency, then states could undermine the sovereignty of the federal government. In declaring the state law unconstitutional, Marshall cast profound doubt on the power of the states to nullify acts of Congress.

Despite the *McCulloch* decision, the doctrine of nullification was not dead. The issue next arose shortly after the tumultuous election of 1828 that elected Andrew Jackson president. His vice-president, John Calhoun, formerly senator from South Carolina, claimed that states had the power to nullify federal laws. The issue involved a tariff, a tax on imports favored by northern manufacturers as a way of protecting local industry from foreign competition. Southerners opposed the tariff, because they wanted to sell their cotton to Europe and buy cheap manufactured products in return.

Calhoun's supporters in South Carolina called a state convention, which declared the tariff null and void in the state. The state even threatened to secede from the union if the federal government attempted to collect the tariff by force. President Jackson prepared to crush the incipient rebellion, but cooler heads prevailed. Congress passed a lower tariff less objectionable to southern interests, and South Carolina agreed to pay the tax.

Though the overt issue was tariffs, the underlying, long-term question involved African Americans. Afraid northerners would abolish slavery, southern leaders continued to espouse the doctrine of nullification and eventually the right to secede from the Union. The issue was brought to a head with the election of Abraham Lincoln in 1860. Lincoln was the candidate of the new Republican party, which opposed the extension of slavery into the western territories and favored its eventual abolition. Seeing the Republicans as a direct challenge to their right to own slaves, white southerners invoked what they saw as their right to secede from the Union, and the United States experienced what Hobbes had most feared: a war between competing sovereigns. Only after a half million soldiers had died and a countryside been laid to waste was the doctrine of nullification finally repudiated. After the Civil War, whatever dual sovereignty meant, it was clear that it did not mean that state legislatures could declare null and void the decisions of the federal government.

■ *McCulloch v. Maryland*
Decision of 1819 in which Supreme Court declares unconstitutional the state's power to tax a federal government entity.

Court Interpretations of the Meaning of Dual Sovereignty

Once the doctrine of nullification had been definitely put to rest, it was up to the federal courts, not state legislatures, to decide the meaning of dual sovereignty. Three clauses in the Constitution have provided much of the basis for the expansion of federal power: the necessary and proper clause, the commerce clause, and the spending clause.

NECESSARY AND PROPER CLAUSE

CONSTITUTION, ARTICLE I: *"Congress shall have power . . . to make all laws which shall be necessary and proper for carrying into execution . . . all other powers vested by this Constitution in the government of the United States."*

The delegated powers of Congress include those items specifically mentioned in the Constitution, such as the power to tax, borrow money, and establish a currency. The **necessary and proper clause** gives Congress the authority to "make all laws which shall be necessary and proper for carrying to execution" its delegated powers. The words "necessary and proper" were first analyzed by Justice Marshall in the same decision that challenged the doctrine of nullification, *McCulloch* v. *Maryland*. Maryland argued that Congress had no authority to establish a national bank, because a bank was not necessary for Congress to carry out its delegated power to coin money; it was only a convenient way of doing so. But Justice Marshall rejected such an interpretation as annihilating Congress's ability to select an appropriate means to carry out a task. "Let the end be legitimate," he said. "Let it be within the scope of the Constitution, and all means which are appropriate, which are plainly adapted to that end, which are not prohibited, but consistent with the letter and spirit of the Constitution, are constitutional."[10] Since this decision, the courts have generally found that almost any means selected by Congress are usually "necessary and proper." As a result, the "necessary and proper" clause has come to be known as the *elastic clause*, which over the centuries has been stretched to fit almost any circumstance.

Even though an elastic interpretation of the necessary and proper clause has given Congress broad powers, the Supreme Court has said, as recently as 1991, that they are not without limit. Adding its voice to the rising political concern over unfunded mandates, the Supreme Court, in *New York* v. *U.S.* (1991), declared that Congress cannot give direct orders to states. Though discussed in the arcane language of dual sovereignty, the case involved one of the most modern of political issues, the disposal of radioactive waste.

Disposal of radioactive waste has become a particularly annoying political problem. Millions of cubic feet need to be buried someplace where it cannot be disturbed for thousands of years.[11] The problem has become an elected official's nightmare: Something needs to be done and there is no way of doing it without making some people angry—really angry. Easily alarmed at the very word *radioactive*, citizens organize protests and demonstrations whenever a town is named as a potential dump. Everyone knows the stuff has to go somewhere but everyone also says "Not In My Back Yard," generally known as the NIMBY problem.

After stewing fitfully over the NIMBY problem, Congress discovered a politically painless solution: It required each state either to find an adequate burial site for its waste or become legally responsible for any damages the waste might cause. Rather than making the tough decisions themselves, Congress decided to place an unfunded mandate on governors and state legislatures.

As a result, the debate over domestic radioactive waste shifted to the states. In no state was the issue more hotly debated than in New York. Whenever state officials identified a potential dump, they were "run off" the site and "burned in effigy."[12] Under the pressure of the federal law, New York officials decided to ignore the opposition and dump the waste in Courtland and Allegheny counties anyway. But the elected boards for the two counties, to keep faith with county voters, filed a suit,

■ **necessary and proper clause** Constitutional clause that gives Congress the power to take all actions that are "necessary and proper" to the carrying out of its delegated powers. Also known as the *elastic clause*.

Easily alarmed at the word *radio-active*, citizens organize protests and demonstrations whenever a town is named as a potential waste dump site.

claiming that the federal law was unconstitutional. Justice Sandra O'Connor, writing for the majority, said Congress could not order states or local governments to bury their nuclear waste. Direct orders to a state violated its sovereignty.[13] It remains to be seen how widely the Court will apply this principle but it seems that the old doctrine of dual sovereignty remains alive and well today.

COMMERCE CLAUSE

CONSTITUTION, ARTICLE I: *"Congress shall have power . . . to regulate commerce . . . among the several states."*

The meaning of the **commerce clause**, which gives Congress the power to regulate commerce among the states, has been the subject of heated dispute. The courts have generally distinguished *interstate* or between-state commerce, which Congress may regulate, from *intrastate* or within-state commerce, which can be regulated only by the states. In the nineteenth century, intrastate commerce was defined as including all commerce that did not overtly cross state lines. So, for example, the Supreme Court in 1895 said, in *United States* v. *E. C. Knight Co.*, that Congress could not break up a monopoly that had a nationwide impact on the price of sugar, because the monopoly refined its sugar within the state of Pennsylvania.[14] The mere fact that the sugar was to be sold nationwide was only "incidental" to its production.

The *Knight* case, which denied the federal government sovereignty over a large portion of economic activity, remained the reigning legal doctrine until the 1930s. But, in 1932, Democrat Franklin D. Roosevelt defeated Herbert Hoover in a bitter presidential election that foreshadowed a period of great expansion of federal power. Campaigning in the midst of a deep depression, Roosevelt promised to use the power of the federal government to get the country going again. He and his Democratic party allies in Congress enacted a series of governmental policies known as the **New Deal,** a wide array of programs that expanded the power of the federal government for the purposes of stimulating economic recovery and creating a national safety-net

■ **commerce clause**
Constitutional provision that gives Congress power to regulate commerce "among the states."

■ **New Deal**
Programs created by the Franklin Roosevelt administration that expanded the power of the federal government for the purpose of stimulating economic recovery and establishing a national safety net.

for those in need. Many Republicans opposed these New Deal policies, in part because they violated long-standing principles of federalism. At first the Supreme Court ruled against any expansion in federal power. But after Roosevelt was re-elected in 1936, the Court's position began to change.

A key decision involved the Wagner Act, a New Deal law that protected union organizers. Despite the fact that the new law regulated activities within a state, Chief Justice Charles Hughes declared it constitutional, saying: "When industries organize themselves on a national scale, . . . how can it be maintained that their industrial labor relations constitute a forbidden field into which Congress may not enter?"[15] Relations between employers and their workers, once declared local, suddenly were said to be part of interstate commerce.

With new appointments to the Court by President Roosevelt, the definition of interstate commerce continued to expand. In 1942, a farmer violated crop quotas imposed under New Deal legislation by sowing twenty-three acres of wheat. The court ruled the law a constitutional regulation of interstate commerce even though the farmer was feeding all the wheat to his own livestock. The court reasoned that the farmer, by not buying the wheat, was depressing the worldwide price of grain.[16] With such an expansive definition of interstate commerce, hardly anything could be characterized as simply local or beyond the scope of Congress to regulate.

This broad interpretation of the commerce clause remained unquestioned until the 1995 case, *U.S.* v. *Lopez*, discussed at the beginning of this chapter. The Lopez decision has opened up an opportunity for the Supreme Court to place new limits on Congress's ability to intervene in state and local affairs. In 1997 the Court declared unconstitutional a federal law which required state and local law enforcement officials to check the backgrounds of those seeking to buy handguns. The Court said that the federal government could not issue orders to state officials without violating state sovereignty, as protected by the Tenth Amendment. It remains to be seen whether the current move toward devolution taking place both in Congress and the Supreme Court will further change the meaning of the commerce clause.

SPENDING CLAUSE

CONSTITUTION, ARTICLE 1: "*Congress shall have power . . . to lay and collect taxes, duties, imposts and excises, to pay the debts and provide for the . . . general welfare of the United States.*"

■ **spending clause**
Constitutional provision that gives Congress the power to collect taxes to provide for the general welfare.

The **spending clause** grants Congress the power to collect taxes to provide for the general welfare. The New Deal Supreme Court considered the meaning of this clause when it ruled on the constitutionality of the Social Security program for senior citizens which was enacted in 1935. The program was challenged by a tax-payer on the grounds that tax dollars were being spent for the specific welfare of the elderly, not for the general welfare. But the Supreme Court, accommodating itself to Roosevelt's enlarged conception of federal power, said it was up to Congress, not the Supreme Court, to decide whether any particular program was for the general welfare. In the words of the Court, "the discretion belongs to Congress, unless the choice is clearly wrong."[17] So far, the Court has never found Congress "clearly wrong."

Not only did the Supreme Court refuse to restrict the purposes for which Congress could spend money, but it conceded to Congress the right to attach any reasonable regulation to the money it spends. Congress in 1984 provided a grant to state governments for highway maintenance, but conditioned some of the funding on state willingness to raise the drinking age from eighteen to twenty-one. The constitutionality of the mandate was challenged on the grounds that teenage drunkenness had only a remote connection to road repair. The Supreme Court rejected this argument.[18] State sovereignty was not violated, the Court concluded, because any state could choose not to accept the money. The regulation proved effective, inasmuch as every state save Louisiana raised its drinking age to twenty-one.

The congressional power to tax and spend has remained one of the broadest federal powers, because it allows Congress to attach whatever regulations it deems appropriate to the grants it gives to states. Upon this power has been founded the theory and practice of cooperative federalism.

★ AT THE STATE & LOCAL LEVEL
Cooperative Federalism

Political scientist Morton Grodzins first propounded the theory of **cooperative federalism** or **marble-cake federalism**, which said all levels of government could and should perform all governmental functions together. Grodzins criticized dual sovereignty theory for viewing government as a layer cake, each level independent of and separate from the other.[19] He pointed out that, in practice, agencies from different levels of government typically work together, combining and intertwining their functions to such an extent that the intergovernmental system resembles a marble cake.

In all policy realms, Grodzins said, one finds many levels of government working together on similar tasks. For example, law enforcement requires cooperation among the Federal Bureau of Investigation, state highway traffic control, the county sheriff's office, and local police departments. According to Grodzins, all levels of government can and should work together for three reasons:

1. Cooperative federalism is democratic. The involvement of all levels of government ensures that many different interests in society are represented.

2. Compromises are reached among officials elected by different constituencies. Federal officials listen to state and local officials, because the latter have influence with members of Congress. Similarly, state officials listen to community leaders, because state legislators, to stay in office, must pay attention to local needs.

3. Professional administrators usually share common values, no matter what level of government they work for. Law enforcement officials have many things in common, whether they work for the FBI or the local police. Most educational administrators, whether federal, state, or local, were once schoolteachers.

The 1964 election of Lyndon Johnson, together with an overwhelming Democratic majority in Congress, provided an opportunity to test Grodzins' theory of cooperative federalism. In the next few years, Congress passed a broad range of legislation that greatly enlarged the number, size, and complexity of **intergovernmental grants**, programs funded in part by the federal government but administered by state and local governments. State and local governments are often asked to provide a matching grant. The typical "match" is 50 percent of total costs, but it can be as

cooperative federalism
A theory stating that all levels of government could work together to solve common problems. Also known as *marble-cake federalism*.

marble-cake federalism
A theory that said all levels of government could work together to solve common problems. Also known as *cooperative federalism*.

intergovernmental grant
Grant from the national government to state or local government.

FIGURE 3.2

Growth and Decline in Federal
Grants to States and Localities:
Expenditures for categorical
grants continue to rise while
expenditures for block grants
have declined.

SOURCE: Paul E. Peterson, *The
Price of Federalism* (Washington,
D.C.: Brookings, 1995), 74.

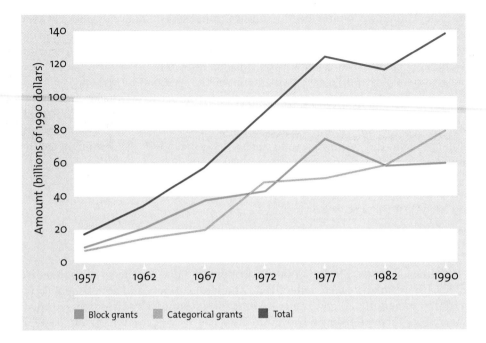

much as 90 percent or as little as 10 percent. Intergovernmental grants have become
a key feature of the federal system. In 1930, only $68 million was spent on intergov-
ernmental grants to local governments.[20] By 1962, grants to state and local governments had grown to $34.7 billion, and by 1977 they had multiplied fourfold to $125.1
billion (see Figure 3.2).[21]

Growth in the number and size of intergovernmental grants was facilitated by
their innate popularity with most members of Congress. Many found they could
profit handsomely from new projects begun in their home constituencies. In Senator Barry Goldwater's words, "I don't care what the piece of equipment is—or how
bad it is—if it's done in his state, the senator has to stand up and scream for it."[22]
Though grants are often criticized as mere "pork barrel" projects that have little or
no value, most grants are well received by the city or town lucky enough to get the
money. As Speaker of the House Thomas Foley once said, "One person's pork barrel project is another person's wise investment in the local infrastructure."[23] For
example, an embankment protecting West Fargo from floods, constructed at the
behest of a North Dakota Senator, was originally condemned as sheer pork. But in
the great 1997 flood of the Red River, the embankment saved the town from disaster.

Representative Joe McDade of Pennsylvania proved to be one of the grand masters of grant-making. From his position as ranking Republican on the House Appropriations committee, McDade secured federal monies to help build a center for the
performing arts, fund a microbiology institute for cancer research at the University
of Scranton, restore an antique aqueduct, construct McDade Park (including a
tourist-friendly museum on the history of coal mining), turn the home of minor
author Zane Grey into a national monument, finance a flood-control project, and
convert a railroad station into a fancy hotel and restaurant. Needless to say,
McDade was extraordinarily popular with his constituents. Though under indictment on charges of "racketeering, conspiracy and accepting about $100,000 in ille-
gal gratuities," McDade's success in winning federal grants for his district enabled
him to win reelection to Congress in 1994.[24]

CATEGORICAL GRANTS

Though Republicans like Representative McDade benefited from federal grants, the theory of cooperative federalism
was particularly well suited to Democratic party philosophy.
Many Democrats saw federal grants as vehicles that could help
the country address needs that state and local governments
had long ignored. To ensure that grants are properly used,
Democrats have generally favored **categorical grants**, which
include regulations that specify the way in which the money is
to be spent. Although some of these categorical grants fund
basic government services, such as the construction of transportation and sanitation systems, most have had social purposes. Categorical grants provide compensatory education for those coming from
disadvantaged backgrounds, fund special educational programs for the disabled,
and train the unemployed. They have been used to construct housing for low- and
moderate-income groups. Food stamps are available for the poor. Rapid transit
operations are subsidized to help reduce commuting costs.

The **War on Poverty**, a wide-ranging program designed to enhance the economic opportunity of low-income citizens, became the most famous and controversial of all categorical grant programs. Enacted in 1964 at the height of the civil rights
movement, the poverty program required involvement of the poor in program
implementation to the maximum extent feasible.

Several accomplishments of the War on Poverty remain evident three decades
later. The popular Head Start program for preschoolers anticipated and paved the
way for a nationwide system of child-care and nursery school programs. Job Corps, a
residential education and training program, paid off in better wages and employment
prospects. Most notably, the poverty program incorporated many minority leaders
into the political fabric. From the ranks of the poverty warriors emerged many minority mayors, state legislators, and members of Congress elected in the eighties and
nineties.

Despite these achievements, the War on Poverty is better known for its warring factions than its substantive results. An annual budget of $5 billion was simply not capable

Food stamps are made available
through categorical grants from
the federal to state and local
governments.

■ **categorical grant**
Federal grants to state and/or
local governments that impose
programmatic restrictions on
use of funds.

■ **War on Poverty**
One of the most controversial
of the Great Society programs.

*RUBE GOLDBERG GETS HIS THINK-TANK
WORKING AND EVOLVES THE SIMPLIFIED
PENCIL-SHARPENER.*

*OPEN WINDOW (A) AND FLY KITE (B).
STRING (C) LIFTS SMALL DOOR (D)
ALLOWING MOTHS (E) TO ESCAPE AND
EAT RED FLANNEL SHIRT (F). AS
WEIGHT OF SHIRT BECOMES LESS, SHOE
(G) STAMPS ON SWITCH (H) WHICH
HEATS ELECTRIC IRON (I) AND BURNS
HOLE IN PANTS (J). SMOKE (K) ENTERS
HOLE IN TREE (L) SMOKING OUT OPOS-
SUM (M) WHICH JUMPS INTO BASKET
(N) PULLING ROPE (O) AND LIFTING
CAGE (P), ALLOWING WOODPECKER (Q)
TO CHEW WOOD FROM PENCIL (R)
EXPOSING LEAD. EMERGENCY KNIFE (S)
IS ALWAYS HANDY IN CASE OPOSSUM OR
THE WOODPECKER GETS SICK AND
CAN'T WORK.*

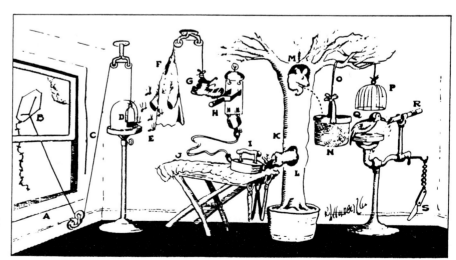

Does it have to be this complicated?

More than three decades after the War on Poverty launched a variety of early intervention programs for disadvantaged preschoolers, Head Start remains the most visible and successful.

■ **implementation**
The way in which grant programs are administered at the local level.

of financing a *war* against poverty. In addition, efforts to coordinate local social services failed dismally. Finally, most of the job-search, worker-readiness, summer-job, and other short-term training programs had only limited long-term benefits.

The main political objection to the War on Poverty was its emphasis on community action. In many cities, poverty warriors antagonized local agencies and elected officials by encouraging protests, demonstrations, legal action, and minority electoral mobilization. Local officials wondered why federal monies should fund political opposition. Some blamed the program for the wave of civil violence that swept through American cities in the two years immediately after its adoption. In 1974, President Richard Nixon, who had campaigned against the poverty war, persuaded Congress to transfer its most popular components to other agencies and shut down the remainder.

PROBLEMS OF IMPLEMENTATION

The War on Poverty was only one of many categorical grant programs that came under tough scrutiny by those who studied their **implementation**, the way in which grant programs are actually administered at the local level. Aaron Wildavsky, Martha Derthick, and other implementation theorists gave three reasons for doubting that many intergovernmental grants were as effective as Grodzins had said:[25]

1. National and local officials, serving different constituencies, often block and check one another, making it impossible to get much done. For example, when Lyndon Johnson tried to build "new towns" for the poor on vacant federal land, he encountered the opposition of local officials who objected to the program's adverse effects on local property values.[26] Virtually no new towns were built.

2. When many are involved, delays and confusion are almost inevitable. It took over four years to get a job-creation program in Oakland, California, under way. Pressman and Wildavsky pointed out that the long delay was dictated at least in part by the sheer number of agencies involved in the decision. The program required seventy separate clearances. Even if each took an average of only three weeks, not an unreasonable length of time, the total delay would be 210 weeks—or over four years.[27]

3. Federal policy makers often raise unrealistic expectations by using exaggerated rhetoric, thereby guaranteeing disappointment. It was a mistake to call the poverty program a "war" against this problem when only limited resources were allocated for this purpose.

The difficulty of achieving intergovernmental cooperation may have been exaggerated by implementation theorists. Most implementation studies focused on problems in federal grant programs during their first two or three years. More recent work has shown that, with the passage of time, many administrative problems were measurably reduced. For example, the federal compensatory education program initially stigmatized disadvantaged students by separating them from their classmates in order to make sure that federal funds were concentrated on the most needy. But once this requirement was found to be educationally counterproductive, federal administrators eliminated it.[28]

TABLE 3.1

The Transformation of Categorical Grants into Block Grants: Some Examples

Categorical Grant		Changed to Block Grant		
Name	Dates Created/Revised	New Name	Dates Transformed/Revised	Date Eliminated
Housing & Urban Development	'34, '49, '65	Housing & Community Development	'74, '81, '87	
Aid to Families with Dependent Children	'35, '50, '88	Temporary Assistance to Families in Need	'96	
Services to Families with Dependent Children	'35	Social Services block grant	'74, '81	
Manpower Development and Training	'62	Comprehensive Employment and Training (CETA)	'74, '81	
War on Poverty	'64	Partly eliminated		'74
		Partly included in social services and CETA grants	'74, '81	
Emergency School Aid (for desegregation)	'70	State Education block grant	'81	
Medicaid	'65, '90	(Remains categorical)		
Compensatory Education	'65	(Remains categorical)		
Food Stamps	'71, '74	(Remains categorical)		
Special Education	'74	(Remains categorical)		
(Never a categorical)		General revenue sharing	'72	'86

BLOCK GRANTS

Despite these more positive findings from recent research, the criticism of categorical grants by implementation theorists proved quite influential. To simplify federal policy, Congress replaced many categorical grants with **block grants**, intergovernmental grants with a broad set of objectives, a minimum of federal restrictions, and maximum discretion for local officials. Some of the programs changed from categorical to block grants are presented in Table 3.1.

The surge toward block grants has had three distinct waves, each influenced by the political circumstances prevailing at the time. The first wave of block grants began under President Nixon. The most comprehensive, **general revenue sharing**, gave state and local governments a share of federal tax revenues to be used for any purpose whatsoever. During the first wave, block grants did not so much replace categorical grants as supplement them. To win support for general revenue sharing and other block grants, Nixon was forced to agree to continue many of the categorical programs that congressional Democrats favored. As a consequence, the total size of the intergovernmental grant program continued to grow throughout the administrations of Richard Nixon and Gerald Ford, and by 1977 they cost more than $125 billion (see Figure 3.2).

The second wave of block grants came at the beginning of the Reagan administration, which, unlike the Nixon administration, enjoyed a Republican majority in

■ **block grant**
Federal grant to state and/or local government that imposes minimal restrictions on use of funds.

■ **general revenue sharing**
The most comprehensive of block grants, it gave money to state and local governments to be used for any purpose whatsoever.

Categorical or Block Grants: Which Is Better?

The debate over categorical and block grants has been intense. Which position do you find more persuasive? Those in favor of block grants and against categoricals argue as follows:

1. Categoricals are inefficient. Federal regulations tie the hands of state and local governments, who have a better feel for local conditions. Montana residents should be able to set their own speed limits, not be tied to federal limits designed for urban areas.

2. Grants are inequitable. Federal grants are handed out to all states on a more or less equal basis, with wealthier states receiving as much or more federal dollars as poorer states.

3. Categoricals create vested interests. Categorical grants typically contain restrictions that focus services on specific groups. These groups support powerful lobbies that perpetuate unneeded policies.

4. Categoricals impose unfunded mandates. Federal funds do not cover the cost of the rules that accompany them. As a result, state budgets are adversely affected and state sovereignty is violated.

Those who defend categoricals make the following case for categoricals and against block grants:

1. Categoricals are necessary to achieve national purposes. Many environmental problems are national in scope. If a state does not clean up its radioactive waste, the resulting pollution can have repercussions far beyond its own boundaries. The federal government needs to attach regulations to its grants to ensure state and local achievement of national objectives.

2. If grants are not categoricals that include regulations, state will "race to the bottom." Federal supervision of Medicaid, food stamps, and other welfare programs is especially important, because states, when not subject to federal regulation, try to shift to other states the burden of serving the needy, the sick, and the poor.

3. Block grants are wasteful. If the federal government provides the money, it has every right and responsibility to make sure the funds are used for federal purposes. Block grants are a dream for local politicians—"free" money to be spent however they want without being held accountable to local taxpayers. When money is "free," it is likely to be wasted.

4. Block grants are simply the first step toward eliminating needed federal programs. Once a program has been converted from a categorical to a block grant, its constituency is less well defined and it becomes harder to sustain the program's political base of support.

the Senate. Reagan succeeded in converting to block grants a broad range of categorical grants in education, social services, health services, and community development. During the second wave, the new block grants not only had fewer restrictions than did the older categoricals,[29] but they became a means by which

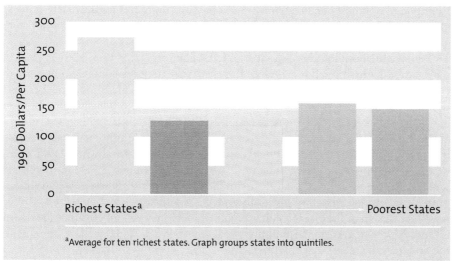

FIGURE 3.3

Block Grants for Traditional
Government Services:
Richer states get as much or more
money than poorer states.

SOURCE: Paul E. Peterson, *The Price of Federalism* (Washington, D.C.: Brookings, 1995), 136.

overall funding levels were reduced. The amount spent on block grants fell from $75 billion in 1977 to $60 billion in 1990 (see Figure 3.2). General revenue sharing was eliminated in 1985, and the community development block grant was cut from $6.1 billion in 1980 to $2.8 billion in 1990.

The third wave of block grants took place after the election of 1994, when Republicans captured control of both congressional chambers. Earlier block grants had left intact large social welfare programs, such as Medicaid and Aid to Families with Dependent Children (AFDC). But in 1996 Congress transformed the AFDC program into a block grant that gave states almost complete discretion over the way in which monies could be used (see Chapter 18). Congress also tried to transform the Medicaid program into a block grant, but this was forestalled by a presidential veto.

Ever since the 1994 election, the debate over categorical and block grants has become a matter of intense political conflict. Each side can make a compelling case for its point of view (see Democratic Dilemma). Perhaps the best argument against both categorical and block grants is that even though they are often defended as a way of equalizing resources across the country,[30] federal grants in fact do not have this effect. Instead, federal grants are handed out to all states on a more or less equal basis, with wealthier states receiving as much or more federal dollars as poorer states (see Figure 3.3).

Election pressures make it difficult for Congress to direct federal dollars to needy parts of the country. Members of Congress fight to get as much money for their home states and districts as possible. If they do not, their election opponent can make it a campaign issue. The experience of Massachusetts Senator Edward Kennedy provides an illuminating example of the political dynamics. In 1988, Kennedy had run on the campaign slogan, "He can do more for Massachusetts," a reference to his many Washington connections dating to the time when his brother had been president. Six years later, when Kennedy ran for reelection in 1994, a study showed that Massachusetts was receiving only 97 cents back for every dollar paid in taxes (instead of the $1.01 it had received in 1988). The finding fetched the following headline in a local newspaper: "State's Share of Federal Dollars Drops: Kennedy's Record in Last Decade, a Campaign Issue." Kennedy's

Republican opponent accused him of not having "done the hard work to do very much [for Massachusetts] at all."[31] Though Kennedy still won reelection, the vote was surprisingly close.

Perhaps the best argument in favor of federal grants is that they are necessary to maintain properly funded social programs. Federal categorical grants, such as medicaid, food stamps, and other welfare programs, are especially important, because states, when not subject to federal regulation, try to shift to other states the burden of serving the needy, the sick, and the poor. In Minnesota, a state with generous programs for the poor, the proportion of new recipients coming from out of state increased from 19 to 28 percent between 1994 and 1995, a time when other states were placing limits on welfare benefits. "We're really concerned," a county official said.[32] A New Jersey official, reporting similar developments, called it "welfare shopping."[33] Fearful of migration from other places, many states feel pressured to offer fewer benefits than their sister states, creating a vicious cycle of cuts that President Clinton called a "race to the bottom." Between 1970 and 1993, welfare benefits in the average state fell by 42 percent.[34]

Though the debate over grants has polarized between those in favor of all kinds of intergovernmental grants and those opposed to any, the most sensible solutions may lie somewhere in the middle. In areas where state and local governments have traditionally concentrated their efforts, including transportation, sanitation, and education, it may be appropriate to keep the federal role to a minimum, because states and localities can be expected to provide these services, whether or not they receive federal aid. But in other areas, such as medicaid and food stamps, it may be important to establish federal standards so that states do not "race to the bottom." In 1966 Congress and the president in fact found it possible to reach compromises at this middle position. They made the biggest cuts in traditional programs. They also changed the AFDC program into a block grant welfare program. But the largest social programs, Medicaid and food stamps, remained federally funded categorical programs.[35]

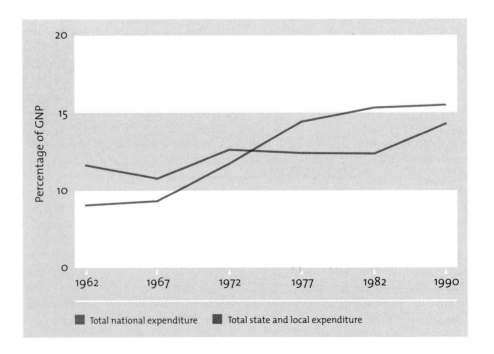

FIGURE 3.4

Domestic Expenditure of Governments: State and local governments spend almost as much as national government does.

SOURCE: Paul E. Peterson, *The Price of Federalism* (Washington, D.C.: Brookings, 1995), Table 3-1.

CHAPTER 3

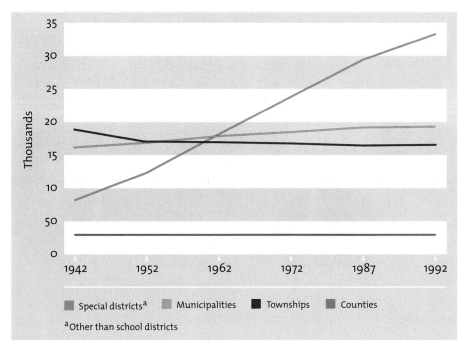

FIGURE 3.5

Number of Local Governments, 1942–1987.

SOURCE: Adapted from Nancy Burns, *The Formation of American Local Governments: Private Values in Public Institutions* (New York: Oxford University Press, 1994), 6; Bureau of the Census, *Statistical Abstract of the United States*, 1993.

★ AT THE STATE & LOCAL LEVEL

Local Government

Because of the recent devolution of responsibilities to state and local governments, these governments play a more important role in the federal system than they have for several decades. Even before the most recent devolution, nearly half of all domestic government expenditure was paid for by taxes raised by state and local governments (see Figure 3.4). This pattern is in keeping with long-standing American traditions. Nearly a century ago, the British scholar, James Bryce, identified the key role played by local governments in the American federal system:

> It is the business of a local authority to mend the roads, to clean out the village well or to provide a new pump, to see that there is a place where straying beasts may be kept till the owner reclaims them, to fix the number of cattle each villager may turn out on the common pasture, [and] to give each his share of timber cut in the common woodland.[36]

Though the nature of the work has been modernized since Lord Bryce wrote, the basic functions remain much the same. Local governments maintain roads, take care of the parks, provide police, fire, and sanitation services, run the schools, and do many, many other things.

THE NUMBER AND TYPES OF LOCAL GOVERNMENTS

In sheer numbers, local governments constitute an overwhelming and growing presence—over 75,000 in 1992, up from 46,000 in 1942 (see Figure 3.5). The type of local government and its exact responsibilities vary greatly from one state to the next. Though the basic unit is, in most states, the county, not all counties are alike.

The basic functions of local government can range from garbage collection to, well, traffic control. A Washington, D.C., police officer on traffic duty with the elephants from ringling Brothers Barnum and Bailey Circus.

In some states they manage school systems, welfare programs, local roads, sanitation systems, a sheriff's office, and an array of other government activities. In other states, they have hardly any duties. Many counties are divided into townships—nearly 17,000 of them—whose duties generally include local road maintenance and other small-scale activities.

As the population has become concentrated in urban areas, the number of municipalities—cities, suburbs, and towns—has increased to nearly 20,000. In most states, these municipal governments have assumed many of the responsibilities once performed by counties.

States, counties, and municipalities have also created an extraordinary array of special districts—nearly 30,000 in all—that have responsibility for some specific governmental function. Some special districts run schools, others manage parks, and still others manage transportation systems. Even as specific a task as mosquito abatement can be the responsibility of a special district.

LOCAL ELECTIONS

In towns like this one in rural New England, town meetings may be scheduled at unpredictable and rather unusual times, in order to obtain citizens' votes on pressing budgetary issues. As a result, turnout may be low.

Most local governments are run by elected officials, though special-district heads are sometimes appointed by other local governments. In the United States as a whole, the total number of elected local officials approaches ½ million people. But despite the large number of elections, actual rates of citizen participation are surprisingly low. If a particularly colorful candidate runs for mayor, or if ethnic or racial issues are raised, large numbers of voters can show up at the polls. But much of the time the local electorate is half the size of the presidential electorate.[37] In small-town and suburban communities, usual voting rates are even less.[38]

The near invisibility of local elections helps to reduce local participation rates. The sheer number of elected officeholders often makes local government elections confusing to many voters. Newspaper coverage is haphazard. Turnout rates are further reduced by the fact that many local governments hold their elections at times that coincide with neither state nor national elections. Many cities and towns hold nonpartisan elections, which do not allow the names of political parties on the ballot, making it more difficult for the voter to figure out which candidate stands for

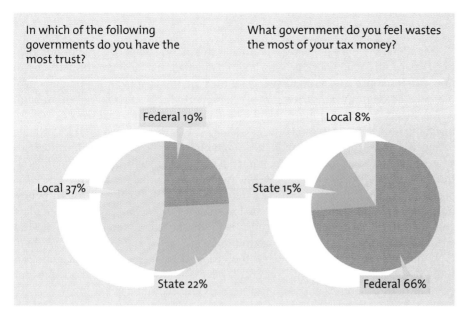

In which of the following governments do you have the most trust?

Federal 19%

Local 37%

State 22%

What government do you feel wastes the most of your tax money?

Local 8%

State 15%

Federal 66%

FIGURE 3.6

Evaluations of Federal, State, and Local Governments: More people trust local government.

SOURCE: Thomas R. Dye, "Federalism: A Return to the Future," *Madison Review* (1) (Fall 1995): 3.

what. Fundamentally, local politics is generally less contentious, except in big cities. Though conflicts break out on occasion, often the voters find little reason to support one candidate over another.[39]

POPULARITY OF LOCAL GOVERNMENT

One might think this extraordinarily diverse, complicated, only half-democratic, seemingly irrational system could not possibly succeed. Yet local government remains very popular (see Figure 3.6). Thirty-seven percent of the population have the most trust in their local government, compared to the only 19 percent who trust the federal government the most. Only 8 percent feel their local government is most wasteful of their tax dollars, as compared to 66 percent who feel this way about the federal government.

One explanation for the apparent popularity of local government, despite the invisibility of its elections, is the ability to "vote with the feet," that is, to move from one community to another, if people are unhappy with their local government. Americans are a mobile people: Over 17 percent move each year.[40] Every local government has to take care that if it is inefficient or unresponsive, its city or town will lose in population and property values. As a result, most local governments have good reason to keep in close touch with constituents, despite low voting rates.

Local governments also serve as **laboratories of democracy**, places where experiments are tried and proved. If successful, the experiment is copied by other town governments. If it fails, the experiment is soon abandoned.

Finally, the wide variety of local governments gives people a choice. Some people favor sex education programs and condom distribution in school; others do not. Some people think refuse collection should be publicly provided; others prefer to recycle their own garbage. Some people think police protection should be intensive; others think intrusive police invade the civil liberties of citizens. By giving people a choice, local government reduces conflict and enhances citizen satisfaction.

■ **laboratories of democracy**
Doctrine that state and local governments contribute to democracy by providing places where experiments are tried and proved.

LIMITS ON LOCAL GOVERNMENT

For all the strengths of local governments, they often do not have the resources to meet the needs of the poor, the sick, and the disabled. If a local government tries to provide substantial services to the needy, it runs the risk of attracting more poor people to its community and driving away the better-off. For example, Framingham, Massachusetts became a convenient place for a broad range of social services, including group homes for recovering drug and alcohol abusers, halfway houses for juvenile offenders, counseling centers, and other programs for the poor. Though the programs were well administered, a growing number of clients eventually provoked complaints from town leaders that the community was becoming "a magnet for everyone else's problems." Complaining that taxpayers were being asked to foot the bill for the education, security, and fire protection of low-income nontaxpayers, one candidate appealed effectively to local voters by insisting, "We can't afford this anymore."[41] Most local governments agree: From their own tax dollars, they spend less than 1 percent of GNP on social programs. (But such is the variety of local government that one can find exceptions to this as to any other rule: San Francisco and New York City, for example, provide a broad range of social services for needy groups.)

Local governments also compete with one another to attract businesses. With state help, one county in Kentucky outbid its neighbors for a Canadian steel mill employing 400 people. It ended up costing the state $350,000 for every job created. Such bidding wars have spread across the country. As one Michigan official put it, "Right now, all we are doing is eating each other's lunch. At some stage we have to start thinking about dinner."[42]

⭐ **AT THE STATE & LOCAL LEVEL**

State Government

When the Constitution was written, the fundamental organization of the federal government was copied from that which existed in most states. Thus it is not surprising that the basic design of most state governments bears a strong similarity to that of the national government. All states have multi-tiered court systems roughly comparable to that of the federal system. The legislatures in all states except Nebraska (which is unicameral) have an upper and lower chamber. Every state has an independently elected governor, whose responsibilities roughly parallel those of the president.

State governments have become increasingly professionalized in recent decades. In many states, fifty years ago, the job of state legislator was little more than a modest distraction from the ordinary business of life. Wyoming legislators, for example, were paid $12 for each day the legislature was in session. But this did not amount to much, since the legislature met every other year for no more than forty days. Legislators came and went. Half the legislature turned over every two years.

But as state government has become more complicated, state legislatures have become professionalized. In 1990, California was among the most modern. Its members remained in legislative session throughout the year, and they received a $41,000 salary, retirement benefits, and handsome per diem expense pay as well as the services of a full-time staff. Turnover rates were half those in Wyoming. During the 1990s, state voters reacted against the professionalization of state government, as many states limited the terms of legislators, cut their staff to the bone, and reduced their salary and benefits.

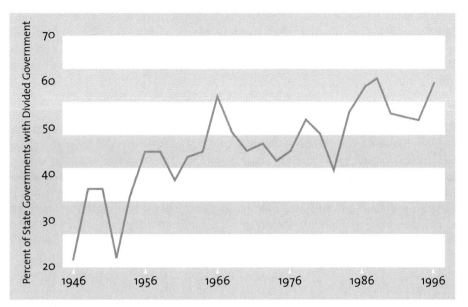

FIGURE 3.7

States with Divided Government: Increasingly, if the governor is one party, the other party has a majority in either the state senate or house.

SOURCE: Morris Fiorina, *Divided Government* (New York: Macmillan, 1992), 31.

STATE ELECTIONS

State elections bear a strong resemblance to national elections. The same two political parties—Republican and Democratic—are the dominant competitors in almost all state elections, though an independent candidate, Lowell Weicker, recently served a term as governor of Connecticut. For many decades following the Civil War, the party of Lincoln, the Republicans, dominated the North, while the South was solidly Democratic. These regional distinctions have broken down in recent years, with Republicans often winning as many southern elections as Democrats. A new trend toward competitive politics and divided government has developed in most states (see Figure 3.7). Democrats have had the advantage in state legislative races, while Republicans more often win the gubernatorial chair. Some scholars think the voters like it this way: Each party can keep a check on the other, and government will drift to neither political extreme.[43]

VARIATION IN STATE GOVERNMENT RESPONSIBILITIES

The size and range of state responsibilities have grown dramatically in recent decades. States bear heavy responsibilities for financing elementary and secondary education as well as for state colleges and universities. They maintain state parks, highway systems, and prisons. They manage welfare and medicaid programs that serve low-income populations. They give grants to local governments to help pay for police, fire, and other basic government services. Overall, state expenditures increased from less than 5 percent of GNP in 1962 to 7.6 percent in 1990.

The amount that states and their local governments spend on government services varies considerably. For one thing, wealthier states spend much more on public services. In 1991, the ten richest states spent an average of $3,750 per person on public services, while the ten poorest states spent, on average, less than $2,000.[44] Many liberals say these differences in spending for education, health, and other public services are inequitable and should be rectified by federal grants. Many conservatives say that it is only to be expected that wealthier people will spend more on public services, just as they spend more for clothes, houses, and cars. In any case, federal grants do very little, if anything, to reduce interstate fiscal inequalities.

Expenditures are also affected by elections. The more Democrats who win election to the legislature, the higher the expenditure for social services. The more Republicans who win, the higher the expenditure for traditional government services.[45] Expenditures are also higher in those states where the legislature has become more professionalized. In 1991, the twenty states with the best-paid legislatures spent $3,160 per person as compared to $2,280 per person in the twenty states with the least well-paid legislature.[46] Conservatives see the higher costs of government in professionalized states as one more reason for imposing term limits. In reply, liberals say that modern society needs a sophisticated, professionally administered system of public services.

Chapter Summary

The Constitution did not clearly define the powers of the federal and state governments. As a result, the nature of American federalism has changed in response to electoral forces and Supreme Court decisions. Much of the debate over federalism has revolved around the meaning of dual sovereignty. The most extreme interpretation of dual sovereignty, the doctrine of nullification, was rejected with the end of the Civil War.

The concept of dual sovereignty was further eroded with the election of Franklin Roosevelt and the enactment of New Deal legislation that greatly enhanced the power of the federal government. Three provisions in the Constitution facilitated the expansion of federal power—the necessary and proper, the commerce, and the spending clauses.

With the election of strong Democratic majorities in the 1960s, there emerged a new theory of federalism known as cooperative or marble-cake federalism, which stated that all levels of government can and should work together. Consistent with this new theory, many new federal grants were given to state and local governments. Many of these grants were categorical in nature; they contained restrictions that specified how the money should be spent. In response to criticism of the implementation of categorical grants, Republican leaders called for the replacement of categorical with block grants that have few federal mandates or restrictions. The two parties remain divided over the merits of categorical and block grants.

Despite the expansion of federal power, state and local governments remain vital components of the federal system. Nearly half the domestic expenditures of the government are paid for out of state and local tax dollars. Though few citizens participate in local elections, local governments are the most popular of all governmental levels, in part because people can "vote with their feet," that is, choose as a place to live the local community they like best.

Key Terms

block grant, p. 85

categorical grant, p. 83

commerce clause, p. 79

cooperative federalism, p. 81

devolution, p. 73

Dillon's rule, p. 71

dual sovereignty, p. 75

federalism, p. 71

general revenue sharing, p. 85

implementation, p. 84

intergovernmental grant, p. 81

judicial review, p. 74

laboratories of democracy, p. 91

marble-cake federalism, p. 81

McCulloch v. Maryland, p. 77

necessary and proper clause, p. 78

New Deal, p. 79

nullification, p. 75

spending clause, p. 80

supremacy clause, p. 74

unfunded mandates, p. 72

unitary government, p. 71

War on Poverty, p. 83

Suggested Readings

Conlan, Timothy. *New Federalism: Intergovernmental Reform from Nixon to Reagan.* Washington, DC: Brookings, 1988. Excellent analysis of changing federal policy.

Dahl, Robert. *Who Governs?* New Haven: Yale University Press, 1961. Classic study of local politics in New Haven.

Dye, Thomas R. *American Federalism: Competition Among Government.* Lexington, MA: D. C. Heath, 1990. Comprehensive account of the way state and local government systems work.

Elkins, Stanley, and Eric McKitrick. *The Age of Federalism.* New York: Oxford, 1993. Account of the first decades of the federal system under the Constitution.

Fiorina, Morris, *Divided Government.* New York: Macmillan, 1992. Explains why control of many state governments is divided between Democratic and Republican parties.

Grodzins, Morton. *The American System: A New View of Government in the United States.* Chicago: Rand McNally, 1966. Classic study of cooperative federalism.

Peterson, Paul E. *The Price of Federalism.* Washington, D.C.: Brookings, 1995. Contrasts the responsibilities of national, state, and local governments.

Pressman, Jeffrey L. and Aaron Wildavsky. *Implementation.* 3rd ed. Berkeley: University of California Press, 1973. Readable, fascinating account of the implementation of a federal program in Oakland, California.

Riker, William H. *Federalism: Origin, Operation, Significance.* Boston: Little, Brown, 1964. Theoretical treatise on federalism.

Rivlin, Alice. *Rethinking the American Dream.* Washington, D.C.: Brookings, 1992. Calls for reorganization of the American federal system.

Smith, Jean E. *John Marshall: Definer of a Nation.* New York: Henry Holt, 1996. Excellent biography of the Chief Justice who helped defined American federalism.

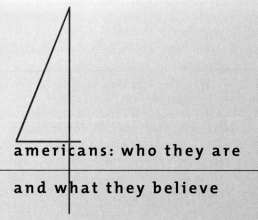

4

americans: who they are

and what they believe

ORE THAN six years of war filled the interval between the Minutemen's stand at Concord that began the American Revolution and the British surrender at Yorktown that ended it. At times the military position of the colonies was desperate, but in the end the newly formed Continental Army and the colonial militias bested the finest standing army in the world.

Well, not exactly. The Americans had a little help from their friends. The French Marquis de Lafayette and the German Baron Johann de Kalb were among Washington's top generals from the beginning (de Kalb died after suffering eleven wounds in hand-to-hand combat).[1] When Washington's army was suffering at Valley Forge and the American cause looked as if it might be lost, another German, Baron Friedrich Wilhelm von Steuben, arrived. An expert in military drill, von Steuben helped transform the untrained Americans into a disciplined force that could stand against the British regulars. A Polish general, Casimir Pulaski, known as the father of the American cavalry,[2] was mortally wounded leading an international unit (Americans, Poles, Irish, French, and Germans) against British fortifications at Savannah. Another Pole, Thaddeus Kosciuszko, designed the defenses at Saratoga, where Americans stopped the British and prevented the separation of New England from the other colonies. (Kosciuszko also designed the fortifications at West Point that the American general and traitor Benedict Arnold tried to deliver to the British.) A Spanish commander in New Orleans, Don Bernardo de Galvez, organized a force of 1200 men, including 80 free blacks and 160 Indians and sailed up the Mississippi, taking British forts as far as Natchez. Then he captured Mobile and Pensacola. In all, de Galvez took about 3000 British soldiers out of the fight.[3] Without this "foreign aid" Americans might still be singing "God Save the Queen" at the start of baseball and football games.

While students read about Lafayette and the support of France in their elementary school history classes, the international character of the "American" Revolution is not sufficiently appreciated. At the time, it was not unusual for soldiers to fight under a foreign flag: recall the story of Washington's midnight raid across the Delaware, where he defeated the Hessians at Trenton. But like the Hessians, foreigners who fought under another flag usually were mercenaries—professional soldiers who fought for pay. In contrast, many of the foreigners who fought in the American revolution volunteered their services (high-ranking army officers were not even paid until after the war). Their motives were mixed, of course. Some, like de Galvez, had the tacit support of their governments, and some had hopes of lands or positions after the war. But many had some degree of commitment to the republican struggle: Kosciuszko donated his military compensation toward the emancipation of the slaves. They came to the colonies, at least in part, because of their attraction to the kind of society that was being created.

n a less grand scale, millions of people have made choices similar to those made by these eighteenth-century foreign officers, and millions more continue to do so today. Carl Friedrich, who immigrated to the United States from Germany, wrote in 1935 that "To be an American is an ideal, while to be a Frenchman is a fact."[4] In the second part of this observation, Friedrich was pointing out that, in most of the world, citizenship is based on race or ethnicity: Members of the dominant racial or ethnic group automatically enjoy the rights and privileges of **citizenship**. If you are not of the appropriate racial or ethnic group, you may not be able to become a citizen even if you were born and have lived your whole life in the country (see International Comparison). This much of Friedrich's observation is simple fact.

What of the first part of Friedrich's assertion—that to be an American is an ideal? Perhaps the easiest way to understand what he meant is to consider the concept of an "unAmerican activity." Americans are clear on this concept. Indeed, from 1945–1969 there was a Congressional Committee—the House Committee on Un-American Activities—that investigated people and organizations suspected of being so engaged.[5] Most of the rest of the world, however, would be unclear on the concept. Why? Consider un-French activities, un-Japanese activities, or un-Egyptian activities. Such concepts make little sense because French, Japanese, or Egyptian refers to the nationality of the people who inhabit the country, not to a set of beliefs and values that can be embraced by people of any ethnic heritage.

Understanding the fundamental beliefs and values of the American people is essential to understanding American government and politics, for even while we emphasize the importance of American institutions, we also emphasize that the operation of these institutions depends on their interaction with the beliefs and values of the citizenry. Imagine, for example, that troubled countries like Bosnia and Burundi were to adopt the United States Constitution and the body of law that has evolved from it. Would their politics look just like ours after they had a few years to become familiar with the new arrangements? Most people intuitively would answer no. The histories, cultures, and economies of countries differ; consequently the beliefs and values of their citizens differ, and it is the interaction of institutions with the larger social and cultural context that produces a country's politics.

Moreover, political institutions are adopted, maintained, and transformed by human beings. And since institutions are human creations, when they conflict with social realities and political practices, they may be replaced, modified, or at a minimum, ignored.

For these reasons, it is important to take a close look at the American people—who we are and what we believe. However, the focus here is not on what Americans believe about the specific personalities and issues of the day; that is what we call public opinion, and we will deal with it in the next chapter. Here we are interested in the deeper beliefs and values of Americans—what they consider to be the purpose of government, how they believe their institutions should work, what authority they consider legitimate, and how they view their rights and responsibilities as well as their duties and obligations. These beliefs and values are the context in which American electoral democracy operates. Some scholars refer to such deep, shared beliefs and values as the **political culture** of a country.

■ **citizenship**
Status held by someone entitled to all the rights and privileges of a full-fledged member of a political community.

■ **political culture**
Collection of beliefs and values about the justification and operation of a country's government and politics.

Any child born in the United States is a citizen. A child born outside the United States is a citizen if either parent is a citizen and has lived in the United States for ten years, two after age fourteen. Legal immigrants can become "naturalized" citizens after five years' residence: They must learn English, demonstrate knowledge of American history and government, renounce their previous citizenship, and swear allegiance to the Constitution and laws of the United States.

Practices in other countries differ considerably. In Germany, for most of the twentieth century, citizenship has been based almost exclusively on ethnicity. In addition to those granted citizenship when the new German Republic was established after World War II, the German Constitution continued an older tradition by defining a German as "a refugee or expellee of German stock or as the spouse or descendant of such a person." Eastern European or Russian residents whose ancestors left Germany centuries ago can migrate to Germany today and quickly assume the rights and privileges of citizenship (as could Americans of German descent if they were of a mind to do so). But the children of a Turkish "guest" worker, born in Germany and speaking German as a first language, are ineligible for citizenship because they are not "German." Germany is an extreme case of ethnically defined citizenship and it has been a matter of considerable controversy in recent years. But most democracies follow practices closer to Germany's than to those of the United States.

The Economist, April 5, 1997: 45–46.

America: Consensus amid Diversity

Many foreign observers find in the American people an intriguing and somewhat puzzling contrast. On the one hand, Americans are—and always have been—more ethnically and religiously diverse than the citizens of other democracies. Most of the world's multicultural democracies have been short-lived—Yugoslavia and Rwanda being two of the latest, tragic examples. Long-lived multicultural societies have not been democracies; rather, they have been authoritarian states like the Austro-Hungarian and Soviet empires, in which central authority repressed ethnic and religious conflicts. The few multicultural democracies that have survived often have done so by decentralizing—giving autonomy to ethnic, religious, or linguistic subgroups. Belgium, for example, is divided into three zones: the city of Brussels, and the Dutch-speaking Flemish and French-speaking Waloon linguistic zones. Within their respective zones each linguistic group controls education and other important policy areas. Strife-torn Burundi and decentralized Belgium are the rule, the United States the exception, an unusual example of diverse people peacefully coexisting under the same democratic government.[6]

On the other hand, generations of European observers have emphasized the homogeneity of American political views, noting that more than in other democracies Americans agree on fundamentals and share basic assumptions about how a good society should be organized. On first hearing, this strikes many Americans as exaggerated, if not wrong, in view of the considerable controversy and disagreement in the United States. But consider that European democracies have major socialist and religious parties—the Social Democrats and Christian Democrats—and until recently, significant Communist and Fascist parties. In the United States, as science fiction writer (and socialist activist) H.G. Wells once observed, "the two great political parties . . . represent only one English party, the middle-class Liberal party, the party of industrialism and freedom . . . All Americans are, from the English point of view, Liberals of one sort or another."7 More

Americans are defined by beliefs, not blood.

recently, the *Economist* (a British newsmagazine) discounted the notion that the 1992 presidential election was about "change." Remarked the British correspondent: ". . not since Herbert Hoover lost to Franklin Roosevelt (and arguably not even then) has there been an American election in which there were real, vivid ideological differences between the parties that were capable of being transmuted into radically different styles of government."8 Even to the relatively uniform English, Americans look unusually homogeneous.

Is it really the case that an ethnically and religiously heterogeneous society somehow developed a homogeneous political culture? If so, how? We will return to that question after considering the social diversity and philosophical unity of the American people.

WORLD IDEOLOGIES NOT COMMON IN THE UNITED STATES

For most of the twentieth century the major competitor of liberal ideology has been **socialism,** a philosophy that supports government ownership and operation of the means of production as well as government determination of the level of social and economic benefits that

people receive. Socialist states can be either democratic or nondemocratic. Social Democratic parties in democratic countries generally espouse some degree of socialist ideology.

Communism is a particular kind of socialism based on the work of Karl Marx, who taught that human history is the product of a class struggle between those who exploit and those who are exploited. Communism is not a democratic ideology as the term is commonly understood.

Fascism is rule by a charismatic dictator supported by a strong party that permeates society. Fascism differs from communism by its support for capital against labor and its frequent association with extreme nationalism.

Clericalism supports the exercise of political power by religious leaders and organizations, such as established churches. Christian Democratic parties in democratic countries often show some degree of clericalist sympathy.

As New York's "Little Italy" illustrates, multiculturalism is nothing new in the United States.

Social Diversity

In *Federalist No. 2* John Jay wrote:

. . . Providence has been pleased to give this one connected country, to one united people; a people descended from the same ancestors, speaking the same language, professing the same religion, attached to the same principles of government, very similar in their manners and customs and who, by their joint counsels, arms and efforts, fighting side by side throughout a long and bloody war, have nobly established their general Liberty and Independence.

Such statements remind us that the *Federalist* was first and foremost a campaign document, for Americans were not nearly as similar—in ethnicity, customs, religious beliefs, or behavior—as Jay alleged. His exaggeration of American cultural and historical unity was a political tactic, an appeal for Americans to rise above the serious divisions that threatened the ratification of the Constitution.

Contrary to Jay's campaign claim, the so-called "New World" was settled by an assortment of different people. While the British were most numerous, the Dutch originally settled New York, and the Swedes established settlements in the area of Delaware and Eastern Pennsylvania. The French were present on the northern and western borders, and the Spanish in the South, although the latter were never very numerous. As for the British, they were not all of a kind. New England was settled by Puritans—dissenters from the Church of England—while Virginians were predominantly loyal to the Church. Maryland was a grant to a Catholic noble, Lord Baltimore, who welcomed his fellow worshippers, and Pennsylvania welcomed Quakers, unwelcome almost everywhere else. Moreover, after 1700 British emigration came increasingly from Scotland, Wales, and Ireland, and the indentured servants (who made up half the population of Pennsylvania, New York, and New Jersey) included thousands of Germans, Scandinavians, Belgians, French, and Swiss. These were

An Illinois mob murders Mormon leader Joseph Smith in 1844. The diversity represented by his religion's polygamist practices was intolerable to Illinois Protestants.

only the voluntary immigrants, of course; the involuntary immigrants—the slaves—were African American. (The Native Americans whose numbers had been decimated by wars and disease, were viewed as separate nations.) All in all, historians estimate that in 1763 only about 50 percent of the population of the colonies was English proper, and nearly 20 percent was African American.[9]

Some students may read the preceding paragraph with skepticism: "A bunch of northern Europeans from different Christian churches is your idea of diversity?" Such a reaction is understandable, but historically naive, for notions of diversity are relative to time and place. During the Thirty Years' War (1618–1648) those northern European Catholics, Calvinists, and Lutherans engaged in pillage, rape, and murder on an incredible scale—one-third the population of what is now Germany died during the conflict. Near the end of that period, the English Civil War (1642–1653) pitted English Puritan dissenters from the Church of England against English Royalist defenders of Church and Crown. Ultimately, the king and archbishop lost their heads. This conflict had a faint echo in Maryland, incidentally, as Catholics, Puritans, and Anglicans for a time engaged in a "minor civil war."[10] For perhaps the most appalling counterexample to the notion that all northern European Christians were alike, consider the St. Bartholomew's Day Massacre, which began on August 24, 1572. After deciding on a "final solution," French Catholics killed 30,000 French Calvinists, moving door-to-door and farm-to-farm, using swords, axes, and crude firearms.

To contemporary Americans **diversity** exists when people of color interact with whites, when people from nonwestern religious traditions interact with those from western traditions, and when people with nontraditional lifestyles interact with those more traditionally oriented. But diversity is a relative concept. In 1640 a German Catholic looked upon a German Protestant with no more understanding (and perhaps less) than an American Catholic or Jew looks upon a Muslim today. In 1844 Illinois protestants murdered Mormon leader Joseph Smith and drove off his followers;

▪ **diversity**
A concept that is relative to time and place; currently refers primarily to ethnic and racial distinctions among people (as opposed to, say, class or occupational differences).

the Mormons practiced polygamy, an intolerable violation of "family values"—as they were understood in that era. And to many Americans of 1900 Greeks and Italians were people of color who detracted from the racial purity of America. *Relative to other countries, and to the times, America has always been diverse.* The national motto, imprinted on the United States Seal and several coins, *E Pluribus Unum*—"out of many, one"—explicitly recognizes that diversity.

In contemporary controversies about multiculturalism—a debate so complex it cannot be defined—both sides exaggerate the homogeneity of the American past, although for different reasons. Both proponents and critics exaggerate the distinctiveness of the present wave of immigration, when in fact, earlier generations of Americans found the immigrants of their eras just as "foreign" as do contemporary generations. Both proponents and critics of multiculturalism exaggerate the ease with which earlier generations of immigrants were assimilated into American society, when, in fact, the existence of distinct ethnic and religious groups and their desire to preserve some part of their distinctiveness underlies much of the history of political conflict in America. Today's debates over multiculturalism, immigration, and related topics are largely a rehash of debates that have occurred in earlier periods. Americans born here always have worried about the capacity of new arrivals to "fit in." Such facts are often overlooked in contemporary political discussion, so it is worthwhile to discuss them in detail here.

___

A Nation of Immigrants Then

After the successful campaign for ratification of the Constitution, the United States maintained the states' existing policy of free immigration, although some concerns were voiced. One of the most cosmopolitan Americans of the time, Benjamin Franklin, expressed his resentment of Germans in several letters:

> *Why should* Pennsylvania, *founded by the* English, *become a colony of Aliens, who will shortly be so numerous as to Germanize us instead of our Anglifying them, and will never adopt our Language or Customs any more than they can acquire our Complexion?" (emphasis in original).*[11]

Despite such misgivings, land was plentiful and labor scarce. The more rapidly the territory could be populated, the more rapidly economic development would follow. Immigration gradually increased, until by mid-century immigrants from England, Ireland, and Germany were arriving in numbers as high as 400,000 per year. Irish immigration became a major political issue. Catholic, and largely poor, they were threatening to many Americans. In the 1854 elections the anti-Catholic "Know-Nothing" party (the party's name comes from its "secret" password: "I know nothing") won 43 seats in Congress—comparable to 80 today. The perception of the Irish as un-American was unfortunately reinforced when tens of thousands of Irish immigrants in New York City rioted during the Civil War after the Lincoln administration attempted to draft them into the Union Army.[12]

Immigration increased considerably in the 1860s and continued at a high rate until World War I. In the 1860s and 1870s the first of an eventual half-million French Canadians began to cross the northern border of the United States, especially in New England, and a couple of million Scandinavians joined a continuing stream of English, Irish, and Germans. Again, today's students may be tempted to view such groups as similar, but many historians argue that the principal basis of state and local political conflict in the late nineteenth century was "ethno-

Americans have never hesitated to impose their values through public laws. The Massachusetts "Blue Laws," which still prohibit liquor sales on Sunday, have sent many a thirsty Massachusetts resident across the New Hampshire border to make a late-weekend purchase. Massachusetts has recently responded by allowing liquor stores near the border to remain open on Sundays.

cultural." In the midwestern battleground states and much of the East, the Republicans had their base in the native stock, Protestant communities, while the Democrats had their deepest roots in the immigrant Catholic communities. Politics revolved around such issues as the prohibition or regulation of alcohol, public funding of Catholic schools, bilingual schools (mostly German, but French in New England), and Sunday "Blue Laws"—laws that restricted commercial and recreational activities on Sundays. The German Lutherans became an important "swing" group in some midwestern states, often voting Republican but swinging to the Democrats when "pietist" Protestants within the Republican Party could not resist the temptation to legislate on cultural and behavioral issues of great sensitivity to immigrants.[13] The Scandinavians, moreover, brought "subversive" notions like socialism to the United States.

Meanwhile, the adoption of the Fourteenth Amendment gave citizenship to 4.6 million African Americans, who constituted about the same proportion of the population in 1865—one-eighth—that they do today. African Americans, of course, differed in one critical respect from other immigrants: they did not choose to emigrate, but were forcibly abducted from their homelands. This fact differentiates the African American experience from that of other immigrants and means that general statements about race and ethnicity must be qualified when considering the history of blacks in America. Nevertheless, it is important to realize that until the "Jim Crow" repression deprived them of fundamental political rights in the 1890s (Chapter 17), African Americans enjoyed significant electoral successes after the Civil War in much of the south.[14]

African Americans were not the only non-Europeans to assume a place in the United States. The Chinese were the first Asians to alter the European character of immigration on a significant scale. More than 20,000 Chinese participated in the California Gold Rush, which began in 1849. (Only two-thirds of the "forty-niners" were Americans, and only two-thirds of the Americans were white; a significant

THE ARGUMENT OF NATIONALITY.
Excited Mob—"We don't want any cheap-labor foreigners intruding upon us native-born citizens."

Immigrant workers have often met with a hostile reception.

number of Cherokee Indians and African Americans panned for gold alongside their white countrymen.[15]) More than one hundred thousand Chinese laborers were recruited to build the western links of the transcontinental railroads. At first these newcomers were viewed positively as peaceful, hard-working, and—of course—cheap labor. Soon, however, a virulent backlash set in. During the Congressional debate on the Chinese Exclusion Act, California Senator John Miller characterized the Chinese as

> *machine-like in every physical characteristic. They are of obtuse nerve, but little affected by heat or cold, wiry, sinewy, with muscles of iron; they are automatic engines of flesh and blood; they are patient, stolid, unemotional, and persistent, with such a marvelous frame and digestive apparatus that they can dispense with the comforts of shelter and . . . grow fat on less than half the food necessary to sustain life in the Anglo Saxon.*

Now, how could white Californians (even in the nineteenth century) compete with such immigrants? In the eyes of many they couldn't:

> *The experiment now being tried in California is to subject American free labor to competition with Chinese servile labor, and so far as it has gone, it has put in progress the displacement of American laborers, and the substitution of Chinese for white men. The process will continue if permitted until the white laborer is driven out into other fields, or until those who remain in the contest come down to the Chinese level.[16]*

Such rhetoric has a familiar ring: cheap foreign labor will undercut the standard of living of "real" Americans—a charge repeatedly leveled at immigrants.

Beginning in the 1880s the character of European immigration changed, as hundreds of thousands of people from southern and eastern Europe followed their northern and western European predecessors. The new immigrants, strange-looking and strange-sounding, were too much for many "real" Americans, who believed that the pre-1880 immigrants "were drawn from the superior stocks of northern and western Europe, while those who came after that date were drawn from the inferior breeds of southern and eastern Europe."[17] In 1916 Madison Grant of the American Museum of Natural History wrote in a best-selling book:

> *The transportation lines advertised America as a land flowing with milk and honey, and the European governments took the opportunity to unload upon careless, wealthy, and hospitable America the sweepings of their jails and asylums . . . the new immigration . . . contained a large and increasing number of the weak, the broken, and the mentally crippled of all races drawn from the lowest stratum of the Mediterranean basin and the Balkans, together with hordes of the wretched, submerged populations of the Polish ghettoes.*

> *With a pathetic and fatuous belief in the efficacy of American institutions and environment to reverse or obliterate immemorial hereditary tendencies, these newcomers were welcomed and given a share in our land and prosperity. The American taxed himself to sanitate and educate these poor helots . . .*

> *The result is showing plainly in the rapid decline in the birth rate of native Americans because the poorer classes of Colonial stock . . . will not bring children into the world to compete in the labor market with the Slovak, the Italian, the Syrian, and the Jew.[18]*

Again, the rhetoric has a contemporary ring: Generous Americans of northern European protestant stock would soon be a minority in their "own" country, submerged by waves of Catholics, Eastern Orthodox, and Jews from southern and eastern Europe. Such sentiments were by no means limited to a small fringe. Reflecting widespread popular concern, a United States Government Commission was established in 1907 to study the immigration situation. It issued an immense report in 1910. Contained in the official report of the U.S. Immigration Commission one finds such "official" observations as

Of the Greeks: "There is no doubt of their nimble intelligence. They compete with the Hebrew race as the best traders of the Orient."

The "south Italian" is "excitable, impulsive, highly imaginative, impracticable . . . an individualist having little adaptability to high organized society."

The Persian "is rather brilliant and poetical than solid in temperament. Like the Hindu he is more eager to secure the semblance than the substance of modern civilization."

The Poles "are more high strung than are the most of their neighbors. In this respect they resemble the Hungarians farther south."

Roumanians are "more emotional than the Slav, less stolid and heavy than the Bulgarian."

The White Russians "are said by travelers to be a distinctly weaker stock than the Great Russians and less prepossessing in appearance."

In Serbo-Croatia, 19th century "savage manners" persist, "illiteracy is prevalent and civilization at a low stage . . . " [19]

This is "insensitivity" on a scale undreamed of today. No one should ever assume that the American "melting pot" in any way resembled Mr. Rogers' neighborhood.

Not all opposition to immigration reflected ethnic or religious bigotry on the one hand, or fear that the immigrants would pollute some uniquely American culture on the other. Some elements of American society opposed further immigration on straightforward economic or political grounds. Although immigrants were well represented in the industrial unions, union leaders believed that continued immigration of cheap labor would undercut the bargaining power of workers. And indeed, American business did encourage immigration as a source of cheap, plentiful labor. The Progressives, a reformist political movement (Chapter 8), opposed further immigration because illiterate immigrants were viewed as the foundation of the corrupt urban political machines. They believed that shutting off immigration would shut off the supply of uninformed, ignorant voters.

For a variety of reasons, then, anti-immigration sentiment grew. After two decades of advocacy, a national literacy test finally was adopted in 1917 (as discussed in Chapter 17, such a device earlier had been used to disenfranchise African Americans and poor whites in the South). Proponents of the test had never disguised their motives. The noted Massachusetts Senator Henry Cabot Lodge observed that the

test will bear most heavily on the Italians, Russians, Poles, Hungarians, Greeks, and Asiatics, and very lightly, or not at all upon English-speaking emigrants or Germans, Scandinavians, and French. In other words, the races most affected by the illiteracy test are those whose emigration to this country has begun with the

"THE MELTING POT"

This famous phrase was popularized by a 1908 play of that name, written by a Jewish immigrant, Israel Zangwill. In the play, David and Vera fall in love, but learn that there is a seemingly unbridgeable gulf between them. David, a talented young violinist, is a Jew, while Vera, a social worker, is the daughter of a Russian officer who supervised the *pogrom* in which David's family was killed. The final scene takes place on a New York rooftop, where David determines that he will live for the American future, not the European past. Here is the ending:

VERA: Look! How beautiful the sunset is after the storm!

DAVID: *[Prophetically exalted by the spectacle]* It is the fires of God round His Crucible. *[He drops her hand and points downward.]* There she lies, the great Melting Pot—Listen! Can't you hear the roaring and the bubbling? There gapes her mouth *[He points east]*—the harbour where a thousand mammoth feeders came from the ends of the world to pour in their human freight. Ah, what a stirring and a seething! Celt and Latin, Slav and Teuton, Greek and Syrian, —black and yellow—

VERA: *[Softly, nestling to him]* Jew and Gentile —

DAVID: Yes, East and West, and North and South, the palm and the pine, the pole and the equator, the crescent and the cross—how the great Alchemist melts and fuses them with his purging flame! Here shall they all unite to build the Republic of Man and the Kingdom of God. Ah, Vera, what is the glory of Rome and Jerusalem where all nations and races come to worship and look back, compared with the glory of America, where all races and nations come to labour and look forward!

[He raises his hands in benediction over the shining city.] Peace, peace, to all ye unborn millions, fated to fill this giant continent—the God of our *children* give you Peace.

SOURCE: Israel Zangwill, *The Melting Pot* (New York: Macmillan, 1912, ©1909).

---

last twenty years and swelled rapidly to enormous proportions, races with which the English-speaking people have never hitherto assimilated, and who are most alien to the great body of the people of the United States.[20]

Contrary to what Senator Lodge anticipated, many would-be immigrants quickly learned to read, so stronger legislation was needed to close the door. A series of laws passed in the 1920s restricted immigration in both a quantitative sense—the total was limited—and in a qualitative sense—legal quotas gave northern and western Europeans preference over peoples from other areas.[21] The Japanese and other Asians joined the Chinese as groups excluded altogether. By 1930 the era of the open door had effectively ended, although Mexicans continued to move into the southwestern states to work in American agriculture (joining those who had been incorporated when the United States took the territory from Mexico), and after World War II, Puerto Ricans in significant numbers emigrated to New York City. But before the United States closed its doors to immigrants, more than 35 million people had left hearth and home to come to America. These immigrants, not to mention their children, were a large component of the growth of the United States from a country of about 10 million inhabitants in 1820, to more than 100 million in 1920 (see Table 4.1).

TABLE 4.1

Population of the United States in 1920

	National Origins Ascribed	Percentage
British (incl. Anglo-Canadian)	42,066	39.5
German	15,489	14.6
Irish	10,653	10.0
Polish	3,893	3.7
Italian	3,462	3.3
French (incl. French-Canadian)	3,029	2.8
Russian	1,661	1.6
Spanish (incl. Spanish-American)	1,313	1.2
Other white	13,140	12.3
Swedish	1,977	1.9
Dutch	1,881	1.8
Norwegian	1,419	1.3
African American	10,463	9.8
Indian	244	0.2
Asian	182	0.2

SOURCE: Adapted from John Hingham, *Send These to Me: Immigrants in Urban America* (Baltimore: The Johns Hopkins University Press, 1984).

Restrictions on immigration were part of a general reactionary movement. In the "Red Scare" that broke out after World War I, immigrants were viewed as carriers of Bolshevik, anarchist, and other subversive foreign ideologies, and the second Ku Klux Klan in the 1920s was based on anti-Catholic and anti-Jewish sentiments more than anti-black sentiments. The reaction to the nomination of Al Smith, a Catholic, in the 1928 election showed that anti-Catholicism was still a virulent force.[22] Gradually, however, ethnocultural tensions died down. Several home-grown Fascist movements with bigoted elements flourished in the 1930s, and on a more ostensibly respectable scale, social, occupational, and educational discrimination against Catholics and Jews was widespread into the 1930s. But all in all, the cumulative effects of economic depression, World War II, revulsion against the Holocaust, and the Cold War led to a general reduction in ethnic and racial tensions that lasted approximately a generation. Today's students should realize, however, that this short period from the early 1930s to the mid-1960s, during which ethnic and religious issues were relatively dormant, was the exception, not the norm. Until the 1930s such issues were major elements of American politics, as they are today.

A NATION OF IMMIGRANTS NOW

As we discuss in Chapter 17, with the rise of the Civil Rights movement in the 1950s, racial issues once more came to the fore. In the 1960s the demands of African Americans for "Black power" stimulated the consciousness of other ethnic groups. Moreover, passage of the Immigration Act of 1965 stimulated yet another surge of immigration and laid the foundation for the current popular controversies over issues like bilingual education and the provision of welfare and medical services to immigrants.

Americans have always worried about the threat immigrants pose to American values. The "Red Scare" of the 1920s evoked a particularly virulent reaction.

FIGURE 4.1

The Population of the United
States Is Becoming Less European
in its Origins

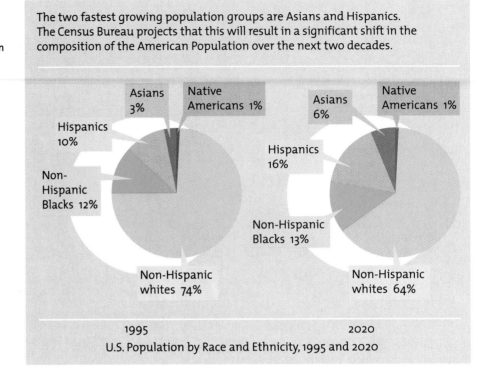

The two fastest growing population groups are Asians and Hispanics.
The Census Bureau projects that this will result in a significant shift in the
composition of the American Population over the next two decades.

1995 — **2020**

U.S. Population by Race and Ethnicity, 1995 and 2020

In 1965 Congress abandoned the national quotas system favoring northern Europeans, with the result that immigration from Latin America and the West Indies increased rapidly. In addition, hundreds of thousands of new immigrants from Vietnam, Korea, Cambodia, India, Iran, the Philippines, and other countries became the first numerically significant Asian immigrant groups since the Japanese in the early years of the twentieth century. In the 1980s the absolute number of immigrants—about 9 million—was higher than in any previous decade, although lower as a proportion of the population than it had been at the turn of the century. Three million came from Mexico, Central America, and the Caribbean, and nearly as many from Asia. Nearly a half million came from South America, and almost 200 thousand from Africa. These figures include legal immigrants only; as many as 4 million people now live in the country illegally.[23] The upshot of this newest wave of immigration was that by 1993 the proportion of the population of European origin had dropped to about 75 percent, and in cities such as Los Angeles, whites of European origin had become a minority (see Figure 4.1).

IMMIGRATION AS A CONTEMPORARY ISSUE

By the early 1990s immigration had once again become a political issue. In 1994 California voters overwhelmingly passed Proposition 187, an initiative that denied state services to illegal immigrants and their children (see Election Connection). And in 1995–96 the question of immigrant eligibility for government services such as welfare was a matter of intense controversy at the national level. Much of this contemporary debate over immigration would sound familiar to Americans of the

early 1900s. Does providing services to immigrants impose unfair financial burdens on local governments? Do immigrants take jobs from Americans already here? Do hard-working immigrant entrepreneurs drive "native" shopkeepers out of business? As we have seen, such fears are not at all new, but that does not mean that they are totally baseless. Four points deserve mention.

First, in contrast to earlier eras of American history, immigrants are not entering a rapidly expanding economy. There is no exploding railroad industry to absorb today's immigrants as it absorbed the Irish and the Chinese. There is no expanding steel industry sending representatives to Italy and Poland to recruit laborers. The American economy is in transition between the old manufacturing economy that absorbed previous generations of immigrants and a new globally integrated service and information economy, and many Americans, especially those lacking skills, are experiencing difficulties in the transition. For struggling Americans trying to make ends meet, immigration is a source of economic competition they don't need.[24]

Second, even though studies show that, in total, immigrants pay more in taxes than they consume in government services—by nearly a two:one ratio according to a 1994 study—all states and localities do not share the burdens and benefits equally.[25] During the 1980s more than 75 percent of new immigrants—who have the greatest need for government assistance—went to six states: California, New York, Texas, Florida, New Jersey, and Illinois. *States and cities* that carry more than a fair share of the fiscal burden of immigration naturally take little consolation in the knowledge that immigrants provide a net gain for the *national* economy.

Even if the economy were expanding more rapidly and new immigrants did not concentrate so heavily in some states, however, immigration would probably be a political issue for a third reason: the benefits and costs of immigration fall on different levels of government. Most of the taxes paid by immigrants are federal income and social security taxes; this revenue does not go to the governors and legislators who pay their welfare and medicaid bills. And within states, most of the taxes that immigrants

Proposition 187

California is on the cutting edge of American social and economic trends. Perhaps for that reason political controversies often surface there first. Such was the case with the immigration issue in 1994. Almost half of the nation's four million illegal immigrants live in California. Taxpayer resentment of the burden of providing services (education, Medicaid, welfare, police) interacted with ethnic antagonisms and the economic slowdown to create a backlash in the form of Proposition 187. This initiative would have denied state and local services to illegal immigrants and their children, and would have instructed all government employees, including school teachers, to report suspected illegals to immigration authorities. Although opponents of the measure charged that it was unconstitutional, and many proponents agreed, both sides felt that it would send an important signal.

During the summer, incumbent Governor Pete Wilson was trailing challenger Kathleen Brown by twenty points in the polls, but Wilson was an experienced politician with a good instinct for important issues. He embraced Prop 187 and led the campaign for its adoption. Brown opposed it. Immigration was not the only issue in the campaign, and Brown was widely viewed as a poor campaigner, but by mid-October Wilson had transformed his double-digit deficit in the polls into a double-digit lead. In the Republican sweep a few weeks later, he thrashed Brown 55%-40%.

Most of Prop 187's provisions indeed were stayed by the courts, and Wilson's attempt to parlay his big victory into the Republican presidential nomination failed. But the campaign demonstrated the political importance of the immigration issue. The new Republican Congress proposed legislation aimed at discouraging illegal

immigration and restricting the benefits legal immigrants could receive. Just before the 1996 elections President Clinton signed a weaker version of the legislation that eliminated most of the provisions dealing with legal immigrants.* A few weeks earlier, however, he had signed a far-reaching welfare reform bill that reduced various benefits for legal immigrants. While these were among the provisions the president had promised to "fix" after the elections, the Republican congressional majority was in no mood to back away from what they had earlier agreed to. Ultimately, some of the cuts were restored in the 1997 budget deal.†

* Dan Carney, "As White House Calls Shots, Illegal Alien Bill Clears," *Congressional Quarterly Weekly Report,* October 5, 1996: 2864-2866.

† George Hager, "Clinton, GOP Congress Strike Historic Budget Agreement," *Congressional Quarterly Weekly Report,* May 3, 1997: 996.

pay are state income taxes, but it is the mayors and city councillors who hire and pay the schoolteachers, social workers, and police officers, and take the blame for the costs of those services. Immigration forces local and state government to cut services, raise taxes, and beg for money from higher levels of government, options that elected officials view as exceedingly undesirable. Many of them have responded by making immigration an electoral issue, trying to shift the blame to federal officials who collect

During the campaign for Proposition 187 some supporters of the initiative denied that they were in any way opposed to immigrants, stating only that they were opposed to *illegal* immigrants, who were the target of the initiative. After all, why should people who are in direct violation of the law be eligible for social welfare services, medical care, and public schooling? While this position seems defensible on its face, its practical application is fraught with problems.

According to the Fourteenth Amendment, all people born in the United States are citizens. This means that children born here of illegal immigrants are citizens. Under the Constitution they cannot be denied any services for which other citizens are eligible—the basis on which opponents asked the courts to strike down Proposition 187. Moreover, what should the authorities do with the parents? Put them in jail? Deport them? Any policy directed against illegals may harm their children, who are citizens if born here.

There are real dilemmas here. On the one hand, every country has a right to control its borders, and practically speaking, completely open borders are not possible—the United States cannot afford it, and American voters would not stand for it. But once immigrants have crossed the border and settled here, practical ways of removing them are lacking. How would you propose to deal with illegal immigration without running afoul of the Constitution or contemporary political realities?

the lion's share of the taxes but plead budget deficits when asked to help pay for the services (see Democratic Dilemma).

Finally, the immigration law adopted in 1965 gives first preference to those with relatives already in the country. In consequence, a higher proportion of dependent immigrants—especially older people—have been admitted in recent years as compared to previous eras.[26] This means that current U.S. immigration policy admits fewer taxpayers and more service recipients than a law that gave preference to productive workers. Even though immigrants as a group pay more in taxes than they consume in services, many American taxpayers ask why any immigrants likely to be dependent on government services should be admitted.

In sum, economic growth, a fairer geographic and political sharing of the costs of immigration, and changes in who receives preference would do much to undermine the economic basis for political opposition to immigration. But economics is not the only basis for opposition. Over and above economic costs, many opponents of immigration regard it as a threat to the American political culture. They believe that immigration by those who speak different languages, attend different churches, and practice different customs threatens American unity. They fear the new immigrants will produce a balkanized country, wherein groups retain their own narrow identities and decline to become part of the larger American whole.[27] They urge the United States to close the door before too much *pluribus* destroys the *unum*. As we have seen, such fears were expressed as far back as the 1850s, if not earlier. Well, then, what does history say about the effects of the earlier immigrations on American unity? To answer that question we need to know just what unity the critics of immigration seek to defend.

Philosophical Consensus

Given that ethnic diversity is relatively greater in the United States than in other countries, it is surprising that numerous foreign observers have noted a philosophical consensus in America that is much stronger than in other countries. From the French visitor Alexis de Tocqueville in the 1830s to the Swede Gunnar Myrdal in the 1940s, visitors have claimed that Americans agree on a common core of beliefs and values that defines what it is to be American. These beliefs and values usually are described as "individualist," and the political culture they produce is generally referred to as a "liberal" political culture.[28]

To avoid confusion, we emphasize that the term *liberal* as used here is not the same as the so-called "L word" used in contemporary political campaigns. The pejorative contemporary usage implies support for big government and lack of respect for traditional values. Small wonder that liberal candidates avoid the term, preferring to call themselves "progressives" or "populists" instead. In contrast, the classical usage of the term "liberal" is more akin to the contemporary term "libertarian," which signifies skepticism of government interference in all spheres of life. These different meanings naturally create confusion; for example, the Nobel Prize winning "conservative" economist, Milton Friedman, considers himself a classical liberal, as did the prominent mid-century Republican Senator, Robert Taft Sr., who was popularly known as "Mr. Conservative."

Classical **liberalism** is a philosophical stance that emerged in Europe as medieval thought disintegrated in the religious wars of the seventeenth century. In contrast to earlier thought that viewed humanity as sinful and in need of tight control by religious and political authority, liberalism elevated and empowered the individual. Liberalism asserted the rights of the individual against the hereditary privilege of the nobility and the religious privilege of the clergy, and liberalism affirmed the autonomy of the individual, first in the religious sphere, then in the political sphere as well. Having elevated the individual in these ways, liberalism made the individual rather than the community the basis for society and government. Instead of regarding individuals as the product of political society—a view that goes back to the Greeks—liberalism makes society the product of individuals. The great "social contract" theorists—Thomas Hobbes, John Locke, and Jean Jacques Rousseau—progressively spelled out this view of political society as a contract between rulers and ruled that specified the rights of each as well as the duties and obligations of one to another.

It was necessary to spell out rights and duties because liberalism viewed human beings as primarily self-interested. Hobbes was the most pessimistic in this respect, but in general, liberal thinkers viewed altruistic and communitarian sentiments as too weak to provide a reliable basis for government.

What kind of political principles are suggested by such a philosophy? The implications are clear. First, individuals have basic rights—religion, thought and expression, and property—that are not to be violated by government. Second, individuals are equal under the law—there are no distinctions based on heredity or religion. Third, to safeguard rights, government must be limited—despite Hobbes' initial defense of an absolutist state, liberal thinkers generally advanced theories of limited government. Fourth, governments are instrumental—the state exists to serve individuals, not as an end or value in itself. In this sense, liberalism stands

liberalism
Philosophy that elevates and empowers the individual as opposed to religious, hereditary, governmental, or other forms of authority.

How Classical Liberalism Became Modern Liberalism

Why is a classical liberal like economist Milton Friedman considered a "conservative" today? How could the same term, *liberal*, have stood for laissez-faire (free market) economics in the nineteenth century, but government regulation of the economy in the twentieth century (at least after Franklin Roosevelt and the New Deal)? The answer lies in the philosophical foundations of liberalism.

Liberalism emphasizes the rights of the individual. At the time of its inception, religion and government were the principal threats to individual rights. Individuals could be free to develop their capacities to the fullest only if they were free from religious or political persecution, and free of burdensome laws and regulations. This concern of liberalism emphasized freedom *from* the interference of larger institutions. Over time, however, as personal and political rights became firmly established, one strand of liberalism became concerned about other obstacles to the de-

velopment of individual capacities. In particular, adverse circumstances such as poverty and discrimination could burden individuals in much the same manner as an oppressive government or church. Some liberal thinkers argued that by alleviating adverse circumstances government could help individuals develop to the fullest. They emphasized the freedom *to* develop one's full capabilities. This line of thought became sufficiently widespread that it appropriated the term "liberal," leaving believers in laissez-faire economics to lead the "conservative" assault on big government.

President John F. Kennedy's famous exhortation on its head. Kennedy urged Americans to "Ask not what your country can do for you, ask what you can do for your country." Classical liberalism suggests the opposite: "Ask not what you can do for government, but what government can do for you."

The preceding should sound familiar, for liberalism provides the philosophical foundation for the American constitutional order. In the *Declaration of Independence* Jefferson wrote:

> *We hold these truths to be self-evident: That all men are created equal, that they are endowed by their Creator with certain inalienable Rights, that among these are Life, Liberty and the pursuit of happiness.*

> *That to secure these rights Governments are instituted among Men, deriving their just powers from the consent of the governed;*

> *That whenever any Form of Government becomes destructive of these ends, it is the Right of the People to alter or to abolish it, and to institute new Government, laying its foundation on such principles and organizing its powers in such form, as to them shall seem most likely to effect their Safety and Happiness.*

These eloquent sentences capture the four tenets of liberal philosophy—political equality, rights, instrumental government, and limited government. Moreover, what is the Constitution and Bill of Rights, after all, if not an elaborate statement of the rights of citizens, the purposes of government, and the limits under which it must operate? And such statements and limits are necessary precisely because neither citizens nor their governors can be trusted—they are self-interested individualists.[29] For this reason the American constitutional tradition often is called a liberal tradition.

To some degree, philosophers and historians have exaggerated the philosophical consensus described in writings about the liberal tradition. Many of them refer to the American "Creed" and the American "Ethos," terms that suggest a more unified and well-defined set of beliefs than probably exists. There is also something of a tendency to romanticize or idealize the liberal tradition by incorporating within it all qualities that anyone would consider desirable, regardless of philosophical or logical consistency. Both kinds of exaggeration may occur together:

> There has been, in a doctrinal sense, only one America. We have debated fiercely, but as men who agreed on fundamentals . . . The American political tradition is basically a liberal tradition . . . its articles of faith, a sort of American Holy Writ, are perfectability, progress, liberty, equality, democracy, and individualism.[30]

■ **civic republicanism**
A political philosophy that emphasizes the obligation of citizens to act virtuously in pursuit of the common good.

Additionally, some skeptical historians argue that writers in the liberal tradition have downplayed the importance of a **civic republicanism** tradition that was strong at the time of the Revolution.[31] That tradition placed more emphasis on the welfare of the community relative to the rights of the individual, but seems to have lost ground to liberalism shortly after the Revolution. Still, the republican tradition certainly has not disappeared, and appeals like President Kennedy's for self-sacrifice periodically enjoy a positive reception.

Other critics note that the rights and privileges exalted in the liberal tradition extended only so far. In particular, they did not extend to African Americans until a century after the Civil War forcibly excised the great contradiction of slavery. Full rights and privileges did not extend to women until even later.[32] And rights of other minority groups such as homosexuals remain matters of political disagreement today.

We agree that there is a danger of exaggerating both the scope and the homogeneity of the "American consensus." But even granting some reservations about the notion of an all-encompassing "liberal tradition," there is plenty of evidence consistent with the assertion that Americans are in widespread agreement on certain basic "liberal" principles, as well as for the assertion that Americans differ in systematic ways from the citizens of other democracies.

AMERICAN INDIVIDUALISM

Perhaps the most striking way in which Americans differ from people elsewhere lies in the balance they strike between individual responsibility on the one hand, and collective—especially governmental—responsibility on the other. In a recent survey of 14 old and new democracies, less than a quarter of the American respondents completely agreed that "It is the responsibility of the state ("government" in the United States) to take care of very poor people who can't take care of themselves." While the wording of the question is demanding (do you *completely* agree?) the proportion of Americans opting for governmental responsibility is only half as large as that in the next closest country (Germany) and barely a third as large as the average of the other 13 democracies (see Figure 4.2). The contrast is not just a product of high rates of agreement in the former Communist countries, which had only recently shed their collectivist systems; their figures are only a bit higher than those of the western European democracies in the sample.

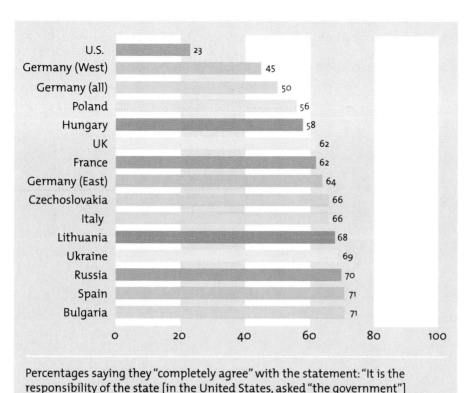

Country	Value
U.S.	23
Germany (West)	45
Germany (all)	50
Poland	56
Hungary	58
UK	62
France	62
Germany (East)	64
Czechoslovakia	66
Italy	66
Lithuania	68
Ukraine	69
Russia	70
Spain	71
Bulgaria	71

Percentages saying they "completely agree" with the statement: "It is the responsibility of the state [in the United States, asked "the government"] to take care of very poor people who can't take care of themselves."

Another international survey of six long-established Western democracies found Americans similarly one-sided in their belief that individuals are responsible for their own welfare. It should come as no surprise that barely a quarter of Americans supported a government-guaranteed income (although on average the citizens of Germany, the United Kingdom, Italy, and the Netherlands supported it), but a majority of Americans even rejected the notion that the government should reduce income inequality. Little more than one-third of Americans felt that the government should provide a decent standard of living for the unemployed, compared to an average of two-thirds in the four European democracies. Interestingly, Australia seems to occupy a middle position between the individual responsibility espoused by Americans and the governmental responsibility espoused by Europeans. Australia, too, is a society of immigrants, and its citizens seem to share some of the predispositions of Americans (see Figure 4.3).

The American emphasis on individual responsibility is reinforced by two general sentiments. First, Americans are suspicious of government power and dubious about government competence. In Samuel Huntington's view, "the distinctive aspect of the American creed is its antigovernment character. Opposition to power and suspicion of government as the most dangerous embodiment of power are the central themes of American political thought."[33] If people doubt the motives and abilities of those who hold office, they can hardly be expected to grant expansive powers and responsibilities to government.

A second reinforcement for the emphasis on individual responsibility is simple: Americans believe that it works. Americans believe that the United States is a

FIGURE 4.3

Americans Are Far Less Supportive of Government Actions to Reduce Economic Inequality than People Elsewhere

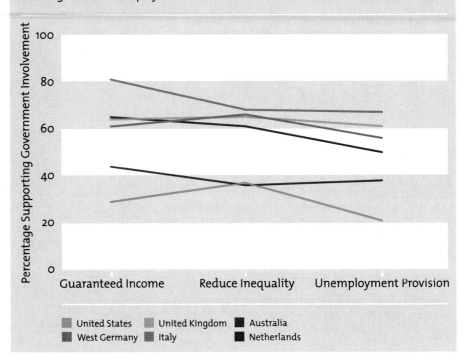

Shows percentage who agree that government should "provide everyone with a guaranteed basic income," "reduce the differences in income between people with high incomes and those with low incomes," and "provide a decent standard of living for the unemployed."

FIGURE 4.4

Americans Are Much More Optimistic about Their Chances of Getting Ahead than People Elsewhere

SOURCE: Everett Carll Ladd, *The American Ideology* (Storrs, CT: The Roper Center, 1994): 76.

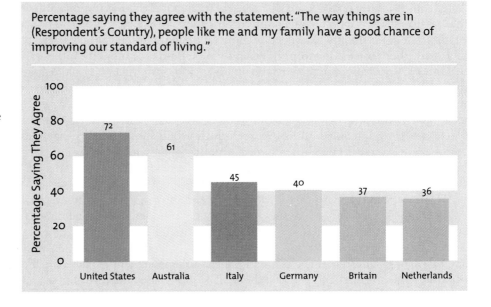

Percentage saying they agree with the statement: "The way things are in (Respondent's Country), people like me and my family have a good chance of improving our standard of living."

Welfare recipients are often stigmatized in a strongly individualistic country like the United States.

country where hard work and perseverance pay off. More than people in other countries, Americans believe that hard work is the key to success; people elsewhere are far less likely to see personal effort as a sure means to better one's life. As a consequence, an overwhelming majority of Americans are optimistic about getting ahead, in contrast to Europeans (see Figure 4.4). (Once again, Australians are more similar to Americans than are Europeans.)

One of the most interesting features of the American belief in individual achievement and responsibility is that it is not closely related to the actual social and economic circumstances in which Americans find themselves. One might expect that those at the bottom of the ladder would be far less individualistic and optimistic than those at the top. But such an expectation has been contradicted repeatedly (see Figure 4.5). Even the very poorest Americans reject a government-guaranteed income, and only the very poorest feel that the government should reduce income differences. There is little or no relationship between one's income and belief in the efficacy of hard work: Two-thirds of the poorest Americans believe in it as do two-thirds of the most affluent. And despite their unfavorable circumstances, two-thirds of poor Americans are optimistic about their chances of getting ahead.

Other studies report that poor Americans are as likely to embrace the "work ethic" as the nonpoor, and as likely as the nonpoor to take personal responsibility for their condition.[34] The poor dislike the progressive income tax as much as the rich.[35] And perhaps the most telling illustration of the pervasive individualist orientation is provided by the attitudes of minorities. African Americans and Latinos clearly partake less in the American dream than do whites. On average they earn less, work in less prestigious occupations, and suffer discrimination in many forms. It comes as no surprise, then, that they are somewhat less likely to embrace the individualist ethic than whites, but it does come as a surprise that they embrace as much of it as they do. In terms of their belief in hard work and individual responsibility, black and Latino Americans are more like white Americans than like Europeans. In sum, even those Americans faring poorly under an individualist regime still offer considerable support for its basic premises [36] (see Figure 4.6).

FIGURE 4.5

Even Less Affluent Americans
Share the Individualistic Values of
the Larger Society

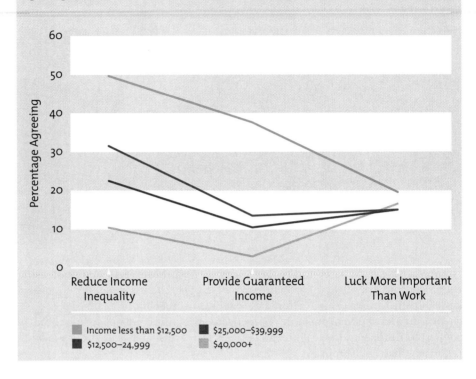

Shows the percentages of people, by income group, who agree respectively that:
(1) government should reduce income inequality, (2) government should
provide a guaranteed income, (3) luck is more important than hard work in
getting ahead.

FIGURE 4.6

Even Racial and Ethnic Minorities
Share the Individualistic Values of
the Larger Society

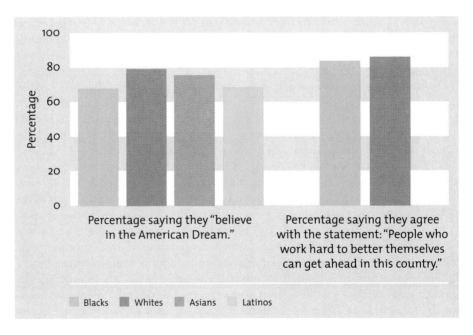

THE TENSION BETWEEN INDIVIDUALISM AND EQUALITY

The findings on American individualism raise an important question: What about equality? Liberal philosophy attaches great importance to equality, and writers in the liberal tradition typically mention it just after liberty—see the quotation on p. 116. Yet great inequalities exist in the United States. For example, the income distribution has changed little during the past six decades, and has actually become slightly less egalitarian since the early 1970s.[37] Nevertheless, popular sentiment does not demand that such inequalities be eliminated or even lessened. The simple fact is that most Americans do not regard economic and social inequality as justification for government action.

At one time there was no great disparity between liberty and equality. Indeed, Tocqueville and other visitors were struck by the extent of social and economic equality in the United States. Liberty and equality were thought to be mutually reinforcing: Free, hard-working people would achieve economic success, and an independent, economically secure middle class would safeguard society and government from extremist threats to liberty. But economic development weakened the association between liberty and equality. For much of its first century the United States was a country of small ("yeoman") farmers, manufacturers, and merchants. But after the Civil War, the industrial revolution produced great concentrations of private wealth on the one hand, and masses of propertyless wage workers on the other. Under such conditions, liberty and equality became detached; indeed, some Americans became disillusioned with a political system that could tolerate such massive social and economic inequalities. But such critical sentiments are not reflected in the beliefs of ordinary Americans, as we have seen, nor have they proved to be a strong stimulus for government action.

The explanation of this seeming inconsistency is that the American political culture supports only a limited kind of equality. Liberalism emphasized equality before the law; one person's rights were the same as another's, regardless of heredity, religious faith, or relationship to some government official. Consistent with this philosophical heritage, Americans display a strong commitment to legal, social, and political equality. The Civil Rights struggle is an excellent example. American society and politics were turned upside down in the 1960s in the effort to extend legal and political equality to African Americans and protect them from social and economic discrimination. But Americans are not committed to economic equality; rather, they agree with Madison, who writes of "the diversity in the faculties of men, from which the rights of property originate."[38] Americans regard economic inequality not only as inevitable, but as fair—the rich deserve to be rich—and reject government action to do much about it.

It is standard today to talk about this distinction in terms of the difference between **equality of opportunity** and **equality of condition**. Americans strongly support equality of opportunity: Everyone should have a fair chance; may the best people—namely, the smartest and hardest working—win. But Americans just as strongly reject attempts to ensure equality of condition, since that may involve rewarding people who are undeserving. Thus, Americans support affirmative action for women and minorities when the survey questions are clear that equal opportunity is the goal:

94 percent agree that "Our society should do what is necessary to make sure that everyone has an equal opportunity to succeed."

equality of opportunity
The notion that individuals should have an equal chance to advance economically through individual talent and hard work.

equality of condition
The notion that individuals have a right to a more or less equal part of the material goods society produces.

79 percent agree that "After years of discrimination, it is only fair to set up special programs to make sure that women and minorities are given every chance to have equal opportunities in employment and education."

But Americans just as strongly oppose affirmative action when the survey questions indicate that equality of outcome is the goal:

86 percent don't think "blacks and other minorities should receive preference in college admissions to make up for past inequalities."

80 percent don't think "blacks and other minorities should receive preference in hiring to make up for past inequalities".[39]

As far as most Americans are concerned, equality of opportunity should be sufficient. The rest is up to the individual. This belief also shows up in government policy. As many critics have pointed out, the United States spends a smaller proportion of its GNP on social welfare than most other democracies. But critics less often note that the United States historically spent a larger proportion of its GNP on education than did other democracies. Education is a means by which individuals improve their skills and make themselves fitter competitors, and Americans resonate with that idea.[40] Direct government assistance, in contrast, looks like "welfare." Americans are uncomfortable with that idea.

Religion and American Individualism: Contradiction or Complement?

There is a further aspect of American beliefs and values that some observers find difficult to square with the notion of a dominant liberal political culture. Put simply, Americans are more religious than people in other developed democracies. Americans are more likely to believe in God, to go to church, and to report that religion plays an important role in their lives (see Figure 4.7). These facts are all the more surprising when one recalls that in a number of European democracies there is an "established" church—a religion that is "official," and often government subsidized. The Anglican Church is the established church in Great Britain, the Catholic Church in Italy, the Lutheran Church in Norway, and the Eastern Orthodox Church in Greece. Yet even the citizens of countries with established churches are not as religious as Americans.

To be sure, much of the original settlement of the United States was carried out by people seeking the freedom to practice their religion. These deeply religious people were trying to escape oppression and even persecution by the established churches of Europe. Of course, they had no problem with established religion in principle, as long as it was *theirs:* The Congregational Church was the established church of Connecticut until 1818, and of Massachusetts until 1833. (Originally the constitutional prohibition of the establishment of religion applied only to the federal government, and even today some state constitutions call for public officials to believe in a deity.[41]) Although the *institutions* of church and state are constitutionally separated in the United States, there is not now and never has been a political wall between religion and politics, as shown by American history in general, and the activities of contemporary religious groups in particular.

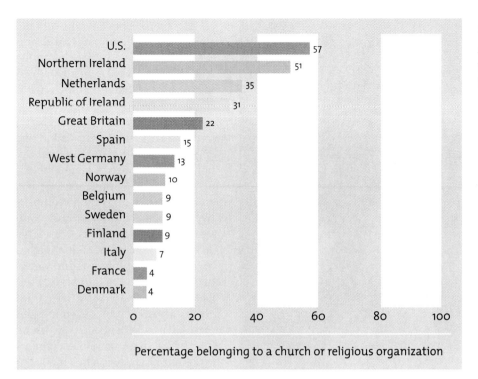

Percentage belonging to a church or religious organization

The religious roots of the United States often are cited as an explanation for the "moralistic" nature of American politics. Throughout history, religiously motivated Americans periodically have attempted to use government to improve society, and even ordinary, less-committed Americans have tended to look at politics in relatively more moralistic terms than have the citizens of other countries.[42]

How can one explain the coexistence of the liberal tradition and religious commitment? Given its origins in a reaction against religious privilege, its emphasis on individual freedom, and its reflection in a capitalist society that celebrates individual achievement, one might think the liberal tradition would inevitably evolve in a secular direction, but there is little indication that it has. Are the religious roots of the original settlers sufficient to explain the persistence of religious sentiment in the United States? Is the influence of the Puritans, Quakers, and others who landed on American shores more than 300 years ago still present in the church-going habits of contemporary Americans?

Many observers doubt that historical origins alone can explain the flourishing of religion in America, especially given all the things that have happened since the early colonial period—the industrial revolution, immigration, and world wars, to name just a few. Several other explanations for the strength and persistence of religion in America have been advanced. One explanation points to the diversity of religion—America's incredible number of churches, branches, and sects. If a person doesn't like one religion, there are numerous others to choose from, and exceptionally hard-to-please worshippers can always start their own. This wide range of options may make it easier to find a comfortable match with some church in America than in other countries where citizens typically face a much narrower range of choices.

Church and state may be separate in the United States, but religion and politics often are not. Here, the Clintons pray at the Democratic National Convention.

A second explanation of the strength of religion in America is related to the first, but focuses on the choices of the clergy rather than those of the congregations. A church that is supported by a government subsidy does not need to cater to its membership to nearly the same extent as one dependent on the voluntary contributions of its members. Because there is no established church in America, and because there is such multiplicity, American churches must compete for members. Thus, the clergy are motivated to adapt their churches to the changing interests and values of their members, and to provide services and auxiliary activities (youth clubs, sports clubs, even singles clubs) that members value. Just as the free market in economics encourages economic enterprise, a free market in religion may encourage religious enterprise: The clergy act as entrepreneurs and try to "sell" their respective religions. Thus, Americans may be more religious than people in other countries because, stimulated by competition, American religion offers them more choices.

Perhaps the most intriguing explanation of the persistence of religiosity in the United States has been proposed by Robert Booth Fowler, who argues that it is wrong to assume that the liberal tradition and religiosity are in conflict. Just the opposite is true—the liberal tradition creates a deep need for religion. People steeped in the liberal tradition jealously guard their rights and hold themselves personally responsible for their successes and failures. They create a society characterized by social and geographic mobility and rapid social and economic change. Fowler suggests that many people find life in such a society precarious, or at least somewhat lonely:

> *Religion has aided liberalism by being a* refuge *from liberalism . . . it provides an escape from liberal culture, a place of comfort where individualism, competition, this worldly pragmatism, and relentless rationalism do not hold sway. In a liberal country with liberal citizens, religion is a place where one can come home . . . and then emerge refreshed for the battles of life in the liberal world.*[43]

Thus, Americans may turn to religion to fill a gap in their lives. In contrast, citizens of other democracies in which communitarian philosophies are stronger do not feel as detached from their fellow human beings and hence feel less need for a religious dimension in their lives.

It is impossible to "prove" theories like these, but especially when considered together, they provide a plausible explanation for the otherwise puzzling persistence of religiosity alongside a social philosophy that emphasizes individual freedom and autonomy.

Why a Liberal Political Culture?

The time has now come to face squarely the apparent contradiction between a population that is strikingly heterogeneous in its ethnic, racial, and religious makeup, but surprisingly homogeneous in the beliefs and values that constitute its political culture. Historically, opponents of immigration have feared that influxes of new, diverse peoples would alter or destroy the American political culture. Why have they been wrong? To examine that question we need to consider in some detail the origins of the American commitment to individualism.

TRADITIONAL EXPLANATIONS

Traditional explanations of American individualism posit an interaction between ideas and social conditions. As suggested by writers like Alexis de Tocqueville and Louis Hartz, the early settlers brought with them liberal ideas. And unlike in Europe, they found nothing in the United States to offer resistance to such ideas. Hartz, in particular, emphasizes the lack of a feudal tradition in the United States. There was no landed, hereditary aristocracy or established church to provide the basis for the kind of conservative and clerical viewpoints that persist even today in Europe. Nor was there an oppressed peasantry that might form the basis for radical agrarian parties.

Perhaps as important as what the United States lacked, however, is what it had. In particular, it had a great deal of land. In contrast to Europe, North America was a sparsely populated continent over which the United States steadily expanded.[44] Some historians suggest that rather than revolt against intolerable economic conditions, struggling citizens found it easier to pack up their belongings, move west, steal some land from Mexico or the Native American tribes, and start again.

So a plentiful supply of land and scarcity of labor meant that ambitious individuals could and did succeed. The individualistic values the early settlers brought with them were reinforced by conditions in the new country. And with little in the way of an historical basis for any competing set of values, a liberal political order and a market economy thrived. As Hartz comments:

> where the aristocracies, peasantries, and proletariats of Europe are missing, where virtually everyone . . . has the mentality of an independent entrepreneur, two national impulses are bound to make themselves felt: the impulse toward democracy and the impulse toward capitalism.[45]

Generations of radical critics of American society have plaintively asked "why no socialism in America?"[46] One simple answer is that Americans never saw much need for it. Under conditions in America individual effort was usually enough to provide an acceptable life for most people.

Still, questions remain. The frontier was officially closed in 1890, more than a century ago, and no one has worried about a labor shortage for more than half a century—just the opposite. So even if social conditions in the nineteenth century reinforced the beliefs and values of the early settlers, of what relevance is that today? Moreover, the millions of immigrants who arrived after the Civil War were not from liberal societies. Most of them came from authoritarian states with established

Political socialization starts at home, as evidenced by this family outing at a demonstration at the Vietnam War Memorial.

■ **political socialization**
The set of psychological and sociological processes by which families, schools, churches, communities, and other societal units inculcate beliefs and values in their members.

churches, and had lived their lives in communal peasant societies. What is the basis for their adherence to the individualist values of the liberal tradition?

Perhaps the answer lies in a process of **political socialization** that continues to instill liberal values long after the objective support for those values has eroded. Certainly, material conditions are not the only factor that determines the ways in which people think and view the world; different cultures socialize their children into different patterns of thinking and different ways of viewing the world, even under similar material circumstances. For example, Robert Putnam shows that modern Italy is characterized by regional subcultures that are more consequential for governmental and economic performance than are material differences.[47] Beginning in the family and continuing in schools, churches, and other organizations, societies inculcate certain values and patterns of thinking in their members. Thus, the explanation for the persistence of the liberal tradition may be a simple one: Socialization perpetuates a consensus established in the eighteenth century, a consensus so dominant that it was able to swallow tens of millions of immigrants who arrived a century and more later.

Many find such an explanation insufficient. For one thing, one of the principal means by which immigrants were integrated into American society was through the efforts of political parties, particularly the urban machines that we discuss in Chapter 8. The machines were interested in controlling governments; to do that they had to win elections, and immigrant votes counted just as much as those of the native-born. Thus, the machines organized each arriving group: In some Eastern cities the Democrats gained an edge by organizing the Irish, so the Republicans countered by organizing the Italians, and so on. But the urban machines were not the embodiment of liberal, individualist values. On the contrary, the machines were something of an anomaly in the larger American political culture; they were collectivist and clannish—with an emphasis on obedience and loyalty, not independence. Because machine politics and immigration are closely associated in American history, we might expect that political socialization would have predisposed the immigrants in a direction different from the liberal tradition.

MORE RECENT EXPLANATIONS

More recent explanations suggest other factors that might have preserved the liberal tradition over a long period and despite the addition of millions of people from nonliberal traditions. Sven Steinmo argues that scholars have exaggerated the causal role of the liberal tradition. In fact, rather than liberal ideas shaping American government and politics, Steinmo suggests the opposite—that the government and politics of the United States create and recreate the ideas.[48] Specifically, he argues that American government is so fragmented and decentralized that it can rarely act in a positive way to improve society. Often it is "gridlocked" or unable to act, and when it does act, it often does so by way of logrolling among special interests. In consequence, successive generations of Americans learn the same basic lesson: Look to yourself because you cannot look to government, and best keep government limited because it will usually act against the general interest. Given their institutions, Americans would have learned this lesson whether they were originally liberal individualists or not, and new waves of immigrants learn what the natives already know.

Although it is somewhat one-sided, Steinmo's argument reminds us that, once established, institutions that were originally the reflection of a particular set of beliefs and values may come to reinforce those beliefs and values. Material conditions in the United States may be far different from those of the nineteenth century, but political institutions are similar and work to preserve the ideas that gave rise to them.

Finally, just as Fowler suggests that there may be no conflict between religion and the liberal tradition, there may never have been any conflict between immigration and the liberal tradition. Just the opposite may be true: Rather than posing a threat to American traditions, as many feared, immigrants reinforced and strengthened American traditions. How could that be the case?

The answer lies in what statisticians refer to as *self-selection*. With the tragic exception of African Americans, no one forced people to emigrate to the United States: They chose to come. True, many came when they were pushed off the land, or when crops failed, or when work was nowhere to be found. Emigration under such circumstances might not seem like much of a choice, *but not everyone chose to emigrate*. Only a small fraction of the potential immigrants—less than 1 percent—actually left their own countries. Many more chose to remain and endure the miserable conditions in which they found themselves.

What kind of person would have been most likely to leave family, friends, and village behind? Remember, emigration through most of history was not a matter of taking a train to Dublin, Frankfurt, or Rome and catching a flight to New York. Before the Civil War the journey usually took months, as immigrants walked to a port, then endured a long journey below deck on a sailing ship. Even after the Civil War, when the steamship shortened the ocean voyage, and the railroad shortened the land journey on both ends, it still took weeks. Many, if not most of the people who booked passage knew that they would never see their relatives or their homes again.[49] What kind of people made such a decision?

By implication, the people who emigrated in all probability already were—relative to their own societies—unusually individualistic. They were more willing to leave the communal order of Europe, more willing to risk all in the hope of bettering themselves—in Hartz's words, more likely to possess "the spirit which repudiated peasantry and tenantry."[50] Bigoted as it was, even the Immigration Commission in 1911 recognized that "emigrating to a strange and distant country, although less of an undertaking than formerly, is still a serious and relatively difficult matter, requiring a degree of courage and resourcefulness not possessed by weaklings of any class."[51] The immigrants probably were more ambitious and more optimistic that they could get ahead through their own efforts. In short, although they had never heard of the liberal tradition, through temperament and experience, immigrants already possessed some of its spirit.

If so, immigrants were never a threat to the liberal tradition. On the contrary, successive waves of immigrants rejuvenated that tradition. Willing to endure hardships, eager to work hard, believing that they could have a better life—such people were hardly the kind who would support an oppressive government or religion. Rather, whatever their skills or education, the immigrants included many of the kind of ambitious, entrepreneurial individuals who already resided in the United States. Those who were not ambitious and entrepreneurial were probably disproportionately represented among the third or more of all immigrants who eventually returned to their home countries.

Some political figures appear to believe that much the same holds true today. During the 1994 campaign over Proposition 187, the California initiative to deny government services to illegal immigrants and their children, Republican leaders William Bennett and Jack Kemp raised eyebrows by publicly opposing the initiative.[52] Similarly, in 1996 Rudolph Giuliani, the Republican Mayor of New York, made news by denouncing congressional attempts to limit immigrant eligibility for welfare and other government services.[53] The positions of these Republicans contradicted the popular image that Republicans were unsympathetic to the poor and disadvantaged, and also seemed to run against their partisan self-interest; after all, the media typically portray minority group members as Democrats.

These Republicans appear to be placing an interesting bet. They are betting that the Mexican laborers, Korean grocers, and Middle-Eastern shopkeepers are the successors to the Irish laborers, Italian grocers, and Jewish shopkeepers of generations past. They are betting that while ethnic activists usually are allied with the Democratic Party, there are many other members of those same ethnic groups who are focused more heavily on economics than on politics. Especially as time passes, such individuals may become much like other middle-class Americans—concerned about their tax rates and their property values, and willing to listen to Republican appeals.

Whatever their motivations, there is support for Bennett's, Kemp's, and Giuliani's general belief that, in the long term, today's immigrants, like yesterday's, will be productive citizens of the United States who will only reinforce the distinctly "American" political culture. For example, Professor Rodolfo de la Garza, reports that

> . . . Anglos and Puerto Ricans who are native born and English dominant and have comparable education and income, are equally patriotic, trusting of government, supportive of economic individualism and willing to allow members of groups they dislike to hold rallies and teach in public schools. Puerto Ricans who express lower support for these values tend to be those who are foreign born and Spanish dominant. As they and their mainland-born children learn English, their support for these values becomes indistinguishable from that of Anglos who find themselves in similar socioeconomic conditions.[54]

De la Garza's studies of Mexican immigrants reach very similar conclusions.[55] And a Gallup study (Figure 4.8) finds that immigrants, even those who have been in the country ten years or less, are virtually indistinguishable from native-born Americans, both in their beliefs about economic opportunity and in their general attitudes about assimilation.[56] Today as previously, immigrants to America are people who already tend to believe what most Americans believe.

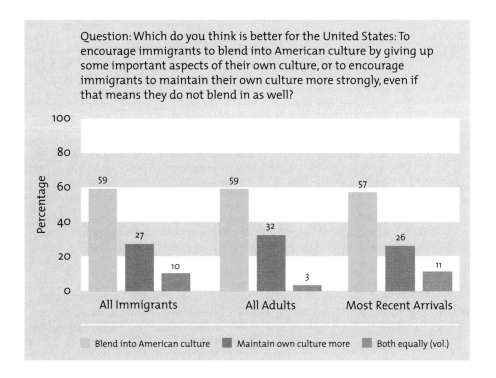

Question: Which do you think is better for the United States: To encourage immigrants to blend into American culture by giving up some important aspects of their own culture, or to encourage immigrants to maintain their own culture more strongly, even if that means they do not blend in as well?

Blend into American culture   Maintain own culture more   Both equally (vol.)

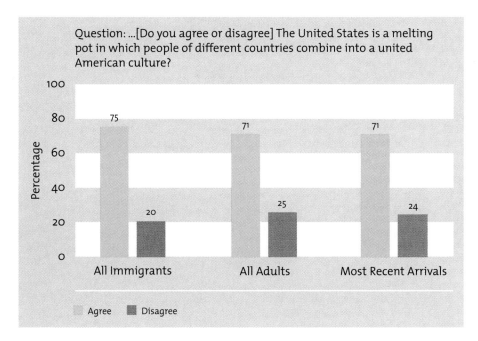

Question: ...[Do you agree or disagree] The United States is a melting pot in which people of different countries combine into a united American culture?

Agree   Disagree

FIGURE 4.8

Contrary to Popular Impressions, Immigrants' Beliefs about American Culture are Strikingly Similar to Those of the Native Born

Chapter Summary

For two centuries the United States has been a study in contrasts. On the one hand, the country always has been socially heterogeneous, containing a wider array of ethnic and religious groups than other countries. On the other hand, the diverse citizenry of the United States long has shown a higher level of agreement on fundamental political principles than in other democracies—Royalist, clerical, and socialist parties have never flourished here. The fundamental political principles that are so widespread in the United States grow out of a classical liberal political philosophy that stresses the rights and liberties of individuals, while giving much less emphasis to their duties and obligations to the community. Today that philosophy is reflected in a greater emphasis on individual responsibility and hard work and a greater suspicion of government than in other countries. Interestingly, this individualistic emphasis coexists with a greater degree of religious commitment than exists in other countries whose citizens are far less individualistic.

Throughout American history many have feared that immigration was a threat to the distinctly American political culture. The debate over immigration today is strikingly similar to debates that have taken place throughout American history. Those already here worry that the new immigrants are too different to fit easily into American society. However, those fears have proved unfounded in the past, and probably will prove unfounded in the future. In all likelihood, immigrants reinforce rather than weaken the spirit of individualism in the United States. The very fact of their immigrating suggests that they possess the ambitious, entrepreneurial orientations that are such a prominent part of the American political culture.

Key Terms

citizenship, p. 99

civic republicanism, p. 116

clericalism, p. 101

communism, p. 101

diversity, p. 103

equality of condition, p. 123

equality of opportunity, p. 123

fascism, p. 101

liberalism, p. 114

political culture, p. 99

political socialization, p. 126

socialism, p. 101

Suggested Readings

Erie, Steven. *Rainbow's End: Irish-Americans and the Dilemma of Urban Machine Politics, 1849-1985.* Berkeley: University of California Press, 1988. Interesting account of the Irish urban machines that played such an important role in American political history.

Fowler, Robert Booth. *Religion and Politics in America.* Metuchen, NJ: American Theological Library Association, 1985. Stimulating discussion of the relationship of religion to political life.

Fuchs, Lawrence. *The American Kaleidoscope: Race, Ethnicity, and the Civic Culture.* Hanover, NH: University Press of New England, 1990. Dispassionate discussion of the problems and prospects of contemporary immigrants and African Americans. Prefers "kaleidoscope" to "melting pot" as a metaphor for the history of ethnicity in America.

Grant, Madison. *The Passing of the Great Race.* New York: Scribner's, 1916. Xenophobic diatribe that was a national best-seller in the second decade of the twentieth century.

Handlin, Oscar. *The Uprooted.* 2nd ed. Boston: Little, Brown, 1973. Sympathetic description of the ordeals experienced by late nineteenth-century immigrants.

Hartz, Louis. *The Liberal Tradition in America.* New York: Harcourt, Brace and Jovanovich, 1955. A classic, if impenetrable, discussion of the liberal tradition. Argues that the absence of feudalism allowed liberal ideas to spread without resistance in the United States.

Kleppner, Paul. *The Cross of Culture.* New York: Free Press, 1970. This example of the "ethnocultural" school of political history provides a detailed account of political conflict in the midwest from the rise of the Republican Party to the end of the nineteenth century.

Ladd, Everett Carll. *The American Ideology.* Storrs, CT: The Roper Center, 1994. A readable data-based discussion of the core beliefs of Americans.

Lipset, Seymour Martin. *American Exceptionalism.* New York: Norton, 1996. The latest work on the distinctively American political culture by an eminent senior scholar who has spent his life studying it.

Mcnendcz, Albert. *Religion at the Polls.* Philadelphia: Westminster Press, 1977. Survey of the association between religion and voting since the founding of the country.

Nicolaus Mills, ed., *Arguing Immigration: Are New Immigrants a Wealth of Diversity ... Or a Crushing Burden?* New York: Simon & Schuster, 1994. This collection of essays provides a good overview of the contemporary immigration debate.

Portes, Alejandro, and Ruben G. Rumbaut. *Immigrant America: A Portrait.* Berkeley, CA: University of California Press. Informative sympathetic account of the post-1965 wave of immigration, but like much contemporary writing, it exaggerates the difference between immigration today and that of a century ago.

Schlesinger, Arthur Jr. *The Disuniting of America.* Knoxville, TN: Whittle, 1991. An eminent senior historian complains about the contemporary influence of multiculturalism.

5

public opinion

N AUGUST 2, 1990, after months of wrangling about oil, territorial boundaries, and war debts, Iraqi troops surged across the Kuwait border and, in a single day, subjugated that small state.[1] In addition to the direct economic damage to countries whose economies depended on imported oil, the Iraqi offensive heightened world uncertainty about what would happen next. Would Iraq's President, Saddam Hussein, now order a move on Saudi Arabia? If that country, with one-quarter of the world's known oil reserves, were to fall under Iraqi domination, the economies of the West would be at the mercy of an unpredictable and unfriendly dictator. Moreover, a powerful Iraq heightened the danger to America's ally, Israel, and threatened the stability of the entire Middle East, if not the world.

President George Bush reacted without hesitation. He warned Iraq in the strongest possible terms, secured a United Nations (UN) resolution condemning the invasion, and sent 200 thousand American troops to Saudi Arabia to bolster the Saudi defensive forces. For the next several months the administration engaged in diplomatic efforts to construct a multinational coalition against Hussein. On November 29 the UN adopted a resolution authorizing member states to use "all necessary means" to expel Iraqi forces from Kuwait if they had not withdrawn by January 15, 1991. This was the first time since the Korean war, a generation ago, that the UN had authorized member states to go to war. By early 1991 a million UN troops lined the Kuwait border facing the Iraqi defenders.

The Bush administration found it a bit tougher to convince the Democratic Congress. While the administration denied that it needed congressional approval to participate in the UN-sponsored war, many in the Congress thought otherwise. In any event, the administration understood that congressional approval would help build domestic support. The Congress began deliberating shortly after the New Year, and on January 12, after an impressive televised debate in the Senate, adopted a resolution authorizing the use of force against Iraq. The vote in the House was 250-183, and in the Senate a closer 52-47. Democrats provided virtually all of the opposition, raising the spectre of Vietnam (pp. 263), charging that a war really would be about oil rather than freedom and aggression, and asking that economic sanctions be given additional time to work. But in the end, enough Democrats (86 in the House and 10 in the Senate) supported the president to give him the victory.

On January 16, the air war began. CNN broadcast from downtown Baghdad during the bombardment, and in the ensuing days Americans were shown impressive military footage of technologically advanced weaponry. On February 24, the ground offensive began. Allied forces outflanked the entrenched Iraqis, and within four days the Iraqis had been driven from Kuwait, with great loss of life — 50 thousand or more dead. The evening news telecasts showed throngs of jubilant Kuwaitis parading through the streets chanting "Bush! Bush! Bush!" On February 27, President Bush declared a cease-fire. On March 6, the president told Congress, "The war is over."

The United States had achieved a stunning military victory, at a cost far lower than most had feared and expected: 89 dead and 38 missing in action. In the aftermath of the war, President Bush's approval ratings soared, reaching unprecedented heights of as much as 90 percent in some polls (see Figure 5.1). Most people conceded his reelection, only a year and a half away. Apparently Bush had been right and the Democrats wrong. Prominent Democrats who had been likely opponents — Majority Leader Gephardt, Senators Sam Nunn and Bill Bradley, Governor Mario Cuomo — all thought better of taking on the seemingly unbeatable Bush. The Democratic first team opted out and left the field of play to "minor leaguers" like Bill Clinton, Jerry Brown, and Paul Tsongas.

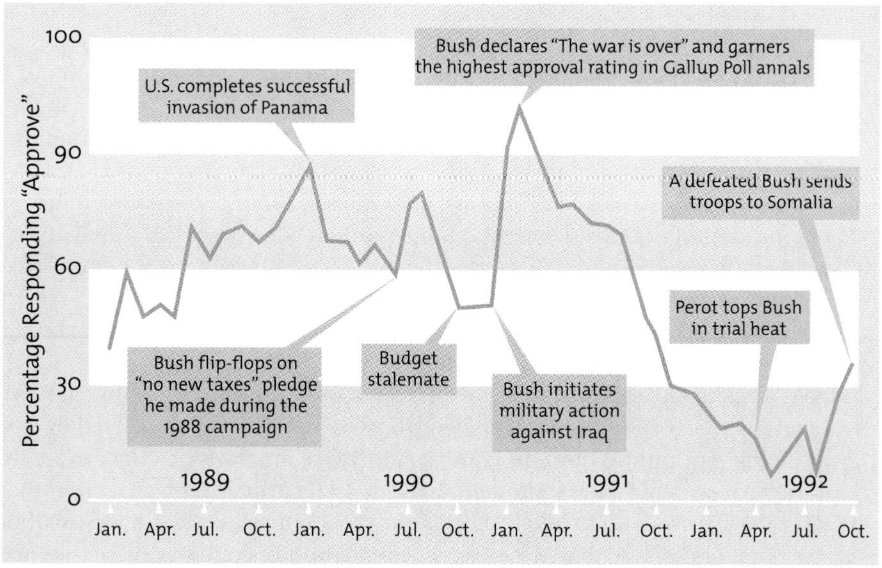

100
90
60
30
0
Percentage Responding "Approve"
U.S. completes successful invasion of Panama
Bush declares "The war is over" and garners the highest approval rating in Gallup Poll annals
A defeated Bush sends troops to Somalia
Perot tops Bush in trial heat
Bush flip-flops on "no new taxes" pledge he made during the 1988 campaign
Budget stalemate
Bush initiates military action against Iraq
1989
1990
1991
1992
Jan. Apr. Jul. Oct. Jan. Apr. Jul. Oct. Jan. Apr. Jul. Oct. Jan. Apr. Jul. Oct.

FIGURE 5.1

The Rise and Decline of President Bush's Approval Ratings

But Bush's fortunes were slipping even as his strongest opponents were conceding him the election. Within a year of his great victory in the Persian Gulf, his approval ratings had dropped by 50 percent (see Figure 5.1). He went into the election as one of the least popular presidents of the past fifty years and lost to Bill Clinton in a three-way race. The explanation for this startling reversal of fortune lies in shifting public opinion: During the eighteen months between the war and Bush's defeat, the American public in effect forgot about the war and turned its focus to the struggling economy (see pp. 280).[2]

George Bush is not the first president to find out that public opinion is not only a powerful force, but a fickle one as well. On the one hand, American politicians and institutions seldom can obstruct an aroused public opinion, but on the other hand, public opinion can shift rapidly from a concern about one subject to concern about a different subject, and political fortunes can shift accordingly. Public opinion is more important in American democracy today than ever before, and modern politicians measure it more and better than ever before. But despite such developments, the role that public opinion plays in determining what government does continues to be as ambiguous and problematic as ever. This chapter examines public opinion—how it arises and why it changes—and considers the problem of governing under its influence.

The Concept of Public Opinion

Although conceptions of democracy vary in important ways, public opinion is an essential element of all of them. As we explained in Chapter 1, democratic theorists tend to fall into two broad camps in their thinking about democracy. In theories that emphasize popular involvement, public opinion plays an active role—it drives the democratic process and determines the outcomes. In theories that emphasize representation and leadership, public opinion plays a more passive role—it constrains the democratic process and the outcomes it produces by establishing bounds within which public officials must operate.

Whether actively or passively, the explanation of why public opinion affects the democratic process is implicit in the definition of public opinion offered by V.O. Key, Jr., for whom **public opinion** consisted of "those opinions held by private persons which governments find it prudent to heed."[3] The principal reason government officials find it "prudent" to heed such opinions, of course, is their concern about their electoral fates. Note that in Key's conception, public opinion can be, but need not be, actively expressed. Even if public opinion is silent or "latent," public officials may act or fail to act because they fear arousing it. This is the so-called "law of anticipated reactions," whereby public opinion influences government even though it does so indirectly and invisibly.[4] When we say "public opinion would not stand for that" we are referring to this latent, constraining function of public opinion. Thus, Key's definition accommodates both the more active role of public opinion in participatory democratic theories and the more passive role in responsible theories.

■ **public opinion**
Those opinions held by private persons that governments find it prudent to heed.

Sources of Public Opinion

The opinions people hold reflect influences too numerous to list, but most of these fall into several broad categories. These categories are not mutually exclusive, of course; often opinions reflect a number of different influences.

SOCIALIZATION

In Chapter 4 we noted that Americans are socialized to value individual responsibility, economic advancement, and other aspects of the liberal tradition. **Socialization** is an imprecise term that encompasses all the ways in which people learn beliefs and values in their families, schools, communities, churches, and workplaces. Sometimes learning is the result of explicit teaching, but often it results from the less conscious observation or imitation of others. For example, studies have found that many children will identify themselves as Democrats or Republicans well before they have any concept of what the parties stand for.[5] And older children are very likely to share the party affiliation of their parents.[6] Thus, a party affiliation forged long ago in a traumatic event like the Great Depression may be passed down through generations of families.

Sometimes socializing agents consciously attempt to influence public opinion. The Catholic Church is officially opposed to abortion, and rank-and-file Catholics are indeed less accepting of abortion than are mainline Protestants and Jews.[7] Most

■ **socialization**
The end result of all the processes by which individuals form their beliefs and values in the home, schools, churches, communities, and workplaces.

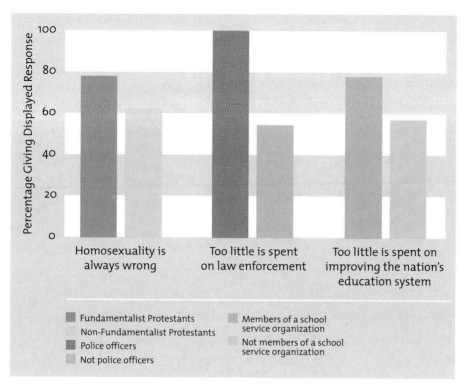

FIGURE 5.2

Examples of Group Differences in
Public Opinion

Fundamentalist Protestant churches officially condemn homosexuality, and rank-and-file members are indeed less tolerant of homosexuality than are mainline protestants.[8] From the 1930s to the 1980s labor unions typically supported the Democratic Party, and union members were indeed typically more Democratic in their voting than other blue-collar workers.[9] Social differences emerge with regularity in survey data on all kinds of issues (see Figure 5.2).

INTERESTS

Some of the opinions people hold are based on their personal interests or the interests of others like them.[10] For example, blue-collar workers are more sensitive to rises in unemployment that throw them out of work, while professionals and managers are more sensitive to rises in inflation that raise interest rates and place a drag on the overall business climate.[11] Homeowners were significantly more likely than renters and public employees to support Proposition 13, the famous 1978 initiative that rolled back property taxes in California.[12] Working women, who must balance the conflicting demands of home and work, are more supportive of gender equality than stay-at-home mothers.[13] Different life experiences give rise to different views on issues that become matters of public policy debate (see Figure 5.3).

EDUCATION

Although schools are socializing agents, and education certainly affects your interests, education belongs in something of a separate category—especially higher education. In general, higher education is associated with a somewhat more tolerant outlook. The more highly educated are more tolerant of minority groups and

FIGURE 5.3

People with Different Life Experiences Hold Different Views about Politics and Government

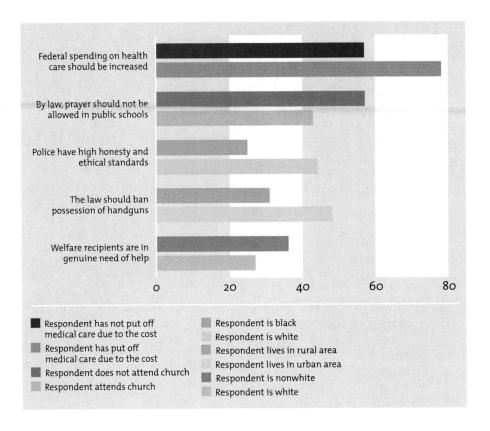

FIGURE 5.4

Higher Education Is Associated with Greater Tolerance of Diversity

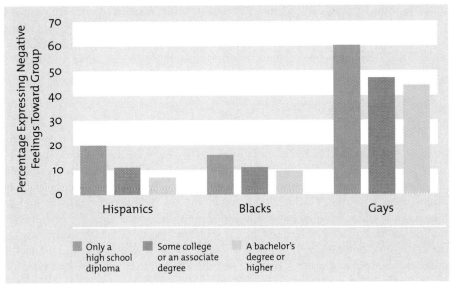

practices. Apparently, the values emphasized in higher education—logical argument, open-mindedness, unemotional analysis—predispose the educated, liberals and conservatives alike, to a somewhat greater acceptance of people and practices different from them and theirs (see Figure 5.4).

Education—in particular, higher education—encourages openness to and toleration of different viewpoints.

THE MEDIA

In recent years many people have expressed the fear that public opinion increasingly is being shaped by the mass media. This is a substantial issue, filled with controversy, and we will treat it at length in Chapter 9. Suffice it to say here that under some circumstances the media can move public opinion, while under other circumstances the media are surprisingly ineffectual. Despite the potential of the mass media to affect public opinion, however, there is little evidence to date to support the worst fears of media critics. For example, an extensive study of opinion change during the 1980 presidential campaign found that, in the aggregate, TV and newspaper exposure had only marginal effects on preexisting views.[14] But, to repeat, we consider this subject at length in Chapter 9.

Measuring Public Opinion: Polling

In the contemporary United States, descriptions and discussions of public opinion are readily available. Gallup is a universally recognized name. Newspapers, magazines, and TV networks sponsor regular polls—NBC News/*Wall Street Journal*, CBS News/*New York Times*, ABC News/*Washington Post*, USA *Today*/CNN—and base major stories on them. Indeed, critics complain that the media become obsessed with polls as the election draws near (see International Comparison). **Exit polls** of people taken as they leave the voting locations even enable the networks to "call" elections before the votes are counted! Given the prominence of public opinion polls, some critics charge that American government has degenerated into "government by opinion poll." Such charges are overstatements, but there is

exit poll
Survey of actual voters taken as they leave the polling stations.

I n the United States, public opinion polling is ubiquitous. The media regularly report the latest polls on the president's standing, the standing of potential challengers, who would win "if the election were held today," and how people feel about the issues of the day. During campaigns, polling reaches a fever pitch as people are deluged with poll results and stories about poll results. As we will discuss in Chapter 9, many critics feel that the American media place too heavy an emphasis on polls, concentrating on who's ahead while giving short shrift to the implications of the election for government and public policy.

Although polling is common in other democracies, many have chosen to limit it to some degree.* For example, Canada allows no polls to be published in the last two days of the campaign. Spain bans publication of polls for the last five days of the cam-paign, and France and Italy for the last seven days. Portugal allows no polls to be published for two weeks prior to election day! In the United Sates, any attempt to impose restrictions like these would be struck down on First Amendment grounds.

*David Butler, "Polls and Elections," in Lawrence LeDuc, Richard Niemi, and Pippa Norris, eds., *Comparing Democracies* (Thousand Oaks, CA: Sage, 1996): 239.

The television networks use exit polls to call the election soon after the voting is over.

legitimate basis for the concerns and criticisms leveled against opinion polling. Although our belief in the importance of public opinion for democratic govern-ments is as strong as anyone's, the problem we see is that public opinion is not some well-defined, stable object that can be easily and accurately measured. Quite to the contrary, public opinion often is mismeasured. A case from the early 1990s provides our first illustration.

A CASE IN POINT

In the spring of 1993 the Holocaust Memorial Museum opened in Washington D.C. Coincident with the dedication of the museum, the American Jewish Committee released startling data from a survey conducted a few months earlier by Roper Starch Worldwide, a respected commercial polling organization. The poll indicated that 22 percent of the American public believed it "possible the Nazi extermination of the Jews never happened," while another 12 percent were unsure. In total, one-third of all Americans apparently entertained doubts that the Nazis had murdered 6 million Jews in World War II.

The news media jumped on the story, which fit the preconceptions of many editorialists and columnists always eager to find shortcomings in their fellow citizens. What was wrong with the American people? Had the educational system failed so miserably? Even worse, was anti-Semitism so widespread and deeply ingrained in the population that Holocaust denials by the lunatic fringe were making headway? In the short span of fifty years, had the greatest genocide in history become a matter of mere opinion, to be believed in or not as one wished? What did this say about the American people?

Very little, it turned out. Social scientists knowledgeable about prejudice and public opinion were immediately suspicious of the poll findings, which seemed far out of line with what other contemporary polls showed about both anti-Semitism and the historical awareness of the American people. The Gallup organization—a Roper business competitor—soon demonstrated that the Roper poll was gravely mistaken, because Roper had asked a confusing question. The exact wording of Roper's question was:

Does it seem possible, or does it seem impossible to you that the Nazi extermination of the Jews never happened?

One of the first rules of **survey research**—the scientific design and administration of public opinion polls—is to keep questions clear and simple. The Roper question fails that test because it contains a double negative—"impossible . . . never happened" —a grammatical construction long known to confuse people.

Gallup conducted a new poll in which one-half of the sample was asked the Roper question with the double negative and the other half an alternative question:

Does it seem possible to you that the Nazi extermination of the Jews never happened, or do you feel certain that it happened?

■ **survey research**
The scientific design and administration of public opinion polls.

The 1993 opening of the Holocaust Memorial Museum was accompanied by a polling embarrassment that underscored the necessity of keeping public opinion poll questions clear and simple. How would you have answered "Does it seem possible, or does it seem impossible to you that the Nazi extermination of the Jews never happened?"

The difference in question wording may seem minor, but it makes a great deal of difference. In the half sample asked the Roper question, one-third of the respondents again replied that it was possible the Holocaust never happened or they were unsure, but in the one-half asked the alternative question, less than 10 percent of the sample were Holocaust doubters. Roper eventually retracted its initial poll results after doing its own follow-up studies. The whole episode had been the product of a simple mistake. Of course, many will find it disturbing that almost 10 percent of the population doubt the occurrence of the Holocaust, but to put that figure in perspective, consider that in a 1995 survey 10 percent of the American people did not know that President Clinton was a Democrat![15]

The Holocaust poll and the resulting controversy illustrate two important points. First, public opinion is extremely important in a democracy. People care deeply about what their fellow citizens believe—in large part because they believe that in the long run public opinion determines what government does. Second, whatever its importance, it is often difficult to know what public opinion is. Our ways of measuring it are far from perfect. With something so important often so uncertain, the interpretation of public opinion is inevitably a matter of controversy.

THE MISMEASUREMENT OF PUBLIC OPINION

Everyone is familiar with the "margin of error" now routinely reported in newspaper and TV stories about polls. Figures such as ±3 percent refer to **sampling error**, the error that results from using a small sample to estimate the characteristics of a larger population. Statistical theory tells us how to calculate the expected accuracy of a sample. For example, if every reader of this book flips a fair coin 15 hundred times, 95 percent of you will get between 47 and 53 percent heads. That is a statistical fact. But despite the attention given to it, in most professionally done surveys sampling is a relatively unimportant source of error.

The reason is that someone's opinion is not like the face of a coin. We can all look at a coin and say without any error or disagreement whether it fell heads or tails. Opinions are different. They are not physical facts, like the two sides of a coin; rather, they consist of subjective beliefs and judgments. Such beliefs and judgments, moreover, often are unconsidered answers to questions the respondent has never really thought about. For that reason, how people answer a poll depends very much on the wording and construction of the questions, the order in which they are asked, and when the poll is conducted. The Holocaust poll is an excellent illustration. No one accused the Roper organization of choosing a bad sample. Roper is a reputable professional organization that undoubtedly selected a sample accurate to within ±4 percent of the American population, as they claimed. But they asked a poorly constructed question that resulted in a bad measurement.

What look like minor variations in question wording can produce significant differences in measured opinion. This is especially likely when the variations involve the substitution of emotionally or politically "loaded" terms for more neutral terms. A well-known example comes from the policy area of government spending on the poor. Consider the following survey question:

We are faced with many problems in this country, none of which can be solved easily or inexpensively. I'm going to name some of these problems and for each one I'd like you to tell me whether you think we're spending too much money, too little money, or about the right amount.[16]

sampling error
The error that arises in public opinion surveys as a result of relying on a small sample that may not be perfectly representative of the larger population.

When the public was asked about "welfare" in the spring of 1994, the responses showed that a large majority of Americans believed that too much was being spent:

Too little: 13 %
About right: 25
Too much: 62

Conservatives would take heart in such a poll and use it to argue that welfare spending should be slashed. But when the *same people* in the *same poll* are asked about "assistance to the poor," a similarly large majority responded that too little was being spent:

Too little   59 %
About right   25
Too much   16

Americans are willing to help the "deserving" poor. If a mother receiving "assistance to the poor" looked like this, would Americans be more favorable than if she looked like a stereotypical welfare recipient?

Liberals would take heart in such a poll and use it to argue that public assistance for the poor should be increased.

While "welfare" and "assistance to the poor" may appear to mean the same thing, many Americans evidently disagree. "Welfare" carries negative connotations; it seems to prompt people to think of lazy and undeserving recipients—the stereotypical welfare cheats. But "assistance to the poor" does not seem to be associated with these negative stereotypes. If anything, people seem to add the modifier "deserving" to poor. Here is clearly a case where careless (or clever) choice of question wording can produce contradictory findings on a major public issue.

Such examples are common. Moreover, loaded questions are far from the only problem. Reputable survey organizations work constantly to identify and eliminate examples like the preceding one concerning public assistance. Responses to opinion polls also vary with question *format*.[17] For example, people tend to give more consistent answers to questions that allow graduated responses (agree strongly, agree somewhat, neither agree nor disagree, disagree somewhat, disagree strongly) than to either/or questions (agree/disagree). More people will choose a "don't know" or "not sure" answer if it is explicitly offered them than if it is not. People respond differently if given supporting arguments than if simply asked to choose between two sides of a question. People respond differently if earlier questions in the survey prompt them to think along certain lines. And people respond differently if surveyed after significant social, economic, or political developments than before.[18]

Characteristics of Public Opinion

Why should the measurement of public opinion be so sensitive to how it is measured? As we commented previously, the reason is that public opinion is not an objective quantity like body weight or temperature that can be measured with a simple physical instrument. On the contrary, the characteristics of public opinion often make it very hard to obtain reliable measurements.

PUBLIC OPINION OFTEN IS UNINFORMED

Americans are obliging people. If asked a question by a pollster, many of them will cooperate by giving an answer, even if they have not thought about the question or have no basis on which to arrive at an answer. A 1989 survey provides an extreme example. People were asked to rate 58 ethnic and nationality groups. Although one group included in the list ("Wisnians") was fictitious, 29 percent of the sample ranked them nevertheless.[19]

On many issues, people have little or no information. The extent of popular ignorance is most obvious when surveys pose "factual" questions. In 1995 only a third of the voting-age population could name their representatives in Congress. Less than half could name either Senator from their state. Barely half could name the Speaker of the House (Newt Gingrich), and only 60 percent could recall the name of the vice-president (Al Gore) (see Figure 5.5).

Elections are not SAT tests, of course; it is not necessary to know the answers to all manner of factual questions in order to vote intelligently. But widespread ignorance extends beyond such factual questions to important matters of government and public policy. During the 1995 federal government shutdown, 40 percent of Americans were unaware that the Republicans controlled both houses of Congress (and 10 percent did not know that the president was a Democrat). And

FIGURE 5.5

Americans Are Not Very Knowledgeable about the Specifics of American Government

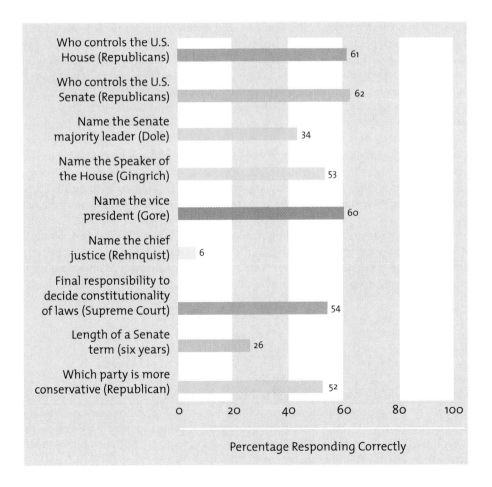

Percentage Responding Correctly

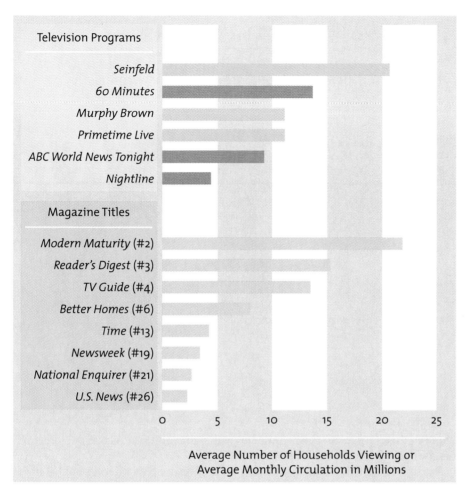

FIGURE 5.6

Interest in Politics is Much Lower
than Interest in Popular Culture
and Entertainment

Television Programs

- Seinfeld
- 60 Minutes
- Murphy Brown
- Primetime Live
- ABC World News Tonight
- Nightline

Magazine Titles

- Modern Maturity (#2)
- Reader's Digest (#3)
- TV Guide (#4)
- Better Homes (#6)
- Time (#13)
- Newsweek (#19)
- National Enquirer (#21)
- U.S. News (#26)

0   5   10   15   20   25

Average Number of Households Viewing or
Average Monthly Circulation in Millions

by more than a 2:1 margin Americans believed—absolutely wrongly—that the federal government spent more on foreign aid than on Medicare. In fact, the United States spends four times more on Medicare than on foreign aid, and the ratio is growing.[20]

Why do people have so little knowledge of basic facts and issues? The answer is that most people, most of the time, pay little attention to politics. News magazines sell far fewer copies than entertainment and lifestyle magazines. Far more Americans watch sitcoms like *Seinfeld* than watch Ted Koppel's *Nightline* (see Figure 5.6).

Upon learning the full extent of popular ignorance, some politically involved students react critically, jumping to the conclusion that ordinary Americans are apathetic and irresponsible people who fall far short of the democratic ideal. While such reactions are understandable, we think they are unjustified because they overlook the reasons why people pay so little attention to public affairs.

The simple fact is that most people have little time for politics; it is something of a luxury interest. They work long and hard to take care of the "necessities"—paying the bills, caring for families, and developing or nurturing personal relationships. Despite the importance of national and international politics, after dropping off and picking up children, commuting, working, and housekeeping, many Americans do not have the time and energy for the *New York Times* and *Nightline*. The

FIGURE 5.7

Higher Education Is Strongly Associated with Greater Knowledge of Politics and Government

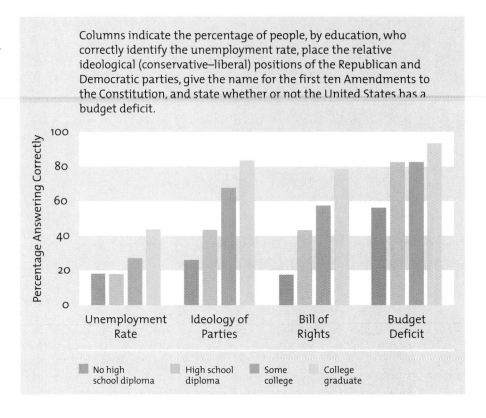

Columns indicate the percentage of people, by education, who correctly identify the unemployment rate, place the relative ideological (conservative–liberal) positions of the Republican and Democratic parties, give the name for the first ten Amendments to the Constitution, and state whether or not the United States has a budget deficit.

information cost
Time and mental effort required to absorb and store information, whether from conversations or the media.

Most Americans are more interested in popular culture than in politics and government.

effort required to stay informed competes with recreation and relaxation, for which many citizens have precious little time.

Those who criticize ordinary citizens for their lack of attention to public affairs often have jobs that enable them to stay informed with minimal effort. For example, in a university environment, political conversation is a common diversion and often relevant to academic pursuits. In such a context, professors and students find it relatively easy to stay informed. Likewise, the jobs of many journalists involve following politics: If they are not informed, they are not doing their job. If all Americans worked for universities or the news media, they would be much better informed. But most do not, a fact academic and journalistic critics would do well to bear in mind.

The general point is that gathering, processing, and storing information is costly. For most Americans, bearing such **information costs** will bring them little in the way of corresponding benefits.[21] Few citizens feel that the resolution of conflicts in Bosnia or Rwanda will be in any way affected by their state of knowledge. And when faced with a costly activity that has no obvious benefit, many of them will decide rationally to minimize their costs. Thus, from a logical standpoint, the puzzle is not that so many Americans are ill-informed; the puzzle is that so many are as well-informed as they are.[22]

Of course, information costs do not fall equally heavily on all people. Education makes it easier to absorb and organize information; thus, it comes as no surprise that more-educated Americans are better informed than less-educated ones (see Figure 5.7). And, as already noted, certain occupations make it relatively easy to stay informed.

In addition, the benefits of information are not the same for all people on all issues. Most people will be better informed on issues that directly affect their lives or livelihoods. Parents and teachers are more knowledgeable than other citizens about school operations and budgets. Human services providers are more knowledgeable about welfare and other public assistance policies and budgets. Auto workers know about and have strong views about foreign imports, as do farmers about cotton and wheat subsidies. Such **issue publics** are different from the large mass of citizens in that their members' occupations or roles make information cheaper to obtain as well as more interesting and valuable.[23]

In addition to varying across people and issues the costs and benefits of information may vary over time as well. When a tax revolt flares or a debate over condom distribution in the schools erupts, information levels surge as people become caught up in the controversy. But after the burning issues are resolved and the controversy subsides, information levels also return to normal.[24]

Of course, some people will bear information costs even when there is little direct benefit from doing so. They may consider it their duty as citizens to be informed—they stay attuned to public affairs simply because they believe it is the "right thing" to do. Other people follow public affairs because they find it intrinsically interesting in the same way that some follow sports or the arts. For such people, following public affairs is a recreational activity; what others view as information costs they view as benefits. Probably most citizens know as much as they do because of considerations like these rather than because there is any personal tangible benefit as a result of being informed.[25]

PUBLIC OPINION OFTEN IS UNCONNECTED

Another characteristic of public opinion that makes it easy to misinterpret is that even when people have reasonably firm views on issues, those views often are surprisingly unconnected to each other. It is common to note that the American people are not very ideological.

An **ideology** is a system of beliefs in which one or more general organizing principles connect your views on a wide range of particular issues. For example, if you are told that Smith is a liberal Democratic congressman, you will infer a great deal about Smith—that he is pro-choice on abortion, favors taxing the rich, and supports a strong government role in health care. Conversely, if you are told that Jones is a conservative Republican congresswoman, you will infer opposite things about her—that she is pro-life, favors low capital gains tax rates, and thinks that health care should be left to the private sector as much as possible. Of course, your inferences will not invariably be correct, but more often than not they will. The reason is that people who are deeply interested in and involved in politics, whether as activists or officeholders (traditionally called **political elites**), tend to have well-structured ideologies that bind together their positions on disparate policy issues. To know that such a person is a "liberal" or "conservative" is to know a good bit about him or her.

Ordinary citizens are another matter. Philip Converse showed long ago that ordinary citizens who are not deeply interested in or involved in politics (tradition-

People who provide or receive a service like family day care represent an "issue public" that tends to know more about policies affecting that service.

■ **Issue public**
Group of people particularly affected by or concerned with specific issues.

■ **ideology**
System of beliefs in which one or more organizing principles connect your views on a wide range of issues.

■ **political elite**
Activists and officeholders who are deeply interested in and knowledgeable about politics.

mass public
Ordinary people for whom politics is a peripheral concern.

closed-ended question
Survey question that asks people to choose their answer from a set of prespecified alternatives.

open-ended question
Survey question that allows people to answer in their own words.

ally called the **mass public**) are nonideological.[26] Ordinary citizens' views on specific issues do not cluster together like those of elites. Rather than believe consistently in either activist or minimal government, citizens favor federal spending in some areas, but oppose it in others. They favor regulation in some areas, but oppose it in others. They favor toleration for some groups and in some situations, but not for other groups in other situations (see Figure 5.8).

Most survey questions are **closed-ended**—they ask people to choose from a set of prespecified alternatives. Sometimes, however, analysts ask **open-ended** questions that allow people to answer in their own words. When responses to such open-ended survey questions were analyzed in depth, Converse and his assistants found that by a strict scoring only 3 percent of the 1950s electorate thought ideologically, a number that could be expanded to a maximum of 16 percent by relaxing the criteria. The most common frame of reference was group allegiances—what kinds of people were the parties and their candidates sympathetic to? The second most common frame of reference was "the nature of the times"—how had the parties and their candidates performed recently when given the chance to govern? Even when generously classified, ideologues were no more numerous than citizens who could articulate virtually nothing of political relevance. In the 1960s there was some increase in ideological thinking, as educational levels rose and the parties became more polarized, but the thought patterns of ordinary Americans remained far less ideologically coherent than elites often presume.[27]

Of course, it is possible that people may find ideological labels useful even if their personal views are not ideologically consistent or they do not articulate an ideological frame of reference when responding to survey questions. But even when the standard for ideological thinking is much weaker, the evidence for widespread ideology is absent. For example, *when given the option* one-quarter to one-third of the population will not even take a position on a liberal–conservative scale, and another one-quarter put themselves exactly in the middle: "moderate, middle of the road."[28] Given these figures, perhaps it is no surprise that in 1995

FIGURE 5.8

Ordinary People Are Much Less Ideological than Political Elites

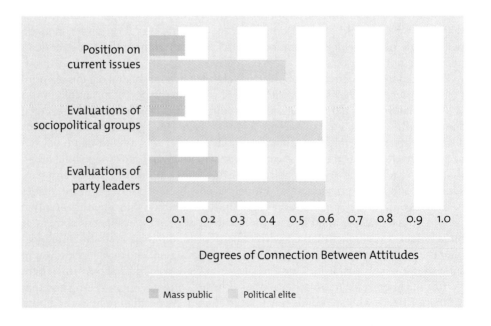

Degrees of Connection Between Attitudes

Mass public   Political elite

only 52 percent of Americans considered the Republicans the more conservative of the two parties, while 17 percent thought the Democrats were, and 30 percent didn't know.[29]

Once again, there is a widespread tendency to cast a negative light on the nonideological thinking of ordinary Americans, and here again, we disagree with such judgments. Maybe it is political elites who should be viewed critically. Because they are ideological, they take that to be the norm and nonideological thinking to be the exception that requires explanation. In our view, ideologies are as much *social* as logical constructions. Personal views aside, can anyone explain the logical connection between supporting low capital gains tax rates, being pro-life, and supporting development of a space station? Positions on such issues may go together for liberal and conservative elites, but *why* do they?

That ideologies are matters of social construction and convention is shown by the way they change over time.[30] From the 1930s through the 1950s "liberal" implied belief in government intervention in the economy in order to control powerful corporations, to provide a safety net for ordinary citizens, and to supply collective goods such as electricity that would not be supplied by the private sector. In the 1960s the terms of political debate shifted. Although present earlier, racial attitudes and opinions about civil rights became much more important components of liberalism than previously. By the time "liberal" became a dirty word in the campaigns of the 1980s and 1990s, the term had become synonymous with support for a hodgepodge of social issues that included tolerance of personal irresponsibility and contempt for traditional values. The economic content of liberalism had greatly receded in importance, and as for government intervention, sometimes it was liberal (affirmative action), while at other times it was "conservative" (restricting abortion).

The American people have a strong pragmatic strain that has often been noted by European observers accustomed to a more ideological style of political discourse. Perhaps the nonideological views of most Americans should be taken as evidence for pragmatic, commonsensical thinking, while the ideological views of elites should be viewed as evidence of rigid, emotional commitment. Whether you regard ideological thinking as good or bad, however, you should bear one point in mind. Because they presume ideological thinking as the norm, party and issue activists, media commentators, and many public officials will conclude too much from opinion polls and voting returns. Support for one variety of government action may indicate nothing about support for another seemingly similar government action. Support for a candidate based on one issue may suggest little or nothing about that candidate's "mandate" to act on seemingly similar issues. The nonideological nature of public opinion means that elites often hear more than the voters are saying.

The most recent example of this common elite mistake was the Federal government shutdown in the winter of 1995–96 (see page 620). Although the new Republican House majority had paid considerable attention to public opinion a year earlier (see Election Connection: 1994), once in office they vastly overestimated the degree of popular support for their program, inferring that their 1994 election victory was a blanket endorsement of balancing the budget, cutting entitlements, and cutting taxes—the things the new majority believed in. When President Clinton refused to accept the Republican plan, and gridlock ensued, public opinion blamed the Republicans more than the president.[31]

Public Opinion and the 1994 Republican Contract

■ **focus groups**
Small groups used to explore how ordinary people think about issues and how they react to the language of political appeals.

Congressional Quarterly described the 1994 congressional elections as an "electoral meteorite that slammed into the American political landscape."* These elections gave Republicans control of both Houses of Congress for the first time in forty years. Although many election observers thought that the Republicans had a chance to win the Senate, few gave them a serious chance to capture the House. When the dust thrown up by the "electoral meteorite" cleared, however, the Republicans had gained 53 seats, giving them a majority of 27 seats, and the pundits now speculated that a new electoral era had dawned.

The architect of the Republican victory was soon-to-be Speaker of the House Newt Gingrich, and his vehicle was the Republican "Contract with Amer-

ica." In late September, Gingrich had more than 350 Republican candidates attend a Washington rally where they signed a contract promising voters that, within 100 days of taking control of Congress, the new House majority would adopt a package of congressional reforms and vote on ten planks dealing with the following issues: balanced budget, crime, welfare, families, a middle-class tax cut, national security, senior citizens' benefits, capital gains taxes, legal reforms, and congressional term limits.† Democrats as well as many nonpartisan commentators scoffed at this Republican media event. Not only did they think that many of the Republican proposals were electoral losers, but conventional wisdom holds that the out-party should simply attack the

in-party, not promise anything specific.

Gingrich and the Republicans stood firm. The criticism of the Contract did not make them back away from it; indeed, they reemphasized it, even publishing it in *TV Guide*, with its popularity and huge circulation. The Republicans were confident in their strategy for a simple reason: The contract had been carefully put together with the aid of modern public opinion research methods. On average, the proposals in the contract were supported by comfortable majorities in national surveys, and the language that was used—the "frames"— had been carefully tested in **focus groups**—small groups of citizens brought together to talk about the proposals.‡ The Republicans believed that the more widely publicized the Con-

PUBLIC OPINION OFTEN IS INCONSISTENT

Given that people often have not thought about issues, and given that most of them do not think ideologically, it should come as no surprise that public opinion often seems inconsistent. For example, in 1980, when Ronald Reagan defeated Jimmy Carter and the Republicans made striking gains in Congress, many in the media interpreted the election results as a "resurgence of conservatism" or a "turn to the right" in American politics. Republican elites were more than happy to accept such interpretations, and Democratic elites feared that such interpretations were correct. The evidence, however, was confusing.[32]

A poll taken in 1978 reported that an overwhelming 84 percent of the citizenry felt that the federal government was spending too much money. A smaller majority thought that the federal government had gone too far in regulating business. Popular sentiments like these appeared to be foretelling the Reagan victory in the next elec-

tract, the better for them it would be. While the Contract was not the only factor in the election, the Republicans' beliefs proved to be more accurate than the Democrats'. In mocking the contract, Democrats were swimming upstream against the current of public opinion. In many cases they were swept away.

If imitation is the sincerest form of flattery, then the 1996 Democrats flattered the 1994 Republicans. In the summer of 1996, Minority Leader Richard Gephardt unveiled a new "Families First" agenda for the Democrats. It provided for tax breaks for child care and health costs, and promised to get tough on crime and balance the budget. This time, the Republicans did the mocking, dismissing "Families First" as "nothing more than a product designed by their pollsters and their elite leadership in Washington."§

* Robert W. Merry, "Voters' Demand for Change Puts Clinton on the Defensive," *Congressional Quarterly Weekly Report*, November 12, 1994: 3207.

† Clyde Wilcox, *The Latest American Revolution* (New York: St. Martin's Press, 1995): 48–56, Appendix A.

‡ On public support for the Contract proposals, see "The Direction Specified in Most of the 'Contract's' Planks Finds High Public Backing," *The Public Perspective,* February/March 1995: 29.

§ John Yang, "'Contract with America,' Meet 'Families First,'", *The Washington Post National Weekly Edition,* July 1–7, 1996: 13.

tion. But then again, the same poll asked the *same people* which domestic programs they favored cutting and which areas of business activity they favored deregulating. Surprisingly, pluralities, often majorities, felt that most domestic activities deserved *higher* funding or *more* regulation.

Findings like these are common. After the Republican congressional victories in 1994, polls reported that large majorities wanted to balance the budget, but not to cut specific programs, especially the large entitlement programs that drive budget deficits.[33] Such contradictory views recall the old maxim that "everybody wants to go to heaven but nobody wants to die." Everyone wants less government spending and interference but not in any particular policy area except welfare and foreign aid.

Obviously, such contradictory views confuse political debate. After his election, President Reagan claimed—with some justification—that he had been elected to cut government spending and deregulate the economy. Democratic leaders in Congress claimed—with some justification—that their party had been returned to power so that they could protect existing spending and regulatory programs. Both claims were plausible given the public opinion data. In 1994 Republican Congressional leaders felt they had a mandate to balance the budget. But when they attempted to slow the growth of Medicare spending, they found out that the mandate did not extend that far. In recent decades the American people have never delivered a clear mandate either for the Republicans to cut and retrench or for the Democrats to tax and expand.[34] One consequence is the gridlock and deficits of the 1980s and 1990s. While gridlock and deficits often are laid at the feet of divided government—Republican presidents and Democratic Congresses—it appears that divided government is a symptom of the conflicting views of the American citizenry as much as a cause of deadlock and deficits.[35]

Why is public opinion so inconsistent? There are many reasons. In the preceding example, most analysts think that the inconsistency arises from two sources. First, people have highly inaccurate views of how much is being spent on programs like "welfare" and foreign aid. Thus, they believe, erroneously, that cutting such unpopular programs will free up sufficient funds to maintain or increase funding for more popular programs. Second, some voters believe that waste and inefficiency are so pervasive that spending could be increased in some policy areas if only government in general were more efficient. Anyone who looks closely at the budget figures realizes that such beliefs are mistaken. We hasten to add, however, that such mistaken impressions are partly the responsibility of elected officials, who, rather than attempt to educate citizens, instead reinforce popular misconceptions for short-term electoral gain.

Not all examples of inconsistency reflect insufficient and inaccurate information, however. Citizens are so consistently inconsistent in their judgments about general principles versus specific applications of those principles that other explanations must be at work. We have seen that they favor cutting spending in general but not specific programs. They also oppose amending the Constitution, but favor a balanced budget, term limitation, and flag-burning amendments. And perhaps most interesting of all, they support fundamental rights but regularly make numerous exceptions.[36] Citizens favor free speech—but not for everyone, and not all the time. They favor freedom of the press and freedom of assembly—but with "reasonable" exceptions. They believe in the separation of church and state—but favor prayer in schools (see Figure 5.9).

It is easy to label such inconsistencies hypocrisy, and some do. Or, they can be viewed as indications that ordinary people do not have a clear understanding of rights—and perhaps they are. But there are other, more positive interpretations as well. To the law professor, the newspaper editor, or the committed political activist, rights may be viewed as absolutes. As a matter of simple logic, to abridge them at all is to destroy them. But despite their commitment to individual rights, few Americans accept such an unconditional perspective. Americans tend to be pragmatists. The constrained thinking of ideology and the absolutist language of rights are foreign to the pragmatic, problem-solving American way of thinking. To the American people, rights are good things, but at times they conflict and must be balanced against other rights and other values.[37] They may very well make such trade-offs on a case-by-case basis.[38] Yes, free speech is a good thing, but should swastika-adorned Nazis be allowed to march down the streets of a neighborhood populated by Holocaust survivors? Many Americans believe free speech doesn't go that far. Yes, the accused have rights against unreasonable searches, but should the courts release murderers on the basis of legal technicalities? Many Americans believe that legal arguments lose sight of the purpose of the legal system—justice. To mature citizens aware of life's conflicts and trade-offs, the legalistic language of rights belongs in the realm of intellectual argument, not the realm of real-world politics. They may feel no contradiction in endorsing a right while simultaneously endorsing significant exceptions.[39]

The first three items show the percentage of people supporting the general principles indicated. The last four items show the percentage of people supporting specific civil liberties for the political or social group they dislike the most. The groups about which people were asked included members of the John Birch Society, the Ku Klux Klan, Black Panthers, as well as Fascists, Communists, socialists, atheists, anti-abortionists, and pro-abortionists.

Entitled to same rights and protections	
Free to win support for opinions	
Free speech for all	
Civil Liberties as General Principles: Yes	
Allowed to be U.S. president	
May teach in public schools	
May hold public rallies	
May make a speech	
Civil Liberties for Most Disliked Groups: No	

0   20   40   60   80   100

Percentage Expressing Tolerance

Governing by Public Opinion

Never before have American politicians had so much data about public opinion. As we have seen, however, given the characteristics of public opinion, trying to measure and interpret it is far from an exact science. Indeed, at times it is more like reading tea leaves than like science. Seldom can a public opinion poll be regarded as conclusive. Any time an interest group—whether it be the American Tobacco Institute or the American Heart Association, Exxon or the Sierra Club—calls a press conference and reports the results of a public opinion poll, citizens should take it with a large heaping of salt. There are very few issues on which a competent pollster cannot deliver a majority on whatever side of the issue the client favors. We are not suggesting that matters actually are as bad as that: There are so many polls that bad ones will be easily identi-

Americans are supportive of free speech in general, but many are willing to restrict hate groups.

fied. Moreover, most polling organizations have professional reputations that they take pains to uphold. What we are suggesting is that the uncertainty surrounding the "true" state of public opinion makes government by public opinion poll immensely difficult, even if that were what everyone wanted. We provide some in-depth illustrations of this point by looking at public opinion on some important contemporary policy issues.

Public Policy and Public Opinion: The 1994 Health Care Debacle

In April of 1991 Republican Senator John Heinz of Pennsylvania was killed in the crash of a small plane.[40] Governor Robert Casey, a Democrat, could appoint someone to serve until a special election in the fall, but Casey found no takers among prominent Pennsylvania Democrats. The reason was that President Bush's Attorney General, Richard Thornburgh, had announced his candidacy for the seat. Thornburgh had been a popular two-term governor of Pennsylvania, and given that the state had not elected a Democratic Senator since 1956, few Democrats were optimistic regarding their chances against him. Eventually Casey appointed Harris Wofford, the bookish president of Bryn Mar, a small liberal arts college near Philadelphia, and seemingly a poor fit for a blue collar state like Pennsylvania. Summer polls showed Wofford trailing Thornburgh by more than 40 points.

Wofford signed consultants Paul Begala and James ("Ragin' Cajun") Carville, who, with the recession eroding President Bush's popularity, set out to run a populist campaign. Wofford made headway with his appeal to working people, but really struck electoral paydirt when he focused attention on health care. His most effective TV spot showed him standing in an emergency room telling voters "If criminals have the right to a lawyer, I think working Americans should have the right to a doctor." To the dismay of the Bush Administration, Wofford overtook Thornburgh, and coasted to an easy win in November.

National Democrats seized on health care as a possible vehicle for electoral victory. All the 1992 Democratic candidates promised serious health care reform of one sort or another. Consultants Begala and Carville signed on with the Clinton campaign, which did to President Bush much the same thing that Wofford had done to Thornburgh. The 1992 exit polls showed that people named health care as the third most important reason for their vote—after the dominant issue, the economy, and just a bit behind the deficit.[41]

Apparently, President Clinton would succeed where Presidents Truman and Johnson had failed—he would complete the New Deal by extending health insurance to all Americans. Clinton named his wife, Hillary Rodham Clinton, to chair a health care task force consisting of some 500 health policy experts. For months they labored, formulating a comprehensive Health Security plan more than 1300 pages long. In September, the plan was presented to Congress. Amid great fanfare Hillary Clinton visited important representatives and senators and appeared before congressional committees to testify for the plan. She received rave reviews from Democrats, and even grudging compliments from some Republicans. Democratic confidence was high. "This is as big as it comes," said one aide. "This is Eleanor Roosevelt time."[42]

One year later, Senate Majority Leader George Mitchell (D-Maine) sounded the death-knell for the Clinton health care plan, blaming "the total obstructionism of Republicans."[43] Despite the importance of the issue for Clinton's election, despite Democratic control of the presidency and both chambers of Congress, and despite seemingly favorable public opinion, the health care initiative had gone down in flames. Five weeks later, the "obstructionist" Republicans captured control of Congress in the 1994 elections.

What had changed between 1992, when national health insurance seemed to be an idea whose time had come, and 1994, when the country would turn to Republicans who had fought health care to the death? Had the electorate undergone some kind of ideological conversion? A review of the public opinion data offers little support for such a change of heart. Rather, many people in and out of politics misinterpreted what the public wanted, and miscalculated about what it would accept.

There is no doubt that the public increasingly had come to view health care as a problem. Health care costs rose faster than inflation in the 1970s and 1980s. The economic restructuring of the 1980s lowered the proportion of the population without health coverage. And the recession of the early 1990s heightened economic insecurities and frustrations. By 1992 some polls reported that a majority of the population felt that the health care system was in crisis and needed to be completely rebuilt (see Figure 5.10).

But agreement about the existence of a problem is no guarantee that people agree about the nature of the problem or what to do about it. In this case, lack of agreement about the basis of the problem and the appropriate solution helped doom the Clinton plan.

Clinton made universal coverage the centerpiece of the plan, threatening to veto any plan that emerged from Congress without universal coverage. There were moral, political, and practical justifications for this emphasis. Most of the nearly 40 million Americans who lack health coverage are members of low-wage working families (senior citizens have Medicare, while the poor have Medicaid). It seemed a matter of simple fairness that such families not be left out. Besides, such families were traditional Democratic voters. But even much of American business favored universal coverage on practical economic grounds.

Along with government officials, businesses were worried about the soaring cost of health care. The United States spends 14 percent of its GNP— one-seventh of the economy—on health care, a figure much higher than in other countries. Paying this bill puts American

Hillary Clinton got the health care initiative off to a good start, testifying on behalf of the plan in Congress.

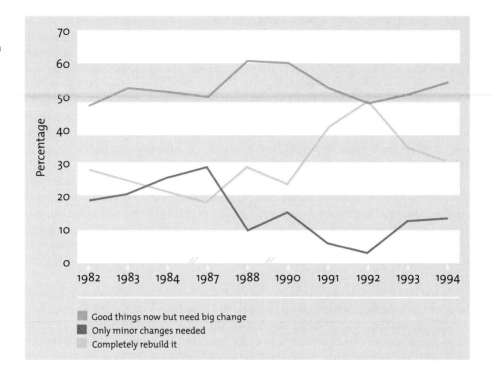

business at a competitive disadvantage in international trade; for example, $700 to $800 of the price of an American car reflects the health care benefits of auto workers.[44] Moreover, within the United States, businesses that incur the costs of providing health insurance to their workers are at a competitive disadvantage compared to those who don't.

The increasing costs of health care make matters worse. As costs rise, more businesses drop coverage, and more workers decline to buy their own. The uninsured tend to forgo preventive care, which is cheap, but eventually many need care for more serious conditions, which is often provided in expensive emergency rooms. Hospitals raise everyone else's rates to recover the costs of those unable to pay. Then, as rates rise further, more workers and businesses drop coverage, and a vicious cycle of spiraling cost and declining coverage ensues. Providing everyone coverage seemed like an essential step in getting health care costs under control.

The American people favored universal coverage—by a 2:1 margin in some polls, but this support was conditional.[45] One Gallup poll showed that nine times more Americans felt cost was a more important problem than access. Moreover, Americans opposed any new tax to pay for national health care. As one public opinion expert commented, "what most people really mean when they say they support universal coverage" is: "We support the president's goal of insurance for all that can never be taken away, but only if the nation can afford it and it doesn't limit choice of doctors or raise taxes or cause employers to cut jobs."[46] Characteristically individualistic, Americans were happy to endorse Clinton's egalitarian priority—but only if it didn't directly cost them anything.

The administration surely knew the details of public opinion. What were they to do? To extend coverage to nearly 40 million people without imposing any new direct tax was a political tightwire act. Part of the answer was to squeeze billions of dollars of waste and inefficiency out of the system. But what looks like waste and inefficiency to a policy expert may look like profits to an insurance or drug company, revenues to a hospital, and income to doctors, nurses, and other employees in the insurance and health care industries, all of whom kept members of Congress informed about their concerns.

Another part of the answer was to force all employers to pay "contributions" (which the public favored), but this set off disputes about the size of contributions and what proportion should be borne by big business, small business, importers, exporters, and so forth. Members of Congress were kept informed about such concerns, also.

The gargantuan Health Security Act was submitted to Congress and referred to five committees and their subcommittees, all of whom set out to improve the plan. Although the administration had consulted widely with organizations representing different parts of the health care industry, deals soon unravelled. Opponents launched attacks on the Clinton plan as too complicated and too bureaucratic, charges that resonated with an uncertain public. Popular support eroded: From nearly a 2:1 majority in favor of the Clinton plan when it was submitted, by summer opinion shifted to a majority against (see Figure 5.11). By Memorial Day Congressional Republicans felt confident enough to announce their complete opposition to any form of national health insurance. In the fall, a plurality of Americans expressed relief when the Clinton plan died.

What is especially telling about this case is that only a year earlier, the entire political establishment—Democratic and Republican members of Congress, the media, and virtually all the pundits—believed that national health insurance was an idea whose time had come. Only the details remained to be worked out. But the American people were less certain. Public opinion was not in agreement with the policy experts about the crux of the problem. The public worried about the cost of a major new government initiative, and it was suspicious of government regulation and government bureaucracy. When the opposition went on the offensive with attacks directed at these concerns, opinion quickly shifted. Public opinion on this issue was fluid and evolved as the debate progressed. An administration that set out to deliver on one of its principal campaign promises ended up suffering one of the worst electoral defeats of the twentieth century.

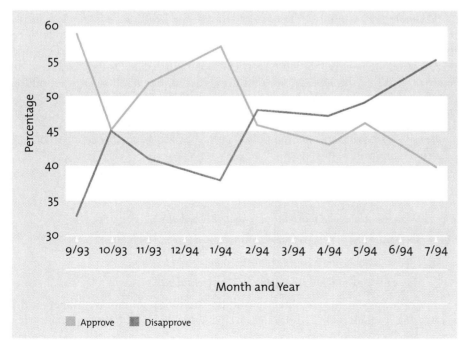

FIGURE 5.11

The Rise and Decline in Popular Support for the Clinton Health Care Plan

THERE...IT'S 100% COVERED...

UNIVERSAL
COVERAGE
1993-1994

Public Policy and Public Opinion: Abortion

In 1992 the United States Supreme Court announced that it would hear a challenge to a Pennsylvania law restricting access to abortion. As a consequence the already heated abortion debate intensified. Pro-choice and pro-life spokespersons alike proclaimed that a large majority of Americans supported their positions. Unless the laws of arithmetic fail to hold in this instance, one side or both apparently were wrong. But neither side was making up its figures.

At the outset we point out that, in contrast to the health care issue, Americans have stable views about abortion. The issue has been on the national agenda since the 1973 *Roe v. Wade* decision, supporting a woman's right to choose abortion, and there is reason to believe that most Americans long ago decided where they stand on the matter. When the *same* survey question is asked repeatedly over time, public opinion is strikingly stable. For example, a National Opinion Research Center (NORC) item reads as follows:

Please tell me whether or not you think it should be possible for a pregnant woman to obtain a legal abortion if

1. *the woman's health is seriously endangered?*

2. *she became pregnant as a result of rape?*

3. *there is a strong chance of serious defect in the baby?*

4. *the family has low income and cannot afford any more children?*

5. *she is not married and does not want to marry the man?*

6. *she is married and does not want any more children?*

After moving in a liberal direction in the late 1960s, opinion stabilized at the time of the Roe decision and has been remarkably constant for two decades (see

Figure 5.12). On average, Americans favor legal abortion in four of six circumstances, with large majorities supporting abortion in the first three so-called "traumatic" circumstances, but pluralities opposing abortion in the second three so-called "elective" circumstances.[47] Opinion changed little after the 1989 *Webster* decision that opened the way for some state regulation of abortion, or the 1992 *Casey* decision that upheld some of the specific restrictions imposed by Pennsylvania. Thus, the complicated picture that follows should not be attributed to uninformed, unconcerned citizens giving haphazard responses to polls. The complications run deeper.

First, consider the effects of question wording shown in two surveys that bracketed the 1989 *Webster* decision.[48] A *Los Angeles Times* poll asked

> *Do you think a pregnant woman should or should not be able to get a legal abortion, no matter what the reason?*

By close to a 2:1 margin (57/34) Americans said no. As the pro-life spokespersons had claimed, Americans were pro-life. Should Democratic campaign consultants have advised their candidates to take a pro-life stand?

Well, probably not. A few months later, a CBS News/*New York Times* survey asked

> *If a woman wants to have an abortion, and her doctor agrees to it, should she be allowed to have an abortion or not?*

By more than a 2:1 margin (58/26) Americans said yes. As the pro-choice spokespersons had claimed, America had a pro-choice majority. Should the Republican campaign consultants have advised their clients to flip-flop to the pro-choice side?

Which poll was right? Probably neither. Upon close examination both survey questions are problematic. Each contains words and phrases that predispose people

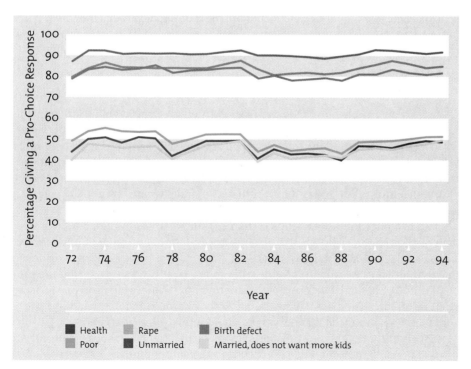

FIGURE 5.12

Popular Attitudes Toward Abortion Have Been Remarkably Stable Since *Roe* v. *Wade* (1973)

Neither the pro-choice nor the pro-life stance represents the nuanced view of abortion held by the American people in general.

to answer in one direction. The first question uses the phrase "no matter what the reason." As shown by the NORC data (Figure 5.12), most Americans are not *unconditionally* pro-choice. Thus, when forced to choose simply yes or no, many say no, believing that some circumstances are not sufficiently serious to justify abortion. The CBS/NYT question leans in the opposite direction. A doctor's approval suggests a reasoned decision based on justifiable grounds.

A more complicated question wording effect is called framing. We discuss this concept at great length in Chapter 9, but briefly, **framing** means that the survey poses the question in such a way that the respondent likely answers it from one point of view rather than another. For example, a CBS/NYT poll asked the following question:

> *Even in cases where I might think abortion is the wrong thing to do, I don't think the government has any business preventing a woman from having an abortion.*[49]

By close to a 3:1 margin (69 to 24 percent) Americans agreed with that sentiment. Apparently, the country is firmly in support of abortion rights. On the other hand, when a 1995 CBS News/*New York Times* poll asked people simply to agree or disagree with the stark claim that "abortion is the same thing as murdering a child," Americans were deeply split (46 percent agreed, 41 percent disagreed), and a plurality or majority of Americans regularly agrees that "abortion is morally wrong" (51 percent agree, 34 percent disagree in the aforementioned CBS News/*New York Times* poll).[50]

The first question uses a "choice" frame. Individualistic Americans favor freedom of choice, especially when it involves freedom from government interference. The second and third questions use an "act" frame. Whatever their views on choice, many Americans are uncomfortable with abortion. It is no surprise that the pro-choice side of the debate consistently employs one frame, while the pro-life side employs another. Nor is it any surprise that an accomplished politician like President Clinton announced that he was pro-choice and against abortion.

Consistently inconsistent, Americans favor the right to choose, but not an unconditional right to choose in every conceivable circumstance. Surveys show that

framing
Stating an argument in such a way as to emphasize one set of considerations and deemphasize others.

rape, birth defects, and threats to the mother's health and life are overwhelmingly viewed as justifiable circumstances. Personal convenience and gender selection are not. Youth, poverty, and marital status divide the population deeply. For this reason Americans oppose overturning *Roe*, but approve state laws that restrict the availability of abortion and prohibit public funding (see Table 5.1). About 60 percent of the public approved the Supreme Court's *Casey* decision, and Democrats were just as likely to approve as Republicans. Political folklore claims that the Supreme Court follows the election returns; in the recent abortion decisions, it can also be said that the Supreme Court followed the opinion polls.

Public opinion on abortion is unlikely to please militants on either side of the issue, because they think in terms of unconditional rights. Pro-choice activists who play an important role in the Democratic Party argue that any infringement on a woman's right to choose is unacceptable, even if that means the occasional abortion of a healthy, viable fetus. Pro-life activists who play an important role in the Republican Party argue that any abortion is unacceptable even if that means the occasional death of a woman. The great majority of the American people reject either extreme position.

Following Public Opinion

As we have seen, even on important, visible public issues like abortion, where public opinion is probably well formed and stable, one can paint very different portraits of public opinion by a careless or clever use of survey questions. Where opinion is less well formed, as on the health care issue, the possibilities are that much greater. Given this state of affairs, our view is that public officials who try to follow public opinion will find the going far more difficult than they might anticipate. Public opinion cannot substitute for leadership (see Democratic Dilemma).

TABLE 5.1

Abortion: With Restrictions

Would you like to see Roe v. Wade *overturned (after explanation)?*

	Oppose	Favor
	65	35

Would you support or oppose the following legislative restrictions (except in threat to mother's life):

	Oppose	Favor
Counseling on dangers and alternatives	9	91
Parental permission	23	77
No public funding	36	64
Fetal viability testing	38	62
No public facilities	33	57
No public employees	56	44

SOURCE: Gallup, July 6–7, 1989.

Public Opinion and Leadership

Public opinion and political leadership coexist uneasily in a democracy. On the one hand, responsiveness to public opinion is viewed as a central feature of democratic government. Public officials who act contrary to public opinion will find themselves characterized as "out of touch" with voters, or even as arrogant elitists in need of a comeuppance at the next election. For example, Democrat Mario Cuomo was elected governor of New York three times, but as the electorate grew increasingly conservative on issues such as taxes and crime, Cuomo steadfastly held to the liberal positions he had always espoused. In the 1994 elections voters rejected him in favor of a little-known Republican state senator, George Pataki.

On the other hand, leaders who change their positions in response to public opinion often find themselves attacked as wishy-washy or unprincipled. For example, shortly after he took office President Clinton called for an end to discrimination against gays in the military. In the face of public opinion polls showing the unpopularity of the proposal, even the Democrats in Congress rebelled, and Clinton was forced to accept a "Don't ask, don't tell" compromise. He was then roundly attacked for changing his positions to accord with public opinion. Critics charged that he lacked the courage of his own convictions.

Thus, elected officials can find themselves damned if they follow public opinion, and damned if they don't follow public opinion. What is an elected official to do?

Elected officials walk a fine line between leadership and responsiveness. Citizens want leaders to articulate and act on their views—to be responsive. But citizens realize that sometimes they are misinformed or wrong, so they also want leaders who will lead—do what they think is right and try to persuade constituents to their point of view. A good politician successfully walks the line, listening and responding to public opinion, but not pandering to it—following his or her own principles, but not to the point at which they are rejected by an aroused public opinion.

Where do you think the line should be drawn? Should it be drawn at the same place for all public officials, all offices, all issues, at all times?

How Important Should Public Opinion Be?

If public opinion is so difficult to measure accurately, you may be tempted to throw up your hands and take the opposite position. Should politicians discount opinion polls and simply implement their own views of good public policy? That would probably be unwise. Given the characteristics of public opinion, polling data should be treated cautiously and with full appreciation of how changeable they may be. But that is far from saying that public opinion polls contain no information. While the opinions of the individuals who make up the public are often poorly informed, unconnected, inconsistent, and changeable, the process of aggregation may cancel out individual error and enable the central tendency to emerge. Think of a grade school orchestra. Individually the young musicians are so unsteady that it is difficult to identify the tune each is playing, but put them together and the audience hears "Twinkle, Twinkle Little Star." So it is with public opinion.

We have noted that individual members of the public are nonideological. But as James Stimson has observed, the collective public understands that the Democrats are to the left of the Republicans on most issues.[51] Moreover, the public understood that Ronald Reagan was farther to the right than Richard Nixon, and George McGovern was farther to the left than Jimmy Carter. It may not be possible to separate the nuances of public opinion from the noise, but the general direction or "mood" of the public may be easier to gauge. Stimson shows, for example, that if hundreds of survey questions are aggregated together, they do indeed yield a portrait of an electorate that was turning to the right in the years leading up to Reagan's election.[52]

In the same vein, Benjamin Page and Robert Shapiro have argued that, viewed *collectively*, the public is reasonably "rational." A compilation of literally thousands of poll questions asked between 1935 and 1980 shows that, in the aggregate, public opinion is more stable than the opinions of individual members of the public, that public opinion generally moves in accordance with events and conditions, and that public opinion reacts to new developments in understandable ways. Moreover, taking such a broad, long-term view, Page and Shapiro find that American public policy follows public opinion. When trends in opinion are clearly moving in one direction, public policy follows, and the more pronounced the trend, the more likely it is that policy will follow it.[53] Similarly, research shows that when federal spending goes up, public preferences for continued increases go down, indicating some broad public recognition of the direction in which government policy has moved.[54]

Of course, not everyone will be pleased with such findings. Some people will take little comfort in evidence that public policy follows public opinion. After all, a Constitution that provides for federalism, the separation of powers, a bicameral legislature, a Bill of Rights, six-year Senate terms, and an electoral college certainly was not designed to translate public opinion directly into public policy. On the contrary, the Constitution sought to insulate senators and presidents from public opinion and allow them to exercise leadership.

As we have noted, differing theories of democracy embody different ideas about the elements of democratic government. The popular model requires ordinary citizens to play a more active, directive role than the responsible model. But Americans are not well informed and, as we will see in the next chapter, often fail to participate even in such a minimal way as voting. Thus, proponents of the popular model are disappointed by the ordinary citizens' modest interest in politics. Too often they forget that the structure and philosophical underpinnings of the American Constitution clearly indicate that the American democratic process reflects the responsible model at least as much as the popular model. But given the structure and philosophical underpinnings of the American Constitution, it is clear that the American democratic process is deeply rooted in the responsible model. Many of the Framers feared and distrusted public opinion, and deliberately chose institutions that would constrain it.

Chapter Summary

Public opinion is a basic element of democratic politics. If you believe that the people "rule," it is their opinions that democratic processes must translate into public laws and policies. If you believe that the people only "consent," it is their opinions that legitimate public policies and allow them to take effect. According to either view, public opinion is a basic force that shapes what a democratic government does.

Public opinion exercises its influence largely through the calculations of public officials who understand that they can and will be challenged in free elections. Clearly, an elected official will hesitate to oppose an aroused public opinion, but even a quiescent public opinion may influence the actions of politicians who fear arousing it.

Despite its importance, governing by public opinion poll is difficult and not to be recommended. Citizens often are not well informed; their views are not firmly held, can change quickly, and often are not connected to other seemingly similar views. For these reasons, poll results often are misleading and often misinterpreted by politicians and journalists. In the long run, American democracy follows public opinion, but in the short run, public opinion moves in fits and starts. Politicians who attempt to govern by public opinion poll will find the going much more difficult than they might imagine.

Key Terms

closed-ended question, p. 148

exit poll, p. 139

focus group, p. 150

framing, p. 160

ideology, p. 147

information cost, p. 146

Issue public, p. 147

mass public, p. 148

open-ended question, p. 148

political elite, p. 147

public opinion, p. 136

sampling error, p. 142

socialization, p. 136

survey research, p. 141

Suggested Readings

Asher, Herbert. *Polling and the Public*, 3rd ed., Washington, DC: CQ Press, 1995. A readable introduction to survey research.

Cook, Elizabeth, Ted Jelen, and Clyde Wilcox. *Between Two Absolutes: Public Opinion and the Politics of Abortion*. Boulder, CO: Westview, 1992. Careful, disinterested description and explanation of American attitudes toward abortion.

Geer, John. *From Tea Leaves to Opinion Polls*. New York: Columbia University Press, 1996. Thoughtful consideration of this chapter's democratic dilemma—do politicians lead public opinion or follow it? Concludes that rational leaders always follow on salient issues, but often lead on less salient ones.

Herbst, Susan. *Numbered Voices: How Opinion Polling Has Shaped American Politics*. Chicago: University of Chicago Press, 1993. An informative historical survey of the growth of opinion polling with a critical examination of its impact on contemporary politics.

Mayer, William. *The Changing American Mind: How and Why American Public Opinion Changed Between 1960 and 1988*. Ann Arbor, MI: University of Michigan Press, 1992. Masterful survey of the changing contours of public opinion over the past generation, with careful dissection of the sources of opinion change.

Page, Benjamin, and Robert Shapiro. *The Rational Public*. Chicago: University of Chicago Press, 1992. Monumental study of public opinion from the 1930s to the 1990s. The authors argue that, viewed as a collectivity, the public is rational, however imperfect the individual opinions members of the public hold.

Ladd, Everett, ed. *The Public Perspective*. Storrs, CT: The Roper Center. This bimonthly periodical is indispensable for any student of public opinion.

Schuman, Howard, and Stanley Presser. *Questions and Answers in Attitude Surveys*. Harcourt, Brace, Jovanovich: Academic Press, 1981. A comprehensive study of the effects of question wording, form, and context on survey results.

Schuman, Howard, Charlotte Steeh, and Lawrence Bobo. *Racial Attitudes in America: Trends and Interpretations*. Cambridge, MA: Harvard University Press, 1985. Thoughtful examination of contemporary racial attitudes. The authors find that Americans have come to accept principles of equal treatment, but remain quite divided about government policies designed to bring about racial equality.

Stimson, James. *Public Opinion in America: Moods, Cycles, & Swings*. Boulder, CO: Westview Press, 1991. Statistically sophisticated examination of American public opinion from the 1960s to the 1990s. The author finds that public opinion was moving in a conservative direction in the 1970s, but reversed direction around the time of Reagan's election.

Zaller, John. *The Nature and Origins of Mass Opinion*. New York: Cambridge University Press, 1992. An influential reinterpretation of public opinion findings that argues that people do not have fixed opinions on many subjects. Rather, their responses reflect variable considerations stimulated by the question and the context.

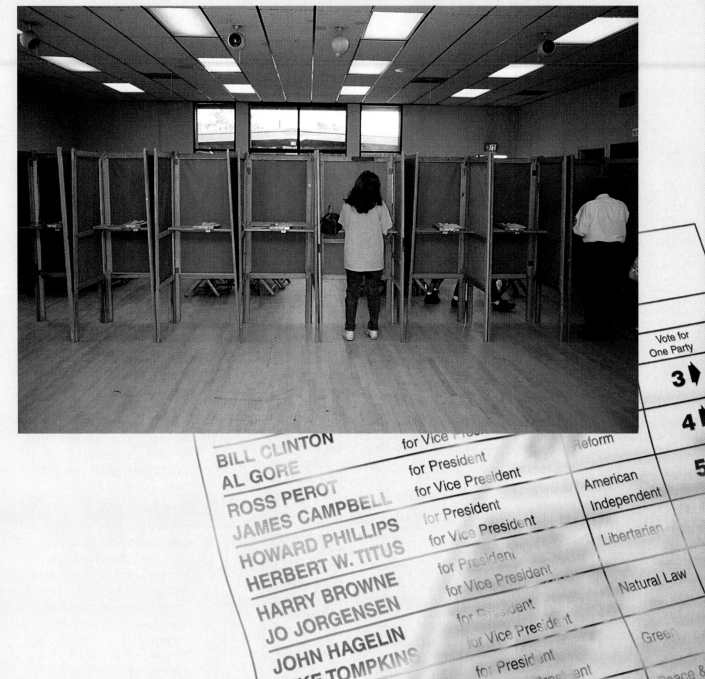

Vote for
One Party

3 ▶

4 ▶

5

BILL CLINTON for Vice Pres... Reform
AL GORE for President
ROSS PEROT for Vice President American
JAMES CAMPBELL for President Independent
HOWARD PHILLIPS for Vice President Libertarian
HERBERT W. TITUS for President
HARRY BROWNE for Vice President Natural Law
JO JORGENSEN for President
JOHN HAGELIN for Vice President Green
MIKE TOMPKINS for President
RALPH NADER for Vice President Peace &
WINONA LADUKE Freedo...
MARSHA FEINLAND for President
KATE MCCLATCHY for Vice President Repu...
BOB DOLE for President
JACK KEMP for Vice President

TURN PAGE TO C...

6

citizen participation

N THE MORNING after the 1992 national elections, the lead headlines summed up the presidential outcome: **Clinton Beats Bush!** But farther down the front page many papers carried another story: **Turnout Rises!** On November 3, 1992, 55 percent of the voting age population cast a presidential vote, a 5 percent increase over 1988. More important than the amount by which the turnout increased was the simple fact that it did: Until 1992 presidential turnout had dropped almost continuously since 1960.

In 1994 the big story was the Republican capture of the Congress for the first time since 1952. But the 3 percent increase in turnout over the 1990 level received some attention, too, for in congressional elections as well, turnout had been declining for a generation, although not as steadily as in presidential elections. Alas, however, in 1996 the story was the opposite. Less than 50 percent of Americans voted for president, the lowest figure since 1924. Indeed, if we set aside the 1920 and 1924 elections because women had just been enfranchised in 1920 and many—especially poor immigrant women—did not immediately exercise their right to vote, the 1996 turnout figure was the lowest since the United States became a mass democracy in 1828.

Foreign observers of American politics undoubtedly have been amused by the attention Americans have given to these recent rises and declines in turnout. After all, more than three-quarters of the British voted when they returned John Major to office in 1992. To Americans, turnout was an almost unimaginable 96 percent in the 1996 Australian parliamentary elections. In 1995 the turnout rate was 79.8 percent in the French presidential elections and 80 percent in the Canadian parliamentary elections. And when the Japanese Liberal Democratic Party in 1993 lost its parliamentary majority for the first time since World War II, the 67 percent turnout rate received wide notice—because it was the lowest ever recorded in Japan !

By the standards of other developed democracies, turnout in American elections is exceptionally low—a little more than half the electorate in presidential elections, and about 40 percent of the electorate in the off-year elections. In primaries and in local elections, turnout ordinarily is even lower. Such anemic levels contrast with most other democracies' turnout rates, which regularly exceed 75 percent. Ironically, here in the United States, where elections occur continually and have a greater impact on government and public policies than in other countries, turnout rates are significantly lower than in most other democracies. Only the Swiss vote as infrequently as Americans, a point to which we will return later.

Many Americans are concerned about turnout levels in the United States, because voting is widely regarded as the fundamental form of democratic participation. Indeed, in modern populous democracies voting is the *only* form of participation for the great bulk of the population. About one-third of Americans report having signed a petition, and a similar number claim to have contacted a government official at one time or another, but substantially fewer make financial contributions to a party or candidate, attend a political meeting or rally, or work in a campaign. Probably two-thirds of Americans do nothing beyond voting.[1]

So, for most people, failure to vote means failure to participate at all. And if a bare majority—or even fewer people—vote, how representative are the public officials they elect, and how legitimate are the actions these officials take? Not very, in the view of some. Benjamin Barber charges that "In a country where voting is the primary expression of citizenship, the refusal to vote signals the bankruptcy of democracy."[2]

merican nonparticipation is an important question which we consider at length later in this chapter. We will begin, however, by considering a history of the franchise in the United States, and why people would participate in politics, then we answer in some detail the comparative and historical questions just introduced:

- Why is turnout lower in the United States than in other democracies?

- Why has turnout varied over the course of American history?

- Why did turnout in the United States decline between 1960 and 1992?

With that background, we then turn to the larger question of whether low participation levels threaten the legitimacy of American government.

A Brief History of the Franchise in the United States

By the 1820s the political system in the young American republic had grown stagnant. After the election of 1800 the Federalists were no longer a serious threat to capture the presidency or the Congress, and the party effectively disappeared after 1816. But the so-called "era of good feeling" was not the happy time the expression suggests. Economic depression, political instability, and popular discontent formed the background for politics during much of the period. National politics was in the hands of a congressional elite, elected by a minority of white male property owners. A congressional caucus, composed of all the Democratic-Republican members of Congress, nominated the presidential and vice presidential candidates who, after 1800, were elected as a matter of course.

But in 1824 the factionalized caucus could not unite behind a single candidate for president. Four candidates vied for the office including Secretary of State John Quincy Adams (son of the second president) and General Andrew Jackson, hero of the War of 1812. Jackson got the largest share of the popular vote for presidential electors, 50 percent more than Adams—his closest competitor—but no one got a majority in the electoral college, so the election went to the House of Representatives, as stipulated by the Constitution. There, Speaker Henry Clay delivered the victory to Adams, who in turn appointed Clay secretary of state. The losers condemned this sequence of events as evidence of a "corrupt bargain" between Adams and Clay.

Outraged, Jackson's supporters redoubled their efforts. Determined to break the grip of the old Virginia elite on national politics, they spread their campaign outward to the newly settled west and downward to the grass roots of the country. In 1824 six of the 24 states had not provided for popular election of presidential electors (the state legislatures selected them), but that number fell to two states by 1828. Turnout increased in all the other states. In total, more than three times as many men voted for presidential electors as had voted in 1824, and Jackson easily defeated Adams.[3]

Despite the tripling of voting turnout between 1824 and 1828, only about 56 percent of the adult male population voted in 1828. As noted, men in two states still could not vote for presidential electors. Property qualifications varied from state to state and were very unevenly enforced, but in various forms they continued into the 1830s, and most

■ **franchise**
The right to vote.

■ **suffrage**
Another term for the right to vote.

states restricted the **franchise**—the right to vote—to taxpayers until the 1850s.[4] Not until the eve of the Civil War can it be said that the United States had universal white male **suffrage** (another term for franchise). And not all voter qualifications were economic; until the 1830s a few states even limited voting to those who professed belief in a Christian god. Jews were not permitted to vote in Rhode Island as late as 1830.

By 1860 all adult white male citizens had the franchise. In fact, white aliens often were permitted to vote, but free black citizens usually were not.[5] The Fifteenth Amendment to the Constitution, adopted in 1870, extended the franchise to black males, who at the time were heavily concentrated in the South. With the Republican Congress providing some protection for the party's newly enfranchised supporters, African-American males were able to exercise their voting rights for almost two decades in some areas.[6] As described in Chapter 17, however, by the mid-1890s a reactionary movement disenfranchised black males by means of poll taxes, literacy tests, white primaries, and other procedures that could be used in discriminatory fashion by white election authorities (backed up by violence and intimidation when necessary). Black Americans were effectively denied their voting rights in many parts of the South until the 1960s. Then, as we discuss in Chapter 17, the Voting Rights Act reestablished the federal oversight of southern elections that had been allowed to lapse in the 1890s. The result has been a steady increase in black voting.

Women had to wait even longer than African Americans for the franchise.[7] Wyoming in 1869 granted women the right to vote in territorial elections, and in 1890 became the first state to extend the franchise to women in national elections. By 1916 eleven other states, mostly in the west, had followed. Finally, in 1920 the Suffrage Movement won its crowning victory when the nineteenth amendment was ratified. In theory, if not in practice, the electorate now was the voting age population, not just the male voting age population.

A smaller extension of the franchise occurred in 1961 when the Twenty-Third Amendment to the Constitution was ratified. This amendment granted the right to vote for presidential electors to residents of the District of Columbia. (The District has no Representatives or Senators, although it elects a Delegate to the House of Representatives.)

In 1870, the Fifteenth Amendment guaranteed African American males the right to vote—at least for 20 years, until discriminatory practices and intimidation began effectively disenfranchising them.

The next and, to date, the last extension of the franchise came in 1971 with the adoption of the twenty-sixth amendment to the Constitution, which extended the right to vote to those between 18 and 21 years of age.[8] In most states, 21 had been the age at which eligibility began. During the Vietnam War the argument that Americans old enough to be sent to fight were old enough to vote gained increasing support, and a Republican president, Richard Nixon, announced his support of the amendment, even though many Republicans feared it would help the Democrats.

The Voting Rights Act of 1961

Daniel H. Lowenstein
UCLA School of Law

The Fifteenth Amendment, added to the constitution in 1870, prohibits denial or abridgement of the right to vote "on account of race, color, or previous condition of servitude." During the Reconstruction period blacks, most of whom lived in the southern states, voted fairly freely and effectively. The right to vote did not end overnight with the end of Reconstruction in 1877. However, over a period of about thirty years, violence, fraud, administrative bias, and legal changes were used to greatly impair the ability of blacks to vote, especially in the deep South.

During the 1930s, there were legal challenges to some of the devices used to deny the franchise to blacks, especially the Democratic Party's "white primary" in states in which winning the Democratic nomination was tantamount to winning the election. Perhaps more importantly, blacks who fought for America in World War II began actively demanding the right to vote when they returned home after the war.

Considerable progress was made, especially in the "outer" South and in big southern cities, but voting rates by blacks remained low in much of the South and were almost nonexistent in deep south states like Alabama and Mississippi. By the 1960s strong voting rights legislation became one of the highest priorities of Martin Luther King and other leaders of the civil rights movement.

Incidents of violence against peaceful demonstrators, especially in Selma, Alabama, created a political climate in which such legislation was politically feasible. After the Selma incident, President Lyndon Johnson made a dramatic demand to Congress for a strong law guaranteeing the franchise, and Congress enacted the Voting Rights Act of 1965.

The Voting Rights Act originally "covered" Alabama, Georgia, Louisiana, Mississippi, South Carolina, Virginia, and large parts of North Carolina. The covered states were prohibited from employing literacy tests as a qualification for voting. At that time, literacy tests could be used to deny the franchise to blacks, partly because most blacks had been poorly educated in southern schools and partly because the tests

were administered unfairly. Other provisions allowed federal officers to register voters in recalcitrant areas. Section 5 of the Act required the covered states to get "preclearance" from the federal Department of Justice before they could make any changes in their electoral procedures or systems. Some have criticized Section 5 as an unprecedented intrusion on state authority, but supporters insisted that it was necessary to prevent the South from repeatedly inventing new devices for denying the franchise.

The Voting Rights Act of 1965 was one of the most successful laws Congress has ever passed. Within two or three years, virtually all impediments to voting by blacks had been eliminated. After allowing for socioeconomic factors that influence the rate of voting, blacks in the South were voting at nearly as high and sometimes a higher rate than whites.

Subsequent amendments extended coverage of the Act to the remaining southern states and many areas outside the South. In addition, the ban on literacy tests was extended to the entire nation and protection of the Act was extended from racial groups to language minorities, such as Hispanics and Asians.

The slow and uneven expansion of the franchise reflects the compromise adopted by the constitutional convention: voting rights were left up to the separate states, which expanded the franchise in different ways at different times. Once the franchise was extended in one state, however, electoral pressures often led to similar extensions in other states. For, in trying to appeal to newly enfranchised voters in one state, national candidates had an incentive to go on record as supporting similar expansions in other states. This dynamic is evident in the case of youth suffrage and black suffrage, but most apparent in the case of women's suffrage.

The most important organization active in the women's rights movement was the National American Women's Rights Association (NAWRA). NAWRA followed a political strategy that in many ways anticipated the strategy used a half-century later by African-Americans to win their civil rights. After establishing a foothold by winning voting rights in a few states, the suffragists then leveraged their voting power to influence the policy positions of the political parties and presidential candidates. With the victory of women's suffrage in California in 1910 and Illinois in 1913, the stage was set for the final push.

Woodrow Wilson had won the 1912 election in a three-way race in which he received only 42 percent of the popular vote. He had not taken a clear position on women's suffrage; indeed, he once dodged the issue by saying that the question had never come to his attention. Many Democratic politicians were opposed to women's suffrage. They believed that women were more conservative than men and would vote against labor unions, against liquor interests, and against machine politicians, all of whom were important Democratic constituencies. Southern Democrats worried, moreover, that granting voting rights to women would raise the aspirations of African Americans for similar rights. Nevertheless by 1916 Wilson was moving to a position in support of women's suffrage, promising to vote in favor in a referendum in New Jersey, his home state.

Wilson's change of heart reflected the fact that by 1916 the electoral votes cast by states in which women had the franchise amounted to one-sixth of the total, which politicians translate as one-third of an electoral college majority. When Republican candidate Charles Evans Hughes announced his support of a constitutional amendment, he put Wilson on the horns of a dilemma. Should Wilson move in a similar direction against the wishes of local Democrats, or risk giving to his opponent one-third of the electoral college votes needed to defeat him? Wilson's political position was precarious, and he could not hope to win if he did not hold the West. Partly on the strength of his new, moderate pro-suffrage position he was able to carry ten of the twelve women's suffrage states and was narrowly reelected.

Although World War I took center stage for a time, the war experience probably contributed to a willingness to consider political change. Seeing victory on the horizon, suffragists dug in and pressed hard for congressional passage of the proposed constitutional amendment, setting 1922 as their target date. NAWRA encouraged women to write letters, make campaign contribu-

The suffragists put considerable pressure on President Woodrow Wilson to support the Nineteenth Amendment.

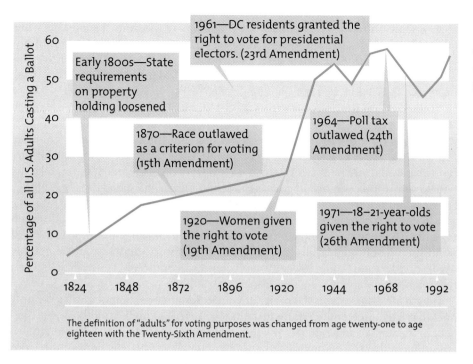

Percentage of all U.S. Adults Casting a Ballot

1961—DC residents granted the
right to vote for presidential
electors. (23rd Amendment)

Early 1800s—State
requirements
on property
holding loosened

1870—Race outlawed
as a criterion for voting
(15th Amendment)

1964—Poll tax
outlawed (24th
Amendment)

1920—Women given
the right to vote
(19th Amendment)

1971—18–21-year-olds
given the right to vote
(26th Amendment)

1824   1848   1872   1896   1920   1944   1968   1992

The definition of "adults" for voting purposes was changed from age twenty-one to age
eighteen with the Twenty-Sixth Amendment.

tions, and use other conventional political tactics, but more militant suffragists
engaged in more confrontational tactics such as protests and demonstrations.
Women's suffrage soon looked to be inevitable, and politicians, fearful of being left
behind, jumped on the bandwagon. Within three years a constitutional amendment
had been passed by Congress and ratified by the states, in time for women in all forty-
eight states to vote in the 1920 presidential election, two years ahead of the suffragists'
original schedule. Interestingly, the United States was far ahead of most of the world
in granting full rights of citizenship to women. France did not allow women to vote
until 1945, and the last Swiss canton did not enfranchise women until 1990![9]

Today every law-abiding, mentally competent citizen over the age of 18 has the
right to vote in the United States (imprisoned felons and the mentally incompetent
are not eligible in many states), although people who move within thirty days of the
election cannot vote in most states (see Figure 6.1). Some have argued, perhaps
tongue-in-cheek, that the right to vote should be further extended to children, perhaps by giving extra votes to their parents. But such proposals are not taken seriously—at least at present.[10]

Why People Participate:
Costs and Benefits

In the weeks leading up to elections, the newspapers, the parties and candidates,
and all manner of organizations exhort Americans to get out and vote. Nonetheless,
even in presidential elections half the potential electorate stays home. After the election, some editorialists criticize the nonvoters for being lazy and uninvolved, while
others criticize the candidates for being uninspiring and unworthy. Undoubtedly

It's the (Non) Voters' Fault

■ **individual motivations for voting**
The tangible and intangible benefits and costs of exercising one's right to vote.

there is some truth in both charges, but the question of why some people vote while others abstain is more complicated than newspaper editorials sometimes imply. Numerous factors influence whether a citizen gets to the polling booth. Professors Steven Rosenstone and Mark Hansen divide such factors into two general categories: individual motivations and outside mobilization.[11]

Individual motivations for voting reflect the personal costs and benefits associated with voting. If you are paid by the hour and you take time off in order to vote, you lose a portion of your wages. If you are a parent who cares for small children, you must pay the cost of a sitter in order to vote. Even if you are a professional who can leave work early or arrive late, you do less work on election day if you take the time to vote. Moreover, not all costs are tangible. When you spend time on political activity you have less time to spend on other, perhaps more attractive or fulfilling activities. And for some people with little education and information, the entire voting situation is confusing and perhaps uncomfortable. Staying home allows them to avoid such psychological discomfort. If it seems surprising that such seemingly small considerations could lower turnout, consider that turnout generally falls when the weather is poor.

There are also benefits to voting, of course. One reason, although not the only one, that late-nineteenth-century turnout levels were so high (usually over 75 percent in the non-South) is that many people were paid to vote. For example, historians estimate that the going price of a vote in New York City elections in the 1880s was $2 to $5 (expressed in 1990s dollars), with prices soaring as high as $25 in particularly competitive circumstances.[12] Material rewards are a much rarer benefit of voting today, but direct payments for voting (sometimes called "walking around money," see page 176) still exist here and there. And for some citizens, elections still directly affect material interests—for example, local government employees vote in low-turnout local elections at higher rates than do people employed in the private sector, and government employees in general vote at higher rates, other things equal.[13] Today, however, most of the benefits of voting are not material, but psychological. Some people take civic norms to heart and feel a duty to vote; they avoid guilt by voting. Others take satisfaction in expressing their preference for a candidate or a position on an issue much as they might enjoy cheering for an

The League of Women Voters is one of many groups that encourage people to get out and vote.

athletic team. Such psychological sources of satisfaction are called **psychic bene-fits of voting.**

Psychic benefits are of critical importance because, in their absence, the personal benefits of voting almost never exceed the costs. The reason is that if you vote, you bear the costs of voting no matter what the outcome, but your vote makes no difference unless it affects the outcome. And your vote affects the outcome only if it creates or breaks a tie between the alternatives being voted on.[14] In all other cases you could stay home and the election would come out the same way. Notice that in a small local committee or board, every member has the potential to be the voter who tips the scale, but in a state or national election, any single voter is insignificant. In the 1996 presidential election, for example, almost 100 million Americans voted. In the 1994 elections for the U.S. House of Representatives an average of 160 thousand citizens voted in each congressional race. Given numbers like these, in most elections the potential voter has every reason to believe that the outcome will be the same whether or not he or she votes.

Thus, psychic benefits are critical. Unless the voter has a strong sense of duty, or takes considerable satisfaction in expressing a preference, the personal benefits of voting generally do not exceed the costs: An individualistic perspective that treats voting as an instrumental act does not support high levels of turnout.[15] As we discussed in Chapter 4, Americans are an individualistic people. Moreover, they are not especially prone to put great weight on their civic duties. The combination of this individualistic outlook with the infinitesimal probability that voting will affect the outcome of a large-scale election has deadly implications for turnout. From a purely individualistic standpoint, the puzzle is not that turnout is so low in the United States, but that turnout is as high as it is.

Why do so many people vote when personal benefits probably do not exceed the costs? Psychic benefits are an important part of the answer because they do not depend on whether you affect the outcome; you get them just by casting your vote. Another important part of the answer is that people are encouraged or mobilized by others who have personal incentives to turn out the vote. **Mobilization** refers to the efforts of parties, groups, and activists to turn out their potential supporters. Campaign workers provide baby-sitters and rides to the polls, thus lessening the individual costs of voting. They apply social pressure by contacting citizens who haven't voted and reminding them to vote. Various groups and social networks to which individuals belong also exert social pressures, playing on the feeling that you have a responsibility to vote. Although pressures and benefits like these may seem small, remember that the costs of voting are relatively small as well. But however small the costs, unless they are balanced out by some benefits, many citizens will opt to stay home.

With some understanding of the general reasons why people vote or fail to vote, we can now address two of the questions raised in the introduction to this chapter. First, why do Americans vote at lower levels than citizens in other countries?

No, It's the System

Can we expect people to turn out when non-responsible political consultants, not only on the presidential level but in campaigns for all other major offices, can think of no tactic too low or too trivial to besmirch the character and reduce the turnout for potential public servants, and when candidates for some of the highest offices in the land lack the character or courage to tell those consultants to shut up and go home?†

† Curtis Gans, "No Wonder Turnout Was Low," *The Washington Post,* November 11, 1988: A23.

■ **psychic benefits of voting**
Intangible rewards such as satisfaction with doing one's duty, feelings of solidarity with the community, and so forth.

■ **mobilization**
The efforts of parties, groups, and activists to encourage their supporters to participate in politics.

DILBERT® by Scott Adams

WAM

A political flap following New Jersey's 1993 state elections reminded Americans that old-time machine politics are not completely dead.* A week after Republican Christine Todd Whitman defeated Democrat Jim Florio in the governor's race, Republican campaign guru Ed Rollins found himself at the center of a political firestorm. At a breakfast with reporters Rollins bragged that a key to winning the election had been paying Democratic precinct workers to stay home, and making "contributions" to black ministers (or their "favorite charities") to urge their congregations not to vote. Although he later recanted, Rollin's boast turned the spotlight on a vestige of machine politics that still exists in major cities—cash spent on election day, called variously "walking-around money" (WAM), "street money," "precinct money," and other terms, depending on the locality.

Campaign workers spend street money on small cash payments, free drinks, coffee and donuts, and other tiny bribes. Money goes to poor people, the homeless, denizens of bars, and other citizens otherwise unlikely to vote. Often the recipient also receives a card suggesting the "right" way to vote. Sometimes too, money is given to community leaders for their endorsements. Typically such payments are made by Democrats, who dominate the urban centers where the practice persists. For example, on election day 1992, Democratic organizations spent about 5 million dollars in street money in fifteen states, according to a source "who asked not to be identified."†

If Rollins was telling the truth, the Republicans had put a new spin on WAM, using it to discourage turnout of minorities likely to vote Democratic. Interestingly, most commentators felt that what the Republicans had purportedly done was ethically more troubling than the Democrats' normal activities. In either case, poor people are the main recipients of street money—as one political operative commented, "it's a little payday for people who don't have much … The underprivileged figure this is their time to screw the big guys out of a few bucks."‡ But paying people to vote seems less corrupt than paying them not to vote, especially if you believe that the Democrats are the party that stands for poor peoples' interests.

* For background see Ceci Connolly, "Use of 'Street Money' Shows Old Ways Remain Potent," *Congressional Quarterly Weekly Report,* November 20, 1993: 3217–3220. John Aloysius Farrell, Brian McGrory and Adrian Walker, "'Street Money' Litters US Politics," *The Boston Sunday Globe,* November 28, 1993: 1, 28–29.

† Farrell, McGrory, and Walker, "Street Money' Litters US Politics": 28.

‡ Quoted in Connolly, "Use of 'Street Money' Shows Old Ways Remain Potent:" 3220.

Republican consultant Ed Rollins, who masterminded Christine Todd Whitman's surprise victory in the New Jersey gubernatorial election, created a flap with his comments about "walking around money." Here he is led to federal court in Newark, to testify about his contradictory remarks on possible vote suppression in the New Jersey governor's race.

International Comparisons of Voting Turnout

More than voters in other countries, Americans are proud of their political institutions and constitutional traditions. It is at least a little surprising, then, to find Americans voting at much lower levels than in most other countries (see Table 6.1), even those where voters are exceedingly cynical about politics—Italy, to cite the most notable example. Yet, while it is clear that American turnout levels trail those in many other countries, the statistical comparisons often published in newspapers are misleading in various respects. Procedures for calculating turnout differ from country to country, and the differences systematically lower American turnout figures relative to those in other democracies.

Turnout would seem to be simple enough to measure. The United States Census Bureau calculates **official turnout** in presidential elections as

$$\frac{\text{\# of people voting for President}}{\text{\# of people in the voting age population}}$$

This definition seems straightforward, but it lowers American turnout as much as five percent relative to other countries. Consider the numerator. If, believing that all the candidates are bums, you don't either vote for president or vote for a recognizable

> **official turnout**
> Defined by the Census Bureau as the number of people voting for president divided by the size of the voting age population.

TABLE 6.1

Americans are Considerably Less Likely to Vote than the Citizens of Many Other Democracies

Average Turnout in Free Elections to the Lower House in 37 Countries, 1960–1995 (in percentages)

Country	Turnout	Country	Turnout
Australia (14)*	95	Costa Rica (8)	81
Malta (6)	94	Norway (9)	81
Austria (9)	92	Israel (9)	80
Belgium (12)	91	Portugal (9)	79
Italy (9)	90	Finland (10)	78
Luxembourg (7)	90	Canada (11)	76
Iceland (10)	89	France (9)	76
New Zealand (12)	88	United Kingdom (9)	75
Denmark (14)	87	Ireland (11)	74
Venezuela (7)	85	Spain (6)	73
Bulgaria (2)	80	Japan (12)	71
Germany (9)	86	Estonia (2)	69
Sweden (14)	86	Hungary (2)	66
Greece (10)	86	Russia (2)	61
Lithuania (1)	86	India (6)	58
Latvia (1)	85	United States (9)	54
Czech Republic (2)	85	Switzerland (8)	54
Brazil (3)	83	Poland (2)	51
Netherlands (83)	83		

* Number of elections in ( ) parentheses.

SOURCE: Adapted from Mark Franklin, "Electoral Participation," in Lawrence Le Duc, Richard Niemi, and Pippa Norris, eds., *Comparing Democracies* (Thousand Oaks, CA: Sage, 1996): 218.

candidate, you are not counted as having voted. Other countries are more liberal. In France, for example, there is a long tradition whereby disaffected voters scribble an offensive suggestion across their ballots (the English translation has initials "F.Y."). French election officials count such ballots, whereas most American officials would not.[16] Or if you cast a "frivolous" write-in vote (actual examples from U.S. elections: "Rambo," "ZZ Top," "Batman"), election officials in many jurisdictions will ignore your vote rather than tabulate it as "other." Such decisions lower U.S. turnout figures by 1 to 2 percent per election.[17]

Factors that affect the denominator are more important. **Voting age population** refers to the number of people over the age of 18, a number that includes some groups legally ineligible to vote: felons, people confined to mental and/or correctional institutions, and most importantly, noncitizens. Counting the entire voting age population rather than only the **eligible voting age population** lowers U.S. turnout figures by another 3 percent.[18]

PERSONAL COSTS AND BENEFITS: REGISTRATION

Far more important than the fact that "voting age population" includes ineligible noncitizens, however, is that other countries use a different denominator in their turnout calculations: Their denominator is registered population. More than 30 percent of the American voting age population is unregistered. When turnout is measured as the number voting among **registered voters**, U.S. figures jump to the mid-range of turnout in industrial democracies.

Before anyone gets too complacent, however, it is important to note that in most of the world registration is automatic; it is a function performed by the central government, like maintaining Social Security records in the United States. Virtually everyone eligible is registered, so turnout rates are essentially the same whether they are measured as a percentage of the voting age population or as a percentage of the registered population. American practice differs in making registration entirely the responsibility of the individual, resulting in scarcely more than two-thirds of the eligible population being registered. The United States is the only country whose figures differ greatly depending on how turnout is measured.

Thus, in theory, one important way to raise U.S. turnout closer to world levels would be to institute an automatic registration system and relieve the individual cit-

voting age population
All people in the United States over the age of 18.

eligible voting age population
All people in the United States over the age of 18 minus those not eligible to vote because of mental illness, criminal conviction, or noncitizenship.

registered voters
Those legally eligible to vote who have registered in accord with the requirements prevailing in their state and locality.

To encourage young people to vote in 1992 and 1996, MTV organized a "Rock the Vote" campaign. Part of the 1996 campaign was a "Rock the Vote" bus, plastered with famous quotations, which toured the country inspiring young voters to register.

THE "MOTOR VOTER" LAW

"Motor Voter" is the nickname for the National Voter Registration Act of 1993, which has four major provisions. First, it requires states to provide for voter registration when residents apply for, renew, or change the address on their driver's licenses (hence the nickname). Given that 90 percent of all people are licensed, and licenses have to be renewed every four years in most states, the provision covers nearly all of the population. A second provision requires states to provide for voter registration at public assistance offices and armed forces recruiting centers, and allows them to provide registration at libraries, schools, and other state and local government offices. A third provision requires all states to provide for mail registration, and a fourth provision restricts their ability to purge the voting rolls for nonvoting.

Although experience with the new law is too limited to permit firm conclusions as yet, registration increased by 9 million in the first year the act was in effect.* As preliminary studies suggested, most of the increase was due to the motor voter provision; other provisions of the law had less impact.† Contrary to Democrats' hopes and Republicans' fears, Republicans appear to have gained slightly more new registrants than Democrats.‡ Despite the increase in registration, however, turnout sank to a modern low in 1996.

* "Motor Voter Law Signs up 9 Million," *USA TODAY*, October 15, 1996: 1A.

† Benjamin Highton and Raymond Wolfinger, "Anticipating the Effects of the National Voter Registration Act of 1993," Paper delivered at the 1995 Annual Meeting of the American Political Science Association, Chicago.

‡ Bob Twigg and Jessica Lee, "Dems Come up Short in Voter Drive," *USA TODAY*, October 16, 1996: 3A.

State-by-state registries of motor vehicles have played a key role in allowing "motor voters" to register to vote at the same time they are renewing licenses or registering their automobiles.

izen of the personal responsibility of registering. One proposal to move in this direction—the "motor voter" law—was enacted in 1993. While such procedural reforms undoubtedly will have some impact, they are not the whole answer. In fact, a few states have no registration or have election day registration at the polling stations. In these states everyone can be considered registered, and while turnout runs 10 to 15 percent higher than the national norm, it still falls well below the levels in many

European countries.[19] Statistical simulations suggest that if every state used the most liberal registration procedures employed in any state, national turnout would be about 9 percent higher than at present.[20]

In sum, registration systems make a big difference; they raise the individual costs of participating for Americans relative to Europeans. But registration is not the entire story.

PERSONAL COSTS AND BENEFITS: COMPULSION

The personal registration system makes voting more costly in the United States. In some other countries, public policy makes *nonvoting* more costly than in the United States. Would you believe that voting is compulsory in many countries (see Democratic Dilemma)? In Australia and Belgium, for example, nonvoters are subject to fines; not only the fine itself but the clear expectation that everyone is legally required to vote helps generate 90+ percent turnout rates. In Italy, nonvoters are not fined, but "Did Not Vote" is stamped on their identification papers, threatening nonvoters with the prospect of unsympathetic treatment at the hands of public officials should they get into trouble or need help with a problem. Turnout in American elections could undoubtedly be raised if people were compelled to vote, but if our students are any indication, Americans consider voting a right they are free to exercise or not.

OTHER PERSONAL COSTS AND BENEFITS

Several additional institutional variations raise the costs of voting for Americans. Elections in America traditionally are held on Tuesdays, an ordinary workday. In most of the rest of the world elections are held on Sundays, or election days are proclaimed official holidays. In Italy, workers receive free train fare back to their place of registration, usually their hometown; in effect the government subsidizes family reunions.

Some observers argue that U.S. turnout is low because Americans are called on to vote so often.[21] In most European countries, citizens vote only two or three times in a four- or five-year period—once for a member of Parliament, once for a representative to the European Union, and perhaps once for a small number of local officials. In contrast, Americans vote in even years for numerous national and state officials, and in odd years (in many states) for numerous local officials. Primaries are held in the spring or summer. Referenda may be held simultaneously with these other elections or decided in special elections of their own. Some have suggested, not completely tongue-in-cheek, that turnout in the United States should be calculated as the percentage who vote at least once during a four-year period, a figure that would be more comparable to turnout figures for other countries. Interestingly, the only other country where voters are called upon to vote with anything close to the frequency that they are in the United States is Switzerland, which has a turnout rate comparable to that in the United States.

Finally, a smaller but interesting disincentive to vote in some areas has recently been identified. Some states use lists of registered voters to select people for jury duty. Statistical studies indicate that in such jurisdictions turnout is 5 to 10 percent lower than it otherwise would be.[22] The fear of losing a day's work or more if a trial is extended (think about the O.J. criminal trial!) is sufficient to motivate some citizens to forfeit their right to vote.

All in all, both intentionally and accidentally American practices raise the costs of voting relative to those in other countries. When some citizens understandably react to those costs by failing to vote, editorialists criticize them for their lack of public spirit.

Compulsory Voting or Freedom to Choose?

After the 1988 elections some disgruntled Democrats grumbled about the legitimacy of the election results. Although George Bush won a comfortable victory over Michael Dukakis, 54 to 46 percent, turnout was only 50.1 percent of the voting age population. To the losers this meant that only 27 percent of the eligible electorate had actually supported Bush. If democracy at a minimum means popular consent, how could such an election be democratic? Can a bare quarter of the electorate consent for a majority?

After the 1992 elections the shoe was on the other foot. Disgruntled Republicans grumbled that Clinton had received only 43 percent of the popular vote. So, even though turnout had risen to 55 percent, less than a quarter of the eligible electorate had supported Clinton. Was this "popular consent?" The 1996 elections underlined that question when less than 50 percent of the voting age population went to the polls.

By ignoring the preferences of nonvoters, the United States treats them as if they had consented to the election outcome, certainly a dubious assumption to make as a general matter. Although some people are content whatever happens, and some are alienated whatever happens, surely many nonvoters would have voted for the loser had they bothered to vote. Thus, to treat the 20 to 25 percent—or less in elections other than presidential ones—of those who voted as consenting on behalf of the majority is at least questionable.

As noted in the text, some democracies make voting compulsory.* Greek electoral law provides for imprisonment of nonvoters for up to twelve months. In practice such penalties are never applied, but other democracies do penalize nonvoters, at least sometimes. Australian law allows for fines of up to $50 for nonvoting without a valid excuse, and estimates are that 4 percent of nonvoters pay fines. In addition to having their papers stamped "Did not Vote," Italian nonvoters have their names posted on communal bulletin boards.

In countries with compulsory voting, questions of consent do not arise. If nearly everyone votes, then by definition the winning party or coalition of parties receives a majority of the vote. Why shouldn't the United States have compulsory voting as in Austria, Belgium, Australia, Italy, and numerous other democracies? Why shouldn't everyone who enjoys the privilege of citizenship be *required* to perform the most basic act of citizenship?

* For an informative discussion of compulsory voting see Richard Hasen, "Voting Without Law," *University of Pennsylvania Law Review* 144(1996): 2135–2179.

Kashmiri turnout was high when armed Indian security men "requested" Kashmiri voters to line up and wait their turn to vote in the 1996 presidential elections.

The Decline of Voting After 1896

In the late nineteenth century, American turnout levels reached all-time highs: in the five elections leading up to 1896, turnout averaged 80 percent of the male voting age population. In the five elections following that of 1896, however, turnout averaged just 65 percent, and it has never since reached the late nineteenth century highs.*

What happened in 1896? As we will explain in Chapter 8, many political historians consider 1896 to be the central election in a "critical era," a period in which the nature of voting alignments changed in significant and lasting ways. The era prior to 1896 was the most electorally competitive in American history: It is sometimes called "the era of no decision" because in the five elections from 1876 to 1892 no presidential candidate ever got more than 51 percent of the popular vote. In this period the parties were stronger than ever before or since. Party organization was so impressive that historians liken the parties of the period to military organizations.† Supported by the patronage system, the parties had ample *resources* to spend to mobilize the electorate. And given the intense electoral competition, the parties had the *incentive* to mobilize the electorate—defeat would throw tens of thousands of party workers out of their jobs. But political developments were undercutting both the resources and incentives that underpinned the strength of the parties.‡

Civil service and other reforms were beginning to eat away at the patronage system, the lifeblood of the parties. And between 1888 and 1896, 90 percent of the states instituted some kind of personal registration system, raising the costs of voting for citizens, and restricting the parties' ability to vote the dead, vote people twice, vote the ineligible, and engage in other corrupt practices that raised turnout.§

Meanwhile, the Populists, a radical third party representing the agricultural West, joined

MOBILIZATION AND TURNOUT

Not only do Americans face higher costs of voting and lower costs of nonvoting, they have less help in overcoming the costs of voting. The chief mobilizing agent in modern democracies is the political party. Parties have incentives to mobilize their supporters; indeed, they have often undertaken that task with excessive enthusiasm, as when urban machines voted the dead, or reported more votes for their candidates than there were residents in their cities. It certainly is no accident that American turnout levels were at their peak in the late nineteenth century when the efficiency of American parties was at a maximum and the ethics of American parties at a minimum. During this period the patronage system was at its strongest. With hundreds of thousands of government jobs at stake in elections, the parties had little trouble motivating their workers, not to mention their relatives and friends. And, unconstrained by conflict of interest or sunshine (government in the open) laws, the parties were quite willing to do whatever it took to gain or keep control of government.

As we will see in later chapters, American parties have declined, at least as mobilizing agents. Voters are less attached to them than at any time in the past, and the parties have less in the way of inducements to turn out the dwindling numbers of

with the Democrats and nominated William Jennings Bryan, who railed that the Republicans would not be allowed to "crucify mankind on a cross of gold." After taking a good look at Bryan, a majority of voters decided to take their chances with the Republican candidate, William McKinley, who won handily. Soon it became apparent that the Republican win had been more than a temporary victory. In large areas of the North and midwest the Democrats were no longer competitive. Now secure in their national majority, the Republicans abandoned the South to the Democrats, who completed their disenfranchisement of black Americans. With party competition greatly reduced in much of the country, the parties no longer had the incentive to mobilize their supporters, and supporters no longer felt it important to vote. Meanwhile reforms continued to take away the material resources the parties had relied on, and party organizations began their long-term decline. Although political historians continue to argue about the relative importance of the procedural and political factors that led turnout to decline, there is little doubt that 1896 was a watershed between a high-turnout, highly competitive electoral era, and a low-turnout era of Republican hegemony. ‖

* Walter Dean Burnham, "The Turnout Problem," in A. James Reichley, ed., *Elections American Style* (Washington DC. Brookings, 1987): Table 5.3.

† Richard Jensen, "American Election Campaigns: A Theoretical and Historical Typology," presented at the 1968 Meetings of the Midwest Political Science Association.

‡ Walter Dean Burnham, *Critical Elections and the Mainsprings of American Politics* (New York: Norton, 1970): Ch. 4.

§ Philip Converse, "Change in the American Electorate," in *The Human Meaning of Social Change*, Angus Campbell and Philip Converse, eds. (New York: Russell Sage, 1972): 263–337.

‖ See the articles, comments, and rejoinders by Walter Dean Burnham, Philip Converse, and Jerrold Rusk in the September 1974 *American Political Science Review*.

faithful than they did in the past.[23] Indeed, as we will discuss in Chapter 8, the lower levels of turnout in this century are associated with the so-called progressive reforms at the turn of the century, reforms that instituted the personal registration system and weakened the parties' control of nominations for office. A significant part of the reason that turnout is lower in the United States than in Europe is that parties are on average much stronger and more active in Europe than they are here (see Election Connections).

Political parties are not the only mobilizing agent in democracies. As we will discuss in Chapter 7, groups and associations are alternative mobilizing agents. But even though more organizations exist in the United States than in other countries, and many of them participate regularly in politics, they are not as deeply rooted in the population as their counterparts in Europe—particularly the unions and the churches, which are foundations of political parties in Europe. Thus, here too, Americans receive less support from collective political actors than in Europe.

Several analysts have statistically dissected the difference in turnout levels between the United States and other countries.[24] All other things being equal, American turnout should actually be somewhat higher than in Europe because of higher educational levels and American civic attitudes that encourage popular participation. But other things are far from equal. Powell estimates that differences in electoral institutions, chiefly registration systems, depress American turnout between 10 and 15 percent relative to Europe, and weaker party and group mobilization depress turnout by about 10 percent. In sum, it costs Americans more to vote, and they receive less support for voting than in most other countries.

OTHER FORMS OF PARTICIPATION

Americans vote at lower levels than citizens in other democracies. Moreover, they are significantly less likely to participate in other ways (see Figure 6.2)—to work in campaigns, to give money, and to attend meetings—than they are to vote. It is perhaps a bit surprising, then, to learn that Americans are *more* likely to engage in these less common forms of participation than are the citizens of some countries where turnout is much higher (see Figure 6.3). That is, even though only minorities of Americans work in campaigns, or contact public officials, more of them do so than citizens in other democracies. The explanation lies in several of the factors just discussed.

(1) Because there are so many elections to fill so many offices, not to mention primaries, initiatives, and referenda, there are far more opportunities for electoral participation in the United States than elsewhere. And because there are far more offices and government bodies in the United States, there are far more opportunities to contact an official, attend a meeting of a government board, and so forth. Even if Americans are less likely to avail themselves of any particular participatory opportu-

FIGURE **6.2**

Americans Are Even Less Likely to Participate in More Demanding Ways than Voting.

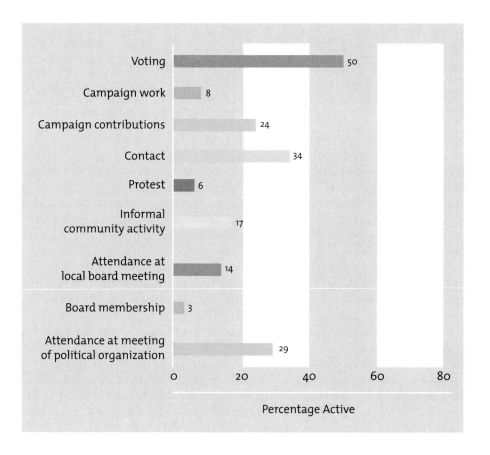

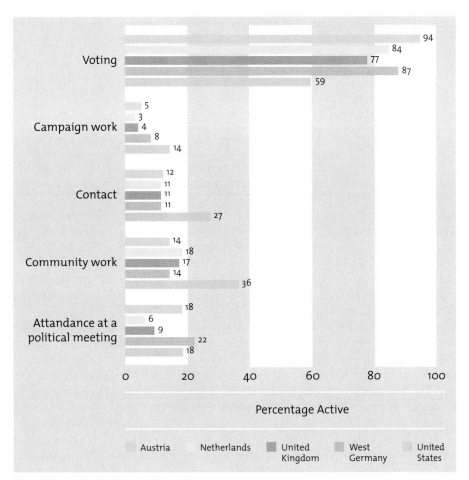

FIGURE 6.3

Americans Are More Likely
than Citizens in Other Democracies to Participate in Ways
More Demanding than Voting

nity, the sheer number of opportunities would give them a higher level of political participation than in other countries where opportunities are more limited.

(2) Our individualistic political culture, with its emphasis on rights and liberties (p. 114), encourages Americans to contact public officials and to protest government actions. In contrast, the political cultures of most other countries are more deferential to authority, and discourage ordinary citizens from taking as active a role in politics as in the United States. Citizens are less likely to protest government decisions, and when they do, their governments are more likely to ignore them.

(3) Because American political parties are weaker today than in earlier eras, candidates construct numerous personal organizations, many of whose members are temporary. In other countries a small cadre of committed party workers takes on most of the burden of campaigning year in and year out, but in the United States campaigns are fought by much larger groups of "occasional activists." These are enthusiastic amateurs who drift in and out of political campaigns, depending on whether particular candidates or issues arouse their enthusiasm.[25]

Consistent with these observations, as American elections have increased in frequency, and governmental bodies have increased in number, some studies have found increases in some kinds of campaign participation. For example, one study found that in the late 1980s, more people claimed that they gave money to candidates and tried to persuade others how to vote, as compared to the late 1960s.[26]

Some people who would not take part in conventional campaign politics participate in less explicitly political ways—by helping out with community projects, for example.

Finally, many Americans participate in politics indirectly by joining or supporting interest groups that take a more direct role. That form of participation is the subject of Chapter 7.

Why Has American Turnout Declined?

For many people the problem is not only that turnout levels in the United States are lower than in Europe, but that turnout has fallen during the past generation (see Figure 6.4). In presidential elections, turnout fell steadily between 1960 and 1988, before hitting a half-century low in 1996. In off-year elections, turnout declined more erratically, but it is significantly lower now than a generation ago. Rosenstone and Hansen report that the minorities of people who work in campaigns or attend a political or governmental meeting also declined in number—although other studies reach slightly different conclusions. Even those who participate in such minimal ways as signing a petition are slightly fewer in number now than a generation ago.[27]

To many observers these declines in popular participation suggest that something is terribly wrong with American politics. This fear was reinforced in the late 1970s when analysts noted that participation was declining at the same time that trust in government was declining (see Fig 6.4). Research soon showed, however, that the two trends were largely unrelated. That is, turnout declined among the trusting and cynical alike, and the former were no more likely to vote than the latter.[28]

What makes the decline in turnout all the more puzzling is that two other developments in the past three decades led to an expectation of *rising* turnout. First, court decisions, federal legislation such as the Voting Rights Act and its amendments, and the Twenty-Fourth Amendment to the Constitution have

FIGURE 6.4

Turnout in America Has Declined Since 1960

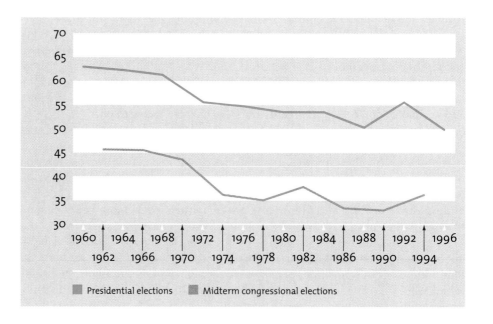

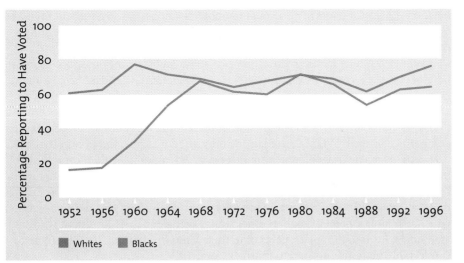

removed numerous institutional and procedural impediments to voting and thus reduced the personal costs. For example, poll taxes and literacy tests were abolished, state and local residency requirements were shortened, registration was made simpler and more convenient, bilingual ballots were permitted, and absentee voting was made easier. Such reforms were especially effective in the South, where they helped to overcome the terrible legacy of racial discrimination. Turnout among black Americans in the South increased sharply between 1960 and 1968 (see Figure 6.5).

Second, socioeconomic change should have raised turnout in the post-1964 period. That the potential electorate was getting younger as the baby boom generation came of age could be expected to lower turnout, since young people traditionally vote at lower levels than older people. But that effect was more than offset by rising educational levels. Education is the single strongest predictor of turnout. Higher educational levels produce a higher sense of civic duty and help people deal with the complexities of registering and voting. Ruy Teixeira estimates that, other things being equal, the net effect of socioeconomic changes, chiefly education, should have been to raise national turnout by about 4 percent.[29]

What, then, explains the turnout decline? There is not as much agreement here as there is on the explanation of turnout differences between Europe and the United States, where, as we have seen, two factors—registration and political parties—dominate the answer. Several factors clearly have contributed to the decline in American turnout, but their precise importance is a matter of debate.

LOWER PERSONAL BENEFITS

One reason that the decline in voting costs did not result in an increase in voting is that the benefits of voting may have declined at an even faster rate. In fact, studies show that Americans today are not as interested in politics, don't care as much about who wins the election, and don't believe that government is as responsive as in times past.[30] Thus, they do not see as much riding on their decisions as in years past, and probably do not get as much intrinsic satisfaction from supporting an admired candidate or party. One must be extremely careful in interpreting such findings, however. Lack of interest in and concern about elections and government might be a cause of nonvoting; but such psychological detachment might also be simply a part of the same syndrome of disengagement as nonvoting.

Another political factor that has lowered the benefits of voting is that elections have become less competitive. As we discuss in Chapter 11, the advantage of incumbency in congressional elections has increased greatly, and a similar process is occurring more slowly in state legislative elections. Many presidential elections in the 1970s and 1980s were landslides, and gubernatorial elections are becoming less competitive as well. When candidates win by large margins, the notion that one's vote actually makes any difference must seem more improbable than ever. Probably more important, however, is that, when elections are closely contested, other mobilizing agents have more incentive to get out the vote. Rosenstone and Hansen find that, in states with competitive gubernatorial campaigns in presidential election years, turnout is 5 percent higher, other things being equal.[31] Consistent with such arguments, turnout dropped 5 percent in 1996 when Bill Clinton led Bob Dole by a comfortable margin from start to finish.

DECLINING MOBILIZATION

Statistical studies find that personal costs and benefits account for less than half of the turnout decline. The larger part of the decline reflects the decreased mobilization efforts of parties, campaigns, and social movements such as the civil rights, antiwar, and other movements that were more active during the turbulent 1960s. Rosenstone and Hansen observe that

> . . . *party mobilization underwrites the costs of political participation. Party workers inform people about upcoming elections, tell them where and when they can register and vote, supply them with applications for absentee ballots, show them the locations of campaign headquarters, and remind them of imminent rallies and meetings. Campaigns drop by to pick up donations, telephone reminders on the day of the election, and drive the lazy, the harried, the immobile, and the infirm to the polls.*[32]

Parties still are active, of course, and candidate organizations are more active than ever. But polling and media advertising are probably not good substitutes for the kind of pound-the-pavement, doorbell-ringing workers who used to dominate campaigns. Voters may be motivated by the entreaties of a campaign worker standing at the front door or telephoning late in the afternoon of election day, but those same voters may not be motivated by an impersonal TV spot urging them to vote.[33] Thus, a change in style from labor-intensive to high-tech campaigning may have indirectly contributed to declining turnout. And the fact that elections have become less competitive would further lower the motivation of campaigns to engage in difficult, time-consuming activity. When the result of an election is a foregone conclusion, the winning side grows complacent, and the losing side sees little reason to make a serious effort.

DECLINING SOCIAL CONNECTEDNESS

When shown a turnout line trending downward, you naturally assume that any given citizen is less likely to vote than a generation ago. Warren Miller has shown such an assumption to be incorrect.[34] The turnout decline is what social scientists

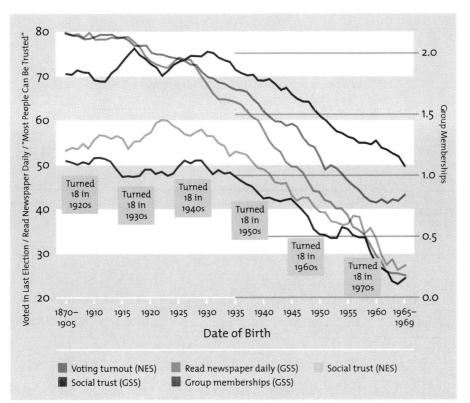

FIGURE 6.6

Younger Generations of Americans Are Less Participatory and Less Trusting

Legend:
- Voting turnout (NES)
- Read newspaper daily (GSS)
- Social trust (NES)
- Social trust (GSS)
- Group memberships (GSS)

call a **compositional effect**: a behavioral change that reflects a change in the make-up or composition of a group rather than a change in the behavior of individuals in the group. Miller finds that older Americans (the pre–New Deal generation) always voted at high levels and continue to do so. Turnout rates of middle-aged Americans (the New Deal generation) were never as high as their elders, but were relatively high and remain so today. In contrast, the turnout rates of younger Americans (the post–New Deal generation) were low when they entered the electorate and remain low today. Turnout is declining because of the simple fact that older Americans accustomed to voting at high rates are dying off and being replaced by younger Americans who vote at lower rates. Miller makes a persuasive case that the causes of the turnout decline must lie in differences among the generations. Robert Putnam argues that declines in other forms of participation, such as group membership, have an analogous generational basis (see Figure 6.6).[35]

One interesting possibility that has received attention is a decline in what sociologists refer to as **social connectedness**. Stephen Knack raises the possibility that common thinking about voting is misconceived. Rather than voting being the fundamental political act, voting may not be a political act as much as a social act. Voting is related to giving blood, donating to charities, doing volunteer work, and other forms of altruistic behavior.[36] Thus, rather than looking for *political* causes of nonvoting, perhaps researchers should look for *social* causes. Interestingly, although turnout is not related to trust in *government*, it is significantly related to trust in *people*[37] (see Figure 6.7).

Social connectedness refers to the extent to which people are integrated into society—their families, neighborhoods, communities, churches, and other social

compositional effect
A change in the behavior of a group that arises from a change in the group's composition, not from a change in the behavior of individuals in the group.

social connectedness
The degree to which individuals are integrated into society—families, churches, neighborhoods, groups, and so forth.

Turnout Is Not Related to Trust in Government, but It Is Related to Trust in People

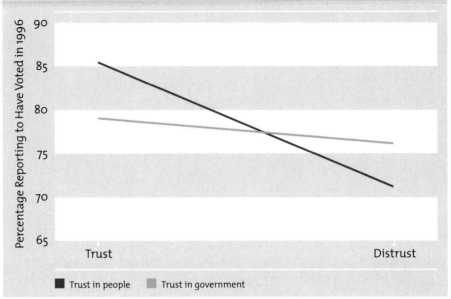

On the left side of the figure, reported turnout is shown for those expressing trust in other people and those indicating that they trust the government "just about always" or "most of the time." On the right side, reported turnout is shown for those expressing distrust in other people and those indicating they trust government "only some of the time" or "none of the time."

Percentage Reporting to Have Voted in 1996

90 — 85 — 80 — 75 — 70 — 65

Trust   Distrust

■ Trust in people   ■ Trust in government

units. Older Americans who grew up in a simpler time—when Americans were less mobile, more religious, and more trusting of their fellow citizens—may be more connected than younger Americans, who have grown up in a highly mobile, secular society where cynicism about the worth of their fellow citizens is widespread. There is always a danger in arguments about the good old days (upon close examination, they often don't look so good), and we doubt that research can ever prove to everyone's satisfaction that people in the pre–New Deal era were more socially connected than today, but given the societal changes that have taken place during the past century, the argument has some plausibility, and there is some research to support it.

Research has examined the social connectedness argument by looking for relationships between measures of social connectedness and turnout. Even relying on such crude indicators as marriage rates, home ownership, church attendance, and length of residence in a community, recent studies find that decreased social connectedness accounts for as much as one-quarter of the decline in presidential turnout.[38] (Interestingly, although being married is associated with higher turnout, being *newly* married is estimated to lower the odds of voting; apparently, voting is not high on the priority list of the newly married.)[39]

In sum, the decline in American voting rates has a number of contributing causes. Today's electorate is younger (although growing older as we write), and less politically committed—less motivated to vote. And these less motivated individuals are less likely to be encouraged to vote by parties or campaign organizations. Moreover, they are also less likely to be stimulated to vote by spouses, church associates and long-time neighbors than the citizens in a less mobile, less atomized, more socially oriented country.

FIGURE 6.8

Group Differences in
Turnout, 1996

The categories for family income corresponded to the following annual figures: poor is less than $10,000; low income is $10,000 to $29,999; middle income is $30,000 to $49,999; and high income is $50,000 or more.

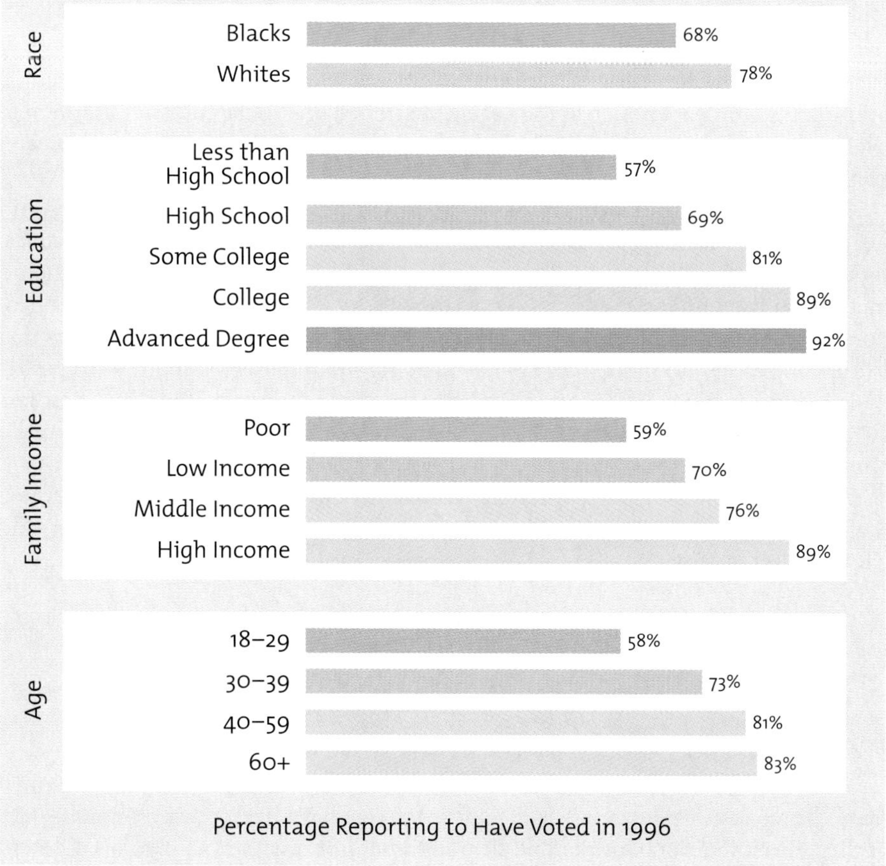

Race

Blacks	68%
Whites	78%

Education

Less than High School	57%
High School	69%
Some College	81%
College	89%
Advanced Degree	92%

Family Income

Poor	59%
Low Income	70%
Middle Income	76%
High Income	89%

Age

18–29	58%
30–39	73%
40–59	81%
60+	83%

Percentage Reporting to Have Voted in 1996

Who Votes and Who Doesn't?

Low voting rates probably would not stimulate as much discussion as they do if all social and economic groups in America had the same rates. But people differ in their ability to bear the costs of voting, in how strongly they feel that voting is a duty, and how often they are the targets of mobilization. Consequently, turnout rates differ considerably across social and economic groups[40] (see Figure 6.8).

Highly educated people are far more likely to vote than people with little formal education. Education instills a stronger sense of duty and gives people the knowledge, analytic skills, and self-confidence to meet the costs of registering and voting. Over and above education, income also has a significant effect. The wealthy are far more likely to vote than the poor. Affluence, too, reflects a set of skills and personal characteristics that help people overcome barriers to voting.

Studies of turnout in the 1970s concluded that, once disadvantages in education and income were factored out, and their younger age considered, blacks were at least as likely to vote as whites.[41] But more recent research finds that blacks are somewhat less likely to vote than whites, even taking into account differences in income and educational levels.[42] One suggestion is that African Americans were disillusioned by the failure of the Jesse Jackson campaigns in 1984 and 1988.[43] Other minorities, such as Latinos and Asians, still face language barriers even if the situation is gradually improving.[44]

Turnout increases with age, until very old age when the trend reverses. People presumably gain experience as they age, experience that makes it easier for them to overcome any barriers to vote. They also become more socially connected, as well as more settled down in a life situation that clarifies their political preferences.

Interestingly, the relationships between socioeconomic characteristics and turnout are consistently stronger in the United States than in other democracies. Indeed, in some countries there is almost no relationship between education and income on the one hand and voting on the other.[45] The reason is not that education and income have different effects than in the United States; the reason is that European parties are much more effective at mobilizing their supporters. In particular, European Social Democratic parties do a far better job of getting their less advantaged potential voters to the polls than does the Democratic party in the United States.

All in all, there is no question that the low turnout rates that exist in the United States result in an electorate that is somewhat wealthier, more educated, older, and whiter than the larger population. What are the implications of that fact?

Is Low Turnout a Problem?

Given who votes and why, should the relatively low turnout rate in the United States be a cause for concern? Quite a few answers have been offered on both sides of this question. To a considerable degree these differing views hinge on different beliefs about the motives for voting. We will briefly sketch three arguments on each side of the debate.

THREE ARGUMENTS FOR WHY LOW TURNOUT IS NOT A PROBLEM

1. A CONSERVATIVE (WITH A SMALL "C") ARGUMENT. Many of those concerned about low turnout implicitly assume that high turnout indicates enthusiasm about politics and commitment to making the political order work. Maybe not. Some skeptics suggest that high turnout may indicate tension or conflict, coupled with a belief that losing would be unacceptable. They cite the experience of Austria and Germany as their democratic governments crumbled and the Fascist parties took power in the 1930s.[46] Turnout in those elections reached very high levels, but probably reflected disillusionment and desperation more than commitment and enthusiasm. The 1992 presidential election is a less extreme case in point. Turnout rose, but did this indicate a healthier political system? On the contrary, by many indications people were "mad as hell"—frustrated and upset with

their government. Similarly, turnout rose a bit in 1994, but according to many pundits it was the year of the "angry white male."

Generalizing from examples like these, some argue that low turnout indicates contentment, not estrangement. If so, low turnout is a sign of the health of a polity, and contributes to political stability. Samuel Huntington goes so far as to argue that ". . . the effective operation of a democratic political system usually requires some measure of apathy and noninvolvement on the part of some individuals and groups."[47]

2. AN ELITIST ARGUMENT. On average, nonvoters are less educated than voters. Studies also show them to be less informed, less interested in, and less concerned about politics. Given these facts, some critics argue that the quality of electoral decisions is higher if no special effort is made to increase turnout. As David Reisman once remarked, "Bringing sleepwalkers to the polls simply to increase turnout is no service to democracy."[48] Columnist George Will provides a more recent illustration of this elitist point of view:

Here comes another campaign to encourage voting, alas. Last weekend, ABC News and Harvard's Kennedy School of Government sponsored a symposium on "the problem of declining voter participation." Problem? As more people are nagged to the polls, the caliber of the electorate declines. The reasonable assumption about electorates is: Smaller is smarter.[49]

Of course, this argument depends on nonvoters staying ignorant and unconcerned even if they were to vote. Alternatively, if the process of encouraging them to vote also informed them and raised their interest, the argument would be undercut.

3. A CYNICAL OR RADICAL ARGUMENT. Some radicals contend that it is not the nonvoters who are cause for concern, but the voters. According to this viewpoint, elections don't matter—they are charades. Real decisions are made by power elites far from the popular arena. If so, voting is merely a placebo that makes the masses feel they have a say in how they are governed. Turnout doesn't matter because elections don't matter.

We disagree strongly with this latter argument. As we stress throughout this book, elections matter a great deal—in some cases, too much. In later chapters we will discuss some of the important issues facing Americans. Those discussions will make it clear that elections have had enormous effects on the shaping of public policy.

THREE ARGUMENTS FOR WHY LOW TURNOUT IS A PROBLEM

1. THE VOTERS ARE UNREPRESENTATIVE. The most obvious concern arising from low turnout is that it produces an unrepresentative electorate. The active electorate is wealthier, whiter, older, and more educated than the potential electorate. Many people naturally assume that such an electorate is more Republican and more conservative than the voting age population. Consequently, elections are biased, and public policies adopted by the winners are correspondingly biased.

Plausible as the argument seems, research suggests that it is overstated. Numerous studies have compared the policy views and the candidate preferences of voters and nonvoters. Typically they differ little. Some studies have even found that at times the conservative candidate was more popular among nonvoters—Ronald Reagan in 1984, for example.[50] In general, nonvoters are less knowledgeable, less interested and less committed, and therefore more susceptible to bandwagons, political advertising, and other transient forces.

After looking at the voting rates of rich and poor, minorities and whites, and so forth, people tend to assume that nonvoters and voters differ more than they do. But in the first place, while minorities and the poor vote less often than whites and the affluent, the difference is only a matter of degree. Thus, blacks were 6 percent less likely to vote than whites in 1988, but only 13 percent of all the nonvoters were black. Similarly, the more highly educated are more likely to vote, but 25 percent of the nonvoters have some college education. Nonvoters are not all poor, uneducated, and members of minorities. Plenty of nonvoters are affluent, well-educated, and white. This is particularly true of movers: According to the Census Bureau, nearly one in five Americans moves during the two-year interval between national elections.[51]

In the second place, few groups are as one-sided in their political inclinations as African Americans, who vote more than 8:1 Democratic. If turnout among most other groups were to increase, the Democrats would get more than half the additional votes, but the Republicans would get some too.

Teixeira provides striking illustrations of these points. If all the Hispanics and African Americans in the country had voted in 1988 at levels 10 percent higher than whites, and all the white poor had voted at levels 10 percent higher than the white rich, Dukakis would still have lost by two and a half million votes.[52] Not all elections are so one-sided, of course, but given the improbability that the disadvantaged could ever be mobilized at such high levels, it is doubtful that realistic increases in turnout would produce a sea change in American politics.

Still, as Marxists might point out, there could be an element of "false consciousness" here: Because present nonvoters are uninformed and uncommitted, they fail to understand or act on their true interests. The political or social changes that could greatly increase their voting also could greatly increase their knowledge and interest and produce a different political outlook. This line of argument can only be settled by greatly increasing turnout and seeing if the preferences of nonvoters change.

2. LOW TURNOUT REFLECTS A "PHONY" POLITICS. This argument emphasizes the character of political issues in present-day America. Essentially, the argument asserts that low turnout among the poor and otherwise disadvantaged reflects a more general disengagement from an American politics that does not address "real" issues of concern to such people. What are real issues? Basically, economic issues: jobs, health care, housing, the income distribution, education. What the United States has is two middle-class parties obsessed with "phony" issues: rights of free expression, gun control, feminism, animal rights, capital punishment, gay rights—issues that have little relevance for the poor, but great relevance for upper middle-class elites. (We refer to such issues as **social issues** to distinguish them from traditional economic issues.) This argument often is made by Democrats who are liberals in the older economic sense. Richard Goodwin, a former aide to President Kennedy, comments:

■ **social issues**
Issues such as obscenity, feminism, gay rights, capital punishment, prayer in schools, and so forth, which reflect personal values more than economic interests.

Now our public leaders are happy to debate the issues of abortion or gay rights or—God save us—"family values" as a welcome diversion from the serious flaws in American life; just as in the 1920s the nation was consumed with a struggle over the right to drink alcohol as the country approached its most serious economic crisis.[53]

In the 1980s a variant of this argument claimed that it was only the Democrats who were obsessed with such issues. Republicans, it was argued, shrewdly used social issues to deflect politics from real issues—like redistribution of the wealth controlled by Republicans! By conducting political campaigns on the basis of more symbolic, lifestyle issues, Democrats fell for the Republicans' bait. But the rise of the Religious Right in the Republican Party leaves little doubt that many activists in both parties are more concerned with social than with economic issues. As a result, some argue, the mass of citizens unconcerned about such issues withdraws from an irrelevant politics based on them.

3. LOW TURNOUT DISCOURAGES INDIVIDUAL DEVELOPMENT. The final argument is in some respects a counter-argument to the elitist argument that low turnout is not a problem. Classical political theorists from Aristotle to John Stuart Mill emphasized that democracy has an important educational component. Participation in democratic politics stimulates individual development. Participants become better citizens and better human beings, which in turn enables them to take politics to a higher level. From the standpoint of this argument, low turnout signifies a lost opportunity to improve both the nonparticipants and politics itself.

Some are skeptical that political participation is such an ennobling experience, and certainly, the argument is more persuasive when applied to participation in intensive personal processes like local board or council meetings than to impersonal processes like voting in a national election.[54] But the argument makes the important point that voting may not only affect who wins and what they do, but may also affect the voters themselves—what manner of people they are and what they want.

CONCLUSION: DOES TURNOUT MATTER?

Evidently there is considerable disagreement about whether low turnout in the United States is a problem, and if so, how serious a problem. Good-intentioned and well-informed people disagree and offer persuasive arguments in support of their positions. For our purposes we point out once again that much of the disagreement arises from different assumptions about what motivates voters and nonvoters. Our view is that nonvoters and voters have diverse motives. Some nonvoters are content while others are estranged, and the same goes for voters. High turnout can indicate either high approval of the political order or serious dissatisfaction with it. Nonvoters have little information, but as we saw in Chapter 5, so do many voters; therefore, raising turnout will not "dilute" the electorate very much. Low turnout does make the actual electorate somewhat less representative than the potential electorate, but not as much as critics often assume. Some potential voters undoubtedly are discouraged by a politics that discusses issues of little relevance for them, but other citizens turn out to vote precisely because of their concern with such issues And while participation fosters citizenship, we are doubtful that the simple impersonal act of casting a vote will foster it very much. In short, we find some validity in each of the arguments presented; we reject in its entirety only the argument that elections don't matter. Low turnout is a cause for concern, yes, a cause for despair, no.

Participation is a broad term that in this chapter we have largely narrowed to voting in elections. In Chapter 7 we broaden the discussion and move on to other, often less direct forms of participation.

Chapter Summary

Popular participation in democratic elections is the essence of democracy. But in most elections a majority of the American electorate stays away from the polls; only in presidential elections does a majority usually turn out, and then, just barely. When it comes to participation in more demanding ways, even fewer people get involved.

Contemporary American turnout levels are significantly lower than in other modern democracies, and lower than they have been even in the recent past. The international difference is not hard to explain. In many ways the United States makes voting more costly than in other countries: Registration is left to the individual, voting is less convenient, and citizens are called on to vote much more often. In addition, mobilizing agents such as parties and unions are weaker in the United States than in other modern democracies; Americans get less encouragement from larger organizations than do citizens of other democracies.

The declining rate of participation in the United States is more difficult to understand. Reforms have lowered the costs of voting, and educational levels have gone up. But Americans seem less interested in politics and less inclined to think that voting makes a difference. The explanation(s) for such disenchantment is a matter of much debate.

Different social and economic groups vote at very different rates. In particular, the poor, the less well-educated, and minorities have lower turnout rates, giving rise to a concern that the actual electorate overrepresents the wealthy, the well-educated, and whites. That is certainly true to some degree, but attempts to measure the actual political effects that would follow an expansion of the electorate suggest that these would be smaller than usually presumed because the nonvoters are not nearly as homogeneous as usually presumed, and do not differ from voters as much as is usually presumed.

Key Terms

compositional effect, p. 189

eligible voting age population, p. 178

franchise, p. 170

individual motivations for voting, p. 174

mobilization, p. 175

official turnout, p. 177

psychic benefits of voting, p. 175

registered voters, p. 178

social connectedness, p. 189

social issues, p. 194

suffrage, p. 170

voting age population, p. 178

Suggested Readings

Ansolabehere, Steven, and Shanto Iyengar. *Going Negative*. New York: Free Press, 1995. Based mostly on experiments, this important study finds that negative ads discourage moderates from voting.

Piven, Francis, and Richard Cloward. *Why Americans Don't Vote*. New York: Pantheon, 1988. Critical Commentary on nonvoting in the United States. Contends that "have-nots" are systematically discouraged from voting.

Rosenstone, Steven, and John Mark Hansen, *Mobilization, Participation, and Democracy in America*. New York: Macmillan, 1993. Comprehensive statistical study of electoral and governmental participation from the 1950s to the 1980s, with particular emphasis on the turnout decline.

Teixeira, Ruy. *The Disappearing American Voter*. Washington, DC: Brookings, 1992. Comprehensive statistical study of turnout from the 1960s to the 1980s, with particular emphasis on the turnout decline and the difference between turnout in the United States and other democracies.

Verba, Sidney, and Norman Nie. *Participation in America: Political Democracy and Social Equality*. New York: Harper & Row, 1972. Classic older study of American participation, with special emphasis on relationship between participation and equality.

Verba, Sidney, Kay Scholzman, and Henry Brady. *Voice and Equality: Civic Volunteerism in American Politics*. Cambridge: Harvard University Press, 1995. A major extension of Verba and Nie. Fascinating discussion of the development of political skills in nonpolitical contexts such as churches. Strong on attention to differences involving race, ethnicity, and gender.

Wolfinger, Raymond, and Steven Rosenstone. *Who Votes?* New Haven, CT: Yale University Press, 1980. A statistical study that relies on huge Census Bureau samples, thus providing the best estimates of the relationships between demographic characteristics and voting, albeit in a limited number of elections (1972, 1974).

7

interest group participation

in american democracy

N FEBRUARY OF 1994, the House Education Committee was hard at work on reauthorization of the 1965 Elementary and Secondary Education Act, an important part of President Lyndon Johnson's Great Society legislation.[1] A subcommittee accepted an amendment by George Miller (D-CA) that would require school districts to have their teachers officially certified in the subjects they teach. Failure to meet this requirement would result in loss of eligibility for some federal education grants. This federal mandate would serve the public interest by boosting teacher qualifications, but there were political considerations as well. Such requirements are favored by the teachers' unions because raising teacher qualifications lowers competition for teaching positions—from unemployed aerospace engineers or computer programmers, for example. Education schools also favor such requirements because they increase the demand for their certification programs. Thus, for reasons of both public and private interest, public education constituencies supported the Miller proposal.

A home school advocate who had been following these obscure committee proceedings contacted Richard Armey (R-TX) to inquire whether the proposed mandate would affect home school teachers. Unknown to many people, including most members of Congress at the time, between 500 thousand and 1 million American children are educated at home, mostly by conservative Christian parents. Uncertain about the impact of the proposal, Armey sought the advice of the Home School Legal Defense Association. After consulting with their lawyers, the association decided that given the tendency of the courts to interpret legislative mandates broadly, there was indeed a danger that the proposed mandate could be interpreted to require formal certification of parents educating their children at home. The reaction was fierce and immediate. In a letter to Congress that illustrates the fevered pitch of political rhetoric today, the Home School Legal Defense Association charged that the House proposal was "the equivalent of a nuclear attack upon the home schooling community." Employing modern communications technologies, the group set out to mobilize the potential constituency of home schoolers and their ideological soul mates. Electronic communications carried the warning to every corner of the United States, and in a matter of days the home school constituency had generated more than a half-million communications to Congress, jamming Capitol Hill switchboards, and overwhelming fax machines. A few days later a second wave of electronic thunder rolled across Capitol Hill after the home school coalition convinced groups representing private schools that they, too, were endangered by the proposed mandate.

In the midst of this constituency explosion, many members of Congress—blithely unaware of what was going on in one of 275 committees and subcommittees—had gone home for the President's Day recess. Some of them were verbally ambushed at town meetings by constituents incensed at what Congress was proposing to do to home schools. And when they tried to reach their offices to find out what was going on, they found the lines jammed! Armey could not get through from Texas, and other members had to call staff at their homes to learn the nature of the problem.

In the face of such an outcry, the House sounded a full retreat. Before galleries packed with home school advocates, the committee offered a floor amendment to kill the Miller provision and add statutory language specifically exempting home schools from the legislation's scope. This passed 424-1, with only Representative Miller voting for his provision. Not completely satisfied, Armey introduced an amendment declaring that the legislation did not "permit, allow, encourage or authorize any federal control over any aspect of any private, religious or home school." Just to be on the safe side, the Democratic-controlled House passed this amendment too, 374-53.

his episode provides a graphic illustration of several features of modern American democracy. First, although most citizens do not participate actively in politics as individuals, many are associated with groups that are very active in politics. Second, mobilizing ordinarily inactive citizens can be a highly effective strategy of political influence. Third, interest groups have adopted state-of-the-art technologies to supplement or even replace the more traditional strategies of group influence—lobbying officeholders in Washington, and working to elect sympathetic candidates. Fourth, elected officials are highly responsive to organized and aroused interests. This chapter explores these and related points.

Interest Groups in the United States

We have seen that, with the exception of voting, only small minorities of Americans participate directly in politics. But large majorities participate indirectly by joining or supporting **interest groups**—organizations or associations that participate in politics on behalf of their members (see International Comparison). Although only half the adult population votes in presidential elections, more than three-quarters of Americans belong to at least one group; on average they belong to two; and they make financial contributions to four.[2]

Of course, not all the groups with which people are associated are political groups—many are social clubs, charities, service organizations, church groups, and so forth—but there are literally thousands of groups that do engage in politics, and even seemingly nonpolitical groups often engage in political activity. For example, parent-teacher organizations involve themselves in school politics; neighborhood associations lobby about traffic, crime, and zoning policies; and even hobby or recreation groups mobilize when they perceive threats to their interests—consider the National Rifle Association!

interest group
Organization or association that engages in politics on behalf of its members.

GROWTH AND DEVELOPMENT OF GROUPS

Americans have a long-standing reputation for forming groups. In his classic work, *Democracy in America*, Alexis de Tocqueville, the nineteenth century French visitor to the United States, noted:

> *Americans of all ages, all stations in life, and all types of disposition are forever forming associations. They are not only commercial and industrial associations in which all take part, but others of a thousand other types—religious, moral, serious, futile, very general and very limited, immensely large and very minute . . . at the head of any new undertaking, where in France you would find the government or in England some territorial magnate, in the United States you are sure to find an association.*[3]

Although Americans are less likely to vote than people in other democracies, they are more likely to join groups. International surveys conducted in the early 1990s found that of nine countries surveyed, only the Dutch joined groups at a rate comparable to that in the United States. In four of the countries surveyed, a majority of citizens reported belonging to no groups.*

Interestingly, the United States differs most from the rest of the world in the proportion of people who belong to religious organizations: nearly half of all Americans report belonging to one. This is consistent with our discussion of the continued importance of religion in American political culture and of the role religion continues to play in American politics. In the countries that score low on group membership, like Mexico, France, Italy, and Spain, the Catholic Church is dominant and respondents seem not to consider membership in the church as a "group" membership. The Dutch score so highly because they are second only to the United States in religious group memberships, and they lead all countries surveyed in membership in educational cultural and environmental organizations.

* Figures drawn from the World Values Surveys, 1990–1993, reported in *The Public Perspective*, April/May, 1995: 21.

	Percent Belonging to No Groups	Percent Belonging to Four or More Groups
Netherlands	15	31
United States	18	19
Germany	33	8
Canada	35	16
Britain	46	9
Italy	59	4
France	61	4
Mexico	64	4
Spain	70	2

Moreover, if James Madison is to be believed, Americans—indeed, all people—come by their associative tendencies naturally. In his famous essay on factions (*The Federalist, no. 10*) Madison writes

> *The latent causes of faction are thus sown in the nature of man . . . the most common and durable source of factions has been the various and unequal distribution of property. Those who hold and those who are without property have ever formed distinct interests in society. Those who are creditors and those who are debtors fall under a like discrimination. A landed interest, a manufacturing interest, a mercantile interest, a moneyed interest, with many lesser interests, grow up of necessity in civilized nations, and divide them into different classes, actuated by different sentiments and views.*

However natural and long-standing the American propensity to form interest groups, there is no doubt that there are more organized groups today than ever before. In fact, one study found that 40 percent of the associations with Washington offices were formed after 1960.[4] Still, group formation in the United States has not been a steady, gradual process. Group formation has occurred in several waves, and most of today's students were born at the tail end of the greatest wave of group formation in American history—the 1960s and 1970s.

The NRA— A Hobby Group?

The NRA is one of the best-known U.S. interest groups.* It was established shortly after the Civil War to promote marksmanship—Union soldiers were considered notoriously poor shots—and grew into an organization of hunters, target shooters, and gun collectors. The NRA's growth was aided by its provision of selective incentives (p. 210) such as low-cost guns and ammunition provided by the federal government out of its stockpiles. By the mid-twentieth century the NRA had become a large service organization that operated firearms and hunter safety programs, and trained law enforcement officers.

But the NRA is far more than a hobby group. With an organizational presence in every state, it takes the lead in opposing gun control legislation of any kind. It has a PAC that is usually one of the top ten contributors to congressional elections. It employs some 80 lobbyists. The NRA is considered one of the best examples of a "single issue group," a group focused on one issue to the exclusion of virtually everything else. Only a politician's position on gun control matters, not whether a politician is generally a liberal or conservative. For example, in 1990 and 1992 the NRA backed Vermont congressional candidate Bernie Sanders, a *socialist* who took a strong anti–gun control position. Sanders twice voted against the Brady handgun control bill, including when it passed in 1993. But when Sanders voted for the assault weapons ban in 1994, the NRA endorsed his opponent and distributed bumper stickers with "Bye, Bye Bernie" printed on them.†

Although Sanders narrowly survived, the NRA was widely credited with playing an important role in the Republican takeover of Congress in 1994. President Clinton was the first president to openly take on the NRA. The organization vociferously opposed the Brady bill, which the Democratic Congress approved, and also the assault weapons ban included in President Clinton's crime bill that passed just a few months before the elections. Gun control became an important issue in many campaigns, and the assault weapons vote was particularly damaging to Democratic incumbents.‡

In recent years the NRA has lost some political support, including the widely publicized resignation of former President Bush, a lifetime member. Its positions are viewed as extreme by many Americans, and some of its for-

mer allies in the law enforcement community have broken with it because of its continued opposition to regulation of assault weapons, armor-piercing bullets (so-called cop-killers), and other products whose human damage seems far out of proportion to any legitimate sporting or recreational value. For their part, activists in the NRA regard any government regulation as a first step down a slippery slope that leads to the eventual outlawing of firearms.

* Much of this profile is taken from Clyde Brown, "National Rifle Association," in L. Sandy Maisel, ed., *Political Parties and Elections in the United States: An Encyclopedia*, vol. 2 (New York: Garland, 1991), 687.

† Michael Barone and Grant Ujifusa, *Almanac of American Politics* (Washington, DC: National Journal, 1995), 1358.

‡ David Brady, John Cogan, Brian Gaines, and Douglas Rivers, "The Perils of Presidential Support: How the Republicans Took the House in the 1994 Midterm Elections" (Stanford, CA: The Hoover Institution, 1995).

Before the Civil War, there were few national organizations in America. Life in general was local. One historian has described the social organization of the United States as one of "island communities" not connected to each other by social and economic links.[5] There was, of course, no national economy; instead, regions produced and consumed much of what they used themselves. This began to change as the railroads connected the country after the Civil War. A national economy developed, and national associations were not far behind. The first two decades after the war saw the birth of national agricultural associations like the Grange, and trade unions like the Knights of Labor and the American Federation of Labor.

Another major wave of group organization occurred during the Progressive era, roughly 1890 to 1917. Many of today's most broad-based or "peak" associations date from that era—the Chamber of Commerce, the National Association of Manufacturers, the American Medical Association, and the American Farm Bureau Federation. These associations have an economic emphasis, but other associations founded during the Progressive era do not; for example, the National Association for the Advancement of Colored People (NAACP) was formed as part of an effort to promote equality for black Americans, and the National Audubon Society was formed to promote conservation.

The 1960–1980 wave of group formation is by far the largest and the most heterogeneous. Thousands of additional economic groups formed, but these tended to be more narrowly based than earlier ones: the American Soybean Association, the National Corn Growers Association, the Rocky Mountain Llama and Alpaca Association, and numerous other specialized organizations joined the more general agricultural associations. Similarly, in the commercial and manufacturing sectors numerous specialized groups have joined the more broad-based older groups.

Numerous nonprofit groups formed as well, many of which represent people working in the public sector. Older national associations of mayors, governors, teachers, and social workers have been joined by newer more specialized associations like the National Association of State and Provincial Lotteries, the Association of State Drinking Water Administrators, and the U.S. Police Canine Association. Similarly, nongovernmental nonprofit sector groups now include all manner of specialized occupational associations. Examples of particular interest to many readers of this book would include the National Association of Student Financial Aid Administrators and the National Association of Graduate Admissions Professionals.

Finally, innumerable shared interest groups have formed in recent decades. Some are actively political, working for specific points of view. Liberal groups like the National Organization for Women (NOW, a feminist group), and People for the American Way (a civil liberties group) are deeply involved in politics, as are conservative groups like the Christian Coalition (which promotes traditional morality) and Operation Rescue (an antiabortion group). Many "citizens" groups, such as Common Cause (a political reform group), Greenpeace (an environmental group), the National Taxpayers' Union (an antitax and antispending group), and numerous other environmental, consumer, and "watchdog" groups are less than a generation old. Other groups are not primarily political, but have a political side. For example, the American Association of Retired Persons (AARP), established in 1958, has become the largest voluntary association that has ever existed, with upwards of 33 million members—and still growing! AARP is a major player whenever Social Security or Medicare are on the political agenda. Under the right circumstances almost any group may become involved in politics. Associations representing those who fish monitor water policy in particular, and natural resources policies in general. Associations representing snowmobilers and mountain bikers make themselves heard when government threatens to restrict their use of public lands.

THE NATURE AND VARIETY OF "INTEREST GROUPS"

Robert Salisbury has called attention to the variety of groups, associations, and organizations included under the term "interest groups."[6] Some have elaborate formal organizations with membership dues, journals, meetings, conventions, and so forth; the American Medical Association is a well-known example. Others are little more than an address where sympathizers send contributions; one study found that of 83 public interest groups examined, 30 had no membership.[7] Some, like Common Cause, are "membership groups" composed of numerous private individuals who make voluntary contributions. Others are associations consisting of corporate or institutional representatives who pay regular dues. Trade associations and associations of universities are examples. Some large corporations maintain their own Washington offices, as do hundreds of state, city, and county governments, and even universities. Institutions, corporations, and governments are not really "groups" in the usual sense, although they certainly are "interests."

Associations representing hobbyists such as mountain bikers make themselves heard when government threatens to restrict their use of public lands.

Jack Walker estimates that almost 80 percent of the interest groups now in existence represent professional or occupational constituencies.[8] For such groups, economic matters are of crucial concern, but these groups are about equally divided between those representing profit-sector constituencies and those representing public and nonprofit-sector constituencies, so they do not exert a uniformly conservative influence on government taxing and spending policies. The other 20 percent of American interest groups reflect the activities of citizens with particular interests, including those spawned by what are called social movements—broad-based reform or protest movements that bring new issues to the agenda. The civil rights movement, the environmental movement, the women's movement, and the religious right are important contemporary examples.

EXPLANATIONS OF THE PROLIFERATION OF INTEREST GROUPS

Several factors underlie the explosion of groups and associations during the past generation. First, the expansion of government activity has given people more reason to form groups. Business groups, for instance, may form in reaction to government activity, or because they see an opportunity to procure a government subsidy. Second, advances in communications technology have made groups easier to form. Simply learning about the existence of other people with common interests was difficult a generation ago. Today, computer databases permit the generation of all manner of specialized mailing lists, and, once identified, people with common interests can communicate easily and cheaply by e-mail and fax. Third, formation of a group to advance some interest may stimulate the formation of other groups opposed to that interest. The pro-life movement formed at least in part because of the activities of the pro-choice movement.[9] The ranching, mining, lumber, and sporting interests who launched the "Sagebrush rebellion" were reacting to the success of the environmental movement.

On closer consideration, however, shared interests, threats from government or other groups, and ease of communications are not sufficient to explain why groups form. Such factors add to the incentive to associate or lessen the obstacles, but they do not explain how a fundamental problem—the free rider obstacle—is overcome.

Getting Americans to contribute to public interest groups is a challenge.

Forming and Maintaining Interest Groups

That so many people belong to so many groups and associations often leads people to overlook the difficulties many groups face.[10] But consider these facts:

- There are approximately 75 million women over the age of 16 in the United States. Polls indicate that more than half have feminist sympathies. But the largest feminist group, NOW, has fewer than 300 thousand members.

- There are approximately 33 million African Americans in the United States, but the NAACP has only about 400 thousand members—including whites.

- More than 40 million American households have at least one gun, but the membership of the NRA is only 2.5 million.

- Majorities of Americans consistently support spending more on the environment, but the combined membership of seven large environmental groups is about 6.5 million (and this double- and triple-counts those who belong to more than one organization).[11]

As these examples suggest, millions of people do *not* join or support associations whose interests they share. Common interest may be a necessary condition for joining a group, but it is very far from a sufficient one.

Why then do people join or decline to join groups? The question is important because the answer bears on how well or how poorly interest groups represent the American citizenry. If some kinds of interests are not fairly represented, politics may be biased, despite the existence of thousands of groups with whom millions of people are affiliated.

Like voting, joining or supporting a group requires some investment of *resources*; that is, it involves costs. Contributing money or paying dues is the most obvious example, but the time required for group activities also can be a significant cost. People who have more resources will find participation easier. Thus, it is no surprise that the affluent contribute more than the poor, and that two-worker families with small children participate less than those whose family situations give them more free time.[12] More generally, a large institution or corporation has more resources to contribute than a solitary citizen. But whether rich or poor, one commits resources only if the *incentive* to do so—the expected benefit—justifies the investment.

Incentives take many forms, and different groups rely on different incentives. James Q. Wilson divides incentives into three categories.[13] The first he calls *solidary*. Some people join a group for social reasons: They simply wish to associate with particular kinds of people. Activity groups and church groups are obvious examples. Where solidary incentives are dominant, membership in the group is an end in itself. Many groups, probably the majority, are composed of individuals who join for solidary reasons, but most such groups are nonpolitical. For example, it is unlikely that people join the National Taxpayers' Union to enjoy the company of other taxpayers, and certainly, people do not send checks to associations without members for social purposes!

The second category of incentives is *material*. Such incentives are economic rather than social: Some people join a group because membership confers tangible benefits. This is obviously the dominant incentive in economic groups and associations. IBM does not belong to various trade associations because its executives like to socialize with other computer executives—they have plenty of other opportunities to do that. IBM belongs because the trade associations are seen as a way of protecting and advancing corporate interests. Material incentives also play a role in some political groups. Those who join taxpayers' associations hope to reduce their taxes. Those who join groups that support government subsidies or services for people like themselves (realtors, the handicapped, the old, farmers) similarly hope to gain material benefits.

Finally, some people join groups for *purposive* reasons: People are committed to and wish to advance the group's social and political goals. They want to save the whales, to bring about a liberal or conservative Congress, to end abortion, or to preserve freedom of choice. Given that many political groups espouse purposive goals, such incentives, along with the previously discussed material incentives, would appear to be the dominant factor underlying the formation and persistence of most of the groups active in politics. Things are not so simple as they appear, however.

THE FREE RIDER PROBLEM

Groups that rely on purposive and material incentives face what is known as the **free rider problem**: many people who share group goals may not join or contribute, but instead will "free ride" on the efforts of others.[14] This problem arises when individuals perceive that attainment of the group goal has little relation to their personal contribution. To explain, if you donate $10 to Greenpeace, does your contribution ensure the survival of some identifiable baby seal? If you donate several hours of your time to march for the end of hunger, does your contribution measurably lessen the amount of malnutrition in the world? If you recycle everything you use and take care to use nonpolluting products, does your personal effort make any measurable difference in the amount of global pollution? Although most well-meaning people are reluctant to admit it, in each case the truthful answer is no.

These examples have two common elements. First, on reflection, people realize that their personal impact is virtually nonexistent. If you don't contribute, just as many baby seals will live or die, world hunger will be no different, and global pollution will be the same. So if your contribution makes no difference, why contribute? The second element makes matters worse: The nature of the benefit is such that individuals receive it whether they contribute or not. If many others do contribute and save some seals, reduce world hunger, or alleviate global pollution, they cannot keep you from enjoying those outcomes, even if you did not contribute. So if you get the same benefit regardless of your actions, why contribute? Together the two conditions pose a major obstacle to group formation and survival. When they hold, the temptation is for individuals to free ride on the contributions of others. If most people feel that way, the group may die, or fail to form in the first place.

Two considerations affect the severity of the free rider problem. First, other things being equal, the larger the group the greater the problem. A few neighbors can pool their efforts to clean up a vacant lot that adjoins their properties. Anyone who fails to show up is easily identified and subject to social pressure. It would be unthinkable, however, for a large city to rely on volunteer effort to maintain city parks. Each resident's personal responsibility is small, and social pressure is less effective where people do not know each other. Thus, cities pay city employees or private contractors to maintain their parks.

free rider problem
Problem that arises when people who share a group's goals do not join or contribute to it because their personal contribution seems too small to make a difference.

Second, other things equal, the free rider problem is more serious with the greater distance and abstractness of the benefit the group seeks to achieve. It is much easier to see one's personal impact on cleaning up a vacant lot than on cleaning the atmosphere. It is much easier to see one's personal impact on feeding the poor in a specific locale than on reducing world hunger.

At issue here are what economists call **public goods**, as distinct from **private goods**. A tomato is a private good. In order to consume it, you must contribute, in the sense that you must grow it or purchase it. Moreover, if you consume it, others cannot. World peace, in contrast, is a public good. In order to enjoy it, you need not contribute. And, if you enjoy it, others are in no way prevented from enjoying it as well. Because free riders can enjoy or consume public goods even if they make no contribution to their provision, economists believe that such goods are typically provided at lower than optimal levels.[15]

It is important to recognize that material goods can be public goods; therefore, groups and associations that seek material benefits also face free rider problems. If Chrysler successfully lobbies for a tariff or quota on Japanese cars, Ford will enjoy the benefits (lower competition, higher prices) even if Ford did not aid Chrysler in the lobbying effort. If members of the Corn Growers' Association pool their efforts to get a higher corn subsidy, even growers who are not members of the association reap the benefit of the higher subsidy. The free rider problem is widespread. Only those groups based on social incentives escape it; since membership itself is the benefit in such groups, there is no incentive to free ride.

The most important implication of the free rider problem for democratic politics lies in the nature of the groups best able to overcome it. Our discussion suggests that, other things being equal, small groups organized for narrow purposes have an organizational advantage over large groups organized for broad purposes. We call the former groups "special" interests, and the latter "general" or "public" interests. For example, a small number of corporations will find it relatively easy to organize an association to lobby for regulations that raise prices; the millions of consumers who buy the products the corporations sell will find it much more difficult to organize an association to lobby against such anticompetitive regulations. The free rider problem implies that, in democratic politics, special interests generally are advantaged relative to general interests.

public goods
Goods that you can enjoy without contributing—by free-riding on the efforts of those who do.

private goods
Goods that you must purchase to enjoy, and your consumption of which precludes that of others.

OVERCOMING THE FREE RIDER PROBLEM

On first learning about the free rider problem, some skeptics protest "what if everyone felt that way?" Well, a great many people do; that is why so many groups mobilize such a small proportion of their potential constituencies. Consumers, taxpayers, environmentalists, conservatives, and liberals all mobilize only a small proportion of the people who sympathize with their goals. Still, there are groups that represent broad purposive interests like these. How do these groups manage to overcome the free rider problem? History reveals a number of useful strategies.

Large numbers of Americans sometimes donate their time and effort to general causes, as in marches to end hunger.

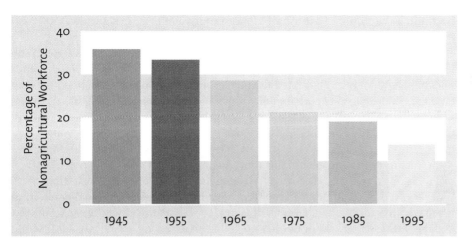

COERCION

If members of a labor union strike for higher wages, how can they prevent nonunion workers from enjoying the results? Historically, the answer has been coercion. Social pressure and even violence have been used to coerce reluctant workers to join unions or prevent them from crossing union picket lines. Because violence is costly to inflict and often brings violence in return, however, unions preferred to rely on a strategy of negotiating "closed shops" with management. Such agreements permit only union members to work, and require workers to join the union as a condition of employment.

Milder forms of coercion are still widespread, although they are often unrecognized. For example, professional and occupational associations may lobby governmental jurisdictions to hire, approve, or certify only their members, thus making membership a condition of working or practicing in that jurisdiction. The practice of law usually requires membership in the state bar, the practice of specialized trades like plumbing may require a state license, and teachers usually must be state-certified to teach in public schools. Such requirements are ways of coercing potential free riders into joining the associations that represent their trades and professions.

While highly effective historically, coercion appears to be a declining means of overcoming the free rider problem. The union movement has fallen on hard times, with membership declining from more than one-third of the workforce to less than one-sixth (see Figure 7.1). Privatization is on the increase, and the general trend toward deregulation opens up occupations to competition.

The Grange was an important nineteenth-century social movement, built at the grassroots by farmers, starting in 1867.

SOCIAL MOVEMENTS

There are times when people do not think individualistically, as they do when they free ride. Consider the Patrons of Husbandry, more commonly known as the Grange. The first Grange chapter was established in 1867. As the railroads expanded after the Civil War, farmers and local communities became increasingly upset with railroad practices. Their discontent soon took organized form. In the spring of 1873 there were 3,360 Grange chapters, by fall the number had more than doubled to 7,325, and less than a year later it had exploded to 20,365. Political institutions yielded to this popular uprising and legislated against the financial power of the railroad corporations. Many states, especially in the Midwest, passed laws (so-called "Granger laws") regulating railroad prices and practices.[16] Even the

Republican-dominated House of Representatives thought it prudent to pass a national law in 1874.[17]

Such **social movements**—broad-based demands for government action on a problem or issue—have a long history in American politics. The abolitionist movement is one of the best known. Dedicated to ending slavery, this movement forced the issue onto the national agenda and played a role in the political upheaval of the 1850s and, ultimately, in the outbreak of the Civil War. Other nineteenth-century social movements included the Populists and labor in the 1880s and 1890s, and the women's suffrage movement, which culminated in passage of the Nineteenth Amendment in 1920.

In modern times the civil rights movement is probably the best-known example of a social movement. As discussed in Chapter 17, the massive demonstrations of the 1960s evolved from a few sit-ins and boycotts in the 1950s. The movement culminated with the adoption of landmark federal legislation, the Civil Rights Act of 1964, and the Voting Rights Act of 1965 (p. 560).

Other movements soon followed. On April 22, 1970, Earth Day marked the sudden eruption of an environmental movement. Within the year there was an Environmental Protection Agency and a Clean Air Act. As discussed in Chapter 17, the women's movement took off at about the same time, flexing its muscle in the 1972–1982 campaign for ratification of the Equal Rights Amendment (ERA), which succeeded in thirty-five states, three short of the three-fourths majority needed to adopt a constitutional amendment.[18] On the other side of the political spectrum, the ranks of the religious right swelled in the late 1970s and contributed to Ronald Reagan's presidential victories in the 1980s and to the Republican congressional resurgence of the 1990s.[19] The movement supports constitutional amendments to outlaw abortion and allow prayer in schools, but, as with the feminists, the religious right has been unable as yet to achieve constitutional change.

Social movements have a significant element of emotional or moral fervor. Many of those active within them dedicate themselves to what they see as a higher cause. When individuals adopt a moral perspective, or think more collectively than individually, they may ignore the considerations that normally would lead them to free ride. As the examples discussed above demonstrate, social movements can be important ways of mobilizing interests and altering the policies and practices of government.

Still, social movements typically mobilize only small proportions of their prospective constituencies. Some people can be induced to think in moral or collective terms, but not many. Moreover, for most people, emotional and moral fervor are temporary conditions that they cannot sustain for long periods. Thus, a social movement has a tendency to "run down," as its emotional basis subsides. Some scholars argue that conservative forces in politics often can stall social movements until they weaken, leaving things much as before. Murray Edelman, for example, suggests that, under pressure from a social movement, Congress may pass a statute that establishes a regulatory agency or commission. But as the movement subsides, the regulators increasingly operate in an environment dominated by the more permanent economic interests they are supposed to regulate. In the end, the payoff to the movement is more symbolic than substantive.[20] For a social movement to exert continued long-term influence, it must find a way to "institutionalize" itself, to spin off organized groups and formal associations that will continue to work for its interests.

SELECTIVE BENEFITS

Many groups that work to achieve collective goods also provide valuable private goods to their members. A professional association may make membership a condition of subscribing to a journal that contains occupationally useful information. A trade association may inform its members about important technological advances. Agricultural associations may provide their membership with information about new varieties of crops, new growing methods, and so forth. In short, people, corporations, and institutions may join associations less to support the collective goods that the association favors than for the specific private goods the association provides—selectively—to members: its **selective benefits**.

The American Association of Retired Persons (AARP) provides the most notable example of this strategy for overcoming the free rider problem. For a mere $8 per year members gain access to the world's largest mail order pharmacy (where volume buying keeps prices low); low-cost auto, health, and life insurance; discounts on hotels, air fares, and car rentals; and numerous other benefits. Even a senior citizen who disagrees with the political positions of AARP finds it hard to forego membership!

Selective benefits are not limited to direct economic ones, or to information that indirectly produces economic benefits. Anything people like that can be selectively provided can be a selective benefit. Some environmental groups produce magazines full of beautiful pictures, organize outings and activities, rate outdoor clothing and equipment, and so forth. These and other benefits of membership often are sufficient to induce people to pay the modest amounts that membership requires.

In short, what you think of as the principal reason for a group's existence may not be the principal reason that many people are members. Just the opposite—the political activity in which the group engages may be a by-product of the selective benefits it provides.

PATRONS AND POLITICAL ENTREPRENEURS

The free rider problem arises in a bottom-up conception of how groups form. The implicit notion is that individual people, corporations, or institutions band together and form associations. Recent research indicates that the process of group formation often is more top-down than bottom-up. Many groups owe their existence to a **political entrepreneur**, an individual or small number of individuals who take the lead in setting up and operating the group.

In the first place, some individuals, institutions, or corporations may be sufficiently rich or have such a stake in the group goal that it is worth their while to act independently or alone. Microsoft, General Motors, the State of California, and many other actors have their own Washington offices or employees because they have a great deal at stake and are sufficiently powerful that their activities and contributions can make a difference. Such large actors do not face a free rider problem; for them, maintaining a lobbying arm is just a good business decision. Sometimes an association will be dominated by a single large firm that bears most of the costs but allows other members to free ride to give the appearance of a broad base of support. Ralston-Purina in the feed industry is an example.

Similarly, a rich individual with a deep commitment to the group goal may be able to make a difference. Your $10 contribution to Greenpeace may have no measurable impact, but if you are in a position to give a million dollars, you can probably save some seals. Foundations also support groups with grants and contracts. The W. Alton Jones Foundation and the Ford Foundation give millions of dollars a year to environmental groups.[21] Similarly, conservative foundations help to fund the Wise Use Movement that opposes traditional environmental groups.

Politicians pay due respect to a politically powerful senior citizens' group like AARP.

■ **selective benefits**
Side benefits of belonging to an organization that are limited to contributing members of the organization.

■ **political entrepreneur**
Someone who is willing to assume the costs of forming and maintaining an organization even when others may free ride on them.

In the second place, political entrepreneurs will often take on the job of setting up and maintaining a group for their own reasons.[22] Their motives are varied. Some feel so strongly about a goal that they are willing to let others free ride on them. We call such people fanatical or dedicated, depending on whether we sympathize with their goals. An ascetic lawyer, Ralph Nader, did more than anyone to organize the consumer movement and has devoted his life to it. A Missouri activist, Phyllis Schlafly, organized the anti-ERA cause. Ross Perot founded and subsidizes a political organization, United We Stand. Many (although not all) such individuals have passed up opportunities to parlay their visibility into riches or political office, suggesting that their commitment to broader goals is genuine.

Of course, some political entrepreneurs do have ulterior motives. They may be aspiring politicians who see an opportunity to use new groups as the basis of future constituencies. Candidates for city and state offices often emerge from neighborhood associations and local protest groups. Perhaps these individuals were just swept along by political tides; on the other hand, their local work may have been a way to position themselves for future election campaigns.

In addition to wealthy patrons, and dedicated or self-interested political entrepreneurs, the government itself did much to organize the new groups of the 1960s and 1970s. As the role of government expanded, federal bureaucracies needed to develop new ways of implementing programs through a decentralized federal system that mixed both public and private elements. One strategy was to stimulate and subsidize organizations: state and local elected officials; state and local employees such as social workers, police, and firefighters; public- and private-sector professionals such as educators, health providers, environmental engineers, and so forth. Once formed, the groups could be used to help develop standards and regulations, and to publicize them and carry them out. In addition to the administrative usefulness of such groups, they were politically useful as well: Not surprisingly, groups and associations that receive federal funds are more than twice as likely to support expanded government activity—and, by implication, the elected officials who expand it—as groups that do not.[23]

Notice, incidentally, that although government has been a prominent source of support for the groups established since 1960, this is by no means a new government role. The Grange, discussed earlier, was founded by an employee of the U.S. Agriculture Department in 1867. The first local chapter was Potomac 1 and was composed of government workers and their wives!

The available evidence suggests that the top-down activities of patrons and political entrepreneurs are a more important means of overcoming the free rider problem than the provision of selective benefits—AARP to the contrary notwithstanding.[24] Wealthy individuals, government agencies, corporations, and private foundations have been important sources of support for nonprofit sector groups, especially citizens groups. About 90 percent of the latter have received such subsidies.

In sum, the free rider problem certainly can be overcome. Not only special interests are represented in American politics; general interests have some representation as well. Still, there is little doubt that the free rider problem creates a bias in the interest group system. Political scientists have long found that the interest group system is dominated by business interests, which remains true today. Indeed, despite the large increase in the number of groups active in politics, including many citizens groups, the most complete data suggest that business dominance of the Washington interest group universe is even more pronounced than it was several decades ago.[25]

How Interest Groups Influence Government

The variety of groups, associations, and institutions that make up the interest group universe engage in an array of political activities. We discuss these under six broad headings and then focus on why groups choose particular tactics over others.

Lobbying

Many interest groups attempt to influence government in the old-fashioned way—by lobbying public officials. **Lobbying** consists of attempts by group representatives to personally influence the decisions of public officials. Groups and associations draft bills for friendly legislators to introduce, testify before congressional committees and in agency proceedings, meet with elected officials and present their cases (sometimes at posh resorts where the official is the guest), and provide public officials with information. In these and other ways, group representatives attempt to personally influence those who make governmental decisions.

People who engage in lobbying are called **lobbyists**, although the term is usually reserved for those who spend most of their time lobbying. Some lobbyists are so-called "hired guns," people who will use their contacts and expertise in the service of anyone willing to pay their price, but some of the best known are closely associated with one party or the other. Many large groups and associations have their own staff lobbyists. Smaller groups or those not often involved in politics may hire lobbyists on a part-time basis or share one with other groups. Some groups simply have their own leaders engage in lobbying, although these individuals typically are not called lobbyists. There are federal and state laws that require all lobbyists to register, but those who register comprise only a fraction of those engaged in lobbying. For example, the *American Lobbyists Directory* lists 65 thousand legally registered federal and state lobbyists, but estimates are that in Washington alone, there are upwards of 90 thousand.[26]

The term *lobbyist* has negative connotations (we doubt that many parents would want their child to grow up to be one). Movies, novels, and even the newspapers often portray lobbyists as unsavory characters who operate on the borders of what is ethical or legal—and often step across them. Research suggests that this is an exaggeration. While there are examples of shady or corrupt behavior by lobbyists, given the number of lobbyists and the amount of lobbying that goes on, such transgressions are hardly the norm. Certainly, most analysts believe that corrupt behavior by interest group lobbyists is less widespread today than in previous eras of American history. Numerous conflict-of-interest laws and regulations, along with an investigative media ever on the lookout for a hint of scandal, make outright corruption in today's politics relatively rare.

For the most part, lobbyists provide public officials with information and supporting arguments. They tend to deal with officials already sympathetic to their position and support those officials' activities. Lobbyists have little incentive to distort information or lie; to do so would destroy their credibility and lessen their future effectiveness. Of course, they emphasize arguments and information favorable to their viewpoint, but they do not want to hurt their political allies by lying, concealing information, or otherwise exposing them to an embarrassing counterattack.

lobbying
Attempts by representatives of groups and associations to directly influence the decisions of government officials.

lobbyist
One who engages in lobbying. *See* Lobbying.

WASHINGTON LOBBYISTS

The term *lobbyist* includes a wide range of people, from poorly compensated public interest lawyers who wear rumpled suits and scuffed shoes, to the wealthy, superlobbyists who wear Armani suits and Gucci shoes. Many of the top Washington lobbyists are lawyers intimately tied to the political system. They contribute generously to congressional candidates and political parties at the same time that they lobby members of congress on behalf of their clients. Unlike many PACs, however, they often are closely tied to one party or the other—probably because their value (contacts and expertise) stems from previous government service in one administration or another.

In 1996, the Center for Responsive Politics tabulated 1995 campaign contributions of more than 300 top Washington lawyers and lobbyists whose firms represented a range of clients (as opposed to in-house lobbyists employed by single industries or firms). In total, these lobbyists gave about equally to the two parties ($1.45 million to Democrats, $1.52 million to Republicans). Individually, a Republican came in first, and a Democrat second.*

1. C. Boyden Gray. Gray represents the firm of Wilmer, Cutler & Pickering. He directed the Task Force on Regulatory Relief in the Reagan Administration, and served as White House Counsel for President Bush. In 1995, Gray and his family contributed $143,910 to Republican committees and candi-

dates, nothing to Democrats.

2. Lawrence F. O'Brien, III. O'Brien served in President Carter's Administration, but his father was a top Democratic Party campaign strategist in the 1960s, having served Presidents Kennedy and Johnson as chief of Congressional Liaison, and he was chairman of the Democratic National Committee at the time of the Watergate break-in. In 1995, the younger O'Brien contributed $77,500 to Democratic candidates and committees, nothing to Republicans.

The # 3 and # 4 finishers, Steve Champlin and Michael Berman of the Duberstein Group gave $49,500 and $46,822, all to Democrats. The #5 finisher, however, split his contributions almost equally between the parties. J. D. Williams, of Williams and Jensen, has been in Washington for more than thirty years. He is especially active on oil matters, hence his contributions to both Republicans and conservative Democrats.

* "Capital Eye: A Close-Up Look at Money in Politics," *Center for Responsive Politics*, May 1, 1996: 4-5.

Lobbyist at work: C. Boyden Gray buttonholes potential supporters for his interest at a Washington, D.C. gathering.

Many political scientists think that lobbyists serve a useful purpose, injecting valuable information into the legislative process. As former Senator and President John Kennedy observed:

> Competent lobbyists can present the most persuasive arguments in support of their positions. Indeed, there is no more effective manner of learning all important arguments and facts on a controversial issue than to have the opposing lobbyists present their case.[27]

With the explosive growth of interest groups during the past generation, there is undoubtedly more old-fashioned lobbying than ever before. Corporate and trade association offices in Washington doubled between 1970 and 1980, and the number of people employed therein tripled. Membership in the District of Columbia Bar Association more than tripled between 1973 and 1983. Registered lobbyists increased sixfold between 1960 and 1980.[28] In part, such developments were stimulated by the democratization of Congress and the expansion of government. Whereas in 1950 a group might lobby only one powerful committee chairman or a key staffer, by 1980 it had to lobby numerous subcommittee chairs as well as the rank and file and many of their staff.

GRASSROOTS LOBBYING

Today, Washington lobbying is often combined with so-called grassroots lobbying: Inside-the-beltway persuasion is supplemented with outside-the-beltway pressure. Whereas lobbying consists of attempts to influence government officials *directly*, **grassroots lobbying** consists of attempts to influence officials *indirectly* through their constituents. The home schooling example that opened this chapter illustrates the process. A Washington association communicates with its grassroots supporters, who in turn put pressure on their elected representatives. As one health care lobbyist put it recently:

> One of the perceptions about lobbying is that you go out drinking, and the guy's your buddy so he does you favors. . . Those days are long gone. That sort of thing may work on tiny things like a technical amendment to a bill, but on big, important issues personal friendships don't mean a thing. . . I'll bet we could have done just as good a job as we did [on influencing health care reform] without ever going to the Hill or ever talking to a member of Congress. It is knowing when and how to ask the troops in the field to do it.[29]

For several reasons, grassroots lobbying probably is more prevalent today than in the past. First, as noted above, Congress is more decentralized. When only a few leaders need to be persuaded, an inside-the-beltway strategy of influence may suffice, but when dozens need to be persuaded, reaching out and touching their constituents may be more effective. Second, government in general is more open than in the past. It is not so easy for Washington insiders to make private deals; it is more important than ever to show that there is popular support for your group's position. Third, as the home schooling example vividly illustrates, the advent of modern communications technology makes grassroots mobilization easier than ever before.

By no means are we saying that grassroots lobbying is a new tactic, however; it has been around for a long time. In a classic study of the anti-Saloon League (a prohibition group), Peter Odegard noted that this group had more than 500 thousand names on its mailing list nearly a century ago—long before dependable long-distance telephone service, let alone computers, the fax, and e-mail![30] Influencing government

THE FIVE COMMANDMENTS OF LOBBYING CONGRESS

1. Tell the truth.
2. Never promise more than you can deliver.
3. Know how to listen so that you accurately understand what you are hearing.
4. Staff are there to be worked with and not circumvented.
5. Spring no surprises.

From Bruce Wolpe and Bertram Levine, *Lobbying Congress* (Washington, DC. CQ Press, 1996), ch. 2.

■ **grassroots lobbying**
Efforts by groups and associations to influence elected officials indirectly, by arousing their constituents.

officials' views by reaching out to their constituents is nothing new, but the decentralized political institutions of the contemporary United States, along with rapid advances in communications technology, have made such a strategy more attractive than ever.

ELECTIONEERING AND PACs

Personal and grassroots lobbying are attempts to influence the views of public officials on specific matters. Another avenue of group influence is to affect the views of public officials in general by influencing who gets elected in the first place. Groups have always been involved in the electoral process, supporting some candidates and opposing others, but as party dominance of campaigns and elections has eroded, and as campaigns have become more expensive, groups have become more active than ever before. Electioneering is probably the fastest growing group tactic, and a principal vehicle of this tactic is the political action committee.

Political action committees (PACs) are specialized organizations for raising and spending campaign funds. Many are associated with an interest group or association. They come in as many varieties as the interests they represent.[31] They represent big economic interests like the realtors' RPAC, and the doctors' AMPAC, but they represent thousands of smaller interests as well—the beer wholesalers, for example, have SixPAC. Numerous PACs represent interests that are at least partly noneconomic. Supporters of Israel donate to AIPAC and NATPAC. Supporters of abortion rights send money to NARAL-PAC, while their pro-life adversaries send money to National Right to Life PAC. (Pro-choice Republicans uncomfortable with the liberal positions of NARAL can give money to WISH LIST.) Gun control supporters contribute to Handgun Control Inc. PAC, while gun control opponents contribute to Gun Owners of America Campaign Committee. In addition to groups, scores of individual politicians have established personal PACs.[32] For example, in 1997 Speaker Newt Gingrich was reprimanded by the House Ethics Committee for lying about activities of his GOPAC that were in violation of tax and campaign finance laws. Like interest groups in general, PACs have enjoyed explosive growth in the past few decades. From a mere handful in 1970, they proliferated rapidly in the 1980s. Reflecting the overall contours of the interest group system, far more PACs represent business and commercial interests than represent labor or citizen interests (see Figure 7.2).

There is widespread public dissatisfaction with the role of PACs in campaign finance (see Democratic Dilemma), although it is ironic that the proliferation of PACs is partly an unintended consequence of early-1970s attempts to reform the campaign finance laws.[33] As their numbers have proliferated, PACs have played an increasingly prominent role in congressional campaign finance. Reflecting their business associations, most PACs tend to give instrumentally, which means donating to the members of key committees regardless of party (see Table 7.1). When the Democrats were in the majority some of their members became highly dependent on business contributions, and critics charged that this dependence affected their legislative judgment.[34] When Democrats became a minority after the 1994 elections, they became much more favorable to campaign finance regulation that restricted PACs.

At the risk of sounding complacent, we suggest that, like interest group corruption in general, the PAC problem in particular is somewhat exaggerated by the popular media. Most PAC contributions are small, and are intended mostly as a way of gaining access to public officials. Most research has failed to establish any significant relationship between contributions and votes.[35] There is even some anecdotal

Political action committees are everywhere, including pro-choice as well as right-to-life advocates.

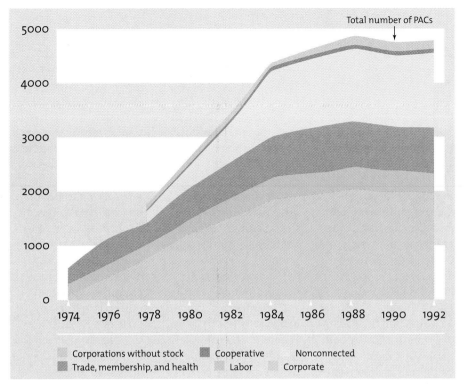

FIGURE 7.2

PACs Formed Rapidly after the
1974 Federal Election Campaign
Act (FECA) Reforms

Total number of PACs

Corporations without stock · Cooperative · Nonconnected
Trade, membership, and health · Labor · Corporate

TABLE 7.1

Business PAC Contributions Tend to Follow Political Power

	Percentage of Contributions to Republications Jan–Feb, 1993 (Democrat majority)	Percentage of Contributions to Republications, Jan–Feb, 1995 (Republican majority)
American Dental Association	27	90
American Bankers Association	52	87
American Hospital Association	53	81
Ameritech	35	79
AT&T	36	79
American Institute of CPAs	45	87
Home Builders	45	71
Realtors	75	91
RJR Nabisco	69	81
United Parcel Service	55	78

SOURCE: Jonathan Salant and David Cloud, "To the 1994 Election Victors Go the Fundraising Spoils," *Congressional Quarterly Weekly Report,* April 15, 1995: 1057.

evidence that politicians extort PACs, pressuring them to buy tickets to fund-raisers and otherwise make contributions as a condition of continued access. For example, a former congressional staffer told one of us the following story:

> *In our office we loved the FEC reports. We'd comb through them and list all the business groups who had contributed to our opponent. Then we'd call them*

Interest Groups and
Campaign Finance

Of all the things that contemporary Americans find unsatisfactory about their politics, campaign finance ranks near the top. People feel that free-spending special interests exercise too much influence over government actions, and that free-spending candidates are able to buy elections. Despite widespread dissatisfaction, however, little has been accomplished by way of reforming campaign finance. At one time or another, both parties and most candidates have condemned the system, but little by way of reform has occurred.

One important aspect of the problem is that any reforms have to be approved by elected officials whose electoral self-interest is at stake. This gives them a view of reform very different from that held by many disinterested citizens. But another large part of the problem is that proposed reforms seem to be at least partly in conflict with constitutional freedoms. For example, in 1996 a proposal to ban PACs achieved considerable support in the House of Representatives, but opponents claimed that such a ban was patently unconstitutional.

In an important 1976 decision, *Buckley* v. *Valeo*, the U.S. Supreme Court held that Congress could not limit spending by either candidates or interest groups: Since it costs money to publicize one's views, limiting spending was equivalent to limiting expression.* Others disagree. Former Senator Bill Bradley argues that "I do not believe that a rich man's wallet is in free-speech terms the equivalent of a poor man's soapbox."† And an expert campaign finance lawyer discounts constitutional arguments and characterizes the contemporary system of campaign finance as "felonious bribery."‡

To what extent is it constitutionally permissible to regulate the campaign finance activities of interest groups? If the courts continue to strike down good faith efforts, should the Constitution be amended to allow regulation of campaign spending? Should some rights of speech and expression be sacrificed to ensure the integrity of the electoral process? How can we distinguish between constitutionally protected contributions to candidates who support the groups' viewpoint, and the tendering of illegitimate bribes? What are some basic principles that might help show where to draw such a line?

* For background on the constitutional issues that arise in campaign finance reform debates, see Beth Donovan, "Constitutional Issues Frame Congressional Options," *Congressional Quarterly Weekly Report*, February 27, 1993, 431–437.

† Adam Clymer, "Senate Kills Measure to Limit Spending in Congress Races," *New York Times*, June 26, 1996, A16.

‡ Daniel Lowenstein, "Political Bribery and the Intermediate Theory of Politics," *UCLA Law Review* 32(1985), 784–851.

up and say, "Hey, we noticed that you contributed to our opponent's campaign. The Congressman just wants you to know that there are no hard feelings. In fact, we're holding a fund-raiser in a few weeks; we hope you'll come and tell us your concerns."

Thus, influence runs in both directions; elected officials are not just pawns to be moved around by interest groups. Campaign finance is a big question and we will say more about it in later chapters.

PERSUADING THE PUBLIC

This interest group strategy overlaps somewhat with grassroots lobbying: The home school story was in one sense an example of interest groups persuading ordinary Americans that congressional actions directly threatened important interests. But many groups communicate with citizens even when no specific legislation or regulation is at issue. Their goal is to build general support for the group and its interests so that it will be more successful in the long run.

Thus, in the 1970s the Mobil Oil Corporation began paying to have columns printed on the Op-Ed page of the *New York Times*. Sometimes these were "advocacy ads" directed specifically at a government activity or proposed law, but more often they were what are now called "infomercials"—attempts to convey information and arguments favorable to business in general and the oil industry in particular.

One communications technique that is a product of modern electronic communications is **direct mail**.[36] Groups compile computerized mailing lists of people who might be favorably disposed to their leader or cause, then send out printed or computer-generated materials soliciting financial contributions. Often, the mailing

■ **direct mail**
Computer-generated letters, faxes, and other communications by a group to people who might be sympathetic to an appeal for money or support.

DIRECT MAIL

Both parties as well as groups from all points on the political spectrum make use of direct mail appeals. Computers generate lists of likely sympathizers who then receive mass-produced correspondence often of an inflammatory character. The appeal is designed to induce a strong response—often anger and anxiety—in the recipient and stimulate a contribution. Here is an excerpt from a pro-environmental group sent in response to congressional efforts to change the Endangered Species Act in 1997.

URGENT WILDLIFE ALERT

"What I should have done is repeal the whole Act... before anybody realized what had happened."

-Rep. Don Young (R-Alaska), Chairman, House Resources Committee, on his intention to eliminate the Endangered Species Act.

Thanks to your help, EDF prevented Don Young and his allies from destroying the Endangered Species Act in 1996.

But Don Young is back in Congress in 1997 with a brand new chance to fulfill his vow: to repeal the law that protects America's most imperiled wildlife. I need your help today to stop him!

Dear EDF Member,

Don Young is back ...

... and he's made no pretense about what he thinks of you and me and the Endangered Species Act that we so cherish.

He's called environmentalists a "self-centered ... Harvard-graduating, intellectual bunch of idiots." He even said, "they are my enemy. They are not Americans." And he doesn't hide his contempt for the Endangered Species Act.

Thanks to your support, EDF helped prevent Don Young from repealing the Endangered Species Act last year. We showed Congress how the Act can be improved and strengthened with steps like EDF's voluntary "Safe Harbor" plan, which gives landowners a new incentive to protect wildlife habitat.

But Don Young is back -- along with dozens of mining interests, oil companies, developers, land speculators, and agribusinesses who backed his anti-wildlife policies in 1996.

And with the Endangered Species Act once again up for reauthorization, we've got a whole new fight on our hands.

That's why I need your immediate help to gain the upper hand with the new 1997 Congress ... and win renewed support for EDF's acclaimed incentives to save wildlife!

Here's what I need you to do:

(over, please...)

Environmental Defense Fund • 257 Park Avenue South • New York, NY 10010

AFF-L   50% Recycled (20% Post-Consumer) Paper

First, I need you to "Cast Your Vote for Wildlife" -- by signing and returning the enclosed Wildlife Protection Ballot.

With your vote in hand, we'll be able to count you among the supporters of our innovative wildlife proposals, including:

·Economic incentives that will win the help of landowners in protecting wildlife on private property.

·Faster action when a species is first at risk -- which lowers the cost of wildlife protection and increases the chances of recovery.

·Clearer wildlife regulations that spell out rights and responsibilities in plain English.

EDF's approach is set out in a new study just featured on the cover of Science magazine, and in an EDF wildlife report called "Rebuilding the Ark," widely acclaimed in the media.

And with your help today, we'll press every new and veteran member of Congress to adopt our innovative Action Plan as they work on wildlife legislation.

I'm confident we'll muster bipartisan support, because we can point to success -- and voluntary landowner cooperation -- in pilot programs that are protecting thousands of acres for Red-cockaded woodpeckers, the Attwater's prairie chicken, and the Aplomado falcon.

But the clock is ticking: Despite the Act's protection, less than 10% of all listed species are known to be recovering ... and, for lack of resources, the Fish and Wildlife Service can't even tell how 30% of all listed species are faring today!

That's why I need you to sign and return your Wildlife Protection Ballot ... and please include a generous contribution that will help us turn our string of successes into the ultimate victory -- a new, improved, and more effective Endangered Species Act.

For the sake of more than 1,000 rare species of American wildlife -- please give generously today!

Sincerely,

Michael Bean
Michael Bean
EDF Wildlife Chairman

P.S. Our well-funded opponents are already maneuvering to influence upcoming Endangered Species legislation in the new 1997 Congress. Help us stop them -- reply today!

A Mobil Oil "infomercial."

■ **direct action**

Everything from peaceful sit-ins and demonstrations to riots and even rebellion.

exaggerates the threat the group faces in an attempt to scare or provoke the recipient into contributing. Some groups depend almost completely on direct mail fund-raising for their budgets. The citizens group, Common Cause, for example, prides itself on its dependence on small contributions.[37]

Finally, any group likes to have favorable media coverage for its activities and points of view. Thus, groups will be on the lookout for opportunities to get such coverage—to plant stories, to associate themselves with popular issues and candidates, and to position themselves as opponents of unpopular issues and candidates. The Center for Science in the Public Interest has received a great deal of media coverage for its exposés of the fat content of movie popcorn and Chinese food, of advertisements for baby foods, and of other colorful subjects. In sum, whether we call it public relations or education, communications with a wider audience is a significant concern for most interest groups.

DIRECT ACTION

As discussed in Chapter 2, the original thirteen colonies cast off British authority in a violent revolution, the constitutional convention was in part stimulated by Shay's Rebellion, and the newly established federal government was tested by the Whiskey Rebellion. But these early conflicts were by no means the end of **direct action** by citizens opposed to government policies. In 1859, John Brown led an abolitionist raiding party against the federal arsenal at Harper's Ferry, Virginia. Urban workers rioted against the Civil War draft in 1863. In the 1880s and 1890s, state or federal troops battled strikers from West Virginia to Idaho, and from Michigan to Texas. In 1932, more than 20 thousand veterans marched on Washington and were dispersed by federal troops. Protest—even violent protest—against social and economic conditions and related government policies is as American as apple pie.[38]

Seen against this background, the boycotts, sit-ins, marches and demonstrations by civil rights, antiwar, feminist, environmentalist, gay rights, pro-choice, pro-life, and other activists are just more recent examples of a long tradition—and for the most part mild ones at that. As these examples suggest, forms of direct action are often used by social movements, given that their members have previously not been organized and lack the access to power and the resources to use other strategies. Direct action typically is used in combination with attempts to persuade larger constituencies. The media—TV in particular—find direct action newsworthy, and thus communicate the protests to locales far beyond where they occur.

LITIGATION

As detailed in Chapter 17, the modern civil rights movement followed a careful legal strategy, selecting cases to litigate that eventually led to the landmark ruling in *Brown* v. *Board of Education of Topeka, Kansas*. Drawing lessons from the success of the civil rights movement, environmentalists, feminists, and advocates for the handicapped, poor people, and other groups followed suit.[39] But litigation strategies are by no means limited to groups ordinarily thought of as liberal. In the 1970s the Pacific Legal Foundation was set up to oppose environmental protection groups. The U.S. Chamber of Commerce established a National Chamber Litigation Center to support business interests in the courts. And the religious right founded the Christian Legal Society, which focuses on issues of church and state.[40] Liberal groups continue to be more active in the courts, perhaps because the past two decades have seen mostly Republican presidents who could effectively block liberal legislation.

In addition to actually litigating cases, which is an expensive activity, interest groups also engage in other activities intended to influence the course of litigation. While it is improper to directly lobby judges, groups do stage demonstrations in front of courthouses, generate letters and telegrams to judges, and file **amicus curiae** (a Latin term meaning "friend of the court") briefs in cases in which they are not otherwise directly involved.

amicus curiae
Latin term meaning "friend of the court." It refers to legal briefs submitted by interested groups who are not directly party to a court case.

WHY GROUPS USE PARTICULAR TACTICS

Different groups use different strategies or mixes of strategies. How they decide to allocate their resources depends both on their own characteristics and on the characteristics of the situation in which they are operating.

GROUP CHARACTERISTICS

How a group decides to deploy its resources depends on what kind of group it is, how much it has in the way of resources, and the kind of resources it has. A trade association representing profitable corporations will have a Washington office with a full-time staff of experts. This gives such associations the wherewithal to maintain close personal contact with government decision makers. A mass membership group may find grass-roots lobbying a more effective use of their resources. A public-interest law firm with no citizen membership will naturally follow a litigation strategy; indeed, the group may have been formed by lawyers precisely because they wished to engage in such activities. A social movement representing a disadvantaged constituency such as the poor may find that direct action is the only means of calling attention to their cause. Wealthy groups of any size or type may find campaign contributions and media campaigns to be useful investments.

Some suggest that groups with a federal structure—local chapters under a national leadership—may have a fund-raising advantage because members get solicited by people personally known to them rather than by an impersonal mailing. In addition, such groups have chapters in many communities and therefore are constituents of a large number of representatives, perhaps giving them an advantage in grassroots lobbying. Interest groups representing realtors, doctors, and banks are good examples.

In sum, size, composition, wealth, organizational structure, and other factors affect the activities in which groups engage; each group allocates its resources in the way that it considers most efficient.

SITUATIONAL CHARACTERISTICS

One of the reasons the civil rights movement adopted a litigation strategy was that more traditional strategies were unavailable. African Americans were disenfranchised in much of the South and politically discriminated against elsewhere. In the Congresses of the 1940s and 1950s the path of civil rights legislation was blocked by senior committee chairmen from the South. African Americans as a group were not wealthy, and they were a small minority of the population. By choosing to litigate, they made a virtue out of necessity. Then, as the movement expanded and gained support, it was able to engage in direct action and later, electioneering, to further advance its goals.

In contrast, an industry or corporation interested in the fine details of a bill or regulation probably will find it better to send an expert representative to discuss the matter with members of congress and their staff, or with regulators. In the former case, a campaign contribution may be a useful investment as well.

Direct mail and other modern advertising and persuasion techniques were developed largely by conservative groups, perhaps because Congress was controlled by Democrats who had little sympathy for their demands. Now that Congress is controlled by the Republicans, perhaps conservative groups are engaging in more direct lobbying. Conversely, having lost their access to the congressional leadership, liberal groups may be forced to shift their resources to alternative methods of influence.

In sum, various situational characteristics—party control of Congress and the presidency, the economic situation, the mood in the country, what your group seeks to achieve—interact with characteristics of interest groups to determine what mix of strategies is adopted.

How Influential Are Interest Groups?

The answer to this question is a matter of enormous disagreement. On the one hand, some critics believe that interest groups dominate American politics. One critic charges that the United States suffers from demosclerosis, a condition in which interest groups clog the veins and arteries of the body politic.[41] Another claims that Americans have the best Congress money can buy.[42] Certainly the number of groups, the volume of their activities, and their massive expenditure of resources amount to strong circumstantial evidence that groups and associations are very influential in politics.

On the other hand, academic research reaches less clear conclusions. Indeed, some of the most expert students of interest group politics contend that a great deal of what groups do is cancelled out.[43] There are so many groups, and so many *opposed* groups, that the efforts of one association's high-priced lobbyist only offset the efforts of another's, one group's media campaign only counteracts the effects of another's, one group's direct mail barrage only cancels out the effects of another's, and so forth.

Also, it is likely that particular interests were more influential in the past than most individual interests are today. The reason is that changes in American politics have undermined the classic "subgovernments" that were dominated by particular interests.

SUBGOVERNMENTS

Observers of American politics in the 1940s and 1950s developed the subgovernment model as a common pattern of policy making in America.[44] In the idealized **subgovernment**, policy was largely determined by three collective actors working hand in hand. A congressional committee provided an executive agency with program authorization and budgetary support, the agency produced outcomes favored by the interest group constituency, and the interest groups provided campaign contributions and votes to the members of the congressional committee. Agriculture, public works, and business regulation were viewed as policy areas dominated by subgovernments. In the most extreme cases, subgovernments were called "iron tri-

■ **subgovernment**
A congressional committee, bureaucratic agency, and a few allied interest groups who combine to dominate policy making in some specified policy area.

angles" (see Chapter 14) in recognition of the difficulty faced by outsiders who wished to influence the decisions of a powerful subgovernment.

The subgovernment model assigns to interest groups an important, if not dominant, role in the policy process. Interests control what members of Congress most need—electoral support—and provide it if the agencies controlled by Congress provide what the interest groups need—favorable policies.

Whatever their importance in the past, subgovernments are less important today. First, as we recount in Chapter 12, Congress has changed. The party caucuses and leadership are stronger and the committees weaker; particular committees no longer have strangleholds on their jurisdictions. Second, there are many more groups now, including many who oppose other groups. In particular, citizens groups representing consumers, environmentalists, and taxpayers are much more active now than they were a half-century ago. They oppose the excesses of special-interest politics and publicize their opposition. Third, as we discuss in Chapter 9, the media are different today. In particular, they are very much on the lookout for stories of special-interest profiteering at the expense of general interests. In the spring of 1996, for example, the media helped kill a quiet attempt by the House Agriculture Committee to aid milk producers in raising prices by burying a helpful regulation in the agriculture bill then under consideration. Dan Rather discussed the "attempted rip-off of the consumer" on his evening news program, and in the wake of the publicity, the attempt collapsed.[45] Subgovernments thrived when they operated quietly, behind the scenes; they shrivel in the glare of publicity.

ISSUE NETWORKS

In the view of many scholars, subgovernments have been superseded by **issue networks**—bigger, broader, and much looser connections of interest groups, politicians, bureaucrats, and policy experts who have a particular interest in or responsibility for a policy area.[46] Given the enormous number and variety of interest groups today, the proliferation of legislative staff and other policy experts, and the interactions between policies in one area with those in another, issue networks are much more open than subgovernments, and much less stable in their composition. In the network model, interests are only one type of actor—competing with elected and appointed officials and experts for influence on public policy.

The academic consensus today clearly leans toward the network model, but not everyone agrees with the consensus, or with each other. On the one hand, some scholars suggest that even the term "network" may exaggerate the degree of organization that characterizes interest group activity in Washington today.[47] But on the other hand, some scholars suggest that the demise of many traditional subgovernments should not make us overlook the influence of organized interests in new policy areas like energy and social regulation. They go so far as to characterize the role of organized interests in these areas as "quasi-corporatist" and "neocorporatist," a reference to European **corporatist** systems in which important interest groups are given official representation in government decision-making bodies.[48] In short, judgments about the general importance of interest groups remain as divided as ever.

Probably the safest conclusion about the influence of interest groups is that influence is conditional: It ranges from weak to strong, depending on the conditions under which groups try to influence politics. Schlozman and Tierney conclude that groups are most influential when they act on low-profile issues, when they attempt to block action rather than originate it, when they are unopposed by other groups or politicians, and when they have plentiful resources.[49] Once again, the real world of American democracy is more complicated than many popular commentators suggest.

■ **issue networks**
A looser constellation of larger numbers of committees, agencies, and interest groups active in a particular policy area.

■ **corporatist**
The official representation of large interest groups in government decision-making bodies.

In the summer of 1983, Ronald Reagan was not a sure bet for reelection. The country was coming out of a serious recession and most of the robust economic growth of Reagan's first term was yet to come. Moreover, the frontrunner for the Democratic nomination was former Senator and Vice President Walter "Fritz" Mondale. Mondale was experienced, respected, and widely regarded as one of the bright spots of the Carter Administration. As the primary season approached, the Mondale campaign busied itself by piling up endorsements from all the groups associated with the Democratic Party.*

Mondale was endorsed by the American Federation of Teachers, the National Organization for Women, and the AFL-CIO. Civil rights groups came out in favor of their long-time ally. Environmental groups and peace groups offered their support, as did newer groups representing other ethnic minorities, and gays. The party's elected officials were solidly behind Mondale. By the start of the primary season, the race for the nomination looked to be all but over.

Such impressions proved wrong. Mondale stumbled badly; indeed, the Mondale bandwagon came perilously close to going off the road. Gary Hart did better than expected in the Iowa caucuses, and, on the strength of the momentum developed there, beat Mondale in New Hampshire. Hart won in Maine, Wyoming, and Vermont, and for a brief time became the front-runner. Finally, Mondale staunched the bleeding with crucial primary victories in Alabama and Georgia. He recovered to win the nomination, but as a humbled and damaged candidate. Reagan buried him in November.

Mondale's endorsement strategy played right into a criticism increasingly leveled at the Democratic Party in the early 1980s—that it had become a party of "special interests." Critics did not mean economic special interests—except for labor unions—but social and cultural special interests represented by liberals, minorities, feminists, welfare recipients, environmentalists, the handicapped, and so forth. While many viewed Mondale's support for

Evaluations of Interest Groups in Politics

Even the generic term *interest group* has a negative connotation, and terms like *pressure group*, *vested interest*, and *special interest* have pronounced negative connotations.[50] Why do contemporary Americans hold interest groups in such low regard? After all, the Constitution protects the rights of citizens to form groups and attempt to influence the government. Consider that the First Amendment not only guarantees freedom of religion, speech, and the press, it also prohibits any law abridging the "right of the people peaceably to assemble and to petition the government for a redress of grievances." Americans have availed themselves of that right since the very beginning of the republic.

Political scientists generally have not held interest groups in as low regard as ordinary citizens. In fact, one mid-century school of thought, **pluralism**, assigned groups to a central place in American politics.[51] The pluralists believed that Amer-

■ **pluralism**
A school of thought holding that politics is the clash of groups that represent all important interests in society and check and balance each other.

these groups as deserved, they attacked him for having no larger vision for America. One of his primary opponents, Senator John Glenn, asked "Will we offer a party that can't say no to anyone with a letterhead and a mailing list?" Mondale underlined the criticism when he gave in to the public demand of the National Organization for Women (NOW) that he choose a woman vice presidential candidate.

Hart portrayed Mondale as a representative of the "old politics." He appealed to a younger, more educated segment of the population that was liberal on social issues, but increasingly skeptical of big government. In November, a third of Hart's primary supporters voted for Reagan.[†]

Some Democrats were well aware that the party had an image problem. Finally, Edward Kennedy (D-MA) a senator with impeccable liberal credentials, felt it necessary to face the harmful public perception squarely. In a widely reported speech he appealed to fellow Democrats:

> As Democrats we must understand that there's a difference between being a party that cares about labor and being a labor party. There's a difference between being a party that cares about women and being a women's party, and we can and must be a party that cares about minorities without being a minority party. We are citizens first and constituencies second.[‡]

In the late 1980s, some Democrats began an organized effort to position the party closer to broad middle-class interests. In 1992, candidate Bill Clinton kept his campaign focused on the national economy, and deliberately picked fights with some of the party's traditional constituency groups. In November he ended the party's twelve-year exile from the White House.

* The following account is based on the essays in Austin Ranney, ed., *The American Elections of 1984* (Durham, NC: Duke University Press, 1985); and Gerald Pomper, ed., *The Election of 1984* (Chatham NJ: Chatham House Publishers, 1985).

† CBS/NYT exit poll, *New York Times*, November 8, 1984: A19.

‡ *New York Times*, March 31, 1985: A24.

ican politics consists of an interplay of numerous interests. Groups compose a dense network in which virtually everyone is represented; no single interest is dominant, and all are required to bargain and compromise. And groups exercise countervailing power; if one interest or set of interests becomes too powerful, others mobilize to counteract it. As a consequence, public policies tend to be moderate and to change incrementally. Thus, the system tends toward an equilibrium that is representative of the broad range of interests in the country.

Pluralism is out of fashion today. Critics find several problems in the pluralist account. We have already discussed the first—the unrepresentativeness of the interest group universe. As critic E.E. Schattschneider once observed, "The flaw in the pluralist heaven is that the heavenly chorus sings with a strong upper class accent"[52] Because of the free rider problem, small special interests have an advantage over large general interests. In particular, economic groups procure narrow economic benefits at the expense of the broader population of consumers and taxpayers. An implicit recognition of this fact is probably one reason the term *interest group* has negative connotations in the popular mind; people see that most groups do not represent the general interests of Americans.

A second objection to the pluralist account is that even if the interest groups were more representative, the interest of the whole nation is not equal to the sum of the interests of the parts. In our discussion of public opinion, we pointed out that majorities of Americans want to cut government spending and reduce government regulation, but majorities oppose specific cuts and reductions. If Congress heeds the wishes of the individual constituencies, it will displease the entire country by maintaining a bigger budget and more intrusive government than a majority desires.

Thus, simply adding up group interests is not enough. Ideally, politics must harmonize and synthesize particular interests and incorporate them into the general interest of the nation. For example, if the government erected a system of trade barriers to protect every American industry from foreign competition, the result would be retaliation against American exports, higher prices for consumers, and slower economic growth, if not worse. As Schattschneider long ago pointed out, a Congress operating according to pluralist principles enacted just such a trade policy in 1930—the Smoot-Hawley tariff—a policy that deepened and lengthened the Great Depression.[53] A more contemporary example is provided by the Democratic party, which in the 1980s became associated in the popular mind with special interests, and suffered electorally because of it (see Election Connection).

A third criticism of pluralism is that a politics dominated by interest groups distorts political discussion and ultimately the political process. The reason is that group processes reinforce extremism and undercut moderation. To explain, ordinary citizens have multiple attachments and affiliations, which generally serve to moderate their outlooks. For example, a retired couple might naturally favor higher Social Security and Medicare expenditures. But if they also are parents and grandparents, they might oppose higher benefits for themselves if the result is higher taxes on their children, or lower government expenditures on their grandchildren's schools. Leaders of interest groups, in contrast, are **fiduciaries**—people whose duty is to act in someone else's interest. Typically they see their job as the maximization of group benefits. Thus, the leadership of a senior citizens group will be more supportive of higher benefits for the elderly than will many of its members. For example, AARP has been attacked as an organization composed of "tax-loving former teachers and government employees" who favor an "age-based welfare state."[54] The attack was levied by the National Taxpayers Union, an opposing interest group concerned with taxes.

This crowding out of moderate demands by more extreme ones is reinforced by the tendency of group activists and leaders to be more zealous in their views and more committed to group goals than nonmembers, or even rank-and-file members. Thus, they will push their demands beyond the point where ordinary members and sympathizers would stop. Activist supporters of the ERA agreed with the charges of the opponents that it would send women into combat on the same basis as men: "combat duty, horrendous as it might seem to all of us, must be assigned to persons on a gender-neutral basis."[55] Most American women and men preferred something less than such full equality. Today, environmental groups speak of a world on the brink of desolation, while their opponents scoff about imaginary threats. The minorities on the extremes of the pro-choice and pro-life debate polarize the debate and drown out the three-quarters of the population who could satisfactorily compromise it. And the Home School Legal Defense Fund accuses Congress of a "nuclear attack" on home schoolers.

fiduciaries
Someone whose duty is to act in the best interest of someone else.

GROUP LEADERS VERSUS OTHERS

The active members of groups and the leaders drawn from them tend to be more extreme in their viewpoints than nonmembers of groups. Since "extreme" is a subjective judgment, a particularly useful way of illustrating such a claim is to compare the views of group leaders with the views of other experts on the issues of interest to the group. A recent study compares the views of 100 top leaders in environmental groups with the views of scientific experts.* Among other things, both sets of people were asked to rate various cancer risks on a 1–10 scale, with ten being the highest. The results are shown below.

As shown, relative to expert judgments, environmentalists systematically overstate the risks of cancer from environmental causes. In a few cases—dioxin, EDBs, DDT—the views of environmentalists are strikingly more extreme than those of scientists.

	Environmentalists	Scientists
Dioxin	8.1	3.7
Asbestos	7.8	6.5
EDB	7.3	4.2
DDT	6.7	3.8
Pollution	6.6	4.7
Dietary fat	6.0	5.4
Food additives	5.3	3.2
Nuclear power	4.6	2.5
Saccharin	3.7	1.6

* Stanley Rothman and S. Robert Lichter, "Environmental Cancer: A Political Disease," *Annals of the New York Academy of Sciences* 775(1996):234–235.

In the end, the general interests of a moderate population can get lost amid the bitter fighting of intense and extreme special interests. No one can deny that groups have a useful and legitimate role to play in articulating the interests of all components of American society, but many feel that groups somehow must be constrained. One of the first pluralists, James Madison, thought factions could be constrained by creating the extended republic, as he explained in *The Federalist, no. 10*. He seems either not to have foreseen or to have underestimated several modern developments.

First is the tremendous expansion of society that contributed to the explosion of groups. The range of interests active today probably would shock someone like Madison, who thought in terms of broad interests like land, labor and commerce, debtors and creditors. Second is the prevalence of logrolling. Rather than check and balance each other, interest groups often cooperate, forming alliances and coalitions to exploit the general interests of consumers and taxpayers by getting higher prices and tax breaks.[56] Logrolling among interests is facilitated by a third development, the rise of professional politicians who, in seeking reelection, broker the group deals in return for the electoral support that interest groups provide.

But what can be done? As the critics look over the experience of democratic governments, they see only one means of controlling group demands that is both democratic and effective. Ironically, it is the institution that George Washington warned the country about—political parties, the subject of the next chapter.

Chapter Summary

Only half the American citizenry votes in presidential elections, and only small minorities engage in other forms of political participation. But most Americans participate indirectly in politics by joining groups that attempt to influence government. In fact, Americans are more likely to participate indirectly through groups than are citizens of other democracies who vote at higher levels.

There has been a major increase in the number of interest groups in the past generation. Successful groups have found ways to overcome the free rider problem—the tendency of people not to join groups if they feel their contribution to group success is too small to matter. Some of the groups rely on selective benefits that are available only to group members, while others depend on the efforts of dedicated or wealthy members who will bear more than a proportionate share of the costs of group maintenance. Some of the groups grew out of social movements composed of morally or emotionally committed members. Still others are not really groups, but rather are the representatives of one or two major members who believe that maintaining a political arm is a sound investment.

Group characteristics and their situations lead them to adopt a variety of political strategies. Grassroots lobbying involves attempts to influence elected officials indirectly by mobilizing constituents, while traditional lobbying involves attempts to influence elected officials directly by speaking personally to them. Increasingly, groups engage in electioneering—contributing money to candidates, or spending money independently to elect officials favorable to their interests and views. Groups also attempt to persuade or educate the public, and some resort to direct action—demonstrations, protests, and the like—to call attention to their positions. Finally, some groups end-run the political process and attempt to influence government through the courts.

Despite extensive study of interest groups, there is wide disagreement about how influential they are. In general, popular commentators view them as more powerful than academic researchers. There is no doubt that groups engage in an incredible amount of political activity, and invest an impressive quantity of money and other resources, but it is difficult to say how effective they are. For every issue that appears to show that interest groups dominated the decision, skeptics can cite another issue where interest groups seemed to be ineffectual or offsetting.

Although interest group activity is constitutionally protected, many worry about its effects. First, special interests are better represented than general interests. Second, even if that were not so, the best interest of the nation as a whole is not merely the sum of the best interests of the particular parts. Third, interest groups overrepresent the more extreme positions in the political debate, and thus polarize political discussion and make the political process needlessly conflictual.

Key Terms

Suggested Readings

Heinz, John, Edward Laumann, Robert Nelson, and Robert Salisbury. *The Hollow Core: Private Interests in National Policy Making.* Cambridge, MA: Harvard University Press, 1993. The most recent major study of the Washington interest group scene. Principal focus is on the characteristics and activities of group representatives and lobbyists.

Hertzke, Allen. *Representing God in Washington.* Knoxville, TN: University of Tennessee Press, 1988. Informative study of lobbying activities of religious groups, including, but not limited to members of the Christian right.

Lowi, Theodore. *The End of Liberalism.* New York: Norton, 1969. Noted critique of "interest group liberalism." Argues that a government of laws has been superseded by a process of bargaining between organized groups and public officials.

Mansbridge, Jane. *Why We Lost the ERA.* Chicago: University of Chicago Press, 1986. Thoughtful discussion of the narrow failure of the women's movement to win passage of the ERA. Argues that the movement overcame the free rider problem by emphasizing the symbolism of the ERA, a strategy that precluded compromises that might have won passage of a weaker version.

Moe, Terry. *The Organization of Interests.* Chicago: University of Chicago Press, 1980. Stimulating discussion of strategies used by political entrepreneurs for organizing and maintaining groups, and the internal politics of groups.

Petracca, Mark, ed. *The Politics of Interests.* Boulder, CO: Westview Press, 1992. Collection of current essays describing and assessing the activities of interest groups in American politics.

Schattschneider, E.E. *The Semi-Sovereign People.* New York: Holt, Rinehart and Winston, 1960. A delightful essay that remains timely. Argues that the pressure system is biased and the result is an artificially constricted range of political conflict in the United States.

Schlozman, Kay, and John Tierney. *Organized Interests and American Democracy.* New York: Harper & Row, 1981. Comprehensive study of the Washington interest group universe circa 1980, as well as its expansion in the 1960s and 1970s.

Sorauf, Frank. *Inside Campaign Finance.* New Haven: Yale University Press, 1992. Thoughtful, balanced and relatively optimistic discussion of contemporary campaign finance.

Truman, David. *The Governmental Process.* New York: Knopf, 1951. Classic interpretation of American democracy as composed of the interplay of interest groups.

Walker, Jack. *Mobilizing Interest Groups in America.* Ann Arbor: University of Michigan Press, 1991. Describes the state of the Washington interest group universe. Noted for discussion of outside support for establishment of groups.

Vote for
One Party

3 ▶
4 ◀
5

BILL CLINTON   for President
AL GORE   for Vice President   Reform

ROSS PEROT   for President
JAMES CAMPBELL   for Vice President   American
                                                Independent

HOWARD PHILLIPS   for President
HERBERT W. TITUS   for Vice President   Libertarian

HARRY BROWNE   for President
JO JORGENSEN   for Vice President   Natural Law

JOHN HAGELIN   for President
MIKE TOMPKINS   for Vice President   Green

RALPH NADER   for President
WINONA LADUKE   for Vice President   Peace &
                                                Freedo

MARSHA FEINLAND   for President
KATE McCLATCHY   for Vice President   Repu

BOB DOLE   for President
JACK KEMP   for Vice President   TURN PAGE TO C

8

political parties

WHEN GEORGE WASHINGTON
left office in 1796, he took the
opportunity to warn his fellow
citizens " ... in the most solemn
manner against the baneful
effects of the spirit of party ...
It agitates the community with
ill-founded jealousies and false
alarms, kindles the animosity of
one part against another,
foments occasional riot and
insurrection." Washington's

warning came too late—the spirit of party already was loose, never to be confined again. Treasury Secretary Alexander Hamilton's ambitious policies—a national bank, federal assumption of the states' revolutionary war debts, and a generally active federal government—produced deep divisions within the Congress, and foreign policy problems encountered by the young republic reinforced these economic and philosophical divisions. Support for Hamilton's program was strongest in New England. It was generally endorsed by commercial interests, and by those philosophically in favor of strong government under a strong executive. By the end of Washington's first term, critics of Hamilton vilified him and his followers as monarchists, Royalists, and British sympathizers.

Opposition to Hamilton was strongest in the South and West, especially among agrarian interests (many of whom were particularly outraged by Hamilton's tax on whiskey). Those philosophically averse to a strong executive also gravitated to the opposition, which was centered in the Virginia congressional delegation led by James Madison. Already called the Madison Party by 1796, Madison and his followers were maligned as Democrats, Jacobins, and French sympathizers. Both Hamilton's and Madison's embryonic parties had their own newspapers (p. 267), which they used to revile each other.[1]

In 1796, John Adams, Washington's vice president, won the presidency. Thomas Jefferson, Washington's secretary of state, came in second in the electoral college voting and thus became the new vice president. Over the course of the next few years, Jefferson and Madison laid the foundations of a new electoral alliance. Jefferson, who regularly glorified the "yeoman farmer," began to reach out to urban interests. In 1800, he and Madison concluded an alliance with the New York Republicans under Governor George Clinton and New York City political operative Aaron Burr. By all accounts a superb organizer, Burr delivered the New York legislature, which chose the presidential electors. New York's twelve electors were the key to the election—Jefferson and Burr finished only eight votes ahead of President Adams.

Thus, within eight years of the adoption of the Constitution, a two-party presidential race had been fought. While the Constitution contains not a word about political parties, they have been active in U.S. national politics almost since the founding. Indeed, some historians claim that the individual colonies had parties even earlier.[2]

■ **political parties**
Groups of like-minded people who band together in an attempt to take control of government.

he simple fact is that all modern democracies have parties. Traditionally defined as groups of like-minded people who band together in an attempt to take control of government, **political parties** dominate the connections between ordinary citizens and the public officials they elect. They nominate candidates for office, they help government administer the electoral process, and they mobilize voters. And after elections have determined the winners, parties also coordinate the actions of elected officials in the government. This chapter examines in greater detail what parties do and how they operate. It also provides an overview of how parties have dominated the electoral history of the United States.

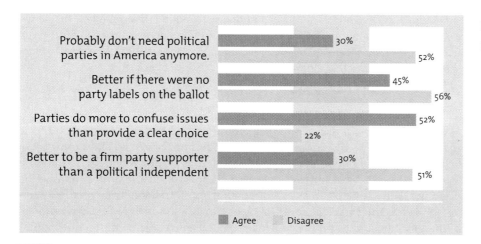

FIGURE 8.1

Public Opinion Toward Parties

Probably don't need political parties in America anymore. — 30% / 52%

Better if there were no party labels on the ballot — 45% / 56%

Parties do more to confuse issues than provide a clear choice — 52% / 22%

Better to be a firm party supporter than a political independent — 30% / 51%

■ Agree   Disagree

What Parties Do

To most political commentators in other advanced self-governed societies, democracy is unimaginable without parties. The European University Institute, a social science research arm of the European Community, recently published a four-volume study on political parties. The study contains such observations as

Political parties have been considered the central institutions of democratic governments at least since the enfranchisement of the working class.[3]

Competitive party systems of government have the special feature of being strongly associated with the values of liberal democracy or perhaps more accurately, to be regarded as its working mechanism.[4]

For contemporary Americans, assertions like these are not self-evident. Americans are more likely to regard representative assemblies as the central institutions of democratic government, and they associate the courts most closely with the values of liberal democracy. Americans inhabit a political world that contains nonpartisan local elections, the initiative, referendum and recall, town meetings, an independent judiciary, and other nonparty institutions that are viewed as important components of democracy. Not surprisingly, when asked directly about parties, most Americans do not sing their praises, and many Americans are more or less indifferent about parties.[5] Indeed, as shown in Figure 8.1, many Americans respond that things would be better if there were none.

In contrast to voters and reformers, many American professors hold views of parties similar to the views of the European professors quoted above. E. E. Schattschneider, for example, devoted much of his life to making the case for the vital role played by political parties. In introducing his classic work, *Party Government*, he wrote: "This volume is devoted to the thesis that political parties created democracy and that modern democracy is unthinkable save in terms of the parties."[6]

HOW PARTIES CONTRIBUTE TO DEMOCRATIC POLITICS

Why are parties so important? What do parties do that make most Europeans and some Americans think they are essential for democratic government? Why could a healthy democracy not have a nonpartisan politics that relied on the activities of individuals and groups? The general answer is that, except at the local level, such a polity would be too disorganized to operate. Politicians create parties to *organize* political life, and they do so by carrying on a series of activities.[7]

ORGANIZING AND OPERATING THE GOVERNMENT

Often Congress is criticized for being disorganized and slow to move. Imagine what it would be like if there were no party leaders or caucuses! Parties bring some degree of coordination to hundreds, indeed thousands, of public officials. At each level of government, executives count on the support of their fellow partisans in the legislature, and legislators trust the information given to them by their fellow partisans in the executive branch. Parties also coordinate across the levels of government, as when Democratic governors convinced some Democratic members of Congress that they should support far-reaching welfare reform proposals in 1995. Similarly, local officials appeal to their partisan allies in the state governments, and the latter appeal to their partisan allies in Congress. However disorderly American government often appears, many believe it would be absolutely chaotic without parties.

FOCUSING RESPONSIBILITY FOR GOVERNMENT ACTION

Beyond shared views on policy issues, a major motivation for politicians to cooperate is summed up in Benjamin Franklin's observation that "we must all hang together, or most assuredly we will all hang separately." Franklin was exhorting colonial representatives to maintain unity or literally be hanged as traitors, and the analogue for parties is the need to maintain unity or suffer electorally. Sharing the same label, party members correctly believe that they will be held to account for their *collective* performance.[8] This, in turn, gives them an incentive to fashion a party record that can be defended at the polls. After the Democrats won full control of national government in 1992, many Democratic members of Congress suspended their own reservations and supported President Clinton's policies because they believed they had to demonstrate to the country that the Democratic Party could govern. Similarly,

The new Republican majority in the 104th Congress rode into office on what Newt Gingrich had called a "Contract with America" —a platform of promised legislative reform and policy initiatives that they felt would show the party's commitment to change.

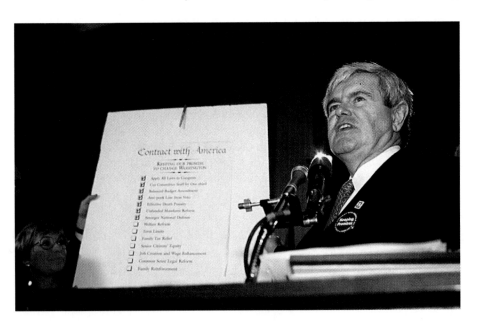

after the elections of 1994, many Republican members of Congress suspended their own reservations and supported the Contract with America because they believed in the importance of their campaign theme: "Promises made, promises kept."

DEVELOPING ISSUES AND EDUCATING THE PUBLIC

Parties engage in a continual struggle for control of public offices, and they develop public issues as weapons in this struggle. They identify problems, publicize them, and advance possible solutions. Much of their motivation is political, of course, and the process is adversarial—somewhat like a court proceeding in which the opposing lawyers present their cases. But the competitive struggle for power generates information, educates the public, and shapes the policy agenda. Where parties are weak, as in the American South during the first half of the twentieth century, politics degenerates, taking on a more personal quality as factions contend for private benefits.[9]

SYNTHESIZING INTERESTS

Earlier (p. 226) we discussed how good public policy in a large, diverse republic must be more than the sum of the demands of individuals and groups. For one thing, some interests conflict; they cannot be simultaneously satisfied but must be compromised in some way. For another thing, satisfying every specific interest may detract from the general interest; granting every individual's spending demand can lead to deficits, inflation, high interest rates, and other national costs. Thus, translating societal demands into public policy must go beyond simple addition to a more difficult and subtle kind of synthesizing or harmonizing of those demands. Because parties compete nationwide, they have incentives to offer platforms that offer a mix of benefits and burdens to all in the hope that a larger good will be the result. When they fail to do so, they suffer electorally. Thus, in 1984 the Democrats suffered because their platform was widely viewed as little more than a series of deals with interest groups (p. 224). Similarly, in 1996, Republicans suffered because groups like the religious right and the NRA were able to demand more extreme commitments than the bulk of the citizenry preferred.

RECRUITING AND DEVELOPING GOVERNMENTAL TALENT

There is an old adage in politics: "You can't beat somebody with nobody." Even if an elected official appears vulnerable, voters may continue that incumbent in office unless offered a plausible alternative—someone with the background and qualifications to hold the office.[10] Thus, parties are always on the lookout for promising candidates. They keep track of the weak links in the opposition and bring along potential replacements in their own ranks. Like predators in the natural environment, parties help to maintain the quality of public officials by weeding out the weak.

SIMPLIFYING THE ELECTORAL SYSTEM

Imagine that there were no parties to winnow the field of candidates. Rather than choosing between two candidates for most offices, voters might be faced with many. Rather than being elected with majority support, the winner of, say, a five-candidate race might be elected by a plurality consisting of as little as 21 percent of the vote. Furthermore, the larger set of candidates would not run with party labels. Although neither major party is completely homogeneous, the labels "Democrat"

Imagine there were no parties to winnow the field of candidates!

and "Republican" nonetheless convey a good bit of information—representing all that some voters use. In the absence of parties, the information costs imposed on voters would multiply manyfold.

How Parties Detract
from Democratic Politics

Despite these valuable organizational functions that political parties can perform, Americans are traditionally suspicious of parties and, since the end of the nineteenth century, have held them in relatively low esteem. There are two general reasons why this is so.

First, that parties *can* perform valuable functions is no guarantee that they *will* perform valuable functions. Politicians do not organize parties because they want to simplify the electoral system, recruit talent, or synthesize interests for their own sake; rather, they are interested in doing these things only insofar as such activities further their chances of winning power and implementing their preferred policies.[11] *Those who organize and operate parties are motivated primarily by the desire to achieve their own political ends.* In particular, the motives for forming parties are primarily electoral: Prospective public officials believe that forming a party will advance their chances of winning office. Thomas Jefferson used a new party that came to be called the Democratic-Republican party, to wrest power from the Federalists. Abraham Lincoln and others used the new Republican party to overthrow the Democratic majority. Theodore Roosevelt established the Bull Moose party because he could not win the nomination of the Republican Party.

Once in office, public officials devote effort to maintaining their parties because parties help them to govern by uniting members behind a single program. Andrew Jackson used the spoils of victory to consolidate his party's majority, as did the Republicans in the aftermath of the Civil War. Franklin Roosevelt used New Deal policies to strengthen the Democratic party in electorally critical local areas.[12] Ronald Reagan actively supported efforts to strengthen the Republican national party, an endeavor that left the Democrats far behind during the 1980s.

While party leaders understandably may view their partisan activities as furthering the public interest, their opponents seldom will agree. For this reason there will always be a natural minority critical of party dominance—namely, the members of the party that is out of power.

But even partisans of the winning party may be critical of parties, for there is a second important reason for the relative unpopularity of parties. Party influence is a double-edged sword: Parties strong enough to perform the functions discussed above are also strong enough to abuse their power. Each of the positive functions that parties can perform can be corrupted and, unfortunately, American history provides numerous such examples.

DICTATING WHAT GOVERNMENTS DO

At a certain point, coordination becomes control. A strong party that controls its component members can become the equivalent of an elected dictatorship, a charge the Progressives leveled at the urban machines that dominated many American cities a century ago (p. 246). While continuing to face periodic elections, the machines kept a stranglehold on office by the calculated distribution of jobs, contracts, and other patronage. Such private payoffs purchased party control over public policy.

CONFUSING RESPONSIBILITY

Because credit for good times and blame for bad times are valuable political currencies, the parties attempt to "manufacture" responsibility. Incumbent administrations are blamed for things they have no control over, just as they, in turn, take credit for things not of their making. Worse, rather than helping to solve a public problem, opposition parties may deliberately act to undercut the governing party's attempts at solution, as the Republicans did with President Clinton's health care plan in 1994, and the Democrats did with the Republican plan to control entitlement spending in 1995. The temptation to torpedo the other party's initiatives is especially strong when **divided government** exists—when one party holds the presidency but does not control Congress. Under such conditions, parties can obstruct action, blaming each other for the failure of government to act, and voters are understandably unsure of who really is responsible.[13] In short, parties often put their own electoral welfare over the good of the nation.

■ **divided government**
Said to exist when a single party does not control the presidency and both houses of Congress.

SUPPRESSING THE ISSUES

For various reasons, parties may choose not to develop new issues. Perhaps the leadership of both parties has grown out of touch and fails to appreciate new developments in society. Or perhaps the internal harmony of parties is threatened by new issues: The parties suppressed the slavery issue during the first half of the nineteenth century, and the Democrats continued to suppress issues of racial equality in the first half of the twentieth. More generally, many historians attribute the periodic eruptions of third parties to popular frustration with the parties' refusal to deal with important issues. Ross Perot's support in the 1992 election came disproportionately from voters concerned about the deficit who believed that neither the Republicans nor the Democrats would do much about it.[14]

Before-and-after views of Sonny Bono: from his heyday as half of Sonny and Cher, and as a U.S. representative from the state of California.

DIVIDING SOCIETY

Rather than synthesize disparate interests into some larger whole, parties may do just the opposite. Seeking electoral advantage, they act divisively, creating or exacerbating cleavages and conflicts among citizens—as Washington warned two centuries ago. During the 1980s, Democrats charged that Republican campaigns subtly inflamed racial resentments. We agree with that charge. For their part, Republicans charged that Democrats divided the country by catering to disparate groups—African Americans, Hispanics, gays, feminists, labor—and had no vision of a larger society. We agree with that charge too.

RECRUITING HACKS AND CELEBRITIES

In theory, parties nominate seasoned members with long experience in office. In practice, parties have often nominated unqualified party hacks. For every Lincoln there was a Garfield, for every Roosevelt a Harding. Moreover, in modern media and money-driven electoral politics, parties increasingly recruit celebrities—NBA (Rep. Tom McMillan, Sen. Bill Bradley) and NFL (Rep. Jack Kemp) players, major league pitchers (Rep. Jim Bunning), movie actors (Sen. Fred Thompson), entertainers (Rep. Fred Grandy, Rep. Sonny Bono), astronauts (Sen. John Glenn, Sen. Harrison Schmitt), and the wealthy (Sen. Herbert Kohl). Well known? Yes. Qualified? Sometimes.

OVERSIMPLIFYING THE ELECTORAL SYSTEM

The voter who must choose between two candidates, one labeled Democrat, one labeled Republican, has a clearer and apparently easier choice than the voter who can choose among many candidates with no labels. But what if she doesn't like that clear but restricted choice? What if she is a pro-choice Republican or a pro-life Democrat? That's just tough. If there are only two parties, she has only two alternatives to choose between. Her choice may be simple, but quite unsatisfactory.

THE BALANCE SHEET

In sum, parties can perform valuable functions, but they also can fail to perform them or even undercut the performance of those functions. Whether they contribute positively or negatively depends on how they see their electoral interest.

Scholars value parties because they *can* make very useful contributions to democratic politics and government. Moreover, when evaluating party performance scholars generally do not examine parties in the abstract; rather, they usually use the standard "relative to having no parties." Even if a party is performing poorly, what's the alternative? Reformers, on the other hand, see that parties often *do not* make useful contributions, and indeed, often abuse their power and detract from democratic government and politics. Moreover, reformers generally apply absolute standards, failing to ask whether there is an alternative institution that could replace parties and do a superior job.

Parties are among the most frequent targets of reform in American politics and, in the view of long-time observers like Austin Ranney and Nelson Polsby, such reforms are often misconceived.[15] In our view, an important reason for such inappropriate reforms is that reformers overlook the reasons that aspiring politicians form and maintain parties. Reformers fail to appreciate that parties will inevitably behave in accord with their political interests. Attempting to force parties to behave contrary to their interests often leads either to reforms that don't work, or to so-called unintended consequences, or both.

Political Parties in American History

Contemporary Americans' comparative lack of enthusiasm for parties is somewhat ironic given that the United States pioneered the mass parties that are such an essential component of politics in modern Europe. When Washington issued his warning, his concern was directed at the political activities of elites, specifically, the followers of leaders like Hamilton and Madison within the national government. Such personal followings or "factions" were the democratic analogue of the "court" parties of monarchical governments—the groups of nobles who engaged in "palace intrigues" (and sometimes paid with their lives for their "treasonous" plotting).

American parties did not stay limited to the Washington elites for very long. During the administration of Andrew Jackson (1828–1836) the Democratic party spread outward from Washington and downward into the grass roots, a movement soon imitated by its adversaries, the Whigs. The kind of mass parties that were contesting American elections by the 1840s and 1850s did not become common in Europe until the end of the nineteenth century. As late as 1889 the famous English political commentator, Lord Bryce, could observe that "In America the great moving forces are the parties. The government counts for less than in Europe, the parties count for more."[16] Today, of course, the first part of the statement remains true: The government counts for less than in Europe—in the sense that the public sector in the United States is smaller. But the second part of Bryce's statement can be turned around: The parties also count for less than in Europe. American parties now are weaker and less active than most of their European counterparts.

Still, above the local level almost all American public officials are elected as Democrats or Republicans (the Nebraska state legislature is formally nonpartisan). Unlike Europeans, Americans may not *believe* that parties are essential to democracy, but in practice, parties seem to be as pervasive as in Europe. Indeed, political historians of the past generation have developed general accounts of American history organized around the concept of "party systems."[17] These accounts provide an indication of the important role the political parties—whether appreciated or not—have played in American history.

The Party-Systems Interpretation of American History

party alignment
The social and economic groups that consistently support each party.

critical election
Election that marks the emergence of a new, lasting alignment of partisan support within the electorate.

realigning election
Another term for a critical election.

According to "critical election" or "realignment" theorists, American political history can be viewed as a succession of electoral eras often referred to as party systems.[18] Within each era, elections are similar, the key points of similarity and dissimilarity being the **party alignment**—the social and economic groups that consistently support each party. The eras themselves are separated by one or more **critical** or **realigning elections** that alter the existing electoral alignment, often in response to some crisis. During these "critical periods" party elites polarize at the same time that intraparty conflicts break out. Third parties appear on the scene. Turnout rises as the general intensity of political life heightens. Some scholars see an additional element—periodicity: They contend that critical or realigning elections come about once a generation, every 35 years or so. Table 8.1 summarizes the party systems interpretation.

THE FIRST PARTY SYSTEM (JEFFERSONIAN)

Some historians date the first party system from the early 1790s to about 1824. The dominating issue during this period was the establishment of a national government and the delineation of its power. The commercial interests in the young republic, especially those located in New England, supported the Federalists,

TABLE

Party-Systems Interpretation of American Electoral History

First (Jeffersonian) Party System: 1796–1824*
    7 Democratic-Republican presidential victories
    1 Fededralist victory

Second (Jacksonian) Party System: 1828–1856
    6 Democratic victories
    2 Whig victories

Third (Civil War and Reconstruction) Party System: 1860–1892
    7 Republican victories
    2 Democratic victories

Fourth (National Republican) Party System: 1896–1928
    7 Republican victories
    2 Democratic victories

Fifth (New Deal) Party System: 1932–1964
    7 Democratic victories
    2 Republican victories

Sixth (Divided Government) Party System: 1968–??
    5 Republican victories
    3 Democratic victories

*Years are approximate.

while the agricultural interests, especially those located in the South and West, supported the Jeffersonians, also called the Democratic-Republicans. The Jeffersonians were the dominant party, winning the presidency seven consecutive times from 1800 to 1824, but the system splintered when Jackson, the popular and electoral vote leader in 1824, was denied the presidency as the result of a so-called "corrupt bargain" (p. 169).

Some historians object to characterizing the Democratic-Republican era as a party system because mass parties did not yet exist. Because property qualifications prevented a majority of white males from voting, and women and slaves could not vote, politics was primarily an elite game between personal factions, especially after the Federalists ceased to be a factor following the War of 1812. In the view of these skeptical historians, no party system, strictly speaking, came into existence until the 1830s.

THE SECOND PARTY SYSTEM (JACKSONIAN DEMOCRACY)

After his defeat in 1824, Jackson and his allies laid the groundwork for another run. An important element of their strategy was to mobilize more of their potential voters. They succeeded with a vengeance: Between 1824 and 1828, turnout in the presidential election tripled, sweeping Jackson into office (pp. 169–170). Jackson's victory over the congressional caucus was complete when in 1832 he had himself renominated by a **national convention** that also chose Martin Van Buren as the vice presidential nominee. To this day, conventions composed of delegates chosen in the states select the presidential nominees and the platforms on which they run.

The Jacksonian Democrats were often called simply the "Democracy." This revitalized, greatly expanded successor to the Jeffersonian Democratic-Republicans was the world's first mass party; one of its principal architects, Martin Van Buren, is sometimes called "the father of parties."[19] Jackson and Van Buren believed in the old adage "to the victors belong the spoils." They freely and openly passed out government jobs and contracts to consolidate their hold on power (p. 455). Until it splintered in the sectional conflicts of the 1850s, the Jacksonian Democracy lost only two presidential elections to the Whigs—in 1840 to William Henry Harrison, and 1848 to Zachary Taylor, both of whom were war heroes. The Democracy also controlled Congress through much of this period.

During this second party system, the dominant issues were economic and territorial (the tariff, the national banks, slavery, and the expansion of the Union), with overarching conflicts over the power of the federal government as opposed to states rights. As the system matured, new issues arose and sectional differences over economics and slavery intensified. By the late 1840s, dissatisfied citizens were challenging the system under the banners of third parties. The "Free Soilers" opposed the expansion of slavery into the territories, and a few years later the "Know Nothings" opposed the immigration of Catholics (p. 104). Ultimately, in 1854–56 a new party, the Republicans, displaced the Whigs as the second major party in the system. The badly split Democracy nominated both northern and southern candidates for president in 1860. Together with the Constitutional Union candidate they received nearly 60 percent of the popular vote, but Abraham Lincoln led all candidates with nearly 40 percent, and with the winner-take-all electoral college system (p. 315) giving the leading candidate in a state its entire electoral vote, Lincoln received a clear electoral college majority.

■ **national convention**
Quadrennial gathering of party officials and delegates who select presidential and vice presidential nominees and adopt party platforms. Extension of the direct primary to the presidential level after 1968 has greatly lessened the importance of the conventions.

The Tammany Machine

One of the most famous machines in American history was the Tammany Hall Machine, which ruled New York City from the 1850s until the 1930s. Newspaper reporter William Riordan wrote a classic little book about George Washington Plunkitt, one of the Tammany ward bosses at the turn of the century. Although the machines were vilified by the Progressives, Riordan's book makes the important point that the machines gained and maintained their power by using it to provide jobs, services, and assistance for thousands of poor constituents. Here is Riordan's description of a typical Plunkitt day:*

2 A.M.: Aroused from sleep by the ringing of his doorbell; went to the door and found a bartender, who asked him to go to the police station and bail out a saloonkeeper who had been arrested for violating the excise law. Furnished bail and returned to bed at three o'clock.

6 A.M.: Awakened by fire engines passing his house. Hastened to the scene of the fire, according to the custom of the Tammany district leaders, to give assistance to the fire sufferers, if needed. Met several of his election district captains who are always under orders to look out for fires, which are considered great vote-getters. Found several tenants who had been burned out, took them to a hotel, supplied them with clothes, fed them, and arranged temporary quarters for them until they could rent and furnish new apartments.

8:30 A.M.: Went to the police court to look after his constituents. Found six "drunks." Secured the discharge of four by a timely word with the judge, and paid the fines of two.

9 A.M.: Appeared in the Municipal District Court. Directed one of his district captains to act as counsel for a widow against whom dispossess proceedings had been instituted and obtained an extension of time. Paid the rent of a poor family about to be dispossessed and gave them a dollar for food.

11 A.M.: At home again. Found four men waiting for him. One had been discharged by the Metropolitan Railway Company for neglect of duty, and wanted the district leader to fix things. Another wanted a job on the road. The third sought a place on the subway and the

The Third Party System (Civil War and Reconstruction)

The third party system was the most competitive electoral era in American history.[20] The Democrats maintained a base in the House of Representatives during the Civil War, and were able to take control of the House in 1874 following the readmission of the South. Throughout the period, however, the Republicans controlled the Senate, partly through the strategy of admitting new western states to the union. These states were very sparsely populated, but their small populations dependably elected Republican senators.[21] At the presidential level, the election results gave rise to the phrase "the period of no decision." From 1876 to 1892, no presidential candidate received as much as 51 percent of the popular vote. In two elections (that of Rutherford Hayes in 1876 and Benjamin Harrison in 1888), the electoral college chose a president who had come in second in the popular vote.

fourth, a plumber, was looking for work with the Consolidated Gas Company. The district leader spent nearly three hours fixing things for the four men, and succeeded in each case.

3 P.M.: Attended the funeral of an Italian as far as the ferry. Hurried back to make his appearance at the funeral of a Hebrew constituent. Went conspicuously to the front both in the Catholic church and the synagogue, and later attended the Hebrew confirmation ceremonies in the synagogue.

7 P.M.: Went to district headquarters and presided over a meeting of election district captains. Each captain submitted a list of all the voters in his district, reported on their attitude toward Tammany, suggested who might be

won over and how they could be won, told who were in need, and who were in trouble of any kind and the best way to reach them. District leader took notes and gave orders.

8 P.M.: Went to a church fair. Took chances on everything, bought ice cream for the young girls and the children. Kissed the little ones, flattered their mothers and took their fathers out for something down at the corner.

9 P.M.: At the clubhouse again. Spent $10 on tickets for a church excursion and promised a subscription for a new church bell. Bought tickets for a baseball game to be played by two nines from his district. Listened to the complaints of a dozen pushcart peddlers who said they were persecuted by the police and assured them he would go to

Police Headquarters in the morning and see about it.

10:30 P.M.: Attended a Hebrew wedding reception and dance. Had previously sent a handsome wedding present to the bride.

12 P.M.: In bed.

A cartoonist's more negative view of the Tammany Hall Machine preying on the innocent.

The dominant issue at the beginning of the period was Reconstruction, but after 1876, economic issues gradually came to occupy center stage. The rise of large business organizations, industrialization and its attendant dislocations, and a long agricultural depression generated the political issues of the period. During this era, party organizations reached their high point. Bitter memories of the Civil War left many people committed to the party of the Union (Republicans) or the party of the rebels (Democrats), and these committed citizens voted a straight party line. Indeed, independents often were viewed contemptuously as "traitors." With feelings so strong and politics so competitive, the parties exerted maximum efforts in campaigns. Moreover, with immigration on the increase, there were thousands of potential new voters to be fed and housed, employed, and marched to the polls. Parties reached such a high level of organization in many cities that they were referred to as **machines**.[22]

machine
A highly organized party under the control of a boss, based on patronage and control of government activities. They were common in many cities in the late nineteenth and early twentieth century.

Once again, the system was unable to contain or adapt to new pressures. Partisan divisions rooted in the Civil War seemed increasingly outmoded as the United States came to be a major player in a global economy. The excesses and corruption of the urban machines spawned reform movements aimed at destroying their influence. The Depression of the 1890s, during the administration of Democrat Grover Cleveland, plunged much of the country into misery. Agricultural protest, common throughout the period, gave rise to a Populist party that seriously challenged the major parties in the South and West, and ultimately fused with the Democrats to nominate William Jennings Bryan in 1896.[23] But the election showed that the electorate viewed the Populist vision of a worker-farmer alliance as less compelling than the Republican vision of a modern industrial state.

THE FOURTH PARTY SYSTEM (NATIONAL REPUBLICAN)

The "critical" election of 1896 inaugurated a period of Republican dominance.[24] The Democrats were reduced to their base in the old Confederacy, while the Republicans became dominant in many areas of the North and West. No longer needing the South for victory, the Republicans abandoned their black supporters and allowed the Democrats to finish erecting the system of political disenfranchisement that persisted into the 1950s.[25] In addition to region, important bases of political cleavage in the fourth party system were religion and ethnicity, as demonstrated in the first-ever major-party nomination and subsequent defeat of a Catholic, Al Smith, in 1928.[26] The Democrats won the presidency only twice during the fourth party system, in 1912 when Woodrow Wilson emerged the victor in a three-way race with President William Howard Taft and ex-President Theodore Roosevelt, and again in 1916 when Wilson was narrowly reelected on a platform of keeping the United States out of World War I (see Election Connection).

The fourth party system was a period of reform in American politics, but as noted in the box on page 246, some commentators see a dark side to the reforms as wealthy and influential corporate and social elites called **Progressives** pushed many ordinary citizens out of politics.[27] Turnout in elections plummeted after the Progressives instituted the personal registration system and the secret ballot. The Progressives aimed body blows at the parties by trying to take away the two principal party resources: control of public employment and control of nominations. Civil Service reforms begun at the national level with the Pendleton Civil Service Act of 1883 were extended wherever possible, diminishing the spoils the parties had available to distribute to their members. The **direct primary** system, which allowed voters to choose nominees for office, weakened party control of nominations, and thus the control parties could exercise over officeholders. The Progressives attacked the urban machines with nonpartisan elections, and provided ways to end-run elected officials with the initiative, referendum and recall. While such reforms were aimed at real corruption, their consequence, intended or not, was to weaken the mobilizing agents that brought many low-income and low-status people into politics.

After World War I, the Progressives' influence declined. For a time the country appeared to have achieved a new, permanent state of prosperity, but then came the great stock market crash of 1929, followed by the Depression of the 1930s with unemployment levels that reached over 20 percent. The Republicans lost the House of Representatives in the midterm elections of 1930, and the "critical elections" of 1932 and 1936 established a new party system.

Progressives
Middle-class reformers of the late nineteenth and early twentieth century who weakened the power of the machines and attempted to clean up elections and government.

direct primary
A method of choosing party candidates by popular vote of all self-identified party members. This method of nominating candidates is virtually unknown outside the United States.

In 1912, the incumbent president, Republican William Howard Taft, finished a distant third in the popular vote, and won only eight votes in the electoral college. Democrat Woodrow Wilson was the winner, and former President Theodore Roosevelt came in second, running as the Progressive party or "Bull Moose" candidate.

The young "Teddy" Roosevelt had become president in 1901, ascending from the vice presidency when President William McKinley was assassinated shortly after his term began. An energetic, colorful, and popular president, Roosevelt managed to straddle the split in the Republican party between the old guard pro-business conservatives, and the emerging progressives. After serving out McKinley's term he was easily elected in his own right in 1904. Although he had not served two full terms, Roosevelt chose not to run in 1908, turning the nomination over to his vice president and friend, Taft, who won a comfortable victory.

Taft was neither as energetic nor as colorful as Roosevelt; worse, he was not a very astute politician. Although his policies originally were little different from Roosevelt's, he antagonized important elements of the party. Moreover, as the party split widened, Taft increasingly allied with the old guard, whereas Roosevelt increasingly favored the progressives.

Roosevelt returned home from safari in 1910 (despite his reputation as a conservationist, he shot over 3000 animals in Africa, including 13 rhinos and five elephants).* Former supporters beseeched him to reenter the political fray and wrest the nomination from Taft. In 1912, Roosevelt hammered Taft in the primaries, but they meant little in that era. At the convention, he was hammered in turn by professional party operatives and southern delegations loyal to Taft. Outraged, a new Progressive party held a convention later in the summer and nominated Roosevelt, who told them that he felt as strong as a bull moose.

The split was fatal to the Republican Party. Although Woodrow Wilson received less than 42 percent of the popular vote, he was elected president as Republicans divided their votes between Taft and Roosevelt. Wilson was reelected in 1916. Wilson's two victories were the only ones by Democratic presidential candidates in the entire fourth party system— 1896 to 1928. During his tenure in office, the Federal Reserve system was established, women received the right to vote in national elections, and the United States entered World War I.

* John Garrity, *The American Nation: A History of the United States* (New York: Harper & Row, 1966): 664.

Teddy Roosevelt, noted conservationist, on safari in 1910.

The Progressives

This reform movement arose in the wake of rapid industrialization and urbanization and was an attempt to bring order to a nearly chaotic society, culminating in major innovation to almost every facet of public and private life in the United States. Progressives sought to improve the political system, the economy, and the standards of everyday living, thereby restoring economic competition and equality of opportunity. In the words of progressive Senator Robert M. La Follette, "The supreme issue, involving all the others, is the encroachment of the powerful few upon the rights of the many."

Owing to the somewhat contradictory nature of the various branches within progressivism, controversy continues today over the membership and goals of this extremely diverse movement. It is viewed by some as primarily an urban middle-class operation designed as a kind of protection against being squeezed out of power by an ever-growing working class on the one hand and the increasing power of big business on the other. Others claim the source of the movement to have been the workers themselves, while still others credit business leadership. Progressives have alternately been called altruistic reformers bent on improving the quality of American life (especially for the disadvantaged), and selfish, condescending meddlers bent more on social control than social reform.

Whatever their motivations, progressives tackled any number of the nation's ills, with varying degrees of success. Although progressives accepted industrial capitalism, they were outraged by some of its consequences. Convinced of their ability to improve these conditions, progressives became active in government reform, notably the destruction of political machines in favor of a more genuine democracy. They employed such measures as direct primaries and elections, and the adaptation of the initiative, the referendum, and the recall. As with most movements within progressivism, this transformation of politics and government originated on the local level and only gradually spread into state and federal arenas.

The great trusts, so powerful as to be immune to the discipline of the individual consumer, were attacked and broken down via regulation and tariff reform. A variety of taxation reforms were introduced in an effort to distribute the nation's wealth more evenly. Additional specific legislative achievements, encompassed such issues as child labor, industrial working conditions, workers' compensation, and women's suffrage.

Following an era of relatively passive chief executives serving as administrators rather than policy shapers and leaders, progressivism marked the return of such strong, active presidents as Theodore Roosevelt and Woodrow Wilson. It was also characterized by strong faith in the ability and skills of professionals to provide answer to society's ills.

SOURCE: Excerpted from Nancy Unger, "Progressivism (circa 1890s to 1917)," in L. Sandy Maisel, ed., *Political Parties and Elections in the United States: An Encyclopedia* (New York: Garland, 1991): vol. 1, pp. 888–889.

The Fifth Party System (New Deal)

The fifth party system was a class-based party alignment that resembled electoral alignments in modern European democracies. After Roosevelt's first term the Democrats became the party of the "common" people—blue-collar workers, farmers, housewives, and minorities, while the Republicans became, more than ever, the party of business and the affluent. The former accounted for quite a lot more voters than the latter, leading to a period of Democratic election dominance not seen since before the Civil War. Only Republican war hero Dwight Eisenhower was able to crack the Democratic monopoly in 1952 and 1956, and only from 1952 to 1954 did the Republicans control Congress as well as the presidency.

During the New Deal system, the United States fought to overcome the Great Depression, defeated Germany and Japan in World War II, and presided over the "cold war" (p. 658) that followed. Foreign policy was formulated in a relatively nonpartisan fashion during this period, leaving politics to revolve around the domestic economic issues that favored Democrats. But, once again, the Democratic party could not deal with the racial issue. In 1936, Roosevelt won repeal of the 104-year-old **two-thirds rule**. By requiring that the Democratic nominee receive a two-thirds majority of the delegates at the national convention, the rule had given the South a veto over the nominee. With its elimination, the South was increasingly unable to resist the growing national pressure for racial justice. Just as the inability to reconcile its northern and southern wings splintered the Jacksonian Democracy in the 1850s, the inability to reconcile its northern and southern wings splintered the New Deal Democrats a century later. By 1968, the Democratic Party was at war with itself and Republican Richard Nixon was elected president.

two-thirds rule
Rule governing Democratic national conventions from 1832 to 1936. It required that the presidential and vice presidential nominees receive at least two-thirds of the delegates' votes.

The Sixth Party System (Divided Government)

For much of the past generation, scholars have debated whether the United States has a sixth party system, and if so, when it arose, and what kind of system it is. What puzzled them was that the Democrats lost five of the six presidential elections from 1968 to 1988, but never lost control of the House of Representatives between 1952 and 1994, and lost the Senate only from 1980 to 1986. While such instances of divided government had been common in the second and third party systems, almost always it had occurred when the incumbent administration lost control of Congress during the mid-term election. What characterizes the sixth party system is a high rate of **ticket-splitting**, with voters supporting the presidential and congressional candidates of different parties in the same election.

In retrospect, 1964 may well have been a critical election in that political alignments changed permanently in its aftermath. While going down to a serious defeat, the Republicans made deep inroads in the Democrats' southern base, inroads that Richard Nixon widened and deepened in 1968 and 1972. Moreover, the third party campaigns of George Wallace revealed how much resentment the racial issue had caused—even in the North. So long as the civil rights movement was aimed at the South, and it worked for political, economic, and social rights and equality of *opportunity*, it enjoyed widespread support. But once it moved north and began demanding some degree of equality of socioeconomic *condition*, large segments of white America withdrew their support. Many blue-collar and urban whites joined southerners in abandoning Democratic presidential candidates.

ticket-splitting
Occurs when a voter does not vote a straight party ticket.

Race was not the only issue that damaged the Democrats, of course. The war in Vietnam led to a popular reaction against the party and spawned a protest movement that split the party internally. And as the first wave of the baby boom entered college, so-called "social" issues began to take on great importance as young people challenged traditional norms about drugs and sexual behavior. Once again, the Democrats were split between their old and new wings, while Republicans allied themselves with more traditional, "middle America."

Today, most commentators believe that the New Deal party system is gone, though they are in less agreement about precisely what has replaced it, or even *whether* it has been replaced. Some scholars like Joel Silbey argue that there can be no further party systems or **realignments** because the American parties have grown too weak to organize the system or to realign. Silbey argues that the United States is now in a nonparty period.[28] Others disagree; while conceding that this is an unusual party system, historically speaking, they believe that the right issue or leader might once again realign the system into one that resembles the earlier party systems.[29]

The Two-Party System

Given the history from Jefferson to the present, Americans understandably regard a **two-party system** as a natural state of affairs. As the survey of party systems showed, for the entire two centuries of the country's history, two major parties have dominated elections for national office. As listed in Table 8.2, third parties regularly arise, and several have played important roles in American elections, but most third parties disappear.[30] Only once has a third party replaced a major party—the Republicans in the 1850s. At best, a third party is absorbed or "co-opted by a major party, as with the Populists in the 1890s, who joined with the Democrats.

But Americans are in a minority as far as the rest of the world is concerned. Most democracies have **multiparty systems** (see International Comparison). A single party rarely wins majority control of government; rather, two or more minority parties that together comprise a legislative majority must form a **coalition government**.

Most scholars believe that an important factor in determining whether a polity has two parties or more is its **electoral system**, the way in which its constitution or laws translate popular votes into control of public offices.[31] At the national and state levels the United States relies almost exclusively on the **single-member, simple plurality (SMSP)** system. Elections for office take place within geographic units (states, congressional districts, cities, and so on), each of which selects the candidate who wins the most votes. When only two candidates run, one candidate will win a majority; when more than two run, a simple plurality determines the winner. This electoral system is characteristic of what are called the "Anglo-American democracies" (England and its former colonies). It is often called the "first past the post" system, since, as in a horse race, the winner is the one who finishes first, no matter how many others are in the race or how close the finish.

In most of the world's democracies, however, the electoral system is some version (there are many variations) of **proportional representation (PR)**. In such systems elections may (Germany) or may not (Israel) take place within geographic units, but even if they do, each unit elects a number of candidates, with each party winning seats in proportion to the vote it receives.

TABLE 8.2

Third Parties in American History

Candidate (Party, Year)	Showing	Subsequent Events
Martin Van Buren (Free Soil Party, 1848)	10.1 percent 0 electoral votes	Party drew 5 percent in 1852; supporters then merged into Republican Party
James B. Weaver (Populist Party, 1892)	8.5 percent 22 electoral votes	Supported Democrat William Jennings Bryan in 1896
Theodore Roosevelt (Progressive Party, 1912)	27.4 percent 88 electoral votes	Supported GOP nominee in 1916
Robert M. La Follette (Progressive Party, 1924)	16.6 percent 13 electoral votes	La Follette died in June 1925
Strom Thurmond (States' Rights Democratic Party, 1948)	2.4 percent 38 electoral votes	Democrats picked slate acceptable to South in 1952
Henry A. Wallace (Progressive Party, 1948)	2.4 percent 0 electoral votes	Party disappeared
George C. Wallace (American Independent Party, 1968)	13.5 percent 46 electoral votes	Ran in Democratic primaries in 1972 until he was injured in assassination attempt
John B. Anderson (National Unity Campaign, 1980)	6.6 percent 0 electoral votes	Withdrew from elective politics
H. Ross Perot (Independent, 1992)	18.7 percent 0 electoral votes	Attempted to form new party to take part in 1996 presidential election

NOTE: The list includes significant third-party candidates who received at least 2 percent of the popular vote. Other third parties that won at least 2 percent of the vote include the Liberty Party (1844); Greenback Party (1880); Prohibition Party (1888, 1892); and Socialist Party (1904, 1908, 1912, 1916, 1920, 1932).

SOURCE: Adapted from Kenneth Jost, "Third-Party Prospects," *The CQ Researcher*, December 22, 1995, 1148.

To illustrate the operation of these differing electoral systems, consider an example. Great Britain has a SMSP system. For decades, a third party, the Liberal Democrats, has competed with the two established parties, the Conservatives and Labour. Suppose the vote were to divide as follows within a parliamentary constituency:

Conservative: 44 %

Labour: 33

Liberal Democrat: 23

The Conservative candidate, having won a plurality, would win the seat with a minority of the overall vote. Labour and the Liberal Democrats would have nothing to show for the 56 percent they won. In reality, in the three elections between 1979 and 1987 that gave Margaret Thatcher's Conservatives large majorities in the Parliament, the Conservatives never received more than 45 percent of the nationwide vote. This is not unusual: *SMSP electoral systems tend to manufacture majorities or at least to exaggerate their size.*

If this hypothetical election had been conducted under a PR electoral arrangement, the geographic unit might have been assigned nine representatives. The Conservatives would have been given four, Labor three, and the Liberal Democrats two, an allocation of seats roughly proportional to the number of votes received. Under PR, governing majorities exist only where voting majorities exist.

Significant Parties	Description	Seats
United States		**1994**
Democratic Party	Favors government assistance for workers, the poor, and minorities; economically and socially left-of-center	204
Republican Party	Favors reliance on individualism and the free market; federalism; economically and socially right-of-center	230
Canada		**1993**
Bloc Québécois	Seeks negotiated sovereignty of the Quebec province	53
Liberal Party of Canada	Favors comprehensive social security and Canadian autonomy	178
New Democratic Party	Social Democrats	9
Progressive Conservative Party	Favors individualism and free enterprise	2
Reform Party	Favors decentralization of federal government and fiscal reform	52
France		**1993**
Rassemblement pour la République (RPR)	Gaullist conservative party	247
Union pour la Democratie Francaise (UDF)	Non-Gaullist centrist coalition	213
Parti Socialiste (PS)	Socialist party	54
Parti Communiste Francais (PCF)	Communist party	23
Mouvement des Radicaux de Gauche (MRG)	Left-wing radical party	0
National Front (FM)	Extreme right-wing Nationalist party	0
Germany		**1994**
Christian Democratic Union (CDU) / Christian Social Union (CSU)	Conservative party (CSU is the Bavarian version of the CDU)	294
Free Democratic Party (FDP)	Centrist party; supports individualism and the free market	47
The Greens	Left-wing party focusing on ecological issues, social justice, and comprehensive disarmament	49
Party of Democratic Socialism (PDS)	Re-formed from the Communist party in areas of the former East Germany; favors public ownership of means of production	30
Social Democratic Party	Socialist party	252

NOTE: The table shows major parties winning seats in the most recent legislative elections. The National Front is included among French political parties because, although it received no seats in the last parliamentary election, it received over 12 percent of the vote in the first round of balloting and has previously held seats.

Significant Parties	Description	Seats
India		**1996**
Bharatiya Janata Party (BJP)	Radical, right-wing Hindu party	186
Indian National Congress	Socialist party; favors government control of industry.	139
National Front-Left Front (NF-LF)	Coalition of the National Front, which includes liberal centrist parties, and the Left Front, which includes Communist parties	111
Israel		**1992/1996**
Hadash	Socialist party	5
Israel Labour Party	Left-of-center party; favors negotiated peace with Arab neighbors and Palestinians in occupied territories	34
Likud ("Consolidation")	Right-of-center party; emphasizes security issues in peace negotiations and favors continued Jewish settlement of occupied territories	32
Meretz ("Vitality")	Favors civil rights, electoral reform, and Palestinian self-determination	9
National Religious Party	Favors strict adherence to Jewish religion and tradition, but moderate by Israeli religious standards	9
Shas (Sephardic Torah Guardians)	Ultra-orthodox Jewish party	10
The Third Way	Centrist party; tries to merge Labor & Likud ideology	4
United Arab List	Muslim Party	4
United Torah Judaism	Jewish religious party	4
Yisrael Ba'aliya	Russian immigrant party	7
Japan	**(1995=upper house seats)**	**1993/1995**
Japanese Communist Party (JCP)	Communist party	15/14
Komei	Centrist party; favors political reform	51/11
Liberal Democratic Party (LDP)	Favors a strong welfare state, government promotion of industry and Japanese culture	223/110
New Frontier Party (NFP)	Amalgamation of 9 opposition parties	/56
Social Democratic Party of Japan (SDPJ)	Seeks collective security system with China, U.S., CIS	70/38
Venezuela		**1993**
Acción Democrática (AD)	Socialist party	55
Partido Social-Cristiano (COPEI)	Christian Democrats	54
Convergencia Nacional (CN) / Movimento al Socialismo	Coalition for national unity against the government in power and corruption; socialist movement	50
Causa Radical	Grassroots, left-wing workers' party	40

In the SMSP electoral system, winning is everything—finishing in any position but first yields nothing. Thus, if small parties have more in common with each other than with the largest party, they have an incentive to join together to challenge the plurality winner, because dividing the opposition among more than one candidate plays into the hands of the largest party. Citizens, in turn, realize that voting for a small party is tantamount to "wasting" their vote, since such a party has no chance of coming in first.[32] Thus, they tend to support one of the two larger parties. These calculations by parties and voters work against third parties.

In PR systems, of course, so long as a party finishes above some legally defined threshold, it wins seats in proportion to its vote. Since it is not necessary to finish first in order to win something, party leaders have more incentive to maintain their separate organizations. And since all votes count, voters are not motivated to abandon small parties. Thus, a multiparty system persists.

As shown in the British example above, the correlation between electoral system and number of parties around the world is not perfect—third parties do survive in SMSP systems. The correlation is strong, however. One study found that the average number of parties in proportional representation systems was 3.7, while the average number in SMSP systems was 2.2.[33]

One of the factors that affects whether third parties can survive in SMSP systems is whether their votes are geographically concentrated. If they receive, say, 20 percent of the nationwide vote, but it is distributed evenly across the country, they win nothing. But if their vote is regionally concentrated, so that they are the first or second party in some constituencies, they may persist indefinitely. For example, modern Canadian elections have been dominated by two major parties, the Liberals and the Progressive Conservatives, which compete nationwide and ordinarily win most of the seats in Parliament. But in recent elections, two smaller parties have established regional footholds. In the French-speaking province of Quebec, the Parti Québécois is the dominant party, and in some western provinces, Reform is the strongest party.

The Current State of American Parties

Ross Perot's strong showing in 1992 certainly was newsworthy, as was his talk about organizing a third party in 1995. But as with other recent challenges, such as those of John Anderson in 1980 and George Wallace in 1968, the two-party system probably will emerge unchanged from the Perot insurrection. The Democrats and Republicans seem to have a monopoly or "lock" on the electoral system.

You may be surprised to learn, then, that much political science scholarship of the past three decades has focused on the decline or death of the parties. In an important 1970 book, Walter Dean Burnham discussed "The Onward March of Party Decomposition."[34] He titled a more popular 1969 article, "The End of American Party Politics."[35] Reflective journalist David Broder titled his 1971 book, *The Party's Over.*[36] This thesis of party decline dominated research on American parties for well over a decade, but by the mid-1980s a revisionist view began to emerge. Xandra Kayden and Eddie Mahe titled their 1985 book *The Party Goes On*, and less than two decades after Burnham first wrote, Professor Larry Sabato published *The Party's Just Begun.*[37] In works with less catchy titles, scholars like Leon Epstein and Joseph Schlesinger claim their colleagues mistake "change" for "decline."[38] How can professional students of politics arrive at such widely divergent viewpoints?

Part of the answer is that people have different conceptions of what a party is. Parties are multifaceted, and although we defined parties earlier, no definition we have ever seen captures all or even most of the facets. Scholars often skirt the definitional problem by subdividing the concept and talking about different aspects, a practice we follow here.[39] In most of the world, party refers to an organization of like-minded people officially united in an effort to elect their members to office. In much of Europe, people join parties in the same way as they join social clubs in the United States. They pay dues, receive official membership cards, and have a right to participate in various party-sponsored activities. In particular, nomination proceedings are open only to those who are official party members. Nonmembers are not welcome.

Party also may refer to the officials elected to government—the members of the parliament and cabinet in most democracies. This is especially the case where elected officials dominate the party leadership and the grass roots, as in the British Conservative party.

Historically, the United States did not have true national party organizations. Rather, what passed for national organizations were temporary associations of state parties that briefly joined together every four years to work for the election of a president, and in the aftermath of the progressive reforms, these state and local organizations themselves declined. Similarly, party members in government have generally not been terribly cohesive. Both parties, but especially the Democrats, have suffered from regional splits, and both parties have incorporated conflicting interests—agricultural versus commercial, and so forth.[40] Thus, modern American commentators have discussed party primarily in a third sense, not as an organization, nor as a united body of elected officials, but as the adherents of the party in the electorate—ordinary citizens who identify themselves as Democrats or Republicans.

For about two decades it appeared that political parties in the United States were in decline—whatever the sense in which one used the concept. By mid-century, state and local party organizations had withered. Meanwhile, party cohesion and presidential support in Congress had declined; in 1963 James MacGregor Burns complained that the United States had a four-party system, with presidential Democrats and Republicans often opposed by congressional Democrats and Republicans.[41] The number of adherents of the two parties began dropping as well: in the mid-1960s the proportion of those calling themselves "independents" rose (p. 320). But by the mid-1980s, the first two of these trends had clearly reversed; party organizations were growing more active again, and party was becoming more important in government. A comparable reversal has not occurred among party in the electorate, though trends have at least bottomed out.

We will discuss party in the electorate in Chapter 10 when we discuss voting behavior. And we will discuss parties in the government when we talk about Congress and the presidency in Chapters 12 and 13. Here we focus on the party organizations, the most common concept of party around the world.

THE DECLINE OF PARTY ORGANIZATIONS

Party organizations were at their strongest at about the time the Progressive Movement began. The decline of American party organizations was in considerable part a consequence of deliberate public policies. As we noted earlier, the two principal resources that party organizations depend on are control of patronage and control of nominations for office. The first was gradually removed from party control by regular expansions of civil service protection (p. 458), and, after World War II, by the unionization of the public sector that gave government workers an additional layer of insulation from partisan politics (the largest union in the AFL-CIO today is the American Federation of State, County and Municipal Employees). Today the president personally controls fewer than 4 thousand appointments.[42] At the height of the spoils system—and with a much smaller federal government—presidents controlled well over 100 thousand appointments.[43] Similarly, governors and big city mayors who once controlled tens of thousands of jobs today control only a few thousand.

Party control over nominations was greatly weakened by the spread of the direct primary, one of the most important progressive reforms. As we note in Chapter 10, the United States is the only world democracy that relies on open, popular elections to decide nominations. In all other systems, much smaller groups of party activists and officials choose party nominees.

Deprived of their principal resources, modern American parties had few sticks and carrots to work with. Electoral defeat did not mean loss of livelihood for thousands of people; hence they were less inclined to work for parties and to support them through thick and thin. Similarly, outsiders could challenge parties for their nominations, and if they won, the parties had no choice but to live with the fact. Controlling neither the livelihoods of ordinary voters nor the electoral fates of public officials, the party organizations atrophied.

However, deliberate political reforms are not the entire explanation for the weakening of American parties. A number of other factors also have contributed to their decline. These were less deliberate actions than they were independent developments that indirectly weakened the parties. For one thing, the communications revolution lessened the need for traditional parties. Candidates could raise funds through direct mail appeals, then use such funds to reach voters directly by computer-generated mail and television. Elections have become less labor-intensive and more capital- and technology-intensive.[44] Technological developments have diminished the need for party workers and party support. In some European countries, the parties have preserved their influence in some part by gaining control of modern communications. In Italy, for example, the Christian Democrats, Social Democrats, and Communists each had their own TV network.

A second development that undercut U.S. parties was the post–World War II increase in mobility—social, economic, and residential. More educated voters had less need of parties to make sense of politics and guide their behavior. In a booming economy, voters had less need of parties to help them get jobs. And as the suburbs grew, the traditional, urban-based parties represented an ever-smaller proportion of the population, while the new, decentralized suburbs went largely unorganized.

Still a third development that may have weakened parties was the so-called "reapportionment revolution," set off by the Supreme Court's "one-person one-vote decisions" in the 1960s.[45] Prior to the Court decisions, political jurisdictions tended to coincide with natural communities. In the lower houses of many state legislatures, for example, every county had a seat. Thus, there would be a natural association between legislators and their local parties. In the aftermath of the reapportionment revolution, however, districting plans often cut across cities, counties, and other jurisdictions in the pursuit of numerical equality, racial balance, and other considerations. Today, legislators might have parts of several counties in their districts. The same is true of cities and towns. Such fragmentation makes each local party less important to the legislator, and in turn, any given local party has less interest in the legislator.

THE REVIVAL OF PARTY ORGANIZATIONS?

Despite the preceding story of decline, by the 1980s it was becoming clear that creative politicians had begun using the nearly empty party vessels for new ends. Most observers credit Republicans like William Brock, chairman of the Republican National Committee from 1976 to 1982, for leading the way. Through most of American history, a traditional organizational chart of American parties would have given a misleading impression. Although it is natural to put the national committees at the apex of the figure, authority in the parties was in no way hierarchical (see Figure 8.2). On the contrary, through most of their 150-year history the national committees were

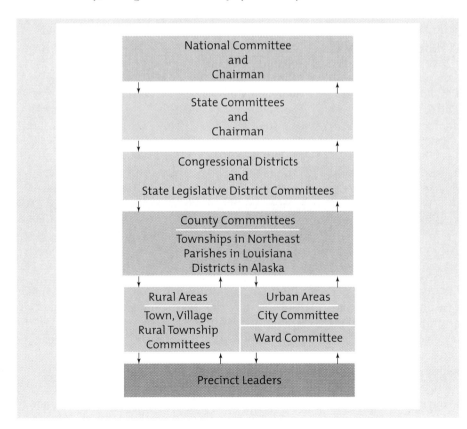

FIGURE 8.2

Party Organizational Chart

"Soft Money" and Campaign Finance

Federal election law limits the amount that can be given to particular candidates. Consider an election for U.S. Representative. Individual contributions are limited to $1,000 per candidate per election. Thus, you can contribute $1,000 to a candidate in the primary and another $1,000 in the general election (and if state law is such that a run-off is necessary after the primary, you can contribute $1,000 in that election too). Group and PAC contributions are limited to $5,000 per candidate per election, so that they can contribute a maximum of $15,000 to a candidate if three elections are necessary. The national and the state party are permitted to contribute another $15,000 in each election. Such limits are easily evaded, however.

As we saw in a previous Democratic Dilemma (p. 218), the courts have held that political contributions are a form of speech. Thus, restrictions on campaign contributions and expenditures potentially violate First Amendment rights of free speech and expression. The courts have compromised the issue by upholding limits on contributions to specific candidates, but not limits on spending for other purposes. The result is that interest groups, PACs, and even wealthy individuals are allowed to spend unlimited amounts of money "independently" of the campaign. They can produce a commercial, publish an ad, or rent a billboard denouncing one candidate, supporting another, or advocating a position, so long as they have not coordinated their activity with a candidate.

Similarly, parties can spend unlimited amounts of money on "generic" political activity. They can conduct polls on behalf of all their candidates. They can mount voter registration drives and "get out the vote" drives. They can pay for producing and broadcasting attack ads denouncing the other party and its candidates and for positive ads praising their own candidates and positions. So long as the ads or other activities are not explicitly coordinated with the candidates' own campaigns, they are legal. Such contributions have come to be known as "soft money," and the amount spent under this rubric has grown rapidly in 1990s campaigns.

Many public interest groups are critical of the expanding role of soft money. According to Ellen Miller of the Center for Responsive Politics, "there are unprece-

the weakest level of party organization, becoming active only during presidential years, when they served as organizing structures for the independent state and city organizations. That has changed greatly in the past quarter century; today, the national committees are active and well-financed, they have been joined by senatorial and congressional committees, and together these national committees have helped rejuvenate party organization at lower levels.

In brief, Brock and the Republicans first saw the possibilities of adapting parties to the modern age. They used direct mail technology to raise large sums of money.

dented amounts of soft money and unprecedented opportunities to abuse the law. Soft money is an addiction; the more there is, the more they want it."* Critics advocate closing the loopholes that permit soft money, even to the extent of supporting proposals that First Amendment lawyers view as unconstitutional. Thus far, they have not been successful. On the contrary, a June 1996 Supreme Court decision not only upheld "soft money" contributions by parties, but affirmed the right of parties to spend unlimited amounts "independently" on behalf of candidates.† Turned loose by that decision, the parties set new records as they raised more than 260 million in the 1996 campaign, three times what they had raised in 1992.‡ Although the Republicans raised a bit more

than the Democrats, the latter got more notice, partly because of a widely publicized $35 million campaign by organized labor against Republican members of Congress, and partly because of questionable contributions from Asian contributors that were revealed the week of the election.§

Naturally enough, the political parties vigorously defend their expanding role in campaign financing. Some political scientists agree, and note that party spending adds a desirable broadening or coordinating force to a campaign finance system that otherwise would be dominated by the contributions of thousands of individual contributors and interest groups, each seeking their particular goals.

What do you think? Is there a need to reduce party spending? Or

does party spending produce an electoral process that is less fragmented and less influenced by interest groups than would be the case if soft money and independent party expenditures were restricted? (See Election Connection, Money in 1996, p. 334, for more on campaign finance reform.)

* Peter Stone, "Some Hard Facts About Soft Money," *National Journal* March 23, 1996, 672.

† Jonathan Salant, "Ruling Loosens Reins on Parties," *Congressional Quarterly Weekly Report*, June 29, 1996, 1857.

‡ Rebecca Carr, "As Soft Money Grows, So Does Controversy," *Congressional Quarterly Weekly Report*, November 16, 1996, 3272–3273.

§ Jonathan Weisman, "Union Leaders Predict Victory Even Before Votes Tallied," *Congressional Quarterly Weekly Report*, November 2, 1996, 3163–3165.

They hired full-time political operatives and experts on polling, fund-raising, campaigning, and the media. They retained lawyers knowledgeable about the campaign finance laws and how to exploit loopholes in them, as well as specialists skilled in computers and other technologies. These consultants and services were made available at low cost to Republican party organizations and candidates nationwide. Moreover, the RNC stretched the boundaries of campaign finance laws to funnel "soft money" to impoverished state and local organizations, rejuvenating them in the process (see Democratic Dilemma). By the late 1980s there were reports of Republican congressional campaign committees actively recruiting candidates for office, a level of national intervention that would have been unthinkable a half century ago. For their part, the Democrats imitated the Republicans, although later and less successfully.

State and local party organizations have become more active as well; indeed, there are data to suggest that the resurgence of local organizations began earlier, in the 1960s.[46] In contrast to a generation ago, most state parties have permanent headquarters, usually in the state capital, and they employ full-time directors and other staff. A number of state organizations now conduct statewide polls. They too provide campaign aid and recruit candidates more actively than a few decades ago. A major study of party organization by John Bibby, Cornelius Cotter, James Gibson and Robert Huckshorn, confirmed by the Advisory Commission on Intergovernmental Relations, leaves no doubt that in terms of personnel and activities, the state and local party organizations have a more tangible existence today than at midcentury.[47] In sum, the process of party decline seems to have been arrested right about the time that the thesis of party decline was promulgated!

Still, the debate is not over. Many knowledgeable observers remain skeptical of the party resurgence thesis. John Coleman asks whether the parties are resurgent, or "just busy."[48] Others grant that the parties are now more active than in earlier decades, but argue that the newer activities do not make them stronger "parties" in any traditional sense. According to these critics, the party organizations essentially have become large campaign consulting firms, taking advantage of economies of scale to provide electioneering services to their associates. But despite increased recruiting efforts, such parties still do not have the control over the candidates that they did in the United States a century ago, or as they do in Europe today; rather, candidates continue to have the upper hand over the parties. The new parties cannot deny anyone a nomination or demand their loyalty once elected. If a party-recruited candidate is defeated in a primary, the party normally supports the victor. And only rarely will "rebels" in office be threatened by loss of party support. Indeed, when Speaker Gingrich suggested in a memo that rebellious freshmen members of the House Agriculture Committee would have their committee assignments changed, it was the Speaker who was forced to back down![49] The reason is obvious. Despite the impressive efforts of the newly constituted parties, they contribute only a fraction of the resources spent on electioneering. Contributions by the parties to members of Congress, for example, make up well under 10 percent of all congressional campaign expenditures (p. 356).

In sum, those skeptical of party renewal argue that what Americans call parties today are not really parties, but giant political action committees—super-PACs—or large campaign consulting firms. You can call these new campaign organizations parties, but that does not make them parties in the traditional sense. The debate goes on.

Parties Versus Interest Groups

Some political theorists believe that the power of interest groups correlates negatively with the power of parties—when parties are strong, groups are weak, and vice versa.[50] The argument follows from two premises: first, that parties have incentives to synthesize and harmonize narrow interests in order to make the broad appeals necessary to win elections; second, that strong parties can provide electoral resources and deliver the vote, thus freeing their candidates from dependence on interest group resources on the one hand, and insulating them from interest group reprisals on the other.

The argument implicitly assumes two-party politics rather than multiparty politics, since in the latter, parties often make very narrow appeals. Indeed, in multiparty systems, there may be very little difference between small parties and large interest groups. But within the two-party context the argument has considerable plausibility. As discussed in the preceding chapter, interest groups proliferated in the Progressive era, when the parties were systematically attacked by reformers, and again in the 1960s and 1970s, when American parties reached their nadir, before their recent recovery. Just as nature is said to abhor a physical vacuum, so it may be that political vacuums cannot persist. If parties do not fill them, groups or some other source of influence will.

If this argument is valid, then the real alternative to party domination of the electoral process is not popular influence, but interest group influence. Rather than reflect the broad appeals of parties, elections will reflect the narrow views of special interests. Of course, interest groups are not the only competitors of parties in modern societies. As we will discuss in Chapter 9, another potential competitor is the media.

Chapter Summary

Although the Constitution contains no mention of them, political parties have been part of American politics from the beginning. Indeed, American political history often is told in terms of "party systems," wherein each party has dependable support among particular social groups, so that elections tend to be similar within each system. Such electoral eras end with "critical" or "realigning" elections that alter the group alignments and usher in a new party system. At present, the United States has a party system that is less stable and more confusing than most of those that have preceded it.

The basic reason that parties have played such an important role in American history — as well as the history of all modern democracies — is that they perform coordinating functions that are essential in large-scale representative democracies. Parties coordinate the actions of numerous officeholders and focus responsibility for their actions. Parties develop issues and educate the public, and synthesize the disparate interests of a heterogeneous nation-state. Parties recruit and develop governmental talent, and simplify the choices of voters who would otherwise be overwhelmed by the task of choosing among numerous candidates for office.

Despite these important functions that parties perform, most Americans do not hold them in especially high regard. One reason is that parties perform their functions as part of the continual struggle for political supremacy. Thus, they act in accord with partisan self-interest and historically have behaved dictatorially, corruptly, and divisively. The question reformers must face, however, is what alternative is there to party influence and activity, however imperfect it may be?

The United States has the world's longest-lived two-party system. In contrast, most modern democracies have multiparty systems. One important reason for the difference is the electoral system common in the United States—the winner-take-all SMSP system, which gives opposition parties incentives to unite and their supporters incentives not to waste their votes on small parties that can't win. Most other democracies, in contrast, have PR systems that give parties seats in parliaments in rough proportion to the votes they receive.

Parties in the United States are not nearly as strong as they were in earlier periods, particularly in the late nineteenth century. Like other American institutions and processes, the parties have been democratized. Few "bosses" remain, party processes are open to all who register, and those elected under the party flag often go their own way when it suits them or their constituents. But despite much discussion of party decline, the Democratic and Republican parties continue to dominate American elections and organize government. And despite periodic third parties, that dominance is likely to continue.

Key Terms

coalition government, p. 248

critical election, p. 240

direct primary, p. 244

divided government, p. 237

electoral system, p. 248

machine, p. 243

multiparty system, p. 248

national convention, p. 241

party alignment, p. 240

political party, p. 232

Progressives, p. 244

proportional representation (PR), p. 248

realigning election, p. 240

realignment, p. 248

single-member, simple plurality (SMSP), p. 248

ticket splitting, p. 247

two-party system, p. 248

two-thirds rule, p. 247

Suggested Readings

Aldrich, John. *Why Parties?* Chicago: University of Chicago Press, 1995. Wide-ranging rational choice account of how and why politicians form and transform political parties.

Bibby, John F. *Politics, Parties, and Elections in America.* 2nd ed. Chicago: Nelson-Hall, 1992. Up-to-date textbook on party politics in the contemporary United States.

Burnham, Walter, D. *Critical Elections and the Mainsprings of American Politics.* New York: Norton, 1970. Influential statement of critical elections theory. Suggests that party decomposition may make classical realignments obsolete.

Epstein, Leon. *Political Parties in the American Mold.* Madison: University of Wisconsin Press, 1986. Capstone work by a prominent student of American parties. Argues that modern parties have adapted and continue to play an important political role, but future prospects are limited by ambivalent feelings in the American electorate.

Jewell, Malcolm E., and David M. Olson. *Political Parties and Elections in the American States.* 3rd ed. Chicago: Dorsey, 1988. Textbook on parties and elections at the subnational level.

Key, V.O., Jr. *Politics, Parties and Pressure Groups.* 5th ed. New York: Crowell, 1964. A classic text. Although dated, it can still be read both for historical interest and for theoretical observations about party politics in a democracy.

Key, V.O., Jr. *Southern Politics.* New York: Vintage, 1949. Another classic. Again, the material is dated, but the theoretical arguments about the nature of politics in systems with weak or nonexistent parties remain relevant today.

Maisel, L. Sandy. *The Parties Respond.* 2nd ed. Boulder, CO: Westview Press, 1994. Up-to-date collection of essays that examines how parties and party politics are changing in the contemporary United States.

Maisel, L. Sandy, ed. *Political Parties and Elections in the United States: An Encyclopedia.* New York: Garland, 1991. Useful reference that provides short discussions of specific topics in the history of party politics in America.

Mayhew, David. R. *Placing Parties in American Politics.* Princeton, NJ: Princeton, 1986. Comprehensive study of state party organization in the twentieth century.

Sundquist, James. L. *Dynamics of the Party System.* Rev. ed. Washington, DC: Brookings, 1983. History of national politics since the 1840s told from a party systems perspective.

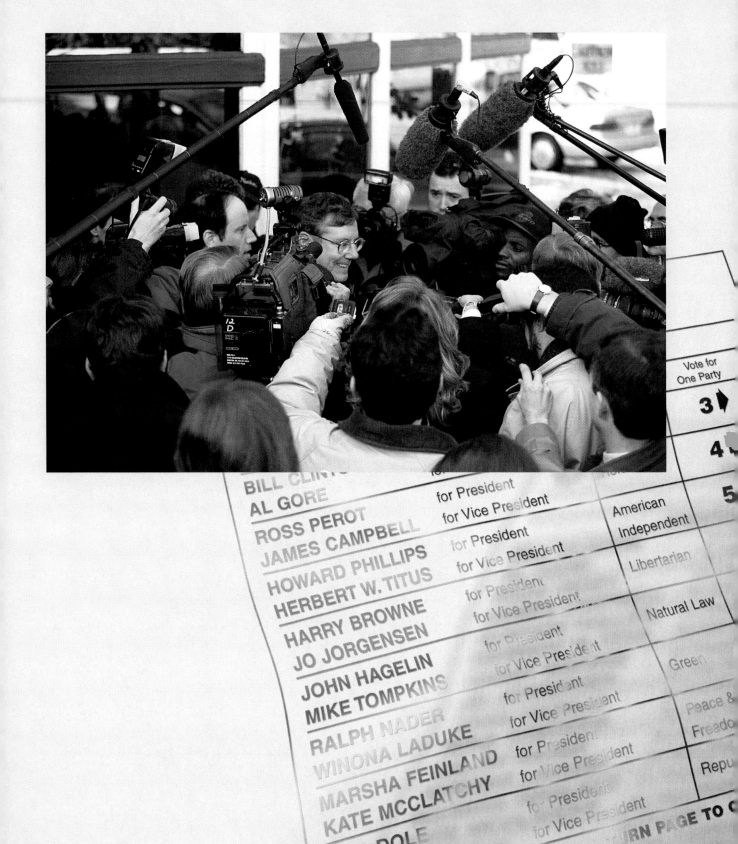

9

the media

HREE DECADES AGO,
hundreds of thousands of young
Americans fought in the Vietnam
war. More than 58,000 died, ten
times that many were wounded,
and American politics was
profoundly affected. Vietnam has
been called the first media war,
and it provides powerful illustrations of the wide range of media
impacts on public opinion.

A TALE OF TWO BATTLES: TET   In the 1964 election, Democrat Lyndon B. Johnson (LBJ) routed Republican Barry Goldwater. Running as the peace candidate, LBJ pledged to keep the United States out of the growing hostilities in Southeast Asia, promising that "Asian boys will fight Asian wars." Step by step, however, American involvement deepened, and by late 1967 more than 500 thousand troops were in Vietnam. With criticism of the war growing, the administration launched a "progress initiative." Top officials announced that they could see "light at the end of the tunnel." The commanding general predicted that troop phase-outs might begin within two years.

And then came Tet. On January 30, 1968, as the Vietnamese new year celebration (Tet) began, the North Vietnamese army and the indigenous Viet Cong guerillas launched coordinated offensives across South Vietnam. They attacked 36 provincial capitals and 64 district capitals, as well as five of the six largest cities and numerous hamlets. Even the U.S. embassy in Saigon nearly was overrun. American forces were rocked by the surprise attacks.

Criticism of the war heretofore had been confined to the fringes of politics, but now it spread to establishment circles. CBS anchorman Walter Cronkite, the most trusted man in America according to the polls, was startled by the Tet footage. He announced that he would go to Vietnam to see the situation for himself.

In the aftermath of the offensive, editorial comment turned pessimistic, and *Newsweek* published a "searching reappraisal." The tone of news coverage turned sharply critical, with increasingly negative stories about low troop morale, drug abuse, and corruption in the South Vietnamese government. Upon returning to the United States, Cronkite broadcast a special report to the nation, reporting that the war had become a bloody stalemate, with no military victory in sight:

> . . . it is increasingly clear to this reporter that the only rational way out, then, will be to negotiate, not as victors, but as an honorable people who lived up to their pledge to defend democracy and did the best they could.[1]

According to some accounts, LBJ turned to his aides and said, "It's all over."[2] A journalist later wrote that, "It was the first time in history that a war had been declared over by an anchorman."[3] Johnson fell eight points in the polls immediately after Tet and continued to slide for six weeks. Popular support for administration policy dropped from 60 percent to 40 percent, and optimism about victory faded. On March 12, Senator Eugene McCarthy (D-MN), a peace candidate, got 42 percent of the vote in the New Hampshire Democratic primary. Four days later, Robert Kennedy announced he would oppose Johnson's renomination. On March 31, LBJ made a nationwide address, calling a partial halt to the bombing of North Vietnam, and withdrawing from the presidential race.

At first glance, this story is encouraging: Adverse developments occurred, the media reported the facts, the public responded, and leaders were replaced—the system worked! But within a few years, some people took a second look and reached a different conclusion.[4] As emotions subsided, as materials were declassified, and as former enemies conferred, revisionists advanced a persuasive case that the media got Tet wrong, that in fact Tet was just what the military said it was at the time—a major defeat for the enemy.[5]

Many in the military had expected the North to launch a last major assault to break the stalemate and force negotiations.[6] Most of the initial assaults were repulsed, with heavy casualties for the attackers. While LBJ's poll numbers plummeted, the North Vietnamese and the Viet Cong suffered nearly 60 thousand combat deaths, compared to 4 thousand for the United States and 5 thousand for the South. The Viet Cong, who bore the brunt of the fighting, were decimated. They had expected a popular uprising, and when it did not occur, they were left exposed and outgunned. But this military defeat was turned into a psychological victory by the spin the media put on the facts. The initial surprise attacks were described as American defeats, even though most ended in bloody retreats. The media ignored the good performance of the South Vietnamese army, and wrongly described the pacification program in the countryside as devastated. Moreover, the media botched several big stories and overlooked others.

Some conservatives accuse the media of losing the war, but more disinterested analysts believe the media's failings reflected inexperience and ignorance, not ideology. The point is simply that the media misconstrued Tet, making it look far worse than it was, just as they misconstrued the prior situation, making it look better than it was. Nevertheless, the evidence suggests that media accounts significantly affected public opinion,[7] supporting the views of those who believe in the awesome power of the media to "create reality."[8]

A TALE OF TWO BATTLES: CHICAGO   The domestic political scene grew increasingly turbulent after Tet. The elimination of graduate student deferments in the spring meant that the draft would now touch the middle class. Partly in consequence, the antiwar movement burgeoned. As the Democratic convention drew near, 10 thousand demonstrators gathered in Chicago to protest the impending nomination of LBJ's vice president, Hubert Humphrey, who had not entered a single primary and who was expected to continue Johnson's policies.

It is difficult to convey to students today the level of tension that existed then. Violence was fully expected—Mayor Richard Daley called out extra police, asked for state and federal troops to go on standby, and announced a hard line toward protesters. After some preliminary skirmishes, violence erupted. In what an investigative commission later described as a police riot, waves of armored police charged demonstrators, often clubbing innocent bystanders in the process. More than 500 protesters needed medical attention. Hard-bitten British reporters who had covered civil war in Northern Ireland wrote that the Chicago police had literally gone berserk.[9]

For the media covering the convention, however, the situation was heaven-sent. There were charges and retreats, snarling police dogs, horses, motorcycles—terrific action and great pictures. Bleeding protesters were eager to vent their spleen over the airwaves. Inside and outside the convention, public figures used the harshest rhetoric: In prime time, from the podium of the convention, Senator Abraham Ribicoff of Connecticut accused Mayor Daley of using Gestapo tactics in the streets outside. It was a night made for TV.

But reporters were not only reporting. By and large their sympathies were with the protesters. As the *New York Times*'s Tom Wicker put it, "these were our children in the streets, and the Chicago police beat them up."[10] Over the course of the evening, the media lost all semblance of balance. Longtime NBC anchor Chet Huntley condemned the police. Walter Cronkite choked back his tears.

Over and above the rhetoric, of course, TV was showing dramatic footage. The scene was hazy because of tear gas, the

The Democrats did not get a positive "bounce" from their 1968 national convention. Outside the convention hall, Chicago police wielded clubs, tear gas, and Mace in pitched battles with thousands of antiwar protesters.

sound of sirens filled the background, and throughout the evening the airwaves carried the continuous chant of the demonstrators: "The whole world is watching, the whole world is watching."

Much of the United States was watching. And most were cheering. When the major poll results came in, American elites were stunned. Popular majorities believed that the Chicago police had acted appropriately; indeed, more felt that the police should have used greater force than thought their actions were excessive![11]

So, with the full power of the media telling them that atrocities were being committed in the streets of Chicago, the American people tuned it all out, stared at their TVs, and cheered for the police. So much for the awesome power of TV. The simple fact was that most Americans didn't like demonstrators, whom they regarded as unpatriotic at best and subversive at worst. The protesters had gone to Chicago looking for trouble, and they had found it, whatever the media thought.

How powerful are the media, then? Are they an overwhelming force that brings down presidents, or a lot of sound and fury that ordinary Americans ignore? The answer is that, depending on the circumstances, the media are both, and everything in between. Media influence is a *contingent influence*; that is, it depends on other conditions present in a situation. Under some conditions, the media can have extremely powerful effects on public opinion, even to the extent of determining who wins elections and what governments do. But under other conditions, media effects are extremely limited. We discuss those contingencies in this chapter, as we discuss the structure, practices, and effects of the modern communications media, an integral part of American electoral democracy.

Evolution of the Mass Media

mass media
Means of communication that are technologically capable of reaching most people and economically affordable to most.

The term **mass media** refers to means of communication that are technologically capable of reaching most people and are economically affordable to most. Failure to meet either criterion will restrict a medium's reach to smaller parts of the population. Mass media have existed for less than two centuries. Their evolution is bound up with the evolution of American democracy: New developments in the media require politicians to adapt as part of a never-ending struggle to control the information that reaches their constituents.

NEWSPAPERS

At the time of the American Revolution most of the colonies' newspapers were weeklies; the first daily paper began publication in Philadelphia in 1783.[12] These early papers were published by printers who, like Benjamin Franklin, also published books, almanacs, and official documents. They reprinted material from European newspapers and from each other, as well as letters and essays from citizens.

As party politics developed, both fledgling parties saw the benefits of having a means of communicating with their constituents. Hamilton and the Federalists established a "house" paper, the *Gazette of the United States*, and the Jeffersonians responded with the *National Gazette*—newspapers that were unabashedly partisan. They printed the party line, viciously attacked the opposition, and depended for economic survival on government printing contracts. Contemporary scholars have noted how modern presidents try to influence voters by "going public," speaking directly to the citizenry through the media. Although early presidents did not speak in their own voice, to the extent that the technology allowed they have been going public since the beginning of the republic.[13]

Improvements in the manufacturing of paper and type and the invention of the steam-driven printing press made it cheaper and easier to publish papers. In 1833 the *New York Sun* began daily publication, selling for a mere penny (before that time the going price for a newspaper was six cents). The rise of the penny press marks the birth of the mass media in the United States. Newspapers now were cheap enough to be purchased and read by millions of ordinary people. Within two years the circulation of the *Sun* was third in the world behind the two largest London newspapers.

As readership expanded, the newspapers began to take on their modern characteristics. The first was an emphasis on local news; the older, more expensive weeklies focused more on national and international news and developments. The second was sensationalism; then, as now, crime and sex sold newspapers. The third was the rise of the human-interest story; more abstract discussions of politics and economics were left to the older weeklies. Still, the new penny papers were overwhelmingly partisan: According to the 1850 census, only 5 percent of the country's newspapers were neutral or independent.[14] Politicians still worked hand in hand with the editors of friendly papers, and they withheld information from those allied with the opposition.

After the Civil War, an independent press began to develop. Horace Greely's New York *Tribune* was a well-known forerunner. One-sided editorial positions remained common, but no longer were most newspapers regularly aligned with one or the other of the parties. Papers took critical stances on many late-nineteenth-century developments and advocated policy changes of various kinds. This was the heyday of the political machine, however, and party bosses were less dependent on or affected by newspapers than previously. They communicated to constituents through their own organizations.

More than ever, late-nineteenth-century newspaper circulation depended on sensationalism. Indeed, the 1890s are remembered for their "yellow journalism"—a term arising from the colorful comics pages of the sensation-seeking papers of the era. But again, conditions were changing.

Around the turn of the century, many newspapers became large enterprises. The great chains—Hearst, Scripps, and others—were being formed around this time. No longer the personal vehicles of lone editors, newspapers were now coming to look much like other American corporations. In addition, the partisanship of newspapers continued to decline and the professionalism of journalists to increase. Some newspapers were important components of the Progressive Movement, publishing "muckraking" exposés of shocking conditions in American industry and corruption in government. Inexpensive magazines that were aimed at the new,

During the Spanish-American War era, "yellow journalism" used sensationalism to inflame readers—and sell newspapers.

SPANIARDS SEARCH WOMEN ON AMERICAN STEAMER

MUCKRAKING

In the late nineteenth century, the new, non-partisan press opened its pages to a group of social critics later called "muckrakers" after Theodore Roosevelt's ambivalent characterization: "Men with the muckrake are often indispensable to the well-being of society, but only if they know when to stop raking the muck."* Roosevelt thought the muckrakers excessively zealous, and was comparing them to the man in *Pilgrim's Progress* (Bunyan's popular nineteenth-century volume) "who was offered a celestial crown for his muckrake but who could neither look up nor regard the crown he was offered but continued to rake to himself the filth of the floor."†

The muckrakers published numerous exposés of the political and economic corruption common in the period, and as with investigative journalists today, some people in politics naturally resented their stories.

Among the best-known muckrakers were Lincoln Steffens, Ida Tarbell, and Upton Sinclair. Steffens's articles in *McClure's Magazine* were later compiled as *The Shame of the Cities*.‡ The flavor of muckraker writing is apparent in the first page of his article on Minneapolis— "The Shame of Minneapolis: The Rescue and Redemption of a City that was Sold Out."

Whenever anything extraordinary is done in American municipal politics, whether for good or for evil, you can trace it almost invariably to one man. The people do not do it. Neither do the "gangs," "combines," or political parties. These are but instruments by which bosses (not leaders; we Americans are not led, but driven) rule the people, and commonly sell them out. But there are at least two forms of the autocracy which has supplanted the democracy here as it has everywhere it has been tried. One is that of the organized majority by which, as in Tammany Hall in New York and the Republican machine in Philadelphia, the boss has normal control of more than half the voters. The other is that of the adroitly managed minority. The "good people" are herded into parties and stupefied with convictions and a name, Republican or Democrat; while the "bad people" are so organized or interested by the boss that he can wield their votes to enforce terms with party managers and decide elections. St. Louis is a conspicuous example of this form. Minneapolis is another. Colonel Ed Butler is the unscrupulous opportunist who handled the non-partisan minority which turned St. Louis into a "boodle town." In Minneapolis "Doc" Ames was the man.

* Address on laying the cornerstone of the House Office Building, April 14, 1906.

† From "Muckraker," in Jay Shafritz, *The HarperCollins Dictionary of American Government and Politics* (New York: HarperPerennial, 1992): 373.

‡ Lincoln Steffens, *The Shame of the Cities* (New York: McClure, 1904).

McClure's Magazine

VOL. XX   *JANUARY*, 1903   NO. 3

THE SHAME OF MINNEAPOLIS

The Rescue and Redemption of a City that was Sold Out

BY LINCOLN STEFFENS

FAC-SIMILE OF THE FIRST PAGE OF "THE BIG MITT LEDGER"

An account kept by a swindler of the dealings of his "Joint" with City Officials, showing first payments made to Mayor Ames, his brother, the Chief of Police and Detectives. This book figured in trials and newspaper reports of the exposure, but was "lost"; and its whereabouts was the mystery of the proceedings. This is the first glimpse that any one, except "Cheerful Charlie" Howard, who kept it, and members of the grand jury, has had of the book

WHENEVER anything extraordinary is done in American municipal politics, whether for good or for evil, you can trace it almost invariably to one man. The people do not do it. Neither do the "gangs," "combines," or political parties. These are but instruments by which bosses (not leaders; we Americans are not led, but driven) rule the people, and commonly sell them out. But there are at least two forms of the autocracy which has supplanted the democracy here as it has everywhere it has been tried. One is that of the organized majority by which, as in Tammany Hall in New York and the Republican machine in Philadelphia, the boss has normal control of more than half the voters. The other is that of the adroitly managed minority. The "good people" are herded into parties and stupefied with convictions and a name, Republican or Democrat; while the "bad people" are so organized or interested by the boss that he can wield their votes to enforce terms with party managers and decide elections. St. Louis is a conspicuous example of this form. Minneapolis is another. Colonel Ed. Butler is the unscrupulous opportunist who handled the non-partisan minority which turned St. Louis into a "boodle town." In Minneapolis "Doc" Ames was the man.

educated middle class also made their appearance. *Cosmopolitan* and *Harper's*, for example, date from this time.

Today, newspapers and magazines continue to be an important part of the mass media: About 11 thousand newspapers and 12 thousand periodicals are published. Large city papers like the *New York Times* and the *Los Angeles Times* have circulations of more than 1 million per day, and the *Wall Street Journal* reaches nearly 2 million. A relatively new entry, *USA Today*, has a circulation of more than 2 million per day. *Time, Newsweek,* and *U.S. News and World Report* each sell about 10 million copies per week. These institutions maintain their own Washington bureaus and send reporters all over the world. But even smaller city papers can get up-to-the-minute national and international news by subscribing to news services like the Associated Press (AP) and Reuters.

The most important modern trends in the newspaper industry are the decline in the number and independence of papers. Afternoon newspapers have all but disappeared. Mergers have resulted in most cities now being served by one or two papers, as opposed to several a half century ago, and chains have continued to gobble up independent newspapers; the largest, Gannett, owns more than ninety papers. Moreover, some conglomerates own TV and radio stations and networks as well as newspapers. Some observers worry that the print media in particular, and the mass media in general, are becoming increasingly homogeneous as a result of common ownership and pressure to make profits for the larger enterprise.

RADIO

In the 1930s, the print monopoly of mass communications began to erode. The first radio stations were established in the 1920s, and the first radio news agencies in the 1930s. Politicians quickly made use of this exciting new technology. Although he was known as "silent Cal," President Coolidge (1924–28) quickly took to the airwaves to reach voters. In the 1930s, Franklin Roosevelt helped calm a worried nation with his famous "fireside" chats, while various radio demagogues, such as the anti-Semitic populist Father Coughlin, exerted a less calming influence. (Roosevelt also established a press relations office in the White House, a clear recognition that an increasingly professional media required an equally professional political response.)

Radio spread rapidly throughout the country. Today there are more than 11 thousand stations that reach 80 percent of the population at some time on an average day. Virtually every household has at least one radio, and the average is five. Additionally, there are millions of cars on the road, nearly all of which contain radios. Because of its local orientation, and because it is relatively cheap, radio continues to be an important means for lower-level public officials to reach people.

At the national level, radio is an increasingly important means of political communication as well. Radio enjoyed something of a resurgence in the 1980s, a resurgence overlooked for a time by observers of the national scene. President Reagan had a regular Saturday broadcast, and President Clinton has followed a similar practice.

Probably the most important recent political development in radio communications is the rapid increase in talk shows. There have been talk shows for almost half a century, but most were local productions. The development of satellite technology and the deregulation of long-distance telephone rates removed the geographic

TALK RADIO

The Republican take-over of Congress in the 1994 elections catapulted talk radio into the forefront of political discussion. According to one popular interpretation, 1994 was the year of the "angry white male," especially disaffected followers of Ross Perot, whom Rush Limbaugh, G. Gordon Liddy, and other Clinton-hating talk radio hosts had mobilized against the Democratic Congress. As San Francisco "shock jock" Geoff Metcalf put it, "I'd vote for PeeWee Herman before I'd vote for Clinton."

Talk radio certainly has blossomed in recent years. And certainly talk radio has a conservative slant—seven of the top nine highest rated shows are hosted by conservatives.* But studies show that the audience for talk radio is more diverse than the popularity of conservative hosts might suggest. A large 1995 survey found that, contrary to the "angry white male" stereotype, 40 percent of the listening audience were female. Similarly contrary to stereotype, the audience was not particularly Republican; Republicans made up 38 percent of the audience, about the same as their percentage of the general population. In all, only half the listening audience consisted of white males and only a fifth were angry white male Republicans.†

Talk show listeners are more highly educated than the general population, and have slightly higher incomes. They are significantly more likely to be registered to vote, and more likely to participate in government in such ways as writing to public officials and attending political meetings. All in all, talk radio appears to be neither as different nor as threatening as some commentators assume.‡ In fact, talk radio was not as prominent in the 1996 election as in 1994, leading some observers to conclude that the political use of talk radio has already peaked.§

* "Survey Profiles Political Talk Radio Fans," The Boston Globe,

† Ibid. These results are consistent with a 1993 *Times-Mirror* survey reported in Diana Owen, "Who's Talking? Who's Listening? The New Politics of Radio Talk Shows," in Stephen Craig, ed., *Broken Contract* (Boulder, CO: Westview, 1996):127–146, and also with the 1994 VNS Exit Poll as reported in Louis Bolce, Gerald De Maio, and Douglas Muzzio, "Dial-In Democracy: Talk Radio and the 1994 Election," *Political Science Quarterly* 111(1996): 457–481, although the listeners who were actual 1994 voters were somewhat more conservative and Republican than the listeners in the other two surveys.

‡ Owen, "Who's Talking? Who's Listening?

§ Ronald Elving, "On Radio, All Politics Is a Lot Less Vocal," *Congressional Quarterly Weekly Report,* May 10, 1997: 1102.

In 1992, candidate Clinton, here interviewed by New York shock jock Don Imus, made extensive use of both talk radio and television—sometimes simultaneously.

limits on such shows, and today many of them are syndicated by large networks. Rush Limbaugh's show is perhaps the best-known example. This conservative commentator began broadcasting nationally in 1988 and now reaches more than 20 million listeners on some 700 stations.[15] Many local stations pair his show with a locally produced one. In recent years, liberals have established more such shows in an attempt to compete for the radio audience, but as noted in the box on the opposite page, conservative viewpoints continue to have a wide edge. The talk show format is now the sixth most popular radio format, just ahead of rock; the five most popular music formats are (1) country and western, (2) adult contemporary, (3) top 40, (4) religious, and (5) oldies.[16]

TELEVISION

Today, the term mass media is associated first and foremost with television. There are more than 1500 television stations in the United States, and about 99 percent of all households have at least one TV set, with an average of four. Like radio, TV is as close to being a universal medium of communications as it is possible to be.

The first TV station went on the air in 1939, but TV grew very slowly during World War II. Afterwards it spread rapidly—by 1960, 90 percent of all households had TVs. The industry was organized under three large networks—NBC, CBS, and ABC—that were established earlier as radio broadcasting networks. The networks produce programs and pay local affiliates to carry them. The affiliates, in turn, make advertising time available for the networks to sell. Of course, the price the networks can charge for advertising time depends critically on ratings, which is why ratings are such an important consideration when it comes to programming decisions.

The Eisenhower campaign was the first to take advantage of TV, producing simple commercials that are amusing when viewed today. But it was the Kennedy administration that elevated TV above the print medium and used it effectively during the campaign (see Election Connection). And during his short presidency, Kennedy held regularly televised press conferences that enabled him to go over the heads of the media and communicate directly with voters. Kennedy once commented to a reporter: "When we don't have to go through you bastards we can really get our story to the American people."[17]

When network TV reached its height in the 1980s, about 85 percent of all the commercial TV stations in the country were affiliated with one of the big three networks. But the network system began to fray after government deregulated the cable industry in the 1970s. The percent of households with cable increased from 20 percent in 1980 to 65 percent by 1995. Prime time network programming has lost more than a quarter of its audience as cable stations have proliferated, leading some scholars to suggest that the United States is in transition from an era of broadcasting to an era of narrowcasting.[18] Still, although the combined ratings of the *ABC*, *CBS*, and *NBC* evening news telecasts have fallen by 30 percent since the mid-1980s, they continue to draw an audience of about 50 million people on an average weekday.[19] While its coverage has declined over the past two decades, network TV continues to be the largest single source of information available to Americans.

A Catholic Wins in 1960

As Dwight Eisenhower's second term drew to a close, it was unclear whether the presidency would revert to the Democratic control that was the norm during the New Deal party system or continue under Republican control. The prospective Republican candidate was Richard Nixon, Eisenhower's vice president and a former senator and representative. On the Democratic side, the identity of the nominee was much less certain. One of the aspiring Democrats was John Kennedy, a young Massachusetts senator.

Kennedy had several liabilities. According to the standards of the time, he was relatively inexperienced, especially in foreign affairs, and he had little by way of substantial accomplishment to show for his years in the Senate. In addition, Kennedy was a Catholic. Every president (and vice president) prior to 1960 had been a Protestant. The only previous Catholic nominee, Al Smith in 1928, had lost badly—even in states in the Democratic "solid south." Although Kennedy was a personable, attractive candidate, many in the party feared that nominating a Catholic was a losing proposition.

Kennedy decided to convince party leaders of his electability by first taking his case to the people, foreshadowing the kind of campaign that is now the norm. In 1960, only 16 states held primaries, and these chose only a small fraction of the convention delegates. Primaries were mostly "beauty contests" in which candidates could show strength and indirectly influence the professionals who would choose the nominee. Kennedy chose to enter seven primaries.

In Wisconsin, Kennedy beat Senator Hubert Humphrey, who had also decided to take the primary route, but the pattern of voting was troublesome. Kennedy lost the protestant congressional districts and won the Catholic districts, fueling fears that a Catholic still could not win a national election in a heavily Protestant country. This set up West Virginia—95 percent Protestant—as the critical battleground. Kennedy met the issue head on, discussing the religious issue in a half-hour statewide TV broadcast. Never giving up the offensive, Kennedy barnstormed the state, but according to Theodore White,

Above all, over and over again there was the handsome, open-faced candidate on the TV screen, showing himself, proving that a Catholic wears no horns. The documentary film on TV opened with a cut of a PT boat spraying a white wake through the black night, and Kennedy was a war hero; the film next showed the quiet young man holding a book in his hand in his own library receiving the Pulitzer Prize, and he was a scholar; then the young man held his golden-haired daughter of two, reading to her as she sat on his lap, and he was the young father; and always, gravely, open-eyed, with a sincerity

NEW MEDIA

During the 1992 campaign, Bill Clinton and Ross Perot irritated the establishment media by appearing on such nontraditional outlets as *Larry King Live*, the *Arsenio Hall Show*, and even *MTV*. Clinton played his sax on *Arsenio Hall*, Perot virtually announced his candidacy on *Larry King Live*, and even President Bush felt

that could not be feigned, he would explain his own devotion to the freedom of America's faiths and the separation of church and state. *

Kennedy beat Humphrey in Protestant West Virginia and went on to win the nomination. TV was not the only explanation for his victory—he had the Kennedy family fortune behind him, and by all accounts, used it freely—but more than any previous candidate he had used TV as a critical part of the campaign.

The next task was to defeat an even more formidable foe, Protestant Vice President Nixon, viewed by many as more knowledgeable and experienced than Kennedy. Nixon and Kennedy agreed to a series of four debates to be carried by radio and, for the first time, TV.

A mythology has grown up about the debates. It is too much to say that they were the key to Kennedy's winning the election, although in a very close election—the closest in American history—any-

thing and everything is key. The audience for the debates was huge—approaching World Series figures. Both candidates performed creditably, and the discussion was more substantive than TV debates in general today. But winning debating points was not Kennedy's aim. Appearing side by side with Nixon, the debates helped Kennedy establish that he belonged in the race. He projected a cool, confident image that contrasted favorably with Nixon's more nervous, less comfortable appearance. Through the debates Kennedy was able to partially offset Nixon's perceived advantage in maturity and experience, and to overcome the hesitation of some Democrats previously reluctant to vote for him.†

In November, Kennedy's Catholicism cost him votes in some areas and gained him votes in others, but the losses were concentrated in the South, where the Democrats had votes to spare. On the plus side, religion may have gained

him the critical states of New Jersey and Illinois, the latter by a thin 9,000 vote margin.‡ Kennedy became the first Catholic president, and the religious issue—at least in its Protestant versus Catholic form—was laid to rest.

* Theodore H. White, *The Making of the President, 1960* (New York: Signet, 1961): 128.

† Nelson Polsby and Aaron Wildavsky, *Presidential Elections: Strategies of American Electoral Politics* (New York: Scribner, 1964): 119-121.

‡ Angus Campbell, Philip Converse, Warren Miller, and Donald Stokes, "Stability and Change in 1960: A Reinstating Election," in *Elections and the Political Order* (New York: Wiley, 1966): Ch. 5.

It is part of American political mythology that John F. Kennedy's confident appearance in the televised debates with Richard Nixon helped him win the election.

compelled to appear on *Larry King* and *MTV* to compete with Clinton. Two years after the election, Vice President Gore returned to *Larry King Live* to debate NAFTA with Ross Perot, and Gore's performance was credited with helping to save the Clinton administration from an embarrassing congressional defeat (see pp. 408–409).

Cable TV is probably the best-known example of what is generally described as the **new media**. The term includes a wide range of technological innovations of the

■ **new media**
Cable TV, fax, e-mail, and the Internet—the consequences of technological advances of the past few decades.

past two decades, including VCRs, fax, cellular phones, satellite dishes, CDs, modems, answering machines, and e-mail.[20] When you surf the Internet via your PC and modem, you are using the new media.

Except for cable TV, the new media cannot yet be considered mass media. For example, as of early 1996, only about 30 percent of American homes had personal computers, and only a fraction of those had modems—although some people have access to the Internet either at work or at various public sites. Surveys indicate that less than one-third of Americans have access to the World Wide Web.[22] Thus, political chat rooms and the *Hotline* are far from the equivalent of radio's Rush Limbaugh, let alone network TV's evening news. The new media are both relatively expensive for many people, and require an investment in knowledge and technical skills beyond what many people are willing to make.

Radio and TV started small as well, however, and grew into the mass media they are today. Many of those involved in politics already are taking advantage of the new media, both to supplement the traditional print and broadcast media, and to obtain coverage they might not get from the traditional mass media. Political use of the Internet, in particular, is growing rapidly.[22] The political parties, prominent politicians, and numerous groups have their own web sites. In one survey conducted after the 1996 election, 9 percent of voters reported that information from the 'Net had influenced their vote.[23]

Network TV has a large, heterogeneous audience. Thus, it encourages politicians to make general appeals. In contrast, the newer media allow politicians to communicate very specific information to specialized audiences. Once again, an innovation in the media realm has altered the existing equilibrium between politicians and the media, this time apparently in favor of politicians. The new media give them a greater capacity to communicate to voters without having their messages constrained and edited by the traditional mass media. The struggle for control of information continues.

GOVERNMENT REGULATION OF THE ELECTRONIC MEDIA

One of the reasons newspapers spread so rapidly in the United States was that freedom of the press was closer to being an absolute doctrine here than in other countries. That was not the case when it came to the electronic media, however. After the invention of radio, it soon became apparent that, left to their own devices, stations would broadcast on the same band lengths and interfere with each other. The result was the creation of the Federal Radio Commission in 1927, followed by the Federal Communications Commission in 1934. These commissions were charged with regulating the industry—issuing licenses to operate and specifying the conditions of operation. When television became commercially viable, Congress added regulation of television to the FCC's responsibilities.

Since the government was allocating a limited public resource, granting it to some and denying it to others, the courts upheld the right of government to regulate what was said over the airwaves in ways that never would have been allowed in the case of print. And politicians certainly had incentives to regulate: After all, to be denied access to radio (later TV) could severely handicap their electoral chances. And to deny access to some points of view could deny those points of view a fair public hearing. Thus, the legislation creating the FCC established an **equal time rule** specifying that, if a station sold time to a legally qualified candidate, it must sell time to all such candidates. Later the rule was expanded, so that, for example, when the networks carry the president's state of the union speech, they also must carry a reply from the opposition. From 1949 to 1987, the FCC also enforced a **fairness doctrine** that required stations to devote a reasonable amount of time to matters of public importance, and to air contrasting viewpoints on those matters. Eventually the doctrine also required stations to grant public figures who were attacked an opportunity to reply.

In the 1970s, technological advances began to undercut the rationale for government regulation. The Bell Telephone monopoly of telecommunications was broken up, and new technologies like fiber optics and microwave transmission made the number of radio and television channels essentially unlimited. In 1987, a deregulation-minded FCC staffed by appointees of President Reagan repealed the "fairness doctrine." But more deregulation was to come.

By the mid 1990s, technological developments had made the 1930s structure of communications regulation hopelessly obsolete. After three years of hard work, the Congress overwhelmingly approved a major telecommunications act in 1996, a genuinely bipartisan effort in the conflict-ridden 104th Congress. As much as practically and politically possible, the act sought to replace government regulation with competition. It created a giant national market for telecommunications services. Previously,

equal time rule
Promulgated by the FCC, required any station selling time to a candidate to sell time to other candidates at comparable rates.

fairness doctrine
Promulgated by the FCC, required stations to carry some public affairs programming and to balance the points of view expressed.

local phone service had been separated from long distance, and both had been separated from cable technology. The new legislation abolished the local phone monopolies but allowed the local companies to compete in offering long distance. Cable rates were deregulated, but telephone companies were permitted to offer video services. As a result of the act's removal of longstanding barriers between sectors of the industry, far-reaching change in the telecommunications field is expected in the years ahead. Today's new media may soon become old media.

What Information Sources Do Americans Use?

Communication is a two-way street. No one can make people read newspapers, listen to radio, watch TV, or visit your home page. Citizens are free to consume or ignore the information provided. When we examine the media choices of ordinary Americans, however, there are few surprises. For the most part, media companies are profit-making enterprises, so their growth and decline should reflect the tastes and choices of the popular audience.

Surveys show that TV supplanted newspapers as the public's principal source of information in the early 1960s (see Figure 9.1) Today, nearly 60 percent of Americans rely primarily on television. A much smaller 20 percent rely primarily on newspapers, with the remaining 20 percent using both. Comparable percentages report TV or newspapers to be the most credible source of information. In short, TV is the dominant provider of information in American society, and its dominance is increasing as the electronic media progress and expand.

FIGURE 9.1A

Primary Sources of News

SOURCE: Data are taken from the Roper Organization, *America's Watching: Public Attitudes Toward Television* (1991).

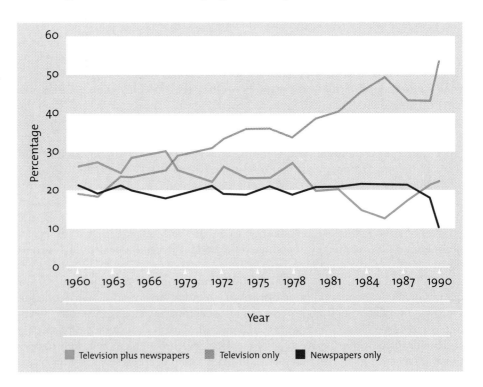

276 CHAPTER 9

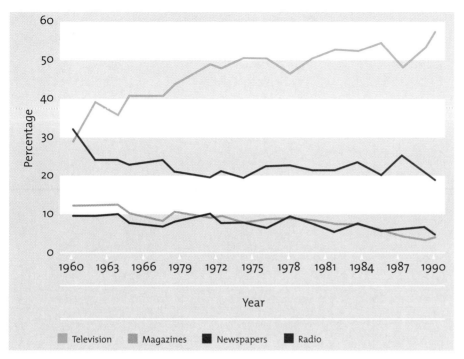

FIGURE 9.1B

Most Credible News Source

SOURCE: Public opinion data are taken from The Roper Organization, *America's Watching: Public Attitudes Toward Television* (1991).

An important qualification to this conclusion about the dominance of TV is that citizens' reliance on different kinds of media varies with the focus of their attention.[24] In presidential campaigns, people rely more on TV than newspapers by a margin of 3:1. But in statewide races for governor and senator, TV's edge is only 5:3. And in local election contests, newspapers have an edge over TV as the principal source of information: The networks are not going to cover local races in small cities and towns (see Figure 9.2). Whether newspapers can maintain their importance in this niche as local cable stations proliferate remains to be seen.

Individuals vary in predictable ways in their absorption of information.[25] Well-educated individuals are relatively more likely to rely on newspapers than less well-educated people. As one would expect, the younger generation is more TV-oriented than its elders, except that older women lead other groups in their attention to television news. Minorities rely on TV and newspapers less than whites (but they pay more attention to racial and ethnic publications and radio stations than whites). Partisans of newspapers have long argued that print is more informative than TV, but research fails to support that argument once the characteristics of the audience (such as education) are taken into account.[26] That is, people of comparable levels of education tend to learn about the same amount, whatever their preferred medium.

Media Effects

The rapid spread of radio in the 1930s coincided with the rise of fascism in Europe. Some worried that the coincidence was more than accidental. Heretofore, political leaders had communicated with constituencies in indirect ways, speaking and writing to lower-level leaders who in turn communicated with the grass roots. Now, demagogues like Hitler and Mussolini were able to talk directly to their audience, giving

FIGURE **9.2**

Distribution of CBS News Coverage
by Type of Election, 1980

SOURCE: Data taken from Harold
Stanley and Richard Niemi,
Vital Statistics on American Politics
(Washington, DC: CQ Press,
1988), p. 52.

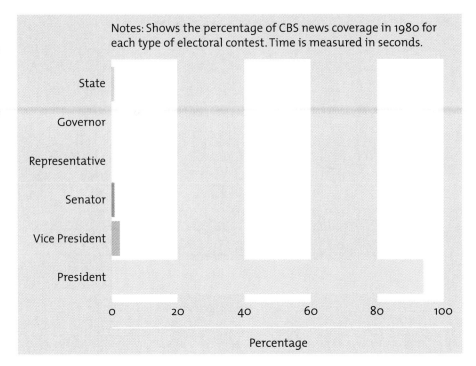

Notes: Shows the percentage of CBS news coverage in 1980 for
each type of electoral contest. Time is measured in seconds.

rise to fears that radio was contributing to the creation of a "mass society" in which charismatic leaders could sway vast numbers of lonely individuals no longer tightly integrated into churches, unions, local communities, and other networks.[27] Stimulated by such concerns, researchers conducted numerous studies of the media's ability to persuade.

Unexpectedly, research on the effects of mass communication proved mostly negative. Americans, at least, were remarkably resistant to attempts to change their views. Many studies found selective perception: People ignored information not consistent with their predispositions and absorbed information that was. Thus, exposure to communications tended more to reinforce than to change what people already believed.[28] By 1960, a **minimal effects thesis** had become widely accepted.[29]

■ **minimal effects thesis**
Theory that the mass media
had little or no effect on public
opinion.

After the rapid spread of TV, however, younger generations of researchers took a new look at the subject. This newer research has documented important media effects, although these effects are more subtle than the kind of mass persuasion the earlier studies had sought to document.

AGENDA-SETTING

Bernard Cohen argued that the media may not tell people *what* to think, but that the media tell people what to think *about*.[30] The media set the agenda, even if they do not determine how the issues will be decided. We know that many people are relatively uninformed about many issues (p. 144). By choosing to focus on one issue or problem rather than another, the media can induce people to think about that issue or problem. For example, in recent years there have been numerous catastrophes in third world countries that have gone largely unnoticed in the developed countries until the media—particularly television—turned its focus on them. In October of 1984, the international community launched a massive relief effort to alleviate famine in Ethiopia after the British Broadcasting Channel (BBC) showed heart-rending footage. In the

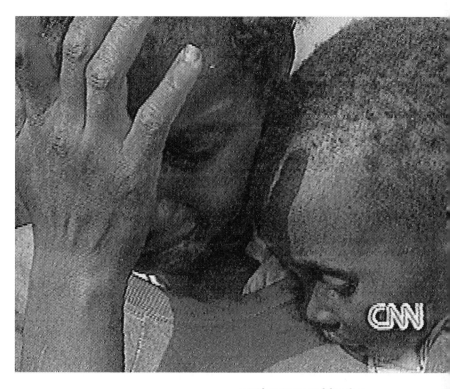

Vivid pictures and familiar correspondents can elevate a faraway situation on the national agenda —the so-called CNN effect.

preceding year the *New York Times* had published four front-page articles on the famine, the *Washington Post* had published three, and the Associated Press (AP) wire service had carried 228 stories.[31] But not until TV decided to cover the story and send tragic pictures into American living rooms did people in great numbers become aware of the problem and support a government effort to help.[32] Similar responses followed media coverage of Somalia, Rwanda, and other scenes of human tragedy. Media analysts have even given such responses a shorthand name, the **CNN effect**, after the tendency for a problem to rise on the agenda once the Cable News Network covers it.

Agenda-setting is well-documented, although much of the evidence is not conclusive.[33] That is, if unemployment rises, the media increasingly focus on unemployment, and people in growing numbers begin to think of unemployment as a major national problem, is this agenda-setting, or are the media and the people both responding to the same reality? Similarly, some careful studies of the CNN effect conclude that the media were enlisted by government officials who were working to place problems on the national and international agendas.[34] Rather than acting independently, the media were used by astute policymakers. Thus, to attribute heightened public concern to media coverage in all cases where the two coexist undoubtedly exaggerates the effect of agenda-setting by the media. Because of such ambiguities, experimental studies that succeed in raising viewer concern about subjects not high on the national agenda provide some of the best evidence of agenda-setting.[35]

- **CNN effect**
  Purported ability of TV to raise a distant foreign affairs situation to national prominence by broadcasting vivid pictures.
- **agenda-setting**
  Occurs when the media affect the issues and problems people think about, even if the media do not determine what positions people adopt.

PRIMING

In the summer of 1990, President Bush sent 200 thousand American troops to Saudi Arabia in reaction to the Iraqi invasion of Kuwait (see p. 133). In February of 1991, the American ground offensive began, and within a week the Iraqis had been driven back across their border, with great loss of life. Bush's approval ratings soared, reaching unprecedented levels—near 90 percent—in the immediate aftermath of the war. However, within a year Bush's ratings had plummeted. What happened? In the spring of 1991, Bush's ratings were based primarily on his handling of the war in the Gulf, but when the war ended, the media turned to other stories, chiefly the struggling economy. Gradually, Bush's ratings became dependent on his handling of the economy, a consideration not nearly as favorable as his handling of the war (see p. 134).[36]

Bush's fall from favor is an example of **priming**, whereby events and the media primed people to evaluate him according to his handling of the war in February 1991, but in terms of the economy later. We emphasize that the media were not totally responsible for this shift in standards of public evaluation. War pushes everything else off the agenda of public opinion—husbands and wives and sons and daughters in danger make all other concerns seem minor in comparison. Thus, both the media and the public were reacting to the reality of the war. Similarly, after the war, both the media and the public were reacting to the reality of the struggling economy. Still, studies suggest that the media overemphasized the economic difficulties facing the country, thus heightening public pessimism as well as the attention people paid to an issue on which President Bush was vulnerable.[37]

Framing and priming are related notions.[38] In Chapter 5 we showed that Americans were more supportive of abortion when it was framed as a question of a woman's freedom to choose, and less supportive when it was framed as the act of destroying a potential life. How issues and arguments are framed can produce important differences in public opinion. For example, if crime is framed as a problem that presidents can and should do something about, it is more likely to have a political impact than if it is framed as an uncontrollable by-product of family and religious breakdown that presidents can do little about. During the 1996 campaign, Robert Dole attacked President Clinton for appointing judges who were soft on criminals. He was attempting to frame the issue in a way that reflected negatively on the president. Inducing people to think along certain lines rather than others can affect their positions on issues and their evaluations of public officials.

- **priming**
  Occurs when the media affect the standards people use to evaluate political figures or the severity of a problem.

- **framing**
  Occurs when the media induce people to think about an issue from one standpoint as opposed to others.

PERSUASION

In 1984, *The New Yorker* published a cartoon in which a man sits up in bed and comments, with feigned surprise, "I went to bed a Democrat, but woke up a Republican."[39] Seldom do people undergo such political conversions, and there is little evidence that the media have the ability to convert people in such dramatic ways, at least in large numbers. Nevertheless, by setting the agenda, priming, and framing, the media can subtly influence people's views and choices. By emphasizing issues that help a party, the media can provide an advantage, and vice versa. By emphasizing some aspect of elected officials' performances, the media can help or hurt them. If persuasion occurs, it is generally the end result of a chain of subtle influences rather than the direct product of media attempts to convert people to an alternative point of view.

HOW STRONG ARE MEDIA EFFECTS?

The strength of such media effects depends on both the characteristics of the audience and the characteristics of the information. People who are uninterested in and uninformed about politics are most susceptible to agenda-setting effects. Since political independents are more likely to be uninformed, they can be more easily swayed as political attention shifts from issue to issue. On the other hand, partisans are more easily primed—encouraged to think in terms of certain issues. One study found that Democrats tend to prime on civil rights and unemployment, while Republicans prime on defense and inflation. Partisans were predisposed to think in terms of issues and problems that were at the core of their party's concerns.[40]

But the characteristics of the information being communicated probably are at least as important as the characteristics of the people receiving it. Bernard Cohen observed that when the problem or event is far away—well beyond personal experience—and the mass media provide the only information we have, their influence will be greater than when information is closer to home and people have some personal basis for arriving at opinions.[41] The Tet and Chicago cases are good illustrations. The media provided the only available information about the events in South Vietnam, and inasmuch as there was no alternative source of information, the media had considerable room to affect the public's view of the war. In the case of Chicago, however, Americans were being shown protestors who had been demonstrating on their college campuses, at public buildings, and in city streets for several years. Many people had developed strong views about protestors and protests, leaving little room for the media's interpretation of the events in Chicago to alter such predispositions. Thus, the media *can* have a major impact on public opinion, but *whether* they do depends both on who they are reaching and what they are focusing on. Media influence is *contingent*; there is no across-the-board or automatic media effect.

Media Biases

Politicians constantly attempt to set the agenda, prime people to think in certain ways, and frame the arguments to the advantage of their side. Those tactics have been used at least since human beings have been able to communicate. The mass media make it possible to extend the reach of such tactics and to use them more quickly. Should that be any cause for concern?

When politicians attempt to change public opinion, we presume that they are biased. They are expected to present one case—theirs—and we can discount their arguments and appeals accordingly. But the modern media purport to be a disinterested force. If, through agenda-setting, priming, and framing, they alter public opinion, it is important that they do so in a neutral way. If they fail to maintain neutrality, they become players in the political process, not disinterested chroniclers of that process. Many observers believe that the media do have characteristic biases, which fall into several general categories.

IDEOLOGICAL BIAS

Conservatives often complain about the "liberal media." In the mid-1980s, some angry conservatives even considered launching a movement to buy CBS and fire news anchor Dan Rather. There is no doubt that liberal viewpoints are overrepresented among practicing journalists, but how much those viewpoints show through in political coverage is far less certain.

Numerous studies report that journalists are more Democratic than the population at large—even George McGovern and Walter Mondale got majorities of the vote among journalists when Republicans Nixon and Reagan were winning by landslides; and more recently, a survey of Washington bureau chiefs and congressional correspondents reported that in 1992, 89 percent had voted for Clinton, 7 percent for Bush, and 2 percent for Perot.[42] More detailed analyses indicate that journalists hold views that are more liberal than other college-educated professionals, especially on so-called social issues—abortion, drugs, crime, the death penalty, feminism, gay rights, and so forth.[43]

But do such biases show through in the news? Some studies find evidence of partisan bias on the part of reporters. For example, a team of researchers carefully watched tapes of the network evening news programs broadcast during the 1984 campaign. Their aim was to evaluate the **spin**—the positive or negative slant—that reporters and anchors put on their reports. They found that President Reagan got ten seconds of bad spin for every second of good spin. Vice President Bush did even worse: He got 1510 seconds of bad spin, but no seconds of good spin! These results contrasted sharply with those for the Democratic candidates, Walter Mondale and Geraldine Ferraro, who had a 3:2 ratio of good to bad spin.[44] In a more humorous vein, a study of the jokes told by Johnny Carson and David Letterman during the 1988 campaign found that Republicans were skewered twice as often as Democrats.[45]

Despite such suggestive findings, there really is not much evidence of a significant liberal bias in media coverage of politics. Although journalists and editors report predominantly liberal sentiments, readers of their newspapers do not perceive a predominantly liberal viewpoint.[46] And, although Democrats got more good spin than Republicans in 1984, more than three-fourths of the coverage had no spin at all. Moreover, there are studies that find pro-Republican biases as well as pro-Democratic biases: An earlier study of the evening news during the 1980 campaign found that Democrats got more bad spin that year.[47] Michael Robinson, who has conducted a number of spin studies, suggests that the media are harder on incumbents (Democrat Carter in 1980, Republican Reagan in 1984) than on challengers. And the studies indicate a tendency to pile on apparent losers (Democrat Carter in 1980, Republican Bush in 1992). Bill Clinton's ups and downs with the national media provide a more recent example of the media's inconsistency. The Gennifer Flowers feeding frenzy nearly destroyed Clinton's nomination hopes. However, after the 1992 campaign, many critics and even some in the media community charged that the media had been overly sympathetic to Clinton and too hard on Bush.[48] But within six months, the press had turned on Clinton again, filing one story after another about scandal, incompetence, and disarray within the administration.[49] The media focused on Clinton's $200 haircuts, partying with sexpot Sharon Stone, Whitewater, Vince Foster's suicide, and other subjects that reflected negatively on the administration, while not recognizing programmatic victories that were genuine accomplishments in the eyes of disinterested observers.[50]

Although given less publicity, critics on the left of the political spectrum also charge that the media are ideologically biased, only they see a conservative bias. After all, even if reporters and editors are liberal, the endorsements of the newspapers they work for go disproportionately to Republican candidates (see Figure 9.3). Since 1930, only Lyndon Johnson and Bill Clinton have been endorsed by more newspapers than their Republican opponents.[51]

Moreover, whatever the personal views of the journalists and editors, the TV stations, major newspapers, and newsmagazines are profit-making enterprises. They are managed by rich executives, they have stockholders who demand a return on their investment, and they must avoid offending major corporations to whom they

spin
The positive or negative slant that reporters or anchors put on their reports.

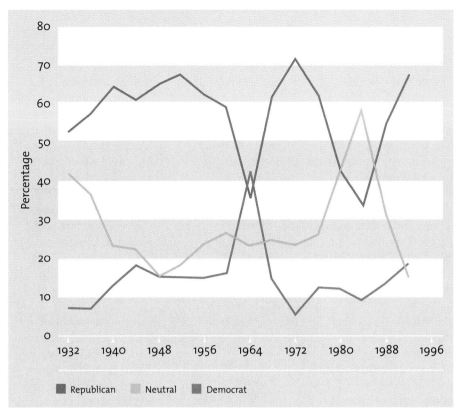

FIGURE 9.3

Newspaper Endorsements of Presidential Candidates

SOURCE: Harold Stanley and Richard Niemi, *Vital Statistics on American Politics*, 5th ed. (Washington, D.C.: CQ Press, 1995): 73.

sell advertising, all of which exerts a conservative pull. The eminent journalist Ben Bagdikian argues that "All of broadcast and printed news is pulled by a dominant current into a continuous flow of business conservatism . . . It has a sufficiently powerful effect to shrink other ideas and news of tax-supported social needs necessary in any self-correcting democracy."[52] In the most recent version of this line of criticism, questions have been raised about whether superstar news media personalities are unduly influenced by corporate interests who pay them honoraria.

Thus, an analysis of network TV and national print coverage of politics will uncover instances of partisan and ideological bias, and probably these favor the liberal side of issues more often than not. But few disinterested observers feel that there is an overwhelming liberal bias in the media. Less often recognized conservative forces exist as well, particularly on economic issues. Moreover, the weakening of the dominance of the big three networks should lessen any existing liberal bias. Local news and public affairs programs are more likely to reflect more conservative local sentiments than the network news operations headquartered in New York, Washington, and Los Angeles. Cable channels broadcast programs produced by conservative and evangelical groups. Talk radio has a conservative slant. The Internet is open to all points of view, and libertarians are especially well-represented there. In short, as network dominance weakens, the communications channels of the future will be more open to alternative points of view than were the airwaves in the past.

Of course, this is not to say that bias is not a serious problem, but only to say that other forms of bias may be more serious than ideological bias. Both liberals and conservatives worry about these.

BUCKRAKING

Journalists and reporters have always been quick to criticize governmental officials who accept honoraria (speaking fees), free transportation, or lodging and expenses to appear at conventions and other meetings of corporations, groups, and associations. Stories in the media imply that the judgment of public officials is compromised by taking money or favors from people who have something to gain or lose from government activity. Under pressure stimulated by the media and public interest groups, Congress adopted ethics reforms that banned the acceptance of honoraria in 1991, then in 1996 extended the ban to gifts of all kinds whose worth exceeds $10.

In recent years, journalists themselves have come under fire for behavior they would condemn in politicians. Some prominent journalists put politicians to shame

ABC's Cokie Roberts at a speaking engagement.

in terms of the amount of money they receive from interest groups.* For example, in 1992, David Gergen, a prominent *U.S. News and World Report* editor, received $466,625 for speeches. In 1993, Cokie Roberts of ABC made more than $300,000. Her colleague at ABC, Sam Donaldson, has earned as much as $30,000 for a single speech!

Journalists disagree about the propriety of such "buckraking."† *Washington Post* editor Ben Bradlee denounces it:

> If the Insurance Institute of America, if there is such a thing, pays you $10,000 to make a speech, don't tell me you haven't been corrupted. You can say you haven't and you can say you will attack insurance issues in the same way, but you won't. You can't.‡

Others defend it. According to David Brinkley, a former NBC anchor, "We are private citizens. We work in the private marketplace."§ And many journalists are conflicted. Ted Koppel, for example, quit accepting pay for speaking engagements after his fee hit $50,000 per speech. Recognizing the potential for conflict of interest, since 1995, the networks

and major newspapers have imposed limitations on fees their reporters can accept from interest groups and other organizations.‖ But they are far less restricted than the politicians they cover.

Journalists stress the public nature of their profession. They are the guardians of democracy, defenders of the people's right-to-know, dispassionate reporters of public affairs. The media sometimes are referred to as the fourth branch of government. If such descriptions are at all accurate, then should political journalists be held to the same standards as politicians? If the judgments of public officials are compromised by accepting favors from interest groups, is not the same true of the judgments of journalists?

* Alicia Shepard, "Talk Is Expensive," *American Journalism Review,* May 1994, 20–42; Ken Auletta, "Fee Speech," *The New Yorker*, September 12, 1994, 40–47; James Fallows, *Breaking the News* (New York: Pantheon, 1996): Ch. 3.

† Michael Kinsley, "Confessions of a Buckraker," *The New Republic*, May 1, 1995.

‡ Quoted in Fallows, *Breaking the News*: 103.

§ Quoted in Auletta, "Fee Speech," 42.

‖ Alicia Shepard, "New Speech Rules Anger TV Vets," *American Journalism Review*, September 1994, 13.

SELECTION BIAS

Periodically, frustrated citizens write to the editor to complain that all the newspaper ever prints is bad news. People working hard and contributing to their communities is not news; one sociopath who runs amok is. Why not more good news? The answer is that to a considerable extent the media *define* news as bad news.[53] A government program that works well is not news; one that is mismanaged, corrupt, or a failure *is* news. An elected official doing a good job is not newsworthy; one who is incompetent or mired in a scandal is newsworthy. Far more pervasive than ideological bias is a bias toward the negative in the media. An emphasis on the negative is a kind of **selection principle**—reporters and editors consider some kinds of stories more newsworthy than others (see International Comparison).

Larry Sabato argues that the negative tone of the media has become much more prominent in recent decades. He contends that presidents from Franklin Roosevelt to John Kennedy enjoyed "kid gloves" treatment by a press with a "lapdog" mentality. Johnson and Nixon received far more scrutiny from a press with a "watchdog" mentality. Succeeding presidents, he maintains, suffer mean treatment from a press with a "junkyard dog" mentality.[54] Some observers believe that the negative tone of press coverage has contributed to the increased cynicism of the American public toward politics and government.[55] The claim is that politics today is no worse than in previous eras—perhaps it is better—but that media treatment makes things seem worse. As we have noted (p. 197), negative "attack ads" are associated with lower turnout.

Another selection bias is that "news" is that which is new, and especially that which is exciting and unusual as well. Thus, events and crises make better news than gradual developments or chronic conditions, which do not lend themselves to the kind of hit-and-run coverage favored by the contemporary media. Heroes and villains are wanted, not abstract social and economic developments. This bias is particularly characteristic of TV, which is even more fast-paced than print. TV needs dramatic events, colorful personalities, bitter conflicts, short snappy comments (sound bites), and above all, compelling pictures—a frequently heard maxim is "if it bleeds, it leads." The result can be insufficient treatment for stories that do not fit the needs of the media, and distorted treatment of stories to make them fit those needs.[56]

> *Our remaining correspondents fly from earthquake to famine, from insurrection to massacre. They land running, as we were all taught to do, and they provide surprisingly good coverage of whatever is immediately going on . . . [But] we miss anticipation, thought, and meaning. Our global coverage has become a comic book: ZAP! POW! BANG-BANG.*[57]

selection principle
Rule of thumb according to which stories with certain characteristic are chosen over stories without those characteristics.

DILBERT® by Scott Adams

How distinctive is the American mass media's conception of news? Does the concept of "news" in the United States differ from that in other countries? Or is "news" pretty much the same everywhere, perhaps because, like other aspects of popular culture, news around the world has become "Americanized?" A 1984 study sheds some light on those questions.*

The study examined nightly television newscasts in eight countries: China, Colombia, India, Italy, Japan, West Germany, the United States, and the former Soviet Union. Telecasts were evaluated for substantive content and tone. Some of the expected differences emerged, although given the wide variation in culture and institutions among the countries, the news telecasts were more similar than might have been expected. Politics was the primary topic of 30 to 40 percent of the stories in all countries. But one-third of the politics stories in the United States were about elections, a figure twice the average of the other five democracies. Moreover, 38 percent of the politics stories in the United States were criticisms of the government, compared to an average of 15 percent critical stories in the other five democracies. (Surprisingly, a quarter of the stories in the former Soviet Union's state-controlled media were critical.) The American telecasts also gave greater attention to accidents and disasters—13 percent of all stories, compared to an average of 5 percent in the other countries. Interestingly, American telecasts were third in attention to crime—behind Japan, where there is little crime, and far behind Italy, where the society's battle with organized crime is an ongoing challenge.

In sum, relative to other democracies, news values in the United States seem to place more emphasis on elections, and on sensational topics like accidents, disasters, and crime. The American news also has a more critical tone. Whether the media in other countries will converge to the American pattern remains to be seen.

* Joseph Straubhaar, Carrie Heeter, Bradley Greenberg, Leonardo Ferreira, Robert Wicks, Tuen-Yu Lau, "What Makes News: Western, Socialist, and Third-World Television Newscasts in Eight Countries," in Felipe Korzenny and Stella Ting-Toomey, eds., *Mass Media Effects Across Cultures* (Newbury Park, CA: Sage, 1992): 89–109.

Numerous observers have pointed to such selection biases as a factor in the largest (in financial terms) policy debacle in American history—the Savings and Loan (S&L) disaster of the 1980s, which is expected to cost taxpayers in the 1990s a total of 200 billion dollars, about $1,000 for every taxpayer in the United States.[58] Democrats and Republicans, Congress and the executive—all share the blame. Beginning in 1981, accountants, prominent economists, and a top government regulator repeatedly issued warnings, eventually declaring the S&L industry bankrupt, but by the time the government finally acted to close down insolvent S&Ls in 1989, many had been operating recklessly for years, realizing that their losses would be covered by the Federal Savings and Loan Insurance Corporation—that is, by taxpayers.

Only after the debacle did the media pick up the story. Why? There are many contributing reasons, but several have to do with the needs of the media. For one thing, the story was about financial policies that journalists themselves found uninteresting, certainly much less interesting than investigating the illicit love affairs of politicians. As one journalist commented, "It was a 'numbers' story, not a 'people' story."[59] For another thing, even if journalists had been interested in the story, it was complex and did not lend itself to short, simple coverage. The problem was particularly acute for TV. It was hard to summarize the developing S&L crisis in a thirty-second story, and interesting pictures were difficult to come by. Not until housing developments were being auctioned off for a song, S&L executives indicted, and members of Congress investigated did the media have the kind of story (and pictures) that it liked.

When the media finally did pick up the story, they distorted it, emphasizing fraud and corruption when, in fact, experts estimate that only a small proportion of the losses were a result of fraud. Most of the problem came from the ordinary operation of the political process.[60] Every congressional district has S&Ls, as well as industries such as real estate and construction that are dependent on them. Together these interests are important components of many local economies. Moreover, S&L executives, realtors, and construction interests are generous contributors to political campaigns. They lobbied Congress and the executive branch, who accommodated them with favorable legislative changes and protected them from regulators when they got into trouble. Economists and other experts warned that the politics would lead to economic disaster; when it did, the press emphasized the corruption of individuals rather than a political process that ignored the predictable long-term effects of policies for short-run electoral gain. Thus, the media even missed the opportunity to draw a useful lesson that might avoid such a problem in the future.

PROFESSIONAL BIAS

A third kind of media bias arises from the demands of the journalism profession today. A few journalists are experts who work specific "beats"—the business reporter, education reporter, health reporter, Supreme Court reporter, and so on. But most reporters and journalists are generalists who lack specific substantive expertise. They operate on tight deadlines and must start from scratch on each new story. Thus, on many subjects more complex than scandals and conflicts they are dependent on experts and other outside sources for information and interpretation. Ironically, despite the image of the investigative reporter, studies find that reporters uncover only a small fraction of the scandals they report—probably less than one-quarter.[61] Government agencies reveal the lion's share, and they generally do so officially, not through surreptitious "leaks."

Moreover, as journalists themselves recognize, the news media have become increasingly entertainment oriented.[62] Especially in the case of TV, looks and personalities are more important today than a generation ago. With the growth of the new media, competitive pressures are greater than ever and have resulted in a race to the bottom as network news becomes more like infotainment—a mixture of news and entertainment, and major newspapers become more like tabloids.

The lack of internal expertise and the competitive pressure for ratings and sales contribute to an unattractive feature of modern political coverage, so-called "pack journalism," wherein reporters unanimously decide something is the big story and attack it like wolves tearing apart a wounded prey. Sabato calls the more extreme manifestations of this behavior "feeding frenzies."[63] Normal people, observing such behavior, are puzzled by the media's obsession with seemingly minor matters, but to journalists under great competitive pressure and lacking the personal stature to stand against the crowd, there is safety in numbers. One can hardly be faulted for working on the same story as other prominent journalists. Far better to focus on what turns out to be an inconsequential story than "run the risk of going down in history as 'the reporter who missed the next Watergate.'"[64] Indeed, there is every indication that the "pack" mentality extends to editorial offices, where each news show or newspaper fears missing a big story.

PROSPECTS FOR CHANGE

However justified, criticisms of the media's coverage of politics and govern-ment miss an important point. The news media in the United States are neither educational institutions nor public institutions; rather, most are private, profit-making enterprises. To complaints that their coverage falls short of what many would like to see, they generally respond that they are trying to provide the kind of coverage people want. Indeed, modern newspapers make frequent use of focus groups and other means of measuring reader interest.[66] If tabloid journalism is on the rise, it is because media executives see that as what the modern public wants.

Of course, the media long have claimed that they are more than profit-making businesses. They claim to be providing an essential public service. When they pub-lish sensitive or private information, they justify their behavior with public interest images—they are the guardians of the First Amendment, the public has a right to know, the free flow of information is the pillar of democracy. Many people believe that such an exalted self-image carries with it the responsibility to give the public what it needs as well as what it wants. (Consider the Democratic Dilemma.)

Perhaps the main hope of citizens is that media executives may be wrong about what people want. Certainly, contemporary Americans are not happy with what the media offer them. The confidence people express in the media has dropped, and as shown in Table 9.1, many citizens are critical of how the media cover politics.

Have the media underestimated the American citizen? During the 1992 presi-dential campaign, people in the media were stunned by the ratings earned by Ross Perot's "infomercials" —as many as 10 million households tuned in.[66] TV produc-ers defend sound-bite journalism with the observation that the average voter has an attention span of less than 30 seconds, but Perot treated voters as intelligent adults and held the interest of many for 30 minutes with lengthy expositions accompanied by charts and figures! As the network system declines, more independent stations begin operation, and the new media continue to advance, we may see the develop-ment of numerous specialized informational channels that reflect values different from the entertainment values that increasingly shape the modern mass media. Thus, the selection biases discussed above might gradually become undermined by technological change.

Much criticism of the mass media reflects the view that the media are not performing the functions critics would like to see the media perform. In particular, many critics view the primary role of the media as educational. They consider their most important function to be the provision of accurate information that citizens can use to inform their opinions and votes. Moreover, the media can present alternative interpretations of the information and its implications for public policy. By doing so the media contribute to democratic deliberation.

To a considerable degree, the media share this view of their role. They emphasize their importance to democracy as indicated by the guarantees in the First Amendment. They defend their aggressive pursuit of news by pointing out that they are the watchdogs in modern democracy—the people have a "right to know" what they have uncovered. But critics charge that the media invade peoples' privacy, report news the people have no need to know, and help weaken democracy by their negativity, emphasis on conflict, and avoidance of detailed issue coverage.

Both points of view have considerable validity. The problem is that while we want them to act like an educational institution, the modern media overwhelmingly consist of profit-making enterprises. All the significant newspapers and news magazines are located in the private sector, as are about three-quarters of the TV stations. And the public broadcasting channels have smaller audiences than the commercial channels. In a nutshell, we are criticizing part of the entertainment industry for not behaving like educational institutions.

Americans are not enthusiastic about public media: The very phrase "government-controlled media" makes people suspicious. The Republican-organized 104th Congress even considered killing the Public Broadcasting Service that produces programs for "educational TV." PBS survived largely because of its identification with popular shows like *Sesame Street, Barney*, and the like.

Many other democracies, however, have a far greater public presence in the mass media. Public ownership and public regulation are common throughout the world. Perhaps Americans should reconsider their cultural and historical bias against public media. Would it be better to greatly expand public TV? If public TV received a government subsidy large enough to put it on an equal footing with the major networks, people unhappy with the entertainment values of network TV could switch over to the more serious elections and campaign coverage as well as the public affairs programming of an expanded PBS. What do you think?

Calvin and Hobbes   by Bill Watterson

TABLE 9.1

Americans Are Critical of the Media

"In presenting the news dealing with political and social issues, do you think that news organizations deal fairly with all sides or do they tend to favor one side?"	
Deal fairly	31%
Favor one side	63

"How often do you think members of the news media let their own political preferences influence the way they report the news?"	
Often	49%
Sometimes	35
Seldom	12
Never	2

"Do you think the news media put too much emphasis on positive news, or too much emphasis on negative news, or do they strike about the right balance between positive and negative news?"	
Too much emphasis on negative	64%
Balance is about right	32
Too much emphasis on positive	3

"Do you think the news media have too much influence over what happens today, too little influence over what happens, or do the news media have just about the right amount of influence over what happens today?"	
Too much influence	59%
Right amount	32
Too little	5

SOURCE: Survey by Princeton Survey Research Associates for the Times Mirror Center for the People & the Press, January 3–6, 1992; survey by Princeton Survey Research Associates for the Time Mirror Center for the People & the Press, September 10–13, 1992; survey by the *Los Angeles Times*, March 6–9, 1993.

The Media and Electoral Politics

Although the media biases just surveyed are general, it is useful to look at them more closely in the specific cases of media coverage of elections and government.

CAMPAIGN COVERAGE

Nowhere do critics of the mass media find more to criticize than in the media's coverage of political campaigns. Numerous studies report that the various production and professional biases of the media come together to produce campaign coverage that is characterized by sins of both omission and commission. We illustrate these in more detail when discussing presidential campaigns in Chapter 10, but we summarize them briefly here.

Critics charge that the media provide too little coverage of policy issues—the nature of social and economic problems, programmatic disagreements between the candidates, accurate appraisals of officials' performance, and so forth. Instead, critics charge that the media devote too much attention to so-called "character" issues having little to do with the ability of the candidates to govern. Thus, the press dwells on whether a candidate was suspended from school, had an extramarital affair, accepted a free vacation from an interest group, and so forth. Such matters are not irrelevant, to be sure, and the media defend their attention to them as providing indications of how the candidate would govern, but that is hardly to say that attention to such matters should crowd out more substantive concerns.

Not only do the media concentrate on character issues at the expense of genuine policy and performance issues, but media interest in such issues stems less from an attempt to evaluate the quality of the candidates than from a wish to handicap the race. Innumerable critics have assailed the media for "horse race" coverage of campaigns: who's leading, who's falling back, and who's coming up on the rail, what the latest polls say, who got what endorsement, and how a new issue announcement will affect the polls are the sorts of things that make up campaign coverage. Any given issue is viewed as a tactical move that can affect the candidate's position in the larger horse race.

This tendency to cover political campaigns as "games" or "horse races" has become much more pronounced over the past generation, and the attention devoted to substance has declined.[67] A study that compared network newscasts in 1968 with those in 1988 found that the average sound bite for presidential candidates who appeared on the news had fallen from 42 seconds to less than 10.[68] Although the media consciously tried to make sound bites longer in 1992 and 1996, candidates still do not receive enough time to explain their positions on complex issues. Modern candidates adapt to media needs and practices by simplifying their appeals accordingly.

Observers of contemporary political campaigns are not the only ones critical of media coverage. The candidates themselves are critical, so much so that they are finding ways to get around the contemporary media. As previously noted, in the 1992 campaign Larry King usurped the role played by the traditional network anchors. In addition, candidates appeared on the *Arsenio Hall Show*, *ABC Prime Time*, and even *MTV*. Establishment reporters complained that the candidates were insulating themselves from the hard questioning of seasoned political reporters, but the candidates enjoyed the opportunity to talk about issues and not the trivia that often fascinates political journalists. Today's candidates increasingly have the means to act on sentiments that candidates probably have felt for decades, if not centuries: Recall President Kennedy's observation about the filtering effect of the media.

THE CONVENTIONS

Before presidential candidates were chosen in the primaries, the national conventions were important political events. Party leaders came together, made deals, hammered out a platform, nominated candidates, and, if successful, left with a unified party prepared to battle the opposition. In recognition of the importance of the conventions, *CBS* and *NBC* provided gavel-to-gavel coverage from 1956 to 1976, and regularly assigned their top anchors and reporters to the events.

Since the primary process for nominating candidates was instituted in 1972, the conventions are not nearly so important as in earlier eras, and media coverage has dropped accordingly (see Figure 9.4). In consequence, the parties now treat the conventions as huge infomercials in an attempt to take advantage of their diminishing time on the screen. Attractive speakers are slotted for prime time, and the entire convention schedule is arranged with the media in mind. The parties showcase

FIGURE 9.4

Network Coverage of National Conventions

SOURCE: Adapted from Harold Stanley and Richard Niemi, *Vital Statistics on American Politics,* 5th ed. (Washington, DC: CQ Press, 1995): 69.

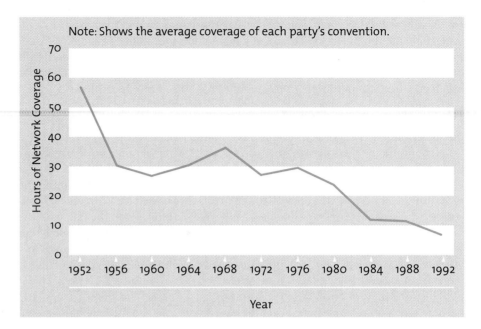

Note: Shows the average coverage of each party's convention.

their candidates in hopes of producing a postconvention "bounce" upward in the polls. Recent conventions that produced large bounces for the candidates were the 1988 Republican convention (for Bush) and the 1992 Democratic convention (for Clinton).[69] Media coverage is a double-edged sword, however; if coverage emphasizes a divided party, or unpopular elements of the party, it will produce a drop in the polls for the candidate. The 1968 Democratic convention discussed at the beginning of this chapter is the classic modern example. Similarly, in 1992 Pat Buchanan's "raw meat" speech to the Republican convention turned off many moderates and hurt President Bush's chances for reelection.

The conventions probably will be even less important in the future. As one commentator observed after the 1996 events, "the more the party managers tried to package their message to please television, the less the major networks were interested."[70] In 1996, Ted Koppel and his *Nightline* team abandoned the Republican convention after two days, the networks cut coverage to about an hour a night, and ratings were off 25 percent from 1992.

THE PRESIDENTIAL DEBATES

One of the high points of modern presidential campaigns is the series of debates between the two, sometimes three, major candidates. No other campaign events earn such high ratings. In fact, more people watch the debates than vote.

The first televised debates were held during the 1960 campaign between candidates Richard Nixon and John Kennedy (see Election Connection, p. 272). One of the surprising findings in studies of the debates was that people who listened to them on the radio had a higher evaluation of Nixon's performance than people who watched them on TV, an indication that visual images could have impacts different from the words with which they were associated.[71] No debates were held in 1964, 1968, or 1972, but they have been held in every election since. Although the format and arrangements usually are matters of considerable controversy, they now appear to be an institutionalized part of presidential campaigns.

There are indications that performance in the debates can sway the undecided voter. For example, in 1984, President Reagan appeared tired and confused in his first debate with Walter Mondale. His unexpectedly poor performance raised the issue of his age (then 73), and resulted in a two-point drop in the polls. Knowing how important the next encounter was, Reagan came in alert, prepared, and full of good humor. He dispelled the concerns raised in the first debate and gained four points in the polls.[72]

As in campaign coverage generally, the first question the media raise about debates is "who won?" If a candidate has misspoken, that often becomes the subject of a "feeding frenzy." In 1992, President Bush and Governor Clinton tried a new format. A media personality, *ABC's* Carole Thomson, moderated a studio show in which uncommitted voters asked questions of the candidates. The questions asked by ordinary citizens were much more substantive than those typically asked by reporters, a salutary development in the eyes of many media critics. But how did the media view it? According to the *New York Times*, "Historic it was. Also responsible, civic-minded, worthwhile, and informative. Also dull as C-SPAN at midnight."[73] Even for the *New York Times*, "responsible, civic-minded, worthwhile, and informative" no longer are sufficient.

CAMPAIGN ADVERTISING

Not everything about politics and government that appears in the media is a result of the decisions of journalists and editors. In addition to such "free" media, politicians pay for the media they desire. In particular, candidates for office spend millions of dollars on campaign ads or "spots." Expenditures for radio and TV spots are probably the largest single expense in contemporary campaigns. TV buys alone account for more than half the total spending in Senate races, and a third of that in House races.[74]

Campaign consultants oversee the expenditure of these large sums of money. These individuals, experts in modern candidate-based campaigns, have replaced the party leaders who supervised older party-based campaigns. Modern campaigns retain pollsters, experts in measuring ups and downs in public opinion. These pollsters are especially interested in opinion movements set in motion by the candidate's actions and statements, the campaign's ads, and the ads run by the opposing campaign. Media consultants design the campaign spots, stage "media events"—appearances designed to allow reporters to get a story, not to meet voters—and schedule the candidate's time so as to maximize coverage. Derided by critics as "handlers" and "hired guns," some campaign consultants have become celebrities in recent decades.

While campaign advertising is widely criticized, studies have consistently found that it is informative, in the sense that those exposed to ads know more about the candidates and where they stand than those not exposed.[75] Indeed, contrary to popular perceptions that everything is getting worse, research suggests that the issue content of ads has increased in recent years.[76]

Another, less-positive recent trend is in the tone of campaign advertising: It has grown increasingly negative.[77] Rather than make the positive case for themselves, candidates make a negative case against their opponents. However, not all negative ads are bad; pointing out the failures and flaws of an opponent is a perfectly legitimate part of the campaign.[78] But too often, the campaign debate is filled with exaggerations, distortions, and, on occasion, outright lies.

Negative advertising seems to work, in the sense that people remember more of what they have seen from negative than from positive spots.[79] Thus, candidates will

■ **campaign consultant**
Expert in the tools of modern candidate-based campaigns—especially polling and the media.

DICK MORRIS

Two faces stared from the cover of *Time* Magazine's September 2, 1996, issue.* Everyone recognized the larger one—a smiling President Clinton, but the smaller face placed next to Clinton's right ear was unknown to most Americans. The face of Dick Morris, President Clinton's chief campaign consultant, was well known to political insiders, however, if not well liked. Many Republicans loathed him as a traitor, while many Democrats resented his conservative influence on the president. But even some of those who disliked him conceded that as a political strategist, he had a touch of genius.

Morris had spent most of his career as a consultant to Republicans. He had managed Massachusetts Governor William Weld's 1990 gubernatorial campaign, and also worked that year for Senator Jesse Helms, a North Carolina Republican, even taking credit for one of Helms's commercials that was widely criticized as racist. As late as December of 1994 he had faxed his associates, addressing them as "My Republican Brethren," and reiterated that he took only Republican clients. A few months later he was working for President Clinton.

Morris and Clinton had long-standing ties. He had worked in Clinton's first Arkansas gubernatorial campaign. Then, after Clinton was defeated in his bid for re-election as governor of Arkansas in 1982, Morris advised him to move to the center, a strategy Clinton followed to the presidency in 1992 (p. 331). Although Clinton fired him during the 1990 gubernatorial campaign, when Clinton's political future looked bleakest after the Republican takeover of Congress in the 1994 elections, he once again called on Morris. Morris is credited with—or blamed, depending on your point of view—for the strategy of "triangulation," according to which President Clinton positioned himself between traditional Democrats in Congress and the new Republican majorities. Thus, Clinton moved away from liberal Democrats in Congress and announced that he was for balancing the budget—but not as quickly, for cutting taxes—but not as deeply, and for welfare reform—but not as radically, as the congressional Republicans proposed. When the Republicans shut down the government in the winter of 1995–96, Clinton became the front-runner. Morris's strategy had worked.

Political fame and fortune are fleeting, however. Campaign consultants rise and fall in accord with their successes in the most recent campaign. In Morris's case, the fall came even before the election and was a result of personal behavior. The same week that *Time* put his face on its cover, it was revealed that Morris, a married man, had a long-standing relationship with a Washington, D.C., call girl. He had even allowed her to listen in on his conversations with the president as he phoned from her apartment. Morris resigned, and signed a large book contract.

* This profile is based on Eric Pooley, "Who Is Dick Morris?" *Time*, September 24, 1996, 24-31.

Clinton campaign guru Dick Morris and his wife Eileen McGann, standing by him shortly after his highly publicized indiscretions with a call girl.

continue to "go negative." What is good for individual candidates, however, has harmful consequences for the larger political process. Much of what people remember may be inaccurate, and, as we have noted previously, attack ads reduce turnout. In particular, they reduce turnout among the independent, more moderate segment of the population. Thus, candidates play to the more committed and more extreme voters, making campaigns more polarized as well as more negative.[80]

Media Coverage of Government

Media coverage of government shows problems and biases similar to those evident in media coverage of campaigns. From the standpoint of the mass media, much of the routine work of government is dull; hence, the media focus on what is less dull. This means a number of things.

EMPHASIS ON THE PRESIDENT (AND OTHER PERSONALITIES)

The president is a single individual with personality and character; therefore, he (so far) is inherently more interesting than a collectivity like Congress, or an abstraction like the bureaucracy. A study of the 1980 *CBS Evening News* found that 60 percent of the shows opened with a story that featured the president.[81] Even in nonelection years, the president receives the lion's share of the coverage. Not only does Congress play second fiddle in terms of media coverage, but coverage of the Congress has declined in recent decades. One study found that congressional stories on network news dropped by two-thirds between the 1970s and the late 1980s.[82]

The problem, of course, is that the president is only one part of the government, and, as we will discuss in Chapter 13, his powers are fairly limited. Thus, the media prime citizens to focus on the president to a degree that is disproportionate to his powers and responsibilities.

The exception to this generalization is one that proves the rule. For six months after the 1994 elections, the media virtually forgot about President Clinton as pack journalism turned its attention to Speaker Gingrich and the new Republican majority in Congress. For once, the media could represent Congress via a single personality. If the Republican takeover of Congress had not been associated with a colorful personality like Gingrich, the media in all likelihood would have devoted less attention to Congress.

This focus of the media on personalities seems to be a universal tendency. Notice that it is similar to building sports coverage around superstars such as Michael Jordan, Junior Griffey, and Deion Sanders. An effective governmental team, like a winning sports team, requires teamwork, but the media find individual heroics and failures to be more compelling stories. Unfortunately, in framing coverage in terms of individuals, the media probably encourage individualism and discourage teamwork, reinforcing tendencies already present in modern entrepreneurial politics. Moreover, such media coverage primes citizens to think about government in terms of the heroic exploits and tragic failures of individuals rather than in terms of institutions and processes that are operating more or less well.[83]

Politicians will often sacrifice their dignity in the interests of media exposure.

QUOTATIONS OF SPEAKER GINGRICH

The mass media rarely quote from the lectures of history or political science professors, but Newt Gingrich is no ordinary professor. As Speaker of the House of Representatives (p. 388) he is, of course, an important figure. But his predecessor, Thomas Foley (D-WA), was not nearly so widely known or quoted. Gingrich's willingness to say whatever crosses his mind makes him a particularly interesting source of material for the media. The following remarks are from a lecture in his course on American Civilization. The comments about women getting infections and men rolling around in ditches and hunting giraffes were quoted around the country in January 1995.*

What does personal strength mean in the age of the laptop? Which, by the way, is a major reason for the rise of women. If upper body strength matters, men win. They are both biologically stronger and they don't get pregnant. Pregnancy is a period of male domination in traditional society. On the other hand, if what matters is the speed with which you can move the laptop, women are at least as fast, and in some ways better. So you have a radical revolution based on technological change and you've got to think that through.

If you talk about being in combat, what does combat mean? If combat means being in a ditch, females have biological problems staying in a ditch for 30 days because they get infections, and they don't have upper body strength. I mean, some do, but they're rela-tively rare. On the other hand, men are basically little piglets, you drop them in the ditch, they roll around in it, doesn't matter, you know. These things are very real. On the other hand, if combat means being on an Aegis class cruiser managing the computer controls for 12 ships and their rockets, a female again may be dramatically better than a male who gets very, very frustrated sitting in a chair all the time because males are biologically driven to go out and hunt giraffes. So you got to look at these kinds of background, what do these transitions mean, how do they apply, what does it mean for personal strength?

* Lois Roman, with Mary Alma Welch, "Gingrich: Big Strong Men on Campus," *The Washington Post*, January 18, 1995, B3.

EMPHASIS ON CONFLICT

Every time Speaker Gingrich makes a controversial comment, he is assured of media coverage. Indeed, because he is so likely to make the kind of comments the media love, and to offer them up in convenient sound bites, they follow him in hopes of being fed.

In 1995, when President Clinton and Speaker Gingrich appeared on the same platform in New Hampshire and engaged in an intelligent, mature discussion, citizens were very receptive, and even Clinton and Gingrich seemed to enjoy it. Journalists found it dull. How could they report an intelligent discussion? They would have preferred the Speaker to level a serious charge or offer a personal criticism that could have provided a ten-second sound bite. According to David Broder, the dean of American political commentators,

It is conflict—not compromise—that makes news. A piece of videotape showing Democratic Rep. Pete Stark of California denouncing the Republicans for "cutting" Medicare will play over and over. Tape of a Democrat praising a Republican for the successful "culmination of a long, bipartisan effort to reexamine and refocus the federal role in the education and training of America's workers" will never make it out of the editing room.[84]

EMPHASIS ON SCANDALS AND GAFFES

However favorable Clinton's election coverage, the honeymoon with the media ended quickly. In the first months of his presidency, the public was bombarded with stories about Whitewater, Vince Foster's suicide, $200 haircuts, parties with Sharon Stone, the White House travel office, Hillary Clinton's investments, and numerous other matters that readers will not remember. The reason you do not remember is that, however important these matters were to the individuals involved, they were not important for the overall operation of government. Hence, they have been forgotten.

The same study that found coverage of Congress to be declining also found that the focus of coverage had changed. Policy stories outnumbered scandal stories by a 13:1 ratio from 1972 to the mid-1980s, but since then the ratio has plunged to 3:1.[85] Is Congress that much worse, or have the media become increasingly interested in scandal?

EMPHASIS ON THE NEGATIVE

A media on the lookout for conflicts, scandals, and gaffes naturally emphasizes the negative. What government does well is less newsworthy than what government does badly. Quiet compromises that improve public policies are less newsworthy than noisy arguments that accomplish nothing.

Thus, network coverage of Congress has gone from highly negative to almost completely negative. According to one count, three of every four evaluations of Congress already were negative in 1972, but that ratio rose to nine of ten by 1992.[86] Again one may ask, has congress become that much worse, or is the change the result of an increasing media emphasis on the negative?

EXAGGERATED CONCERN WITH THE PRESS

Because the press has become the principal link between citizens and their government, in their concern about the channel, elected officials often lose sight of the people. According to a former Clinton White House official,

When I was there, absolutely nothing was more important than figuring out what the news was going to be. . . .

There is no such thing as a substantive discussion that is not shaped or dominated by how it is going to play in the press. . . .

When you put together a press that is only interested in "horse race" and "inside baseball" and a White House staff that is interested only in the press, you've got the worst of both worlds.[87]

In sum, the struggle for control of information continues, as ever, and many are uncertain whether the outcome of this struggle will work to the benefit of the American people.

Chapter Summary

The mass media are less than two centuries old. Newspapers have been superseded by TV as the most important form of mass communication, but recent technological developments have produced new media that are changing the shape of that medium, weakening the traditional broadcast system and encouraging various forms of narrowcasting aimed at smaller, more specialized audiences. Trends in the print medium seem to be going in the opposite direction, with mergers reducing the number of papers, large chains absorbing others, and larger conglomerates absorbing media corporations.

The mass media can have important effects on public opinion, but such effects are contingent—they depend on other conditions present in the situation. For example, where people have strong predispositions, the effects of the mass media are limited. Also, where people have alternative sources of information, such as their personal experience, media effects are limited.

Media effects on public opinion fall into several categories. Agenda-setting occurs when media coverage affects what issues or problems people think about. Priming occurs when the media encourage people to evaluate political figures in terms of one set of considerations rather than another. Framing occurs when the media present problems or issues in such a way that people are stimulated to think about them in terms of one frame of reference rather than another. Finally, outright persuasion occurs when the media change people's minds about issues or candidates—whether suddenly or as the result of more complicated processes of agenda-setting, priming, and framing.

Frequently, critics charge the media with one or another form of bias. While surveys show that reporters and editors are more Democratic and liberal than the population, research finds little reason to believe that media coverage of elections and government has a significant liberal bias. Moreover, other critics charge that economic considerations lead the media in a conservative direction, at least on economic issues. More important than ideological biases are biases that arise from the definition of what is news, and especially what is considered good TV news. The media reflect an emphasis on the negative and an emphasis on conflict. The media focus on dramatic incidents and colorful personalities rather than more abstract forces and developments, even where the latter are far more important than the former. The media oversimplify complex situations and reduce complicated arguments and positions to sound bites. Such media biases are understandable. In contrast to the situation in many other countries, the media in the United States are organized and operated from the private sector. This means that, like other private enterprises, the media must look at the bottom line—what will sell. Thus, the role of the mass media in serving the public interest exists in constant tension with their role as profit-making enterprises serving their stockholders.

In addition to free media news coverage, candidates and elected officials also pay for media. They produce positive ads that praise their own capacities and achievements, and more and more frequently, negative ads that denigrate the capacities and achievements of their opponents. The increasingly important role of the media, especially TV, in American politics has led to the development of a new political actor, the media consultant, who is knowledgeable about the needs of the media and their methods of operation. The consultant positions his or her candidates to take maximum advantage of the media. Insofar as managing campaigns goes, the media and other campaign consultants of today have taken the place of the party leaders of a century ago.

Key Terms

agenda-setting, p. 279

campaign consultant, p. 293

CNN effect, p. 279

equal time rule, p. 275

fairness doctrine, p. 275

framing, p. 280

mass media, p. 266

minimal effects thesis, p. 278

new media, p. 273

priming, p. 280

selection principle, p. 285

spin, p. 282

Suggested Readings

Ansolabehere, Steven, Roy Behr, and Shanto Iyengar, *The Media Game*. New York: Macmillan, 1993. A readable survey of the influence of television in modern American politics.

Graber, Doris, *Processing the News*. 2nd ed. New York: Longman, 1988. Intensive study of how Americans process the news they receive from TV and print sources. Finds that while attention is haphazard, most people learn about important political matters.

Iyengar, Shanto, and Donald Kinder, *News That Matters*. Chicago: University of Chicago Press, 1987. An exemplary experimental study that demonstrates the existence of agenda setting and priming.

Jamieson, Kathleen, *Packaging the Presidency*. New York: Oxford University Press, 1996. Impressive critical survey of the evolution of presidential campaign advertising from the Eisenhower years to the present.

Neumann, W. Russell, *The Future of the Mass Audience*. Cambridge, England: Cambridge University Press, 1991. Thoughtful study that considers the effects of technological change on mass communications. Concludes that new media will not fragment the audience as much as many think.

Patterson, Thomas, *Out of Order*. New York: Vintage, 1994. A critical discussion of the way the print media defines news when they cover presidential campaigns. Recommended by President Clinton.

Sabato, Larry. *Feeding Frenzy*. New York: Free Press, 1991. Entertaining critique of the most extreme manifestations of "pack journalism."

West Darrell, *Air Wars*. Washington, DC: Congressional Quarterly, Inc., 1993. Readable study of evolution and consequences of television advertising in campaigns since 1952.

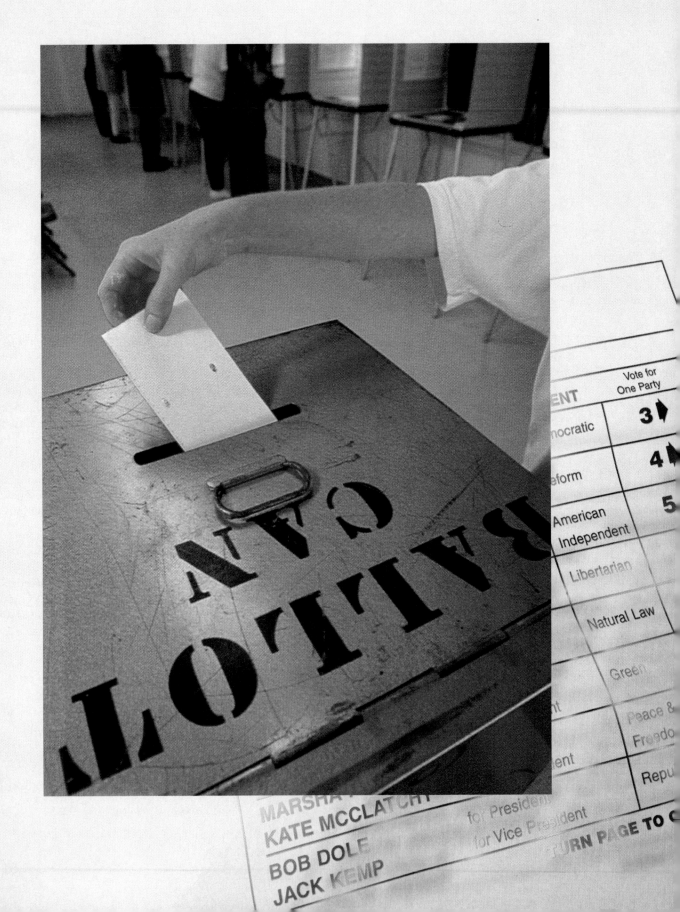

10

choosing the president

N 1992, BILL CLINTON was elected to a four-year term as president. Although the election marked the end of one campaign, it is only a slight exaggeration to say that it also marked the beginning of the next one. Realizing that the new president had received only 43 percent of the popular vote, the Republicans in Congress quickly served notice that they would oppose his agenda. Led by Minority Leader Robert Dole, the Senate Republicans killed Clinton's economic stimulus program by refusing to allow it to come to a vote. Then Senate and House Republicans voted *unanimously* against Clinton's budget, which passed by only one vote in each chamber—Representative Margolies-Mezvinsky's suicidal vote (pp. 342–343) in the House and Vice President Gore's tie-breaking vote in the Senate.[1]

In September 1993, Clinton delivered on his campaign promise to submit to Congress a plan for national health insurance. Although most observers anticipated some kind of bipartisan compromise, congressional Republicans soon decided that their best electoral strategy was to oppose any and all health care plans that were on the table. With the Democrats themselves divided, national health care officially was pronounced dead in September 1994 (p. 155).

As the Republicans had foreseen, the public did not blame them for killing the health care plan. The Democrats, in contrast, did take the blame. Given that they controlled the presidency and both houses of Congress, the complete failure of health care reform suggested that the Democrats were incapable of governing. In a stunning reversal, they lost control of both the House and Senate in the 1994 elections. Six days after the elections, one Republican senator, Arlen Specter (PA), already was campaigning in New Hampshire, and another, Phil Gramm (TX), had filed a statement of candidacy. Republicans thought Clinton was a goner.

But Clinton was not called "the comeback kid" for nothing. By early 1996, he had recovered politically and never trailed in the 1996 trial heats. Because the election was a foregone conclusion, many insiders began to speculate about the 2000 election before the 1996 elections had even been held! Would Vice President Al Gore be the next nominee, or would his way be blocked by Minority Leader Richard Gephardt? The 1996 campaign began within a week of the 1994 elections, but the race for the 2000 nomination began even *before* the 1996 elections!

Traditionally, newly elected presidents enjoy a **honeymoon**, a period in which the opposition and the media suspend criticism and allow the new president a chance to organize his administration and begin governing. If President Clinton's 1993 honeymoon was brief, his 1997 honeymoon was nonexistent. Because he had waged a cautious campaign and avoided major issues, he could not lay claim to any **mandate** to offer major initiatives. And because divided government continued, with Republicans still in control of both chambers of Congress, it was unlikely that he could win passage of any major policies. Members of both parties accepted that a standoff existed, and began looking ahead to the off-year elections of 1998, which probably would further weaken the President—and ultimately to the election of 2000.

Although Clinton's honeymoons were briefer than most, modern presidents have little more than a year—the first year after election—in which electoral considerations do not dominate the national arena. In the second year of the administration, members of Congress are gearing up for their own campaigns, and in the third and fourth years of the administration, the prospective presidential candidates are gearing up for theirs. Nearly everything a president proposes after the first year is given an electoral spin by media eager for an exciting contest and by competitors for the presidential nomination.

honeymoon
Period early in a president's term when partisan conflict and media criticism are minimal.

mandate
Implied authorization by the electorate to govern boldly in a certain way.

his chapter takes an in-depth look at how Americans choose their presidents. We begin with the nomination process, considering its various pros and cons. Then we turn to the general election, showing how the factors that determine how people vote make the campaign itself less determinative than journalists and pundits often presume. Before considering the 1996 presidential election, we review recent electoral history in order to understand the string of Democratic losses that Bill Clinton overcame in 1992 and again in 1996. Finally, we look at how Americans chose in 1996 and consider what their choice suggests for the future.

The Primary Process

Americans are unique in the degree to which ordinary citizens can participate in the choice of candidates. In most other democracies, candidates for office are chosen by party activists and leaders—a small minority of dues-paying, card-carrying, meeting-attending *members* of the party. In the United States every citizen, whatever his or her history of party support, has an equal right to participate in a **caucus**—a meeting of party activists—or a **primary**—a preliminary election within the party—to choose a presidential candidate. These contests, which also select delegates to the national conventions, begin in the spring of the president's fourth year, but serious candidates begin organizing for these contests a year in advance.

GROWTH OF THE PRIMARY PROCESS

The direct primary, in which ordinary citizens choose the political parties' nominees, is an American invention, a Progressive reform (p. 246) that swept across the United States in the early twentieth century. Between 1902 and 1917, all but four states adopted primary systems for nominating candidates for state and local offices. Somewhat strangely, in retrospect, it was another half century before presidential nominations were determined by primaries.[2] As late as 1968, Vice President Hubert Humphrey received the Democratic nomination without entering a single primary. Although some states had held presidential primaries since the turn of the century, these generally were viewed as "beauty contests" in which a prospective candidate might demonstrate popular appeal to party leaders (p. 272). These leaders—mayors, governors, and other public and party officials—controlled the delegates to the national conventions where candidates were nominated.

Humphrey's nomination created an uproar within the Democratic Party. Many Democratic activists had supported candidates like Eugene McCarthy and Robert Kennedy who opposed the war in Vietnam.[3] These candidates had won most of the primaries that were held, driving President Lyndon Johnson from the race in the process (p. 264), and their supporters—already stunned by Robert Kennedy's

■ **caucus**
Meeting of party activists, especially one that chooses delegates to a state or national convention.

■ **primary**
Preliminary election in which all registered party voters are eligible to vote to select a party's nominee.

PRIMARIES AND CAUSES

The modern presidential selection process consists of a mixture of primary elections and caucuses. Nearly three-quarters of the states choose their national convention delegates in primary elections held in the spring of the election year, while the other quarter choose them in caucuses. Primaries are familiar to most Americans; nearly everyone has heard of the famous New Hampshire Primary—traditionally the first of the presidential election season. Caucuses, however, are much less well known and understood.

In caucus states, supporters of the respective candidates in each precinct gather at a specified time to begin the process of delegate selection. Generally they gather in public places like town halls or public schools, but sometimes they meet on private property such as in a restaurant. The precinct gatherings are only the beginning, however, because the process has a number of stages, or "tiers." For example, the Iowa caucuses in February of the election year are the first major test of the candidates' respective strengths. But these caucuses only choose delegates to the county conventions in March, which in turn choose delegates to the congressional district conventions in May and the state convention in June!

Democratic caucuses are constrained by national party rules that mandate proportional representation for the supporters of different candidates, as well as equal numbers of male and female delegates, where possible. Any registered Democrat is eligible to participate. Republican caucuses are more independent. Some limit participation to party officials and workers, and some continue to use winner-take-all voting procedures.

While primary turnout is generally lower than turnout in general elections, caucus turnout is extremely low—in the low single-digits in most cases. The 12 percent turnout in the 1988 Iowa caucuses, when both parties had competitive nomination contests, probably was the highest caucus turnout ever recorded. Caucus participants of both parties are unrepresentative of the general population in terms of income and education, and ideologically they tend to be more extreme than their party's larger base of identifiers. Recent studies, however, find that many caucus participants are long-time party workers, and inclined to temper their personal views with pragmatic political considerations, such as the electability of the respective candidates.

SOURCE: Jay McCann, "Presidential Nomination Activists and Political Representation: The View from the Active Minority Studies," and William Mayer, "Caucuses: How they Work, What Difference They Make," both in William Mayer, ed., *In Pursuit of the White House* (Chatham, NJ: Chatham House, 1996).

Attending the Democratic caucus was important to Rachelkle Tsachor, who had time after work only for a quick stop at home. Tsachor packed her dinner and ate it at Longfellow School in Iowa City as the caucus began.

assassination—were outraged that the nomination went to Johnson's vice president. The antiwar faction gained the upper hand in the party and created the process we now have.[4] The Republicans already had been moving in the same direction. In 1964, the insurgent from Arizona, Barry Goldwater, clinched the nomination by edging New York Governor Nelson Rockefeller, the candidate of the eastern establishment, in the California primary.[5]

By 1976, when the previously unknown Jimmy Carter won the Democratic nomination, three-quarters of the delegates were chosen in primaries. And although the Republicans had not moved quite so far, Ronald Reagan fell just short of taking the nomination away from President Gerald Ford in the 1976 Republican primaries. Carter was probably the first to see that adoption of the primary process had transformed presidential politics; in many ways his campaign became a model for those that followed.

The past two decades have seen much tinkering with the rules, but the broad outlines of the system have not changed. In 1996 about 73 percent of the Democratic delegates and 85 percent of the Republican delegates were chosen in primaries. The Democrats also reserved 20 percent of their slots for elected officials and party leaders. There is a premium on building extensive organizations in the states where the first caucuses and primaries are held. Here the emphasis is on "retail politics," face-to-face contact with voters, which resembles the dealings of neighborhood merchants with their customers. Candidates strive to exceed "expectations" and to build "momentum" so that they can raise money and thereby qualify for federal **matching funds** to continue their campaigns in later, more expensive contests.[6] While it is certainly possible that the primary season could end with no candidate's

■ **matching funds**
Public moneys (from $3 check-offs on income tax returns) that the Federal Election Commission distributes to primary candidates and the general election nominees according to a formula.

MATCHING FUNDS

Federal election law provides public subsidies to candidates for the party nominations. The money for the subsidies comes from voluntary checkoffs on Americans' income tax returns, and the subsidies are distributed by the Federal Elections Commission (FEC). Qualifying candidates have their fund-raising matched dollar for dollar, up to a specified maximum limit, hence the name matching funds. Eligibility is not automatic, however. To be eligible, a candidate must raise at least $5,000 in each of twenty states, in contributions no larger than $250, in the year in which he or she announces or

in the preceding year. Obviously, most serious candidates do not find it very difficult to raise $100,000 in twenty states. Even minor party candidates have qualified, although they generally do not raise much money after they do.

To stay eligible, and continue to receive matching funds throughout the primary season, candidates must adhere to preset spending limits in each state, and they must be at least minimally successful. A candidate who fails to receive at least 10 percent of the vote in two consecutive primaries loses eligibility and can regain it only by getting 20 percent or more of the vote in a later primary. Thus, a struggling cam-

paign may find itself bereft of funds just when it most needs them.

The FEC provided about $55 million in matching grants during the 1996 primary season. Nearly all candidates take advantage of matching funds, but a notable exception occurred in 1996 when millionaire Steve Forbes declined to accept matching funds so that he would not be subject to the spending limits that accompany them. Forbes blanketed the early primary states with expensive TV campaigns, and his opponents were limited in their ability to respond.

SOURCE: Stephen Wayne, *The Road to the White House*, 1996 (New York: St. Martin's Press, 1997): Ch. 2.

having a majority of delegates, by the time of the conventions one candidate in each party always has won enough delegates in the primaries and secured enough commitments from those not chosen in the primaries to be assured of the nomination. As we discussed in Chapter 9, the conventions today do not choose the nominees; rather, they are media events. Party leaders today use the conventions to showcase their stars and potential stars, and to unify the party by compromising on the platform, and giving the losers a chance to speak.

Strengths and Weaknesses of the Primary Process

Despite its participatory nature, many observers are critical of the presidential primary process.[7] Their concerns fall into two broad categories, one procedural, the other political.

Procedural Concerns

The primary process is sequential: Candidates organize and campaign in one state, then pack up and move on to the next one. The problem, critics complain, is that the process starts too early and lasts too long. Unlike presidential candidates, ordinary Americans are not preoccupied with elections. Candidates may be sending messages 18 months before the general election, but no one may be tuned in to receive them. Consequently, some candidacies die before anyone knows they are alive. At a minimum, this concern suggests that the process be compressed into a few regional primaries or even a national primary held much closer to the general election.

Others reply that it is just the long, drawn-out character of the process that allows outsiders a chance to compete. Jimmy Carter was the former governor of a medium-sized state, Jesse Jackson a civil rights leader, Pat Buchanan a political pundit, Bill Clinton governor of a small state. If the existing primary process is helpful to the candidacies of those outside establishment party and government circles, then, depending on what you think of such candidacies, you may view this feature of the primary process either as a positive or a negative.

Those who believe that the primary process starts too early naturally also believe that it lasts too long. By the time the process is over, the candidates have been pounding on each other for months. Every personal imperfection and mistake has been exposed by the media and the negative campaigning of rivals, and the voters have grown tired of and disillusioned with the candidates. The nominees already are "damaged goods," and they have yet to face the candidate of the other party! Is it any surprise that many Americans are unhappy with the presidential candidates among whom they must choose?

The obvious response is that the process shines a bright light on candidates and reveals a great deal of information about them. Is it better that voters not know about cheating on spouses, alcohol or drug abuse, questionable business dealings, and other shortcomings that often went unknown before the primary process? The reply to this response is that since no one is perfect, the process surely discourages good people who are unwilling to give up every shred of personal privacy. Indeed, some have suggested—tongue in cheek—that anyone willing to expose every aspect of his or her life to media scrutiny is not the kind of person Americans should want to elect.

And so the procedural argument goes, back and forth. The structure of the pri-

A HUMOROUS LOOK AT THE NOMINATION PROCESS

Even as you read these words, leading Republicans are tromping all over Iowa and New Hampshire, fawning over voters, feigning great interest in their opinions, pretending that they actually care what some pig farmer thinks about the Mexican-peso bailout.

They're doing these things because that's how we make people run for president in this country: We make them go through a lengthy and embarrassing process that a person with even the tiniest shred of dignity would never get involved in. It's analogous to the ice-breaking party game Twister, wherein somebody spins a pointer, and the players have to put their hands and feet on whatever colored circles it points to, thus winding up in humiliating positions. When this game is hauled out at a party, a self-respecting person like you immediately wanders off to get a beer. But those who want to be president have to play. If the spinning pointer of political necessity points to "Suck Up to Unions," they have to put their left hands on that circle; if the spinner points to "Suck Up to Religious Nuts," they have to put their right feet on *that* circle. And so on, month after month, with candidates dropping out one by one as the required contortions become too difficult, until, finally, there's only one candidate left—some sweaty, exhausted, dignity-free yutz in a grotesquely unnatural pose. Then the rest of us swig our beers, burp, and declare this person to be the President of the United States.

SOURCE: Excerpted from Dave Barry, "Running on Empty," *The Boston Globe Magazine*, April 2, 1995, 20–21.

---

mary process has positive and negative aspects, and any change is soon criticized. For example, in 1996 the primaries were "front-loaded"; many states moved their primaries to dates earlier in the season in hopes that the nomination contests would be decided more quickly and the winners would have more time to unify their parties and plan for the fall election campaign[8] (see Figure 10.1). Critics charged that this front-loading gave an advantage to well-known establishment candidates like Robert Dole who could raise large sums of money to pay for a national campaign; outsider and dark horse candidates like Pat Buchanan and Lamar Alexander were correspondingly disadvantaged.

POLITICAL CONCERNS

A second set of concerns about the primary process focuses on the *politics* of the process. The reformers who instituted the process spoke of giving "power to the people." Supposedly, the new nomination process would empower ordinary citizens at the expense of the party "bosses." As we observed in our discussion of political parties and interest groups (p. 258), however, taking power away from one organization seldom empowers unorganized citizens. Rather, other organized entities more often are the beneficiaries. Thus, weaker parties may mean stronger interest groups, not empowered citizens. In the case of the nomination process, many commentators fear that taking power from party and government officials who were viewed as unrepresentative may only have empowered two groups who are equally or more unrepresentative.

FIGURE 10.1

Front-Loading In 1996: More Delegates Were Chosen Earlier than in Previous Years

SOURCE: Adapted from William Mayer, *The Divided Democrats* (Boulder, CO: Westview Press, 1996): (Table 2.1).

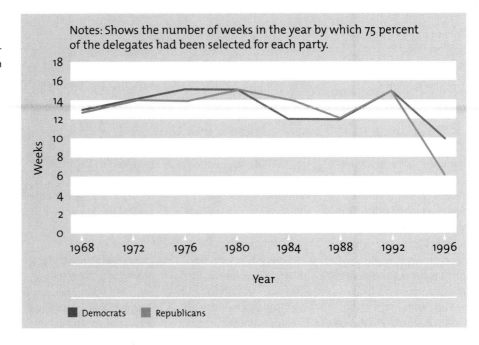

Notes: Shows the number of weeks in the year by which 75 percent of the delegates had been selected for each party.

■ Democrats   ■ Republicans

■ **political activists**
People who voluntarily participate in politics; they are more interested in and committed to particular issues and candidates than are ordinary citizens.

1. POLITICAL ACTIVISTS. The first interest to gain influence from the primary process consists of those called **political activists**. These are people who are more interested in and committed to political issues than are ordinary citizens. Primary turnout is generally lower than general election turnout, and caucus turnout is lower still—typically in single digits. Being more dedicated, activists naturally are more likely to turn out than are ordinary citizens. Even more importantly, the activists work in campaigns and give money to candidates. They are people who help mobilize other voters (p. 182). None of this would be a cause for concern if the activists resembled everyone else, but in some important respects the activists are different. Not only are their views more intense than those of nonactivists, but often their views are more extreme as well (see Table 10.1).

Thus, pundits doubt that it was any coincidence that a pro-life Baptist like minority Leader Richard Gephardt became pro-choice shortly before deciding to seek the Democratic nomination in 1988. Could any pro-life candidate possibly win a majority of delegates in Democratic caucuses and primaries in which feminist and other pro-choice activists play a major role? Conversely, was it any coincidence that the socially tolerant, Yale-educated George Bush of the 1970s became pro-life as he anticipated entering a Republican nomination process in which religious right and other conservative activists play a major role?

There are some striking examples of the influence of political activists in nomination politics. Although the Reverend Jesse Jackson won the Michigan caucuses in 1988, Jackson could not have won a statewide race; only 3 percent of the Michigan electorate came out for the caucuses, and these activists were not a representative sample of Michigan voters. Similarly, the Reverend Pat Robertson surprised everyone by beating out Vice President Bush for second place in the 1988 Iowa Republican caucuses. Despite exaggerated media talk about Robertson's "secret army," Robertson could not have carried the state; only 12 percent of the Iowa electorate came out for the caucuses, and the "religious right" supporters of Robertson were not a representative sample of Iowa voters.

TABLE 10.1

Party Activists Are Not Moderates

Surveys find that, on most issues, Democratic activists tend to be more liberal than Democratic identifiers, and Republican activists more conservative than Republican identifiers. Here is how national convention delegates compared to their parties' supporters in 1996. Democratic delegates were more extreme than identifiers on eight of ten issues, Republican delegates more extreme on nine of ten issues:

Issue	Democratic Delegates	Democratic Identifiers	Republican Identifiers	Republican Delegates
Government should do more to				
solve the nations' problems	76%	53	20	4
regulate the environment and				
safety practices of business	60	66	37	4
promote traditional values	27	41	44	56
Abortion should be permitted				
in all cases	61	30	22	11
Assault weapons should be banned	91	80	62	34
Necessary to have laws to protect				
racial minorities	88	62	39	30
Affirmative Action programs should				
be continued	81	59	28	9
Organized prayer should be				
permitted in public schools	20	66	69	57
Trade restrictions are necessary to				
protect domestic industries	54	65	56	31
Children of illegal immigrants should				
be allowed to attend public school	79	63	46	26

SOURCE: From *New York Times*/CBS News Poll results distributed by Michael Kagay, at the Annual Meeting of the American Political Science Association, San Francisco, August 31, 1996.

The fact that participation in primaries, and especially caucuses, is so low means that small groups of dedicated political activists can exercise more influence in the nomination contests than they do in general elections, where turnout is much higher. Consequently, some worry that the primary process advantages candidates who appeal to activists by taking positions far from the center of the political spectrum where the mass of Americans is located. Thus, Democratic candidates generally are more liberal and Republican candidates generally are more conservative than the average voter, and whoever is elected is between a rock and a hard place; they must either attempt to fulfill unpopular platform commitments, or flip-flop and go back on those commitments.[9] In the former case they antagonize voters, and in the latter case they antagonize activists.

While examples are easy to cite, some research suggests that the preceding argument is exaggerated. Primary electorates, at least, do not appear to be significantly unrepresentative, even if convention delegates and campaign workers may be.[10] And even convention delegates may temper their views in the interests of winning.[11] Certainly, neither the Democrats nor the Republicans have yet nominated any

Democratic presidential candidate Jesse Jackson campaigns in 1988. Jackson's "rainbow coalition" was strong enough to win low-turnout state caucuses, but not statewide elections.

"extremists." Even George McGovern's actual positions were less out-of-the-mainstream than often portrayed, and while Ronald Reagan was viewed by some as an extremist, the American public evidently did not agree.[12] The evidence is not conclusive, however; and even if presidential primaries are not terribly unrepresentative in most states, it seems likely that, in most caucuses and in the money-raising game, unrepresentative activists exercise disproportionate influence.[13]

Another consequence of the enhanced influence of activists in the nominating process is that they skew the political debate. To someone following the primaries it might seem that the most important problems facing the United States are so-called hot-button issues such as abortion, gun control, capital punishment, gay rights, and so forth. While not denigrating in any way the concerns of any readers, it should be pointed out that ordinary voters do not view these as the most important issues facing the country. Yet such issues often drive out general and far-reaching issues of concern to all Americans—social harmony and economic prosperity.

2. THE MEDIA. The second group advantaged by the primary process are the media—the sum total of TV, radio, and newspaper reporters, editors, and commentators who interpret confusing primary and caucus developments for the American people. As discussed in Chapter 9, there is widespread dissatisfaction with media coverage of elections, especially the primaries.

A first criticism is that the press trivializes elections by focusing on matters other than public policies and government performance. The press focuses on the "horse race," who is ahead and by how far, who is coming up on the rail, and who is fading from contention. Is the campaign play-by-play more important than the implications of the campaign for the country? Recall the concept of "framing" discussed in Chapter 9. Thomas Patterson has documented a striking shift in how the media "frame" campaigns. In the 1960s, just before the primary era, media coverage was about evenly split between a "policy" frame and a "game" frame. In 1972, the first year of the new system, coverage shifted to the game frame by a proportion of 2:1. Since 1976, the proportion has been 4:1.[14] For the media, campaigns are increasingly the political equivalent of "March Madness."

Not only do the media focus on the race, but in explaining who is winning and why, the media tend to focus on what many observers regard as trivia—scandals, gaffes, and campaign feuds. Accounts of recent presidential campaigns are littered with stories like Jimmy Carter's revelation to *Playboy* magazine that he had felt "lust in his heart," Gary Hart's frolics on the yacht *Monkey Business*, and, of course, Bill Clinton's alleged affair with Gennifer Flowers. Critics charge that today's press is more concerned with sleaze than with real questions of government policy. Voters seem to agree (see Table 10.2).

Of course, there is a response to these criticisms of media behavior: Newspapers, newsmagazines, and television networks cannot be expected to behave like nonprofit educational enterprises, because they are profit-making enterprises, which must compete for advertising dollars. If they focus on the horse race and sleaze, it is because that is what voters want to hear and read about. Despite what voters tell pollsters, who gets higher ratings—the long, informative newscasts on public television or the tabloid shows? Look in the mirror, defenders of the media say, "the media only give us what we want."

A second criticism of the media is that the pressure to provide news often leads the media to *manufacture* news by exaggerating the importance of many campaign events and developments. Thus, Iowa, the first caucus state, and New Hampshire, the first primary state, usually receive an inordinate amount of news coverage (see

TABLE 10.2

What Citizens Say They Want Differs from What They Say the Media Give Them

	Very Interested in	Media Devotes Too Much Attention to
Candidates' stances on issues	77%	8
How election affects people like you	72	11
Third party and independent candidates	27	10
Campaign strategies and tactics	26	33
Which candidates are ahead	22	46
Personal lives of candidates	14	68

SOURCE: Kenneth Dautrich and Jennifer Necci Dineen, "Media Bias: What Journalists and the Public Say About It," *The Public Perspective,* October/November, 1996, 12. Personal communication from Kenneth Dautrich, February 7, 1997.

Figure 10.2). Some critics ask whether two sparsely populated, rural, mostly white states should play such an important role in determining whether candidacies are viable, or indeed in determining who is the front-runner.

Finally, many observers are troubled by the fact that the media no longer are merely chroniclers of the primary process, but have become important players in that process. Again, in the 1960s, Patterson found that 20 percent or fewer of all campaign stories could be categorized as "interpretive"; the remainder were "descriptive." In 1972, the ratio shifted to 50:50, and in the 1988 and 1992 elections, the ratio shifted further to 80 percent interpretative and 20 percent descriptive.[15] Rather than tell Americans what the political participants think, the media now tell Americans what the media think.

For example, in every campaign there is a widely publicized "expectations" game. The question is not so much whether candidates win or lose, but how they do relative to "expectations." And who sets these expectations? The media, the critics answer. Thus, in 1972, Senator Edmund Muskie's campaign never recovered from his showing in the New Hampshire Primary. Muskie won the primary over George McGovern 46 percent to 37 percent. But New Hampshire was next to Muskie's home state—Maine—so the media expected him to do well, while they thought that South Dakotan McGovern's showing was surprisingly strong. The momentum that McGovern took out of New Hampshire carried him to the Democratic nomination.

The response to this charge is that by interpreting campaign events the press performs a legitimate and useful task. The media are not the only ones who put a spin on campaign developments, but they may be the only ones without a vested interest in putting a personal spin on the results. After all, how do we define victory in an election where numerous candidates are running and no one wins a majority? The candidates and their managers are the ones who start the expectations game, downplaying their strength and exaggerating that of their competitors in an effort to foster low expectations that they can easily exceed. The media counteract the more biased and self-interested spin of the campaigns.

In sum, the establishment of the primary process for selecting presidential nominees has given increased influence to the media. Some critics regard this as a minus, believing that the media are neither qualified nor motivated to cover campaigns in a way that would inform the American public. Others believe that this is an unreasonable standard by which to measure media behavior, and point out that

FIGURE 10.2

The United States from Different
Perspectives

SOURCE: William Adams,
"As New Hampshire Goes ...,"
in Gary Orren and Nelson Polsby,
eds., *Media and Momentum:
The New Hampshire Primary and
Nomination Politics* (Chatham
House, NJ: Chatham House, 1987)

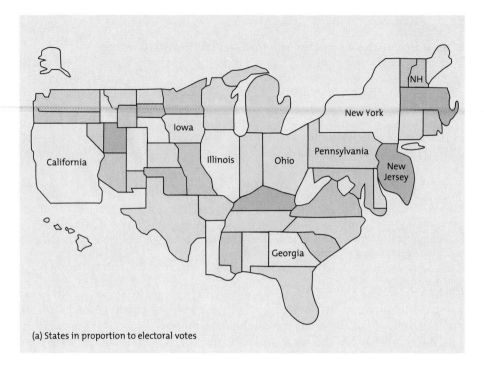

(a) States in proportion to electoral votes

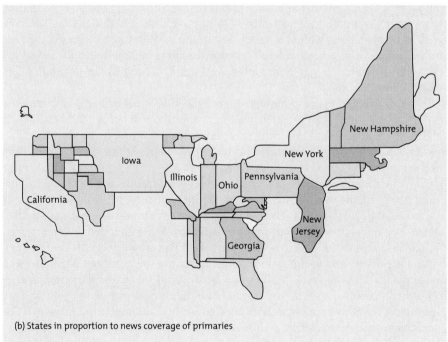

(b) States in proportion to news coverage of primaries

the media in fact perform a number of positive functions. The question is not whether the media are performing well or badly according to some absolute standard, but how their performance compares with any practical alternative.

Whatever your view of the pros and cons of the primary process, it is now well established and unlikely to change except in marginal ways in the foreseeable future.

The system "works" in the most basic sense of determining a winner for each party, and it is democratic in the basic sense that the nominees have always been the candidates who won the largest share of the popular vote and the largest share of the delegates in their parties' primaries. At the conclusion of the process, each party has a nominee.

WHO NOMINATES THE VICE PRESIDENT?

Since 1968, the primary process has concluded with one candidate in each party holding a majority of delegates. Only in 1976 on the Republican side was the nomination in any doubt, and enough uncommitted delegates shifted between the primaries and the convention to assure President Ford of the nomination. For this reason the conventions no longer are the important party meetings they were in earlier eras. They are media events, and the media increasingly find them unimportant (Chapter 9).

Before the establishment of the primary process, the conventions chose the vice presidential candidates as well as the presidential candidates. The choice usually was an effort to "balance" the ticket ideologically or geographically, and the convention often chose the runner-up for the presidential nomination, who, by definition, was supported by a significant fraction of the party. Today, the choice of vice presidential candidates is completely in the hands of the presidential nominees, although they still attempt to choose a nominee who will help the ticket, or at least not hurt it.[16] The presidential nominees simply announce their choices, and the conventions accept them. Often the presidential nominees keep the choice secret,

Republican presidential candidate Robert Dole hoped that his preconvention announcement of Jack Kemp as his 1996 running mate would help energize a flagging campaign.

hoping to bring some excitement to an otherwise dull convention, but in 1996 Senator Dole even announced his choice of Jack Kemp prior to the convention, hoping to energize the delegates. Given that vice presidents quickly become viewed as serious presidential candidates, the relatively haphazard way of choosing them is a matter of concern to some people[17] (see Democratic Dilemma).

The General Election Campaign

The campaign for the presidency is fully under way by Labor Day and dominates the news for the two months until election day—the first Tuesday after the first Monday in November.[18] The media typically portray the election as a genuine horse race; even if one candidate trails badly, the media emphasize the "what ifs" that might make it a close race again. Moreover, the media interpret every campaign development as one that potentially determines the outcome—like moves in a game of chess played by grand masters.

The reality often is different. Some elections—such as 1984 and 1996—are never in doubt, and many campaign decisions and developments make little or no difference. In fact, there is good reason to believe that the campaigns in general, and the media in particular, do not influence voters in November elections as much as they do in the spring primaries. This assertion runs somewhat counter to popular wisdom, but it is understandable in light of the factors that affect how Americans decide to vote. These factors determine a candidate's chances of constructing an electoral college majority, which is where we must begin.

THE ELECTORAL COLLEGE

popular vote
The total vote cast for a candidate across the nation.

The candidate who wins the most votes—in the so-called **popular vote**, or the total actual votes cast—does not necessarily become president. Indeed, three times in American history—with the elections of John Adams in 1824, Rutherford Hayes

Nominating Vice Presidents

The vice presidency is traditionally the butt of jokes and derision. Texan John Nance Garner, vice president in Franklin Roosevelt's first term, once commented that the vice presidency "was not worth a bucket of warm spit." Nevertheless, the office is extremely important. Under the Constitution, the vice president is first in line to succeed the president should the latter die or otherwise be unable to serve—not an infrequent occurrence. In just the past half century, Harry Truman became president on FDR's death in 1945, Lyndon Johnson became president after the assassination of John Kennedy in 1963, and Gerald Ford became president after Richard Nixon resigned in 1974.

Furthermore, even when presidents survive their terms, vice presidents frequently become presidential contenders in later years. Thus, Richard Nixon was Eisenhower's vice president. Vice President Hubert Humphrey was the 1968 Democratic presidential nominee. Former Vice President Walter Mondale became the Democratic presidential nominee in 1984. George Bush was Ronald Reagan's vice president. And today, Vice President Gore is one of the favorites for the Democratic nomination in 2000.

Given this history, many are perturbed by the seemingly haphazard way in which the presidential nominees choose vice presidential running mates. Some of the recent choices clearly have been questionable. In 1968, Richard Nixon chose Maryland Governor Spiro Agnew, who resigned in 1973 when faced with corruption charges. In 1972, Democratic nominee George McGovern chose Senator Tom Eagleton of Missouri. When it was revealed that Eagleton had been treated for emotional problems, he was dropped from the ticket, an episode that damaged the already struggling McGovern campaign. In 1984, Walter Mondale felt obliged to choose a woman, but the excitement generated by the choice of Representative Geraldine Ferraro evaporated in the face of questionable financial dealings by her and her husband. In 1988, George Bush chose Dan Quayle, a young, relatively inexperienced senator from Indiana, who was a liability in the campaign, and thereafter.

Although presidential campaigns have been more thorough in checking the backgrounds of vice presidential possibilities in recent years, many feel that the process is unsatisfactory. Some propose that the candidate with the second highest number of delegates automatically be the vice presidential nominee. Others suggest a separate nominating process in which candidates vie for the nomination.

What do you think? Should the occupant of such an important office be determined entirely by the personal preferences and political calculations of the presidential nominee? Is there a better way?

Doonesbury

BY GARRY TRUDEAU

in 1876, and Benjamin Harrison in 1884—the candidate who came in second became president. How? Recall that the Constitution stipulates that the president and vice president are chosen by the electoral college, a fictitious body composed of electors chosen by the voters (pp. 54–57). In the electoral college, each state receives an **electoral vote** equal to the number of its House seats plus two votes for its Senate seats (the District of Columbia gets three votes, under the terms of the Twenty-Third Amendment). Thus, Hayes and Harrison became presidents because they won a majority of this electoral vote despite losing the popular vote. If no one receives a majority of the electoral vote, the election is decided by the House of Representatives, which is how Adams defeated Jackson (p. 169).

Because every state has two senators, whereas House seats are apportioned according to population, the electoral college gives a theoretical advantage to small states. For example, with two senators but only one seat in the House, Wyoming has three electoral votes—approximately one per 151 thousand residents. With 52 seats in the House but two senators, California has 54 electoral votes, approximately one per 551 thousand residents, a ratio only one-third as large as Wyoming's.

But most observers agree that, in practice, the electoral college has a large state bias that easily offsets the small state bias just described. The reason is the traditional **winner-take-all** voting feature. In the electoral college, the candidate who wins the state receives *all* of the state's electoral vote (except for Maine and Nebraska, where the winner of each congressional district gets one electoral vote and the statewide winner gets the two other votes). So, if you carry a large state by a single vote, you get all of its electoral vote, whereas even if you win a small state by a landslide, you get only a few electoral votes. This is why candidates often win much bigger electoral college majorities than their popular majorities (see Figure 10.3). In 1996, Clinton won 49 percent of the popular vote, but 70 percent of the electoral

electoral vote
Cast by electors, with each state receiving one vote for each of its members of the House of Representatives and one vote for each of its Senators.

winner-take-all
Refers to any voting procedure in which the side with the most votes gets all of the seats or delegates at stake.

FIGURE **10.3**

Bill Clinton Won an Overwhelming Electoral College Majority in 1996 Despite Winning Only 49 Percent of the Popular Vote

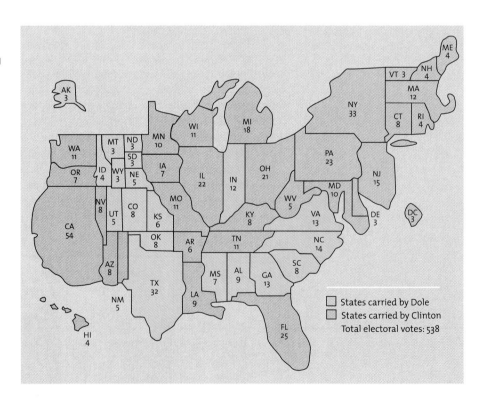

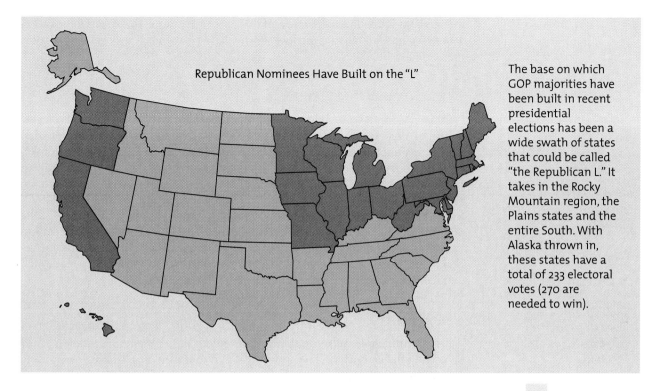

Republican Nominees Have Built on the "L"

The base on which GOP majorities have been built in recent presidential elections has been a wide swath of states that could be called "the Republican L." It takes in the Rocky Mountain region, the Plains states and the entire South. With Alaska thrown in, these states have a total of 233 electoral votes (270 are needed to win).

FIGURE 10.4

The Republican "L."

SOURCE: "Republican Nominees Have Built on the 'L'." *Congressional Quarterly Guide to the 1996 Republication National Convention,* August 3, 1996, 9.

vote. And this is also the reason why, in a tight election, the popular vote winner might lose in the electoral college.

Even though it has been more than a century since the popular vote winner has not become president, some observers continue to believe that there is a real possibility that the electoral college will produce the "wrong winner."[19] Although various reform schemes have been proposed, none has received strong support, and probably none will until some future date when a "wrong winner" is selected.[20]

The media and interested voters naturally think of the campaign in terms of the popular vote, but the campaigns are focused on the electoral vote. It does not matter if you are ahead in the national polls if you are not ahead in states that compose an electoral college majority. In fact, the electoral college was particularly unkind to the Democrats throughout the 1970s and 1980s. Between 1968 and 1988, 21 states with 191 electoral votes voted six consecutive times for the Republican candidate. Another 17 states with 176 electoral votes voted five times (with the exception of 1976) for the Republicans. Only the District of Columbia, with three electoral votes, was as loyal to the Democrats. This base in the electoral college—the Republican "L" (see Figure 10.4)—was the basis for the much talked-about Republican "lock" on the Presidency.[21] Although they were often competitive in national polls, Democratic candidates in each election had to formulate a plan to win all the states outside the Republican base and perhaps chip a few out of it.

VOTING BEHAVIOR IN PRESIDENTIAL ELECTIONS

Why is it that some states consistently support one party or the other for long periods of time? The reason is that there is a significant element of continuity in how citizens vote. This continuity or "electoral inertia" is why the impact of campaigns and the media is limited in the context of the general election. To explain these observations we need to take a close look at when and how Americans decide to vote for presidential candidates.

WHEN AMERICANS DECIDE

Many people decide how they will vote before the campaign begins. Typically, a third to a half of the electorate reports deciding how to vote *before the primaries*. This is easy enough for people who always vote the party line, but easy, too, for voters who know the identity of at least one of the nominees—most obviously an incumbent president who seeks reelection. Another portion of the electorate reports deciding how to vote between the primaries and the conventions. All told, from one-half to two-thirds of the electorate decides how to vote by the end of the conventions—before the campaign gets under way. The figure was 53 percent in 1988, when no incumbent ran, and 65 percent in 1984, when Reagan sought reelection.[22] So, a large fraction of the electorate, typically more than half, is not much attuned to the campaign, already having made up their minds.

HOW AMERICANS DECIDE

How can people make up their minds before policies and programs are ever debated in the campaign? The answer is simply that Americans decide how to vote not only on the basis of the short-term considerations—the candidates and the positions they advocate—that dominate the campaign, but also on the basis of longer-term considerations arising years before the campaign gets under way. The various forces that determine how Americans vote fall into four general categories.

■ **party identification**
A person's subjective feeling of affiliation with a party.

1. PARTY LOYALTIES. About two-thirds of the American electorate view themselves as Democrats or Republicans, the remainder as Independents. Political scientists call this allegiance to one party or the other **party identification**, or party ID for short.[23] Party ID is a long-term force that provides continuity from election to election. For example, the Civil War and Reconstruction created many "yellow-dog" Democrats in the South—people who wouldn't vote for a Republican if the Democratic nominee were a yellow dog. Similarly, the Great Depression left many northerners intensely committed to the New Deal Democratic Party of Franklin Roosevelt. Such deeply held allegiances underlie the "party systems" that we discussed in Chapter 8.

Party identification underlies the well-known tendencies of various groups to support candidates of one party or the other. For example, African Americans and Jews are very heavily Democratic in their voting at all levels. Union members, urban residents, southerners, and Catholics traditionally have been Democratic groups, although their support has declined in recent decades, particularly white southerners. On the other hand, businesspersons, small-town residents, midwesterners, and Evangelical Protestants tend to be Republican (see Table 10.3).

At one time, party ID was considered to be much like a religious affiliation. It was learned early in childhood and was quite resistant to change. Moreover, such early party ID had little policy or ideological content. Just as children learn to call themselves Catholics, Jews, or Muslims before they know the doctrines of their religion, so children learned to call themselves Democrats or Republicans before knowing what the party stands for. Today, it is recognized that party ID responds to political events and conditions, although it is a "lagging indicator."[24] Some south-

TABLE 10.3

Groups Differ in Their Support for the Parties

Groups	Percentage Voting for Clinton in 1996
Whites	53
Hispanics*	79
Blacks	99
Wealthy (family income>$90,000)	42
Poor (family income<$10,000)	81
Evangelical Protestant	43
Other Protestant	52
Catholic	58
Jewish	94
Southern Whites	49
Northeastern Whites	62
Executive/Manager	53
Government Employee	65
Union household	75
Suburban	53
Rural	57
Urban	66

* The category "hispanics" is an ethnic self-identification that includes people identifying racially as "black" or "white," so the hispanic category is not mutually exclusive of the racial categories.

erners continued to call themselves Democrats, for example, long after they had begun voting for Republicans. There is some evidence, too, that older people are less likely to change their party ID than younger people.[25] Consistent with this evidence, during the 1980s, younger Americans led the resurgence of identification with the Republican party.[26]

Between the 1936 and 1984 elections, more Americans consistently considered themselves Democrats than Republicans (see Figure 10.5). Republican candidates like Eisenhower and Nixon were able to win by getting a majority of the Independents and by inducing some Democrats to defect. After Reagan's election in 1980, the gap between the parties began to close, especially after 1984. Taking into account that Republicans are more likely to vote than Democrats, Democratic and Republican nominees today begin the campaign roughly even. For the strongest partisans, the campaign is irrelevant; come hell or high water they will vote their party ID.

2. PUBLIC POLICIES. For the most politically active voters, policy is the essence of politics. There are problems and conflicts in American society and in the world at large. Problems call out for solutions and conflicts require resolutions. Elections determine which solutions and resolutions will be adopted. For people with this view of politics, the campaign is a long-running debate—a chance to educate the

FIGURE 10.5

The Democrats Continue to
Enjoy a Slight Edge in Party
Identification

SOURCE: American National Election Studies.

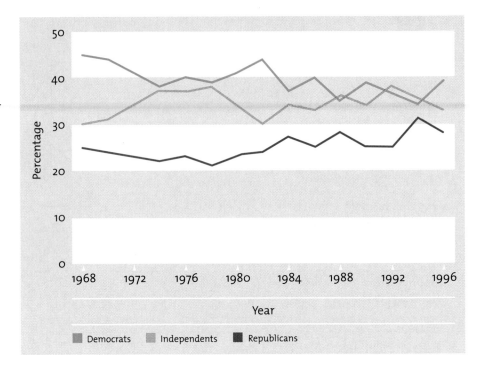

electorate about alternative paths the country might take, and to persuade voters to
follow one of them.

Surprisingly, research has found that, while policy concerns are important, in
most elections they are not a dominant factor.[27] The reason is that public policy
debates often are complex, and people have limited information. To cite one recent
example, President Clinton's 1993 health care proposal required 1342 printed pages,
and that was just one of the competing proposals! How could voters possibly have
been expected to have detailed views about such a complex issue?

Moreover, voters often are unsure where the candidates stand, because candidates equivocate and otherwise confuse voters about their positions. Research on
the 1968 election, for example, found that views of U.S. policy in Vietnam
(whether to escalate, maintain the status quo, or withdraw) were only minimally
related to the presidential vote. How could that be true when disagreement about
the war was tearing the country apart? The answer was that the positions of the candidates gave the voters no basis on which to choose. The Democratic nominee,
Humphrey, supported the status quo, but he kept wavering; and the Republican,
Nixon, refused to reveal his position, saying that he had a "secret plan" to end the
war. In the end, befuddled voters guessed that both candidates supported the same
policy.[28]

While some may find it troubling that preferences about specific policies do
not dominate presidential elections, it really depends on what theory of democracy
you hold. Recall that, in our discussion of popular and responsible theories in
Chapter 1, popular theories treat elections as expressions of the popular will and
assume that election outcomes provide mandates for those elected. In order for
elections to work that way, citizens must decide how to vote on the basis of policy
issues. In contrast, responsible theories view elections as occasions when citizens

endorse or reject parties and leaders. Election outcomes provide opportunities for leadership, not mandates. In such theories, citizens can vote largely on the basis of successful or unsuccessful performance rather than on the basis of the policies that underlie that performance.

There are some important exceptions to the finding that public policies are not the dominant factor in most elections. The first involves issues that are variously called "social" or "cultural." Candidates announce that they favor the death penalty and prayer in schools, or that they oppose abortion and gun control. Such issues are "easy" in the sense that the desired outcome and the policy that achieves it are one and the same: execute murderers, pray in schools, stop abortions, eliminate gun control.[29] Such issues are different from policy issues such as health insurance, where a complex chain of actions is required to bring about a particular outcome.[30] Social issues are as much about values held by different groups in society as they are about specific public policies. Such values often are incorporated into the party identifications of citizens—they are part of the **party images**, those continuing associations that voters make between the parties and particular issues.[31] Campaign appeals based on such issues serve to solidify a candidate's base and reach out to sympathetic members of the other party.

Second, voters may be upset about a problem and eager for government to do something about it. Thus, in recent elections, candidates have talked about "getting tough on crime," "cleaning up the welfare mess," "providing health care for all," and "creating good jobs at decent wages." These are important political issues, to be sure, but often they do not involve much by way of specific policy proposals; rather, voters are asked to choose between general approaches such as "soft" versus "tough." Moreover, such issues at least implicitly reflect voters's unhappiness with the government *performance* that has allowed such problems to fester.

3. GOVERNMENT PERFORMANCE. Real elections are a mix of the considerations emphasized in popular and responsible theory, but a great deal of research verifies the importance of government performance as emphasized in responsible theory.[32] Policy voting demands more of voters than performance voting. To make judgments about performance, voters do not have to watch C-SPAN or read the *New York Times*. Voters can make judgments about economic conditions from their own experiences and those of their friends and neighbors. They can make judgments about many other social conditions by observing the conditions of their communities, schools, and workplaces. Just as students do not need to know how to fix a car in order to judge whether a mechanic has been successful in a repair, so voters do not need to know what specific policies work best in order to judge whether a president is governing satisfactorily.

Voting on the basis of performance often outweighs voting on the basis of policy. In the 1984 campaign, for example, surveys revealed that, on many issues, more voters were closer to the Democratic nominee, Walter Mondale, than to President Reagan. A majority believed tax increases were inevitable (Mondale's position), a majority were dubious about "Star Wars" (the missile defense system dear to Reagan's heart), a majority rejected Reagan's call for further increases in defense spending, and a majority were doubtful about Reagan's Central American Policy.[33] Nevertheless, Reagan carried 49 states. Was this just an expression of his winning personality? Probably not. Analysis of the election returns showed that a majority of voters approved of Reagan's performance as president, regardless of many of the specific policies he followed.

party image
A set of widely held associations between a party and particular issues and values.

Voters can hardly be blamed for adopting shortcuts like performance voting. The future is uncertain, the experts disagree, and time is limited, so how can one make an intelligent decision about complex policy alternatives? Moreover, candidates are not always crystal clear about their intentions. At least good performance by government suggests competent leadership, and voters certainly are behaving reasonably in voting for competence.[34]

From the perspective of our discussion of voting behavior, the important point to remember is that government performance is a medium-term consideration. It is something that reflects four years of activity, not something that suddenly arises when the campaign begins. The campaign can attempt to put some "spin" on government performance, but it is difficult to make an economic recession or unsuccessful war into a positive accomplishment for the incumbent administration, no matter how good the media experts and campaign consultants.

4. THE CANDIDATES. Not surprisingly, the individual candidates are the major source of change in how people vote from election to election.[35] Not since 1956, when Adlai Stevenson fought a rematch with Dwight Eisenhower, have Americans had the same choice of candidates in two presidential elections. Winners generally get to run a second time, but not always—witness Lyndon Johnson, who was forced to withdraw in 1968—while losers typically fade from serious contention. In a coun-

TABLE 10.4A

What Americans Liked and Disliked about Clinton and Dole in 1996
What Americans Most *Liked* about the Candidates

	Bill Clinton	Robert Dole
Experience/Ability		
"good man"; general ability	23	32
general experience	12	60
military record	0	98
record in public service	9	51
government/political experience	25	115
Leadership Qualities		
inspiring; "a leader"	26	11
Personal Qualities		
honest; man of integrity	40	213
man of high principles	3	56
hard-working	21	13
intelligent	29	11
likeable	23	7
positive reference to wife	26	38
young	57	1
Government Management		
efficient; balanced budget	54	39
has done/would do a good job	154	17

try that exhorts voters to "support the person not the party," the qualities of the candidates are extremely important influences on how people vote. But several caveats are important.

First, when we say that candidate qualities are important influences on how people vote, we are not using "qualities" as a synonym for "personalities." Personality is overrated, especially by the losers. It is more comforting to blame your loss on the winning personality of your opponent (as Walter Mondale did in 1984) than to admit that voters reject what you believe in or think that you are incompetent. In fact, detailed analyses of what people like and dislike about the candidates show that most of the qualities they mention have some legitimate relevance for governing—intelligence, integrity, decisiveness, experience, character, and their opposites (see Table 10.4).

Second, after the election, there is a tendency to downgrade the loser's personal qualities and upgrade the winner's. For example, in the spring of 1988, many Democrats considered Michael Dukakis to be just what the doctor ordered. They felt that their immediately preceding candidates—McGovern, Carter, Mondale—were viewed as somewhat whiny men who had contributed to a "wimpy" image of

TABLE 10.4B

What Americans Liked and Disliked about Clinton and Dole in 1996
What Americans Most *Disliked* about the Candidates

	Bill Clinton	Robert Dole
Experience / Ability		
"bad man"; general ability	17	31
lack of/poor military record	75	0
record in public office/voting record	9	64
has not fulfilled/kept promises	42	12
Leadership Qualities		
indecisive; waffles	131	54
uninspiring; not a leader	9	21
too much of a (Washington) politician	34	45
doesn't think before speaking	5	19
Personal Qualities		
dishonest; lacks integrity	279	58
lacks principles	129	6
negative reference to wife	98	15
age; too old	2	299
Government Management		
inefficient; budget deficit	22	15
has done/would do a poor job	35	17

NOTE: The table shows the number of people who mentioned a specific quality as something they liked/disliked about the candidate.

SOURCE: American National Election Studies.

1988 Democratic presidential nominee Mike Dukakis, shown here in an uncomfortable moment in St. Louis, was reassessed by pundits and found "nerdy" after he lost the election.

the Democratic party. Dukakis, in contrast, was a hard-headed technocrat, a tough, competent manager. That was in the spring. After he lost the election, Dukakis's personality was reassessed. Now, pundits savaged him as a nerdish policy wonk who lacked passion: they called him the "Iceman," "Mr. Spock," and "Zorba the Clerk." Dukakis hadn't really changed, but many in the Democratic Party found it easier to blame their messenger than to admit that the electorate had rejected their message, a tendency reinforced by the media's tendency to explain politics in personal terms.

Robert Dole provides the most recent example. After his defeat in 1996, many pundits concluded that Dole was a terrible candidate, behind the times, who had run an uninspired and uninspiring campaign. While there is some truth to such charges, everyone seemed to forget that Dole had been viewed very differently less than two years earlier. In the aftermath of Gingrich's elevation to Speaker and Clinton's drop from sight, Dole was viewed as the "grown-up" in Washington, a mature, responsible, experienced public official who would fill the leadership vacuum, broker the necessary compromises, and keep the government functioning. Reports mentioned his quick wit, and warm—if private—personality. Did Dole change in two years? No, he was the same Dole, but a national presidential campaign calls for different strengths than Washington negotiations, and even more importantly, he was trying to unseat an incumbent who had peace and prosperity behind him.

There are some striking contrasts between what voters actually thought of the candidates in a given campaign and how popular history views the candidates. The 1960 contest between John F. Kennedy and Richard Nixon is the best example. Although revisionist historians have debunked much of the Kennedy mystique, students probably are familiar with the Kennedy legend—the charismatic leader of a new "Camelot," struck down in his prime. On the contrary, 1960 data show that Nixon was more favorably regarded as a candidate than Kennedy.[36] Kennedy owed his narrow victory primarily to the fact that he was a Democrat, and at the time there were more Democrats in the country than Republicans.[37]

Are we saying that Nixon had a more attractive personality than Kennedy? Not at all. What we are saying is that Nixon was more experienced, and citizens perceived him as more qualified for the job. But what lives on in political folklore about the candidates may have little resemblance to the reality of citizen opinions when they voted.

Finally, we should remember that what people think about the candidates is partly based on the other considerations already discussed. Citizens with a strong Democratic party ID probably are going to like the Democratic candidate—any Democratic candidate; people with strong positions on certain policies probably are going to like any candidate who shares those policy commitments and dislike those who do not; people who think the president has performed very well probably are going to like him as a president, whether they'd like him as a neighbor, or not.

In sum, the identities of the candidates and the qualities they embody are important influences in how people vote for president. But there is a tendency to overestimate the independent effect of the candidates because (1) we tend to rewrite history in terms of the personalities on the political stage at a particular time, and (2) impressions of the candidates are significantly influenced by the policies they advocate and their performance records, as well as by the partisanship of the voters.

LIMITS ON MEDIA INFLUENCE ON PRESIDENTIAL ELECTIONS

The popular view of the influence of the mass media in presidential campaigns tends to be exaggerated. Certainly, the media are less influential in the general election campaign than in the primaries. In Chapter 9, we pointed out that media influence is *contingent*. The primaries, especially the early primaries, maximize the opportunity for media influence, but in the general election media coverage runs up against voter predispositions—the party identifications many hold, and the impressions of government performance they have been forming for four (or even eight) years, not just the few months of the campaign.[38] In the primaries, neither predisposition exists. Primary voters choose only among Democrats or only among Republicans, so party ID is not relevant. Nor is presidential performance of any use: Normally, all the candidates in the incumbent party's primaries defend the president's record, while all the candidates in the other party's primaries criticize his record. Consequently, citizens use other information to choose among the candidates, and the media in most cases provide it. The general election differs in that many voters have all the information they need—their own partisan identification and that of groups they like or dislike, and their impressions of government performance.

Why should there be an exaggerated view of media influence in the general election? One reason is that many people have incentives to exaggerate the impact of the media. In the first place, members of the media like to believe that they play an indispensable role and bear an awesome responsibility. With numerous people telling them they are stars whose words make and break candidates, why should they doubt that they are? Similarly, the campaign consultants who rake in millions of dollars from the presidential campaigns have a personal financial interest in perpetuating the belief that elections are won or lost by their expertise in conducting modern media campaigns.[39] Finally, as we mentioned earlier, candidates themselves—especially losing candidates (nearly half of all who run, given that some offices are uncontested)—have incentives to blame the media for determining the election. How often do you hear the losing candidate say "I wasn't remotely qualified, and the voters understood that"? Honest sentiments like these are seldom expressed. What you hear, instead, are words like "I fought for the public interest, but the cunning media campaign of my opponent smeared me and distorted my views."

Much the same thing can be said about the importance of the campaign itself, which is increasingly fought in the mass media. Contrary to what the media imply, many elections are decided before the campaign begins: Conditions in the preceding four years and the government's response to them determined the outcome. The 1964, 1972, 1984, and 1996 campaigns are clear examples, but even in 1980 and 1988, the outcome was largely predetermined.

We emphasize that nothing we have said implies that campaigns do not matter.[40] Rather, instead of the narrow and exaggerated view that campaigns determine election outcomes, we offer a broader and more complex view that campaigns themselves are determined by larger forces. They affect elections but are themselves affected by what goes on between elections. A card game provides a good analogy. Who wins a hand depends on both the skill with which you play, but also on the deal of the cards. No matter how skillfully you play, it may not be sufficient to overcome a bad draw.

The contemporary U.S. presidential campaign is a grueling physical and mental test of the candidates' endurance.

In politics, some cards are dealt years, even decades, before the election. The Democrats drew the Herbert Hoover Depression card in 1932 and played it until the 1960s. The Republicans drew the McGovern "liberal" card in 1972 and were still attempting to play it in 1996. Other cards are drawn in the four years since the last election. Good economic conditions are aces dealt to the incumbent party; poor conditions are aces dealt to the other party. The same is true for international embarrassments and costly wars.

The deal of the cards strongly affects the campaign. We praise and criticize campaigns while often forgetting that the candidates and their managers were limited in what they could do by social and economic realities. Did the fact that Dukakis lost to Bush in 1988 while Clinton beat Bush in 1992 indicate that Dukakis ran a poor campaign while Clinton ran a brilliant one? To some extent, maybe so. In retrospect, Dukakis surely could have done some things better.[41] But Clinton's brilliant campaign probably also reflects the fact that the Bush administration was a much easier target in 1992 than was the Reagan-Bush administration in 1988.

The Dole campaign in 1996 is the most recent example of this confusion of political cause and effect. Despite suggestions in the media, Robert Dole did not lose the election because he ran a poor campaign.[42] The opposite is more nearly true: His campaign was lousy because he had no chance to win the election. As noted below, the economy and the image that the Republican Party projected in 1995-96 put Dole well behind before the campaign ever began.

The importance of the campaign in presidential elections is on the margins. If, based on party ID and presidential performance, the race is about even when the campaign begins, then the campaign will determine the outcome by winning over the marginal, or undecided voters. Under such conditions, the favorability of media coverage and the expertise of media advisers may in fact win or lose the election. But the point to remember is that many elections, such as in 1996, do not begin as even contests. Rather, what elected officials have done between elections has largely determined the outcome.

1992: Picking the Republican Lock on the Presidency

Democratic presidential fortunes plummeted in the mid-1960s under the pressures of social and economic change, as well as the war in Vietnam. After being trounced in 1964, the Republicans won five of the next six presidential elections, losing only in 1976 after Nixon's forced resignation. The Democrats' presidential predicament during the 1970s and 1980s stemmed from a series of reinforcing developments.

THE ECONOMY

Perhaps most fundamentally, in the late 1970s the Democrats lost their advantage on economic issues. For almost half a century Americans viewed Democrats as the party of prosperity (see Figure 10.6). But the post–World War II economic expansion ended in the early 1970s, giving way to an inflationary era that began when President Johnson failed to ask for tax increases sufficient to pay for both the war in Vietnam and the Great Society. Republican Presidents Nixon and Ford did little to halt the inflation, but it reached frightening levels (13 percent) under Democratic President Carter.

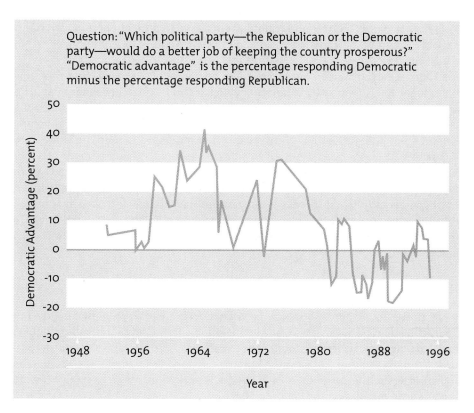

Question: "Which political party—the Republican or the Democratic party—would do a better job of keeping the country prosperous?" "Democratic advantage" is the percentage responding Democratic minus the percentage responding Republican.

FIGURE 10.6

Until the 1980s the Democrats Generally Had Been Viewed as the Party of Prosperity

SOURCE: Harold Stanley and Richard Niemi, *Vital Statistics on American Politics*, 5th ed. (Washington, DC: CQ Press, 1995): 156.

An economically pinched electorate naturally became less generous—less supportive of government programs to aid the needy, and less willing to tolerate a tax burden they found increasingly onerous. By the late 1970s, a tax revolt had begun. As the party that stood for government spending, and the party in power when economic conditions hit bottom, the Democratic party was placed on the defensive by the downturn in the economy.

DEFENSE AND FOREIGN POLICY

While Americans at mid-century viewed Democrats as the party of prosperity, they often viewed Republicans as more competent in the realm of international affairs. Events in the 1960s reinforced that view. Vietnam split the Democratic Party and strengthened its pacifist wing. Americans are not imperialists. They tend to be skeptical of international involvements, but throughout the 1970s, the United States faced a succession of foreign challenges, and voters were not confident that the Democratic party was strong enough to deal with them. The final humiliation came when Iranian militants seized 90 hostages from the American embassy in Teheran and held them for more than a year. This hostage crisis destroyed any remaining hopes for President Carter's reelection.

RACE

Slavery split the Democratic party in the 1850s, and the continuing issue of race helped do so again a century later. When President Johnson signed the 1964 Civil Rights Act he commented that he was "giving the South to the Republicans for a long time to come." Johnson may not have realized that his support of civil rights not only would hurt Democratic candidates in the South, but would hurt them in the North as well.

There is great disagreement today about the nature of the racial issue. One side holds that white support of Republican candidates and white opposition to policies aimed at helping blacks simply shows the continued virulence of racism in the United States.[43] Another side disagrees, arguing that racial prejudice has greatly declined but policies such as affirmative action, proposed to help minorities, are inconsistent with traditional American values.[44] Certainly, there is a gulf between black and white opinion. Whites feel that enormous progress has already been made and, to a lesser degree, that African Americans fail to recognize how much has been accomplished. Blacks see continued racism and focus on how much remains to be accomplished before racial equality is a reality (see Figure 10.7). To their electoral misfortune, the Democrats have been caught in the middle of such disagreements.

MODERN LIBERALISM: SOCIAL ISSUES

As noted in Chapter 5, the New Deal Democratic party was a liberal party, but liberal then had primarily economic connotations. In the 1960s, liberalism took on new connotations, becoming more closely associated with racial issues such as busing, affirmative action, and welfare. At about the same time, liberalism began to be linked to sexual permissiveness and drug abuse. Feminism and gay rights were incorporated into liberalism somewhat later.

A majority of Americans took "conservative" stances on such issues, and the more prominent such issues became, the more fertile ground they provided for a popular reaction. That reaction came in the late 1970s in the form of the "new right," a socially conservative movement often associated with evangelical religious groups. Given that culturally liberal points of view had found a warmer welcome in the Democratic Party than in the Republican, the reaction typically took an anti-Democratic form.

THE 1992 CAMPAIGN

In 1992, Bill Clinton was elected with 43 percent of the vote in a three-way election. Although analysts disagree somewhat on whether Ross Perot cost Clinton or Bush more votes, there is little doubt that Clinton still would have won in a two-way race.[45] Each of the four factors just discussed contributed to Bush's defeat.

Most fundamentally, by presiding over a recession, Bush rejuvenated the Democrats' image as the party of economic prosperity. "The Economy, Stupid" was the foundation of Clinton's campaign. He promised to get the economy moving again, and appealed to middle-class anxieties with his support of health care for all. Fortunately for Clinton, the end of the Cold War meant that foreign threats would not interfere with the voters' preoccupation with the economy. With the demise of the Soviet threat, voters ignored the Republican advantage in foreign and defense policy.

Meanwhile, Clinton moved to the center on race, distancing himself from prominent black leaders like Jesse Jackson, and even criticizing an African American entertainer Sister Souljah for the lyrics in some of her songs. And he defused the social issues by aligning himself with "Middle America." He talked about personal responsibility and family values, promised "to end welfare as we know it," prayed,

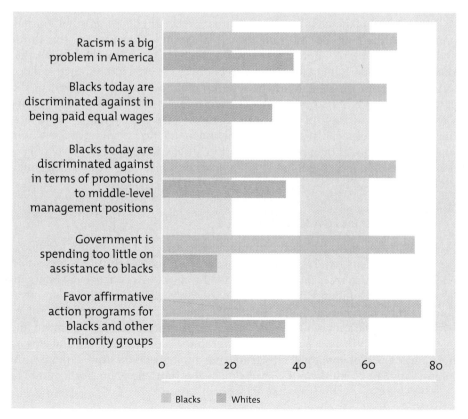

FIGURE 10.7

Blacks and Whites Differ Greatly in their Views about Race Relations and Racial Policy

SOURCE: "An American Dilemma (Part II), *The Public Perspective,* March/April, 1996, 20, 23, 26.

allowed a convicted murderer in Arkansas to be executed, and in other ways tried to dispel the cultural liberal image that had dogged the Democrats for a generation.

The 1996 Presidential Election

After Republicans captured Congress in 1994, President Clinton looked electorally dead. He maintained a low profile, and followed such a reactive strategy that, in a press conference in April of 1995, one reporter had the audacity to ask him if he was "still relevant" to American politics. Within a year, however, Clinton had risen from the political grave. Throughout 1996, Clinton's reelection never seemed in doubt, and he won handily. Clinton's reversal of fortune was based on a number of favorable developments.

THE ECONOMY

An irony of George Bush's 1992 defeat was that the economy had actually been growing for eighteen months prior to the election, although the rate of growth was slow.[46] The economy continued to grow steadily throughout Clinton's first term, and by the 1996 elections, most Americans were economically optimistic—indeed, as optimistic as they had been in 1984 when they overwhelmingly reelected Republican Ronald Reagan.[47] Both inflation and unemployment were very low, and the stock market was at an all-time high. Incumbents who run during times of economic prosperity tend to be very successful, and Clinton was no exception.

Thus, twice as many voters thought their personal economic situation had improved in the past year as thought their situation had worsened. Two-thirds of the former voted for Clinton, whereas Dole won a narrow majority of the latter. Perceptions of the health of the national economy were even more strongly related to the vote. Four times as many people thought that it had improved in the past year as thought it had worsened. Three-quarters of the former voted for Clinton, while two-thirds of the latter voted for Dole (see Figure 10.8). These relationships were especially strong among independents, a plurality of whom supported Clinton, as they had in 1992. All in all, the relatively high level of economic satisfaction meant that the Dole campaign was paddling upstream against a strong current.

THE REPUBLICAN CONGRESS

Even the Republican national chairman admitted that the Republican Congress overplayed its hand during 1995–96, reading too much into the election returns, as new majorities often do (p. 149).[48] By attacking restrictive environmental regulations, Congress exposed the Republican party to the charge that it was antienvironment, a charge that is especially damaging among independent voters. By passing a welfare reform bill with numerous provisions viewed as punitive, the new Congress exposed the party to the charge that it was mean-spirited and lacking in compassion, a charge especially damaging among women. And perhaps most importantly, the Republican Congress made a serious tactical error in shutting

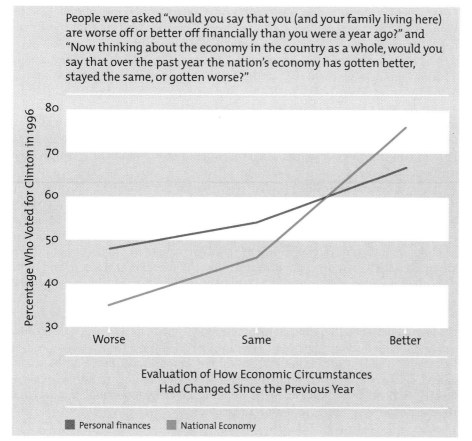

People were asked "would you say that you (and your family living here) are worse off or better off financially than you were a year ago?" and "Now thinking about the economy in the country as a whole, would you say that over the past year the nation's economy has gotten better, stayed the same, or gotten worse?"

Evaluation of How Economic Circumstances Had Changed Since the Previous Year

■ Personal finances   ■ National Economy

FIGURE 10.8

Clinton Was Rewarded for the Healthy Economy in 1996

down the government in the winter of 1995–96, when President Clinton would not accept their budget. Not only did the action strike many Americans as juvenile, but it also allowed Clinton to levy a damaging charge against the Republicans—that they were trying to force him to cut medicare in order to provide tax cuts for the wealthy. Despite the exaggeration of Clinton's charge—Clinton himself will have to do something about Medicare (p. 587)—the polls indicated that Congress lost the budget battle, and quite probably any chance of winning the election. Clinton took the position that it was necessary to reelect him in order to check and balance the Republicans in Congress. Ironically, by the end of the campaign, the Republican Party was running ads arguing that it was necessary to reelect Congressional Republicans in order to check and balance Clinton![49]

THE GENDER GAP

During the campaign, many analysts pointed out that if only men were voting, Bob Dole would be running neck-and-neck with Bill Clinton. Since the 1980 election, women have been more likely than men to vote Democratic for President and to express a Democratic party identification (see Figure 10.9). But the gap was larger in 1996 than ever before.

The gender gap is widely misunderstood. Given the growing influence of the Women's Movement in the 1970s, the near-successful campaign for the Equal Rights Amendment (ERA), and the rise of the abortion issue, many pundits understandably attributed the emergence of the gender gap to different male and female positions on "women's issues." On the contrary, men and women differ little in their views of abortion and women's equality issues.[50] Rather, differences in voting appear to arise more from long-standing gender differences on issues of military force, the use of violence, and government activities in support of the disadvantaged.[51] Note, for example, that in the 1950s, women were more likely to favor Republican Eisenhower, who ended the Korean War and declined to become involved in Vietnam.

There is considerable disagreement about why women and men differ on some issues. Some argue that women's values are different from men's. If so, do they reflect childhood socialization, the maternal experience, biology, or some combination of factors?[52] From an electoral standpoint, the origins of gender differences are less important than the fact that they exist. Women are more supportive of the disadvantaged than men, less supportive of force and coercion than men, and more likely than men to favor an activist government (see Table 10.5). Given the general images of the contemporary Republican and Democratic parties, the gender gap follows.[53]

The actions of the Republican Congress in 1995–96 helped to widen the gender gap and indirectly contributed to Dole's loss. By adopting an approach to welfare that was viewed by many as punitive, by taking an aggressive stance on Medicaid and Medicare reform, and by proposing cutbacks in environmental and safety regulation—in these and similar ways the Republicans heightened the attention that voters gave to issues that divided men and women.

FIGURE 10.9

The Democrats Have Received More Support from Women than from Men since 1980

SOURCE: Janet Clark and Cal Clark, "The Gender Gap: A Manifestation of Women's Dissatisfaction with the American Polity?," in *Broken Contract?* edited by Stephen Craig (Boulder, CO: Westview, 1996): 168.

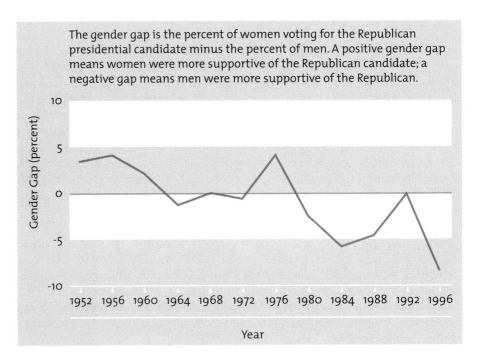

The gender gap is the percent of women voting for the Republican presidential candidate minus the percent of men. A positive gender gap means women were more supportive of the Republican candidate; a negative gap means men were more supportive of the Republican.

TABLE 10.5

Men and Women

	Women	Men
Consider self conservative	29%	43
Government should provide fewer services	30	45
Poverty and homelessness are among the country's most important problems	63	44
Government should see that every person who wants work can find a job	69	57
Government should guarantee medical care for all	69	58
Favor affirmative action programs for blacks and other minority groups	53	41
American bombers should attack all military targets in Iraq including those in heavily populated areas	37	61
Handguns should be illegal except for use by police and other authorized persons	48	28
Favor death penalty	76	82
Approve of caning the Singapore teenager who committed acts of vandalism	39	61

SOURCE: *The Public Perspective,* August/September 1996, 10–27; *The Public Perspective,* July/August 1994, 96.

In addition, the close association between the Republican party and the religious right probably served to widen the gender gap. Although the religious right emphasizes family values, their ideal seems to be the patriarchal family with a stay-at-home mother. While appealing to some women, such an ideal is not appealing to others, a large number of whom are unmarried or divorced, and most of whom work. The gender gap was wider among single men and women as opposed to married men and women.[54]

THE ISSUES THAT WEREN'T

Almost as interesting as the issues that swayed votes are the issues that did not play a role in the campaign. Where was crime, an issue that Republicans used to define Democrats—negatively—in the 1970s and 1980s? What about "hot-button" issues like welfare, immigration, race, and affirmative action? Part of the reason that such issues did not loom large in the campaign was that President Clinton had co-opted them, moving close enough to the Republicans to neutralize the issues. He was roundly criticized by liberals in the Democratic party for this strategy of "triangulation"—positioning himself between liberal congressional Democrats and conservative congressional Republicans—but the campaign and election suggest that his strategy was effective.[55]

Money in 1996

For most of the 1996 campaign, President Clinton appeared headed for an easy win—a double-digit margin according to most of the polls. But in the end, Clinton's margin of victory was only eight points, and he failed to reach the psychologically important 50 percent mark. Once again he was a "minority president."

One school of thought held that the polls persistently underestimated Republican strength, although that charge was hotly denied by poll spokespersons.* A more widely held explanation pointed to the campaign finance scandal that began to break in the last week of the election. Asian Americans had made large "soft money" contributions to the Democratic National Committee. There is nothing illegal about that, and the Clinton defense at first implied that critics were bigoted. But a number of the contributions looked suspiciously as if foreign corporations were fun-neling money through American citizens, and that *is* illegal under existing campaign law (U.S. subsidiaries of foreign corporations may contribute). The Democratic National Committee began returning questionable contributions, and even Vice President Al Gore, known as a straight arrow, found himself entangled in a series of flip-flops associated with his fund-raising activities. In the aftermath of the election, embarrassing new revelations filled the media. Potential large contributors had been taken along on U.S. trade missions, invited to White House coffees, and in some cases, even invited to stay a night in the Lincoln bedroom. Both parties had essentially "sold" photo-ops and invitations to social functions where high-level politicians were present.

When the final reports were filed, it turned out that the party commit-tees had raised about $260 million in the 1995–96 campaign season, with the Republicans taking in about 140 million, and the Democrats about 120 million.† These sums were three times higher than the corresponding amounts in the 1992 campaign, a rather clear indication that the June 1996 Supreme Court decision (p. 257) had opened the floodgates.

Postelection stories began to link large contributions and White House policy changes, giving rise to an outcry for reform. In his February State of the Union Address, President Clinton endorsed a bipartisan campaign finance bill. The McCain-Feingold Bill, named after its sponsors Arizona Senator John McCain, a Republican, and Wisconsin Representative Russell Feingold, a Democrat, proposed to eliminate soft money, prohibit PAC contributions, and provide low-cost broadcast time to candidates who accept spending limits. Congress had

MONEY

Not all issues in the 1996 campaign were substantive. President Clinton's solid win was marred at the end by a series of campaign finance scandals involving large illegal contributions on behalf of foreign interests. Many Democratic politicians felt that the late revelations were sufficiently damaging to enable the Republicans

killed an earlier version of the bill in June of 1996.

Whatever the fate of the McCain-Feingold bill, it is unlikely to settle the debate over campaign finance. The debate is a perennial one, and every step toward reform seems to create a new problem. As noted earlier (p.216), PACs were a response to the 1974 FECA amendments, and soft money is actually a product of a 1979 law designed to give the parties a greater role in the campaign process.‡ The problem is especially difficult because attempts to restrict spending may run afoul of free speech considerations, and any proposed regulation or restriction threatens the electoral self-interest of incumbents and the partisan self-interest of the contending parties. Whatever is done about campaign finance between 1997 and 2000, we suspect that the issue will live on. Former Senator Bill Bradley is right: "Money invades politics like ants in the kitchen—without closing all the holes, there is always a way in."§ Given the American constitution and the incentives facing politicians, it will never be possible to close all the holes.

* See the exchange among Everett Ladd, Frank Newport, and Kathleen Frankovic in *The Public Perspective*, December/January 1997.

† Rebecca Carr, "As Soft Money Grows, So Does Controversy," *Congressional Quarterly Weekly Report*, November 16, 1996, 3272.

‡ Jonathan Salant, "Despite Attempts, Loopholes in Law Remain Unplugged," *Congressional Quarterly Weekly Report*, November 16, 1996, 3274–3275.

§ Carr, "As Soft Money Grows," 3272.

to keep control of the House by a narrow margin. After the election, the media reported new revelations of presidential fund-raising that apparently resulted in privileged access to major economic interests in return for large contributions (see Election Connection).

Although campaign finance is a perennial issue in the United States, it is not much of an issue in most other democracies. There are a number of reasons for this contrast.

In the first place, much more money is spent—even relative to the size of the electorate—here than in most other countries. Nationwide, the total amount spent in the 1996 elections was more than $3 billion. Only Japan comes close to spending as much (relative to the size of its electorate). The total cost of campaigns is determined by both the number of campaigns and the amount spent on each. As we have noted, there are far more elections in the United States than elsewhere, because there are more offices and terms of office are short. Additionally, the cost of campaigns is higher. A major factor is the candidate-centered electoral system. Like the United States, high-spending Japan has candidate-centered elections: each candidate constructs a personal organization that funds the campaign. Most other democracies have party-centered elections. The national party and its leaders conduct a single campaign on behalf of all the party candidates. Rather than having hundreds of individual candidates running duplicate campaigns, the parties take advantage of economies of scale.

Another factor contributing to the expense of American campaigns is that increasingly they are fought over the airwaves, and TV campaigns are expensive—not only the time itself, but the services of the consultants, ad people, and so forth.* In most other democracies, candidates still rely more on the campaign work of party members than attempt to reach voters directly through broadcasting.

A second reason campaign finance is a lesser concern in other democracies is that spending is heavily regulated. Britain is an extreme case. Indi-

Under the terms of the 1974 Federal Elections Campaign Act, presidential elections are publicly funded. The Federal Elections Commission gives major-party candidates a subsidy—approximately $62 million each in 1996—and in return the candidates agree not to raise and spend more. What campaigns increasingly do, however, is to exploit the soft money loophole (p. 257). The money is not given to the candidates, but to party committees, which legally can take contributions of any size and spend as much as they take in. Thus, large contributions were made to the Democratic National Committee, not to the Clinton campaign, which formally adhered to the FEC limit. In the aftermath of the campaign, pressure for campaign finance reform once again mounted. This is a perennial problem in the United States, a by-product of the First Amendment, private sector media, and traditionally weak parties. In few other countries is campaign finance such a perennial issue (see International Comparison).

vidual candidates are not permitted to buy television or radio time! Even the parties cannot make media buys. They are limited to a small number of publicly financed addresses by national party leaders. Campaigning in Britain mostly involves putting up signs, distributing campaign literature, and personally talking to voters, none of which costs very much. Of course, if limits such as these were imposed in the United States, the courts would strike them down as violations of the First Amendment right of free speech.

Finally, many other democracies provide at least some degree of public financing of all elections.† For example, in Austria, Belgium, Denmark, Finland, Germany, Mexico, Sweden, and Turkey, the parties receive public subsidies in proportion to the number of votes they received in the last election or the number of seats they hold in parliament. In-kind subsidies, especially free media time, also are common. Many democracies even provide subsidies for the major parties *between* elections. In the United States, public financing has progressed only as far as presidential elections; attempts to extend it even to Congress have been futile. Imagine the popular reaction if anyone were to propose that the Democratic and Republican National Committees were to receive public subsidies between elections!

In sum, the Constitution, the structure of electoral processes, and popular attitudes all interact to create a campaign finance problem more severe in the United States than elsewhere.

* "Money and Politics," *The Economist*, February 8, 1997, 23.

† Richard Katz, "Party Organizations and Finance," in Lawrence LeDuc, Richard Niemi, and Pippa Norris, eds. *Comparing Democracies* (Thousand Oaks, CA: Sage, 1996): 129–132.

PROSPECTS FOR 2000

Our view is that the elections of the 1990s are sufficiently different from those of the 1970s and 1980s to suggest that what was called the sixth party system has evolved into something new. We think that politics today looks much like the so-called "era of no decision" that prevailed from the 1870s to the 1890s. During that period—an era of social and economic change—presidential elections were won and lost by the narrowest of margins, and control of Congress shifted back and forth. No dependable majority existed.

The situation today looks similar. As we note in Chapters 19 and 20, tax revenues, budget deficits, and federal spending are the major pieces of an economic puzzle that no longer fit together. But as both parties have learned in recent decades, there is no majority in favor of raising taxes, and as the Republicans learned in 1996, it is very dangerous to support reforms of entitlement programs like Medicare. Events will force actions, and it appears that both parties will suffer at times for the policies they are forced to adopt. As close as it is, it is difficult to predict the political situation in the year 2000.

Chapter Summary

The United States is unique among the world's democracies for its long, drawn-out process of nominating the candidates for chief executive—a British correspondent calls it "a bizarre ritual."[56] In contrast to most countries, the process gives "outsider" candidates a chance by enabling them to contest the early, smaller primaries and caucuses. The process advantages party activists, as it does in most countries, but also advantages the media, in contrast to most countries. Whatever its pluses and minuses, the system is now well established, and unlikely to change except at the margins.

The presidential campaign is often misunderstood. It is not an independent force that determines election outcomes; rather, the campaign itself is shaped by events and conditions in the years leading up to the election. Candidates who run good campaigns usually are those who have good records that are easy to defend, or those whose opponents have bad records that are hard to defend. Candidates who run bad campaigns are generally those who face the opposite situations.

The reason that campaigns are limited in their impact is that most voters do not make up their minds on the basis of the campaign. Many of them decide well before the campaign ever begins. They do so on the basis of long-standing party identifications, of evaluations of government performance, and of the associations between the parties and particular values and positions. Only a few people decide how to vote late in the campaign and as a result of the particular candidates and the particular things they say. Campaigns determine outcomes when party identification, government performance, and the deeper issues leave both candidates relatively evenly matched. The 1996 election was not such a case, despite what many pundits said. Even a far more personable candidate than Robert Dole would have lost to a president running with a strong economy and a contented country.

Key Terms

caucus, p. 303

electoral college, p. 316

electoral vote, p. 316

honeymoon , p. 302

mandate, p. 302

matching funds, p. 305

party identification, p. 318

party image, p. 321

political activist, p. 308

popular vote, p. 314

primary, p. 303

winner-take-all, p. 316

Suggested Readings

Abramson, Paul, John Aldrich, and David Rohde. *Change and Continuity in the 1996 Elections.* Washington, DC: CQ Press, 1998. This quadrennial publication provides a comprehensive overview of voting behavior in national elections.

Asher, Herbert. *Presidential Elections and American Politics,* 5th ed. New York: Dorsey, 1992. An excellent survey of presidential campaigns and how voters reacted to them in the second half of the twentieth century.

Brown, Clifford, Lynda Powell, and Clyde Wilcox, *Serious Money.* Cambridge, England: Cambridge University Press, 1995. A detailed empirical study of who contributes to presidential campaigns and why.

Carmines, Edward, and James Stimson. *Issue Evolution: Race and the Transformation of American Politics.* Princeton: Princeton University Press, 1989. An important argument about the importance of race for realigning American politics in the 1960s.

Holbrook, Thomas. *Do Campaigns Matter?* Thousand Oaks, CA: Sage, 1996. A scientifically rigorous study of the impact of presidential campaigns.

Mayer, William, ed. *In Pursuit of the White House: How We Choose Our Presidential Nominees.* Chatham, NJ: Chatham House, 1996. An informative collection of essays covering all facets of the contemporary nominating process.

Miller, Arthur, and Bruce Gronbeck, eds. *Presidential Campaigns and American Self Images.* Boulder, CO: Westview, 1994. This collection of essays presents a balanced and sophisticated view of campaigns.

Polsby, Nelson, and Aaron Wildavsky. *Presidential Elections,* 9th ed. Chatham, NJ: Chatham House, 1995. A classic text that covers all aspects of presidential elections.

Wayne, Stephen. *The Road to the White House, 1996.* New York: St. Martin's, 1997. Provides useful background on all stages of the presidential nomination and election process, along with specific discussions of how the 1996 campaigns played out.

Businesswoman
TOM CONDIT
Writer

JACK FOREM
Writer

Natural Law

STATE SENATOR

Natural Law

Ninth District

CAROL FLYER PRETTIE
Businesswoman

Republican

THOMAS N. HUDSON
Trust Attorney

Peace &
Freedom

ROBERT J. EVANS
Criminal Defense Lawyer

Democ

BARBARA LEE
member/Business Woman

Vote for
One

13

14

15

16

TURN PAGE TO CO

choosing the congress

N AUGUST 5, 1993, the fate of the Clinton presidency lay in the hands of a freshman Democrat from Pennsylvania, Representative Marjorie Margolies-Mezvinsky. The final version of the president's deficit reduction plan lay before Congress. A sweeping package of spending cuts and tax increases, the plan would chart the course of government economic policy for the next five years. Earlier in the year the Clinton plan had passed the House and Senate without a single Republican vote. A conference committee (see Chapter 12) had ironed out the differences in the two chambers' versions of the legislation, and now final passage was at hand. Or was it?

Again, not a single Republican would support the plan: The income tax increases were unacceptable, and even though these tax increases fell entirely on affluent Americans, some Democrats were opposed to the plan because of small increases in gasoline taxes and other particular elements of the plan. Democratic leaders worked feverishly to muster a majority. Speaker Thomas Foley exhorted his partisans: "Tonight is the time for courage. Tonight is the time to put away the old, easy ways. Tonight is the time for responsibility. Tonight is the night to vote." [1]

President Clinton himself worked the phones, calling undecided Democrats and telling them that he had to have their vote—his presidency was at stake. For Representative Margolies-Mezvinsky, the situation was a political nightmare. She had been elected only seven months earlier, in the "year of the woman." Her margin of victory was less than 1 percent and her affluent Philadelphia suburban district had a 2:1 Republican registration edge; she was the first Democrat to be elected from the district in 76 years. Already she had voted against each of President Clinton's three important economic proposals, including the deficit reduction package that was once again on the floor. On that earlier occasion she had announced: "I promised the voters of Montgomery County that I would not vote for an across-the-board tax increase — and tonight I kept that promise." [2] She had told her constituents that she would continue to oppose the plan. Now she was under intense pressure from the president and Democratic leaders to reverse her stand.

At the conclusion of electronic voting, the tally stood at 216-216. A majority of the full house (218 of 435) is required to pass the budget. Pat Williams, a Democrat from Montana, had agreed to support the president, if necessary, so the vote of Representative Margolies-Mezvinsky would decide whether the plan passed or failed, and by implication, the fate of the Clinton presidency. Surrounded by supportive Democrats and "with the demeanor of someone being marched to her own hanging" she approached the well of the house to cast a written vote, while gleeful Republicans chanted "Goodbye, Marjorie!" [3] Margolies-Mezvinsky's "profile in courage" saved the Clinton presidency, but the cost was her political life.

President Clinton himself appeared in her district, and the Democratic leadership helped her raise more than $1,600,000 in campaign funds; but it wasn't enough. The Republican whom Margolies-Mezvinsky defeated in 1992 ran against her again in 1994. Although he raised less than two-thirds as much money as she did, she could not overcome her damaging vote and the national Republican tide. She received only 45 percent of the vote.

ongress is the most electorally sensitive of American political institutions. Members of the House of Representatives put their fates on the line every second November, but even that two-year interval between elections is deceptive. Many representatives face primaries in the spring of election years, so primary campaigns are under way scarcely more than a year after members have taken the oath of office. In response to such realities, representatives campaign for reelection more or less continuously.

Surprisingly, the situation isn't that different for senators. Although elected for six-year terms, one-third are elected every two years, so at any given time one-third of the Senate is operating with the same short time horizon as members of the House. Moreover, Senate campaigns are so expensive that senators must raise an average of $15,000 every week for six years, a time-consuming, psychologically draining activity that keeps all of them aware of their need to maintain political support, even if their actual reelection campaign is some years away.

The great majority of congressional incumbents win reelection, but as the unhappy experience of Representative Margolies-Mezvinsky illustrates, the advantage of incumbency is not automatic. Even if you are an incumbent and even if you spend much more than your challenger, you may still lose. That simple fact colors all aspects of congressional life. This chapter examines how contemporary representatives and senators seek and achieve reelection.

The Electoral Evolution of the Congress

An electorally sensitive House of Representatives was the clear intent of the Founders. Madison wrote that the House should have "an immediate dependence on, and an intimate sympathy with, the people. Frequent elections are unquestionably the only policy by which this dependence and sympathy can be effectually secured."[4] An electorally sensitive Senate, however, was not the Founders' intent. The Constitution originally provided for Senators to be chosen by state legislatures, not elected by the people. According to Madison, the electorally insulated, elite Senate was "to consist in its proceeding with more coolness, with more system, and with more wisdom, than the popular branch."[5] Not until adoption of the Seventeenth Amendment to the Constitution in 1913 did all Senators face popular election, although many states adopted various popular procedures as early as the mid-nineteenth century.

Thus, the Framers were half right (the House) and half wrong (the Senate) in their general expectations about the electoral sensitivity of the Congress. As for the actual history of the two chambers, however, neither has worked out as the Framers planned. At first, the House was the *amateur* political body the Framers expected. Unstable in its membership and tumultuous in its operation, the House operated more or less according to plan. More than 40 percent of the members of the First Congress did not return for the Second. In fact, turnover levels often were as high as

Young Representative Abraham Lincoln (Whig–IL) in 1846.

Term Limits

In the early 1990s, a popular movement to limit legislative terms swept across the country. By the 1996 elections the electorates of 25 states had approved referenda limiting the terms members of their legislatures could serve, usually to six or eight years of consecutive service.* Many of the same states limited members of Congress as well, but in *U.S. Term Limits, Inc.* v. *Thornton* (1995) the Supreme Court held state limits on federal officials to be unconstitutional. (Both the 104th and 105th Congresses considered constitutional amendments to limit congressional terms, but failed to pass them.)

Poll after poll in the early 1990s found that term limits enjoyed widespread support, typically with two-thirds or larger majorities in favor. The movement no doubt had roots in multiple causes. Like syndicated columnist George Will, some voters longed for a simpler age when "citizen legislators" served briefly, then returned to their homes and occupations.† Rather than citizen legislators, American legislators increasingly have become full-time professionals.‡ Ordinary Americans, meanwhile, have been getting steadily more suspicious of government (p. 11), and incumbents seemed harder than ever to defeat: In the

House elections of 1986 and 1988, 98 percent of all incumbents who ran were reelected. Many citizens thought that it was becoming impossible to defeat long-term incumbents supported by special interests. There was some partisan motivation as well, given that most state legislatures were Democratic. But majorities of both Democrats and Republicans supported limits, although Democrats were somewhat less enthusiastic.§

The courts generally upheld the right of state electorates to limit the terms of their own legislatures, but in 1995 a Federal District Court agreed to hear a suit seeking to

---

50 percent until after the Civil War.[6] But contrary to Madison's pronouncement, frequent elections were not the cause. Until the late nineteenth century, many more Representatives quit than were defeated. In the first place, job conditions were not very attractive, especially after the national government moved to Washington, D.C., an uninhabited, swampy area with a less than desirable climate.[7] Many members found life in Washington less comfortable than life in the cities and towns of their home states. In the second place, the national government was not very important in the early years of the Republic. Ambitious politicians, especially outside the South, often found state governments to be better outlets for their energies than the small and limited national government.[8] Even those members willing to serve multiple terms sometimes were prevented from doing so by **rotation** practices, whereby the counties, towns, or political factions in a congressional district "took turns" holding the congressional seat. Abraham Lincoln, for example, was elected to the House in 1846 but stepped down after one term in accord with local rotation agreements.[9] The result of these and other lesser considerations was that average service in the House of Representatives did not reach three years until after 1900.

Also contrary to Madison's expectations, the early Senate was not much different from the House. Far from being a continuing body whose members served for long

rotation
The practice whereby a member of Congress stepped down after a term or two so that someone else could have the office.

overturn California's state term limits, which imposed a lifetime ban on legislators after their allotted six (House) or eight years (Senate). While 52 percent of the California electorate had approved term limits in 1990, a 63 percent majority of Representative Tom Bates's district had rejected them. When Bates was "termed out" of office, he and his constituents filed suit, claiming that their First and Fourteenth Amendment rights of free expression and association were violated.‖

When First and Fourteenth Amendment rights are in question, courts impose a test of strict scrutiny, which among other things requires a state to demonstrate a compelling interest if it is to restrict liberties. Most political scientists oppose term limits and doubt that they would accomplish any good (p. 411); partly as a result, California was unable to demonstrate a compelling interest for imposing its lifetime ban, and in 1997 the court overturned California term limits in *Bates v. Jones*.

What do you think? In today's complex world are professional legislators bad? Should voters in other districts be able to decide that someone in your district cannot represent you? What business is it of theirs? Are there compelling interests that justify denying you your right to vote for whomever you please?

* Everett Carl Ladd, ed., *America at the Polls, 1994* (Storrs, CT: The Roper Center, 1996): 122.

† George Will, *Restoration: Congress, Term Limits, and the Recovery of Deliberative Democracy* (New York: Free Press, 1992).

‡ Morris Fiorina, "Divided Government in the American States: A Byproduct of Legislative Professionalism," *American Political Science Review* 88(1994): 304-316.

§ "Term Limits," *The Public Perspective* (January/February 1993): 97.

‖ Joseph Remcho, et. al., "Bates v. Jones, Plaintiffs' Trial Brief," U.S. District Court, Northern District of California, C95 2638 CW.

periods, between the beginning of the Republic and 1800, more than one-third of the Senators failed to serve out their terms, and until 1820 more Senators resigned during their term than were denied reselection by their state legislatures. Though they had the opportunity to stay longer than members of the House, for the reasons noted earlier, many chose to pass it up.[10]

Today, things are much different. The Congress is the world's foremost example of what political scientists call a **professional legislature**: Its members are full-time legislators who stay for long periods (see Figure 11.1). Relatively few members quit voluntarily, and many intend to remain in Congress indefinitely. In fact, many people in the United States think that the membership of Congress is *too* stable, and support institutional changes such as term limits in order to shake up what they see as an unresponsive institution (see Democratic Dilemma). Such views conflict with our description of Congress as an electorally sensitive if not hypersensitive institution. Given the electoral advantage contemporary incumbents appear to have, how can anyone argue that Congress is such an electorally sensitive institution? The conflict is more apparent than real, because the reason contemporary incumbents do so well is precisely because they are so electorally sensitive. Moreover, paradoxical as it may seem, the reason that citizens are so frus-

professional legislature
Legislature whose members serve full-time and for long periods.

FIGURE 11.1

Congress Became a Career in the Twentieth Century

SOURCES: Nelson W. Polsby, "The Institutionalization of the U.S. House of Representatives," *American Political Science Review* (March 1968): 146. Norman J. Ornstein et al., eds., *Vital Statistics on Congress, 1995–1996* (Washington, DC: Congressional Quarterly, 1996): 60

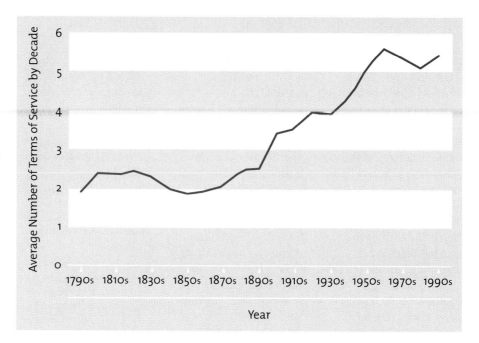

trated with the Congress, as well as with other legislatures, is that the members of these institutions are so electorally sensitive. This chapter and the next explain and support these claims.

★ AT THE STATE & LOCAL LEVEL
Reapportionment and Redistricting

The Constitution specifies that a census be held every decade. After the census, the 435 seats in the House of Representatives are apportioned among the states according to their populations; hence the term **reapportionment**, which refers to the new allocation of seats as a result of population shifts. After the states learn the number of House seats to which they are entitled, they set to work **redistricting**— drawing the boundaries of the new districts. In a majority of the states the legislature does the work, but in a large minority of states a bipartisan commission does the job. The process is often highly contentious, since political careers depend on how the lines are drawn. Charges of **gerrymandering**—drawing the lines for partisan or other political advantage—are hurled back and forth, and often the courts are drawn into the process.

In *Wesberry v. Sanders* (1964), the U.S. Supreme Court held that congressional districts should be based on population (previously districts varied widely in population), and subsequent decisions have refined the standard to one of precise numerical equality. In practice, court standards are often ludicrously precise, since the census data themselves are only approximate, especially some years after the census.

In recent decades, northeastern states have lost House seats and southern and southwestern states have gained them as population has shifted from the frostbelt to

reapportionment
The allocation of House seats to the states after each decennial census.

redistricting
Drawing new boundaries of congressional districts, usually after the decennial census.

gerrymandering
Drawing boundary lines of congressional districts in order to advantage some partisan or political interest.

the sunbelt. Given the political leanings of the regions, the net effect has been to strengthen Republican representation in the House.

In the Senate, things are simpler and never change. The Constitution gives every state two senators, regardless of population, and this provision can be amended only with the consent of every state (Article 5). Since smaller states cannot be expected to give up a political advantage, equal representation in the Senate is essentially an amendment-proof feature of American democracy.

Contemporary Congressional Elections: The House Incumbency Advantage

Journalists and politicians often comment that incumbency is the single most important factor in House elections. That is not quite right. Party long has been and continues to be the single most important factor in House elections. Most strikingly, the Democrats maintained unbroken control of the House of Representatives between 1954 and 1994, even while all but three of their 1954 incumbents departed.[11] In many House districts it is almost inconceivable that a member of the party other than that of the present incumbent could win. Indeed, one reason that Senate elections are generally more competitive than House elections is that the parties are more evenly matched in most states than in many of the smaller, more homogeneous congressional districts.[12]

Of course, as discussed in Chapter 8, the parties do not control nominations and campaigns as they did in earlier periods of American history, and as discussed in Chapter 10, voters are not as influenced by party when deciding how to vote as in earlier times. But to say that party is not as important as in earlier periods is not to say that party is unimportant or even less important than other factors, but only to say that party no longer is as dominant a factor as it once was.

One reason that party remains the most important factor in House elections is that many voters know little, if anything, about the candidates. Compared to presidential, senatorial, or even most gubernatorial elections, House elections are "low information" elections. Only a third of the citizenry can recall the name of the incumbent, and even fewer can remember anything he or she has done for the district. Only 10 percent or so can remember how the incumbent voted on a particular bill. Challengers are much less well known. Having little information on which to base a vote, many uninformed voters simply vote for the candidate of the party with which they generally sympathize. In House elections, 70 percent or more of all voters who identify with a party typically support the House candidate of that party.[13]

If not the single most important factor in House elections, incumbency clearly is the second most important factor; moreover, incumbency has grown in importance while party has declined. Statistical studies of House elections have found that the **incumbency advantage**—the electoral benefit of being an incumbent after controlling for their other relevant political characteristics—has grown from about 2 percent before 1964 to as much as 12 percent today.[14] The increase has not been smooth; rather, the incumbency advantage surged in the mid- to late 1960s, and stayed roughly constant thereafter (see Figure 11.2). A number of factors underlie this development.

■ **incumbency advantage**
The electoral gain from being an incumbent over and above other personal and political characteristics of the candidate.

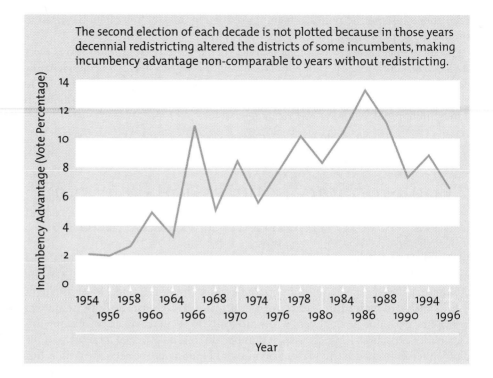

The second election of each decade is not plotted because in those years decennial redistricting altered the districts of some incumbents, making incumbency advantage non-comparable to years without redistricting.

PARTY DECLINE

Although 70 percent of all party identifiers support the candidate of their party today, the figure was more than 80 percent until 1964—and more voters had a party identification in the 1950s than do today.[15] As party affiliations weakened, voters became more "available," more susceptible to other sorts of appeals.[16] Thus, party decline created a context in which other factors, such as the incumbent's personal characteristics and activities, could exert a stronger influence.

Moreover, realizing that voters were "up for grabs" more so than previously, the behavior of incumbents adjusted to fit the new reality. In the first place, their own partisan constituencies became somewhat less secure; realizing that they could no longer rely on rock-solid partisan support, they moved to offer voters additional, personal reasons to support them. In the second place, the partisan constituencies of the opposition became somewhat more vulnerable; realizing that opposition party voters would not automatically go to the challenger, some incumbents began to court them. The result is that challenger party identifiers began to defect to incumbents at much higher rates in the late 1960s, and since then their defection rates have often been close to 50 percent. In contrast, defection rates of incumbent party identifiers have stayed below 10 percent.[17]

★ AT THE STATE & LOCAL LEVEL

CHANGING REPRESENTATIONAL ROLES

Most students think of members of Congress primarily as *lawmakers*. This is indeed the principal business of Congress, and the major responsibility that the Constitution bestows on the Congress. But members of Congress do many other things besides make laws. Indeed, the official title of members of the House is "Representative," and at least in the contemporary era, representation involves other activities in addition to making national laws.[18]

One activity that occupies a great deal of the time and effort of members of Congress is **district service**—making sure that their congressional districts get a fair share (or more) of federal programs, projects, and expenditures.[19] Some members of Congress are famous for their efforts to bring such economic benefits to their districts, although the most famous of all is a senator—Robert Byrd of West Virginia. Although critics of Congress often use the pejorative term "pork barrel" to refer to such activities, it appears that constituents generally approve when their own representatives and senators "bring home the bacon," and reward them at the ballot box for their successes.

Members of Congress diligently keep in touch with their constituents, as Tillie Fowler demonstrates in her office.

Another activity to which modern representatives devote a great deal of attention is **constituent assistance**, or more colloquially, "casework." Citizens, groups, and businesses frequently encounter difficulties in qualifying for government benefits or subsidies, or in complying with federal regulations. When their problems are not solved through normal channels, they appeal to a members of Congress for assistance. About one in six voters reports having contacted a Representative for information or help with a problem. In overwhelming numbers they report satisfactory resolution of their problems, and, again, show their gratitude at the polls.[20] In other countries such assistance is often provided by an administrative official called an **ombudsman**; in the United States, members of Congress act as ombudsmen.[21]

District service and constituent assistance often are included together under the general term **constituency service**. The activities share two important characteristics that shed some light on the advantage of incumbency. First, they are nonpartisan and nonideological. Road projects and grants to schools and local governments are neither liberal nor conservative, Democrat nor Republican. Similarly, Democratic incumbents willingly help Republican businesses deal with federal regulators, and Republican incumbents willingly help Democratic constituents qualify for federal benefits. When members of Congress take positions on issues, they please some groups and antagonize others; on controversial issues their positions may lose them as many votes as they gain. But when incumbents bring home an economic benefit or help a constituent, nearly everyone approves. Such activities carry significant electoral benefits, but little, if any, electoral cost. Small wonder that by a 5:1 margin House administrative assistants ranked constituency service over their members' legislative records as the most important factor in maintaining their electoral base.[22]

The second important characteristic shared by both forms of constituency service is that they have grown in importance. As the federal government expanded, subsidizing and regulating more and more activity, the contacts between individual citizens, groups, and firms and their government multiplied. Thus, the opportunities for

district service
Efforts of members of Congress to make sure their districts get a share of federal projects and programs.

constituent assistance
Efforts of members of Congress to help individuals and groups when they have difficulties with federal agencies.

ombudsman
Official whose job is to mediate conflicts between citizens and government bureaucracies.

constituency service
The totality of Congress members' district service and constituent assistance work.

SENATOR ROBERT BYRD, PORK-MEISTER

Democratic Sen. Robert C. Byrd of West Virginia, who vowed to steer $1 billion homeward after becoming the powerful chairman of the Appropriations Committee in 1989, is exceeding his best expectations.

Robert Byrd

Byrd has met his five-year goal in less than three years, and he continues to deliver almost unprecedented federal largesse to West Virginia.

At least $510.8 million in projects and earmarked funds for his rural home state already have cropped up in fiscal 1992 spending bills moving through the Senate. The money comes from various agencies and programs and not just the Interior appropriations that Byrd oversees as a subcommittee chairman.

A rundown of the funding for West Virginia in key Senate appropriations bills this year includes:

Transportation

■ $165 million for a Corridor G highway improvement project to "demonstrate methods of eliminating traffic congestion and to promote economic benefits" for western West Virginia.

■ $12.3 million for a highway demonstration construction project for a $185 million FBI complex, which Byrd had earlier won for Clarksburg. The bill also allots $600 thousand for a study.

■ $14 million for an upgraded approach radar system for the Eastern West Virginia Airport in Martinsburg.

Defense, Military Construction

■ $32.9 million to begin moving 21 CIA offices to Harpers Ferry and to Prince William County, VA.

■ $9.6 million to build a Guard and reserve center at Huntington Air Force Base and $25.1 million to house C-130 cargo airplanes at Martinsburg Air Force Base.

■ $5.4 million to alter the operations center at the Naval Radio - Telescope Observatory in Green Bank.

members of Congress to engage in constituency service increased correspondingly. In 1978, for example, three times as many citizens reported having contacted their representative for assistance as reported having done so in 1958.[23] Thus, at the same time that strength of party affiliation was declining, an expanding federal government was stimulating constituent demand for assistance that members of Congress were able and willing to provide. These activities enabled them to reinforce their own base and make inroads into the opposition's base.

Commerce, Justice, State

- $48 million to develop and install in 1995 an automated fingerprint identification system for the new FBI headquarters in Clarksburg.

Agriculture

- $600 thousand for two West Virginia research services to study a replacement for lime fertilizer and to develop sensors to cut the costs of handling fruit.

- $750,000 for the Appalachian Export Center for Hardwoods at West Virginia University in Morgantown.

- $9 million for the construction of North and South Mill Creek Dam No. 7.

- $3.5 million for the Huntington area hit by spring floods.

Treasury, Postal Service

- $25 million for the construction of a federal building and courthouse in Beckley.

Energy and Water

- $58 million for corridors G and H.

- $26 million for two flood control projects in Mingo County that are part of an ongoing Army Corps of Engineers program in West Virginia and Kentucky.

- $2.4 million for Army Corps of Engineers water project studies on several West Virginia and Kentucky sites.

- $2 million to build a riverfront park in Charleston.

Interior

- $4.5 million to Mercer County as the second Forest Service grant for the Hardwoods Training and Flexible Manufacturing Center.

- $13.7 million in Bureau of Land Management funds for construction of the Harpers Ferry National Educational Training Center and $2 million to acquire the site.

- $2.5 million to restore the current funding level for the Generic Center for Respirable Dust.

VA, HUD, Independent Agencies

- $22.5 million for the National Technology Center at the Wheeling Jesuit College.

- $7.5 million for construction and an educational program at Wheeling Jesuit College using multimedia aids such as simulated space missions and a video library.

- $10 million for a validation center for NASA computer software at West Virginia University in Morgantown.

- $2.1 million to convert abandoned buildings into a job training center in Elkins, an Alzheimer's clinic and adult day-care center in Parkersburg, and a rural health-care clinic in McDowell County.

SOURCE: Excerpted from "Byrd's Eye View," *Congressional Quarterly Weekly Report,* September 21, 1991, 2682.

In sum, representatives present themselves to constituents as guardians of district economies and ombudsmen for constituents, as well as framers of national laws. An expanding federal government increased the demand for constituency service, and thereby the opportunity for members of Congress to respond to such demands. Since such activities are generally applauded, incumbents were able to add to their reservoir of goodwill and undercut their natural opposition.

Congressional staffs have grown considerably in the past generation. Here, Tillie Fowler speaks with one staff member during a meeting with several others in her Washington office.

■ **frank**
Name given to representatives' and senators' free use of the U.S. mail for sending communications to constituents.

EXPANDING MEMBER RESOURCES

In recent years, members of Congress have been likened to CEOs (chief executive officers) of small businesses.[24] Each member heads an office system—one in Washington and one or more in the district—and directly employs an average of 18 personal staff assistants, more than 40 percent of whom are assigned to district offices.[25] (Senators have even bigger staffs, although their size depends on their states' population.) Although these offices have many responsibilities, no one doubts that much of their effort is directed toward the reelection of their members. Indeed, it has been said that Capitol Hill is the headquarters of 535 political machines.

Such was not always the case. In 1950, the average representative had three staff employees. And as late as 1960, nearly a third of the representatives did not have a permanent district office. The 1960s and 1970s were a period of great growth in congressional resources (see Figure 11.3). Besides office and staff, travel subsidies and other perks expanded greatly.[26] In 1960, members were reimbursed for only three trips to their districts per year, by 1976 the number had increased to 26, and today there is no limit except the overall budget allocated to each member. Of course, before the jet plane few members could go home every weekend, as they do today, and many went home only once or twice a session. A technological advance made possible a change in behavior, and Congress authorized the funds to support that change in behavior.

Use of the **frank**—the free use of the U.S. mail for official business—too, has expanded. Although Congress has long subsidized its communication with constituents, technological advances such as computerized mailing lists have allowed members to take greater advantage of the privilege in recent years. Use of franked mail has increased much faster than the rate of population increase or the increase in incoming mail that must be answered. Not surprisingly, congressional mailings to constituents are much higher in even-numbered (election) years than in odd-numbered years. (see Figure 11.4).

FIGURE 11.3

The Personal Staffs of Representatives and Senators Have Expanded

SOURCE: Norman J. Ornstein et al., eds., *Vital Statistics on Congress, 1995–1996* (Washington, DC: Congressional Quarterly, 1996): 133.

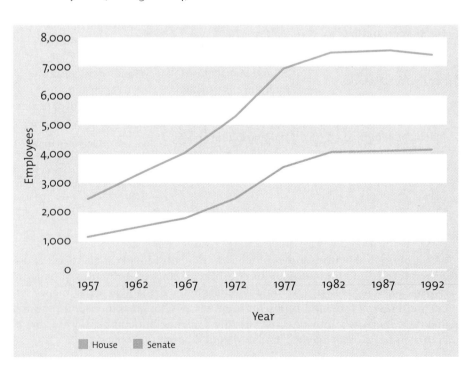

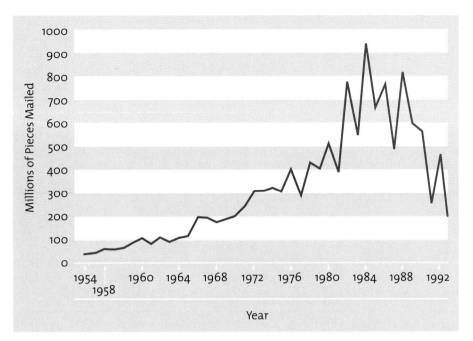

FIGURE **11.4**

Use of the Frank Exploded in the 1980s Before Being Restricted by Recent Congresses

SOURCE: Norman J. Ornstein et al., eds., *Vital Statistics on Congress, 1995–1996* (Washington, DC: Congressional Quarterly, 1996): 170.

In recent years, members have been criticized for providing themselves with many of these resources—often called "perks," for perquisites of office. Attention thus far has focused largely on smaller, personal items like subsidized haircuts and gym memberships. Under pressure from public interest groups, Congress has adopted some restrictions on the use of the frank. For example, newsletters cannot be mailed within 90 days of an election, and members cannot have more than two personal photos per page. No one has seriously suggested that cutbacks of staff, offices, or travel be imposed, however.

The increased resources enjoyed by representatives are intimately related to two of the factors discussed above: the weakening of party and the changes in congressional

A day in the life of a member of Congress. Here, Senator Dianne Feinstein (D–CA) has a working lunch with staffers at the Twin Palms restaurant in Pasadena.

roles. As members realized that traditional party organization was becoming increasingly unreliable, they had incentives to vote themselves the resources to substitute for the declining organizations. Similarly, as they realized that reliance on traditional partisan voting was becoming increasingly unreliable, they had incentives to vote themselves the resources necessary to meet the increasing demand for constituency service. Thus—at least at first—the growth in congressional resources probably was more a consequence of these other factors than a cause of the increasing incumbency advantage. But once available, of course, resources could be put to other uses, chiefly the promotion of the members and the advertisement of their activities. An incumbent representative today receives resources that would cost as much as $1 million per year if purchased on the open market.[27] This level of support undoubtedly contributes to the advantage of incumbency.

CAMPAIGN FUNDS

Few aspects of elections receive more attention in the media than the campaign "war chests" raised and spent by members of Congress. Indeed, House elections have become increasingly expensive: Average total spending in each House race was over $900 thousand in 1996, with more than 75 candidates spending over a million dollars.[28] Moreover, the gap between incumbent spending and that of their challengers is wide and has widened steadily since 1980 (see Figure 11.5). For many critics of Congress, the explanation of the advantage of incumbency is simple and self-evident: money.

There is no doubt that money affects candidate visibility and that congressional challengers are seriously underfunded. Nevertheless, research on the influence of money in congressional elections produces a surprisingly complicated picture. It is

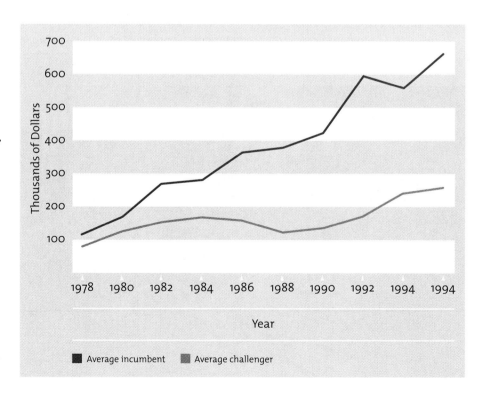

FIGURE 11.5

Challengers Are Falling Farther and Farther Behind Incumbents in Their Campaign Spending

SOURCE: Norman J. Ornstein et al., eds., *Vital Statistics on Congress, 1995–1996* (Washington, DC: Congressional Quarterly, 1996): 81.

certainly the case that money makes a significant contribution to the electoral advantage that incumbents enjoy, but it is almost equally certain that its contribution to the advantage of incumbency often has been exaggerated.

In the first place, a great deal of research has found that the influence of money in elections illustrates what economists refer to as *diminishing returns*: The more a candidate spends the less impact an additional dollar of spending has. In particular, incumbents already receive so much in the way of free resources (as much as a million dollars a year) that an extra $100 thousand has less impact, certainly much less impact than if spent by a challenger who lacks the resource base of an incumbent. That is why sophisticated advocates of campaign finance reform oppose low spending limits: Such limits would hurt challengers, who have little name recognition, much more than incumbents who already enjoy the visibility and perquisites of office.[29]

In the second place, the timing of the surge in the incumbency advantage (the mid-1960s) does not match the changes in campaign finance. Recall from Chapter 7 that the growth of PACs came after the adoption of campaign finance reform laws in 1974. House elections in the late 1960s and early 1970s were not nearly as expensive as they are today. Indeed, heavy spending by an incumbent was often regarded less as a sign of electoral strength than a sign of electoral weakness—an incumbent in trouble.[30] While there is no doubt that spending levels are now so high that incumbents benefit from spending, even if they get less bang for the buck than do challengers, if campaign spending were slashed to nothing tomorrow, there is every reason to believe that 90 percent of all incumbents would still be reelected.

Possibly the most important impact of campaign funds today is the one that is most difficult to observe, let alone measure. Because it takes so much money for a challenger to mount a serious campaign—$600 thousand in the estimation of Gary Jacobson—many potentially strong challengers probably are discouraged from entering the race.[31] If the incumbent has a widely advertised million-dollar "war chest," the prospect of a challenge is all the more daunting. Why mortgage your house and your children's college educations for what is at best a long shot? Thus, incumbents' ability to raise substantial campaign funds may be most important as a deterrent: Money may serve to scare potential opponents out of the arena more than actually buy the election if a strong challenger has not been otherwise scared off.[32]

This deterrent effect of campaign funds probably has been exacerbated by the decline of parties. In today's candidate-centered system the individual candidate bears the full risk of running and losing. A losing challenger may have given up her job, exhausted her savings, and gone deeply into debt. In earlier party-centered systems the party assumed such risks, allowing candidates to run and lose without suffering financial and political ruin. Once again, the weakening of parties creates a context in which other factors take on greater importance, other factors that advantage incumbents.

In recent years the topic of campaign finance reform has received enormous attention, and members of Congress have grappled with a wide variety of reform proposals. Even if it is true that the negative effects of the present system are somewhat exaggerated, there seems to be little doubt that citizens are disgusted with the present system of campaign finance and cynical about government in general and the Congress in particular as a result of it. Some reform is appropriate, but thus far little has been accomplished.

The problem is that the reforms that would probably do the most good have the least likelihood of adoption. Many observers believe that public financing of congressional elections is the most constructive proposal that could be adopted. By relieving members of the burden of fund-raising, it would give them more time to spend on more publicly productive activities, and it would insulate them from the influence of special interests. The problem is that if campaign subsidies are set too low, they will benefit incumbents, who already have high visibility and the perks of office. But setting subsidies high enough to make challengers credible (perhaps half a million dollars in House races, not counting primaries) would no doubt be too large for a cynical public to accept—not that incumbents would ever vote to give their challengers that much funding anyway.[33]

In 1996, the focus of dissatisfaction shifted from PAC contributions to incumbents to independent expenditures by interest groups like the AFL-CIO, and so-called "soft money" contributions to the parties who then contributed to congressional candidates (see Election Connection). While many people were troubled by these developments, one thing that can be said in their favor is that they help to redress the balance between incumbents and challengers. Parties and interest groups can target large sums into campaigns where credible challengers are running, thus helping to offset incumbents' large advantage in PAC and individual contributions.

MORE RESPONSIVE INCUMBENTS

Many popular critics of Congress believe that there is something illegitimate about high rates of reelection. That is true if members' electoral success reflects the operation of some illegitimate factor—selling out to PACs, for example. But as we have seen, one reason for members' success is that they work very hard at aiding their constituents and serving their districts. Another source of their success, although difficult to measure, is that they are extremely sensitive to the wishes of their constituents, perhaps even more so than members of Congress from earlier eras.

In the first place, members of Congress today have more and better information than members of Congress did previously. Not only do their offices have WATS lines, fax machines, e-mail, World Wide Web pages, and other technologies undreamt of a generation ago, but the members physically return to their districts 30 to 50 times a year. Only a generation ago, one often heard a derisory term, "the Tuesday to Thursday Club," applied to a minority of East Coast members who lived close enough to Washington to go home to their districts on Friday and return to the capitol on Monday. Today, jet transportation enables most of the Congress to belong to the Tuesday to Thursday club. Important business is rarely scheduled for Mondays or Fridays because so many members are in the friendly skies on those days. With members spending so much time in their districts, is it any surprise that they are highly attuned to the sentiments of constituents?

Moreover, members have access to survey research today. Again, as recently as a generation ago, only a few well-heeled interest groups ever conducted a poll in a congressional district, and then usually only to gauge the chances of a candidate. Today, with telephone interviewing and a great deal more money flowing through the system, members can conduct surveys to learn the views of constituents. Today's members probably make fewer mistakes based on bad information than did their predecessors.

In the second place, contemporary members of Congress probably have more incentive to act in accordance with the superior information they now have. In the modern Congress, every vote cast is closely watched by interest groups who rate members; moreover, years after a vote, opponents engaged in opposition research

Independent Expenditures in the 1996 House Elections

For nearly two decades, PACS (p. 216) occupied center stage in congressional campaign finance debates. The 1996 campaign was different: PACs and their activities barely made the radar screen. The reason was the large independent expenditure (p. 256) campaigns mounted on behalf of congressional candidates. Like "soft money" contributions to the parties (p.256, 334), independent expenditures have become more important as parties and interest groups push the envelope of campaign finance practices, and the courts decline to restrain them.

Most of the action was in House campaigns; it was generally conceded that the Republicans would hold the Senate, but Democrats felt that they had a reasonable shot at recapturing the House. Anticipating hard fights, House candidates raised and spent over $400 million, a 25 percent increase over the previous record set in 1994. But although candidate expenditures made up the lion's share of what was spent, they were not what got the publicity.

In early 1996, the AFL–CIO announced that it would spend $35 million dollars in an attempt to defeat Republican House candidates.* The union organization targeted many of the freshmen first elected in 1994, as well as seats with no incumbent in 1996. The campaign included negative ads attacking Republican positions on the so-called M^2E^2 issues—Medicare and Medicaid, the environment and education—as well as other issues such as health care and the minimum wage. The ads stayed on the right side of the law by not explicitly asking people to vote against the targeted candidates.

The Republicans responded, of course. The Republican National Committee spent millions of dollars on its own ads, attacking "big labor bosses" who were trying to "buy Congress." The U.S. Chamber of Commerce organized a coalition of 31 organizations that spent $7 million on ads designed to offset the union ads. Conservative religious groups spent a reported $10 million. (The image of a national war between two well-organized coalitions should not be overdrawn, however; some of the Republican candidates on the national "hit list" received contributions and support from individual union PACS!† House elections continue to be predominantly decentralized, district-oriented affairs.)

In the end, the AFL–CIO effort fell a bit short, and ironically, it may have been the campaign finance scandals that erupted during the last two weeks of the campaign that prevented the Democrats from winning the few additional seats they needed to recapture the House. Whatever the 1996 electoral impact, however, the dramatic increases in soft money contributions and independent expenditures signal the end of the campaign finance system that prevailed between 1976 and 1996.‡

* The following account is drawn from Anthony Corrado, "Financing the 1996 Elections," in Gerald Pomper et. al., eds., *The Elections of 1996* (Chatham, NJ: Chatham House, 1997): 162–164.

† Jonathan Salant, "Some on Labor 'Hit List' Get Labor Contributions," *Congressional Quarterly Weekly Report*," October 5, 1996, 2884–2885.

‡ Corrado, "Financing the 1996 Elections."

Congresswoman Nancy Pelosi
California's 8th District
San Francisco

NEW! What's New

About Rep. Pelosi

Constituent Services

Internship Opportunities

Email Rep. Pelosi

Guest Register

I Love San Francisco

Pelosi in Congress

AIDS Resources

China and Human Rights

Government Guide

Presidio

Grants

Women's Issues

This page was last updated on July 29, 1997

Free Speech Online
Blue Ribbon Campaign

President appoints a  **Board of Trustees!**

Links found on Representative Pelosi's Web site are provided as a service to visitors to this Web page. Congresswoman Nancy Pelosi does not control the content or functionality of these links.

Paid for by the funds authorized by the House of Representatives for the 8th Congressional District of California.

Many members of Congress are taking full advantage of new technologies to communicate with constituents.

may bring it up. In the House, far more votes are public today than a generation ago. Until 1971, representatives cast many votes by standing, voice (aye-nay), and "tellers" (depositing colored cards in boxes)—voting procedures that hid their individual positions. But rules changes that year made it easy to demand a roll call. This change more than doubled the number of roll calls held in an average session of the House. A damaging roll call vote need not be a highly visible one that saves a president, as in Representative Margolies-Mezvinsky's case. An obscure vote may come back to haunt a member years later if the policy supported proved a failure or had some unforeseen negative consequence.[34] More recorded votes mean more electoral danger.

Interest Group Ratings

Many interest groups offer evaluations of the voting records of members of the House and Senate. Each group adopts positions on crucial votes relevant to their interests and then calculates ratings for senators and representatives based on the percentage of votes they cast in agreement with the positions adopted by the group. For example, if an interest group gave a senator a rating of 75, it would mean that the senator had voted in accord with the group's position on 75 percent of the key votes identified by the group.

Over fifty different interest groups offer this type of rating—ranging from broad ideological organizations to very specialized single-interest lobbying organizations. Some examples of these groups, their self-descriptions, and their ratings for a small selection of senators and representatives that served in the 104th Congress are offered below. If you are interested in additional ratings, they are available on the World Wide Web homepage of Vote Smart (www.vote-smart.org/ congress).

American Conservative Union (ACU)

"A defense, foreign policy and economic lobbying group that seeks to mobilize conservatism and further the general cause of conservative issues."

Americans for Democratic Action (ADA)

"A liberal, domestic and foreign policy political action and lobbying organization." Its ratings offer a generally accepted measure of liberalism.

National Abortion and Reproductive Rights Action League (NARAL)

An organization that "supports action to keep abortion safe, legal and accessible to all women."

National Rifle Association (NRA)

An organization that "protects and defends the Second Amendment rights of citizens. Encourages civilian marksmanship,

compiles statistics, sponsors research and education programs, and lobbies."

American Federation of Labor–Congress of Industrial Organizations (AFL–CIO)

A labor union that accounts for approximately three-quarters of national union membership, with more than 13 million affiliated members.

League of Conservation Voters (LCV)

An organization that "seeks to elect pro-environment candidates to Congress and to educate voters on the voting records of their elected officials."

Selected Interest Group Ratings for Members of the 104th Congress (1995–1996)

	ACU	ADA	NARAL	NRA	AFL–CIO	LCV
Senator Edward M. Kennedy (D–MA) (Very Liberal Senator)	4	100	100	0	100	100
Senator Tom Daschle (D–SD) (Senate Minority Leader)	4	95	99	0	100	100
Representative Richard Gephardt (D–MO) (House Minority Leader)	12	85	80	0	100	77
Senator Ernest F. Hollings (D–SC) (Moderate Democrat)	35	75	100	50	75	86
Senator Arlen Specter (R–PA) (Moderate Republican)	36	55	100	50	33	50
Representative Dick Armey (R–TX) (House Majority Leader)	92	0	0	100	0	0
Senator Trent Lott (R–MS) (Senate Majority Leader)	96	0	0	100	0	0
Senator Jesse Helms (R–NC) (Very Conservative Senator)	100	0	0	100	0	0

SOURCE: All group self-descriptions and ratings were gathered from the World Wide Web homepage of Vote Smart (www.vote-smart.org/congress).

The third reason members may be more responsive today than in the past is that there are fewer constraints that might keep members from acting on the information and the incentives they have. Once again, party decline is an important factor here. Except under the most exceptional circumstances, such as Rep. Margolies-Mezvinsky encountered, members of Congress are not forced to cast votes that will damage them in their districts. When party and constituency collide, constituency trumps party—except in truly exceptional circumstances. This is in contrast to the late nineteenth century, when strong parties organized Congress. When members were forced to toe the party line, they were much more likely to be defeated when constituents disagreed with the party position or disapproved of the president's performance, because congressional party unity left constituents with no choice but to vent their disagreement or disapproval on the party as a whole. Today, members of Congress distance themselves from their party and president whenever they think it politically advantageous. Fewer are defeated in part because fewer give their constituents such reasons to defeat them.

As we will discuss in Chapter 13, the gap between presidential and congressional election results makes presidential leadership of Congress more difficult. Even when the president's party controls Congress, as in 1993-94, fewer members believe they have much to gain electorally from supporting the president and fewer believe they have much to lose electorally from opposing the president. The weakening of these electoral connections makes the partisan division of Congress more stable over time. Ironically, as individual members become more responsive to their districts, the Congress as a whole becomes less responsive to shifts in partisan sentiment than in earlier eras.[35]

Contemporary Congressional Elections: The Perils of the Senate

No informed observer would claim that incumbency is the single most important factor in Senate elections. While incumbent senators are elected more often than not, they are defeated much more frequently than are representatives, and in a few elections such as 1980, barely more than half survive (see Figure 11.6). Despite their six-year terms, the average length of time a senator serves is the same as the average tenure of a representative—about 11 years.[36] There are a number of important respects in which Senate elections differ from House elections; each of these makes the position of Senate incumbents relatively more perilous than that of House incumbents.

PARTY COMPETITION

The two parties compete on a relatively more even basis in Senate races than in House races.[37] Each senator has a state for a constituency, and in general, states are more heterogeneous than the smaller congressional districts included in them. This is significant because social and economic diversity provides a basis for party competition.[38] For example, an urban, heavily minority House district will be dominated by the Democrats, and a rural, white district in the North usually will be dominated by the Republicans. But if a state includes both kinds of districts, each party has a natural base on which to compete for the Senate seats. Partisanship figures indicate that in statewide elections few states are reliably "safe" for either party, whereas a

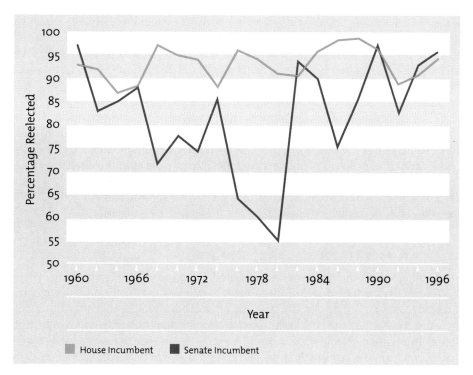

FIGURE 11.6

Representatives Get Reelected More Often than Senators

SOURCE: Norman J. Ornstein et al., eds., *Vital Statistics on Congress, 1995–1996* (Washington, DC: Congressional Quarterly, 1996); 60–61.

majority of the smaller, more homogeneous House districts are "safe" seats. Thus, part of the reason senators lead less secure electoral lives than representatives is simply that they have larger, more diverse constituencies that are more difficult to please.

UNCONTROLLED INFORMATION

Senators receive far more media coverage than representatives. One study found that the average senator appeared on the network evening news 33 times during the course of a session, compared to 5 times for the average representative. Every senator had at least one appearance, whereas a quarter of the House got no coverage whatsoever.[39] Given the image of politicians as uninhibited publicity-seekers, this greater media exposure might seem like a good thing for senators, but things are not always what they seem to be. Almost all the information that constituents receive about House incumbents comes *from* House incumbents—newsletters, press releases, and so forth.[40] Naturally, such information has an entirely positive slant; representatives certainly are not going to circulate negative information about themselves. Senators also would like their constituents to get nothing but positive information about them, but the media are not under Senate control; the media publicize controversial statements, personal peccadilloes, and fights with the president and other politicians: Controversy and conflict are newsworthy (Chapter 9). And such coverage inevitably puts the senator in a negative light in the eyes of at least some constituents.

BETTER CHALLENGERS

The office of senator enjoys a higher status than the office of representative. After all, the Senate is commonly referred to as the "upper" chamber while the House is referred to as the "lower" chamber (reflecting sensitive House feelings, members of

Congress refer to the "other" chamber). Thus, more potential challengers would be willing to risk a race for the more prestigious Senate than a race for the less prestigious House. Moreover, Senate seats are scarce. Every two years, all 435 House seats are available, compared to 33 or 34 Senate seats; a state with 20 House seats has 40 House elections in a four-year period, but only 2 Senate elections. Thus, far fewer credible challengers are needed in order to make Senate races competitive.

The combination of greater attractiveness and greater scarcity produces Senate challengers who are on average much stronger than House challengers.[41] Senate challengers are better known and better liked than House challengers, and the gap between incumbents and challengers is smaller, partly because the challengers are more highly regarded, and partly because the incumbents are apt to be less highly regarded (because they have less control of press coverage and more heterogeneous constituencies, as explained earlier).

HIGH AMBITIONS

Another reason that senators are associated with more controversial matters than representatives is that many of them have higher ambitions. Pundits have commented that every senator looks in the mirror and sees a president. The political system depends, of course, on ambitious office-seekers putting themselves on the line.[42] But higher ambition has its risks. No senator can seek the presidential nomination solely on the basis of the projects brought home to his or her state. Presidential ambitions require senators to take on larger national and international issues to demonstrate vision, expertise, and leadership. But again, such issues are controversial and will offend some constituents; moreover involvement with broader issues leaves senators vulnerable to the charge that they are neglecting their states. In recent years, senators have been defeated partly as a result of charges that they had become the "Senator from Angola" or were "more interested in Africa than Iowa."[43] And when senators do make the race for president, they can be so damaged in the process that their Senate careers also come to an end: witness Gary Hart's retirement after the sex scandals revealed during the course of his unsuccessful bid for the 1988 Democratic nomination.

SENATE ELECTIONS AND ELECTORAL MANDATES

We conclude this discussion of Senate elections with a caution. After every election, pundits and politicians pore over the vote returns in an attempt to divine the meaning of the voting. What was the voters' message? This is always a hazardous enterprise, since voters always send numerous messages, many of which are in conflict. But interpreting Senate election returns is an especially ticklish business because state electorates differ wildly in size. For example, in the 1992 elections, California cast more than 10.5 million votes in electing Diane Feinstein, whereas neighboring Nevada cast only half a million in electing Harry Reid, a vote ratio of 21:1. Such disparities in state size make the gap between votes and victories wider in Senate elections than in others. Consider the arrival and departure of the "Reagan revolution" of the 1980s. In the 1980 elections, the Republicans gained 12 Senate seats. Objectively, this had a major impact—it made Bob Dole the majority leader of the Senate, and more subjectively, the election results contributed to the belief that the election gave a mandate to Ronald Reagan. But the impact of the Senate elections was far out of proportion to the reality of the voting. As disgruntled Democrats observed, their party actually got 3 million more Senate votes nationally than the

Republicans, but the Republicans won narrow victories in a number of small states. In 1986, the shoe was on the other foot. The Republicans lost eight seats and Bob Dole went back to being minority leader; many commentators viewed the election results as the end of the Reagan era. But, once again, perception and reality were only tenuously related. The Republicans actually *increased* their percentage of the national Senate vote over 1980, but this time the Democrats won narrow victories in a number of small states. So, with about 48 percent of the national vote in 1980 the Reagan era began, and with about 50 percent of the vote in 1986 the Reagan era ended. As has been observed before, things are not always what they seem to be.

House and Senate Elections Compared

So, Senate elections are different from House elections in that they are more competitive between the two parties and less favorable for incumbents. In most states, both parties can make a credible attempt to win Senate elections. And incumbency is far less of an advantage in the Senate—even though their terms are three times as long, the average senator serves only about as long as the average representative. In terms of party competition and the advantage of incumbency, House and Senate elections show important differences. But Senate elections are similar to House elections in other important respects.

Like House elections, Senate elections have become individualized. Programmatic and ideological concerns may be more important, but it is the *candidates'* programmatic and ideological commitments that matter, more so than those of their party or the president. As in House elections, more voters split their tickets between presidential and senatorial candidates now than previously. In addition, there has been a sharp upsurge in the proportion of "split" states, states that send one senator from each party to Washington.[44] In the 105th Congress (1997–1998) 19 states had a senator from each party. The bottom line is that just as contemporary House races are local, not national contests, so contemporary Senate races are state, not national contests.

National Forces in Congressional Elections: 1994

Former Speaker of the House Thomas P. "Tip" O'Neill (D-MA) once commented that "all politics is local." O'Neill's remark partly reflected the parochial politics of Massachusetts, but its broader significance lies in the reminder that, although members of Congress are national lawmakers, they are elected and reelected by people in thousands of localities, to whom they owe their ultimate responsibility.

The tendency of today's representatives and senators to distance themselves from locally unpopular party and presidential positions makes modern congressional elections less subject to the kind of **national forces**—across-the-board electoral effects of popular presidents, party performance, and economic conditions—that were common in the American past.[45] Presidential **coattails**—the tendency

■ **national forces**
Electoral effects felt across most states and congressional districts. Most often they reflect especially strong presidential candidates, party performance, or the state of the economy.

■ **coattails**
Positive electoral fallout of a popular presidential candidate on congressional candidates of the party.

of presidents to carry members of Congress of their own party into office—have declined in strength.[46] Far more voters split their tickets between presidential and congressional choices than in the past.[47] Moreover, as parties have weakened and incumbency has strengthened, fewer voters seemed to treat off-year elections as referenda on the performance of the president. In every off-year election since the Civil War except one (1934) the party of the president has lost House seats—and usually Senate seats as well—but fewer are lost today than in earlier periods (see Figure 11.7) That is why the 1994 elections came as such a surprise—they were reminiscent of the kind of electoral tides that flowed regularly in earlier eras.

As we have seen, beginning in the mid-1960s, congressional incumbents developed entrepreneurial politics to a fine art. They voted themselves perks to replace the resources formerly provided by local party organizations, they used constituency service to construct a nonpartisan, nonideological layer of support, and they developed fund-raising capacities that dwarfed those of potential opponents. When combined with research showing that presidential coattails and midterm effects were declining, members of the House appeared to be well on their way to insulating themselves from the kinds of national forces that in earlier times often determined which party controlled Congress.

The 1994 elections upset that view. The 57-seat loss suffered by the Democrats was the largest since 1946 and seemed more in keeping with late-nineteenth-century electoral conditions than late-twentieth-century conditions. A strong national tide seemingly had destroyed the insulation of the Democratic Congress—notwithstanding the perquisites of office, constituency service, and the advantage in campaign finance. With the benefit of two years of hindsight it now appears that, although national forces were more important in 1994 than in most other elections of the past generation, the changes were somewhat exaggerated.[48]

Although incumbent losses in 1994 were severe, and entirely on the Democratic side, 90 percent of incumbents who ran were reelected. Estimates of the incumbency advantage continued to be significant, although higher for Republicans than for Democrats. Some of the new Republicans announced that they

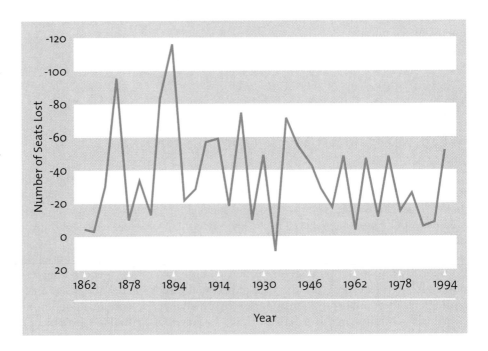

FIGURE 11.7

Incumbent Administrations Do Not Lose as Many House Seats in Mid-Term Elections Today as in the Past

SOURCES: Norman J. Ornstein et al., eds., *Vital Statistics on Congress, 1995-1996* (Washington, DC: Congressional Quarterly, 1996); 55.

intended to act as courageous lawmakers and not engage in mundane political activities like bringing home the bacon. Representative Michael Flanagan (R-IL), who had upset a scandal-ridden incumbent, "practically bragged that he would bring home less federal largesse, saying: 'Pork has not served this district well.'"[49]

A year later, after the Republican Congress had overplayed its hand and its control of the House seemed in danger, Rep. Flanagan had changed his tune: His press release read "These are good projects, not pork."[50] Representative Mark Neumann (R-WI) was a diehard deficit hawk, but he was in the minority as Republican colleagues on the Appropriations Committee doled out projects for members in need of electoral credit.[51] In the end, Flanagan's about-face could not save him—his district was too Democratic, but there is little doubt that the Republicans saved their majority in 1996 by time-honored techniques—putting distance between themselves and an unpopular leader (Newt Gingrich) and highlighting their activities on behalf of their districts.[52] In the 1996 elections, the Republican majorities pulled through as ticket-splitting and the incumbency advantage helped 91 Republican House candidates to win districts carried by President Clinton. The 1994 elections now appear to be as much an exception as a new beginning, as the new Republican majority comes to appreciate the value of the electoral techniques developed by the old Democratic one.

Is Congress a Representative Body?

By various objective measures as well as the more subjective judgments of long-time observers, members of Congress are highly qualified people. In contrast to times past, today's Congress contains few political "hacks." Current members are hard-working, well-educated, bright, and personally interested in public policy. Moreover, despite the impressions the media gives to the public, today's Congress is less corrupt than ever before. Although scandals are more common news now than in the past, that probably reflects changing perspectives in the media—the rise of the "junkyard dog" mentality—rather than increased corruption in the Congress (see p. 285).

Still, some people look at the membership of Congress and are troubled. They see a supposedly representative body that does not mirror the diversity of today's United States. The Congress is overwhelmingly composed of white male professionals. The 105th House has only 51 women—albeit a historical high-water mark—and the 37 African American, 18 Hispanic, and five Asian members are less than their proportions of the larger population.[53] Comparable proportions of the Senate are much lower: nine women, one African American, no Hispanics, and two Asian Americans (the senators from Hawaii). The numbers have been rising in recent decades, but at a slow rate except for the 1992 elections (see Figure 11.8). The subject of the gender, racial, and ethnic diversity of the Congress has been a matter of considerable controversy in recent years.

The concept of representation means different things to different people. For some, the personal characteristics (gender, race, religion) of the representative are unimportant: So long as he is responsive to the needs and aspirations of constituents, they are well represented.[54] Others disagree. They contend that by definition a male representative cannot be responsive to the needs and aspirations of women ("They just don't get it!") and that white representatives cannot be

FIGURE 11.8

The Presence of Women and Minorities in Congress Has Increased Significantly Since 1990

SOURCES: Stanley, Harold W., and Richard G. Niemi, *Vital Statistics in American Politics,* 4th ed. (Washington DC: CQ Press, 1994): 21.

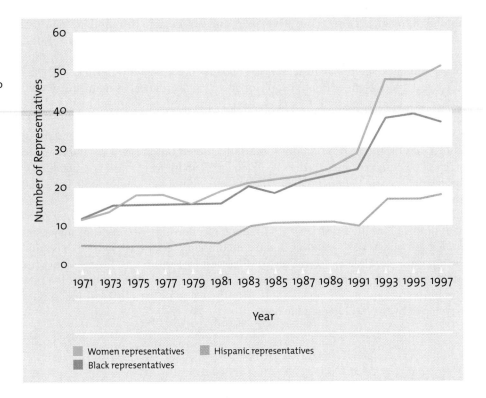

responsive to the needs and aspirations of blacks and other minorities. Those who hold such views believe that Congress must be *descriptively* similar to the country in order to be truly a representative body. Still others concede that white male representatives might be able to represent women and minorities, but believe nonetheless that women and minority representatives have important symbolic value. If they have a visible presence in the councils of government, they will both provide valuable role models for women and minorities in the population and enhance the legitimacy of government actions.[55]

Those who believe in either the actual or the symbolic importance of diversifying the Congress are not likely to see their frustration alleviated very soon. For the Congress is not like a business that hires employees or a university that admits students. Its members are chosen by millions of citizens voting independently (and secretly) in hundreds of elections. Voters can be urged to practice affirmative action, but such appeals are unlikely to be very effective. Because the political problems faced by women and minorities are different, they require separate discussions.

WOMEN

In terms of the proportion of women in the national legislature, the United States ranks quite low among world democracies (see International Comparison). But societal prejudice against women serving in public office is diminishing (see Figure 11.9). White males, after all, have mothers, wives, sisters, and daughters, all of whom can make the case for women's equality and all of whom stand to benefit from greater equality. Not surprisingly, white males are less negative toward affirmative

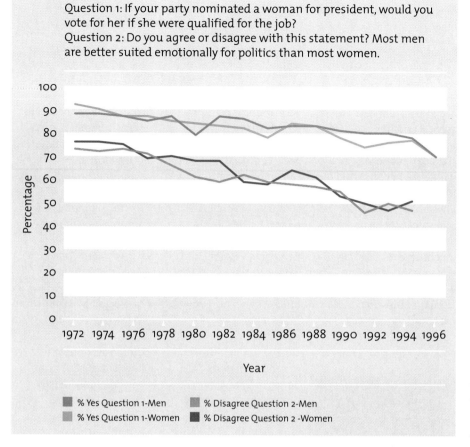

Question 1: If your party nominated a woman for president, would you vote for her if she were qualified for the job?
Question 2: Do you agree or disagree with this statement? Most men are better suited emotionally for politics than most women.

Year

- ■ % Yes Question 1-Men
- ■ % Yes Question 1-Women
- ■ % Disagree Question 2-Men
- ■ % Disagree Question 2 -Women

FIGURE 11.9

Changing Attitudes toward Women in Public Office

SOURCE: "Americans Rate Their Society and Chart Its Values," *The Public Perspective*, February/ March 1997, 25. © The Public Perspective, a publication of the Roper Center for Public Opinion Research, University of Connecticut, Storrs. Reprinted by permission.

Although women like Representative Barbara Mikulski from Maryland and her colleagues are now part of a historical highwater mark —60 women—Congress is still composed largely of white males.

action for women than toward affirmative action for minorities.[56] The former bestows some advantage on their loved ones, whereas the latter usually bestows advantages on strangers.

Women suffer politically in that they have only recently gained admission to the networks that move politicians upward to higher office—men have a long head start. Despite some well-publicized examples of TV anchors and other personalities moving laterally into Congress, these are the exceptions, not the rule. Winning a seat is usually the result of a series of successful efforts, beginning with a local office or community organization, moving through state office, and ultimately winning an open seat or defeating a vulnerable incum-

Women in Politics

Women are even rarer in the Japanese Diet than in the U.S. Congress.

Since the 1950s, the role of women in the United States has undergone a revolutionary change. There are still apparent gender inequalities, such as the salaries and wages women earn compared to men, and the unequal division of housework and child care responsibilities between wives and husbands, but the expectations of young women today are similar to those of young men, and the career opportunities of today's young women far exceed those of their mothers, let alone their grandmothers. In few other countries are women less subject to educational and occupational barriers.

There is one realm, however, in which American women continue to trail women in other countries—politics. A recent study found that, in comparison to other democracies, American women are considerably less likely to hold national office. The accompanying table shows the proportion of women elected to the lower (more important) house of a country's parliament, compared to the proportion of women in the U.S. House of Representatives.

The United States trails all but a few of the advanced industrial democracies, occupying a cluster that includes Belgium, the United Kingdom, and Australia.

Only France and Japan are significantly lower. Undoubtedly there are many factors that contribute to the differences, but one seems to be the electoral system. The countries with highest proportions of women tend to have some version or another of proportional representation (p. 248). In such systems, party leaders submit lists of candidates who will be elected in proportion to the party's vote. Judging by the results, these lists appear to have significant numbers of highly ranked women. Countries with simple plurality (p. 248) or related systems tend to have lower proportions of women. Apparently, women are not as successful where they have to contend for a specific geographically defined seat.

bent. Along the way, the member-to-be of Congress learns the art of politics, makes valuable political allies, becomes acquainted with those who bankroll campaigns, and generally acquires the experiences, characteristics, and resources that comprise the "qualifications" that someday will make her a "credible" challenger. The most common base for congressional candidates is the state legislature.[57] Women are making rapid progress in this arena (see Figure 11.10), and as the pool of women in state legislatures and other lower offices grows, their representation in Congress will follow.

Thus, we believe that the underrepresentation of women in Congress will naturally lessen as women's educational and career patters become more like those of men. To be sure, some feminists will reject this analysis, believing that women

Women Legislators in the Lower House

Country	Year of Election	Women MPs (Percentage)	Electoral System
Sweden	1994	40.3	PR
Norway	1993	39.4	PR
Finland	1991	39.0	PR
Denmark	1990	33.0	PR
Netherlands	1994	31.3	PR
Germany	1994	26.3	Other
Austria	1990	21.3	PR
New Zealand	1993	21.2	Plurality
Canada	1993	18.0	Plurality
Switzerland	1991	17.5	PR
Argentina	1993	16.3	PR
Spain	1993	16.0	PR
Italy	1994	15.1	Other
Costa Rica	1994	14.0	PR
Poland	1993	13.0	Plurality
Ireland	1992	12.1	Other
Columbia	1994	11.0	PR
Hungary	1994	10.9	Other
United States	1994	10.8	Plurality
Philippines	1992	10.6	Plurality
Bangladesh	1991	10.3	Plurality
Czech Republic	1992	10.0	PR
Russia	1993	9.6	PR
Belgium	1991	9.4	PR
Israel	1992	9.2	PR
United Kingdom	1992	9.2	Plurality
Portugal	1991	8.7	PR
Australia	1993	8.2	Other
Mexico	1991	7.6	Other
India	1991	7.3	Plurality
France	1993	6.1	Other
Uruguay	1989	6.1	PR
Brazil	1990	6.0	PR
Japan	1993	2.7	Other

SOURCE: Adapted from Pippa Norris, "Legislative Recruitment," in Lawrence LeDuc, Richard Niemi, and Pippa Norris, eds., *Comparing Democracies* (Thousand Oaks, CA: Sage, 1996): 191-92

should strive to be elected as *women*, not because they have learned to play the game the same way that men do. We recognize this viewpoint, but in our view such a strategy will not succeed, simply because American women are unlikely to vote as a block rather than as a complex combination of their other identities. Progress will be gradual, not rapid, and many women naturally will feel frustration. We encourage impatient women students to put their impatience to a positive use: get involved in politics and help expand the pool of women candidates.

FIGURE 11.10

More and More Women Are Being
Elected to State Legislatures, a
Stepping Stone to Congress

SOURCES: "The Gender Story,"
The Public Perspective, August/
September 1996, p. 7.

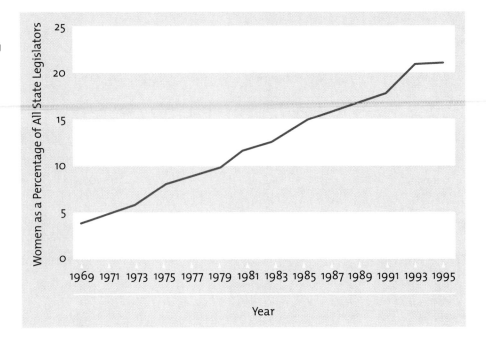

MINORITIES

The prospects for further lessening of minority underrepresentation in Congress are less favorable than for women, especially the prospects for African Americans. The critical fact is that, in racially diverse constituencies, **block voting**—whereby racial groups vote as blocks—often does occur. When it does, a black candidate can be elected only where African Americans are a majority of the electorate. In the 103rd Congress, for example (the first Congress after the redistricting following the 1990 census), 32 of the 39 black members came from districts in which African Americans were in the majority, and in five of the remaining seven districts African Americans plus Latinos made up a majority. Similarly, 15 of the 17 Latino members of the 103rd Congress came from majority Latino districts; none came from districts with a white majority.

Given this fundamental fact, efforts to increase minority representation in Congress have been made largely through the redistricting process. The 1982 amendments to the Voting Rights Act and subsequent court decisions have been interpreted to require the creation of **majority-minority districts** wherever possible. In such districts, a racial or ethnic minority constitutes a majority of the population. Given the lower turnout rates that prevail among minority groups, the rule of thumb is that 65 percent of the population in such districts should belong to minority groups.

Efforts to create majority-minority districts, sometimes called **affirmative-action redistricting**, have generated considerable controversy. Some of the districts that have been created have taken on unusual shapes, sometimes uniting areas of different cities connected only by a freeway. This has given rise to charges of racial gerrymandering. In 1993, the Supreme Court ruled in *Shaw* v. *Reno* that majority-minority districting had its limits: A district created on no basis other than to include a majority of minorities might raise constitutional questions. And in 1995 and 1996, the Court declared redistricting plans in Georgia, North Carolina, and Texas to be unconstitutional racial gerrymanders.

block voting
Voting in which nearly all members of one group (i.e., African Americans) vote for a candidate of their race whereas nearly all members of another group (i.e., whites) vote against that candidate.

majority-minority districts
District in which a minority group is the numerical majority.

affirmative-action redistricting
The process of drawing district lines to maximize the number of majority-minority districts.

MAJORITY-MINORITY DISTRICTING

In the 1980s, the Voting Rights Act (p. 171) was put to a new use. With the right of minorities to cast a vote seemingly secure, civil rights activists turned their attention to the outcomes of elections.* Although barriers to voting had been overturned, in many areas racially polarized voting prevented minorities from actually winning any elections. The proposed remedy came to be the creation of majority-minority districts.

Congress encouraged such districts in 1982 amendments to the act, and the Supreme Court continued in the same direction in a 1986 decision, *Thornburg* v. *Gingles*. Ultimately, the Justice Department began to deny approval to redistricting plans that did not provide for creation of the maximum number of majority-minority districts.

In 1993, the Court began to draw back. A North Carolina plan contained two districts with unusual shapes. As shown in the figure, one followed Interstate 95 across the state to pick up black residential areas in the state's major cities. In *Shaw* v. *Reno*, a splintered Court sent the plan back to the lower courts, expressing concern over "bizarrely shaped" districts drawn only to include people of a particular race. In 1995, the Court went further in *Miller* v. *Johnson*. By a 5-4 majority the court ruled that Georgia's plan was a "racial gerrymander" that violated the equal protection clause of the Constitution.† In 1996, the Court affirmed *Miller* in *Shaw* v. *Hunt*, striking down the North Carolina plan that a lower court had approved.‡ The decision again was by a 5-4 majority. While the Court has not explicitly rejected the use of racial considerations in redistricting, it appears that the current Court will reject plans that use race as a "predominant factor" in drawing districts. However, the Court has left itself a loophole because it has shown no inclination as yet to strike down the large amount of race-dominated districting that is required by its own interpretation of the Voting Rights Act in *Thornburg*. Furthermore, the current majority is fragile, with one law professor commenting that the current state of the law depends "on Justice O'Connor's personal opinion about when race-consciousness goes too far."§

* This discussion is partly based on personal communications with Daniel Lowenstein, Professor of Law, UCLA.

† Holly Idelson, "Court Takes a Harder Line on Minority Voting Blocs," *Congressional Quarterly Weekly Report*," July 1, 1995), 1944–46.

‡ Holly Idelson, "Minority-District Decisions Lay No Clear Guidelines," *Congressional Quarterly Weekly Report*, June 15, 1996, 1679–81.

§ Pamela Karlan, quoted in Ibid., 1679.

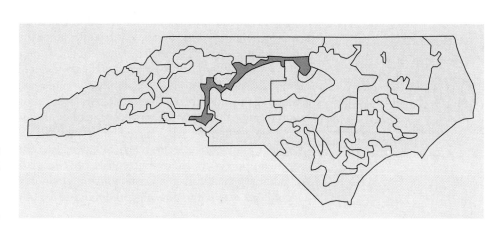

Even racial liberals are not all of the same mind on the issue of majority-minority districting. On the pro side they value the increased representation of African American and Latino representatives. On the con side they are naturally cautious about something supported by Republicans and likely to work against Democrats. During the Bush administration, the Justice Department aggressively pushed majority-minority redistricting plans, and Republicans have typically joined minorities in challenging plans on grounds that they did not create the maximum number of such districts. The political logic is clear, of course. Republicans believe that by concentrating minority groups in urban districts they can push white Democratic incumbents outward into the suburbs where they are more vulnerable to Republican challengers. Republicans understandably prefer fewer Democrats to more Democrats, regardless of race.

The dilemma posed by majority-minority districting became exceptionally clear after the 1996 elections. Were it not for the majority-minority districting after the 1990 census, the Democrats might have won control of the House.[58] Democrats ask whether it is better to have somewhat fewer African Americans who would all be subcommittee and committee chairs in a Democrat-controlled House, or to have somewhat more African-American members who are all back-benchers in a Republican-controlled House?

Whatever one's view of such trade-offs, there is an upper limit on the number of majority-minority districts that can possibly be created—racial minorities by definition consist of *minorities* of people, and redistricters cannot cross state boundaries to concentrate them. Indeed, given the recent court decisions, we may already be near that limit. If the maximum number of majority-minority districts that can be created is roughly the same as the number that currently exist, then the upper limit for minority representatives will be correspondingly low unless minorities can break through and win in districts where they are not majorities. From that standpoint, the kind of racial block voting assumed in and perhaps even encouraged by majority-minority districting works against the long-term prospects for minority candidates to win in nonminority districts. That is, the floor for minority representation assured by majority-minority districting might at the same time be a ceiling on the number of minority representatives. Thus, many were encouraged when two black incumbents whose districts were redrawn were able to win reelection in white majority districts in 1996.[59]

A second potentially negative effect of affirmative-action redistricting is that it may work to marginalize minority members of Congress, putting them in a kind of political ghetto. The risk is especially serious for black representatives. The homogeneity of African-American views should not be overstated.[60] Nevertheless, blacks are overwhelmingly Democratic in their allegiance, more liberal in general, and far more supportive of federal social welfare programs in particular.[61] Representatives of such a group will probably be correspondingly liberal. Indeed, members of the Congressional Black Caucus (CBC), all of whom are Democrats in the 105th Congress, are among the most liberal members of Congress, as measured by numerous interest group ratings. But liberal records compiled by them as U.S. Representatives may well preclude them from being credible challengers in gubernatorial, senatorial, and ultimately presidential elections, where statewide constituencies are much more heterogeneous in general, and more conservative in particular. A minority member of the House who faithfully represents a majority-minority district may thereby compile a record that makes it impossible for him or her to contend by state or nationwide.

In sum, the subject of minority representation in Congress is a troubling one, and existing court-imposed methods of encouraging more minority representation are controversial. Each person must decide whether the gains from assuring some level of minority representation exceed the costs. Unfortunately, the latter are highly uncertain. Thus, people of good faith may well disagree.

ELECTIONS, PARTIES, AND SUBGROUP REPRESENTATION

Before concluding this discussion, we note two additional points. First, some part of the difficulty entailed by increasing minority representation stems from the simple fact that the single-member district simple plurality (SMSP) electoral system (p. 248) is not designed to produce a descriptively representative legislative body. The SMSP system disadvantages minorities—racial and otherwise. If you get less than the leading candidate, even if you get 49 percent of the vote, you win nothing. Republicans in Democratic districts or vice versa, liberals in conservative districts or vice versa, African Americans in white districts or vice versa, pro-lifers in pro-choice districts or vice versa—all are unrepresented if the majority elects a representative who shares the majority sentiment. In a sense, U.S. courts have been trying to coax a more proportional result from an electoral system never designed to be proportional. It should be no surprise that their efforts have met with limited success. Recognizing these realities, some academic critics have raised questions about the electoral system itself. President Clinton's 1993 nomination of Lani Guanier to the office of assistant attorney general for civil rights would have provided an opportunity for the general public to hear some of this debate, but some of her proposals proved too controversial and her nomination was withdrawn before hearings were held.

Second, it is interesting to speculate whether minorities (and women) might be better represented if the old-style party machines were still in existence. After all, the "balanced ticket" was a common strategy of the political party: To construct a coalition of diverse groups, the party recognized each group when putting together a slate of candidates. Historians believe that, because of racial prejudice, minorities generally did not fare as well as whites in the urban machines, which were based largely on white ethnic groups. Still, it is at least arguable that if every city in the United States still had a respectable machine, there would be more African Americans in Congress. As Professor V.O. Key, Jr., argued in his classic work, *Southern Politics*, a disorganized politics advantages the economic "haves" and disadvantages the economic "have nots." The urban machines integrated earlier ethnic groups into the American political structure, but the machines were crumbling when the large post–World War II migration of African Americans from the rural South to northern cities took place. Today, party organization has weakened and candidates fend for themselves. The demise of the machines and the rise of candidate-centered politics may be an additional disadvantage imposed on African Americans.

Chapter Summary

Members of the House of Representative are reelected at very high rates, more than 90 percent in all recent elections, including the Republican landslide of 1994. Upon close examination, this does not really represent any violation of the Founders' plan for an electorally sensitive House. On the contrary, because representatives are so electorally sensitive, they work very hard at serving their districts, try very hard to represent constituents' policy concerns, and in general attempt to eliminate any basis for a strong challenge against them. Contrary to the charges of many critics, electoral success does not lead members of the House to be lazy and unresponsive; just the opposite. Members are reelected *because* they are so hard-working and responsive.

Senators too are hard-working and responsive—probably more so than the Framers intended—although they do not enjoy the same electoral success as members of the House. On average, their constituencies—states—are more competitive than House districts; they face stronger challengers; and their very prominence makes them the object of media coverage that they do not control and exposes them to expectations and ambitions that carry risks as well as rewards.

But if representatives and senators are so hard-working and responsive, why are many citizens so dissatisfied with Congress? The reason is that in politics, as in life, all good things do not go together. In particular, as we will explain in the next chapter, high responsiveness to congressional districts may detract from the ability of Congress to achieve other valuable goals, not the least of which is the national interest.

The single-member district simple plurality electoral system provides strong incentives for representatives to be *responsive* to the wishes of majorities in their district. But the system in no way ensures that the composition of the Congress will be *descriptively representative* of the diversity of the country's population. On the contrary, if people vote as ethnic or racial blocs, the system will not elect a proportional number of ethnic and racial minorities. The courts have encouraged districting arrangements that would produce more proportional outcomes, but with limited success and via procedures such as majority-minority districting that are highly controversial and politically divisive, especially within the Democratic party. At this time, such procedures may be the only way to ensure some reasonable representation of minorities, but it may be that in the long run they work against minority representation by encouraging block voting and becoming ceilings on minority representation rather than floors.

As for women, the problems are different and the primary solution is time: As women increasingly win lower offices, the pool of qualified women candidates inevitably expands. As the pool expands, the proportion of women candidates for Congress will increase.

Key Terms

affirmative-action redistricting, p. 370

block voting, p. 370

coattails, p. 363

constituency service, p. 349

constituent assistance, p. 349

district service, p. 349

frank, p. 352

gerrymandering, p. 346

incumbency advantage, p. 347

majority-minority districts, p. 370

national forces, p. 363

ombudsman, p. 349

professional legislature, p. 345

reapportionment, p. 346

redistricting, p. 346

rotation, p. 344

Suggested Readings

Brady, David. *Critical Elections and Congressional Policy Making*. Stanford, CA: Stanford University Press, 1988. Prize-winning account that ties together congressional elections, processes, and policy-making.

Butler, David and Bruce Cain. *Congressional Redistricting*. New York: Macmillan, 1992. Readable account of the redistricting process, with comparisons to practices in other democracies.

Campbell, James. *The Presidential Pulse of Congressional Elections*. Lexington, KY: University of Kentucky Press, 1993. Detailed analysis of national forces operating in midterm elections.

Canon, David. *Actors, Athletes, and Astronauts*. Chicago: University of Chicago Press, 1990. Interesting study of how political amateurs run for and occasionally win a seat in Congress.

Fenno, Richard. *Home Style*. Boston: Little, Brown, 1978. Influential study of how House members interact with constituents, earning their trust, and explaining Washington activity.

Fiorina, Morris. *Congress—Keystone of the Washington Establishment*. 2nd ed. New Haven: Yale University Press, 1989. A critical look at the implications of constituency service for national policy making.

Grofman, Bernard and Chandler Davidson, eds. *Controversies in Minority Voting*. Washington, DC: Brookings, 1992. This collection of essays offers a balanced perspective on the uses to which the Voting Rights Act has been put.

Jacobson, Gary. *The Politics of Congressional Elections*. 4th ed. New York: Longman, 1997. The definitive text on modern congressional elections.

Hernsonn, Paul. *Congressional Elections*. 2nd ed. Washington, DC: CQ Press, 1997. The most up-to-date study of congressional campaigns.

Hibbing, John. *Congressional Careers*. Chapel Hill: University of North Carolina Press, 1991. Detailed study of career development of modern U.S. representatives after their initial election.

Mayhew, David. *Congress—The Electoral Connection*. New Haven: Yale, 1974. Influential work that shows how much of congressional structure and behavior can be explained by the assumption that reelection is the most important goal of members.

Thernstrom, Abigail. *Whose Votes Count? Affirmative Action and Minority Voting Rights*. Cambridge, MA: Harvard University Press, 1987. Critical study of majority-minority districting and other uses to which the Voting Rights Act, as amended, has been put.

ote for
One

13

14

15

16

Businesswoman
TOM CONDIT
Writer   Natural Law

JACK FOREM
Writer   STATE SENATOR

Natural Law

Ninth District   Republica
CAROL FLYER PRETTIE
Businesswoman
                                                      Peace
THOMAS N. HUDSON   Freedo
Trust Attorney
                                                      Dem
ROBERT J. EVANS
Criminal Defense Lawyer

BARBARA LEE
ember/Business Woman   TURN PAGE TO CO

the congress in operation

N APRIL OF 1992 a California jury acquitted four Los Angeles police officers who had been filmed brutally beating an African American, Rodney King, after an early morning chase. The acquittal triggered violent rioting in south central Los Angeles that resulted in sixty deaths and a billion dollars in property damage. Originally mischaracterized by the media as a simple race riot, the disturbances soon were recognized as a multiethnic conflict reflecting the tensions of urban poverty and joblessness, exacerbated by ethnic and racial rivalries. Understandably, many Americans turned to the national government to do something about "the crisis of the cities." Whatever their personal views, with an election only six months away, many in Congress felt compelled to respond.[1]

Jack Kemp, secretary of Housing and Urban Development in the Bush administration, had been pushing an urban policy based on the concept of "enterprise zones." These are specified areas in which favorable tax treatment is given to investors in hopes of stimulating economic development in run-down areas otherwise unattractive to private investors. While the program had previously received a less than enthusiastic reception in the Democratic Congress, which favored more direct government involvement, it now became the vehicle through which Congress would respond to the urban crisis. The Democrats proposed new government spending in the zones to reinforce the tax incentives, and the legislative dance began.

The House passed a bill providing for 50 zones, 25 of which were to be located in rural areas. The Senate decided that a total of 115 zones was a better idea, with 40 allocated to rural areas, and an additional 40 to cities of less than 500 thousand population. Were these appropriate responses to the "crisis of the cities?" Why so many zones, and why zones in rural areas and small cities (as well as Indian reservations, in one version of the Senate bill)? Simple — you cannot expect senators and representatives from rural states and districts to support a bill that provides nothing for *their* constituencies. In conference committee the House position prevailed: 50 zones split evenly between urban and rural. The bulk of the direct spending was allocated to the urban zones, but much of it was earmarked for smaller cities, rather than the great urban concentrations people think of when they hear the phrase "crisis of the cities."

By this time the legislation had become thoroughly enmeshed in election-year politics. Six months after the King beating, and a week before the elections, Congress included the urban legislation in an omnibus tax bill that it submitted to President Bush. By bundling together a number of controversial pieces of legislation, the Democratic Congress hoped to force Bush to accept provisions he opposed in order to get those things he wanted. The strategy failed: Bush vetoed the omnibus bill. The crisis of the cities would have to wait.

his episode displays several characteristic features of the United States Congress. On the one hand, members of Congress are quick to respond to a societal problem that rises on the agenda. On the other hand, the collective Congress is slow to decide what to do about the problem, in considerable part because individual members struggle for constituency advantage. The struggle distorts the purpose of the legislation, and when all is said and done it is not clear that the legislative response would make a major contribution if it were enacted. This chapter examines and explains this characteristic difficulty, as well as the workings of our most powerful, most complex, and most democratic political institution.

Congress—The First Branch

More so than people in other democracies, Americans are proud of their political institutions. They revere the Constitution, honor the law, and respect the presidency and the courts. But there is a noteworthy exception to the observation that Americans hold their institutions in high esteem—the Congress. As Rodney Dangerfield might say, "Congress don't get no respect." Examples are commonplace. American humorist Mark Twain once observed that "it could probably be shown with facts and figures that there is no distinctly native American criminal class except Congress."[2] Congress has been defined as "a creature with 535 bellies, and no brain." Periodically one hears the remark that "the opposite of progress is Congress."

Disrespect for Congress is nothing new, as this 1798 print of the congressional floor shows.

These disparaging quips are quite representative of popular sentiment. Surveys consistently report that only a minority of Americans trust the Congress to do what is right or have confidence in Congress, and they view generic members as having ethical standards only a bit higher than car salespersons (see Figure 12.1). The reputation

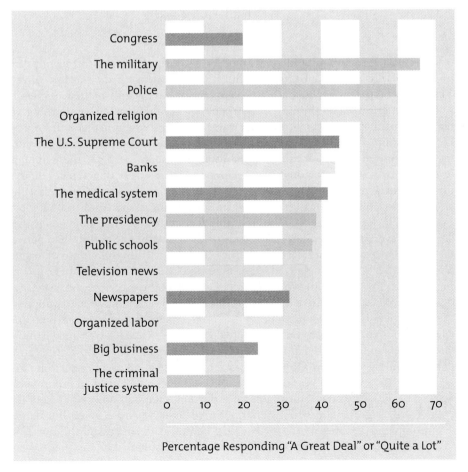

Percentage Responding "A Great Deal" or "Quite a Lot"

FIGURE 12.1 A

Public Confidence in Congress Trails Confidence in Many Other Institutions

SOURCE: The Gallup Poll, May 28-29, 1996.

FIGURE 12.1B

The Public Rates the Honesty
and Ethics of Members of
Congress Lower than That of
Other Occupations

SOURCE: The Gallup Poll,
October 19–22, 1995.

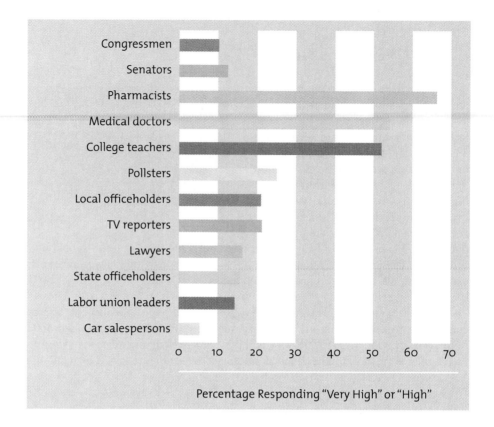

Percentage Responding "Very High" or "High"

of Congress has been repeatedly tarnished by a variety of scandals. Ironically, this most electorally sensitive institution is the one whose image is the most negative.[3] Majorities of the represented doubt the competence and integrity of the Congress.[4]

Why Americans hold the Congress in such low regard is somewhat puzzling. As discussed in Chapter 11, Congress is the world's foremost example of a professionalized legislature. Most of its members are capable and hard-working and consider legislative service to be their career. They put in hours comparable to those of high-level executives and professionals, but receive far less by way of material compensation. Moreover, as Nelson Polsby observes, there is little doubt that Congress is the world's most powerful legislature, with policy-making responsibilities far more extensive than elsewhere.[5] Most of the world's legislatures are subordinate to parties and executives, and membership in many of them is more honorific than active; their members vote as party leaders instruct, and typically do little more than support or oppose the programs advanced by the Prime Minister and his or her supporting coalition. Not only is the Congress independent of the executive, but insofar as domestic policy is concerned, the Congress is more powerful than the executive.

The generally negative perception of Congress becomes even more puzzling when contrasted with the generally positive view Americans have of their particular members of Congress. After all, at the same time popular majorities express doubts about the collective Congress, they reelect 90 percent or more of all incumbents who run; even in a year of upheaval like 1994, 90 percent of all incumbents won.[6] This disparity between support for individual members and criticism of the collective Congress is so striking that political scientists have given it a name, "Fenno's paradox," after Professor Richard Fenno, who first asked the question "Why do we hate our Congress, but love our Congressman?"[7] Fenno pointed out

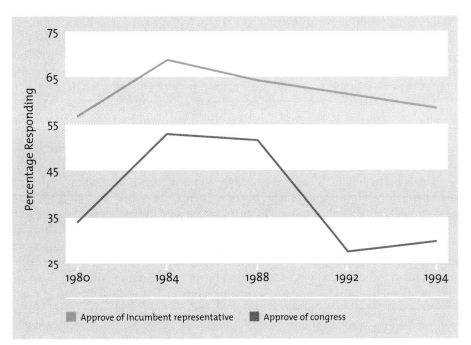

FIGURE 12.2

Americans Rate Their Representative Much More Positively than the Congress

SOURCE: American National Election Studies

that citizens invariably rate their members of Congress far more favorably than the Congress as a whole (see Figure 12.2). Members can take advantage of this disparity by adopting an unusual electoral strategy: "Members run *for* Congress by running *against* Congress."[8]

Fenno's observations are not so puzzling once you have a good understanding of the operation of the Congress and the incentives underlying Congressional operations. The Congress is a complicated institution, however, and it will take some time to lay the groundwork for that understanding.

THE STRUCTURE OF CONGRESS

Like many of the world's parliaments, Congress is **bicameral**; it consists of two chambers, the House of Representatives and the Senate. Unlike most of the world's legislatures, however, both chambers have roughly equal powers. Elsewhere, upper chambers of parliament typically have only ceremonial duties—or, at most, powers that are much weaker than those of the lower chamber.

The near equal power of the two chambers in the United States gives rise to a certain amount of inter-chamber rivalry. Speaker of the House, Thomas Reed (p. 388) once commented that "The Senate is a nice quiet place where good Representatives go when they die."[9] The Senate has a pat response to such jibes: only one Senator in history has given up a Senate seat to run for the House, and that was in 1811 (Henry Clay). For understandable reasons the House dislikes referring to the Senate as the "upper" chamber, preferring the neutral term "other" chamber.

Historically, although their constitutional powers are roughly equal, the political power and importance of the two chambers has waxed and waned. In the decades prior to the Civil War, when turnover in the House was very high (p. 344), the Senate was clearly the more important body. The country's most prominent statesmen—Henry Clay, John C. Calhoun, Daniel Webster, Stephen Douglas, and others—spent their time in the Senate. After the Civil War, political leadership moved to the

bicameral
Description of a legislature that contains two chambers.

Behind Speaker Gingrich is a competent and dedicated staff. In addition to his personal staff, the Speaker oversees a leadership staff of about 150 people.

House, where shifting party control more accurately reflected national sentiments, and where strong Speakers (see later discussion) mobilized their party majorities.

For most of the twentieth century the two chambers have been equal in power and importance. Political circumstances may make one chamber enjoy greater prominence for a time, but eventually the equal power of the other chamber asserts itself. For example, after the Republican takeover of Congress in the 1994 elections, national attention fixated on the successful efforts of House Republicans to pass the Contract with America. Ultimately, however, only 10 of 21 specific proposals in the Contract were adopted by Congress, a pointed reminder that the Congress is genuinely bicameral.

The legislative branch consists of people and institutions in addition to the 535 members of the House and Senate. Beyond the members' personal staffs (p. 352), who number more than 7 thousand in the House and 4 thousand in the Senate, each chamber hires thousands of staff members to support the committees. While many of these individuals do primarily clerical work, others are policy experts who play an important role in the shaping of legislation, especially long-time staff who speak for important members. Additional staff support the party leadership. All in all, there are about 17 thousand people employed as congressional staff (see Table 12.1).

Moreover, in addition to those who work for members and committees, thousands of people work in various support agencies of Congress. The Library of Congress employs nearly 5 thousand, as does the General Accounting Office (GAO), the watchdog agency of Congress that oversees the operation of the executive branch. A smaller number of people work for the Congressional Budget Office (CBO). This

TABLE 12.1

The Legislative Branch

House	
Committee staff	2,147
Personal staff	7,400
Leadership staff	137
Officers of the House staff	1,194
Senate	
Committee staff	994
Personal staff	4,138
Leadership staff	100
Officers of the Senate staff	1,165
Joint Committee Staffs	145
Support Agencies	
General Accounting Office	4,958
Congressional Research Service	814
Congressional Budget Office	230
Miscellaneous	
Architects	2,060
Capitol police	1,159

SOURCE: Adapted from Norman Ornstein, Thomas Mann, and Michael Malbin: *Vital Statistics on Congress: 1995-96* (Washington, DC: Congressional Quarterly Inc, 1996): 131–132.

agency provides Congress with expert economic projections and budgetary information that is independent of the Office of Management and Budget, which works for the president (p. 475). In total, the legislative branch of government consists of some 30 thousand people.

Numbers and expertise are not synonymous with power, however. At the top of the legislative branch pyramid sit the 535 members, who with the advice of their most trusted staffs, make the decisions.

Congress—The Context

To a considerable extent, politics and policy making in the modern Congress are products of an interaction among geography, professionalism, and electoral independence. Together these factors create the incentive and the opportunity to serve specific constituencies, the hallmark of the modern Congress.

Geography and Constituencies

Geography is an element in the politics of all countries simply because socioeconomic interests and the values associated with them tend to be territorially concentrated rather than evenly distributed. Seaports are built on the water, not scattered around the countryside; farms and ranches are located in sparsely populated areas, not in the cities and suburbs; racial and ethnic minorities tend to live in clusters rather than distribute themselves evenly across a country. Thus, politics everywhere has geographic and regional dimensions that reflect underlying differences in social and economic interests and values.

But electoral institutions can either reinforce or minimize the importance of geography. To explain, suppose that policy analysts in the Department of Commerce estimate that a trade agreement will cost 1,000 jobs in an industry, with the impact likely to be felt in a factory closing in either Ohio or Illinois. Electorally speaking, the president is indifferent to where the impact is felt—both states are electorally competitive and have almost the same number of votes in the Electoral College. Most assuredly, however, the members of Congress from Ohio and Illinois are *not* indifferent to where the impact is felt. The members of Congress from each state will wheel and deal, threaten and beg in attempts to make sure the negative impact of the trade agreement concession is not felt in their state. Do they feel that workers in their state are any more deserving than those in the other state? Not at all, but members of Congress (MCs) are the products of the single-member district simple plurality (SMSP) electoral system (p. 248). They are reelected if and only if

they can defeat all the challengers in their particular districts (if they are representatives) or states (if they are Senators). From an electoral standpoint, Illinois workers simply are of no consequence to Ohio members of Congress, and vice versa.

In contrast, members of parliament elected under proportional representation (p. 248) have little incentive to concentrate on a particular geographic area; their fates depend on party leaders who decide how high they are ranked on the party list. Members elected under proportional representation consider themselves to be representatives of major interests, social classes, and ethnic or religious groupings that constitute their party's base of support. Both electorally and philosophically, such an electoral system dampens the importance of geographic considerations.[10] To return to our example, if the United States elected members of Congress by proportional representation (PR), they would be more likely to consider job losses in any state to be as electorally serious as job losses in any other state.

PROFESSIONALISM AND CONSTITUENCIES

Even if members of Congress in the United States were "citizen legislators" who did not care about—or were not eligible for—reelection, the preceding argument would have some force. Members still would be more sensitive to friends and neighbors than to unknown people in other districts and states. Moreover, individuals are shaped by where they grow up and where they live, so members still would bring local perspectives to Congress, even in the absence of electoral motivations.

But today's members of Congress are not "citizen legislators"; they are *professionals* who care, and care deeply, about reelection. And the more concerned they are about reelection, the more attentive they must be to the needs, interests, and values of their districts. At the height of Newt Gingrich's power in the 104th Congress, the party's revision of agricultural policy ("Freedom to Farm") was torpedoed in the Agriculture Committee by Republicans whose agricultural districts were threatened by the legislation. When Gingrich threatened to sanction the defectors, he was forced to back down.[11] Important constituency interests trump other forces, be they party, ideology, or, indeed, the national interest. It has been said of contemporary members of Congress that they understand the national interest only when it speaks to them in a local dialect, an illuminating, if slightly exaggerated comment (see Democratic Dilemma).

For former Speaker Thomas P. "Tip" O'Neill, all politics was local.

Not only does the SMSP system render voters outside your district irrelevant to your chances of reelection, but it also encourages a philosophy of representation that holds that it is the representative's proper function—indeed his or her duty as a representative—to work first and foremost for the people in their districts. Thus, most MCs, much of the time, in genuine good conscience, will work to advance the interests of their districts even at the expense of the districts of other MCs.*

The debate over *whom* a representative should represent—the constituency or the whole country—goes back centuries in political philosophy. It is often intertwined with another debate about *how* the representative should act.† Edmund Burke posed the question most sharply in a classic speech in 1774.‡ Is it the representative's duty to act as a **delegate** of the constituency, who follows the wishes of those who have elected him or her, or as a **trustee**, who decides according to his or her own best judgment? Many people have difficulty maintaining consistency when they think about this question. Here is a simple thought experiment.

> *Representative A believes that the United States should constitutionally prohibit abortion, but represents a suburban district with a pro-choice majority. Should she vote for or against a constitutional amendment prohibiting abortion?*

> *Representative B believes the Constitution includes a right to abortion, but represents a Catholic district with a pro-life majority. Should she vote for or against a constitutional amendment prohibiting abortion?*

Our classroom experiments show that some pro-choice students want the representative to behave as a delegate in the first example, and as a trustee in the second, whereas some pro-life students have the opposite preference.

What do you think? Should members of Congress generally act as delegates or as trustees? Does the issue under consideration make a difference?

* For a critical evaluation of such a philosophy of representation, see Dennis Thompson, *Ethics in Congress* (Washington, DC: Brookings, 1995): chs. 3-4.

† Heinz Eulau, John Wahlke, William Buchanan and Leroy Ferguson, "The Role of the Representative: Some Empirical Observations on the Theory of Edmund Burke," *American Political Science Review* 53(1959): 742–756.

‡ "Speech to the Electors of Bristol," Peter Standlis, ed., *Selected Writings and Speeches* (New York: Doubleday, 1963).

■ **delegate**
Role of representative who follows the wishes of those who have elected him or her.

■ **trustee**
Role of representative who decides according to his or her own best judgment.

ELECTORAL INDEPENDENCE AND CONSTITUENCIES

A final important element that shapes the behavior of MCs is *electoral independence*. Other democracies such as Britain have both SMSP electoral systems and members of parliament (MPs) who wish to be reelected. But British MPs are not nearly as able to shape policy to serve their constituencies as are members of Congress. The reason is that party leaders prevent them from doing so, and party-line voting among British voters prevents them from being rewarded for doing so.[12]

Members of Congress are far more independent of party leaders, and in the United States electoral politics is candidate-centered. As discussed in Chapter 8, in most areas, parties no longer control nominations and finance campaigns, and voters no longer vote loyally for parties. More than ever before, candidates' fates depend on their personal qualifications, characteristics, and activities. In particular, members of Congress do not find ready-made constituencies; rather, they construct them.

Fenno observes that we are only using shorthand when we speak of members representing their districts. The congressional district is a legal entity (as is the senatorial district—a state). But while the winning candidate is officially the representative of the district, he or she actually has been elected by a subset of the district. That subset is the member's *reelection constituency*. Where party ties are strong, the reelection constituency may be based largely on party supporters, but in this day and age most reelection constituencies also depend on members' personal views, service to constituents, and even their personalities and styles. Fenno suggests that each member's reelection constituency can be further partitioned. The *primary constituency* consists of the member's original supporters, contributors, workers, and strongest allies; it is the member's base if he or she is challenged in a primary. The *personal constituency* contains the member's most intimate friends and loyal supporters. They provide the representative with his or her closest link to what is going on in the district.[13]

Fenno was writing in 1978, before the proliferation of PACs and the explosive growth in congressional campaign spending (p. 216). Twenty years later another constituency should appear on the list—the *contributor constituency* consisting of interest groups and PACs that contribute to the MC's campaign coffers. This constituency is most prominent in the case of senior members who chair important committees and subcommittees. Unlike the other constituencies, it is not confined to the members' districts, although many groups and PACs have local chapters or affiliates.

Where party support is strong and dependable, members need not concern themselves as much about personal policy positions, service, style, and campaign contributions. But where party support is weak and uncertain, members depend on personal positions, service, style, and contributions as instruments of constituency maintenance. Given that parties generally have grown weaker over time, members have become more dependent on their own efforts to construct and maintain constituencies that will keep them in office.

Inside Congress

What would you expect from career legislators with personally constructed constituencies largely defined in territorial terms? In the absence of countervailing pressures, you would expect them to organize Congress to enable them to do things for their constituencies—to bestow government benefits on them and protect them from the costs of government actions—and just as importantly, to claim credit for any benefits received and avoid blame for any costs imposed. As David Mayhew remarks, "if a group of planners sat down and tried to design a pair of American national assemblies with the goal of serving members' electoral needs year in and year out, they would be hard pressed to improve on what exists."[14] There are two major organizational features of the Congress, the party structure and the committee structure.

The constitution says nothing about parties or committees. These structures have been developed by elected officials to meet their needs. Both are more important in the House than in the Senate. The House is much larger; hence, it needs more internal organization to enable it to do its work. The House operates in a more hierarchical, more follow-the-rules fashion than the Senate, which, being much smaller, can operate more by way of informal coordination and negotiation.[15] While parties and committees are important in the Senate, they do not dominate Senate operations to quite the same degree that they dominate House proceedings.

THE CONGRESSIONAL PARTIES

Although parties do not dominate Congress to nearly the extent that they dominate the parliaments of other democracies, they are still the principal organizing force in the Congress (see Table 12.2).

TABLE 12.2

Party Organization and Leaders at the Start of the 105th Congress

Leadership Position	Occupant
House Republicans	
Speaker	Newt Gingrich, R–GA
Majority Leader	Dick Armey, R–TX
Majority Whip	Tom DeLay, R–TX
Conference Chairman	John A. Boehner, R–OH
Conference Vice Chairman	Susan Molinari, R–NY
Conference Secretary	Jennifer Dunn, R–WA
House Democrats	
Minority Leader	Richard A. Gephardt, D–MO
Minority Whip	David E. Bonior, D–MI
Caucus Chairman	Vic Fazio, R-CA
Caucus Vice Chairman	Barbara B. Kennelly, D–CT
Senate Republicans	
Majority Leader	Trent Lott, R–MS
Assistant Majority Leader	Don Nickles, R–OK
Conference Chairman	Connie Mack, R–FL
Conference Secretary	Paul Coverdell, R–GA
Chief Deputy Whip	Judd Gregg, R–NH
Senate Democrats	
Minority Leader and Conference Chairman	Tom Daschle, D–SD
Minority Whip	Wendell H. Ford, D–KY
Conference Secretary	Barbara A. Mikulski, D–MD
Chief Deputy Whip	John B. Breaux, D–LA
Assistant Floor Leader	Byron L. Dorgan, D–ND

SOURCE: "Players, Politics and Turf of the 105th Congress," *Congressional Quarterly Committee Guide,* March 22, 1997.

Joseph "Boss" Cannon.

WHEN SPEAKERS RULED THE HOUSE

During the latter part of the nineteenth century the House of Representatives was arguably the most powerful of the three branches of government. Presidents of the period were undistinguished, and the public image of the Senate was poor, owing partly to its unrepresentative partisan balance (p. 242), and partly to its unrepresentative membership, which included numerous party bosses and millionaire industrialists. In this context, a series of strong Speakers organized their party members into energetic, cohesive, lawmaking majorities.*

First was James G. Blaine (R–ME), who from 1869–1875 raised party loyalty to a moral principle and ruthlessly manipulated committee assignments to maintain discipline and pass the legislation he wanted. Republicans had no monopoly on strong leadership, however. In the 1880s, Speaker John Carlisle (D–KY) claimed for the Speaker absolute discretion in the power to recognize members to make speeches or offer amendments. This authority of the Speaker to control floor proceedings is one of the few powers that has persisted almost unchanged to the present.

Thomas "Czar" Reed (R–ME) is considered by many to be the greatest Speaker ever. In the 1890s he raised the power of the House majority to new heights. Soon after taking office, Reed destroyed the ability of the minority to obstruct House floor action via delaying motions and "disappearing quorums." According to the Constitution, in order to act, a *quorum* of the House—one-half plus one—must be present. In Reed's time, members of the minority would offer some trivial motion, then refuse to vote, thus appearing to be "absent." Since some members of the majority party were invariably absent as well, the House could not proceed because of the apparent lack of a quorum. First, Reed announced that he would no longer entertain "dilatory motions." Then, he instructed the Clerk of the House to record Democrats in the Chamber who didn't vote as "present." An uproar ensued. Democrats reacted by leaving the chamber so that they were physically absent. Reed countered by

---

SPEAKER OF THE HOUSE

The Constitution stipulates that the House shall elect a *Speaker*. While technically a constitutional officer, in practice the **Speaker** is always the leader of the majority party in the House and is usually elected on a straight party-line ballot. Despite being a partisan leader, the Speaker ordinarily does not vote. Only on close contests involving matters vital to the party does the Speaker descend to the floor of the House and vote. In 1995, for example, even with the Republicans in control of the House for the first time in forty years, Speaker Gingrich participated in only 58 of 845 recorded votes.[16]

Until the late nineteenth century the Speaker was the only formal party leader in the House. Indeed, from the end of Reconstruction to the turn of the century, the Speaker often rivaled the president as the most powerful public official in the United States. Many scholars refer to this period of congressional history as a period of "party government." Powerful Speakers awarded the chairmanships of important committees to their close allies, made all committee assignments, and punished disloyal members when their behavior displeased the Speaker by removing them from committees on which they had previously served.[17] Moreover, as both the presiding officer of the House and the chairman of the Rules Committee, the Speaker controlled the floor. Speakers ruled. Then came the revolt.

ordering the sergeant at arms to lock the doors. Eventually, the Democrats acquiesced, and when they returned to majority status, Speaker Charles Crisp (D–GA) took full advantage of "Reed's rules."

Reed also adapted the Rules Committee as a powerful tool of the Speaker. With himself as chair, the three majority members would construct floor procedures that paved the way for their legislative program, then Reed reportedly would announce to the two minority members, "Gentlemen, we have decided to perpetuate the following outrage."

Joseph "Boss" Cannon, was the last of the great Speakers. Pushing the envelope of all the powers he had inherited, Cannon dominated the House in the first decade of the twentieth century. But the times were changing. The Republican party was split between regular and progressive wings (p. 245), and maintaining party discipline led Cannon to an increasingly punitive use of his appointment powers.† Dissident Republicans who chafed under the iron rule of the majority eventually joined with Democrats in a revolt that stripped the Speaker of several of the most important powers that underpinned the power of the office.‡ In 1910–1911 the Speaker lost the power to make committee assignments and was removed from the Rules Committee. Procedural reforms also guaranteed ordinary members some rights to have their proposals considered.

When Newt Gingrich moved boldly in the weeks following the 1994 elections, elevating some members with lower seniority to committee chairmanships over members with higher seniority, some commentators likened his behavior to that of Reed and Cannon. But such comparisons ceased as the underlying power of individual members soon circumscribed what Gingrich and the leadership could do.

* For colorful accounts of these congressional leaders see, Neil McNeil, *Forge of Democracy* (New York: McKay, 1963).

† Nelson Polsby, Miriam Gallagher, and Barry Rundquist, "The Growth of the Seniority System in the U.S. House of Representatives," *American Political Science Review* 63(1969): 787-807.

‡ Charles Jones, "Joseph G. Cannon and Howard W. Smith: An Essay on the Limits of Leadership in the House of Representatives," *Journal of Politics* 30(1968): 617-646.

▪ **majority leader**
Leader of the majority party, the Speaker's chief lieutenant in the House, and the most important office in the Senate. He or she is responsible for managing the floor.

In 1910 a coalition of minority Democrats and dissident Republicans removed "Boss" Cannon from the Rules Committee, expanded the committee, and gave to the House as a whole the power to elect the members.[18] A year later, after the Democrats captured the House, they stripped the Speaker of the power to make committee assignments and vested it in the House as a whole—although practically speaking, in the majority party. The office of Speaker never regained the powers removed at this time. In the months immediately following the 1994 elections, Speaker Gingrich moved boldly and decisively, in a way reminiscent of late-nineteenth-century Speakers. But the appearance was deceptive. The new Republican majority allowed Gingrich to exercise more authority than he formally possessed. As the session wore on, Gingrich's ability to rule the House diminished.[19]

In 1995, Newt Gingrich was the most powerful Speaker since Cannon.

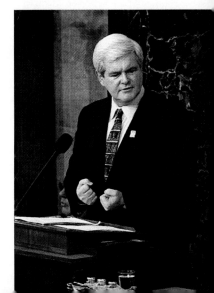

PARTY LEADERSHIP: HOUSE

The first official **majority leader**—leader of the majority party—in the House was appointed in 1899; prior to that time a lieutenant of the Speaker, often the chair of the Ways and Means Committee, served as the unofficial floor leader.[20] The Democratic rank and file began electing their majority leader in 1911, and the

Republicans in 1923. Unlike the Speaker, the majority leader votes. Contemporary majority leaders are responsible for the day-to-day leadership of the party—scheduling legislation, coordinating committee activity, negotiating with the president, the Senate, and the minority, and otherwise working to build and maintain the coalitions required to pass legislation. The analogous office of **minority leader**—the leader of the minority party—was created somewhat earlier, in 1883, as a counterpart to the powerful Speakers emerging on the majority side. While we generally think of the floor leaders as principally occupied with all the work needed to build coalitions to pass or obstruct legislation, Barbara Sinclair stresses that another important job of the leaders is simply to maintain "peace in the family." Both parties contain a variety of points of view, and it falls to the leadership to prevent minor spats and quarrels from developing into destructive feuds.[21]

The majority and minority leaders are assisted by **whips**, whose job is to link the leadership to the party rank and file. The whip communicates leadership positions and strategies, counts votes, and carries back rank-and-file views to the heads of the party. The whip offices are rather large, with deputy, assistant, regional, and zone whips (upwards of 25 in the Democratic party, about 20 in the Republican party). While their title conjures up an image of party leaders "whipping" their members into line (the title derives from "whippers-in" of the hounds in a fox hunt), in practice the whips engage far more in communication and cajolery than in coercion.

Many party members participate in the leadership via the whip organizations. Others participate via membership in the Democratic Steering and Policy Committee and the Republican Policy Committee and the Republican Steering Committee. These party committees provide a forum for discussion of the issues and development of a party program, and occasionally they endorse legislation. When the Democrats are in the majority, the Speaker chairs the Democratic Steering Committee and appoints many of its members. Given that this committee appoints the members of the standing committees, it gives the Speaker an important lever for influencing the behavior of members in their committees. In contrast, the Republicans elect a chair of their Policy Committee, and also a chair of their Steering Committee, which makes their committee assignments.

Finally, in both parties all members participate in party **caucuses** (the Republicans call theirs the **Conference**). These meetings of the full party membership elect the party leadership and approve the slates of committees nominated by the Steering Committees. At times they debate policies and attempt to develop party positions on policies. In Woodrow Wilson's time they would even adopt resolutions binding party members to support particular policy proposals, although this power is rarely used in modern times.

PARTY LEADERSHIP: SENATE

The situation in the Senate is simpler. With a hundred members—an even number—some tie-breaking mechanism is necessary, and the Constitution obliges by making the vice president the president of the Senate and giving him a tie-breaking vote, *when necessary*. The Constitution also provides for a **President pro-tempore**, who presides in the absence of the vice president, which is almost all the time. This office is mainly honorific—without real power; ordinarily it goes to the most senior member of the majority party. Both parties established official leader and whip positions in 1911-13.

Senate leaders today are not as strong as those in the House. Indeed, one of the main jobs of the leader is to hammer out **unanimous consent agreements**. So

minority leader
Leader of the minority party, who speaks for the party in dealing with the majority.

whips
Members of Congress who serve as informational channels between the leadership and the rank and file, conveying the leadership's views and intentions to the members, and vice versa.

caucus
All Democratic members of the House or Senate. Members in caucus elect the party leaders, ratify the choice of committee leaders, and debate party positions on issues. *See also* Conference.

conference
What Republicans call their caucus.

president pro-tempore
President of the Senate, who presides in the absence of the vice president.

unanimous consent agreement
Agreement that sets forth the terms and conditions according to which the Senate will consider a bill; these are individually negotiated by the leadership for each bill.

In the classic form of a filibuster, a lone senator holds the floor and prevents the Senate from acting on any other business. The filibuster record is currently held by Strom Thurmond, who filibustered the 1957 Civil Rights Act for 24 hours, 18 minutes.

called because they are agreed to by all senators with any interest in a proposal, these agreements specify the terms of debate—what amendments will be in order, how long they will be debated, when votes will be taken, and so forth.[22] The necessity for such agreements arises from the fact that (unbelievable as it may sound) a single member can hold up consideration of a bill or resolution. The reason is the Senate's tradition of unlimited debate—the **filibuster**. According to present rules, debate cannot be ended unless a **cloture** motion is adopted, and that takes an affirmative vote of 60 members. This is not an easy matter, as illustrated by the fact that the 54 Senate Democrats were unable to break a Republican filibuster that blocked President Clinton's first major legislative proposal, an economic stimulus package, in the spring of 1992. The existence of the filibuster means that a simple majority of senators is not necessarily a winning coalition. A minority of forty-one can prevent the Senate from acting on a measure.

filibuster
Delaying tactic by which one or more senators refuse to allow a bill or resolution to be considered, either by speaking indefinitely or by offering dilatory motions and amendments.

cloture
Motion to end debate; requires 60 votes to pass.

UPS AND DOWNS OF CONGRESSIONAL PARTIES

While the congressional party leadership today is not as strong as it was in the period before the revolt against Cannon, it is stronger than it was for a half century after the revolt. From the 1920s to the 1960s the Speakers were far weaker and less active than they had been. The most important Speaker of the era, Sam Rayburn (D-TX), relied more on his personal prestige than on his limited formal powers. The balance of power in the mid-century Congress is suggested by the fact that many scholars refer to this period of congressional history as the era of "committee government."[23] But beginning in the mid-1970s a series of reforms and developments strengthened the Speakership in particular and the party leadership in general.

In 1975 the Democratic Caucus, augmented by a large number of freshmen members—the "class of '74"—deposed three standing committee chairmen, two of them because their arrogant and arbitrary styles were found unacceptable. For example, when the freshmen invited the chair of the Armed Forces Committee, F. Edward Hebert (D-LA), to speak to them, he patronized them, reportedly addressing them as "boys and girls."[24] His arrogance cost him his position.

Shortly thereafter, the power to make committee assignments was given to a reconstituted Steering Committee in which the leadership was highly influential. Moreover, the Speaker was given the power to appoint the Democratic members of the Rules Committee, making it virtually an adjunct of his office. Paralleling these institutional changes, party unity in roll call voting recovered from the low levels to which it had sunk in the 1960s (Figure 12.3).

When the Republicans took control of Congress in 1994, partisanship surged. They had chafed under Democratic control for decades and now turnabout was fair play. Democrats personally disliked Speaker Gingrich and opposed his program. Republicans united in support of the leader who had brought them majority status, and Democrats united to oppose him. The Congressional parties looked stronger in the mid-1990s than they had looked at any time since Woodrow Wilson's day.

How do we explain the waning and waxing of party power in Congress? At least two factors appear to be important. First, the revolt against the Speaker in 1910 probably had something to do with the growth of careerism. Congressional turnover had been dropping steadily in the late nineteenth century as the power and importance of the federal government grew. More members came to see Congress as an attractive career, and after the realignment of the 1890s, a congressional career became a feasible option since large areas of the country were rendered electorally "safe" for one party or the other.[25] During this period there were some little-noticed but suggestive developments in Congress that are consistent with rising careerism. For example, the power to appropriate money was removed from the tight-fisted appropriations committees and given to more generous policy committees. This movement began in the areas of rivers and harbors, and agriculture—areas of special interest to many congressional districts—and spread to other policy areas.[26] Consistent with Mayhew's observation, careerist members became increasingly resistant to life under powerful party leaders who could hinder attempts to serve their constituencies, arbitrarily remove them from their committees, and force them to cast locally unpopular votes.

A second factor uncovered by recent scholarship can explain both rising and falling party strength. When parties are relatively homogeneous, members are willing to cede more power to party leaders because they have little fear that the leaders will act in such a way as to endanger their electoral prospects. That is, if all agree

FIGURE 12.3

The Congressional Parties Are More Unified Today than a Generation Ago

SOURCE: Norman J. Ornstein, Thomas E. Mann, and Michael J. Malbin, *Vital Statistics on Congress, 1995–1996* (Washington, DC: Congressional Quarterly, Inc., 1996), 208.

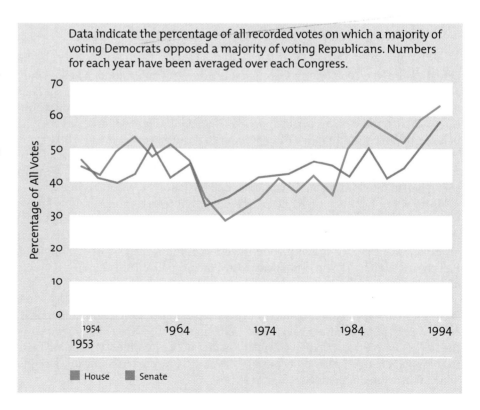

Data indicate the percentage of all recorded votes on which a majority of voting Democrats opposed a majority of voting Republicans. Numbers for each year have been averaged over each Congress.

■ House ■ Senate

about some issue, anyone can decide for all. But when the parties are heterogeneous, members are reluctant to cede power to party leaders who may act in ways opposed by many of the rank and file—and electorally dangerous to them.[27]

Thus, David Brady argues that an important factor underlying the strong congressional parties of the late nineteenth century was the homogeneity of their constituencies.[28] The parties represented different kinds of interests, and neither had many members who represented the kinds of interests represented by the other party. Only when the Republican party split into progressive and regular wings (p. 245) did the move to weaken the Speakership gain momentum. Conversely, the weak parties of the mid-twentieth century in part reflect the division of the parties—especially the majority Democrats—into regional factions. After labor and liberal elements gained control of the presidential wing of the Democratic party during the New Deal, and especially after Civil Rights split the party in the 1960s, southern Democrats became unwilling to accept party leadership that would reflect the view of the northern majority. After the split over Vietnam and the emergence of the "social issues" (p. 329), the cohesion of the party and the willingness of the southerners to accept northern leadership hit bottom.[29]

What changed that situation was largely what had caused it—the Civil Rights revolution and, especially, the 1965 Voting Rights Act guaranteeing everyone—particularly southern African Americans—the right to vote. In the aftermath, the electoral influence of southern African Americans increased, with two effects. First, some southern Democrats moderated their views to accommodate newly enfranchised black constituents: Southern Democrats in the 1990s are not as different from northern Democrats as were southern Democrats in the 1960s. Second, some white southern voters reacted to black empowerment (and the social issues) by voting Republican and replacing Democratic members of Congress with Republicans: The Democratic House contingent from southern and border states was twice as large in the 1960s as it is today. The upshot of these changes is that both congressional parties are more homogeneous now than a generation ago and consequently more willing to support strong leaders committed to particular national policies.[30] Especially in the House, the Democrats are now a liberal, urban party, while the Republicans are a conservative, suburban and rural party.

But why would today's members of Congress be willing to tolerate *any* party constraints at all? After all, members are elected by the citizens of states and districts far from Washington, where the congressional leadership has no influence. Nor does the local party have much influence. Forty years ago Speaker Sam Rayburn could phone a local party boss like Chicago's Mayor Daley and request his help in getting the Chicago House delegation to support Rayburn. Daley had the power—nominations, workers, money—to deliver. But in few areas today does the local party organization—such as it is—have much influence over the member of Congress. Why then would members tolerate party institutions that constrain them in any way? Does the fact that they do contradict Mayhew's assertion (p. 385)?

Part of the answer is that while the electoral fates of members of Congress are largely dependent on their personal efforts, they are not completely so. An effective congressional party contributes to members' electoral prospects in two ways. First, although presidential coattails have weakened, they still exist, and a successful president provides coattails that can help members running for reelection. Similarly, as the Democrats found to their sorrow in 1994, an unsuccessful president can hurt his party, especially in the mid-term elections. An effective congressional party that passes a president's program contributes to his perceived success, while an ineffective congressional party that fails to pass his program contributes to his perceived failure. Thus, members of the president's party have an incentive to work together to help him succeed, and members of the opposing party have an incentive to work together to make him fail. The second way that an effective congressional party helps individual members arises from the fact that only half the voters know anything about their representative; the rest vote on the basis of impersonal factors, including party images (p. 347). An ineffective congressional party contributes to the impression that the party is incompetent, and thereby costs all party members votes.

Thus, members of Congress are willing to tolerate party constraints partly because such constraints contribute indirectly to their electoral prospects. Just as most people feel that they are better off obeying stop signs and red lights that add a few minutes to their travel time, so members of Congress feel that they are better off by giving the parties some authority over them in exchange for general support provided for the party and/or the president.

Finally, another reason electorally independent members willingly accept some party discipline is that they see it as necessary to achieve other ends. For some, reelection is an end in itself, but most wish to accomplish something while in office and view party organization as necessary to accomplish anything in a body as unwieldy as Congress. Furthermore, if parties are too weak to accomplish anything, the collective image of the institution deteriorates, and the members' job satisfaction lessens. Thus, effective parties make the office worth more to many representatives; consequently, they are willing to accept some restrictions on their individual freedom of action in return for enhanced institutional performance.

THE COMMITTEE SYSTEM

During the mid-twentieth-century period of "committee government" many observers agreed with the young Woodrow Wilson's comment that "I know not how better to describe our form of government in a single phrase than by calling it a government by the chairmen of the Standing Committees of Congress."[31] In retrospect, Wilson's comment was far less true at the time he made it (1885) than it became a generation later. For, as we have noted, party leaders dominated committees at the time Wilson was a critical young graduate student.

Congress does its business through its committees. Virtually all bills and resolutions that are introduced are referred to committees for consideration, and most proposals die there. For example, since 1980, 6 to 8 thousand bills have been introduced in each two-year session of the House of Representatives, but only 10 to 15 percent eventually passed. While a few unsuccessful proposals die on the floor, most of the 85 to 90 percent that failed never made it out of committee. Floor majorities can discharge a proposal from a recalcitrant committee via a rarely used **discharge petition**, which requires 218 signatures, but in most cases favorable action by a committee is a necessary condition for a proposal to become law.

Standing committees have fixed memberships and jurisdictions, and persist from one Congress to another. Standing committees contrast with **select committees**, which are temporary committees created to deal with specific issues. By 1825 both houses of Congress had standing committee systems in place.[32] The number of committees grew steadily until 1919 when the Senate cut them by more than half and the House stabilized at about fifty. Still, by 1946 there were 47 committees in the House and 33 in the Senate, and members increasingly felt that the committee system was unwieldy and poorly aligned with contemporary problems. The Legislative Reorganization Act of 1946 rationalized the committee system and gave it the shape that it largely retains today—more than half a century later. In the 105th Congress (1997–98) there are 19 standing committees in the House and 17 in the Senate (see Table 12.3).

◼ **discharge petition**
Means by which a House majority (218) may take a bill out of a committee that refuses to report it.

◼ **standing committee**
Committee with fixed membership and jurisdiction, continuing from Congress to Congress.

◼ **select committee**
Temporary committee appointed to deal with a specific issue or problem.

TABLE 12.3

Standing Committees at the start of the 105th Congress (1997–1999)

Committee	Size (Party Ratio)	No. of Subcoms.	Chairman	Ranking Member
Senate				
Agriculture	18 (R 10/D 8)	4	Richard Lugar, R–IN	Tom Harkin, D–IA
Appropriations	28 (R 15/D 13)	13	Ted Stevens, R–AK	Robert Byrd, D–WV
Armed Services	18 (R 10/D8)	6	Strom Thurmond, R–SC	Carl Levin, D–MI
Banking, Housing and Urban Affairs	18 (R 10/D 8)	5	Alfonse M. D'Amato, R–NY	Paul S. Sarbanes, D–MD
Budget	22 (R 12/D 10)	—	Pete V. Domenici, R–NM	Frank R. Lautenberg, D–NJ
Commerce, Science & Transportation	20 (R 11/D 9)	7	John McCain, R–AZ	Ernest F. Hollings, D–SC
Energy and Natural Resources	20 (R 11/D 9)	4	Frank H. Murkowski, R–AK	Dale Bumpers, R–AR
Environment and Public Works	18 (R 10/D 8)	4	John H. Chafee, R–RI	Max Baucus, D–MT
Finance	20 (R 11/D 9)	5	William V. Roth Jr., R–DE	Daniel Patrick Moynihan, D–MA
Foreign Relations	18 (R 10/D 8)	7	Jesse Helms, R–NC	Joseph R. Biden Jr., D–DE
Governmental Affairs	16 (R 9/D7)	3	Fred Thompson, R–TN	John Glenn, D–OH
Indian Affairs	14 (R 8/D 6)	—	Ben Nighthorse Campbell, R–CO	Daniel K. Inouye, D–HI
Judiciary	18 (R 10/D 8)	6	Orrin G. Hatch, R–UT	Patrick J. Leahy, D–VT
Labor and Human Resources	18 (R 10/D 8)	4	James M. Jeffords, R–VT	Edward M. Kennedy, D–MA
Rules and Administration	16 (R 9/D 7)	—	John W. Warner, R–VA	Wendell H. Ford, D–KY
Small Business	18 (R 10/D 8)	—	Christopher S. Bond, R–MO	John Kerry, D–MA
Veterans' Affairs	12 (R 7/D 5)	—	Arlen Spector, R–PA	John D. Rockefeller IV, D–WV
House				
Agriculture	50 (R 27/D 23)	5	Bob Smith, R–OR	Charles W. Stenholm, D–TX
Appropriations	60 (R 34/D 26)	13	Robert L. Livingstone, R–LA	David R. Obey, D–WI
Banking and Financial Services	53 (R 29/D 24)	5	Jim Leach, R–IA	Paul Henrey B. Gonzalez, D–TX
Budget	43 (R 24/D 19)	—	John R. Kasich, R–OH	John M. Spratt Jr., D–SC
Commerce	51 (R 28/D 23)	5	Thomas J. Bliley, R–VA	John D. Dingell, D–MI
Education and the Workforce	45 (R 25/D 20)	5	Bill Goodling, R–PA	William L. Clay, D–MO
Government Reform and Oversight	44 (R 24/D 19/I 1)	7	Dan Burton, R–IN	Henry A. Waxman, D–CA
House Oversight	8 (R 5/D 3)	—	Bill Thomas, R–CA	Sam Gejdenson, D–CT
International Relations	47 (R 26/D 21)	5	Benjamin A. Gilman, R–NY	Lee H. Hamilton, D–IN
Judiciary	35 (R 20/D 15)	5	Henry J. Hyde, R–IL	John Conyers Jr., D–MI
National Security	55 (R 30/D 25)	7	Floyd D. Spence, R–SC	Ronald V. Dellums, D–CA
Resources	50 (R 27/D 23)	5	Don Young, R–AK	George Miller, D–CA
Rules	13 (R 9/D 4)	—	Gerald B.H. Solomon, R–NY	Joe Moakley, D–MA
Science	6 (R 25/D 21)	4	F. James Sensenbrenner Jr., R–WI	George E. Brown Jr., D–CA
Small Business	35 (R 19/D 16)	4	James M. Talent, R–MO	John J. LaFalce, R–NY
Standards of Official Conduct	—	—	James V. Hansen, R–UT	Howard L. Berman, D–CA
Transportation and Infrastructure	73 (R 40/D 33)	6	Bud Shuster, R–PA	James L. Oberstar, D–MN
Veterans' Affairs	29 (R 16/D 13)	3	Bob Stump, R–AZ	Lane Evans, R–IL
Ways and Means	39 (R 23/D 16)	5	Bill Archer, R–TX	Charles B. Rangel, D–NY

SOURCE: "Players, Politics and Turf of the 105th Congress," *Congressional Quarterly Committee Guide,* March 22, 1997.

NOTE: The House Standards of Official Conduct Committee was temporarily suspended at the start of the 105th Congress.

Most of the business of Congress is accomplished in committee. It was a committee—the U.S. Senate Judiciary Committee—that held confirmation hearings for Supreme Court nominee Clarence Thomas in 1991.

There are also 4 "joint" committees with membership from both houses, and a small number of select committees.

HOUSE COMMITTEES

House committees vary in importance. Both parties agree that the Rules, the Appropriations and the Ways and Means Committees are very important. The Democrats refer to them as *exclusive* committees and the Republicans as "red" committees. The Republicans also include Commerce in this category. The Rules Committee is the right arm of the Speaker. By granting or withholding rules it controls the flow of legislation to the floor and the conditions of debate. The other two committees deal with spending and taxing, broad powers that enable them to affect nearly everything government does. A member who serves on such a committee is ordinarily allowed no other assignment, except for eligibility to serve on the Budget Committee. Major policy committees (referred to as "major" by the Democrats and "white" by the Republicans) deal with important policy areas—agriculture, armed services, energy, and so forth. Again, a member ordinarily serves on only one such committee, along with another less important committee. These less important committees (called "nonmajor" by the Democrats and "blue" by the Republicans) include "housekeeping" committees like Government Reform and Oversight, and committees with narrow policy jurisdictions like Veterans' Affairs. A member may serve on two such committees. The Budget Committee has something of a special status. Members can serve for only four years in any ten-year period, and its membership is drawn from other committees and from the leadership.

SENATE COMMITTEES

The Senate committee system is simpler, with committees divided into A (major) and B (minor) categories. Like their House equivalents, Appropriations and Finance are major committees, but the Senate Rules Committee is a minor committee with nothing like the power of its House counterpart—the Senate leadership itself discharges the tasks performed by the House Rules Committee. Budget is also a major committee, as is Foreign Affairs, reflecting the constitutional responsibilities of the chamber in that area. Power is widely spread: Chairs of major committees cannot chair any other committee or subcommittee, and chairs of minor committees can chair only one other panel. Each senator may serve on two major and one minor committee, and every senator gets to serve on one of the four major committees. On average, senators sit on more committees. In part this reflects the fact that the Senate has nearly as many committees as the House but less than one-fourth as many members to staff them. In addition, senators represent entire states, which are typically more heterogeneous than congressional districts; thus, they cannot afford to focus their attention on one or two subjects, as many representatives can. Having more committee assignments creates conflicting loyalties and makes it difficult to specialize in a few subjects, as many House members do. As a result, senators' legislative lives are not as closely oriented around a particular committee as are the lives of representatives.[33]

The Budget Committees are among the most important committees in Congress. Here House Budget Committee members mull over the nation's finance.

HOW COMMITTEES ARE FORMED

The committee system is formally under the control of the majority party in the chamber. Each committee has a majority-minority ratio at least as favorable to the majority as the overall division of the chamber. The more important committees are "stacked" in favor of the majority. In the 105th Congress, for example, the Republicans had a 9:4 advantage over the Democrats on the House Rules Committee, a ratio far greater than their 227:207 edge in the chamber. In contrast, the party ratio on the less important Judiciary Committee was 20:15. Party committees nominate members for assignment, and party caucuses approve those assignments, so the potential for party control of committees exists. But, in practice, the committees exercise a considerable degree of independence.

Part of the reason is the use of **seniority** to choose committee chairs: The majority party member with the longest continuous service on the committee almost invariably is chair of the committee. Often called a "norm" because the use of seniority is not an official rule and is nowhere written down, seniority became the mode of selecting Senate committee chairs in the 1880s and House chairs after the 1910 revolt. The practice of seniority also entails the "right" to continued reappointment to a committee. Thus, once a member is initially appointed to a committee, he or she rises automatically up its seniority ladder. Given sufficient longevity, members eventually become chairs, perhaps decades after their initial appointment. Physically or mentally failing members occasionally are moved aside, and on occasion the caucus will reject a nomination for chair (p. 391), but the system gives committee chairs in particular, and committee members in general, a considerable degree of independence or autonomy.

After the 1994 elections gave Republicans control of Congress for the first time in forty years, Speaker Gingrich passed up the most senior committee member when he named the Republican chairs of Appropriations, Commerce, and Judiciary.[34] Whether this represents a one-time deviation from seniority because of an electoral upheaval or a long-term move away from seniority is something to watch in the years ahead.

seniority
Practice by which the majority party member with longest continuous service on a committee becomes the chair.

By the 1950s, party influence in Congress had become so weak that many observers believed the standing committee chairs held the real power. A few of them behaved autocratically, creating and abolishing subcommittees and varying their jurisdictions; monopolizing subcommittee chairmanships; controlling committee staff and budgets; and even refusing to call meetings and to consider legislation they opposed. To make matters worse, because members from safe southern seats had built up considerable seniority, many of the chairs were more conservative than the younger, mostly northern Democrats who held more liberal views.[35] Eventually, the rank and file, operating through the party caucuses, curbed the power of the standing committee chairs and injected more democracy into the committee system. Much of this effort took place in the Democratic caucus.[36]

In the early 1970s a caucus resolution limited House committee chairs to holding one subcommittee chair—previously some committee chairs hoarded subcommittee chairs as well. A "subcommittee bill of rights" guaranteed subcommittees their existence, jurisdictions, budgets, and staff. Moreover, power was distributed by allowing the Democratic members of the committee to choose among available subcommittee chairs in order of their seniority on the committee—subject to a vote of all committee Democrats. The Senate had treated junior members somewhat better since the 1950s, but it, too, moved in the same direction as the House, spreading power more evenly across the membership.

Many contemporary observers were unsure whether the preceding changes were in fact reforms. Did Congress simply decentralize power from approximately 40 standing committees to approximately 300 standing committees and subcommittees, many of them as small as eight or nine members? Did a period of "committee government" give way to one of even more decentralized "subcommittee government?"[37] For more than a decade, political scientists debated the reforms. Today the prevailing view is that the reforms adopted in the late 1970s to strengthen the party leadership (p. 391) more than offset the subcommittee reforms. In the 1990s the committees appear to be more responsive to party influence than they were a generation ago. At the least, an out-of-the-mainstream chair of an important committee or subcommittee would run a greater risk of being overthrown today than at any time since the revolt against Cannon.

THEORIES OF THE COMMITTEE SYSTEM

Why does the standing committee system exist at all? Members of Congress are elected as equals. Why would a majority willingly give a minority exceptional influence in a policy area—the power to decide whether legislation should be considered at all, the power to shape the legislation if it is considered, and the power to review its implementation? Why not consider everything on the chamber floor (the so-called *Committee of the Whole*), where all members might participate on an equal basis? And if the size of the membership would make that process too unwieldy, why not consider legislation in select committees specifically created for the particular bill or resolution? Why give a (perhaps unrepresentative) minority more-or-less permanent influence over a policy area? There are two major answers to these questions; these are interpretations or theories of the committee system.

The first theory views the committee system as the formal expression of a comprehensive **log-rolling** process in which members implicitly trade votes.[38] Accord-

log-rolling
Colloquial term given to politicians' trading of favors, votes, or generalized support for each other's proposals.

ing to this interpretation, members select committees in order to satisfy constituency interests. For example, members from urban districts seek membership on committees that deal with banking, housing, labor, and other matters, whereas members from rural districts have little interest in such matters and opt instead for committees that deal with agriculture and resources. Once appointed to committees whose work is relevant to their constituencies, members are in a position to use the process to bestow benefits on those constituencies. Studies have documented how districts and states whose members serve on particular committees receive a disproportionate share of projects and grants from programs in the jurisdictions of those committees.[39] And to cite more anecdotal evidence, Senator Robert Byrd (D-WV) became infamous for using his chairmanship of the Senate Appropriations Committee to lavish federal largess on his state. According to this **distributive theory** of the committee system: Members join committees that deal with matters important to their constituencies, then use their strategic position to deliver for those constituencies. Members give disproportionate influence to committees that deal with issues they care little about because they expect others to reciprocate when their own committee reports to the floor on an issue they do care about.

An alternative interpretation is that committees serve primarily a knowledge function.[40] This **informational theory** stresses that members frequently are uncertain about the outcomes that policies will produce. Hence, they wish some members to become experts in each subject area and to reveal the results of their research to the broader membership. The way to do this is to give committees disproportionate influence, subject to the condition that they do their job conscientiously and not abuse their power. Committee members can utilize their position to gain a bit extra for themselves, but only to the extent that they specialize and give the chamber useful, reasonably reliable information.

These two theories are not incompatible. Each captures an important aspect of the committee system. Indisputably, members wish to serve their constituencies and regard committees as important means for doing so (although certainly not the *only* means). But just as certainly, members often are unsure of just how they can best serve their constituencies. If they adopt the wrong policy and the results are disastrous, it could come back to haunt them in a future campaign.[41] Hence, members need and value information. The distributive theory appears most applicable to the committees that deal with straightforward matters like handing out money—subsidies, grants, funding for projects, and so forth. Here members of Congress will allow interested colleagues to turn public institutions into private fiefdoms, so long as they receive similar privileges in areas of importance to their constituencies. In contrast, where policy making involves great uncertainty and/or large costs and benefits—telecommunications and environmental regulation, for example—members will wish to have reliable information and will hold committees to a higher standard.

The distributive theory also seems somewhat less applicable today than in the period of "committee government." When government revenues were rising steadily and congressional party influence was weak, there was little to prevent members from using the committee system for their narrow ends. But with the tight budgets that arrived with the Reagan era, with stronger congressional parties, and with considerable uncertainty surrounding much of the policy agenda (health care, welfare reform, environmental protection), committee members are less free to pursue their narrow constituency interests. The incentives still are present, but the opportunities are more restricted.

■ **distributive theory**
Theory that sees committees as a standing log-roll in which members get to serve on the committees of most importance to them.

■ **informational theory**
Theory that sees committees as means of providing reliable information about the actual consequences of the legislation members could adopt.

How a Bill Becomes a Law

It is Congress's constitutional responsibility to make the laws that govern the United States. Section 8 of Article 1 lays down an impressive list of legislative powers that Congress shall exercise, and finishes with the "necessary and proper" clause—that Congress has power "to make all laws which shall be necessary and proper for carrying into execution the foregoing powers, and all other powers vested by this Constitution . . . " How do the two chambers, the four parties, and the over 250 committees and subcommittees get together and pass laws? Although no flowchart can possibly convey the complexity of getting a bill through Congress, we will here outline the process, describing the stages that any major piece of legislation goes through (see Figure 12.4). Any particular bill or resolution will have a somewhat different and often more complicated history.

To start things off, a bill or resolution is introduced by a congressional **sponsor** and one or more cosponsors. The House Speaker or Senate presiding officer, advised by the chamber's parliamentarian (an expert on rules and procedures), refers the proposal to an appropriate committee. In some cases sponsors are not serious—they are acting only to please some constituency or interest group. If they are serious, they may draft their bill so as to raise the likelihood of its being referred to a friendly committee—often theirs—rather than to an alternative, less friendly one. This strategic possibility exists because committee jurisdictions often overlap. In recent years the Speaker of the House has made increasing use of **multiple referrals**—sending the bill simultaneously to more than one committee, and/or dividing it up among several committees. Complex legislation and overlapping committee jurisdictions raise the likelihood of multiple referral.

Once the bill goes to committee it is referred to an appropriate subcommittee by the committee chair. Here the work begins. If the subcommittee takes the bill seriously, the staff will schedule hearings at which witnesses will speak in favor of or in opposition to the bill. Witnesses can be other members of Congress, members of the executive branch, representatives of groups and associations, or ordinary citizens. Sometimes hearings are genuinely disinterested attempts to gather information. More often, hearings are carefully choreographed: The subcommittee staff stacks the witness list in favor of the position of the subcommittee chair. As one study observed, "committees neither seek nor receive complete information. Rather, they seek to promote certain views of their issues to bolster their abilities to produce favorable legislation."[42]

After hearings, the subcommittee begins **markup** of the bill—revising it, adding and deleting sections, and preparing it for report to the full committee, assuming that a majority of the subcommittee supports it. The full committee may repeat the process, holding its own hearings and conducting its own markup, or it may largely accept the work of the subcommittee.[43] If a committee majority supports the bill after committee markup, the bill is ready to be reported to the floor—but not quite.

Let's consider what happens in the House first. Bills that are uncontroversial, because they either are trivial or have extremely narrow impact, can be called up at specified times and passed unanimously with little debate. Many somewhat more important bills are considered under a fast-track procedure called **suspension of the rules**. On being recognized, the committee chair may move to consider a bill under suspension. If a two-thirds majority of those voting agrees, the bill will be considered. Debate is limited to 40 minutes, no amendments are in order, and a two-thirds majority is required for passage. There is some risk in considering a bill under

---

sponsor
Representative or senator who introduces a bill or resolution.

multiple referrals
Said to occur when party leaders give more than one committee responsibility for the consideration of a bill.

markup
Process in which a committee or subcommittee considers and revises a bill that has been introduced.

suspension of the rules
Fast-track procedure for considering bills and resolutions in the House; debate is limited to 40 minutes, no amendments are in order, and a two-thirds majority is required for passage.

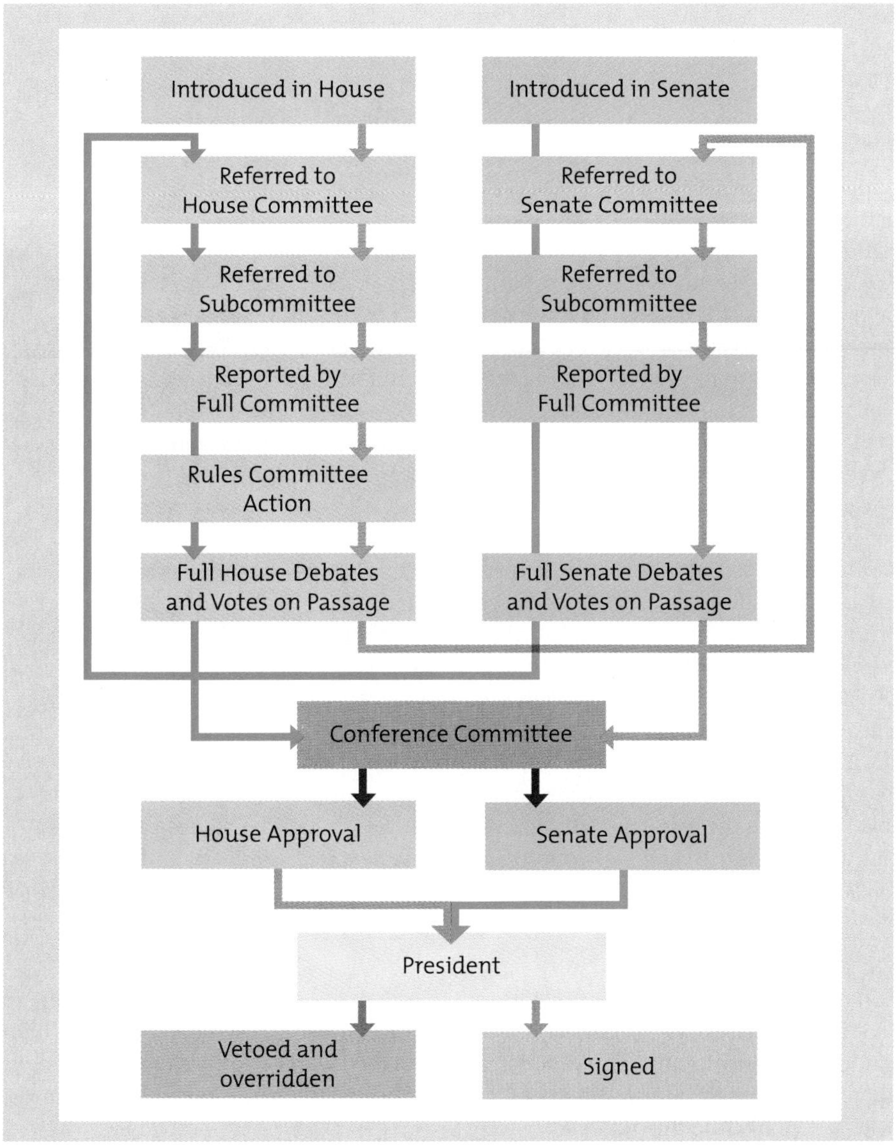

FIGURE 12.4

How a Bill Becomes a Law

Introduced in House | **Introduced in Senate**

Referred to House Committee | Referred to Senate Committee

Referred to Subcommittee | Referred to Subcommittee

Reported by Full Committee | Reported by Full Committee

Rules Committee Action

Full House Debates and Votes on Passage | Full Senate Debates and Votes on Passage

Conference Committee

House Approval | Senate Approval

President

Vetoed and overridden | Signed

suspension—even if a majority supports it, it could fail because the majority is less than two-thirds. Indeed, opponents of the bill sometimes support the motion to suspend the rules precisely in order to raise the threshold for passage to two-thirds.

Legislation that is important, and therefore usually controversial, goes to the Rules Committee before going to the floor. The Rules Committee, too, may hold hearings, this time on the type of **rule** it should grant. In these hearings only members of Congress may testify. The rule specifies the terms and conditions of debate. A rule allocates the time that will be allowed the supporters and opponents to speak, and may prohibit any amendments (a *closed rule*), allow any and all amendments (an *open rule*), or specify the amendments that are in order (a *restrictive rule*). In recent years three-quarters of all bills that come from the Rules Committee have been granted restrictive rules. Sometimes rules are quite interesting. For example, so-called *king of the mountain rules* allow a number of (often conflicting) amendments to be offered, but specify that only the last amendment that receives a majority is

■ **rule**
Specifies the terms and conditions under which a bill or resolution will be considered on the floor of the House; in particular, how long debate will last and how time will be allocated, and the number and type of amendments that will be in order.

President Hoover's defeat in 1932 ushered in a long period of unified Democratic control of the national government. For 14 years the Republicans labored in opposition, until in the 1946 elections they gained 55 seats in the House and 12 in the Senate to capture both chambers of Congress. The election outcome reflected post-war inflation, labor strife, and the unpopularity of Harry Truman, who had succeeded to the presidency on Roosevelt's death. But as politicians often do (p. 149), congressional Republicans read more into it, treating the election as a mandate to halt or even roll back the New Deal and prepare the way for recapturing the presidency in 1948.

Congress passed the Taft-Hartley Labor Relations Act, over Truman's veto. Named after "Mr. Conservative," Robert Taft, of Ohio, the Senate Majority Leader, and Fred Hartley, a New Jersey Republican who chaired the House Education and Labor Committee, the act was bitterly opposed by organized labor. Congress passed three tax cuts, all of which were vetoed; the third veto was overridden. Congress twice overrode Truman vetoes of bills that prevented extensions of Social Security coverage. Then a young congressman, future President Richard Nixon, got his start as the House Un-American Activities Committee (p. 99) held hearings in which ex-Communist Whittaker Chambers testified about the existence of Washington spy rings during the war. (In contrast to the domestic strife, however, Congress worked with the president to construct a bipartisan postwar foreign policy.) On the negative side, Congress refused to pass a health care bill— as the Democratic Congresses had refused earlier—or any further extensions of the New Deal.*

A few months before the 1948 elections, President Truman appeared to be a goner, facing not only

actually adopted. Naturally, the committee orders the permissible amendments so that the one it favors goes last. This kind of rule allows some members to play a little game with constituents. The member can vote for several conflicting amendments, thereby earning credit from each of the supporters, all the while knowing that the last vote is the only one that matters.

Assuming that the Rules Committee recommends a rule, the floor then chooses to accept or reject the rule. Rules rarely are rejected, but that does not mean that the floor goes along with anything the Rules Committee proposes. Rather, in shaping the rule the committee anticipates the limits of what the floor will accept. Sometimes committee members miscalculate and are embarrassed when a floor majority rejects the rule. Most of the time the rule is approved and the bill is finally under consideration by the full chamber. After debate and voting on amendments, the floor then decides whether to adopt the "perfected" bill.

In the Senate, the process is a bit simpler. A motion to pass a bill by unanimous consent is sometimes all that is necessary for uncontroversial legislation. More important and controversial legislation will require the committee and party leaders to negotiate unanimous consent agreements that are complicated bargains analogous to the rules granted by the House Rules Committee. Assuming that they succeed and thereby avoid a filibuster, the bill eventually comes to a floor vote.

If a majority votes to adopt the bill, are we at the end of the process? Not at all. Before the bill can be sent for the president's signature, it must pass both chambers in

a Republican challenger, Thomas Dewey (governor of New York), but a third-party candidate on his right, Strom Thurmond (then a *Democratic* Senator from South Carolina), and a fourth-party candidate on his left, Henry Wallace (Roosevelt's second vice President). But Truman did not concede defeat. He mounted a vigorous campaign against the "Do nothing 80th Congress" and barnstormed the country, repeatedly attacking the Republican congress. The truth is that the Congress had actually done quite a bit, but Truman vetoed much of it. And much of what became law was passed over Truman's veto; the only President overridden more often by Congress was Andrew Johnson, who became president when Lincoln was assassinated.† It was the extreme positions taken by Congress that provoked vetoes and resulted in apparent stalemate.

The day after the election, Democrats were elated and Republicans crushed to learn that Truman had squeaked through. Perhaps even worse, the Democrats gained 75 seats in the House and 9 in the Senate to retake both chambers of Congress. The Republicans had read too much into their 1946 landslide and paid the consequences.

Still, there were enough conservative Democrats in the new Congress that, together with Republicans, they were able to block repeal of the significant legislation passed by the Republicans in the 80th Congress. The Taft-Hartley Law is still on the statute books today. And the anti-Communist hearings continued under Democratic Congressional control, eventually developing into McCarthyism (p. 525). Two years of Republican control had made a difference.

* For background see *Congressional Quarterly Almanac* (Washington, DC: Congressional Quarterly, 1948).

† Harold Stanley and Richard Niemi, *Vital Statistics on American Politics*, 5th ed. (Washington, DC: CQ Press, 1995): 258.

identical form. But the bill may have started in one chamber before going to the other, or it may have proceeded simultaneously through both. In either case, it is extremely unlikely that the House and Senate have passed exactly the same bill. In fact, their versions of the legislation may be in serious conflict. Sometimes, with less controversial matters, one house will simply adopt the other's version as is. Sometimes the two chambers may send proposals back and forth (called "messaging") and iron out the points of difference. But for really important and controversial legislation, each chamber appoints conferees to participate in a **conference committee**.

One participant-observer likens a bill making it to conference to a college basketball team's making it to the "Final Four." Only, according to Paul Light, "conferences have very few rules and absolutely no referees. Games almost never start on time, and no one gets called for travelling."[44] Each chamber's conferees ostensibly are committed to their chamber's version of the legislation, but in practice this is not likely. Conferences for some complex bills involve hundreds of members who support some parts of the bill, oppose other parts, and care little about still other parts. This makes the situation ideal for bargaining and vote-trading. When a majority of each chamber's conferees agree to the final compromise, the bill is reported back to the parent chambers, where another floor vote in each chamber is required for passage.[45]

Now, you may think that we have finally reached the end of the process. The bill will be sent to the president, and assuming he does not veto it, it will become law (see Election Connection). While this is formally true, it does not guarantee that the bill

conference committee
Group of representatives from both the House and Senate who iron out the differences in the two chambers' versions of a bill or resolution.

will have any effect. The reason is that we have been describing only the **authorization process**. All government action must be authorized—paying subsidies, issuing regulations, buying bombers, inspecting workplaces—whatever; there must be statutory authority for the government's activity. That authority is contained in the bills passed by the authorization process. But before the government can actually carry out its activities, money must be appropriated for it to do so.

The Constitution grants Congress the power of the purse, and makes the House the lead actor: All tax bills must originate in the House, and by custom and tradition, all appropriations bills do too. The **appropriations** process parallels the authorization process. Thirteen powerful appropriations subcommittees in each chamber hold hearings and mark up the bill (the subcommittee chairs are commonly referred to as "the Cardinals of Capitol Hill").[46] The full committees may also do so, but usually defer to their subcommittees. In the House, appropriations bills are privileged; they take precedence over other legislation, and a motion to take up an appropriations bill can be offered at any time. But in practice, appropriations bills, too, usually pass through the Rules Committee. Thus, appropriations subcommittees in both chambers must report bills, the rank and file in both chambers must pass them, and a conference committee must agree on every dollar before the government actually has any money to spend.

In sum, before Americans feel the impact of a new government policy it must run the legislative gauntlet four times (an authorization process in both House and Senate and an appropriations process in both House and Senate), the two chambers must agree on the results of each process, and the president must accept the agreements. Small wonder that of approximately 12 thousand bills introduced in each recent Congress, only about 600 ultimately became law, and even fewer were funded at the levels their proponents believed necessary.

Criticisms of Congress

By now the first criticism of the congressional process should be obvious to every reader: *It is lengthy and inefficient.* Legislation may take months or even years to wend its way through the process, and there is much duplication of effort—both within and between the chambers. Moreover, after all is said and done, Congress often produces a compromise that leaves no one satisfied. To those with a penchant for quick, decisive action, Congress-watching is enough to put their teeth on edge. Of course, that is what the Framers intended. They wished to ensure that government could act only after proposals had been thoroughly considered and majorities were convinced that they were needed.

This brings us to a second criticism: *the congressional process works to the advantage of policy minorities, especially those content with the status quo.* Proponents of legislation must build many winning coalitions—in subcommittee, full committee, appropriations committee, and conference committee, on the floor, in both chambers. Opponents, in contrast, need win only once to defeat a bill. If a minority controls only one stage of the process, it may be able to frustrate the majority. Granted, a determined majority cannot be stopped indefinitely, except by a Senate filibuster, but it can be delayed for a crushingly long time. Moreover, potential majorities sometimes are deterred from acting, calculating that the costs of overcoming all the obstacles are not worth the effort and that their resources and energy should be saved for other battles. Since changing the status quo requires positive action, the congressional process hinders majorities who support change and helps minorities who are content to block change. In a word, the congressional process is *conservative* with a small *c*. Most of the time congressional enactments make only minor or *incremental* changes in the status quo, simply because the obstacles to major changes are so formidable.

Two other criticisms focus on what Congress does when it acts, rather than on its failure to act or to act promptly. First, given that members are trying to please reelection constituencies, *they will be constantly tempted to use their positions to extract constituency benefits*, even when important national legislation is at stake. Jimmy Carter got so upset with trying to deal with Congress on national energy policy that he wrote in his diary, "Congress is disgusting on this particular subject."[47] President Clinton's lobbying campaign on behalf of the North American Free Trade Agreement (NAFTA) was likened to an "oriental bazaar." Members not only demanded special treatment for constituency interests, but even traded votes for concessions on unrelated issues. Besides its appearing highly unseemly (unless *you* are part of the constituency getting the concession), many observers charge that Congress defeats, distorts, and otherwise damages national interests in pursuit of its members' parochial interests. Of course, others point out that such favor-trading may simply be the price of passing any general national legislation.[48] As long as the president and congressional leadership do not "give away the store," it is just a standard feature of legislative politics.

Finally, the nature of the congressional process is such that *sometimes the very process of passing legislation ensures that it will not work*. This is especially true of legislative initiatives that involve targeting resources at small portions of the population. For example, in the aid-to-the-cities effort described in the introduction to this chapter, the process of getting the legislation through Congress spread the available resources across small cities and rural areas, leaving too little to make much difference to the major cities—had it been enacted.[49]

"BOY,,, DID I DO SOME HORSE TRADING OR WHAT?"

Congress Acts Slowly: The Telecommunications Act of 1996

For six decades, modern electronic communications in the United States was regulated under the provisions of the Communications Act of 1934, as amended and supplemented. But as cable and satellite technology developed, the old regulatory system increasingly came to be seen as a means of protecting established industries and a hindrance to technological progress.* By 1982, court decisions had broken up the long-standing communications monopoly of American Telephone and Telegraph (AT&T), and as technology raced ahead, it became increasingly clear that Congress would have to construct a new regulatory structure that would balance the conflicting interests of new and old technologies, as well as the interests of producers and consumers.

Congress deregulated the cable industry in 1984, and partially reregulated it in 1992, but it was clear that a much broader approach would be needed. Congressional Democrats began work on a comprehensive bill in 1993. In 1994 the House passed a bill, but the effort died in the Senate. After the 1994 elections the Republican Congress took up the task. In 1995 both chambers passed a bill but House Republicans refused to accept the conference report. Finally, to make a very long and complicated story very short, in early 1996 Congress passed a comprehensive bill— three years after first taking up the subject in a serious way.

The legislation attempted to create one integrated market for telecommunications services—replacing the existing division of the market into local telephone service, long-distance, and cable TV. For the most part, barriers to competition were broken down, although various interested parties received various protections. Consumer groups (doubtful that the bill was truly pro-competitive), civil libertarians (opposed to censorship), and rural areas (fearful of lower quality and higher-priced services) all were dubious. The legislation was such a delicate com-

---

Another example was provided by the House when it moved in 1992 to reauthorize programs created by the Elementary and Secondary Education Act of 1965, a landmark piece of Great Society legislation. The Chapter 1 program then gave about $6 billion annually to 95 percent of the school districts in the country, a large sum in absolute terms but only about 3 percent of what the districts collectively spend. Under existing law, 10 percent of the Chapter 1 money was reserved for the poorest districts. President Clinton proposed a reallocation that would reserve 50 percent of the money for the poorest districts and give no money to the richest districts. While the proposed legislation was praised by advocates of the poor, over half the counties in the country would have lost money under the redistribution, a fact that led to its rejection by the Subcommittee on Elementary, Secondary, and Vocational Education of the House Education and Labor Committee, one of the more liberal committees in the House.

Explained committee chairman William Ford (D-MI), "I can't get the votes to do anything that does that much to that many people on the floor." Jack Reed (D-RI), who represents a poor district, criticized the committee decision as one of

promise that, two days before the two chambers approved the conference report, the key congressional negotiators were unsure that the legislation would pass.† In the end, however, the choice was surprisingly easy. If the contending interests did not accept the compromise, three years of political effort would go down the drain and everyone would have to start over. To most people's surprise, both chambers overwhelmingly adopted the conference report.

On the one hand, many find it maddening that it took Congress three years to legislate while American investors were betting billions of dollars on an uncertain future, and that Congress ultimately produced a compromise that no one could sup- port enthusiastically. On the other hand, should Congress have moved more rapidly when billions of dollars and the technological position of the United States in the next century were at stake? In government, as in everything else, there is a trade-off between speed of decision and quality of decision, and reasonable people dis- agree about how much of one to trade off for a quantity of the other.

* Glen Robinson, "The Federal Communications Commission: An Essay on Regulatory Watchdogs," *Virginia Law Review* 64(1978): 169–262.

† Dan Carney, "Congress Fires its First Shot in Information Revolution," *Congressional Quarterly Weekly Report*, February 3, 1996: 289.

Bill Clinton holds up a V-chip, symbolic of the signing of the Telecommunications Act of 1996.

"pork over policy." Ford replied "You can talk philosophy, but philosophy doesn't buy you votes on the floor." Ranking minority member, Bill Goodling (R-PA) admitted that "I don't disagree with what they're saying, that you need to target the poorest." But he went on to say that he opposed any proposal that would take money away from his district. In the end, the House passed a bill that provided for some limited targeting, conditional on greatly increased appropriations, which no one expected to be forthcoming. In the Senate a similar attempt to target spending in the poorest districts was defeated on a voice vote in the liberal Labor and Human Resources Committee. In the end, Congress adopted a conference report that directed "slightly more money" to low-income children.[50]

Examples like these illustrate the charge that Congress regularly shows a **distributive tendency**. Every member wants a "fair share" of the federal pie for his or her district. Even if the district is relatively affluent or does not have the problem a program addresses, the member is reluctant to pass up an opportunity to deliver local benefits. Taken to extremes, this tendency can be almost comical. Consider,

distributive tendency
Penchant of Congress for spreading the benefits of any program widely across the districts of the members.

THE NAFTA BAZAAR

As the first year of Bill Clinton's presidency drew to a close, Washington politics reached a fever pitch. Clinton had submitted the North American Free Trade Agreement (NAFTA) for congressional approval and now faced the real possibility of an embarrassing defeat at the hands of his own party. The agreement would remove trade barriers among the United States, Canada, and Mexico, encouraging expanded trade among the three countries, and was viewed as a possible precursor to a broader agreement that would extend to South America.

Economic opinion was heavily in favor of the agreement, contending that, although there would be winners and losers in each country, in the aggregate all three countries would benefit from expanded trade. American unions feared that their members would be among the losers, agreeing with Ross Perot that "that giant sucking sound you hear" would be the sound of high-wage American jobs going south to low-wage Mexico. Environmental and consumer groups also were concerned that strict U.S. environmental and safety regulations might be considered unfair trade barriers and consequently invalidated. Thus, many congressional Democrats were under pressure to oppose the agreement. Indeed, Majority Leader Gephardt opposed it, and the opposition was led by the Democratic Whip, David Bonior of Michigan (see International Comparison). Other representatives—of both parties— whose districts depended on particular threatened commodities—also were opposed.

The Clinton administration considered NAFTA a must-win situation. Following on repeated first-year stumbles, to suffer a major congressional defeat at the hands of their own party would crystallize a damaging image of political incompetence and weak leadership. Moreover, such a defeat would weaken Clinton's hand in the upcoming battle over national health care. As the vote drew near, some pundits intoned that Clinton's presidency hung in the balance.

President Clinton had no intention of losing. As *Congressional Quarterly* described the situation:

> NAFTA supporters clearly have a big advantage. They have the White House and all its political currency to spend in the bazaar of congressional vote-trading: Phone calls from the president. Visits to the White House. The undivided attention of Cabinet officials. Promises of Clinton's support in the 1994 elections.
>
> And the White House has the kinds of dealmaking powers that anti-NAFTA legislators can only dream of.
>
> To win support in the Louisiana delegation, the administration cut a deal with Mexico

to protect U.S. markets from being flooded with Mexican sugar imports. That agreement could also help win the vote of Maryland Democrat Benjamin L. Cardin, whose Baltimore district is home to a huge sugar refinery.

To snare support of Democratic Rep. Lewis F. Payne Jr., whose southern Virginia district includes the textile center of Danville, the administration backed protections for the U.S. textile industry.

To reassure the many members nervous about job losses, the administration devised a worker retraining program.

Administration officials also have tried to woo uncommitted members of the Florida delegation by making agreements with Mexico designed to protect the U.S. citrus and fresh-vegetable growers.*

Although most Republicans were ideologically in favor of free trade (and the treaty originally had been negotiated by the Bush Administration), they played their cards close to their vests, not wishing to help a president whom they hoped to defeat a few years later. Minority Leader Gingrich promised to provide half the votes necessary to pass the treaty. The rest would be up to Clinton.†

In the end, Clinton won handily: 234–199.‡ The administration's efforts had helped to bring along 102 of 258 Democrats, not quite as many as Gingrich had demanded, but three-quarters of the House Republicans supported the treaty either on its merits or because of general hostility to unions and environmentalists. Thus, NAFTA was approved, although, for many Democrats, the crucial consideration was a side deal they had cut with the administration rather than the economic implications of the

agreement for the United States.

NAFTA is a more important and more visible case than most, but it is not at all unusual. Because American institutions encourage such a strong local orientation among members of Congress, the critical consideration in adopting legislation often comes down to the local benefits and costs rather than the national benefits and costs. Congress is more sensitive to the former than the president, an important part of the ever-present tension between the two institutions.

* Janet Hook, "The Uphill Battle for Votes Produces a Whirl of Wooing and Wheedling," *Congressional Quarterly Weekly Report*, November 6, 1993: 3015.

† Barbara Sinclair, "Trying to Govern Positively in a Negative Era," in Colin Campbell and Bert Rockman, eds., *The Clinton Presidency* (Chatham, NJ: Chatham House, 1996: 109–111.

‡ David Cloud, "Decisive Vote Brings Down Trade Walls with Mexico," *Congressional Quarterly Weekly Report*, November 20, 1993: 3174–3179.

for example, another legacy of the Great Society, the Economic Development Administration created to subsidize the construction of infrastructure—roads, utilities, industrial parks, and so forth—in depressed areas. By the time the program was killed by the Reagan administration it had been repeatedly expanded by Congress to the point that more than 80 percent of all the counties in the United States were officially classified as "economically depressed" to make them eligible for federal subsidies.[51]

The distributive tendency reflects the difficulty Congress has with redistribution. All too often, federal programs are not targeted on the most needy areas or focused on people for whom they would do the most good. Instead, members want a piece of the action whether their districts really need it or not. Federal programs distribute money based on complex formulas that include population, economic conditions, physical characteristics of the people or area, and so forth. These formulas are of great importance to members of Congress. Indeed, members' staffs use state-of-the-art spreadsheets to show how much their districts would gain or lose under alternative formulas. In the end, though, all the bargaining over formulas seems to result in government policies that distribute funds on roughly a *per capita* basis.

Bashing federal programs is a popular sport. Sometimes it is warranted—programs may be badly designed, poorly implemented, or ineptly administered. But federal programs often fail because they were born to fail: They are not focused on where they will do the most good, and resources are not sufficiently concentrated to have a major impact. Consequently, money is spent and the citizenry sees little to show for it. But the reason is not incompetence or corruption. The reason is that resources are spread so broadly and thinly that they have little impact. And they are spread so broadly and thinly because members of Congress, ostensibly working in their constituents' interest, deliberately do it.

Why Americans Don't Like Congress

We have traveled a long and circuitous route, but the solution to Fenno's paradox is now in sight. Why do Americans hate their Congress but love their senators and representatives and reelect the great majority of them? The answer is simply that Americans hold the collective Congress and the individual member up against different, largely conflicting standards.[52] The Congress is judged according to how well it actually solves the major problems and meets the serious challenges that face the country. Polls show that Americans generally take a dim view of how well the Congress solves those problems and meets those challenges. The Congress, they believe, rarely meets its collective responsibilities. Moreover, citizens take an equally dim view of how they think Congress operates—sluggishly, conflictually, inefficiently, and sometimes corruptly. The key to the puzzle, however, is that citizens reward their representatives and senators for doing the very things that make the collective Congress perform poorly. Members respond to narrow interests that are part of their constituencies, they look for opportunities to channel benefits to constituencies, they go to bat for constituents seeking exemptions from general policies, and they attempt to extract constituency concessions from major legislative efforts. Even though many of these activities detract from the national good, local constituencies appreciate them and reward members for doing them (p. 349).

But the collective good suffers. An old country maxim states that "if you want to make an omelet, you've got to break some eggs." Constituents want the omelets, but they oppose contributing any of their eggs, and indeed, applaud when their members of Congress steal eggs from other districts and states. Fenno's puzzle is just another example of the widely discussed "tragedy of the commons." A timber company would rather log the national forest than pay private landowners, but if all do so, the national forest is desolated. Every fisherman would like to take the maximum catch, but if all do so, the national fishery is depleted. In the modern Congress, electoral incentives tempt members to maximize benefits to their constituencies. If most succumb to the temptation, the nation suffers.

CURING WHAT AILS CONGRESS: LIMIT TERMS?

In the early 1990s a reform proposal swept over much of the United States. The proposal was that public officials, especially legislators, be limited by law to some maximum number of terms, usually amounting to 8 to 12 years of service. Observers consider this the most significant reform movement since the Progressive era (p. 246). The strength of the movement reflects popular frustration with American government in general, and legislative bodies in particular. In the 1992 elections, 14 states joined three that had acted earlier in imposing limits on how long incumbents could serve in their state legislatures. By 1997, 21 states had limited the terms of their state legislators. Twenty-three states also attempted to limit congressional service in similar fashion, but the Supreme Court in *U.S. v. Thornton* (1995) held such attempts to be unconstitutional. Still, some candidates elected to Congress have pledged to support congressional term limits, Ross Perot's United We Stand organization supports limits, and congressional limits are still the announced position of the Republican party, so it is possible that Congress could be pressured into approving a constitutional amendment.

Whether Republican or Democratic, conservative or liberal, few political scientists favor term limits.[53] They do not deny the existence of popular frustration, or even that it is justified, but they generally believe that term limits would accomplish little good and would likely do some bad. In their view, term limit advocates misunderstand what is wrong with Congress in particular and legislatures in general.

The argument for term limits assumes that incumbents are virtually unbeatable, and that their electoral success is illegitimate—the product of responsiveness to special interests. Thus, a mechanism like term limits is needed to turn incumbents out of office and increase legislative responsiveness to popular majorities. As we discussed in Chapter 10, however, incumbents are not unbeatable and their success is not illegitimate. Rather, incumbents win so often because they work so hard. In large part they succeed because they are so responsive to constituents and work diligently in their behalf.

The popular perception is that legislatures are performing poorly. But legisla*tures* often perform poorly because legisla*tors* perform so well, at least in terms of responding to their constituencies. That is the irony underlying Fenno's puzzle: If individual members single-mindedly serve their constituencies, they create the tragedy of the commons. People understandably blame Congress for fouling the commons but fail to see the role of their own members—and themselves. This oversight generates the support for term limits. If your member is deserving, simple logic implies that the problem must be everyone else's member, and since you cannot vote in other districts, term limits is the only way to get rid of other districts' members. The problem is that every constituency is a special interest from the standpoint of other constituencies, and your member is a pork-barreling tool of special interests from the standpoint of other districts.

Would term limits change that? Advocates believe that careerists interested in reelection would be replaced by "citizen legislators" who would deliberate and take a broad view of the public interest. As syndicated columnist George Will argues: "Term limits would increase the likelihood that people would come to Congress from established careers, with significant experience in the private sector."[54] This argument is unpersuasive. What kind of people can devote six to ten years to serve in Congress? It will not be the professionals, proprietors, and business executives that Will imagines. How can they sacrifice years out of their careers? In all likelihood, Congress would still be populated with professional politicians. However, they would not be professional members of Congress; rather, professionals would probably rotate from municipal to state to federal offices and back. Would the responsiveness of such people to special interests—and local constituencies—be less than it is today? It might be even greater than now since the professionals would be continually worried about their next positions. Another source of temporary legislators might be special interests—corporate, ideological, and other—who could subsidize employees to serve temporary stints in Congress, then return to their permanent employment. Would that be an improvement?

Term limits would not be the end of the world. Both the advocates and the opponents exaggerate the likely effects. But term limitation does not address the real problem with Congress. The real problem is that professional politicians chosen in single-member districts by simple pluralities have compelling incentives to please the special interests of their districts, and—as campaign funds become increasingly important—special interests outside their districts. They have much less compelling incentives to consider the consequences of their activities for the larger, more general interests of the country. In fact, only one elected official of the 500 thousand who hold office in America has an electoral incentive to consider the good of the entire country: the president. Partly for that reason, Americans make that office the principal focus of their expectations. Can the presidency support the weight of those expectations? (See International Comparison.)

The United States is one of the distinct minority of world democracies that have a presidential form of government, meaning that the chief executive of the government is elected directly by the people rather than chosen by the legislature. Most world democracies are parliamentary in form, meaning that the parliament chooses the chief executive from among its members. (A few countries, such as France, have hybrid systems).

Legislatures are much stronger and more independent in presidential systems. In parliamentary systems, legislatures tend to be mainly arenas that choose the executive, then do little more than rubber-stamp the executive's program. Indeed, in parliamentary systems, legislatures generally are not called legislatures, since they do little legislating: They are called parliaments. To highlight the difference between the two systems, consider again the case of NAFTA (p. 408).

In the United States the opposition to NAFTA was led by the Democratic Whip, David Bonior of Michigan, *the number 3 person in the Democratic congressional leadership*. Few American commentators found this terribly disturbing or noteworthy. Bonior represents a Michigan, rust-belt district in which unions are strong. His position was a natural reflection of his constituency. But in, say, Britain, the world's oldest example of a parliamentary democracy, Bonior's actions would have been unthinkable.

In a parliamentary democracy, once the prime minister and cabinet decide on an important party policy, they expect virtually unanimous support from the party rank and file in parliament. A high-ranking member like Bonior who opposed the policy would have been expected to resign his party position, or, failing that, would have been cashiered. And rather than buy off opponents, as Clinton did, the executive would have threatened to punish them.

One important reason that the executive can impose such discipline is that, in most parliamentary systems, elections do not occur at fixed time intervals as in the United States. Rather, the government chooses when to call elections, subject to some constitutional provision that they must occur at least once within some interval. Thus, a prime minister could declare a vote on a proposal like NAFTA a "vote of confidence," meaning that if it fails to pass, he or she will dissolve parliament and call a new parliamentary election. (Alternatively, when the government suffers a serious defeat, the opposition may offer a "vote of no confidence." If it passes, a new election is held.)

While a serious defeat for the president can cripple his presidency, there is no way to replace him or elect a new Congress before the next scheduled election— a full three years for Clinton in the NAFTA case. Citizens of other democracies consider this a strange feature of American democracy.

Chapter Summary

The United States Congress is the world's most powerful legislature. It is also the most professionalized—its members are full-time, professional legislators, whose incomes derive almost entirely from Congressional service. Despite these facts, citizens hold Congress in relatively low esteem, in much lower esteem than they hold their individual representatives and senators, whom they reelect regularly.

The explanation of this discrepancy lies in the interaction between the electoral system and the members' careerism. Because members of Congress depend for their elections on specific constituencies, they have strong incentives to serve those constituencies; and those incentives often are inconsistent with behavior that would best serve the larger interest of the nation. In particular, members organize the committee system not just to deal efficiently and effectively with major national problems, but in part to enable them to serve their constituencies. Members hesitate to give the leadership enough power to produce an efficient and effective response to national problems in part because that power might be used to prevent them from serving constituency interests or even to force them to oppose constituency interests. The structure of Congress is an uneasy compromise between what is needed to get the job done and what is needed to get reelected.

The result is that Congress is slow and inefficient, and what emerges from the complex legislative process may not be very effective policy. This makes citizens frustrated with Congress, but they fail to see that it is precisely the efforts of their own representatives to serve their specific interests that makes it so difficult for Congress as a whole to serve the national interest. Citizen frustration has produced a powerful reform movement that seeks to limit the terms of legislators. Most political scientists are skeptical, believing that term limits are not an appropriate solution to what ails Congress. Members have powerful incentives to behave as they presently do, and term limits do not specifically attack those incentives.

Key Terms

appropriations, p. 404

authorization process, p. 404

bicameral, p. 381

caucus, p. 390

cloture, p. 391

conference, p. 390

conference committee, p. 403

delegate, p. 385

discharge petition, p. 394

distributive tendency, p. 399

distributive theory, p. 407

filibuster, p. 391

informational theory, p. 399

log-rolling, p. 398

majority leader, p. 389

markup, p. 400

minority leader, p. 390

multiple referral, p. 400

president pro-tempore, p. 390

rule, p. 401

select committee, p. 394

seniority, p. 397

Speaker , p. 388

sponsor, p. 400

standing committee, p. 394

suspension of the rules, p. 400

trustee, p. 385

unanimous consent agreement, p. 390

whips, p. 390

Suggested Readings

Arnold, R. Douglas. *The Logic of Congressional Action*. New Haven, CT: Yale, 1990. An excellent discussion of how the incentives members face interact with characteristics of public policy problems to shape legislation.

Cox, Gary, and Mathew McCubbins. *Legislative Leviathan*. Berkeley, University of California Press, 1993. Important revisionist work that argues parties were more significant in the mid-century congresses than most analysts believed.

Davidson, Roger, and Walter Oleszek. *Congress and Its Members*, 5th ed. Washington, DC: 1996. A comprehensive and readable text that relates the electoral and institutional arenas.

Deering, Christopher, and Steven Smith, *Committees in Congress*. Washington, DC: CQ Press, 1997. The most thorough and up-to-date discussion of the congressional committee system.

Dodd, Larry, and Bruce Oppenheimer, eds., *Congress Reconsidered*, 6th ed. Washington, DC: CQ Press, 1996. An excellent collection of articles on Congress. Many pieces in earlier editions still merit reading.

Kingdon, John. *Congressmen's Voting Decisions*, 3rd ed. Ann Arbor: University of Michigan Press, 1989. Classic study of how representatives decide to vote on the floor.

Oleszek, Walter. *Congressional Procedures and the Policy Process*, 4th ed. Washington, DC: CQ Press, 1995. The most accessible treatment of the myriad rules and procedures that govern the national legislative process.

Ornstein, Norman, Thomas Mann, and Michael Malbin, *Vital Statistics on Congress, 1995-96*. Washington, DC: Congressional Quarterly Inc., 1996. This biennial compilation of congressional statistics is to Congress-watchers what *The Bill James Baseball Abstract* is to baseball fans.

Rohde, David. *Parties and Leaders in the Post-Reform House*. Chicago: University of Chicago Press, 1991. Important work that traces the apparent strengthening of the congressional parties in recent decades.

Sinclair, Barbara. *Legislators, Leaders, and Lawmaking: The U.S. House of Representatives in the Postreform Era*. Baltimore: Johns Hopkins University Press, 1995. Organized around an argument similar to that of Cox and McCubbins, this is the most up-to-date treatment of Democratic leadership in the modern House.

Smith, Steven. *Call to Order: Floor Politics in the House and Senate*. Washington, DC: Brookings, 1989. Detailed study of increasing importance of the chamber floors in the contemporary Congress.

Smith, Steven. *The American Congress*, 2nd ed. Boston: Houghton Mifflin, 1995. The newest comprehensive textbook on Congress. Incorporates changes following Republican control in 1994.

BILL CLINTON   for President
AL GORE   for Vice President   Reform

ROSS PEROT   for President
JAMES CAMPBELL   for Vice President   American
                                                                Independent

HOWARD PHILLIPS   for President
HERBERT W. TITUS   for Vice President   Libertarian

HARRY BROWNE   for President
JO JORGENSEN   for Vice President   Natural Law

JOHN HAGELIN   for President
MIKE TOMPKINS   for Vice President   Green

RALPH NADER   for President
WINONA LADUKE   for Vice President   Peace &
                                                                Freedom

MARSHA FEINLAND   for President
KATE MCCLATCHY   for Vice President   Repub

BOB DOLE   for President
JACK KEMP   for Vice President

Vote for
One Party

3

4

5

TURN PAGE TO C

the presidency: powers and practice

HE MORNING after winning a presidential election is a dangerous moment. Euphoria can sweep aside caution. As President Calvin Coolidge once said, "One of the first lessons a president has to learn is that every word he says weighs a ton."[1]

The day after Bill Clinton first won the presidency, he was asked whether he would issue an executive order allowing gays to join the armed forces. Unhesitatingly, the president-elect said, "yes."[2] With that one word, the president-elect had created a political problem for himself. Though gays thought his stand morally courageous, Clinton paid a political price for his policy commitment.

The political miscalculation was in some ways understandable. Gays had by 1992 become a significant political force. By taking pro-gay positions, Clinton had received as much as $3.5 million in campaign dollars from the gay community and gained an estimated 72 percent of its vote.[3] That Clinton, as president, had the legal authority to permit gays in the military also seemed beyond question. Congress had never passed a law on the subject, and the ban was based solely on an order issued by President Reagan.

But Clinton still might have thought more about the political consequences before responding positively to the reporter's question. Gay access to the military had marginal popular appeal. Though it was acceptable to 45 percent of the electorate, 47 percent remained opposed. Of those opposed, eight out of ten said they held strong opinions.[4]

With no military experience, Clinton was vulnerable on defense policy issues. Further, the president-elect's promise to gays annoyed senior military officers, who were quoted as saying the policy would "wreck morale" and "undermine recruiting."[5] General Colin Powell, a Persian Gulf war hero, said "the presence of homosexuals in the force would be detrimental to good order and discipline."[6] The president-elect could, of course, simply ignore opposition from within the military. After all, he was **commander in chief**, and the armed forces had to obey executive orders. But these orders can be overturned by congressional legislation.

Attention shifted to Capitol Hill, where members of Congress quickly sensed the emergence of a controversial issue. In a single day the congressional switchboard was swamped by nearly half a million phone calls, mainly in opposition.[7] Delighted at the president's predicament, one Republican legislator exclaimed, "You would think that someone who has not served a day in uniform would be particularly careful to consult his military chiefs."[8] Senator Sam Nunn, chair of the Senate Armed Services Committee, also expressed doubts, and Nunn's opposition was critical. Popular in his socially conservative home state of Georgia, he was the leading Democratic spokesman on military questions, a man many thought should have been elected president.

Clinton appointed a presidential task force to review the issue. The recommendation of the task force was a compromise formula known as "Don't ask, don't tell." Although individuals were not to be asked questions about their sexual preferences when joining the armed forces, gays could be asked to leave the armed services if they told anyone they were gay or if they were observed engaging in impermissible behavior. The compromise was more satisfactory to Nunn than to gay rights advocates. The number of individuals dismissed for homosexual activity actually increased. One political commentator wondered whether "there is *any* principle for which Bill Clinton will fight."[9]

■ **commander in chief**
The President in his constitutional role as head of the armed forces.

residents often seem unprincipled, because they frequently are unable to carry out their campaign pledges. Their problems are due both to the constituency pressures they face and to the limits on their powers. In this chapter we shall first examine presidential constituencies. We shall then look at the ways in which presidents have exercised their constitutional powers. We conclude by considering the factors that make for successful presidents.

Presidential Constituencies

Presidents also often find it challenging to find the right balance between their national constituency, created by the general election, and their partisan constituency, shaped by presidential primaries. President Clinton's desire to allow gays to serve in the armed forces was popular with many elements within his own party, yet the policy did not have the broad national support that a presidential proposal generally needs. Both national and partisan constituencies play a role in presidential decision making.

NATIONAL CONSTITUENCY

Presidents have one unique political asset: They fill the only position elected by a national constituency. Only presidents can persuasively claim to be speaking for the country as a whole and they can use this national constituency to powerful effect. When President Clinton and Congress could not agree on the 1996 federal budget, the deadlock shut down many parts of the federal government. National parks were closed and government bills went unpaid. In the midst of the crisis, the president asked Congress to place the national interest above partisan objectives. Speaker of the House Newt Gingrich replied by saying it was the president who should put the country's future ahead of his own. Each appealed to a national constituency, but the president, in part because he was the *president*, proved to be more persuasive. According to polls, most Americans sided with the president and blamed Congress for the deadlock.

Though the president's national constituency is a great political asset, it creates dangers as well. In the eyes of the voters, presidents are held responsible for many things over which they have little control. Presidents are expected to conduct foreign policy, manage the economy, administer a complex bureaucracy, promote desired legislation, respond to disasters, and address an endless variety of real and imagined social problems.[10]

Though presidents are sometimes given credit for good things that happen, they are more often blamed when things go bad. President Bush, for example, enjoyed a succession of foreign policy successes equalled by only a few of his predecessors. He oversaw the fall of the Berlin wall, the collapse of the Soviet Union, and a spectacular victory in the Persian Gulf War. Yet when the economy faltered, Bush was chased from office. And, in his first year in office, Bill Clinton presided over a recovering

Most Americans seem to have blamed, not President Clinton, but the Congress for the massive budget deadlock that shut down the federal government—from parks to national shrines like the Washington Monument—in 1996.

FIGURE **13.1**

Partisan Support for the President in Congress

Each party in Congress supports its own president more often.

SOURCE: This figure is based on data for the period 1954–94 taken from Norman J. Ornstein, Thomas E. Mann, and Michael J. Mablin, *Vital Statistics on Congress, 1995-96* (Washington, DC: Congressional Quarterly 1996), pp. 206–07.

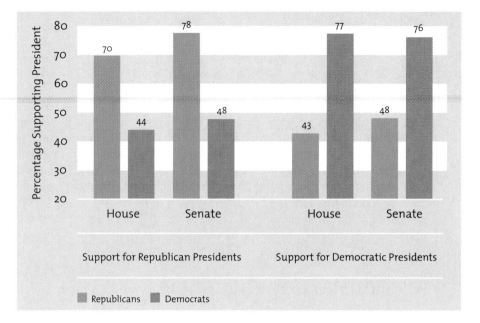

Every presidential administration has its gadflies, including conservative Pat Buchanan, who took the likes of George Bush to task for not being conservative enough.

economy and persuaded Congress to take a major step toward balancing the budget. But when he failed to win congressional support for his health care reform, Clinton's popularity fell and Republicans swept to power in the mid-term elections.

PARTISAN CONSTITUENCIES

In addition to a national constituency, presidents have a party constituency to which they must be responsive. They need to keep the support of their party's most active members who work in and help finance their campaigns. If they do not attend to their party constituency, they may encounter difficulties with the party faithful in presidential primaries. When Jimmy Carter was thought to have moved too far away from traditional Democratic positions, in his attempt at a second term, he was challenged by Edward Kennedy in the Democratic primaries. When George Bush was thought to have been insufficiently conservative, he was challenged by Pat Buchanan.

A party constituency usually takes more extreme issue positions than does the national constituency. Republican activists support tighter controls on abortion than do most voters. Democratic activists support more generous welfare benefits than the typical voter does. Presidents have to find some way of responding to the demands of their most ardent supporters without offending the general-election voter who determines the outcome of national elections.

PARTISAN SUPPORT IN CONGRESS

Party connections are especially important when the president tries to work with Congress. On most issues, presidents gain more support from members of their own party than from the opposition. As can be seen in Figure 13.1, party members in both the House and Senate vote with presidents somewhere between 70 and 80 percent of the time. Opposition party members vote with presidents somewhere between 40 and 50 percent of the time. As a consequence, the bigger the president's

British prime ministers receive the support of nearly every party member in parliament on all major issues. Over 90 percent of the time, party members go along with the prime minister. These extraordinary high levels of party support are due to a rule that forces prime ministers to resign from office if they fail to get a majority on critical votes. When that happens, a new election is usually called and members of parliament must immediately run for reelection, something they usually like to delay for as long as possible.

Since American presidents can lose in Congress and still remain president, members of Congress balance party loyalty against their own convictions as well as constituency and interest group pressures. Jimmy Carter failed to get his party to enact most of his energy policy. Clinton could not persuade his party to pass his health care reform. Had they been British prime ministers, they could have forced either passage or new elections.

source: Jack Brand, *British Parliamentary Parties: Policy and Power* (New York: Oxford, 1992), Ch. 2.

partisan majority in Congress, the more likely he is to get his proposed legislation approved.[11]

Recent events provide a clear illustration of the importance to presidents of a party majority in Congress. During the first two years of President Clinton's presidency, he enjoyed a Democratic party majority in both the Senate and the House. During this time Congress approved several presidential proposals, including two international trade bills, as well as laws that eased registration requirements, provided medical and family leave, and reduced the budget deficit. After Democrats lost their majority at the mid-term elections, Clinton was able to secure passage of almost no additional items in his legislative agenda. Instead, he was forced to accept Republican welfare proposals with which he did not altogether agree (see Chapter 1).

Partisanship is not as all-pervasive as it is in many European countries (see International Comparison). Still, political scientists have debated whether it is a good or bad thing to have divided government, the control of the presidency by one party and the control of one or both Houses of Congress by the other. Some think a president needs a partisan majority in Congress in order to solve national problems. Others think each party keeps a check on the other, when government is divided (see Democratic Dilemma).

Separate Institutions Sharing Power

Divided government raises important issues, because most of the important constitutional powers of the president are shared with Congress. Presidents are seldom in a position to force members of Congress to support them; they usually have to coax, beg, plead, and compromise to gain the necessary votes. Even when the same

Democratic Dilemma

Is Divided Government Good or Bad?

Republican Speaker of the House Newt Gingrich and Democratic President Bill Clinton, contemporary embodiments of divided government.

When Government is divided ..., the normal and healthy partisan confrontation that occurs during debates in every democratic legislature spills over into confrontation between the branches of the government, which may render it immobile .... When the president sends a recommendation to the opposition-controlled Congress, the legislators are virtually compelled to reject or profoundly alter it; otherwise they are endorsing the president's leadership.... [and] strengthening him or his party for the next election.

The separation of powers is far more likely to lead to debilitating governmental deadlock when the organs of government are divided between the parties. [One] measure give[s] promise of discouraging the ticket-splitting that produces divided government.... *Four-year House terms and eight-year Senate terms....* The midterm election now gives the electorate an opportunity to express its objections if an administration performs poorly but it gives them no chance to remedy the situation, for the president remains in office.... [Let's] eliminate that election...."

—James Sundquist

If ... ticket-splitting [between the two parties] of a significant proportion of the citizenry reflects a lack of confidence in the elites of both parties, who are we to recommend that they make a clear choice? ... If citizens believe that Republicans wish to redistribute from poor to rich, while Democratic elites have never met a tax they didn't like, should they be forced to give either party unfettered control of economic affairs? If citizens think Republicans are tough on crime but dismiss acid rain as a figment of the liberal imagination, while Democrats are good on the environment but believe that there are no criminals, only oppressed victims of society, should citizens be forced to make a clear choice? ... If ... the citizenry choose to split control of government so as to frustrate both parties, should they be blamed? On the contrary, perhaps they should be praised for frustrating the arrogant, cynical, and self-serving elites who wish to govern them.

—Morris Fiorina

Scholars disagree on the issue of divided government. What do you think?

SOURCES: James L. Sundquist, *Constitutional Reform and Effective Government* (Washington, DC: Brookings, 1986), pp. 75–76, 240. Morris Fiorina, *Divided Government* (New York: Macmillan, 1992), pp. 128–29.

party controls both the presidency and Congress, presidents do not find it easy to get their proposals approved. Jimmy Carter failed to persuade a Democratic Congress to enact most of his energy policy.[12] Clinton, as stated earlier, could not get his party to back his health care reform proposals.[13] Over 80 percent of the time presidents either fail to secure passage of their major legislative agendas or must make important compromises to win congressional approval.[14] As presidential scholar Charles Jones has observed, "Presidents don't pass laws; they work with, alongside of, or against the House and Senate."[15]

When President Clinton was unable to open the military to gays, he was not the first president to be frustrated by Congress. Theodore Roosevelt sighed, "Oh, if I could only be president and Congress too for just ten minutes."[16] Harry Truman expressed the frustration of many presidents when he predicted what would happen to his successor, Dwight Eisenhower: "He'll sit here and he'll say, 'Do this! Do that!' *And nothing will happen.* Poor Ike—it won't be a bit like the Army. He'll find it very frustrating."[17] Or, in the words of George Bush, "I don't want to sound sanctimonious about this, but I was elected to govern."[18]

Those who wrote the Constitution ensured that presidents would govern only with the help of Congress (see Chapter 2, Table 2.4). Most delegates to the Constitutional Convention wanted to strengthen the executive branch beyond what was provided for by the Articles of Confederation. Alexander Hamilton even proposed electing a president for life. But most delegates realized that voters would never ratify a constitution that created a strong executive who might become another King George. The result is a "government of separated institutions which share power."[19] We now turn to the many ways in which the Constitution has shaped presidential power and practice. (Our emphasis in this chapter will be on the president's powers with respect to domestic affairs; his foreign policy powers are the subject of Chapter 20.)

THE POWER TO INFORM AND PERSUADE

PRESIDENTIAL POWER: *The President "shall from time to time give to the Congress Information of the State of the Union."*

CONGRESSIONAL CHECK: *None*

The Constitution requires presidents to give Congress information on the state of the Union. Since the line between information and persuasion is thin, presidents have interpreted this requirement as authority to persuade Congress and the public at large to adopt their policies. The president relies on hundreds of public speeches during the year to set forth his vision of the country's future, but the most prestigious and formalized address is the **State of the Union address**, given annually, usually in late January or early February.

■ **State of the Union address**
In fulfillment of the constitutional obligation of reporting to Congress on the state of the Union.

EARLY USE OF PERSUASION POWER

The power to persuade is used much more publicly today than it was in the early years of the Republic (see Figure 13.2). Early presidents seldom spoke in public, and when they did, their remarks were of a general nature. When Thomas Jefferson reported on the state of the Union, he did so by means of a written communication, read by the Speaker of the House. Not until Woodrow Wilson did it become a regular practice for presidents to address personally a joint session of both Houses of Congress.[20] Some early presidents found other ways of persuading Congress. Thomas Jefferson, a master politician, invited members of Congress to the Executive Mansion for dinners at which he would persuade them to support his political agenda.[21] He also communicated his views through friendly newspaper editors.

FIGURE 13.2

Growth in Presidential
Speech-Making

SOURCES: Data on Presidents
Washington through McKinley are
taken from Jeffrey Tulis, *The Rhetor-
ical Presidency* (Princeton: Prince-
ton University Press, 1987), p. 64; for
Theodore Roosevelt, see Robert V.
Friedenberg, *Theodore Roosevelt
and the Rhetoric of Militant
Decency* (New York: Greenwood
Press, 1990); for Taft, see *Presiden-
tial Addresses and State Papers of
William Howard Taft*, Vol.1, 1910
(New York: Doubleday, Page & Co.);
for Wilson, see Albert Shaw, ed.,
*Messages and Papers of Woodrow
Wilson*, Volumes 1 and 2 (New York:
Review of Reviews Corporation,
1924); for Coolidge, see Claude M.
Fuess, *Calvin Coolidge: The Man
from Vermont* (Hamden, CT: Archon
Boojs, 1965); for Presidents Truman
through Reagan, see Roderick Hart,
The Sound of Leadership (Chicago:
The University of Chicago Press,
1987); for Hoover, Bush, and Clinton,
information is taken from *The
Public Papers of the President*,
various compilations.

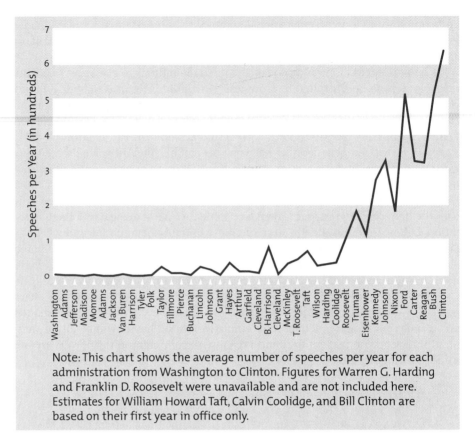

Note: This chart shows the average number of speeches per year for each
administration from Washington to Clinton. Figures for Warren G. Harding
and Franklin D. Roosevelt were unavailable and are not included here.
Estimates for William Howard Taft, Calvin Coolidge, and Bill Clinton are
based on their first year in office only.

Woodrow Wilson, here shown
(right of center) in 1916, the first
U.S. president to regularly
address joint sessions of both
houses of Congress.

Though active behind the scenes, early presidents avoided open involvement in day-to-day politics.[22]

In fact, the unwritten rule against presidential rhetoric was at one time so strong that it became a basis for presidential impeachment. President Andrew Johnson, who succeeded to the presidency upon the assassination of Abraham Lincoln, personally criticized specific members of Congress. In the list of impeachment charges brought against Johnson, one stands out:

> That said Andrew Johnson, President of the United States, unmindful of the high duties of his office and the dignity and propriety thereof . . . did . . . deliver with a loud voice certain intemperate, inflammatory, and scandalous harangues, and did therein utter loud threats and bitter menaces . . . against Congress.[23]

MODERN PERSUASION POWER

More than any other single president, Theodore "Teddy" Roosevelt changed the definition of what was permissible in presidential rhetoric. Roosevelt liked to achieve results by using what he called the "**bully-pulpit**" available to presidents, even more than preachers. (The phrase combines the images of high school "bully" with that of the president in the pulpit preaching to the country as a congregation.) He mobilized support through bold gestures, forceful speeches, presidential trips, and dramatic turns of phrase. Roosevelt's rhetoric may have been his most lasting contribution to presidential politics. As one historian has noted, "the number of laws [Roosevelt] inspired was certainly not in proportion to the amount of noise he emitted."[24] Yet Roosevelt's popular appeal was such that, after a cartoon depicted the president sparing the life of a bear cub while hunting, the "Teddy Bear" was named after him.

Although he was an avid hunter, President Theodore "Teddy" Roosevelt's popular appeal gave him household-word status (through the term *"Teddy" bear*) when he supposedly spared the life of a bear cub on a 1902 hunting trip.

■ **bully-pulpit**
The use of the presidential platform to persuade the public to support the president's policies.

Presidents since Teddy Roosevelt have increasingly used the bully pulpit to persuade Congress and the public (see Figure 13.2).[25] Franklin Delano Roosevelt's "fireside chats" over the radio enabled him to vault over the print media, which he accused of being controlled by Republican publishers. John Kennedy had a compelling rhetorical style that both inspired and challenged his audience. In his Inaugural speech the young president challenged Americans to "ask not what your country can do for you, ask what you can do for your country."[26]

President Reagan, the first president with experience as a professional actor, used television more effectively than any of his predecessors. Reagan knew "precisely how to give a twenty-eight-minute television address in twenty-eight minutes, to use a TelePrompTer without seeming to read, to look at a camera as though it were a person, to use cue cards without fumbling, [and] chalk marks without stumbling." He understood there is but "a thin line between politics and theatricals."[27] Pictures were worth a thousand words, and body language spoke more convincingly than verbal formulations.[28] As Reagan once said, " I've wondered how people in positions of this kind . . . manage without having had any acting experience."[29]

THE VETO POWER

PRESIDENTIAL VETO POWER: *Before any law "shall take effect," it must be "approved by" the president.*

CONGRESSIONAL CHECK: *Unless "repassed by two thirds of the Senate and the House of Representatives."*

- **veto power**
  Presidential rejection of congressional legislation. May be overridden by two-thirds vote in each congressional chamber. Most state governors also have the veto power over their legislatures.
- **override**
  Congressional passage of a bill by a two-thirds vote over the president's veto.

The president's **veto power** is a good deal more concrete than the power to inform: It gives presidents the capacity to prevent bills passed by Congress from becoming law. Before the Civil War, the veto was seldom used. Washington cast the presidential veto twice. The average number cast by presidents between Madison and Lincoln was only a little more than four. As can be seen in Figure 13.3, modern presidents are much more willing to use the veto power.

This presidential power to say "No" is not unconditional. But Congress usually fails to muster the necessary two-thirds vote in each chamber to pass an **override**, which makes the bill a law despite the president's opposition. Since the Kennedy administration, the veto has been overridden approximately one out of every ten times a veto has been cast.[30]

The veto power is of little help to presidents in their attempts to initiate policy change. Carter wanted an energy policy that was the "moral equivalent of war" but, when confronted by opposition from senators from Texas, Louisiana, and other oil-producing states, Carter was forced to sign a law much altered from his original proposals. Carter might have vetoed the legislation, but once having put the issue on the agenda, he could hardly block the action Congress saw fit to take.

Though the veto can seldom be used to initiate policy, it can sometimes be successfully employed in a negative way. In his confrontation with the Republican Congress over the 1996 budget, President Clinton used the veto to stall Republican tax and spending cuts. Not only did Clinton achieve many of his policy objectives,

FIGURE 13.3

Growth in Presidential Use of the Veto Power

SOURCES: Figures for 1989–1995 are taken from Lyn Ragsdale, *Vital Statistics on the Presidency* (Washington, DC: CQ Press, 1996); Figures for 1996 are taken from *Congressional Quarterly Weekly Report*, various issues.

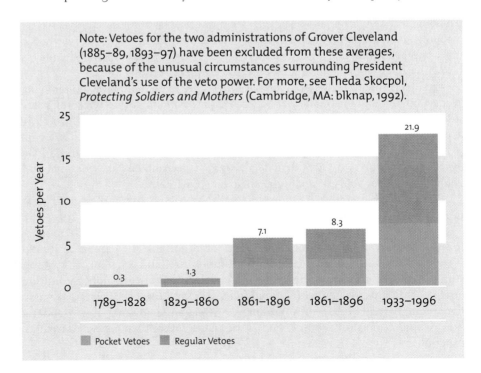

Note: Vetoes for the two administrations of Grover Cleveland (1885–89, 1893–97) have been excluded from these averages, because of the unusual circumstances surrounding President Cleveland's use of the veto power. For more, see Theda Skocpol, *Protecting Soldiers and Mothers* (Cambridge, MA: blknap, 1992).

Vetoes per Year

| | 0.3 | 1.3 | 7.1 | 8.3 | 21.9 |
| 1789–1828 | 1829–1860 | 1861–1896 | 1861–1896 | 1933–1996 |

■ Pocket Vetoes   ■ Regular Vetoes

he gained political support as well. Before the conflict, Clinton was seen by many as a weak leader lacking in principle. By casting vetoes, Clinton conveyed the impression of a president committed to standing up to a recalcitrant Congress.

If Congress enacts a law ten days before it adjourns, a president may exercise a **pocket veto** simply by not signing the bill into law. Congress has no opportunity to override a pocket veto. Almost all of President Reagan's vetoes were pocket vetoes that could not be overriden—one of the devices that he used to convey the impression of a strong president. But the pocket veto strategy works only at the very end of a Congressional session; if Congress remains in session for more than ten days after passing a bill, the president must explicitly cast a veto to prevent the bill from becoming law. As the distinction between campaigning and governing has disappeared, Congress has remained in session virtually throughout the entire year, giving Bush and Clinton few opportunities to cast pocket vetoes, still another illustration of the way in which elections influence American government.

In still another way of countering presidential veto power, Congress often incorporates policies that presidents oppose into large bills that contain items presidents feel they must approve. When faced with such a package, the president finds it difficult to cast a veto. Clinton reluctantly signed a bill requiring the discharge of HIV-positive soldiers because the provision was incorporated into an important defense bill.

Because Congress can artfully package laws so as to make the veto unusable, many people favor giving the president the **item veto**, the authority to negate particular provisions of a law while letting the remainder stand. The item veto became a popular idea among congressional Republicans during the Reagan and Bush Administrations, a time when a Democratic Congress was packaging laws in ways that Republican presidents found difficult to veto. In 1995 the shoe was slipped unto the other foot: an item veto would give Democratic President Bill Clinton the power to veto expenditures approved by a Republican Congress. Clinton endorsed the item veto, but Republicans became less enthusiastic. In the spring of 1996, the two sides compromised by enacting legislation that allowed presidents to veto specific items that affected fewer than one hundred individuals or entities. In the summer of 1997 President Clinton exercised the item veto by rejecting legislation giving tax loopholes to big agricultural co-operatives and financial companies with overseas investments. He also vetoed a special medicaid spending provision that benefitted only the State of New York. Congress can override these vetoes by a simple majority, but if the president vetoes the items a second time, a two-thirds vote is necessary to override.

Originally, item veto proposals involved amending the Constitution. When supporters could not get the two-thirds vote in Congress for a constitutional amendment, they agreed to a simple piece of legislation that has just been discussed. Now that President Clinton has exercised the item veto, its constitutionality will be challenged on the grounds that it transfers law-making authority from Congress to the president. It remains to be seen whether the Supreme Court will agree with this argument or whether the president will at last exercise an item veto.

■ **pocket veto**
Presidential veto after congressional adjournment, executed by not signing a bill into law.

■ **item veto**
Recently enacted presidential authority to negate particular provisions of a law.

THE APPOINTMENT POWER

PRESIDENTIAL POWER: *The president "shall appoint ambassadors, other public ministers and consuls . . . and all other offices of the United States."*

CONGRESSIONAL CHECK: *Appointments are subject to the "advice and consent of the Senate," which is taken to mean that a majority must approve the nomination.*

The appointment power enables presidents to appoint thousands of public officials to positions of high responsibility within their **administration**, those responsible for directing the executive branch of government.

THE CABINET

The president's **cabinet** consists of the key members of the administration. Most are heads of government departments and carry the title **secretary**. The terms are leftovers from the days when secretary referred to a confidential assistant who kept secrets under lock and key in a wooden cabinet. Originally, the president's cabinet had but four departments, and the secretaries met regularly with the president and gave him confidential political guidance on a broad range of policies. It was in cabinet meetings, for example, that Abraham Lincoln developed his strategy for fighting the Civil War.

Over the years, government began to perform a much broader range of functions. As the number of departments grew from four to fifteen (see Chapter 14), the cabinet lost its capacity to provide confidential advice to presidents. In President Nixon's words, "Cabinet government is a myth and won't work . . . no [president] in his right mind submits anything to his cabinet."[31] Today it meets only occasionally, mainly for ceremonial purposes or to help the president make some kind of political statement.

THE WHITE HOUSE STAFF

Many of the president's closest current advisers are not cabinet secretaries but White House aides who deal in matters with utmost confidentiality. At one time the president's personal staff was small and informal. Abraham Lincoln had but two young assistants; otherwise, he communicated personally with his cabinet. Even President Franklin Roosevelt originally had only a small handful of personal assistants. To address organizational problems caused by the growing size of the federal government, Roosevelt in 1936 asked a committee of three specialists in public administration headed by Louis Brownlow to recommend ways in which the organization of the federal government could be improved. Saying "the President needs help," the Brownlow Committee recommended sweeping changes throughout the government, including additional appointments to the president's personal staff.

FIGURE 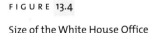 **13.4**

Size of the White House Office

SOURCES: White House Office staff, 1943–93, from Harold W. Stanley, and Richard G. Niemi, *Vital Statistics on American Politics*, 4th ed. (Washington, DC: CQ Press, 1994), p. 267–9; staff figures for 1994–1996 taken from U.S. Office of Personnel Management, *Federal Civilian Workforce Statistics*.

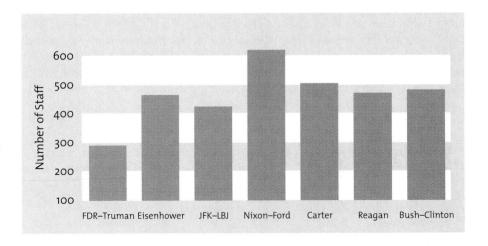

TABLE 13.1

Executive Office of the President

	Budget[a] (millions)	Staff[a]
Office of Management and Budget	$56.5	572
White House Office	38.8	430
Administration	25.0	190
U.S. Trade Representative	20.6	191
National Drug Control	11.7	25
National Security Council	6.6	147
Policy Development	5.1	50
Science and Technology	4.4	46
Council of Economic Advisers	3.4	35
Council of Environmental Quality	.4	None

[a] As of 1994.

SOURCE: John Hart, *The Presidential Branch*, 2nd ed. (Chatham, NJ: Chatham House, 1995), p. 46.

Brownlow said they "should be possessed of high competence, great physical vigor, and a passion for anonymity." Though Congress rejected most of the other Brownlow recommendations, it agreed to enlarge the White House staff.[32]

Brownlow envisioned only a "small number of executive assistants," but the president's staff has steadily evolved in size and complexity.[33] The number of aides has grown from 48 in 1944 to over 400 today (see Figure 13.4). Its organization is now so complex that even informed citizens have trouble keeping everything straight. One basic distinction to keep clear is the difference between the **White House Office**, the main subject under discussion here, and the much larger **Executive Office of the President (EOP)**. Although the names make it seem as if they are much the same thing, the White House Office is just one component of the EOP, which also includes other important coordinating bodies as well as operating agencies (see Table 13.1).

In Roosevelt's day, no single person headed the White House staff. Even as late as the Carter administration, White House aides worked together as "spokes in a wheel," each having their own direct access to the president. But today presidents usually place one person in charge.[34] This person, the **chief of staff**, meets with the president several times a day and communicates decisions to other staff, cabinet officers, and members of Congress.

The best chiefs are usually Washington insiders. Though little acclaimed, Ronald Reagan's last chief, Howard Baker, was one of the most powerful and effective. A former Senate majority leader and presidential aspirant, Baker served at a time when he had forsaken all political ambition. Skilled at reaching compromises, Baker helped boost Reagan's popularity, despite the fact that the aging president himself had lost much of his former vitality.

Newcomers to Washington are not always as successful. Instead, they often become lightning rods, people to be blamed when things go wrong. John Sununu, former governor of New Hampshire, was forced to leave the job of chief of staff when he was blamed for urging President Bush to sign an unpopular tax increase.[35] Thomas McLarty from Arkansas resigned when he was blamed for the Clinton Administration's poor beginning.[36]

White House Office
Political appointees who work directly for the president, many of whom occupy offices in the White House.

Executive Office of the President (EOP)
Agency that houses both top coordinating offices and other operating agencies.

chief of staff
Head of White House staff and often regarded as the second most powerful person in the executive branch. Has continuous, direct contact with president.

This group portrait of President Clinton's staff shows their average age to be around twenty-something.

Although Brownlow expected White House aides to have "no power to make decisions," the tighter connection between campaigns, elections, and government decision making has made the White House staff increasingly influential.[37] Here, more than anywhere else, presidents can count on the loyalty of those around them. Unlike departmental secretaries, staff careers are closely intertwined with that of the president.

In addition, presidents have more need for political help than ever before. Presidents today need pollsters who can keep them in touch with changes in public opinion.[38] They also need assistants who can help them communicate with the media, interest groups, and members of Congress. Once a major piece of legislation arrives for consideration by the chamber floor, White House aides will be in regular contact with many legislators. As part of the White House effort to pass Clinton's national service plan, one aide personally contacted sixty-seven Senate offices.[39] So intense is the work inside the White House, most staff jobs demand seven-day, one-hundred-hour-plus work weeks. As a result, many positions are given to those young in age and spirit.

Quite apart from the president's genuine need for lots of political "help," the White House staff is an excellent place to reward loyal campaign workers. After the presidency has been won, those who worked on the campaign expect their reward. As one old-time politician put it, folks "ain't in politics for nothin'. They want to get somethin' out of it."[40] The White House Office is a convenient place for the president to put campaign workers, because the president has exclusive control over appointments to his personal staff. Only the chief of staff must be confirmed by the Senate.

During presidential election years, the number of people working at the White House provokes strong criticism from the opposition party. When running for president, Bill Clinton promised to cut the White House staff by 25 percent. But when it came time to make the cuts, Clinton found his White House Office too valuable to be the target of cost-cutting efforts. So the president made the staff cuts elsewhere in the Executive Office of the President. Because of the confusion in the public's mind between the White House Office and the EOP, it was difficult for Republicans to criticize him for breaking this campaign promise.[41]

SCANDALS IN THE WHITE HOUSE OFFICE

The highly personal and partisan nature of the White House staff can be a weakness as well as a strength. A White House full of personal friends and fellow partisans has at times so protected presidents from external criticism that presidents have lost touch with political reality. And sometimes staff members have used the power of the presidential office for improper—even illegal—purposes, paving the way for scandals of presidential proportions.

Linda Purdue holds a sign referring to "Zippergate," the sexual harassment lawsuit against President Clinton, and to other scandals that have dogged him, in front of the Supreme Court in early 1997. The Court had begun hearing arguments on whether the lawsuit, filed by former Arkansas state employee Paula Jones, should be deferred until after Clinton left office.

Scandals are hardly new to American politics. When lawmakers discovered that Abraham Lincoln's wife and her assistants outspent housekeeping funds, the president, in secret session, pleaded with them not to carry out an investigation but to secretly appropriate more money.[42] But the intensity and significance of White House scandals have escalated in recent decades.[43] Three major and many more minor scandals have both captured the attention of the nation and carried the potential for presidential impeachment.

- The most serious was the Watergate scandal during the Nixon Administration. At the instigation of members of the White House staff, several men broke into Democratic party headquarters at the Watergate condominium in Washington, DC, apparently to obtain information on Democratic party campaign strategies. President Nixon's chief of staff, Bob Haldeman, knew that "hush money" was paid to keep the burglars from revealing White House involvement. When tapes of President Nixon's own conversations indicated that the president himself had been involved in the "cover-up," impeachment proceedings were initiated and he was forced to resign.

- In the Iran-Contra scandal, arms were illegally sold to the Iranian government and the profits from the sale were given, also illegally, to a group of guerrillas known as "Contras" who were trying to overthrow a left-wing government in Nicaragua. White House aides were prosecuted and Chief of Staff Donald Regan resigned when a presidential task force said he had mishandled the situation. Some Democrats talked of impeachment, but no direct evidence implicating the president was found.

■ President Clinton's White House staff were implicated in what became known as the Whitewater scandal when they allegedly withheld information from investigators concerning financial transactions in Arkansas that involved Bill and Hillary Clinton. After the 1996 election, the scandal widened to include campaign contributions from foreign companies and even, allegedly, the Chinese government. Several White House aides resigned from office and one, Harold Ickes, released vast quantities of his personal papers concerning campaign contributions to congressional investigators. Independent Counsel Kenneth Starr interviewed the president and the First Lady concerning some of the charges and made strong efforts to gain information from White House aides to see whether impeachment was warranted. The scandal adversely affected Clinton's popularity at the beginning of his second term, and threatened to hold a cloud over his remaining years in office.

The outcome of the multi-faceted Whitewater scandal may very well depend on court decisions concerning the range and extent of executive privileges enjoyed by presidents. In two cases decided in the mid-1990s, the courts have ruled against the president. First, a federal appeals court ruled in 1996 that notes from conversations between the president, the First Lady, and their attorneys could not be kept from the independent counsel, because the presence of White House attorneys at these meetings voided the usual right to privacy enjoyed by conversations between clients and their attorneys.

The Supreme Court chose not to review the appeals court decision, forcing White House lawyers to turn over the transcripts to the independent counsel, Kenneth Starr. It remains to be seen whether Starr will use these documents to allege presidential efforts to "cover up" wrong-doing.

Secondly, the Supreme Court decided in 1997 that a private individual may bring a president to trial while in office for alleged wrongful conduct that was not part of his presidential duties. The case was brought by Paula Jones, who accused the president of sexual harassment when he was governor of Arkansas. It remains to be seen whether this case will be settled out of court, subjected to further legal delays, or whether a sitting president of the United States, for the first time, will be forced to wage a court room defense in a civil suit.

These are only the most prominent of a host of scandals involving members of the White House staff. No other agency of the federal government is so repeatedly charged with misconduct and wrongdoing. Several factors seem to make the White House staff particularly prone to scandal.

■ News organizations and opposition leaders have a vested interest in uncovering a White House scandal. Any misdoing by the White House Office immediately embarrasses the president and could lead to presidential defeat, resignation, or impeachment.

■ Many White House aides often have a strong interest in seeing the president reelected. They are thus tempted to use governmental power for partisan purposes and sometimes overreach their authority. As an exasperated congressman exclaimed upon learning that a Clinton aide (formerly a campaign aide) had erroneously obtained FBI files on prominent Republicans, "we have political operatives, incompetents and even teen-agers involved in this process."[43]

- Presidential campaigns often attract young, bold, ambitious risk-takers. They may not necessarily be most suited to exercise responsibility in an office of such visibility that great care and caution are always in order.

THE POWER TO RECOMMEND

PRESIDENTIAL POWER: *The president may recommend to Congress for "their consideration such Measures as he shall judge necessary and expedient."*

CONGRESSIONAL CHECK: *Only Congress may enact measures into law.*

The power to recommend gives to the president the power of initiation, the power to set the political agenda.[44] Presidents can shut down old policy options, create new possibilities, and change the political dialogue. Ronald Reagan placed budget and tax cuts on the policy agenda; Bill Clinton proposed major health care reform.

However, this power does not go unchecked. Congress can—and often does—ignore a presidential recommendation. Nor is the power to initiate limited to the president. In 1994, congressional Republicans under the leadership of House Speaker Newt Gingrich campaigned on a "Contract with America" that set the policy agenda for the next two years, though only a small portion became law.

EARLY USE OF POWER TO RECOMMEND

Presidential use of the power to recommend was exercised with great restraint in the decades preceding the Civil War.[45] Presidents were expected to remain silent on any issue, once deliberations had begun on Capitol Hill.[46] The very unity of the country required a low-key presidency. Since the president was the symbol of the nation as a whole, and since the nation was divided into free and slave states, presidents could not talk about slavery, the most important political question of the period.

MODERN USE OF POWER TO RECOMMEND

The presidential power to recommend expanded rapidly after the end of the Civil War. The country was growing swiftly, and many social and economic problems were becoming national in scope. The nation's strongest presidents have had their greatest impact not so much by making decisions as by opening up new possibilities. For example, Theodore Roosevelt made conservation a major public concern. Franklin Delano Roosevelt called for a New Deal that would protect Americans from economic downturns and persuaded Congress to pass dozens of bills within **one hundred days** of his inauguration (see Election Connection). Reagan focused attention on reducing the size of government.

- **one hundred days**
  The first days a president is in office, during which time great legislative accomplishments are expected.

TIMING PRESIDENTIAL INITIATIVES

Presidents have the best chance of initiating policy in the first months after their election. As can be seen in Figure 13.5, presidents make most new proposals at the very beginning of their first term. This is the time when presidential popularity is at a peak and both Congress and the country are eager to hear what solutions the new president is bringing to the country's problems. As one of Lyndon Johnson's top aides noted, "You've got to give it all you can that first year. . . . You've got just one year when they treat you right . . . . You can't put anything through when half of the Congress is thinking about how to beat you. So you've got one year."[47]

Roosevelt's First Hundred Days

When Roosevelt campaigned for president in 1932 in the midst of the Great Depression, he promised the voters to bring "Recovery, Relief and Reform." As soon as he became president he called Congress into special session and persuaded it to pass within one hundred days dozens of new laws, including the following legislation which provided the foundation for what became known as the New Deal:

Emergency Banking Relief Act

Unemployment Relief Act (Civilian Conservation Corps)

Agricultural Adjustment Act

Tennessee Valley Authority Act

Federal Securities Act

Home Owners' Refinancing Act

National Industrial Recovery Act, creating the

National Recovery Administration and

Public Works Administration

Glen Steagall Banking Recovery Act

One senator declared that if the president had asked Congress "to commit suicide tomorrow, they'd do it."

Although some of the legislation proved to be hastily drawn, Roosevelt's bill-passing record has haunted presidents ever since. At the end of every president's first one hundred days, newspaper reporters compare his bill-passing record to Roosevelt's. The comparison is inevitably unfavorable.

SOURCES: Thomas Bailey, *The American Pageant* (Boston: D.C. Heath, 1956), p. 836; William E. Leuchtenburg, *In the Shadow of FDR: From Harry Truman to Bill Clinton* (Ithaca, NY: Cornell University Press, 1993).

---

transition
The period after a presidential candidate has won the November election but before the candidate assumes office as President on January 20.

Since the beginning of a presidential term is so important, the **transition** period between the previous and the new presidency is critical. Transitions are the approximately seventy-five days between election day (the first Tuesday after the first Monday in November) and January 20, Inauguration Day. It is the one moment when incoming presidents have power without responsibility. They cannot be blamed for anything that happens, but those who want something from government are eager to cooperate. If the transition is well organized, this is the best of all times for building public support.

In a highly successful transition, Reagan asked his top advisers to prepare an extensive array of tax cuts, increases in the defense budget, domestic expenditure cuts, and cuts in government regulation. Bill Clinton's transition was much more painful. The gays in the military issue dogged him throughout, and his nominee for attorney general asked that her name be withdrawn because of a controversy surrounding her failure to pay social security taxes for a household employee.

The transition period is typically followed by the presidential honeymoon, the first several months of a presidency when reporters are kinder than usual, Congress more inclined to be cooperative, and the public receptive to new approaches.[48] Ronald Reagan's reputation as a strong president owes much to his accomplishments during his honeymoon period. Controlled by the opposition party, Congress

at first seemed prepared to defy his wishes, but when Reagan survived an assassin's bullet with spirit and self-confidence, presidential popularity soared and Congress acquiesced to many of his requests.

Some have wondered whether presidential honeymoons have gone the way of LP records and wooden tennis rackets. As public expectations have risen and presidents have become ever more exposed to media scrutiny, chief executives may no longer count on a period of good will before facing determined opposition.[49] Certainly, Bill Clinton's honeymoon hardly lasted the time it took him to traverse the Inauguration Day parade route from the Capitol to the White House. "By Memorial Day," one scholar has noted, "Clinton gave an address at the Vietnam War memorial that was met by a highly vocal and hostile crowd."[50] Only later did Clinton recover somewhat from one of the most "shallow and brief" of presidential honeymoons.[51] Presidents sometimes enjoy a brief second honeymoon after their reelection. Ronald Reagan managed to use this moment to initiate a major tax reform. Clinton used his second honeymoon to achieve a balanced budget.

Clinton suffered different transition and "honeymoon" periods: (left) Bill Clinton announcing his position on gays in the military, before taking office in 1993; and (right) protesters at his Vietnam Memorial speech on Memorial Day 1993.

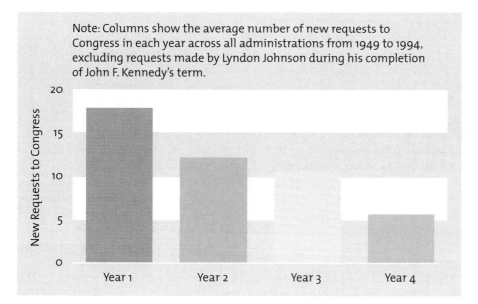

Note: Columns show the average number of new requests to Congress in each year across all administrations from 1949 to 1994, excluding requests made by Lyndon Johnson during his completion of John F. Kennedy's term.

New Requests to Congress

Year 1   Year 2   Year 3   Year 4

FIGURE 13.5

The Presidential Legislative Agenda: It's Largest in First Year

SOURCES: Calculations are based on data drawn from Lyn Ragsdale, *Vital Statistics on the Presidency* (Washington, DC: CQ Press, 1996).

At times, particularly when being upstaged by the national turkey at Thanksgiving, it is difficult for a president to maintain his dignity.

■ efficient aspect
Distinct from the dignified aspect, according to Walter Bagehot, the aspect of government that involves making policy, administering the laws, and settling disputes.

■ dignified aspect
According to Walter Bagehot, the aspect of government, including royalty and ceremony, that generates citizen respect and loyalty.

THE PRESIDENT AS CHIEF OF STATE

PRESIDENTIAL POWER: *The President "shall receive Ambassadors and other public Ministers. . . and shall Commission all the Officers of the United States."*

CONGRESSIONAL CHECK: *None.*

One of the very few unchecked powers granted to the president, this constitutional clause seems to say little more than that presidents may welcome visitors and administer oaths of office. Yet the words endow presidents with an invaluable political resource, the capacity to act with all the dignity countries give their heads of state. In many countries the political leader and the head of state are institutionally separated (see International Comparison). In the United States the president fulfills both roles.

According to Walter Bagehot, an analyst of British politics, governments have both **efficient** and **dignified aspects**.[52] The efficient aspect of government involves the making of policy, the administration of the laws, and the settling of political disputes. This is the nuts and bolts of day-to-day policy making, the kind of activity enjoyed by the Washington insider, often derisively called a "policy wonk". It is also hard work that often generates conflict. But government also has a dignified aspect that Bagehot thought equally important to long-term effectiveness. Governments must express the unity of the people, their high moral purposes, their hopes for the future, and their capacity to defend themselves against foreign aggressors. Ceremonial occasions provide opportunities for expression of the dignified aspect of government that help sustain public trust and loyalty.

The dignified aspect of the presidency has always stood in tension with the egalitarian ideals of American democracy. One of the issues discussed in the very first Congress was the manner by which President George Washington should be addressed. A Senate committee recommended that he be addressed as "His Highness the President of the United States of America, and Protector of their Liberties." When the House of Representatives objected to the royal language, the Senate agreed to address Washington simply as "the President of the United States." Washington himself preferred the simpler language. He wrote privately to a friend: "Happily the matter is now done with, I hope never to be revived."[53] To this day, the simpler form of address remains in use.

Early American presidents were expected to play only a limited role in the efficient aspect of government so that they could enhance the dignity of the national government and serve as a unifying symbol for a far-flung country. By remaining distant from day-to-day legislative politics, presidents tried to retain the respect and admiration of citizens from throughout the country. As presidents have become increasingly engaged in the efficient aspect of government, it has at times made it difficult for them to maintain their dignity. In the words of one novelist, presidents must learn to "appreciate the gentle absurdity of Dignity skating on the thinnest of ice with the placid sang-froid of the truly courageous."[54]

The Watergate crisis during the presidency of Richard Nixon took a particularly severe toll. As president, Nixon enjoyed the pomp and circumstance of office. He liked to listen to the presidential song, "Hail to the Chief," and to review at strict attention ranks of marching soldiers. Nixon's vaguely royal pretensions seemed harmless enough until many people felt that an all-too-royal president was endangering democratic practice.

After Nixon's resignation, his successors deemphasized the splendor of the office. Gerald Ford adopted a folksy, informal manner. Jimmy Carter wore a sweater, carried his own suitcases, and remained on a nickname basis with ordinary

In many countries the political leader and the chief of state are institutionally separated. In Great Britain, for example, the dignified chief of state is the Queen. She symbolizes the unity of the nation and represents her country on formal international occasions. She presides over national holidays. The efficient aspect of British government is headed by the country's prime minister. Though powerful, prime ministers lack royal dignity. Their residence is a modest home tucked away in a small London side street. Before assuming ministerial responsibilities, they must first accept on bended knee Her Majesty's request that they form a government.

The division of political responsibilities in Japan is much the same. The Emperor of Japan is the dignified chief of state; the elected prime minister is—in ceremonial terms—nothing more than the Emperor's efficient minister. Of course, the dignified Queen and Emperor have very little real power, but their presence as a symbol of the unity of the nation reminds people that the ministers can be ejected by the voters at any time.

In the United States, presidents are expected to combine in their one person both the efficient and dignified aspects of government. In addition to their political and policy tasks, presidents are expected to be the symbol of national unity. When Queens and Emperors assemble, the United States is represented by its president. On days of national celebration, such as Independence Day and Thanksgiving, it is the president who is called upon to express national hopes and dreams. Presidents live in the White House, which though modest by the standards of European and Japanese castles, has become an increasingly grand focal point of Washington society. An invitation to a White House dinner party, jazz concert, or movie preview is for many Washingtonians the quintessential social achievement. Some people gave large campaign contributions in 1996 just to sleep in the Lincoln bedroom.

voters. At the same time, Carter became deeply involved in the efficient aspects of government, working late into the night on policy issues and foreign policy crises. Carter's concession to presidential dignity had its costs. When American diplomats were taken hostage in Iran, many blamed the president for appearing too weak.

Ronald Reagan worked assiduously to restore grandeur to the presidential office. White House social events once again became formal affairs. The unveiling of a restored Statue of Liberty was carefully designed to celebrate the country's past and future. At the same time, Reagan withdrew from day-to-day legislative politics. By emphasizing the dignity of the office, Reagan acquired the title, "Teflon President," because bad news seemed not to stick to him.

In the first year of his presidency, Bill Clinton took quite the opposite tack. Instead of emphasizing broad themes, he became known as a policy wonk. Toward the end of his first year in office, President Clinton met with a group of scholars who advised him "to pull back from the immediate details of policies and programs . . . and to explain what is at stake morally and politically in these policies." The president responded by making a series of speeches condemning violence on television and crime in the

President Jimmy Carter was a regular guy even when meeting with international chiefs of state. He donned his trademark sweater for meetings with Anwar Sadat at Camp David.

streets, and calling for an end to the "great crisis of the spirit that is gripping America today."[55] The change helped him gather greater public support in subsequent years. In short, a president's dignity, if not carried to royalist extremes, can be a valuable political asset.

THE FIRST LADY

■ **First Lady**
Traditional title of the president's spouse.

Historically, the role of the president's spouse, traditionally called the **First Lady,** was to reinforce the dignified aspect of the presidency. In keeping with the traditional role women have played in American society, First Ladies typically hosted social events, visited the sick, promoted children's issues, and loyally stood by their husbands in times of trouble. Yet some were able to use this dignified role to make contributions that will long be remembered. Jackie Kennedy invigorated Washington art and culture and restored the White House. Lady Bird Johnson committed herself to the beautification of Washington. Nancy Reagan's "Just Say No" educational program may have done more to reduce drug use than billions of dollars spent in anti-drug enforcement efforts.[56]

Few First Ladies were as effective at managing the dignified aspect of the presidency as Barbara Bush. Her large family, graying hair, unflappable demeanor, and genuine concern for other people, together with her relentless refusal to comment on any policy question, gave her a grandmotherly appeal that crossed all political boundaries. Her book on her dog, Millie, became a national best-seller, out-selling her husband's memoirs by a wide margin.

Not all First Ladies have been content to confine themselves to the dignified aspect of the presidency, however. Eleanor Roosevelt promoted civil rights and other social causes supported only off-handedly by her husband.[57] But it has been Hillary Rodham Clinton who has given the role of the First Lady a dramatically new definition. She became known as the president's top adviser and she was asked to lead the presidential health care task force.[58] Her policy involvement has won the praise of some, but, together with her alleged involvement in the Whitewater scandal, it has taken a toll on her popularity with the public in general. As can be seen in Figure 13.6, Hillary Clinton was less popular than her predecessor, Barbara Bush. On the other hand, her activist definition of the First Lady role made her noticeably

FIGURE 13.6

Popularity of the First Lady

SOURCE: Data are from polls taken by the Gallup Organization on January 24–26, 1989 (for Barbara Bush) and April 22–24, 1993 (for Hillary Clinton).

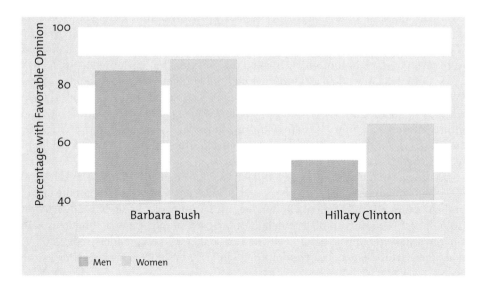

more popular among women than men. To enhance her public image, Hillary Clinton began deemphasizing her policy responsibilities and enlarged her dignified role by concentrating on children's issues.

It remains to be seen whether Hillary Clinton's assumption of political and policy responsibilities will permanently redefine the role of the First Lady. Her involvement in politics and policy is consistent with the increased acceptance of women as equal participants in political life. Yet presidents incur a special risk when they ask the First Lady to assume policy responsibilities. The role will be redefined most profoundly when the position is referred to as First Gentleman.

THE VICE PRESIDENT

Traditionally, the vice president's efficient impact on policy has been so limited that the office suffered in dignity as well. The nation's first vice president, John Adams, wrote to his wife, "My country has in its wisdom contrived for me the most insignificant office that ever the invention of man contrived. . . . I can do neither good nor evil." Franklin Roosevelt's vice president, John Garner, claimed the job "isn't worth a pitcher of warm spit." Harry Truman, when vice president, allowed it was "about as useful as a cow's fifth teat."[59]

Jokes about the vice presidency have a basis in reality. The only formal responsibility is to preside over the United States Senate and cast a vote in case of a tie. Otherwise, the vice president's responsibilities and influence depend entirely upon the will of the president. As Vice President Hubert Humphrey put it, "He who giveth can taketh away and often does."[60]

Presidents have traditionally been reluctant to delegate responsibility to vice presidents, because they inherently constitute a potential political problem. Presidents cannot fire their vice presidents, unlike other aides. If a vice president decides to criticize the president or pursue an independent policy line, the president can do little about it. When Nelson Rockefeller pushed more liberal policies than those favored by Gerald Ford, he proved an embarrassment to the president. Some even claim the Rockefeller controversy cost Ford his re-election.

The vice-presidential selection process accentuates the potential for conflict, because vice presidents often come from a wing of the party opposite that of the president.[61] An aide to John Kennedy admitted that Lyndon Johnson was picked for vice president because "he was the leader of that segment of the party where Kennedy had very little strength—the South."[62] Carter's assistant said, "Mondale was chosen to run . . . precisely *because* he . . . was from a different area of the country and represented the other wing of the Democratic party."[63]

But if presidents have powerful incentives to limit the vice presidential role, one can no longer dismiss vice presidents as political lightweights. For one thing, no person is more likely to become president of the United States than the vice president, either through death, by resignation, or by winning the next election. Twelve of the 41 presidents of the United States held the office of vice president, and no less than half of the last eight presidents were vice presidents.

Perhaps because of the greater awareness that the vice president may one day gain the highest office, the role of the vice president has steadily increased. Perhaps the biggest change has occurred in the dignification of the office. Vice presidents now travel extensively in foreign countries, attend state funerals, speak at political party and interest group conventions, and act as substitutes for the president on state occasions. Their efficient role has also been enhanced. For example, Vice President Albert Gore has been key to shaping the Clinton Administration's environmental policy.

Barbara Bush's book about her dog, Millie, outsold her husband's memoirs by a wide margin.

INHERENT EXECUTIVE POWER

PRESIDENTIAL INHERENT EXECUTIVE POWER: *"The executive power shall be vested in a President."*

The Constitution says that "the executive power shall be vested in a President." Some have said this statement adds nothing to presidential power beyond the specific powers granted to the president. But many presidents have found in this clause the basis for a claim to additional rights and privileges. Presidential claims to **inherent executive power** have been invoked most frequently in making foreign policy (see Chapter 20). But presidents have asserted inherent executive power on other occasions as well. Teddy Roosevelt placed 46 million acres of public land into the National Forest just before signing a bill denying presidents the power to place any more land in the National Forest.[64] After leaving office, Roosevelt admitted: "My belief was that it was not only the [president's] right but his duty to do anything that the needs of the Nation demanded unless such action was forbidden by the Constitution or by its laws."[65]

EXECUTIVE ORDER

One way in which presidents use their inherent executive powers is by issuing **executive orders**, directives that carry the weight of law even though they were not enacted by Congress. After the Supreme Court said in 1936 executive orders were constitutional, they have increased in frequency and importance.[66] Executive orders were used by Harry Truman to desegregate the armed forces, by Lyndon Johnson to institute the first affirmative action program and by Ronald Reagan to forbid homosexuality in the military. These orders may not run contrary to congressional legislation and they may be overturned by congressional statute. When President Clinton proposed to issue an executive order reversing the ban on gays in the military, it was the threat of congressional action reversing the proposed order that forced the president to reach the "don't ask, don't tell" compromise discussed in the opening section of this chapter.

EXECUTIVE PRIVILEGE

The most controversial invocation of inherent executive powers has been the doctrine of **executive privilege**, the right of the president to deny Congress information it requests on the grounds that executive-branch conversations must be kept confidential. George Washington was the first to invoke executive privilege when he refused to provide Congress information on an ill-fated military expedition on the grounds that its "disclosure . . . would injure the public."[67] Ever since, presidents have claimed authority to withhold from Congress information on executive decision making. The Watergate scandal brought the question before the Supreme Court, which sanctioned the doctrine of executive privilege, saying that privileged communication among aides to the president was "fundamental to the operation of government and inextricably rooted in the separation of powers under the Constitution."[68]

Although Congress could not simply demand access to any and all conversations taking place among the president's advisers, the Supreme Court went on to say that executive privilege could not be invoked to cover up criminal conduct. Communication that might be privileged under other circumstances loses that status when wrongdoing occurs. Nor can it be left to the executive branch to decide whether the communication is part of a coverup. The disputed documents must be

---

inherent executive power
Presidential authority inherent to the executive branch of government, although not specifically mentioned in the Constitution.

executive order
A presidential directive that has the force of law, though it is not enacted by Congress.

executive privilege
The right of members of the executive branch to have private communications among themselves that need not be shared with Congress.

submitted to the court for its examination behind closed doors. When the Supreme Court examined the Watergate documents, sufficient evidence of criminal conduct was found that President Nixon was forced to release the documents. Because of this ruling, the Clinton Administration has reluctantly released many, but not all, documents connected with the Whitewater scandal.

THE IMPEACHMENT POWER

CONGRESSIONAL IMPEACHMENT POWER: *Presidents may be impeached by a majority of the House of Representatives for "high crimes and misdemeanors." The president is removed from office if the Senate convicts by a two-thirds vote.*

Nothing makes more clear the subordination of presidents to Congress than the fact that the House of Representatives can impeach and the Senate can convict and remove presidents from office. Though seldom used, the constitutional power of **impeachment** is no dead letter. Andrew Johnson was impeached in 1865, though the Senate, by one vote, failed to convict him.[69] Richard Nixon resigned in the face of almost certain impeachment in 1974.

The permanent establishment of the office of **independent counsel** in 1978 has enhanced the impeachment power of Congress. An independent counsel (called special prosecutor when originally set up during the Watergate Scandal) may be appointed whenever allegations of criminal conduct are made against high-ranking officials of the executive branch. Appointed by judges, the counselors are independent in the sense that they are entirely independent of any other executive branch official. No less than seventeen independent counsel investigations have taken place since 1974.[70] The Nixon precedent suggests that any time an independent counsel finds the president worthy to be charged with criminal conduct, it is likely that the House of Representatives will initiate impeachment proceedings. It is entirely possible that investigations and threats of impeachment will become regular features of presidential politics. Such a climate is an integral part of the election-driven, media-influenced political world of contemporary presidential politics.

■ **impeachment**
Recommendation by a majority of the House of Representatives that a president, other executive branch official, or judge of the federal courts be removed from office; removal depends upon 2/3 vote of Senate.

■ **independent counsel (originally called special prosecutor)**
Legal officer appointed by the court to investigate allegations of criminal activity against high-ranking members of the executive branch.

Presidential Expectations and Presidential Performance

Presidents are expected to be strong, yet presidential powers are limited. As a result, presidents seldom satisfy the hopes and aspirations of the voting public. Presidential successes are quickly forgotten, while their failures are often magnified by time. To sustain their reputation and effectiveness, presidents are forced to act with Machiavellian cleverness.

Presidents in the past were often able to cover ruthless actions with a cloak of dignity that the role of chief of state allowed them to wear. But as the life of the president becomes more open to the media, it grows ever more difficult to keep the cloak of dignity tightly wrapped. As Bill Clinton said one year into his presidency, "It is difficult for people to function in an environment in which they feel that their character, their values, and their motives are always suspect, and where the presumption here is against them."[71]

Niccolo Machiavelli

Lincoln, the Great Machiavellian

Presidents often find themselves in tough situations not much different from the circumstances faced by sixteenth-century rulers of northern Italian cities, who were constantly threatened by foreign invasions and internal coups. The strategic advice the great theorist Niccolò Machiavelli gave these rulers has remarkable applicability to modern presidents. Most Americans believe Lincoln to be their greatest president, but few realize he was also the greatest Machiavellian. Machiavelli's advice can be reduced to three maxims, all of which Lincoln followed:

Maxim I: Be energetic, decisive, and sudden.

At the very beginning of his presidency, Lincoln perceived the benefits that came from acting suddenly and decisively. Even before he had taken the Oath of Office, seven southern states had seceded from the Union. Lincoln knew that the longer the Confederate states had to organize an armed force, the more likely the secession would become permanent. Lincoln was also concerned that Congress would be reluctant to initiate military action. Following Machiavelli's advice, Lincoln moved quickly while Congress was in recess. Just days after his Inauguration, he, in his role as commander in chief, ordered the U.S. Navy to resupply South Carolina's Fort Sumter. The Confederates, claiming the fort as theirs, shot at northern ships as they entered the harbor. Blaming the southerners for having started the war (though he had invited the attack), Lincoln appealed to northerners to join a volunteer army. Now that blood had been shed, new recruits poured into Washington.

Maxim II: Make plans in secret

Lincoln wrote the Emancipation Proclamation that freed the slaves two months before announcing it, and he chose not to announce the proclamation until the Union army had won a significant victory. Otherwise the proclamation might have appeared to be an act of desperation and perhaps even caused loyal slave states, such as Kentucky and Missouri, to defect to the Confederacy.

Maxim III: Only one ruler is possible

According to ancient legends, Rome was founded by two brothers, Romulus and Remus. When the two became rulers of the city, Romulus killed Remus. Machiavelli thought the killing was justified, because the existence of two rulers invites a contest for power.

When Lincoln assumed office, he was thought to be little more than a lightweight, storytelling attorney from a small, frontier town. Most cabinet members thought they were more qualified to serve as president than Lincoln. But he proved tougher and more shrewd than any of the others. On one occasion, when every member of the cabinet opposed him, he declared the vote as follows: "Seven nays, one aye—the ayes have it."

SOURCES: Harvey Mansfield, Jr., *Taming The Prince: The Ambivalence of Modern Executive Power* (New York: Free Press, 1989); James McPherson, *The Battle Cry of Freedom: The Civil War Era* (New York: Oxford University Press, 1988), pp. 264–75, 505; Frederic Austin Ogg and P. Orman Ray, *Introduction to American Government,* 10th ed. (New York: Appleton-Century-Crofts, 1951), p. 394.

PRESIDENTIAL REPUTATIONS

To meet public expectations with limited power, presidents need to protect their professional reputation among members of Congress and other **beltway insiders**, the politically influential people who live inside the beltway surrounding Washington, D.C.[72] Presidential reputations inside Washington are shaped by the quality of the people surrounding the presidents and the frequency with which presidents win political contests. They also depend on the ability to let go of issues that cannot be won. As Lincoln put it, "When you have got an elephant by the hind legs and he is trying to run away, it is best to let him run."[73]

The epitome of the active-negative president, grimly determined to do his duty until the end, Richard Nixon doggedly repeats his "V for victory" sign upon leaving office on August 9, 1974.

PRESIDENTIAL POPULARITY

In addition to guarding their professional reputation, presidents need to maintain their **presidential popularity** with the general public. As Abraham Lincoln shrewdly observed, "With public sentiment, nothing can fail; without it, nothing can succeed."[74] Presidential popularity is measured by asking the adult population how well they think the president is doing at his job. Since the question is now asked on an almost weekly basis, it provides a reasonably decent barometer of the public's current assessment of presidential performance.

All presidents experience considerable fluctuations in popularity over the course of their term. Their support rises and falls with changes in the country's economic conditions (see Chapter 19) and in response to foreign policy crises (see Chapter 20). But in addition to these external factors, presidential popularity tends to slide over time as public expectations go unfulfilled.[75] A study of the first term of eight recent presidents indicates that, separate and apart from any specific economic or foreign policy events, their popularity fell by nearly eight points in their first year in office and by 15 points by the middle of their third year (see Figure 13.7). Their popularity recovered in their fourth year, when a presidential campaign is under way, probably because presidents make special efforts to communicate positive news about their administration. Presidents regain popularity when reelected for a second term, but once again it tails off.

President Clinton had less public support at the beginning of his first term, but it did not decay over time. During his first year, only 48 percent of Americans thought he was doing a good job; the percentage rose slightly to 52 percent in his second and third years, and to 53 percent his fourth year.[76] The usual tendency for presidential support to drop was probably offset in this case by steady economic growth.

Presidential popularity and professional reputation were at one time regarded as two quite separate phenomena. Unpopular presidents could still have the respect of beltway insiders, if they husbanded their political resources carefully. But as public opinion presses ever more insistently on Washington decision making, the distinction between popularity and reputation has become clouded.[77] Presidents are the focus of seemingly inexhaustible but utterly exhausting television, radio, and newspaper

- **beltway insider**
  Person living in Washington metropolitan area who is engaged in, or well informed about, national politics and government.
- **presidential popularity**
  Evaluation of president by voters, usually as measured by a survey question asking adult population how well they think the president is doing his job.

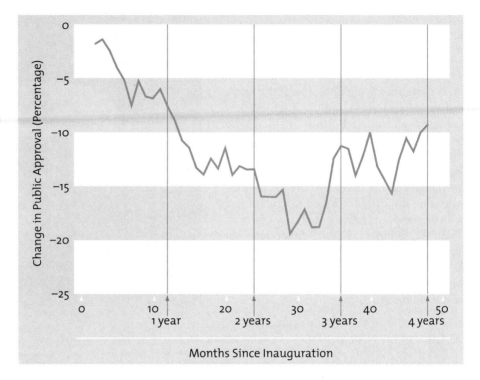

FIGURE 13.7

Decline in Presidential Popularity over the First Term. President's popularity typically declines until year before election.

SOURCE: This figure is taken from Paul Brace and Barbara Hinckley, *Follow the Leader: Opinion Polls and the Modern Presidents* (New York: Basic Books, 1992), p. 33, Figure 2.3.

coverage. They are the objects of what has been called the "politics of high exposure." As soon as they have addressed one problem, they are urged to resolve the next. As one commentator put it, "Getting the public's attention, particularly on a subject that the polls show is already gnawing at people, is no trick for a President. . . . The trick is holding that attention."[78]

The one kind of attention presidents are likely to hold is the kind they don't want. When George Bush became nauseous at a state dinner in Tokyo, the consequences were fully reported in news headlines. When Bill Clinton apparently held up traffic at the Los Angeles airport to get a $200 haircut, the incident became grist for TV comics.

If these kinds of incidents cause a president's popularity to slip, weekly polling results transmit this information to beltway insiders. If the president's reputation is slipping in Washington, the news media just as quickly communicates insider opinions to the wider public. As a result, the president now has to work both the inside and the outside of the beltway at the same time.[79]

GREAT PRESIDENTS

All presidents are challenged by problems and opponents both at home and abroad, and all find it difficult to preserve both professional reputation and public popularity throughout their term of office. Yet some presidents are remembered as "Great Presidents," because they achieve many of the objectives they set for themselves; others are seemingly unable to tackle the problems they face. Why do some succeed and others fail?

In a study of presidential character, James Barber argued that certain personality traits make for successful presidents (see Figure 13.8).[80] He said effective presidents both like their job and readily adapt their policies to changing circumstances. He called these presidents "active-positives." For Barber, Franklin Roosevelt was the ideal active-positive president. He loved his job as president, and he brought great

How the President Feels about What He Does	How Much Energy the President Has	
	High	Low
Enjoys	Active-Positive Examples Jefferson F.D. Roosevelt	Passive-Positive Examples Madison Eisenhower
Is Discouraged	Active-Negative Examples John Adams L.B. Johnson Nixon	Passive-Negative Examples Washington Coolidge

FIGURE 13.8

Presidential Character: Does Presidential Effectiveness Depend on Presidential Attitudes and Energy?

SOURCE: Adapted from James Barber, *The Presidential Character: Predicting Performance in the White House* (Englewood Cliffs, NJ: Prentice-Hall, 1992).

energy to it. He changed his mind frequently, but always with an eye to solving governmental problems. No wonder he was reelected three times.

Barber argued that most other modern presidents lacked one or the other of these two character traits. President Eisenhower brought a positive attitude toward his job, but Barber thought he was too passive. Instead of taking the initiative, he waited for others to pose solutions to problems. Barber claimed that both Lyndon Johnson and Richard Nixon brought an active-negative attitude to the job. Both were grimly determined to do their duty to the end. Though both brought energy to the job, neither could adapt to new circumstances. As a result, each pursued a policy position long after a more adaptive president would have changed course. Johnson led the country ever more deeply into the Vietnam War; Nixon tried to "cover up" Watergate misdeeds when he may have been better advised to let the problem come immediately to the surface.

Critics of Barber's schema say he placed too much emphasis on presidential activity.[81] Jimmy Carter and Bill Clinton have both been active policy wonks, but they have not always been successful in achieving their goals. Eisenhower appeared to be passive, but presidential analyst Fred Greenstein shows that he governed with a "hidden hand."[82] Though Ike let others grab the headlines, he steered the ship from behind, staying out of controversy and preserving his popularity. Reagan was hardly a policy wonk—on the contrary, he seldom let the presidency interfere with a good afternoon nap.[83] Yet his use of the power of the dignified presidency, together with his focus on fundamental goals, made him a powerful political force.

Presidential success may depend less on personality than on the circumstances under which the newly elected come into office.[84] Presidential scholar Stephen Skowronek says that most are so hemmed in by the checks placed upon them they simply cannot accomplish the job the public expects. As a result, presidents become "great" only when a political realignment allows them to repudiate the past (on political realignment, see Chapter 8, p. 240). The act of repudiation allows them to break through the institutional fetters that ordinarily limit presidential action.

Franklin Roosevelt is once again the archetypal effective president. Running for office in 1932 in the midst of the recession, he declared "these unhappy times call for…plans…that build from the bottom up and not from the top down, that put their faith once more in the forgotten man." After an election that realigned the American party system, Roosevelt pushed through major legislation in his first one hundred days in office.

Roosevelt was not the first effective president who profited by a political realignment (see Table 13.2). Thomas Jefferson rejected the program of John Adams and the Federalist party, a party so badly defeated it never returned to national power. Republican Abraham Lincoln repudiated the Democratic party and its defense of slavery. Ronald Reagan rejected the growth in government under his predecessors, saying "Government is not the solution to our problem. Government is the problem."[85]

Skowronek's model is not perfect. Many people think Theodore Roosevelt was one of the country's most successful presidents, but he became president not through a realigning election but only because his predecessor, William McKinley, had been assassinated. And some people think other presidents—Eisenhower (for managing the Cold War) and Johnson (for initiating the Great Society)—deserve inclusion at the top of the list of presidents. But Skowronek does show that presidents are often most effective when they exercise their power to initiate new approaches. It is often left to others to bring things to a conclusion.

TABLE 13.2

Failure, Realignment, and Effective Presidents in American Politics:
Effective Presidents Assume Office after Electoral Realignments

Failure	Realignment/Election	Effective President
Articles of Confederation	1789	Washington
John Adams	1800	Jefferson
John Q. Adams	1828	Jackson
Buchanan	1860	Lincoln
Hoover	1932	Roosevelt
Carter	1980	Reagan

SOURCE: Based upon a study by Stephen Skowronek, *The Politics Presidents Make* (Cambridge, MA: Harvard University Press, 1993).

Chapter Summary

Presidents must meet the high expectations of their national and partisan constituencies, despite the fact that Congress checks many of their most important powers. Presidents can initiate legislation, but Congress often rejects or substantially modifies their proposals. Presidents can appoint executive and judicial officers, but the Senate must approve them. Presidents may invoke inherent executive power, including the right of executive privilege, but Congress can impeach them. Though the president can veto congressional bills, presidential leadership depends most heavily on the power of the chief executive to initiate and persuade, capacities that come as much from the dignity of the office as from any specific clauses in the Constitution.

To achieve their goals, presidents must preserve their professional reputation and their political popularity. Because their popularity tends to slip over time, it is at the beginning of their presidency—during the transition and honeymoon periods—that they have the greatest capacity to initiate change. Great presidents emerge not so much because they have the right personal qualities as because they come to office when the country thinks it is time for a change.

Key Terms

administration, p. 428

beltway insider, p. 443

bully-pulpit, p. 425

cabinet, p. 428

chief of staff, p. 429

commander in chief, p. 418

dignified aspect, p. 436

efficient aspect, p. 436

Executive Office of the President (EOP), p. 429

executive order, p. 440

executive privilege, p. 440

First Lady, p. 438

impeachment, p. 441

independent counsel (originally called special prosecutor), p. 441

inherent executive power, p. 440

item veto, p. 427

one hundred days, p. 433

override, p. 426

pocket veto, p. 427

presidential popularity, p. 443

secretary, p. 428

State of the Union address, p. 423

transition, p. 434

veto power, p. 426

White House Office, p. 429

Suggested Readings

Barber, James. *The Presidential Character: Predicting Performance in the White House.* Englewood Cliffs, NJ: Prentice-Hall, 1972. Premise is that presidential character affects presidential success.

Jones, Charles. *The Presidency in a Separated System.* Washington, DC: Brookings, 1994. Examines the role of the president under divided government.

Kernell, Samuel. *Going Public: New Strategies of Presidential Leadership.* Washington, DC: Congressional Quarterly, 1986. Describes the increasing tendency of presidents to use popular appeals to influence legislative processes.

Korn, Jessica. *The Power of Separation: American Constitutionalism and the Myth of the Legislative Veto.* Princeton: Princeton University Press, 1996. Identifies the many ways power is shared between Congress and the executive.

Moe, Terry. "The Politicized Presidency," in John Chubb and Paul E. Peterson, eds., *The New Direction in American Politics.* Washington, DC: Brookings, 1985. Insightful essay on the evolution of the White House staff.

Nelson, Michael, ed., *The Presidency and the Political System,* 4th ed. Washington, DC: Congressional Quarterly, 1994. Important contemporary essays on the presidency.

Neustadt, Richard E. *Presidential Power and the Modern Presidents.* New York: Free Press, 1990. Modern classic on the limits to presidential power.

Skowronek, Stephen. *The Politics Presidents Make: Leadership from John Adams to George Bush.* Cambridge, MA: Harvard, 1993. Provocative analysis of the historical development of the presidency.

Sundquist, James L. *The Decline and Resurgence of Congress.* Washington, DC: Brookings, 1981. Authoritative description of the growth in presidential powers and responsibilities as well as congressional response to same.

Tulis, Jeffrey. *The Rhetorical Presidency.* Princeton: Princeton University Press, 1987. Contrasts modern presidential rhetoric with that of early presidents. Argues against a rhetorical presidency.

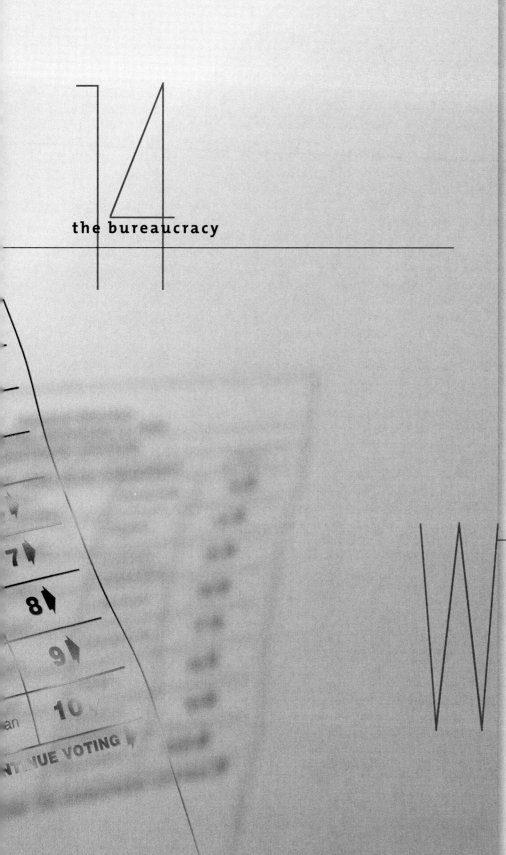

14
the bureaucracy

E CAN NO LONGER afford to pay more for—and get less from—our government," declared Bill Clinton and Al Gore in their first presidential campaign. "It is time ... to shift from top-down bureaucracy to entrepreneurial government."[1] To do this, Vice President Gore issued a report on "reinventing government," containing hundreds of proposals expected to save over $100 billion. The federal government would no longer order "designer bug sprays" or pay more for computer discs than those who buy at discount stores.[2] Gore's plan was well received. According to one poll, 95 percent of the public believed that the government wasted "a great deal" or "quite a lot" of the taxpayers' dollars.[3] "Make no mistake about this," the president said. "This is one report that will not gather dust in a warehouse."[4]

Among other things, Gore proposed to "transfer [the] law enforcement functions of the Drug Enforcement Administration [DEA] and the Bureau of Alcohol, Tobacco and Firearms [ATF] to the Federal Bureau of Investigation [FBI]." The missions of the three overlapped. ATF enforced laws regulating the sale and use of alcohol, tobacco, and firearms, DEA enforced the drug laws, and the FBI's job included all these responsibilities and many more. In 1992, DEA received $758 million to fight narcotics; the FBI got $205 million.

Duplication of efforts was not just inefficient; it was dangerous. "It is not uncommon for agents from one . . . agency to believe the other to be the criminal element," said a draft version of the Gore study. It concluded that "this . . . could result in life-threatening situations."[5] In part because ATF and FBI had overlapping responsibilities, in 1993 they bungled an attempt to capture arms held by the Branch Davidians, a heavily armed religious sect living in Waco, Texas. When agents sought to overrun the dwelling, the sect's leaders set fire to the building, causing death by immolation to fifty-one adults and children.

Despite the president's commitment, Gore's proposal failed to get off the ground. Within days of its announcement, the idea was scuttled by bureaucratic and congressional opponents. ATF was located within the Department of the Treasury, headed by Secretary Lloyd Bentsen—the most powerful member of the first Clinton cabinet—who let it be known he did not want to give up part of his turf. The DEA also had its supporters. Representative Charles Rangel, head of the House Caucus on Drugs, said the merger "would be a monumental mistake."[6] To anyone familiar with the culture of DEA and the FBI, a merger between the two seemed inconceivable. DEA agents often arrived at work in jeans, ponytails, and earrings, while the FBI wore the garb of Wall Street bankers. Said one DEA agent, "An FBI guy's idea of undercover is to loosen his tie."[7] In the end, the reorganization was abandoned.

President Clinton is not the first president to have tried—and failed—to reform the federal bureaucracy. As one member of Congress observed, "We all know that the toughest things in Washington are the turf wars. . . . No [congressional] committee likes their authority cut back."[8]

hough an essential part of government, bureaucracies have bedeviled many presidents. The problem is caused partly by characteristics inherent to all bureaucracies, but it is also caused in part by a connection between bureaucracies and elections that is particularly American. Though the origins of these connections are buried deep in American history, they continue to affect contemporary practice. Control of government bureaucracies is divided between Congress and the president, making coherent administration more difficult. Most American bureaucracies nonetheless somehow muddle through.

The Bureaucracy Problem

Bureaucracies, organizations designed to perform a particular set of tasks, are essential to governmental action. Laws become effective only when a government agency implements them. Without some kind of organization, government cannot build roads, operate schools, put out fires, fight wars, send out social security checks or do the thousands of other things Americans expect from their government. When performing their tasks, bureaucracies necessarily have great **administrative discretion**, the power to interpret their legislative mandates. Congress can enact general rules but it cannot anticipate every circumstance, nor can it apply these rules to every individual case. Congress may decide to provide benefits to the disabled, but it is up to a bureaucrat, in this case an official within the social security agency, to decide whether a particular handicap precludes employment.[9] Congress may decide to give loans to college students from families of moderate income, but it is up to a bureaucrat, in this case an officer within the Department of Education, to decide what family resources count as income.

As the range of governmental responsibilities has grown, the number of bureaucrats in the United States has also greatly increased. The greatest growth has occurred at state and local levels, where are employed the vast majority of civilian government workers, including school teachers, police officers, and sanitation workers (see Figure 14.1). In addition, many private contractors perform tasks paid for by government agencies. Though the number of employees who work directly for the federal government is smaller, we shall focus most of our attention on federal bureaucracies, because their policies and regulations are far-reaching and their impact is felt throughout the country.

The **agency**, also known as the *office* or *bureau*, is the basic organizational unit of the federal government. It is the entity specifically assigned by Congress to carry out a task. There are 181 federal agencies within the executive branch.[10] Some 80 of the 400 agencies are free-standing entities that report either to the president or to a

> ■ **bureaucracy**
> Organization designed to perform a particular set of tasks.

> ■ **administrative discretion**
> Power to interpret a legislative mandate.

> ■ **agency**
> Basic organizational unit of federal government. Also known as *office* or *bureau*.

Unexpected bureaucrats: these handlers feeding sea lions at the National Zoo are as much members of the federal bureaucracy as IRS employees.

board; the remainder are grouped into **departments**, collections of related agencies that report to a secretary who serves in the president's cabinet.

In theory, agencies and departments are modern bureaucracies that are rationally organized so they can achieve their objectives efficiently. People hired to work in the bureaucracy are selected for their ability to do the job. Each reports to his or her superior, with ultimate authority exercised by the head of the agency. The bureaucracy supplies each worker with the necessary materials and supplies to get the job done. The ideal is best exemplified by soldiers on parade, marching together in lockstep formation. When all works perfectly, bureaucracies have tremendous unity, focus, and power.[11] But many factors inhibit perfection. Bureaucracies face impossible tasks, their performance is difficult to measure, they have an urge to expand, they are slow to change, and they are often mired in red tape. Taken together, these factors create what is known as the bureaucracy problem.[12]

IMPOSSIBILITY OF TASKS

Most governmental tasks are extremely hard to accomplish. If they were easy, someone other than the government would have undertaken the job. Tasks are usually complex and potentially unlimited.[13] Schools are expected to teach students—but there is no end to what students might learn. Transportation agencies are expected to achieve smooth-flowing traffic—but to avoid all bottlenecks in most large cities, one would have to pave almost everything. The Environmental Protection Agency is supposed to protect the environment from pollutants—but almost all human activity increases pollution in some way.

FIGURE **14.1**

Government Employment, 1946–1992

SOURCE: Data are taken from the U.S. Bureau of the Census, *Historical Statistics of the United States: Colonial Times to 1970* (Washington, DC: GPO, 1975), 1100, 1141; Advisory Commission on Intergovernment Relations, *Significant Features of Fiscal Federalism 1994* (Washington, DC: 1994), Table E; Harold W. Stanley and Richard G. Niemi, *Vital Statistics on American Politics*, 4th ed. (Washington, DC: CQ Press, 1994), 359–60.

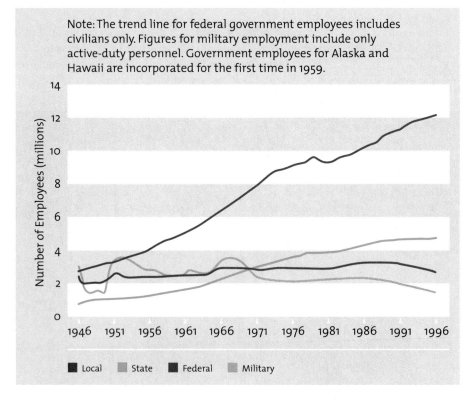

Note: The trend line for federal government employees includes civilians only. Figures for military employment include only active-duty personnel. Government employees for Alaska and Hawaii are incorporated for the first time in 1959.

The Environmental Protection Agency (EPA) faces one of the most impossible of bureaucratic tasks: protecting the environment from all manner of pollutants.

MEASURING PERFORMANCE

It is often difficult to measure the performance of government bureaucracies.[14] If the streets and parks are strewn with garbage and litter, one is tempted to criticize the government. But the garbage problem usually has more to do with the habits of residents than with the efficiency of the sanitation bureau. Since it is hard to measure the performance of most government bureaucracies, it is difficult for supervisors to tell whether work is being performed carefully and promptly. As a result, government bureaucracies often have a reputation for inefficiency.

EXPANSIONARY TENDENCIES

Once they are created to address a problem, bureaucracies generally try to expand so they can better address it. Government agencies almost always feel they need more money, more personnel, and more time to perform their tasks effectively.[15] There is nothing new about this propensity. "You may blame the War Department for a great many things," General Douglas MacArthur said back in 1935, "but you cannot blame us for not asking for money. That is one fault to which we plead not guilty." In much the same vein, the head of the Forest Service once exclaimed to a congressional committee: "Mr. Chairman, you would not think that it would be proper for me to be in charge of this work and not be enthusiastic about it and not think that I ought to have more money, would you? I have been in it for thirty years, and I believe in it."[16]

SLUGGISHNESS

Any large governmental organization has standard procedures through which it makes its decisions. And most standard procedures are absolutely essential if large numbers of people are to work toward some common end in a coordinated manner. If procedures were not standardized, those working within the bureaucracy would be so confused they would soon be unable to do anything.

Standard procedures nonetheless make bureaucracies sluggish, slow to adjust to new circumstances.[17] Schools still provide long summer holidays originally allowed so that children could help harvest crops on the family farm. The U.S. customs service issued forms in the 1970s that "have not changed to any great extent since 1790, and merchant vessels today are required to report on the number of guns mounted."[18] As one humorist observed, "Bureaucracy defends the status quo long past the time when the quo has lost its status."[19]

RED TAPE

Everyone complains about government red tape, but, as one analyst has observed, "one person's red tape may be another's treasured procedural safeguard."[20] People often complain, for example, that it takes forever to get a bridge repaired. But bridge repair can be politically complicated: The design of the replacement bridge must be acceptable to neighbors. If the bridge is regarded as a historical landmark—and a surprising number of bridges are so designated—the approval of an historical commission must be obtained. After the design is approved, the agency, when letting contracts, must advertise the job and allow time for the submission of bids. To avoid accusations of political favoritism, the choice of contractors must be made deliberately and according to published criteria. And the repairs themselves must be subject to careful inspection to make sure the bridge does not collapse upon completion.

After the 1994 Los Angeles earthquake destroyed many bridges and roadways, seriously crippling metropolitan traffic, the Department of Transportation waived the usual procedural safeguards and promised the contractor extra payment, if the work could be done ahead of schedule. The end result: a record-breaking restoration of key roadways within eighty-five days.[21] But red tape was eliminated in this case only because the public insisted that time was of the essence.

American Bureaucracies: Particularly Political

The bureaucracy problem can be found in all countries, but American bureaucracies have special characteristics rooted in their country's unusual political history. As a result, U.S. bureaucracies have several distinctive qualities. They had a difficult beginning, were built with patronage, and were slowly modernized by a "bottom-up" civil service reform.

DIFFICULT BEGINNINGS

American bureaucrats lack the royal blood that runs through the veins of those in Europe and Japan, where government departments evolved out of the household of the King, Queen, or Emperor. King Louis XIV constructed a great French administration within the Palace of Versailles. Japan's powerful bureaucracy owes its prestige to an historic relationship to the Emperor. The extraordinarily efficient German administration, which became a model for the world, descended from the household of the King of Prussia. The lineage of federal bureaucrats in the United States is less distinguished. As one scholar has pointed out, "In England, France and Germany, . . . it is considered an honor simply to serve the state. . . . . In the United States civil servants, instead of being regarded with honor, are often considered tax eaters, drones, grafters, and bureaucrats."[22]

The original bureaucratic planners of the District of Columbia seemed doomed from the start. They had visions of Versailles (left), but the location they chose to work with was so swampy (above) that few people opted to live there.

The American Revolution was fought against the King's bureaucrats. At the time the Constitution was being written, the framers could not even agree on where to put the people who were to run the national government. Finally, as part of a compromise, they agreed to locate the District of Columbia, the new home of the federal government, on the Maryland–Virginia border near the small town of Washington—on land so swampy and unusable that at the time only a few people had chosen to live there. When federal officials arrived in Washington, D.C., in 1800, they considered the city utterly despicable. According to one political scientist, early residents found the:

> climate intolerable. The place was a menace to health, pervaded with "contaminated vapour" which brought on all sorts of "auges and other complaints." The public buildings were "large naked ugly buildings" surrounded with fences "unfit for a decent barnyard." [23]

⭐ **AT THE STATE & LOCAL LEVEL**

MOUNTAINS OF PATRONAGE

Not only did the disreputable appearance of the District of Columbia reinforce early American suspicion of the federal government, but bureaucrats received a second blow when President Andrew Jackson, after the election of 1828, handed out to political followers political **patronage,** consisting of government jobs, contracts, and other favors (see Election Connection). The practice of hiring workers on the basis of party loyalty became known as the **spoils system** when New York Senator William Marcy attacked President Andrew Jackson for seeing "nothing wrong in the rule that to the victor belong the spoils."[24]

Politicians in both political parties quickly discovered that the spoils system suited their needs.[25] Local, state, and national elections occurred frequently, making campaign tasks many and time-consuming. By handing out patronage, party politicians found it easier to find campaign workers to take on such thankless jobs as passing out pamphlets, organizing rallies, and getting people out to vote. The New York machine politician George Washington Plunkitt explained the logic of patronage this way: "You can't keep an organization together without patronage. Men ain't in politics for nothin'. They want to get somethin' out of it."[26] Patronage

patronage
Jobs, contracts, or favors given to political friends and allies.

spoils system
A system of government employment in which workers are hired on the basis of party loyalty.

The Election of 1828 and the Spoils System

President Andrew Jackson's use of the spoils system was immediately lampooned by political cartoonists.

With the election of Andrew Jackson in 1828, patronage was made a staple of American national politics. Jackson replaced 2000 government workers with his own supporters, creating what came to be known as the spoils system. Jackson saw patronage as critical for building his campaign organization, but he also elevated patronage to the level of political principle. In Jackson's view, one person was as good as the next. Almost anyone could do government work. Everyone should take a turn. Government offices should rotate, giving new people a chance to learn the duties of citizenship.

By replacing learned experts with ordinary citizens, Jackson felt he was making government democratic. The spoils system ensured that the government administrators were in tune with the views of the people. It also got rid of malcontents who might frustrate the new government. But it meant appointment of unsavory political cronies to positions such as New York customs collector, a job with a wealth of patronage opportunities. Jackson's appointee absconded to England when it became apparent that his account was short a million dollars.

also made it easier for parties to raise the large amounts of cash that frequent elections required. Every Pennsylvania state employee received the following letter from the Republican State Committee: "Two percent of your salary is _____. Please remit promptly. At the close of the campaign we shall place a list of those who have not paid in the hands of the head of the department you are in."[27] Further, these practices were not conducted in secret; politicians felt they were a natural part of politics. As one delegate to a national convention once shouted out, "What are we here for, except for the offices [government jobs]?"[28]

Plunkitt defended patronage politics by making the fine distinction between dishonest and honest graft. Dishonest graft wasted the taxpayers' money. Honest graft simply paid a friend to build a bridge or roadway that needed to be constructed anyway. Or as the patronage-prone Mayor of Chicago, Richard J. Daley, once said, when asked to explain why he had given the city's insurance business to one of his sons, "If a man can't put his arms around his sons, then what kind of a world are we living in?. . . I make no apologies to anyone. There are many men in this room whose fathers helped them, and they went on to become fine public officials."[29] (Mayor Daley's eldest son, Richard M. Daley, is today mayor of Chicago.)

Looking back on American political history, many scholars have found much to praise in the old spoils system.[30] For one thing, it helped immigrant Americans adjust to the realities of urban life. "I think there's got to be in every ward somebody that any bloke can come to— no matter what he's done—and get help," said one Boston politician. "Help, you understand; none of your law and your justice, but help."[31] Some of the help took the form of jobs in city government. Irish immigrants were particularly good at using politics as a way of getting ahead. In Chicago, the percentage of public-school principals of Irish background rose from 3 percent in the 1860s to 25 percent in 1914. In San Francisco, it climbed from 4 percent to 34 percent over a similar period of time.[32]

The Mayors Richard Daley, father and son, in a moment of family resemblance.

Contemporary affirmative action programs have many of the same pluses and minuses as the old-fashioned spoils system. When African Americans became part of urban governing coalitions, they gained better access to government jobs by invoking the principle of affirmative action.[33] Nationwide, African Americans are more likely to get a job in government than in the private sector (see Figure 14.2a), a sign that politics still seems to help some disadvantaged groups get a toehold on

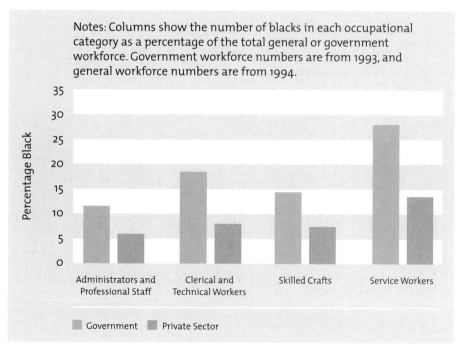

Notes: Columns show the number of blacks in each occupational category as a percentage of the total general or government workforce. Government workforce numbers are from 1993, and general workforce numbers are from 1994.

FIGURE 14.2A

Black Representation in State and Local Government Compared to Private Sector

SOURCE: Data for the private sector are for the U.S. workforce as a whole and are taken from the U.S. Bureau of the Census, *Statistical Abstract of the United States 1995* (Washington, DC: Government Printing Office), Table No. 649; data for the government workforce are taken from the U.S. Equal Employment Opportunity Commission, *Job Patterns for Minorities and Women in State and Local Government 1993* (Washington, DC: EEOC, 1994), Table 2.

the ladder to success. However, government employment for Hispanics still lags behind their role in the private sector, probably because the percentage of Hispanics who vote and otherwise participate in politics remains comparatively low (see Figure 14.2b).

If the spoils system helped incorporate immigrants into American politics and society, it nonetheless contributed to the negative image suffered by American bureaucracies. Education, training, and experience counted for little, and jobholders changed each time a new party came to power. As one Democratic leader joked after his party had been in power for years, a bureaucrat was "a Democrat who holds some office that a Republican wants."[34] Max Weber, the great German theorist of bureaucracy, said Americans told him they "prefer having people in office whom we can spit upon, rather than a caste of officials who spit upon us, as is the case with you [Europeans]."[35]

In many European countries, bureaucrats are more likely to "spit" on citizens, because government officials are much less subject to electoral pressures. Political parties have little patronage, and administrative matters are left to a **civil service**, professionally qualified public officials recruited for a career in government. Members of the civil service are expected not to have an overt allegiance to any particular party.

Though the U.S. spoils system was also eventually replaced by a civil service (see next section), the many decades of patronage politics have left an antibureaucratic legacy that continues to the present day. Many Americans agree with Neville Shute, who said "a civil servant is still to me an arrogant fool until he is proved otherwise."[36] Three-fourths of all Americans think "people in the government waste a lot of money we pay in taxes (see Figure 14.3)."[37] When Americans were asked how

■ **civil service**
Government employees chosen according to their educational qualifications, performance on examinations, and work experience.

FIGURE **14.2B**

Hispanic Representation in Local/State Government Workforce Compared to the Private Sector

SOURCE: Data for the private sector are for the U.S. workforce as a whole and are taken from the U.S. Bureau of the Census, *Statistical Abstract of the United States 1995* (Washington, DC: Government Printing Office), Table No. 649; data for the government workforce are taken from the U.S. Equal Employment Opportunity Commission, *Job Patterns for Minorities and Women in State and Local Government 1993* (Washington, DC: EEOC, 1994), Table 2.

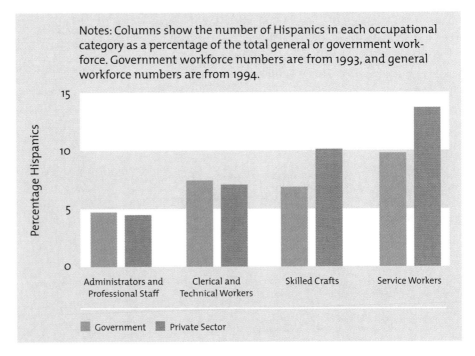

Notes: Columns show the number of Hispanics in each occupational category as a percentage of the total general or government workforce. Government workforce numbers are from 1993, and general workforce numbers are from 1994.

NATHANIEL HAWTHORNE'S DESCRIPTION OF LIFE IN A CUSTOM HOUSE

The great American author Nathaniel Hawthorne held a top patronage job between 1847 and 1849, when he served as the surveyor for the Custom House for the Port of Salem, Massachusetts. A loyal Democrat, he was fired from his job when the Whigs captured the presidency. Hawthorne was accused of paying his Democratic employees more than Whig workers.* In the introduction to his novel, *The Scarlet Letter*, Hawthorne described life at the Custom House in the following words:†

> On ascending the steps [to the Custom House], you would discern a row of venerable figures, sitting in old-fashioned chairs, which were tipped on their hind legs back against the wall. These old gentlemen were Custom House officers.

> They were ancient sea-captains, for the most part, who, after being tost [sic] on every sea had finally drifted into this quiet nook; with little to disturb them, except the periodical terrors of a presidential election.

> Two or three of their number, being gouty and rheumatic, or perhaps bedridden, never dreamed of making their appearance at the Custom House during a large part of the year; but, after a torpid winter, would creep out into the warm sunshine of May or June, go lazily about what they termed duty, and, at their own leisure and convenience, betake themselves to bed again.

> They spent a good deal of time, also, asleep in the accustomed corners, with their chairs tilted back against the wall; awaking, however, once or twice in a forenoon, to bore one another with the several thousandth repetition of old sea-stories, and mouldy jokes.

> Mighty was their fuss about little matters, and marvelous, sometimes, the obtuseness that allowed greater ones to slip between their fingers! Whenever such a mischance occurred,—when a wagon-load of valuable merchandise had been smuggled ashore, at noonday, perhaps, and directly beneath their unsuspicious noses,—nothing could exceed the vigilance and alacrity with which they proceeded to lock and double lock and secure with tape and sealing-wax, after the mischief had happened.

* James R. Mellow, *Nathaniel Hawthorne in His Times* (Boston: Houghton Mifflin, 1980), 289-97.

† Selected with ellipses deleted.

SOURCE: Nathaniel Hawthorne, *The Scarlet Letter* (Boston: Houghton Mifflin, 1885), 21, 28-31.

Nathaniel Hawthorne and the men of the Salem Custom House.

they would rate the "ethical and moral practices" of federal government workers, only 33 percent came up with a rating of good or excellent. (Americans were otherwise quite lenient in their evaluations; even college professors got a rating of 69 percent! See Figure 14.4).

FIGURE 14.3

Public Opinion on Waste in
Government

SOURCE: Data are taken from the
National Election Study, 1952–1994
(cumulative data file), conducted
by the Center for Political Studies
at the University of Michigan.

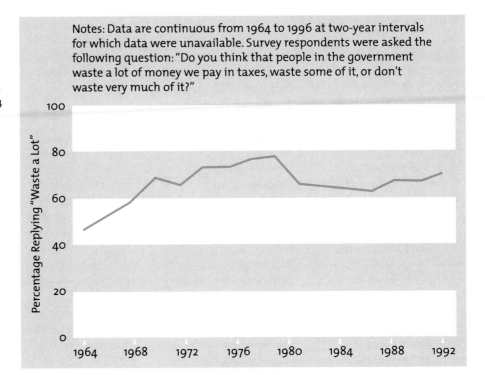

Notes: Data are continuous from 1964 to 1996 at two-year intervals for which data were unavailable. Survey respondents were asked the following question: "Do you think that people in the government waste a lot of money we pay in taxes, waste some of it, or don't waste very much of it?"

FIGURE 14.4

Ratings of the Ethical and
Moral Practices of Government
Workers Compared to Other
Occupational Groups

SOURCE: Gary King and Lyn
Ragsdale, *The Elusive Executive:
Discovering Statistical Patterns in
the Presidency* (Washington, DC:
CQ Press, 1988), 368. (Data shown
are taken only from the 1985
column of Table 6.21.)

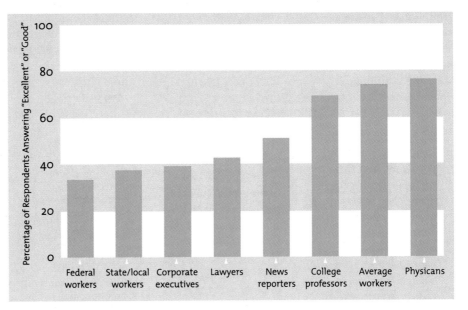

mugwumps
A group of civil service reformers
organized in the 1880s who said
government officials should be
chosen on a merit basis.

EROSION OF THE SPOILS SYSTEM

The mountains of patronage created by the spoils system were gradually eroded by civil service reformers who, in the 1880s, were called **mugwumps**. A group of professors, journalists, clerics, and businessmen, mugwumps said government officials should be chosen on the basis of merit, not for their political connections.

Originally a term of abuse, the name is a modification of a Native American word meaning "holier than thou." Mugwumps were also scorned for refusing to back either party. It was said that their "mugs" peered over one side of the fence while their "wumps" stuck out over the other. Mugwumps, in turn, accused politicians of appointing political hacks. One clergyman accused the mayor of Boston of appointing saloon keepers and bartenders to public office.

If the mountains of patronage did not erode easily, mugwumps won a succession of modest victories that gradually changed the system. Their first major breakthrough came in 1881 when President James Garfield was assassinated by a madman said to be a disappointed office-seeker. Public scrutiny focused on the new president, Chester Arthur, who had once served as the New York customs collector and seemed the very personification of the spoils system. As the demand for reform swept the country, Congress passed—and Arthur signed—the **Pendleton Act**, which created a Civil Service Commission to set up qualifications, examinations, and procedures for getting many government jobs.

■ **Pendleton Act**
Legislation in 1881 creating the Civil Service Commission.

Civil service reform was bottom up. Requirements initially applied mainly to ordinary jobs—those who swept the floors and typed government forms. Gradually, more positions were incorporated into the civil service; additions were especially plentiful when the party in power expected defeat. By making a job part of the civil service, soon-to-be-defeated presidents "blanketed in" their supporters, making it impossible for their successors to replace them with patronage workers from the other party. Eventually, civil service reform became so complete that in 1939 Congress passed the **Hatch Act**, which prohibited federal employees from political campaigning and solicitation. The mountains of patronage were all but worn away.

■ **Hatch Act**
1939 law prohibiting federal employees from political campaigning and solicitation.

POLITICAL APPOINTEES TODAY

In the deserts of Arizona and New Mexico one can find mesas—often called islands in the desert—that tower over surrounding flatland. All that remain of ancient mountains, long eroded by wind and water, mesas are ecologically distinct from the surrounding desert.

Just as one finds geological mesas in the deserts of the West, one can locate patronage mesas that have survived decades of civil service reform. One of the most populated patronage mesas is also the most prestigious, for it includes thousands of policy makers at the top levels of the federal government. It consists of most members of the White House staff, the heads of most departments and agencies, and the members of most government boards and commissions. Political appointees also predominate in offices bearing such titles as deputy secretary, undersecretary, deputy undersecretary, assistant secretary, deputy assistant secretary, and special assistant.

This high-level patronage mesa is becoming increasingly crowded. The estimated number of top-level agency appointees grew from less than 500 in 1960 to nearly 2500 in 1992 (see Figure 14.5). Adding the White House staff, the total number of high-ranking patronage positions is estimated to be close to 3 thousand.[38] No other industrial democracy gives its leader as much patronage power (see International Comparison).

The president's ability to hire political allies for the top echelon of government has both advantages and disadvantages. On the positive side, it allows presidents-elect to bring many new people with innovative ideas into government. For example,

FIGURE 14.5

High-Level Patronage Appointments in the Average Government Department

SOURCE: Paul Light, *Thickening Government* (Washington, DC: Brookings, 1995), 12, Table 1.3.

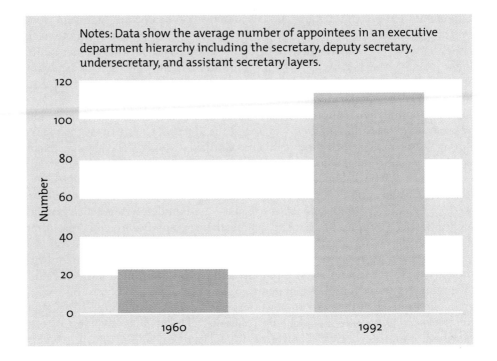

Notes: Data show the average number of appointees in an executive department hierarchy including the secretary, deputy secretary, undersecretary, and assistant secretary layers.

President Reagan's dramatic tax and expenditure cuts were designed by think-tank experts and leaders from business and industry. The wholesale changeover in personnel also helps presidents introduce their political agendas with minimal resistance from an entrenched bureaucracy. President Clinton's economic recovery package and health reforms were designed without the aid or obstruction of leftover Bush advisers. Indeed, it is the presidential appointive power that makes presidents the most dynamic element in the American political system.

Yet the arrival of so many new faces at about the same time complicates government coordination. European and Japanese governments are marked by close, informal, long-time associations among leading administrators. In the United States, the average presidential appointee leaves office after only a little more than two years; almost a third leave in less than 18 months.[39] A member of Woodrow Wilson's cabinet admitted that "the average head of a department is not highly competent and has not first-rate executive ability, "[40] a view echoed three decades later by public administration expert Leonard White, who observed: "The previous experience of federal Secretaries does not usually prepare them to exercise quick and effective leadership."[41]

The turnover in high-level governmental personnel is so pervasive that it has been called a government of **in-and-outers**, people who come in, go out, and come back in again with each change in administration.[42] Because they cannot count on long-term employment with the government, most political appointees begin planning ways of making a satisfactory departure shortly after arrival. For some people, it will mean returning to their old positions in the business, legal, or academic worlds before losing their contacts there. For others, it will be a matter of using connections inside the beltway to win new financial opportunities in the private or nonprofit sectors. One deputy secretary leaving the Clinton administration

■ **in-and-outers**
Political appointees who come in, go out, and come back in again with each change in administration.

Most high-level administrative positions in Europe and Japan are occupied by well-educated, highly experienced, professional civil servants who refrain from participating actively in politics. Most achieve their positions by studying in prestigious training programs and spending years, even decades, in dedicated government service.

In the United States, high government officials often get their jobs only after gaining prominence outside government in business, law, medicine, education, or a policy institute. Usually, they will have worked in a presidential campaign, made financial contributions, or given other evidence of party loyalty. For example, Clinton's first two secretaries of commerce were not long-time government experts on trade policy but Ron Brown and Mickey Kantor, well-known Washington attorneys who had played key roles in the Clinton campaign. Similarly, President George Bush, when selecting his secretary of transportation, turned not to a long-time government servant who had worked on roads or airports but to Andrew Card, who had managed his political campaign in Massachusetts. Secretary Card, in turn, chose as his special assistant a loyal political aide who had been a member of the Massachusetts state legislature. Secretary Card admitted that his aide could not answer any questions on transportation policy but would nonetheless be an invaluable adviser because he was "a politician in the very positive sense of the word." As one wag put it, "One of the principal qualifications for a political job is that the applicant know nothing much about what he is expected to do."

The less professional, more political orientation of high-level appointees in the United States is due in part to the fact that the bureaucracy must respond to both president and Congress. In most other industrial democracies, the legislative branch has less direct influence over the bureaucracy. Where the bureaucracy has only one master, bureaucrats can be professionals instead of politicians.

SOURCES: Harry Eckstein, "The British Political System," in Samuel Beer and Adam Ulam, eds., *Patterns of Government: The Major Political Systems of Europe* (New York: Random House, 1962), 158–68; Hugh Heclo, *Modern Social Politics in Britain and Sweden: From Relief to Income Maintenance* (New Haven: Yale University Press, 1974); Paul Pierson, *Dismantling the Welfare State* (New York: Cambridge University Press, 1994); Kent Weaver, Bert Rothman, and Terry M. Townsend, as quoted in Henning, *Wit and Wisdom of Politics*, 11.

just one year after joining it was asked whether he had any regrets. "Yes," he replied. "I should have rented," instead of incurring the costs of buying a house in Washington.

These rapid changes in personnel leave government without the continuity necessary for sustained policy focus (see Democratic Dilemma). The newcomers bring energy and ideas, but by the time their ideas are turned into plans that can be brought

Should Bureaucratic Leaders Be Professional Experts or Loyal Partisans?

Presidents often must choose between knowledgeable professionals and long-time political associates. The first bring more expertise to the task of government, the second are more loyal to presidents. Presidential scholars differ as to what presidents need most. With whom do you agree?

Neutral competence consists of giving one's cooperation and best independent judgment to a succession of partisan leaders.

Neutral competence is valuable in a number of ways. For one thing, it improves the capacity of elected leadership to get what it wants out of the government machine. [It] accumulates informal sources of information within the bureaucracy, sources otherwise unavailable to transient political appointees. [It] has a vested interest in continuity. Agencies and officials with this attribute temper boldness with the recognition that they will have to live with the consequences of misplaced boldness.

—Hugh Heclo[a]

Presidents are up against institutional arrangements purposely designed to limit and obstruct the very leadership presidents are trying to exercise. The president [can] mitigate these problems [by] two strategies: he can politicize and he can centralize.

Presidents [can politicize] by using their appointment authority to place their own people—loyal, ideologically compatible people—in pivotal positions to ensure that important bureaucratic decisions are placed in the hands of presidential agents.

Presidents can [also] try to see that most of the important decisions are not made "out there" at all, but inside the presidency proper. They can shift the locus of effective decision authority to the center by building presidential organizations whose job it is to make and enforce rules [that] have the effect of limiting agency discretion and shifting decision-making power to the president.

The bureaucracy does not want to be controlled, is structured to prevent it, and has resources to resist. The continuing problem for presidents is that they have far too little control, not too much.

—Terry Moe[a]

[a] Passages excerpted, ellipses deleted.

SOURCES: Hugh Heclo, "OMB and the Presidency—the Problem of 'Neutral Competence,'" *Public Interest* 38 (Winter 1975), 80–98; Terry Moe, "Presidents, Institutions and Theory," in George C. Edwards III, John H. Kessel, and Bert A. Rockman, eds., *Researching the Presidency: Vital Questions, New Approaches* (Pittsburgh: Pittsburgh University Press, 1993), 337–86.

to fruition, they are gone, only to be succeeded by another energetic group with an altogether different set of priorities. The newcomers also run the risk of trying to make too many changes at once. Clinton's inexperienced health policy experts tried to introduce such massive changes that their efforts collapsed under the weight of their own ambitions.[43]

With rapid change in personnel, governmental memory becomes as limited as that of an antiquated computer. One Japanese trade specialist who negotiated with the United States observed that the Japanese "look at politics in their historical perspective. . . . However, in the case of the U.S., almost all of their negotiators seem like they came in just yesterday."[44] At one point in 1994, the differing styles of top Japanese and U.S. bureaucrats created a relationship so abrasive that the two countries broke off trade negotiations on the eve of a summit meeting between their leaders.

Worst of all, the denial of most top-level positions to nonpolitical civil servants makes government service a less attractive career for intelligent, ambitious young people. In Japan, many of the top students graduating from the country's most prestigious law school go directly into government service, and the most gifted reach the highest levels of government. The peak of the U.S. government is not part of a large mountain that employees can gradually ascend a lifetime career. Instead, the top-level positions are ordinarily cut off from the surrounding civil service desert, reachable only by a patronage-filled presidential helicopter.

If young people knew that loyal government service could eventually be rewarded by promotion to high-level policy positions, many more might consider this an attractive career option. But the best advice that can be given to a young person who wants to achieve a high policy-making position is to do an internship with a member of Congress, build connections with a political party, achieve distinction outside the government, and wait for the right moment to *rent* a Washington home.

Congress and the Bureaucracy

It is a truism that no one should have more than one "boss." If two or more people can tell someone what to do, signals get confused, delays ensue, and accountability is undermined. Government bureaucrats in Japan and most European countries generally abide by this rule. Members of the civil service report to the heads of their departments, who report to the head of the government. Members of parliament have little to say about administrative matters.

Officially, federal bureaucrats in the United States have only one boss—the president, who according to the Constitution is the head of the executive branch. But they are also bossed by many in Congress. One House subcommittee chair declared, quite frankly, "I've been running the medicare system, or our committee has, for the past nine years. We're its board of directors."[45] With Congress divided into House and Senate, and each chamber divided into many committees, bureaucrats often find themselves with multiple committees all considering themselves "boards of directors." Further, the pressures on bureaucracies have intensified in an era of high exposure and perpetual campaigns. As Martha Derthick has observed, "while the U.S. Constitution has not changed . . . the presidency ha[s] become much more vigilant and intrusive . . . [while] Congress has become more critical."[46]

SENATE CONFIRMATIONS

Congressional influence begins with the very selection of executive department officers. The Senate's confirmation power has long given senators a voice in

senatorial courtesy
An informal rule that the Senate will not confirm nominees within or from a state unless they have the approval of the senior senator of the state from the president's party.

administrative matters, traditionally by the practice of **senatorial courtesy**. This courtesy consists of an informal rule that the Senate will not confirm nominees for positions within a state unless they have the approval of the senior senator of the state from the president's party. For example, Clinton's nomination of Massachusetts governor, William Weld, as Mexican ambassador in 1997 needed the approval of Massachusetts senior senator, Edward Kennedy. In this way, senators can protect their political base by controlling patronage and administrative practices within their state.

In recent years, the mass media have joined together senatorial confirmations and election strategies even more closely. In an age when strong visual images are needed for the television screen, confirmation processes make for good political theater. Nominees have private lives to be examined. They can be asked embarrassing questions during their confirmation hearings. Conflicts between nominees and senators can elevate a previously little-known senator to the national stage.

Because the confirmation process has greater election potential than ever before, senators want more than just the usual "courtesy" traditionally extended to senators from the nominee's home state. Senators now want to be assured that presidential nominees take acceptable policy positions, do not have private investments that conflict with their public duties, have not violated any laws, and have not acted contrary to conventional moral norms. The Senate rejected George Bush's nomination of John Tower as secretary of defense because he was known to have a drinking problem. It forced Bill Clinton to withdraw the nomination of Zoe Baird as attorney general because she had not paid social security taxes for her housemaid. It denied confirmation of Henry Foster as Clinton's surgeon-general because he had performed thirty-nine abortions when he originally recalled having conducted only a dozen. Governor Weld's nomination as Mexican ambassador was held up in 1997 because the governor, when district attorney, had allegedly not aggressively prosecuted drug dealers.

Senate rejections of presidential nominees are still the exception, not the rule. Yet the new, more election-driven confirmation process has had important consequences for government administration. To ensure that a nominee will not be rejected by the Senate, the White House must interview the potential nominee at length, ask the FBI to undertake an extensive check, and defend the nominee against exhaustive senatorial scrutiny. When John Kennedy was president, the average nominee was confirmed in less than two and one-half months after the president was inaugurated. The confirmation of Bill Clinton's average nominee required eight and one-half months (see Figure 14.6).

Prolonging the confirmation process strengthens congressional control over administrative matters. As long as agency heads await confirmation, they hesitate before taking actions that might offend members of Congress. Bill Clinton was without half his administrative team throughout much of his first year as president, the very year in which he was expected to give the country a new direction.

recess appointment
An appointment made when the Senate is in recess.

Under Article II of the Constitution, presidents may make **recess appointments** without Senate confirmation "during the Recess of the Senate." Recess appointees may serve until the end of the next session of Congress, at which point they must resign, if they have not been confirmed. Chief Justice Earl Warren, a recess appointment of President Eisenhower in the fall of 1953, served as Chief Justice even before he was confirmed by the Senate. Nothing in the Constitution precludes presidents from reappointing someone as a recess appointment, even if the

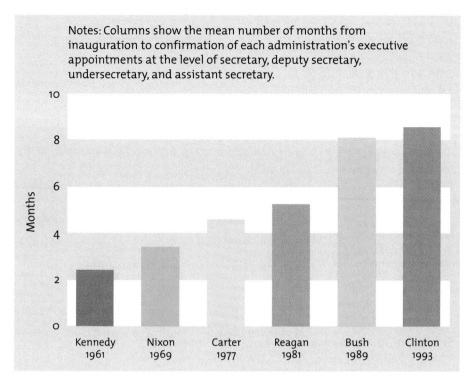

Notes: Columns show the mean number of months from inauguration to confirmation of each administration's executive appointments at the level of secretary, deputy secretary, undersecretary, and assistant secretary.

FIGURE 14.6

Average Time It Takes Presidential Appointees to Be Confirmed

SOURCE: Paul Light, *Thickening Government* (Washington, DC: Brookings, 1995), 68.

appointee is never confirmed. When Theodore Roosevelt could not secure confirmation of an African American as a customs collector in Charleston, South Carolina, the president reappointed him to the office during Senate recesses. Congress has since placed a check on the recess appointment power by passing legislation prohibiting payment of salary for service prior to Senate confirmation. As a result, presidents today seldom exercise this power over Congressional objections.[47]

CONGRESSIONAL TURF

In addition to influencing the appointments of agency heads, congressional subcommittees fight to keep jurisdictional control over agencies for which they have legislative responsibility.[48] As a result, they typically resist governmental reorganization, no matter how duplicative or antiquated existing organizational structures might be. For example, Jimmy Carter wanted to shift worker training programs from the Department of Labor to a newly created Department of Education. But powerful senators defeated the proposal because they wanted to keep the programs within their committee's jurisdiction.[49]

LEGISLATIVE DETAIL

The committees exercise their powers in part by writing detailed legislation. In European countries, most legislation is enacted in a form close to the draft prepared by the executive departments.[50] In Japan, 90 percent of all successful legislation is drafted by an executive agency.[51] In the United States, most legislation proposed by presidents is extensively revised by Congress.[52]

Even if the statute itself does not dwell on administrative issues, agency operations can be influenced by committee reports accompanying the legislation. The reports are considered by the courts as evidence of congressional intent and have frequently been given the force of law. Even in the absence of court action, agencies pay attention to committee reports. In the words of one observer, "That language [in the reports] isn't legally binding, but the agencies understand very well what happens if they ignore it."[53]

BUDGETARY CONTROL

Congress also controls agencies by means of the budget process. Every year each agency prepares a budget for the president to submit to Congress. Each agency must defend its budget before an appropriations subcommittee in both the House and Senate, and those who offend committee members put their funding in jeopardy. To ensure that agencies spend monies in ways consistent with congressional preferences, significant portions of many agency budgets are subject to an **earmark**, a very specific designation as to the way money is to be spent, sometimes specifying particular congressional districts. Earmarking seems to be on the increase. At one time Congress let the scientific research community decide national research priorities; but between 1980 and 1995, the amount of research dollars earmarked for specific projects skyrocketed from $11 million to $875 million,[54] often for pet projects at a representative's home university. The greatest "earmarker" of all time may be the former chair of the Senate Appropriations Committee, Robert Byrd, beloved by his constituents for earmarks requir-

■ **earmark**
A specific congressional designation as to the way money is to be spent.

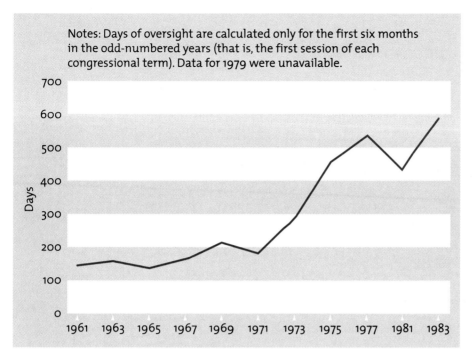

FIGURE **14.7**

Growth in the Number of Days of Congressional Oversight Hearings

SOURCE: Joel Aberbach, *Keeping a Watchful Eye* (Washington, DC: Brookings, 1990), 38.

Notes: Days of oversight are calculated only for the first six months in the odd-numbered years (that is, the first session of each congressional term). Data for 1979 were unavailable.

ing numerous agencies to locate their operations in his home state of West Virginia. He once slipped into an emergency bill a provision that shifted the 2,600-employee FBI fingerprinting center from downtown Washington to Clarksburg, West Virginia.[55]

LEGISLATIVE OVERSIGHT

Congressional committees have in recent decades expanded their control over administrative practice by holding more legislative oversight hearings. The number of days each year that committees hold oversight hearings nearly quadrupled between the 1960s and the 1980s (see Figure 14.7). At these hearings members of the administration are asked to testify on agency experiences and problems. Outside groups are given opportunities to praise or criticize the bureaucrats. Through the oversight process, committees obtain information that can be used to revise existing legislation or modify agency budgets.

IRON TRIANGLES AND ISSUE NETWORKS

Congressional influence is such a pervasive part of bureaucratic politics that many agencies—simply in order to survive—have found it necessary to build close connections to powerful interest groups. The connections among agencies, interest groups, and congressional committees have become so intimate that some political scientists say government in the United States is run by **iron triangles**.[56] Interest groups form the base of the triangle, because they have the membership and money that can influence the outcome of congressional elections, and agen-

■ **iron triangle**
Close, stable connection among agencies, interest groups, and congressional committees.

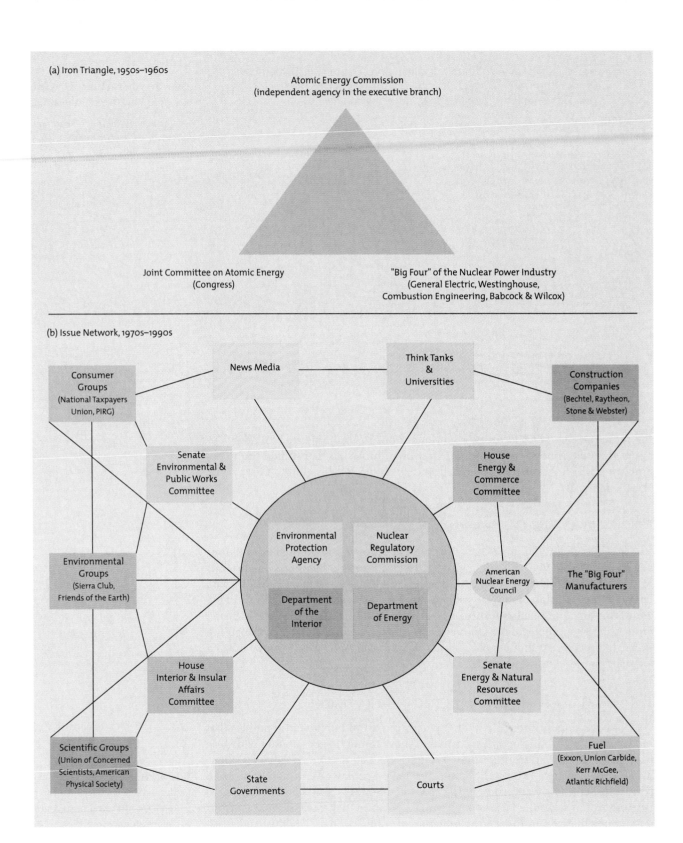

(a) Iron Triangle, 1950s–1960s

Atomic Energy Commission
(independent agency in the executive branch)

Joint Committee on Atomic Energy
(Congress)

"Big Four" of the Nuclear Power Industry
(General Electric, Westinghouse,
Combustion Engineering, Babcock & Wilcox)

(b) Issue Network, 1970s–1990s

Consumer Groups
(National Taxpayers Union, PIRG)

News Media

Think Tanks & Universities

Construction Companies
(Bechtel, Raytheon, Stone & Webster)

Senate Environmental & Public Works Committee

House Energy & Commerce Committee

Environmental Protection Agency

Nuclear Regulatory Commission

Department of the Interior

Department of Energy

American Nuclear Energy Council

Environmental Groups
(Sierra Club, Friends of the Earth)

The "Big Four" Manufacturers

House Interior & Insular Affairs Committee

Senate Energy & Natural Resources Committee

Scientific Groups
(Union of Concerned Scientists, American Physical Society)

State Governments

Courts

Fuel
(Exxon, Union Carbide, Kerr McGee, Atlantic Richfield)

cies listen to group demands to obtain committee backing (see Figure 14.8a). One agency head claimed he "could pick up the phone and find out more in ten minutes about what was happening on the Hill than the current White House staff could in a week."[57]

The relationship is said to be an *iron* triangle, because the connections among the threesome remain a lot more stable than the proverbial love triangle. In the case of the iron triangle, each of the three parties can deliver something the other needs. Compromises are readily arranged because interests are mutual. Most oversight hearings are in fact three-way love feasts. Agency work is adored by the groups it serves, and members of Congress add words of endearment. When a congressional scholar asked congressional committee staff whether they considered their committee to be agency advocates, nearly two-thirds said "yes." In response to this question, one staff person replied,

> *I think any subcommittee . . . whatever its subject is, they're advocates. I mean the Aging Subcommittee is advocating for aging programs, the Arts for arts, you know, Education for education, Health for health. They wouldn't be doing their work if they weren't interested.*

Added another:

> *The trouble of it is we get in bed with agency people in some respects. We're hoping that they'll distribute good projects in our state, you know, and it's a kind of a working with them so that, you know, there'll be more, more and better of everything for everybody.*[58]

This research was undertaken when Democrats controlled Congress. With the Republican takeover in 1995, the House leadership initially placed tight restrictions on committees in order to weaken the committee–agency relationship. Infuriated at the loss of committee power, Democrats on one committee complained "the Republican leadership has decided that the considered judgment of expert committees no longer matters."[59] But within a year the Republican leadership found it necessary to loosen its controls, and the natural tendency for committees to support "their" agencies began to assert itself. For example, House Republican leaders in 1995 proposed elimination of all funding for the public broadcasting corporation. "We were read our last rites," said the corporation's president. But after Republican members of the key congressional subcommittee were beseiged by letters and faxes from constituents, who feared the demise of "Sesame Street" and "Mister Rogers' Neighborhood," they voted to keep the agency alive, though at a reduced level of funding.[60]

Some iron triangles are no longer as rigid as they once were. As the number of interest groups and policy experts has expanded, congressional committees and government agencies have become bombarded with competing demands from multiple sides, which together form **issue networks** (see Figure 14.8b).[61] For example, nuclear energy policy was at one time of interest mainly to just four companies who built nuclear reactors and the utility companies that used the electricity. After an accident at the Three Mile Island reactor in Pennsylvania, the subject attracted the attention of environmental, safety, and antinuclear groups, all of whom pressed for tighter regulation of nuclear reactors. With the interests of the groups divided, the media took a greater interest in the issue, and conflict between congressional committees and the Department of Energy intensified.[62]

FIGURE 14.8 (opposite page)

Change of Nuclear Energy Policy Arena from Iron Triangle to Issue Network

SOURCE: Based on information in Seong-Ho Lim, "Changing Jurisdictional Boundaries in Congressional Oversight of Nuclear Energy Regulation: Impact of Public Salience." (Paper presented before the Annual Meeting of the American Political Science Association, 1992); Frank R. Baumgartner and Bryan D. Jones "Agency Dynamics and Policy Subsystems," *Journal of Politics* 53 (November 1991): 1044–74.

■ **issue networks**
Loose, competitive relationship among policy experts, interest groups, congressional committees, and government agencies.

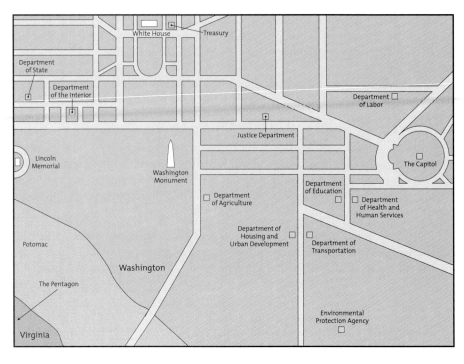

The appropriately baroque seat of the Office of Management and Budget, the Executive Office Building adjacent to the White House.

A Map with Location of Key Buildings in Washington

The physical location of the headquarters of the inner cabinet suggests the comparatively close ties these departments have to the president. Treasury is located next door to the White House. The walks from State and Justice are also shorter to the White House than to Capitol Hill. Defense, almost a world unto itself, is headquartered in the Pentagon in nearby Virginia.

Many of the departments of the outer cabinet are located at the foot of Capitol Hill. Here they hunker, almost on bended knee, faceless and humorless, in the shadow of the magnificent Capitol building shining brilliantly above them. Transportation, Education, Agriculture, Housing and Urban Development, and Health and Human Services all stumble over one another near the Hill's left foot in an unappealing corner of Washington that the tourist seldom sees. Labor pays its homage at the Hill's right foot. The Envi-

ronmental Protection Agency, though housed in a bedraggled part of town, still sits on a spot closer to the Hill than the White House. The Department of the Interior stands as an exception to this pattern. It is located close to the White House, despite its close ties to the interest group community.

The Office of Management and Budget (OMB) stands at the president's side, physically as well as metaphorically. When facing the front facade of the White House, one can see to the right a gargantuan Victorian building in which OMB's offices are to be found. Its ornate exterior gives a hint of the complexities of the budgetary processes taking place behind its doors.

Managing the Bureaucracy

Although most federal agencies must pay a good deal of attention to Congress, they are formally responsible to the president. Presidents exercise their control primarily by appointing political allies to top positions. But allies, once they become agency heads, can become more closely identified with their turf than with the president's program. As FDR's top budget adviser put it, "Cabinet members are vice presidents in charge of spending, and as such they are the natural enemies of the President." [63]

THE CABINET

Most federal agencies are located in one of the major departments. The secretaries for these departments, plus a few other top-ranking officials, form the president's cabinet (see Chapter 13). The four original departments are known as the **inner cabinet**, because their secretaries typically have easy access to the president.[64] These departments are:

- State, responsible for foreign policy

- Defense, originally called War, responsible for the military

- Treasury, responsible for tax collections, payments, and debt service

- Justice, headed by the Attorney General, who is responsible for law enforcement

A major function of the remaining departments of the cabinet, known as the **outer cabinet**, is to provide interest-group access into the executive branch of government.[65] The Interior Department's job was originally to regulate the use of federal land, particularly in the West. Today, it maintains close ties to ranchers, timber companies, mining interests, and others who depend on federal lands for their livelihood. The Agriculture Department serves farmers; the Commerce Department helps business and industry, especially with overseas contracts; Labor defends unions; Health and Human Services heeds the American Association for Retired Persons; and Education pays attention to teacher organizations (see Table 14.1).

The connections between departments and interest groups can change overnight, however, if an event activates the public spotlight. During the first Clinton Administration, the Department of Commerce worked hard to open up foreign markets to U.S. businesses. Secretary Ronald Brown, formerly chair of the Democratic Party, routinely escorted prominent corporate executives on trade missions throughout the world. In 1996, he literally gave his life to the cause when a military plane crashed in Bosnia, killing Brown, 13 business leaders, and other government officials. The trip was expected to yield U.S. contracts to help rebuild that war-torn country. Brown's trade missions had won applause in business circles, but his successor terminated them when the practice became tainted by reports that many of those accompanying Brown were contributors to the Clinton campaign.[66]

INDEPENDENT REGULATORY AGENCIES

Not all agencies are members of cabinet departments. Some of the most important of these, the **independent regulatory agencies**, have quasijudicial regulatory

inner cabinet
Four original departments (State, Treasury, Justice, and Defense) whose secretaries typically have the closest ties to the president.

outer cabinet
Newer departments with fewer ties to president and more influenced by interest group pressures.

independent regulatory agencies
Agencies that have quasi judicial responsibilities

TABLE 14.1

Establishment Year of Each Cabinet Department and Group Allies

Department	Year	Group Allies
Inner Cabinet		
State	1789	
Treasury	1789	
Justice (Attorney General)	1789	
War (Defense)	1789	
Outer Cabinet		
Interior	1849	Timber, miners, ranchers
Agriculture	1889	Farm Bureau and other farm groups
Commerce	1913	Chamber of Commerce
Labor	1913	AFL-CIO
Health and Human Services	1953	American Association of Retired Persons
Housing and Urban Development	1965	League of Cities
Transportation	1966	Auto manufacturers, truckers, airlines
Energy	1967	Gas, oil, nuclear interests
Education	1979	Teacher unions
Veterans Affairs	1987	American Legion, VFW
Environmental Protection Agency	1990	Sierra Club and other environmental groups

responsibilities, which are to be carried out in a manner free of presidential interference. These agencies are generally headed by a several-member board or commission appointed by the president and confirmed by the Senate. Independence from the president is achieved by giving board members appointments that last for several years (see Table 14.2). In a number of cases, presidents may not be able to appoint a majority of board members until well into their second term of office.

Most independent regulatory agencies were established in response to widespread public pressure to protect workers and consumers from negligent or abusive business practices. The Federal Trade Commission was created in 1914 in response to the discovery of misbranding and adulteration in the meatpacking industry. It was given the power to prevent price discrimination, unfair competition, false advertising, and other unfair business practices. The Securities and Exchange Commission was formed in 1934 to root out fraud, deception, and inside manipulation on Wall Street after the stock market crash of 1929 left many Americans suspicious of speculators and financiers.

When originally formed, most regulatory agencies aggressively pursued their reform mandates. But as the public's enthusiasm for reform fades, many agencies find their most interested constituents to be members of the very community they are expected to regulate. Thus, the independent commissions, too, have tended to become part of the world of iron triangles.[67] In one recent instance, a regulator's legal fight to keep his job was financed by those subject to his regulation. The three-person board of the National Credit Union Administration has responsibility for overseeing the nation's 12 thousand credit unions. When the term of board member Robert Swan

TABLE 14.2

Independent Agencies and their Group Allies

Independent Agency	Board Size	Length of Term	Group Allies
National Credit Union Administration	3	6	Credit Unions
Federal Reserve Board	7	14	Banks
Consumer Product Safety	5	5	Consumers Union
Equal Employment Opportunity	5	5	Civil rights groups
Federal Deposit Insurance Corporation	3	6[a]	Banks
Federal Energy Regulatory Commission	4	4	Oil/gas interests
Federal Maritime Commission	5	5	Fisheries
Federal Trade Commission	5	7	Business groups
National Labor Relations Board	5	5	Unions
Securities and Exchange Commission	5	5	Wall Street
Tennessee Valley Authority	3	9	Regional farmers and utilities

[a] One member, Comptroller of the Currency, has a five-year term.

expired, President Clinton nominated another to take his place. Arguing that he should keep his job until the new member was confirmed by the Senate (itself delayed by partisan bickering), Swan, with the financial help of the members of the National Association of Federal Credit Unions, filed suit in federal court. In the words of one critic: If Swan wins the suit, "He will be . . . beholden to the very people about whom he casts judgment." Swan nonetheless won strong support on Capitol Hill, with Speaker Newt Gingrich's writing the president that Swan's ouster might violate "laws relating to the tenure of government employees in independent agencies."[68] (For more on regulatory agencies, see Chapter 18, p. 599-608).

OFFICE OF MANAGEMENT AND BUDGET

Before 1921, every federal agency sent its own budget to Congress to be examined by an appropriations subcommittee. Without anyone to review all the requests, no one, not even the president, knew whether agency requests exceeded government revenues. When President Woodrow Wilson asked for a bureau to coordinate agency requests, Congress at first refused, saying such a bureau encroached on congressional authority. However, when federal deficits ballooned during World War I, Congress, under pressure to make government more efficient, relented and gave the president the needed help.

Originally known as the Bureau of the Budget, it is now called the **Office of Management and Budget (OMB)**, a name that reflects its enlarged set of responsibilities. Although development of the president's budget is still its most important responsibility, OMB also sets personnel policy and reviews every piece of proposed legislation submitted to Congress to see that it is consistent with the president's agenda. Agency regulations, too, now have to get OMB approval. Even preliminary drafts have to be reviewed by OMB before they are unveiled to the public. One bureau chief claimed OMB has "more control over individual agencies than . . . [the departmental] secretary or any of his assistants."[69]

■ **Office of Management and Budget (OMB)**
Agency responsible for coordinating work of executive branch departments and agencies.

Alice Rivlin, OMB director during President Clinton's first administration, en pointe.

end-run
Effort by agencies to avoid OMB controls by appealing to allies in Congress.

Congressional Budget Office (CBO)
Congressional agency that evaluates the president's budget as well as the budgetary implications of all other legislation.

OMB was once considered a professional group of technicians, who searched for budget cuts. But OMB has become more political as budget deficits have reached the center stage of electoral politics.[70] Former Congressman David Stockman, Reagan's OMB director, led the fiscal side of the Reagan revolution.[71] Bush's OMB director, Richard Darman, developed such a subtle, indirect style that politicians coined the word "darmonesque" to mean someone too clever to be believed. Clinton's initial OMB director, Leon Panetta, also a former member of Congress, became the White House chief of staff. Panetta's successor, Alice Rivlin, was more reminiscent of the professionals of the past: respected for her directness but disparaged by some for her green-shaded view of spending proposals. As the Clinton administration began its second term, the job was taken over by another well-respected Washington insider, Franklin Raines.

Although OMB has given presidents greater control over agencies, they can still make **end-run**s around OMB by appealing to their allies on Capitol Hill. When OMB tried to cut the budget of the Customs Service, the chair of the House subcommittee responsible for its appropriations objected:

> Sometimes after all of these years, I am getting the feeling there is somebody in the Office of Management and Budget that is carrying on an endless vendetta against the U.S. Customs Service.[72]

To check OMB's growing power, in 1974 Congress created the **Congressional Budget Office (CBO)**, which evaluates the president's budget as well as the budgetary implications of all other legislation. CBO's influence in Washington has grown to the point at which it now stands as a strong rival to OMB. In the health care policy debate, for example, it proved to be a "critical player in the game" whose estimates of the costs of health care reform doomed both presidential and congressional proposals.[73]

Elections and Administrative Performance

For more than a century, reformers have tried to separate politics from administration. Government should serve the people, not the special interests. Departments should make decisions according to laws and regulations, not in response to political pressure. Agencies should treat every applicant alike, not respond more favorably to those who contribute to political parties.

These reform principles are worthy of respect. When politics interfere, bureaucracies are often inefficient and ineffective. The post office, long a patronage reserve, is said to deliver snail mail. The customs service, its name once synonymous with political spoils, is still slow to report international economic transactions. The Department of Housing and Urban Development, always a political thicket, has at times so badly mismanaged its property it has had to blow up buildings it constructed.[74]

Many of the more effective federal bureaucracies are less politically charged.[75] The National Aeronautics and Space Agency was able to put men on the moon, because it originally operated with few political constraints. The National Science Foundation, protected by a board from political pressures, is known for the integrity with which it allocates dollars among competing scientific projects. Schools are more effective when they are freed of regulations and political interference.[76] The Federal Bureau of Prisons does a better job than many state prisons of maintaining security without depriving prisoners of rights; it has succeeded in part because members of Congress, respectful of prison leadership, have left the agency alone.[77]

BUREAUCRATIC SECRECY

Bureaucracies generally like to protect their secrets. Inside knowledge is power. Secrecy can cover mistakes. In Europe, where administrators are less exposed to electoral pressure, they work hard to guard their private information. In Britain, it is a crime for civil servants to divulge official information, and political appointees swear themselves to secrecy upon taking office.

Electoral pressures have sharply curtailed the amount of secrecy in American government. In the view of one specialist, "secrecy has less legitimacy as a governmental practice in the United States than in any other advanced industrial society with the possible exception of Sweden," in large part because "Congress has done a great deal to open up the affairs of bureaucracy to greater outside scrutiny."[78] The **sunshine law**, passed in 1976, required that federal government meetings be held in public, unless military plans, trade secrets, or personnel questions are under discussion. Under the Freedom of Information Act of 1967, citizens have the right to inspect unprotected government documents. If the government feels the requested information needs to be kept secret, it must bear the burden of proof when arguing its case before a judge.

Secrecy is hard for agencies to preserve, even when it is both permitted and essential. The tear-gas attack on Branch Davidians was announced ahead of time by an enterprising reporter for a Waco, Texas, radio station, who had gleaned the information from federal officials. Because the attack was no longer a surprise, the leaders of the Branch Davidians had time to organize their self-immolation (see chapter opening).

General Norman Schwarzkopf did a better job at preserving secrecy when U.S. troops invaded Kuwait in 1991. The army planned an end-run around Iraqi forces, surprising the enemy from behind. The surprise depended on keeping not only the enemy but the international press from finding out.

Some think that news management was one of General Norman Schwarzkopf's greatest military achievements during the Gulf War.

■ **sunshine law**
1976 law requiring federal government meetings to be held in public.

BUREAUCRATIC COERCION

Bureaucracies are often accused of using their coercive powers harshly and unfairly. Police stop young drivers for traffic violations that are often ignored when committed by older drivers. Bureaucratic zealots trap sales clerks into selling cigarettes to heavily bearded seventeen-year-olds. Disabled people are refused benefits because they do not fill out their applications correctly.

Although such abuses occur, they happen less frequently because agencies are held accountable to the electorate. For example, the Internal Revenue Service planned in 1995 to pick the names of thousands of people out of a hat and audit their tax returns, even though they had no reason to suspect any errors or misdeeds. The unlucky winners of this upside-down lottery were to explain their every financial transaction and document all deductions. The procedure, IRS said, would enable the agency to get a good estimate of the amount and kind of tax-cheating taking place. But when the plan was presented to Congress, members objected that innocent taxpayers should not be subjected to great inconvenience, intimidation, and expense just to satisfy IRS's desire to have good estimates. Under political pressure, IRS scaled back its plans.

AGENCY EXPANSION

Though agencies generally try to increase their budgets, elections brake such tendencies, if only for the reason that politicians get blamed for raising taxes. "As a general rule," says analyst Martha Derthick, "Congress likes to keep bureaucracy lean and cheap."[79] Keeping with that policy, Congress has in recent years cut expenditures on all domestic programs other than social security and medicare.[80] The number of people working for the federal government, as a percentage of the workforce, has also declined (see Figure 14.1), in good part because elected officials are under public pressure to cut bureaucracy.

ADMINISTRATOR CAUTION

Federal agencies are sometimes accused of going beyond their legislative mandates. But most federal agencies are more likely to err on the side of caution. For any agency, the worst thing that can happen is to make a major mistake that captures national attention. As one official explained, "The public servant soon learns that successes rarely rate a headline, but government blunders are front-page news. This recognition encourages the development of procedures designed less to achieve successes than to avoid blunders."[81]

In 1962 it was discovered, to everyone's horror, that thalidomide, a sedative available in Europe, increased the probability that babies would be born with serious physical deformities. Congress immediately passed a law toughening the procedures the Food and Drug Administration (FDA) needed to follow before approving prescription drugs for distribution.[82] Two decades later, in keeping with this policy, FDA refused to approve the sale of several experimental drugs to terminally ill people suffering from AIDS. Patients desperate to try anything did not share the FDA's concern for ascertaining proven effectiveness. When the FDA's refusal to allow experimentation became a public issue, the agency began to allow AIDS patients to try the untested drugs, once again responding to potential electoral pressures.

COMPROMISED CAPACITY

Agency effectiveness is often undermined by the very terms of the legislation that created it. For legislation to pass Congress, it is necessary to build a broad coalition of support. To do this, proponents must strike deals with those who are at best lukewarm to the idea. Such compromise can cripple a program at birth.[83]

The politics of charter schools illustrate the restraint that compromises can place on organizational effectiveness. School reform advocates have begun to establish charter schools—new schools free of most state regulations. Reformers expect charter schools to provide alternatives to and competition for traditional public schools. School boards and teacher organizations oppose the establishment of these schools, claiming they will undermine public education by attracting students away from their local schools. Many state legislatures, under pressure from both sides, have compromised the issue by passing legislation allowing charter schools but restricting their number, funding, and autonomy. It remains to be seen whether charter schools can prosper within the constraints imposed by these legislative compromises.[84]

MUDDLING THROUGH

American bureaucracies do not do as badly as most Americans think. One survey examines the actual experiences of clients encountering government bureaucracies, then compares their reactions to these experiences with the impressions that these same people have of government bureaucracies in general. The differences between actual experiences and general impressions are striking:

> *Seventy-one percent of all the clients said that their [own] problems were taken care of, but only 30 percent think that government agencies [generally] do well at taking care of problems. Eighty percent said that they were treated fairly, but only 42 percent think that government agencies treat most people fairly.*

> *In other words, most Americans . . . decide that their [good] experiences represent an exception to the rule. People who have had* bad *experiences, however, are likely . . . to think that everyone else is getting unfair treatment too.*[85]

When all the pluses and minuses are added up, the average government bureaucracy probably deserves something like a B minus. A few agencies, like NASA during the race to the moon, are A plus winners. A few others, like the customs service, don't deserve a passing grade. But the general tendency is toward a bland, risk-free mediocrity. Too much imagination generates too much controversy, which invites political retribution. The best way to survive politically is to try to muddle through.[86]

The forest service, responsible for managing most of the millions of acres owned by the federal government, does a pretty good job of muddling along. Although its rangers are professionally trained, talented individuals, its political problems are vexing. Ranchers, miners and timber companies want to exploit the land's natural resources. Others want to use the land for hiking, camping, and fishing. Environmentalists want to salt as much of the land as they can into wilderness areas for the benefit of future generations.

To balance these pressures, the forest service came up with the doctrine of multiple use. It proposed to manage the land in such a way that its multiple uses could be blended together and harmonized. Timber harvests should be accompanied by reforestation. Especially scenic areas should be preserved for recreational activities. Mining should be as inconspicuous as possible.

But the doctrine of multiple use did not so much resolve conflicts as legitimate them. As a result, the forest service is under continuous pressure. Ranching, timber, and mining interests have clout at the local level, where local political leaders make the potent claim that the local economy will suffer unless these interests are protected. Environmentalists have the greatest influence on those chosen in elections affected by the national media, which dramatically depicts the desecration of the American landscape.

Any attempt to balance these interests antagonizes one or more sides to the dispute. Only by muddling through can the forest service survive politically and manage the federal lands as well as it does.[87]

Chapter Summary

Government bureaucracies and bureaucratic problems are inevitable. But American bureaucracies have specific troubles that owe much to the electoral climate in which they have evolved. Federal agencies suffer an opprobrium that goes back to their very founding in a mosquito-infested swamp called the District of Columbia. With the creation of the spoils system, bureaucrats were often regarded as slow, inefficient, corrupt political hacks. Gradually, civil service reforms eliminated the worst of the abuses. But the reforms were bottom-up, not top-down. The highest levels of government continue to be filled with political appointees—generally capable but not always experienced government administrators.

Congress influences federal agencies by means of the confirmation process, legislative enactments, the budget process, oversight, and casework. To survive, agencies build ties to key interest groups, who form the base of what are known as iron triangles.

Elections influence agencies in diverse ways. On the one hand, they keep agencies from becoming too secretive and coercive. On the other hand, they can also make agencies too cautious or force them to operate under compromised laws that undermine their effectiveness. Most of the time, agencies respond to politics by muddling through, for which they deserve more credit than they usually get.

Key Terms

Suggested Readings

Chubb, John, and Terry Moe. *Politics, Markets and America's Schools*. Washington, DC: Brookings, 1990. Brilliant, controversial account of the way in which politics interferes with effective management of public schools.

DiIulio, John. *Governing Prisons: A Comparative Study of Correctional Management*. New York: Free Press, 1987. Shows how politics affects the management of prisons.

Heclo, Hugh. "Issue Networks and the Executive Establishment," in Anthony King, ed. *The New American Political System*. Washington, DC: American Enterprise Institute, 1978. Describes the shift from iron triangles to issue networks.

Kaufman, Herbert. *The Forest Ranger*. Baltimore: Johns Hopkins University Press, 1981. Classic study of a government agency.

Light, Paul. *Thickening Government: Federal Hierarchy and the Diffusion of Accountability*. Washington, DC: Brookings, 1995. Identifies and explains the growth in higher-level governmental positions.

Niskanan, William A. *Bureaucracy and Representative Government*. Chicago: Aldine-Atherton, 1971. Develops the argument that says government bureaucracies seek to maximize their budgets.

Wilson, James Q. *Bureaucracy: What Government Agencies Do and Why They Do It*. New York: Basic Books, 1989. Comprehensive treatment of public bureaucracies.

Young, James. *The Washington Community 1800–1828*. New York: Harcourt, Brace, 1966. Engaging, insightful account of political and administrative life in Washington during the first decades of the nineteenth century.

For Associate Justice
of the Supreme Court

Shall **JOYCE L. KENNARD**
be elected to the office for the term
prescribed by law?

For Associate Justice
of the Supreme Court

Shall **ARMAND ARABIAN**
be elected to the office for the term
prescribed by law?

For Associate Justice
of the Supreme Court

Shall **MARVIN BAXTER**
be elected to the office for the term
prescribed by law?

For Associate Justice
of the Supreme Court

Shall **EDWARD A. PANELLI**
be elected to the office for the term
prescribed by law?

For Associate Justice
of Appeal

Shall **WILLIAM D. STE**
be elected to the office for the term
prescribed by law?

13

14

YES **15**

NO **16**

YES **17**

NO 1

YES

NO

Y

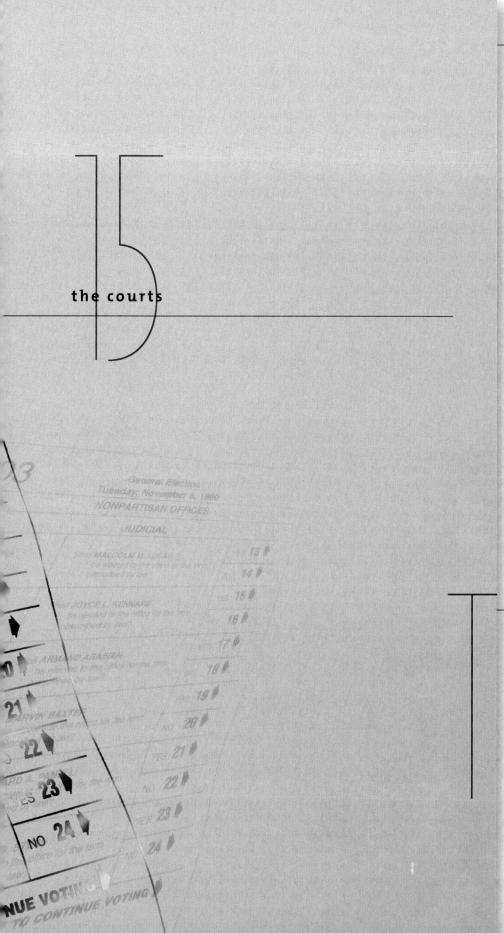

15

the courts

HURGOOD MARSHALL, the Supreme Court's first black justice, once jested, "I have a lifetime appointment and I intend to serve it. I expect to die at 110, shot by a jealous husband."[1] He nonetheless resigned in June 1991, reluctantly concluding that at age 83 he could no longer continue a civil rights struggle he had fought for decades. Clearly worried about his successor, he gruffly warned President Bush against "picking the wrong Negro" to replace him.[2]

Ignoring Marshall's plea, Bush nominated Clarence Thomas, a man who had brought a conservative definition of equal opportunity to his work as chair of the Equal Employment Opportunity Commission. He was opposed to quotas and preferential treatment for minorities because "they assume that I am not the equal of someone else, and if I'm not the equal, then I'm inferior."[3]

The Senate majority vote needed for Thomas's Senate confirmation was problematic. The Democratic-controlled Senate viewed Thomas with great suspicion. And just three years earlier, the Senate had refused to confirm an equally conservative Reagan nominee, Robert Bork.

At first it seemed that Thomas would escape much criticism. Unlike Bork, Thomas had not publicly expressed his views on controversial constitutional questions, thereby making it more difficult for his opponents to make an issue of his nomination. Thomas also had political savvy that Bork had lacked. Whereas Bork, a former Yale Law School professor, had naively supposed that he could impress the senators with his legal erudition, Thomas realized that silence was golden. Anything said might be used in opposition. At his Senate confirmation hearings, when Thomas was asked no less than seventy times for his opinion on the constitutionality of laws against abortion, his replies were studiously ambiguous. To Senator Leahy's question as to whether he had ever discussed the constitutional issue, Thomas replied, "If you're asking me whether I ever debated the contents . . ., the answer to that is no, senator."[4] By refusing to respond to questions like these, Thomas took from his opponents weapons they needed to defeat his candidacy.

Still another factor was significant. Civil rights groups and liberal Democrats were uneasy in their opposition to Thomas, hesitant to denounce an African American when they had so frequently called upon presidents to appoint more minorities. Moreover, opinion polls indicated that three-quarters of the black population supported Thomas's appointment, despite his conservative views.[5] Senator Edward Kennedy, opposed as he was to the Thomas nomination, was forced to admit, "In many ways he exemplifies the promise of the Constitution and the American ideal of equal opportunity."[6]

But Thomas ended up being involved in a political uproar after all—as the result of testimony by a soft-spoken woman named Anita Hill. An attorney and former employee of Thomas's at the EEOC, Hill had left the high-pressure world of Washington politics to assume a professorial position in her home state of Oklahoma. She had left Washington, she told a friend, because she had been sexually harassed. Hill came under increasing pressure to report her encounter with Thomas to Senate staff members and newspaper reporters. Eventually, in hearings televised across the country, millions had an opportunity to hear Hill's account of the exact lewd and suggestive phrases she claimed to have heard from the mouth of a future justice of the Supreme Court. Thomas categorically denied all charges and called the Senate exploitation of the Hill allegations nothing less than a "high-tech lynching."[7]

The confirmation battle spilled out of the Washington beltway to involve men and women of all races and creeds in every city and hamlet. For the fourteen senators forced to listen to the sensational testimony, it was a political nightmare. In some strange twist of politics, it was not just Thomas, but the Senate itself, that was on trial. When one senator explored Anita Hill's credibility through close cross-examination, women's groups attacked him for his unfair, aggressive style.

In the end, Thomas was confirmed by a close vote. More people believed Thomas than Hill, and a clear majority continued to favor Thomas's confirmation.[8] The strong support Thomas received from African-American voters was particularly significant.[9]

Though Thomas was confirmed, the process had a dramatic effect on the next election. The more women thought about the outcome, the more unhappy they became. The percentage of women who believed Thomas had harassed Hill increased from 27 to 51 percent over the course of the coming year, a year that became known as the "year of the woman."[10] For the first time in history, forty-six women were elected to the House of Representatives and four more women were elected to the Senate. In the presidential election, Bush's support among women was 5 percentage points less than his support among men, enough of a difference to cost Bush the election.[11] It was the costliest nomination to the Supreme Court a president had ever made.

n this chapter we will discuss the ways in which the selection of Supreme Court justices has become more tied to electoral considerations, the antidemocratic potential of the power of judicial review, the way in which the Supreme Court conducts its business, the political role of lower court judges, and the checks that other branches of government place on the courts.

The Politics of Supreme Court Nominations

U.S. CONSTITUTION: *The President "shall nominate . . . by and with the Advice and Consent of the Senate . . . Judges of the Supreme Court."*

The judicial system is supposed to be politically blind. Justice is expected to fall, like the rain, equally, on rich and poor, Democrat and Republican, black, white, Latino, Asian, and Native American. Judges are appointed for life because they are expected to approach each case that comes before them with an open mind. They are expected to avoid discussing cases in public or with friends and acquaintances other than their judicial colleagues. Chief Justice Warren E. Burger went so far as to claim that "Judges . . . rule on the basis of law, not public opinion, and they should be totally indifferent to pressures of the times."[12] Should judges do otherwise, they are potentially subject to congressional impeachment. Consistent with this understanding of the role of the justice, most Supreme Court nominees, like Thomas, say they cannot discuss or testify on issues that might come before the court. Anything they may say in testimony might prejudge a case before it is heard.

Not many years ago, presidential nominations to the Supreme Court were approved by the Senate as a matter of course. Most were approved quietly without testimony before the judiciary committee. One of Harry Truman's nominees declined an invitation to testify before the judiciary committee but was confirmed anyway.[13] Earl Warren, the Eisenhower appointee who would write the opinion in the landmark 1954 school desegregation decision, *Brown* v. *Board of Education*, was also confirmed without giving testimony.[14]

This long-time separation of Supreme Court nominations from political disputes owed a great deal to the efforts of William Howard Taft. Taft was the only person ever to serve both as president (1909–13) and as chief justice on the Supreme Court (1921–30). Before Taft, political factors openly affected the confirmation decisions. In the nineteenth century, the Senate rejected a third of the presidents' nominees.[15] But Taft worked hard both as president and as chief justice to enhance the quality of nominees, minimize the significance of confirmation procedures, and elevate the prestige of the Supreme Court. He also made sure the Supreme Court building looked like a Greek temple, so that Americans would respect their laws in the same way Greeks venerated their gods.

Taft was so successful that until 1968 every twentieth-century nominee but one was confirmed by the Senate, most without significant dissent. But in recent years the Senate's propensity to reject presidential nominees has steadily increased. One of the most celebrated cases involved Robert Bork, the Reagan nominee rejected by the Senate in 1987. Bork's rejection had in fact given American politics a new word, **borking,** which means to raise the political significance of the confirmation process by means of a major media campaign. Even judicial appointments had become so election-oriented that pundits had to invent a new word to explain what was happening. Both Congress and the media now subject each nomination to scrutiny. Few nominations win unanimous Senate approval; no fewer than six have been rejected (see Table 15.1).

Not every Supreme Court nomination will be borked. If the same party controls both Congress and the presidency, borking is less likely. So, for example, Bill Clinton was able to appoint both Ruth Bader Ginsberg and Stephen Breyer without significant controversy. Even so, Clinton had to be careful to pick moderates rather than well-known liberals. Although Ginsberg was one of the first to develop a legal case for women's rights, as a lower-court judge she had taken moderate positions on regulatory issues, making her acceptable to conservatives. Ginsberg was gently questioned by the Senate Judiciary Committee and confirmed by the overwhelming margin of 98 to 2.

Borking is more likely if the president's party does not control the Senate. Both Bork and Thomas were nominated by Republican presidents, then borked by a Democratic Senate. To avoid borking, presidents facing a hostile Senate may choose a nominee whose views are unknown, a stealth strategy named after the bomber that cannot easily be detected by radar. President Bush nominated stealth candidate David Souter, a New Hampshire state supreme court justice who had never written any opinion or treatise on any major constitutional question. Souter was easily confirmed because Washington insiders could not be sure where he stood on most issues. On the Court, he was at first a moderating influence, more recently a member of the activist bloc.

Although many think the borking of judicial nominations destroys "the public's belief in the fairness of those on the bench and . . . undermine[s] confidence in the

Originally designed by President and Chief Justice William Howard Taft to instill public respect for the courts, the Supreme Court building resembles a Greek temple built to house ancient gods.

borking
Raising the political and electoral significance of a confirmation process by means of a media campaign.

TABLE 15.1

Presidential Nominees to Supreme Court
Not Confirmed by Senate, 1900–1997

Nominee	Date	President	Main Reason for Rejection or Withdrawal
John Parker	1930	Hoover	Anti-labor
Abraham Fortas	1968	Johnson	Too liberal; alleged financial abuses
Homer Thornberry	1968	Johnson	No vacancy when Fortas not confirmed for chief justice
Clement Haynsworth	1970	Nixon	Alleged financial abuses
Harold Carswell	1970	Nixon	Racially conservative
Robert Bork	1987	Reagan	Too conservative
Douglas Ginsberg	1987	Reagan	Smoked marijuana

Should the Confirmation Process Be Politicized?

When the Court is perceived as a political rather than a legal institution, nominees will be treated like political candidates, campaigns will be waged in public, lobbying of senators and the media will be intense, the nominee will be questioned about how he will vote, and he will be pressed to make campaign promises.

This is a logical development as law becomes politicized. We have been moving in this direction for a long time. [But] no legal system can produce increasingly political results without at some point ceasing to be a legal system. If the court comes to seem illegitimate, the legitimacy of law itself declines and the moral obligation to obey it is cast into doubt. What the future holds in this respect is unclear. What is clear is that we have come close to a tipping point and we must draw back.*

—Robert Bork, Supreme Court Nominee

Both law and politics are at heart about what society values. To discourage citizens from participating in the confirmation process of a Supreme Court Justice flies in the face of what the Constitution is all about. There is no better way to celebrate [the Constitution] than for citizens to let their Senators know their views on Bork's nomination. It sure beats reading about the Constitution on the backs of cereal boxes.†

—Linda Monk, legal analyst

* Robert Bork, *The Tempting of America* (New York: Free Press, 1990), 348–49.

† Michael Pertschuk and Wendy Schaetzel, *The People Rising* (New York: Thunder's Mouth Press, 1989), 272–73.

Both passages excerpted with ellipses deleted.

Court"[16] (see Democratic Dilemma), future trends seem clear. The United States is unlikely to go back to the older way of selecting Supreme Court justices. Modern methods of communication—the televised hearings, fax machines, 800 numbers, radio talk shows, and interactive television—ensure that the public will be involved in the making of major political decisions such as the appointment of a justice of the Supreme Court. By a "five-to-one margin," Americans think the "Senate should carefully scrutinize a presidential nominee."[17] The selection of Supreme Court justices is likely to continue to be strongly affected by electoral considerations.

Judicial Review

CONSTITUTION, ARTICLE VI: *This Constitution, and the Laws of the United States which shall be made in Pursuance thereof. . . shall be the supreme Law of the Land.*

■ **judicial review**
Power of the courts to declare null and void laws of Congress and of state legislatures they find unconstitutional.

Many Americans believe Supreme Court nominees should be carefully scrutinized, in part because the Supreme Court's great political authority includes the power of **judicial review**, the power of the courts to declare null and void laws of Congress and of state legislatures they find unconstitutional. The significance of the power of judicial review for a democratic society can hardly be overestimated. Judicial review gives judges, appointed for life, the power to veto laws passed by a majority of the elected representatives of the people, causing Senator George W. Norris to complain, "The people can change Congress but only God can change the Supreme Court."[18]

Although the Constitution says it is the "supreme law of the land," it says nothing explicit about judicial review. The Founders provided for a Supreme Court but said little about its powers (see Chapter 2, p. 57). From what little was said at the convention, it seems the delegates did not expect it to be a particularly powerful institution. As political scientist Robert McCloskey once observed, "The United States began its history . . . with a Supreme Court whose birthright was most uncertain."[19]

ORIGINS OF JUDICIAL REVIEW

Despite its uncertain status during the first years of the new Republic, the Supreme Court, in 1803, successfully asserted its power of judicial review in the most important of all Supreme Court decisions, **Marbury v. Madison.** The case was profoundly shaped by an intense conflict then dividing the two main political parties, the Federalists and the Jeffersonians (see Chapter 3, pp. 75-77). William Marbury, one of several last-minute appointments made by defeated Federalist President John Adams in 1801, was appointed a justice of the peace for the District of Columbia. When through an oversight Marbury failed to receive the commission officially appointing him justice of the peace, Jefferson's secretary of state, James Madison, used this as an excuse to refuse Marbury the job. Chief Justice John Marshall used a small question of political patronage as an occasion to assert that the Supreme Court could declare laws of Congress null and void. It has been acknowledged and accepted ever since.

In asserting the power of judicial review, Marshall's reasoning was simple and straightforward. Any new law supersedes older laws on the same subject, except when the older law has been issued by a higher governmental entity. If a town changes its speed limit from thirty to forty miles an hour, the new law takes effect, unless a state law prohibits speeds in towns from exceeding thirty miles an hour. Then the law of the higher level of government, even though of an earlier date, takes precedence. The highest law of the land, according to Marshall, was the Constitution. It was established by the people, and no entity subject to the Constitution, not even Congress itself, can enact legislation that contravenes the will of the people, as expressed in the Constitution.

THREE THEORIES OF CONSTITUTIONAL INTERPRETATION

The reasoning is impeccable as long as one assumes that judges only examine a law of Congress, compare it to the Constitution, and determine whether or not the law runs contrary to constitutional language. The simplest case, perhaps, would be a law that postponed a constitutionally mandated election day. But very few issues of constitutionality are that simple. To help decide which laws are unconstitutional, the Supreme Court has developed three distinct theories of constitutional interpretation that help decide whether a law is or is not constitutional—original intent, living constitution, and plain meaning of the text.

The first is the theory of **original intent**, which determines the constitutionality of a law by ascertaining the intentions of those who wrote the Constitution. To find out the intentions of the Founders, judges examine such documents as the notes

> **Marbury v. Madison**
> Supreme Court decision (1803) in which the court first exercised the power of judicial review.

> **original intent**
> A theory of constitutional interpretation that determines the constitutionality of a law by ascertaining the intentions of those who wrote the Constitution.

that James Madison wrote down at the constitutional convention, the *Federalist Papers*, and the speeches made during the ratifying campaign. Among today's sitting justices, it is Justice Thomas who relies most frequently on the theory of original intent. For example, he favors overturning *Roe* v. *Wade* because he finds nothing in the Constitution that gives women the right to choose an abortion. On the contrary, he says that at the time the Constitution was ratified many states outlawed abortion, making it clear the framers had no intention of denying the states this authority.

Critics of original-intent theory say that many issues now before the courts were never contemplated by those who wrote the Constitution. And even if they were, should the views of the Founders count? Should the opinions of fifty-five men gathered together in Philadelphia in the summer of 1787 constrain the actions of the U.S. government more than 200 years later?

Those who criticize original intent theory offer instead a **living-Constitution theory** of judicial review, which says that a law is to be judged constitutional in light of the entire history of the United States as a nation. The determining factor should not be just the opinions expressed at the time the Constitution was written but also ideas and judgments shaped by American experience since then. In the words of Justice Oliver Wendell Holmes Jr., constitutional questions must be "considered in the light of our whole experience and not merely in that of what was said a hundred years ago."[20] The living-Constitution theory is practical and helps the Constitution adapt to modern circumstances; however, it reduces constitutional interpretation to the judge's personal understanding of the meaning of American history. Since no two judges' interpretations of the country's living history are likely to be the same, constitutional interpretation becomes highly subjective.

These difficulties have given risen to what has been called the **plain meaning of the text** theory of constitutional interpretation, which determines the constitutionality of a law in light of what the words of the Constitution obviously seem to say. Justice William Douglas pointed out that the First Amendment requires that "Congress shall make no law . . . abridging freedom of speech," adding "The First Amendment is couched in absolute terms—freedom of speech shall not be abridged . . . No leeway is granted."[21]

Plain meaning has two clear advantages. Unlike original-intent theory, it does not require extensive inquiry into obscure debates undertaken in the distant past. The constitutional text itself is taken as a guide to action. Nor does this approach require that judges evaluate the meaning of the totality of the American experience and apply it to the case at hand.

But plain meaning theory has its own limitations. The Constitution is a very short document that left many issues undecided and used ambiguous language in order to win ratification. Even words that appear plain do not always have a clear meaning. Even Justice Black agreed to some limitations on free speech—for example, he agreed that one private person cannot libel another with impunity.

More recently, Sandra O'Connor relied on plain-meaning theory to overturn a federal law on the grounds that the federal government cannot give orders to the states. She said no such power could be found in the Constitution, and the Tenth Amendment "made explicit" that all powers not delegated to Congress are reserved to the states. But Justice John Stevens, dissenting from O'Connor's opinion, pointed out that Congress under the Articles of Confederation had the authority to compel states to take certain actions.[22] He said the Constitution was written to strengthen, not weaken, the powers of Congress. If two noted jurists, O'Connor and Stevens, do not agree on the content of the Tenth Amendment, its meaning can hardly be plain and clear.

JUDICIAL REVIEW IN PRACTICE

Not only is judicial review theory controversial, judicial review has problems in practice as well. In three celebrated instances the Supreme Court created constitutional crises by defying the declared will of Congress and the president.

The first case, Dred Scott (1857), declared unconstitutional the Missouri Compromise, passed in 1820.[23] The law drew a line coinciding with the Arkansas–Missouri border, north of which there could never be slavery (see Figure 15.1). Missouri, the exception, was allowed to have slaves. The Missouri Compromise had been so successful at preventing a breakup of the union, few thought the Supreme Court would dare call it unconstitutional. But instead of respecting Congress's capacity to find satisfactory compromises, the Supreme Court said masters could take their slaves with them throughout the United States. Few Supreme Court decisions have been more disastrous. If it did not by itself cause the Civil War, it certainly kindled fiery sentiments. The Dred Scott decision convinced northerners that slavery would be extended throughout the Union. For southerners, it helped justify secession. This was probably the most disastrous instance when judicial review was exercised.

In the late nineteenth century, the Supreme Court once again unwisely used its power of judicial review to declare a law unconstitutional, this time to block legislation designed to protect workers from the raging industrial capitalism of the day. In *Lochner* v *New York* (1905) the Supreme Court said the State of New York could not regulate the number of hours women and children worked because to do so deprived them of the right to work as long and as hard as they pleased. In his dissent from this decision, Oliver Wendell Holmes insisted that the Constitution be interpreted as a living document, saying

Dred Scott

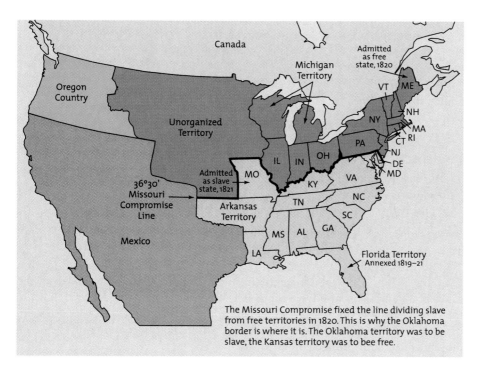

The Missouri Compromise fixed the line dividing slave from free territories in 1820. This is why the Oklahoma border is where it is. The Oklahoma territory was to be slave, the Kansas territory was to bee free.

FIGURE 15.1

The Missouri Compromise

The Impact on the Supreme Court of Roosevelt's Reelection in 1936

In 1936, seven of the nine Supreme Court justices had been appointed by Republican presidents, most of whom initially resisted Roosevelt's efforts to expand federal power. As late as 1935, the Supreme Court, in Schechter, declared unconstitutional a federal regulation of economic activity within a state.

The Roosevelt Democrats were furious at decisions that seemed to deny the country's elected officials the right to govern. Never before had judicial review placed the Supreme Court in such direct conflict with the president and Congress. But Roosevelt overplayed his hand. Instead of trying to change Supreme Court views gradually by appointing judges who shared his New Deal philosophy, he tried to "pack the court" by adding six new judges over and above the nine already on the court (one for each of those over 70 years old who refused to retire). Although the Constitution does not specify the number of justices that shall serve on the Supreme Court—its actual size had varied between five and ten— many felt the courts should not be subjected to such direct political manipulation. Roosevelt's court-packing scheme went nowhere in Congress.

Although Roosevelt lost the battle, he won the war. Shortly after his great reelection victory in 1936, Chief Justice Charles Hughes and Justice Owen Roberts, who had previously voted to restrict federal power, changed their views. This time the issue involved the recently passed Wagner Act, a New Deal law that protected union organizers.† Despite the fact that the new law regulated activities within a state, a court majority, in a 5-4 vote, declared it constitutional.

The change of heart by Hughes and Roberts has been called "the switch in time that saved nine." The New Deal majority that emerged on the court was soon augmented and solidified by Roosevelt's own appointees. The meaning of interstate commerce was extended to include almost all commerce, whether taking place between states or not.‡

* *Schechter Poultry Corp.* v. *United States* (1935). The Court also said Congress could not delegate its power to regulate to the executive branch, unless clear standards were established. This rule was also overturned by later Court decisions.

† *NLRB* v. *Jones & Laughlin Co.* (1937).

‡ *Wickard* v. *Filburn* (1942).

This case is decided upon an economic theory which a large part of the country does not entertain. A Constitution is not intended to embody a particular economy theory. It is made for people of fundamentally differing views.[24]

Holmes' dissent in *Lochner* eventually becomes the view of the Supreme Court. Today, it is accepted that government can regulate people's right to work.

The third controversial use of the power of judicial review occurred after Franklin Delano Roosevelt became president in 1933. Coming to power in the midst of a depression, the Democrats passed a host of new legislation, known as the New Deal, which was designed to help stimulate economic recovery. Republicans felt that New Deal policies interfered with the natural workings of the economy and would only prolong the depression.

The Supreme Court, which included a majority of justices appointed by Republican presidents, declared many of the New Deal laws unconstitutional. In *Schechter*

Some scholars say courts must have the power of judicial review to protect civil liberties; others say such power is anti-democratic. What do you think?

Majoritarian democracy is the core of our entire system. [But] that cannot be the whole story, since a majority with untrammeled power to set government policy is in a position to deal itself benefits at the expense of the minority. [By means of judicial review], courts must police inhibitions on expression and other political activity because we cannot trust elected officials to do so: ins have a way of wanting to make sure the outs stay out. Constitutional law appropriately exists for those situations where representative government cannot be trusted.*

—John Ely

It is the very power and scope of modern judicial review that is both its greatness and its main danger to American life. If judicial review is a means to check legislative encroachments, what means exist to check the encroachments of the judiciary, a judiciary that has increasingly taken on itself the attributes and powers of legislation? What checks can we devise in order to superintend a judiciary with final power over policies involving abortion, welfare, schools, police, racial balance, busing, employment? The proclamations of judicial review as the nation's security against anti-constitutional abuses rings hollow unless we give some thought to the problem of unreviewed judicial legislation as well.† —John Agresto

* John H. Ely, *Democracy and Distrust: A Theory of Judicial Review* (Cambridge, MA: Harvard University Press, 1980), 7, 106, 183. Excerpted with ellipses deleted.

† John Agresto, *The Supreme Court and Constitutional Democracy* (Ithaca, New York: Cornell University Press, 1984), 163. Excerpted with ellipses deleted.

Poultry Corp. v. *United States* (1935) the Supreme Court found the National Industrial Recovery Act an unconstitutional intrusion on the power of the states to regulate intrastate commerce.[25] In what was known as the "sick chicken" case, the Court, with all the precision of a medieval theologian calculating the number of angels that can dance on the head of a pin, said the law regulated the sale of poultry after it arrived within the State of Illinois, not while the chicks were being transported across a state line. Since Congress could only regulate commerce between states, not commerce within a state, the court declared the law unconstitutional (see Chapter 3, pp. 79-80). The decision placed the Supreme Court at odds with the president and Congress, creating a constitutional crisis that was not fully resolved until Roosevelt was able to appoint judges of his own persuasion to the Supreme Court (see Election Connection).

Instances such as *Dred Scott*, *Lochner*, and *Schechter Poultry* have led some to argue that judicial review should be abandoned. But others see judicial review as a valuable protection against majority infringement on minority civil rights and civil liberties (see Democratic Dilemma). Despite the controversy, judicial review has become a well-established part of American government. It survives in part because it is seldom used to defy the strongly held views of the president and Congress. On only 106 occasions between 1803 and 1974 did the Supreme Court decide that a law was unconstitutional.[26] Most of these decisions affected old laws no longer supported by either a majority of Congress or the president. Political scientist Robert Dahl has gone so far as to claim: "The Supreme Court is inevitably a part of the dominant political leadership. The main task of the Court is to confer legitimacy on [the government's] fundamental policies."[27] Though some scholars think the court is less sensitive to political pressure than Dahl claims, a recent study has identified changes in Supreme Court policy that parallel swings in public opinion. The policy shifts by the Supreme Court are not as marked as those in Congress, the study finds, but justices still seem to pay "attention to what the public wants."[28] The *Dred Scott* and *Schechter Poultry* cases are the exception, not the rule. Bartender Mr. Dooley, the Irish cartoon figure, was not wide of the mark when he observed years ago "th' supreme court follows th' illiction returns."

The Supreme Court in Action

The Supreme Court decided in its 1995-96 term only 75 cases out of the more than 27 million criminal trials and civil suits brought yearly before the state and federal courts.[29] Yet Supreme Court decisions provide the framework for the country's entire judicial system.

STARE DECISIS

A few decisions can have a far-ranging impact because lower federal and state courts are expected to follow the principle of **stare decisis**. The phrase means literally "stable decisions": All court decisions must be consistent with **precedents**, prior decisions as well as their written justification, known as court **opinions**. Jonathan Swift used his biting satire to define *stare decisis* somewhat differently:

> *Whatever has been done before may legally be done again; and therefore [judges] take special care to record all the decisions formerly made against common justice and the general reason of mankind. These, under the name of precedents, they produce as authorities, to justify the most iniquitous of opinions.*

Despite Swift's lampoon, *stare decisis* is a powerful judicial principle that can be ignored only at risk to the stability of the legal system: Only if court decisions are consistent with one another can a country live under a rule of law, where citizens know what it is that they are expected to obey. In the words of one judge, "We cannot meddle with a prior decision [unless it] strikes us as wrong with the force of a five-week-old unrefrigerated dead fish."[30] And only by means of the principle of *stare decisis* can the Supreme Court provide the broad framework within which all other courts decide the legal issues before them.

When reaching a decision that seems contrary to a prior decision, courts try to find a **legal distinction** between the case at hand and earlier court decisions, usually by emphasizing that the facts of the current case differ. The process of drawing a legal distinction can in some cases become a refined art, finding a distinction when others can see no difference. As one wit has put it, the Supreme Court "could find a loophole in the Ten Commandments."[31] Or, as an attorney once bragged, "Law school taught me one thing: how to take two situations that are exactly the same and show how they are different."[32] If the legal distinctions drawn by a lower court seem unconvincing to the losing side, it may file an **appeal** to the next higher court asking for a reversal of the lower court decision. If the higher court thinks the lower court has strayed too far from legal precedents, it may decide on a **reversal**, or overturning, of the lower court decision.

---

stare decisis
In court rulings, reliance on consistency with precedents. *See also* precedent.

precedent
Previous court decision or ruling applicable to a particular case.

opinion
In legal parlance, a court's explanation for its decision.

legal distinction
The legal difference between a case at hand and previous cases decided by the courts.

appeal
The procedure whereby the losing side asks a higher court to overturn a lower-court decision.

reversal
The overturning of a lower court decision by an appeals court or the Supreme Court.

When interpreting statutes, British judges exercise much less discretion than American ones. British judges have less leeway, because they operate within a less fragmented governmental system. In Britain, the party of the prime minister exercises effective control over Parliament. Every piece of legislation passed by the party in power is carefully examined by specialists, who ensure that new legislation is internally coherent and consistent with existing laws. If a judge says government administrators have misinterpreted the law, the party in power can also, if it chooses, quickly pass new legislation. Political scientist Shep Melnick points out that, as a result, "it is not surprising that British judges seldom question the interpretive authority of administrators."*

American judges work within a more decentralized governmental context. To get a majority, members of Congress, when writing legislation, are tempted to use ambiguous language that may include phrases that come close to contradicting one another. In Melnick's words: "The openness and messiness of the legislative process in the United States ensures that when judges scrutinize a statute and its history, they will seldom discover a single, coherent purpose or intent."† In the voting rights legislation of 1982, for example, Congress forbade electoral arrangements that gave minorities "less opportunity than other members of the electorate to elect representatives of their choice," but a few sentences later said that nothing in the legislation required minorities be elected "in numbers equal to their proportion in the population." The "less opportunity" forbidden in the first phrase seemed permitted by the second phrase saying that "equal numbers" need not be elected.‡

When courts are asked to sort out the meaning of this kind of vague and potentially contradictory language, the office of the solicitor general may express the opinion of the presidential administration. But if the courts ignore the solicitor general, the administration must try to persuade Congress to enact a new law, a more difficult task for American presidents than for British prime ministers. Knowing this, U.S. courts feel free to interpret laws in any way not "plainly contrary to the content of Congress." As Supreme Court Justice William Brennan once said, "the Court can virtually remake congressional enactments."§

* R. Shep Melnick, *Between the Lines: Interpreting Welfare Rights* (Washington, DC: Brookings, 1994), 13. (Ellipses deleted.)

† Melnick, *Between the Lines.*

‡ As quoted in Bernard Grofman, Lisa Handley, and Richard G. Niemi, *Minority Representation and the Quest for Voting Equality* (New York: Cambridge University Press, 1992), 39. (Ellipses deleted.)

§ Melnick, *Between the Lines,* 13.

KEY POWERS OF THE COURTS

Judicial review is only the most sweeping and controversial of judicial powers. The courts also engage in **statutory interpretation**, the application of the laws of Congress and of the states to particular cases. The courts have great discretion in exercising this power, much more than their counterparts in Great Britain (see International Comparison). For example, Congress passed a vague and general law

■ **statutory interpretation**
The judicial act of interpreting and applying the law to particular cases.

protecting endangered species in 1973. The Supreme Court gave this law sharp teeth by saying that Congress intended to protect all species, the tiny snail darter as well as the eagle. In reaching this decision, Chief Justice Warren Burger wrote that "it may seem curious to some that the survival of a relatively small number of three-inch fish among all the countless millions of species extant would require the permanent halting of a virtually completed dam for which Congress has expended more than $100 million." But the law, Burger said, required "precisely that result." [33] Though dissenting Justice Powell thought it was "absurd" to think Congress had any such intention, all the Court pretended to do in this instance was to interpret and apply an act of Congress. Yet its decision has had far-reaching consequences.

If a court finds that an injury has been suffered, it is up to the court to fashion a **remedy**, the compensation for the injury. Often the remedy simply involves monetary compensation to the injured party. But a judge may also direct the defendant to alter future behavior. To overcome racial segregation in schools, courts have ordered school boards to institute magnet schools, to set up special compensatory programs, and to bus children from one part of the city to another. As Justice Lewis Powell put it, courts have the right, if racial segregation is sufficiently severe, to "virtually assume the role of school superintendent and school board." [34]

THE CHIEF JUSTICE

The members of the Supreme Court consist of eight **associate justices** and the **chief justice**, who heads the Court and is responsible for organizing its work. Though the chief justice has only one vote and many of the chief's tasks are of a ceremonial or housekeeping nature, certain responsibilities give the office added influence. For one thing, the chief justice, if voting with the majority, assigns the responsibility for writing the majority opinion. Since the court opinion is often as important as the actual decision, this assignment power can have important consequences, since some cases are "destined for the history books," while others are, in [former Justice Lewis] Powell's term, 'dogs.'" Powell's biographer tells us that Warren Burger, not the most popular of chief justices, was suspected by his colleagues of voting with the court majority, even when privately opposed, simply in order to exercise his assignment power. [35]

Some chief justices have used their position to facilitate compromise and achieve consensus. In the case of *Brown* v. *Board of Education of Topeka, Kansas* (1954), the landmark decision desegregating schools, Chief Justice Earl Warren was able to win the support of two judges initially inclined to dissent. To achieve the unanimity he thought crucial, Warren agreed to write a less than completely forthright opinion. *Brown* banned segregation in schools but not in other public places, and it specified delay in the implementation of the ruling. Warren was willing to make these compromises, because he thought only a unanimous court could order such a major social change—which at the time ran contrary to strongly held opinions of many southern whites. [36]

DECISION MAKING

Before reaching its decisions, the Supreme Court first considers **briefs**, written legal arguments submitted by the opposing sides. (Unfortunately for judges, briefs are often anything but brief.) The justices then listen to oral arguments from attorneys on both sides in a **plenary** session (one that is attended by all justices), the chief justice presiding. Open to the public, these plenary sessions are held on Mondays, Tuesdays, and Wednesdays from October through May. If a controversial case is to be heard,

remedy
Court-ordered action designed to compensate plaintiffs for wrongs they have suffered.

associate justice
One of the eight Justices of the Supreme Court who are not the chief justice.

chief justice
Head of Supreme Court.

brief
Written arguments presented to the court by lawyers on behalf of clients.

plenary
Activities of a court in which all judges participate.

such as one involving abortion rights, the courtroom will overflow and, outside, "competing protesters [will] square . . . off at the courthouse steps, chanting, singing and screaming at each other."[37] In the one hour the attorneys for each side usually have to present their case, they may find themselves interrupted by searching questions from the bench. Former law professor Antonin Scalia is especially well known for his willingness to turn the plenary session into a classroom seminar. Yet it is not always clear how closely the justices attend to the responses. As Justice John Marshall said many years ago, "The acme of judicial distinction means the ability to look a lawyer straight in the eye for two hours and not hear a damned word he says."[38]

After hearing the oral argument, the justices usually reach a preliminary decision the same week in a private conference presided over by the chief justice. There are "three levels of elbow room about the conference table." The most ample are for the chief justice and senior associate justice, who sit at opposite ends. The next best is grabbed by the three most senior justices sitting on one side, leaving the four most junior crowded together across from them. No outsiders, not even a secretary, are permitted to attend. The only record consists of handwritten notes taken by individual justices.

From the outside, it may appear that the private conferences are opportunities for great minds to gather and discuss fundamental legal questions. But in most instances the justices already will have discussed the issues with their law clerks and enter the conference room with their intentions firmly fixed. The justices express their views and preliminary votes in order of seniority, beginning with the chief justice.[39] If the chief justice is in the minority, the writing of the opinion is assigned by the senior associate justice in the majority.[40]

The justice assigned the responsibility for preparing the court opinion circulates a draft version among the other eight. Revisions are then made in light of comments received from the other justices. On rare occasions, the justice writing the opinion has "lost a court," meaning that one or more justices voting with the majority at the first conference have changed their minds. To keep a majority, the justice writing the opinion may produce an extremely bland opinion that gives little guidance to lower court justices. In a 1993 sexual harassment case, *Harris* v. *Forklift*, the majority hardly created any precedent at all, saying only that the court would look at the "totality of the circumstances" in order to decide whether harassment in the workplace had occurred.[41]

Justices who vote against the majority may prepare a **dissenting opinion** that explains their disagreement. **Concurring opinions** may be written by those members of the majority who disagree with some aspect of the reasoning included in the majority opinion or who wish to elaborate some further considerations. Two hundred years ago, when John Marshall was chief justice, the court was usually unanimous, and the chief justice wrote most opinions. Today the court is seldom unanimous in its judgment, and, quite apart from the dissenting opinions, so many concurring opinions are filed that it is sometimes difficult to ascertain exactly what the majority has decided. For example, in an important case involving racial quotas, only the judge who wrote the majority opinion, Justice Lewis Powell, took the middle position allowing affirmative action programs but forbidding racial quotas.[42] The other eight justices expressed in their concurring and dissenting opinions views that were either more conservative or more liberal than Powell's (see discussion in Chapter 17, pp. 564–565). As a result, it has never been clear exactly what the Supreme Court decided in this case.

Though the proliferation of dissenting and concurring opinions has sown considerable confusion about overall court rulings, these opinions themselves often have a clearer, and more convincing style than majority opinions—in part because they are signed by only one or two justices, making compromise language unnecessary. In

■ **dissenting opinion**
Written opinion presenting the reasoning of justices who vote against the majority.

■ **concurring opinion**
A written opinion prepared by judges who vote with the majority but who wish to disagree with or elaborate some aspect of the majority opinion.

Harris v. *Forklift*, the sexual harassment case mentioned above, Justice Ginsberg, though agreeing with the decision, wrote a crisp concurring opinion that proposed a simple straightforward standard for ascertaining whether harassment had occurred: Harassment exists whenever it is more difficult for a person of a particular gender to perform well on a job. Convincingly written concurring and dissenting opinions, such as Ginsberg's, sometimes become even more influential than majority opinions.

Once a decision has been reached by the court, it usually sends or **remands** the case to a lower court for implementation. Since the Supreme Court regards itself as responsible for establishing general principles and an overall framework, it seldom becomes involved in the detailed resolution of particular cases. This leaves a great deal of legal responsibility in the hands of the lower courts (see pp. 506–508).

VOTING ON THE SUPREME COURT

Justices of the court divide into quite predictable voting blocs—an exception to this pattern, Justice John Stevens, has "long been considered a maverick" who has often "confound[ed] the categorizers."[43] But the remainder of the judges currently serving on the Supreme Court divide into three fairly well-defined blocs.

The liberals, consisting of Souter and the two Clinton appointees, Ruth Bader Ginsberg and Stephen Breyer, favor a certain amount of **judicial activism**, a doctrine that says the principle of *stare decisis* should sometimes be sacrificed in order to adapt the Constitution to changing conditions. Ginsberg and Breyer contend that too rigid an application of the principle of *stare decisis* would place the country in a straitjacket, unable to incorporate the emerging rights of women and minorities into the country's legal code. Judicial activists are also concerned about the tyranny of the majority, and they see the Court as a mechanism for preserving minority rights and fundamental freedoms that may be trampled upon by electoral majorities.

A second bloc, consisting of three conservative **restorationists**, including Thomas, Scalia, and Rehnquist, believe in overturning earlier liberal decisions. They think the only way the original meaning of the Constitution can be restored is by ignoring the doctrine of *stare decisis* until earlier liberal decisions have been reversed. For example, they favor reversing *Roe* v. *Wade*, the decision declaring unconstitutional laws forbidding abortion.

The moderates who hold the balance of power in the Court, Justices Sandra Day O'Connor and Anthony Kennedy favor **judicial restraint**, a doctrine that says courts should, if at all possible, avoid overturning a prior court decision. If the law is to be changed, it should be changed not by the courts but by the people's elected representatives. O'Connor and Kennedy are willing to uphold prior decisions even when they do not necessarily agree with them. Specifically, although they do not necessarily agree that *Roe* v. *Wade* was a correct decision, these justices have expressed a reluctance to reverse it.

Most of the time, justices vote along lines anticipated by those who nominated and confirmed them. Both statements made in testimony before Congress and other information available at the time the justice is confirmed generally provide a pretty clear indication of the justice's future voting pattern.[44] That the future behavior of the typical justice is predictable may suggest that the justices do not decide each case on its facts and merits. But predictability does allow elected officials—both presidents and Senators—to shape the future direction of the Supreme Court, thereby maintaining some degree of popular control of the courts.

Not every prediction of future behavior is correct, however. The one justice who most surprised those who favored his selection was Harry Blackmun, thought to be a

remand
The request by a higher court to a lower court to determine the best way of implementing the higher court's decision.

judicial activism
Doctrine that says the principle of *stare decisis* should sometimes be sacrificed in order to adapt the Constitution to changing conditions.

restorationist
Judge who thinks that the only way the original meaning of the Constitution can be restored is by ignoring the doctrine of *stare decisis* until liberal decisions have been reversed.

judicial restraint
Doctrine that says courts should, if at all possible, avoid overturning a prior court decision.

judicial conservative. Yet Blackmun wrote the famous opinion in *Roe v. Wade* declaring unconstitutional state laws forbidding abortion. Blackmun himself once said: "Having been appointed by a Republican President and being accused now of being a flaming liberal on the court, the Republicans think I'm a traitor, I guess, and the Democrats don't trust me. And so I twist in the wind. . . beholden to no one, and that's just exactly where I want to be."[45]

In this composite, the justices of the Supreme Court are pictured from left to right according to their judicial philosophies. On the left are John Paul Stevens, David Souter, Ruth Bader Ginsberg, and Stephen Breyer. In the middle are Anthony Kennedy and Sandra Day O'Connor. To the right are Chief Justice William H. Rehnquist, Antonin Scalia, and Clarence Thomas.

CERTS

At one time the Supreme Court was, by law, forced to review many appeals, but the workload became so excessive that Congress gave the Court the power to refuse review of almost any case it did not want to consider. Today almost all cases argued before the Court arrive upon the grant of what is known as a **cert** by court insiders. Cert is a shorthand of the Latin phrase **writ of *certiorari***, which means "to be informed of."[46] Certs are issued when four members of the Supreme Court agree that there is some issue raised by a lower court decision that the Supreme Court should resolve. Approximately 95 percent of the time, the Supreme Court denies cert to a filed petition. The Court rejects most certs because it is burdened by the number of cases on its docket. As one clerk for a Supreme Court justice put it, " You almost get to hate the guy who brings the cert petitions around. He is really a nice guy, but he gets abuse all the time."[47]

The number of certs granted by the Supreme Court has fallen markedly in recent years. In the 1970s the Supreme Court decided as many as 400 cases annually.[48] But as previously mentioned, in the 1995-96 term, only 75 cases were decided. After a period in which many controversial decisions were issued, the Court seems to want to reduce its visibility in American politics.

Certs are granted only for those cases that raise the most important legal or constitutional issues. As the old saying goes, the Supreme Court cares less about justice than about the law. In the words of one chief justice:

> *The Supreme Court is not, and never has been, primarily concerned with the correction of errors in lower court decisions. . . . To remain effective the Supreme*

■ **cert**
See writ of *certiorari*.

■ **writ of *certiorari* (cert)**
A document issued by the Supreme Court indicating that the Court will review a decision taken by a lower court.

Drew Day III, Bill Clinton's first solicitor general, presented the government's position on cases coming before the Supreme Court.

■ **solicitor general**
Government official responsible for presenting before the courts the position of the presidential administration.

Court must continue to decide only those cases which present questions whose resolution will have immediate importance far beyond the particular facts and parties involved." [49]

To issue a cert requires the vote of four justices. The justices look for a nebulous quality known as certworthiness when considering which cases to accept for full-scale argument before the Court. The mere fact that an issue is controversial does not necessarily mean the Court will grant a cert. The justices may decide to let the issue percolate in the lower courts for a few years until the matter is ripe for decision.

The case for cert is strongest if two lower courts have reached opposite conclusions on cases where the facts seem virtually identical. In such cases, the Supreme Court feels a responsibility to clarify the law so that its effect is uniform throughout the United States. But even lower-court disagreement does not guarantee issuance of a cert.

In 1997 a district court judge in North Carolina said that the Food and Drug Administration could not regulate tobacco billboard advertising, even though an appeals court in another circuit had previously said Baltimore could do so, with the Supreme Court denying cert. If the North Carolina decision forbidding the regulation of tobacco is upheld by the court of appeals for North Carolina, the Supreme Court will need to issue a cert or else it will leave standing two quite different court interpretations of the right of tobacco companies to advertise.

The Solicitor General

The case for cert is also strengthened if the request for a cert is backed by the **solicitor general**, the government official responsible for presenting before the courts the position of the presidential administration. Involvement of the solicitor general is a signal that the president and attorney general have strong views on the subject, raising its visibility and political significance. Seventy percent of the solicitor general's cert petitions are accepted by the court. [50]

Although the solicitor general reports to the attorney general, the political head of the Department of Justice, the solicitor general, who is always carefully selected for his professional legal skills, is "in fact what the Attorney General is in name—the chief legal officer of the United States government as far as the courts are concerned." [51] The solicitor general presents the case for the government whenever it is party to a suit. In other important cases, the solicitor general may submit an *amicus curiae* brief, literally, a brief submitted by a "friend of the court." (*Amicus curiae* briefs can also be submitted by others who wish to inform the court of a legal issue presented by a particular case.) When the office of the solicitor general files an *amicus curiae* brief, it finds itself on the winning side approximately three-quarters of the time, a batting average envied by even the most successful private attorneys. [52]

■ **law clerk**
Young, influential aide to a Supreme Court justice.

Clerks

Much of the day-to-day work within the Supreme Court building is the job of **law clerks**, young, influential aides hired by each of the justices. Recently out of law school, most will have spent a year as a clerk with a lower court before being asked to help a Supreme Court justice. Each justice will have somewhere between two and four law clerks. [53] The role of the law clerk has grown in recent years: Not only do clerks initially review certs, but they also draft many court opinions. As a result, says one critic, "the standard opinion style has become that of the student-run [law] reviews: colorless, prolix, platitudinous, always error on the side of inclusion, full of lengthy citations and footnotes—and above all dull."[54] The role of the law clerk has grown to the point at which some claim that a junior Supreme Court of bright but unseasoned attorneys, unconfirmed by the Senate or anybody else, is the true "Supreme Court" of today. Others reply that well-trained graduates from the country's most prestigious law schools may be better judges than aging Titans who refuse to leave office well beyond the age of normal retirement. The truth probably lies between these two extremes: The brilliance of the young clerks and the political and legal experience of the justices are probably better in combination than either would be without the other.[55]

The Federal Court System

CONSTITUTION, ARTICLE III, SEC 1: *The judicial power . . . shall be vested in one supreme Court, and in such inferior Courts as the Congress may from time to time ordain and establish."*

The Constitution established a Supreme Court, leaving it to Congress to decide what lower federal courts were needed in addition to the state courts already in existence. The first Congress enacted the Judiciary Act of 1789, which though updated in many ways still provides the basic framework for the modern federal court system. Although the Supreme Court provides the linchpin for the nation's system of courts, the day-to-day work of the courts is carried out at lower tiers. Lower courts are less visible political institutions than the Supreme Court, but they are no less affected by political and electoral forces. Judges and prosecutors are either appointed by elected officials or, in some cases, are themselves elected. If they ignore strongly held views, their decisions can be checked by other parts of the government.

The main responsibility of the lower-court judges is to hold trials for alleged violations of the civil and criminal code. The **civil code** regulates relations among individuals. Alleged violations of the civil code are stated by individuals, who ask the court to award damages and otherwise offer relief for injuries they claim to have suffered. For example, you can act as **plaintiff**, the person bringing the suit, and sue your landlord for not supplying heat to your apartment. You can ask for monetary damages and a guarantee this will not happen in the future. In these civil cases, redress for injury depends on your taking legal action against the **defendant**, the person against whom the complaint is made. One cannot be imprisoned for violating the civil code (though one can be imprisoned for noncompliance with a court-order issued in conjunction with a civil suit).

civil code
Laws regulating relations among individuals. Alleged violators are sued by presumed victims, who ask courts to award damages and otherwise offer relief.

plaintiff
One who brings legal charges against another.

defendant
One accused of violating the civil or criminal code.

Although O.J. Simpson was found not guilty of violating the *criminal* code, he was found guilty in the *civil* suit against him. Here, pro-and anti-Simpson demonstrators crowd the courthouse to express their views.

FIGURE 15.2

Federal and State Court
Systems

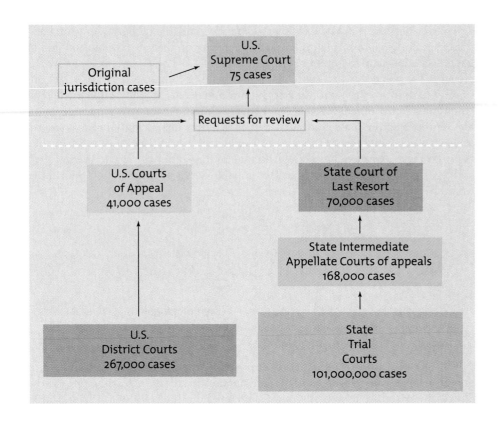

Laws regulating relations
between individuals and
society. Alleged violators are
prosecuted by government.

Violations of the **criminal code** are violations against society as a whole and are enforced by the government itself acting as plaintiff and initiating charges against suspects. If convicted, the criminal owes a debt to society, not just to the injured party. The debt may be paid either by fine, imprisonment, or, in the case of capital crimes, execution.

The same act can simultaneously be a violation of both the criminal and civil code. When former football star O. J. Simpson was found not guilty of criminal charges in conjunction with the murder of his ex-wife, Nicole Brown Simpson, her relatives filed civil charges, alleging that the family had suffered injuries at his hands for which they should be compensated. The plaintiffs were able to secure a guilty verdict in the civil suit despite the finding of not guilty in the criminal prosecution, because, in civil suits, the accused can be forced to testify and standards of proof are lower. In civil suits, one is not considered innocent until proven guilty beyond a reasonable doubt. Juries have only to consider the weight of the evidence.

DISTRICT AND APPEALS COURTS

■ **federal district court**
The lowest level of the federal
court system and the court
in which most federal trials
are held.

Most federal suits are initially filed in one of the 94 **federal district courts**, the lowest tier of the federal court system (see Figure 15.2). Alternatively, suits are filed in certain specialized courts responsible for particular legal questions. Federal district courts hold trials for violations of the federal criminal and civil codes, for civil suits that involve citizens from more than one state, and for suits against federal agencies.

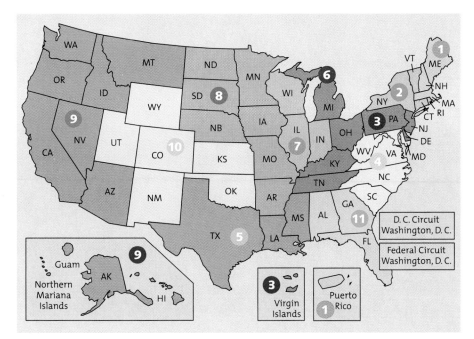

FIGURE 15.3

Appellate Court Boundaries

SOURCE: Robert A. Carp and Ronald Stidham, *The Federal Courts,* 2nd ed. (Washington, D. C.: CQ Press: 1991), 18.

The federal district courts are organized into 13 circuits, including eleven numbered circuits, a D.C. circuit, and a federal circuit, each of which has a **circuit court of appeals**, the court to which all district court decisions may be appealed (see Figure 15.3). Originally, circuit judges literally traveled by stage coach from district to district, listening to appeals from lower-court decisions. Depending on the size of the circuit, the circuit courts have between 6 and 28 justices. Usually, the senior justice of the circuit court assigns three justices to review each case that has been appealed. In exceptionally important cases, a plenary session may be held in which all of the appeal judges in the circuit participate. Courts of appeal typically confine their review to points of law under dispute; they ordinarily take as given the facts of the case, as stated in the trial record and decided by district judges. Though decisions by the appeals court may be taken up by the Supreme Court, most circuit court decisions are final.

■ **circuit court of appeals**
Court to which decisions by federal district courts are appealed.

SELECTION OF JUDGES

All federal judges hold lifetime positions after their nomination by the president and confirmation by the Senate. Because of long-standing agreements among senators, known as senatorial courtesy, any presidential nominee must be acceptable to the senior senator, of the state involved, who is of the same political party as the president (see Chapter 14, pp. 465–466). Political and electoral considerations play a major role in the selection of federal judges. Most share the same partisan identification as the president who nominates them (see Figure 15.4). Ninety-four percent of Ronald Reagan's nominees were Republican, 90 percent of Jimmy Carter's nominees were Democratic.[56] Though most judges would not acknowledge the fact publicly, political loyalty is often the key to appointment. As one judge admitted:

> *I worked hard for Franklin Roosevelt. . . . In 1939 I began running for the Senate, and the party convinced me it would be best if there wasn't a contest for the*

FIGURE 15.4

Partisan Affiliation of District Judges

SOURCE: Sheldon Goldman, "Reagan's Judicial Legacy: Completing the Puzzle and Summing Up," *Judicature* 72 (April–May, 1989): 321–322.

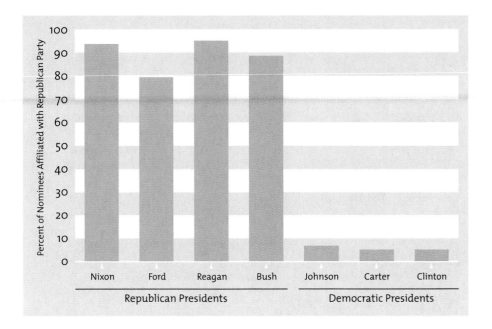

Democratic nomination. So I withdrew . . . . They gave this judgeship as sort of a consolation prize. . . . " [57]

Although most lower court nominees are confirmed, rejections do occur. Rejection is usually a result of some financial or personal problem uncovered during the confirmation process. Ideological and partisan considerations play a minor role. Robert Bork, for example, was easily confirmed as an appeals court justice even though he was later rejected as a nominee to the Supreme Court. But ideological battles over lower-court judges have become increasingly important. Clinton did not nominate a liberal Washingtonian, Peter Edelman, as an appeals court judge, even though he was a close personal friend, because Republicans in the Senate said they would block the appointment. When Daniel Manion was nominated by Ronald Reagan to serve on an appeals court, Democrats chose to oppose the appointment on the grounds that he had once had connections with the extremely conservative John Birch society. His confirmation was secured by just one vote, which Vice President George Bush cast in Manion's favor.

In the spring of 1997, some Republicans in Congress began giving serious consideration to voting against all of Clinton's nominees to Circuit Court of Appeals unless a majority of Republicans from states served by the Circuit approved the appointment. If this rule is adopted by the majority party in the Senate, judicial appointments will become even more controversial.

Although district judge decisions must be within the guidelines handed down by the Supreme Court, they nonetheless reflect the political orientation of the president who nominated the particular judge. According to one study, Reagan-appointed judges were tougher towards those accused of crime than were Carter-appointed judges.[58] More generally, judges appointed by Democratic presidents were more likely to hand down liberal decisions than are those appointed by Republican presidents (see Figure 15.5).

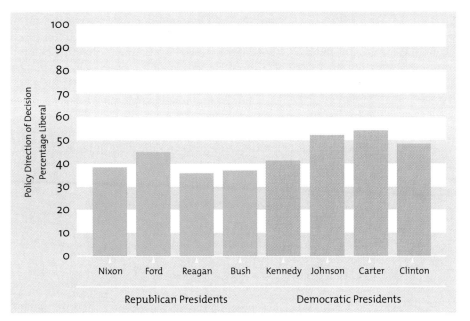

FIGURE 15.5

Decision Making by Democratic and Republican Judges

SOURCE: Robert A. Carp and Ronald Stidham, *The Federal Courts*, 2nd ed. (Washington, DC: Congressional Quarterly 1991), 116; *U.S. News and World Report*, May 26, 1997, 24.

Judges can be threatened with impeachment if their decisions run contrary to dominant opinion. Few judges have been impeached, and successful impeachments have almost always been for financial abuse of the office. But movements to impeach judges who handed down unpopular decisions have regularly surfaced. Those opposed to school desegregation campaigned for years for the impeachment of Earl Warren. As the connection between courts and elections grows closer, it is possible that calls for impeachment or resignation will increase (see Chapter 16, p. 537).

DECIDING TO PROSECUTE

Suspected violations of the federal criminal code are usually investigated by the Federal Bureau of Investigation, though other federal agencies, such as the Secret Service and the Alcohol, Tobacco and Firearms agency, also exercise investigatory powers. The evidence collected is given to prosecutors in the office of a federal **district attorney**, who is responsible for prosecuting violations of the federal criminal law. If persuaded that a prosecution is warranted, district attorneys ask grand juries, consisting of 16 to 23 citizens, to indict, or bring charges against, the suspect. Since accused people cannot defend themselves before the grand jury, the district attorney's advice pretty much determines the outcome. As one wit observed, "Under the right prosecutor, a grand jury would indict a ham sandwich."[59]

Federal district attorneys hold a particularly high political profile. Appointed by and operating under the overall direction of the attorney general, they usually share the president's party affiliation, and, though expected to be incorruptible, they often are sensitive to the political needs of their superiors in Washington. Since routine law enforcement is left in the hands of state officials, federal district attorneys concentrate on high-visibility, attention-grabbing activities. If they are particularly successful, they may become candidates for higher office. New York Mayor Rudolph Giuliani achieved prominence as a federal district attorney who successfully prosecuted Wall

district attorney
Person responsible for prosecuting criminal cases.

Street inside-trader Ivan Boesky and tax-evading hotel magnate Leona Helmsley. Sometimes one can get ahead politically simply by initiating a high-profile investigation. Governor William Weld of Massachusetts won fame as the district attorney by investigating the mayor of Boston. He launched the investigation, he later admitted, because "I had picked up enough anecdotal stuff to persuade me there was a spiritual" violation of the law. Though the investigation attracted widespread media attention, boosting Weld toward the governorship, he eventually dropped the charges when no actual crime could be identified.[60] But it was Thomas Dewey who turned the office of district attorney to greatest political advantage. After winning fame by prosecuting labor racketeers, he became governor of New York and, in 1948, won the Republican presidential nomination, though he lost to Harry Truman.[61]

★ AT THE STATE & LOCAL LEVEL

State Courts

Every state has its own judicial arrangements, but in most the basic structure has the same three tiers found in the federal system: trial courts, courts of appeals, and a court of last resort, usually called the state supreme court. Decisions of state supreme courts may be appealed to the federal Supreme Court, if the issue involves a federal statute or the interpretation of the federal Constitution. In an early key decision, **McCulloch v. Maryland** (1819), the Supreme Court made it clear that the power of judicial review applied to state as well as federal laws (see Chapter 3, p. 77.). Maryland had imposed a tax on the congressionally chartered Bank of the United States. When bank cashier, McCulloch, refused to pay the tax, he was convicted of violating the law. But the Supreme Court overturned the conviction, Chief Justice Marshall saying the power to tax involves "the power to destroy" and no state had the power "to retard, impede, burden or in any manner control, the operations of the constitutional laws enacted by Congress."[62]

The Supreme Court's power to review state laws and decisions of state courts is essential for maintaining basic uniformity in the laws of the United States. Over the decades, the Supreme Court has found over 600 state statutes and state constitutional provisions contrary to the federal constitution.[63] The judicial power to declare state laws unconstitutional is much less controversial than the power to declare laws of Congress unconstitutional. As Justice Holmes once said,

> I do not think the United States would come to an end if we lost our power to declare an act of Congress void. I do think the Union would be imperilled if we could not make that declaration as to the laws of the several states. For one in my place sees how often a local policy prevails with those who are not trained to national views.[64]

STATE TRIAL COURTS: THE JUDICIAL WORKHORSE

Most judicial activity takes place within state trial courts under the control of state and local governments, which go by many different names in the various states (district courts, county courts, common pleas courts, and so forth). In fact, 99 percent of all civil and criminal cases originate in these courts.

▦ **McCulloch v. Maryland**
Decision (1819) in which Supreme Court first declared a state law unconstitutional.

John Marshall, appointed by John Adams to serve as Chief Justice, 1801–1835, was also a revolutionary war soldier, supporter of the Constitution at the Virginia ratifying convention, Federalist member of Congress, and secretary of state under Adams.

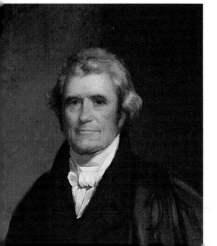

State courts are influenced by electoral considerations at least as much as federal ones. In 37 of the 50 states, both appellate and trial judges are subject to election. In the remaining states, judges are appointed by the state legislature, the governor, or some governmental agency. In New York, trial court judges are elected but appellate judges are appointed.[65] In Georgia it is the reverse.

Though most state judges are subject to election, most judicial campaigns "are waged in obscurity, with the result that most voters are unfamiliar with the names, not to speak of the issues, involved in the campaign."[66] As a result, judicial elections have traditionally been dominated by organized groups and party politicians interested in controlling court patronage. During the 1960s, 73 out of Chicago's 80 circuit court judges were active in Democratic party politics. Political scientist Milton Rakove described how the party–judicial connection worked:

> Without question the surest and safest road to a seat on the bench is through the party organization. Having a judge on the bench from his ward organizations gives the precinct captains access to the county judicial system which can be used on behalf of the ward's constituents. Many sitting judges continue to attend ward organization meetings and ward fund-raising affairs.[67]

It is not only in big-city politics that party and judicial affairs are interconnected. Before the civil rights movement changed Alabama politics, the "probate judge [was] generally the leader of the dominant faction within the county." In Louisiana the "sheriff [was] generally the kingpin of local politics."[68] However, parties seem to have a bigger impact on court patronage than on lower-court judicial decisions; most studies find few differences between the decisions of Democratic and Republican state judges.[69]

PROSECUTING STATE CASES

Acting on information provided by local police, prosecutors in the office of the local district attorney determine whether the evidence warrants presentation before a grand jury for prosecution. In large cities the district attorney has enormous responsibilities. In Los Angeles, for example, the office prosecutes 300 thousand cases a year.

Because they are responsible for the prosecution of all criminal cases, some of which have high visibility in local news media, many prosecutors earn recognition that wins them election or appointment to the judiciary. About 10 percent of all judges once worked in the district attorney's office.[70] Many local district attorneys are interested in moving to other higher offices as well. For example, the decision to try the Los Angeles police officers accused of beating motorist Rodney King in 1991 was made by District Attorney Ira Reiner. Less than a year previously Reiner had run for state attorney general, a steppingstone to the governor's mansion. He hoped prosecution of the police officers would help his reelection campaign. When the jury failed to convict the police officers, the voters blamed Reiner for a sloppy prosecution and, at the earliest opportunity, threw him out of office.

RELATIONS BETWEEN STATE AND FEDERAL COURTS

Most cases are heard in state courts, but any case can be shifted to a federal court if it can be shown that a federal law or constitutional principle is involved. The federal courts have higher prestige than do state courts; to become a federal judge is to hold a position of great honor. But as Justice Sandra Day O'Connor, herself a former state judge, acutely observed, "When the state court judge puts on his or her federal court robe, he or she does not become immediately better equipped intellectually to do the job."[71]

The same act can simultaneously constitute a violation of both state and federal laws. Although the Fifth Amendment to the Constitution forbids **double jeopardy**—being tried twice for the same crime—something very close to double jeopardy can occur if a person is tried in both federal and state courts for the same action. In 1897 the Supreme Court permitted dual prosecutions, saying "an act denounced as a crime by both national and state sovereignties is an offense against the peace and dignity of both."[72] In recent years the chances for such prosecution has been rising, because Congress, under pressure to do something about crime, has passed new laws essentially duplicating state laws.

Despite the recent wave of anti-crime legislation, dual state and federal prosecutions remain unusual. Most of the time, federal and state officials reach an agreement allowing one or the other to take responsibility. Generally speaking, the federal government takes over the prosecution only when the case has national implications. (From this comes the popular phrase, "Don't make a federal case out of it.") For example, the 1995 bombing of a federal building in Oklahoma, in which 168 people lost their lives, constituted a violation of both state and federal laws. Though state officials began the investigation, federal investigators quickly took charge and the accused, Timothy McVeigh was convicted in a federal courtroom.

If the state prosecution fails to result in a conviction in a sensational case where a federal law has been broken, the federal district attorney may also bring charges. In 1992, the State of California, as mentioned above, was unable to win a conviction in the trial of four police officers charged with beating Rodney King, which had been videotaped. The failure to convict officers for what seemed to be a well-documented offense provoked three days of civil disorder in Los Angeles's minority communities.

To help calm the city, the federal district attorney decided to bring federal charges against the officers, despite the fact that the state had already tried them once for the alleged offense. After hearing all the evidence, the jury in the federal trial convicted two officers and acquitted the other two. The decision to hold a second trial was almost certainly affected by electoral considerations. Though the decision was made by the federal district attorney serving Los Angeles, it was made only at the request of the attorney general and with the apparent approval of President Bush. The president was at that moment in the midst of the presidential election—in which his opponent, Bill Clinton, was accusing Bush of having helped create the racial climate leading to a failure to convict in the first trial.

Checks on Court Power

Though court decisions have great impact, their consequences can be limited by others. As political scientist Jack Peltason has put it, "Judicial decision making is one stage, not the only nor necessarily the final one.[73] Alexander Hamilton, writing in the *Federalist Papers*, explained why this was to be expected under the Constitution:

> *The judiciary will always be the least dangerous to the political rights of the Constitution. The executive not only dispenses honors but holds the sword of the*

double jeopardy
Placing someone on trial for the same crime twice.

community. The legislature not only commands the purse, but prescribes the rules. The judiciary, on the contrary, has no influence over either the sword or the purse. It may truly be said to have neither force nor will, but merely judgment; and must ultimately depend on the aid of the executive arm even for the efficacy of its judgments.[74]

Other branches of government can alter or circumscribe court decisions in three important ways: by constitutional amendment, statutory revision, and by nonimplementation.

CONSTITUTIONAL AMENDMENT

The power to amend the Constitution is the formal constitutional check on the Supreme Court's power of judicial review. But this constitutional check has been used on only a few occasions. The Eleventh Amendment overturned an early Court decision that gave citizens of one state the ability to sue another state. The Sixteenth Amendment allowing an income tax was prompted by a Court decision that seemed to deny Congress this authority. Many amendments under consideration by Congress today have been generated by Supreme Court decisions, including amendments to ban abortions, allow school prayer, and prohibit flag-burning. It is unclear whether any of these proposed amendments will win the necessary support to become part of the Constitution, since supporters must ordinarily win a two-thirds vote in Congress and the backing of three-quarters of the states (see Chapter 2, pp. 60–61). In practice, the complexities of the amendment process make it the weakest check on court power.

STATUTORY REVISION

Congress can reverse court decisions without resorting to a constitutional amendment, if the court decision involves only the interpretation of a statute. In such cases, Congress can simply pass a clarifying law that reverses a court interpretation of earlier legislation. In the case of *Wards Cove v. Antonio*, for example, the Supreme Court gave a narrow interpretation to a congressional law banning race and gender discrimination. The court said that Congress intended that women and minorities bringing the complaint had to bear the burden of proof, a difficult assignment in these kinds of cases. Under pressure from women's groups and civil rights organizations, Congress in 1991 responded by saying the burden of proof had to be borne by business, thereby reversing the Supreme Court decision.

Although passing new legislation is much easier than amending the Constitution, it still is only a partial check on court power. Republicans in Congress tried in 1995 to amend the Endangered Species Act so as to narrow its impact. But a storm of protest from environmentalists and a threatened presidential veto weakened Republican resolve, and the legislation, as interpreted by the courts, remains on the books unscathed (see Chapter 18, pp. 605–607).

NONIMPLEMENTATION

Court decisions can also be checked simply by being ignored. When told of a court decision he did not like, President Andrew Jackson reportedly replied: "Justice Marshall has made his decision, now let him enforce it."[75] Although outright refusal to obey a Supreme Court decision by a president is today unlikely, strong resistance to lower-court decisions by state and local governments is not unknown. After the Supreme Court declared Bible-reading in public schools unconstitutional, the practice in most Tennessee school districts continued hardly unchanged. As one school board attorney explained, "My personal conviction is that the Supreme Court decisions are correct, and I so told the Board and Superintendent, but I saw no reason to create controversy. If the Board had made public a decision abolishing devotional exercises, there would have been public outcry."[76]

Public opposition also frustrated the implementation of a New Jersey state supreme court ruling that required every school district in the state to spend the same amount of money per pupil. Committed to equal educational opportunity and feeling obliged to obey the court decision, Democratic Governor James Florio and his Democratic colleagues in the state legislature passed a new law carrying out the decision by shifting funds from wealthier school districts to poorer ones. Parents and teachers in the communities who lost money responded by voting the governor and his allies in the legislature out of office and electing a new governor, Christine Todd Whitman, who promptly signed legislation repealing some of the shift in funds. The court decision was not fully implemented.

To ensure implementation of judicial orders, courts sometimes appoint a **receiver**, an official who has the authority to see that judicial orders are carried out. For example, in 1996 a Massachusetts judge found the State Department of Mental Retardation guilty of willfully abusing its authority over a school that served severely disabled students. Since the state agency had a long history of misusing its authority over this school, the judge, to prevent future abuse, replaced state supervision of the school with that of a court receiver.

But even the monitoring power of the courts can be checked by elected officials. For two decades, the Correction Department in the city of New York had been overseen by a court monitor who enforced judicial orders ensuring respect for the civil rights of prisoners. Judge Harold Baer Jr., reluctantly withdrew the monitor in 1995 after Congress and the president, concerned that the rights of the guilty were taking precedence over the rights of victims, enacted a law limiting court authority in such matters. "Although the court's [my] concerns with this new legislation are myriad," Judge Baer wrote, "I am constrained under the law to uphold it."[77]

receiver
Court official who has the authority to see that judicial orders are carried out.

Finding officials of the State of Massachusetts guilty of "bad faith," Judge Elizabeth LaStaiti appointed a receiver to oversee a school for the disabled.

Litigation as a Political Strategy

The courts have increasingly been used by advocacy groups to place issues on the political agenda, particularly when elected officials have not responded to group demands. This strategy was initiated by civil rights groups, a topic discussed in detail in Chapter 17 (pp. 555–558). But the strategy has since spread and become a common political phenomenon,[78] fully consistent with de Tocqueville's observation over a century and a half ago, "there is hardly a political question in the United States which does not sooner or later turn into a judicial one."[79]

Disabled Americans owe much of their current inclusion in American politics to an extraordinarily successful use of litigation as a political strategy. As late as 1970 many families with disabled children were told by school officials that their children were not qualified to attend public school. Challenging such denial of equal educational opportunity, advocacy groups won, in 1972, two federal courts rulings saying the disabled had a right to an "appropriate education." Anticipating further litigation, many school officials felt that a federal law might clarify the situation. Under pressure from advocacy groups and with the acquiescence of those representing local school officials, Congress within two years passed sweeping federal legislation that became the "most significant child welfare legislation" of the decade. Although President Ford had opposed the legislation, passage in both House and Senate was by such lopsided margins that he signed it into law, fully aware that a veto was futile.[80]

To advance an issue, advocacy groups often file **class action** suits on behalf of all individuals in a particular class, whether or not they are actually participating in the suit. For example, both individual and class action suits were brought against the Ford Motor Company during the 1980s on behalf of all those who had bought Pinto cars which had gas tanks located in a dangerous place. Ford paid around $20 million "as a result of settlements of court verdicts."[81] Class action suits are justified on the grounds that the issue affects many people in essentially the same way, and it should not be necessary for each member of the class to participate in the litigation in order to secure relief.

Attorneys have been accused of abusing their power to file class action suits by filing problematic claims, then reaching settlements that mainly benefit lawyers, not clients. In 1989 a pop duo, Milli Vanilli and Arista, issued a best-selling record and video of their hit song, "Girl You Know It's True." When it became known that the duo had not truly sung the tune but had only lip-synched, attorneys, shouting fraud, filed class action suits, naming their own children as defendants. Some two years later, the case was settled when the distributor agreed to rebate customers $1 for each single record, $2 for each video cassette, and $3 for each compact disc, provided they had a sales receipt (something only the most compulsive sales-slip collector was likely to possess). The distributor also agreed to make a modest contribution to some charities. The big winners: a few lawyers who collected $670,000 in fees.[82]

■ **class action**
Suit brought on behalf of all individuals in a particular class, whether or not they are actually participating in the suit.

Chapter Summary

The courts are the branch of government most removed from political influences. Federal judges are appointed for life. They are expected only to apply the law, not revise it. Constrained by the principle of *stare decisis*, they are expected to rely upon legal precedents when reaching their decisions. They have been accused of using the power of judicial review to frustrate the popular will. In the famous *Dred Scott* and *Schechter Poultry* cases, the Supreme Court may well have done so.

Yet the courts are not immune to electoral pressures. When justices are selected for the Supreme Court, their political and judicial philosophies are closely evaluated by both presidents and Congress. Once appointed, most Supreme Court justices decide cases in ways that are consistent with views known at the time of their selection. Most of the time, court decisions are broadly responsive to contemporary political currents. If court decisions challenge deep-seated political views, they may be modified by new legislation, frustrated by nonimplementation, or even reversed by constitutional amendment.

Although the most important political issues eventually reach the Supreme Court, the day-to-day work of the judiciary is carried out by lower federal and state judges, who interpret the civil and criminal code. Many state judges and district attorneys are elected officials, and in many other ways political factors also influence the operation of the lower courts.

The judicial system may not work perfectly, but it is probably better than most alternatives. If the law were more removed from politics, the law would control people instead of the reverse. But if federal judges did not have the distance from politics that lifetime appointment gives many of them, justice could be perverted to narrow, partisan ends.

Key Terms

appeal, p. 494

associate justice, p. 496

borking, p. 487

brief, p. 496

cert, p. 499

chief justice, p. 496

circuit court of appeals, p. 503

civil code, p. 501

class action, p. 511

concurring opinion, p. 497

criminal code, p. 502

defendant, p. 501

dissenting opinion, p. 497

district attorney, p. 505

double jeopardy, p. 508

living Constitution theory , p. 490

federal district courts, p. 502

judicial activism, p. 498

judicial restraint, p. 498

judicial review, p. 488

law clerk, p. 500

legal distinction, p. 494

Marbury v. *Madison*, p. 489

McCulloch v. *Maryland*, p. 506

opinion, p. 494

original intent, p. 489

plain meaning of the text, p. 490

plaintiff, p. 501

plenary, p. 496

precedent, p. 494

receiver, p. 510

remand, p. 498

remedy, p. 496

restorationist, p. 498

reversal, p. 494

solicitor general, p. 500

stare decisis, p. 494

statutory interpretation, p. 495

writ of *certiorari*, p. 499

Suggested Readings

Agresto, John. *The Supreme Court and Constitutional Democracy.* Ithaca: Cornell University Press, 1984. Makes a powerful case against judicial review.

Bork, Robert. *The Tempting of America.* New York: Free Press, 1990. Bork's defense of his legal position and his interpretation of the Senate confirmation process.

Bronner, Ethan. *Battle for Justice: How the Bork Nomination Shook America.* New York: W. W. Norton, 1989. Fascinating case study of the Senate refusal to confirm Robert Bork's nomination to the Supreme Court.

Carp, Robert A., and Ronald Stidham, *The Federal Courts,* 2nd ed. Washington, DC: Congressional Quarterly, 1991. Lucid description of federal court system and its political context.

Jeffries, John C. Jr., *Justice Lewis F. Powell, Jr.: A Biography.* New York: Charles Scribner, 1994. Superb biography by Powell's law clerk that provides inside information on the thinking that went into some of the most important Supreme Court decisions.

Massaro, John. *Supremely Political: The Role of Ideology and Presidential Management in Unsuccessful Supreme Court Nominations.* Albany, New York: State University of New York Press, 1990. Engaging account of the politics of Supreme Court nominations.

McCloskey, Robert G. *The American Supreme Court.* Chicago: University of Chicago Press, 1960. Excellent, though somewhat dated, analysis that shows the close connection between public opinion and court decisions.

Melnick, R. Shep. *Between the Lines: Interpreting Welfare Rights.* Washington, D. C.: Brookings, 1994. Insightful analysis of the Court's role in the interpretation and elaboration of statutory law.

Murphy, Walter F. *Elements of Judicial Strategy.* Chicago: University of Chicago Press: 1964. A political analysis of the courts.

O'Brien, David M. *Storm Center: The Supreme Court in American Politics.* New York: Norton, 1996. 4th edition. Up-to-date account of the political role of the Supreme Court.

Perry, H. W., Jr. *Deciding to Decide: Agenda Setting in the United States Supreme Court.* Cambridge, MA: Harvard University Press, 1991. Comprehensive explanation of the process by which the Supreme Court decides whether to review a case.

Pritchett, C. Herman. *The American Constitution.* New York: McGraw-Hill, 1959. Dated, but still authoritative, account of constitutional issues.

Simon, James F. *The Center Holds: The Power Struggle Inside the Rehnquist Court.* New York: Simon & Schuster, 1995. Describes the recent split between conservative and moderate justices.

TURN PAGE TO

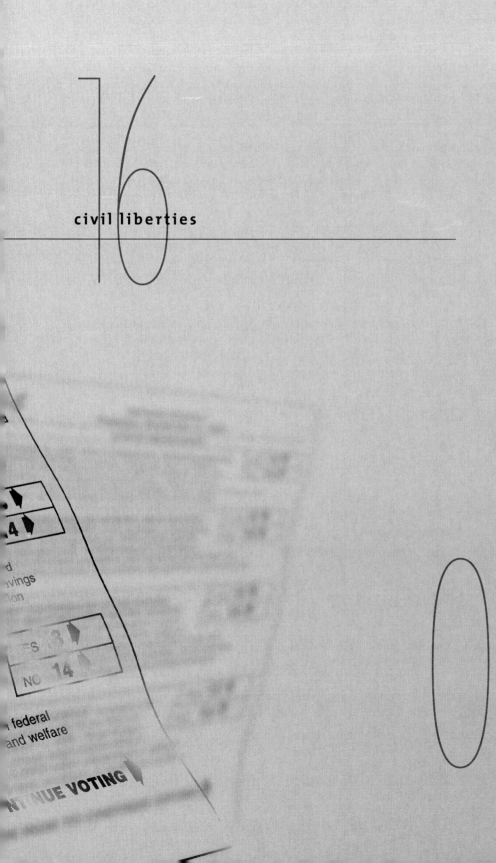

16

civil liberties

N A C R I S P January night in 1993, a group of African-American students at the University of Pennsylvania were celebrating. Unfortunately, their ardor invited only a stream of invective from the windows above that included racial and sexually demeaning slurs. Someone was said to have yelled, "Shut up, you black water buffaloes! Go back to the zoo where you belong!" When the women complained to campus administrators, an ensuing investigation identified only one individual, Eden Jacobowitz, who admitted to having participated in the outcry. Jacobowitz, an Israeli, denied any racial animosity and claimed he was upset only because the women failed to acquiesce to urgent demands to be quiet. He admitted to calling the women "water buffalo," but said the term was nothing more than a translation of a "mild Hebraic epithet for a rude person." When invited to join the party below, he admitted replying, "If you're looking for a party, there's a zoo a mile from here!"[1] The university's Judicial Inquiry Office felt that the campus code prohibiting racial epithets had been violated; Jacobowitz objected that the university's code violated his right of free speech.

At almost the same time, Professor Leonard Jeffries complained that his right of free speech had been violated by the City College of New York. Jeffries, the head of the college's African-American studies department, had claimed there was a "conspiracy, planned and plotted and programmed out of Hollywood," a conspiracy that included Jews and the Mafia, to cause "the destruction of black people." A month after these statements had been made, the president of City College sent a letter to the university community stating that Jeffries's speech "contained clear statements of bigotry and anti-Semitism." Some time later, the Board of Trustees removed Jeffries as head of African-American studies. He sued to be reinstated as departmental chair on the grounds that his right to free speech had been infringed. The jury found in favor of Jeffries.[2]

In an effort to promote an atmosphere of tolerance and respect for men and women from diverse racial and religious backgrounds, many colleges and universities have established guidelines that limit the use of "fighting words" on sensitive topics. The desirability of such regulations has been a subject of national debate.

■ **civil liberties**
Fundamental freedoms that together preserve the rights of a free people.

n this chapter we place such debates in a larger constitutional context by describing the evolution of civil liberties under the U.S. Constitution. The concept of **civil liberties**, the fundamental freedoms that together preserve the rights of a free people, is never mentioned in the Constitution, nor has it ever been explicitly defined by the Supreme Court. But specific rights that together make up the civil liberties of U.S. citizens are to be found in the Bill of Rights, the first ten amendments to the Constitution, and, again in amendments added to the Constitution after the Civil War. The number of rights and freedoms protected by the Constitution has been greatly enlarged over the centuries, and the United States probably does more to protect its citizens' liberties than any other nation. In this chapter we shall focus on the most important of these liberties. Three of them are almost universally regarded as fundamental: freedom of speech, freedom of religion, and the rights of those accused of a crime. A fourth right, the right of privacy, remains a subject of political dispute.

Origins of Civil Liberties
In the United States

The evolution of civil liberties in the United States has been shaped by Supreme Court decisions. But as we shall see, these liberties have also been affected by political debates and election outcomes. Civil liberties have not been created simply by a small number of justices but reflect basic values shared by most citizens (see Chapter 4, pp. 114–122).

ORIGINS OF THE BILL OF RIGHTS

The liberties of Americans were among the rallying cries of the revolution. Not only did the Declaration of Independence declare a fundamental "right to life, liberty and the pursuit of happiness," but many states incorporated similar principles into their laws and constitutions. For example, the Virginia assembly passed a bill of rights a month before the proclamation of the Declaration of Independence. Among its provisions was the pronouncement that "freedom of the press" was "one of the great bulwarks of liberty." [3]

Despite their expressed commitment to basic freedoms, the colonial revolutionaries trampled on the liberties of the Tories, who opposed the revolution. They closed Tory newspapers, threatened well-known Tory editors, confiscated their property, and so intimidated those opposed to the revolution that some 80 thousand people fled to Canada, England, and the West Indies. Even John Adams, future president of the United States, vowed that "the [Tory] presses will produce no more seditious or traitorous speculations." [4]

Nor did those who drafted the Constitution include explicit protection for individual civil liberties. When Anti-Federalist Charles Pinckney offered a motion to guarantee freedom of the press at the constitutional convention, the Federalist

Not much free speech. Many a Tory editor was hung in effigy before and during the American Revolution.

The driving force behind the Bill of Rights in the first Congress was James Madison. Madison's willingness to defer to the desire of others can be explained by the same constituency pressures that shape the views of modern-day members of Congress. Though a Federalist, Madison came from Virginia, the home state of the acclaimed Virginia Bill of Rights and the country's most influential Anti-Federalists, George Mason and Patrick Henry. Henry had successfully fought to prevent Madison from being selected as one of Virginia's two Senators, and Madison had won a seat in the House of Representatives only by promising to work for the passage of a Bill of Rights.

That Madison was influenced more by election pressures than by constitutional scruples is evident from the fact that at the constitutional convention itself he had seen little need for such a document. Even after the convention, Madison wrote, "I have never thought the omission [of a bill of rights] a material defect, nor been anxious to supply it even by subsequent amendment, for any other reason than that it is anxiously desired by others."

In Madison's hands, the meaning of the Bill of Rights underwent a significant transformation. Whereas the Anti-Federalists had wanted amendments that would protect states rights, the Bill of Rights, as written by Madison, mention states rights in only two of the eight amendments, focus-

ing all the other amendments on the rights of individuals. By focusing on the rights of individuals, Madison avoided the central issue of contention between Federalists and anti-Federalists—the balance of power between the states and the new national government. The ten amendments were quickly and quietly ratified in 1791 by all but two states, apparently because few people thought they would have much practical effect.

SOURCES: Robert A. Rutland, *The Birth of the Bill of Rights* (Chapel Hill: University of North Carolina Press, 1955); Stanley Elkins and Eric McKitrick, *The Age of Federalism* (New York: Oxford University Press, 1993); Thornton Anderson, *Creating the Constitution: The Convention of 1787 and the First Congress* (University Park: Pennsylvania State University Press, 1993) p. 176.

majority voted the motion down—on the grounds that regulation of the speech and press was a state responsibility.[5] Only when ratification of the Constitution seemed in danger did Federalists agree to add a Bill of Rights in the form of ten amendments to the Constitution (see Chapter 2, pp. 58–59). The first Congress reluctantly approved the Bill of Rights in 1790 only at James Madison's insistence (see Election Connection). Most voted for the ten amendments, it seems, because they thought the provisions would have little effect.

FEW LIBERTIES BEFORE THE CIVIL WAR

The Bill of Rights was a virtual dead letter for sixty years, mainly because the first ten amendments were applied only to the national, not state, government. The First Amendment, for example, focused solely on the national government, saying that *Congress* shall not abridge speech or religious practice. No limitations were placed on state governments. As a result, the Episcopalian Church remained the state church in Virginia, and the Puritan religion remained the established religion in Massachusetts.

Many of the other provisions in the Bill of Rights did not specifically mention either the national or the state governments, leaving open the possibility that they applied to both. For example, the Fifth Amendment said "no person shall . . . be deprived of life, liberty, or property, without due process of law." But when the owner of Barron's Wharf complained that the City of Baltimore had deprived his company of property without "due process of law," the Supreme Court, in 1833, said the Fifth Amendment limited the powers of the federal government but not those of the states. The Bill of Rights, said John Marshall "contain[s] no expression indicating an intention to apply them to the state governments. This court cannot so apply them."[6]

It would have been difficult for Marshall to apply the Bill of Rights to the states prior to the Civil War, because doing so would have raised the slavery issue in acute form. Were slaves people who had liberties, or were they property that belonged to their masters? These questions would eventually provoke the Civil War, but during the early 1800s, both the Supreme Court and most elected leaders avoided the issue.

The main use of the Bill of Rights prior to the Civil War, ironically enough, was to justify continued enslavement. In the extraordinary *Dred Scott* decision, Justice Roger Taney reached the conclusion that the Fifth Amendment precluded Congress from denying Dred Scott's master his right of property. As for Dred Scott, the slave, he was not regarded as a person within the meaning of the Fifth Amendment.

⭐ **AT THE STATE & LOCAL LEVEL**

APPLYING THE BILL OF RIGHTS TO STATE GOVERNMENTS

CONSTITUTION, FOURTEENTH AMENDMEN*t*: [No] *state shall deprive any person of life, liberty, or property, without due process of law.*

The Civil War transformed the spirit, meaning, and application of the Bill of Rights. Once slavery had been abolished, the words in the first ten amendments could begin to be applied to all Americans. To give the Bill of Rights new meaning, the Constitution was altered by three **Civil Rights Amendments**, Amendments 13, 14, and 15, which abolished slavery, redefined civil rights and liberties, and guaranteed the right to vote to all adult male citizens. Ordinarily, the complex procedures for amending the Constitution would have made it impossible to enact amendments that changed the Constitution in such a fundamental manner. But the Civil Rights amendments were approved at a time when those who had fought for the South were excluded from political participation. Congress was controlled by those who had remained loyal to the Union, and southern states were denied readmission to the Union until they had ratified these amendments.

Of all the provisions in the Civil Rights Amendments, the one that has had the greatest significance for civil liberty is the **due process clause** of the Fourteenth Amendment, which says that a person cannot be deprived of life, liberty, or property without due process of law. As mentioned above, the phrase was already to be found in the Fifth Amendment, but the Fourteenth Amendment greatly expanded civil liberties by making one apparently minor change—saying that no *state* may "deprive any person of life, liberty, or property, without due process of law." By

■ **Civil Rights Amendments**
Amendments 13, 14, and 15, which abolished slavery, redefined civil rights, and guaranteed the right to vote to all adult male citizens.

■ **due process clause**
Found in the Fifth and Fourteenth Amendments to the Constitution, forbids deprivation of life, liberty, or property without due process of law.

specifically mentioning state governments, the due process clause of the Fourteenth Amendment guaranteed that civil liberties were to be protected from interference by the states as well as by the federal government.

Despite the explicit language in the Fourteenth Amendment in applying the due process clause to the states, the Supreme Court has never interpreted this clause as saying that states must abide by each and every provision of the Bill of Rights. Instead, the Court has taken an approach known as **selective incorporation**, a process by which the courts decide on a case-by-case basis whether a particular denial of a liberty listed in the Bill of Rights is also a violation of the due process clause of the Fourteenth Amendment. Over the years, almost all of the provisions in the Bill of Rights have been incorporated. But a few exceptions remain, such as the Second Amendment, which says that inasmuch as "a well-regulated militia" is necessary to "the security of a free state, the right of the people to keep and bear arms shall not be abridged." Although the National Rifle Association has argued that laws banning the use of guns are contrary to the Constitution, the Supreme Court has said this provision only guarantees state governments' right to have a militia.

■ **selective incorporation**
The case-by-case incorporation by the courts of the Bill of Rights into the due process clause of the Fourteenth Amendment.

Freedom of Speech, Press, and Assembly

CONSTITUTION, FIRST AMENDMENT: *Congress shall make no law . . . abridging the freedom of speech, or of the press; or the right of the people peaceably to assemble, . . .*

Of the liberties listed in the Bill of Rights, one trio stands paramount: freedom of speech, press, and assembly. Though each has its own nuance, the three are closely intertwined. If free speech is to be effective, it must be communicated through a free press. Unless an audience can be assembled to listen, speakers might as well keep silent. Because of the close connection among the three liberties, we shall treat them as one—which we refer to as free speech.

FREE SPEECH AND MAJORITARIAN DEMOCRACY

Free speech is vital to the workings of free elections in a democratic society. In the absence of free speech, public opinion can be molded by government officials without fear of contradiction. Elections have little meaning when candidates cannot express their opinions without fear of punishment.

Yet, elections are won by candidates backed by a majority of the voters, and majorities can at times be as tyrannical as single-minded despots. Indeed, the greatest threat to the rights of the people, said James Madison, is the **tyranny of the majority**, the suppression of minority opinions by those voted into power by a majority.[7] Its very size enhances the conviction with which the majority holds its views as well as its capacity to identify those who dissent. As Lord Acton once said, "The one pervading evil of democracy is the tyranny of the majority, or rather of that party, not always the majority, that succeeds, by force or fraud, in carrying elections."[8]

The classic defense of free speech was provided by the English civil libertarian, John Stuart Mill, who insisted that, in the free exchange of ideas, truth would eventually triumph over error. Galileo's declaration that the Earth was not at the center

■ **tyranny of the majority**
Stifling of dissent by those voted into power by the majority.

When I was in sixth grade, my teacher gave us the word "slavery" in a spelling test. He recited a sentence to clarify its meaning: "Sharon is lucky she is not in slavery." As my stomach began to lurch, my hands held tighter to my pencil. My friends began to hiss and boo in disgust at his thoughtlessness. My teacher merely smiled; he never apologized.

That was the first time I experienced racism. It changed my life.... If I was hurt in a situation of that level, think of how the person who is the target of a racial epithet must feel....

During freshman orientation week a dean told us that education should advance society. I agree. Yet promoting ideas of hatred only serves to hinder this advancement.

    —Sharon Gwyn,
Stanford University*

My father, Carl Foreman, a Hollywood screenwriter, was blacklisted in the 1950s for refusing to cooperate with the House Committee [on Un-American Activities.] His decision forced him to live in exile in Britain for 30 years....

I am a senior in college at a time when the freedom to voice, indeed even to think, controversial thoughts is under assault in American universities. One can't ignore the similarity between those accused in the 1950s of being disloyal and those accused today of failing to be politically correct....

There are stories from all over the country of liberal professors who have been denounced for crimes as big as teaching a controversial theory, or as small as using the "wrong" adjective.... America cannot remain a free country if the rights of its citizens are taken away. It's something the universities have yet to learn.

    —Amanda Foreman,
Sarah Lawrence College†

* *New York Times*, May 12, 1989, I, B12.

† *New York Times*, March 29, 1991, A29.

of the universe eventually became accepted as true, though informed opinion initially regarded his claims as preposterous. Fifty years ago, geologists laughed at Alfred Wegner's suggestion that the world's continents drifted over long distances. Hardly a decade ago, the claim that dinosaurs were destroyed by an asteroid was dismissed out of hand by paleontologists.

But some truths seem beyond dispute. It is not easy to accept the idea of people enjoying the freedom to spread doctrines of racial hatred (see Democratic Dilemma). Are their beliefs not founded on false premises that could never be shown to be true? To such contentions, Mill replied that "he who knows only his own side of the case, knows little of that."[9] Mill argued further that error repressed becomes more powerful by virtue of its suppression. Only if error is allowed to express itself can its proponents be denied the privilege of a false martyrdom.

ORIGINS OF FREEDOM OF SPEECH

Speech and press during the early colonial period were governed by the **prior restraint doctrine**, which said the government could not censor an article before it was published. However, the prior restraint doctrine did not prevent prosecution after the fact. Instead, the publisher could be convicted for bringing the government's

prior restraint doctrine
Legal doctrine that gives individuals the right to publish without prior restraint—that is, without first submitting material to government censor.

"dignity into contempt," even if what he said were true. So when Peter Zenger in 1734 published a true and accurate critique of an incompetent, unprincipled New York governor, the governor put Zenger in jail at excessive bail for ten months while awaiting trial. In one of the great early victories for the freedom of the press, the jury found Zenger innocent after his attorney argued that the issue at stake was "the Liberty—both of exposing and opposing arbitrary Power . . . by speaking and writing Truth."[10]

EVOLUTION OF FREE SPEECH DOCTRINE

Even though the beginnings of free speech date back to the colonial period, the doctrine of free speech, as we know it today, is not as deeply entrenched a part of the American tradition as Fourth-of-July speakers often proclaim. Despite the First Amendment, people have been jailed for expressing controversial thoughts as long ago as 1798 and as recently as 1968. The development of free speech in the United States is not a hoary story from the ancient past; most of the important developments have taken place in recent decades.

Nor is the story of free speech a story of the Supreme Court protecting the rights of citizens from the tyranny of the majority. In moments when popular passions are intense and minorities are endangered, the least democratic institution, the judicial system, is often called upon to protect individual rights from the momentary rage of the public and the elected leaders beholden to them. But as we shall see, for many years the judiciary did not provide minorities much protection. Instead, the Supreme Court has moved along at about the same speed—or perhaps a little slower—than the rest of the country. In the words of one scholar, "the Court has seldom lagged far behind or forged far ahead of America."[11] Nonetheless, progress toward free speech in the United States can best be traced by noting the evolution in court doctrine.

CLEAR AND PRESENT DANGER DOCTRINE

In its first major decision affecting freedom of speech, the Supreme Court, in *Schenck* v. *United States* (1919), enunciated the **clear and present danger doctrine**, a principle that said people should have complete freedom of speech unless their language gives rise to a clear and present danger. In the midst of World War I, members of Congress passed the Espionage Act, which outlawed obstruction of recruitment into the armed forces. Socialist Charles Schenck was convicted under this law for mailing anti-conscription pamphlets to draft-age men.

At the time, most people thought that Schenck's conviction was entirely proper. Wartime creates conditions under which civil liberties are likely to be tested; elected officials are often under public pressure to identify pacifists or other dissenters as enemies of the country. As Alexis de Toqueville wrote, " All those who seek to destroy the liberties of a democratic nation ought to know that war is the surest and shortest means to accomplish it."[12]

It was thus up to the courts to protect the right of free speech under these wartime conditions. The Supreme Court, no more sympathetic to socialists than Congress had been, upheld Schenck's conviction. Yet the Schenck case ironically became the occasion for the enunciation of the clear and present danger doctrine. Justice Oliver Wendell Holmes observed that no person has the right to falsely cry "Fire" in a crowded theater: Such a cry creates a clear and present danger. His example seemed to capture succinctly the appropriate balance between the right of free speech and the need to maintain social order.

The meaning of clear and present danger, however, is open to many interpretations. If this standard is applied to the college campuses discussed at the beginning of this chapter, many might decide that in neither case was anything said that was tantamount to crying "Fire" in a crowded theater. Others might reply that, if racial and ethnic slurs come to be standard practice, they constitute a clear and present danger to society; to keep that from happening, speech should be restricted now before the danger becomes too present.

Holmes himself took the more restrictive point of view. He said that Schenck's actions constituted a clear and present danger to the successful prosecution of the war, because, if successful, the mailing of anti-draft pamphlets to draft-age men could endanger the war effort.[13] Holmes ignored the fact that few paid much attention to Schenck and his associates.

But even though Holmes initially used the clear and present danger doctrine to suppress dissent, the doctrine became the foundation upon which a free speech tradition was gradually built. During the 1930s, when the public was more tolerant of dissenting opinion, the Supreme Court, reflecting the changing political climate, explicitly defended the civil liberties of minorities. Two cases decided in 1931, *Stromberg* v. *California* and *Near* v. *Minnesota*, were particularly important, because for the first time they gave court protection to extremely unpopular opinions. Yetta Stromberg had encouraged children attending a camp operated by the Young Communist League to pledge allegiance to the flag of the Soviet Union, a violation of California's "red-flag" law.[14] The Supreme Court overturned her conviction, saying that the law limited "free political discussion." Also in 1931, the Supreme Court, in *Near* v. *Minnesota*, overruled the Minnesota legislature when it shut down a newspaper for publishing malicious and defamatory material. The action of the legislature was regarded by the court as "the essence of censorship."[15] Since neither Stromberg nor the Minnesota newspaper constituted a clear and present danger, their civil liberties should not be curtailed.

FIGHTING WORDS DOCTRINE

The toleration that emerged during the 1930s did not survive the onset of World War II. In 1940 Congress responded to public outrage against fascism by enacting the Smith Act which forbade advocating the overthrow of the government by force. Even university administrators forbade demonstrations against the draft. Columbia University President Nicholas Butler justified the ban in these words: "Before academic freedom comes university freedom to pursue its high ideals, unembarrassed by conduct which tends to damage its reputation."[16]

The Supreme Court, instead of acting as a bulwark against majority tyranny during World War II, endorsed these limitations on free speech. In *Chaplinsky* v. *New Hampshire*, the court enunciated the **fighting words doctrine** that said some words constitute violent acts. Walter Chaplinsky, a member of the Jehovah's Witnesses religious group, had asked a policeman to guard him from a threatening crowd objecting to his pacifist address. When the policeman gave him no protection but instead cursed him and asked him to "come along," Chaplinsky called the policeman "a God damned racketeer" and "a damned Fascist." Enunciating the fighting words doctrine, the Supreme Court upheld Chaplinsky's conviction on the grounds that Chaplinsky had used threatening words that are not speech but "by their very utterance inflict injury or intend to incite an immediate breach of the peace."[17] In sum, the new fighting words doctrine developed during World War II seriously qualified the court's earlier inclination to give some protection to free speech under

■ **fighting words doctrine**
Supreme Court writing in *Chaplinsky* v. *New Hampshire* (1942), saying some words constitute violent acts.

CIVIL LIBERTIES ARE OFTEN THE FIRST CASUALTY OF WAR: THE EXPERIENCE OF JAPANESE AMERICANS IN WORLD WAR II

Responding to public concern that Japanese Americans might act as spies for Japan, President Franklin Roosevelt ordered 70 thousand Japanese-American citizens and another 40 thousand resident Japanese to leave their homes and live in "relocation centers." Those who swore loyalty to the United States were released but, if they lived close to either the East or West Coast, told they could not return home. Earl Warren, the California attorney general and later the chief justice of the Supreme Court, gave a racial rationale for these actions: "When we are dealing with the Caucasian race we have methods that will test the loyalty of them.... But when we deal with the Japanese ... we cannot form any opinion that we believe to be sound." *

Discriminatory actions by elected officials at a time when popular opinion was ferociously anti-Japanese is perhaps understandable. More difficult to rationalize is the inability of the Supreme Court to protect a minority against the tyranny of the majority. In *Korematsu* v. *United States* (1944), the Court found relocation centers constitutional. In his dissent, Justice Murphy said the relocation was "one of the most sweeping and complete deprivations of constitutional rights in the history of this nation."† To rectify the injustice, Congress in 1988 finally voted to compensate many Japanese Americans who had been relocated.

* Robert Goldstein, *Political Repression in Modern America: 1870 to the Present* (New York: Schenkman, 1978), 266–67.

† 323 US 244.

---

the clear and present danger doctrine. It was this fighting words doctrine that many university administrators invoked in the early 1990s when they tried to enforce ethnic tolerance on campus (see pp. 515–516).

BALANCING DOCTRINE

The end of World War II did not automatically restore civil liberties to dissident groups. Instead, those who were regarded as Communist sympathizers were harassed by government officials responding to public concern about the growing conflict between the United States and the Soviet Union. Senator Joseph McCarthy of Wisconsin gained political popularity by accusing artists, teachers, and government officials of having ties to the Communist party. As part of the anti-Communist crusade, Congress voted to require that all employees of the federal government take an oath swearing loyalty to the United States. Students also had to take this oath when applying for student loans.

Once again, it was up to the courts to protect the free speech of minority dissidents. But the Supreme Court, instead of taking special care to protect free speech, enunciated the **balancing doctrine**, which said that freedom of speech had to be balanced against other competing public interests at stake in particular circumstances. In *Dennis* v. *United States* (1951), the Court said the "balance ... must be struck in favor" of the governmental interest in resisting subversion when it declared constitutional

■ **balancing doctrine**
Supreme Court enunciation that freedom of speech must be balanced against other competing public interests at stake in particular circumstances.

the conviction of eleven leaders of the Communist party under the Smith Act for joining a political party that espoused the revolutionary overthrow of the government. The balancing doctrine was used to limit the clear and present danger doctrine. The court explicitly said that clear and present danger "cannot mean that before the Government may act, it must wait until . . . the [revolutionary] plans have been laid and the signal is awaited."[18]

It was elected political leaders, not judges, who resisted the threat that McCarthyism posed to the country's civil liberties. President Eisenhower refused to act on McCarthy's most outrageous accusations, and McCarthy's Senate colleagues finally inquired into the senator's methods of operation, finally censuring him for his inappropriate conduct.

Senator Joseph McCarthy, at the hearings that bore his name, which investigated alleged Communist sympathizers in the early fifties.

FUNDAMENTAL FREEDOMS DOCTRINE

After McCarthy's political power had been undermined by an elected president and Congress, public opinion became increasingly supportive of the free speech rights of radicals and Communists (see Figure 16.1) Reflecting these changes in public opinion, the Supreme Court gradually became committed to

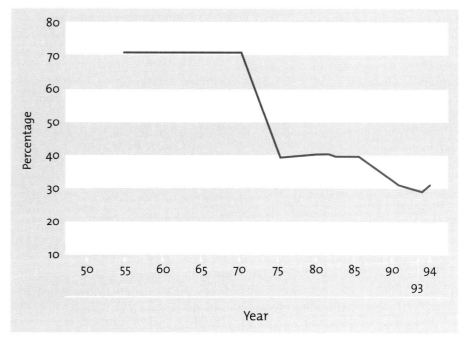

FIGURE **16.1**

Percentage Opposed to Allowing Communists to Make a Speech:

The public has become more tolerant.

SOURCES: Benjamin I. Page and Robert Y. Shapiro, *The Rational Public: Fifty Years of Trends in Americans' Policy Preferences* (Chicago: University of Chicago Press, 1992): 87; National Opinion Research Center, General Social Survey.

Gregory Johnson, whose conviction for torching the American flag in 1984 was overturned by the Supreme Court. Johnson later challenged President George Bush to debate Bush's proposal of a constitutional ban on flag burning.

■ **fundamental freedoms doctrine**
Court doctrine stating that laws impinging upon the freedoms fundamental to the preservation of democratic practice—speech, press, assembly and religion—are to be scrutinized by the courts more closely than other legislation. These are also termed the *preferred freedoms.*

the **fundamental freedoms doctrine**, which said that some constitutional provisions were to be given special preference because they are basic to the functioning of a democratic society. The doctrine had its origins in a footnote to a Supreme Court opinion written in 1938 by Justice Harlan Stone, who said that some freedoms, such as freedom of speech, have a "preferred position" in the Constitution; any law threatening these freedoms must be given strict scrutiny by the Supreme Court.[19]

Although no one court case specifically set forth the fundamental freedoms doctrine, it became the Court's governing doctrine during the 1960s in the midst of the Vietnam war. Under its guidance, the Supreme Court did a better job of defending dissenters against government repression than in any previous war. As one civil libertarian wrote in 1973, "The truly significant thing in recent years has not been the attempt of the current administration to suppress criticism, but rather the marked inability of the administration to do so effectively."[20] In virtually every case that came before it, the Court ruled against efforts to suppress free speech. For example, it overturned the expulsion of a student from the University of Missouri who was distributing a newspaper containing a picture of a policeman raping the Statue of Liberty. Said the Court: The mere dissemination of ideas—no matter how offensive to good taste—on a state university campus may not be shut off in the name of decency.[21]

In one of its most significant decisions, *New York Times* v. *United States* (1971), the Supreme Court rejected an attempt by the Nixon Administration to prevent, on national security grounds, the *New York Times* from publishing the "Pentagon Papers," a Defense Department document revealing many wartime mistakes made by government officials. The newspaper objected that the government was trying to exercise prior restraint, a violation of the freedom of the press outlawed since the days of Peter Zenger (see p. 522). The Supreme Court ruled in favor of the *New York Times* on the grounds that the "Pentagon Papers" did not in fact include highly sensitive material.

The fundamental freedoms doctrine has now become firmly established. Nothing better illustrates the contemporary Supreme Court's strong commitment to this principle than its rulings with respect to flag-burning.[22] During the 1984 Republican national convention, Gregory Johnson burned an American flag to protest the policies of the Reagan Administration. Five years later, Johnson's conviction came before the Supreme Court. The Court, in *Johnson* v. *Texas* (1989), overturned his conviction, saying the principal purpose of free speech is to invite dispute and the mere burning of the flag did not breach the peace.

Unlike earlier court decisions, the Supreme Court in the flag-burning case went well beyond popular opinion of the day. President George Bush called for a constitutional amendment that would prohibit flag desecration, and over 70 percent of the public supported him. Almost immediately, Congress passed a law making it a federal offense to burn the flag. The very day the law was passed, flags were set fire in Seattle and Washington, D.C., preparing the ground for another court decision. The next year the Supreme Court, in *Eichman* v. *United States* (1990), declared the new law unconstitutional.[23] Many thought it especially significant that Antonin Scalia, one of the Court's most conservative justices, voted with the majority.

If anything, Supreme Court conservatives have become champions of free speech. In *R.A.V.* v. *City of St. Paul* (1990), Scalia wrote a majority opinion that gave protection to speech criticizing other ethnic groups. The City of St. Paul had passed an ordinance forbidding the placement on public or private property of a symbol

An extraordinary contribution to American civil liberties arose out of the Watergate debacle that took place during President Nixon's reelection campaign in 1972. Watergate clarified for many Americans the danger that executive power could pose to fundamental freedoms.

As part of its electoral campaign to remain in office, the Nixon administration engaged in a wide variety of activities that violated the privacy of prominent political opponents. Telephone lines were tapped without court authorization, income tax returns were examined for politically motivated reasons, and, worst of all, an effort was made to burglarize the Democratic party headquarters at the Watergate Hotel in Washington, D.C. Over a year after the burglars were caught, when it became clear that the burglary had been authorized by the president and his top aides, Richard Nixon was forced to resign as president of the United States.

Richard Nixon was not the first president to have authorized actions that violated people's civil liberties. But the public outrage prompted by the Watergate revelations placed civil liberties on more solid ground than ever before. President Nixon's party was overwhelmingly defeated in the congressional elections in 1974 and it lost control of the White House in 1976. Elected officials became aware that serious violations of civil liberty could provoke adverse electoral consequences.

---

that "arouses anger, alarm or resentment in others on the basis of race, color, creed, religion or gender." When on the summer solstice of 1990 a group of teenagers were caught placing a "crudely made cross" made of "broken chair legs" inside the fence of the yard of a black neighbor, the City of St. Paul charged them of violating the city ordinance. The Supreme Court unanimously agreed with the defendants that the ordinance violated their right of free speech, saying ordinary trespassing laws were adequate to deal with the alleged intrusion on a person's property.[24]

WATERGATE

The Watergate scandal was probably as important to the preservation of free speech and other civil liberties as any court decision. When taped evidence revealed that President Richard Nixon had helped plan a burglary against his political opposition, bipartisan public outrage forced his resignation. The incident left a strong impression on elected officials, who were warned that violations of civil liberties, if discovered, could have a high electoral cost (see Election Connection).

LIMITATIONS ON FREE SPEECH

Though free speech has now been firmly established as one of the country's fundamental freedoms, this does not mean that all speech is free of government control. In particular, three types of speech can be subjected to regulation: commercial speech, libel, and obscenity.

Commercial speech may be regulated. Though no regulation ever barred this Joe Camel ad, the company eventually dropped its highly effective sales animal, which protesters charged was aimed directly at young people.

■ **commercial speech**
Advertising or other speech made for business purposes; may be regulated.

■ **libel**
False statement defaming another.

Commercial Speech—advertising or other speech made for business purposes—may be regulated. The court says regulation of commercial speech is needed so that customers are not provided false or misleading information. Also, commercial speech can be controlled to discourage the consumption of substances the government regards as harmful. For example, cigarette advertising on television and radio is forbidden, despite the complaints by tobacco companies that it interferes with their right to free speech.

Libel, that is, a false statement defaming another, is not constitutionally protected, if made by one private person about another. But what if press reports about public figures are erroneous? Can a newspaper then be successfully sued? This issue was raised by a fund-raising advertisement placed in the *New York Times* on March 29, 1960, by a civil rights group. The advertisement, running ten paragraphs long, reported on student demonstrations against segregation in Montgomery, Alabama. The advertisement contained a number of factual errors: The students sang the National Anthem, not "My Country 'Tis of Thee." The students had been expelled from college by the State Board of Education for sitting at a white lunch counter, not for leading a demonstration. For these and other errors, Montgomery County Commissioner L. B. Sullivan sued for libel, and an all-white Alabama jury found the *New York Times* guilty to the tune of half a million dollars per allegation.[25]

The Supreme Court's decision in this case reflected national public opinion, which at the time was very supportive of the civil rights movement. In *Sullivan* v. *New York Times* (1963), the Court held that untruthful statements made about public figures were not actionable for libel unless the errors were made knowingly or with reckless disregard for the truth. In the Court's view, the errors in the advertisement were reasonable mistakes that showed no reckless disregard for truth.

Some wonder whether the *Sullivan* decision, by freeing the media from legal responsibility for "accidental" errors and falsehoods, has granted it too much power. Certainly, the news media have acquired an aggressive, investigative style which at times has led them to make erroneous accusations. In 1993, a CBS news magazine program, "Eye to Eye," placed at risk severely disabled students by placing an employee with a hidden camera in their school, seeking (but not finding) evidence of wrong-doing. The year before, ABC's show, "Primetime Live," had its employee, again with a hidden camera, submit a fake resume to gain a job in the meat section of a grocery store that it accused of selling doctored fish. Though a federal jury found ABC's misrepresentation fraudulent, it is too soon to know whether the media's potential liability for misrepresentation will curb recent tendencies toward excessive sensationalism.

Obscenity—publicly offensive language or portrayals of no redeeming social value—is not protected under the First Amendment. Whether explicit sexual material is obscene depends on whether it has some social or cultural purpose. The Warren Court, in *Redrup* v. *New York* (1967), came close to saying that it would not uphold any conviction unless the obscenity involved a juvenile, was forced upon unwilling adults, or "pandered" to the most disgusting of prurient interests. But just a few years later a more conservative court said in *Miller* v. *California* (1973) that obscenity is a matter to be settled according to local community standards, though this was later qualified to mean local standards as long as they take into account the "national consensus of protected expression."[26] Overall, the Court seems to have said that local communities may, if they wish, ban hard-core pornography. Less explicit sexual material may not be outlawed, particularly if presented within an artistic or literary context.

Although the media are constitutionally free from legal responsibility for spreading misinformation through accidental errors and falsehoods, the media has its own checks. Popular reporter Connie Chung was dismissed by CBS after she received sharp criticism for excessive sensationalism. Here Chung interviews Faye Resnick, a close friend of O.J. Simpson's late wife, Nicole, in footage that was never aired.

■ **AT THE STATE & LOCAL LEVEL**
Freedom of Religion

CONSTITUTION, FIRST AMENDMENT: *Congress shall make no law respecting an establishment of religion, or prohibiting the free exercise thereof.*

Freedom of religion is guaranteed by two clauses in the First Amendment. The **establishment of religion clause** denies the government the power to establish any single religious practice as superior. The **free exercise of religion clause** protects the right of individuals to practice their religion. When interpreting these clauses, the Supreme Court, as we shall see, has often been influenced by the political and electoral context in which its decisions have been made.

■ **obscenity**
Publicly offensive language or portrayals with no redeeming social value.

■ **establishment of religion clause**
Denies the government the power to establish any single religious practice as superior.
■ **free exercise of religion clause**
Protects the right of individuals to practice their religion.

(right) President Clinton discussing the new television rating system that warns viewers about sex and violence, with Westinghouse CEO Michael Jordan (center) and Turner Broadcasting CEO Ted Turner.
(left) An on-screen example of the rating for a children's cartoon program.

Mr. Michael Jordan
Westinghouse Electric Corporation

Mr. Ted Turner
Turner Broadcasting

No Establishment of Religion Clause

Religious issues often arise in conjunction with the provision of public education, in good part because many think schools need to teach not only reading and arithmetic but morals and values as well. When Massachusetts passed the nation's first compulsory schooling law in 1852, the legislation was enacted because many Protestants felt something had to be done about the waves of Catholic immigrants arriving in Boston from Ireland and Germany. Distressed by the changing composition of the city's population, the Boston School Committee urged that

> We must open the doors of our school houses and invite and compel them to come in. There is no other hope for them or for us. . . . In our schools they must receive moral and religious teaching, powerful enough if possible to keep them in the right path amid the moral darkness which is their daily and domestic walk.[27]

Catholic parents did not think they were allowing their sons and daughters to live in "moral darkness" and saw little reason why their children should acquire their moral and religious training in public schools run by Protestants. So they requested instead public monies to help fund Catholic schools. But Catholic demands for government financing only heightened Protestant fears of immigrants and "the power of the Catholic pope." The anti-Catholic forces were so strong that in 1875 they nearly passed a constitutional amendment that explicitly forbade state aid to religious schools (for more on fears of immigrants, see pp. 104–113).[28]

Although the proposed amendment failed to pass, Supreme Court decisions interpreting the establishment of religion clause reflected the views of the Protestant majority, which opposed aid to religious schools. As a result, the Court has pretty much followed Thomas Jefferson's **separation of church and state doctrine**, which says that a wall should separate the government from religious activity. For example, in *Meek* v. *Pittenger* (1975), the Court struck down most forms of aid that Pennsylvania provided religious schools as part of its federally funded compensatory education program.[29] The Court said public monies cannot be used to pay religious-school teachers, for curricular materials, or for any other expense, except for textbooks and the cost of transporting students to school.

■ **separation of church and state doctrine**
Principle that a wall should separate the government from religious activity.

For many years, Protestant religious celebrations in public schools were observed, despite the separation of church and state doctrine. But in recent years the doctrine has been quite rigorously applied to most forms of state-supported religious activity. School prayer, a sacred moment of silence, reading from the Bible as a sacred text, and the celebration of religious holidays have all been banned.[30]

These Court decisions provoked efforts to amend the Constitution so as to permit prayer in school. A majority of the public have said they support such an amendment,[31] and Republican presidential candidates have generally campaigned in favor of its adoption. But supporters have been unable to win the necessary two-thirds vote in Congress. Yet, in 1990, a more conservative Supreme Court relaxed somewhat the ban on prayer in school, saying students may form Bible-reading or school prayer clubs as long as other clubs are allowed to use school property.[32] Banning religious groups while allowing secular ones to organize was said to infringe upon students' right to freely exercise their religion. In 1997 a five-member majority of the Supreme Court, in *Agostini* v. *Felton* (1997), ruled that public school teachers could provide remedial and other specialized, non-religious instruction in religious schools, as long as this instruction is "made available generally without regard to the sectarian–nonsectarian or public–nonpublic nature of the institution benefitted" and that any aid to individuals occurred "only as a result of the genuinely independent and private choices of individuals." By justifying its decision in terms of the "private choices of individuals," the Court once again showed a concern for the right to the free exercise of religion, the subject to which we now turn.

Separation of state and religion are evident in the lack of religious symbolism at an elementary school celebration of neither Christmas nor Hanukkah nor Kwanza, but the "winter holidays."

FREE EXERCISE OF RELIGION CLAUSE

The Supreme Court has protected private religious schools from hostile action by state legislatures. During the 1920s anti-immigrant sentiments were so strong in Nebraska that the legislature tried to close private religious schools that provided instruction in a foreign language. The Supreme Court in 1923 said that this violated the free exercise clause of the First Amendment, because it prevented parents from exercising "the right of the individual to . . establish a home and bring up children [and] to worship God according to the dictates of his own conscience."[33]

But with war breaking out in Europe and patriotic fervor on the upsurge, the Court, in 1940, upheld a West Virginia statute requiring that Jehovah's Witnesses salute the flag in public school ceremonies, despite the fact that it was against the group's religion to salute a secular symbol. The Court said that schools could interfere with religious liberty in this case, because saluting the flag promoted "national unity, [which] is the basis of national security."[34] Yet just three years later the Supreme Court, apparently realizing they had curbed religious liberty, reversed the West Virginia decision. "Compulsory unification of opinion," wrote Justice Jackson in the midst of the war against Nazism, "achieves only the unanimity of the graveyard."[35]

Do School Vouchers Establish a Religion or Permit the Free Exercise of Religion?

Those for Vouchers Say:

Vouchers are consistent with the free exercise of religion clause, because they allow families to choose the moral and religious milieu in which their children are to be raised. The absence of prayer in school conveys as distinctive a religious message as its presence. Since schools cannot avoid providing religious and moral instruction, parents should be given a choice among schools. For example, they should be allowed to choose a school that teaches sex education programs in a manner with which they agree.

Apart from constitutional questions, vouchers will force schools to respond to the needs and interests of the young people who attend them, not the adults who work there. Schools will become more effective, because the competition among them would drive inefficient, ineffective schools out of business.

Those against Vouchers Say:

Tuition voucher plans violate the establishment of religion. By allowing parents to use state-provided vouchers to pay for the cost of education in religious schools, the government provides financial support to religious groups, some of which may be exclusionary and divisive.

Quite apart from constitutional questions, vouchers are bad policy. The contribution that the public school has made to democracy will be undermined. Schools will no longer serve as a melting pot that blends together students from diverse racial and religious backgrounds. Voucher plans would turn public schools into charity schools reserved for poor minorities. Middle-class parents will add their own monies to tuition vouchers in order to educate their children in ethnically and socially isolated settings.

Extending this line of reasoning, the Court, in 1972, disallowed the application of a compulsory attendance law to two Amish children, whose parents opposed on religious grounds their continued attendance in a public school.[36]

ESTABLISHMENT OF RELIGION OR FREE EXERCISE?

The debate over school choice, which divided presidential candidates in 1996, involves weighing the establishment of religion clause against the free exercise clause.[37] Republican presidential candidate Robert Dole favored giving families vouchers that would allow parents to choose among public and religious schools. President Clinton said choice should be limited to public schools.

The Supreme Court has yet to decide whether school vouchers establish a religion or simply permit its free exercise (see Democratic Dilemma). But the Court, in *Mueller* v. *Allen* (1983), said tax breaks can be given to families who send their children to religious schools, provided the same tax breaks are available to families sending their children to public schools.[38] It remains unclear whether the Supreme Court will extend the *Mueller* decision and permit families to use vouchers to send their children to religious schools. Some observers think the outcome may turn on the next appointment to the Supreme Court. If so, politics continues to affect Court interpretations of the meaning of freedom of religion.

Law, Order, and the Rights of the Accused

Elections also affect court interpretations of the procedural rights of the accused. These procedural rights are often thought to come into conflict with the need for government to maintain social order. Many public officials think procedural obstacles protecting the rights of suspects unduly handicap the police in their efforts to find and prosecute criminals. They seem to share the view of the ancient jurist who once said, "The judge is condemned when the criminal is absolved."[39] But others think that unless procedural safeguards are carefully observed, innocent people will be unjustly convicted. "I think it a less evil," said Justice Hughes, "that some criminal should escape than that the government should play an ignoble part."[40]

ELECTION POLITICS AND CRIMINAL JUSTICE

Politics affects criminal justice routines, because almost everyone worries about being a victim of a crime. According to the Federal Bureau of Investigation, 83 percent of all Americans will become victims of a crime at some point in their lifetime.[41] Most of these crimes—thefts, burglaries, and robberies—take place in the United States at more or less the same rate as in other major industrial countries. But many people in the United States today are especially afraid of personal injury and violent death and their fears are not unfounded. The murder rate in the United States is far in excess of that of most other countries (see International Comparison).

In recent years, the news media have magnified public concern about crime. Murders, rapes, carjackings, and muggings fill the six o'clock news shows now more than ever before (see Figure 16.2). Even if these stories do not touch most people

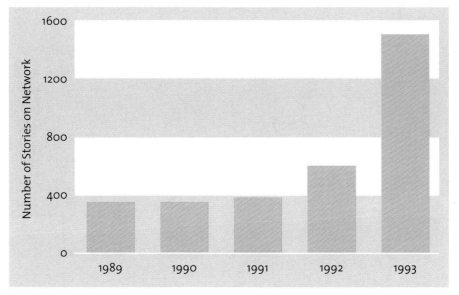

FIGURE 16.2

Television Coverage of Crime Is Increasing

SOURCE: Media Monitor of Washington, DC, as reported in *Boston Globe*, April 4, 1994, 16.

United States Has Much Higher Murder, but Not Burglary Rates, than Most Other Countries.

SOURCE: *International Criminal Police Organization, Interpol, 1991.*

All data are based on police statistics, not judicial statistics. Comparisons among nations should be interpreted with caution, due to different definitions and methods of calculation.

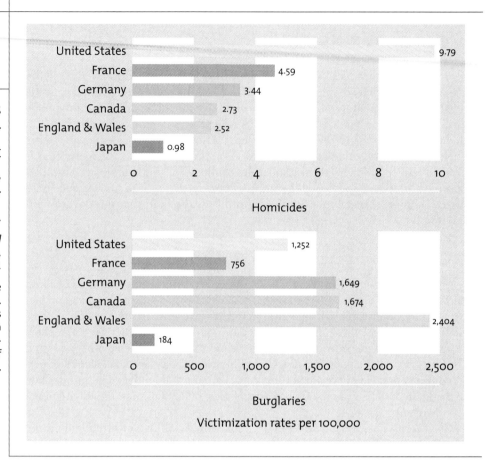

United States — 9.79
France — 4.59
Germany — 3.44
Canada — 2.73
England & Wales — 2.52
Japan — 0.98

0   2   4   6   8   10

Homicides

United States — 1,252
France — 756
Germany — 1,649
Canada — 1,674
England & Wales — 2,404
Japan — 184

0   500   1,000   1,500   2,000   2,500

Burglaries
Victimization rates per 100,000

FIGURE 16.3

Homicide Rates in the United States: In Early 1990s, Rates Increased for Young People, Declined for Older People

SOURCE: Bureau of Justice Statistics 1993 (Table 3.130); Statistical Abstract, 1993 (No.314); ?

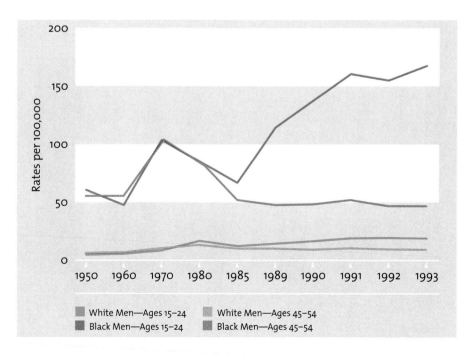

Rates per 100,000

200

150

100

50

0

1950   1960   1970   1980   1985   1989   1990   1991   1992   1993

■ White Men—Ages 15–24   ■ White Men—Ages 45–54
■ Black Men—Ages 15–24   ■ Black Men—Ages 45–54

directly, they create an atmosphere in which many feel that they are witnessing a crime rate that is escalating out of control. In response to clamors to solve the problem, politicians often feel they must "do something." As one senator remarked, "There is a mood here that if someone came to the floor and said we should barb-wire the ankles of anyone who jaywalks, I suspect it would pass."[42]

Whether crime rates are actually rising or falling is not so easy to determine, because many crime statistics are notoriously unreliable. The best evidence on trends in crime rates comes from statistics on homicides, because most murders are reported and are correctly classified. Most victims of homicides are men. Black men are more likely to be murdered than white men. But for older men, both black and white, the murder rate has been falling since the 1980s. On the other hand, the murder victimization rate among younger men, especially younger black men, rose steeply in the early 1990s (see Figure 16.3), though it began to decline in the late 1990s.

THE RIGHTS OF THE ACCUSED

The way in which the police and the courts treat suspects was severely scrutinized during the 1960s, when civil rights groups focused public attention on the rights of the disadvantaged. Influenced by political currents at the time, the Supreme Court, under the leadership of Chief Justice Earl Warren, issued a series of decisions, discussed below, that substantially extended the meaning of the Bill of Rights.

As the rights of the accused were being extended by these Warren Court decisions, many law enforcement officials claimed that the courts had forgotten about the rights of victims. An increasing number of voters agreed with these sentiments; popular support for capital punishment also increased (see Figure 16.4). Court procedures soon became a campaign issue, with many candidates for office calling for tougher law enforcement. Richard Nixon's successful 1968 campaign was the first to become known as the "law and order" election. Since then, the issue has arisen in

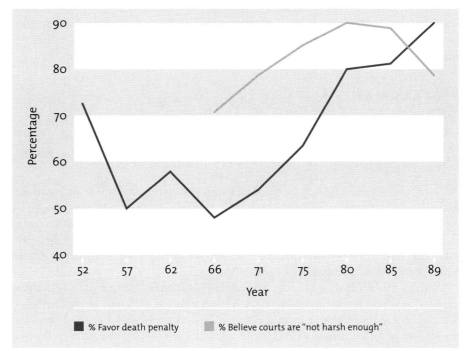

FIGURE 16.4

More People Think Courts Should Be Tougher on Criminals

SOURCE: Benjamin I. Page and Robert Y. Shapiro, *The Rational Public: Fifty Years of Trends in Americans' Policy Preferences* (Chicago: University of Chicago Press, 1992); 92.

TABLE 16.1

Key Changes in the Rights of the Accused

Constitutional Provision	Amendment	Extensions by Warren Court	Limitations by Post-Warren Court
Search and Seizure	4	*Mapp* v. *Ohio*, '61 Improperly collected evidence cannot be introduced in court	*Washington* v. *Chrisman*, '82 But campus dorm rooms can be searched
No Self-Incrimination	5	*Miranda* v. *Arizona*, '66 Officers must tell suspects their rights before questioning	*Harris* v. *New York*, '71 But if suspect testifies, evidence can be introduced
Impartial Jury	6	*Sheppard* v. *Maxwell*, '66 Establishes guidelines to protect jurors from biased news coverage	*Nebraska Press Association* v. *Stuart*, '76 But pre-trial publicity does not necessarily preclude a fair trial
Legal Counsel	6	*Gidean* v. *Wainwright*, '63 Poor person guaranteed legal counsel	No limitation
No Double Jeopardy	5	*Benton* v. *Maryland*, '69 Applies to state as well as federal trials	No limitation

both national and local campaigns. In 1996, both Clinton and Dole campaigned as "law and order" candidates. Although most anticrime talk is tough, New York Mayor Ed Koch found a way of making his case in a more humorous vein: "A judge I helped elect was mugged recently. And do you know what he did? He called a press conference and said: 'This mugging of me will in no way affect my decisions in matters of this kind.' And an elderly lady got up in the back of the room and said: 'Then mug him again.'"[43]

After the retirement of Earl Warren in 1969, the Supreme Court, responding to changing political circumstances, began to qualify the rights of those accused of a crime. Yet the post-Warren Court, as we shall see in the next section, did not reverse but only qualified the major Warren Court decisions (see Table 16.1). Most debate over the rights of those suspected of criminal activity has focused on five constitutional provisions: (1) search and seizure, (2) immunity against self-incrimination; (3) impartial jury; (4) legal counsel; and (5) double jeopardy, the topics of this section.

SEARCH AND SEIZURE

CONSTITUTION, FOURTH AMENDMENT: *The right of the people to be secure in their persons, houses, papers, and effects, against unreasonable searches and seizures, shall not be violated, and no Warrants shall issue, but upon probable cause.*

Your house cannot be searched without your permission unless a search warrant, based on a showing that a crime has probably been committed, is properly issued by a court. The Supreme Court, under Earl Warren, decided in **Mapp v. Ohio** (1961) that any improperly obtained evidence cannot used in court.[44] But in *Washington* v. *Chrisman* (1982), a more conservative court ruled that this protection did not extend to a dormitory room on a college campus.[45]

Whether this rule should apply to evidence obtained from automobiles became an issue in the 1996 election campaign. A federal judge originally denied, as inadmissible evidence, eight pounds of cocaine, because police officers had obtained the drugs from the trunk of a car without a search warrant after seeing men throw a

■ **Mapp v. Ohio**
Court decision saying that any evidence obtained without a proper search warrant may not be introduced in a trial.

bag in the car and run away. Pointing out that the judge had been appointed by Clinton, Dole criticized the judge for letting constitutional scruples interfere with police work. Clinton, sensitive to the charge of being soft on crime, initially called for the judge's resignation, though he later withdrew the suggestion. Meanwhile, the federal judge in New York reversed his decision and let the evidence be introduced. Cars can still be searched by the police without a warrant, if they have good reason to think they contain evidence of a crime.

IMMUNITY AGAINST SELF-INCRIMINATION

CONSTITUTION, FIFTH AMENDMENT: *Nor shall [one] be compelled in any criminal case to be a witness against himself.*

The Fifth Amendment protects individuals from torture and coerced confessions by saying that persons cannot be forced to testify against themselves. In *Miranda v. Arizona* (1966), the Warren Court put teeth into this constitutional provision by requiring police officers to tell suspects, before questioning them, that they need not reply and that they may request the presence of an attorney. Otherwise, any information obtained may not be presented in court. After Richard Nixon made the *Miranda* decision an issue in his 1968 presidential campaign, the Supreme Court softened the ruling when it decided, in *Harris v. New York* (1971), that information gathered in violation of the *Miranda* decision may be introduced in evidence, if defendants testify in their own defense.

IMPARTIAL JURY

CONSTITUTION, SIXTH AMENDMENT: *The accused shall enjoy the right to a speedy and public trial, by an impartial jury.*

The requirement that a jury be impartial is difficult to ensure when a crime becomes newsworthy, because jurors may be biased by media accounts of the alleged crime both before and during the trial. The Warren Supreme Court considered these issues in *Sheppard v. Maxwell* (1966), a case growing out of the trial of medical doctor Sam Sheppard, accused of murdering his wife. Sheppard complained about the excessive news coverage to which jurors were exposed, including the fact that the media were positioned in the courtroom in such a way they could listen in on his conversations with his attorneys.[46] The Supreme Court overturned his conviction and set forth the following guidelines to preserve impartial juries in the future:

1. Trials should be postponed until public attention has subsided.

2. Jurors should be questioned to screen out those with detailed knowledge or fixed opinions.

3. Judges should instruct jurors emphatically to consider only the evidence presented in the courtroom, not any evidence obtained from an external source.

4. Jurors may be **sequestered** during a trial, that is, kept away from all sources of trial information other than that presented in the courtroom.[47]

5. Courts should consider changing a **trial venue**, the place where the trial is held, in order for the case to be heard by a jury less exposed to pre-trial publicity.

Enesto Miranda, the namesake of the "Miranda rights" read to all suspects before questioning. Accused of kidnap and rape, Miranda was interrogated by police for two hours until he confessed his guilt—without being told of his right not to answer any questions. Although he was ultimately found guilty, Miranda's confession was held inadmissible by the U.S. Supreme Court in *Miranda v. Arizona*.

■ *Miranda v. Arizona*
Court decision stating that persons must be told by police that they need not testify against themselves.

■ **sequestered**
Housing jurors privately, away from any information other than that presented in the courtroom.

■ **trial venue**
Place where a trial is held.

A French judge subjected 10 photographers to investigation for alleged involuntary homicide in conjunction with the Parisian car accident that killed British Princess Diana in August 1997. When originally questioned, the photographers had no right to legal counsel, as in the U.S. If they are brought to trial, the procedures to be followed will differ sharply from those in high profile U.S. cases. The trial will not be televised, nor last for months, as in the O.J. Simpson case. Instead a secret investigation will be followed by a sedate two or three day trial in which most of the questioning is conducted by judges, not by lawyers for the two sides. Conviction, if it occurs, will not occur by jury but by three professional judges. To prove guilt, the prosecution need not persuade all judges "beyond a reasonable doubt" but only a majority that guilt is "more likely than innocence."

According to defense attorney Gerald Shargel, "Local U.S. district attorneys, most of whom are elected, probably would be sensitive to public demands for punishment, making it more likely that they would charge the photographers with the most severe crime possible.... French prosecutors and judges, by contrast, are all nationally appointed professionals, generally thought to be less vulnerable to popular pressure."

SOURCE: Thomas Kamm and Paul M. Barrett, "How Would Paparazzi Who Stalked Diana Fare in French Court," *Wall Street Journal* September 2, 1997, pp. A1, A8.

Although these constitutional safeguards designed to prevent the jury from becoming biased have never been reversed, the post-Warren Court, in *Nebraska Press Association* v. *Stuart* (1976), handed down a decision reflecting the country's more conservative political mood. It said that "pre-trial publicity—even pervasive, adverse publicity—does not inevitably lead to an unfair trial."[48]

Sometimes a change in venue to avoid publicity can have a dramatic effect on the outcome of a trial. In 1992, black motorist Rodney King was videotaped by an amateur cameraman as he was beaten by Los Angeles police after he tried to get away when asked to stop by a police officer. When the officers were brought to trial, a state appeals court ordered a change of venue to escape the racial passions that had been aroused in Los Angeles. The trial court judge chose as the new venue a state court in Simi Valley, on the northwestern fringe of the Los Angeles metropolitan area. The judge picked Simi Valley because its docket was short and extra space was available for the expected avalanche of reporters. Since many residents of Simi Valley were former police officers and army personnel, the jury ended up consisting of several people associated with law enforcement. The jury found three of the four officers innocent of all charges, and it could not agree on charges against the fourth.

LEGAL COUNSEL

CONSTITUTION, SIXTH AMENDMENT: . . . *and to have Assistance of Counsel for his defense.*

The Warren Supreme Court ruled in ***Gideon v. Wainwright*** (1963) that all citizens accused of serious crimes, even the indigent, are constitutionally entitled to legal representation. If the accused is too poor to hire an attorney, then the court must assign one.

It was easier to enunciate this right than to put it into practice. At one time, courts asked private attorneys to donate their services in order to defend the poor. But donating time to help suspected crooks was not popular among the members of the legal profession. As a result, most states have created the office of **public defender**, an attorney whose full-time responsibility is to provide for the legal defense of indigent criminal suspects. When the public defender was originally established, it was thought that full-time, paid attorneys would provide higher-quality representation. But this solution, too, has had its problems. For one thing, the job of a public defender is thankless, pay is bad, and defenders are forced to deal with "rotten case after rotten case."[49] One of the public defenders' biggest problems is winning respect from those with whom they work. From the perspective of the police, defenders simply throw up roadblocks that prevent conviction of the guilty. Surprisingly, defendants are hardly more grateful. Defendants, as do most other people, think anything free probably is not worth much. One felon, when asked by a judge if he had an attorney, replied, "No, I had a public defender."[50] Public prosecutors probably appreciate the work of the public defender more than anyone else. As fellow attorneys, they know that those working on the other side are just doing their job. Still, there is a general impression, perhaps unfair in many cases, that public defenders are "crummy lawyers . . . dreck . . . an inferior breed."[51]

DOUBLE JEOPARDY

CONSTITUTION, FIFTH AMENDMENT: *Nor shall any person be subject for the same offence to be twice put in jeopardy of life or limb.*

The Warren Supreme Court said in *Benton v. Maryland* (1969) that states cannot try a person twice for the same offense, thereby placing the defendant in **double jeopardy**. Despite this rule, the Supreme Court, in an old decision that has never been overturned, has said that a person can be tried in federal courts, even though acquitted in a state court. "An act denounced as a crime by both national and state sovereignties is an offense against the peace and dignity of both."[52] Both may prosecute without putting the defendant in double jeopardy.

Prosecution by both federal and state governments is most likely in high-visibility cases. For example, when the State of California was unable to win a conviction in the trial of the four police officers charged with beating Rodney King, the officers were tried under federal law.

The decision to bring the officers to a second trial was undoubtedly influenced by electoral considerations. Three days of civil disorder broke out in Los Angeles's minority communities after the initial failure to win a conviction. In his campaign for president, Bill Clinton blamed the rioting on the Bush Administration for creating an atmosphere that fostered racial conflict. Although the decision to bring a second prosecution was made by the federal district attorney serving Los Angeles, it was made only at the request of the attorney general (likely with the approval of President Bush). With the decision to prosecute a second time, the city calmed and the

■ *Gideon v. Wainwright*
Supreme Court decision in 1963 giving indigent people accused of crimes the right of court-appointed counsel.

■ public defender
Attorney whose full-time responsibilities are to provide for the legal defense of indigent criminal suspects.

■ double jeopardy
Fifth Amendment provision that prohibits prosecution for the same offense twice.

United States Has Higher Incarceration Rates than Other Countries

SOURCES: March Mauer, *Americans Behind Bars: The International Use of Incarceration, 1992–1993* (Washington DC: The Sentencing Project, September 1994); James Austin, *An Overview of Incarceration Trends in the United States and Their Impact on Crime* (San Francisco: The National Council on Crime and Delinquency, January 1994).

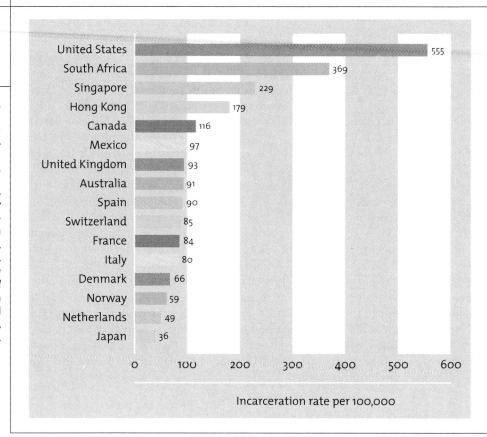

Country	Incarceration rate per 100,000
United States	555
South Africa	369
Singapore	229
Hong Kong	179
Canada	116
Mexico	97
United Kingdom	93
Australia	91
Spain	90
Switzerland	85
France	84
Italy	80
Denmark	66
Norway	59
Netherlands	49
Japan	36

Incarceration rate per 100,000

issue dropped out of the presidential campaign. In the federal trial, the jury split the difference, convicting two officers while acquitting the other two.

RIGHTS IN PRACTICE: THE PLEA BARGAIN

If a case is newsworthy, constitutional procedures will generally be observed: The public is looking on and political pressures must be taken into account. But the reality of justice in most criminal cases is very different. Hardly anyone accused of a crime is actually tried by a jury, and almost all those convicted of a crime testify against themselves. The accused have their rights, to be sure, but very few of the accused actually choose to exercise them. Most of the time it is to their advantage *not* to do so.[53]

Trial court judges depend on the willingness of prosecutors and defenders to settle cases before going to trial. The number of people accused of crimes is high, the number of cases on the court docket is seemingly endless, court personnel resources are limited, and court time is precious. Judges are expected to administer efficient court rooms, settle cases quickly, and keep the court docket short. To speed the criminal justice process, defenders and prosecutors are usually expected to try to arrange a **plea bargain**, an agreement between prosecution and defense that the

■ **plea bargain**
Agreement between prosecution and defense that the accused will admit to a crime, provided that other charges are dropped and the recommended sentence is shortened.

accused will admit to a crime, provided other charges are dropped and a reduced sentence is recommended. The Supreme Court is not unhappy with this transformation of the rights of the accused into chips that can used "to cop a plea." In the words of Justice Burger, plea bargaining is "an essential component of the administration of justice. Properly administered, it is to be encouraged."[54]

Extensive use of the plea bargain has become an issue in electoral politics, with many candidates insisting that those convicted serve longer sentences. One popular proposal, enacted in a number of states, is known as "three strikes and you're out." After conviction of three felonies, a convict must receive life imprisonment, whether or not a plea bargain is struck. As a result of these new tough laws, incarceration rates are rising and prison costs are becoming one of the fastest growing items in state budgets. The United States now seems to have the largest incarceration rate in the world (see International Comparison). Whether a higher incarceration rate is the best way to reduce crime has become a matter of considerable debate.

★ AT THE STATE & LOCAL LEVEL
The Right of Privacy

CONSTITUTION, NINTH AMENDMENT: *The enumeration in the Constitution, of certain rights, shall not be construed to deny or disparage others retained by the people.*

The civil liberties discussed thus far are explicitly mentioned in the Bill of Rights. In addition, the Supreme Court has enunciated an additional liberty, the **right of privacy**, the right to be free of government interference in those aspects of one's personal life that do not affect others. Although the right of privacy is not explicitly mentioned in the Constitution, the Ninth Amendment says that some rights may be retained by the people even though not explicitly mentioned in the Constitution.

Some constitutional scholars feel the judicial power to identify any right not explicitly mentioned in the Constitution should be exercised cautiously, because abuse of this power gives a nonelected judiciary the power to overrule the will of elected public officials, who presumably are carrying out the will of the majority. "Where constitutional materials do not clearly specify [a right]," Robert Bork has said, "the judge must stick close to the text and history, and their fair implications, and not construct any new rights."[55]

REGULATION OF SEXUAL BEHAVIOR

Despite such caution, a right of privacy was constructed by the courts in *Griswold* v. *Connecticut* (1965).[56] Estelle Griswold, executive director of Planned Parenthood, was fined $100 for violating a Connecticut law prohibiting the use of any instrument for the purpose of contraception. Declaring the law unconstitutional, Justice William Douglas discerned "a right of privacy older than the Bill of Rights." "Would we allow the police to search the sacred precincts of marital bedrooms for telltale signs of the use of contraceptives? The very idea is repulsive to the notions of privacy surrounding the marriage relationship."[57] In dissent, Justice Stewart declared the Ninth Amendment "but a truism" that could hardly be used to "annul a law passed by the elected representatives of the people."

right of privacy
Right to keep free of government interference those aspects of one's personal life that do not affect others.

Can Crime Be Reduced While Protecting Civil Liberties?

The best way of lowering crime rates is a matter of great dispute. Four quite different approaches have been suggested.

1. James Wilson says crime is best reduced by incarcerating repeat offenders. "Wicked people exist," he frankly asserts. "Nothing avails except to set them apart from innocent people." He calls for a strategy of "incapacitating a larger fraction of the convicted serious robbers" and other criminals.* Wilson recommends more money for police, courts, and prisons so that the necessary resources are made available to find, convict, and imprison serious criminals.

2. Sociologist William J. Wilson argues that crime can be reduced in minority communities only when job opportunities are enhanced.† In many central cities, nearly half the male workforce is unemployed. Starved of legitimate economic opportunities, young men steal, commit burglaries, and sell drugs to get the cash they need. Once they have acquired a criminal record, these young men find it even more difficult to obtain a job within the economic mainstream. Without jobs, they do not have the resources or self-esteem to form stable family relationships.

3. Still others blame violence and murder on the ready availability of guns in American society, which they would subject to strict regulation. They point out that the victims of most violent crimes know their assailants. Violence is usually not premeditated or a by-product of a professional robbery, but the result of actions taken in anger. Easy access to guns has increased the deadliness of angry encounters. Opponents of gun control argue that gun laws are obeyed only by the law-abiding; besides, they deprive citizens of their Second Amendment rights.

4. Finally, many blame high rates of crime and violence on the widespread availability and use of illegal narcotics. Police estimate that one-third of all major crimes are drug-related. Some people feel that the crime-related consequences of drug use can best be reduced through the legalization of drugs. Joycelyn Elders, when she was the surgeon general, said "we would markedly reduce our crime rate if drugs were decriminalized."‡ But her statement was immediately rebutted by President Clinton, and she soon resigned her position. Drug decriminalization remains highly controversial, with virtually no mainstream political support.

* James Q. Wilson, *Thinking About Crime* (New York: Basic Books, 1975), 199, 205, 209.

† William J. Wilson, *The Truly Disadvantaged: The Inner City, the Underclass, and Public Policy* (Chicago: University of Chicago Press, 1987).

‡ *Dayton Daily News*, November 27, 1994, 16A.

Despite Stewart's dissenting comment, there seems little doubt that a national majority agreed with the Supreme Court that a married couple should have the right to use contraceptives. But would the Supreme Court be equally protective of the right of privacy when the actions in question were not approved by a majority

Does the right to privacy include gay marriages? Its legality is currently at issue in several states.

of the public? This question arose in 1986 in *Bowers* v. *Hardwick*, when the court was asked to declare unconstitutional a Georgia law prohibiting sodomy under which two homosexuals had been convicted. Noting that laws against sodomy existed at the time the Constitution was written, the court majority found no reason to think the writers of the Ninth Amendment intended to exempt homosexual behavior from state regulation. In dissent, Justice Blackmun said the freedom to enjoy intimate associations is "central to any concept of liberty."[58]

Whether or not one can find any consistency in the Court's reasoning in these two quite different interpretations of the right to privacy, the two decisions indicate court sensitivity to the political context in which the cases were decided. In both instances, the court majority decided in a manner consistent with the views of a majority of voters.

RIGHT TO LIFE OR RIGHT TO CHOOSE?

While the court has left uncertain the range of sexual acts to which the right of privacy extends, it ruled, in *Roe* v. *Wade* (1973), that the right of privacy was broad enough to include at least a partial right of abortion. The case arose out of a request from Norma McCorvey, using the pseudonym Jane Roe, who, seeking to terminate a pregnancy, asked for a judgment declaring unconstitutional the Texas law prohibiting abortion. Writing for the court majority, Justice Blackmun said that the woman's right of privacy was so fundamental it could be infringed only when the state interest in doing so was compelling. Dissenting justices objected to judicial interference with a state legislature's right to balance the rights of women against the welfare of her unborn child.

Roe v. *Wade* launched two powerful political movements that have helped to shape American politics in the twenty-five years since the Court decision. The "right to life" crusade was organized by Catholic and other religious groups

Shown here in 1973, when *Roe* v. *Wade,* was decided, Norma McCorvey (whose privacy at the time was protected by the use of the pseudonym Jane Roe) in 1995 made the surprise announcement that she had become a pro-life advocate.

COURT REASONING IN *ROE* V. *WADE*

The right of privacy ... is broad enough to encompass a woman's decision whether or not to terminate her pregnancy. The detriment that the State would impose upon the pregnant woman by denying this choice altogether is apparent.

—Justice Blackmun,
majority opinion,
Roe v. *Wade*

The Court apparently values the convenience of the pregnant mother more than the continued existence and development of the life or potential life which she carries. ... I find no constitu-tional warrant for imposing such an order of priorities on the people and legislatures of the States. In a sensitive area such as this, I cannot accept the Court ... interposing a constitutional barrier to state efforts to protect human life.

—Justice Byron White,
dissenting in *Roe* v. *Wade*

SOURCE: *Roe* v. *Wade,* 410 US 113 (1973).

opposed to abortion on two grounds. These groups believe that, inasmuch as human life begins at conception, abortion cannot be distinguished from infanticide. They also believe human sexuality is and should always be intimately connected with procreation. If the two are separated, the moral basis of family and society are undermined. In short, opponents of abortion do not regard the issue as a question of a woman's personal preference; the welfare of both the fetus and society are also at stake.

These "right-to-life" supporters became actively engaged in state and national politics, asking legislatures to impose as many restraints on abortion as the courts would allow. Responding to right-to-life groups, Congress in 1976 enacted legislation preventing coverage of abortion costs under government health insurance programs, such as Medicaid. In 1980, the Republican party promised to restore the "right to life," and, in subsequent years, Republican presidents began appointing justices to the Supreme Court who were expected either to reverse *Roe* v. *Wade* or to limit its scope.

In response to these political pressures and with a change in its membership, the Supreme Court began to declare constitutional certain restrictions on abortion practice. The Court in 1980 said the congressional law preventing public funding of abortions was constitutional.[59] In 1989 it said that states could require the doctor to ascertain the viability of a fetus before permitting an abortion, if the woman is twenty or more weeks pregnant.[60] By 1990 it was thought that four justices on the Supreme Court were prepared to overturn *Roe*, and that any new appointee by a Republican president would create the majority needed to reverse the decision.

Opposition to "right-to-life" groups was at first weak and uncertain, mainly because many of those defending a woman's constitutional "right of choice" thought it had been permanently protected by the Supreme Court decision. But as the "right-to-life" movement gained in strength, and the possibility that *Roe* v. *Wade* would be overturned became ever more likely, the "right-of-choice" movement gained in strength and aggressiveness. By 1984, it was able to secure the Democratic party's commitment to the "right-of-choice" principle.

Both sides to the controversy waited anxiously for the 1992 court decision in *Planned Parenthood* v. *Casey*.[61] The organization challenged a Pennsylvania law that placed a number of restrictions on the right to abortion—which went well beyond what seem permissible under *Roe* v. *Wade*. Right-to-life groups saw the case as an opportunity to return to the states the authority to decide whether abortions were legal. Right-to-choose groups feared that many, if not all, of the recently enacted impediments to abortion would be declared constitutional. The Court majority satisfied neither side entirely, finding a compromise that upheld some of the Pennsylvania restrictions on abortion, but left intact the principle that states cannot simply outlaw all abortions.

The majority based its decision on nothing other than the principle of *stare decisis*, the rule stating that court decisions, once made, should, if at all possible, be followed by subsequent judges (see Chapter 15, p. 494). To do otherwise is to make a mockery of the law. In the words of Judge Sandra O'Connor, "Where . . . the Court decides a case in such a way as to resolve the sort of intensely divisive controversy reflected in *Roe* . . . the promise of constancy, once given, binds its maker for as long as . . . the understanding of the issue has not changed so fundamentally as to render the commitment obsolete." In other words, the Court said it was not changing its mind.

Either by accident or design, the Court majority once again adopted a position very close to that of the average American voter (see Chapter 5, pp. 158–161). It permitted restrictions, such as the need for teenagers to obtain parental consent, which are endorsed by a majority of voters, but rejected those most people think unwarranted, such as the need for a married woman to obtain the consent of her husband. Even in matters as sensitive as the right of privacy, the court seems to be influenced by majority opinion, as expressed in the outcome of recent elections.

Chapter Summary

The Bill of Rights remained pretty much a dead letter until the Civil War ended slavery. Only as key provisions of the Bill of Rights were selectively incorporated into the due process clause of the Fourteenth Amendment did they become an effective component of the country's constitutional makeup.

Although the courts are expected to protect civil liberties against majority tyranny, most of the time the Supreme Court has followed, not led, public opinion. In 1919 the Supreme Court said speech could not be prohibited unless it created a clear and present danger, but it initially applied the doctrine in such a way as to convict a socialist. Though it protected minority dissent during the 1930s, later, it elaborated the fighting words doctrine, which declared certain phrases to be the equivalent of violent acts. Not until McCarthyism had been rejected by elected officials did a Court majority say free speech was a fundamental freedom that required special protection.

Freedom of religion is protected by two separate clauses in the First Amendment. The establishment of religion clause prohibits the propagation of religious beliefs by public institutions and direct aid to churches, religious schools, and other religious institutions. The free exercise of religion clause prevents the government from interfering in the religious activities of citizens. At times, the two clauses come into apparent conflict. For example, the Supreme Court has yet to decide whether school vouchers that permit families to choose between religious and secular schools violate the establishment clause or are permitted under the free exercise clause.

When balancing the rights of the accused against the need to maintain social order, Supreme Court decisions have fluctuated with changes in public opinion. During the 1960s, the Warren court expanded rights by tightening rules under which police and prosecutors could obtain evidence, question suspects, and hold trials. After "law and order" became a campaign issue, the Supreme Court modified, though it did not reverse, many of these decisions.

The Court has discerned a right of privacy, despite the fact that it is not mentioned explicitly in the Bill of Rights. The right of privacy is broad enough to include a woman's right to terminate a pregnancy. But it is not absolute. As interpreted by the Court, the right of privacy does not preclude regulation of abortions, especially among children and after the first trimester of pregnancy. Nor has it been extended to homosexual acts. The right of privacy discerned by the court comes very close to the viewpoint held by most Americans. The country's definition of civil liberties seems to depend as much on the thinking of its citizens as on its judicial system.

Key Terms

balancing doctrine, p. 524

civil liberties, p. 516

Civil Rights Amendments, p. 519

clear and present danger doctrine, p. 522

commercial speech, p. 528

double jeopardy, p. 519

due process clause, p. 539

establishment of religion clause, p. 529

fighting words doctrine, p. 523

free exercise of religion clause, p. 529

fundamental freedoms doctrine, p. 526

Gideon v. *Wainwright*, p. 538

libel, p. 528

Mapp v. *Ohio*, p. 536

Miranda v. *Arizona*, p. 537

obscenity, p. 529

plea bargain, p. 540

prior restraint doctrine, p. 521

public defender, p. 539

right of privacy, p. 511

selective incorporation, p. 520

separation of church and state doctrine, p. 530

sequestered, p. 537

trial venue, p. 538

tyranny of the majority, p. 520

Suggested Readings

Bork, Robert H. "Neutral Principles and Some First Amendment Problems," *Indiana Law Journal* 47 (1971): 1–35. Argues for a narrow definition of constitutional rights that limits the majority will.

Casper, Jonathan D. *American Criminal Justice: The Defendant's Perspective.* Englewood Cliffs, NJ: Prentice-Hall, 1972. Discusses the day-to-day realities of the criminal justice system.

Friedman, Lawrence M. *Crime and Punishment in American History.* New York: Basic Books, 1993. Readable overview of the changing nature of the American system of criminal justice.

Garrow, David J. *Liberty and Sexuality.* New York: Macmillan, 1994. Comprehensive account of the legal debate over abortion before and after *Roe.*

Goldstein, Robert. *Political Repression in Modern America: 1870 to the Present.* New York: Schenkman, 1978. Comprehensive account of violations of freedom of speech, press, and assembly in the United States.

Goldstein, Robert. *Saving "Old Glory": The History of the Desecration Controversy.* Boulder, CO: Westview, 1995. Authoritative political and constitutional history of the flag-burning controversy.

Lewis, Anthony. *Make No Law: The Sullivan Case and the First Amendment.* New York: Random House, 1992. Excellent, readable case study of the politics of the *Sullivan* decision and the evolution of free speech doctrine.

Macedo, Stephen. *The New Right v. The Constitution.* Washington, DC: Cato Institute, 1987. Thoughtfully asserts the responsibility of the courts to protect all liberties, not just fundamental freedoms, from legislative intrusion.

McIntyre, Lisa J. *The Public Defender: The Practice of Law in the Shadows of Repute.* Chicago: University of Chicago Press, 1987. Careful sociological study of this little-appreciated courtroom player.

Meiklejohn, Alexander. *Free Speech and Its Relation to Self-Government* New York: Harper, 1948. Influential, early statement of absolutist position.

Pritchett, C. Herman. *Constitutional Civil Liberties.* Englewood Cliffs, NJ: Prentice-Hall, 1984. Definitive, if somewhat dated, discussion of civil liberties constitutional law in a political context.

Rosenberg, Gerald N. *The Hollow Hope: Can Courts Bring about Social Change?* Chicago: University of Chicago Press, 1991. Casts doubt on the proposition that the courts play a major, independent role in shaping policy.

Skolnick, Jerome. *Justice Without Trial.* New York: John Wiley and Sons, 1966. Classic study of the way in which police and courts resolve low-visibility criminal cases.

Wilson, James Q. *Thinking About Crime.* New York: Basic Books, 1975. Makes a persuasive, realistic, conservative case for ways of controlling crime.

Wilson, William J. *The Truly Disadvantaged: The Inner City, the Underclass, and Public Policy.* Chicago: University of Chicago Press, 1987. Places urban crime in the context of economic deprivation and social dislocation.

COLORED

CON
erential treatment
public employment, education, a
local programs that currently cost well in exce
would depend on various factors (such as future
actions by government entities).

210 MINIMUM WAGE INCREASE. INITIATIVE STATUTE Increases the
state minimum wage for all industries to $5.00 one hour on
March 1, 1997, and to $5.75 per hour on March 1, 1998. Fiscal Impact:
Unknown impact on government revenues. Annual wage-related costs to
state and local governments of 120 million to $300 million (decreasing
action), partly offset by net savings, in the low tens of millions, in
grams.

TURN PAGE

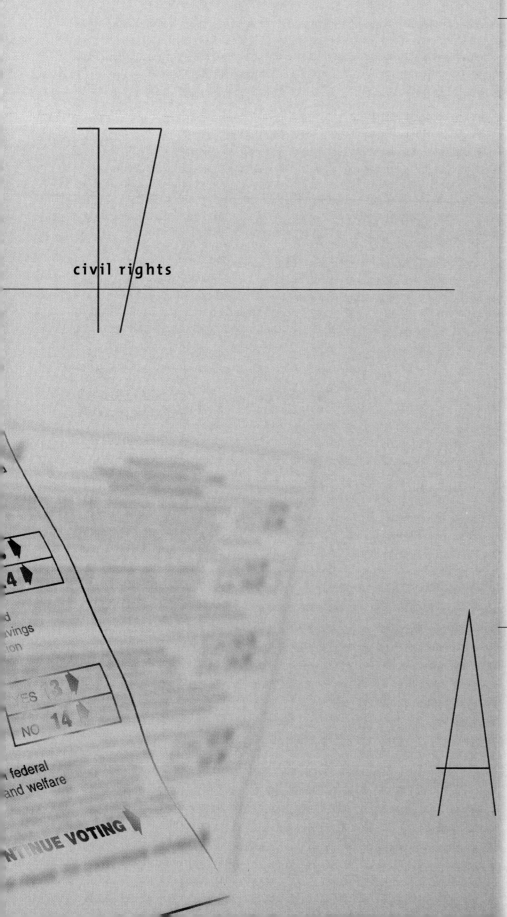

17

civil rights

FOOTBALL GAME triggered
the incident. The Fiesta Bowl had
been criticized for scheduling
its 1990 holiday game in Arizona,
a state yet to declare Martin
Luther King's birthday a legal holiday. To placate critics, Fiesta Bowl
sponsors announced that
$100,000 in minority scholarship

aid would be given in King's name to each of the two universities participating in the game.

Fiesta Bowl organizers thought they had thrown a touchdown; instead they found themselves in their own end zone. Michael Williams, a conservative African American who headed the Department of Education's Office for Civil Rights, said that even though attempts to help minority students were to be applauded, such programs had to be "color-blind." They should not make race or ethnicity a determining factor in granting aid. But the National Association for the Advancement of Colored People (NAACP) said the Education Department's criticism "stymies efforts to increase diversity and chills motivation to eliminate the vestiges of past discrimination."

President Bush set the Department's decision to one side. Even though he opposed giving minorities the right to a specific number of jobs, he did not feel the same way about minority fellowships. As one Republican strategist observed, "It's one thing to tell blue-collar workers you're protecting their jobs against racial quotas. It's quite another to take a college scholarship away from an 18-year-old black kid."

By not backing his own appointee in the Department of Education, Bush successfully defused the Fiesta Bowl incident. Clinton chose not to make the matter an issue in the election campaign. The Fiesta Bowl sponsors nonetheless redesigned their fellowship program so that it would assist all students from disadvantaged backgrounds regardless of race. Not long thereafter, Arizona finally declared King's birthday a legal holiday.

he minority fellowship incident raises broader questions. What does it mean to say the Constitution is color-blind? When may people be legally classified by race, ethnicity, or gender? Do the courts define the issues, and then elected officials follow? Or is it the other way around? In this chapter we shall discuss the struggle for civil rights for African Americans, other minority groups, women, and the disabled. In most cases we shall find that the Supreme Court followed trends first established by electoral politics. As Justice Ruth Bader Ginsburg once observed, "With prestige to persuade, but not physical power to enforce, and with a will for self-preservation, the Court generally follows, it does not lead, changes taking place elsewhere in society."[1] Nonetheless, the Supreme Court has played a major role by codifying civil rights policy into constitutional doctrine. This interplay between electoral forces and constitutional doctrine, as interpreted by the Supreme Court, provides the focus for this chapter.

Origins of Civil Rights

FOURTEENTH AMENDMENT: *"No state shall . . . deny to any person within its jurisdiction the equal protection of the laws."*

Although civil rights and civil liberties are often used interchangeably, it is possible to distinguish between them. Civil liberties refer to the fundamental freedoms that together preserve the rights of a free people (see p. 516). **Civil rights** refers to the right to equal treatment under the law. In Chapter 16 we emphasized how important the due process clause of the Fourteenth Amendment has been to the protection of civil liberties in the United States. The civil rights of Americans are guarded by a no less important provision in the Fourteenth Amendment, the **equal protection clause**, which says that no state can deny any of its people equal protection under the law.

Differing interpretations of the meaning of the equal protection clause have generated intense political controversy. Many people have strong opinions about civil rights questions, in part because relationships among races, genders, and ethnic groups affect them in their daily lives.[2] Many members of minority groups rely on this clause as a primary protection of their right to equal opportunity. But the meaning of civil rights for disadvantaged groups is shaped as much by majority opinion as by minority demands, because elected leaders, though often sensitive to the rights of minorities, never forget they are elected by majorities.

Since minorities, by definition, cannot by themselves control the outcome of elections, they have often pursued a legal strategy by bringing apparent violations of civil rights to the attention of the courts. But legal strategies do not always work. Judges, too, are concerned about preserving credibility with majorities. If courts on occasion move ahead of public opinion, they take such steps cautiously; if public opinion does not follow, the courts are unlikely to continue to forge onward. If the courts persist in deviating from the majority perspective, elected officials will eventually appoint judges willing to reverse the direction the courts have taken. As a result, the Supreme Court has not provided steady leadership on civil rights questions. As one legal scholar has noted, "For every case destructive of racial segregation, other cases can be cited with greater force to support the view of judicial power as fundamentally unfriendly to civil rights, unnecessarily illiberal in its judgment, and oppressive in its results."[3]

THE EARLY CIVIL RIGHTS STRUGGLE

At the end of the Civil War, some southern states passed **black codes**, laws that applied to newly freed slaves but not to whites. "Persons of color . . . must make annual written contracts for their labor," one of the codes said, adding that if blacks ran away from their "masters" they had to forego a year's wages.[4] Other black codes denied African Americans access to the courts or the right to hold property, except under special circumstances. Northern abolitionists, who thought the fight against slavery had been won, urged Congress to override these black codes. Congress responded by passing the Civil Rights Act of 1866, which gave citizens "of every race and color . . . the same right . . . to full and equal benefit of all laws." Almost the same words were later incorporated into the equal protection clause of the Fourteenth Amendment.

These laws were imposed on southern whites during **Reconstruction**, a period after the Civil War when southern states were subject to a military presence. During this period, blacks exercised their right to vote, while it was denied to many whites who had participated in the Confederate cause. In addition, Congress established a Freedman's Bureau, which provided blacks with education, immediate food relief, and land from former plantations.[5]

Reconstruction was motivated both by moral outrage at racial injustice and by northern postwar bitterness toward the Confederacy. But as the years progressed, moral commitment evaporated and war memories faded. The Freedman's Bureau

civil rights
Right to equal treatment under the law.

equal protection clause
Fourteenth Amendment clause specifying that no state can deny any of its people equal protection under the law.

black codes
Laws that applied to newly freed slaves but not to whites.

Reconstruction
Period after the Civil War when the military was present in most southern states.

ultimately proved to be a disappointment to many blacks and abolitionists. Northerners were thrown on the defensive by southern charges of fraud, corruption, and mismanagement. Though not always justified, complaints were effectively leveled against both black elected officials and new arrivals from the North—derisively called carpetbaggers, after the luggage in which they kept their clothing.

The extraordinarily close election of 1876 brought Reconstruction to an end. Republican presidential candidate Rutherford B. Hayes claimed victory, but the outcome depended on allegedly fraudulent vote counts reported by several southern states. The compromise resolving the dispute gave each side what it most wanted. Republicans were given the presidency, but Democrats won removal of the Union army from the South and control of future southern elections.

With the ending of Reconstruction, whites gradually restored many of the old racial patterns.[6] Although black men were still voting in significant numbers as late as the 1880s, the Ku Klux Klan, a fraternity dedicated to white supremacy, intimidated many to keep them from voting by holding great parades of hooded figures, by burning crosses, and by lynching those they accused of crimes.

These tactics were reinforced by formal restrictions on the right to vote. Voters were asked to pass a literacy test, meet strict residency requirements, and pay a **poll tax**, a fee that allowed one to vote. While the laws themselves avoided specific mention of African Americans, they were in fact the target. As the chair of the suffrage committee in Virginia frankly said: "I expect the examination with which the black men will be confronted to be inspired by the same spirit that inspires every man in this convention. I do not expect an impartial administration of this clause."[7] States also enacted what became known as a **grandfather clause** which exempted men from voting restrictions if their fathers and grandfathers had voted before the Civil War. Of course, only whites benefitted from this exemption.

The most successful restriction on the right to vote was known as the **white primary**, elections held by the Democratic party that excluded nonwhites from participation. Since Democrats at that time won nearly all southern elections, the winner of the white primary almost always won the general election.[8] As a result of these restrictions, only 10 percent of adult African American males in 1910 were registered to vote in most of the states of the old Confederacy.[9]

African Americans were also subject to **Jim Crow laws**, state laws that segregated the races from each other. The name comes from a stereotypical, belittling characterization of African Americans in minstrel shows popular at the time. Jim Crow laws required African Americans to attend segregated schools, sit in separate areas in public trains and buses, eat in different restaurants, and use separate public facilities.

★ **AT THE STATE & LOCAL LEVEL**

EARLY COURT INTERPRETATIONS OF CIVIL RIGHTS

With little public support for civil rights, the Supreme Court of the day took a very restrictive view of the equal protection clause. Two post-Reconstruction Court decisions were of particular significance. In a decision that has been given the ironic title, the *Civil Rights Cases* (1883), the court declared the Civil Rights Act of 1875 unconstitutional.[10] This law, written just before Reconstruction came to an end, had abolished segregation in restaurants, train stations, and other public places. In declaring the law unconstitutional, the Supreme Court developed the

poll tax
Fee that allowed one to vote.

grandfather clause
Racially restrictive southern laws permitting a man to vote if his father or grandfather could have voted.

white primary
Primary elections, held by the Democratic party, that excluded nonwhites from participation in many southern states.

Jim Crow laws
Laws passed by southern states, after Reconstruction, enforcing segregation.

Tear gas clouds, laid by the Mississippi Highway Patrol, bring confusion to early civil rights marchers in Canton, Mississippi.

state action doctrine, a rule that says only the actions of state and local governments, not those of private individuals, must conform to the equal protection clause. The Court said Congress could prevent state and local governments from discriminating against blacks, but that it had no constitutional authority to tell private individuals whom to serve in their restaurants, railroads, and hotels. The Court maintained that, by attempting to do so, the Civil Rights Act of 1875 unconstitutionally violated the right of property.

The second major decision by the courts, ***Plessy v. Ferguson*** (1896), had even more sweeping consequences.[11] It developed the **separate but equal doctrine**, a rule that said that segregated facilities were constitutional as long as they were equivalent. Plessy had challenged a Louisiana law that required separation of the races in buses, railroad cars, and waiting rooms at train stations. Plessy argued that his inability to use white facilities denied him equal protection before the law. But the Supreme Court majority said the Louisiana statute was constitutional, because the mere fact that the racial groups were being separated did not stamp African Americans with a "badge of inferiority." In a famous dissent, Justice Harlan protested that "our Constitution is color-blind." In Harlan's view, the Constitution forbids states from making any distinctions based on race.

BLACKS GET ELECTORAL POWER

Because of the court decisions in the *Civil Rights Cases* and *Plessy v. Ferguson*, legally sanctioned segregation remained intact until well into the 1970s. Significant gains in dismantling the old system of segregation took place only after African Americans gained electoral clout by moving in large numbers from southern

state action doctrine
Rule stating that only the actions of state and local governments, not those of private individuals, must conform to the equal protection clause.

Plessy v. Ferguson
Court decision declaring separate but equal public facilities constitutional.

separate but equal doctrine
A rule that said that the equal protection clause was not violated simply by the fact of racial segregation, if the separated facilities were equal.

FIGURE 17.1

Percentage of African Americans Living Outside South by Decade, 1910 to 1997.

SOURCE: U.S. Bureau of the Census, Census of Population.

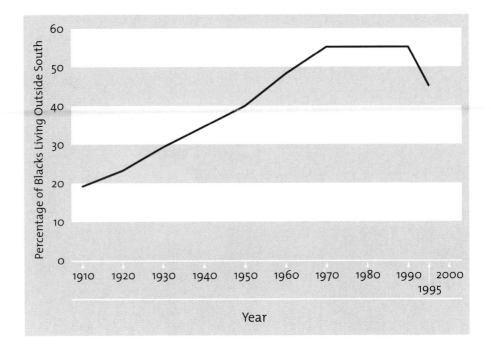

states, where they could not vote, to northern states, where they could. World War I created a labor shortage in northern cities, and many African Americans gave up sharecropping in Mississippi and Alabama for factory work in the sweatshops of New York, Chicago, and Detroit. When World War II created another labor shortage, blacks left southern farms for big-city tenements in even larger numbers (see Figure 17.1).

Northerners were not much more tolerant of blacks than were southerners. Most northern blacks attended segregated schools, ate in segregated restaurants, and shopped in segregated stores. Housing was even more segregated in the North than in the South. But African Americans at least could vote.

Unlike those who governed the South, northern machine politicians who dominated big city politics were not fussy about the color or religion of the votes they organized (see pp. 456–458). Machine politicians had long represented poor, downtrodden, immigrants who had little in the way of material wealth or social prestige. Any warm body who could walk into a voting booth was good enough for a machine politician. (Indeed, some politicians, in an illegal practice known as mobilizing the graveyard vote, voted bodies no longer warm but lying in the cold, cold ground.) The tough, shrewd machine politician knew that black votes counted as much as the vote of any other newcomer to the city.[12]

By the 1930s, African Americans used their votes to win a small place in the politics of a few big cities. African-American politicians won election to city councils and became neighborhood leaders in party organizations, obtaining jobs and other benefits for their constituents.[13] By 1944, two African Americans, William Dawson of Chicago and Adam Clayton Powell of New York, had been elected to the House of Representatives. But the biggest political breakthrough for African Americans occurred in 1948, when many gave them credit for casting the decisive votes electing Harry Truman as president (see Election Connection).

Blacks Help Elect Harry Truman in 1948

In 1948, African Americans had their first opportunity to shape presidential politics. For many decades, partly because Republican President Abraham Lincoln had issued the Emancipation Proclamation, African Americans had favored Republican party candidates. But during the thirties, the Republican stranglehold on the black vote began to loosen. Franklin Roosevelt's programs for the poor had induced many black voters to switch to the Democratic party. By 1948, it was no longer clear which party would gain the most black votes.

The 1948 election was hotly contested, and the outcome was decided by just a few thousand votes. Since the African American vote might go to either political party and could prove decisive for the outcome of the election, appeals to the black voter became an explicit part of Truman's campaign strategy. In the words of his top political analyst: "the northern Negro vote today holds the balance of power in Presidential elections for the simple arithmetical reason that the Negroes not only vote in a block but are geographically concentrated in the pivotal, large and closely contested electoral states such as New York, Illinois, Pennsylvania, Ohio, and Michigan."

Truman himself had never been known as a civil rights enthusiast. On the contrary, he came from the former slave state of Missouri, and his private language was sprinkled with racial slurs. But Truman had exceptional political instincts. The election year had hardly begun before Truman delivered the strongest civil rights message any president had ever presented. He called for the abolition of poll taxes, more effective protection of black voting rights, the creation of a Fair Employment Practices Commission with authority to stop racial discrimination, an end to racial segregation in interstate travel, and he brought to an end racial segregation within the armed forces.

Some have claimed that Truman's civil rights strategy was responsible for his reelection. The two-thirds support he received from African Americans helped him carry the "large, pivotal" states of Ohio by 7,000 votes, Illinois by 33,000 and California by 17,000. Had he lost these states, Dewey would have been elected. Although no one factor determines the outcome of any presidential election, African Americans had for the first time since 1876 become a significant force in national politics.

Significantly, it was in that same year the NAACP began to win key Supreme Court decisions.

SOURCES: David McCullough, *Truman* (New York: Simon & Schuster, 1992): 586–90; Patricia Gurin, Shirley Hatchett, and James S. Jackson, *Hope and Independence: Blacks' Response to Electoral and Party Politics* (New York: Russell Sage, 1989): 36–38.

AWAKENING THE SUPREME COURT TO CIVIL RIGHTS

The legal case against segregation was gradually developed by the **National Association for the Advancement of Colored People (NAACP)**, a civil rights organization that relied heavily on a legal strategy to pursue its objectives. Formed in 1909, the NAACP bears a name that strikes readers today as odd but is rooted in the historical moment when it was established. The NAACP chose the courtroom

National Association for the Advancement of Colored People (NAACP)
Civil rights organization, dating from 1909, that relied heavily on a legal strategy to pursue its objectives.

EVOLUTION OF CIVIL RIGHTS ACCOMPANIED BY CHANGES IN LANGUAGE

The well-known newspaper columnist, Miss Manners, tells us that it is respectful to refer to people by the name they wish to be called. This can readily be done for individuals, but when members of a group cannot themselves agree upon the name by which they wish to be called, selecting a respectful reference is more difficult.

In the case of the descendants of immigrants to the United States from Africa, the name deemed respectful has evolved over the years. At the turn of the century, "colored people" was preferred by many, and so the National Association for the Advancement of Colored People took a name that now seems unusual. When colored people came to be used by some whites in an abusive way, "Negro" became the respectful reference, and so Martin Luther King, referred to the Negro in his "I Have a Dream" oration. But at the very moment King was speaking, Negro was beginning to be regarded as a deprecatory reference, and the simpler word, black, was frequently substituted. Thus, King, in the same "Dream" speech, also refers to blacks. Significantly, he uses "Negro" when referring to the past, "black" to dream about the future:

Five score years ago, a great American, in whose symbolic shadow we stand, signed the Emancipation Proclamation. This momentous decree came as a great beacon light of hope to millions of Negro slaves.... But ... we must face the tragic fact that the Negro is still not free....

I have a dream that ... little black boys and black girls will be able to join hands with little white boys and white girls as brothers and sisters."

Recently, "African American" has become the identification preferred by many; it places more emphasis on national origins than skin color. Since the preferred designation may (or may not) be changing, we are following the lead of Martin Luther King by using both the established referent, black, as well as the African American referent that may be replacing it.

---

strategy because it thought that the electoral strength of African Americans was too small to achieve anything other than legal victories.

But a legal strategy carried out without the support of black votes was not very effective. Despite the care with which cases were prepared by the NAACP's lead attorney, Thurgood Marshall (who later became the first black Supreme Court Justice), the organization initially had but few successes in the courtroom. It could get neither the poll tax nor educational requirements outlawed. The Court did strike down one version of the white-primary in 1927,[14] but it did so in such a convoluted way that its decision had no practical consequence. For all of the legal efforts of the NAACP, only 12 percent of the *southern* black adult population was registered to vote in 1947.[15]

Later, as blacks moved North and gained the right to vote, NAACP's legal strategy became more potent. In an important 1944 case, *Smith* v. *Allwright*, the Court outlawed the all-white primary, saying parties were not private organizations but integral parts of a state electoral system.[16] After this decision, black voting in the South began to increase.

In 1948, the very year blacks helped elect Harry Truman, the Court outlawed **restrictive housing covenants**, legal promises by those buying houses that they

■ **restrictive housing covenant**
Legal promise by home buyers that they will not resell to an African American, declared unconstitutional by Supreme Court.

would not resell to an African American. Under the state action doctrine enunciated by the court in the *Civil Rights Cases*, the contract seemed a private matter, not subject to constitutional scrutiny. But in 1948 the Supreme Court held, in *Shelley* v. *Kraemer*, that inasmuch as a contract had meaning only if it were enforced by a state court, the contract involved state action.[17] By making this decision, the Court greatly narrowed the range of activities in which segregation could be legally practiced.

Linda Brown, in whose case the Supreme Court declared racial segregation unconstitutional, stands in front of the school that refused to admit her.

Redefining the Equal Protection Clause

Civil rights groups tried hard to reverse the separate but equal doctrine set forth in *Plessy* v. *Ferguson*, but for decades the Supreme Court resisted. In one extraordinary case, the Court admitted that educational facilities for blacks and whites were unequal, because the whites were allowed to keep their high school in operation after a black high school had been shut down.[18] Yet the Court allowed the white school to continue to operate, saying that blacks would gain little from a decision to shut down a white school, and ignoring the possibility that blacks and whites might share the same facility.

The NAACP seemed more successful in 1938 when it won a suit on behalf of a black law student denied access to Missouri's all-white law school but who could have his tuition paid if he attended a law school in another state.[19] When the Court decided against Missouri, it and other southern states responded by creating all-black law schools of inferior quality, leaving blacks worse off than they were before the decision.

After blacks demonstrated their electoral influence in the 1948 presidential election, the NAACP proved to be more effective in the courtroom, as the Supreme Court began to reconsider the separate but equal doctrine enunciated in *Plessy*. First, the Court, in 1950, declared that an all-black law school was inherently unconstitutional because it could not be an effective "proving ground for legal learning and practice."[20] By focusing on law schools, the NAACP, in this case, had shrewdly aimed at the weakest point in the separate but equal doctrine. Supreme Court justices were all attorneys, and they all knew from personal experience the importance of a law school's reputation for one's subsequent career.

Once the law school decision provided an opening wedge, the NAACP attacked the separate but equal doctrine directly by encouraging Oliver Brown to file suit saying his daughter, Linda, was being denied equal protection by Topeka, Kansas, despite the fact that the black schools of Topeka seemed as good as those whites enjoyed. This suit led to the **Brown v. Board of Education of Topeka, Kansas** decision in 1954 that finally declared racial segregation unconstitutional.[21]

Chief Justice Earl Warren, a former California governor, was keenly aware of the political significance of the *Brown* decision, so he asked the justices to delay it for a year in order to try to get a unanimous vote. At first it seemed that unanimity could not be achieved, because two members of the court thought a decision to reverse *Plessy* v. *Ferguson* would violate the principle of *stare decisis*, a rule that says courts should adhere to the doctrines set forth in prior decisions (see Chapter 15, p. 494). But Warren argued that the *Brown* decision could be distinguished from the *Plessy* decision, because the *Plessy* case had involved buses and trains, not schools.

To distinguish segregation in school from segregation in train stations, Warren cited psychological studies to show that racial separation created a sense of inferiority

■ **Brown v. Board of Education of Topeka, Kansas**
1954 court decision declaring racial segregation in schools unconstitutional.

among black children. One study showed, for example, that black children favored white dolls over black ones.[22] By focusing on the particularly harmful effects of segregation on children, Warren was able to limit his opinion to schools, thereby avoiding a direct repeal of *Plessy*. By so limiting the effect of the decision, Warren was able to obtain a unanimous vote from the justices, but in pursuing a legal doctrine, Warren might have done better to have followed Harlan's dissent in *Plessy* that simply said, "the Constitution is color blind." The constitutionality of racial segregation should depend not on its psychological effects, which may vary from person to person, but on whether racial criteria are valid grounds for classifying individuals.

Some years later, the Supreme Court did provide just this rationale for its finding that segregation was unconstitutional. It said that any distinction based on race or other ethnic group that had been discriminated against in the past was a **suspect classification**, which would be closely scrutinized by the courts to make sure that its use did not violate the equal protection clause of the Constitution. This concept soon became crucial for ensuring that racial and ethnic minorities received equal protection before the law.[23]

Warren realized he could not get a unanimous court to back such a sweeping statement outlawing segregation in the *Brown* decision, and so he settled for less. Also to preserve court unanimity, Chief Justice Warren postponed consideration of the exact way in which school boards were to rectify their segregated practices. The next year, the Court called for school desegregation "with all deliberate speed," a phrase that was interpreted by southern school boards to mean as little desegregation as possible.

In spite of its deficiencies, most scholars believe *Brown* to be among the most important decisions the Supreme Court has ever made.[24] In this decision, the Supreme Court declared unconstitutional a system of racial segregation that from the earliest colonial settlements had organized social life in a large part of the United States. Within two years, the border states of Maryland, Kentucky, and Missouri, as well as Kansas and the District of Columbia, eliminated formal segregation in their schools.

CIVIL RIGHTS AFTER *BROWN*

Brown also changed the country's political dynamics. The impact on young people and church leaders was particularly noticeable. Immediately after the decision, three new civil rights organizations, the Congress of Racial Equality (CORE), the Student Nonviolent Coordinating Committee (SNCC), and the Southern Christian Leadership Conference (SCLC), rose to prominence. Consisting mainly of college students and ministers, the groups held demonstrations, led boycotts, undertook voter registration drives, and appealed to the federal government for intervention into southern racial practices.[25]

One year after *Brown*, a more militant phase of the civil rights movement erupted. Rosa Parks, of Montgomery, Alabama, engaged in an extraordinarily successful act of **civil disobedience**—a peaceful, well-publicized violation of a law designed to dramatize its injustice. When Parks refused to vacate her seat in the white section of a bus, her arrest induced a boycott led by a young Baptist minister, Martin Luther King, who had the resourcefulness and rhetorical capacity necessary to give the event national significance.[26] Using boycotts, protests, and acts of civil disobedience, the southern civil rights movement gained strength by winning sympathetic coverage in the northern press.[27]

suspect classification
Categorization of a particular group that will be closely scrutinized by the courts to see if its use is unconstitutional.

civil disobedience
A peaceful, well-publicized violation of a law designed to dramatize its injustice.

The civil rights movement met intense opposition from southern government officials. In March 1956, nearly every southern member of Congress signed the Southern Manifesto, committing each official to resist by every legal means the implementation of the *Brown* decision. Southern resistance to court-ordered integration was so consistent and complete that, in the states of the Old Confederacy, hardly any school desegregation actually occurred. When school began in the fall of 1964, ten years after the *Brown* decision, only 2.3 percent of black students in the states of the Old Confederacy attended integrated schools.[28]

Yet the protests and demonstrations gradually had their effect. For one thing, southern African Americans were registering to vote. The percentage registered more than doubled from 12 percent in 1947 to 28 percent in 1960 (see Figure 17.2). At the same time, African Americans were becoming an ever increasing political factor in the large industrial states of the North. With civil rights demonstrators focusing national attention on racial issues, presidential candidates had to balance southern resistance against the need to get black votes in the big northern states.

John Kennedy's defeat of Richard Nixon in the breathtakingly close election of 1960 owed much to his success at attracting the black vote. In the summer of 1960, when Kennedy captured the Democratic presidential nomination, his civil rights credentials remained in doubt—in part because he had won the nomination only after defeating Hubert Humphrey and Adlai Stevenson, both of whom had stronger civil rights records. To strengthen his support in the black community, Kennedy, in the middle of the campaign, placed a phone call to Coretta Scott King expressing sympathy for the plight of her husband, Martin Luther King, who had been locked for four months in a Birmingham jail. The phone call electrified Kennedy's supporters in the black community, and Kennedy captured enough black votes to win such crucial states as Ohio, Michigan, and Illinois.

Rosa Parks

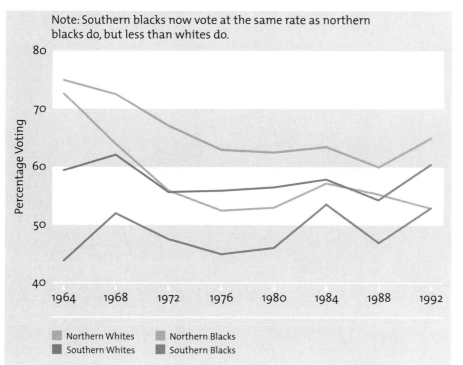

Note: Southern blacks now vote at the same rate as northern blacks do, but less than whites do.

FIGURE 17.2

Changes in Black and White Participation in Presidential Elections, by Region.

SOURCE: U.S. Bureau of the Census, *Current Population Reports.* South is defined as the states that formed the Confederacy.

Northern Whites Northern Blacks
Southern Whites Southern Blacks

Kennedy's victory further encouraged civil rights demonstrators. In the largest demonstration of all, 100 thousand black and white demonstrators marched on the Washington Mall in the summer of 1963, calling for jobs and freedom. Martin Luther King gave his powerful and moving "I Have a Dream" oration. Civil rights suddenly was regarded by a plurality of Americans as the country's most important problem.[29] Kennedy's assassination just a few months later generated an outpouring of moral commitment to racial justice unseen since the closing years of the Civil War (see Figure 17.3).

Elected political leaders responded quickly to this transformation in the public mood. The new president, Lyndon Johnson, though himself a southerner, called upon Congress to memorialize the dead president by enacting civil rights legislation. After intense congressional debate, a majority of both Republican and Democratic members of Congress voted in favor of the Civil Rights Act of 1964, a law more sweeping than any passed since the days of Reconstruction. Segregation was banned in all places of public accommodation, no federal money could be used to support segregated programs, and black job opportunities were given formal federal protection. The legislation brought about major changes in race relations throughout the South. Backed by federal money facilitating school desegregation and enforced by federal bureaucrats, many southern schools desegregated. The percentage of black students in southern schools that included whites increased dramatically from 2.3 percent in 1964 to 91.3 percent in 1972.

Buoyed by economic prosperity and his civil rights achievements, Lyndon Johnson won a sweeping election victory in the fall of 1964. Not one to rest on his accomplishments, Johnson immediately pushed through Congress the Voting Rights Act of 1965, which guaranteed black voting rights by placing federal officials in southern registration halls and polling places.[30] As a result, the percentage of southern black adults registered to vote jumped upward (see Figure 17.2),[31] and the number of elected officials of African-American descent rose from less than 500 in 1965 to over 8,400 in 1996.[32]

FIGURE **17.3**

Evaluation of Civil Rights as Country's Most Important Problem

SOURCE: Gerald Jaynes and Robin M. Williams, Jr., eds. *A Common Destiny: Blacks and American Society* (Washington, DC: National Academy Press, 1989), 224.

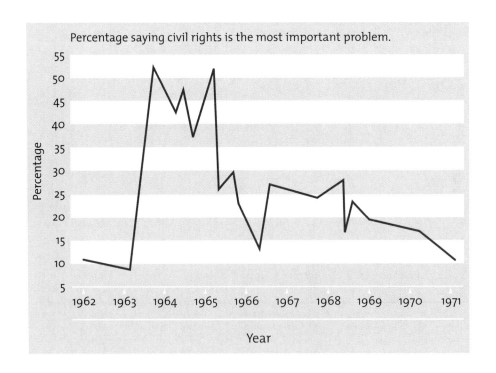

Martin Luther King, Jr., delivers his "I Have a Dream" speech at the March on Washington in August of 1963.

DECLINE IN STRENGTH OF CIVIL RIGHTS MOVEMENT

Segregation and discrimination were not limited to the South. Most northern blacks lived in racially isolated neighborhoods, sent their children to predominantly black schools, and found it difficult to find good jobs. Even as Congress was passing the Voting Rights Act of 1965, Martin Luther King changed the focus of the civil rights movement by mounting a series of civil rights demonstrations in Chicago.[33] This decision changed political dynamics in unanticipated ways. As school busing and job discrimination became a northern issue as well, support for civil rights protests among many northern whites dwindled.[34] At the same time, new black leaders, such as Malcolm X, took a black nationalist position, affirming black culture and denying the value of integration. Civil violence began to break out in black neighborhoods, beginning in Los Angeles in 1964 and spreading to other cities over the next three years. When Martin Luther King was assassinated by a white man in Memphis, Tennessee, in the spring of 1968, violent racial disturbances broke out simultaneously in dozens of cities throughout the country. National guard and army units were called upon to quell wholesale theft and property destruction.

After these events, civil rights was no longer regarded by the white majority as the country's most important problem (see Figure 17.3). As long as civil rights issues were being addressed by nonviolent demonstrations in the South, African Americans appealed successfully to the moral instincts of northern whites. But once whites realized that the problem was national in scope, and that civil disobedience could turn violent, many had second thoughts. Opposition to busing, affirmative

FIGURE 17.4

Percentage of Delegates to Republican and Democratic National Conventions Who Are African American.

Percentage of black delegates to Democratic convention has risen rapidly, while Republican percentage has remained steady.

SOURCE: "The Democratic Delegates," *San Francisco Examiner*, August 27, 1996, p. A-9; Robert Zauser, "Small Number of Black Delegates Illustrates Problem for Republicans," *Philadelphia Inquirer*, August 16, 1996, p. A22.

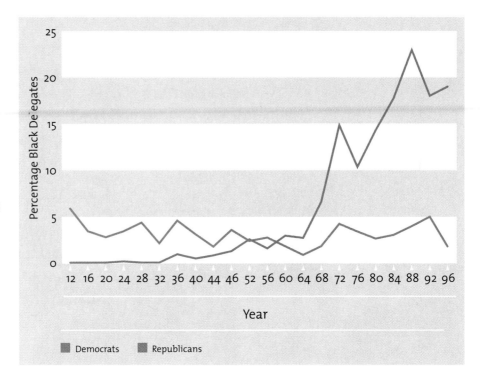

action, and other programs of racial integration split the biracial political coalition that had elected Harry Truman and John Kennedy.

Race issues now began to divide the two political parties. When Senator Barry Goldwater voted against the Civil Rights Act of 1964, he was among a minority of Republicans to do so. But by 1968, Republicans were pursuing what was known as a "southern strategy," an appeal to all those who thought the civil rights movement had gone too far. Meanwhile, blacks began to identify even more closely with the Democratic party.[35] The percentage of blacks attending the Democratic convention grew from 6.7 to 14.6 percent between 1968 and 1972 (see Figure 17.4).

SUPREME COURT NO LONGER FORGES AHEAD

Encountering increasing popular resistance to further legislative initiatives, civil rights groups once again turned to the courts for assistance. African-American leaders hoped the Supreme Court would remain a bulwark against this shift in public opinion. But the courts followed in the more conservative direction that the rest of the country was moving. For example, the Supreme Court drew a distinction between two types of segregation. *De jure* segregation, the legal separation of the races practiced in the South, was said by the Court to violate the equal protection clause of the Constitution. But segregation in the North was said to be *de facto* segregation, occurring as the result of private decisions made by individuals—such as their choice of residence. In *Milliken v. Bradley* (1974), the Supreme Court considered the constitutionality of the most pervasive form of *de facto* segregation.[36] Milliken argued that the State of Michigan tolerated racial segregation by allowing virtually all-white suburban school districts to surround the City of Detroit, whose schools were predominantly black. In rejecting Milliken's claim, the Supreme

■ *de jure* segregation
Racial segregation that is legally sanctioned.

■ *de facto* segregation
Segregation that occurs as the result of decisions by private individuals.

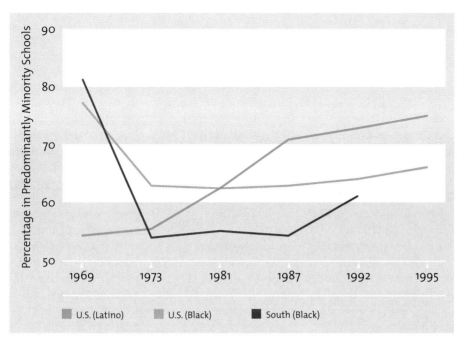

FIGURE **17.5**

Percentage of African-American and Latino Students in Desegregated Schools, 1968–1992.

SOURCE: U.S. Department of Education Office for Civil Rights Data as reported in Gary Orfield et al., "Deepening Segregation in American Public Schools," Report of the Taubman Center for State and Local Government, Harvard University, 1997.

Court ruled that suburban school districts in the North had never practiced *de jure* racial segregation. The segregation that had occurred was *de facto*, simply the result of private decisions to live in Detroit or its suburbs. Writing for the majority, Warren Berger, who had replaced Earl Warren as chief justice, said that the lower courts, in calling for metropolitan-wide desegregation, were trying to produce "the racial balance which they perceived as desirable." But the Constitution only forbids segregation; it "does not require any particular racial balance." Dissenting from the decision, Thurgood Marshall, the former NAACP attorney now serving on the Supreme Court, responded: "Negro students will continue to perceive their schools as segregated educational facilities and this perception will only be increased when whites flee . . . to the suburbs to avoid integration." After the 1974 *Milliken* decision, very little additional school desegregation took place in either the North or South. School segregation among Latinos actually increased during the 1980s (see Figure 17.5).

AFFIRMATIVE ACTION

Civil rights groups also called upon government agencies, universities, and businesses to rectify past discriminatory practices by taking affirmative steps to provide increased educational and job opportunities for African Americans. In response to these demands, many organizations have developed programs based on **affirmative action**, that is, programs designed to enhance opportunities for groups that have suffered discrimination in the past, be they ethnic- or gender-based groups. Affirmative-action activities vary in their size and significance. An action may be nothing more than special advertising, recruitment, and counseling programs designed to help members of the disadvantaged group learn about available opportunities. Another may take the person's membership in a disadvantaged

affirmative action
Programs designed to enhance opportunities for groups that have suffered discrimination in the past.

The Case Against Affirmative Action

The Constitution is color-blind and gender-neutral. When race or gender is used as a criterion for allocating educational and job opportunities, this confers advantages on some individuals at the expense of others. Those who are helped are regarded with suspicion, because they are thought to have got their opportunity for reasons other than their individual merit. As a result, affirmative action perpetuates group antag-onisms as well as feelings of group superiority and inferiority. In the end, ethnic and gender classi-fication is self-defeating. If it is difficult to fire people because they are members of a particular group, they will not be hired in the first place.

The Case For Affirmative Action

The Constitution has been neither color-blind nor gender-neutral: It per-mitted the slave trade and counted slaves as only three-fifths of a person. It permitted the denial of the vote to women. Racism and sexism per-meate institutions and practices so thoroughly that the only way discrim-ination can be alleviated is through race-conscious and gender-explicit poli-cies that are designed to reverse past practices. The equal protection clause of the Fourteenth Amend-ment does not preclude classification by race. The clause only requires that race classifications not harm those groups against whom discrimi-nation has historically been practiced.

---

group as one factor among many to be considered when hiring a person. The strongest form of affirmative action involves setting aside a quota, or a spe-cific number of positions, for members of disadvantaged groups (see Democratic Dilemma).

The constitutionality of affirmative action programs was considered by the Supreme Court in 1978 in a case that involved Allen Bakke, a Norwegian–American, who sued for admission to the medical school of the University of California at Davis.[37] Bakke had been denied a place among the 84 positions open to all applicants. He complained that he had been denied equal protection of the law, because he was not allowed to compete for the 16 places reserved for minority students.

The four dissenting judges in *Regents of the University of California* v. *Bakke* said the Constitution allowed quotas when needed to remedy "past societal discrim-ination." But the five-member majority agreed with Bakke's complaint and allowed him to enter Davis and eventually become a physician.

Four of the justices who formed the five-member majority said they opposed all forms of affirmative action. They said Bakke should be admitted because a racial **quota**, a specific number of positions set aside for a specific group, constituted an unconstitutional classification. They also opposed all other forms of affirma-tive action, including diversity programs. Any distinctions based on race not specif-ically required to offset *de jure* segregation were in violation of the Civil Rights Act of 1964.

But Justice Lewis Powell, who cast the fifth and decisive vote, took a middle posi-tion. He agreed with the other four members of the majority that Davis could not

■ **quota**
Specific number of positions set aside for a specific group, said by Supreme Court to constitute an unconstitutional classification.

establish a quota, because Davis itself had never been involved in *de jure* segregation. But Powell went on to say that some affirmative action programs passed the constitutionality test. He said that preserving "diversity" was a legitimate college objective. A college or university had a justifiable interest in having a diverse group of students, and decisions ensuring such diversity were constitutional as long as specific racial quotas were not established.

Though Powell was the only justice to take this position, it has remained guiding Court doctrine, in large part because it took a middle position that seemed to have broad public support. A majority of Americans have supported diversity programs but opposed quotas.

During the 1990s, all forms of affirmative action came under increasing criticism. Whereas Republican President Bush supported minority fellowships in 1990 (see the introduction to this chapter, p. 550), Republican presidential candidate Dole opposed them during his 1996 campaign. Dole's opposition may have been influenced by the debate over affirmative action that took place in California in 1995. Amidst considerable controversy, the Board of Regents of the University of California, at the request of Governor Pete Wilson, voted to end all affirmative action admissions and fellowships programs. The next year, California voters approved an initiative banning all forms of affirmative action. The initiative is currently being challenged in the courts. In response to these developments, President Clinton has said that affirmative action programs should be "mended, not ended," a middle-of-the-road position not unlike Powell's. It remains to be seen whether Powell's position in Bakke will be modified by the Supreme Court so that not just quotas but other forms of affirmative action are banned.

At the time of his Supreme Court case, many white Americans sympathized with Allen Bakke's fight against racial quotas. Bakke won the case, was admitted to medical school, and is now a doctor.

Elections, Courts, and Civil Rights: An Appraisal

Although African Americans made striking progress after World War II, the process of racial change has slowed in recent years. Blacks have continued to make political gains, winning an increasing number of mayoral elections, state legislative races, and seats in Congress, and they have also made noticeable educational gains. The percentage of blacks between the ages of 16 and 24 who dropped out of high school fell from 22 percent in 1970 to 10 percent in 1994. The percentage of blacks with four or more years of college increased from 4 to 13 percent. Between 1980 and 1992, the reading scores of black high school seniors increased by 18 points (as compared to a gain among whites of only 4 percent).[38]

But these political and educational gains have not been translated into wide-reaching economic progress for many black Americans. The percentage of black men and women in professional and managerial positions increased markedly in the twenty years after the passage of the Civil Rights Acts.[39] But these gains have been limited to upper-middle-class black Americans with a college education. Less well-educated blacks were actually worse off in the 1990s than they were in 1970. The percentage of less than high-school-educated black males participating in the labor force fell from 67 to 42 percent between 1970 and 1991.[40] (The percentage of similar placed white males without a job also dropped—but only by 3 percentage points). Poverty among blacks has hardly changed since 1970. Thirty-one percent of the black population was poor in 1994, only 3 percentage points less than in 1970.[41] Similar problems persist in other multiracial nations (see International Comparison).

Explanations for the persistence of black unemployment and poverty vary. Civil rights groups say that racism remains a pervasive feature of American society, and

British sociologist Stephen Small:

When I first arrived in the United States in 1984 to begin graduate study at the University of California, Berkeley, I met an African American graduate student. Surprised that I had come to study in the United States, he said something to the effect of "you must be mad coming to study here. Black people are catchin' hell in this racist society. In fact, things are so bad I even thought why not go to England to study." "Why not go to England to study?" I replied, "I'll tell you why not! Because they probably won't let you into the country if you're black. And if they do let you in

then you'll have more trouble than any white person finding a job, a place to live and getting an education for your kids. Black people are getting kicked in the teeth in England."

Small continues:

Blacks in England [who total about 4 percent of the population] have faced a number of distinct problems not faced by African Americans. One problem is the racialized nature of immigration legislation which has increasingly restricted their entry to the country. Another problem is the perception on the part of white English people that black people are somehow "not English" even if

born in England. Englishness and blackness are seen as incompatible, though the English are sometimes ambivalent. American essayist Paul Theroux captures the hypocrisy involved in English terminology about blacks:

"Convicted criminals were 'West Indian,' and purse snatchers were 'nig-nogs.' But when a black runner came first in a race against foreigners, he was 'English.' If he came second, he was 'British.' If he lost, he was 'colored,' if he cheated he was 'West Indian.'

Excerpted, without ellipses, from Stephen Small, *The Black Experience in the United States and England in the 1980s* (New York: Routledge, 1994): 61-62, 178.

that affirmative action programs have never been implemented. Conservatives argue that enhanced welfare programs have given poor people incentives not to look for jobs. They also say that affirmative action programs have proven counterproductive, because businesses are reluctant to hire black workers for fear of being accused of discrimination if they discharge them.

Civil Rights of Other Ethnic Minorities

Most of the civil rights issues and rulings discussed thus far apply as much to other racial and ethnic groups as they do to African Americans. The civil rights of other ethnic groups nonetheless become of distinctive legal and political significance under two circumstances: (1) when groups eligible for affirmative action need to be defined, and (2) when language or other issues arise.

The Supreme Court has never specifically delineated the groups in American society whose historic treatment makes them eligible for affirmative action. Neither the 1964 nor 1965 civil rights legislation identified any groups other than blacks as deserving affirmative action to redress historic grievances. But after the civil rights movement defined many issues in terms of equal protection under the Constitution, groups representing other ethnic minorities began to make similar civil rights claims, and Congress, in voting rights legislation, has given them recognition.

LATINOS

Latinos have in recent years been numerically the most rapidly growing minority group in the United States. Today, they constitute nearly 9 percent of the U.S. population, only somewhat less than the 11 percent that is African American; but for several reasons they have not been as politically effective. A sizeable percentage of the Latino population lacks citizenship, and even among Latino citizens, voting rates are much lower than among African Americans, partly because most Latinos have not experienced a prolonged civil rights struggle. Building a broad-based political coalition is further complicated by the fact that Latinos come from many different countries and differ from one another in important respects. The largest group of Latinos, Mexicans, want to be able to move freely back and forth across the border. Puerto Ricans, who already are U.S. citizens, tend to be darker-skinned and suffer more from racial discrimination. Cubans are primarily concerned about the restoration of democracy in their home country and are much more likely to vote Republican than other Latinos. Those from other parts of Latin America are more likely to be recent immigrants who have yet to acquire citizenship.

Yet, in recent years, Latinos have become increasingly active and influential in politics. One of the earliest groups to draw attention to the civil rights concerns of Latinos was the Mexican American Legal Defense and Education Fund (MALDEF) which has focused on voting, education, and immigration issues (see Chapter 4, pp. 109–113 for discussion of immigration). In response to MALDEF complaints, the Supreme Court, in 1974, interpreted the Civil Rights Act to mean that schools must provide special educational programs for those not proficient in the English language.[42] MALDEF and other advocacy groups also argued that Latinos and other language minorities were discriminated against because ballots and other voter registration materials were published only in English. Congress responded to these demands in 1982 by requiring that ballots be printed in the language of any protected minority constituting more than 5 percent of a county's population, extending protection not only to Latinos but also to Asian Americans and members of indigenous tribes.[43]

ASIAN AMERICANS

Asian Americans have not emphasized a political strategy as part of their struggle for assimilation into the mainstream of American society. They constitute only 2 percent of the population and they are less likely than blacks and Latinos to live in ethnically homogeneous neighborhoods. They are internally divided among many different nationalities who have differing, even conflicting, foreign policy concerns. Asians are also less likely to support affirmative action programs and more likely to vote Republican than other ethnic minorities.[44] Five Asian Americans have been elected to Congress, and in 1996 the first Asian was elected governor of a state (Washington). The major Asian-American civil rights victory in recent years has been the compensation paid to Japanese Americans for their internment in relocation camps during World War II (see p. 524).

INDIGENOUS PEOPLE

The rights and liberties of descendants of indigenous tribes do not seem to be protected by the Bill of Rights, because at the time of the writing of the Constitution these people were considered members of a foreign nation. As one authority on Indian rights has put it, "No constitutional protections exist for Indians in either a tribal or an individual sense."[45]

The relations between indigenous people and the government are instead governed by laws of Congress and by the many treaties that have been signed by the United States and Native American tribes. Although, over the long course of American history the United States government, under political pressure from those migrating westward, ignored or broke many of the treaties it made with indigenous tribes, the Supreme Court today still interprets some of these treaties as binding.[46] As a result, members of these tribes have certain rights and privileges not available to other groups. For example, court interpretations of treaties have given tribes in the Pacific Northwest special rights to fish for salmon.

One economically significant tribal right recognized in recent years has been the authority to provide commercial gambling on tribal property. The Court has said that tribal grounds are governed by federal, not state law. Federal law does not disallow gambling on tribal grounds, except if forbidden everywhere within a state.

Most of the rights contained in the Bill of Rights have been applied to members of tribes through congressional legislation. To protect tribal religious freedom, Congress in 1978 passed the American Indian Religious Freedom Resolution. Tribal leaders have argued that the resolution gives them special access to traditional religious sites in national parks and other government-owned lands. But the federal courts have interpreted the resolution narrowly, saying it does not make indigenous Americans "supercitizens" but provides them with comparable, but no additional, religious freedoms beyond those granted to other citizens.[47]

Women's Rights

Although gender is not mentioned in the equal protection clause of the Fourteenth Amendment, the meaning of the clause has been gradually redefined to refer to equal rights for women as well as for racial and ethnic groups. As one constitutional scholar has written, "It is in the very nature of ideas to grow in self-awareness, to work out all their implications over time. . . . The very content of the great clauses of the Constitution, their coverage, changes."[48] But the changes in the meaning of the equal protection clause were not won simply by actions taken in courtrooms. They were part of a broad struggle for women's rights played out as much among the electorate as in the legal arena.

The first struggle for women's rights focused on the right to vote (see pp. 170–173). Once that was achieved in 1920, the women's movement became dormant for

Women's rights across the century. (left) Women's rights issues in the United States at first focused on women's right to vote. (right) In August 1970, 50 years after women had won the franchise, 10,000 women's liberationists marched to a "Women's Strike for Equality" rally at New York City's Bryant Park.

nearly fifty years, finally to be awakened in the late sixties by the civil rights movement.[49] Since the late sixties, women's groups have achieved four civil rights objectives: the right to equal treatment before the law; tough enforcement of this right; the right not to be sexually harassed in the workplace; and access to state-funded military academies. In the following discussion, it will be shown that achievement of these objectives required both electoral involvement and courtroom presentations.

THE RIGHT TO EQUALITY BEFORE THE LAW

As unlikely as it may seem, it was a conservative southerner, Howard Smith of Virginia, who proposed an amendment to Title VII of the Civil Rights Act of 1964 that would prohibit discrimination on the basis of sex as well as race, religion, or national origin. Though the amendment passed overwhelmingly, the National Organization for Women (NOW) was formed because activist women became concerned that Title VII would not be enforced. To guarantee enforcement of women's civil rights, NOW, together with other women's organizations, backed the **Equal Rights Amendment**, a proposed amendment to the Constitution that banned gender discrimination. This amendment was expected to give the courts the tools necessary to strike down gender inequities.

At first it looked as if women's groups would succeed in winning passage of a constitutional amendment. Responding to its female constituency, Congress passed the ERA by overwhelming majorities by the spring of 1972. Within a year, a majority of states had voted to ratify it.[50] But at the very moment the ERA was about to become a part of the U.S. Constitution, it encountered increasing resistance led by groups of conservative women who were concerned, among other things, that the amendment would require government funding of abortions and the application of the military draft to women.[51] With women divided, the amendment was ratified by 35 states but failed to win approval from the three additional legislatures needed to achieve the three-fourths necessary to ratify a constitutional amendment.

As discouraging as the ERA defeat was for supporters at the time, in retrospect it seems that they won the war by losing the battle. Fifty years earlier, the women's movement had collapsed immediately following the passage of the constitutional amendment giving women the right to vote. This time, the women's movement

■ **Equal Rights Amendment (ERA)** Proposed amendment to the Constitution which banned gender discrimination.

The Civil Rights of Women and African Americans: Cooperation and Conflict

From its very beginning, the struggle for women's civil rights has been shaped by the African American struggle for equal rights. Many of those who first fought for women's rights came out of the struggle for equality for black Americans. Yet the two causes have come into conflict on two critical occasions.

1. Elizabeth Stanton organized the first public meeting on behalf of women's rights in Seneca Falls, New York, in 1848, because she had been refused the right to participate in an antislave convention. Because she included in her demands the women's right to vote, her own husband—who would later become Abraham Lincoln's secretary of state—refused to participate in the meeting. Their first efforts to petition for equal property rights in New York were received by an all-male legislative committee in the following words: "Ladies always have the best place and choicest tidbit at the table.... [Yet men] have presented no petitions for redress." To which Sojourner Truth, an ex-slave who became the first black advocate for women's rights, responded "Nobody ever ... gives me the best place—and aren't I a woman?" Raising her work-weary arm, she cried, "I have ploughed and planted and gathered into barns—and aren't I a woman?... I have borne thirteen children, and seen most of 'em sold into slavery, and when I cried out with my mother's grief, none but Jesus heard me— and aren't I a woman?"

Stanton tried to get members of Congress to forbid gender discrimination and to give women the right to vote when they wrote the Fourteenth and Fifteenth Amendments at the end of the Civil War, but she was unsuccessful. So bitter was she about the exclusion of women from the rights guaranteed by the two amendments, she campaigned against them.

---

continued to forge on, perhaps in part because the Equal Rights Amendment did not pass. Because the prolonged campaign for the ERA became a lengthy political and educational struggle, the movement did not wither away. In the twenty-five years after the ERA campaign began in earnest, women's place in politics changed more dramatically than in any previous quarter century. More women were being elected to public office in the 1990s than ever before.[52] In 1997, the House of Representatives included 49 women, the Senate had nine, and two of the nine Supreme Court justices were female.

Initial Court Response to Women's Rights

The ERA also had its impact on the Supreme Court. Before the ERA campaign, the court had done little, if anything, for women's rights. As late as 1961, the Supreme Court, in an opinion signed by Earl Warren, unanimously upheld a Florida law that made a clear gender distinction. It said that men were to be asked to serve on juries, but women were to serve on a jury only if they volunteered for duty.[53]

2. The modern women's movement was also shaped by race politics. Ironically enough, it was a conservative southerner's tactical effort to deflect the civil rights movement that constituted the initial stimulus. In the heat of the debate over the Civil Rights Act of 1964, Representative Howard Smith, one of the most shrewd and effective opponents of the civil rights movement, offered an amendment adding "sex" to the Title VII provision of the legislation that prohibited discrimination on the basis of race, religion, or national origin.

Just as Radical Republicans had kept women's rights out of the Fourteenth Amendment one hundred years earlier, so liberals opposed the Smith Amendment to Title VII of the Civil Rights Act of 1964 on grounds that it would weaken the racial focus of the civil rights legislation. But unlike the situation in 1867, women in 1964 had the vote, and most members of Congress dared not vote to prohibit discrimination on the basis of gender. So amidst great hilarity— one representative said that in his household he always had the last two words, "yes, dear"— and with little appreciation of the significance of what they were about to enact, the Civil Rights Act of 1964 banned gender as well as racial discrimination.

When the head of the Federal Equal Employment Opportunity Commission was called upon to enforce Title VII and refused to do so, calling it a "fluke" that was "conceived out of wedlock," a number of women working within the commission urged the formation of a national organization that would campaign for its enforcement and persuaded Betty Friedan, author of the recently published book, *The Feminine Mystique,* to head it. Friedan persuaded the founders to call the organization the National Organization for Women (NOW).

SOURCES: Eleanor Flexner, *Century of Struggle: The Women's Rights Movement in the United States* (Cambridge, MA: Harvard University Press, 1975): Ch. 5; Jo Freeman, *The Politics of Women's Liberation* (New York: Longman, 1975): 53–54; *Congressional Record,* House, February 8, 1964, 257.

Court opinions changed after the House of Representatives had voted overwhelmingly in favor of the ERA's passage. The Supreme Court, in *Craig* v. *Boren* (1976), declared unconstitutional an Oklahoma law that allowed women to drink at age 18 but denied that privilege to men until the age of 21. Oklahoma defended the law on the grounds that young men were more likely than young women to drive when drunk and more likely to have accidents. But the Supreme Court rejected as irrelevant the statistical evidence Oklahoma had presented on the grounds that the law constituted "invidious gender-based discrimination" that constituted "a denial [to males] of equal protection of the laws in violation of the Fourteenth Amendment."[54] (Oklahoma subsequently made the age of 21 the legal drinking age for both men and women.)

Although the Supreme Court said that gender discrimination violates the equal protection clause, it has never said gender, like race, is a suspect classification, that will be strictly scrutinized by the courts to see if its use is constitutional. Instead, the Court has said only that it "will strike out any gender classification absent a *substantial* relationship to an *important* objective."[55]

National defense remains the most important arena in which classifications by gender remain intact. According to federal law, men must register for the draft but women need not, and men carry out combat assignments while women are not allowed (though many "noncombat" positions now assigned to women may actually place women in danger of enemy fire). The Supreme Court ruled gender distinctions within the military constitutional in *Rostker* v. *Goldberg* (1981) on the grounds that on military matters "Congress' constitutional power" is broad and "the lack of competence on the part of the courts is marked."[56] The court ruling was consistent with the view of a majority of the voters, who favored certain restrictions on female participation in the military combat.[57]

DISCRIMINATION IN THE WORKPLACE

The Supreme Court has said that "business necessity" may at times make it difficult to recruit and retain members of disadvantaged groups. The court has reasoned that some types of positions must be performed by a person of a particular gender or that qualified persons of disadvantaged groups are not readily available for the type of work that needs to be performed.[58] The Court, in *Wards Cove* v. *Antonio* (1989), also said that Congress, in Title VII of the Civil Rights Act of 1964, intended that those discriminated against bear the burden of proof when showing that race or gender discrimination, not business necessity, caused a particular employment practice.[59] Although the case involved Alaskan salmon workers, women's organizations believed that the case had broad implications for gender discrimination as well. Though burden of proof may seem a technical detail, it is not a small matter in discrimination cases, because it is often difficult to provide conclusive evidence one way or another.

Justice Blackmun, in his dissenting opinion, denounced the restrictive interpretation given Title VII by the Supreme Court in *Wards Cove* v. *Antonio* in the strongest possible language, saying, "One wonders whether the majority [of the Court] still believes that . . . discrimination is a problem in our society, or even remembers that it ever was."[60] Sharing Blackmun's concern about the decision, women's and civil rights groups pressed Congress to shift the burden of proof from plaintiffs to businesses, thereby overturning the Supreme Court decision. Congress responded to these demands and enacted them into law as part of the Civil Rights Act of 1991, signed by George Bush. In sum, it was elected officials, not the Court, that took the lead on this gender discrimination issue.

SEXUAL HARASSMENT

The Supreme Court did not rule on the meaning of sexual harassment in the workplace until *Meritor Savings Bank* v. *Vinson*, a case decided in 1986.[61] In this case Michelle Vinson said that she had been psychologically damaged as a result of sexually abusive language used in her presence. In deciding in Vinson's favor, Justice Rehnquist in 1986 wrote a very narrow opinion that strongly implied that sexual harassment would be considered illegal only if it caused psychological damage to the victim. In other words, the Court said sexual harassment had to be experienced as personally devastating before it constituted a violation of Title VII.

In 1991, sexual harassment became a major political issue when Clarence Thomas was nominated to serve on the Supreme Court (see Chapter 15, pp. 483–485). The issue so energized the women's movement that 1992, the election year that followed, became known as the year of the woman; 46 more women were elected to the House of Representatives and 4 more to the Senate. Responding to the change in the political atmosphere, the Supreme Court, in a unanimous 1993 decision, *Harris* v. *Forklift Systems*, expanded its definition of sexual harassment.[62] Teresa Harris resigned her position at Forklift Systems, a heavy equipment rental firm, because her employer called her "a dumb ass woman" and made other derogatory remarks. Although she had complained and he had promised to restrain his remarks, her boss subsequently suggested in front of other employees that Hardy had had intercourse with a client in order to land a contract. She quit and sued. Lower courts denied her compensation, because no psychological damage could be shown. But Justice O'Connor said that Title VII "comes into play before harassing conduct leads to a nervous breakdown." Ruth Ginsburg went further, saying in her concurring opinion that gender discrimination exists whenever it is more difficult for a person of a particular gender to perform well on a job. Once again, the Supreme Court moved forward under the force of public pressure and political events.

SINGLE-SEX SCHOOLS AND COLLEGES

Single-sex education has long been a significant part of American education. As late as the 1950s, well-known private colleges, such as Princeton and Yale, limited their admissions to men. Although these colleges now admit approximately equal numbers of men and women, single-sex education survives at many private women's colleges. These colleges assert that women learn more in an environment where they can assume leadership roles that on co-educational campuses have often become the prerogative of male students. First Lady Hillary Rodham Clinton, who graduated from Wellesley, a women's college, said it "was very, very important to me and I am so grateful that I had the chance to go to college at a place where women were valued and nurtured and encouraged."[63] Similar arguments have recently been made for all-male education as well. In 1989 the Dade County, Florida, school system established an all-male elementary school serving African-American boys.[64] The school system claims the school has succeeded in increasing student attendance and test scores while reducing hostility among the students. Despite the claims of those who favor single-sex education, many feel that education that is separated by gender cannot be equal.

Although the pros and cons of single-sex education are still under debate, the Supreme Court in 1996 cast doubt on its constitutionality in *United States* v. *Virginia*, the Court said that women must be admitted to Virginia Military Institute (VMI), even though the state had recently established a separate military education program for women.[65] The Supreme Court said the newly established military training program for women did not match the history, reputation, and quality of VMI. It remains unclear, however, whether the Court will extend its decision to private schools or to state programs beyond those that prepare young people for military careers.

Women were finally admitted to the Citadel in 1996. However, in one of many difficult situations for the new cadets, the female students were reprimanded for trying to cut their hair to look like that of male students. Here, in the front row, Petra Lovetinska, Jeanie Mentavlos, and Kim Messer in their new haircuts.

The Future of Women's Rights

Despite many gains, the women's movement has not yet realized all of its civil rights agenda. Sexual harassment remains a burning issue within the military and in many business firms. Only a few women have broken through what is known as the glass ceiling, the invisible barrier that has limited their opportunities for advancement to the highest ranks of politics, business, and the professions. Very few women are chosen as college presidents, heads of major corporations, or as partners in major law firms. And no woman has yet been nominated for president by either major political party.

The changing American family has also left many women in difficult circumstances. The percentage of children raised in single-parent families headed by a woman has increased sharply in the past quarter century, and these households are much more likely to be poor than households headed by males or couples. Women's issues are likely to remain an important feature in American politics in the twenty-first century.

Americans with Disabilities

Disabled people constitute about 9 percent of the working-age population.[66] Ironically, they have one political advantage that both women and minorities lack: Every person runs the risk of someday becoming disabled. The rights of disabled people thus have broad appeal. Yet, this advantage is offset by a number of political limitations. Disabilities differ in kind and severity, making coordinated efforts more difficult. The disabled are also more scattered and less visible than ethnic minorities. The more severely mentally disabled neither vote nor engage directly in politics, leaving them dependent on others to defend their rights. The cost of helping people with disabilities is another drawback. It is estimated that the annual cost of disability payments and health care services for this group totals more than $275 billion.[67] Although many people are, in principle, sympathetic to the needs of the disabled, they do not necessarily like to pay the taxes needed to fund appropriate services.

Only after the civil rights movement of the 1960s sensitized the country to the needs of minorities were the civil rights of the disabled taken seriously. Previously, programs for the disabled were seen as charitable activities, to be supported by private donations. Mentally disabled people were closeted away in "insane asylums" and "homes for the incurable." Organizations representing the disabled were fragmented into those interested in the blind, deaf, mentally retarded, and so forth.

The needs of the disabled were first successfully cast in civil rights terms not by an interest group but by one individual, Hugh Gallagher, a wheelchair-bound polio victim who in the mid-sixties served as a legislative aide to Alaska Senator E. L. Bartlett. Gallagher constantly faced great difficulty using public toilets and obtaining access to such buildings as the Library of Congress. At his prodding, Congress enacted in 1968—just four years after the 1964 Civil Rights Act—a law requiring that all future public buildings built with federal monies provide access for the disabled. Similar language was subsequently inserted into the mass transportation act of 1970.[68]

Once elected officials had responded to the demands of the disabled, the courts, too, became more sensitive. Previously, many retarded children were denied access to public education on the grounds that they were not mentally competent. But in the early seventies, federal courts in Pennsylvania and the District of Columbia required that states provide disabled children with equal educational opportunity.[69] These decisions generated a nationwide movement for equal educational opportunity for the disabled, culminating in the passage of federal legislation in 1975 that guaranteed all handicapped children the right to an appropriate education.[70]

Encouraged by both judicial and legislative victories, groups representing the physically and mentally challenged became increasingly energetic and assertive. Legislative victories in education, transportation, and construction of public buildings finally culminated in the Americans with Disabilities Act of 1991, signed by George Bush. The Act made it illegal to deny employment to individuals on the grounds that they are handicapped. To the extent feasible, the workplace is to be adapted to the capacities of the disabled person.

Wheelchair-bound veteran Max Cleland (D–GA) toasts his staff with iced tea as they celebrate his 1996 Senate victory in winning the seat of retiring Senator Sam Nunn (D–GA).

Because of these legislative changes, opportunities for the disabled have greatly increased. Twenty years ago, public toilets for the handicapped hardly existed; sidewalks and staircases had no ramps; buses and trains were inaccessible to the handicapped; colleges and universities were designed in ways that all but precluded attendance by the physically challenged; and mentally retarded children were denied a public education. Unlike President Franklin Roosevelt, who fifty years ago felt it necessary to avoid being photographed in the wheelchair to which he was confined, Robert Dole referred constantly to his disabled arm during his 1996 campaign. Meanwhile, Georgia voters elected wheelchair-bound Max Cleland to the Senate and President Clinton appointed a blind person, David Tatel, to a federal appeals court.

Most of the expansion in the rights of the disabled have occurred as the result of congressional legislation rather than court interpretation. The courts have shown considerable reluctance to interpret the rights of the disabled in sweeping terms. For example, the Supreme Court unanimously ruled in 1979 against a nearly deaf woman, who complained that she had been denied admission to a nurses' training program for which she was otherwise qualified. The court ruled that deafness might preclude the woman from understanding instructions in a hospital setting, just as blindness fundamentally limits an otherwise qualified bus driver.[71]

Yet the disabled, too, have begun to encounter increasing political resistance. Educators complain that too many school dollars are set aside for special education programs. Architectural changes in public buildings and adaptations in transportation are said to be far too expensive to justify the limited amount of usage they receive. Ordinary citizens grumble at empty parking spots reserved for the disabled. It remains to be seen whether such complaints are a sign that the rights of the disabled are soon to be subjected to more limits or whether the extensions made in recent years will continue.

Chapter Summary

Civil rights groups have achieved many of their advances by persuading majority populations of the justice of their cases through participation in political demonstrations and electoral politics.[72] The 1954 *Brown* decision, to be sure, had an impact of its own, though even this decision came only after blacks had demonstrated political clout in the 1948 presidential election. Otherwise, the Supreme Court has usually followed the moods and swings of the rest of the country. When the country abandoned Reconstruction in the latter part of the nineteenth century, the Supreme Court, in *Civil Rights Cases* and *Plessy* v. *Ferguson*, ruled against civil rights demands. When blacks moved north and thereby acquired the right to vote, the Supreme Court reversed these decisions and redefined the equal protection clause, banning discrimination against African Americans, Latinos, Asians, and other minority groups. Yet the most notable progress toward racial desegregation occurred as the result of legislation passed by bipartisan majorities in Congress in 1964 and 1965.

When civil rights groups called for metropolitan-wide desegregation and affirmative action programs in the north, many northern whites, no less than southern whites, felt threatened by racial change. Supreme Court decisions in the 1970s reflected this new mood. The Court said *de facto* segregation was unconstitutional, and it forbade quotas as part of affirmative action programs.

The modern women's rights movement grew out of the civil rights movement. Once women's groups became active, they achieved striking changes in legal doctrine, even though they did not succeed in securing passage of the ERA. The Supreme Court outlawed most forms of gender discrimination, though women are not allowed in combat positions within the military. The Court has declared gender discrimination and sexual harassment in the workplace contrary to the Civil Rights Act of 1964 and has ruled state-funded, single-sex military training unconstitutional.

The civil rights movement also spawned new attention to the rights of the disabled. Once again, the most important steps forward were taken not by the courts but by Congress, which acted in response to electoral-based political pressure.

Key Terms

affirmative action, p. 563

black codes, p. 551

Brown v. *Board of Education of Topeka, Kansas,* p. 557

civil disobedience, p. 558

civil rights, p. 551

de facto segregation, p. 562

de jure segregation, p. 562

equal protection clause, p. 551

Equal Rights Amendment, p. 569

grandfather clause, p. 552

Jim Crow laws, p. 552

National Association for the Advancement of Colored People (NAACP), p. 555

Plessy v. *Ferguson,* p. 553

poll tax, p. 552

quota, p. 564

Reconstruction, p. 551

restrictive housing covenant, p. 556

separate but equal doctrine, p. 553

state action doctrine, p. 553

suspect classification, p. 558

white primary, p. 552

Suggested Readings

Browning, Rufus, Dale Rogers Marshall, and David H. Tabb. *Protest Is Not Enough: The Struggle of Blacks and Hispanics for Equality in Urban Politics.* Berkeley: University of California Press, 1984. Excellent analysis of the importance of electoral politics for black advances.

Deloria, Jr., Vine. "The Distinctive Status of Indian Rights," in Peter Iverson, ed., *The Plains Indians of the Twentieth Century.* Norman: University of Oklahoma Press, 1985, 237–48. Discusses the constitutional status of the rights of indigenous peoples.

Flexner, Eleanor. *Century of Struggle: The Women's Rights Movement in the United States.* Cambridge, MA: Harvard University Press, 1975. Engaging history of suffragist movement.

Foner, Eric. *A Short History of Reconstruction.* New York: Harper, 1990. An abridgment of Foner's classic historical study of Reconstruction.

Ginsburg, Ruth Bader. "Employment of the Constitution to Advance the Equal Status of Men and Women," in Shlomo Slonim, ed., *The Constitutional Bases of Political and Social Change in the United States.* New York: Praeger, 1990, 186–96. Succinct overview of court interpretations of women's rights.

Higgenbotham, Jr., A. Leon. *Shades of Freedom: Racial Politics and Presumptions of the American Legal Process.* New York: Oxford University Press, 1996. Sharp critique by former jurist of the racial bias in American legal practice.

Hochschild, Jennifer L. *The New American Dilemma.* New Haven: Yale University Press, 1984. Identifies the tension between racial desegregation and electoral politics in the United States.

Katzman, Robert A. *Institutional Disability: The Saga of Transportation Policy for the Disabled.* Washington, DC: Brookings, 1986. Discusses the ways in which legislative and judicial policy making for the disabled have interacted.

Katznelson, Ira. *Black Men, White Cities.* New York: Oxford University Press. Compares the political involvement of blacks in American and English cities.

Key, V. O., Jr. *Southern Politics.* New York: Random House, 1949. Classic study of effects of racial conflict on southern politics.

Lipsky, Michael. "Protest as a Political Resource," *American Political Science Review* LXII (December 1968), 1144-58. Shows the limits of protest as a political bargaining tool.

Lublin, David. *The Paradox of Representation: Racial Gerrymandering and Minority Interests in Congress.* Princeton, New Jersey: Princeton Press, 1997. Discusses dilemmas of affirmative action in redistricting.

Mandel, Ruth B. "The Political Woman," in Sherri Matteo, ed., *American Women in the Nineties: Today's Critical Issues.* Boston: Northeastern University Press, 1993, 34–65. Describes the increasing involvement of women in politics.

Mansbridge, Jane J. *Why We Lost the ERA.* Chicago: University of Chicago Press, 1986. Insightful, readable case study.

Rosenberg, Gerald N. *The Hollow Hope: Can Courts Bring About Social Change?* Chicago: University of Chicago Press, 1991. Argues that courts are generally unable to act contrary to majority opinion.

Skerry, Peter. *Mexican Americans: The Ambivalent Minority.* New York: Free Press, 1993. Engaging but controversial book that questions the effectiveness of Mexican-American political leadership.

Skocpol, Theda. *Protecting Soldiers and Mothers: The Political Origins of Social Policy in the United States.* Cambridge, MA: Harvard University Press, 1992. Analyzes the way in which women's groups have influenced U.S. social policy.

Tate, Kathryn. *From Protest to Politics.* Cambridge, MA: Harvard, 1993. Explains black political choices in the 1980s.

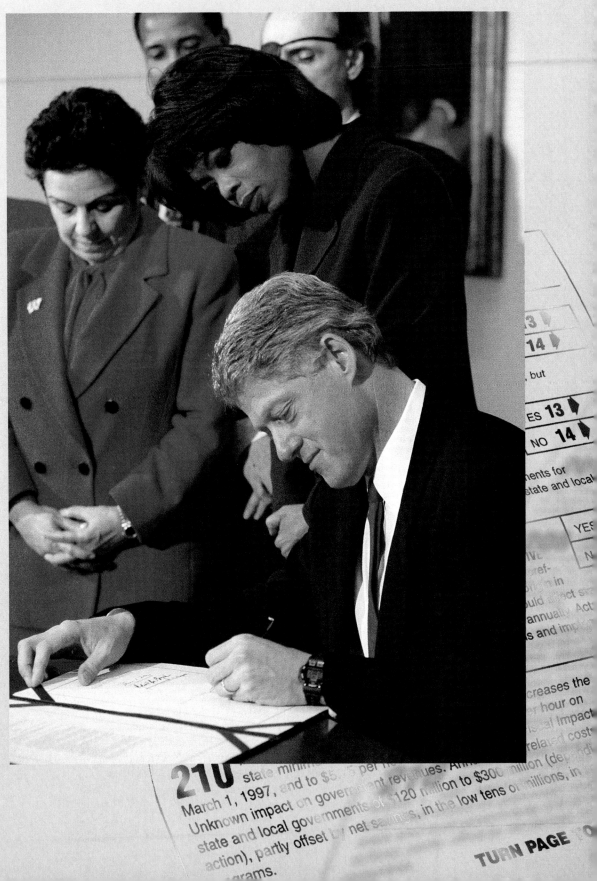

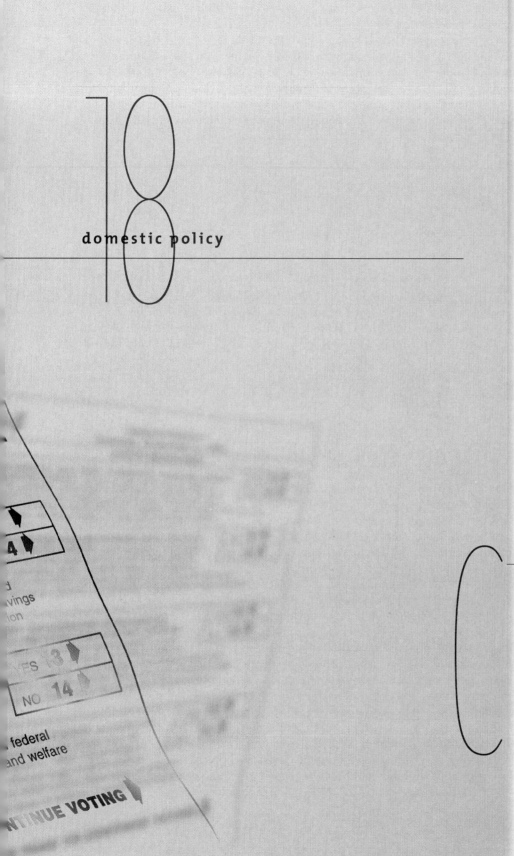

18

domestic policy

ONGRESSIONAL Republicans,
enjoying their first majority in
both House and Senate in fifty
years, vowed in 1995 to cut
back government programs and
take steps toward balancing
the budget.[1] Programs for both
senior citizens and for poor
families with children were the
target of some of the largest
proposed cutbacks. Although

President Clinton agreed to some, he opposed many others in a bitter, two-year confrontation, which on two separate occasions closed all but vital operations of the federal governments.

When the smoke cleared at the end of this prolonged battle, two decisions stood out. First, virtually all programs serving senior citizens, including very expensive health care programs, remained in place. Second, Congress passed and the president signed several pieces of legislation that cut benefits to poor families with children, including a program that turned welfare responsibility over to the states. These cuts in programs for families with poor children became law, despite the fact they cost much less than the programs serving senior citizens.

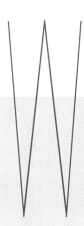

hy did budget cuts fall more heavily on programs for families with children than on more elaborate programs for senior citizens? Are the elderly's social needs greater? Are families with children less deserving? Or are senior citizens better organized and exercise more voting power? To provide a way of thinking about these questions, this chapter will examine the electoral and political forces that shape domestic policy.

Policy and Policy Making

domestic policy
Government programs and regulations that directly affect those living within a country.

Domestic policy consists of all government programs and regulations that directly affect those living within a country. It includes everything from education and health care to transportation and garbage collection—hundreds of different kinds of governmental activity. Domestic policy is the opposite of foreign policy, which involves relations with other nations (see Chapter 20). However, the distinction between domestic and foreign policy is not always sharp and clear. Some domestic policies, such as immigration, affect relations with other countries. Some foreign policies, such as foreign trade, have major domestic consequences.

Most policies, whether domestic or foreign, come about as the result of a complex process known as the policy-making round. After describing the process, we shall examine the political forces that shape three important domestic policies—social, educational, and regulatory. Economic policy is discussed in the next chapter.

The making of policy is a complex, never-ending round of events. To clarify what is often a very messy process, political scientists have divided the policy-making round into six stages (See Figure 18.1). At each stage, electoral forces are at work.

The first stage is agenda setting, making an issue visible enough that important political leaders take it seriously.[2] When elected officials think a problem is serious and might even affect an election, the issue has reached the agenda stage. The second stage consists of **policy deliberation**, the debate and discussion over issues placed on the policy agenda.[3] At this stage, groups and policy experts try to convince

policy deliberation
Debate and discussion by groups and political leaders over issues placed on the policy agenda.

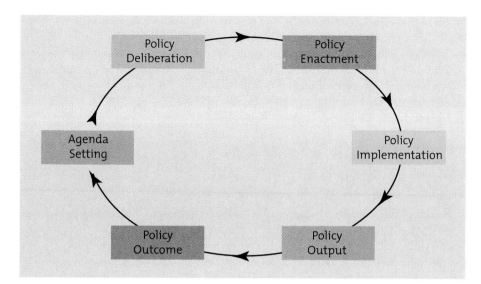

FIGURE **18.1**

Policy-making Stages

Policy Deliberation → Policy Enactment → Policy Implementation → Policy Output → Policy Outcome → Agenda Setting → Policy Deliberation

leaders not only that their proposals are a good way to deal with the problem but also that they are popular with the electorate. Next comes **policy enactment**, the passage of a law by public officials. Enactment may involve passage by Congress, a state legislature, or a city council and signing into law by a president, governor, or mayor. Elected officials who vote for the law usually expect that its passage will enhance their popularity, though there are celebrated instances when political leaders sacrifice their career for what they see as the good of the country. The fourth stage is **policy implementation**, the translation of the legislation into an actual set of government programs or regulations.[4] When fashioning the details, bureaucrats must exercise care so as to carry out the intentions of the legislative branch and not to stray too far from what is politically acceptable. At the fifth stage, government produces **policy outputs**, the provision of services to citizens or the regulation of their conduct. Beneficiaries usually think well of those who established the program; those hurt by the policy outputs probably feel otherwise. Finally, **policy outcomes** are the effect of policy outputs on individuals and businesses.[5] These outcomes often given rise to new issues, which are then placed on the policy agenda, completing the policy-making round.

The enactment of the 1996 welfare reform law, **Temporary Assistance for Needy Families (TANF)**, illustrates the way in which politics affects the various stages of the policy round. The first stage, placing the issue on the policy agenda, occurred when Bill Clinton scored points in his 1992 campaign for president by promising to end "welfare as we know it." The second stage, policy deliberation, occurred when interest groups, policy experts, members of Congress, and the media debated many different ways of redesigning welfare policy. Throughout the debate, polls reported that a majority of the public supported welfare reform, increasing the likelihood that something would be approved. The third stage, policy enactment, transpired when Congress devolved responsibility for welfare policy to state governments. President Clinton signed the bill into law, even though he had expressed strong reservations about many provisions, in part because voters supported the idea. The fourth stage, policy implementation, began in early 1997 when many state governments began revising their welfare plans, often in response to electoral pressures at the state level. The fifth stage, policy outputs, took place when many

- **policy enactment**
Passage of a law by public officials.

- **policy implementation**
Translation of legislation into a set of government programs or regulations.

- **policy output**
Provision of services to citizens or regulation of their conduct.

- **policy outcome**
Effect of policy outputs on individuals and businesses.

- **Temporary Assistance for Needy Families (TANF)**
Welfare reform law passed by Congress in 1996.

families left or were removed from the welfare rolls. Little is known thus far about the sixth stage, policy outcomes. Will people without welfare benefits try harder to find jobs? Will they obtain more education? Are they more likely to marry? Or will they become absolutely destitute? These questions are currently being researched and debated; answers to them could place welfare reform back on the policy agenda, producing a new policy-making round.[6]

Social Policy

■ **social policy**
Programs designed to help those thought to be in need of government assistance.

Social policy consists of programs designed to help those thought to be in need of government assistance. People may be regarded as needy because they are old, infirm, young, disabled, unemployed or poor, or some combination of these. One of the central issues in the making of social policy is finding an appropriate balance between government assistance to the elderly and to the young. As the opening story emphasizes, the elderly have done particularly well in securing government help.

The different effects of social policy on the young and the old is evident from some basic facts concerning changes in the nation's poverty rate. Poverty among senior citizens fell from 25 percent in 1970 to 12 percent in 1994, but poverty among families with children increased from 15 percent to 21 percent over this same period of time (see Figure 18.2). The poverty rate among families with children in the United States is twice as high as in most other advanced industrial societies;[7] the poverty rate among senior citizens is about the same in the United States as elsewhere.[8]

FIGURE 18.2

U.S. Poverty Rates for Senior Citizens and Children, 1970–1994.

Poverty rates are falling for seniors, but climbing for children.

SOURCE: *Annual U.S. Statistical Abstracts, 1972–1996.*

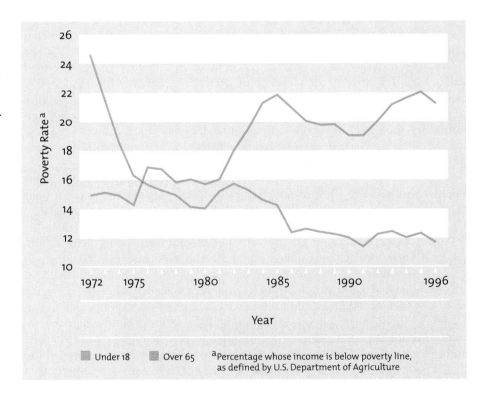

Year

■ Under 18   ■ Over 65   [a]Percentage whose income is below poverty line, as defined by U.S. Department of Agriculture

It is not just a matter of money. The chances for good health are also different for senior citizens and children. Of the seven countries with the largest economies, the United States has the highest infant mortality rate. But if one actually becomes a senior citizen, one has a better chance of living longer in the United States than in any of the other six countries. As one analyst put it, the United States is the "healthiest place to grow old but the riskiest [in which] to be born."[9]

Social Insurance for Senior Citizens

The improvement in the well-being of senior citizens today is due in good part to the country's social policy. As the population has aged, government has expanded programs to meet the retirement income and medical needs of the elderly. The amount spent on social programs for senior citizens grew from under $3,000 per senior citizen in 1960 to over $13,000 in 1995. (Unless otherwise indicated, all dollar figures in this chapter are expressed in 1990 dollars so as to adjust for inflation.)

ORIGINS AND DEVELOPMENT
OF SOCIAL INSURANCE PROGRAMS

Demands for aid to senior citizens escalated during the Great Depression of the 1930s, when poverty among the elderly was particularly acute. Approximately 5 million senior citizens rallied behind the proposals of Dr. Francis E. Townsend, a Californian who promised to end the depression by giving everyone over the age of sixty $200 a month, provided they spent it immediately.[10] Always quick to recognize potential electoral threats, President Franklin Roosevelt checked Townsend's soaring popularity by appointing an advisory committee to consider the problem. The committee recommended a program of **social insurance**, a program that provides benefits in return for contributions made by workers. Consistent with the committee's recommendations, Congress enacted in 1935 the landmark Social Security Act, which created a broad range of social programs, including a social insurance program for senior citizens generally known as **social security**.[11]

Social security initially cost the government very little. Most of those who first retired under the program received minimal benefits, because they had paid into the program only for a limited number of their working years. Also, retirement costs were limited by the fact that, in 1935, average life expectancy for those reaching the age of 65 was only 12.6 years, as compared to over 17 years today.

Gradually, the program expanded. The number of people covered went up; so did the length of their retirement. Benefits increased in size and cost. Two milestones deserve particular emphasis. In 1965, the year after Democrats won an overwhelming election victory against Barry Goldwater, a presidential candidate accused of opposing social security, Congress enacted **medicare**, which provides social security recipients a broad range of medical benefits (see Election Connection). In 1972, an election year, Congress gave senior citizens a large increase in their monthly social security check and indexed this amount to the cost of living. If inflation goes up 10 percent, so does the paycheck.[12]

■ **social insurance**
Program that provides benefits in return for contributions made by workers.

■ **social security**
Social insurance program for senior citizens.

■ **medicare**
Program that provides social security recipients a broad range of medical benefits.

President Lyndon B. Johnson signs the Medicare bill in 1965, as Hubert H. Humphrey and Harry Truman look on.

The popularity of both social security and medicare is due in part to the fact that they are based on the insurance principle, which provides benefits to people in return for contributions they have made. People become eligible for benefits by paying a payroll tax to social security during their working years. To get social security benefits, beneficiaries need only prove they are over the age of 65 (or, if they agree to a lower monthly check, the age of 62). Because of the insurance principle, a retiree does not have to show a need. People can receive benefits even if they own a vacation house overlooking the ocean and have millions in the bank.

Although social security is called an insurance program, it differs from a true insurance program in one fundamental respect: It operates at a loss. For all other insurance, most people pay more in initial payments and foregone interest than they receive in benefits; were it not so, the insurance company could not make a profit. But, from the beginning, social security has given most people more in benefits than they contributed in their social security tax. A couple who retired in 1995 can expect to receive about $435,000 in social security and medicare benefits over the remaining years of their lives, even though the worker in the family made tax contributions of only $175,000. The windfall for the average single person is less, but even this retiree is to get back $106,000 more than the amount contributed in taxes.[13]

How is this magic possible? How can benefits exceed contributions? Why have social security and medicare not gone broke? Up until now, three economic facts of life have done the trick:

■ Workers have grown in number, as women and baby boomers have entered the workforce. This means more people are contributing to the social security program.

■ Workers today produce more and earn more than their predecessors did. This means that more money is available.

■ Workers today pay a higher percentage of their earnings in social security taxes than their predecessors did. Essentially, every generation is being asked to pay more to cover the costs of the previous one. As economist Lester Thurow has pointed out, "the current generation of retirees . . . did not have to pay [much] into the system but gets benefits financed by those behind them."[14] The practice is not new. Jonathan Swift saw the same thing happening in England three centuries ago. "'Tis pleasant to observe," he said, "how free the present Age is in laying taxes on the next."[15]

Unfortunately, these three circumstances may all be disappearing:

Social policy was set on a new course after the election of Lyndon Johnson over Barry Goldwater in 1964. When Goldwater suggested that social security be made a voluntary program, Democrats accused him of seeking to destroy it. Though Goldwater denied wanting to do anything other than strengthen the program, both election analysts and Goldwater himself thought the issue did him more harm than any other issue.

Johnson won 60 percent of the vote, and the Democratic party captured a large majority of both houses of Congress. Although other factors also contributed to Johnson's overwhelming victory, the outcome was interpreted as providing a mandate for more social insurance. Over the next two years, Congress passed the medicare program for senior citizens, the medicaid program for low-income families, and an educational program for low-income children and, in general, laid the groundwork for a rapid expansion of the welfare state over the next dozen years.

SOURCES: John D. Pomfret, "Campaign Issues–VI" *New York Times*, October 30, 1964, 24; "Goldwater Sees Signs of Victory" November 1, 1964, 75.

■ The number of workers is not expected to increase much in the next couple of decades. As the baby boomers retire, the number of retirees will grow faster than the number of workers.

■ Rates of growth in economic productivity may be slowing down. Workers in the future may not be producing enough more to cover the much higher cost of social security caused by the retirement of the baby boomers.

■ Workers may be less willing to pay higher taxes. The much smaller X generation may not be willing to pay the huge taxes that may be required to cover the retirement costs of the baby boomers.

Unless something is changed, the social security fund is expected to be running a deficit by the time today's college sophomores are 50 years of age. To finance social security and medicare at the current level, workers may have to bear a social security tax of somewhere between 36 and 60 percent of their earnings, as compared to just over 16 percent in 1997 (see Figure 18.3). Even in the best of circumstances,

DILBERT® BY SCOTT ADAMS

FIGURE 18.3

Projected Cost of Social Insurance
for Senior Citizens.

Costs of programs for senior
citizens expected to rise rapidly.

SOURCE: Neil Howe and Richard
Jackson, *Entitlements and the
Aging of America* (Washington,
DC: National Taxpayers' Union
Foundation, 1994).

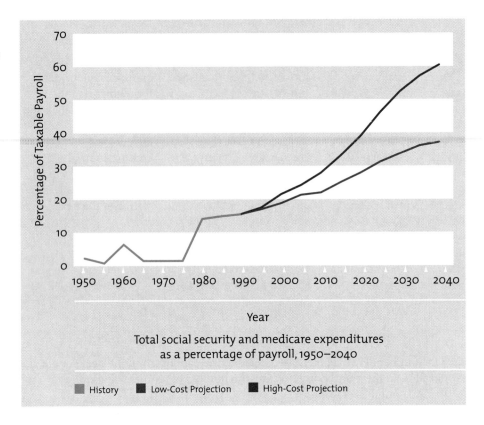

Total social security and medicare expenditures
as a percentage of payroll, 1950–2040

young people today will have to pay more than twice as much in taxes just to keep
social security benefits at their current levels.

Most analysts believe that if disaster is to be avoided, adjustments in social security are essential.[16] Most young people also realize that their retirement future is not
as rosy as their grandparents' has been. According to one survey, 62 percent of
younger adults think benefits will be cut before they retire.[17]

POLITICS OF SOCIAL INSURANCE

Electric trains once required dangerous, middle or "third" rails that provided the
electricity that drove the train. Social security and medicare are said to be the "third
rail" of American politics—"touch it and you die." Richard Morin put it another
way: "The bottom line on the public's attitude is: Spend whatever is needed—particularly on me—just don't bill us for it." [18]

THE RISKS OF CHANGE TO SOCIAL SECURITY

Most public officials worry they will be punished by the voters if they are perceived to threaten social security programs. In 1981, President Ronald Reagan suggested off-handedly that budget savings might be achieved by placing limits on the
growth in social security. Two days later, the Senate condemned the idea. Every
senator, both Republican and Democrat, disavowed the president's position. Even
so, Republicans lost control of the Senate the following year, and a number of pun-

dits attributed the loss to Reagan's misstatement on social security (though a down-turn in the economy was also a factor).

Only once, in 1983, did Congress make significant cuts in social security benefits. A commission that included leaders from both political parties recommended cuts that would become effective, for the most part, only in the distant future.[19] Because the recommendations were bipartisan and because cuts were postponed into the next century, the reductions did not produce an electoral fall-out. But at all other times, presidential candidates, leaders in Congress, and both parties have opposed cutting social security, despite the fact that it is the largest item in the federal budget. In 1995, both Republican House Speaker Newt Gingrich and Democratic President Clinton called for massive budget cuts in almost every aspect of the federal budget. Yet both leaders insisted that social security be completely spared from the budgeteers' ax.

COMPLEXITIES OF MEDICARE

The politics of medicare are much the same, making it difficult to keep the cost of the program from growing rapidly. The program, which cost little more than $25 billion in 1970, grew to nearly $160 billion in 1995.[20] Numerous factors contribute to the rapidly rising cost of medicare. Though doctors and hospitals are often accused of price-gouging, other factors play a more important role. The number of elderly is growing rapidly, increasing the demand for medical services. Doctors can now diagnose and treat more crippling injuries and life-threatening diseases (through CAT scans, magnetic resonance imaging, bone-marrow transfusions, and other high-tech, high-cost procedures). Hospitals and doctors try to offer the latest in technology and service. Patients expect error-free medicine, and they sue doctors when mistakes are made, driving up doctors' insurance costs (and the fees to cover them).

Congress has tried to control some of these costs by placing limits on doctor and hospital fees, ending the duplication of high-cost technologies, refusing to pay for expensive, highly experimental treatments, and encouraging the formation of health maintenance organizations (HMOs)—which have strong incentives to rein in costs. But these actions only slowed, not halted, the rising cost of medicare.

Stronger proposals, such as raising medical premiums and requiring patients to pay a larger share of the costs, have provoked political controversy. When Republicans made these suggestions in 1995, they said they were doing so only to save the program from bankruptcy. They claimed that President Clinton's failure to reduce cuts doomed medicare over the long run. Clinton and his Democratic allies in Congress responded that Republicans were cutting medical services in order to cut rich people's taxes. Cuts in medicare became a central issue in the 1996 election. President Clinton was able to use the issue so successfully that he carried Florida, a normally Republican state but one to which many retirees have migrated.

THE INFLUENCE OF SENIOR CITIZENS

The electoral impact of the social security issue is likely to continue. At a time when voter turnout has been declining, senior citizen turnout rates have been climbing. Between 1964 and 1988, voting rates among young voters between the ages of 21 and 24 fell by 13 percent, while voting rates among those over 75 climbed by 5.5 percent.[21] Sixty-four percent of those between ages 65 and 74 said they voted

The social security issue is particularly important to senior citizens, like this group demonstrating against medicare cuts.

in the 1994 congressional elections, but only 22 percent of those between the ages of 21 and 24 reported voting. Senior citizens are also more likely than young people to back up their vote by other political actions, such as writing letters to elected officials and contributing money to political campaigns.[22]

Many senior citizens have joined an organization that effectively presents their point of view. Some 33 million people are members of the American Association for Retired Persons (AARP), the largest interest group in the United States. Once the age of 50, any person can join AARP for $8. Members are eligible for a wide range of travel and other discounts worth much more than their annual dues. They also receive a magazine that keeps them up to date on proposals that might affect their social security and medicare benefits. AARP employs 1,700 people and has a budget that runs as high as $450 million.[23]

BROAD SUPPORT

AARP has the advantage of promoting a cause that very few voters strongly oppose. In fact young people are just about as likely to support social security as those over the age of 65. Only 7 percent of younger adults think the elderly are getting more than their fair share of government benefits, while 48 percent think the elderly are getting *less* than their fair share (see Figure 18.4).

FIGURE **18.4**

Both Young and Old Support Senior Citizen's Programs.

SOURCE: Survey by the Luntz Research Companies/Mark A. Siegal and Associates, September 8–10, 1994; *The Public Perspective: People, Opinions, & Polls,* February/ March 1995.

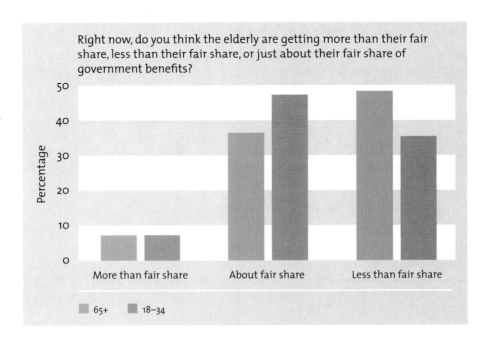

At least three factors contribute to broad support for social security. First, most people hope to benefit from social security and medicare someday themselves. In addition, many have parents who currently receive these benefits, relieving their children of financial responsibility for their parents' well-being. Finally, most people think that since senior citizens contributed to social security, they now deserve the benefits they are getting back. On the other hand, few are aware that these benefits are usually in excess of the contributions.

Public Assistance to Poor Families

If the interests of the elderly are well protected by AARP and both political parties, the same cannot be said for the interests of poor families with children. Programs designed for poor families are neither as lavish nor as user-friendly as those designed for the elderly. Neither political party is strongly committed to expanding them, and no association comparable to the AARP defends the interests of poor families with children.

ORIGINS AND DEVELOPMENT OF PUBLIC ASSISTANCE PROGRAMS

Public assistance consists of programs that provide low-income households with limited income and access to essential goods and services. Together, the programs form what is often known as the "safety net" that helps those who fall into financial difficulty. The sheer number of major public assistance programs actually exceeds the number of major programs for the elderly. Public assistance programs include the following:

TEMPORARY ASSISTANCE FOR NEEDY FAMILIES (TANF)

This program, passed by Congress in 1996, devolved the responsibility for designing income-maintenance programs for poor families to the states. However, state programs are subject to certain limitations. For example, no family may receive more than two consecutive years of assistance, and no family may receive more than five years of assistance altogether.

TANF has replaced the long-standing public assistance program, **Aid to Families with Dependent Children (AFDC)**, which was established in 1935 as part of the Social Security Act. Known as "the welfare program," AFDC was criticized by liberals and conservatives alike. Conservatives felt that it discouraged recipients from working.[24] Liberals felt the benefits were too low and program eligibility and administrative restrictions were too harsh: Recipients lost their benefits as soon as they earned more than a very minimal amount, and administrators inquired into the personal lives of the poor.[25]

FOOD STAMPS

This public assistance program provides recipients with stamps that can be used to purchase food. Enacted by Congress on an experimental basis in the early seventies, it has been gradually enlarged so that today it is larger than TANF.

public assistance
Programs that provide to low-income households limited income and access to essential goods and services.

Aid to Families with Dependent Children (AFDC)
Public assistance program established in 1935 as part of the Social Security Act; replaced in 1996 by Temporary Assistance to Needy Families (TANF).

food stamps
Public assistance program that provides recipients with stamps that can be used to purchase food.

EARNED INCOME TAX CREDIT (EITC)

This program returns the taxes paid to those who have little income. Initially proposed by Republicans in the early seventies as a way of helping the working poor, EITC was greatly expanded during the first year of the Clinton administration. One who fills out a tax return can receive an EITC reimbursement even if no taxes have been paid. In 1995, a family of four could receive a credit of as much as $3,560 a year.[26]

SUPPLEMENTAL SOCIAL INSURANCE (SSI)

This program provides disabled people of low income with income assistance. Created in the early seventies, SSI succeeds programs of aid to the blind and the deaf established by the Social Security Act of 1935.

RENT SUBSIDIES

This policy helps low-income families pay their rent, provided they select designated housing. The program was established in the early seventies to replace public housing programs, which had been criticized for encouraging racial segregation and large concentrations of poverty.

MEDICAID

This program pays for medical services for the poor. One becomes eligible only if one has no more than a minimal income and few assets other than a home. Medicaid was established in 1965 at the same time as medicare, in response to Republican objections to medicare on the grounds that it was designed to serve the middle class but not the poor. The cost of medicaid benefits has risen rapidly—from around $10 billion in 1970 to close to over $90 billion in 1995.

Applying for food stamps at a Department of Human Services office. The food stamp program is currently larger than TANF.

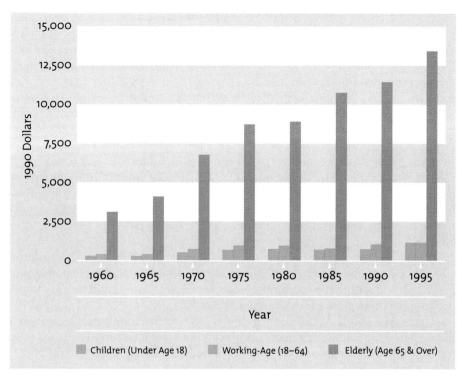

FIGURE **18.5**

Federal Entitlement Expenditures by Beneficiary Age Group, Per Capita, 1960–1995.

Much more money is spent on programs for elderly than for children.

SOURCE: Neil Howe and Richard Jackson, *Entitlement and the Aging of America* (Washington, DC: National Taxpayers' Union Foundation, 1994).

Although medicaid serves poor families, regardless of age, over one-quarter of all medicaid costs cover the medical expenditures of low-income senior citizens,[27] making medicaid an important supplement to the more well-known medicare program discussed earlier.

DRAWBACKS OF PUBLIC ASSISTANCE PROGRAMS

This list of public assistance programs that help poor families with children seems impressive, but actual expenditures are only one-tenth as much as what is spent on the elderly. Federal social programs for the elderly amounted to over $13,000 per capita in 1990, whereas public assistance programs for families with children amounted to little more than $1,300 per capita (see Figure 18.5). In addition, programs for families with children are more restrictive than programs for senior citizens. Six factors make programs for families with children less user-friendly.[28]

FEWER CASH BENEFITS In 1990, the elderly received two-thirds of their benefits in cash,[29] as compared to 41 percent of the benefits received by poor families with children.[30] Most people prefer cash income to benefits that come in the form of goods or services. Cash income enables one to purchase what one wants, when, where, and from whom one wants.

LESS INDEXATION Almost all benefits to the elderly, including social security and other retirement pensions, are indexed to changes in the cost of living. Although some programs for families with children are also indexed, the main welfare program, TANF (previously AFDC) is not. Benefits under this program, instead of keeping pace with increases in the cost of living, fell by 43 percent between 1975 and 1993 in the average state.

ASSISTANCE, NOT INSURANCE Unlike social security, which distributes benefits according to age and contributions made, programs for families with children are not paid out of an insurance fund. To become eligible for benefits, a low-income family must demonstrate that it has virtually no other means of livelihood. To show minimal income, the family head must visit a government agency, wait patiently in line with appropriate documents in hand, and then reveal to a government official the family's complete fiscal record. To receive cash benefits, the potential recipient must document that the family does not own a home, has virtually no savings, and has hardly any income.

STATE, NOT NATIONAL, PROGRAMS Families with children receive benefits that vary from one state to another. Only EITC benefits are uniform throughout the country. For the other major programs—TANF, food stamps, SSI, housing assistance, and medicaid—eligibility rules and benefit levels vary from state to state. In the case of TANF, the benefits can be five times as much in one state as in another.[31]

Because public assistance programs are state-operated, families with children who move from one state to another have to reconnect to public assistance programs. This means that poor families may not be able to respond quickly to job opportunities or changing family circumstances.[32]

These restrictions do not apply to senior citizens, because social security is a national program. Senior citizens can move from New Jersey to Florida (or even overseas) without jeopardizing the amount or delivery of their social security check.

BENEFITS CANNOT SUPPLEMENT INCOME Programs for poor families with children substitute for other income; they do not supplement it. In most states, families are not eligible for income assistance if they have savings of more than $1000, a car worth more than $1500, or anything other than a very modest home (the exact value varies from state to state). Under the AFDC program, families lost their benefits more quickly if they earned more money. The exact rules are now changing under TANF, but, if the old pattern holds, a recipient whose combined income is at the poverty line will continue to suffer a $.51 loss in benefits (from AFDC, food stamps and EITC combined) for every dollar earned over the first $2400.[33]

By comparison, senior citizen benefits supplement the recipient's own resources. Senior citizens may receive their medicare and social security benefits, even if they have savings, earn dividends and interest on their investments, and are homeowners.

POLITICS OF PUBLIC ASSISTANCE

Programs for poor families with children are poorly funded and restrictively designed because, unlike the elderly, children do not exercise direct political power. Instead, they are dependent upon a weak network of interest groups who fight among themselves, policy analysts who offer competing explanations for the persistence of poverty, a divided public, and opportunistic political parties.

GROUP ORGANIZATION

No group speaking on behalf of children has a mass membership of a size remotely comparable to that of the AARP. Instead, many small, competing groups take stances as varied as the alternative explanations for rising poverty rates. The most significant liberal group, the Children's Defense Fund, headed by Marion Wright Edelman, fought welfare reform to no avail. Though it had a budget in 1995 of $13 million and a staff of 150, it lacks a large membership that can effectively lobby Congress.[34] (By comparison, AARP has 33 million members, employs 1,700 people and spends as much as $450 million; see p. 588.)

On the conservative side, Gary L. Bauer has built the Family Research Council into a 250,000-member organization committed to the protection of family values. The group favored the welfare reform bill, in the conviction that welfare programs discourage fathers from assuming family responsibilities.

Groups with larger memberships do take positions on children's issues, but these groups are also divided about policy choices. For example, the Christian Coalition and Planned Parenthood both take stands on issues relevant to children, but inasmuch as they disagree on abortion policy and many other issues, they generally work at cross-purposes.

Still other groups adopt positions on issues affecting children's welfare, but these groups typically have other objectives more central to their mission. For example, the Urban League has long emphasized the importance of youth-oriented programs, but its fundamental objective remains the protection of the civil rights of African Americans. The AFL-CIO supports most child-oriented legislation, but its main concern is protection of the interests of labor. Though many women's groups care about children's issues, they tend to remain focused on issues of gender discrimination and harassment. In short, the interest group chorus on children's issues sings separate songs in different keys. They are unable to focus on a common cause in the way the AARP does.

Marion Wright Edelman, founder of the Children's Defense Fund.

POLICY DEBATE

Policy experts in this arena are in no more agreement than are interest groups. Three different explanations for the rising poverty rate among families with children have influenced the welfare debate.

First, liberals argue that poverty rates among children have risen because the government has not maintained an adequate level of governmental assistance. Sociologist Theda Skocpol advocates the establishment of a family allowance that would guarantee all families with children a basic stipend not unlike the social security check the elderly receive. She points out that lower poverty rates in European countries are due in part to family-allowance programs.[35]

Conservatives find the explanation for rising poverty rates in what they identify as a "culture of poverty" found in urban centers, in which young people are encouraged to place short-term pleasures ahead of long-term goals. Flashy clothes, adventure, crime, and sexual promiscuity are allowed to displace the study, patience, and hard work necessary for long-term success. Policy analyst Charles Murray has argued that this culture of poverty has been strengthened and reinforced by welfare policies that reward sloth and promiscuity. The work ethic is undermined by government programs that give as much money in welfare benefits as can be obtained from an entry-level job. Responsible parenting is undermined by the availability of aid for those who bear children out of wedlock.[36]

Conservatives point out that between 1970 and 1991, the percentage of women with children who were living without a mate more than doubled—from 11 percent to 27 percent. These female-headed families are particularly at risk of living in poverty. Many women find it difficult to both work and raise children. Mothers who do work find it hard to get full-time jobs at good wages. Nearly two-thirds of all children living in poverty are living in single-parent families headed by a woman.[37] Liberals respond by noting that poverty rates among families with children are

Data from other countries suggests that cultural forces have a more powerful effect on family life than do either welfare policy or employment opportunities. Over half the babies are born out of wedlock in Swe-

den, a country with a waning religious tradition. Only 6 percent of newborns are to unmarried women in Italy, a Catholic country that places heavy emphasis on family ties. In Japan, an even more traditional society, babies are almost

never born out of wedlock. The United States falls between these extremes with a rate roughly comparable to that of Canada, France, Britain, and Germany.

SOURCE: *Statistical Abstract*, 1992, Table 1365, 828.

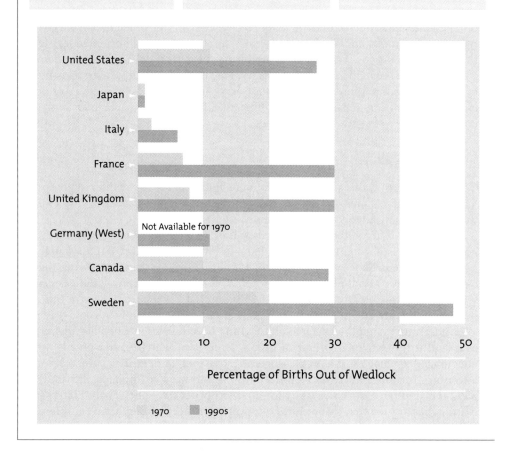

Percentage of Births Out of Wedlock

1970   ■ 1990s

much lower in other countries, despite the fact that the frequency of out-of-wedlock births is often just as high (see International Comparison). Apparently, the availability of family allowances softens the economic impact on single-parent families.

Offering a third explanation, sociologist William J. Wilson attributes a growing culture of poverty to changes in the post-industrial economy. Physically demanding blue-collar jobs, which can be performed by unskilled workers with minimal education, are declining in number. These jobs have been lost to technology or have moved overseas.[38] As a result, unemployment rates among young men without a high school degree have exploded, climbing from 8 percent in 1969 to 22 percent in 1985.[39] According to Wilson, when young men cannot find work, they refuse to take on the responsibilities of marriage and child-rearing. Young women don't want to marry men with few prospects.

PUBLIC OPINION

The general public wavers between liberal and conservative explanations for rising poverty rates. In 1992, when the country was emerging from a recession, half the population thought poverty was mainly due to circumstances beyond a person's control, while less than a third thought it was mainly due to a lack of effort. But just two years later, when the economy was booming, more people thought poverty was due to a lack of effort than to circumstances beyond a person's control.[40]

POLITICAL PARTIES

Because public opinion on the question fluctuates, so do the positions of the political parties. Most of the time, the Democratic party takes a more liberal position, while Republicans adopt the more conservative one. Hillary Clinton, for example, was once a member of the liberal Children's Defense Fund's board of directors. Gary Bauer of the Family Research Council is a former Reagan adviser.[41] But despite these underlying partisan differences, party leaders often search for the middle ground. As a result, their positions shift over time, and they do not always disagree. In fact both parties have adjusted their positions over the years, largely in response to changes in the public mood.

When the country was building the Great Society in the 1960s and 1970s, Democrats took the lead, but Republicans were not far behind. Republican presidents signed into law several welfare programs for children. President Nixon proposed the food stamp and SSI programs. Republicans proposed and President Ford signed the law creating the Earned Income Tax Credit. Republicans in Congress initiated the medicaid program.

As the public mood shifted in a conservative direction, the positions of both parties altered accordingly. In 1995, it was the Republicans who took the lead, proposing cuts in many of the programs they had once sponsored.[42] Although some Democrats opposed the cuts, a majority voted in favor of welfare reform and President Clinton signed the bill into law.

In sum, social policy is the product of powerful political influences. Senior citizens benefit from social policy, because they have constructed a powerful political coalition that can influence the outcome of elections. Poor families with children have done much less well, because they have less clout.

★ **AT THE STATE & LOCAL LEVEL**
Educational Policy

Historically, Americans have supported a large, well-financed educational system. Equal opportunity meant equal access to good schools. But the commitment to public schools, though still strong, has waned somewhat in recent years.

S tudent math scores
are lower in the
United States than
in other industrial
countries, yet Americans

pay more for schools than
many other countries.

a 1994–95 school year.

b 1991 (or closest available
   year.)

SOURCES: U.S. Department
of Education, *National Center
for Education Statistics,* 1994,
430; Millicent Lawton,
"U.S. Students About Average
in Global Study," *Education
Week* November 27, 1996, 32.

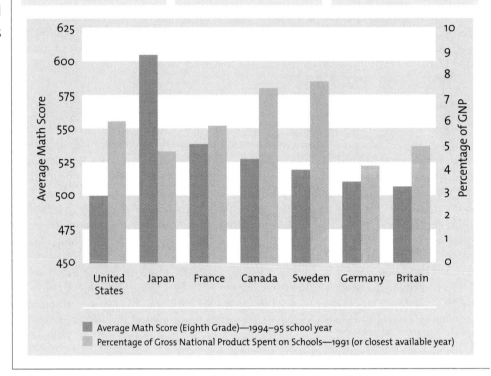

Average Math Score (Eighth Grade)—1994–95 school year

Percentage of Gross National Product Spent on Schools—1991 (or closest available year)

DEVELOPMENT OF PUBLIC EDUCATION

The public's commitment to its schools is deeply rooted. Although the Constitution says nothing about education, Congress in 1785 set aside one-sixteenth of the land west of the Appalachian Mountains to help pay for "the maintenance of public schools."[43] Support for public schools intensified with the flood of immigrants that arrived in the nineteenth century. As immigrants gained the right to vote, they demanded and won more or less equal access to public education. In Chicago and San Francisco, for example, children from immigrant backgrounds were no more likely to suffer from crowded classrooms than were children from native-born families. On the other hand, where racial minorities lacked adequate political representation, they were given second-class schools. Before gaining the right to vote, African Americans in the South and Chinese in California were segregated into badly maintained, inferior schools.[44]

Despite the discriminatory treatment of racial minorities, public schools did much to build American democracy. The percentages of young people enrolled in American schools far surpassed those in European countries. Public schools helped foster a common language out of a people from disparate parts of the world. Offering at least the appearance of equal opportunity, they reinforced a distinctive American identity built around the concepts of liberty and equality. They educated the workforce that operated the new machines that were to make the country the world's greatest industrial power.

Most of these changes occurred as the result of decisions taken by state and local officials. Even today, 95 percent of the cost of public education is paid for out of state and local budgets, each contributing approximately half the cost (though the exact percentage paid varies widely from one state to another). The 5 percent contribution by the federal government is spent mainly on programs enhancing equal opportunity: Clearly, federal programs hastened the pace of school desegregation. Federal dollars, today, are spent mainly on special education for the disabled and compensatory programs for disadvantaged children.[45] Core educational programs are generally paid for out of state and local dollars.

SCHOOL POLICY TODAY

Despite the strength of the American educational tradition, Americans no longer remain so committed to their public schools. Within the United States itself, financial support for elementary and secondary education (as a percentage of GNP) has increased only slightly over the past twenty-five years.[46] Teacher salaries, relative to salaries in other occupations, have hardly improved at all.[47]

Other industrial nations, once far behind in financial terms, have now nearly caught up. The United States spends 6 percent of its Gross National Product on elementary and secondary education. Although this is still more than most other countries (see International Comparison), the difference is narrowing. Many other countries spend almost as much, and Canada and Sweden spend more.

Not only are American schools losing their financial edge, but they seem to be doing an inferior job at converting dollars into schools that help students learn.[48] Students in American schools are learning less in reading, science, math and geography than are students in most other industrial countries (see International Comparison). Not surprisingly, the public's assessment of the quality of its schools has slipped. The percentage who give American schools a grade of D or F increased from 14 percent in 1987 to 28 percent in 1997 (see Figure 18.6).[49]

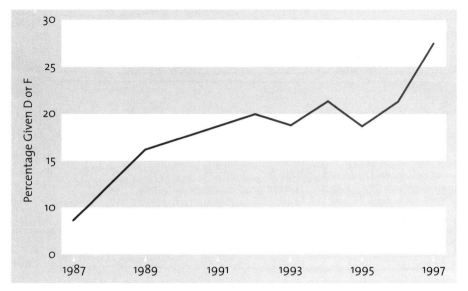

FIGURE 18.6

More Americans Giving Schools a Low Grade.

SOURCE: Polls by Gallup Organization and *Wall Street Journal/NBC News*, March 1997, as reported in *Wall Street Journal*, March 14, 1997, R1.

As in other social policy areas, liberals and conservatives diagnose the problem differently and offer competing solutions. Liberals argue that schools could be more effective if they were given more resources.[50] Maintaining educational expenditures at the same level as in the past is not enough. Liberals point out that between 1965 and 1995 the country more than doubled its spending on health care from 7 to 15 percent of GDP.[51] Its commitment to education increased from only 5 to 6 percent.[52] In other words, government has committed itself to helping pay more of the costs of medical care in order to extend the last years of life, while doing little additional to enhance the capacities of those in the first years of life. Some say this is another sign that domestic policy is skewed to the advantage of the elderly.

Conservatives respond by saying that money is neither the problem nor the solution. They cite studies showing that the amount young people learn in school is seldom affected by the amount of money a school has.[53] The problem is not financial but bureaucratic. Lacking goals, public schools have become cafeterias, where students take whatever courses they want. Lacking competition, public schools have gone stale. They better serve the interests of the adults teaching in and administering the school than the students who are its presumed clientele.

Critics of American education offer two widely contrasting solutions. Some propose national standards, together with a national curriculum, that clearly define the country's educational goals.[54] An effort to create such national standards was begun by the Bush Administration. The project ran into difficulty when it attempted to define exactly what students should learn in school. Do students need to learn about Paul Revere's ride? Or about the traditions and way of life of indigenous tribes? When committees of experts were created to resolve these kinds of issues,

they decided to ask students to learn nearly everything any expert recommended. Although this helped the committees reach a consensus, the end result was a curriculum so comprehensive even a Ph.D. student could not master it. The project eventually collapsed under the weight of its own ambitions, but the issue continues to percolate. In 1997 President Clinton once again called for the establishment of national standards.

Other critics recommend redesigning the educational system so that students and parents have their choice of schools, just as senior citizens, under medicare, have their choice of doctor and hospital.[55] The government would give each family a voucher, which could then be used to purchase education from any school they preferred. Those opposed to the idea say it will enhance racial, religious, and ethnic divisions and make it more difficult for students from disadvantaged backgrounds to achieve equal educational opportunity (see Chapter 16, p. 532).[56]

POLITICS OF EDUCATION

In the past, public schools were, like motherhood and apple pie, beyond partisan dispute. But in recent years, the two political parties have begun to disagree over a broad range of educational issues. Republicans have given increasing support to alternative ways of organizing the country's educational system, while Democrats have won strong support from the two largest teacher groups, the National Education Association and the American Teachers Federation, by maintaining a steadfast commitment to public schools as currently organized.

If any one moment can be regarded as the time when educational issues took on a partisan flavor, it was the campaign of 1976, when candidate Jimmy Carter promised to create a Department of Education, a commitment he fulfilled. Teachers flocked to the Carter bandwagon; they constituted 20 percent of the delegates to the Democratic national convention that year. Meanwhile, many Republicans became increasingly critical of the influence of teacher unions and called for merit pay instead of automatic salary increases.

Yet a majority of Republicans, especially those elected at state and local levels, have continued to support public schools. For all the current discontent, Americans still think schools are crucial for achieving the American dream. As long as the electorate feels this way, schools will continue to have bipartisan support.

Regulation

On May 11, 1996, one hundred ten people boarded ValuJet's Flight 592 from Miami to Atlanta, many of them students returning from spring break. Over one hundred oxygen generators, mislabeled as empty, were also loaded onto the plane. Shortly after take-off, a fire broke out in a cargo hold. The oxygen generators exploded, fueling the fire, and the plane nose-dived into the Florida Everglades, killing all aboard.

The oxygen generators never should have been loaded onto the plane. According to regulations issued by the Federal Aviation Administration (FAA), ValuJet was not authorized to carry hazardous materials.[57] Hours after the Florida Everglades disaster, Anthony Broderick, an FAA administrator, assured the public that ValuJet was a safe airline. But several weeks later, investigators discovered that the company

Searchers look for bodies and wreckage of the ill-fated ValuJet DC-9 Flight 592, which crashed in the Everglades. The crash led to heightened scrutiny of federal regulations affecting airline safety.

had not followed FAA procedures. Broderick was fired, all 51 ValuJet aircraft were grounded, and Congress began a massive investigation.

The ValuJet disaster raises questions about the government's regulatory policies. Does the federal government have the responsibility to ensure the public safety? What other kinds of activities should be regulated? How should this responsibility be exercised? In the remainder of this chapter, we discuss why and how the federal government regulates many aspects of our social life.

THE RISE OF FEDERAL REGULATION

■ **regulation**
Rules and standards that control economic, social, and political activities.

Government **regulation** consists of rules and standards that control economic, social, and political activities. Regulation dates back to feudal times. For example, businesses in sixteenth-century England "were required to set prices and render service in a socially responsible manner."[58] In the United States, the most important basis for federal regulation is found in the Constitution, which gives Congress the power "to regulate Commerce." Regulations under the authority of the commerce clause were originally applied to the railroad industry, with the passage of the Interstate Commerce Act of 1887. They have since been applied by Congress to regulate everything from civil rights regulation to national insurance standards. Since the New Deal, the Supreme Court has generally found regulatory policies constitutional (see Chapter 3, pp. 79–81).[59]

Government regulations increased in number and significance at three distinct periods in the country's history, the progressive era, the New Deal era, and the Great Society era. Each period is marked by a strong political movement that identified major abuses in certain sectors of society, and each produced legislation that created a host of new government agencies (see Figure 18.7).

During the progressive era, a series of exposes created a public revulsion against the worst abuses of industrialization. Initially, the spotlight was turned on the power of large corporations, such as Standard Oil Company, which exercised almost complete control over the oil industry. When the public demanded antitrust legislation,

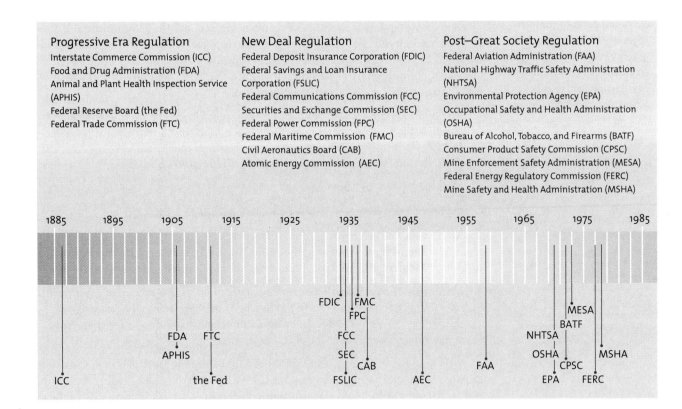

Progressive Era Regulation
Interstate Commerce Commission (ICC)
Food and Drug Administration (FDA)
Animal and Plant Health Inspection Service (APHIS)
Federal Reserve Board (the Fed)
Federal Trade Commission (FTC)

New Deal Regulation
Federal Deposit Insurance Corporation (FDIC)
Federal Savings and Loan Insurance Corporation (FSLIC)
Federal Communications Commission (FCC)
Securities and Exchange Commission (SEC)
Federal Power Commission (FPC)
Federal Maritime Commission (FMC)
Civil Aeronautics Board (CAB)
Atomic Energy Commission (AEC)

Post–Great Society Regulation
Federal Aviation Administration (FAA)
National Highway Traffic Safety Administration (NHTSA)
Environmental Protection Agency (EPA)
Occupational Safety and Health Administration (OSHA)
Bureau of Alcohol, Tobacco, and Firearms (BATF)
Consumer Product Safety Commission (CPSC)
Mine Enforcement Safety Administration (MESA)
Federal Energy Regulatory Commission (FERC)
Mine Safety and Health Administration (MSHA)

FIGURE 18.7

Establishment of Major Federal Regulatory Agencies Occurred in Three Waves.

SOURCE: Marcia Lynn Whicker, *Controversial Issues in Economic Regulatory Policy* (Newbury Park, CA: SAGE Publications, 1993).

Congress enacted the Sherman Act (1890), which made it a crime to "restrain" or "monopolize" trade. Journalists and writers known as muckrakers then publicized other abuses, leading to the creation of additional regulatory agencies. For example, Upton Sinclair's best-selling novel, *The Jungle*, detailed horrible sanitation conditions in the meat-packing industry, resulting in the passage of the Meat Inspection Act of 1906.

The second regulatory wave occurred during the 1930s, when the government tried to prevent practices that were thought to have caused the depression. The eight major new regulatory agencies created at this time, as listed in Figure 18.7, formed an important component of Franklin Roosevelt's New Deal. The new agencies included the Civil Aeronautics Board, the predecessor to FAA, which later played the controversial role in the ValuJet disaster (pp. 599–600).

The third wave of regulatory innovation took place during the 1960s and 1970s as part of the Great Society. During this period, the issues were consumer safety, occupational safety, and environmental protection. Ralph Nader wrote a best-selling book, *Unsafe at Any Speed*, which revealed serious safety problems with a popular sports car, the Corvair. His efforts were so effective that General Motors halted production, and government regulations required manufacturers to install seat belts in all cars. Nader hired young people known as "Nader's Raiders," who found safety problems in many domains, including other consumer products, occupational hazards, and the environment. Congress passed sixty-one new significant pieces of regulatory legislation and established or substantially enhanced the role of nine regulatory agencies. Nader has remained politically active; in 1996, he ran for president as the candidate of the Green Party but received only a little more than a half million votes.

■ **Environmental Protection
Agency (EPA)**
Agency responsible for issuing
regulations designed to protect
the environment from
unwanted pollutants.

The most important of the new agencies formed was the **Environmental Protection Agency (EPA)**, which has the main responsibility for issuing regulations designed to protect the environment from unwanted pollutants. Its controls on air and water pollution have done much to improve air and water quality in many metropolitan areas. As one analyst has pointed out,

> Air pollution from lead, by far the worst atmospheric poison, declined 89 percent during the 1980s; from carbon monoxide, also poisonous, went down 31 percent. In 1992, the number of Americans living in counties that failed some aspect of air-quality standards was only half [those] who lived in dirty air in 1982.[60]

JUSTIFICATIONS FOR REGULATION

As the result of these waves of regulatory expansion, many aspects of economic and social life have now become the subject of government regulation. According to Murray Weidenbaum, a former chairman of the Council of Economic Advisors,

> No business, large or small, can operate without obeying a myriad of government rules and restrictions. Costs and profits can be affected as much by a directive written by a government official as by a management decision in the front office or a customer's decision at the checkout counter.[61]

Why have the regulatory responsibilities of government expanded so dramatically during the past century? Scholars have identified three broad types of circumstances in which they find government regulation most easily justified—natural monopoly, externalities, and protection of the uninformed.

NATURAL MONOPOLY

■ **natural monopoly**
A situation in which a public
service is best provided by a
single company.

In a situation known as a **natural monopoly** a public service is best provided by a single company. To make sure that the company does not take advantage of its monopoly and charge consumers unnecessarily high prices, natural monopolies are usually subject to regulation. For example, regulations control the charges set by telephone companies that have exclusive rights in a particular region. Regulations also control the prices of gas, electricity, cable television, and other utilities that have exclusive rights in a particular state or locality. Otherwise, it is likely that these companies would charge excessively.

EXTERNALITIES

■ **externalities**
Consequences of activities that
do not directly affect those
engaged in them.

The government may also regulate to prevent or adjust for **externalities**, consequences of activities that do not directly affect those engaged in them. One of the best examples of an externality is air pollution. A company may try to keep its costs low by using cheap fuel, even though it emits black soot into the air. The black soot does not directly affect the company, though it threatens the health of, and creates a nuisance for, those living nearby. To prevent companies from imposing this externality on others by polluting their environments, EPA has imposed numerous regulations on industry to control the emission of pollutants.

One of the most celebrated pollution controversies took place at Love Canal, New York, in the mid-1970s. Over the course of almost 25 years, Hooker Chemical and Plastics Corporation had used the Love Canal as an industrial landfill. In 1953, they sold the land to a local school board for $1. The sale was hardly a bargain, because Hooker, without telling the school board or anyone else, had buried in the landfill tons of toxic waste. The school board built a grammar school and residential development on the land. It had no idea it was sitting on a ticking environmental disaster.

At first, signs of trouble were periodic and faint. Occasionally the ground caved in and revealed rotting chemical drums. Record rainfalls accentuated the problem in 1976. Chemicals leaked from drums and were washed into neighborhood yards. Corroded toxic containers surfaced in residential backyards. Fence posts were eaten away. A pungent odor pervaded the neighborhood. Toxic chemicals oozed into basements. Sores and burns developed on humans and animals. Over 250 chemical compounds and 42.5 million pounds of chemical wastes were discovered. Many of these chemicals were responsible for genetic damage, birth defects, cancer, neurological disorders, and liver damage.[62]

New York Health Commissioner Robert Whalen released a report which declared Love Canal a "great and imminent peril" to the health of local residents.[63] President Carter declared Love Canal a federal disaster area. The government evacuated hundreds of families, and the EPA found 263 homes unlivable. In response to public outrage, Congress quickly passed legislation designed to regulate the disposal of hazardous wastes.

In one of the nation's most notorious pollution controversies, the EPA found 263 homes at New York's Love Canal unlivable because of hazardous industrial pollution.

PROTECTING THE UNINFORMED

Regulations are used to protect those who cannot be expected to be well-informed, most notably consumers. For example, many government rules forbid the marketing of unsafe products or the use of deceptive advertising and labeling.

The need for regulation is especially great in the case of medications. When citizens catch the flu, they cannot be expected to research the side effects of every cold medication on the market. Government regulation, consequently, is required to ensure that drugs sold over the counter meet specified safety standards.

Regulation of drugs began during the progressive era. In 1906, Congress created the Food and Drug Administration (FDA), which was given the power to regulate the production and labeling of goods sold in interstate commerce. The initial legislation gave the FDA only limited powers. To garner public support for stronger regulatory authority, the FDA established in the 1920s a museum known as the Chamber of Horrors that contained such atrocities as:

Samples seized from goods on public sale—samples of patent medicines to cure every known disease, with testimonials from their users, accompanied by copies of their death certificates; and samples of cosmetics—eye-lash beautifiers containing poisonous aniline dyes, hair removers containing thallium acetate, and hair tonics, freckle removers, ointments, and salves containing mercury or other dangerous ingredients—together with photographs of women who had been blinded, paralyzed, or permanently disfigured by their use.[64]

The museum effectively aroused public concern. The FDA now monitors the production of everything from drugs to cosmetics to therapeutic devices, such as muscle developers and sun lamps.

POLITICS OF REGULATION

When and how regulation takes place is a political decision. Regulations are thus shaped by election pressures on Congress, government agencies, and even the courts.

CONGRESS

Members of Congress often create regulatory agencies in order to escape criticism when things go wrong. Laws are often passed in response to a well-publicized incident or disaster. In 1984, the Union Carbide explosion in Bhopal, India, killing thousands, resulted in the Emergency Planning and Community Right-to-Know Act. The oil spill in 1989 in the pristine waters of an Alaskan bay, caused by an accident aboard the oil tanker *Exxon Valdez*, sparked the enactment of the Oil Pollution Act of 1990. With each disaster, congressional representatives demonstrate their responsiveness to public concerns by passing yet another regulatory act. The end result is that regulations often duplicate and overlap one another.

Though regulation may help reassure a public after a crisis or a disaster has occurred, it is inherently unpopular with at least some. The essence of regulation is telling some people they must follow certain procedures in order to avoid injuring others. For example, regulations that prevent the emission of dirty smoke may win the approval of environmentalists but they almost certainly will alienate the companies forced to install less-polluting furnaces. Because compelling people to do something is likely to make them upset or angry, members of Congress usually employ a strategy known as **blame avoidance**, a set of political techniques political leaders use to disguise their actions and shift the blame to others. In the case of regulatory policy, Congress avoids blame by not directly imposing the regulations but by giving that job to a regulatory agency.

When creating a regulatory agency, Congress often defines its task in general terms. As one group of policy analysts said about EPA, its "discretion was truly enormous. It produced hundreds of pages of regulations, embodying dozens of significant policy choices, all on the basis of the most elliptical statutory language and the sparsest of legislative records."[65] Leaving the terms of reference vague can be justified on the grounds that Congress cannot anticipate every circumstance requiring regulatory action. It can be correctly claimed that only those who know the facts in detail can come up with the appropriate regulation. But Congress has also discovered that it can avoid "unpleasant truths" by keeping regulatory legislation broad and general.[66] Different members of Congress may then interpret the law in contrasting ways. Some may claim they have satisfied the concerns of environmentalists and consumers, while others will insist they have not placed undue burdens on business and industry.

■ **blame avoidance**
Set of political techniques employed by political leaders to disguise their actions and shift the blame to others.

When Congress deliberated over the Clean Air Act of 1990, it could have decided to greatly reduce air pollution by making one or two clear decisions, such as raising substantially the tax on gasoline (thereby discouraging unnecessary consumption) or subjecting minivans, four-wheelers, and other light trucks to the same antipollution standards that have been imposed on passenger cars (thereby reducing the rapid growth in pollution caused by the growth in the number of these vehicles). But had Congress taken either step, members would have been blamed for raising taxes or driving up the cost of light trucks. To avoid blame, Congress chose to state in general terms the clean-air goals that it wanted to achieve, then to ask the EPA to figure out ways of achieving them.

When Congress has been blamed for writing ambiguous legislation, it has sometimes responded by identifying specific goals (though without saying how to achieve them), then including a **hammer**, a harsh penalty, if those goals are not met. For example, the Clean Air Act of 1990 says that if certain goals are not met in particular metropolitan areas by a specific deadline, the "sale of all gasoline in the designated area must cease."[67] Such draconian rules make Congress appear tough but in fact they are utterly impractical.

hammer
Harsh penalty set by Congress if a regulatory agency does not achieve a statutory objective.

AGENCY DISCRETION

Because of the ambiguity of much congressional legislation, agencies often enjoy considerable freedom when deciding how to execute their mandates. When the EPA was asked by Congress to improve air quality in metropolitan areas, it had to decide the following kinds of questions: Should automobile manufacturers be required to build and sell some electric cars within ten years? Should every vehicle be checked at a state-run inspection station? Should inner-city highways be subject to a toll during rush hour? Should states be told they cannot build new roads? Although EPA officials have considered each of these difficult questions, nothing in the Clean Air Act of 1990 provides them with a precise answer.

The autonomy afforded to regulatory agencies is not limitless. There exists a **zone of acceptance**, a range within which Congress will accept whatever an agency decides is the correct interpretation of the statutes.[68] When an agency goes beyond the zone, political opposition arises and the agency backtracks. For example, all of the clean-air options mentioned above provoked controversy, and, as a result, the EPA has been slow to implement any of them.

zone of acceptance
Range within which Congress allows agencies to interpret and apply statutes.

Sometimes an agency's zone of acceptance can be rapidly redefined. When Democrats controlled Congress, the EPA developed close ties to senior Democrats on key congressional committees. But this strategy left the agency in trouble when Republicans gained control of Congress in 1995.[69] Initially, the Republican Congress cut the EPA's budget by 21.1 percent. President Clinton vetoed these cuts, but he subsequently signed legislation reducing the EPA's budget by 9.8 percent.[70]

COURTS

Although regulatory policies are enacted by Congress and executed by agencies, courts interpret the meaning of congressional statutes and decide whether their application in specific cases conforms to congressional intent. Courts exercise considerable discretion when performing this role, because they are often asked to interpret vague, even contradictory, laws passed by Congress.

COURT INTERPRETATION OF THE CONGRESSIONAL REGULATION: THE SPOTTED OWL DISPUTE

Court interpretations of the 1973 Endangered Species Act provide dramatic examples of the ways in which congressional legislation is open to interpretation by the courts. One of the most controversial disputes has involved the northern spotted owl. This small creature lives in the old-growth forests of the Pacific Northwest, and only 3,000 pairs remain. The species can be saved from extinction only by preserving forests whose habitat is dark enough to allow the spotted owl to evade its main predator, the great horned owl.

Environmentalists called for the protection of the spotted owl because they can, at the same time, preserve from logging the old-growth forests, with their marvelous redwoods, cedars, and Douglas firs. Only 10 percent of the original forests remain. To safeguard these, environmentalists asked the Fish and Wildlife Service to declare the spotted owl an endangered species. After extensive investigation, the Fish and Wildlife Service announced that logging on federally owned ancient forests would have to be reduced by 50 percent.

Timber interests prized these great trees for the quality of the wood they produced. Each year they sold billions of board feet to Japan, a country starved for high-quality lumber. The industry saw little need to protect an owl that few had ever seen. "There are millions of owls in the world," said their political ally, Oregon Republican Representative Denny Smith. "This little puppy just happens to be a passive kind of owl that's being run over by the great horned owl." The thousands of workers in the industry cherished not only their jobs but the logging way of life to which they had become accustomed. Bumper stickers appeared, calling upon the reader to "Save a Logger. Kill a Spotted Owl." Local taverns advertised "Spotted Owl Stew" for dinner. In response to growing logger complaints, the Bush administration modified the Fish and Wildlife Service plan so that logging would be reduced by only 20 percent.

The issue came before federal judge William Dwyer. Environmentalists told Dwyer that the government had failed to comply with the provisions of the Endangered Species Act. Dwyer issued

---

Court interpretations of the 1973 Endangered Species Act provide dramatic examples of the ways in which federal judges influence public policy. The law protects any species on federal lands found by the U.S. Fish and Wildlife Service to be threatened with extinction. The species' natural habitat is to be safeguarded from threatening human activity, no matter what the economic consequences of such protection. In voting for this legislation, most members of Congress probably thought they were protecting large mammals and birds, such as wolves, whooping cranes, and eagles. And, indeed, the Endangered Species Act has been successful in protecting the American bald eagle. In 1963 there were only 417 nesting pairs; by 1994, the numbers increased to over 4,000, allowing the Fish and Wildlife Service to reclassify the bald eagle from "endangered to threatened."[71] However, the Fish

an injunction halting all logging on federally owned, old-growth forests until the government offered a clear plan that would protect the spotted owl.

The spotted owl became a major campaign issue in the 1992 presidential election, in part because Bush and Clinton both considered Washington and Oregon to be important swing states. Bush called the Endangered Species Act a "broken law," asserting "it's time to put people ahead of owls." Governor Clinton sought votes from both environmentalists and loggers by accusing the Bush Administration of not coming up with a reasonable plan to resolve the conflict.

After the Clinton victory in both states and in enough others to become president, officials in the administration, after meeting with both sides,

reduced by two-thirds the logging operations and restricted logging entirely in over 3 million acres of ancient forestry. At the same time, the federal government allocated over $1 billion for retraining programs for loggers and to stimulate the economy of distressed logging communities.

Both sides found it difficult to accept the compromise. Environmentalists condemned loopholes in the plan, while timber interests claimed the aid was simply a way of paying off displaced loggers. But Judge Dwyer found the compromise consistent with the requirements of the Endangered Species Act.

Subsequently, a Republican Congress voted in favor of allowing the timber industry to carry out a two-year program that salvaged fallen trees. Despite the intense opposition of environmental-

ists, Clinton signed the bill, though he later said he regretted doing so. The issue is not likely to disappear soon.

SOURCES: Timothy Egan, *The Good Rain* (New York: Random House, 1991); *New York Times*, June 23, 1990, A1; *New York Times*, January 9, 1992, A14; *New York Times*, May 22, 1990, A20; *New York Times*, September 15, 1992, A25. See also Kathie Durbin, *Tree Huggers* (Seattle: Mountaineers Books, 1996).

and Wildlife Service greatly expanded the scope of the legislation when it found nearly 1,000 species in danger of extinction. And the federal courts have interpreted the law as applicable to even little-known species. Judges have halted the growth of suburbs in order to protect desert kangaroo rats; they have prevented the construction of a billion-dollar dam in order to save a tiny snail darter; and they have halted logging operations in order to safeguard the spotted owl.

DEREGULATION

Although regulation is an inevitable part of modern society, it can be carried to an excess. Regulations intended to protect consumers may have the opposite effect. For example, regulating drugs may prevent some patients from getting the treatment they need (see Democratic Dilemma). Also, regulation is expensive. Salaries for bureaucrats, lawyers, and investigators generate an annual price tag that runs in the billions of dollars. Regulatory policies may also limit the ability of businesses to compete in international markets. The additional paperwork, inspections, procedures, and mandates imposed by regulatory agencies can make the difference between a corporation that thrives and provides good jobs to Americans and one that cannot remain solvent and is forced to let go its workforce. Many firms relocate to foreign countries in order to avoid the regulatory burdens imposed by the American government.

To address these concerns, Congress has introduced in many areas policies of **deregulation**, the removal of government rules that once governed an industry. In a series of legislation, it has authorized the partial deregulation of the trucking, banking, and communications industries.[72] No longer must banks abide by strict lending and investment restrictions. No longer must trucks charge specific amounts for particular routes.

■ **deregulation**
Removal of government rules that once controlled an industry.

Perhaps the most celebrated deregulation occurred within the airline industry. At one time, a government agency determined the air fare that could be set for every route a plane flew. Though originally established to prevent price gouging by airlines that had a natural monopoly in a particular city, many policy analysts claimed that the effect of the law was precisely the opposite of its intent: Regulators were letting airlines charge excessively high prices. Deregulation of the airlines was placed on the political agenda by President John F. Kennedy, when he called for "greater reliance on the forces of competition and less reliance on the restraints of regulation" in the airline industry.[73] Alfred Kahn pushed the issue forward when he was appointed chair of the Civil Aeronautics Board by Jimmy Carter. Opposed to the regulation of airline prices and flight patterns, Kahn announced his intention to eliminate many regulations, ending the need for the agency to which he had just been appointed. Kahn stripped away many of the pricing regulations that had governed the airline industry for decades.[74] The action led to the enactment of the Airline Deregulation Act.

Most policy outcomes were favorable. Airline competition increased, companies became more efficient, service to remote areas increased, and air fares fell.[75] Though some worried about the effect on safety,[76] the number of deaths per passenger mile also declined. Yet the ValuJet crash suggests that some regulation must remain in place to ensure that new airline companies, in their search for profits, do not cut corners too closely.[77] Complete deregulation is unlikely, because the public will always expect government to act in response to crises and disasters.

How Much Regulation Is Needed?

At what point do government regulations become excessive? The contemporary debate over the FDA drug approval policy indicates how difficult it is to answer this question.

Since 1981, upwards of 40 thousand Americans have died from AIDS. In 1988 the average AIDS patient lived only eighteen months after diagnosis; more than 85 percent died within three years. However, there existed only one FDA-approved drug on the market, Azidothymidine (AZT), to combat this deadly disease. Pharmaceutical companies were investing millions of dollars to develop new drugs, but partially due to the lengthy approval process, these drugs were slow to reach AIDS patients. This sparked outrage by AIDS activists across the country. Patsy Stewart, who contracted AIDS in the early 1990s, expressed their view:

> I believe that pharmaceutical research offers the best hope of beating this disease. But it now takes nearly 15 years to develop a new drug, in part because the FDA micro-manages the development process.

When David Kessler became the head of the FDA in 1991, he initiated numerous programs to streamline the drug-approval process. A succession of new drugs were quickly approved: Dideoxycytidine (ddC), (DDI), (3TC), and (D4T). The FDA permitted patients in the advanced stages of AIDS to undergo experimental treatment with certain drugs, such as Pentamidine. Pharmaceutical companies proposed new "Home Testing Devices" to help combat the spread of the disease.

Recently, growing numbers of patient advocates have criticized the FDA for this relaxation of government regulations. Some denounce the FDA for lowering their standards and allowing the widespread use of untested new mechanisms, most notably the Home Testing Devices. Proposals to privatize the drug-approval process have met staunch opposition. Geraldine Burress, who nearly died when a mechanical valve inside her heart suddenly broke in half, spoke to Congress in 1996 about the dangers of relaxing federal drug approval standards. Legislation aimed at easing requirements for manufacturers to sell and promote new therapies, she argued, would undo "protections that were won the hard way . . . with the lives of people like me and the lives of people who were not as lucky as I was."

Should FDA regulations be further relaxed, thereby improving the life-chances of some AIDS patients? Or do these regulations serve as important measures against the proliferation of potentially dangerous drugs?

SOURCES: Margaret S. Rivas, "The California AIDS Initiative and the Food and Drug Administration: Working at Odds with Each Other?" *Food Drug Cosmetic Law Journal*, January 1991, 107; Patsy Stewart, "Reform FDA's Lengthy Drug Approval Process," *The Tampa Tribune*, May 31, 1996, 14; Lauran Neergaard, "Opponents of FDA Overhaul Take Case to Congress," *Tulsa World*, July 28, 1996, A4.

Chapter Summary

Domestic policy involves government spending on social and education policies as well as government regulation of many social and economic activities. Many domestic policies divide the two political parties. Democrats typically want to spend more on social and education policy and they usually favor more regulation. Republicans typically think government spends and regulates too much. In 1995 and 1996, a Republican Congress passed legislation that cut the EPA's budget and reduced spending on a broad range of social programs.

But even though the parties take distinctive positions on many social policies, the intensity of their disagreement lessens substantially whenever a clear majority among the voters begins to emerge. In 1996, neither party was willing to cut social security, and a majority of the members of Congress from both parties voted in favor of welfare reform. In 1997, leaders of both parties said they favored spending more on education. Leaders of both parties promise to protect the environment and promote consumer safety in the transportation industry. To do otherwise is to commit political suicide, something successful politicians learn to avoid.

If there is a bias in the system, it is a bias against the next genera-tion, a bias against those who cannot vote. Programs for the elderly are financed lavishly; those for children are not. The amount spent on the social services needed by older people, such as health care, has greatly increased. The amount spent on education has barely edged upward. Young people have the most to lose from a deterio-rating environment, but they seldom help shape antipollution policies. These biases in social policy may be due to the fact that, while older people cast ballots, children cannot and young people often fail to do so. An electoral democracy responds to those who vote.

Key Terms

Aid to Families with Dependent
  Children (AFDC), p. 589

blame avoidance, p. 604

deregulation, p. 608

domestic policy, p. 580

Earned Income Tax Credit
  (EITC), p. 590

Environmental Protection Agency
  (EPA), p. 602

externalities, p. 602

food stamps, p. 589

hammer, p. 605

medicaid, p. 590

medicare, p. 583

natural monopoly, p. 602

policy deliberation, p. 580

policy enactment, p. 581

policy implementation, p. 581

policy outcome, p. 581

policy output, p. 581

public assistance, p. 589

regulation, p. 600

rent subsidy, p. 590

social insurance, p. 583

social policy, p. 582

social security, p. 583

Supplemental Social Insurance
  (SSI), p. 590

Temporary Assistance for Needy
  Families (TANF), p. 581

zone of acceptance, p. 605

Suggested Readings

Burtless, Gary, ed. *Does Money Matter? The Effect of School Resources on Student Achievement and Adult Success.* Washington, DC: Brookings. Excellent collection of essays that debate current state of public education.

Derthick, Martha and Paul Quirk. *The Politics of Deregulation.* Washington, DC: Brookings, 1985. Engaging accounts of the political circumstances that enable the federal government to eliminate existing regulations.

Jencks, Christopher and Paul E. Peterson, eds. *The Urban Underclass.* Washington, DC: Brookings, 1991. Collection of essays analyzing and providing information on the underclass debate.

Kingdon, John. *Agenda, Alternatives and Public Policies.* Boston: Little Brown, 1984. Discusses the policy-making process, with particular attention to how problems become issues on the political agenda.

Landy, Marc K., Marc J. Roberts, and Stephen R. Thomas. *The Environmental Protection Agency: Asking the Wrong Questions from Nixon to Clinton,* expanded edition. New York: Oxford University Press, 1994. Thorough, critical analysis of EPA policymaking.

Melnick, R. Shep. *Regulation and the Courts.* Washington, DC: Brookings, 1983. Case studies of the central role courts play in interpreting government regulations.

Murray, Charles A. *Losing Ground: American Social Policy: 1950–1980.* New York: Basic Books, 1984. Makes the case that government welfare benefits help to create poverty. Suggests ending welfare.

Pierson, Paul. *Dismantling the Welfare State?: Reagan, Thatcher and the Politics of Retrenchment.* New York: Cambridge University Press, 1994. Insightful analysis of political battles over cuts in welfare expenditure.

Skocpol, Theda. *Protecting Soldiers and Mothers: The Politics of Social Provision in the United States.* Cambridge, MA: Harvard University Press, 1993. Fascinating, comprehensive historical analysis of the evolution of the U.S. welfare state.

Tyack, David. *The One Best System: A History of Urban Education.* Cambridge, MA: Harvard University Press, 1974. Classic historical account of the expansion of public education.

Weidenbaum, Murray L. *Business, Government and the Public.* Englewood Cliffs, N.J.: Prentice-Hall, 1990. Examines when and how the government interferes with business affairs.

Whicker, Marcia. *Controversial Issues in Economic Regulatory Policy.* Newbury Park, CA: Sage Publications, 1993. Provides a comprehensive summary of the arguments for and against government regulation.

Wilson, James Q. *The Politics of Regulation.* New York: Basic Books, 1980. Comprehensive text of regulatory politics and policy.

Wilson, William J. *The Truly Disadvantaged: The Inner City, the Underclass, and Public Policy.* Chicago: University of Chicago Press, 1987. Argues that poverty has been caused by the internationalization of the economy and the disappearance of blue-collar jobs. Says government should provide jobs.

YES 13
NO 14
...but

YES 13
NO 14

to impose ... probably not significant, ...

208 CAMPAIGN CONTRIBUTIONS AND SPENDING LIMITS. LOBBYISTS. INITIATIVE STATUTE. Limits campaign contributions to $500 statewide elections, $250 large districts, $100 smaller districts. Incentives for voluntary spending limits. Prohibits lobbyist contributions. Fiscal Impact: Costs of up to $4 million annually to state and local governments for implementation and enforcement; unknown, but probably not significant, state and local election costs.

YES
NO

209 PROHIBITION AGAINST DISCRIMINATION OR PREFERENTIAL TREATMENT BY STATE AND OTHER PUBLIC ENTITIES. INITIATIVE CONSTITUTIONAL AMENDMENT. Generally prohibits discrimination or preferential treatment based on race, sex, color, ethnicity, or national origin in public employment, education, and contracting. Fiscal Impact: Could affect state and local programs that currently cost well in excess of $125 million annually. Actual savings would depend on various factors (such as future ... decisions and ... actions by government entities).

210 MINIMUM WAGE INCREASE. INITIATIVE STATUTE. Increases the state minimum wage for all industries to $5.00 ... hour on March 1, 1997, and to $5.75 per hour on March 1, 1998. Fiscal Impact: Unknown impact on government revenues. Annual wage-related costs state and local governments of $120 million to $300 million (depending ... action), partly offset by net savings, in the low tens of millions, in ... programs.

TURN PAGE ...

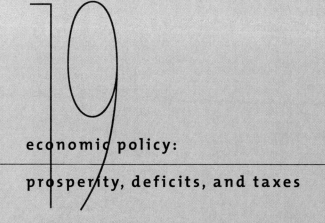

19

economic policy:

prosperity, deficits, and taxes

EAD MY LIPS. No new taxes," proclaimed Vice President George Bush, upon accepting the Republican presidential nomination in the summer of 1988. "And the Congress will push me to raise taxes," he declared, "and I'll say no, and they'll push, and I'll say no, and they'll push again, and I'll say to them, 'Read my lips. No new taxes.'"[1]

Repeating these words almost like a mantra in the campaign that followed, Bush swept to victory over Michael Dukakis, his Democratic opponent, whom Bush accused of being just another "tax and spend liberal." Some pundits credited Bush's victory to his stand on the tax question, although it is likely that Bush benefited more from six consecutive years of economic growth while he was Ronald Reagan's vice president.

During the initial months of the Bush administration, the economy continued to grow. Sunny economic skies were clouded only by a rising federal deficit. Bush tried to persuade Congress to reduce the deficit through spending cuts but was unable to do so. Finally, in the fall of 1990, facing deficits that were the largest in American history, both Congress and the administration decided that something had to be done about the deficit in order to reassure the financial markets. After lengthy and torturous negotiations, Bush agreed to a compromise budget that provided for modest tax increases along with cuts in spending programs.

Many disinterested observers judged the compromise to be a good one that served the public interest.[2] In their view, Bush's decision to support some tax increases was statesmanlike. But many Republicans were outraged. Newt Gingrich, the minority leader at the time, led the House Republicans in opposition. He bitterly chastised then–Senate Minority Leader Robert Dole, who had helped broker the compromise, as "the tax collector for the welfare state."[3]

When Bush ran for reelection in 1992, his old campaign slogan came back to haunt him. His primary challenger, Pat Buchanan, taunted him with the slogan, "No new taxes—and I really mean it." In his acceptance speech to the Republican convention, Bush apologized for his decision to allow a tax increase, saying, "Two years ago I made a bad call on the Democrats' tax increase . . . Well, it was a mistake to go along with the Democratic tax increase."[4] Despite the apology, the political damage had been done. Bush had bitterly disappointed Republicans and given away an issue that they had long used against the Democrats.

Bush's problems were greatly aggravated by the fact that the campaign took place during a period of economic hard times. In early 1990, the country entered a **recession**, a slowdown in economic activity. It was fairly mild by historical standards, lasting only nine months, and produced a relatively small drop in **gross national product** (**GNP**), the official measure of the total value of economic activity. But the well-publicized financial problems of large American corporations like General Motors and IBM, the stagnation of personal incomes, and a rising unemployment rate kept the economy at the top of the electorate's list of concerns. Clinton's campaign manager posted a sign in the Little Rock campaign headquarters reading "It's the Economy, Stupid!" to remind everyone that the campaign must stay focused on the economy.[5] Although the economy was growing throughout the campaign, especially during the fourth quarter of the year, when the election occurred, the improvement was too little and too late for Bush. Assaulted by Perot on one side, and Clinton on the other, George Bush was turned out of office by an economically unhappy electorate.[6]

■ **recession**
A slowdown in economic activity, officially defined as a decline that persists for 2 quarters (6 months).

■ **gross national product (GNP)**
The monetary value of all goods and services produced by a nation during a given year.

Unemployment, inflation, taxes, budgets, deficits, and economic growth are major factors in national elections. Indeed, with the exception of wars (see Chapter 20), economic questions are the primary forces that shape presidential contests year in and year out, as captured by the old political maxim that "you can't beat a sitting president when the country is at peace and the economy is prosperous." Economic conditions affect other elections as well. And because economic conditions and concerns are so politically important, elected officials place great emphasis on formulating and implementing the policies that affect economic conditions. In this chapter, we examine the tools at officials' disposal, how the use of those tools is constrained by the political, economic, and international environment, and how the American political system has been dealing with two major contemporary economic issues—deficits and taxes.

Prosperity and Political Fortunes

When times are hard, people tend to blame those in charge. President Bush's approval ratings fell 40 percentage points during the economic slowdown in the second half of his administration—from 78 percent in July 1990, when the rate of unemployment first began to rise, to 38 percent two years later, when unemployment peaked (p. 135).

Bush is not the only president to have lost popularity when the economy faltered. Presidents Eisenhower, Nixon, and Carter suffered similar fates, losing significant public support when recessions hit. Some of his critics called Ronald Reagan the "Teflon President" because they believed that none of the usual political dirt and grease stuck to him; but even Ronald Reagan's popularity dropped precipitously during the 1981–82 recession.[7]

Herbert Hoover was president when the United States plunged into the Great Depression, and Republicans suffered from being portrayed as "the depression party" for decades thereafter.

Terrible economic times in American history are associated with massive election losses for the party of the president. The Depression of the 1890s ushered in an era of Republican hegemony, and the Great Depression of the 1930s did the same for the Democrats (pp. 244, 247). Indeed, Republican President Herbert Hoover (1929–33) became one of history's most unpopular presidents simply because he was in office when the Great Depression occurred. For decades afterwards, Democrats ran against the party of Hoover, using the issue to help win the next five elections.

FIGURE 19.1

How Americans Feel About the
Economy Is a Good Predictor of
What They Think About the
President

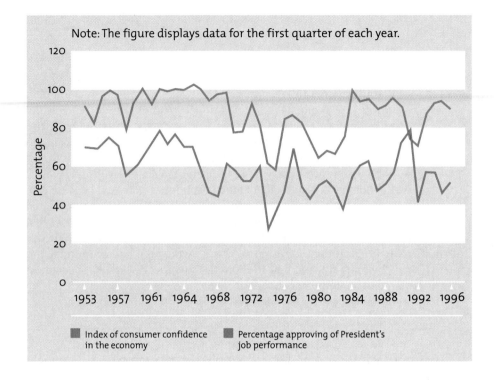

Note: The figure displays data for the first quarter of each year.

■ Index of consumer confidence   ■ Percentage approving of President's
in the economy   job performance

Prosperity, in contrast, strengthens a president's position for reelection (see Figure 19.1). Riding booming economies, Lyndon Johnson trampled Barry Goldwater in 1964, Richard Nixon crushed George McGovern in 1972, and Ronald Reagan trounced Walter Mondale in 1984. Of course, a healthy economy does not guarantee presidential popularity. For example, prosperity did not keep Johnson's popularity from falling sharply in response to the rising casualty rate in Vietnam.[8]

inflation
A sustained rise in the price level so that people need more money to purchase the same amount of goods and services.

unemployment
Describes the circumstance when people who are willing to work at the prevailing wage cannot get jobs.

Inflation—a rise in the price level—diminishes the purchasing power of everyone a bit. In contrast, **unemployment**—when people willing to work at prevailing wages cannot find jobs—harms a smaller number of people but in ways that are marked and visible. For a long time, the two conditions were thought to be closely, and negatively, related—lower unemployment necessarily meant higher inflation, and vice versa.[9] But economists no longer believe the relationship is so close. In fact, President Carter disproved the relationship: He had the misfortune to run for reelection at a time of "stagflation," when both inflation and unemployment were high. He suffered a humiliating defeat. For the next three elections Republicans ran against the Carter Democrats (see Election Connection).

National economic conditions are important influences on the outcome of congressional elections also.[10] In 1930, Democrats captured control of Congress when voters blamed Republicans for the onset of the Great Depression. The Eisenhower recession of 1958 inflated the narrow Democratic majorities in the House and Senate. The huge Democratic majorities of 1974 were due both to the Watergate scandal and to economic downturn.[11] When the economy dragged Carter under in 1980, the Republicans took control of the Senate and made large gains in the House. As we saw in Chapter 11, economics is not the only force at work in national elections.

In 1980, Jimmy Carter became the first (elected) president since Herbert Hoover to lose his bid for reelection. Ironically, the struggling economy that helped him win office in 1976 led to his defeat in 1980.

In 1976, Carter added the inflation and unemployment rates and named the resulting sum the "misery index," suggesting that it was a measure of the misery suffered by the average American. The misery index in 1976 was 12.5, up from 8.9 in 1972. Partly as a result of the poor economic conditions summarized by the index, Carter narrowly defeated the unelected incumbent, Gerald Ford.

By all accounts, Carter was a decent and intelligent man, but he was unlucky to hold office during the 1970s, an era of "stagflation"—low growth and high inflation. During his administration, inflation raged at double-digit levels, interest rates exceeded fifteen percent, and even the unemployment rate seemed stuck at a relatively high level. In the late 1970s, the Gallup Poll reported that the Democrats had lost their traditional advantage as the party best able to keep the country prosperous. In 1980, the misery index stood at 18.2, one-third higher than when Carter defeated Ford.

Ronald Reagan campaigned across the country asking crowds "are you better off today than you were four years ago?" And the crowds yelled back "NO!" In the final days of the campaign, undecided voters moved decisively to Reagan and he won easily. In the next few years, Reagan's policies smashed inflation. But in the process, taxes were cut and defense spending was increased, creating huge deficits.

SOURCE: Data are taken from *OECD Economic Outlook*, no. 58, December 1995 (Paris: Organisation for Economic Co-Operation and Development).

The Democrats suffered serious congressional losses in 1966, although the economy was fine. That election turned on Vietnam and racial tensions. Similarly, the Republicans captured control of both the House and Senate in 1994, despite the fact that unemployment fell during Clinton's first two years.

Although it may seem surprising, the condition of the national economy also affects state election outcomes. If times are bad, the party of the president suffers significant losses in gubernatorial and state legislative elections.[12] Even though there is little that state officials can do about national economic conditions, unhappy voters take out some of their frustration on members of the president's party throughout government. Thus, state elected officials are highly interested in the economic policies followed by national officials of their party.

But the economy is most critical for presidential elections, so it is the president who pays the closest attention to economic policy. Traditionally, presidents try to shape economic conditions by using two major governmental tools—**fiscal policy**, the sum total of government taxation and spending, and **monetary policy**, adjusting interest rates by varying the supply of money. We discuss these two policies in turn.

fiscal policy
The sum total of government taxing and spending decisions, which determines the level of the deficit or surplus.

monetary policy
Consists of the actions taken by government to affect the level of interest rates.

Government Management of the Economy: Fiscal Policy

John Maynard Keynes, responsible for the school of macroeconomics that came to be called "Keynesianism," with his wife in 1945.

■ **deficit**
When government spending exceeds revenues.

■ **surplus**
When government spending is less than revenues.

■ **Keynesianism**
Economic policy based on the belief that governments can control the economy by manipulating aggregate demand, running deficits to expand it and surpluses to contract it.

■ **Council of Economic Advisors (CEA)**
Three economists who head up a professional staff that advises the president on economic policy.

Between the administrations of FDR and Ronald Reagan, presidents and congresses actively tried to influence the rate of economic growth through the economic policies they adopted—particularly fiscal policies, which they directly controlled. A government's fiscal policy determines whether the budget is balanced or not. When yearly spending exceeds tax receipts, government runs a **deficit**. When the amount collected in taxes exceeds spending, government enjoys a **surplus**. According to an influential English economist of the 1920s, John Maynard Keynes, there is nothing sacred about a balanced budget; on the contrary, fiscal deficits can lift an economy out of a recession. If government spends money when no one else does, it can jump-start the economy, which then can keep growing on its own. Following this line of reasoning, which came to be called **Keynesianism**, Franklin Roosevelt broke with the traditional belief in a balanced budget (held by Herbert Hoover and most economists of the time) and ran large deficits during the 1930s in an attempt to get the country moving again.

After World War II, Keynesian thinking became widely accepted. In 1946, Congress established a **Council of Economic Advisors (CEA)**, composed of three prominent economists who would advise the president about the state of the national and international economy, present economic forecasts, and make recommendations about the budget. Because deficits were thought to create jobs, while surpluses held prices down, these expert economists could help presidents "fine-tune" the economy to ensure steady prosperity. On the recommendation of the CEA to stimulate a sluggish economy, John Kennedy urged Congress to pass a deficit-creating tax cut. Some credit the cut, passed in 1964, for stimulating the mid-1960s economic boom.[13] Conversely, to slow down the inflation rate, Lyndon Johnson followed CEA advice and persuaded Congress to pass a tax increase in 1968. In this case, inflation continued, largely because the tax increase was not big enough to offset the effects of increased spending for the Vietnam war.[14]

Administrations today are much less likely to use fiscal policy as a tool for managing the economy than they were during the Kennedy-Johnson era. The CEA has declined in importance, so much so that some Republicans in the House of Representatives proposed its abolition in 1995. Several factors have contributed to the decline in the economic significance of fiscal policy.

DIVIDED GOVERNMENT

An economic policy must be implemented quickly if it is to address the economic conditions it is aimed at. But the rise of divided government has made it especially difficult to adjust fiscal policy quickly in response to changing economic conditions. Fiscal policy is a product of the taxing and spending decisions recommended by presidents and passed by Congress. Even under the most favorable conditions, it takes considerable time for the two institutions to iron out their differences and adopt a budget. Getting them to work together when each is controlled by different parties is that much more difficult.[15] In the divided government administrations of the 1980s, it typically took eight months for Congress to act on a president's annual budget, then it would take many more months for the taxing and spending decisions to take effect. But the economy can change direction in a matter of a few months. Thus, the economic conditions that seem to call for a new fiscal policy often have changed by the time a policy takes effect. Among other things, Bush's 1990 tax increase was supposed to keep inflation in check, but it took effect in the midst of a recession.

MONETARISM

A school of economic thinking known as **monetarism** (because of its central claim that only monetary policy influences the economy) undercut the Keynesian theoretical claim that fiscal policy could fine-tune the economy. Monetarists argued that deficits are paid for by borrowing money from investors. Thus, every dollar the government spends is one less dollar to be invested. Deficits do not add any extra stimulus—they just transfer available dollars from the private sector to the public sector.

Even Keynesians favored only short-term deficits; they did not believe that a government budget could be continually in deficit. A nation's economy can grow over the long run only if people save money and invest it in productive enterprises. High savings rates in Japan, Taiwan, and South Korea generally are credited for the phenomenal growth these countries have enjoyed in recent decades. The problem is that, if a government borrows money, it soaks up some of the country's savings, and with less savings to finance investment, economic growth slows. Thus, most economists agree that it is counterproductive to run deficits for very long; more government spending in the present will result in a smaller economy to support government spending in the future.

THE DEFICIT AND THE DEBT

In the 1960s, when fiscal policy enjoyed its greatest support, the federal **debt**—the cumulation of annual deficits—was still declining from the peak to which it had climbed in World War II. Thus, modest adjustments in fiscal policy could be made from one year to the next without undermining the long-term savings rate of the country. But social welfare spending commitments made in the 1960s soon outpaced tax revenues. The 1970s saw consistently large deficits, and, in the 1980s, **supply-side economics**, implemented by the Reagan administration, exacerbated the situation.[16] The central tenet of supply-side economics (called "Reaganomics" by his critics) held that lowering tax rates would stimulate so much additional economic activity that the government would raise more in taxes even while it taxed economic activity at lower rates. The theory proved incorrect. Large tax cuts enacted during the 1980s coupled with massive increases in defense spending and the failure to control entitlements (pp. 586–589) led to sustained deficits unprecedented in American history (see Figure 19.2, p. 622). Approximately 15 percent of the federal budget consists of interest paid to holders of the national debt.

In this environment, aggressive fiscal policies have become politically infeasible. Even if Keynes's theory were correct, and even if presidents and Congress could quickly agree on a mix of tax and spending changes, lowering the deficit is such a priority today that deficit-raising actions are viewed as outside the range of feasible policies.

> **monetarism**
> An economic school of thought that rejects Keynesianism, arguing that only monetary policy affects the state of the economy.

> **debt**
> The cumulation of yearly deficits.

> **supply-side economics**
> Economic policy based on belief that governments can keep the economy healthy by supplying the conditions, especially low taxes and minimal regulation, that encourage private economic activity.

The Federal Budget Process

The practice of developing and adopting the federal budget is a long and complicated process; the adjective "labyrinthine" is frequently used to describe it.* To illustrate, consider the process of constructing the federal budget for fiscal year 1996, which, by law, began on October 1, 1995.

On the executive side, the budget process is governed by the Budget and Accounting Act of 1921. The process starts a year and a half before the beginning of the fiscal year. Thus, budgeting for fiscal year 1996 began in the spring of 1994, when agency budget offices sent preliminary guidelines to the bureaus and other units. The latter submitted their budget requests during the summer. These were compiled and submitted to the Office of Management and Budget (OMB). During the fall of 1994, OMB reviewed the requests and made modifications. This is a period of negotiation between the departments and OMB,

with final decisions made by the President.†

The law requires that the president's budget be submitted to Congress no later than the first Monday in February. But no law requires Congress to pay any attention to it, and in early 1995 the new Republican Congress was not inclined to pay much heed to the president's budget. As in the 1980s, when Presidents Reagan and Bush faced Democratic congresses, the congressional majority treated the president's budget as DOA—dead on arrival.

The procedures Congress follows are laid down in the 1974 Budget and Impoundment Control Act, modified in the light of subsequent practice. The authorizing committees submit their estimates to the budget committees by March 15. The 1974 law requires the Congress to adopt a concurrent Budget Resolution by April 15. Constructed by the budget committees with the aid of the Congressional Budget Office (CBO) (see p. 476), this resolution specifies the total amount that the government plans to raise and spend in each

of the next five fiscal years, and allocates funding in the next fiscal year to 20 broad functional categories of spending.

The Budget Resolution is a matter of considerable controversy because it also provides for reconciliation: it tells the authorizing committees that they must alter existing law to adopt spending and tax changes that will reconcile government policy with the resolution. In recent decades, this has required program and spending cutbacks that committees often resist. Conflict is heightened by the fact that, since the Budget Enforcement Act of 1990, the process operates under a PAYGO (pay-as-you-go) rule: any proposal to cut taxes or increase spending must be coupled with an offsetting proposal to increase taxes so that the overall proposal does not raise the deficit. This procedure forces members of Congress to accept the blame for tax increases as well as the credit for spending increases. The difficulty of adopting the budget resolution is evident from the fact that Congress has met the statutory deadline for adoption only once since the 1974 law went into effect.

In principle, the appropriations subcommittees take the budget resolution adopted on April 15 and work through the summer on the thirteen appropriations bills, which Congress passes by October 1, the start of the fiscal year. In practice, this almost never happens, and parts of the government operate under continuing resolutions, stopgap resolutions passed by congress to keep the government going, generally at current levels. By October 1, 1995, the Republican Congress had passed only two appropriations bills, one of which Clinton vetoed. In November, they sent two continuing resolutions to the president, which he also vetoed, prompting a partial shutdown of the government.‡

Because reconciliation involves changes in existing law, it must be approved by both houses of Congress and the president. The required changes are packaged in an omnibus reconciliation bill that in the present era is often called a deficit-reduction bill—another occasion for conflict and delay. In 1995, the government was already shut down when, on November 17, the Republican House and Senate were finally able to agree on a huge reconciliation bill that proposed balancing the budget in seven years. President Clinton vetoed this bill, too, objecting to its changes in the medicaid (health care for the poor) system, and for cuts in medicare (health care for the aged). Short-term continuing resolutions reopened the government, but after Congress was unable to override Clinton's veto, the government shut down again. Social security and other checks kept flowing, but many "nonessential" government workers were laid off, and their activities suspended.

Finally, on January 25, 1996, after months of partisan wrangling, and poll results showing that the Republican Congress had been blamed for the budget debacle, Congress abandoned the fight and passed a large continuing resolution that was acceptable to the president. This was nearly four months after the beginning of the fiscal year.

While this example is extreme in the amount of bickering that occurred, bitter conflicts and long delays also occurred in 1985, 1987, and 1990. Thus, the 1996 budget battle is not that far out of the ordinary in terms of how long the process dragged on. All-in-all, given the length, complexity, and unpredictability of the federal budget process, it is understandable why fiscal policy has ceased to be an important means of managing the national economy.

* The following summary account is drawn from Allen Schick, *The Federal Budget* (Washington, DC: Brookings, 1995); Steven Smith, *The American Congress* (Boston: Houghton-Mifflin, 1995): Ch. 11.

† Aaron Wildavsky, *The New Politics of the Budgetary Process* (Glenview, IL: Scott, Foresman, 1988); Ch. 3.

‡ George Hager, "Budget Battle Came Sooner Than Either Side Expected," *Congressional Quarterly Weekly Report,* November 18, 1996: 3503-3509.

FIGURE **19.2**

The Federal Deficit in Modern
Times

SOURCE: "The Deficit Over the
Years," *Congressional Quarterly
Weekly Report* (March 23, 1996):
755. (Data are originally from the
president's fiscal 1997 budget but
updated due to 1997 legislation.)

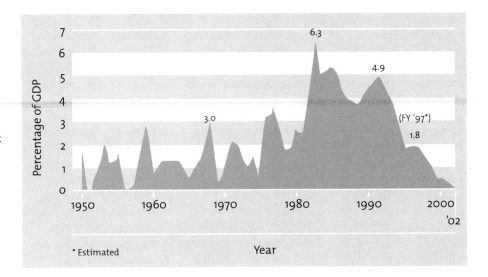

INTERNATIONALIZATION

In the 1970s, another school of economic thinking developed. Called "rational expectations," the central notion was that firms, investors, and other private economic actors would rationally anticipate what government planned to do, then act in ways that would offset what the government did.[17] For example, if the government budget provided for a deficit in order to stimulate the economy, rational investors would anticipate inflation, and would protect their investments by demanding a higher interest rate on government bonds and other investments. But higher interest rates dampen economic growth, which counteracts the intended stimulus effect of the budget deficit. If such calculations were widespread, the only way government policy could dependably affect the economy would be to "surprise" private economic actors.

Of course, people are not perfectly informed, and even professional economic forecasters cannot predict economic developments all that well; but there was enough truth in rational expectations arguments to raise doubts about the ability of government to manage the economy, especially through the lengthy public process of setting fiscal policy. These doubts were reinforced by other developments such as the communications revolution and the internationalization of the economy.

Advances in computer technology made it possible to store and analyze vast quantities of information. Moreover, communications advances allowed economic actors to analyze and react to economic developments faster than ever before; it became possible to move millions of dollars literally overnight. Certainly, it is not possible to "surprise" firms and investors with fiscal policies that are public and messy in their formulation, policies that may take a year or more to implement.

Moreover, as economic activity became increasingly international, the reactions of economic actors to government policies were no longer limited to reactions in their own countries. If American investors do not like something the government is doing, they can move billions of dollars to markets in Europe or Asia. Investors in other countries can do the same. Thus, communications advances have enabled investors to penalize governments for their economic policies. If a government adopts policies that investors dislike, they can vote with their money and move it to more accommodating countries, thus imposing economic costs on the government that adopts unfavorable policies. James Carville, President Clinton's 1992 campaign manager, offered a humorous recognition of this fact when he commented that "I used to think if there was reincarnation, I wanted to come back as the president or the Pope . . . but now I would like to come back as the bond market. You can intimidate everybody." [18]

Maintaining Prosperity: Monetary Policy

While Keynesian thinking recognized the usefulness of monetary policy, it clearly trailed fiscal policy in importance, particularly during Democratic administrations. Today, however, monetary policy is the government's most important tool for managing the economy. The essence of monetary policy is raising or lowering interest rates, which governments do by subtracting or adding money to the economy. When the supply of money is increased, its price—interest rates—comes down, which encourages people to borrow more. As they spend and invest the borrowed money, the economy grows, and unemployment falls. Conversely, when the supply of money goes down, interest rates go up, and people borrow less. With less to spend and invest, the economy slows, and inflationary pressures ease.

Monetary policy is thought to be an effective tool for managing the economy partly because, in contrast to fiscal policy, it can be altered quickly in response to changing economic circumstances. Interest rates can be adjusted on a monthly, weekly, or even daily basis as the need arises (although it may take months before the policy change actually affects economic conditions).

THE FEDERAL RESERVE SYSTEM

Commonly referred to as the "Fed," the **Federal Reserve System** is responsible for managing the government's monetary policy. Created in 1913, the Fed (see Figure 19.3) is headed by a board consisting of seven governors, each of whom holds office for 14 years. The Fed acts on the economy through the operations of its 12 regional banks, each of which oversees member banks in its part of the country.

Often the Fed is said to be—next to the Executive Office of the President—the most powerful agency in the government. Its decisions affect interest rates, employment levels, and growth rates. The great American humorist, Will Rogers, once remarked that "there are two things that can disrupt the American economy. One is a war. The other is a meeting of the Federal Reserve Board." Surprisingly, in view of its importance, the Fed's activities are relatively unknown to many Americans.

The most important decisions affecting the day-to-day workings of the economy are made by the Fed's Open Market Committee. This committee decides whether interest rates are too high or too low and what adjustments should be made. The committee consists of the seven governors, all of whom vote, and the twelve regional bank presidents, only five of whom have a vote (the New York Bank president always has a vote; the remaining four votes rotate among the other eleven banks).

■ **Federal Reserve System ("Fed")** The country's central bank, which executes monetary policy by manipulating the supply of funds that lower banks can lend.

FIGURE 19.3

The Structure of the Federal
Reserve System

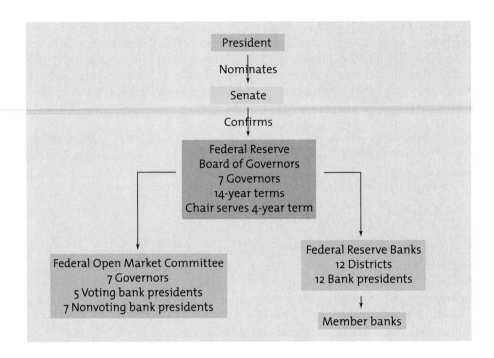

THE FED CHAIR

If the Fed is the second most powerful agency in Washington, the chair of the Federal Reserve Board, currently Alan Greenspan, may well be the second most powerful person in government. The chair's great power derives from close ties to the president, direct access to up-to-date economic information supplied by Fed staff, and the power to approve the appointment of the twelve presidents of the Federal Reserve Banks (upon the recommendation of the member banks in each region). In addition, the chair inherits a job held in the past by powerful, prestigious people. Martin Eccles, head of the Fed during the 1930s, is acclaimed for taking actions to get the country out of the depression, William McChesney Martin received credit for keeping the American economy on an even keel after World War II, and Paul Volcker is remembered for bringing the double-digit inflation of the late 1970s to an end. Greenspan is adding to this tradition by becoming known as the person who managed the economic growth of the 1990s.

WHO CONTROLS THE FED?

Surprisingly, in this elections-dominated political system, this important government agency is relatively insulated from electoral pressures. The Fed's power, independence, and objectivity are symbolized by its Washington home, a magnificent quasi-palace fronted by a remote—almost forbidding—facade, located two miles from Capitol Hill, next door to the National Academy of Sciences. Of course, the Fed is not immune to political pressure, but it is more insulated than most government agencies, including the so-called "independent commissions" that we discussed in Chapter 14.

The Second Most Powerful Man in the United States

Most Americans cannot name the man pictured below, but there are those who feel that, next to the president, he is the most powerful man in the country. He is Alan Greenspan, the current chair of the Fed.

Greenspan was appointed by President Reagan, and was reappointed to a second four-year term by President Bush in 1992. Greenspan's second term would end in 1996. Would President Clinton reappoint this life-long conservative Republican who had served Presidents Nixon, Reagan, and Bush?

Greenspan had many critics in the Democratic party who felt that he had been too concerned about inflation, that he had kept economic growth needlessly slow by holding interest rates higher than necessary to avert inflation. Senator Thomas Harkin (D–IA) opposed Greenspan's reappointment, charging that "Under the Greenspan Fed, job growth and the living standards of average Americans have been sacrificed on the altar of high interest rates and slow-growth policies."* Certainly, the political importance of the appointment was widely appreciated. According to columnist Robert Kuttner:

It used to be said that the chairman of the Federal Reserve held the second most powerful job in the country. There is a good case that his job is the most powerful.

Consider: Jimmy Carter lost his job when Fed chairman Paul Volcker slammed on the money brake in 1979–80. Ronald Reagan won a handy reelection when Volcker obligingly eased up in 1983–84. George Bush crashed when Alan Greenspan took too long to allow a recovery in 1992. And in 1996, Bill Clinton, far from criticizing the Fed, is being very, very deferential to Greenspan. Wouldn't you? †

Greenspan enjoyed wide support in the financial community, and in the Republican Congress. Democratic President Clinton reappointed Republican Chairman Greenspan. His term runs through the year 2000.

* Andrew Taylor, "Greenspan, Rivlin Confirmed," *Congressional Quarterly Weekly Report*, June 22, 1996, 1746.

† Robert Kuttner, "Forget Flat Tax; Reform the Fed," *The Boston Globe*, February 5, 1996, 11.

Alan Greenspan

Like all other government agencies, the Fed was created and its powers defined by congressional statutes. Nominees to the Federal Reserve Board must be approved by the Senate, and the Fed must make quarterly reports to the banking committees of the House and the Senate.

But despite these legal obligations to Congress, the Fed is remarkably free of congressional influence. For one thing, the Fed's budget is not congressionally determined. Instead, the Fed raises its own revenue by creating money—almost literally—and using this money to buy U.S. Treasury bonds, from which it earns interest. Creating money and buying Treasury bonds are a necessary part of the Fed's job—they are among the ways the Fed puts money into and takes money out of the economy. But Fed investments have a side benefit for the agency. Every year Fed investments earn billions of dollars ($18 billion in 1993). Most of this money is turned over to the federal Treasury, but the Fed keeps about a tenth for its own operations.[19] As a result, the Fed does not need to ask Congress for an appropriation in the way most agencies do. The Fed owns squash courts in its building near the Washington Monument and bowling alleys on Wall Street, the most expensive real estate in the world—a reflection of the fact that it can literally manufacture its own money.

The Fed is also relatively free of congressionally determined salary schedules and personnel controls. Consequently, it is able to hire a better trained, more professional, more prestigious staff than other government agencies. In fact, the Fed is the one agency of the United States government that has a civil service that resembles the type found in Europe and Japan (see Chapter 13). Instead of political appointees that rotate in and out of office, the Fed staff consists of expert, career appointees.

In general, congressional influence on the Fed takes place indirectly. Congress "jawbones" the Fed when it feels that monetary policy is not appropriate for prevailing conditions. Individual members make critical speeches, and committees hold hearings at which the Fed chair is asked to testify. In these ways, liberal Democrats make known their belief that monetary policy is too restrictive, or conservative Republicans announced their belief that monetary policy is too loose. There is an implied warning that if the Fed is not responsive, more serious attempts to influence the Fed may be forthcoming.

Although it is generally agreed that—in contrast to much of the federal bureaucracy—Congress does not exercise significant control over the Fed, there is less of a consensus on the influence of other groups and individuals. Three distinct interpretations of Fed operations have been offered: banker dominance, presidential control, and Fed independence.

BANKER DOMINANCE

The first interpretation, held by many liberal Democratic critics of the Fed, holds that the banks control the Fed.[20] Just as interest groups underpin other iron triangles, so the banking industry, with a huge stake in Fed decisions, forms the primary base of support for the Fed. Bankers influence the appointment of the Board of Governors, and they nominate the Federal Reserve bank presidents, who cast five votes on the Open Market Committee.

As evidence of the banker dominance interpretation, proponents point to the apparent policy bias of the Fed, which is generally viewed as being less concerned about reducing unemployment than about lowering inflation rates. Alternatively, the Fed seems to be worried more about rising prices than about staving off recessions. The Fed "can't stand prosperity." When jobs are plentiful and people are spending freely, the Fed typically responds by raising interest rates and slowing down the economy: "Just when the party gets going, the Fed takes away the beer." [21]

The Fed defends itself against such accusations of policy bias by saying that unless inflation is checked quickly, much stronger action will eventually have to be taken, creating more hardship in the long run. The Fed offers as evidence its policy in the late 1970s, when it mistakenly let inflation get out of control. Only after the deep and painful recession of 1981–82 were inflation and interest rates brought down to an acceptable level.

Meeting of the Federal Reserve's Open Market Committee.

PRESIDENTIAL DOMINANCE

Most observers believe that the president, who appoints its members and chairs, has more influence than Congress over the Fed.[22] But how much influence do presidents have, and further, to what ends do they use it?

Some political scientists suggest that presidents try to manipulate Fed policy for their own political purposes. These scholars note that the chair of the Board, in order to win reappointment, must be sensitive to signals from the White House. Even more importantly, the Fed's very desire to appear nonpolitical creates a dependency on the president. If the president publicly criticizes the Fed, it becomes the subject matter of news commentaries and talk shows because the Fed's actions have become matters of partisan controversy. The best way for the Fed to appear independent is for its chair to listen carefully to suggestions coming from presidential advisors and to avoid acting in such a way as to provoke controversy.

Two versions of the presidential control interpretation—the partisan and the election cycle—have been proposed.[23] The **partisan interpretation** distinguishes between the constituencies of Republican and Democratic presidents.[24] The Republican constituency includes more upper-income business and professional people, who traditionally are less worried about unemployment—which less frequently strikes them—than inflation. The Democratic constituency includes more lower-income, blue-collar workers traditionally more concerned about rising unemployment, which normally hits them hardest. Consistent with these constituency preferences, studies show that inflation rates tend to rise under Democratic presidents and fall under Republican presidents, and that stocks and bonds earn higher returns under Republican administrations.[25]

The differences between the two parties should not be exaggerated, of course. Most citizens, regardless of income, occupation, or partisan affiliation, dislike both rising unemployment and rising prices; they don't want to lose their jobs, but

partisan interpretation
The argument that Democratic administrations set economic policy to benefit lower-income, wage-earning groups, and that Republican administrations set economic policy to benefit higher-income business and professional groups.

neither do they want to see the purchasing power of their wages eroded by inflation. Similarly, investors dislike inflation, but if growth slows and unemployment rises, their investments will earn lower returns. Thus, whatever their party, presidents are better off striking a balance between the two goals rather than focusing on either one to the neglect of the other. Nevertheless, Democrats and Republicans strike different balances, reflecting their different constituencies. Republican administrations favor keeping money tighter and are more willing to accept a little higher unemployment in order to avoid inflation. Democrats strike the opposite balance. They favor keeping money a little looser and are more likely to accept somewhat higher inflation in order to avoid unemployment. To keep from provoking presidents, the Fed probably tends to slant its decisions in the direction of these well-known partisan preferences. But the effect is too small to call it presidential control.

> **election-cycle interpretation**
> The argument that, whatever their party, presidents attempt to slow the economy early in their terms, then expand it as their reelection approaches.

In contrast to the preceding partisan interpretation, the **election-cycle interpretation** suggests that presidents deliberately manipulate the economy to engineer their reelections. They tolerate slow growth, even a recession, early in their term of office so they can step on the gas and "rev up" the economic engine when the election pay-off is the greatest.

Richard Nixon's first term is a clear example of presidential manipulation. Edward Tufte documents how the Nixon administration pulled out all the stops and achieved a huge increase in per capita disposable income during the election year, 1972.[26] Nixon was reelected overwhelmingly. Reagan's first term is another example consistent with presidential manipulation of the economy. During the first two years of his administration, the country suffered a deep recession as the Fed squeezed high inflation out of the economy. During the last two years, the Fed lowered interest rates and the economy took off. Economic growth in the election year of 1984 was the best in the entire decade, and Reagan was overwhelmingly reelected.

But if Nixon's and Reagan's first terms fit the election-cycle interpretation, Carter's and Bush's directly contradict it. Carter may have tried to increase growth, but the economy was stagnant throughout his administration, and the year of the election was a recession year. Bush seems to have done things exactly backwards. At the beginning of his term, the country enjoyed steady growth, but the economy reversed, and Bush's fortunes shifted with it. Convincing statistical proof that the recession was over did not appear until after election day. Bush's timing could not have been worse.

Combining information for all years since World War II, there is some evidence, but not a lot, that presidents manipulate the economy to their political advantage. In years when presidents themselves are running for reelection, growth rates are somewhat higher, but not a lot, than in other years (see Figure 19.4).

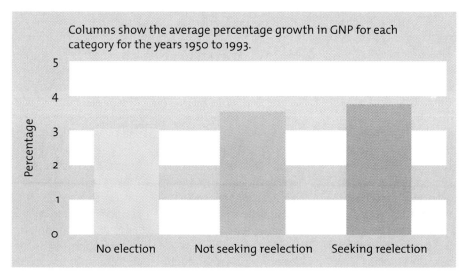

FIGURE 19.4

Presidential Elections and
Economic Growth

SOURCE: Data are calculated
from *The Economic Report of the
President*, February 1994
(Washington, DC: Government
Printing Office).

AN INDEPENDENT FED

Fed supporters says the agency is independent of both politics and external pressure groups.[27] The independence of the Fed is guaranteed by the fact that board members are appointed for fourteen-year terms. They can be removed only through the impeachment process. Because board members serve such long terms, presidents may not be able to appoint a majority of the board until they have been in office six years. And because the chair of the Fed serves a four-year term, in the worst case a president may not be able to appoint a new chair until the fourth year of the administration.

Various other factors reinforce the Fed's independence. Business confidence in government economic policy is strengthened by the belief that Fed decisions are above politics. The Board acts on the advice of a strong, independent staff. The chair is usually more knowledgeable about economic policy than any other presidential appointee. Monetary policy is too arcane to engage the general public; consequently, Fed-bashing is not a very effective campaign tactic.

Further, those who say the Fed is independent usually consider this is a good idea. They say that an independent Fed has improved the management of the economy. In particular, they emphasize that the country has had fewer and shorter recessions since establishing the Fed than it had earlier in history.

It may be that it is impossible to conclude that anyone tightly controls the Fed. The Fed operates with a considerable amount of independence, mainly because it tries to achieve not only what presidents want but also what nearly everyone desires—steady economic growth. Presidents need good economic news their first year, because that is when they are getting their political agenda off the ground. They need good economic news their second year to help the congressional candidates of their party. It is dangerous for a president to encourage a recession in the third year because it could spill over into the election campaign, and of course, no president wants a recession in the election year. The Fed's emphasis on steady, moderate growth is pretty much what the president wants, so the president can usually leave the Fed alone. Perhaps the Fed is an example of the proposition that good public policy in a democracy is not necessarily produced by the most democratic processes (see Democratic Dilemma).

An Independent Federal Reserve

In Homer's *Odyssey,* when the hero's ship passes the Isle of the Sirens, Odysseus orders his crew to block their ears, lest they be lured by the Sirens' irresistible singing and wreck the ship on the rocks. But Odysseus himself wants to hear the Sirens, so he has the crew tie him to the mast so that he can hear the singing but not be able to steer the ship toward the rocks. (If he orders the crew to untie him, they won't hear him because their ears are covered—a little far-fetched, but a neat story.)

The moral of this epic poem is that people sometimes are better off by preventing themselves from doing what they would otherwise like to do. Some people view the Federal Reserve in these terms. They argue that while it is undemocratic to have monetary policy set by a small elite that is not subject to election or even oversight by Congress, that's the whole point of an insulated, independent agency. Before the Federal Reserve was established, monetary policy was a subject of intense political controversy. Battles over tight money versus loose money, paper versus metal, gold versus silver, and so on were important parts of nineteenth-century history.* (In 1896, William Jennings Bryan thundered that "you shall not crucify mankind on a cross of gold!") According to defenders of the Fed, only when monetary policy was taken out of politics was it possible to set policy rationally and with a long-term view. If the Federal Reserve were subject to democratic control, they argue, politicians would be tempted to manipulate policy for short-term electoral gain, and in the long run the country would be worse off.

What do you think? In a democracy, can citizens democratically decide that some policies will not be made democratically?

* James Livingston, *Origins of the Federal Reserve System* (Ithaca, NY: Cornell University Press, 1986).

Dealing with the Deficit

Since the early 1980s, the deficit has been a major issue in American politics. Ross Perot made it the centerpiece of his independent campaign for the presidency in 1992, and disagreement about how to balance the budget led President Clinton and the Republican Congress to shut down the federal government several times in the winter of 1995–96.

Eliminating the deficit requires that taxes be raised or spending be reduced. Either choice is unpopular. Most people would like to pay less in taxes (see p. 633), but they enjoy government programs and services. The only programs that majorities wish to cut are welfare, foreign aid, and the space program, and not nearly enough money is spent in these areas to eliminate the deficit. This perennial inconsistency in public opinion has lead elected officials to search for blame-avoidance techniques—strategies that deal with deficits while avoiding any blame for the consequences.

It's Not Whether You Win or Lose, It's How You Place the Blame

Since taxes are unpopular, elected officials think carefully about how to get the money the government needs without offending their constituents. As a French economist once observed, "The art of taxation consists in so plucking the goose as to obtain the largest possible amount of feathers with the smallest amount of hissing."[28] Avoiding blame for raising taxes or cutting benefits is even more important to elected leaders than claiming credit. When politicians take credit for something that happens, many voters will remain skeptical. But voters are unlikely to forgive an official whom they blame for a harm they have suffered.

To avoid being blamed, elected officials naturally try to disguise the connections between their actions and the harms that occur.[29] At one time, blame could be avoided by letting inflation raise taxes and cut benefits; the process was invisible but highly effective. Government benefits were reduced by allowing inflation to eat away the purchasing power of the monthly check sent to senior citizens, the poor and disabled, and others dependent on government support. At the same time, taxes were increased by allowing inflation to push people into higher tax brackets, forcing them to pay a higher percentage of their **real income**—their income adjusted for inflation—in taxes. For example, if the inflation rate is running at 5 percent, a union contract might provide for workers to get a compensating 5 percent increase in wages, often called a cost-of-living adjustment, or COLA. This is not a real raise, but just an adjustment to offset the lower value of the dollar due to inflation. But the raise might push the worker into the next higher tax bracket, resulting in higher taxes although real income has not increased. This disguised way of raising taxes is called **bracket creep**.

Bracket creep was such an effective blame-avoidance mechanism that Congress hardly ever raised income tax rates during the first decades of the Cold War, even though federal spending was continually rising. Lyndon Johnson obtained a temporary 10 percent surtax (a move that added to his unpopularity), but almost all other tax legislation cut nominal rates. This was the best of all possible worlds for elected officials; they appeared to be cutting taxes while inflation was actually raising them.

Just as Congress hardly ever increased taxes, so it seldom cut benefits. Instead, Congress simply waited for inflation to cut benefits. This neat blame-free process that kept federal spending and revenues roughly in balance came to an end with **indexing**, the practice of adjusting benefit and tax levels to the inflation rate. Today, when inflation erodes the purchasing power of a senior citizen's social security check, the amount received is raised to compensate for the inflation rate. Similarly, tax brackets are redefined yearly to adjust for inflation. Given difficulties in measuring inflation, the process is not perfect, but indexing keeps government benefit levels and tax rates constant in the face of inflation.

Indexing and the End of Blame-Avoidance

Indexation first appeared in 1962 and 1963, when increases in pensions for civil service and military personnel were pegged to the cost of living. Military pay was indexed in 1967, and coal miner's disability insurance was included in 1969. The politics of indexation accelerated in the early seventies. The salaries of white-collar federal employees were indexed to inflation in 1970, food stamp benefits were

real income
Income adjusted for inflation, that is, the value of the dollar; often expressed as "income in constant dollars."

bracket creep
Hidden tax increases made possible by not indexing taxes for inflation; thus, cost of living raises push people into higher tax brackets even though their real incomes (that is, adjusted for inflation) are unchanged.

indexing
Adjusting tax brackets, benefit levels, and so forth for inflation.

indexed in 1971, and social security and medicare insurance in 1972.[32] In nearly every case, the period upon which the index was based was an interval when government benefits had reached an all-time high.

TAX INDEXATION AND DEFICITS

Indexation of benefits was fiscally tolerable so long as taxes were not indexed. As inflation pushed benefits up, it pushed taxes up as well. But in 1981, the game changed. A decade of inflation had subjected Americans to continually rising income taxes (as they were pushed into higher tax brackets), and periodic property tax increases (as the assessed value of their homes increased). In the late 1970s, a "tax rebellion" frightened elected officials. Beginning with California's Proposition 13, which slashed property tax rates, citizens in 18 states put tax-cut or tax-limitation initiatives on the ballot.[33] In this changed political climate, Robert Dole, the new majority leader in the Senate, saw the 1981 tax bill as an opportunity to enact tax indexation. And just as indexation of benefits came at a point when benefits had reached a high, indexation of taxes came when rates had been cut to their lowest point since before World War II.

After indexation, elected officials found it more difficult to avoid blame for tax increases. The Budget Compromise of 1990, the law that contained the tax increase Bush's lips said would never take place, proved politically costly (see p. 614). Later, the Clinton administration raised taxes modestly again in 1993, with every Republican member of Congress voting against the increase. Not entirely coincidentally, the Republicans captured control of Congress in the next election.

In 1997, however, Clinton and a Republican Congress finally agreed on a balanced budget. But the achievement was due almost entirely to unexpected economic growth that by itself dramatically cut budget deficits. All of a sudden, it became relatively easy to balance the budget in five years while at the same time cutting taxes and increasing social spending. President Clinton and Republican leaders put their bickering to one side and reached a popular compromise.

Senators Warren B. Rudman (R–NH), Phil Gramm (R–TX), and Ernest F. Hollings (D–SC), cosponsors of the 1985 Gramm-Rudman-Hollings Act to stem the deficit.

The "T" Word: Taxes

Hardly anyone likes to pay taxes. Most people think that their tax bill is too high (Figure 19.5) and that governmental officials waste much of what is paid in taxes (p. 460). As a result, tax policy is a major issue today, with various aspects of the American tax system subject to heated debate.[35]

THE TAX BURDEN

Although tax receipts as a percentage of the nation's GNP did rise from 19 percent in 1950 to 27 percent in 1970, they scarcely increased between 1970 and 1990.[36] Federal tax receipts as a percentage of GNP did not increase at all during this latter period, but there was a marginal increase in state tax receipts. Some advocates of higher government spending complain that Americans have become selfish over the course of the past generation, and are increasingly unwilling to tax themselves for good purposes. Others defend taxpayers and point to the stagnation of personal incomes beginning in the early 1970s. So long as standards of living were rising, people were willing to absorb higher taxes, but once living standards stagnated, frustrated citizens increasingly vented their unhappiness on the tax system. At any rate, Americans have come to feel that the tax burden is too high, and elected officials have responded—from President Bush's "no new taxes," to President Clinton's signing of the 1997 tax cut.

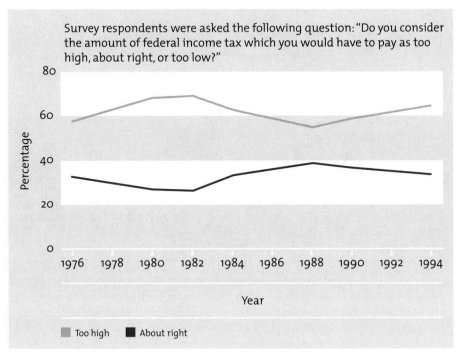

Survey respondents were asked the following question: "Do you consider the amount of federal income tax which you would have to pay as too high, about right, or too low?"

FIGURE 19.5

Public Opinion About Taxes

SOURCE: Surveys by the National Opinion Research Center.

THE TAX BASE

tax base
Those type of activities, types of property, or kinds of investments that are subject to taxation.

The income, property, wealth or economic activity that is taxed is called the **tax base**. Economists argue that taxes are less intrusive if they are imposed on all economic activity at the same rate. Thus, the amount you pay in income taxes should depend only on the amount you make, not on how you make it: Whether you make your money growing crops, making movies, writing wills, or running a charity should not matter. Nor should the amount you pay in sales taxes depend on whether you spend money on groceries, cars, beer, or medical insurance. If everything is taxed alike, then tax policy will not distort the economy—it will not influence the choices people make.

tax preferences
Activities, properties, or investments that receive special tax treatment.

Broad-based taxes are more easily recommended than enacted into law, however. Often, good reasons can be given for not taxing some particular activity, and there are numerous organized groups that offer such good—and often not-so-good—reasons to persuade elected officials to give favorable treatment to the activities of their members. In response to these pressures, national and state legislators have enacted thousands of **tax preferences** that exempt particular types of economic activity from taxation. Reformers regularly target tax preferences in the federal income tax code that cost the government billions of dollars in forgone revenues. Here are some major examples:

■ Deductions for college tuition. In 1997, Congress allowed a tax deduction for college tuition, a tax break popular with college students. Critics say colleges will simply boost tuition.

■ Deductions for mortgage interest and real estate taxes ($55 billion). Developers and brokers claim that this tax preference encourages home-ownership, said to be good for families and community stability. Critics say the preference primarily benefits higher-income people who can afford huge mortgages and subsidizes their over investment in big houses and vacation homes.

■ Deductions for state and local taxes ($37 billion). This tax preference exempts money used to pay state and local taxes. State and local governments say people should not have to pay taxes on money that already has been taxed away. Critics say the tax preference is a subsidy that encourages state and local governments to provide more services than taxpayers would choose if they were faced with the true cost. Congressional representatives from high-tax states fiercely defend this tax break: Its abolition would eliminate a major deduction for their constituents.

- Deductions for charitable contributions ($18 billion). Defenders of this tax preference claim that it encourages public support for the arts, education, and the needy. Critics say many charities are actually businesses that provide services to those "giving" them money.

Tax preferences are the classic "slippery slope." Once government grants them to any group, it abandons the principle of neutral taxation and encourages other groups to lobby for their own preferences. Tax preferences distort the economy by encouraging people to make economic decisions on the basis of tax considerations. Moreover, granting preferences to some activities requires that taxes be higher on other activities that do not have defenders strong enough to get their own tax break.

TAX PROGRESSIVITY

Taxes are said to be **progressive taxes** if people with higher income pay a higher tax rate. The most important progressive tax is the federal income tax. In 1997, individual taxable incomes up to $24,650 were being taxed at a 15 percent rate. Incomes between $24,650 and $60,000 were being taxed at a 28 percent rate. Above that figure rates rise to 31 percent, then to 36 percent, until at $271,000 a surcharge and the phase-out of deductions and personal exemptions was bringing the marginal rate to about 43 percent.

Taxes that require low-income people to pay a higher rate are called **regressive taxes**. The payroll or social security tax is a regressive tax, because it is levied only on the first $65,400 a person earns. Because all earnings in excess of that figure are exempt from the tax, higher-income people pay a smaller share of their income for social security than do lower-income people.

Progressive taxes traditionally have been defended by liberals who claim that progressive rates reduce income inequality in the society. Thus, Bill Clinton and the congressional Democrats pushed through an increase on high-income taxpayers over united Republican opposition in 1993. Progressive taxes traditionally have been opposed by conservatives who claim that progressive rates discourage investment and hard work by the most productive members of society. Thus, the tax cut passed by a Republican Congress in 1997 made bigger reductions in taxes paid by high-income groups.

There are numerous taxes levied in the United States. The federal personal income tax and some state personal income taxes are progressive. Social security and state sales taxes are regressive. Property taxes vary a great deal, but generally fall in between. When all taxes levied by federal, state and local governments are taken into account, it is difficult to say whether the tax structure in the United States is progressive or not.[37]

TAX REFORM

Debates over tax reform traditionally focus on the breadth and progressivity of the tax system. In 1986, Congress passed a widely acclaimed reform that lowered individual income tax rates, raised corporate rates, and broadened the tax base by eliminating many tax preferences. The federal income tax burden for a typical family of four dropped from 10.5 to 8.9 percent of total income, without reducing government revenue.[38]

In recent years, many members of Congress have proposed even more sweeping tax reforms. The best known is the **flat tax**, a family of proposals that would eliminate

- **progressive tax**
  A tax structured so that higher-income people pay a larger proportion of their income in taxes.

- **regressive tax**
  A tax structured so that higher-income people pay a smaller proportion of their income in taxes.

- **flat tax**
  A tax that is neither progressive nor regressive: Everyone pays at the same rate.

The VAT Tax

As still more radical proposal for tax reform is to change the basis of taxation. Most European countries rely on consumption taxes in addition to income taxes. A sales tax is a consumption tax—how much you pay depends on what you buy. The value-added tax (VAT) is the best-known consumption tax. This is essentially a national sales tax imposed at each level of the manufacturing and distribution process. Such a tax has been opposed by both liberals and conservatives in the United States. Liberals oppose the VAT because it is not progressive. Conservatives oppose it because it is "hidden" in the prices of goods and services and thus allows governments to raise money easily and quietly. Recently, however, some tax reformers have argued that it is possible to design consumption taxes that are as progressive and as visible as the existing income tax, thus meeting the objections of both liberals and conservatives to consumption taxes like the VAT.

To explain this new proposal, consider two single taxpayers, alike in education and occupation, who earn identical salaries. Person one is a party animal who has borrowed every dollar the banks will loan him to pay for a beachfront condominium, a fancy sports car, luxury vacations, and various controlled substances. He has no savings, only debts. Person two is a sober, hard-working individual who rents a modest apartment and drives an old car that is fully paid for. She saves 10 percent of her income every month. What disturbs many people is this: At year's end, spendthrift person one will pay less in income taxes than thrifty person two. The reason is that person one can deduct all his first- and second-mortgage interest from his taxable income, while person two not only does not have such deductions, but she must pay additional taxes on her interest and dividend earnings. In effect, person two's savings subsidize person one's play.

In the early 1990s, Senators Sam Nunn (D-GA) and Pete Domenici (R-NM) argued that the present tax system rewards consumption and penalizes savings and investment.[41] Obviously, if low savings in the United States is a problem, the tax system should be corrective. People should get credit (deductions) for whatever they save or invest, not for what they spend. If such a system were in effect, person two in the preceding example could deduct the 10 percent of her income that she saves, but person one would not be able to deduct his interest expenses. Person two's thrifty behavior would be rewarded, not penalized. Tax rates could still be progressive, satisfying liberals, and the tax you pay would still be visible, satisfying conservatives, but taxable income would be reduced by saving and investing, not by consuming. Such a reversal of policy would help to raise the low savings rate in the United States.

the progressive features of the income tax and tax all income groups above a certain minimum at the same rate.[39] Advocates argue that it is unfair to require some people to pay a higher percentage of their income in taxes than others. Supporters of a flat tax also defend it on the grounds of efficiency—the more progressive taxes are, the greater the incentive for the wealthy to hire accountants, lawyers, and lobbyists to help them avoid taxes. Indeed, the wealthy are not the only ones who pay: As of 1990, a majority of Americans used professional tax preparers, and taxpayers spent at least $75 billion a year on record-keeping, filling out forms, complying with audits, and paying for accountants and lawyers.[40]

In the 1996 Republican primaries, *Fortune* magazine publisher Steve Forbes based his presidential campaign on his advocacy of the flat tax. While he enjoyed some early success, and helped publicize the idea of a flat tax, the philosophy was dismissed by most of the other candidates in the race. But Forbes was undeterred. In early 1997 he was out on the campaign trail building grass roots support for a flat tax.

The debate over tax reform is fractious and many-sided because people want to use the tax system to achieve different goals—goals that often conflict. They want to raise revenue, to reduce income inequality, to discourage some kinds of behavior, to encourage other kinds of behavior, to benefit some kinds of people, and to punish other kinds.

Steve Forbes has based his campaigns for the Republican presidential nomination on a radical reform of the tax system: replacing the graduated income tax with a "flat tax."

What is clear is that Americans are unhappy with the system that exists. Perhaps surprisingly, much of that unhappiness focuses on the federal income tax, the most progressive and therefore, the "fairest" tax in the view of many liberals. Citizens believe the income tax is far too complex. They believe that the wealthy find ways to evade the progressivity of the tax. They resent the heavy-handed tactics of the IRS. And many of them do not share the belief that progressive rates are fair. As we saw in Chapter 4, even the poor have no great love for the progressive income tax. Rather, many Americans view such rates as penalizing hard work and accomplishment. Whether this underlying dissatisfaction can be mobilized behind a sweeping reform of the tax system remains to be seen.

The U.S. Economy in Comparative Perspective

While we have focused on government and the economy, the truth is that the extent to which the economy can be controlled by government is limited, and has become much more so in recent years. The Fed loosens or tightens the money supply, but it does so in reaction to national and global economic forces, forces that may overcome its best efforts. Indexation exacerbated the deficit problem, but other broad economic and demographic forces also contributed to the rising imbalance between spending and revenues. Taxes can be raised, lowered, or altered, but any change sets in motion economic reactions that may not be anticipated. Indeed, all over the world, countries with very different political systems are struggling to deal with economic challenges similar to those in the United States. And given the steady diet of bad news the media throw at the American public, citizens might be reassured to know that, relative to other advanced democracies, the United States is dealing reasonably well with its economic challenges and difficulties.

PROSPERITY

In the early 1990s, the unemployment rate in Western Europe was stuck around 12 percent—about twice the rate in the United States. In the 1980s, the workforce in the Western world expanded rapidly as the entire baby boom reached working age and women moved into the workforce in greater numbers, especially in the United States. The American economy absorbed these new workers far more successfully than did European economies, creating three times more jobs per 1000 people than did France and West Germany. Moreover, European countries were able to keep their unemployment rates as low as they did in part by policies that would be unacceptable in the United States. For example, policy in Germany and Switzerland induced so-called "guest" workers to return to their countries of origin. The United States, in contrast, allowed immigration to increase during the 1980s. Some countries absorbed new workers by expanding their public sectors. The Swedes, for example, dealt with the surge of women into the labor force by doubling public-sector employment.[42] In the United States, public sector employment grew very slowly in the antibureaucratic 1980s.

Some critics complain that the jobs that have been created are low-skill, low-paying "McJobs," but the evidence suggests that such claims are exaggerated. According to an extensive jobs study by the Organization of Economically Developed Countries (OECD), four-fifths of the net job increase in the United States came in the professional, technical, managerial, and administrative categories—again, a performance far superior to western European democracies.[43]

Compared to most other countries, the American economy is less restricted by government policies and regulations. This gives it a greater capacity to adapt to changing economic conditions. No one can deny that changes in the world economy have had costly, even tragic consequences for individuals and communities in the United States during the past two decades. But it would be equally hard to argue that the aggregate consequences of economic change have been any worse here than elsewhere. Indeed, the case appears to be the contrary. And as we explained in Chapter 18, many of the European economies are facing futures that look more difficult than ours.

DEBTS AND DEFICITS

Two hundred billion dollars, the size of deficits in the early 1990s, sounds like a huge number. Four trillion dollars, the size of the national debt, is an almost unimaginable number. But such numbers are meaningful only relative to baselines, and the natural baseline—the size of the American economy—is an even more unimaginable number. Relative to the size of the economy, the deficits and the public debt in the United States are moderate. For example, as a proportion of **gross domestic product (GDP)**, the total value of all goods and services produced and sold in a country, Italy's national debt is over twice as large as that of the United States (see International Comparison).

Certainly, this is not to say that concern about deficits and the debt is unnecessary. That so much debt accumulated in such a short period of time is worrisome, but in the last quarter of the twentieth century the debt in other democracies increased even

■ **gross domestic product (GDP)** Same as GNP except that goods and services produced outside the specific nation are excluded and revenues received by foreign corporations are included.

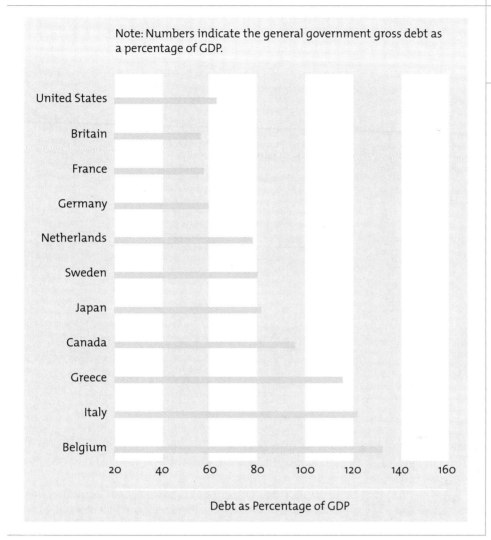

Note: Numbers indicate the general government gross debt as a percentage of GDP.

Debt as Percentage of GDP

more rapidly. In sum, looking around the world, there is little evidence that the political systems in other countries are consistently dealing with their economic problems any more effectively than is the American political system. The economic challenges facing the world today are serious and their causes complex; all political systems have difficulty dealing with them.

TAXES

The tax burden in the United States compares very favorably with that in the world's other developed countries. As of 1990, the tax burden in the United States was the lowest of 13 OECD countries, about 30 percent of GDP. At the other

FIGURE 19.6

Tax Burden in Democracies

SOURCE: Data are taken from
OECD in *Figures: Statistics on the
Member Countries*, 1995 edition
(Paris: Organisation for Economic
Co-Operation and Development).

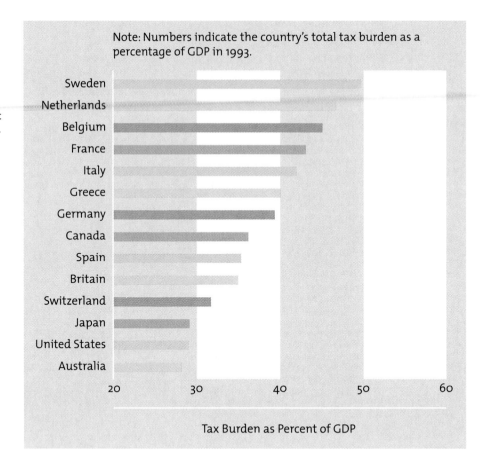

Note: Numbers indicate the country's total tax burden as a percentage of GDP in 1993.

Tax Burden as Percent of GDP

extreme the public sector in Sweden taxes away more than half the country's GDP. Taxes in Holland, Belgium, France and Italy all exceed 40 percent of GDP (see Figure 19.6).

To be sure, other countries provide more services in exchange for the money they extract in taxes. The most important example is health care; about half of it is paid for by the private sector in the United States, whereas it is almost entirely government-provided in the other OECD countries.

If their tax rates and the overall tax burden are the lowest in the developed world, and falling, why then are Americans so unhappy with taxes? European observers of the United States frequently ask that question. A former French foreign minister once commented that "it's hard to take seriously [the proposition] that a nation has deep problems if they can be fixed with a 50-cent-a-gallon gasoline tax."[44] As in most of the rest of the world, gasoline taxes are high in France—the equivalent of $2.85 per gallon, as compared to an average $.38 in the United States. If Americans were not so averse to taxes, they could wipe out the deficit with a gasoline tax much smaller than that which already exists in other developed countries!

We doubt that there is any single explanation for the American aversion to taxes. Part of the answer may lie in the nature of the American tax system. The United

States relies more heavily than most other countries on income and payroll taxes to raise revenues; nearly two-thirds of total tax revenues come from such sources, a figure exceeded only by Switzerland and Belgium. Other countries rely more heavily on consumption taxes such as the VAT, which are hidden in the prices of goods and services. Thus, their voters may not realize the full tax cost of the services they receive. Ironically, Sweden, Germany, and Italy—with their large welfare states— rely heavily on a tax that American liberals view as regressive. Only Japan, with its minimal provision of social services, relies less on consumption taxes than the United States.

But we suspect that a larger part of the answer lies simply in the historic preferences of Americans. In Chapter 4 we saw that, more so than in other countries, Americans are economic individualists who wish to keep the role of government limited. Fewer services and lower taxes are desired. The price of this preference is greater inequality. Compared to other advanced democracies, income inequality in the United States is higher (see Figure 19.7). Moreover, after declining between 1930 and 1970, inequality has since risen until by some measures it is higher than at any time since the 1930s. Some social critics see in such trends a "class war" of the rich against the poor,[45] but there seems to be no great popular demand for government to intervene directly to reverse the trend toward inequality. Candidates who advocate a greater role for government and a greater degree of income redistribution regularly run for office, but the American people have not elected them in recent decades, and have not demanded such policies from their representatives in Congress and the state legislatures.

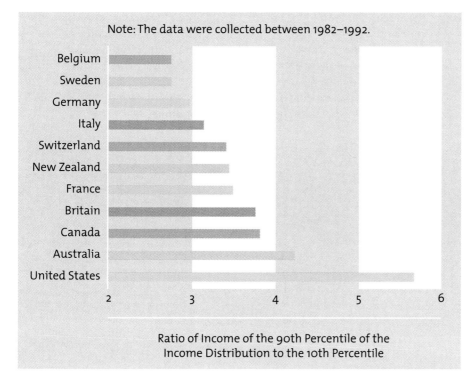

Note: The data were collected between 1982–1992.

Ratio of Income of the 90th Percentile of the Income Distribution to the 10th Percentile

FIGURE 19.7

Income Inequality

SOURCE: Data was taken from Timothy M. Smeeding and Peter Gottshalk, "The International Evidence on Income Distribution in Modern Economies: Where Do We Stand?" Luxembourg Income Study Working Paper #13, December 1995.

Chapter Summary

People care a lot about whether they can find a job and what they have to pay for the things they buy. If times are bad, the president takes the blame. If times are good, the president usually—but not always—gets the credit. Presidents' popular standing and their odds of reelection are significantly influenced by national economic conditions. To a somewhat lesser extent, this is also true of members of Congress and even state-level elected officials.

Given these political facts of life, presidents give economic policy top priority. Ironically, they do so most effectively by giving the agency responsible for monetary policy, the Federal Reserve, a good deal of independence. Although they try to shape policy on the margins, presidents realize that the Fed needs independence to do its job well. And when the Fed does a good job by keeping economic growth steady, the president usually gets the credit.

For half a century, presidents tried to use fiscal policy—the management of budget deficits and surpluses—to manage the economy. But the importance of fiscal policy for managing the economy has been reduced by a combination of factors, including divided government, declining faith in Keynesian theory, a rising public debt, and the globalization of economic activity.

Growth in the public debt has been accelerated by the indexation of taxes and benefits. Because such a large proportion of government expenditures were put on automatic pilot, and because inflation-induced tax increases were eliminated, Congress must now openly discuss and plan ways of reducing benefits and increasing taxes. One result is that recent congresses have given much more attention to proposals for tax reform.

Debates over tax reform typically involve discussion of whether tax preferences should be eliminated in order to broaden the tax base, whether the progressivity of the tax system needs to be raised or lowered, and whether the basis of the tax system should be shifted away from a heavy reliance on income and toward a greater reliance on consumption.

Despite the prominence of the deficit in contemporary American politics, deficits in the United States are not especially high, relative to those in other democracies. Moreover, given that taxes are significantly lower in the United States than elsewhere, the capacity of the economy to deal with the deficit is higher than in other democracies where government already extracts significantly more resources from their economies.

Key Terms

bracket creep, p. 631

Council of Economic Advisors (CEA), p. 618

debt, p. 619

deficit, p. 618

election-cycle interpretation, p. 628

Federal Reserve System ("Fed"), p. 623

fiscal policy, p. 617

flat tax, p. 635

gross domestic product (GDP), p. 638

gross national product (GNP), p. 614

indexing, p. 631

inflation, p. 616

Keynesianism, p. 618

monetarism, p. 619

monetary policy, p. 617

partisan interpretation, p. 627

progressive tax, p. 635

real income, p. 631

recession , p. 614

regressive tax, p. 635

supply-side economics, p. 619

surplus, p. 618

tax base, p. 634

tax preferences, p. 634

unemployment, p. 616

Suggested Readings

Birnbaum, Jeffrey H., and Alan S. Murray. *Showdown at Gucci Gulch*. New York: Random House, 1987. Fast-paced case study of the passage of the 1986 tax reforms.

Bradford, David F. *Untangling the Income Tax*. Cambridge, MA: Harvard University Press, 1986. Everything you ever wanted to know about income taxes, presented in a reasonably comprehensible fashion.

Greider, William. *Secrets of the Temple*. New York: Simon & Schuster, 1987. Long, well-researched, engagingly written, if uneven, book on the history of the Federal Reserve Board.

Hibbs, Douglas, A., Jr. *The American Political Economy*. Cambridge, MA: Harvard University Press, 1987. Provides detailed statistical evaluations of partisan and electoral cycle interpretations of presidential management of the economy.

Kettl, Don. *Deficit Politics*. New York: Macmillan, 1992. Short, readable book on budget deficits.

Krugman, Paul. *Peddling Prosperity*. New York: Norton, 1994. Written for the noneconomist, this critique of many of those who have influenced recent economic policy provides a comprehensible discussion of schools of economic thought and an overview of economic trends of the past several decades.

Weaver, R. Kent. *Automatic Government: The Politics of Indexation*. Washington, DC: Brookings, 1988. Explains how government benefits came to be indexed.

Weir, Margaret. *Politics and Jobs: The Boundaries of Employment Policies in the United States*. Princeton: Princeton University Press, 1992. Broad historical and political analysis of government efforts to guarantee full employment.

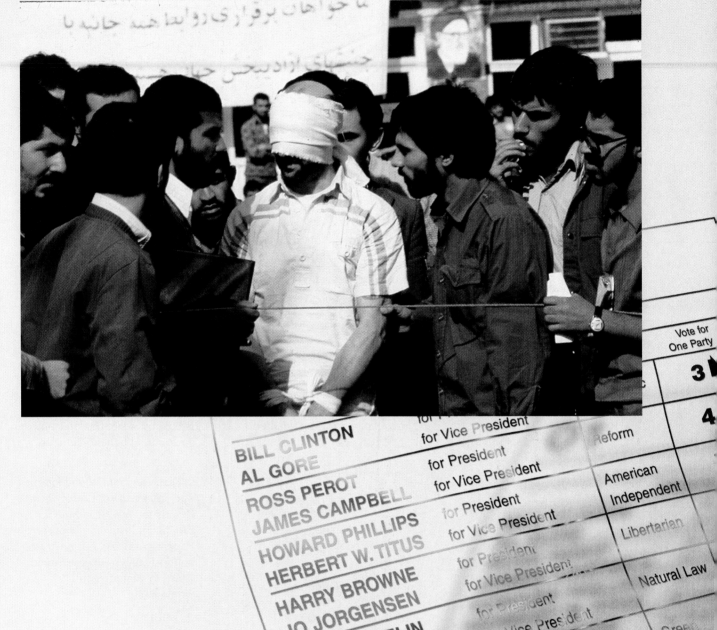

20

foreign and defense policy

UT FOREIGN affairs first, the Italian thinker Machiavelli advised his prince. If you fail at foreign policy, nothing you do in the domestic sphere will matter. If living today, Machiavelli might have added that in matters of war and peace, military success is not enough. In the world of the modern, exposed presidency, leaders must not only succeed but do so quickly. As the following story shows, voters don't have much patience.

The Iranian Shah, Mohammed Reza Pahlavi, was regarded by the Carter administration as the most reliable political leader in the oil-rich but politically unstable Persian Gulf region. Though known for his ruthless suppression of internal dissent, the Shah was anti-communist and thought to be capable of using his country's oil wealth to modernize its industry and economy. Muslim fundamentalists, led by Ayatollah Ruhollah Khomeini, who were demonstrating in the streets of Teheran, were thought to be little more than a political irritant. But almost overnight, the Muslim revolutionaries seized power, forcing the Shah to flee to the United States (for medical care, it was said). On the night of November 4, 1979, demonstrators marched into the U.S. Embassy in Teheran, taking more than five hundred American officials hostage.

Invading a foreign embassy and taking diplomatic personnel hostage transgresses the most ancient and fundamental principle of international law. For hundreds of years, countries have established diplomatic ties with one another—so that they can learn about each other, communicate differences, and reach agreements. The residence of the ambassador, known as the embassy, is respected as the sovereign territory of the guest nation. Its privacy is not to be violated by the host nation—even if war breaks out between the two countries. When that occurs, each side breaks diplomatic relations, and each side allows the other's ambassador and staff to depart peacefully. To do otherwise would only invite retaliation against its own diplomatic personnel.

Revolutionaries are not known for their respect for law, domestic or international. When they seize power, they act first, then think about the possible ramifications of their actions. The Muslim revolutionaries of Teheran refused to return the U.S. ambassador and other diplomatic personnel until the Shah had been returned and Iran had been paid reparations.

Demanding the return of the hostages, President Jimmy Carter broke diplomatic relations with Iran, imposed a trade embargo, and froze all Iranian economic assets in the United States, expecting that these strong actions would force the Iranians to recognize their international obligations. After five months passed without release of the hostages, Carter ordered a secret rescue operation, which failed when a U.S. helicopter and its crew were lost in a desert sandstorm. Carter decided that any further military action would only endanger the lives of the hostages.

Time and economic pressure finally had their effect. The hostages were released fourteen months after they had been taken, but Carter paid a high price for his patience. At the beginning of the crisis, public opinion rallied around the president. His standing in the polls jumped by as much as 27 points. Several months into the crisis, Carter was still strong enough to defeat Senator Edward Kennedy's challenge in several Democratic presidential primaries. But as the crisis persisted into the summer and fall of an election year, the president himself seemed to have been taken hostage. The individual personalities of the hostages became known through TV interviews with family members. Yellow badges, banners, and bumper stickers expressed public concern, and the news media began counting the number of days the hostages had been held. As the president seemed unable to bring the problem to resolution, his support in opinion polls fell dramatically. On election day, Carter carried only seven states and won but

40 percent of the popular vote. Few television scenes were more ironic than those showing hostages leaving Teheran while Ronald Reagan was viewing his inaugural parade. Carter's economic sanctions finally forced the release of the hostages, but his success had come too late.

n this chapter, we shall discuss the preeminent role that presidents play in the making of foreign policy. We begin by discussing the extent to which voters hold presidents responsible for conducting the country's foreign affairs, and then see how the Constitution, as interpreted by the courts, has also given the president special authority in this area. We next discuss the most important agencies that assist presidents in carrying out their foreign policy responsibilities. The chapter concludes by discussing the way in which the United States currently interprets and applies its democratic traditions to foreign policy issues.

Elections, Presidents, and Foreign Policy

Foreign policy is the conduct of relations among nation states. The most important foreign policy issues involve war and peace. Of all foreign policy objectives, the most critical is to prevent the country from being attacked or invaded by a foreign power. But foreign policy also involves economic trade among nations as well as such mundane matters as issuing passports to citizens who wish to travel abroad.

In a classic essay, political scientist Aaron Wildavksy developed what has become known as **two-presidency theory**, which explains why presidents exercise greater power over foreign affairs than domestic policy.[1] On domestic matters, presidents are usually subject to pressure politics and congressional checks. On foreign policy questions, presidents are given a degree of autonomy that enables them to manage the external relations of the country fairly free of short-term political pressures. In this section we describe four factors that differentiate foreign from domestic policy: (1) the need for fast action; (2) the voters' focus on presidents; (3) the limited role of interest groups; and (4) the congressional role.

■ foreign policy
Conduct of relations among nation states.

■ two-presidency theory
Theory that explains why presidents exercise greater power over foreign affairs than over domestic policy.

NEED FOR FAST ACTION

Foreign policy questions often require fast action. As Alexander Hamilton observed, governments require a single executive leader in order to achieve "decision, activity, secrecy, and dispatch."[2] Or, in the words of Artemis Ward, "Thrice is he armed that has his quarrel just—And four times he who gets his fist in first."[3] Following this principle, President Bush in 1991 quickly placed U.S. troops in Saudi Arabia to forestall an invasion by Iraq (see Figure 20.1). Congress did not consider the issue until six months later (see Election Connection).

Foreign Policy Success Comes Too Soon

The Gulf War stirred a wave of patriotic fervor, boosting President Bush's short-term popularity ratings to the highest levels achieved by a modern president.

Foreign policy successes, no matter how spectacular, are quickly forgotten. For presidential reelection strategies, it is the timing of foreign policy success that is all important.

A decade after President Carter's Iranian hostage debacle, a second crisis exploded in the Persian Gulf. Iran's neighbor, Iraq, had long coveted the oil riches of Kuwait, its small, defenseless neighbor, and Saddam Hussein, Iraq's shrewd, unpredictable leader, often asserted historic claims to Kuwait. But when the Iraqi army overran Kuwait on the night of August 2, 1990, the United States was caught by surprise.

With the capture of Kuwait, Hussein controlled 10 percent of the world's oil reserves. With his army poised to march into neighboring Saudi Arabia, Hussein was within reach of another 10 percent (see Figure 20.1).

The Saudis were alarmed, and Israel, frightened at the potential of an Arabia united under Hussein, threatened to intervene.

At the request of the Saudis, President Bush first ordered 200 thousand troops to Saudi Arabia, then succeeded in winning United Nations support for a trade embargo against Iraq. Bush's advisors next debated the wisdom of taking offensive military action.

Carter's experience in Iran came immediately to their minds. From that experience, it was clear that it would take months, maybe years, for economic sanctions to cripple the Iraqi economy. And the stalemate would undoubtedly undermine Bush's political popularity. Yet Bush also had to consider the price of military action. If American soldiers were to die by the tens of thousands in an all-out war far from U.S. borders, the public might not forgive the president who initiated the action.

For Bush the choice was not difficult. He persuaded the United Nations to demand departure of Iraqi troops from Kuwait by January 15, 1991, a date that postponed the final decision to go to war until after the November congressional elections. In the new Congress, heav-

ily Democratic, most Democratic congressional leaders recommended that the president delay military action until the effectiveness of economic sanctions could be tested. One critical senator said, "It doesn't pass my Dover, Delaware, test. How many bodies will be coming back through Dover?"* One Republican senator accused Democratic leaders of "wanting it both ways. If it works, they want to be with the President. If not, they want to be against him."

Despite the opposition of the Democratic leadership, a majority of both the House and Senate voted in favor of Bush's ultimatum. Within days of the key votes on Capitol Hill, American planes bombed Baghdad and Iraqi troops adjacent to the Saudi border. General Norman Schwarzkopf, the field commander, faked a naval landing and attacked Iraqi troops from behind, encircling and virtually destroying the enemy army. The United States suffered fewer than 2,000 combat fatalities. Only the decision not to march to Baghdad and capture Saddam Hussein himself made the victory less than complete.

The victory boosted Bush's popularity ratings to the highest levels ever achieved by a modern

American president (see Figure 20.4). As the summer of 1991 approached, Bush seemed politically invincible. Democrats openly wondered whether their opposition to the use of armed force would "keep us out of the White House forever." The White House chief of staff gloated, "I can't believe that [Democrats] are going to expect everyone to ignore the vote they cast on the most impor-tant issue this country has had to deal with in 40 years." But within a year, public memories of the Persian Gulf war had faded. The news media turned its attention to domestic problems. The economy was languishing. The deficit was burgeoning. Success in foreign affairs had come too early, too quickly, and too easily to propel President Bush into a second term.

* Senator John Glenn of Ohio, as quoted in Jill Zuckman, "In Congress, Big Majority Isn't Voting for Invasion," *Boston Globe,* May 18, 1994, 7.

SOURCES: James Baker III with Thomas M. DeFrank, *The Politics of Diplomacy: Revolution, War, and Peace, 1989–1992* (New York: G. P. Putnam & Sons, 1995); "Parties Split into Postwar Camps after Giving Victory Cheer," *Congressional Quarterly,* Vol. 49, March 9, 1991, 611. *New York Times,* January 4, 1991, 1. *Washington Post,* December 7, 1990, A25.

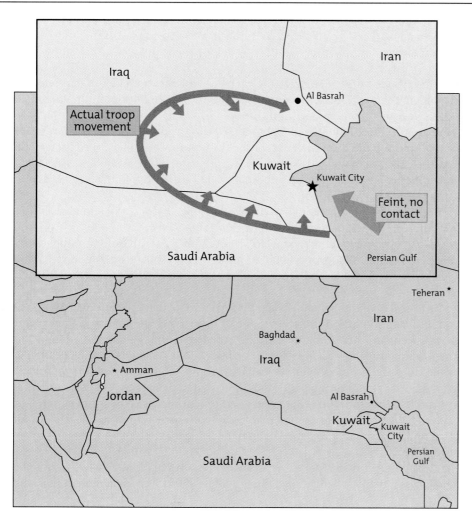

FIGURE 20.1

Persian Gulf During the Hostage Crisis and Gulf War Periods

VOTERS FOCUS ON PRESIDENTS

Wildavksy points out that voters "expect the president to act in foreign affairs and reward him with their confidence."[4] In the early days of a crisis, voters generally ignore those who criticize presidential actions. When Edward Kennedy ran against Carter for the Democratic nomination during the first months of the hostage crisis, he made little political headway. When members of Congress criticized President Bush for issuing an ultimatum to the Iraqis, they ran the risk of seeming unpatriotic.

■ **"rally 'round the flag"**
The tendency among the public to back presidents in moments of crisis.

The tendency among the public to back presidents in moments of crisis, often called the **"rally 'round the flag"** effect, shows up in opinion polls in almost every instance when the United States becomes involved in a foreign policy emergency.[5] Support for the president almost always goes up in the first days of a conflict with another nation. Between 1950 and 1992, public support for presidents increased by an average of 8 percentage points in the month after a foreign policy crisis occurred (see Figure 20.2). But if voters support presidents in times of crisis, they nonetheless demand quick results. Though Carter won initial public backing in the first month of the hostage crisis, his popularity later took a nosedive (see Figure 20.3).

The public seems especially ready to hold presidents to account when war breaks out. Entry into both the Korean and Vietnam wars initially received broad public support. But when the wars dragged on, both Harry Truman, in the case of the Korean war, and Lyndon Johnson, in the Vietnam case, lost so much public support they announced they would not run for reelection and the opposition party won the next election.[6]

Not only do voters demand quick results, but they quickly forget victories. Presidents get credit for achievements in the short run, but not in the long run. Unless a foreign policy accomplishment immediately precedes an election, there are few electoral dividends. Voters instead turn to domestic concerns. For example, during the first three years of the Bush presidency, the United States won both the Cold War and the Persian Gulf War. Yet one year later, the voters, deciding that domestic issues were more important, voted Bush out of office (see Election Connection).

As presidents are increasingly exposed to media coverage, the number of crises have increased and grace periods have shortened. With satellite television, the world has become smaller and events move from one phase to another more quickly. Struggles unknown or ignored in the past are now regularly served along with TV dinner. Conflict and suffering in distant lands are now visually evident and often intensely personal.

Bush sent troops to Somalia to end internal warfare that was causing mass starvation. Explanation for public acceptance of the policy, said foreign policy expert George Kennan, "lies primarily with the exposure of the Somalia situation by the American media, above all, television. . . . The [public] reaction was . . . occasioned by the sight of the suffering of the starving people."[7] Similarly, President Clinton felt responsible for resolving political disorder that was causing widespread suffering in Haiti. He sent in troops to enforce a settlement mediated by former President Carter. In the words of one commentator, decisions such as these are "less the result of a rational weighing of need or what is remediable than it is of what gets on nightly news shows."[8]

At the same time that pressure to intervene has risen, presidents seem not to be enjoying as much of a benefit from doing so. President Clinton has not received the

Bill Clinton did not seek congressional approval for deploying troops to Bosnia, leading some to call the War Powers Resolution a "dead letter." Here, a U.S. Army soldier hands out leaflets explaining his mission to a villager near Tuzla Air Base.

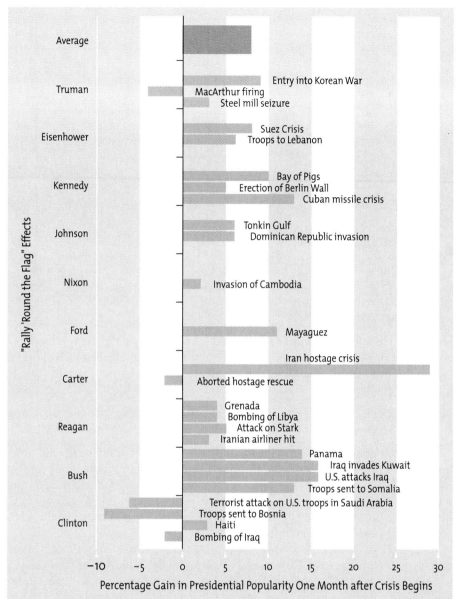

FIGURE 20.2

"Rally 'Round the Flag" Effects

Presidents' gains in popularity average 8 percentage points.

"Rally 'Round the Flag" Effects (y-axis label)

Percentage Gain in Presidential Popularity One Month after Crisis Begins (x-axis label)

Chart categories and events:

Average

Truman — Entry into Korean War; MacArthur firing; Steel mill seizure

Eisenhower — Suez Crisis; Troops to Lebanon

Kennedy — Bay of Pigs; Erection of Berlin Wall; Cuban missile crisis

Johnson — Tonkin Gulf; Dominican Republic invasion

Nixon — Invasion of Cambodia

Ford — Mayaguez

Carter — Iran hostage crisis; Aborted hostage rescue

Reagan — Grenada; Bombing of Libya; Attack on Stark; Iranian airliner hit

Bush — Panama; Iraq invades Kuwait; U.S. attacks Iraq; Troops sent to Somalia

Clinton — Terrorist attack on U.S. troops in Saudi Arabia; Troops sent to Bosnia; Haiti; Bombing of Iraq

same "rally 'round the flag" boost enjoyed by his predecessors. For the four major foreign policy crises of the first Clinton Administration—Saudi Arabia, Haiti, Bosnia, and Iraq—Clinton's popularity averaged a downward shift of an average of three points (instead of a gain of eight).

Not only do voters seem increasingly reluctant to rally around the flag, but they now seem to expect results within a year after the United States becomes deeply involved in a crisis. They become especially unhappy if U.S. soldiers are dying in foreign fields for more than a year without any "light at the end of the tunnel." When President Clinton kept soldiers in Somalia for more than a year, the death of just eighteen soldiers cost the president public support, and U.S. troops were withdrawn shortly thereafter. When President Clinton sent troops to Bosnia in 1995, he

FIGURE 20.3

Shifts in Carter Popularity During
the Hostage Crisis

SOURCE: Michael Nelson, ed.,
*Congressional Quarterly Guide to
the Presidency, 1989* (Washington,
DC: Congressional Quarterly
Inc.), 1471.

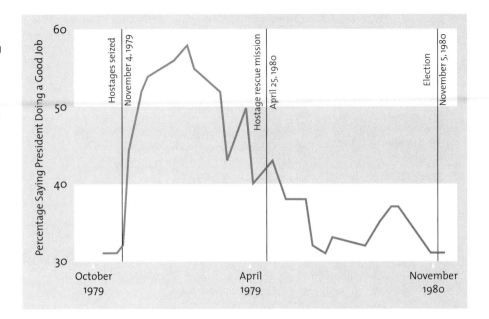

promised to remove them within a year, a date conveniently set just beyond the date of the next presidential election. Immediately after his reelection, Clinton, no longer under as much electoral pressure, announced the troops would have to remain for another year.

LIMITED ROLE OF INTEREST GROUPS

Wildavksy points out that, on foreign policy questions, "the interest group structure is weak, unstable, and thin."[9] The most important group influencing foreign affairs is the Council on Foreign Relations, a prestigious group that includes former secretaries of state, former ambassadors, foreign policy experts, and prominent business leaders. But the organization influences government action by the quality of its advice, not by its ability to mobilize votes.

On some occasions, organized groups capable of mobilizing large numbers of voters play a role in foreign policy issues. For example, the hundreds of thousands of people living in Florida whose families fled Cuba in the 1950s when communist leader Fidel Castro came to power have persuaded the U.S. government not to recognize the legitimacy of the Castro regime for forty years, despite the fact that nearly every other country now does. By directly appealing to their foreign policy concerns, President Clinton won enough Cuban votes to win the state of Florida in 1996.

Middle East policies are also shaped by group pressures. James Baker, Bush's secretary of state, has observed that the conflict between Israel and Palestine is "a perpetual fixture of domestic politics" due to "the political power of the American Jewish community."[10] Because a strong domestic constituency is vitally interested, Congress regularly becomes actively engaged. With strong support in Congress, Israel receives 20 percent of all U.S. foreign aid.[11] But although U.S. Middle East policies are, in the words of one former State Department official, influenced by "what we can get through [Capitol] Hill,"[12] they are also shaped by the country's interest in protecting access to oil reserves located in Arab countries. As a result, U.S. support for Israel seldom is as complete as Jewish organizations prefer, and relations between the United States and Israel are often tense and uneasy.

But these examples are "exceptions that prove the rule." Most nationality groups are not large enough or concentrated enough or sufficiently attentive to events overseas to have a decisive effect on U.S. foreign policy. Civil rights groups have long taken an interest in race relations in South Africa, but they have never been as effective at mobilizing supporters for the South African cause as for domestic issues.

CONGRESSIONAL ROLE

Wildavsky argues that members of Congress follow a "self-denying ordinance. They do not think it is their job to determine the nation's defense policies."[13] Wildavksy's observations were particularly correct for the early 1960s. At that time Congress was only a peripheral participant in the making of foreign policy, in part because it had done so little to prepare the country for World War II. Just four months before the Japanese attacked Hawaii's Pearl Harbor, a bill requiring young men to register for service in the armed forces passed the House of Representatives by only a single vote. After the war, Congress, realizing its earlier mistakes, let many foreign policy decisions be made by the executive. Writing at the time, political scientist Samuel Huntington concluded that "strategic programs are determined in the executive rather than the Congress," adding "just as power to legislate strategic programs was at one time, at least in theory, shared by [the] President and Congress, so it is now, very much in practice, shared by the President and a variety of agencies within the executive branch."[14] A few years later, Robert Dahl reached the same conclusion: "The President proposes, the Congress disposes. . . . [But] in a very large number of highly important decisions about foreign policy, the Congress does not even have the opportunity to dispose."[15]

After the Vietnam War, Congress played a more assertive foreign policy role, as conflict between the branches intensified.[16] For example, Congress began to cut the defense requests of Republican presidents by an average of 5 percent (see Figure 20.4). Congress also called for more strenuous efforts to secure arms reduction agreements with the Soviet Union. Congressional leaders even opposed the use of force against Iraq in the Persian Gulf War, though a majority of Congress eventually backed the president.

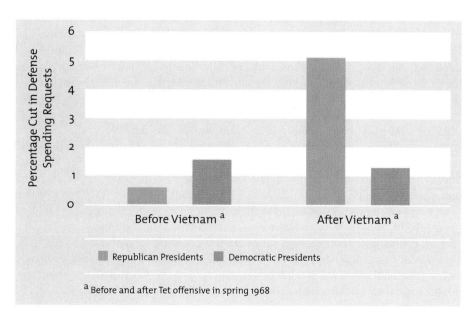

FIGURE 20.4

Growing Partisanship: After Vietnam, Democratic Congresses Cut Republican Presidential Defense Spending Requests, 1947–1991.

SOURCE: Ralph Carter, "Budgeting for Defense" in Paul E. Peterson, ed., *The President, the Congress, and the Making of Foreign Policy* (Norman, OK: Oklahoma University Press, 1993): 165.

The great victory in the Persian Gulf has erased some of the bad memories from the Vietnam War and helped boost the prestige of the executive. In recent years, Congress has begun to defer somewhat more to the president on foreign policy questions. For example, it acquiesced to the placement of troops in Somalia under Bush and in Bosnia under Clinton.[17]

Constitutional Responsibilities of President and Congress

WAR POWER

CONSTITUTION, ARTICLE 1, SECTION 8: *The Congress shall have power to ... declare war, ... raise and support armies, ... provide and maintain a navy, ... [and] make rules for the government and regulation of the land and naval forces.*

CONSTITUTION, ARTICLE 2, SECTION 2: *The President shall be commander in chief of the army and navy.*

CONSTITUTION, ARTICLE 2, SECTION 1: *The executive power shall be vested in a President of the United States.*

"Of all the concerns of government," wrote Alexander Hamilton, "the direction of war most peculiarly demands the exercise of power by a single hand."[18] Yet the Constitution gives to Congress the authority to declare war and to raise and maintain the armed forces. The president's constitutional powers are less clearly defined, the Constitution saying only that the president is commander in chief and exercises executive power. John Marshall interpreted these powers broadly: "The President is the sole organ of the nation in its external relations, and its sole representative with foreign nations."[19] But Thaddeus Stevens, the great defender of congressional prerogatives, proclaimed that "though the president is commander-in-chief, Congress is his commander, and God willing, he shall obey."[20] The issue has been debated ever since.

Prior to the Civil War, presidents seldom acted on their own on military matters. President James Madison refused to attack Great Britain in 1812 until Congress had declared war. And in 1846, President Polk, though he provoked war by placing troops in disputed territory, did not actually order troops into battle against Mexico until Congress had declared war.

Faced with a national emergency, Abraham Lincoln was the first to give an expanded interpretation of the role of commander in chief. When the southern states seceded from the Union, Lincoln proclaimed a blockade of southern ports and enlisted 300 thousand volunteers before Congress had convened. A few decades later, Theodore Roosevelt further expanded the role of commander in chief by exercising executive powers in a much less urgent situation. He sent naval ships to Japan even when Congress refused to appropriate enough money for the trip. He said that the president, in his role as commander in chief, would send the ships. Congress, if it wished, could appropriate enough funds to get them back. Congress did.

Presidents ever since have felt free to initiate military action even in the absence of congressional approval. President Truman fought the Korean War without any congressional declaration whatsoever. More recently, President Bush ordered troops into Somalia and President Clinton ordered troops into Bosnia without securing congressional approval.

Two major Supreme Court decisions have set forth the parameters within which presidents exercise their authority as commander in chief. In 1936, the court was asked, in **U.S. v. Curtiss-Wright**, whether Congress could delegate to the president the power to determine whether arms could be sold to Bolivia and Paraguay, countries engaged in a border dispute. In his decision in favor of presidential power, Justice George Sutherland said that the authority of the presidents on foreign policy questions was greater than their authority on domestic issues. Sutherland referred to "the very delicate, plenary and exclusive power of the president as the sole organ of the federal government in the field of international relations." He went on to say that the President had "a degree of discretion and freedom from statutory restriction which would not be admissible were domestic affairs alone involved."[21]

Curtiss-Wright was qualified by the 1951 **Youngstown** case, in which the Supreme Court placed limits on the executive power of the president. Trade unions in the steel industry had gone on strike during the Korean War. President Truman used his executive power to order the strikers back to work, ignoring procedures for handling strikes recently approved by Congress. When the steel companies disputed Truman's claim to have executive power in this case, the Supreme Court ruled against the president, saying he should have instead observed congressionally defined procedures. Justice Jackson wrote that when a president "takes measures incompatible with the expressed or implied will of Congress, his power is at its lowest ebb."[22]

When the *Curtiss-Wright* and *Youngstown* cases are considered together, the Court seems to have said that presidents have more constitutional discretion with respect to foreign than domestic questions. However, presidents may not act contrary to the will of Congress.[23]

WAR POWERS RESOLUTION

The issue of executive authority arose again during the Vietnam War. Both Presidents Eisenhower and Kennedy had sent soldiers to Vietnam to serve as "advisors" to the South Vietnamese army without explicit congressional authorization. As the war intensified, U.S. military personnel became ever more directly involved. Then, in the summer of 1965, North Vietnam attacked several U.S. ships sailing in Tonkin Bay off the coast of Haiphong, Vietnam's second largest city. President Johnson denounced the action as an unlawful attack on U.S. ships sailing in international waters. He asked Congress for a resolution authorizing the president to respond with armed force. Congress passed the **Tonkin Gulf Resolution**, which gave the president the authority to send troops to Vietnam. The resolution became the legal basis for a war that would last for eight more years. Only much later was it revealed that Johnson had misled Congress by inaccurately claiming that the U.S. had avoided North Vietnam's territorial waters.

To prevent future usurpation of congressional prerogatives, Congress in 1973 passed, over President Ford's veto, the **War Powers Resolution**, which required that the president formally notify Congress any time he orders U.S. troops into military action. If the president makes no report, Congress may itself take notice that U.S. troops are engaged in combat. The resolution further specifies that troops must be withdrawn unless Congress approves the presidential decision within sixty days after Congress has been formally notified or itself taken formal notice by passing a resolution.

Other than George Bush, who asked for congressional authorization of the Persian Gulf War, no president has asked for congressional authorization for military action.

U.S. v. Curtiss-Wright
Supreme court decision in which Congress is given the authority to delegate foreign policy responsibilities to the president.

Youngstown
Case in which the Supreme Court placed limits on the executive power of the president.

Tonkin Gulf Resolution
Congressional resolution giving the president the authority to send troops to Vietnam.

War Powers Resolution
1973 congressional resolution requiring the president to formally notify Congress any time he orders U.S. troops into military action.

Ten years before U.S. troops would leave Vietnam, U.S. military advisors were slowly becoming involved in the fight against communism in Southeast Asia.

President Reagan invaded Grenada, bombed Libya, and placed military troops in Lebanon without notifying Congress. President Bush attacked Panama and moved troops into Somalia. President Clinton bombed Iraq and deployed troops in Bosnia without reference to the War Powers Resolution.

Some analysts believe that presidential refusal to notify Congress of military engagements has made the War Powers Resolution a dead letter without any constitutional significance. But other analysts have pointed out that Congress can, by majority vote, take formal notice of any military engagement, and once it has done so, the sixty-day clock begins to tick, after which troops must be withdrawn. Congress itself has never been willing to challenge presidential refusal to invoke the War Powers Resolution by itself taking formal notice. Until such a direct conflict takes place between the president and Congress, the exact significance of the War Powers Resolution will remain unclear.

TREATY POWER

CONSTITUTION, ARTICLE II, SECTION 2: *The President shall have power, by and with the advice and consent of the Senate, to make treaties, provided two-thirds of the Senators present concur.*

■ **treaties**
Official agreements with foreign countries that are ratified by the Senate.

The power of the president to negotiate **treaties**, official agreements with foreign countries that are ratified by the Senate, is the most circumscribed of all presidential powers. A treaty does not take effect until it wins approval by a two-thirds Senate vote. Since this super-majority can be difficult to achieve, unless a treaty has overwhelming public support, presidents have often felt fettered by senatorial pressures when negotiating with foreign countries. Prior to 1928, the Senate rejected or withheld approval of 14 percent of the treaties presidents had negotiated.[24]

No president was more frustrated than Woodrow Wilson by this constitutional check on presidential power. When negotiating the Versailles treaty that ended World War I, President Wilson pursued one objective above all others: the establishment of a **League of Nations**, an international organization created to settle international disputes, which became the precursor to the United Nations. Wilson felt that such an organization was essential if future world wars were to be avoided.

■ **League of Nations**
International organization created after World War I to settle international disputes; became the precursor of the United Nations.

Wilson's ideas were accepted by the other nations at the Versailles conference and had considerable public support. But the Senate voted down the treaty, primarily on the grounds that the League of Nations would undermine U.S. sovereignty. The United States, alone among the countries who had fought in the war, did not add its signature to the document and remained outside the League of Nations. Shocked and dismayed, Wilson lost both his political efficacy and his personal health.

A half century later, President Carter faced similar difficulties with Congress. In 1977, the president signed the Strategic Arms Limitation Treaty II (SALT II) with the Soviet Union, which halted the development and deployment of a broad range of nuclear arms. The agreement had broad public support and was backed by a majority of the Senate. Yet opposition exceeded the one-third-plus-one needed under the Constitution to prevent the ratification of the agreement. So the United States and the Soviet Union informally agreed to abide by the treaty, though officially none existed.

The ability of a third-plus-one of the Senate to block treaties eventually induced presidents to negotiate **executive agreements**, legal contracts with foreign countries that require only a presidential signature. Though nothing in the Constitution explicitly gives the president the power to sign executive agreements, the practice is long established. The first executive agreement—limiting the size of both countries' naval forces on the Great Lakes—was signed by President James Monroe with Great Britain in 1817. In 1937, the Supreme Court affirmed the constitutionality of executive agreements.[25] Since that decision, presidents have increasingly relied upon executive agreement as a vehicle for negotiating with other nations. Favorite topics for executive agreements include routine matters such as trade and tax questions. But executive agreements can also be used to implement major foreign policy decisions. For example, President Bush relied upon executive agreements to coordinate with other countries the sending of troops to suppress ethnic conflict in Somalia.[26] In recent years, ten executive agreements have been signed for every treaty submitted to the Senate for its approval (see Figure 20.5).

executive agreement
Agreement with foreign countries that requires only a presidential signature.

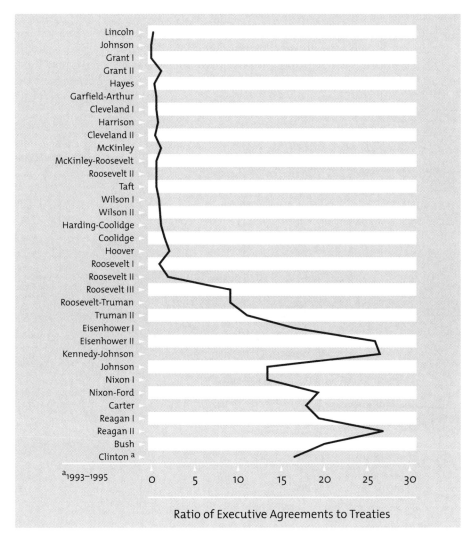

FIGURE 20.5

Growing Presidential Power: Executive Agreements are Replacing Treaties

SOURCES: Gary King and Lyn Ragsdale, *The Elusive Executive: Discovering Statistical Patterns in the Presidency* (Washington, DC: CQ Press, 1988): 131–140; U.S. Bureau of the Census, *Statistical Abstracts* (U.S. Government Printing Office, 1996), Table 1294, 792; FAX from Randall J. Snyder, Law Librarian, Office of the Legal Advisor, Department of State, Washington, DC, December 1996.

Ratio of Executive Agreements to Treaties

The Foreign Policy Government

Cold War

The forty-three-year period (1946–1989) during which the United States and the Soviet Union threatened one another with mutual destruction by nuclear warfare.

iron curtain

Armed barrier during Cold War that prevented movement across national borders between communist East Europe and democratic West Europe.

The country's greatest foreign policy challenge came with the beginning of the **Cold War,** a forty-three-year period (1946–1989) during which the United States and the Soviet Union threatened one another with mutual destruction by nuclear warfare. A few months after the end of World War II, the armed forces of the Soviet Union occupied Eastern Europe and parts of the Korean peninsula, imposing communist rule on half the globe. By 1949, a communist army with Soviet backing seized power in China. Germany was divided into eastern and western parts and Korea was carved into a North and South, one half of each country under western influence, the other within the communist domain. Armed barriers preventing movement across national borders that became known as the **iron curtain** divided Europe into East and West (see Figure 20.6). The term was coined in 1946 by British Prime Minister Winston Churchill, when he said "From Stettin in the Baltic to Trieste in the Adriatic an iron curtain has descended across the Continent."[27] Eventually, a huge concrete wall would be built through the middle of Berlin, dramatically symbolizing the division of the world into its communist and western parts.

The Cold War began at a time when the prestige of the executive branch had been greatly enhanced by its successful prosecution of World War II. As a result, President Truman was able to mobilize bipartisan support for his foreign policy and to recruit to key positions the most talented group of foreign policy advisors the

FIGURE **20.6**

Spread of Communism after World War II

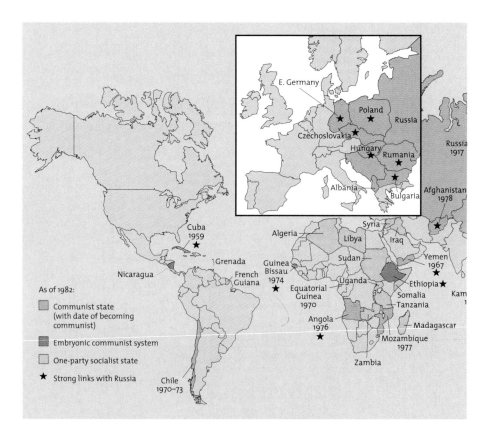

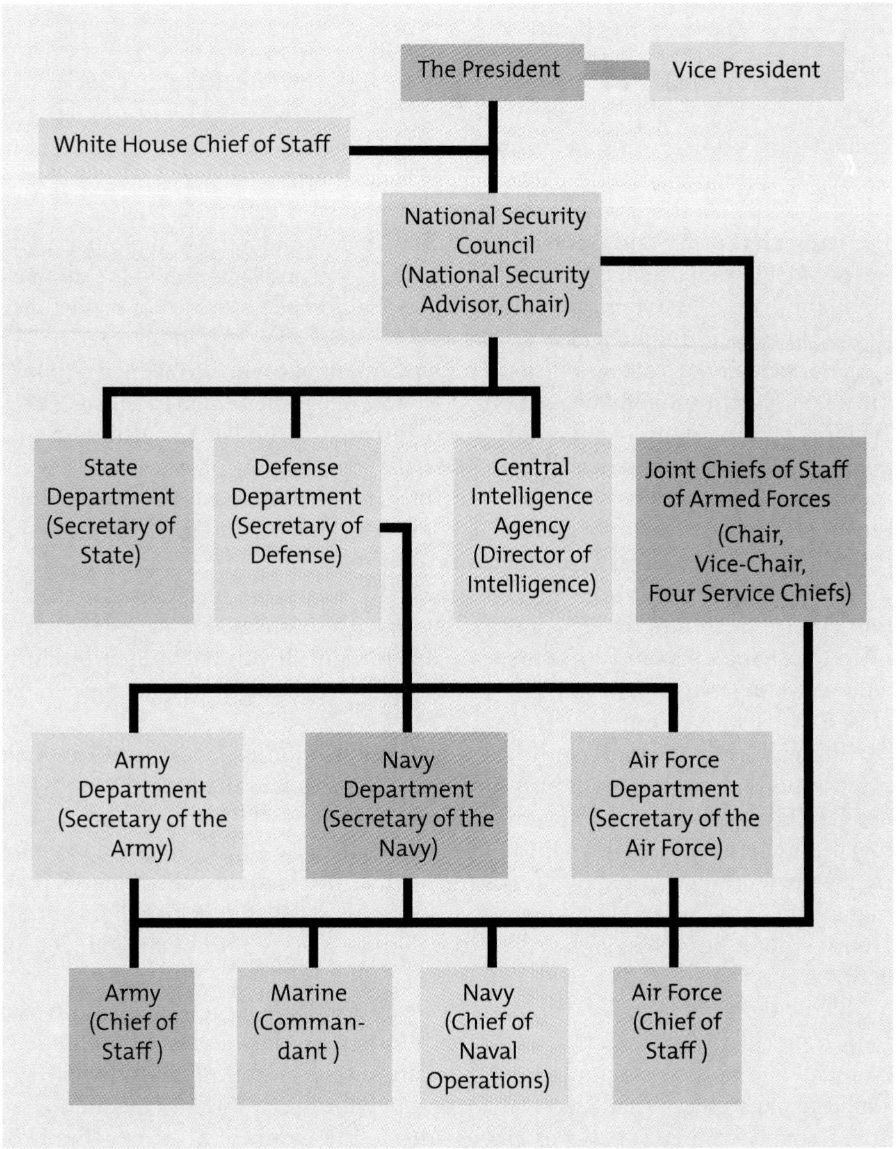

FIGURE 20.7

The Foreign Policy Institutions

```
The President ──── Vice President

White House Chief of Staff ──┐
                             │
              National Security
              Council
              (National Security
              Advisor, Chair)
```

State Department (Secretary of State)	Defense Department (Secretary of Defense)	Central Intelligence Agency (Director of Intelligence)	Joint Chiefs of Staff of Armed Forces (Chair, Vice-Chair, Four Service Chiefs)

Army Department (Secretary of the Army)	Navy Department (Secretary of the Navy)	Air Force Department (Secretary of the Air Force)

Army (Chief of Staff)	Marine (Commandant)	Navy (Chief of Naval Operations)	Air Force (Chief of Staff)

country had ever assembled. They designed a policy of **containment**, a policy that attempted to stop the spread of communism in the expectation that this system of government would eventually collapse on its own. The policy, designed by George Kennan, a brilliant state department specialist, won bipartisan support.[28] Though it took fifty years, containment proved successful. Unrest began in the communist-dominated countries of East Europe during the 1980s and it spread to the Soviet Union by the end of the decade. When the Berlin wall was torn down by demonstrators in 1989, the Cold War finally came to an end. Truman's top policy advisors also established or modernized most of the critical institutions that are today responsible for foreign policy, including the modern State Department, the Defense Department, the Central Intelligence Agency, and the office of the National Security Advisor, the organizations discussed in this section (see Figure 20.7).

containment
U.S. policy that attempted to stop the spread of communism in the expectation that this system of government would eventually collapse on its own.

STATE DEPARTMENT

The **secretary of state** is officially the president's chief foreign policy advisor. In most administrations, the secretary of state is also the nation's chief diplomat. For example, the secretary of state during the first term of the Clinton administration, Warren Christopher, played a major role in negotiating a peace agreement between Israel and the Palestinians. The job of chief diplomat is extremely challenging. As former Secretary of State George Marshall once commented, "In diplomacy, you never can tell what a man is thinking. He smiles at you and kicks you in the stomach at the same time."[29] Or as one pundit put it, "Diplomacy is the art of saying 'nice doggie' until you can find a rock."[30]

The secretary of state also heads the Department of State, the agency responsible for conducting diplomatic relations. The state department is often called "Foggy Bottom" because of its location near the foggy banks of the Potomac River. (Some people think the name especially apt, given the foggy quality of many state department memos.) Reporting to the secretary of state are **ambassadors**, who head the diplomatic delegations to major foreign countries. Ambassadors are responsible for the management of major U.S. **embassies** abroad, which house diplomatic delegations in the capital cities of foreign countries. Consulates are maintained in important cities that are not foreign capitals. If you wish to travel abroad, you will first need to obtain a passport from the state department. If you encounter difficulty while traveling in a foreign country, your first phone call might well be made to the closest embassy or consulate.

Although embassies and consulates help American tourists and businesses, their most important political responsibility is to report back to the State Department detailed information on the government and politics as well as the economic and social conditions of the host country. The ambassador also conveys to the host country the views of the United States government, as instructed by the State Department. The job of an ambassador requires special skills. As the British diplomat Sir Henry Wotton put it "an ambassador is an honest man sent to lie abroad" for his country.[31]

Before the Cold War, U.S. embassies were as important for rewarding those who helped presidents win election as for the information they collected on the host country. The most prestigious ambassadorships were given to long-time political supporters who had raised large sums of money for the president's election. The grandest appointment of all was ambassador to the Court of St. James, the U.S. Embassy in London. The holder of this distinguished position could be expected to be invited to the most elegant of the Queen's official gatherings.

Appointments to the Court of St. James often went to truly worthy public figures who happened also to be loyal partisans. But many other ambassadorial and diplomatic positions were handed out to individuals with considerably less diplomatic skill. As one historian put it, "Most diplomats earned their appointments through party affiliation, personal wealth, or social position, seldom through training. Many lacked knowledge; some lacked dignity, although few were as tactless as John Randolph, who allegedly commented, when presented to the Czar in 1830, 'Howaya Emperor? And how's the madam?'"[32] Even today, some ambassadorial positions remain frankly political. President Clinton named an early political supporter with no diplomatic experience ambassador to the Vatican, and he appointed as ambassador to Ireland the sister of influential Senator Edward Kennedy, despite the fact that she had little foreign policy experience.

But patronage today is more the exception than the rule. Those appointed to less prestigious diplomatic positions are almost always trained career officers who have more familiarity with the language and customs of the host country. Ever since the 1920s they have been organized into a **foreign service**, which consists of the diplomats who staff U.S. embassies and consulates. But it would take decades before the foreign service would become a predominantly professional organization.

Important steps in this direction were taken as part of the effort to fight the Cold War. George Marshall delegated administrative responsibilities to his undersecretary of state, Dean Acheson, a career officer who strengthened the department's professional competence and elan. A reporter at the time declared: "For the first time in the memory of living man, the American foreign office comes somewhere near being adequate to the needs of the country."[33]

Madeleine Albright greets staffers on the day she took office as the country's first female secretary of state.

■ **foreign service**
Diplomats who staff U.S. embassies and consulates.

The State Department and the foreign service are today key, if rather stodgy, components of the foreign policy system. Diplomatic service tends to place a higher premium on etiquette than imagination. Historian Arthur Schlesinger once wrote: "At times it almost looked as if the [Foreign] Service inducted a collection of spirited young Americans at the age of 25 and transmuted them in 20 years into bland . . . denizens of a conservative men's club."[34] Schlesinger's suggestion that the foreign service tended to be a men's club was on target, for as recently as 1995 only about one-quarter of foreign service positions were held by women.[35] With the appointment by William Clinton of Madeleine Albright as the country's first female secretary of state, one may see more changes in the gender composition of the state department.

DEFENSE DEPARTMENT

At the close of World War II, the Army and Navy were two separate departments, each with its own air force and each with its own seat in the president's cabinet. With the beginning of the Cold War, it soon became clear that the armed forces needed to be reorganized because, for the first time in its history, the United States would have in peacetime a large standing army. To better coordinate civilian control of the armed forces, the 1947 National Security Act created a single **Department of Defense** that contained within it the Departments of Army, Navy, and Air Force, each with their own civilian secretary appointed by the president, thereby providing for civilian control of the military. The secretaries for the Army and the Air Force are each responsible for their respective branch of the armed services. The secretary of the Navy is responsible for both the naval forces and the marines. All three secretaries report to the **secretary of defense**, the president's chief civilian advisor on defense matters and overall head of all three departments, army, navy, and air force.

■ **Department of Defense**
Cabinet department responsible for managing U.S. armed forces.

■ **secretary of defense**
President's chief civilian advisor on defense matters and overall head of all three departments, army, navy, and air force.

In addition to the civilian leadership provided by the secretary of defense and the other three secretaries, the armed forces are headed by military professionals. At one time, each armed force acted more or less independently of the other; before World War II, for example, both the army and navy had their own air force. To achieve better coordination, Congress, building on wartime experience, formally created a **Joint Chiefs of Staff** in 1947. The Joint Chiefs consist of the heads of each military service—the army, navy, air force, and marine corps—together with a chair and vice-chair nominated by the president and confirmed by the Senate. Its establishment was explained to Congress by the first chair, Omar Bradley, as necessary to achieve a unified, effective military force: "Our military forces are one team—in the game to win regardless of who carries the ball. This is no time for 'fancy dans' who won't hit the line with all they have on every play, unless they can call the signals."[36]

Despite the unification of the services, each has retained its own identity and each reports to its own civilian secretary. Each has its favorite, big-ticket weapon systems for which it seeks funding from the president and the Congress. The navy thinks it needs more aircraft carriers and nuclear submarines; the air force wants quieter bombers and missiles; and the army demands more sophisticated tanks. To help persuade president and Congress to fund the project, each department enlists the support of retired army personnel as well as prospective defense contractors. So persistent were these demands during the Cold War, Representative Pat Schroeder once exclaimed: "However useless a defense contract, however premature its implementation, however extravagant its cost, an argument to proceed is deemed conclusive [by the armed services] on one of two grounds; either the Russians are doing it so we must do it to avoid falling behind, or the Russians are not doing it and therefore we must do it to stay ahead."[37]

Rivalries among the armed services have been so intense that it took decades to achieve what Omar Bradley promised in 1949, but eventually a unified command structure was created in each of the major operating theaters of the world. This unified structure proved extraordinarily effective during the Persian Gulf War when General Schwarzkopf, an army general, directly controlled the actions of not only the army but also those of the navy, air force, and marines, achieving one of the most coordinated military attacks the United States has ever mounted.

The success of the armed forces during the Persian Gulf War helped dispel the memory of Vietnam, one of the country's worst foreign policy disasters. For years presidents declared victory in Vietnam was around the corner. Indeed, President Kennedy gave an optimistic account eleven years before U.S. troops left Vietnam: "We don't see the end of the tunnel, but I must say I don't think it is darker than it was a year ago, and in some ways lighter."[38] Nearly 58 thousand soldiers were killed in combat. It was in Vietnam that television, modern communication, and election pressures began to play a new role in shaping U.S. foreign policy. Vietnamese deaths made for ghastly television visuals and disconcerting headline news (see Chapter 9, pp. 263–265.) When defeat came, it came close to being complete. The South Vietnamese government fell shortly after U.S. forces had been withdrawn. North Vietnam assumed complete control of the country, and the bordering nations of Laos and Cambodia also fell under communist control.

Public support for military engagements declined significantly after the Vietnam War. At the beginning of the Cold War, the United States invested heavily in its armed forces. Throughout the 1950s, approximately 10 percent of the total GNP was devoted to defense expenditures. During the Korean War, the percentage

Joint Chiefs of Staff
Heads of each military service—the army, navy, air force, and marine corps—together with a chair and vice-chair nominated by the president and confirmed by the Senate.

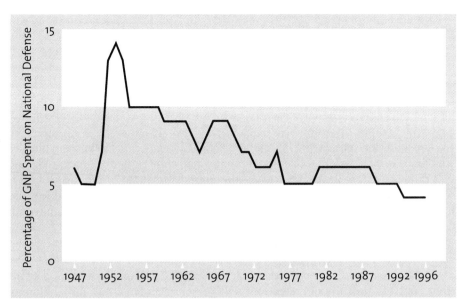

FIGURE 20.8

Defense Expenditures as a
Percentage of GNP, 1945–1996

SOURCES: "Historical Statistics of
the U.S., Colonial Times to 1970,
1971–83," *Statistical Abstract*, 1984;
SA, 1990; 1990–95, SA 1996;
"Historical Statistics of the United
States 1971–1995," *Statistical
Abstract*, 1996.

increased to as high as 14 percent. In response to public pressures, Congress began to cut the defense budget. With the end of the Cold War, defense expenditures have fallen to less than 4 percent of GNP (see Figure 20.8).

CENTRAL INTELLIGENCE AGENCY

"I only regret that I have but one life to lose for my country," said the revolutionary war hero Nathan Hale, after he had been caught spying and was about to be hung by the British. Hale's memory is honored today by a statue at the entrance of the main offices of the **Central Intelligence Agency (CIA)**, the agency primarily responsible for gathering and analyzing information about the political and military activities of other nations. The subject of many a spy novel, it is lovingly referred to as the "Company" or the "Pickle Factory" by members of the intelligence community.[39]

But if spying is an ancient and honorable practice, its organization into an independent agency that reports directly to the president is of fairly recent vintage. The need for better organized intelligence became fully manifest on December 7, 1941, at Pearl Harbor, called a "day of infamy" by President Roosevelt. It was a day of particular disrepute for the intelligence community inasmuch as naval officers at Pearl Harbor were completely unaware that Japan had either the intention or capability of destroying half the U.S. naval force. (The chief naval official in Hawaii had an appointment with the Japanese envoy on that infamous day.)

Haphazard efforts to improve intelligence capabilities were subsequently undertaken, but it was not until the Cold War began that a systematic, centralized system of intelligence was set up. When Congress finally decided to coordinate political and military intelligence, the CIA was made independent of both the Departments of State and Defense. Although State and Defense (as well as other departments) continue to have their own sources of intelligence, the 1947 statute establishing the CIA gave it responsibility both for gathering intelligence and for conducting secret operations abroad at the request of the president.

■ **Central Intelligence Agency (CIA)**
Agency primarily responsible for gathering and analyzing information about the political and military activities of other nations.

It is the authority to conduct clandestine operations that has been the source of the most serious controversies concerning the CIA. Its most notorious covert operation was the ill-fated attempt in 1961 to dislodge communist leader Fidel Castro from Cuba.[40] To overthrow Castro, the CIA helped Cuban exiles plan an invasion on the shores of the **Bay of Pigs** that was expected to foment a popular insurrection. President Kennedy approved the invasion attempt but decided against giving it naval or air support. The effort failed, leaving in doubt the CIA's ability to conduct large-scale military operations.

The following year, Soviet Premier Nikita Khrushchev decided to place missiles with nuclear capability in Cuba. In an intelligence error of the first magnitude, the CIA failed to detect the secret arrival and rapid deployment of the missiles until some had become operational. All of a sudden, John Kennedy had stumbled into the greatest crisis of the Cold War, a potentially lethal nuclear confrontation with the Soviet Union.

Though begun with an intelligence error, the **Cuban missile crisis**—the Soviet effort to place missiles in Cuba—ended with a victory for the United States. The Soviet Union withdrew its missiles under the threat of a naval blockade and an air strike. The triumph all but erased Kennedy's embarrassment at his mishandling of the Bay of Pigs invasion. Only many years later did it become known that Kennedy had secretly agreed to withdraw missiles in Turkey in exchange for Soviet withdrawal of the Cuban missiles. By agreeing to a secret deal, the Soviet Union had accommodated an American president's political need to appear totally victorious.[41] It is not clear whether a secret of this significance could be kept today.

Despite intelligence errors and flawed operations in Cuba and elsewhere, the CIA has become one of the pillars of the foreign policy establishment. It recruited brilliant analysts whose interpretations of Soviet intentions informed U.S. Cold War policy. It recruited as informers people holding high-ranking positions within the Soviet government. It placed spies inside terrorist cells throughout the world. And though the CIA has many critics, it played a crucial role throughout the Cold War.[42] Its main responsibility today is to identify and squelch potential terrorist operations.

NATIONAL SECURITY COUNCIL

Because so many departments and agencies must work together to formulate U.S. foreign policy, the president needs a coordinating mechanism to help resolve differences in viewpoints. The **National Security Council (NSC)**, formed inside the White House in 1947, is responsible for the coordination of U.S. foreign policy. Meetings of the NSC are generally attended by the president, the vice president, the secretary of state, the secretary of defense, the head of the Central Intelligence Agency, the chair of the military Joint Chiefs of Staff, the president's chief of staff, and such other persons as the president designates.[43] The council is assisted by a staff under the direction of the National Security Advisor (NSA). The NSA has often played simply a coordinating role, someone who reconciles interagency disagreements, or, if that proves impossible, reports them to the president. But inasmuch as the NSA has more access to the president than any member of the foreign policy team, the advisor can wield great influence. During the Nixon Administration, National Security Advisor Henry Kissinger became the president's most influential aide, overshadowing the influence of the secretary of state. Clinton's NSAs have played a more modest, coordinating role.

Bay of Pigs
Location of CIA-advised effort by Cuban exiles in 1961 to invade Cuba and overthrow Fidel Castro.

Cuban missile crisis
Soviet effort to place missiles in Cuba in 1962.

National Security Council (NSC)
White House agency responsible for coordinating U.S. foreign policy.

The office of the NSA has not escaped controversy. The most notorious event in which it played a major role has become known as the **Iran-Contra scandal**, an allegedly illegal diversion of funds from an Iranian arms sale to an anti-government group in Nicaragua known as the Contras. The issue was a byproduct of a bitter confrontation between the president and Congress. The Reagan administration, in the words of one foreign policy expert, "came into office believing that [Nicaraguan leaders] were communists, opposed to free elections, and intent on aiding [communist] guerrillas throughout" Central America.[44] To dislodge Nicaraguan leaders from power, Reagan supported the organization and funding of the Contras. However, many members of Congress thought the United States should not become involved in what they perceived to be another Vietnam, and in 1984 Congress passed a law that its author said "clearly ends U.S. support for the war in Nicaragua." At this point, President Reagan privately asked his NSA Robert MacFarlane to "assure the Contras of continuing administration support [and]—to help them hold body and soul together—until the time when Congress would again agree to support them."[45] Telling President Reagan "I certainly hope none of this discussion will be made public in any way," MacFarlane then solicited contributions for the Contras from wealthy individuals and from small, oil-rich countries in the Persian Gulf dependent on U.S. support.[46] MacFarlane and his assistant Oliver North, working with the CIA, arranged the sale of arms. North diverted the profits from the sale to the Contras in Nicaragua.

The issue escalated to a constitutional crisis in 1987 in the Iran-Contra scandal. The diversion of profits seemed to be an illegal attempt to circumvent clear congressional policy to discontinue support for the Contras. Congress held hearings on the scandal and an independent prosecutor was appointed, though no convictions withstood court appeals.

A presidential commission recommended that, in the future, the office of the NSA limit itself to a coordinating role and not involve itself in covert operations. By following these guidelines and playing a lower-profile role, the NSA has since avoided political controversy.

■ **Iran-Contra scandal**
An allegedly illegal diversion of funds from the sale of arms to Iran to a guerrilla group in Nicaragua.

The American Foreign Policy Tradition

The way in which the president and his advisors resolve foreign policy questions is shaped by a long-standing tension that exists between American ideals and the country's practical need to defend itself against foreign aggression. Alexander Hamilton, in the *Federalist Papers*, made the best case for placing the highest priority on the country's practical interests: "No Government [can] give us tranquility and happiness at home, which [does] not possess sufficient stability and strength to make us respectable abroad."[47] The idealist point of view was best expressed by Abraham Lincoln, who reminded his fellow citizens that one purpose of the American experiment was to spread liberty throughout the world. "The Declaration of Independence . . . [gave] liberty, not alone to the people of this country, but hope to the world for all future time."[48]

Under the best of circumstances, as in the waging of World War II, ideals and practical interests were readily combined. But at other times, as we shall see, the United States has been forced to make hard choices.

DEMOCRATIZATION

U.S. foreign policy has not been so naive and innocent that its affirmation of democratic ideals is unconnected to its underlying national interests. The country acquired land and possessions when opportunities were ripe. The United States drove indigenous tribes from their homeland, coming close to committing genocide in the process. It has defended itself against attack and threat of attack by other world powers. But the United States, more than most nations, has expressed its national interest in a language that identifies its cause with that of people throughout the world.

Its idealism is rooted in its revolutionary, anticolonial heritage. The United States is founded not on the racial or ethnic characteristics of its people but on the ideals that inspired the Declaration of Independence and the Bill of Rights. Liberty, democracy, and inalienable rights help define what it is to be an American. So important are these ideals to the country's self-definition they cannot be ignored when framing its relations with other countries.

The **Monroe Doctrine**, declaring the Western Hemisphere to be free of European colonial influence, provides an early example of U.S. identification of its self-interests with worldwide aspirations. Announced in 1823, at a time when European countries were establishing colonies throughout the world, President Monroe declared that "The American continents . . . are henceforth not to be considered as subjects for future colonization by any European power."[49] The Monroe Doctrine was particularly idealistic, because it was enunciated at a time when the United States lacked the military power to make the doctrine effective.

The United States cloaked its relentless expansion to the West in the idealistic language of **manifest destiny**, which said it was inevitable the United States would spread democracy throughout the North American continent. "Our manifest destiny," asserted a newspaper columnist in 1846, "is to overspread the continent allotted by Providence for the free development of our yearly multiplying millions."[50] The phrase at once expressed the country's aspirations for continental domination and its tradition as a haven for refugees from Europe. The liberties to be extended by the American people seemed both to justify a war in 1846 to acquire Mexican territory and to legitimate what was an undeniably ruthless suppression of the indigenous population of the West.

Finally, both world wars were fought in the name of American democracy. When asking his countrymen to enter World War I, President Woodrow Wilson claimed it was necessary because "the world must be made safe for democracy."[51] He promised people that this would be the war to end all wars, but unfortunately, it was not. When World War II broke out, the United States was asked, this time by President Roosevelt, to fight for the four freedoms: "freedom of speech . . . —everywhere in the world; freedom . . . to worship God . . . in his own way—everywhere in the world; freedom from want . . . —everywhere in the world; and freedom from fear . . . —anywhere in the world."[52] All in all, Woodrow Wilson may have been right when he said, "Sometimes people call me an idealist. Well, that is the way I know I am an American. America is the only idealist nation in the world."[53]

ISOLATIONISM

Though American ideals have helped shape and justify the country's foreign policy, it has also been the product of the country's practical self-interests. One of

Monroe Doctrine
Policy that declared the Western Hemisphere to be free of European colonial influence (1819).

manifest destiny
Belief in the inevitability that the United States would spread democracy throughout the North American continent.

The Forgotten War

Most Americans think that Vietnam was the one and only war the country ever lost. But, it is difficult to call the outcome of the War of 1812 against the British anything other than a defeat for the United States. The causes of the war were several. The British navy had been stopping American ships on the high seas and dragooning American sailors into the service of its navy for its war against France. Americans also disputed British claims to land north of the Great Lakes, which contained valuable Canadian timber and fur as well as indigenous tribes, which the United States wanted to push further west. These lands seemed ripe for plucking at a time when the British were fighting the French.

At the prompting of President Madison, Congress in 1812 declared war on the world's greatest naval power. Lacking both an army and a navy, the United States was ill-equipped to fight. On two occasions, states were asked to raise militia for the purpose of invading Canada; both attempts failed. In the meantime, the British burned Washington, D. C., forcing the president and his wife to flee into the Virginia countryside, Dolly Madison loyally lugging along George Washington's portrait. Fortunately for the United States, the British were so pleased at defeating the French that they demanded little in reparation from the United States. Britain simply took for Canada all the disputed land north of the Great Lakes.

---

the oldest ideological positions in American foreign policy is in fact explicitly self-centered. This position is known as **isolationism**, which advocates a foreign policy that keeps the United States separate from the conflicts taking place among other nations. Isolationists often quote a phrase from George Washington's Farewell Address, made when he retired from the presidency: "Tis our true policy to steer clear of permanent alliances, with any portion of the foreign world." [54] Washington meant to say that our alliances should not be permanent, but he was often interpreted as saying that alliances should not be made at all.

For more than a century after Washington made this speech, the United States pursued an essentially isolationist foreign policy. Until airplanes and nuclear-tipped missiles shrank the size of the globe, the United States was, in the words of Winston Churchill, "splendidly isolated." Asian wars took place across the wide Pacific, making them all but irrelevant to U.S. concerns. Even the narrower Atlantic Ocean placed the United States months apart from most European controversies. When the United States did enter a war, it usually emerged successful shortly afterward, seeming to prove that the United States did not need the help of others (see International Comparison). Most Americans conveniently ignore the poor performance of the United States in the War of 1812.

Isolationist sentiments were so widely shared that the United States became involved in World Wars I and II only reluctantly and belatedly. World War I broke out in August 1914, but the United States remained, for over two and one-half years, as "splendidly isolated" from the European tangle as it possibly could. In language reminiscent of George Washington's Farewell Address, Woodrow Wilson initially

> **isolationism**
> A foreign policy that keeps the United States separate from the conflicts taking place among other nations.

solationist sentiments have been fed by the country's wartime successes, which have fostered the belief that the United States is invincible. Until the Vietnam War, the United States, after the War of 1812, had a victory record that would make a Superbowl team proud. The Mexican, Spanish-American, and World Wars I and II all ended in overwhelming victories. Few, if any, other world powers have enjoyed such an unbroken string of successes. Japan and Germany can never forget their humiliating defeats in World War II. The French cannot forget the ease with which German troops captured Paris in both 1870 and 1940. The Russians cannot readily dislodge the memory of their defeat by Japan in 1905 or the collapse of their army in 1917. Only the British have nearly as enviable an historical record as the Americans, and even Britain suffered more than one defeat at the hands of the French.

Not only has the United States won its wars, but it has done so quickly. The Mexican War, though spread over three years, consisted of three short and decisive campaigns. The Spanish-American war was over in eight months. Even U.S. involvement in the two world wars was of relatively short duration. Within six months of the arrival of U.S. troops in Europe, an armistice brought World War I to an end. The pattern was not altogether different in World War II. Little more than a year after U.S. troops landed in Normandy, Germany was defeated. Japan struggled for an additional two months until nuclear bombs dropped over Hiroshima and Nagasaki forced surrender.

American civilians have never suffered significantly from foreign attack. Not since the British burning of Washington, D. C., in 1814 has the mainland of the United States been invaded by foreign troops. Apart from the bombing of Pearl Harbor, the United States has been free of aerial raids. All of the other major powers of the World have suffered enormous civilian casualties and disruptions to their economy. During World War II, German tanks overran Europe and Russia, German airplanes bombed Britain, and U.S. airplanes all but destroyed German and Japanese cities. As the

called for the United States to be "neutral in fact as well as in name. . . . We must be impartial in thought as well as in action."[55] The United States did not declare war until the Germans began torpedoing U.S. commercial ships delivering supplies to Britain.

At the beginning of World War II, the United States once again declared its neutrality. In his campaign for reelection in the fall of 1940, FDR promised American "mothers and fathers" that the country's neutrality would be preserved: "I have said this before, but I shall say it again and again and again: Your boys are not going to be sent into any foreign wars."[56] But soon, after the election, FDR lent arms to the British and began to make preparations for war, declaring "we must be the great arsenal of democracy."[57]

figure below shows, even U.S. troop casualties have been small.

SOURCES: R. Ernest Dupuy and Trevor N. Dupuy, *The Harper Encyclopedia of Military History: From 3500 B.C. to the Present* (New York: Harper Collins Publishers, 1993); Y. Takenob, *The Japan Year Book: 1919–20* (Tokyo: Japan Year Book Office, 1921); B. R. Mitchell, *International Historical Statistics: Europe 1750–1988* (New York: Stockton Press, 1992); B. R. Mitchell, *International Historical Statistics of the Americas: 1750– 1988* (New York: Stockton Press, 1993); B. R. Mitchell, *International Historical Statistics: Africa and Asia* (New York: New York University Press, 1982); Raymond E. Zickel, ed., *Soviet Union: A Country Study* (Washington, DC: U.S. Government Printing Office, 1991).

(Population figures were from the following years: France, 1911, 1936; Germany, 1910, 1939; U.K. (incl. Scotland), 1911, 1931; U.S., 1910, 1940; Russia, 1913 (estimated), 1939; Japan, 1913, 1940.)

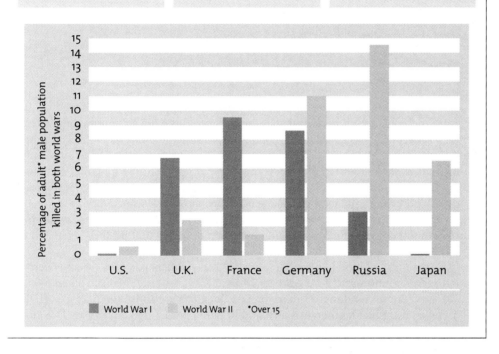

LATIN AMERICA

American foreign policy toward Latin America was also shaped more by the nation's practical self-interests than by its democratic ideals. It is best characterized by Theodore Roosevelt's slogan, "Speak softly but carry a big stick."

As the country gained in industrial strength, it was increasingly capable of putting sharp teeth into the once idealistic Monroe Doctrine. In 1846, President Polk came to the aid of the Texas independence movement by declaring war on Mexico. The war was a complete mismatch between an emerging industrial power and a still technologically backward nation. The United States won easily.

Fifty years later, when the Cubans revolted against a weak Spanish government, President McKinley rallied to the support of the Cubans. Once again, the battle was hardly a contest. The United States had become one of the most powerful industrial countries of the world, while Spain's days of glory had long passed. Teddy Roosevelt won fame in 1898 by leading the "Rough Riders" to victory up San Juan Hill. More importantly, a decisive naval victory in Manila gave the United States new possessions, including Puerto Rico, Guam, and the Philippines.

The United States also repeatedly used military force to impose its will on weaker countries in the Caribbean and Latin America. The most significant case in point occurred when Theodore Roosevelt wanted to build the Panama Canal, which would shorten the distance ships needed to travel between the East Coast and California. The land belonged to Colombia, which resisted Roosevelt's requests to build the Canal. To get around Colombian opposition, President Roosevelt fomented a rebellion by Panamanians living in northern Colombia, then ordered naval ships to support the Panamanian revolt against Colombia. Panama became an independent country and the Canal was dug.

Idealism and Realism in Contemporary Foreign Policy

As long as the Cold war was continuing, U.S. foreign policy was shaped by its commitment to containment. But after the collapse of the Soviet Union, the United States needed to redesign its foreign policy in as fundamental a way as it did in the first years of the Cold War. In the current debate over foreign policy, two competing perspectives draw on different aspects of the American political tradition. Relying upon the sentiments first expressed in the Declaration of Independence, **idealists** say that U.S. foreign policy should be guided primarily by democratic principles—the spread of liberty, equality, human rights, and respect for international law throughout the world. **Realists** say that U.S. foreign policy best protects democracy when it guards its own economic and military strength.

One can find both idealists and realists in each political party and in all government agencies, and some people are idealistic on one issue, yet realistic on another. But some general tendencies seem to exist. Idealists are more likely to associate themselves with the Democratic party, and Republicans tend to be realists. The idealists are more likely to be found in the State Department, the realists in the Defense Department.

The two perspectives provide different assessments of four major foreign policy issues that face the United States: (1) unilateralism versus multi-lateralism; (2) intervention in regional conflicts; (3) policies toward Eastern Europe and the former Soviet Union; and (4) human rights policies.

UNILATERALISM VERSUS MULTILATERALISM

At the end of World War II, the victorious nations agreed to establish the **United Nations (UN)**, an organization of all nation states whose purpose is to preserve world peace and foster economic and social development throughout the world. Though the United Nations has been more successful than its predecessor, the ill-starred League of Nations, idealists and realists within the United States often find themselves at odds concerning the usefulness of the United Nations and other international orga-

idealists
Those who say that U.S. foreign policy should be guided primarily by democratic principles—the spread of liberty, equality, human rights, and respect for international law throughout the world.

realists
Those who say that U.S. foreign policy best protects democracy when it guards its own economic and military strength.

United Nations (UN)
Organization of all nation states whose purpose is to preserve world peace and foster economic and social development throughout the world.

UN peacekeeping force in Somalia.

nizations as vehicles for the conduct of U.S. foreign policy. Idealists recommend that the United States work through the United Nations and other international organizations in order to achieve closer international cooperation. Idealists argue that these goals not only place American foreign policy on a high ethical plane but they are a practical way of defending the interests of the United States. If countries work together in international organizations, they are less likely to engage in warfare.[58] Realists are reluctant to concede to the United Nations or to other international organizations responsibility for the conduct of U.S. policy. Decisions to intervene in world affairs must be predicated not on some vague ideal but on a calculation of the extent to which the United States has a substantial and visible interest at stake.[59]

INTERNATIONAL LEADERSHIP VERSUS ISOLATIONISM

Although the United States is no longer locked into a Cold War with a powerful adversary, serious disputes among countries continue to develop into military confrontations. For example, the break-up of Yugoslavia at the end of the Cold War has provoked bitter strife among Bosnians, Serbs, and Croatians. Idealists support the Clinton administration's decision to send troops to separate the warring parties in Bosnia. By using whatever force it takes to bring regional conflicts under control, the U.S. keeps them from escalating.

According to realists, the United States should avoid heavy involvement in regional conflicts unless U.S. interests are directly at stake. The United States cannot become the world's police force without stretching its own economic and military resources too far. They opposed Bush's decision to send troops into Somalia, and Clinton's decision to send them to Bosnia. If the United States keeps making these kinds of decisions, the U.S. will eventually find itself bogged down in a regional conflict in which it has little stake, and will earn the enmity of other countries for little practical reason.

POLICIES TOWARD EASTERN EUROPE
AND THE FORMER SOVIET UNION

Idealists favor developing close ties with Russian reformers, who are seeking to establish democratic practices and a market economy. Only if the United States consistently supports Russian reformers, they say, will these reformers be able to manage the difficult transition from a communist to a market economy. These idealists favor U.S. aid and loans to Russia. Realists question whether the United States can influence developments inside Russia. They are concerned that either Communists or authoritarian nationalists could easily gain power. If either faction should become dominant, the Soviet Union might very well use its nuclear arsenal and economic clout to threaten its immediate neighbors. To hem in any aggressive Russian government that might appear in the future, realists think the United States should form close ties with the countries of eastern Europe, the Ukraine, and other former republics of the Soviet Union. If these ties are built now, realists argue, Russia will be more contained, making it more difficult for it to become once again the leading adversary to the United States.

HUMAN RIGHTS

Basic human rights and democratic procedures are regularly violated in many countries throughout the world. The South African government for decades suppressed the antiapartheid movement. The Chinese government suppressed the student demonstrators in Tiananmen Square. The Serbian government practiced a policy of "ethnic cleansing" in Bosnia.

Idealists say that the United States must use its economic and military muscle to promote human rights throughout the world. South Africa is moving away from apartheid and toward the direct involvement of blacks in its governing arrangements only because of prolonged international pressure. South Korea, Taiwan, and other countries in Asia have established more democratic regimes in response to expressed U.S. concerns. So have many countries in Latin America. U.S. support for human rights must be as vigorous after the end of the Cold War as it was when the United States was fighting communism.

Realists recommend that the United States exercise caution before supplementing diplomatic efforts to promote human rights with economic or military pressure. They argue that progress toward democracy is achieved largely through internal political struggle. It can seldom be imposed successfully from abroad. They argue further that violations of human rights and democratic norms are so frequent and widespread that consistent application of an interventionist doctrine would compel constant U.S. involvement in the affairs of other countries (see Democratic Dilemma).

Changing Impact of Foreign Policy on U.S. Elections

Foreign policy issues can effect election outcomes. During the 1980s, a majority of the electorate voted Republican in presidential elections—in part because most voters favored the tougher position toward the Soviet Union taken by Republicans.

Should U.S. Foreign Policy Focus on Promoting Human Rights and Democratic Practices or on Defending U.S. Interests?

Basic human rights and democratic procedures are regularly violated in many countries throughout the world. Particularly egregious violations of human rights are regularly practiced by China's authoritarian government. Since 1950, China has forced many Tibetans, including the revered Dalai Lama, to seek refuge abroad. During the Tiananmen Square massacre of 1989, over 700 student protesters were killed, 10 thousand dissidents were arrested, and 31 leaders were tried and executed. The families of each of those executed received a bill for the cost of the bullet used to kill their kin. Harry Wu, who spent 19 years in a Chinese labor reform camp, has chronicled their dual function: "Politically, they suppress dissidents to reinforce the system of dictatorship, while economically they exploit prisoners to earn foreign exchange for the Chinese Communist regimes."*

Idealists and realists differ in their response to these human rights violations. Idealists argue that the United States should abet the cause of human rights by placing an embargo on Chinese products. In the words of one commentator, "Americans are troubled that their country contributes heavily to oppression. They know that the profits of Chinese goods sold in the United States, and the benefits of American investments, go in substantial part directly to the Chinese Army, policy and politburo."† In part because of China's dismal human rights record, the International Olympic Committee rejected China's bid to host the Summer Games in the Year 2000.

Realists say that trade embargoes would only isolate U.S. businesses from one of the world's largest and fastest growing markets. The best way to foster human rights in China is to tie its economy closely to ours. They claim that when free markets develop, democratization soon follows. Secretary of Commerce Mickey Kantor explained the Clinton doctrine toward China in the following terms: "Not mutually assured destruction and a policy of containment, but mutually assured prosperity and a policy of engagement."‡ Clinton's policies differ little from those of previous presidents: China has enjoyed ready access to U.S. markets since 1980.

* Harry Wu, *Bitter Winds: A Memoir of My Years in China's Gulag* (New York: John Wiley & Sons, 1996): 284.

† A. M. Rosenthal, "What Can I Do," *New York Times*, December 6, 1995, A23.

‡ David Nyhan, "Clinton Wields the Velvet Glove on China," *Boston Globe*, November 29, 1996, A31.

In 1988, Michael Dukakis, the Democratic candidate for president, tried to counter this Republican advantage by trying to convince the voters that he was a strong defense supporter. As part of this strategy, he ran a television ad showing himself riding in a tank. The ad backfired when Republicans convinced the voters that the image was inconsistent with Dukakis's experiences and policy positions.

With the end of the Cold War, Republicans lost some of the political advantages that came from their foreign policy positions. As long as the United States was confronting the nuclear power of the Soviet Union, the public expected the president to

Despite his ride in a General Dynamics tank during the 1988 presidential campaign, Michael Dukakis could not convince voters that he was a strong defense candidate.

be a strong foreign policy leader. As long as the potential for nuclear holocaust hovered in the air, the public wanted a president whose dependability and reliability could not be questioned. But with the end of the Cold War, Americans became more interested in domestic issues. With the collapse of the Soviet Union, it no longer seemed as important as it once did that the president be capable of dealing with foreign aggression. No other country had the military might to attack the United States.

The effect of the end of the Cold War on American politics is best shown by the rapid rise in popularity of Ross Perot, a businessman who had no governmental and very limited foreign policy experience. Had the Soviet Union still been challenging the United States, voters would probably have felt Perot could not be trusted with the awesome responsibility of deciding whether to launch a nuclear attack. His propensity to make outrageous statements, to accuse others of malicious actions, and, in general, to shoot from the hip would have made him seem utterly inappropriate as president. But with the end of the Cold War, economic issues—not issues of global warfare—became paramount. Perot's demands that the United States balance its budget and put its economic house in order captured public attention, and, in 1992, he won nearly 20 percent of the vote, without the support of either major political party.

The Clinton campaign benefited even more from the ending of the Cold War. Had the Soviet Union still been challenging the United States, the voters would probably have been reluctant to vote George Bush out of office. After all, Bush had served as a naval pilot, minister to China, head of the CIA, vice president and president. Having held governmental office almost continuously for over thirty years, he knew every world leader personally. As a Republican, Bush represented the party

Two Generals, Different Decisions

Since the end of the Cold War, it has become more difficult to persuade qualified leaders that their country needs their service. Nothing better illustrates the political change that has occurred than the reactions of two generals, General Dwight D. Eisenhower and General Colin Powell, to the request that they run for president.

Eisenhower had led the country to victory in World War II. Though reluctant to run for public office, he was nonetheless persuaded in 1952 that the country needed his services. The United States was bogged down in the Korean War, and the Soviet Union was rapidly arming itself with nuclear weapons. Eisenhower was persuaded that new, strong leadership was necessary. He won handily after promising that he himself would "go to Korea" to seek a peace.

Forty-four years later, General Colin Powell, who led the country to victory in the Persian Gulf War, was asked by Republican leaders if he would seek the presidency. But except for regional conflicts in Bosnia, Somalia, and the Middle East, there was little in foreign affairs that required new leadership. The campaign issues involved taxes, budget deficits, health care, education, narcotics, and honesty in government. Powell's family members, fearful that he might be the target of an assassination, urged him not to run. Though Powell gave the matter careful thought, he gave family considerations higher priority than public service. Had the nation still been involved in a Cold War, he might well have made the opposite decision.

General Dwight D. Eisenhower.

that had stressed the critical importance of national defense. By comparison, Governor Clinton had never served in the army, had opposed the Vietnam War, and had never been responsible for the conduct of foreign policy. As a Democrat, he could be tainted with the charge that he was not sufficiently protective of American defense needs. It was exactly this contrast in 1988 between Bush and his opponent Michael Dukakis, a governor from a small state who had no wartime service, that made the Dukakis tank advertisement such a devastating campaign miscalculation. Inasmuch as the Soviet Union was still a force with which to be reckoned, the country in 1988 was not willing to entrust an inexperienced Democrat with White House responsibilities. But just four years later, the public mood had changed. Domestic issues were of greater importance. Clinton edged President Bush from office and won reelection in 1996.

Chapter Summary

Electoral considerations alone help account for the fact that presidents dominate policy making on foreign policy questions more than on domestic ones. Voters expect presidents to take the lead. In the short run, they tend to support presidents in crises no matter what action is taken. Only later, if things do not turn out well, do voters penalize presidents for choosing the wrong policy.

Other factors reinforce the presidents' dominant role in foreign policy. Fast action is often needed; interest group pressures are less intense than on domestic issues; the Supreme Court has interpreted the powers of the president broadly; and Congress tends to defer to the executive. However, Congress became more assertive and foreign policy became more partisan in the years following the end of the Vietnam War when it passed the War Powers Resolution, which attempted to place controls on the president's role as Commander in Chief.

The three agencies shaping U.S. foreign policy, the Department of State, Department of Defense, and the Central Intelligence Agency, together with the head of the Joint Chiefs of Staff, all sit on the National Security Council, which is managed by a National Security Advisor responsible to the president for overall foreign policy coordination.

Both idealistic and realistic factors help shape American foreign policy. On the one side, the United States feels responsible for promoting the democratic experiment abroad. On the other hand, the United States, like any other country, has its own interests to protect. Idealist and realist considerations both play a role in current debates over unilateralism versus multilateralism, regional conflicts, policy toward the former Soviet Union, and human rights versus national self-interests.

Key Terms

ambassador, p. 660

Bay of Pigs, p. 664

Central Intelligence Agency (CIA), p. 663

Cold War, p. 658

containment, p. 659

Cuban missile crisis, p. 664

Department of Defense, p. 661

embassy, p. 660

executive agreement, p. 657

foreign policy, p. 647

foreign service, p. 661

idealists, p. 670

Iran-Contra scandal, p. 665

iron curtain, p. 658

isolationism, p. 667

Joint Chiefs of Staff, p. 662

League of Nations, p. 656

manifest destiny, p. 666

Monroe Doctrine, p. 666

National Security Council (NSC), p. 664

"rally 'round the flag," p. 650

realists, p. 670

secretary of defense, p. 661

secretary of state, p. 660

Tonkin Gulf Resolution, p. 655

treaties, p. 656

two-presidency theory, p. 647

United Nations (UN), p. 670

U.S. v. *Curtiss-Wright*, p. 655

War Powers Resolution, p. 655

Youngstown, p. 655

Suggested Readings

Allison, Graham. *Essence of Decision*. Boston: Little Brown, 1971. Fascinating account of the Cuban missile crisis, the closest the United States and the Soviet came to nuclear confrontation.

Baker, James III, with Thomas M. DeFrank. *The Politics of Diplomacy: Revolution, War, and Peace, 1989–1992*. New York: G. P. Putnam & Sons, 1995. Thoughtful reflections of George Bush's secretary of state.

Corwin, Edward S. *Total War and the Constitution*. New York: Knopf, 1947. Classic, if dated, discussion of constitutional arrangements as they affect foreign policy.

Jeffreys–Johnes, Rhodri. *The CIA and American Democracy*. New Haven: Yale University Press, 1989. A solid history of the CIA.

Johnson, Loch K. *America's Secret Power: The CIA in a Democratic Society*. New York: Oxford University Press, 1989. Informed critique of CIA power and tactics.

Huntington, Samuel. *The Clash of Civilizations*. New York: Simon & Schuster, 1996. Argues that future world conflicts will be between clusters of nations that share a common cultural heritage.

Koh, Harold Hungju. *The National Security Constitution: Sharing Power after the Iran-Contra Affair*. New Haven: Yale University Press, 1990. Analyzes the constitutional authority of the president and Congress on matters of foreign policy.

Leffler, Melvyn P. *A Preponderance of Power: National Security, the Truman Administration, and the Cold War*. Stanford, CA: Stanford University Press, 1992. Historical account of the establishment of U.S. Cold War strategy under Truman.

Mann, Thomas E., ed. *A Question of Balance: The President, the Congress and Foreign Policy*. Washington, DC: Brookings, 1990. Essays arguing that too much power over foreign policy has shifted from president to Congress.

Peterson, Paul E., ed. *The President, the Congress, and the Making of Foreign Policy*. Norman, OK: Oklahoma University Press, 1994. Essays describing changes in presidential and congressional policy-making roles.

Silverstein, Gordon. *Imbalance of Powers: Constitutional Interpretation and the Making of American Foreign Policy*. New York: Oxford University Press, 1996. Argues that president's constitutional authority over foreign policy has not been ceded to Congress.

Wildavsky, Aaron. "The Two Presidencies." In Steven A. Shull, ed., *The Two Presidencies: A Quarter Century Assessment*. Chicago: Nelson-Hall, 1991. Pp. 11–25. Explains how politics differs between foreign and domestic issues.

Weissman, Stephen R. *A Culture of Deference: Congress's Failure of Leadership in Foreign Policy*. New York: Basic Books, 1995. Argues that Congress defers too much to presidential authority in foreign affairs.

The Declaration of Independence

In Congress, July 4, 1776
The Unanimous Declaration of the Thirteen United States of America

WHEN IN THE COURSE of human events it becomes necessary for one people to dissolve the political bands which have connected them with another, and to assume, among the powers of the earth, the separate and equal station to which the Laws of Nature and of Nature's God entitle them, a decent respect to the opinions of mankind requires that they should declare the causes which impel them to the separation.

We hold these truths to be self-evident, that all men are created equal, that they are endowed by their Creator with certain unalienable Rights, that among these are Life, Liberty and the pursuit of Happiness. That to secure these rights, Governments are instituted among Men, deriving their just powers from the consent of the governed. That whenever any Form of Government becomes destructive of these ends, it is the Right of the People to alter or to abolish it, and to institute new Government, laying its foundation on such principles and organizing its powers in such form, as to them shall seem most likely to effect their Safety and Happiness. Prudence, indeed, will dictate that Governments long established should not be changed for light and transient causes; and accordingly all experience hath shewn that mankind are more disposed to suffer, while evils are sufferable, than to right themselves by abolishing the forms to which they are accustomed. But when a long train of abuses and usurpations, pursuing invariably the same Object evinces a design to reduce them under absolute Despotism, it is their right, it is their duty, to throw off such Government, and to provide new Guards for their future security. —Such has been the patient sufferance of these Colonies; and such is now the necessity which constrains them to alter their former Systems of Government. The history of the present King of Great Britain is a history of repeated injuries and usurpations, all having in direct object the establishment of an absolute Tyranny over these States. To prove this, let Facts be submitted to a candid world.

He has refused his Assent to Laws, the most wholesome and necessary for the public good.

He has forbidden his Governors to pass Laws of immediate and pressing importance, unless suspended in their operation till his Assent should be obtained; and when so suspended, he has utterly neglected to attend to them.

He has refused to pass other Laws for the accommodation of large districts of people, unless those people would relinquish the right of Representation in the Legislature, a right inestimable to them and formidable to tyrants only.

He has called together legislative bodies at places unusual, uncomfortable, and distant from the depository of their Public Records, for the sole purpose of fatiguing them into compliance with his measures.

He has dissolved Representative Houses repeatedly, for opposing with manly firmness his invasions on the rights of the people.

He has refused for a long time, after such dissolutions, to cause others to be elected; whereby the Legislative Powers, incapable of Annihilation, have returned to the People at large for their exercise, the State remaining in the mean time exposed to all the dangers of invasion from without, and convulsions within.

He has endeavored to prevent the population of these States; for that purpose obstructing the Laws of Naturalization of Foreigners; refusing to pass others to encourage their migration hither, and raising the conditions of new Appropriations of Lands.

He has obstructed the Administration of Justice, by refusing his Assent to Laws for establishing Judiciary powers.

He has made Judges dependent on his Will alone, for the tenure of their offices, and the amount and payment of their salaries.

He has erected a multitude of New Offices, and sent hither swarms of Officers to harass our people, and eat out their substance.

He has kept among us, in times of peace, Standing Armies without the Consent of our legislatures.

He has affected to render the Military independent of and superior to the Civil power.

He has combined with others to subject us to a jurisdiction foreign to our constitution, and unacknowledged by our laws, giving his Assent to their Acts of pretended Legislation:

For quartering large bodies of armed troops among us:

For protecting them, by a mock Trial, from punishment for any Murders which they should commit on the Inhabitants of these States:

For cutting off our Trade with all parts of the world:

For imposing Taxes on us without our Consent:

For depriving us in many cases, of the benefits of Trial by Jury:

For transporting us beyond Seas to be tried for pretended offences:

For abolishing the free System of English Laws in a neighboring Province, establishing therein an Arbitrary government, and enlarging its Boundaries so as to render it at once an example and fit instrument for introducing the same absolute rule into these Colonies:

For taking away our Charters, abolishing our most valuable Laws, and altering fundamentally the Forms of our Governments:

For suspending our own Legislatures, and declaring themselves invested with power to legislate for us in all cases whatsoever.

He has abdicated Government here, by declaring us out of his Protection and waging War against us.

He has plundered our seas, ravaged our Coasts, burnt out towns, and destroyed the lives of our people.

He is at this time transporting large Armies of foreign Mercenaries to compleat the works of death, desolation and tyranny, already begun with circumstances of Cruelty and perfidy scarcely paralleled in the most barbarous ages, and totally unworthy the Head of a civilized nation.

He has constrained our fellow Citizens taken Captive on the high Seas to bear Arms against their Country, to become the executioners of their friends and Brethren, or to fall themselves by their Hands.

He has excited domestic insurrections amongst us, and has endeavored to bring on the inhabitants of our frontiers, the merciless Indian Savages, whose known rule of warfare, is an undistinguished destruction of all ages, sexes and conditions.

In every stage of these Oppressions We have Petitioned for Redress in the most humble terms: Our repeated Petitions have been answered only by repeated injury: A Prince, whose character is thus marked by every act which may define a Tyrant, is unfit to be the ruler of a free people.

Nor have We been wanting in attention to our British brethren. We have warned them from time to time of attempts by their legislature to extend an unwarrantable jurisdiction over us. We have reminded them of the circumstances of our emigration and settlement here. We have appealed to their native justice and magnanimity; and we have conjured them by the ties of our common kindred to disavow these usurpations, which would inevitably interrupt our connections and correspondence. They too have been deaf to the voice of justice and consanguinity. We must, therefore, acquiesce in the necessity, which denounces our Separation, and hold them, as we hold the rest of mankind, Enemies in War, in Peace Friends.

We, therefore, the Representatives of the United States of America, in General Congress, Assembled, appealing to the Supreme Judge of the world for the rectitude of our intentions, do, in the Name, and by Authority of the good People of these Colonies, solemnly publish and declare, That these United Colonies are, and of Right ought to be Free and Independent States; that they are Absolved from all Allegiance to the British Crown, and that all political connection between them and the State of Great Britain, is and ought to be totally dissolved: and that as Free and Independent States, they have full power to levy War, conclude Peace, contract Alliances, establish Commerce, and to do all other Acts and Things which Independent States may of right do. And for the support of this Declaration, with a firm reliance on the protection of divine Providence, we mutually pledge to each other our Lives, our Fortunes and our sacred Honor.

JOHN HANCOCK

NEW HAMPSHIRE
Josiah Bartlett,
Wm. Whipple,
Matthew Thornton.

MASSACHUSETTS BAY
Saml. Adams,
John Adams,
Robt. Treat Paine,
Elbridge Gerry.

RHODE ISLAND
Step. Hopkins,
William Ellery.

CONNECTICUT
Roger Sherman,
Samuel Huntington,
Wm. Williams,
Oliver Wolcott.

NEW YORK
Wm. Floyd,
Phil. Livingston,
Frans. Lewis,
Lewis Morris

NEW JERSEY
Richd. Stockton,
In. Witherspoon,
Fras. Hopkinson,
John Hart,
Abra. Clark.

PENNSYLVANIA
Robt. Morris,
Benjamin Rush,
Benjamin Franklin,
John Morton,
Geo. Clymer,
Jas. Smith,
Geo. Taylor,
James Wilson,
Geo. Ross.

DELAWARE
Caesar Rodney,
Geo. Read,
Tho. M'kean.

MARYLAND
Samuel Chase,
Wm. Paca,
Thos. Stone,
Charles Caroll of
Carollton.

VIRGINIA
George Wythe,
Richard Henry Lee,
Th. Jefferson,
Benjamin Harrison,
Thos. Nelson, jr.,
Francis Lightfoot Lee,
Carter Braxton.

NORTH CAROLINA
Wm. Hooper,
Joseph Hewes,
John Penn.

SOUTH CAROLINA
Edward Rutledge,
Thos. Heyward, Junr.,
Thomas Lynch, jnr.,
Arthur Middleton.

GEORGIA
Button Guinnett,
Lyman Hall,
Geo. Walton.

The Constitution of the United States of America

WE THE PEOPLE of the United States, in Order to form a more perfect Union, establish Justice, insure domestic Tranquility, provide for the common defence, promote the general Welfare, and secure the Blessings of Liberty to ourselves and our Posterity, do ordain and establish this Constitution for the United States of America.

ARTICLE I

SECTION 1. All legislative Powers herein granted shall be vested in a Congress of the United States, which shall consist of a Senate and House of Representatives.

SECTION 2. The House of Representatives shall be composed of Members chosen every second Year by the People of the several States, and the Electors in each State shall have the Qualifications requisite for Electors of the most numerous Branch of the State Legislature.

No person shall be a Representative who shall not have attained to the Age of twenty five Years, and been seven Years a Citizen of the United States, and who shall not, when elected, be an Inhabitant of that State in which he shall be chosen.

Representatives and direct Taxes shall be apportioned among the several States which may be included within this Union, according to their respective Numbers which shall be determined by adding to the whole Number of free Persons, including those bound to Service for a Term of Years, and excluding Indians not taxed, three fifths of all other Persons. The actual Enumeration shall be made within three Years after the first Meeting of the Congress of the United States, and within every subsequent Term ten Years, in such Manner as they shall by Law direct. The Number of Representatives shall not exceed one for every thirty Thousand, but each State shall have at Least one Representative; and until such enumeration shall be made, the State of New Hampshire shall be entitled to chuse three, Massachusetts eight, Rhode-Island and Providence Plantations one, Connecticut five, New-York six, New Jersey four, Pennsylvania eight, Delaware one, Maryland six, Virginia ten, North Carolina five, South Carolina five, and Georgia three.

When vacancies happen in the Representation from any State, the Executive Authority thereof shall issue Writs of Election to fill such Vacancies.

The House of Representatives shall chuse their speaker and other Officers; and shall have the sole Power of Impeachment.

SECTION 3. The Senate of the United States shall be composed of two Senators from each State chosen by the Legislature thereof, for six Years; and each Senator shall have one Vote.

Immediately after they shall be assembled in Consequence of the first Election, they shall be divided as equally as may be into three Classes. The Seats of the Senators of the first Class shall be vacated at the Expiration of the second year, of the second Class at the Expiration of the fourth Year, and of the third Class at the Expiration of the sixth Year, so that one third may be chosen every second Year and if Vacancies happen by Resignation, or otherwise, during the Recess of the Legislature of any State, the Executive thereof may make temporary Appointments until the next Meeting of the Legislature, which shall then fill such Vacancies.

No Person shall be a Senator who shall not have attained to the Age of thirty Years, and been nine Years a Citizen of the United States, and who shall not, when elected, be an Inhabitant of that State for which he shall be chosen.

The Vice President of the United States shall be President of the Senate, but shall have no Vote, unless they be equally divided.

The Senate shall chuse their other Officers, and also a President pro tempore, in the Absence of the Vice President, or when he shall exercise the Office of President of the United States.

The Senate shall have the sole Power to try all Impeachments. When sitting for that Purpose, they shall be on Oath or Affirmation. When the President of the United States is tried, the Chief Justice shall preside: And no Person shall be convicted without the Concurrence of two thirds of the Members present.

Judgment in Cases of Impeachment shall not extend further than to removal from Office, and disqualification to hold and enjoy any Office of honor, Trust or Profit under the United States; but the Party convicted shall nevertheless be liable and subject to Indictment, Trial, Judgment and Punishment, according to Law.

SECTION 4. The Times, Places and Manner of holding Elections for Senators and Representatives, shall be prescribed in each State by the Legislature thereof; but the Congress may at any time by law make or alter such Regulations, except as to the Places of chusing Senators.

The Congress shall assemble at least once in every Year, and such Meeting shall be on the first Monday in December, unless they shall by Law appoint a different Day.

SECTION 5. Each House shall be the Judge of the Elections, Returns and Qualifications of its own Members, and a Majority of each shall constitute a Quorum to do Business; but a smaller Number may adjourn from day to day, and may be authorized to compel the Attendance of absent Members, in such Manner, and under such Penalties as each House may provide.

Each House may determine the Rules of its Proceedings, punish its Members for disorderly Behaviour, and with the Concurrence of two thirds, expel a Member.

Each House shall keep a journal of its Proceedings, and from time to time publish the same, excepting such Parts as may in their judgment require Secrecy; and the Yeas and Nays of the Members of either House on any question shall, at the Desire of one fifth of those present, be entered on the Journal.

Neither House, during the Session of Congress, shall, without the Consent of the other, adjourn for more than three days, nor to any other Place than that in which the two Houses shall be sitting.

SECTION 6. The Senators and Representatives shall receive a Compensation for their Services, to be ascertained by Law, and paid out of the Treasury of the United States. They shall in all Cases, except Treason, Felony and Breach of the Peace, be privileged from Arrest during their Attendance at the Session of their respective Houses, and in going to and returning from the same; and for any Speech or Debate in either House, they shall not be questioned in any other Place.

No Senator or Representative shall, during the Time for which he was elected, be appointed to any civil Office under the Authority of the United States, which shall have been created, or the Emoluments whereof shall have been encreased during such time; and no Person holding any Office under the United States, shall be a Member of either House during his Continuance in Office.

SECTION 7. All Bills for raising Revenue shall originate in the House of Representatives; but the Senate may propose or concur with Amendments as on other Bills.

Every Bill which shall have passed the House of Representatives and the Senate, shall, before it become a Law, be presented to the President of the United States; If he approves he shall sign it, but if not he shall return it, with his Objections to that House in which it shall have originated, who shall enter the Objections at large on their journal, and proceed to reconsider it. If after such Reconsideration two thirds of that House shall agree to pass the Bill, it shall be sent, together with the Objections, to the other House, by which it shall likewise be reconsidered, and if approved by two thirds of that House, it shall become a Law. But in all such Cases the Votes of both Houses shall be determined by Yeas and Nays, and the Names of the Persons voting for and against the Bill shall be entered on the Journal of each House respectively. If any Bill shall not be returned by the President within ten Days (Sundays excepted) after it shall have been presented to him, the Same shall be a Law, in like Manner as if he had signed it, unless the Congress by their Adjournment prevent its Return, in which Case it shall not be a Law.

Every Order, Resolution, or Vote to which the Concurrence of the Senate and House of Representatives may be necessary (except on a question of Adjournment) shall be presented to the President of the United States; and before the Same shall take Effect, shall be approved by him, or being disapproved by him, shall be repassed by two thirds of the Senate and House of Representatives, according to the Rules and Limitations prescribed in the Case of a Bill.

SECTION 8. The Congress shall have Power To lay and collect Taxes, Duties, Imposts and Excises, to pay the Debts and provide for the common Defence and general Welfare of the United States; but all Duties, Imposts and Excises shall be uniform throughout the United States;

To borrow Money on the credit of the United States;

To regulate Commerce with foreign Nations, and among the several States, and with the Indian Tribes;

To establish a uniform Rule of Naturalization, and uniform Laws on the subject of Bankruptcies throughout the United States;

To coin Money, regulate the Value thereof, and of foreign Coin, and fix the Standard of Weights and Measures;

To provide for the Punishment of counterfeiting the Securities and current Coin of the United States;

To establish Post Offices and post Roads;

To promote the Progress of Science and useful Arts, by securing for limited Times to Authors and Inventors the exclusive Right to their respective Writings and Discoveries;

To constitute Tribunals inferior to the supreme Court;

To define and punish Piracies and Felonies committed on the high Seas, and Offences against the Law of Nations;

To declare War, grant Letters of Marque and Reprisal, and make Rules concerning Captures on Land and Water;

To raise and support Armies, but no Appropriation of Money to that Use shall be for a longer Term than two Years;

To provide and maintain a Navy;

To make Rules for the Government and Regulation of the land and naval Forces;

To provide for calling forth the Militia to execute the Laws of the Union, suppress Insurrections and repel Invasions;

To provide for organizing, arming, and disciplining, the Militia, and for governing such Part of them as may be employed in the Service of the United States, reserving to the States respectively, the Appointment of the Officers, and the Authority of training the Militia according to the discipline prescribed by Congress;

To exercise exclusive Legislation in all Cases whatsoever, over such District (not exceeding ten Miles square) as may, by Cession of particular States, and the Acceptance of Congress, become the Seat of the Government of the United States, and to exercise like Authority over all Places purchased by the Consent of the Legislature of the State in which the Same shall be for the Erection of Forts, Magazines, Arsenals, dock-Yards, and other needful Buildings;—And

To make all Laws which shall be necessary and proper for carrying into Execution the foregoing Powers, and all other Powers vested by this Constitution in the Government of the United States, or in any Department or Officer thereof.

SECTION 9. The Migration or Importation of such Persons as any of the States now existing shall think proper to admit, shall not be prohibited by the Congress prior to the Year one thousand eight hundred and eight, but a Tax or duty may be imposed on such Importation, not exceeding ten dollars for each Person.

The Privilege of the Writ of Habeas Corpus shall not be suspended, unless when in Cases of Rebellion or Invasion the public Safety may require it.

No Bill of Attainder or ex post facto Law shall be passed.

No Capitation, or other direct, Tax shall be laid, unless in Proportion to the Census or Enumeration herein before directed to be taken.

No Tax or Duty shall be laid on Articles exported from any State.

No Preference shall be given by any Regulation of Commerce or Revenue to the Ports of one State over those of another; nor shall Vessels bound to, or from, one State, be obliged to enter, clear, or pay Duties in another.

No Money shall be drawn from the Treasury, but in Consequence of Appropriations made by Law; and a regular Statement and Account of the Receipts and Expenditures of all public Money shall be published from time to time.

No Title of Nobility shall be granted by the United States: And no Person holding any Office of Profit or Trust under them, shall, without the Consent of the Congress, accept of any present, Emolument, Office, or Title, of any kind whatever, from any King, Prince, or foreign State.

SECTION 10. No state shall enter into any Treaty, Alliance, or Confederation; grant Letters of Marque and Reprisal; coin Money; emit Bills of Credit; make any Thing but gold and silver Coin a Tender in Payment of Debts; pass any Bill of Attainder, ex post facto Law, or Law impairing the Obligation of Contracts, or grant any Title of Nobility.

No State shall, without the Consent of the Congress, lay any Imposts or Duties on Imports or Exports, except what may be absolutely necessary for executing its inspection Laws: and the net Produce of all Duties and Imposts, laid by any State on Imports or Exports, shall be for the Use of the Treasury of the United States, and all such Laws shall be subject to the Revision and Controul of the Congress.

No State shall, without the Consent of Congress, lay any Duty of Tonnage, keep Troops, or Ships of War in time of Peace, enter into any Agreement or Compact with another State, or with a foreign Power, or engage in War, unless actually invaded, or in such imminent Danger as will not admit of delay.

ARTICLE II

SECTION 1. The executive Power shall be vested in a President of the United States of America. He shall hold his Office during the Term of four Years, and, together with the Vice President, chosen for the same Term, be elected as follows.

Each State shall appoint, in such Manner as the Legislature thereof may direct, a Number of Electors, equal to the whole Number of Senators and Representatives to which the State may be entitled in the Congress; but no Senator or Representative, or Person holding an Office of Trust of Profit under the United States, shall be appointed an Elector.

The Electors shall meet in their respective States, and vote by Ballot for two Persons, of whom one at least shall not be an Inhabitant of the same State with themselves. And they shall make a List of all the Persons voted for, and, of the Number of Votes for each; which List they shall sign and certify, and transmit sealed to the Seat of the Government of the United States, directed to the President of the Senate. The President of the Senate shall, in the Presence of the Senate and House of Representatives, open all the Certificates, and the Votes shall then be counted. The Person having the greatest Number of Votes shall be the President, if such Number be a Majority of the whole Number of Electors appointed; and if there be more than one who have such Majority, and have an equal Number of Votes, then the House of Representatives shall immediately chuse by Ballot one of them for President; and if no Person have a Majority, then from the five highest on the List the said House shall in like Manner chuse the President. But in chusing the President, the Votes shall be taken by States, the Representation from each State having one Vote; A quorum for this Purpose shall consist of a Member or Members from two thirds of the States, and a Majority of all the States shall be necessary to a Choice. In every Case, after the Choice of the President, the Person having the greatest Number of Votes of the Electors shall be the Vice President. But if there should remain two or more who have equal Votes, the Senate shall chuse from them by Ballot the Vice President.

The Congress may determine the Time of chusing the Electors, and the Day on which they shall give their Votes; which Day shall be the same throughout the United States.

No Person except a natural born Citizen, or a Citizen of the United States, at the time of the Adoption of this Constitution, shall be eligible to the Office of President; neither shall any Person be eligible to that Office who shall not have attained to the Age of thirty five Years, and been fourteen Years a Resident within the United States.

In Case of the Removal of the President from Office, or of his Death, Resignation, or Inability to discharge the Powers and Duties of the said Office, the Same shall devolve on the Vice President, and the Congress may by Law provide for the Case of Removal, Death, Resignation or Inability, both of the President and Vice President, declaring what Officer shall then act as President, and such Officer shall act accordingly, until the Disability be removed, or a President shall be elected.

The President shall, at stated Times, receive for his Services, a Compensation, which shall neither be encreased nor diminished during the Period for which he shall have been elected, and he shall not receive within that Period any other Emolument from the United States, or any of them.

Before he enter on the Execution of his Office, he shall take the following Oath or Affirmation—"I do solemnly swear (or affirm) that I will faithfully execute the Office of President of the United States, and will to the best of my Ability, preserve, protect and defend the Constitution of the United States."

SECTION 2. The President shall be Commander in Chief of the Army, and Navy of the United States, and of the Militia of the several States, when called into the actual Service of the United States; he may require the Opinion, in writing, of the principal Officer in each of the executive Departments, upon any Subject relating to the Duties of their respective Offices, and he shall have Power to grant Reprieves and Pardons for Offences against the United States, except in Cases of Impeachment.

He shall have Power, by and with the Advice and Consent of the Senate, to make Treaties, provided two thirds of the Senators present concur; and he shall nominate, and by and with the Advice and Consent of the Senate, shall appoint Ambassadors, other public Ministers and Consuls, Judges of the supreme Court, and all other Officers of the United States, whose Appointments are not herein otherwise provided for, and which shall be established by Law: but the Congress may by Law vest the Appointment of such inferior Officers, as they think proper, in the President alone, in the Courts of Law, or in the Heads of Departments.

The President shall have Power to fill up all Vacancies that may happen during the Recess of the Senate, by granting Commissions which shall expire at the end of their next Session.

SECTION 3. He shall from time to time give to the Congress Information of the State of the Union, and recommend to their Consideration such Measures as he shall judge necessary and expedient; he may, on extraordinary Occasions, convene both Houses, or either of them, and in Case of Disagreement between them, with Respect to the Time of Adjournment, he may adjourn them to such Time as he shall think proper; he shall receive Ambassadors and other public Ministers; he shall take Care that the Laws be faithfully executed, and shall Commission all the Officers of the United States.

SECTION 4. The President, Vice President and all civil Officers of the United States, shall be removed from Office on Impeachment for, and Conviction of, Treason, Bribery, or other high Crimes and Misdemeanors.

SECTION 1. The judicial Power of the United States, shall be vested in one supreme Court, and in such inferior Courts as the Congress may from time to time ordain and establish. The Judges, both of the supreme and inferior Courts, shall hold their Offices during good Behaviour, and shall, at stated Times, receive for their Services, a Compensation, which shall not be diminished during their Continuance in Office.

SECTION 2. The judicial Power shall extend to all Cases, in Law and Equity, arising under this Constitution, the Laws of the United States, and Treaties made, or which shall be made, under their Authority;—to all Cases affecting Ambassadors, other public Ministers and Consuls;—to all Cases of admiralty and maritime Jurisdiction;—to Controversies to which the United States shall be a Party;—to Controversies between two or more States;—between a State and Citizens of another State;—between Citizens of different States,—between Citizens of the same State claiming Lands under Grants of different States,—and between a State, or the Citizens thereof, and foreign States, Citizens of Subjects.

In all Cases affecting Ambassadors, other public Ministers and Consuls, and those in which a State shall be Party, the supreme Court shall have original Jurisdiction. In all the other Cases before mentioned, the supreme Court shall have appellate Jurisdiction, both as to Law and Fact, with such Exceptions, and under such Regulations as the Congress shall make.

The Trial of all Crimes, except in Cases of Impeachment, shall be by Jury; and such Trial shall be held in the State where the said Crimes shall have been committed; but when not committed within any State, the Trial shall be at such Place or Places as the Congress may by Law have directed.

SECTION 3. Treason against the United States, shall consist only in levying War against them, or in adhering to their Enemies, giving them Aid and Comfort. No Person shall be convicted of Treason unless on the Testimony of two Witnesses to the same overt Act, or on Confession in open Court.

The Congress shall have Power to declare the Punishment of Treason, but no Attainder of Treason shall work Corruption of Blood, or Forfeiture except during the Life of the Person attainted.

ARTICLE IV

SECTION 1. Full Faith and Credit shall be given in each State to the public Acts, Records, and judicial Proceedings of every other State. And the Congress may by general Laws prescribe the Manner in which such Acts, Records and Proceedings shall be proved, and the Effect thereof.

SECTION 2. The Citizens of each State shall be entitled to all Privileges and Immunities of Citizens in the several States.

A Person charged in any State with Treason, Felony, or other Crime, who shall flee from Justice, and be found in another State, shall on Demand of the executive Authority of the State from which he fled, be delivered up, to be removed to the State having Jurisdiction of the Crime.

No Person held to Service or Labour in one State under the Laws thereof, escaping into another, shall, in Consequence of any Law or Regulation therein, be discharged from such Service or Labour, but shall be delivered up on Claim of the Party to whom such Service or Labour may be due.

SECTION 3. New States may be admitted by the Congress into this Union; but no new State shall be formed or erected within the Jurisdiction of any other State; nor any State be formed by the Junction of two or more States, or Parts of States, without the Consent of the Legislatures of the States concerned as well as of the Congress.

The Congress shall have Power to dispose of and make all needful Rules and Regulations respecting the Territory or other Property belonging to the United States; and nothing in this Constitution shall be so construed as to Prejudice any Claims of the United States, or of any particular State.

SECTION 4. The United States shall guarantee to every State in this Union a Republican Form of Government, and shall protect each of them against Invasion, and on Application of the Legislature, or of the Executive (when the Legislature cannot be convened) against domestic Violence.

ARTICLE V

The Congress, whenever two thirds of both Houses shall deem it necessary, shall propose Amendments to this Constitution, or, on the Application of the Legislatures of two thirds of the several States, shall call a Convention for proposing Amendments, which, in either Case, shall be valid to all Intents and Purposes, as Part of this Constitution, when ratified by the Legislatures of three fourths of the several States, or by Conventions in three fourths thereof, as the one or the other Mode of Ratification may be proposed by the Congress; Provided that no Amendment which may be made prior to the Year One thousand eight hundred and eight shall in any Manner affect the first and fourth Clauses in the Ninth Section of the first Article; and that no State, without its Consent, shall be deprived of its equal Suffrage in the Senate.

ARTICLE VI

All Debts contracted and Engagements entered into, before the Adoption of this Constitution, shall be as valid against the United States under this Constitution, as under the Confederation.

This Constitution, and the laws of the United States which shall be made in Pursuance thereof; and all Treaties made, or which shall be made, under the Authority of the United States, shall be the supreme Law of the Land; and the Judges in every State shall be bound thereby, any Thing in the Constitution or Laws of any State to the Contrary notwithstanding.

The Senators and Representatives before mentioned, and the Members of the several State Legislatures, and all executive and judicial Officers, both of the United States and of the several States, shall be bound by Oath or Affirmation, to support this Constitution; but no religious Test shall ever be required as a Qualification to any Office or public Trust under the United States.

ARTICLE VII

The Ratification of the Conventions of nine States, shall be sufficient for the Establishment of this Constitution between the States so ratifying the Same.

Done in Convention by the Unanimous Consent of the States present the Seventeenth Day of September in the Year of our Lord one thousand seven hundred and Eighty seven and of the Independence of the United States of America the Twelfth. In witness whereof we have hereunto subscribed our Names,

Go. WASHINGTON
Presid't. and deputy from Virginia

Attest
WILLIAM JACKSON
Secretary

Articles in addition to, and amendment of the Constitution of the United States of America, proposed by Congress and ratified by the Legislatures of the several states, pursuant to the Fifth Article of the original Constitution.

(The first ten amendments were passed by Congress on September 25, 1789, and were ratified on December 15, 1791.)

AMENDMENT I

Congress shall make no law respecting an establishment of religion, or prohibiting the free exercise thereof; or abridging the freedom of speech, or of the press; or the right of the people peaceably to assemble, and to petition the Government for a redress of grievances.

AMENDMENT II

A well regulated Militia, being necessary to the security of a free State, the right of the people to keep and bear Arms, shall not be infringed.

AMENDMENT III

No Soldier shall, in time of peace be quartered in any house, without the consent of the Owner, nor in time of war, but in a manner to be prescribed by law.

AMENDMENT IV

The right of the people to be secure in their persons, houses, papers, and effects, against unreasonable searches and seizures, shall not be violated, and no warrants shall issue, but upon probable cause, supported by Oath or affirmation, and particularly describing the place to be searched, and the persons or things to be seized.

AMENDMENT V

No person shall be held to answer for a capital, or otherwise infamous crime, unless on a presentment or indictment of a Grand Jury, except in cases arising in the land or naval forces, or in the Militia, when in actual service in time of War or public danger; nor shall any person be subject for the same offence to be twice put in jeopardy of life or limb; nor shall be compelled in any criminal case to be a witness against himself, nor be deprived of life, liberty, or property, without due process of law; nor shall private property be taken for public use, without just compensation.

AMENDMENT VI

In all criminal prosecutions, the accused shall enjoy the right to a speedy and public trial, by an impartial jury of the State and district wherein the crime shall have been committed, which district shall have been previously ascertained by law, and to be informed of the nature and cause of the accusation; to be confronted with the witnesses against him; to have compulsory process for obtaining witnesses in his favor, and to have the assistance of counsel for his defence.

AMENDMENT VII

In Suits at common law, where the value in controversy shall exceed twenty dollars, the right of trial by jury shall be preserved, and no fact tried by a jury, shall be otherwise re-examined in any Court of the United States, than according to the rules of the common law.

AMENDMENT VIII

Excessive bail shall not be required, nor excessive fines imposed, nor cruel and unusual punishments inflicted.

AMENDMENT IX

The enumeration in the Constitution, of certain rights, shall not be construed to deny or disparage others retained by the people.

AMENDMENT X

The powers not delegated to the United States by the Constitution, nor prohibited by it to the States, are reserved to the States respectively, or to the people.

AMENDMENT XI
(Ratified on February 7, 1795)

The Judicial power of the United States shall not be construed to extend to any suit in law or equity, commenced or prosecuted against one of the United States by Citizens of another State, or by Citizens or Subjects of any Foreign State.

AMENDMENT XII
(Ratified on June 15, 1804)

The Electors shall meet in their respective states, and vote by ballot for President and Vice-President, one of whom, at least, shall not be an inhabitant of the same state with themselves; they shall name in their ballots the person voted for as President, and in distinct ballots the person voted for as Vice-President, and they shall make distinct lists of all persons voted for as President, and of all persons voted for as Vice-President, and of the number of votes for each, which lists they shall sign and certify, and transmit sealed to the seat of the government of the United States, directed to the President of the Senate;—The President of the Senate shall, in the presence of the Senate and House of Representatives, open all the certificates and the votes shall then be counted;—The person having the greatest number of votes for President, shall be the President, if such number be a majority of the whole number of Electors appointed; and if no person have such majority; then from the persons having the highest numbers not exceeding three on the list of those voted for as President, the House of Representatives shall choose immediately, by ballot, the President. But in choosing the President, the votes shall be taken by states, the representation from each state having one vote; a quorum for this purpose shall consist of a member or members from two-thirds of the states, and a majority of all the states shall be necessary to a choice. And if the House of Representatives shall not choose a President whenever the right of choice shall devolve upon them, before the fourth day of March next following, then the Vice-President shall act as President, as in the case of the death or other constitutional disability of the President.—The person having the greatest number of votes as Vice-President, shall be the Vice-President, if such number be a majority of the whole number of Electors appointed, and if no person have a majority, then from the two highest numbers on the list, the Senate shall choose the Vice-President; a quorum for the purpose shall consist of two-thirds of the whole number of Senators, and a majority of the whole number shall be necessary to a choice. But no person constitutionally ineligible to the office of President shall be eligible to that of Vice-President of the United States.

AMENDMENT XIII
(Ratified on December 6, 1865)

SECTION 1. Neither slavery nor involuntary servitude, except as a punishment for crime whereof the party shall have been duly convicted, shall exist within the United States, or any place subject to their jurisdiction.

SECTION 2. Congress shall have power to enforce this article by appropriate legislation.

AMENDMENT XIV
(Ratified on July 9, 1868)

SECTION 1. All persons born or naturalized in the United States, and subject to the jurisdiction thereof, are citizens of the United States and of the State wherein they reside. No State shall make or enforce any law which shall abridge the privileges or immunities of citizens of the United States; nor shall any State deprive any person of life, liberty, or property, without due process of law; nor deny to any person within its jurisdiction the equal protection of the laws.

SECTION 2. Representatives shall be apportioned among the several States according to their respective numbers, counting the whole number of persons in each State, excluding Indians not taxed. But when the right to vote at any election for the choice of electors for President and Vice President of the United States, Representatives in Congress, the Executive and Judicial officers of a State, or the members of the Legislature thereof, is denied to any of the male inhabitants of such State, being twenty-one years of age, and citizens of the United States, or in any way abridged, except for participation in rebellion, or other crime, the basis of representation therein shall be reduced in the proportion which the number of such male citizens shall bear to the whole number of male citizens twenty-one years of age in such State.

SECTION 3. No person shall be a Senator or Representative in Congress, or elector of President and Vice President, or hold any office, civil or military, under the United States, or under any State, who, having previously taken an oath, as a member of Congress, or as an officer of the United States, or as a member of any State legislature, or as an executive or judicial officer of any State, to support the Constitution of the United States, shall have engaged in insurrection or rebellion against the same, or given aid or comfort to the enemies thereof. But Congress may by a vote of two-thirds of each House, remove such diability.

SECTION 4. The validity of the public debt of the United States, authorized by law, including debts incurred for payment of pensions and bounties for services in suppressing insurrection or rebellion, shall not be questioned. But neither the United States nor any State shall assume or pay any debt or obligation incurred in aid of insurrection or rebellion against the United States, or any claim for the loss or emancipation of any slave, but all such debts, obligations and claims shall be held illegal and void.

SECTION 5. The Congress shall have power to enforce, by appropriate legislation, the provisions of this article.

AMENDMENT XV
(Ratified on February 3, 1870)

SECTION 1. The right of citizens of the United States to vote shall not se denied or abridged by the United States or by any State on account of race, color, or previous condition of servitude.

SECTION 2. The Congress shall have power to enforce this article by appropriate legislation.

AMENDMENT XVI
(Ratified on February 3, 1913)

The Congress shall have power to lay and collect taxes on incomes, from whatever source derived, without apportionment among the several States, and without regard to any census or enumeration.

AMENDMENT XVII
(Ratified on April 8, 1913)

The Senate of the United States shall be composed of two Senators from each State, elected by the people thereof, for six years; and each Senator shall have one vote. The electors in each State shall have the qualifications requisite for electors of the most numerous branch of the State legislatures.

When vacancies happen in the representation of any State in the Senate, the executive authority of such State shall issue writs of election to fill such vacancies: Provided, That the legislature of any State may empower the executive thereof to make temporary appointments until the people fill the vacancies by election as the legislature may direct.

This amendment shall not be so construed as to affect the election or term of any Senator chosen before it becomes valid as part of the Constitution.

AMENDMENT XVIII
(Ratified on January 16, 1919)

SECTION 1. After one year from the ratification of this article the manufacture, sale, or transportation of intoxicating liquors within, the importation thereof into, or the exportation thereof from the United States and all territory subject to the jurisdiction thereof for beverage purposes is hereby prohibited.

SECTION 2. The Congress and the several States shall have concurrent power to enforce this article by appropriate legislation.

SECTION 3. This article shall be inoperative unless it shall have been ratified as an amendment to the Constitution by the legislatures of the several States, as provided in the Constitution, within seven years from the date of the submission hereof to the States by the Congress.

AMENDMENT XIX
(Ratified on August 18, 1920)

The right of citizens of the United States to vote shall not be denied or abridged by the United States or by any State on account of sex.

Congress shall have power to enforce this article by appropriate legislation.

AMENDMENT XX
(Ratified on February 6, 1933)

SECTION 1. The terms of the President and Vice President shall end at noon on the 20th day of January, and the terms of Senators and Representatives at noon on the 3d day of January, of the years in which such terms would have ended if this article had not been ratified; and the terms of their successors shall then begin.

SECTION 2. The Congress shall assemble at least once in every year, and such meeting shall begin at noon on the 3d day of January, unless they shall by law appoint a different day.

SECTION 3. If, at the time fixed for the beginning of the term of the President, the President elect shall have died, the Vice President elect shall become President. If a President shall not have been chosen before the time fixed for the beginning of his term, or if the President elect shall have failed to qualify, then the Vice President elect shall act as President until a President shall have qualified; and the Congress may by law provide for the case wherein neither a President elect nor a Vice President elect shall have qualified, declaring who shall then act as President, or the manner in which one who is to act shall be selected, and such person shall act accordingly until a President or Vice President shall have qualified.

SECTION 4. The Congress may by law provide for the case of the death of any of the persons from whom the House of Representatives may choose a President whenever the rights of choice shall have devolved upon them, and for the case of the death of any of the persons from whom the Senate may choose a Vice President whenever the right of choice shall have devolved upon them.

SECTION 5. Sections 1 and 2 shall take effect on the 15th day of October following the ratification of this article.

SECTION 6. This article shall be inoperative unless it shall have been ratified as an amendment to the Constitution by the legislatures of three-fourths of the several States within seven years from the date of its submission.

AMENDMENT XXI
(Ratified on December 5, 1933)

SECTION 1. The eighteenth article of amendment to the Constitution of the United States is hereby repealed.

SECTION 2. The transportation or importation into any State, Territory, or possession of the United States for delivery or use therein of intoxicating liquors, in violation of the laws thereof, is hereby prohibited.

SECTION 3. This article shall be inoperative unless it shall have been ratified as an amendment to the Constitution by conventions in the several States, as provided in the Constitution, within seven years from the date of the submission hereof to the States by the Congress.

AMENDMENT XXII
(Ratified on February 27, 1951)

No person shall be elected to the office of the President more than twice, and no person who has held the office of President, or acted as President, for more than two years of a term to which some other person was elected President shall be elected to the office of the President more than once. But this Article shall not apply to any person holding the office of President when this Article was proposed by the Congress, and shall not prevent any person who may be holding the office of President, or acting as President, during the term within which this Article becomes operative from holding the office of President or acting as President during the remainder of such term.

AMENDMENT XXIII
(Ratified on March 29, 1961)

SECTION 1. The District constituting the seat of Government of the United States shall appoint in such manner as the Congress may direct:

A number of electors of President and Vice President equal to the whole number of Senators and Representatives in Congress to which the District would be entitled if it were a State, but in no event more than the least populous State; they shall be in addition to those appointed by the States, but they shall be considered, for the purposes of the election of President and Vice President, to be electors appointed by a State; and they shall meet in the District and perform such duties as provided by the twelfth article of amendment.

SECTION 2. The Congress shall have power to enforce this article by appropriate legislation.

SECTION 1. The right of citizens of the United States to vote in any primary or other election for President or Vice President, for electors for President or Vice President, or for Senator or Representative in Congress, shall not be denied or abridged by the United States or any State by reason of failure to pay any poll tax or other tax.

SECTION 2. The Congress shall have power to enforce this article by appropriate legislation.

AMENDMENT XXV
(Ratified on February 10, 1967)

SECTION 1. In case of the removal of the President from office or of his death or resignation, the Vice President shall become President.

SECTION 2. Whenever there is a vacancy in the office of the Vice President, the President shall nominate a Vice President who shall take office upon confirmation by a majority vote of both Houses of Congress.

SECTION 3. Whenever the President transmits to the President pro tempore of the Senate and the Speaker of the House of Representatives his written declaration that he is unable to discharge the powers and duties of his office, and until he transmits to them a written declaration to the contrary, such powers and duties shall be discharged by the Vice President as Acting President.

SECTION 4. Whenever the Vice President and a majority of either the principal officers of the executive departments or of such other body as Congress may by law provide, transmit to the President pro tempore of the Senate and the Speaker of the House of Representatives their written declaration that the President is unable to discharge the powers and duties of his office, the Vice President shall immediately assume the powers and duties of the office as Acting President.

Thereafter, when the President transmits to the President pro tempore of the Senate and the Speaker of the House of Representatives his written declaration that no inability exists, he shall resume the powers and duties of his office unless the Vice President and a majority of either the principal officers of the executive department or of such other body as Congress may by law provide, transmit within four days to the President pro tempore of the Senate and the Speaker of the House of Representatives their written declaration that the President is unable to discharge the powers and duties of his office. Thereupon Congress shall decide the issue, assembling within forty-eight hours for that purpose if not in session. If the Congress, within twenty-one days after receipt of the latter written declaration, or, if Congress is not in session, within twenty-one days after Congress is required to assemble, determines by two-thirds vote of both Houses that the President is unable to discharge the powers and duties of his office, the Vice President shall continue to discharge the same as Acting President; otherwise, the President shall resume the powers and duties of his office.

AMENDMENT XXVI
(Ratified on July 1, 1971)

SECTION 1. The right of citizens of the United States, who are eighteen years of age or older, to vote shall not be denied or abridged by the United States or by any State on account of age.

SECTION 2. The Congress shall have power to enforce this article by appropriate legislation.

AMENDMENT XXVII
(Ratified on May 7, 1992)

No law varying the compensation for the services of Senators and Representatives shall take effect until an election of Representatives shall have intervened.

The Federalist No. 10

November 22, 1787
James Madison

TO THE PEOPLE OF THE STATE OF NEW YORK.

Among the numerous advantages promised by a well constructed Union, none deserves to be more accurately developed than its tendency to break and control the violence of faction. The friend of popular governments, never finds himself so much alarmed for their character and fate, as when he contemplates their propensity to this dangerous vice. He will not fail therefore to set a due value on any plan which, without violating the principles to which he is attached, provides a proper cure for it. The instability, injustice and confusion introduced into the public councils, have in truth been the mortal diseases under which popular governments have every where perished; as they continue to be the favorite and fruitful topics from which the adversaries to liberty derive their most specious declamations. The valuable improvements made by the American Constitutions on the popular models, both ancient and modern, cannot certainly be too much admired; but it would be an unwarrantable partiality, to contend that they have as effectually obviated the danger on this side as was wished and expected. Complaints are every where heard from our most considerate and virtuous citizens, equally the friends of public and private faith, and of public and personal liberty; that our governments are too unstable; that the public good is disregarded in the conflicts of rival parties; and that measures are too often decided, not according to the rules of justice, and the rights of the minor party; but by the superior force of an interested and over-bearing majority. However anxiously we may wish that these complaints had no foundation, the evidence of known facts will not permit us to deny that they are in some degree true. It will be found indeed, on a candid review of our situation, that some of the distresses under which we labor, have been erroneously charged on the operation of our governments; but it will be found, at the same time, that other causes will not alone account for many of our heaviest misfortunes; and particularly, for that prevailing and increasing distrust of public engagements, and alarm for private rights, which are echoed from one end of the continent to the other. These must be chiefly, if not wholly, effects of the unsteadiness and injustice, with which a factious spirit has tainted our public administrations.

By a faction I understand a number of citizens, whether amounting to a majority or minority of the whole, who are united and actuated by some common impulse of passion, or of interest, adverse to the rights of other citizens, or to the permanent and aggregate interests of the community.

There are two methods of curing the mischiefs of faction: the one, by removing its causes; the other, by controlling its effects.

There are again two methods of removing the causes of faction: the one by destroying the liberty which is essential to its existence; the other, by giving to every citizen the same opinions, the same passions, and the same interests.

It could never be more truly said than of the first remedy, that it is worse than the disease. Liberty is to faction, what air is to fire, an aliment without which it instantly expires. But it could not be a less folly to abolish liberty, which is essential to political life, because it nourishes faction, than it would be to wish the annihilation of air, which is essential to animal life, because it imparts to fire its destructive agency.

The second expedient is as impracticable, as the first would be unwise. As long as the reason of man continues fallible, and he is at liberty to exercise it, different opinions will be formed. As long as the connection subsists between his reason and his self-love, his opinions and his passions will have a reciprocal influence on each other; and the former will be objects to which the latter will attach themselves. The diversity in the faculties of men from which the rights of property originate, is not less an insuperable obstacle to a uniformity of interests. The protection of these faculties is the first object of Government. From the protection of different and unequal faculties of acquiring property, the possession of different degrees and kinds of property immediately results: and from the influence of these on the sentiments and views of the respective proprietors, ensues a division of the society into different interests and parties.

The latent causes of faction are thus sown in the nature of man; and we see them every where brought into different degrees of activity, according to the different circumstances of civil society. A zeal for different opinions concerning religion, concerning Government and many other points, as well of speculation as of practice; an attachment to different leaders ambitiously contending for pre-eminence and power; or to persons of other descriptions whose fortunes have been interesting to the human passions, have in turn divided mankind into parties, inflamed them with mutual animosity, and rendered them much more disposed to vex and oppress each other, than to cooperate for their common good. So strong is this propensity of mankind to fall into mutual animosities, that where no substantial occasion presents itself, the most frivolous and fanciful distinctions have been sufficient to kindle their unfriendly passions, and excite their most violent conflicts. But the most common and durable source of factions, has been the various and unequal distribution of property. Those who hold, and those who are without property, have ever formed distinct interests in society. Those who are creditors, and those who are debtors, fall under a like discrimination. A landed interest, a manufacturing interest, a mercantile interest, a monied interest, with many lesser interests, grow up of necessity in civilized nations, and divide them into different classes, actuated by different sentiments and views. The regulation of these various and interfering interests forms the principal task of modern Legislation, and involves the spirit of party and faction in the necessary and ordinary operations of Government.

No man is allowed to be a judge in his own cause; because his interest would certainly bias his judgment, and, not improbably, corrupt his integrity. With equal, nay with greater reason, a body of men, are unfit to be both judges and parties, at the same time; yet, what are many of the most important acts of legislation, but so many judicial determinations, not indeed concerning the rights of single persons, but concerning the rights of large bodies of citizens, and what are the different classes of legislators, but advocates and parties to the causes which they determine? Is a law proposed concerning private debts? It is a question to which the creditors are parties on one side, and the debtors on the other. Justice ought to hold the balance between them. Yet the parties are and must be themselves the judges; and the most numerous party, or, in other words, the most powerful faction must be expected to prevail. Shall domestic manufactures be encouraged, and in what degree, by restrictions on foreign manufactures? are questions which would be differently decided by the landed and the manufacturing classes; and probably by neither, with a sole regard to justice and the public good. The apportionment of taxes on the various descriptions of property, is an act which seems to require the most exact impartiality; yet, there is perhaps no legislative act in which greater opportunity and temptation are given to a predominant party, to trample on the rules of justice. Every shilling with which they over-burden the inferior number, is a shilling saved to their own pockets.

It is in vain to say, that enlightened statesmen will be able to adjust these clashing interests, and render them all subservient to the public good. Enlightened statesmen will not always be at the helm: Nor, in many cases, can such an adjustment be made at all, without taking into view indirect and remote considerations, which will rarely prevail over the immediate interest which one party may find in disregarding the rights of another, or the good of the whole.

The inference to which we are brought, is, that the causes of faction cannot be removed; and that relief is only to be sought in the means of controlling its effects.

If a faction consists of less than a majority, relief is supplied by the republican principle, which enables the majority to defeat its sinister views by regular vote: It may clog the administration, it may convulse the society; but it will be unable to execute and mask its violence under the forms of the Constitution. When a majority is included in a faction, the form of popular government on the other hand enables it to sacrifice to its ruling passion or interest, both the public good and the rights of other citizens. To secure the public good, and private rights, against the danger of such a faction, and at the same time to preserve the spirit and the form of popular government, is then the great object to which our enquiries are directed: Let me add that it is the great desideratum, by which alone this form of government can be rescued from the opprobrium under which it has so long labored, and be recommended to the esteem and adoption of mankind.

By what means is this object attainable? Evidently by one of two only. Either the existence of the same passion or interest in a majority at the same time, must be prevented; or the majority, having such co-existent passion or interest, must be rendered, by their number and local situation, unable to concert and carry into effect schemes of oppression. If the impulse and the opportunity be suffered to coincide, we well know that neither moral nor religious motives can be relied on as an adequate control. They are not found to be such on the injustice and violence of individuals, and lose their efficacy in proportion to the number combined together; that is, in proportion as their efficacy becomes needful.

From this view of the subject, it may be concluded, that a pure Democracy, by which I mean, a Society, consisting of a small number of citizens, who assemble and administer the Government in person, can admit of no cure for the mischiefs of faction. A common passion or interest will, in almost every case, be felt by a majority of the whole; a communication and concert results from the form of Government itself; and there is nothing to check the inducements to sacrifice the weaker party, or an obnoxious individual. Hence it is, that such Democracies have ever been spectacles of turbulence and contention; have ever been found incompatible with personal security, or the rights of property; and have in general been as short in their lives, as they have been violent in their deaths. Theoretic politicians, who have patronized this species of Government, have erroneously supposed, that by reducing mankind to a perfect equality in their political rights, they would, at the same time, be perfectly equalized and assimilated in their possessions, their opinions, and their passions.

A republic, by which I mean a government in which the scheme of representation takes place, opens a different prospect, and promises the cure for which we are seeking. Let us examine the points in which it varies from pure democracy, and we shall comprehend both the nature of the cure and the efficacy which it must derive from the union.

The two great points of difference, between a democracy and a republic, are, first, the delegation of the government, in the latter, to a small number of citizens, elected by the rest; secondly, the greater number of citizens, and greater sphere of country, over which the latter may be extended.

The effect of the first difference is, on the one hand, to refine and enlarge the public views, by passing them through the medium of a chosen body of citizens, whose wisdom may best discern the true interest of their country, and whose patriotism and love of justice, will be least likely to sacrifice it to temporary or partial considerations. Under such a regulation, it may well happen, that the public voice, pronounced by the representatives of the people, will be more consonant to the public good, than if pronounced by the people themselves, convened for the purpose. On the other hand the effect may be inverted. Men of factious tempers, of local prejudices, or of sinister designs, may by intrigue, by corruption, or by other means, first obtain the suffrages, and then betray the interest of the people. The question resulting is, whether small or extensive republics are most favorable to the election of proper guardians of the public weal, and it is clearly decided in favor of the latter by two obvious considerations.

In the first place, it is to be remarked that, however small the republic may be, the representatives must be raised to a certain number, in order to guard against the cabals of a few; and that however large it may be, they must be limited to a certain number, in order to guard against the confusion of a multitude. Hence, the number of representatives in the two cases not being in proportion to that of the constituents, and being proportionally greatest in the small republic, it follows, that if the proportion of fit characters be not less in the large than in the small republic, the former will present a greater option, and consequently a greater probability of a fit choice.

In the next place, as each Representative will be chosen by a greater number of citizens in the large than in the small Republic, it will be more difficult for unworthy candidates to practise with success the vicious arts, by which elections are too often carried; and the suffrages of the people being more free, will be more likely to center on men who possess the most attractive merit, and the most diffusive and established characters.

It must be confessed, that in this, as in most other cases, there is a mean, on both sides of which inconveniences will be found to lie. By enlarging too much the number of electors, you render the representatives too little acquainted with all their local circumstances and lesser interests; as by reducing it too much, you render him unduly attached to these, and too little fit to comprehend and pursue great and national objects. The Federal Constitution forms a happy combination in this respect; the great and aggregate interests being referred to the national, the local and particular, to the state legislatures.

The other point of difference is, the greater number of citizens and extent of territory which may be brought within the compass of Republican, than of Democratic Government; and it is this circumstance principally which renders factious combinations less to be dreaded in the former, than in the latter. The smaller the society, the fewer probably will be the distinct parties and interests composing it; the fewer the distinct parties and interests, the more frequently will a majority be found of the same party; and the smaller the number of individuals composing a majority, and the smaller the compass within which they are placed, the more easily will they concert and execute their plans of oppression. Extend the sphere, and you take in a greater variety of parties and interests; you make it less probable that a majority of the whole will have a common motive to invade the rights of other citizens; or if such a common motive exists, it will be more difficult for all who feel it to discover their own strength, and to act in unison with each other. Besides other impediments, it may be remarked, that where there is a consciousness of unjust or dishonorable purposes, communication is always checked by distrust, in proportion to the number whose concurrence is necessary.

Hence it clearly appears, that the same advantage, which a Republic has over a Democracy, in controlling the effects of faction, is enjoyed by a large over a small Republic—is enjoyed by the Union over the States composing it. Does this advantage consist in the substitution of Representatives, whose enlightened views and virtuous sentiments render them superior to local prejudices, and to schemes of injustice? It will not be denied, that the Representation of the Union will be most likely to possess these requisite endowments. Does it consist in the greater security afforded by a greater variety of parties, against the event of any one party being able to outnumber and oppress the rest? In an equal degree does the increased variety of parties, comprised within the Union, increase this security? Does it, in fine, consist in the greater obstacles opposed to the concert and accomplishment of the secret wishes of an unjust and interested majority? Here, again, the extent of the Union gives it the most palpable advantage.

The influence of factious leaders may kindle a flame within their particular States, but will be unable to spread a general conflagration through the other States: a religious sect, may degenerate into a political faction in a part of the Confederacy but the variety of sects dispersed over the entire face of it, must secure the national Councils against any danger from that source: a rage for paper money, for an abolition of debts, for an equal division of property, or for any other improper or wicked project, will be less apt to pervade the whole body of the Union, than a particular member of it; in the same proportion as such a malady is more likely to taint a particular county or district, than an entire State.

In the extent and proper structure of the Union, therefore, we behold a Republican remedy for the diseases most incident to Republican Government. And according to the degree of pleasure and pride, we feel in being Republicans, ought to be our zeal in cherishing the spirit, and supporting the character of Federalists.

Publius

The Federalist No. 51

February 6, 1788
James Madison

TO THE PEOPLE OF THE STATE OF NEW YORK.

To what expedient then shall we finally resort for maintaining in practice the necessary partition of power among the several departments, as laid down in the constitution? The only answer that can be given is, that as all these exterior provisions are found to be inadequate, the defect must be supplied, by so contriving the interior structure of the government, as that its several constituent parts may, by their mutual relations, be the means of keeping each other in their proper places. Without presuming to undertake a full development of this important idea, I will hazard a few general observations, which may perhaps place it in a clearer light, and enable us to form a more correct judgment of the principles and structure of the government planned by the convention.

In order to lay a due foundation for that separate and distinct exercise of the different powers of government, which to a certain extent, is admitted on all hands to be essential to the preservation of liberty, it is evident that each department should have a will of its own; and consequently should be so constituted, that the members of each should have as little agency as possible in the appointment of the members of the others. Were this principle rigorously adhered to, it would require that all the appointments for the supreme executive, legislative, and judiciary magistracies, should be drawn from the same fountain of authority, the people, through channels, having no communication whatever with one another. Perhaps such a plan of constructing the several departments would be less difficult in practice than it may in contemplation appear. Some difficulties however, and some additional expense, would attend the execution of it. Some deviations therefore from the principle must be admitted. In the constitution of the judiciary department in particular, it might be inexpedient to insist rigorously on the principle; first, because peculiar qualifications being essential in the members, the primary consideration ought to be to select that mode of choice, which best secures these qualifications; secondly, because the permanent tenure by which the appointments are held in that department, must soon destroy all sense of dependence on the authority conferring them.

It is equally evident that the members of each department should be as little dependent as possible on those of the others, for the emoluments annexed to their offices. Were the executive magistrate, or the judges, not independent of the legislature in this particular, their independence in every other would be merely nominal.

But the great security against a gradual concentration of the several powers in the same department, consists in giving to those who administer each department, the necessary constitutional means, and personal motives, to resist encroachments of the others. The provision for defense must in this, as in all other cases, be made commensurate to the danger of attack. Ambition must be made to counteract ambition. The interest of the man must be connected with the constitutional right of the place. It may be a reflection on human nature, that such devices should be necessary to control the abuses of government. But what is government itself but the greatest of all reflections on human nature? If men were angels, no government would be necessary. If angels were to govern men, neither external nor internal controls on government would be necessary. In framing a government which is to be administered by men over men, the great difficulty lies in this: You must first enable the government to control the governed; and in the next place, oblige it to control itself. A dependence on the people is no doubt the primary control on the government; but experience has taught mankind the necessity of auxiliary precautions.

This policy of supplying by opposite and rival interests, the defect of better motives, might be traced through the whole system of human affairs, private as well as public. We see it particularly displayed in all the subordinate distributions of power; where the constant aim is to divide and arrange the several offices in such a manner as that each may be a check on the other; that the private interest of every individual, may be a sentinel over the public rights. These inventions of prudence cannot be less requisite in the distribution of the supreme powers of the state.

But it is not possible to give to each department an equal power of self defense. In republican government the legislative authority, necessarily, predominates. The remedy for this inconveniency is, to divide the legislature into different branches; and to render them by different modes of election, and different principles of action, as little connected with each other, as the nature of their common functions, and their common dependence on the society, will admit. It may even be necessary to guard against dangerous encroachments by still further precautions. As the weight of the legislative authority requires that it should be thus divided, the weakness of the executive may require, on the other hand, that it should be fortified. An absolute negative, on the legislature, appears at first view to be the natural defense with which the executive magistrate should be armed. But perhaps it would be neither altogether safe, nor alone sufficient. On ordinary occasions, it might not be exerted with the requisite firmness; and on extraordinary occasions, it might be prefidiously abused. May not this defect of an absolute negative be supplied, by some qualified connection between this weaker department, and the weaker branch of the stronger department, by which the latter may be led to support the constitutional rights of the former, without being too much detached from the rights of its own department?

If the principles on which these observations are founded be just, as I persuade myself they are, and they be applied as a criterion, to the several state constitutions, and to the federal constitution, it will be found, that if the latter does not perfectly correspond with them, the former are infinitely less able to bear such a test.

There are moreover two considerations particularly applicable to the federal system of America, which place that system in a very interesting point of view.

First. In a single republic, all the power surrendered by the people, is submitted to the administration of a single government; and usurpations are guarded against by a division of the government into distinct and separate departments. In the compound republic of America, the power surrendered by the people, is first divided between two distinct governments, and then the portion allotted to each, subdivided among distinct and separate departments. Hence a double security arises to the rights of the people. The different governments will control each other; at the same time that each will be controlled by itself.

Second. It is of great importance in a republic, not only to guard the society against the oppression of its rulers; but to guard one part of the society against the injustice of the other part. Different interests necessarily exist in different classes of citizens. If a majority be united by a common interest, the rights of the minority will be insecure. There are but two methods of providing against this evil: The one by creating a will in the community independent of the majority, that is, of the society itself, the other by comprehending in the society so many separate descriptions of citizens, as will render an unjust combination of a majority of the whole, very improbable, if not impracticable. The first method prevails in all governments possessing an hereditary or self appointed authority. This at best is but a precarious security; because a power independent of the society may as well espouse the unjust views of the major, as the rightful interests, of the minor party, and may possibly be turned against both parties. The second method will be exemplified in the federal republic of the United States. While all authority in it will be derived from and dependent on the society, the society itself will be broken into so many parts, interests and classes of citizens, that the rights of individuals or of the minority, will be in little danger from interested combinations of the majority. In a free government, the security for civil rights must be the same as for religious rights. It consists in the one case in the multiplicity of interests, and in the other, in the multiplicity of sects. The degree of security in both cases will depend on the number of interests and sects; and this may be presumed to depend on the extent of country and number of people comprehended under the same government. This view of the subject must particularly recommend a proper federal system to all the sincere and considerate friends of republican government: Since it shows that in exact proportion as the territory of the union may be formed into more circumscribed confederacies or states, oppressive combinations of a majority will be facilitated, the best security under the republican form, for the rights of every class of citizens, will be diminished; and consequently, the stability and independence of some member of the government, the only other security, must be proportionally increased. Justice is the end of government. It is the end of civil society. It ever has been, and ever will be pursued, until it be obtained, or until liberty be lost in the pursuit. In a society under the forms of which the stronger faction can readily unite and oppress the weaker, anarchy may as truly be said to reign, as in a state of nature where the weaker individual is not secured against the violence of the stronger: And as in the latter state even the stronger individuals are prompted by the uncertainty of their condition, to submit to a government which may protect the weak as well as themselves: So in the former state, will the more powerful factions or parties be gradually induced by a like motive, to wish for a government which will protect all parties, the weaker as well as the more powerful. It can be little doubted, that if the state of Rhode Island was separated from the confederacy, and left to itself, the insecurity of rights under the popular form of government within such narrow limits, would be displayed by such reiterated oppressions of factious majorities, that some power altogether independent of the people would soon be called for by the voice of the very factions whose misrule had proved the necessity of it. In the extended republic of the United States, and among the great variety of interests, parties and sects which it embraces, a coalition of a majority of the whole society could seldom take place on any other principles than those of justice and the general good; and there being thus less danger to a minor from the will of the major party, there must be less pretext also, to provide for the security of the former, by introducing into the government a will not dependent on the latter; or in other words, a will independent of the society itself. It is no less certain than it is important, notwithstanding the contrary opinions which have been entertained, that the larger the society, provided it lie within a practicable sphere, the more duly capable it will be of self government. And happily for the republican cause, the practicable sphere may be carried to a very great extent, by a judicious modification and mixture of the federal principle.

Publius

Presidents of the United States

President	Year	Party	Most Noteworthy Event
George Washington	1789-1797	Federalist	Establishment of Federal Judiciary
John Adams	1797-1801	Federalist	Alien-Sedition Acts
Thomas Jefferson	1801-1809	Dem.-Republican	First President to Defeat Incumbent/Louisiana Purchase
James Madison	1809-1817	Dem.-Republican	War of 1812
James Monroe	1817-1825	Dem.-Republican	Monroe Doctrine/ Missouri Compromise
John Quincy Adams	1825-1829	Dem.-Republican	Elected by "King Caucus"
Andrew Jackson	1829-1837	Democratic	Set up Spoils System
Martin Van Buren	1837-1841	Democratic	Competitive Parties Established
William H. Harrison	1841	Whig	Universal White Male Suffrage
John Tyler	1841-1845	Whig	Texas Annexed
James K. Polk	1845-1849	Democratic	Mexican-American War
Zachary Taylor	1849-1850	Whig	California Gold Rush
Millard Fillmore	1850-1853	Whig	Compromise of 1850
Franklin Pierce	1853-1857	Democratic	Republican Party Formed
James Buchanan	1857-1861	Democratic	Dred Scott Decision
Abraham Lincoln	1861-1865	Republican	Civil War
Andrew Johnson	1865-1869	Republican	First Impeachment of President
Ulysses S. Grant	1869-1877	Republican	Reconstruction of South
Rutherford B. Hayes	1877-1881	Republican	End of Reconstruction
James A. Garfield	1881	Republican	Assassinated by Job-seeker
Chester A. Arthur	1881-1885	Republican	Civil Service Reform
Grover Cleveland	1885-1889	Democratic	Casts 102 Vetoes in One Year
Benjamin Harrison	1889-1893	Republican	McKinley Law Raises Tarrifs
Grover Cleveland	1893-1897	Democratic	Depression / Pullman Strike
William McKinley	1897-1901	Republican	Spanish-American War
Theodore Roosevelt	1901-1909	Republican	Conservation / Panama Canal
William H. Taft	1909-1913	Republican	Judicial Reform
Woodrow Wilson	1913-1921	Democratic	Progressive Reforms / World War I
Warren G. Harding	1921-1923	Republican	Return to Normalcy
Calvin Coolidge	1923-1929	Republican	Cuts Taxes / Promotes Business
Herbert C. Hoover	1929-1933	Republican	Great Depression
Franklin D. Roosevelt	1933-1945	Democratic	New Deal / World War II
Harry S Truman	1945-1953	Democratic	Beginning of Cold War
Dwight D. Eisenhower	1953-1961	Republican	End of Korean War
John F. Kennedy	1961-1963	Democratic	Cuban Missile Crisis
Lyndon B. Johnson	1963-1969	Democratic	Great Society / Vietnam War
Richard M. Nixon	1969-1974	Republican	Watergate Scandal
Gerald R. Ford	1974-1977	Republican	War Powers Resolution
James Earl Carter	1977-1981	Democratic	Iranian Hostage Crisis
Ronald Reagan	1981-1989	Republican	Tax Cut / Expenditure Cuts
George Bush	1989-1993	Republican	End of Cold War / Persian Gulf War
William J. Clinton	1993-	Democratic	Deficit Reduction

Glossary

administration
The president and his political appointees responsible for directing the executive branch of government.

administrative discretion
Power to interpret a legislative mandate.

advice and consent
Support for a presidential action by a designated number of senators.

affirmative action
Programs designed to enhance opportunities for groups that have suffered discrimination in the past.

affirmative-action redistricting
The process of drawing district lines to maximize the number of majority-minority districts.

agency
Basic organizational unit of federal government. Also known as *office* or *bureau*.

agenda setting
Occurs when the media affect the issues and problems people think about.

Aid to Families with Dependent Children (AFDC)
Public assistance program established in 1935 as part of the Social Security Act; replaced in 1996 by Temporary Assistance to Needy Families (TANF).

ambassadors
The heads of the diplomatic delegations to major foreign countries.

amicus curiae
Latin term meaning "friend of the court." It refers to legal briefs submitted by interested groups who are not directly party to a court case.

Annapolis Convention
1786 meeting to discuss constitutional reform.

Anti-Federalists
Those who opposed ratification of the Constitution.

appeal
The procedure whereby the losing side asks a higher court to overturn a lower-court decision.

appropriations
Process of providing funding for government activities and programs that have been authorized.

aristocracy
Government by a few leaders made eligible by birthright.

Articles of Confederation
The United States's first basic governing document (1781- 1789) and forerunner to the Constitution.

associate justice
One of the eight Justices of the Supreme Court who are not the chief justice.

authorization process
Term given to the process of providing statutory authority for a government program or activity.

balancing doctrine
Supreme Court enunciation that freedom of speech must be balanced against other competing public interests at stake in particular circumstances.

Bay of Pigs
Location of CIA-advised effort by Cuban exiles in 1961 to invade Cuba and overthrow Fidel Castro.

beltway insider
Person living in Washington metropolitan area who is engaged in, or well informed about, national politics and government.

bicameral
Description of a legislature that contains two chambers.

Bill of Rights
The first ten amendments to the Constitution that protect individual and state rights.

black codes
Laws that applied to newly freed slaves but not to whites.

blame avoidance
Set of political techniques employed by political leaders to disguise their actions and shift the blame to others.

block grant
Federal grant to state and/or local government that imposes minimal restrictions on use of funds.

block voting
Voting in which nearly all members of one group (i.e., African Americans) vote for a candidate of their race whereas nearly all members of another group (i.e., whites) vote against that candidate.

borking
Raising the political and electoral significance of a confirmation process by means of a media campaign.

bracket creep
Hidden tax increases made possible by not indexing taxes for inflation; thus, cost of living raises push people into higher tax brackets even though their real incomes (that is, adjusted for inflation) are unchanged.

brief
Written arguments presented to the court by lawyers on behalf of clients.

Brown v. *Board of Education of Topeka, Kansas*
1954 court decision declaring racial segregation in schools unconstitutional.

bully-pulpit
The use of the presidential platform to persuade the public to support the president's policies.

bureaucracy
Organization designed to perform a particular set of tasks.

cabinet
The combined heads of all executive-branch departments.

campaign consultant
Expert in the tools of modern candidate-based campaigns-especially polling and the media.

categorical grant
Federal grants to state and/or local governments that imposes programmatic restrictions on use of funds.

caucus
All Democratic members of the House or Senate. Members in caucus elect the party leaders, ratify the choice of committee leaders, and debate party positions on issues. *See also* Conference.

Central Intelligence Agency (CIA)
Agency primarily responsible for gathering and analyzing information about the political and military activities of other nations.

cert
See writ of *certiorari*.

checks and balances
Division of power into several branches by the Constitution, giving each branch the power to block the actions of the others.

chief justice
Head of Supreme Court and federal judiciary.

chief of staff
Head of White House staff. Has continuous, direct contact with president.

circuit court of appeals
Court to which decisions by federal district courts are appealed.

citizenship
Status held by someone entitled to all the rights and privileges of a full-fledged member of a political community.

civic republicanism
A political philosophy that emphasizes the obligation of citizens to act virtuously in pursuit of the common good.

civil code
Laws regulating relations among individuals. Alleged violators are sued by presumed victims, who ask courts to award damages and otherwise offer relief.

civil disobedience
A peaceful, well-publicized violation of a law designed to dramatize its injustice.

civil liberties
Fundamental freedoms that together preserve the rights of a free people.

civil rights
Right to equal treatment under the law.

Civil Rights Amendments
Amendments 13, 14, and 15, which abolished slavery, redefined civil rights, and guaranteed the right to vote to all adult male citizens.

civil service
Government employees chosen according to their educational qualifications, performance on examinations, and work experience.

class action
Suit brought on behalf of all individuals in a particular class, whether or not they are actually participating in the suit.

clear and present danger doctrine
Principle stating that people should have complete freedom of speech unless their language causes a danger to the nation, as in cases of espionage.

clericalism
Exercise of political power by religious leaders and organizations, such as established churches.

closed-ended question
Survey question that asks people to choose their answer from a set of prespecified alternatives.

cloture
Motion to end debate; requires 60 votes to pass.

CNN effect
Purported ability of TV to raise a distant foreign affairs situation to national prominence by broadcasting vivid pictures.

coalition government
Occurs when two or more minority parties must join together in order to elect a prime minister. Such governments are common in multiparty systems.

coattails
Positive electoral fallout of a popular presidential candidate on congressional candidates of the party.

Cold War
The forty-three-year period (1946-1989) during which the United States and the Soviet Union threatened one another with mutual destruction by nuclear warfare.

colonial assembly
Lower legislative chamber elected by male property owners in a colony.

colonial council
Upper legislative chamber appointed by British officials, upon the recommendation of the governor.

commander in chief
The President in his constitutional role as head of the armed forces.

commerce clause
Constitutional provision that gives Congress power to regulate commerce "among the states."

commercial speech
Advertising or other speech made for business purposes; may be regulated.

communism
A particular kind of socialism based on the work of Karl Marx, who taught that human history is the product of a class struggle between those who exploit and those who are exploited.

Compositional effect
A change in the behavior of a group that arises from a change in the group's composition, not from a change in the behavior of individuals in the group.

concurring opinion
A written opinion prepared by judges who vote with the majority but who wish to disagree with or elaborate some aspect of the majority opinion.

conference
What Republicans call their Congressional caucus.

conference committee
Group of representatives from both the House and Senate who iron out the differences in the two chambers' versions of a bill or resolution.

Congressional Budget Office (CBO)
Congressional agency that evaluates the president's budget as well as the budgetary implications of all other legislation.

Connecticut Compromise
Constitutional convention proposal that created a House proportionate to population and a Senate in which each state was represented equally.

constituency
Those legally entitled to vote for a public official.

constituency service
The totality of Congress members' district service and constituent assistance work.

constituent assistance
Efforts of members of Congress to help individuals and groups when they have difficulties with federal agencies.

Constitution
Basic governing document for the United States.

containment
U.S. policy that attempted to stop the spread of communism in the expectation that this system of government would eventually collapse on its own.

cooperative federalism
A theory stating that all levels of government could work together to solve common problems. Also known as *marble-cake federalism.*

corporatist
The official representation of large interest groups in government decision-making bodies.

Council of Economic Advisors (CEA)
Three economists who head up a professional staff that advises the president on economic policy.

criminal code
Laws regulating relations between individuals and society. Alleged violators are prosecuted by government.

critical election
Election that marks the emergence of a new, lasting alignment of partisan support within the electorate.

Cuban missile crisis
Soviet effort to place missiles in Cuba in 1962.

debt
The cumulation of yearly deficits.

Declaration of Independence
Document signed in 1776 declaring the United States to be a country independent of Great Britain.

***de facto* segregation**
Segregation that occurs as the result of decisions by private individuals.

defendant
One accused of violating the civil or criminal code.

deficit
When government spending exceeds revenues.

***de jure* segregation**
Racial segregation that is legally sanctioned.

democracy
System in which governmental power is widely shared among the citizens, usually through free and open elections.

department
Organizational unit into which many agencies of federal government are grouped.

Department of Defense
Cabinet department responsible for managing U.S. armed forces.

deregulation
Removal of government rules that once controlled an industry.

devolution
Return of governmental responsibilities to state and local governments.

dignified aspect
According to Walter Bagehot, the aspect of government, including royalty and ceremony, that generates citizen respect and loyalty.

Dillon's rule
Legal doctrine that local governments are mere creatures of the state.

direct action
Everything from peaceful sit-ins and demonstrations to riots and even rebellion.

direct democracy
Type of democracy in which ordinary people are the government, making all the laws themselves.

direct mail
Computer-generated letters, faxes, and other communications by a group to people who might be

sympathetic to an appeal for money or support.

direct primary
A method of choosing party candidates by popular vote of all self-identified party members. This method of nominating candidates is virtually unknown outside the United States.

discharge petition
Means by which a House majority (218) may take a bill out of a committee that refuses to report it.

dissenting opinion
Written opinion presenting the reasoning of justices who vote against the majority.

distributive tendency
Penchant of Congress for spreading the benefits of any program widely across the districts of the members.

distributive theory
Theory that sees committees as a standing log-roll in which members get to serve on the committees of most importance to them.

district attorney
Person responsible for prosecuting criminal cases.

district service
Efforts of members of Congress to make sure their districts get a share of federal projects and programs.

diversity
A concept that is relative to time and place; currently refers primarily to ethnic and racial distinctions among people (as opposed to, say, class or occupational differences).

divided government
Said to exist when a single party does not control the presidency and both houses of Congress.

divine right
Doctrine that says God selects the sovereign for the people.

domestic policy
Government programs and regulations that directly affect those living within a country.

double jeopardy
Placing someone on trial for the same crime twice.

dual sovereignty
A theory of federalism saying that both levels of government are sovereign within their own sphere.

due process clause
Found in the Fifth and Fourteenth Amendments to the Constitution, forbids deprivation of life, liberty, or property without due process of law.

earmark
A specific congressional designation as to the way money is to be spent.

Earned Income Tax Credit (EITC)
Provision that gives back tax payments to those who have little income.

efficient aspect
Distinct from the dignified aspect, according to Walter Bagehot, the aspect of government that involves making policy, administering the laws, and settling disputes.

election-cycle interpretation
The argument that, whatever their party, presidents attempt to slow the economy early in their terms, then expand it as their reelection approaches.

Electoral College
Those chosen to cast a direct vote for president by a process determined by each state.

electoral incentive
Desire to obtain or remain in an elected office.

electoral system
A means of translating popular votes into control of public offices.

electoral vote
Cast by electors, with each state receiving one vote for each of its members of the House of Representatives and one vote for each of its Senators.

eligible voting age population
All people in the United States over the age of 18 minus those not eligible to vote because of mental illness, criminal conviction, or noncitizenship.

embassies
House ambassadors and their diplomatic aides in the capital cities of foreign countries.

end-run
Effort by agencies to avoid OMB controls by appealing to allies in Congress.

Environmental Protection Agency (EPA)
Agency responsible for issuing regulations designed to protect the environment from unwanted pollutants.

equal protection clause
Fourteenth Amendment clause specifying that no state can deny any of its people equal protection under the law.

Equal Rights Amendment (ERA)
Proposed amendment to the Constitution which banned gender discrimination.

equal time rule
Promulgated by the FCC, required any station selling time to a candidate to sell time to other candidates at comparable rates.

equality of condition
The notion that individuals have a right to a more or less equal part of the material goods society produces.

equality of opportunity
The notion that individuals should have an equal chance to advance economically through individual talent and hard work.

establishment of religion clause
Denies the government the power to establish any single religious practice as superior.

executive agreement
Agreement with foreign countries that requires only a presidential signature.

Executive Office of the President (EOP)
Agency that houses both top coordinating offices and other operating agencies.

executive order
A presidential directive that has the force of law, though it is not enacted by Congress.

executive privilege
The right of members of the executive branch to have private communications among themselves that need not be shared with Congress.

exit poll
Survey of actual voters taken as they leave the polling stations.

externalities
Consequences of activities that do not directly affect those engaged in them.

fairness doctrine
Promulgated by the FCC, required stations to carry some public affairs programming and to balance the points of view expressed.

fascism
Rule by a charismatic dictator supported by a strong party that permeates society.

federal district court
The lowest level of the federal court system and the court in which most federal trials are held.

Federal Reserve System ("Fed")
The country's central bank, which executes monetary policy by manipulating the supply of funds that lower banks can lend.

federalism
Division of fundamental governmental authority between at least two different levels of government.

Federalist Papers
Essays written in support of the Constitution's ratification that have become a classic argument for the American constitutional system.

Federalists
Those who wrote and campaigned on behalf of the ratification of the Constitution.

fiduciaries
Someone whose duty is to act in the best interest of someone else.

fighting words doctrine
Supreme Court writing in *Chaplinsky* v. *New Hampshire* (1942), saying some words constitute violent acts.

filibuster
Delaying tactic by which one or more senators refuse to allow a bill or resolution to be considered, either by speaking indefinitely or by offering dilatory motions and amendments.

First Continental Congress
The first quasi-governmental institution that spoke for nearly all the colonies (1774).

first lady
Traditional title of the president's spouse.

fiscal policy
The sum total of government taxing and spending decisions, which determines the level of the deficit or surplus.

flat tax
A tax that is neither progressive nor regressive: Everyone pays at the same rate.

focus groups
Small groups used to explore how ordinary people think about issues and how they react to the language of political appeals.

food stamps
Public assistance program that provides recipients with stamps that can be used to purchase food.

foreign policy
Conduct of relations among nation states.

foreign service
Diplomats who staff U.S. embassies and consulates.

framing
Stating an argument in such a way as to emphasize one set of considerations and deemphasize others.

franchise
The right to vote.

frank
Name given to representatives' and senators' free use of the U.S. mail for sending communications to constituents.

free exercise of religion clause
Protects the right of individuals to practice their religion.

free rider problem
Problem that arises when people who share a group's goals do not join or contribute to it because their personal contribution seems too small to make a difference.

fundamental freedoms doctrine
Court doctrine stating that laws impinging upon the freedoms fundamental to the preservation of democratic practice-speech, press, assembly and religion-are to be scrutinized by the courts more closely than other legislation. These are also termed the *preferred freedoms*.

general election
Final election that selects the officeholder.

general revenue sharing
The most comprehensive of block grants, it gave money to state and local governments to be used for any purpose whatsoever.

gerrymandering
Drawing boundary lines of congressional districts in order to advantage some partisan or political interest.

Gideon* v. *Wainwright
Supreme Court decision in 1963 giving indigent people accused of crimes the right of court-appointed counsel.

government
The institution in society which has a "monopoly of the legitimate use of physical force".

grandfather clause
Racially restrictive southern laws permitting a man to vote if his father or grandfather could have voted.

grassroots lobbying
Efforts by groups and associations to influence elected officials indirectly, by arousing their constituents.

gross domestic product (GDP)
Same as GNP except that goods and services produced outside the specific nation are excluded and

revenues received by foreign corporations are included.

gross national product (GNP)
The monetary value of all goods and services produced by a nation during a given year.

hammer
Harsh penalty set by Congress if a regulatory agency does not achieve a statutory objective.

Hatch Act
1939 law prohibiting federal employees from political campaigning and solicitation.

honeymoon
Period early in a president's term when partisan conflict and media criticism are minimal.

idealists
Those who say that U.S. foreign policy should be guided primarily by democratic principles-the spread of liberty, equality, human rights, and respect for international law throughout the world.

ideology
System of beliefs in which one or more organizing principles connect your views on a wide range of issues.

impeachment
Recommendation by a majority of the House of Representatives that a president, other executive branch official, or judge of the federal courts be removed from office; removal depends upon 2/3 vote of Senate.

implementation
The way in which grant programs are administered at the local level.

in-and-outers
Political appointees who come in, go out, and come back in again with each change in administration.

incumbency advantage
The electoral gain from being an incumbent over and above other personal and political characteristics of the candidate.

independent counsel (originally called special prosecutor)
Legal officer appointed by the court to investigate allegations of criminal activity against high-ranking members of the executive branch.

independent regulatory agency
Agencies that have quasi judicial responsibilities.

indexing
Adjusting tax brackets, benefit levels, and so forth for inflation.

individual motivations for voting
The tangible and intangible benefits and costs of exercising one's right to vote.

inflation
A sustained rise in the price level so that people need more money to purchase the same amount of goods and services.

information cost
Time and mental effort required to absorb and store information, whether from conversations or the media.

informational theory
Theory that sees committees as means of providing reliable information about the actual consequences of the legislation members could adopt.

inherent executive power
Presidential authority inherent to the executive branch of government, although not specifically mentioned in the Constitution.

inner cabinet
Four original departments (State, Treasury, Justice, and Defense) whose secretaries typically have the closest ties to the president.

interest group
Organization or association that engages in politics on behalf of its members.

intergovernmental grant
Grant from the national government to state or local government.

initiative
Proposed laws or state constitutional amendments placed on the ballot by citizen petition.

Iran-Contra scandal
An allegedly illegal diversion of funds from the sale of arms to Iran to a guerrilla group in Nicaragua.

iron curtain
Armed barrier during Cold War that prevented movement across national borders between communist East Europe and democratic West Europe.

iron triangle
Close, stable connection among agencies, interest groups, and congressional committees.

isolationism
A foreign policy that keeps the United States separate from the conflicts taking place among other nations.

issue networks
Loose, competitive relationship among policy experts, interest groups, congressional committees, and government agencies in a particular policy area.

Issue public
Group of people particularly affected by or concerned with specific issues.

item veto
Recently enacted presidential authority to negate particular provisions of a law.

Jim Crow laws
Laws passed by southern states, after Reconstruction, enforcing segregation.

Joint Chiefs of Staff
Heads of each military service, the army, navy, air force, and marine corps-together with a chair and vice-chair nominated by the president and confirmed by the Senate.

judicial activism
Doctrine that says the principle of *stare decisis* should sometimes be sacrificed in order to adapt the Constitution to changing conditions.

judicial restraint
Doctrine that says courts should, if at all possible, avoid overturning a prior court decision.

judicial review
Power of the courts to declare null and void laws of Congress and of state legislatures they find unconstitutional.

Keynesianism
Economic policy based on the belief that governments can control the economy by manipulating aggregate demand, running deficits to expand it and surpluses to contract it.

laboratories of democracy
Doctrine that state and local governments contribute to democracy by providing places where experiments are tried and proved.

law clerk
Young, influential aide to a justice.

League of Nations
International organization created after World War I to settle international disputes; became the precursor of the United Nations.

legal distinction
The legal difference between a case at hand and previous cases decided by the courts.

libel
False statement defaming another.

liberalism
Philosophy that elevates and empowers the individual as opposed to religious, hereditary, governmental, or other forms of authority.

living-Constitution theory
A theory of constitutional interpretation that places the meaning of the Constitution in light of the total history of the United States.

lobbying
Attempts by representatives of groups and associations to directly influence the decisions of government officials.

lobbyist
One who engages in lobbying. *See* Lobbying.

log-rolling
Colloquial term given to politicians' trading of favors, votes, or generalized support for each other's proposals.

machine
A highly organized party under the control of a boss, based on patronage and control of government activities. They were common in many cities in the late nineteenth and early twentieth century.

majority
50 percent plus one.

majority leader
Leader of the majority party, the Speaker's chief lieutenant in the House, and the most important officer in the Senate. He or she is responsible for managing the floor.

majority-minority districts
District in which a minority group is the numerical majority.

mandate
Implied authorization by the electorate to govern boldly in a certain way.

manifest destiny
Belief in the inevitability that the United States would spread democracy throughout the North American continent.

Mapp v. Ohio
Court decision saying that any evidence obtained without a proper search warrant may not be introduced in a trial.

marble-cake federalism
A theory that said all levels of government can work together to solve common problems. Also known as *cooperative federalism*.

Marbury v. Madison
Supreme Court decision (1803) in which the court first exercised the power of judicial review.

markup
Process in which a committee or subcommittee considers and revises a bill that has been introduced.

mass media
Means of communication that are technologically capable of reaching most people and economically affordable to most.

mass public
Ordinary people for whom politics is a peripheral concern.

matching funds
Public moneys (from $3 checkoffs on income tax returns) that the Federal Election Commission distributes to primary candidates and the general election nominees according to a formula.

Mayflower Compact
First document in colonial America in which the people gave their expressed consent to be governed.

McCulloch v. Maryland
Decision of 1819 in which Supreme Court declares unconstitutional the state's power to tax a federal government entity.

medicaid
Program that provides medical care to those of low income.

medicare
Program that provides social security recipients a broad range of medical benefits.

minimal effects thesis
Theory that the mass media have little or no effect on public opinion.

minority leader
Leader of the minority party, who speaks for the party in dealing with the majority.

Miranda v. Arizona
Court decision stating that persons must be told by police that they need not testify against themselves.

mobilization
The efforts of parties, groups, and activists to encourage their supporters to participate in politics.

monetarism
An economic school of thought that rejects Keynesianism, arguing that only monetary policy affects the state of the economy.

monetary policy
Consists of the actions taken by government to affect the level of interest rates.

Monroe Doctrine
Policy that declared the Western Hemisphere to be free of European colonial influence (1819).

mugwumps
A group of civil service reformers organized in the 1880s who said government officials should be chosen on a merit basis.

multi-party system
System in which more than two parties compete for control of government. Most of the world's democracies are multi-party systems.

multiple referrals
Said to occur when party leaders give more than one committee responsibility for the consideration of a bill.

National Association for the Advancement of Colored People (NAACP)
Civil rights organization, dating from 1909, that relies heavily on a legal strategy to pursue its objectives.

national convention
Quadrennial gathering of party officials and delegates who select presidential and vice presidential nominees and adopt party platforms. Extension of the direct primary to the presidential level after 1968 has greatly lessened the importance of the conventions.

national forces
Electoral effects felt across most states and congressional districts. Most often they reflect especially strong presidential candidates, party performance, or the state of the economy.

National Security Council (NSC)
White House agency responsible for coordinating U.S. foreign policy.

natural monopoly
A situation in which a public service is best provided by a single company.

necessary and proper clause
Says Congress has the power to do whatever is necessary and proper to carry out its other powers.

New Deal
Programs created by the Franklin Roosevelt administration that expanded the power of the federal government for the purpose of stimulating economic recovery and establishing a national safety net.

New Jersey Plan
Small-state proposal for constitutional reform.

new media
Cable TV, fax, e-mail, and the Internet —the consequences of technological advances of the past few decades.

nullification
A doctrine developed by John Calhoun saying that states have the authority to declare acts of Congress unconstitutional.

obscenity
Publicly offensive language or portrayals with no redeeming social value.

Office of Management and Budget (OMB)
Agency responsible for coordinating work of executive-branch departments and agencies.

official turnout
Defined by the Census Bureau as the number of people voting for president divided by the size of the voting age population.

oligarchy
Government by a few who gain office by means of wealth, military power, or membership in a single political party.

ombudsman
Official whose job is to mediate conflicts between citizens and government bureaucracies.

one hundred days
The first days a president is in office, during which time great legislative accomplishments are expected.

open-ended question
Survey question that allows people to answer in their own words.

opinion
In legal parlance, a court's explanation for its decision.

original intent
A theory of constitutional interpretation that determines the constitutionality of a law by ascertaining the intentions of those who wrote the Constitution.

outer cabinet
Newer departments with fewer ties to president and more influenced by interest group pressures.

override
Congressional passage of a bill by a two-thirds vote over the president's veto.

partisan interpretation
The argument that Democratic administrations set economic policy to benefit lower-income, wage-earning groups, and that Republican administrations set economic policy to benefit higher-income business and professional groups.

party alignment
The social and economic groups that consistently support each party.

party caucus
Meeting of party activists, especially one that chooses delegates to a state or national convention.

party identification
A person's subjective feeling of affiliation with a party.

party image
A set of widely held associations between a party and particular issues and values.

Patriots
Political group defending colonial American liberties against British infringements.

patronage
Jobs, contracts, or favors given to political friends and allies.

Pendleton Act
Legislation in 1881 creating the Civil Service Commission.

permanent campaign
The next election campaign begins as soon as the last one has ended.

plain meaning of the text
A theory of constitutional interpretation that determines the constitutionality of a law in light of what the words of the Constitution obviously seem to say.

plaintiff
One who brings legal charges against another.

plea bargain
Agreement between prosecution and defense that the accused will admit to a crime, provided that other charges are dropped and the recommended sentence is shortened.

plenary
Activities of a court in which all judges participate.

Plessy v. Ferguson
Court decision declaring separate but equal public facilities constitutional.

pluralism
A school of thought holding that politics is the clash of groups that represent all important interests in society and check and balance each other.

pocket veto
Presidential veto after congressional adjournment, executed by not signing a bill into law.

policy deliberation
Debate and discussion by groups and political leaders over issues placed on the policy agenda.

policy enactment
Passage of a law by public officials.

policy implementation
Translation of legislation into a set of government programs or regulations.

policy outcome
Effect of policy outputs on individuals and businesses.

policy output
Provision of services to citizens or regulation of their conduct.

political action committee (PAC)
Specialized organization for raising and contributing campaign funds.

political activists
People who voluntarily participate in politics; they are more interested in and committed to particular issues and candidates than are ordinary citizens.

political culture
Collection of beliefs and values about the justification and operation of a country's government and politics.

political elite
Activists and officeholders who are deeply interested in and knowledgeable about politics.

political entrepreneur
Someone who is willing to assume the costs of forming and maintaining an organization even when others may free ride on them.

political parties
Groups of like-minded people who band together in an attempt to take control of government.

political socialization
The set of psychological and sociological processes by which families, schools, churches, communities, and other societal units inculcate beliefs and values in their members.

poll tax
Fee that allowed one to vote.

popular model of democracy
Type of representative democracy in which ordinary people participate actively and closely constrain the actions of public officials.

popular vote
The total vote cast for a candidate across the nation.

precedent
Previous court decision or ruling applicable to a particular case.

President pro-tempore
President of the Senate, who presides in the absence of the vice president.

presidential popularity
Evaluation of president by voters, usually as measured by a survey question asking adult population how well they think the president is doing his job.

primary election
Preliminary election in which all registered party voters are eligible to vote to select a party's nominee.

priming
Occurs when the media affect the standards people use to evaluate political figures or the severity of a problem.

prior restraint doctrine
Legal doctrine that gives individuals the right to publish without prior restraint-that is, without first submitting material to government censor.

private goods
Goods that you must purchase to enjoy, and your consumption of which precludes that of others.

professional legislature
Legislature whose members serve full-time and for long periods.

progressive tax
A tax structured so that higher-income people pay a larger proportion of their income in taxes.

Progressives
Middle-class reformers of the late nineteenth and early twentieth century who weakened the power of the machines and attempted to clean up elections and government.

proportional representation (PR)
Electoral system in which parties receive a share of seats in parliament that is proportional to the popular vote they receive.

proprietary colony
Colony governed either by a prominent English noble or by a company. See royal colony.

psychic benefits of voting
Intangible rewards such as satisfaction with doing one's duty, feelings of solidarity with the community, and so forth.

public assistance
Programs that provide to low-income households limited income and access to essential goods and services.

public defender
Attorney whose full-time responsibilities are to provide for the legal defense of indigent criminal suspects.

public goods
Goods that you can enjoy without contributing-by free-riding on the efforts of those who do.

public opinion
Those opinions held by private persons that governments find it prudent to heed.

quota
Specific number of positions set aside for a specific group, said by Supreme Court to constitute an unconstitutional classification.

"rally 'round the flag"
The tendency among the public to back presidents in moments of crisis.

real income
Income adjusted for inflation, that is, the value of the dollar; often expressed as "income in constant dollars."

realigning election
Another term for a critical election.

realignment
Occurs when the pattern of group support for political parties shifts in a significant and lasting way, such as in the last half of the twentieth century, when the white South shifted from Democratic to Republican.

realists
Those who say that U.S. foreign policy best protects democracy when it guards its own economic and military strength.

reapportionment
The allocation of House seats to the states after each decennial census.

recall election
Attempt to remove an official from office before the completion of the term.

receiver
Court official who has the authority to see that judicial orders are carried out.

recess appointment
An appointment made when the Senate is in recess.

recession
A slowdown in economic activity, officially defined as a decline that persists for 2 quarters (6 months).

Reconstruction
Period after the Civil War when military present in most southern states.

redistricting
Drawing new boundaries of congressional districts, usually after the decennial census.

referendum
A law or state constitutional amendment proposed by a legislature or city council that does not go into effect unless the required majority of voters approve it.

registered voters
Those legally eligible to vote who have registered in accord with the requirements prevailing in their state and locality.

regressive tax
A tax structured so that higher-income people pay a smaller proportion of their income in taxes.

regulation
Rules and standards that control economic, social, and political activities.

remand
The request by a higher court to a lower court to determine the best way of implementing the higher court's decision.

remedy
Court-ordered action designed to compensate plaintiffs for wrongs they have suffered.

rent subsidies
Help in paying rent for low-income families, provided they select designated housing.

representative democracy
An indirect form of democracy in which the people choose representatives who determine what government does.

responsible model of democracy
A type of representative democracy in which public officials have considerable freedom of action but are held accountable by the people for the decisions they make.

restorationist
Judge who thinks that the only way the original meaning of the Constitution can be restored is by ignoring the doctrine of stare decisis until liberal decisions have been reversed.

restrictive housing covenant
Legal promise by home buyers that they will not resell to an African American, declared unconstitutional by Supreme Court.

reversal
The overturning of a lower court decision by an appeals court or the Supreme Court.

right of privacy
Right to keep free of government interference those aspects of one's personal life that do not affect others.

rotation
The practice whereby a member of Congress stepped down after a term or two so that someone else could have the office.

royal colony
Colony governed by the king's representative upon the advice of an elected assembly. See proprietary colony.

rule
Specifies the terms and conditions under which a bill or resolution will be considered on the floor of the House; in particular, how long debate will last and how time will be allocated, and the number and type of amendments that will be in order.

sampling error
The error that arises in public opinion surveys as a result of relying on a small sample that may not be perfectly representative of the larger population.

Second Continental Congress
Political authority that directed the struggle for independence beginning in 1775.

secretary
Head of a department within executive branch.

secretary of defense
President's chief civilian advisor on defense matters and overall head of three departments, army, navy, and air force, located in the Department of Defense.

secretary of state
Officially, the president's chief foreign policy advisor and head of the Department of State, the agency responsible for conducting diplomatic relations.

select committee
Temporary committee appointed to deal with a specific issue or problem.

selection principle
Rule of thumb according to which stories with certain characteristic are chosen over stories without those characteristics.

selective benefits
Side benefits of belonging to an organization that are limited to contributing members of the organization.

selective incorporation
The case-by-case incorporation by the courts of the Bill of Rights into the due process clause of the Fourteenth Amendment.

senatorial courtesy
An informal rule that the Senate will not confirm nominees within or from a state unless they have the approval of the senior senator of the state from the president's party.

seniority
Practice by which the majority party member with longest continuous service on a committee becomes the chair.

separate but equal doctrine
A rule that said that the equal protection clause was not violated simply by the fact of racial segregation, if the separated facilities were equal.

separation of church and state - doctrine
Principle that a wall should separate the government from religious activity.

separation of powers
A system of government in which different institutions exercise different components of governmental power.

sequestered
Housing jurors privately, away from any information other than that presented in the courtroom.

Shays's Rebellion
Uprising in western Massachusetts in 1786 led by revolutionary war captain Daniel Shays.

single-issue voter
Voter who cares so deeply about some particular issue that a candidate's position on this one issue determines his or her vote.

single-member simple plurality (SMSP)
Electoral system in which the country is divided into geographic districts, and the candidates who win the most votes within their districts are elected.

social connectedness
The degree to which individuals are integrated into society-families, churches, neighborhoods, groups, and so forth.

social insurance
Program that provides benefits in return for contributions made by workers.

social issues
Issues such as obscenity, feminism, gay rights, capital punishment, prayer in the schools, and so forth, which reflect personal values more than economic interests.

social movement
Broad-based demand for government action on some problem or issue, such as civil rights for blacks and women, or environmental protection.

social policy
Programs designed to help those thought to be in need of government assistance.

social security
Social insurance program for senior citizens.

socialism
A philosophy that supports government ownership and operation of the means of production as well as government determination of the level of social and economic benefits that people receive.

socialization
The end result of all the processes by which individuals form their beliefs and values in the home, schools, churches, communities, and workplaces.

solicitor general
Government official responsible for presenting before the courts the position of the presidential administration.

Speaker
The presiding officer of the House of Representatives; normally the Speaker is the leader of the majority party.

special prosecutor)
See independent counsel.

spending clause
Constitutional provision that gives Congress the power to collect taxes to provide for the general welfare.

spin
The positive or negative slant that reporters or anchors put on their reports.

spoils system
A system of government employment in which workers are hired on the basis of party loyalty.

sponsor
Representative or senator who introduces a bill or resolution.

Stamp Act Congress
A meeting in 1765 of delegates from nine colonies to oppose the Stamp

Act; the first political organization that brought leaders from several colonies together for a common purpose.

stamp tax
Passed by Parliament in 1765, it required people in the colonies to purchase a small stamp to be affixed to legal and other documents.

standing committee
Committee with fixed membership and jurisdiction, continuing from Congress to Congress.

stare decisis
In court rulings, reliance on consistency with precedents. *See also* precedent.

state action doctrine
Rule stating that only the actions of state and local governments, not those of private individuals, must conform to the equal protection clause.

State of the Union address
In fulfillment of the constitutional obligation of reporting to Congress on the state of the Union.

statutory interpretation
The judicial act of interpreting and applying the law to particular cases.

subgovernment
A Congressional committee, bureaucratic agency, and a few allied interest groups who combine to dominate policy making in some specified policy area.

suffrage
Another term for the right to vote.

sunshine law
1976 law requiring federal government meetings to be held in public.

Supplemental Social Insurance (SSI)
Provides disabled people of low income with income assistance.

supply-side economics
Economic policy based on belief that governments can keep the economy healthy by supplying the conditions, especially low taxes and minimal regulation, that encourage private economic activity.

supremacy clause
Says the Constitution is the supreme law of the land, to which all judges are bound.

surplus
When government spending is less than revenues.

survey research
The scientific design and administration of public opinion polls.

suspect classification
Categorization of a particular group that will be closely scrutinized by the courts to see if its use is unconstitutional.

suspension of the rules
Fast-track procedure for considering bills and resolutions in the House; debate is limited to 40 minutes, no amendments are in order, and a two-thirds majority is required for passage.

tax base
Those type of activities, types of property, or kinds of investments that are subject to taxation.

tax preferences
Activities, properties, or investments that receive special tax treatment.

taxation without representation
Levying of taxes by a government in which the people are not represented by their own elected officials.

Temporary Assistance for Needy Families (TANF)
Welfare reform law passed by Congress in 1996.

three-fifths compromise
When calculating representation in the House of Representatives, it counted slaves as three-fifths of a person; repealed by the Fourteenth Amendment.

ticket-splitting
Occurs when a voter does not vote a straight party ticket.

Tonkin Gulf Resolution
Congressional resolution giving the president the authority to send troops to Vietnam.

Tories
Those who opposed independence from Great Britain.

transition
The period after a presidential candidate has won the November election but before the candidate assumes office as President on January 20.

treaties
Official agreements with foreign countries that are ratified by the Senate.

trial venue
Place where a trial is held.

two-party system
System in which only two significant parties compete for office. Such systems are in the minority among world democracies.

two-presidency theory
Theory that explains why presidents exercise greater power over foreign affairs than over domestic policy.

two-thirds rule
Rule governing Democratic national conventions from 1832 to 1936. It required that the presidential and vice presidential nominees receive at least two-thirds of the delegates' votes.

tyranny of the majority
Stifling of dissent by those voted into power by the majority.

unanimous consent agreement
Agreement that sets forth the terms and conditions according to which the Senate will consider a bill; these are individually negotiated by the leadership for each bill.

unemployment
Describes the circumstance when people who are willing to work at the prevailing wage cannot get jobs.

unfunded mandates
Federal regulations that impose burdens on state and local governments without appropriating enough money to cover costs.

- **unitary government**
  System under which all authority is held by a single, national government.
- **United Nations (UN)**
  Organization of all nation states whose purpose is to preserve world peace and foster economic and social development throughout the world.
- *U.S. v. Curtiss-Wright*
  Supreme court decision in which Congress is given the authority to delegate foreign policy responsibilities to the president.
- **veto power**
  Presidential rejection of congressional legislation. May be overridden by two-thirds vote in each congressional chamber. Most state governors also have the veto power over their legislatures.
- **Virginia Plan**
  Constitutional proposal supported by convention delegates from large states.

- **voting age population**
  All people in the United States over the age of 18.
- **War on Poverty**
  One of the most controversial of the Great Society programs.
- **War Powers Resolution**
  1973 congressional resolution requiring the president to formally notify Congress any time he orders U.S. troops into military action.
- **Whigs**
  Political opposition in eighteenth-century England that developed a theory of rights and representation.
- **whips**
  Members of Congress who serve as informational channels between the leadership and the rank and file, conveying the leadership's views and intentions to the members, and vice versa.
- **White House Office**
  Political appointees who work directly for the president, many of

whom occupy offices in the White House.
- **white primary**
  Primary elections, held by the Democratic party, that excluded non-whites from participation in many southern states.
- **winner-take-all**
  Refers to any voting procedure in which the side with the most votes gets all of the seats or delegates at stake.
- **writ of *certiorari* (cert)**
  A document issued by the Supreme Court indicating that the Court will review a decision taken by a lower court.
- *Youngstown*
  Case in which the Supreme Court placed limits on the executive power of the president.
- **zone of acceptance**
  Range within which Congress allows agencies to interpret and apply statutes.

End Notes

TO OUR COLLEAGUES

1. *Pluralist Democracy in the United States: Conflict and Consent* (Chicago: Rand McNally, 1967).

2. Robert A. Dahl, *The New American Political (Dis)Order* (Berkeley, CA; IGS Press, 1994): 1.

3. *Ibid.*, 5.

4. Gabriel Almond, "The Civic Culture: Prehistory, Retrospect, and Prospect," Center for the Study of Democracy Research Monograph No. 1, University of California, Irvine, 1996: 14.

5. James Stimson, "Opinion and Representation," *American Political Science Review* 89(1995): 181.

CHAPTER 1

1. For an informative collection of public opinion data on welfare see "Welfare: the American Dilemma," *The Public Perspective*, February/March 1995, 39–46.

2. For a dispassionate academic work, see Lawrence Mead, *The New Politics of Poverty* (New York: Basic Books, 1992). The most prominent conservative critiques were those of George Gilder, *Wealth and Poverty* (New York: Bantam, 1981); and Charles Murray, *Losing Ground: American Social Policy, 1950–1970* (New York: Basic Books, 1984).

3. Martin Gilens, "Race and Poverty in America: Public Misperceptions and the American News Media," *Public Opinion Quarterly* 60 (1996): 515–541.

4. For background on Clinton's promises and actions, see "Clinton, Congress Talk of Welfare Reform," *1993 CQ Almanac* (Washington, DC:

Congressional Quarterly Inc., 1994): 373–375; "Welfare Reform Takes a Back Seat," *1994 CQ Almanac* (Washington, DC: Congressional Quarterly Inc., 1995): 364–365.

5. Details of the 1995–96 welfare reform debate appear in "Welfare Bill Clears Under Veto Threat," *1995 CQ Almanac* (Washington, DC: Congressional Quarterly Inc., 1996): 7–35 to 7–52.

6. Jeffrey Katz, "After 60 Years, Most Control Is Passing to States," *Congressional Quarterly Weekly Report*, August 3, 1996: 2190.

7. Ibid.: 2195.

8. "Half a Million Voters' Choices," *Governing* (April 1995): 15.

9. Herbert Jacob and Kenneth Vines, "Courts," in Virginia Gray, Herbert Jacob, and Kenneth Vines, eds., *Politics in the American States: A Comparative Analysis*, 4th ed. (Boston: Little Brown, 1983): 238.

10. As quoted in Chuck Henning, *The Wit and Wisdom of Politics: Expanded Edition* (Golden, CO; Fulcrum, 1992): 216.

11. Thomas Cronin, *Direct Democracy* (Cambridge, MA: Harvard University Press, 1989); David Magleby, *Direct Legislation* (Baltimore: John Hopkins, 1984).

12. Anthony King, *Running Scared: Why America's Politicians Campaign Too Much and Govern Too Little* (New York: Free Press, 1996): 2–3.

13. Joseph S. Nye, Jr., Philip D. Zelikow, and David C. King, eds., *Why People Don't Trust Government* (Cambridge, MA: Harvard University Press, 1997).

14. H. H. Gerth and C. W. Mills, trans., *From Max Weber* (New York: Oxford University Press, 1946): 78.

15. Chuck Henning, *The Wit and Wisdom of Politics: Expanded Edition* (Golden, CO: Fulcrum, 1992): 91.

16. The novel by Anonymous, *Primary Colors*, in which the main character is modeled on Bill Clinton, emphasizes this dimension of the Clinton personality.

17. Jimmy Carter, *A Government as Good as Its People* (New York: Simon and Schuster, 1977): 102.

18. *Federalist 51*.

19. Hobbes, *Leviathan* (New York: Dutton, 1973): 65.

20. Henning, *Wit and Wisdom*: 89.

21. Jane Mansbridge, *Beyond Adversary Democracy* (New York: Basic Books, 1980): Chs. 4–11.

22. "How to Run a Referendum," *The Economist*, November 23, 1996: 66.

23. Good surveys of democratic theory include J. Roland Pennock, *Democratic Political Theory* (Princeton, NJ: Princeton University Press, 1979); Giovanni Sartori, *The Theory of Democracy Revisited* (Chatham, NJ: Chatham House, 1987), Two volumes.

24. James Marone, *The Democratic Wish: Popular Participation and the Limits of American Government* (New York: Basic Books, 1990): 5. Marone is summarizing the claims of others; he himself is a critic of popular democracy.

25. Benjamin Barber, *Strong Democracy* (Berkeley, CA: University of California Press, 1984).

26. Alexis de Tocqueville, *Democracy in America*, 2nd ed., Henry Reeve, trans., 2 vols. (Cambridge, MA: Sever & Francis, 1863), I: 318–19, as quoted in Marone, *The Democratic Wish*: 86.

27. John Adams, *The Political Writings of John Adams*, George Peek Jr. ed., (New York: Macmillan, 1985): 89.

28. Marone, *The Democratic Wish*: 5–6.

29. We are grateful to Anthony King for conversations that helped us think about these issues.

30. *Federalist 51*.

31. Sidney Blumenthal, *The Permanent Campaign* (New York: Simon & Schuster, 1982).

32. Jerry Gray, "Breaking Ranks, Gephardt Says He'll Fight Clinton Budget Deal," *The New York Times*, May 21, 1997: A1, A22.

33. Richard Boyd, "Decline of U.S. Voter Turnout: Structural Explanations," *American Politics Quarterly* 9(1981): 133–159.

34. Frank Sorauf, *Political Parties in the American System* (Boston: Little, Brown, 1964); Martin Wattenberg, *The Decline of American Political Parties, 1952–1984* (Cambridge, MA: Harvard University Press, 1986).

35. Gary Jacobson finds that national swings in House elections are much more heterogeneous than at mid-century. See "The Marginals Never Vanished: Incumbency and Competition in Elections to the U.S. House of Representatives, 1952–1982," *American Journal of Political Science* 31(1987): 126–141.

36. Larry Sabato, *Feeding Frenzy* (New York: Free Press, 1991).

37. Journalist Richard Reeves, as quoted in Henning, *Wit and Wisdom*: 207.

38. Quoted in John Geer, *From Tea Leaves to Opinion Polls* (New York: Columbia University Press, 1996): vii.

39. R. R. Alford and E. C. Lee, "Voting Turnout in American Cities," *American Political Science Review* 61 (1968): 796–813; Heinz Eulau and Kenneth Prewitt, *Labyrinths of Democracy* (Indianapolis, IN: Bobbs Merrill, 1973): 380.

40. Susan A. Macmanus, *Young v. Old: Generational Combat in the 21st Century* (Boulder, CO; Westview Press, 1996): Ch. 2.

41. Cook, "Primary Season Concludes without Much Drama," *Congressional Quarterly*, June 15, 1996.

42. Robert Dahl, *Who Governs?* (New Haven: Yale University Press, 1961); David Truman, *The Governmental Process* (New York: Alfred Knopf, 1951).

43. As quoted in Henning, *Wit and Wisdom*: 216.

44. R. Douglas Arnold, *The Logic of Congressional Action* (New Haven: Yale University Press, 1990).

45. Terry Moe, "The Politics of Bureaucratic Structure," in John Chubb and Paul Peterson, eds., *Can the Government Govern?* (Washington, DC: Brookings, 1989): 267–329.

46. John Dewey, as quoted in Marone, *The Democratic Wish*: 322.

47. Marone, *The Democratic Wish*.

48. Michael Wines, "Cabinet Memoir Discovers Humans in Masks of Power, *New York Times*, March 30, 1997, 11.

49. Henning, *Wit and Wisdom*: 94.

50. Henning, *Wit and Wisdom*: 58.

51. Charles Masters, "Riviera Tramps Run Risk of 'Tourist Cleansing' Round-Ups," *The Daily Telegraph*, July 27, 1996, International Section: 15.

CHAPTER 2

1. Herbert J. Storing, ed., *The Complete Anti-Federalist: Maryland and Virginia and the South*, Vol. 5 (Chicago: University of Chicago Press, 1981), p. 210.

2. Storing, *Complete Anti-Federalist*, p. 207.

3. James Madison, "Federalist 10," in Alexander Hamilton, John Jay, and James Madison, writing under the pseudonym Publius, *The Federalist Papers* (Baltimore: Johns Hopkins University Press, 1981), pp. 16, 23.

4. Owen S. Ireland, *Religion, Ethnicity and Politics: Ratifying the Constitution in Pennsylvania* (University Park, PA: Pennsylvania State University Press, 1995).

5. Thomas A. Bailey, *The American Pageant: A History of the Republic* (Boston: D. C. Heath, 1956).

6. Gordon S. Wood, *The Radicalism of the American Revolution* (New York: Alfred Knopf, 1992), p. 80.

7. Jack P. Greene, "The Role of the Lower Houses of Assembly in Eighteenth-Century Politics," in Jack P. Greene, ed., *The Reinterpretation of the American Revolution 1763–1789* (New York: Harper & Row, 1968), p. 86–109.

8. Wood, *Radicalism*, p. 55.

9. Merrill D. Peterson, *Thomas Jefferson and the New Nation* (New York: Oxford University Press, 1970), pp. 22–23.

10. J. Franklin Jameson, *The American Revolution Considered as a Social Movement* (Princeton: Princeton University Press, 1926).

11. Edmund S. Morgan and Helen M. Morgan, *The Stamp Act Crisis: Prologue to Revolution*. (Chapel Hill: University of North Carolina Press, 1953), p. 106.

12. Morgan and Morgan, *Stamp Act Crisis*, p. 106.

13. Bernard Bailyn, *The Origins of American Politics* (New York: Alfred Knopf, 1968), p. 12.

14. Thomas Hobbes, *Leviathan* (New York: Oxford University Press, 1996). Originally published in 1651.

15. John Locke, *Two Treatises on Civil Government* (London: Dent, 1924). Originally published in 1690.

16. J. H. Plumb, *The Origins of Political Stability* (Boston: Houghton Mifflin, 1967).

17. For a discussion of the influence of James Harrington on colonial thought, see Samuel H. Beer, *To Make a Nation: The Rediscovery of American Federalism* (Cambridge, MA: Harvard University Press, 1993).

18. Thomas Paine, *Common Sense* (New York: Penguin, 1986). Originally published in 1776.

19. C. L. Becker, *Freedom and Responsibility in the American Way of Life* (New York: Knopf, 1945), p. 16, as quoted by Louis Hartz, *The Liberal Tradition in America* (New York: Harcourt, Brace, 1955), p. 61.

20. Robert J. Dinkin, *Voting in Revolutionary America: A Study of Elections in the Original Thirteen States, 1776–1789* (Westport CT: Greenwood Press, 1982); Robert J. Dinkin, *Voting in Provincial America: A Study of Elections in the Thirteen Colonies, 1689–1776* (Westport CT: Greenwood Press, 1977).

21. Willi Paul Adams, *The First American Constitutions: Republican Ideology and the Making of the State Constitutions in the Revolutionary Era* (Chapel Hill: University of North Carolina Press, 1980), pp. 245, 308–11.

22. Adams, *First American Constitutions*. p. 207.

23. Bailey, *American Pageant*, p. 136.

24. Charles A. Beard, *An Economic Interpretation of the Constitution of the United States* (New York: Free Press, 1913).

25. Robert E. Brown, *Charles Beard and the Constitution* (Princeton: Princeton University Press, 1956); Forrest McDonald, *We the People* (Chicago: University of Chicago Press, 1958).

26. John P. Roche, "The Founding Fathers: A Reform Caucus in Action," *American Political Science Review* 55 (December 1961): 799–816.

27. Winton U. Solberg, ed., *The Federal Convention and the Formation of the Union of the American States* (New York: Bobbs-Merrill, 1958), p 79.

28. Solberg, *Federal Convention*, p. 78.

29. Solberg, *Federal Convention*, pp. 131–34.

30. Max Farrand, *The Framing of the Constitution of the United States* (New Haven: Yale University Press, 1913), p. 113.

31. Thornton Anderson, *Creating the Constitution: The Convention of 1787 and the First Congress* (University Park, PA: Pennsylvania State Press, 1993).

32. Arthur M. Schlesinger, Jr., ed., *History of American Presidential Elections, 1789–1968*, Vol. 2 (New York: McGraw-Hill, 1971), p. 1244.

33. Anderson, *Creating the Constitution*, p. 148.

34. Anderson, *Creating the Constitution*, p. 148.

35. Henry Steele Commager, ed., *Documents of American History* (New York: Appleton-Century-Crofts, 1958), p. 104; Willi Paul Adams, *The First American Constitutions: Republican Ideology and the Making of the State Constitutions in the Revolutionary Era* (Chapel Hill: University of North Carolina Press, 1980).

36. Arthur M. Schlesinger, *Prelude to Independence* (New York: Alfred Knopf, 1958), p. 299.

37. C. M. Kenyon, "Men of Little Faith: The Anti-Federalists on the Nature of Representative Government." In Jack P. Greene, *The Reinterpretation of the American Revolution, 1763–1789* (New York: Harper, 1968), pp. 526–67; Herbert J. Storing, ed.,

The Anti-Federalist (Chicago: University of Chicago Press, 1986).

38. John Jay, Alexander Hamilton, and James Madison, writing under the pseudonym, Publius, *The Federalist Papers* (New York: New American Library, 1961).

39. Jane Mansbridge, *Why We Lost the ERA* (Chicago: University of Chicago Press, 1986).

40. Charles A. Beard, *An Economic Interpretation of the Constitution of the United States* (New York: Free Press, 1913).

41. Bernard Bailyn, *The Ideological Origins of Revolution* (Cambridge, MA: Harvard, 1967); Gordon S. Wood, *The Creation of the American Republic, 1776–1787* (Chapel Hill: University of North Carolina Press, 1969).

42. Beard, *Economic Interpretation*, Ch. 9.

43. Second Inaugural Address, 1865, as quoted in John Bartlett, *Familiar Quotations*, 16th ed. (Boston: Little, Brown, 1992), p. 450.

CHAPTER 3

1. *U.S.* v. *Lopez* 514 U.S. 549 (1995), as quoted in "Is there Hope for the Supreme Court?" *Madison Review* I (Fall, 1995), 22–23.

2. John Bartlett, *Familiar Quotations: Revised and Enlarged.*, 15th ed. (Boston: Little, Brown, 1980), p. 452.

3. Alexis de Tocqueville, *Democracy in America*, Vol. I, ed. by Philips Bradley (New York: Knopf, 1945), 169.

4. Gregory S. Lashutka, "Local Rebellion: How Cities Are Rising Up against Unfunded Mandates," *Commonsense* 1 (Summer 1994): 66.

5. Timothy Conlan, "And the Beat Goes On: Intergovernmental Mandates and Preemption in an Era of Deregulation," *Publius* 21 (Summer 1991): 57.

6. On the costs of environmental mandates, see Richard C. Feiock, "Estimating Political, Fiscal and Economic Impacts of State Mandates: A Pooled Time Series Analysis of Local Planning and Growth Policy in Florida." Paper prepared for the annual meeting of the American Political Science Association, 1994.

7. Colleen M. Grogan, "The Influence of Federal Mandates on State Policy Decision-Making." Paper

prepared for the annual meeting of the American Political Science Association, 1994; Teresa Coughlin, Leighton Ku, and John Holahan, *Medicaid Since 1980* (Washington, DC: Urban Institute, 1994); John Holahan and others, "Explaining the Recent Growth in Medicaid Spending," *Health Affairs* 12 (Fall, 1993): 177–93.

8. Jean E. Smith, *John Marshall: Definer of a Nation* (New York: Henry Holt, 1996), 440–46.

9. *McCulloch* v. *Maryland* (1819), 4 Wheaton 316, as reprinted in Henry Steele Commager, ed., *Documents of American History*, 6th ed. (New York: Appleton-Century-Crofts, 1949), 217.

10. *McCulloch* v. *Maryland* (1819), as reprinted in Commager, 217.

11. Dan M. Berkovitz, "Waste Wars: Did Congress 'Nuke' State Sovereignty in the Low-Level Radioactive Waste Policy Amendments Act of 1985?" *Harvard Environmental Law Review*, 11, 1987, 437–40.

12. *New York Times*, January 18, 1991.

13. *New York* v. *U.S.*, 112 *Supreme Court Reporter*, 2414–47 301 U.S. 1 (1991).

14. *United States* v. *E. C. Knight Co.* (1895).

15. *NLRB* v. *Jones & Laughlin Co.* 317 U.S. 111 (1937).

16. *Wickard* v. *Filburn*, (1942).

17. *Helvering* v. *Davis*, 301 U.S. 548, 599 (1937).

18. *South Dakota* v. *Dole*, 483 U.S. 203 (1987).

19. Morton Grodzins, *The American System: A New View of Government in the United States*, ed. Daniel J. Elazar (Chicago: Rand McNally, 1966).

20. Calculated from data in Ester Fuchs, *Mayors and Money* (Chicago: University of Chicago Press, 1992), 210.

21. Unless otherwise indicated, all amounts in this chapter are calculated in 1990 dollars.

22. Chuck Henning, comp., *The Wit and Wisdom of Politics: Expanded Edition.* (Golden, CO: Fulcrum, 1992), 208.

23. Ibid., 208.

24. James M. Perry, "GOP Congressman Shows How to Keep Power, Even While Under Indictment for Corruption," *Wall Street Journal*, June 14, 1994, A16.

25. Jeffrey L. Pressman and Aaron Wildavsky, *Implementation*, 3rd ed.

(Berkeley: University of California Press, 1984); Martha Derthick, *New Towns in Town: Why a Federal Program Failed* (Washington, DC: Urban Institute, 1972); Eugene Bardach, *The Implementation Game*, 4th ed. (Cambridge, MA: MIT Press, 1982).

26. Derthick, *New Towns in Town*.

27. Pressman and Wildavsky, *Implementation*, 118.

28. Paul E. Peterson, Barry Rabe, and Kenneth Wong, *When Federalism Works* (Washington, DC: Brookings, 1986).

29. Timothy Conlan, *New Federalism: Intergovernmental Reform from Nixon to Reagan* (Washington, DC: Brookings, 1988).

30. David McKay, *Domestic Policy and Ideology: Presidents and the American State, 1964–1987* (New York: Cambridge University Press, 1989), Ch. 4.

31. Peter J. Howe, "State's Share of Federal Dollars Drops," *Boston Globe*, July 2, 1994, 17.

32. Lynda McDonnell, "Will Our State be a Magnet for Poor from Across Nation?" *Pioneer Press*, December 31, 1995, 1A, 10A.

33. Iver Peterson, "Do Poor Shop for Welfare? New Jersey Officials Say Yes and No," *New York Times*, December 9, 1995, 29.

34. Paul E. Peterson and Mark Rom, *Welfare Magnets: A New Case for a National Standard* (Washington, DC: Brookings, 1990).

35. Peterson, *The Price of Federalism*.

36. James Bryce, *Modern Democracies* (New York: Macmillan, 1921), Vol. I, 132.

37. Robert R. Alford and Eugene C. Lee, "Voting Turnout in American Cities," *American Political Science Review* 62 (September 1968): 796–813.

38. Village politics are well described in A. J. Vidich and J. Bensman, *Small Town in Mass Society* (New York: Harper & Row, 1972). For descriptions of courthouse gangs in the county politics of the South, see V. O. Key, *Southern Politics* (New York: Random House, 1949).

39. Paul E. Peterson, *City Limits* (Chicago: University of Chicago Press, 1981).

40. *Statistical Abstract of the United States*, 1992, Table 22.

41. Greta Anand, "Circling of the Welcome Wagons: Selectman Candidates Rip Social Programs," *Boston Globe*, West Weekly Section, March 19, 1995, 1, 8.

42. "Money to Burn," *Economist*, August 14, 1993, 23.

43. Morris Fiorina, *Divided Government* (New York: Macmillan, 1992).

44. Paul E. Peterson, *The Price of Federalism* (Washington, DC: Brookings, 1995), 92. Data on state expenditures combine expenditures by state and local governments. Since the sharing of responsibilities by state and local governments varies widely from state to state, any interstate comparison that looks at state government expenditures alone can be quite misleading.

45. Peterson, *Price of Federalism*, 105.

46. Peterson, *Price of Federalism*, 103.

CHAPTER 4

1. Joseph B. Mitchell, *Military Leaders of the American Revolution* (McLean, VA: EPM Publications, 1967): 138–149.

2. Jan Stanislaw Kopczewski, *Kosciuszko and Pulaski* (Warsaw: Impress Publishers, 1976).

3. Louis des Cognets, Jr. *Black Sheep and Heroes of the American Revolution* (Princeton: Cognets, 1965): Ch. 15.

4. Carl J. Friedrich, *Problems of the American Public Service* (New York: McGraw-Hill, 1935): 12.

5. The committee's name was changed to the Committee on Internal Security in 1969, and it was abolished in 1975.

6. See Alvin Rabushka and Kenneth Shepsle, *Politics in Plural Societies* (Columbus, OH: Merrill, 1972).

7. H.G. Wells, *The Future in America* (New York: Harper, 1906): 73–74.

8. *The Economist*, October 17, 1992: 38.

9. John A. Garrity and Peter Gay, eds., *The Columbia History of the World* (New York: Harper & Row, 1972): 673.

10. Garrity, *The Columbia History of the World*: 669–670.

11. Quoted in Marc Shell, "Babel in America; or, The Politics of Language Diversity in the United States," *Critical Inquiry* 20(1993): 109.

12. James McCague, *The Second Rebellion: The Story of the New York City Draft Riots of 1863* (New York: Dial Press, 1968).

13. Richard Jensen, "The Religious and Occupational Roots of Party Identification: Illinois and Indiana in the 1870s," in Joel Silbey and Samuel McSeveney, eds. " *Voters, Parties, and Elections* (Lexington, MA: Xerox, 1972): 169. Paul Kleppner, *The Third Electoral System, 1853–1892: Parties, Voters, and Political Cultures* (Chapel Hill, NC: 1979).

14. J. Morgan Kousser, *The Shaping of Southern Politics* (New Haven, Yale University Press, 1974).

15. On the multicultural character of California after it was annexed to the United States, see Ronald Takaki, *A Different Mirror* (Boston: Little, Brown, 1993): Ch. 8.

16. Senator John Miller, "Chinese Exclusion Act," *Congressional Record—Senate* 1882, 13, pt. 2: 1484–85.

17. This is Oscar Handlin's sardonic characterization. See his *Race and Nationality in American Life* (Boston, Little, Brown, 1957): 95.

18. Madison Grant, *The Passing of the Great Race* (New York: Scribner's, 1916): 80–81.

19. *Abstracts of Reports of the Immigration Commission* (Washington, DC: Government Printing Office, vol. 1, 1911). The quoted words can be found on p. 244, 251, 259, 259, 261, 265, 229, respectively. The characterization of southern Italians is based on work by an Italian (presumably northern) sociologist, but the commission clearly agrees with the description.

20. Senator Henry Cabot Lodge, "Immigration Restriction," *Congressional Record-Senate* 1896, 28, pt. 3: 2817.

21. "Emergency" immigration restrictions passed in 1921 were fine-tuned and formalized in the National Origins Act of 1924, and the National Origins Quota Act of 1929.

22. Alan Lichtman, *Prejudice and the Old Politics: The Presidential Election of 1928* (Chapel Hill, NC: University of North Carolina Press, 1979).

23. Spencer Rich, "A 20-Year High Tide of Immigration," *Washington Post National Weekly Edition*, September 4–10, 1995: 30.

24. George Borhas, "The New Economics of Immigration," *The*

Atlantic Monthly, November 1996: 72–80.

25. A widely publicized 1994 study by the Urban Institute concluded that immigrants currently pay about $70 billion per year in taxes, while using $40–45 billion in services. *Immigration and Immigrants: Setting the Record Straight* (Washington, DC: The Urban Institute, 1994).

26. David Kennedy, "Can We Still Afford to Be a Nation of Immigrants?" *The Atlantic Monthly*, November 1996: 67.

27. Arthur Schlesinger, Jr. *The Disuniting of America* (Knoxville, TN: Whittle, 1991).

28. Louis Hartz, *The Liberal Tradition in America* (New York: Harcourt, Brace, Jovanovich, 1955).

29. On Madison's pessimistic view of human nature, see Richard Matthews, *If Men Were Angels* (Lawrence, KS: University of Kansas Press, 1995): esp. Ch. 3.

30. Clinton Rossiter, *Conservatism in America* (New York: Knopf, 1962): 67, 71.

31. Bernard Bailyn, *The Ideological Origins of the American Revolution* (Cambridge, MA: Harvard University Press, 1967).

32. Rogers Smith, "Beyond Tocqueville, Myrdal and Hartz: The Multiple Traditions in America," *American Political Science Review* 87(1993): 549–566. These inconsistencies were not lost on earlier thinkers, to be sure. Recall Jefferson's pessimistic predictions in his *Notes on the State of Virginia 1781–1785*. Also see Alexis de Tocqueville, *Democracy in America*, J.P. Mayer, ed. (New York: Harper, 1969): 340–363.

33. Samuel Huntington, *American Politics: The Promise of Disharmony* (Cambridge, MA: Harvard University Press, 1981).

34. I. A. Lewis and William Schneider, "Hard Times: The Public on Poverty," *Public Opinion*, June/July 1985: 2–8, 59–60.

35. "Income Tax Irritation." *Public Perspective* (July/August, 1990): 86.

36. Stanley Feldman, "Structure and Consistency in Public Opinion: The Role of Core Beliefs and Values," *American Journal of Political Science* 32(1988):416–440.

37. Paul Krugman, *Peddling Prosperity* (New York: Norton, 1994): Ch. 5.

38. Madison, *Federalist 10*.

39. Everett Carll Ladd, *The American Ideology* (Storrs, CT: The Roper Center, 1994): 56–57.

40. Sidney Verba and Gary Orren, *Equality in America* (Cambridge, MA: Harvard University Press, 1985).

41. "In (Blank) We Trust," *The Economist*, October 12, 1996: 32.

42. Seymour Martin Lipset, *American Exceptionalism* (New York: Norton, 1996):

43. Robert Booth Fowler, *Religion and Politics in America* (Metuchen, NJ: American Theological Library Association, 1985): 27.

44. Frederick Jackson Turner, *The Frontier in American History* (New York: Holt, 1920).

45. Hartz, *The Liberal Tradition*: 89.

46. For a discussion, see Seymour Martin Lipset, "Why No Socialism in the United States?" in Seweryn Bialer and Sophia Sluzar, eds. *Sources of Contemporary Radicalism* (New York: Westview Press, 1977):

47. Robert Putnam, *Making Democracy Work* (Princeton, NJ: Princeton University Press, 1993).

48. Sven Steinmo, "American Exceptionalism Reconsidered," in Larry C. Dodd and Calvin Jillson, eds. *The Dynamics of American Politics* (Boulder, CO: Westwood, 1994): 106–131.

49. For a sympathetic description of the trials and ordeals of the immigrants, see Oscar Handlin, *The Uprooted*, 2nd ed. (Boston: Little, Brown, 2nd ed. 1973).

50. Hartz, *The Liberal Tradition*: 18.

51. *Abstracts of Reports of the Immigration Commission*, p. 170.

52. William Bennett and Jack Kemp, "The Fortress Party?" *The Wall Street Journal*, October 21, 1994: A14.

53. David Firestone, "Mayor Seeks Immigration Coalition," *The New York Times*, October 11, 1996: B-3.

54. "The Effects of Ethnicity on Political Culture," in Paul Peterson, ed., *Classifying by Race* (Princeton, NJ: Princeton University Press, 1995): 351–352.

55. Rodolfo de la Garza, Angelo Falcon, and F. Chris Garcia, "Will the Real Americans Please Stand Up: Anglo and Mexican American Support of Core American Political Values,"

American Journal of Political Science 40(1996): 335–351.

56. Lydia Saad, "Immigrants See United States as Land of Opportunity," *The Gallup Poll Monthly*, July 1995: 19–33.

CHAPTER 5

1. For background on the Gulf War see "Gulf Crisis Grows into War with Iraq," *1990 Congressional Quarterly Almanac* (Washington, DC: Congressional Quarterly Inc., 1991): 717–756; "1991 Begins with War in the Mideast," *1991 Congressional Quarterly Almanac* (Washington, DC: Congressional Quarterly Inc., 1992): 437–450.

2. Jon Krosnick and Laura Brannon, "The Impact of the Gulf War on the Ingredients of Presidential Evaluations," *American Political Science Review* 87(1993): 963–975.

3. *Public Opinion and American Democracy* (New York: Knopf, 1961.

4. Carl Friedrich, *Man and His Government* (New York: McGraw-Hill, 1963): 19–215.

5. Fred Greenstein, *Children and Politics* (New Haven, CT: Yale, 1969): Ch. 4.

6. M. Kent Jennings and Richard G. Niemi, *Generations and Politics* (Princeton, NJ: Princeton, 1981): 51.

7. Elizabeth Cook, Ted Jelen, and Clyde Wilcox, *Between Two Absolutes: Public Opinion and the Politics of Abortion* (Boulder, CO: Westview Press, 1992).

8. David Leege, Kenneth Wald, and Lyman Kellstedt, "The Public Dimension of Private Devotionalism," in David Leege and Lyman Kellstedt, eds., *Rediscovering the Religious Factor in American Politics* (Armonk, NY: Sharpe, 1993): 139–156; Alan Hertzke and John Rausch, "The Religious Vote in American Politics: Value Conflict, Continuity, and Change," in Stephen Craig, ed., *Broken Contract* (Boulder, CO: Westview Press, 1996): 188.

9. Warren Miller and Santa Traugott, *American National Election Studies Data Sourcebook, 1952–1986* (Cambridge, MA: Harvard University Press, 1990): 316, 332.

10. For a survey of positive and negative findings see Jack Citrin and Donald Green, "The Self-Interest Motive in American Public Opinion,"

Research in Micropolitics, vol. 3, (Greenwich, CT: JAI Press, 1993): 1–28.

11. Douglas Hibbs, *The American Political Economy* (Cambridge, MA: Harvard University Press, 1987): Ch. 5.

12. David Sears and Jack Citrin, *Tax Revolt* (Cambridge, MA: Harvard University Press, 1985): Chs. 6–7.

13. David Sears and Leonie Huddy, "On the Origins of Political Disunity Among Women." in L. Tilly and P. Gurin, eds., *Women, Politics, and Change* (New York: Russell Sage, 1990): 249–277.

14. Larry Bartels, "Messages Received: The Political Impact of Media Exposure," *American Political Science Review* 87(1993): 267–285.

15. "Survey Looks at Political Insight," *The Boston Globe*, February 11, 1996: 32, citing results of a *Washington Post* survey conducted in November 1995.

16. Tom Smith, "Public Support for Public Spending, 1973–1994, *The Public Perspective* 6(April/May 1995): 2.

17. Jon Krosnick and Matthew Barent, "Comparisons of Party Identification and Policy Preferences: The Impact of Survey Question Format," *American Journal of Political Science* 37(1993): 941–964.

18. On these topics, see Howard Schuman and Stanley Presser, *Questions and Answers in Attitude Surveys* (New York: Harcourt, Brace, and Jovanovich: Academic Press, 1981); and the essays in Thomas Mann and Gary Orren, eds., *Media Polls in American Politics* (Washington, DC: Brookings, 1992).

19. Tamar Lewin, "Study Points to Increase in Tolerance of Ethnicity," The *New York Times*, January 8, 1992: A12.

20. For a comprehensive breakdown of federal spending, see *Congressional Quarterly*, *Where the Money Goes*, December 11, 1993.

21. Anthony Downs, *An Economic Theory of Democracy* (New York: Harper & Row, 1957): Chs. 11–13.

22. Morris P. Fiorina, "Information and Rationality in Elections," in John Ferejohn and James Kuklinski, eds., *Information and Democratic Processes* (Urbana: University of Illinois Press, 1990): 329–342.

23. John Krosnick, "Government Policy and Citizen Passion: A Study of Issue Publics in Contemporary America," *Political Behavior* 12(1990): 59–92. Peter Natchez and Irvin Bupp, "Candidates, Issues, and Voters, *Public Policy* 1(1968): 409–437.

24. Anthony Downs, "Up and Down with Ecology—The Issue Attention Cycle," *The Public Interest* 28(1972): 38–50.

25. Fiorina, "Information and Rationality."

26. "The Nature of Belief Systems in Mass Publics," in David Apter, ed., *Ideology and Discontent* (New York: Free Press, 1964): 206–261.

27. There is a huge literature debating the size of the increase in ideological thinking. See *inter alia*, Norman Nie and Kristie Andersen, "Mass Belief Systems Revisited: Political Chance and Attitude Structure," *Journal of Politics* 36(1974): 540–580; John Field and Ronald Anderson, "Ideology in the Public's Conceptualization of the 1964 Election," *Public Opinion Quarterly* 33(1969): 380–398; John Sullivan, James Piereson, and George Marcus, "Ideological Constraint in the Mass Public: A Methodological Critique and Some New Findings," *American Journal of Political Science* 22(1978): 233–249.

28. Miller and Traugott, *American National Election Studies Data Sourcebook*, 94.

29. *The Washington Post*/Kaiser Family Foundation/Harvard University Survey Project, *Why Don't Americans Trust the Government?* (Menlo Park, CA: The Kaiser Foundation, 1996): 9.

30. Vernon Van Dyke, *Ideology and Political Choice* (Chatham, NJ: Chatham House Publishers, 1995): Chs. 3–5.

31. David Moore and Lydia Saad, "Budget Battle Now a Political Standoff," *Gallup Poll Monthly*, January 1996: 15–16.

32. James A. Davis, "Changeable Weather in a Cooling Climate Atop the Liberal Plateau," *Public Opinion Quarterly* 56(1992): 261–306. Morris P. Fiorina, "The Reagan Years: Turning to the Right or Groping Toward the Middle?" in Barry Cooper, Allan Kornberg, and William Mishler, eds., *The Resurgence of Conservatism in Anglo-American Democracies* (Durham, NC: Duke University Press, 1988): 430–459.

33. "Public Expects GOP Miracles," *Times-Mirror News Release*, December 8, 1994.

34. Morris P. Fiorina, *Divided Government* 2nd ed. (Boston: Allyn & Bacon, 1995): 173–177.

35. Ibid.

36. Samuel Stouffer, *Communism, Conformity, and Civil Liberties* (New York: Doubleday, 1955); James Prothro and Charles Grigg, "Fundamental Principles of Democracy: Bases of Agreement and Disagreement," *Journal of Politics* 22 (1960): 176–194.

37. For evidence that peoples' opinions reflect a smaller number of "core beliefs" that may conflict with each other or situational characteristics, see Stanley Feldman, "Structure and Consistency in Public Opinion: The Role of Core Beliefs and Values," *American Journal of Public Opinion* 32(1988): 416–440; Stanley Feldman and John Zaller, "A Simple Theory of the Survey Response: Answering Questions versus Revealing Preferences," *American Journal of Political Science* 36(1992): 579–616.

38. R. Michael Alvarez and John Brehm, "American Ambivalence Toward Abortion Policy," *American Journal of Political Science* 39(1995): 1055–1082.

39. On the effects of posing political conflicts as matters of conflicting rights see Mary Anne Glendon, *Rights Talk: The Impoverishment of Political Discourse* (New York: Free Press, 1991).

40. For a good account of the events discussed here, see Theda Skocpol, *Boomerang* (New York: Norton, 1996). Professor Skocpol is not responsible for our interpretations, of course.

41. "Issues They Care About," *Newsweek Special Election Issue*, November/December 1992.

42. Quoted in Maureen Dowd, "Clinton's Health Plan," The *New York Times*, September 29, 1993: A18.

43. Dana Priest, "Democrats Pull the Plug on Health Care Reform," *The Washington Post*, September 27, 1994: A1.

44. Alissa Rubin, "Leap of Faith," *Health Care's Hour*, Congressional Quarterly, September 25, 1993: 8.

45. Unless otherwise noted, public opinion data cited in the text are drawn from "The Public Decides on Health Care Reform," *The Public Perspective*, September/October 1994: 23–28.

46. Daniel Yankelovich, "The Debate That Wasn't: The Public and

the Clinton Plan," *Health Affairs* (1995): 7–23.

47. Cook, Jelen, and Wilcox, *Between Two Absolutes*: Ch. 2.

48. "Abortion: Overview of a Complex Opinion," *The Public Perspective*, (November/December, 1989): 19, 20.

49. Ibid. 20.

50. "Abortion," *The American Enterprise* (July/August 1995): 107.

51. "A Macro Theory of Information Flow," in John Ferejohn and James Kuklinski, eds., *Information and Democratic Processes* (Urbana, IL: University of Illinois Press, 1990): 345–368.

52. James Stimson, *Public Opinion in America: Moods, Cycles, and Swings* (Boulder, CO: Westview Press, 1991).

53. Benjamin Page and Robert Shapiro, *The Rational Public* (Chicago: University of Chicago Press, 1992).

54. Christopher Wlezien, "The Public as Thermostat: Dynamics of Preferences for Spending," *American Journal of Political Science* 39(1995): 981–1000.

CHAPTER 6

1. Steven Rosenstone and John Mark Hansen, *Mobilization, Participation, and Democracy in America* (New York: Macmillan, 1993): 51.

2. Benjamin Barber, *Strong Democracy: Participatory Politics for a New Age* (Berkeley and Los Angeles, University of California Press, 1984): xiii.

3. John Aldrich, *Why Parties?* (Chicago: University of Chicago Press, 1995): 106–107.

4. Chilton Williamson, *American Suffrage from Property to Democracy: 1760–1860* (Princeton, NJ: Princeton University Press, 1960).

5. Ibid., 277.

6. On Republican withdrawal from the South after the realignment of the 1890s see Richard Vallely, "National Parties and Racial Disenfranchisement," in Paul Peterson, ed., *Classifying by Race* (Princeton, NJ: Princeton University Press, 1995): 188–216. On black exercise of voting rights see J. Morgan Kousser, *The Shaping of Southern Politics*

(New Haven, CT: Yale University Press, 1974).

7. Eleanor Flexner, *Century of Struggle*, rev. ed., (Cambridge, MA: Harvard University Press, 1975). Anne Scott and Andrew Scott, *One Half the People* (Philadelphia: Lippincott, 1975).

8. "18-Year-Old Vote: Constitutional Amendment Cleared," *Congressional Quarterly Almanac* (Washington, DC: Congressional Quarterly, 1972): 475–477.

9. For a comparative study of the American and Swiss suffrage movements see Lee Ann Banaszak, *Why Movements Succeed or Fail* (Princeton, NJ: Princeton University Press, 1996).

10. Paul Peterson, "An Immodest Proposal," *Daedalus* 121 (1992): 151–174.

11. Rosenstone and Hansen, *Mobilization, Participation, and Democracy*: Ch. 2.

12. John Milholland, "The Danger Point in American Politics," *North American Review* 164(1897).

13. Raymond Wolfinger and Steven Rosenstone, *Who Votes?* (New Haven, CT: Yale University Press, 1980): 101.

14. John Ferejohn and Morris Fiorina, "The Paradox of Not Voting: A Decision Theoretic Analysis," *American Political Science Review* 68(1974): 525–535.

15. Anthony Downs, *An Economic Theory of Democracy* (New York: Harper and Row, 1957): Ch. 14.

16. Howard Rosenthal and Subrata Sen, "Electoral Participation in the French Fifth Republic," *American Political Science Review* 67(1973): 29–54.

17. Wolfinger and Rosenstone, *Who Votes*: 116.

18. Ruy Teixeira, *The Disappearing American Voter* (Washington, DC: Brookings, 1992): 10.

19. Martha Angle, "Low Voter Turnout Prompts Concern on Hill," *Congressional Quarterly Weekly Report*, April 2, 1988: 864. Stephen Bennett, "The Uses and Abuses of Registration and Turnout Data," *PS: Political Science and Politics* 23(1990): 166–171.

20. Wolfinger and Rosenstone, *Who Votes*: 88.

21. Richard Boyd, "Decline of U.S. Voter Turnout: Structural Explanations," *American Politics Quarterly* 9(1981): 133–159.

22. Stephen Knack, "The Voter Participation Effects of Selecting Jurors from Registration Lists," Working Paper No. 91–10, University of Maryland, Department of Economics.`

23. Martin Wattenberg, *The Decline of American Political Parties, 1952–19*. Interestingly, the percentage of voters who reported being contacted by a party rose from 1956 to 1982, but declined thereafter. Party efforts would appear to have met with very limited success inasmuch as turnout was falling throughout the period. See Rosenstone and Hansen, *Mobilization, Participation, and Democracy*: 163.

24. G. Bingham Powell, "American Voter Turnout in Comparative Perspective," *American Political Science Review* 80(1986): 17–43; Robert Jackman, "Political Institutions and Voter Turnout in the Industrial Democracies," *American Political Science Review* 81(1987): 405–423.

25. David Nexon, "Asymmetry in the Political System: Occasional Activists in the Democratic and Republican Parties, 1956–1964," *American Political Science Review* 65(1971): 716–730; Warren Miller and M. Kent Jennings, *Parties in Transition* (New York: Russell Sage, 1986): Ch. 2.

26. Sidney Verba, Kay Schlozman, and Henry Brady, *Voice and Equality* (Cambridge, MA: Harvard University Press, 1995): 72.

27. Rosenstone and Hansen, *Mobilization, Participation, and Democracy*: 63–70. There is some conflict between their figures and those reported by Verba, Schlozman, and Brady in *Voice and Equality*: 69–74. Part of the explanation may be that the survey items relied on by Rosenstone and Hansen generally have more specific referents (e.g., this year's elections), while the items relied on by Verba, Schlozman, and Brady ask more generally about activity in the last year or two years. Thus, the Verba, Schlozman and Brady figures may reflect the increasing number of opportunities.

28. Jack Citrin, "Comment: The Political Relevance of Trust in Government," *American Political Science Review* 68(1974): 973–988.

29. Teixeira, *The Disappearing American Voter*: 49.

30. Richard Brody, "The Puzzle of Political Participation in America," in Anthony King, ed., *The New American Political System* (Washington, DC: American Enterprise Institute, 1978: 287–324; Paul Abramson and John Aldrich, "The Decline of Electoral Participation in America," *American Political Science Review* 76(1982): 502–521.

31. Rosenstone and Hansen, *Mobilization, Participation, and Democracy*: 183.

32. Ibid.: Ch. 7, p. 175.

33. Marshall Ganz, "Motor Voter or Motivated Voter," *The American Prospect*, September-October, 1996: 46–48; Marshall Ganz, "Voters in the Crosshairs," *The American Prospect*, Winter 1994: 100–109.

34. Warren Miller, "The Puzzle Transformed: Explaining Declining Turnout," *Political Behavior* 14(1992): 1–43.

35. Robert Putnam, "Tuning In, Tuning Out: The Strange Disappearance of Social Capital in America," *PS: Political Science and Politics* 28(1995): 664–683.

36. Stephen Knack, "Civic Norms, Social Sanctions, and Voter Turnout," *Rationality and Society* 4(1992): 133–156.

37. Eric Uslaner, "Faith, Hope, and Charity: Social Capital, Trust, and Collective Action" (College Park, MD: University of Maryland, unpublished manuscript).

38. Rosenstone and Hansen, *Mobilization, Participation, and Democracy*: Ch. 7, Teixeira, *The Disappearing American Voter*: Ch. 2.

39. Laura Stoker and M. Kent Jennings, "Life-Cycle Transitions and Political Participation: The Case of Marriage," *American Political Science Review* 89 (1995): 421–433.

40. For detailed analyses of the relationship between demographic characteristics and voting see Raymond Wolfinger and Steven Rosenstone, *Who Votes?* (New Haven: Yale University Press, 1980); Rosenstone and Hansen, *Mobilization, Participation, and Democracy*: Ch. 5.

41. Verba and Nie, *Participation in America: Political Democracy and Social Equality* (New York: Harper & Row, 1972): 170–171; Wolfinger and Rosenstone, *Who Votes*: 90.

42. Rosenstone and Hansen, *Mobilization, Participation, and Democracy in America*: Ch. 5.

43. Katherine Tate, "Black Political Participation in the 1984 and 1988 Presidential Elections," *American Political Science Review* 85(1991): 1159–1176.

44. On language and political participation, see Sidney Verba, Kay Schlozman, and Henry Brady, *Voice and Equality: Civic Volunteerism in American Politics* (Cambridge, MA: Harvard University Press, 1995).

45. Russell Dalton, *Citizen Politics in Western Democracies* (Chatham, NJ: Chatham House, 1988): 51–52.

46. Herbert Tingsten, *Political Behavior: Studies in Election Statistics* (London: King & Son, 1937): 225–226.

47. "The Democratic Distemper," *The Public Interest* 41 (1975): 36–37.

48. Quoted in Seymour Martin Lipset, *Political Man* (New York: Anchor, 1963): 228, note 90.

49. George Will, "In Defense of Nonvoting," in George Will, ed., *The Morning After* (New York: Free Press, 1986): 229.

50. Stephen Bennett and David Resnick, "The Implications of Nonvoting for Democracy in the United States," *American Journal of Political Science* 34(1990): 771–802.

51. U.S. Bureau of the Census, *Current Population Reports*, P20–485: Table B. For a general discussion see Peverill Squire, Raymond Wolfinger, and David Glass, "Residential Mobility and Voter Turnout," *American Political Science Review* 81(1987): 45–65.

52. Teixeira, *The Disappearing American Voter*: 92.

53. "A Three-Party Election Won't Address Issue of Economic Injustice," *The Boston Globe*, July 26, 1996: A17.

54. Political theorist Benjamin Barber refers to the former as an example of "strong democracy," and the latter as an example of "thin democracy." See Barber, *Strong Democracy*.

CHAPTER 7

1. The following account is based on Phil Kunz, "Home Schooling Movement Gives House a Lesson," *Congressional Quarterly Weekly Report*, February 26, 1994: 479–480.

2. There is some controversy about how to measure group membership and consequently about the exact figures. For differing viewpoints see Frank Baumgartner and Jack Walker, "Survey Research and Membership in Voluntary Associations," *American Journal of Political Science* 32(1988): 908–928; Tom Smith, "Trends in Voluntary Group Membership: Comments on Baumgartner and Walker," *American Journal of Political Science* 34(1990): 646-661; and Baumgartner and Walker, "Response to Smith's 'Trends in Voluntary Group Membership,'" *American Journal of Political Science* 34(1990): 662–670.

3. Alexis de Tocqueville, *Democracy in America*, ed. J.P. Mayer (New York: HarperPerennial, 1969), 513.

4. Kay Schlozman and John Tierney, *Organized Interests and American Democracy* (New York: Harper & Row, 1981), 75.

5. Robert Wiebe, *The Search for Order, 1877–1920* (New York: Hill and Wang, 1967).

6. "Interest Representation: The Dominance of Institutions," *American Political Science Review* 78(1984): 64–76.

7. Jeffrey Berry, *Lobbying for the People* (Princeton: Princeton University Press, 1977).

8. *Mobilizing Interest Groups in America* (Ann Arbor: University of Michigan Press, 1991), 10.

9. Kristen Luker, *Abortion and the Politics of Motherhood* (Berkeley: University of California Press, 1984), Chs. 5–6.

10. An excellent source of basic information about groups and associations in the United States is the *Encyclopedia of Associations*, Carol Schwartz and Rebecca Turner, eds. (Detroit: Gale Research, Inc., annual editions).

11. These figures represent the combined membership of the Sierra Club, Environmental Defense Fund, Friends of the Earth, Audubon Society, National Wildlife Federation, Natural Resources Defense Council, and the Wilderness Society (*Encyclopedia of Associations*, 1995 edition).

12. Henry Brady, Sidney Verba, and Kay Schlozman, "Beyond SES: A Resource Model of Political Participation," *American Political Science Review* 89(1995): 271–294.

13. *Political Organizations* (New York: Basic, 1973), Ch. 3.

14. Mancur Olson, *The Logic of Collective Action* (Cambridge, MA: Harvard University Press, 1965).

15. R. Cornes and T. Sandler, *The Theory of Externalities, Public Goods and Club Goods* (Cambridge, England: Cambridge University Press, 1986), Ch. 6.

16. George Miller, *Railroads and the Granger Laws* (Madison: University of Wisconsin Press, 1971).

17. The law, known as the McCrary bill after its sponsor, George McCrary (R-IA), died in the Senate. As the Founders intended, the House yielded to popular passion, while the Senate resisted.

18. Jane Mansbridge, *Why We Lost the ERA* (Chicago: University of Chicago Press, 1986).

19. Kenneth Wald, *Religion and Politics in the United States* 2nd ed. (Washington, DC: CQ Press, 1992), Ch. 7.

20. Murray Edelman, *The Symbolic Uses of Politics* ((Urbana IL: University of Illinois Press, 1964), Ch. 2.

21. "As Green Turns to Brown," *The Economist*, March 5, 1994: 28.

22. The term is from Richard Wagner, "Pressure Groups and Political Entrepreneurs," *Papers in Nonmarket Decision Making* 1(1966): 161–70. For extended discussions see Norman Frolich, Joe Oppenheimer, and Oran Young, *Political Leadership and Collective Goods* (Princeton: Princeton University Press, 1971); Terry Moe, *The Organization of Interests* (Chicago: University of Chicago Press, 1980), Chs. 3–4.

23. Walker, *Mobilizing Interest Groups in America*, 98–99.

24. Jack Walker, "The Origins and Maintenance of Interest Groups in America," *American Political Science Review* 77(1983): 390–406.

25. Schlozman and Tierney, *Organized Interests and American Democracy*, Ch. 4.

26. *American Lobbyists Directory*, Robert Wilson ed. (Detroit: Gale Research Inc., 1995). The estimate of Washington lobbyists is that of James Thurber, cited in Burdett Loomis, *The Contemporary Congress* (New York: St. Martin's, 1996), 35.

27. Chuck Henning, *The Wit and Wisdom of Politics* (Golden, CO: Fulcrum Publishing, 1992), 137.

28. For figures see Mark Petracca, ed., *The Politics of Interests* (Boulder, CO: Westview Press, 1992), 14–15. Edward Laumann, John Heinz, Robert Nelson, and Robert Salisbury, "Washington Lawyers—and Others: The Structure of Washington Representation," *Stanford Law Review* 37(1985): 465–502.

29. Lobbyist Michael Bromberg, quoted in Eleanor Clift and Tom Brazaitis, *War Without Bloodshed: The Art of Politics* (New York: Scribner, 1996), 100.

30. *Pressure Politics: The Story of the Anti-Saloon League* (New York: Columbia University Press, 1928), 76.

31. Frank Sorauf, *Inside Campaign Finance* (New Haven: Yale University Press, 1992), Ch. 4. A basic reference on PACs is *The PAC Directory* (Cambridge, MA: Ballinger, various editions).

32. Ross Baker, *The New Fat Cats: Members of Congress as Political Benefactors* (New York: Priority Press, 1989); Eliza Carney, "PAC Men," *National Journal*, October 1, 1994: 2268–2273.

33. See Edward Epstein, "Business and Labor Under the Federal Election Campaign Act of 1971," in Michael Malbin, ed., *Parties, Interest Groups, and Campaign Finance Laws* (Washington, DC: American Enterprise Institute, 1980), 107–51.

34. Thomas Ferguson and Joel Rogers, *Right Turn: The Decline of the Democrats and the Future of American Politics* (New York: Hill and Wang, 1986).

35. For a discussion, see Richard Hall and Frank Wayman, "Buying Time: Moneyed Interests and the Mobilization of Bias in Congressional Committees," *American Political Science Review* 84(1990): 797–820.

36. R. Kenneth Godwin, *One Billion Dollars of Influence* (Chatham, NJ: Chatham House Publishers, 1988).

37. Andrew McFarland, *Common Cause: Lobbying for the People* (Chatham, NJ: Chatham House Publishers, 1984), 74–81.

38. For elaboration, see Hugh Graham and Ted Gurr, *The History of Violence in America* (New York: Bantam: 1969).

39. For an analysis of the expansion by the judiciary of federal programs for the handicapped and the poor, see R. Shep Melnick, *Between the Lines* (Washington, DC: Brookings, 1994).

40. Karen O'Connor and Bryan McFall, "Conservative Interest Group Litigation in the Reagan Era and Beyond," in Mark Petracca, ed., *The Politics of Interests* (Boulder, CO: Westview Press, 1992), 263–281.

41. Jonathan Rauch, *Demosclerosis* (New York: Random House, 1994).

42. Philip Stern, *The Best Congress Money Can Buy* (New York: Pantheon, 1988).

43. John Heinz, Edward Laumann, Robert Nelson and Robert Salisbury, *Representing Interests: Structure and Uncertainty in National Policy Making* (in press).

44. J. Leiper Freeman, *The Political Process*, rev. ed. (New York: Random House, 1965); Grant McConnell, *Private Power and American Democracy* (New York: Knopf, 1966); Theodore Lowi, *The End of Liberalism* (New York: Norton, 1969).

45. David Hosansky, "House and Senate Assemble Conflicting Farm Bills," *Congressional Quarterly Weekly Report*, February 3, 1996: 298.

46. Hugh Heclo, "Issue Networks and the Executive Establishment, in Anthony King, ed., *The New American Political System* (Washington, DC: Brookings, 1978), 87–124.

47. Robert Salisbury, John Heinz, Robert Nelson, and Edward Laumann, "Triangles, Networks, and Hollow Cores: The Complex Geometry of Washington Interest Representation," in Mark Petracca ed., *The Politics of Interests* (Boulder, CO: Westview Press, 1992), 130–149.

48. John Chubb, *Interest Groups and the Bureaucracy* (Stanford, CA: Stanford University Press, 1983), 249–265. Richard Harris, "Politicized Management: The Changing Face of Business in American Politics," in Richard Harris and Sidney Milkis, eds., *Remaking American Politics* (Boulder, CO: Westview Press, 1989), 261–286.

49. Schlozman and Tierney, *Organized Interests and American Democracy*, 314–317.

50. John Hibbing and Elizabeth Theiss-Morse, *Congress as Public*

Enemy (New York: Cambridge University Press, 1995), 63–65, 147.

51. Earl Latham, *The Group Basis of Politics* (New York: Cornell University Press, 1952); David Truman, *The Governmental Process* (New York: Knopf, 1958).

52. *The Semisovereign People* (New York: Holt Rinehart and Winston, 1960), 34–35.

53. *Politics, Pressures, and the Tariff* (New York: Prentice-Hall, 1935).

54. "The Gerontocrats," *The Economist* (May 13, 1995): 32.

55. Mansbridge, *Why We Lost the ERA*, 73.

56. Peter Aranson and Peter Ordeshook, "A Prolegomenon to a Theory of the Failure of Representative Democracy," in Aranson and Ordeshook, eds., *American Re-evolution* (Tucson: University of Arizona, 1977), 23–46.

CHAPTER 8

1. This short account is based on James MacGregor Burns, *The Deadlock of Democracy* (Englewood Cliffs, NJ: Prentice-Hall, 1964): Ch. 2.

2. Jackson Turner Main, *Political Parties Before the Constitution* (New York: Norton, 1973).

3. Richard Katz, "Party Government: A Rationalistic Conception," in F. Castles and R. Wildenmann, eds. *Visions and Realities of Party Government* (Berlin: deGruyter, 1986): 31.

4. Geoffrey Smith, "The Futures of Party Government," ibid.: 206.

5. Martin Wattenberg, *The Decline of American Political Parties, 1952–1992* (Cambridge, MA: Harvard University Press, 1994).

6. *Party Government* (New York: Farrar and Rinehart, 1942): 1.

7. John Aldrich, *Why Parties?* (Chicago: University of Chicago Press, 1995): Ch. 2.

8. See, for example, James Campbell, *The Presidential Pulse of Congressional Elections* (Lexington: University Press of Kentucky, 1993).

9. V.O. Key, Jr., *Southern Politics* (New York: Knopf, 1949).

10. Richard Fenno, *Home Style* (Boston: Little, Brown, 1978): Ch. 3.

11. Anthony Downs, *An Economic Theory of Democracy* (New York: Harper and Row, 1957).

12. Gavin Wright, "The Political Economy of New Deal Spending: An Econometric Analysis," *Review of Economics and Statistics* 56(1974): 30–38.

13. Morris Fiorina, *Divided Government*, 2nd ed. (Boston: Allyn & Bacon, 1996): 107–110.

14. R. Michael Alvarez and Jonathan Nagler, "Economics, Issues, and the Perot Candidacy: Voter Choice in the 1992 Presidential Election," *American Journal of Political Science* 39(1995): 714–744.

15. Austin Ranney, *Curing the Mischiefs of Faction* (Berkeley: University of California Press, 1975); Nelson Polsby, *Consequences of Party Reform* (New York: Oxford University Press, 1983).

16. James Bryce, *The American Commonwealth*, 4th ed. (London: Macmillan, 1910): vol. 2, p. 5.

17. See, for example, William Chambers and Walter Dean Burnham, eds. *The American Party Systems: Stages of Political Development* (New York: Oxford University Press, 1975).

18. The seminal contribution was V.O. Key, Jr., "A Theory of Critical Elections," *Journal of Politics* 17(1955): 3–18. The most influential elaborations and extensions of the idea are Walter Dean Burnham, *Critical Elections and The Mainsprings of American Politics* (New York: Norton, 1970), and James Sundquist, *Dynamics of the Party System*, rev. ed. (Washington, DC: Brookings, 1983).

19. Robert Remini, *Martin Van Buren and the Making of the Democratic Party* (New York: Columbia, 1959); Donald Cole, *Martin Van Buren and the American Political System* (Princeton: Princeton University Press, 1984).

20. For a recent history of the period, see Paul Kleppner, *The Third Electoral System, 1853–1892: Parties, Voters, and Political Cultures* (Chapel Hill: University of North Carolina Press, 1979).

21. Charles Stewart and Barry Weingast, "Stacking the Senate, Changing the Nation: Republican Rotten Boroughs, Statehood Politics, and American Political Development," *Studies in American Political Development* 6 (1992): 223–271.

22. Harold Gosnell provides a classic study of a machine. See his *Machine Politics: Chicago Model* (Chicago: University of Chicago Press, 1937). For a more recent study see M.C. Brown and C. N. Halaby. "Machine Politics in America, 1870–1945," *Journal of Interdisciplinary History* 17(1987): 587–612.

23. John D. Hicks, *The Populist Revolt* (Minneapolis: University of Minnesota Press, 1931).

24. E.E. Schattschneider, "United States: The Functional Approach to Party Government," in Sigmund Neumann, ed. *Modern Political Parties* (Chicago: University of Chicago Press, 1956): 194–215.

25. Richard Vallely, "National Parties and Racial Disenfranchisement," in Paul Peterson, ed., *Classifying by Race* (Princeton: Princeton University Press, 1995): 188–216.

26. Alan Lichtman, *Prejudice and the Old Politics* (Chapel Hill: University of North Carolina Press, 1979).

27. Richard Hofstadter, *The Age of Reform* (New York: Vintage, 1955); Gabriel Kolko, *The Triumph of Conservatism* (New York: Free Press, 1963).

28. Joel Silbey, "Beyond Realignment and Realignment Theory," in Byron Shafer, ed. *The End of Realignment?* (Madison: University of Wisconsin Press, 1991): 3–23.

29. Walter Dean Burnham believes that a realignment did indeed occur in the early 1990s. See his "Realignment Lives: The 1994 Earthquake and Its Implications," in Colin Campbell and Bert Rockman, eds. *The Clinton Presidency: First Appraisals* (Chatham, NJ: Chatham House Publishers, 1996): 363–395.

30. Steven Rosenstone, Roy Behr, and Edward Lazarus, *Third Parties in America* (Princeton: Princeton University Press, 1981).

31. Maurice Duverger, *Political Parties: Their Organization and Activity in the Modern State* (New York: Wiley, 1963): Book II, Ch. 1.

32. Ibid. For elaboration see Thomas Palfrey, "A Mathematical Proof of Duverger's Law," in *Models of Strategic Choice in Politics*, Peter Ordeshook, ed. (Ann Arbor: University of Michigan Press, 1989): 69–91.

33. Douglas Rae, *The Political Consequences of Electoral Laws*, rev. ed. (New Haven: Yale University Press, 1971): 98. Cf. Arend Lijphart, who argues that Rae's figures exaggerate the

difference; see Lijphart, "The Political Consequences of Electoral Laws, 1045–1985," *American Political Science Review* 84 (1990): 481–496.

34. *Critical Elections*, Ch. 5.

35. *Trans Action* 7(1969): 12–22.

36. *The Party's Over: The Failure of American Politics* (New York: Harper and Row, 1971).

37. Xandra Kayden and Eddie Mahe, Jr., *The Party Goes On: The Persistence of the Two-Party System in the United States* (New York: Basic, 1985); Larry Sabato, *The Party's Just Begun: Shaping Political Parties for America's Future* (Glenview, IL: Scott, Foresman, 1988.

38. Leon Epstein, *Political Parties in the American Mold* (Madison: University of Wisconsin Press, 1986); Joseph Schlesinger, "The New American Party System," *American Political Science Review* 79(1985): 1152–1169.

39. The following classification of parties as organizations, parties in the electorate, and parties in government is a standard one developed most fully in Frank Sorauf's text, *Party Politics in America* (Boston: Little, Brown, various editions).

40. Julius Turner, *Party and Constituency: Pressures on Congress* (Baltimore, MD: Johns Hopkins University Press, 1951).

41. *The Deadlock of Democracy*.

42. Writing in the 1970s Hugh Heclo put the number at 3,000. See his *A Government of Strangers* (Washington, DC: Brookings, 1977). By 1992, Thomas Weko put the number at about 3700. See *The Politicizing Presidency* (Lawrence: University of Kansas Press, 1995): 161.

43. Stephen Skowronek, *Building a New American State* (New York: Cambridge University Press, 1992): 69.

44. Stephen Frantzich, *Political Parties in The Technological Age* (New York: Longman, 1989).

45. Gordon Baker, *The Reapportionment Revolution* (New York: Random House, 1966).

46. Cornelius Cotter, James Gibson, John Bibby and Robert Huckshorn, *Party Organizations in American Politics* (New York: Praeger, 1984).

47. Ibid.

48. John Coleman, "Resurgent or Just Busy? "Party Organizations in Contemporary America," in John Green and Daniel Shea, eds., *The State*

of the Parties, 2nd ed. (Lanham, MD: Rowman and Littlefield, 1996): 312–326.

49. David Hosansky, "House Torn on Agriculture; Senate Makes Progress," *Congressional Quarterly Weekly Report,* September 30, 1995, 2980–2984.

50. Robert Dahl, *Dilemmas of Pluralist Democracy* (New Haven: Yale, 1982).

CHAPTER 9

1. Quoted in Peter Braestrup, *Big Story,* abridged edition (New Haven, CT: Yale University Press, 1983): 134.

2. Austin Ranney, *Channels of Power: The Impact of Television on American Politics* (New York: Basic Books, 1983): 4.

3. David Halberstam, *The Powers That Be* (New York: Knopf, 1979): 514.

4. Don Oberdorfer, *Tet!* (New York: Doubleday, 1971).

5. Braestrup provides the most ambitious account, comparing the reality of the war to the news coverage in *Big Story*.

6. In December, the chairman of the Joint Chiefs of Staff noted the possibility of an all-or-nothing offensive such as the Battle of the Bulge launched by the Germans as they retreated during World War II. Ibid., 54.

7. For a thoughtful treatment of media impact, see Braestrup, *Big Story*: 505-507.

8. David Altheide, *Creating Reality: How TV News Distorts Events* (Beverly Hills, CA: Sage, 1976).

9. Lewis Chester, Godfrey Hodgson, and Bruce Page, *An American Melodrama* (New York: Viking, 1969): 582.

10. Ibid., 592.

11. The American National Election Study asked a finer-grained question some months later: 19 percent said too much force had been used, compared to 25 percent who said not enough force had been used. Thirty-two percent said the right amount of force had been applied, and 25 percent said they couldn't remember or hadn't heard about the disturbances.

12. Frank Luther Mott, *American Journalism* (New York: Macmillan, 1950).

13. Samuel Kernell, *Going Public: New Strategies of Presidential Leader-*

ship (Washington, DC: Congressional Quarterly Press, 1986). Cf. Mel Laracey, "The Presidential Newspaper: The Forgotten Way of Going Public" (Manuscript, Harvard University, 1993).

14. Mott, *American Journalism,* p. 216.

15. "Talk Radio," *The Public Perspective,* September/October 1993, 96.

16. James C. Roberts, "The Power of Talk Radio," *The American Enterprise,* May/June 1991, 57–61.

17. Mary Ann Watson, *The Expanding Vista: American Television in the Kennedy Years* (New York: Oxford University Press, 1990): 76.

18. Austin Ranney, "Broadcasting, Narrowcasting, and Politics," in Anthony Kind, ed. *The New American Political System,* second version (Washington, DC: AEI Press, 1990): 175–201.

19. Frederic Biddle, "Many Drop the Network News Habit," *The Boston Globe,* October 1, 1996, 1.

20. William Mayer, "The Rise of the New Media," *Public Opinion Quarterly* 58(1994): 124–146.

21. "Caught in the Net," *The Public Perspective,* June/July 1996, 36.

22. Paul Starobin, "On the Square," *National Journal,* May 26, 1996, 1145–1149.

23. Rajiv Chandrasekaran, "Trolling for Votes in Cyberspace," *The Washington Post National Weekly Edition,* December 9–15, 1996, 34.

24. William Mayer, "Trends in Media Usage," *Public Opinion Quarterly* 57(1993): 597, 610.

25. See, for example, Doris Graber, *Mass Media and American Politics* (Washington, DC: CQ Press, 1993): Ch. 7.

26. Russell Neuman, Marion Just, and Ann Crigler, *Common Knowledge: News and the Construction of Political Meaning* (Chicago: University of Chicago Press, 1992); Jeffrey Mondak, "Newspapers and Political Awareness," *American Journal of Political Science* 39(1995): 513–27.

27. William Kornhauser, *The Politics of Mass Society* (New York: Free Press, 1959).

28. An example is the study of the 1940 presidential campaign reported in Paul Lazarsfeld, Bernard Berelson, and Hazel Gaudet, *The People's Choice* (New York: Columbia University Press, 1948).

29. Joseph Klapper, *The Effects of Mass Communication* (New York: Free Press, 1960).

30. Bernard Cohen, *The Press and Foreign Policy* (Princeton: Princeton University Press, 1963): 13.

31. Presentation by Steven Livingston at the John F. Kennedy School of Government, Harvard University, March 1996.

32. Robert Rotberg and Thomas Weiss, eds., *From Massacres to Genocide* (Washington, DC: Brookings, 1996).

33. M. McCombs and D. Shaw, "The Evolution of Agenda-Setting: Twenty-Five Years in the Marketplace of Ideas," *Journal of Communications* 43(1993): 58–67.

34. Steven Livingston and Todd Eachus, "Humanitarian Crises and U.S. Foreign Policy: Somalia and the CNN Effect Reconsidered," *Political Communication* 12(1995): 413–429.

35. Shanto Iyengar and Donald Kinder, *News That Matters: Television and American Opinion* (Chicago: University of Chicago Press, 1987).

36. Jon Krosnick and Laura Brannon, "The Impact of the Gulf War on the Ingredients of Presidential Evaluations," *American Political Science Review* 87(1993): 963–975.

37. Everett Carll Ladd, "As Much about Continuity as Change: As Much about Restoration as Rejection," *The American Enterprise* (January/February, 1993): 49–50. Marc Hetherington, "The Media's Role in Forming Voters' National Economic Evaluations in 1992," *American Journal of Political Science* 40(1996): 372–395.

38. The most extensive study of framing is by Shanto Iyengar, *Is Anyone Responsible?* (Chicago: University of Chicago Press, 1991).

39. *Public Opinion*, December/January 1985: 39.

40. Iyengar and Kinder, *News That Matters*, Ch. 6, 10.

41. Cohen, *The Press and Foreign Policy*. See also Lutz Erbring, Edie Goldenberg, and Arthur Miller, "Front-Page News and Real-World Clues: A New Look at Agenda-Setting by the Media," *American Journal of Political Science* 24(1980): 16–49.

42. S. Robert Lichter and Stanley Rothman, "Media and Business Elites," *Public Opinion*, October/ November 1981, 43. Freedom Forum survey cited

in Jill Zuckman, "Dole Says Media Overplay GOP View on Abortion," *The Boston Globe*, June 25, 1996, 10.

43. William Schneider and I.A. Lewis, "Views on the News," *Public Opinion*, August/September 1985, 6–11; "Ordinary Americans More Cynical Than Journalists: News Media Differs with Public and Leaders on Watchdog Issues" (Washington, DC: Times Mirror Center on People and the Press, May 22, 1995).

44. Maura Clancy and Michael Robinson, "The Media in Campaign '84: General Election Coverage, Part I," *Public Opinion*, December/January 1985, 49–54, 59.

45. Daniel Amundson and S. Robert Lichter, "Heeeeeree's Politics," *Public Opinion*, July/August 1988, 46.

46. Schneider and Lewis note that in the *Los Angeles Times* study, "Views on the News" they report on, one-quarter of the readership thought their papers were conservative, one-quarter liberal, one-quarter moderate, and one-quarter didn't know.

47. Michael Robinson, "The Media in Campaign '84: Part II," *Public Opinion*, February/March 1985, 43–48.

48. Thomas Palmer, "Reputation for Bias Seems Well Earned," *The Boston Globe*, January 3, 1993, 65, 68.

49. For an example of the media's tone after the election see Robert Woodward, *The Agenda: Inside the Clinton White House* (New York: Simon and Schuster, 1994).

50. David Mayhew, "The Return to Unified Party Control Under Clinton: How Much of a Difference in Lawmaking?" in Dryan Jones, ed., *The New American Politics* (Boulder, CO: Westview Press, 1995): 111–121.

51. Harold Stanley and Richard Niemi, *Vital Statistics on American Politics* 5th ed. (Washington, DC: CQ Press, 1995): 73.

52. Ben Bagdikian, *Double Vision* (Boston: Beacon Press 1995): 48.

53. G.C. Stone and E. Grusin, "Network TV as Bad News Bearer," *Journalism Quarterly* 61(1984): 517–523; R.H. Bohle, "Negativism as News Selection Predictor," *Journalism Quarterly* 63(1986): 789–796; D.E. Harrington, "Economic News on Television: The Determinants of Coverage," *Public Opinion Quarterly* 53(1989): 17–40.

54. Larry Sabato, *Feeding Frenzy* (New York: Simon and Schuster, 1991).

55. Michael Robinson, "Public Affairs Television and the Growth of Political Malaise," *American Political Science Review* 70(1976): 409–432. On TV making people more negative about human nature generally, see George Comstock, *The Evolution of American Television* (Newbury Park, CA: Sage, 1989): 265–269.

56. A widely cited study of what constitutes news is provided by Herbert Gans, *Deciding What's News: A Case Study of CBS Evening News, NBC Nightly News, Newsweek and Time* (New York: Vintage, 1979).

57. Quoted in James Fallows, *Breaking the News* (New York: Pantheon, 1966): 137.

58. The following account is based on Thomas Romer and Barry Weingast, "Political Foundations of the Thrift Debacle," in Alberto Alesina and Geoffrey Carliner, eds., *Politics and Economics in the 1980s* (Chicago: University of Chicago Press, 1981): 175–214.

59. Ellen Hume, "Why the Press Blew the S&L Scandal," *New York Times*, May 24, 1990: A25.

60. Mark Rom, *Public Spirit in the Thrift Tragedy* (Pittsburgh: University of Pittsburgh Press, 1996).

61. John David Rausch, Jr. "The Pathology of Politics: Government, Press, and Scandal," *Extensions: A Publication of the Carl Albert Congressional Research and Studies Center* (Norman, OK: Carl Albert Congressional Research and Studies Center, Fall, 1990): 11-12.

62. A Gallup survey of former Nieman Journalism Fellows found that more than three-quarters believe that traditional journalism is being replaced by tabloid journalism. See "The State of the Public Media Today" (Nieman Foundation, Cambridge, MA: April 1995).

63. Sabato, *Feeding Frenzy*.

64. Fallows, *Breaking the News*, 132.

65. Alison Carper, "Paint-by-Numbers Journalism: How Reader Surveys and Focus Groups Subvert a Democratic Press" (Barone Center on the Press, Politics and Public Policy, Harvard University Kennedy School of Government, Discussion Paper D–19, April 1995).

66. Peter Canellos, "Perot Ad Announcement is Also-Ran Against Reruns," *The Boston Globe*, September 13, 1996, A24.

67. Thomas Patterson, *Out of Order* (New York: Knopf, 1993): Ch. 2.

68. Kiku Adatto, *Picture Perfect* (New York: Basic, 1993): Ch. 25.

69. Ibid.

70. Pippa Norris, "Editorial," *Press/Politics* 2(1997): 1.

71. Elihu Katz and Jacob Feldman, "The Debates in the Light of Research: A Survey of Surveys," in Sidney Kraus, ed., *The Great Debates* (Bloomington: University of Indiana Press, 1962): 173–223.

72. Thomas Holbrook, "Campaigns, National Conditions, and U.S. Presidential Elections," *American Journal of Political Science* 38(1994): 973–998.

73. Quoted in Matthew Kerbel, *Remote & Controlled* (Boulder, CO: Westview Press, 1995): 93.

74. Dwight Morris and Murielle E. Gamache, *Handbook of Campaign Spending* (Washington, DC: Congressional Quarterly, 1994).

75. Thomas Patterson and Robert McClure, *The Unseeing Eye: The Myth of Television Power in National Elections* (New York: Putnam, 1976); Stephen Ansolabehere and Shanto Iyengar, *Going Negative: How Attack Ads Shrink and Polarize the Electorate* (New York: Free Press, 1995).

76. Darrel West, *Air Wars: Television Advertising in Election Campaigns, 1952–1992* (Washington, DC: Congressional Quarterly, 1993).

77. Edwin Diamond and Stephen Bates, *The Spot*, 3rd ed. (Cambridge, MA: MIT Press, 1992).

78. William Mayer, "In Defense of Negative Campaigning," *Political Science Quarterly* 111(1996): 437–455.

79. Craig Brians and Martin Wattenberg, "Campaign Issue Knowledge and Salience: Comparing Reception from TV Commercials, TV News, and Newspapers," *American Journal of Political Science* 40(1996): 172–193.

80. Ibid.

81. Michael Robinson and Margaret Sheehan, *Over the Wire and on TV* (New York: Russell Sage, 1983).

82. S. Robert Lichter and Daniel Amundson, "Less News Is Worse News: Television News Coverage of Congress, 1972–92," in Thomas Mann and Norman Ornstein, eds. *Congress, the Press, and the Public* (Washington, DC: American Enterprise Institute, 1994): 131–140.

83. Iyengar, *Is Anyone Responsible?* passim.

84. David Broder, "The Heroism of Hard Work," *Boston Globe*, October 18, 1995, 23.

85. Lichter and Amundson, "Less News Is Worse News."

86. Ibid.

87. Quoted in Fallows, *Breaking the News*: 187–188.

CHAPTER 10

1. For a fuller discussion see Barbara Sinclair, "Trying to Govern Positively in a Negative Era: Clinton and the 103rd Congress," in Colin Campbell and Bert Rockman, eds., *The Clinton Presidency: First Appraisals* (Chatham, NJ: Chatham House, 1996): 101–109.

2. On the history of the presidential primary see James Davis, *Springboard to the White House* (New York: Crowell, 1967).

3. Nelson Polsby, *Consequences of Party Reform* (New York: Oxford University Press, 1983): Ch. 1.

4. For a participant observer's account of the post-1968 reforms, see Austin Ranney, *Curing the Mischiefs of Faction* (Berkeley: University of California Press, 1975).

5. John Kessel, *The Goldwater Coalition* (Indianapolis: Bobbs-Merrill, 1968): ch. 3.

6. On primary dynamics see John Aldrich, *Before the Convention* (Chicago: University of Chicago Press, 1980), and Larry Bartels, *Presidential Primaries and the Dynamics of Public Choice* (Princeton: Princeton University Press, 1988).

7. John Haskell, *Fundamentally Flawed* (Lanham, MD: Rowman & Littlefield, 1996).

8. Larry Sabato, "Presidential Nominations: The Front-Loaded Frenzy of '96," in Larry Sabato, ed., *Toward the Millennium: The Elections of 1996* (Boston: Allyn & Bacon, 1997): 37–91.

9. On popular perceptions of Democratic and Republican presidential versus congressional candidates see Robert Erikson, "Roll Calls, Reputations, and Representation in the U.S. Senate," *Legislative Studies Quarterly* 15(1990): 630.

10. See John G. Geer, *Nominating Presidents* (New York: Greenwood Press, 1989): Ch. 2. Barbara Norander, "Nomination Choices: Caucus and Primary Outcomes, 1976–1988," *American Journal of Political Science* 37(1993): 343–364.

11. James McCann, "Presidential Nomination Activists and Political Representation: A View from the Active Minority Studies," in William Mayer, ed., *In Pursuit of the White House* (Chatham, NJ: Chatham House, 1996): 72–104.

12. On McGovern, see Samuel Popkin, et. al., "Toward an Investment Theory of Voting Behavior: What Have You Done For Me Lately?" *American Political Science Review* 70(1976): 779–805.

13. On presidential fund-raising see Clifford Brown, Lynda Powell, and Clyde Wilcox, *Serious Money* (Cambridge, England: Cambridge University Press, 1995).

14. Thomas Patterson, *Out of Order* (New York: Vintage, 1994): 74.

15. Ibid., 82.

16. Most research finds only small electoral impacts for the vice presidential nominees. See Steven Rosenstone, *Forecasting Presidential Elections* (New Haven: Yale University Press, 1983): 64–66, 87–88.

17. *A Heartbeat Away: Report of the Twentieth Century Fund Task Force on the Vice Presidency* (New York: Priority Press, 1988).

18. During the last two months of the presidential campaigns of 1976–1988, about 40 percent of the lead stories on the CBS evening news were about the election, as were 20 percent of all the stories reported. See Stephen J. Rosenstone and John Mark Hansen, *Mobilization, Participation, and Democracy in America* (New York: Macmillan, 1993): 178, n. 26.

19. David Abbott and James Levine, *Wrong Winner* (New York: Praeger, 1991).

20. For a discussion, see Nelson Polsby and Aaron Wildavsky, *Presidential Elections*, 9th ed. (Chatham, NJ: Chatham House, 1995): 291–299.

21. Rhodes Cook, "Dole's Job: To Convince His Own Party,"

Congressional Quarterly Weekly Report," August 3, 1996, 9–10.

22. For time of voting decisions since 1952, see Warren Miller and Santa Traugott, *American National Election Studies Data Sourcebook* (Cambridge, MA: Harvard University Press, 1989): 319.

23. Although the general notion of "partisanship" has been around for centuries, the social-psychological concept of party ID was advanced in the pioneering work of Angus Campbell, Philip Converse, Warren Miller, and Donald Stokes, *The American Voter* (New York: Wiley, 1960): Ch. 6–7.

24. Morris Fiorina, *Retrospective Voting in American National Elections* (New Haven: Yale University Press, 1981); Michael MacKuen, Robert Erikson, and James Stimson, "Macropartisanship," *American Political Science Review* 83(1989): 1125–42.

25. Charles Franklin and John Jackson, "The Dynamics of Party Identification," *American Political Science Review* 77(1983): 957–973.

26. Helmut Norpoth, "Under Way and Here to Stay: Party Realignment in the 1980s?" *Public Opinion Quarterly* 51(1987): 381–87.

27. The classic demonstration appears in Campbell et al., *The American Voter*, Ch. 8, although there is general agreement that the picture presented there is overstated. For balanced treatments of policy issues in recent campaigns, see the series of *Change and Continuity* volumes by Paul Abramson, John Aldrich, and David Rohde, published by CQ Press.

28. Benjamin Page and Richard Brody, "Policy Voting and the Electoral Process: The Vietnam War Issue," *American Political Science Review* 66(1972): 979–995.

29. Edward Carmines and James Stimson, "The Two Faces of Issue Voting," *American Political Science Review* 74(1980): 78–91.

30. Ibid., Also see R. Douglas Arnold, *The Logic of Congressional Action* (New Haven: Yale University Press, 1990: Ch. 2.

31. Richard Trilling, *Party Image and Electoral Behavior* (New York: Wiley, 1976).

32. Fiorina, *Retrospective Voting*.

33. Scott Teeter, "Public Opinion in 1984," and Gerald Pomper, "The Presidential Election," both in Gerald

Pomper, et. al., *The Election of 1984* (Chatham, NJ: Chatham House, 1985).

34. Samuel Popkin, *The Reasoning Voter* (Chicago: University of Chicago Press, 1991): 60–67.

35. Donald Stokes, "Some Dynamic Elements of Contests for the Presidency," *American Political Science Review* 60(1966): 19–28.

36. Stokes, "Some Dynamic Elements," 222.

37. Indeed, by some calculations, Kennedy ran worse than a "generic" Democrat for that time. See Angus Campbell, Philip Converse, Warren Miller and Donald Stokes, "Stability and Change in 1960; A Reinstating Election," in *Elections and the Political Order* (New York: Wiley, 1966): 78–95.

38. Thus, an important correlate of support for Bush in 1988 was what citizens thought of *Reagan's* performance as President. See Paul Abramson, John Aldrich, and David Rohde, *Change and Continuity in the 1988 Elections* (Washington, DC: CQ Press, 1990): Ch. 7.

39. For recent examples of the genre, see Edward Rollins, with Tom DeFrank, *Bare Knuckles and Back Rooms* (New York: Bantam Doubleday, 1996), Dick Morris, *Behind the Oval Office* (New York: Random House, 1997).

40. See Thomas Holbrook, *Do Campaigns Matter?* (Thousand Oaks, CA: Sage, 1996).

41. For a discussion, see Marjorie Hershey, "The Campaign and the Media," in Gerald Pomper, et. al., *The Election of 1988* (Chatham, NJ: Chatham House, 1989): Ch. 3.

42. See, for example, Adam Nagourney and Elizabeth Kolbert, "Missteps Doomed Dole from the Start," *New York Times*, November 8, 1996, A1.

43. Donald Kinder and Lynn Sanders, *Divided by Color* (Chicago: University of Chicago Press, 1996).

44. Paul Sniderman and Thomas Piazza, *The Scar of Race* (Cambridge, MA: Harvard University Press, 1993).

45. Paul Abramson, John Aldrich, and David Rohde, *Change and Continuity in the 1992 Elections* (Washington, DC: Congressional Quarterly Inc., 1994); Herbert Weisberg and David Kimball, "Attitudinal Correlates of the 1992 Presidential Vote: Party Identification and Beyond," in Herbert Weisberg, ed.,

Democracy's Feast: Elections in America (Chatham, NJ: Chatham House, 1995): 72–111.

46. Marc Hetherington, "The Media's Role in Forming Voters' National Economic Evaluations in 1992," *American Journal of Political Science* 40(1996): 372–395.

47. Everett Ladd, "The Public's Views of National Performance," *The Public Perspective*, October/November 1996, 17–20.

48. Rhodes Cook, "Race of Muted Differences Has the Nation Yawning," *Congressional Quarterly Weekly Report*, October 119, 1996, 2950.

49. Peter Canellos, "New TV Ad Mentions a GOP Unmentionable," *The Boston Globe*, October 29, 1996, A23.

50. Jane Mansbridge, "Myth and Reality: The ERA and the Gender Gap in the 1980 Election," *Public Opinion Quarterly*, 49(1985): 164–178.

51. Emily Stoper, "The Gender Gap Concealed and Revealed," *Journal of Political Science* 17(1989): 50–62; Tom Smith, "The Polls: Gender and Attitudes Toward Violence," *Public Opinion Quarterly* 48(1984): 384–396.

52. For discussions, see Pamela Conover, "Feminists and the Gender Gap," *Journal of Politics* 50(1988): 985–1010; Elizabeth Cook and Clyde Wilcox, "Feminism and the Gender Gap—A Second Look," *Journal of Politics* 53(1991): 1111–1122.

53. "Where the Parties Are," *The Public Perspective*, March/April 1994, 78–79. "Which Party Is Better on Which Issues?" *The Public Perspective*, June/July 1996, 65.

54. Exit poll results or 1996 ANES study, when either is available for analysis.

55. Robert Merry, "A Rule for Presidents: Go Centrist or Perish," *Congressional Quarterly Weekly Report*, October 26, 1996, 3106.

56. "Fresh Light on Primary Colours," *The Economist*, February 24, 1996, 23.

CHAPTER 11

1. Quoted in George Hager and David Cloud, "Democrats Tie Their Fate to Clinton's Budget Bill," *Congressional Quarterly Weekly Report*, August 7, 1993, 2123.

2. Martha Angle, "Tallying Up the Thank-Yous," *Congressional*

Quarterly Weekly Report, May 29, 993, 1344.

3. Hager and Cloud, "Democrats Tie Fate to Clinton's Budget Bill," 2127, 2125.

4. "Federalist # 52," *The Federalist Papers*, Clinton Rossiter, ed., (New York: Mentor, 1961): 327.

5. Max Farrand, ed., *The Records of the Federal Convention of 1787* (New Haven: Yale University Press, 1966): Vol. 1, 151.

6. Morris Fiorina, David Rohde, and Peter Wissel, "Historical Change in House Turnover," in Norman Ornstein, ed., *Congress in Change* (New York: Praeger, 1975): 24–57. Nelson Polsby, "The Institutionalization of the U.S. House of Representatives," *American Political Science Review* 62(1968): 144–168.

7. James Young, *The Washington Community, 1800–1828* (New York: Harcourt, Brace, 1966): Ch. 2.

8. The South was primarily agricultural and had fewer high-status career opportunities outside of politics From the very beginning, southern members of Congress stayed longer than northerners. Fiorina, Rohde, and Wissel, *Historical Change in House Turnover*, 34–38.

9. Robert Struble Jr., "House Turnover and the Principle of Rotation," *Political Science Quarterly* 94(1979–80): 660.

10. Douglas Price, "The Congressional Career—Then and Now," in Nelson Polsby, ed., *Congressional Behavior* (New York: Random House, 1971): 14–27.

11. On the failure of incumbency to provide a complete explanation of Democratic dominance during this era see Morris Fiorina, *Divided Government*, 2nd ed. (Boston: Allyn & Bacon, 1995): 18–23.

12. Alan Abramowitz and Jeffrey Segal, *Senate Elections* (Ann Arbor: University of Michigan Press, 1992).

13. Norman Ornstein, Thomas Mann, and Michael Malbin, *Vital Statistics on Congress, 1993–1994* (Washington, DC: Congressional Quarterly Inc., 1994): 67–68.

14. Robert Erikson, "Malapportionment, Gerrymandering and Party Fortunes in Congressional Elections," *American Political Science Review* 66(1972): 1234–1245. Gary King and Andrew Gelman, "Systemic Consequences of Incumbency Advantage in U.S. House Elections," *American Journal of Political Science* 35(1991): 110–138.

15. Ornstein, Mann, and Malbin, *Vital Statistics*, 67–68.

16. John Ferejohn, "On the Decline of Competition in Congressional Elections," *American Political Science Review* 71(1977): 172–174.

17. Gary Jacobson, *The Politics of Congressional Elections*, 4th ed. (New York: Longman, 1997).

18. Heinz Eulau, "Changing Views of Representation," in Heinz Eulau and John Wahlke, eds., *The Politics of Representation* (Beverly Hills, CA: Sage, 1978): 31–53.

19. Morris Fiorina, *Congress—Keystone of the Washington Establishment*, 2nd ed. (New Haven: Yale University Press, 1989).

20. Ibid., Ch. 10. See also Bruce Cain, John Ferejohn, and Morris Fiorina, *The Personal Vote* (Cambridge, MA: Harvard University Press, 1987): Ch. 2.

21. Walter Gellhorn, *Ombudsmen and Others: Citizens' Protectors in Nine Countries* (Cambridge, MA: Harvard University Press, 1966).

22. Richard H. Shapiro, *Frontline Management* (Washington, DC: Congressional Management Foundation, 1989): 94.

23. Morris Fiorina, "Congressmen and Their Constituents: 1958 and 1978," in Dennis Hale, ed., *The United States Congress: Proceedings of the Thomas P. O'Neill, Jr., Symposium* (Leomaster, MA: Eusey Press, 1982): 33–64.

24. Burdett Loomis, "The Congressional Office as a Small Business: New Members Set Up Shop," *Publius* 9(1979): 35–55.

25. Ornstein, Mann, and Malbin, *Vital Statistics*, 126, 130.

26. Glenn Parker, *Homeward Bound* (Pittsburgh, PA: University of Pittsburgh Press, 1986).

27. Roger Davidson and Walter Oleszek, *Congress and Its Members*, 4th ed. (Washington, DC: CQ Press, 1994): 149.

28. Totals in 1996 from preliminary FEC releases. Jonathan Salant, "Million-Dollar Campaigns Proliferate in 105th," *Congressional Quarterly Weekly Report*, December 21, 1996, 3448–3451.

29. Gary Jacobson, "Practical Consequences of Campaign Finance Reform: An Incumbent Protection Act?" *Public Policy* 42(1976): 1–32.

30. Gary Jacobson, *Money in Congressional Elections* (New Haven: Yale University Press, 1980).

31. Jacobson, *Politics of Congressional Elections*, 40.

32. Kenneth Bickers and Robert Stein, "The Electoral Dynamics of the Federal Pork Barrel," *American Journal of Political Science* 40 (1996): 1300–1326.

33. David Magleby and Kelly Patterson, "The Polls—Poll Trends: Congressional Reform," *Public Opinion Quarterly* 58(1994): 420–21.

34. Douglas Arnold, *The Logic of Congressional Action* (New Haven: Yale University Press, 1990): Ch. 2.

35. Stephen Ansolabehere, David Brady, and Morris Fiorina, "The Vanishing Marginals and Electoral Responsiveness," *British Journal of Political Science* 22(1992): 21–38.

36. Amihai Glazer and Bernard Grofman, "Two Plus Two Equals Six: Tenure in Office of Senators and Representatives, 1953–1983," *Legislative Studies Quarterly*, 12(1987): 555–564.

37. Abramowitz and Segal, *Senate Elections*, 34–35.

38. Morris Fiorina, *Representatives, Roll Calls, and Constituencies* (Lexington, MA: Heath, 1974): 90–100.

39. Joe Foote and David Weber, "Network Evening News Visibility of Congressmen and Senators," presented to the Association for Education in Journalism and Mass Communication, August 1984.

40. Glenn Parker, "Interpreting Candidate Awareness in U.S. Congressional Elections," *Legislative Studies Quarterly* 6(1981): 219–233.

41. Abramowitz and Segal, *Senate Elections*, 228–231. Jonathan Krasno, *Challengers, Competition, and Reelection: Comparing Senate and House Elections* (New Haven, CT: Yale University Press, 1995).

42. Joseph Schlesinger, *Ambition in Politics* (Chicago: Rand McNally, 1966).

43. These were charges leveled at Senator John Tunney of California in his losing 1976 race, and Senator Dick Clark of Iowa in his losing 1978 race.

44. Catherine Shapiro, David Brady, Richard Brody, and John Ferejohn, "Linking Constituency

Opinion and Senate Voting Scores: A Hybrid Explanation," *Legislative Studies Quarterly* 15(1990): 603.

45. David Brady and Morris Fiorina, "Ruptured Legacy: Presidential– Congressional Relations in Historical Perspective," in Larry Berman, ed., *Looking Back on the Reagan Presidency* (Baltimore: Johns Hopkins University Press, 1989): 268–287.

46. John Ferejohn and Randall Calvert, "Presidential Coattails in Historical Perspective," *American Journal of Political Science* 28(1984): 127–146.

47. Morris Fiorina, *Divided Government* (Boston: Allyn & Bacon, 1996): 14.

48. David Brady and Morris Fiorina, "Local and National Forces in Post-War House Elections," in David Brady, ed., *Contemporary Congressional Elections*, in press.

49. Janet Hook, "Freshmen in Congress Find Uses for Pork as they Seek Reelection, *The Boston Globe*, July 2, 1996, 6.

50. Hook,"Freshmen in Congress…"

51. Jon Healey, "'Projects' Are His Project," *Congressional Quarterly Weekly Report*, September 21, 1996, 2672.

52. Healey, "'Projects' Are His Project." Also see Jonathan Salant, "Some Republicans Turned Away from Leadership," *Congressional Quarterly Weekly Report*, December 7, 1996, 3352–3354; Andrew Taylor, "GOP Pet Projects Give Boost to Shaky Incumbents," *Congressional Quarterly Weekly Report*, August 3, 1996, 2169–2173.

53. "Minorities in Congress," *Congressional Quarterly Weekly Report*, January 4, 1997, 28.

54. Carol Swain, *Black Faces, Black Interests: The Representation of African Americans in Congress* (Cambridge, MA: Harvard University Press, 1993).

55. For a thoughtful treatment of these and related issues, see Jane Mansbridge, "In Defense of Descriptive Representation," working paper, Harvard University, 1997.

56. "Affirmative Action, Welfare, and the Individual," *The Public Perspective*, June/July 1995, 33.

57. David Canon, *Actors, Athletes, and Astronauts* (Chicago: University of Chicago Press, 1990): 53–56

58. David Lublin, "Racial Redistricting and Public Policy in the U.S. House of Representatives," unpublished manuscript.

59. Juliana Gruenwald, "Incumbents Survive Redistricting," *Congressional Quarterly Weekly Report*, November 9, 1996, 3229.

60. Lee Sigelman and Susan Welch, *Black Americans' Views of Racial Inequality* (Cambridge, England: Cambridge University Press, 1991).

61. Donald Kinder and Lynn Sanders, *Divided by Color* (Chicago: University of Chicago Press, 1996): Ch. 2.

CHAPTER 12

1. The blow-by-blow is recounted in various issues of *Congressional Quarterly Weekly Report* published in 1992: pages 1605–06, 1860–61, 1927–30, 2154, 2251–53, 2354–57, 2435–36, 3020–22, 3134, 3556.

2. Chuck Henning, *The Wit and Wisdom of Politics* (Golden, CO: Fulcrum, 1992), 39.

3. For institutional comparisons, see John Hibbing and Elizabeth Theiss-Morse, *Congress as Public Enemy* (New York: Cambridge University Press , 1995), Ch. 2.

4. Kelly Patterson and David Magleby, "Trends: Public Support for Congress," *Public Opinion Quarterly* 56(1992): 539–551.

5. Nelson Polsby, "Legislatures," in Fred Greenstein and Nelson Polsby, eds., *Handbook of Political Science*, vol. 5 (Reading, MA: Addison-Wesley, 1975): 257–319.

6. One hundred percent of Republican incumbents and 85 percent of Democratic incumbents won, for an average of 90 percent. See Dave Kaplan and Juliana Gruenwald, "Longtime 'Second' Party Scores a Long List of GOP Firsts," *Congressional Quarterly Weekly Report*, November 12, 1994: 3232. For further evidence that 1994 was not as much a break with the past as often portrayed in the media, see Gary Jacobson, "The 1994 House Elections in Perspective," in [Jacobson] *Political Science Quarterly* 111(1996): 203–223.

7. Richard Fenno, "If, as Ralph Nader says, Congress is the 'Broken Branch,' How Come We Love Our Congressmen So Much?" in Norman Ornstein, ed., *Congress in Change* (New York: Praeger, 1975), 277–287.

8. Richard Fenno, *Home Style: House Members in Their Districts* (Boston: Little, Brown, 1978), 168.

9. Neil McNeil, *Forge of Democracy* (New York: McKay, 1963).

10. Bruce Cain, John Ferejohn, and Morris Fiorina, *The Personal Vote: Constituency Service and Electoral Independence* (Cambridge, MA: Harvard University Press, 1987).

11. David Hosansky, "House Torn on Agriculture: Senate Makes Progress," *Congressional Quarterly Weekly Report*, September 30, 1995: 2980–2984.

12. For a comparison of the electoral payoffs of constituency activities for British MPs and members of the United States Congress see Cain, Ferejohn, and Fiorina, *The Personal Vote*.

13. Fenno, *Home Style*, Ch 1.

14. David Mayhew, *Congress: The Electoral Connection* (New Haven: Yale University Press, 1974), 81–82.

15. Richard Fenno, *The United States Senate: A Bicameral Perspective* (Washington, DC: American Enterprise Institute, 1982).

16. "Voting Participation: House," *Congressional Quarterly Weekly Report*, January 27, 1996: 256.

17. Nelson Polsby, Miriam Gallagher, and Barry Rundquist, "The Growth of the Seniority System in the U.S. House of Representatives," *American Political Science Review* 63(1969): 787–807.

18. For a more extensive discussion see Charles Jones, "Joseph G. Cannon and Howard W. Smith: An Essay on the Limits of Leadership in the House of Representatives," in Nelson Polsby, ed., *Congressional Behavior* (New York: Random House, 1971), 203–224.

19. Jackie Koszczuk, "For Embattled GOP Leaders, A Season of Discontent," *Congressional Quarterly Weekly Report*, July 20, 1996: 2019–2023. Jackie Koszczuk, "Unpopular, Yet Still Powerful, Gingrich Faces a Critical Pass," *Congressional Quarterly Weekly Report*, September 14, 1996: 2573–2579.

20. Randall Ripley, *Party Leaders in the House of Representatives* (Washington, DC: Brookings, 1967).

21. Barbara Sinclair, *Majority Leadership in the U.S. House* (Baltimore: Johns Hopkins University Press, 1983).

22. For a full discussion see Steven S. Smith and Marcus Flathman, "Managing the Senate Floor: Complex Unanimous Consent Agreements Since the 1950s," *Legislative Studies Quarterly* 14(1989): 349–374.

23. Lawrence Dodd and Richard Schott, *Congress and the Administrative State* (New York: Wiley, 1979), Ch. 3. For further discussion see Kenneth Shepsle, "The Changing Textbook Congress," in John Chubb and Paul Peterston, eds., *Can the Government Govern?* (Washington, DC: Brookings, 1989).

24. "Democrats Oust Hebert, Poage; Adopt Reforms," *Congressional Quarterly Weekly Report*, January 18, 1975: 114.

25. H. Douglas Price, "The Congressional Career—Then and Now," in Nelson Polsby, ed., *Congressional Behavior* (New York: Random House, 1971), 14–27.

26. David Brady and M.J. Morgan, "Reforming the Structure of the House Appropriations Process: The Effects of the 1885 and 1919–20 Reforms on Money Decisions," in Mathew McCubbins and Terry Sullivan, eds., *Congress: Structure and Policy* (New York: Cambridge University Press, 1987), 207–234.

27. Barbara Sinclair, *Legislators, Leaders, and Lawmaking: The U.S. House of Representatives in the Postreform Era* (Baltimore: Johns Hopkins University Press, 1995).

28. David Brady, *Congressional Voting in a Partisan Era* (Lawrence: University of Kansas Press, 1973).

29. Gary Cox and Mathew McCubbins, *Legislative Leviathan* (Berkeley: University of California Press, 1993).

30. David Rohde, *Parties and Leaders in the Postreform House* (Chicago: University of Chicago Press, 1991).

31. Woodrow Wilson, *Congressional Government* (Cleveland: Meridian, 1956), 82.

32. Gerald Gamm and Kenneth Shepsle, "Emergence of Legislative Institutions: Standing Committees in the House and Senate, 1810–1825,"

Legislative Studies Quarterly 14(1989): 39–66. Joseph Cooper, *The Origins of the Standing Committees and the Development of the Modern House* (Houston, TX: Rice University Studies, 1970).

33. Richard Fenno, *Congressmen in Committees* (Boston: Little, Brown, 1973), 172.

34. Karen Foerstel, "Gingrich Flexes His Power in Picking Panel Chiefs," *Congressional Quarterly Weekly Report*, November 19, 1994: 3326.

35. Mark Ferber, The Formation of the Democratic Study Group," in Nelson Polsby, ed., *Congressional Behavior* (New York: Random House, 1971), 249–267.

36. Norman Ornstein, "Causes and Consequences of Congressional Change: Subcommittee Reforms in the House of Representatives, 1970–1973," in Norman Ornstein, ed., *Congress in Change* (New York: Praeger, 1975), 88–114. Roger Davidson and Walter Oleszek, *Congress Against Itself* (Bloomington: Indiana University Press, 1977).

37. Dodd and Schott, *Congress and the Administrative State*: 124. Roger H. Davidson and Walter J. Oleszek, *Congress and Its Members*, 2nd ed. (Washington, DC: CQ Press, 1985), 228–230).

38. Barry Weingast and William Marshall, "The Industrial Organization of Congress," *Journal of Political Economy* 91(1988): 132–163.

39. John Ferejohn, *Pork Barrel Politics* (Stanford, CA: Stanford University Press, 1974); R. Douglas Arnold, *Congress and the Bureaucracy* (New Haven: Yale University Press, 1979).

40. Keith Krehbiel, *Information and Legislative Organization* (Ann Arbor: University of Michigan Press, 1991).

41. Morris Fiorina, *Representatives, Roll Calls, and Constituencies* (Lexington, MA: Heath, 1974), Chs. 2–3; R. Douglas Arnold, *The Logic of Congressional Action* (New Haven: Yale University Press, 1990), Chs. 2–4.

42. Jeffrey Talbert, Bryan Jones, and Frank Baumgartner, "Nonlegislative Hearings and Policy Change in Congress," *American Journal of Political Science* 39(1995): 391–2.

43. For a detailed study of how and why individual members partici-

pate at these various stages of the legislative process, see Richard Hall, *Participation in Congress* (New Haven, CT: Yale University Press, 1996).

44. Paul Light, *Forging Legislation* (New York: Norton, 1992), 199.

45. On the conference committee in recent years see Stephen Van Beek, *Post-Passage Politics: Bicameral Relations in Congress* (Pittsburgh: University of Pittsburgh Press, 1995).

46. Richard Munson, *The Cardinals of Capitol Hill* (New York: Grove Press, 1993).

47. Quoted in Stephen Skowronek, *The Politics Presidents Make* (Cambridge, MA: Harvard University Press, 1993), 389.

48. Diana Evans, "Policy and Pork: The Use of Pork Barrel Projects to Build Policy Coalitions in the House of Representatives," *American Journal of Political Science* 38(1994): 894–917.

49. The Model Cities case provides an older, similar example. See Douglas Arnold, *Congress and the Bureaucracy* (New Haven, Yale University Press, 1979), Ch. 8.

50. Robert Wells, "House Gives Its Approval to School Aid Measure," *Congressional Quarterly Weekly Report*, October 1, 1994: 2807. For background, see 1994 *Congressional Quarterly Weekly Reports*: 70–73, 246–47, 328–331, 552, 746, 1632, 2256–58, 2691, 2807–08, 2884–85.

51. Harrison Donnelly, "Reagan Opposition Threatens EDA Development Program," *Congressional Quarterly Weekly Report* 40(1982): 2295–2296.

52. Glenn Parker and Roger Davidson, "Why do Americans Love Their Congressman So Much More Than Their Congress? *Legislative Studies Quarterly* 4(1979): 52–61.

53. Mark Petracca, "Predisposed to Oppose: Political Scientists and Term Limitations," *Polity* 24(1992): 657–672.

54. George F. Will, *Restoration: Congress, Term Limits, and the Recovery of Deliberative Democracy* (New York: Free Press, 1992).

CHAPTER 13

1. As quoted in Chuck Henning, *The Wit and Wisdom of Politics:*

Expanded Edition (Golden, CO: Fulcrum Publishing, 1992), 214.

2. *Atlanta Journal and Constitution*, November 12, 1992.

3. "Gay Activists' Cash, Votes Ride on Ban Decision," *Congressional Quarterly*, July 10, 1993; p. 1815.

4. *New York Times*, January 27, 1993; 14.

5. *New York Times*, January 23, 1993; 1.

6. *New York Times*, January 27, 1993; 1.

7. *New York Times*, January 28, 1993; 1.

8. *Congressional Quarterly Weekly Report*, January 30, 1993; 229.

9. *New York Times*, July 18, 1993; sect. 4, p. E19.

10. Terry Moe, "The Politicized Presidency," in John Chubb and Paul E. Peterson, eds., *The New Direction in American Politics* (Washington, DC: Brookings, 1985).

11. Mark Peterson, *Legislating Together: The White House and Capitol Hill from Eisenhower to Reagan* (Cambridge, MA: Harvard University Press, 1990), Ch. 6; Jon R. Bond and Richard Fleisher, *The President in the Legislative Arena* (Chicago: University of Chicago Press, 1990), Ch. 4.

12. Pietro S. Nivola, *The Politics of Energy Conservation* (Washington, DC: Brookings, 1986).

13. Theda Skocpol, *Boomerang: Clinton's Health Security Effort and the Turn Against Government in U.S. Politics* (New York: W. W. Norton, 1996); Haynes Johnson and David S. Broder, *The System: The American Way of Politics at the Breaking Point* (Boston: Little, Brown, 1996).

14. Peterson, *Legislating Together*, 1990, 157.

15. Charles O. Jones, "Campaigning to Govern: The Clinton Style," in Colin Campbell and Bert A. Rockman, *The Clinton Presidency: First Appraisals* (Chatham, NJ: Chatham House, 1996), 16. Also, see Michael L. Mezey, *Congress, the President and Public Policy* (Boulder, CO: Westview, 1989).

16. As quoted in Henning, *Wit and Wisdom of Politics*, 240.

17. Bradley H. Patterson, Jr., *The Ring of Power: The White House Staff and Its Expanding Role in Government* (New York: Basic Books, 1988), 31.

18. Henning, *Wit and Wisdom of Politics*, 212.

19. Richard E. Neustadt, *Presidential Power and the Modern Presidents* (New York: Free Press, 1990), 19.

20. Daniel Stid, *The Statesmanship of Woodrow Wilson: Responsible Government under the Constitution* (Lawrence, KS: University Press of Kansas, forthcoming), ch. 6.

21. Benjamin Ginsberg and Martin Shefter, *Politics by Other Means: The Declining Importance of Elections in America* (New York: Basic Books, 1990).

22. James S. Young, *The Washington Community 1800–1828* (New York: Columbia University Press, 1966).

23. Jeffrey Tulis, *The Rhetorical Presidency* (Princeton: Princeton University Press, 1987), 91.

24. Thomas Bailey, *The American Pageant* (Boston: D. C. Heath, 1956), 669.

25. Samuel Kernell, *Going Public* (Washington, DC: Congressional Quarterly Press, 1986).

26. Inaugural Address, January 20, 1961, as quoted in *Bartlett Familiar Quotations, Revised and Enlarged*, (Boston, MA: Little, Brown, 1980), 15th ed., 890.

27. Neustadt, *Presidential Power*, 274.

28. Denis G. Sullivan and Roger D. Masters, "Happy Warriors: Leaders' Facial Displays, Viewers' Emotions and Political Support," *American Journal of Political Science* 32 (1988): 345–68.

29. Henning, *Wit and Wisdom of Politics*, 240–41.

30. Norman C. Thomas, Joseph A. Pika, and Richard A. Watson, *The Politics of the Presidency*, 3rd ed. (Washington, DC: Congressional Quarterly Press, 1993), 204.

31. As quoted in James P. Pfiffner, *The Modern Presidency* (New York: St. Martin's Press, 1994), 114.

32. John Hart, *The Presidential Branch: From Washington to Clinton*, 2nd. ed. (Chatham, NJ: Chatham House, 1995), 26–30.

33. See Matthew Dickinson, *Bitter Harvest: FDR, Presidential Power, and the Growth of the Presidential Branch* (New York: Cambridge University Press, 1997).

34. Paul Quirk, "Presidential Competence," in Michael Nelson, ed., *The Presidency and the Political System*, 4th ed., (Washington, DC: Congressional Quarterly; 1994), 171–221; John P. Burke, *the Institutional Presidency* (Baltimore: Johns Hopkins University Press, 1992), 40–42.

35. Colin Campbell, "Management in a Sandbox," in Colin Campbell and Bert A. Rockman, *The Clinton Presidency: First Appraisals* (Chatham: Chatham House, 1996), 60.

36. Charles O. Jones, "Campaigning to Govern: The Clinton Style," in Campbell and Rockman, *The Clinton Presidency*, 16.

37. Terry Moe, "The Politicized Presidency."

38. Bruce E. Altshuler, *LBJ and the Polls* (Gainesville: University of Florida Press, 1990); Lawrence R. Jacobs, "The Recoil Effect: Public Opinion in the U.S. and Britain," *Comparative Politics* 24 (1992): 199–217.

39. *Wall Street Journal*, December 22, 1993, A4.

40. George Washington Plunkitt, as quoted in Henning, *Wit and Wisdom of Politics*, 11.

41. Hart, *The Presidential Branch*, 120–22.

42. Jack Mitchell, *Executive Privilege: Two Centuries of White House Scandals* (New York: Hippocrene Books, 1992), 89–90.

43. John Farrell, "Embattled Security Official Quits, Calls Getting FBI Files a 'Mistake,'" *Boston Globe*, June 27, 1996: 12.

44. John W. Kingdon, *Agendas, Alternatives and Public Policies* (Boston: Little, Brown, 1981).

45. Tulis, *Rhetorical Presidency*, Ch. 3.

46. Tulis, *Rhetorical Presidency*, Ch. 3.

47. Harry McPherson, *A Political Education* (Boston: Little, Brown, 1972, 268), as quoted in Paul C. Light *The President's Agenda: Domestic Policy Choice from Kennedy to Reagan* (Baltimore: Johns Hopkins University Press, 1991), 13.

48. Stephen Hess, *Organizing the Presidency* (Washington, DC: Brookings, 1988), 11–18.

49. Richard Brody, *Assessing the President: The Media, Elite Opinion*

and *Public Support* (Stanford: Stanford University Press, 1991), 40.

50. Rockman, "Leadership Style and the Clinton Presidency," in Campbell and Rockman, *The Clinton Presidency*, 334.

51. Rockman, "Leadership Style and the Clinton Presidency," 334.

52. Walter Bagehot, *The English Constitution* (London: Fantana, 1993).

53. Stanley Elkins and Eric McKitrick, *Age of Federalism* (New York: Oxford University Press), 48.

54. The phrase is taken from Margery Allingham's *The Estate of the Beckoning Lady* (New York: Doubleday), 2.

55. Gerald F. Seis, "Soul on High: Clinton Strikes Deeper Chords, *Wall Street Journal*, December 15, 1993.

56. Lou Cannon, *President Reagan: The Role of a Lifetime* (New York: Simon & Schuster, 1991), 25.

57. Doris Kearns Goodwin, *No Ordinary Time: Franklin and Eleanor Roosevelt: The Home Front in World War II* (New York: Simon & Schuster, 1994).

58. Rockman, "Leadership Style and the Clinton Presidency," 334–36.

59. Henning, *Wit and Wisdom of Politics*, 261–62.

60. Paul C. Light, *Vice Presidential Power* (Baltimore: Johns Hopkins University Press, 1984), p. 258.

61. Sidney Milkis, *The President and the Parties: The Transformation of the American Party System Since the New Deal* (New York: Oxford University Press, 1993), 81.

62. Theodore Sorensen, as quoted in M. Miller, *Lyndon: An Oral Biography* (New York: Putnam, 1980), 254–55.

63. *New Republic*, June 6, 1983, as quoted in Light, *Vice Presidential Power*, 137.

64. Stephen Skowronek, *The Politics Presidents Make: Leadership from John Adams to George Bush* (Cambridge, MA: Harvard University Press, 1993), 250.

65. As quoted in James L. Sundquist, *The Decline and Resurgence of Congress* (Washington, DC: Brookings, 1981), 31.

66. *United States v. Belmont* 301 US 324 (1936); Harold Bruff and Peter Shane. 1988. *The Law of Presidential Powers: Cases and Materials.*

(Durham, NC: Carolina Academic Press), 88; Joseph Paige. 1977. *The Law Nobody Knows: Enlargement of the Constitution—Treaties and Executive Orders.* (New York: Vantage Press), 63.

67. Louis Fisher, *Constitutional Conflicts between Congress and the President*, 3rd ed., rev. (Lawrence: University of Kansas, 1991), 154.

68. *United States v. Nixon*, 418 U.S. 683, 709 (1974).

69. The man who cast the decisive vote provided subject matter for John F. Kennedy's *Profiles in Courage* (New York: Harper and Row, 1964).

70. *Arkansas Democrat-Gazette*, March 10, 1996; 4J.

71. *Wall Street Journal*, December 22, 1993; A1.

72. Neustadt, *Presidential Power*, Ch. 4.

73. Henning, *Wit and Wisdom of Politics*, 219.

74. As quoted in Henning, *Wit and Wisdom of Politics*, 222.

75. The significance of time on presidential support is stressed by Paul Brace and Barbara Hinckley, "The Structure of Presidential Approval: Constraints Within and Across Presidencies," *Journal of Politics* 53 (November 1991); 993–1017; John Mueller, "Presidential Popularity from Truman to Johnson," *American Political Science Review* (March 1970): 18–24. For contrasting views, which stress events rather than time, see Brody, *Assessing the President*; Samuel Kernell, "Explaining Presidential Popularity," *American Political Science Review* (June 1978): 506–22. Also, see Michael MacKuen, "Political Drama, Economic Conditions, and the Dynamic of Public Popularity," *American Journal of Political Science* (May 1983): 165–92; Charles Ostrom and Dennis Simon, "Promise and Performance: A Dynamic Model of Presidential Popularity," *American Political Science Review* (June 1985): 334–58; James Stimson, "Public Support for American Presidents," *Public Opinion Quarterly* 1976: 401–21.

76. These are averages for the Gallup polls taken throughout each year.

77. Samuel Kernell, *Going Public*, 2nd ed. (Washington, DC: Congressional Quarterly Press, 1993), Ch. 5.

78. Anthony King, *The Vulnerable Politician* (New York: Free Press, forthcoming).

79. George C. Edwards III, *At the Margins: Presidential Leadership of Congress* (New Haven: Yale University Press), 1989, 120–24; Calvin Mouw and Michael MacKuen, "The Strategic Configuration, Political Influence, and Presidential Power in Congress" (Paper prepared for the annual meeting of the Midwest Political Science Association, Chicago, 1989); Terry Sullivan, "Headcounts, Expectations and Presidential Coalitions in Congress," *American Journal of Political Science* 32 (1988): 567–89.

80. James Barber, *The Presidential Character: Predicting Performance in the White House* (Englewood Cliffs, NJ: Prentice-Hall, 1972).

81. For criticism of Barber's analysis, see Michael Nelson, "The Psychological Presidency," in Michael Nelson, ed., *The Presidency and the Political System*, 4th ed. (Washington, DC: Congressional Quarterly, 1994), 198–224; Alexander George, "Assessing Presidential Character," *World Politics* 26 (January 1974): 234–82; Jeffrey Tulis "On Presidential Character," in Jeffrey Tulis and Joseph M. Bessette, eds., *The Presidency in the Constitutional Order* (Baton Rouge: Louisiana State University Press, 1981); Erwin C. Hargrove, "Presidential Personality and Leadership Style," in George C. Edwards III, John H. Kessel, and Bert A. Rockman, eds., *Researching the Presidency: Vital Questions, New Approaches* (Pittsburgh: Pittsburgh University Press, 1993), 93–98.

82. Fred Greenstein, *The Hidden-Hand Presidency: Eisenhower as Leader* (New York: Basic Books, 1982).

83. Charles O. Jones, "The Separated Presidency—Making It Work in Contemporary Politics," in Anthony King, ed., *The New American Political System*, Second Version (Washington, DC: American Enterprise Institute Press, 1990), 24.

84. Stephen Skowronek, *The Politics Presidents Make: Leadership from John Adams to George Bush* (Cambridge, MA: Harvard University Press, 1993).

85. Henning, *Wit and Wisdom of Politics*, 92.

CHAPTER 14

1. Bill Clinton and Al Gore, *Putting People First: How We Can All Change America* (New York: Times Books, 1992).

2. *New York Times*, September 9, 1993: D20.

3. *New York Times*, September 8, 1993: B10.

4. *New York Times*, September 8, 1993: B10.

5. *Washington Post*, August 12, 1993: A6.

6. *New York Times*, September 5, 1993: sec I, p. 39.

7. *New York Times*, September 5, 1993: sec. I, p. 39.

8. *New York Times*, September 9, 1993: D20.

9. Martha Derthick, *Agency Under Stress: The Social Security Administration in American Government* (Washington, DC: Brookings, 1990).

10. Private correspondence from Patrick Wolf, Department of Political Science, Columbia University. In addition, there are independent government corporations, interagency commissions, and advisory committees. See also Patrick Wolf, "What History Advises About Reinventing Government: A Case Meta-Analysis of Bureaucratic Effectiveness in U.S. Federal Agencies" (Ph.D. dissertation, Department of Government, Harvard University, 1996).

11. Max Weber, *Essays in Sociology* (New York: Oxford University Press, 1958); Max Weber, *Economy and Society* (Berkeley: University of California Press, 1978).

12. James Q. Wilson, "The Bureaucracy Problem," *The Public Interest* (Winter 1967): 3–9.

13. Michael Lipsky, *Street-Level Bureaucracy: Dilemmas of the Individual in Public Services* (New York: Russell Sage, 1980).

14. Lipsky, *Street-Level Bureaucracy.*

15. William A. Niskanen, *Bureaucracy and Representative Government* (Chicago: Aldine-Atherton, 1971), Ch. 2–4.

16. Aaron Wildavsky, *The New Politics of the Budgetary Process* (Boston: Little, Brown, 1988), 84–85.

17. Graham Allison, *Essence of Decision: Explaining the Cuban Missile Crisis* (Boston: Little, Brown, 1971), Ch. 3.

18. Herbert Kaufman, *Red Tape: Its Origins, Uses and Abuses* (Washington, DC: Brookings, 1977), as reprinted in Francis E. Rourke, *Bureaucratic Power in National Policy Making*, 4th ed. (Boston: Little, Brown, 1986), 442.

19. Laurence J. Peter, as quoted in Chuck Henning, *The Wit and Wisdom of Politics: Expanded Edition* (Golden, CO: Tulcrum Publishing, 1992), 16.

20. Kaufman, *Red Tape*, 434.

21. Virginia Ellis, "I-10 Is Repaired—But Spans Need Retro-fitting," *Los Angeles Times*, April 12, 1994, A1; "Accelerated Earthquake Repair Allows I-5 to Reopen Early," *Los Angeles Times*, May 18, 1994, p. B6; Henry Chu, "Quake-Damaged Freeway Link Opens," *Los Angeles Times* July 8, 1994: B1.

22. Lucius Wilmerding as quoted in Herman Finer, "Better Government Personnel," *Political Science Quarterly* 50 (1936): No. 4, p. 577.

23. James Young, *The Washington Community 1800–1828* (New York: Harcourt, Brace, 1966), 49. Ellipses deleted.

24. John Bartlett, *Familiar Quotations: Revised and Enlarged*, 15th ed., (Boston, MA: Little, Brown, 1980), 455.

25. Seymour J. Mandelbaum, *Boss Tweed's New York* (New York: John Wiley and Sons, 1965).

26. As quoted in Henning, *Wit and Wisdom of Politics*, 11.

27. A. James Reichley, *The Life of the Parties* (New York: Free Press, 1992), 157–58.

28. Thomas A. Bailey, *The American Pageant: History of the Republic* (Boston: D. C. Heath, 1956), 504.

29. Eugene Kennedy, *Hurrah! The Life and Times of Mayor Richard J. Daley* (New York: Viking, 1978), 255, 274.

30. Robert Dahl, *Who Governs?* (New Haven: Yale University Press, 1961); Raymond E. Wolfinger, *The Politics of Progress* (Englewood Cliffs, NJ: Prentice-Hall, 1974), Ch. 4; Edward Banfield and James Q. Wilson, *City Politics* (New York: Random House, 1963); Robert K. Merton, *Social Theory and Social Structure* (Glencoe, IL: Free Press, 1957), 71–81.

31. Quoted in Reichley, *Life of the Parties*, 212.

32. Paul E. Peterson, *The Politics of School Reform, 1870–1940* (Chicago: University of Chicago Press, 1985), 86–87.

33. Rufus P. Browning, Dale Rogers Marshall, and David H. Tabb, *Protest Is Not Enough: The Struggle of Blacks and Hispanics for Equality in Urban Politics* (Berkeley: University of California Press, 1984), Ch. 5.

34. Alben W. Barkley, vice president of the United States, 1949–53, as quoted in Henning, *Wit and Wisdom of Politics*, 17.

35. H. H. Gerth and C. Wright Mills, eds., from *Max Weber: Essays in Sociology* (New York: Oxford University Press, 1946), 110.

36. As quoted in Henning, *Wit and Wisdom of Politics*, 18.

37. Margaret Weir, *Politics and Jobs: The Boundaries of Employment Policy in the United States* (Princeton: Princeton University Press, 1992), 159.

38. Paul Light, *Thickening Government: Federal Hierarchy and the Diffusion of Accountability* (Washington, DC: Brookings, 1995), Ch. 1.

39. G. Calvin MacKenzie, "The Presidential Appointment Process: Historical Development, Contemporary Operations, Current Issues" (Background paper for the Twentieth Century Fund Panel on Presidential Appointments, March 1, 1994; 1).

40. David Houston, secretary of agriculture from 1913 to 1920 and secretary of the treasury from 1920 to 1921, as quoted in Richard F. Fenno Jr., *The President's Cabinet* (Cambridge, MA: Harvard University Press, 1959), 221.

41. Leonard White, *Introduction to the Study of Public Administration*, 4th ed. (New York: Macmillan, 1955), 80.

42. As quoted in G. Calvin MacKenzie, *The In- and Outers: Presidential Appointees and Transient Government in Washington* (Baltimore: Johns Hopkins University Press, 1987).

43. Haynes Johnson and David Broder, *The System: The American Way of Politics at the Breaking Point* (Boston: Little Brown, 1996).

44. *Wall Street Journal*, February 9, 1994; 1.

45. Johnson and Broder, *The System*, 397.

46. Derthick, *Agency Under Stress*, 200.

47. Frederic Ogg and P. Orman Ray, *Introduction to American Government* 10th ed. (Appleton-Century-Crofts; 1951), 405

48. David King, "The Nature of Congressional Committee Jurisdictions," *American Political Science Review* 88 (March 1995): 48–62.

49. Beryl A. Radin and Willis D. Hawley, *The Politics of Federal Reorganization: Creating the U.S. Department of Education* (New York: Pergamon Press, 1988).

50. James Q. Wilson, *Bureaucracy: What Government Agencies Do and Why They Do It* (Basic Books, 1989), 295–314; Ezra N. Suleiman, *Politics, Power and Bureaucracy in France: The Administrative Elite* (Princeton: Princeton University Press, 1974).

51. T. J. Pempel, "The Bureaucratization of Policymaking in Postwar Japan," *American Journal of Political Science* 18 (November 1974): 64.

52. R. Shep Melnick, *Regulation and the Courts: The Case of the Clean Air Act* (Washington, DC: Brookings, 1983).

53. Robert L. Park, director of the Washington office of the American Physical Society, as quoted in Graeme Browning, "Fiscal Fission," *National Journal*, June 8, 1996, 1259.

54. Graeme Browning, "Fiscal Fission," 1259.

55. Bill McAllister, "Byrd's Big Prize: Bringing Home the FBI," *Washington Post*, March 13, 1991, p. A1.

56. Grant McConnell, *Private Power and American Democracy* (New York: Alfred Knopf, 1966); Theodore Lowi, *The End of Liberalism*, 2nd ed. (New York: W. W. Norton, 1979); Mark P. Petracca, ed., *The Politics of Interests: Interest Groups Transformed* (Boulder, CO: Westview, 1992).

57. Herbert Kaufman, *The Administrative Behavior of Federal Bureau Chiefs* (Washington, DC: Brookings, 1981), 166, n. 51.

58. Joel Aberbach, *Keeping a Watchful Eye* (Washington, DC: Brookings, 1990), 162–64, 166.

59. Graeme Browning, "Fiscal Fission," 1260.

60. "Public Broadcasting Develops Dialogue with House GOP," *Congressional Quarterly*, March 23, 1996, p. 791.

61. Hugh Heclo, "Issue Networks and the Executive Establishment," in Anthony King, ed., *The New American Political System* (Washington, DC: American Enterprise Institute, 1978), 87–124.

62. John E. Chubb, *Interest Groups and the Bureaucracy* (Stanford: Stanford University Press, 1983); John Chubb "U.S. Energy Policy: A Problem of Delegation." in John E. Chubb and Paul E. Peterson, eds., *Can the Government Govern?* (Washington, DC: Brookings, 1989); Seong-Ho Lim, "Changing Jurisdictional Boundaries in Congressional Oversight of Nuclear Energy Regulation: Impact of Public Salience" (Paper presented before the annual meeting of the American Political Science Association, 1992); Frank R. Baumgartner and Bryan D. Jones, "Agenda Dynamics and Policy Subsystems," *Journal of Politics* 53 (November 1991): 1044–74.

63. Kermit Gordon, *Reflections on Spending* (Washington, DC: Brookings, 1967), 15.

64. Thomas E. Cronin, *The State of the Presidency*, 2nd ed. (Boston: Little, Brown, 1980).

65. Jefferson Cohen, *The Politics of the U.S. Cabinet* (Pittsburgh: University of Pittsburgh Press, 1988).

66. Martha M. Hamilton, "For Executives, Search for Business Turns to Tragedy," *Washington Post*, April 4, 1996, p. A26.

67. Marver H. Bernstein, *Regulating Business by Independent Commission* (Princeton: Princeton University Press, 1955): Harold Seidman, *Politics, Position and Power: The Dynamics of Federal Organization*, 2nd ed. (New York: Oxford University Press, 1975); George J. Stigler, "The Theory of Economic Regulation," *Bell Journal of Economics and Management Science* 2 (Spring 1971): 3–21; Terry Moe, "Regulatory Performance and Presidential Administration," *American Journal of Political Science* 16 (May 1982), 197–224; B. R. Weingast and M. J. Moran, "Bureaucratic Discretion or Congressional Control? Regulatory Policymaking by the Federal Trade Commission," *Journal of Political Economy* 91 (1983, no. 5): 765–800; B. R. Weingast, "The Congressional-Bureaucratic System: A Principle-Agent Perspective (With Application to the SEC)," *Public Choice* 44 (1984, no. 1): 147–91.

68. Robyn Meredith, "Credit Unions Help Finance a Bid for Reinstatement by a Dismissed Federal Regulator," *New York Times*, July 20, 1996; 7.

69. Herbert Kaufman, *The Administrative Behavior of Federal Bureau Chiefs*, 183, n.8.

70. Hugh Heclo, "OMB and the Presidency—the Problem of 'Neutral Competence,'" *Public Interest*, 38 (Winter 1975): 80–98; Karen Hult, "Advising the President," in George C. Edwards, John H. Kessel, and Bert A. Rockman, *Researching the Presidency: Vital Questions, New Approaches* (Pittsburgh: University of Pittsburgh Press, 1992), 126.

71. David Stockman, *The Triumph of Politics* (New York: Harper & Row, 1986).

72. As quoted in Kaufman, *Administrative Behavior of Federal Bureau Chiefs*, 169–70.

73. Johnson and Broder, *The System*, 116.

74. Paul E. Peterson, Barry G. Rabe, and Kenneth K. Wong, *When Federalism Works* (Washington, DC: Brookings, 1986), Ch. 8; John J. Harrigan, *Political Change in the Metropolis*, 2nd ed. (Boston: Little, Brown, 1981): 267–68, 350–51; Rochelle L. Stanfield, "Communities Reborn," *National Journal*, June 22, 1966: 1371.

75. Wolf, "What History Advises."

76. John Chubb and Terry Moe, *Politics, Markets and America's Schools* (Washington, DC: Brookings, 1990).

77. John DiIulio, *No Escape: The Future of American Corrections* (New York: Basic Books, 1991), 19–26.

78. Francis Rourke, "Executive Secrecy: Change and Continuity," in Rourke, *Bureaucratic Power in National Policy Making*, 536–37.

79. Martha Derthick, *Agency Under Stress*, 87.

80. John E. Dawson and Peter J. E. Stan, *Public Expenditures in the United States: 1952–1993* (Santa Monica, CA: Rand Corporation, 1995), 51, Figure 3.4a.

81. Former Bureau of the Budget Director Kermit Gordon, as quoted in Kaufman, *Administrative Behavior*, 1981, 443.

82. Paul J. Quirk, "Food and Drug Administration," in James Q. Wilson, *The Politics of Regulation* (New York: Basic Books, 1980), 199.

83. Terry Moe, "The Politics of Bureaucratic Structure," in John E. Chubb and Paul E. Peterson, *Can the Government Govern?* (Washington, DC: Brookings, 1988).

84. Brian Hassel, "Charter Schools: Designed to Fail?" (Ph.D. dissertation, John F. Kennedy School of Government, Harvard University, 1997).

85. Robert L. Kahn, Barbara A Gutek, Eugenia Barton, and Daniel Katz, "Americans Love their Bureaucrats," *Psychology Today* (1975), as reprinted in Rourke, *Bureaucratic Power in National Policy Making*, 290.

86. Charles Lindblom, "The Science of 'Muddling Through,'" *Public Administration Review* XIX (Spring 1959): 79–88.

87. Herbert Kaufman, *The Forest Ranger: A Study in Administrative Behavior* (Baltimore: Johns Hopkins University Press, 1960).

CHAPTER 15

1. As quoted in Chuck Henning, *The Wit and Wisdom of Politics* (Golden, CO: Fulcrum Publishing, 1992), 250.

2. Maureen Dowd, "The Supreme Court: Conservative Black Justice, Clarence Thomas, is Named to Marshall's Court Seat, *New York Times*, July 2, 1991, A1.

3. David Brock, *The Real Anita Hill: The Untold Story* (New York: Free Press, 1993), 66.

4. Paul Simon, *Advice and Consent* (Washington, DC: National Press Books, 1992), 89.

5. Ibid, 93.

6. Bob Dart, "Abortion Key to Hearing Today," *Atlanta Journal and Constitution*, Sept. 11, 1991, A1.

7. Simon, *Advice and Consent*, Chs. 5–6.

8. Ibid., 122.

9. Ibid., 122.

10. Brock, *The Real Anita Hill*, 17.

11. Gerald Pomper, "The Presidential Election," in Gerald M. Pomper et al., *The Election of 1992: Reports and Interpretations* (Chatham, NJ: Chatham House, 1993), 138.

12. As quoted in Henning, *Wit and Wisdom*, 107.

13. Carl B. Swisher, *American Constitutional Development*, 2nd ed.

(Boston: Houghton Mifflin, 1954), 1075–79.

14. Simon, *Advice and Consent*, 275.

15. Henry J. Abraham, *Justices and Presidents: A Political History of Appointments to the Supreme Court*, 3rd ed. (New York: Oxford University Press, 1992).

16. Twentieth Century Fund, *Judicial Roulette* (New York: Priority Press, 1988), 10–11.

17. Ethan Bronner, *Battle for Justice: How the Bork Nomination Shook America* (New York: W.W. Norton, 1989), 158–59.

18. Henning, *Wit and Wisdom*, 250.

19. Robert G. McCloskey, *The American Supreme Court* (Chicago: University of Chicago Press, 1960), 14.

20. *Lochner v. New York* 195 U.S. 45 (1905).

21. *Beau harnais v. Illinois* 343 U.S. 250 (1952).

22. *New York v. U.S.* 112 Supreme Court Reporter (1993), 2446–47.

23. *Dred Scott v. Sandford* 19. How. 393 (1857).

24. *Lochner v. New York* 198 U.S. 45 (1905). Ellipses deleted from excerpt.

25. *Schechter Poultry Corp.* v. *United States* 295 U.S. 495 (1935).

26. Jonathan D. Casper, "The Supreme Court and National Policy Making," *American Political Science Review*, 70 (March 1976): 50.

27. Excerpted with ellipses deleted. Robert A. Dahl, "Decision-making in a Democracy: The Supreme Court as a National Policy-Maker," *Journal of Public Law* 6 (Fall 1957): 293–94. See also Richard Y. Funston, "The Supreme Court and Critical Elections," *American Political Science Review* 69 (1975): 795–811.

28. James A. Stimson, Michael B. Mackuen, and Robert S. Erikson, "Dynamic Representation," *American Political Science Review* 89 (September 1995): 555. Also see William Mishler and Reginald S. Sheehan, "The Supreme Court as a Counter-Majoritarian Institution? The Impact of Public Opinion on Supreme Court Decisions," *American Political Science Review* 87 (1993): 87–101; Helmut Norpoth and Jeffery Segal, "Popular Influence on Supreme Court Decisions," *American Political Science Review* 88 (September 1994): 711–24.

29. Linda Greenhouse, "Legacy of a Term," *New York Times*, July 3, 1996: A1.

30. *Parts and Electric Motors* v. *Sterling Electric* 866 F. 2d 288 (1988).

31. Hennig, *Wit and Wisdom*, 213.

32. Hart Pomerantz, as quoted in Henning, *Wit and Wisdom*, 250.

33. John C. Jeffries Jr., *Justice Lewis F. Powell, Jr: A Biography* (New York: Charles Scribner, 1994), 248.

34. Jeffries, Jr., *Justice Lewis Powell, Jr.*, 323.

35. Jeffries, *Justice Lewis F. Powell Jr.*, 248.

36. Bernard Schwartz, A *History of the Supreme Court* (New York: Oxford University Press, 1993), Ch. 13.

37. Simon, *Advice and Consent*, 128.

38. As quoted in Henning, *Wit and Wisdom*, 106.

39. Jeffries, *Justice Lewis F. Powell Jr.*, 247.

40. Jeffries, *Justice Lewis F. Powell Jr.*, 245–47.

41. *Harris v. Forklift* 508 U.S. 938 (1993).

42. *Regents of the University of California v. Bakke*, 438 U.S. 265 (1978).

43. James F. Simon, *The Center Holds: The Power Struggle Inside the Rehnquist Court* (New York: Simon & Schuster, 1995): 227, 229.

44. Jeffrey A. Segal and Albert D. Cover, "Ideological Values and the votes of U.S. Supreme Court Justices," *American Political Science Review* 83 (June 1989): 557–65.

45. Henning, *Wit and Wisdom*, 250.

46. H. W. Perry Jr., *Deciding to Decide: Agenda Setting in the United States Supreme Court* (Cambridge, MA: Harvard University Press, 1991), 27.

47. Perry, *Deciding to Decide*, 218–19.

48. Perry, *Deciding to Decide*, 99.

49. Address of Chief Justice Vinson before the American Bar Association, September 7, 1949, as quoted in Perry, *Deciding to Decide*, 36.

50. This was true for the period 1958 to 1967; with the reduction in the number of certs accepted, this percentage has undoubtedly declined. Robert Scigliano, *The Supreme Court and the Presidency* (New York: Free Press, 1971) as quoted in Rebecca M. Salokar, *The*

Solicitor General: The Politics of Law (Philadelphia: Temple University Press, 1992), 3.

51. Scigliano, *Supreme Court and The Presidency*, 162.

52. Jeffrey A. Segal, "*Amicus Curiae* Briefs by the Solicitor General During the Warren and Burger Courts: A Research Note," *Western Political Quarterly* 41 (March 1988): 135–144.

53. Perry, *Deciding to Decide*, 71.

54. Schwartz, *History of the Supreme Court*, 372.

55. Perry, *Deciding to Decide*; Schwartz, *History of the Supreme Court*, Ch. 16.

56. David O'Brien, "Background Paper," in Twentieth Century Fund, *Judicial Roulette* (New York: Priority Press, 1988), 37.

57. As quoted in Robert A. Carp and Ronald Stidham, *The Federal Courts*, 2nd ed. (Washington, DC: Congressional Quarterly, 1991), 97.

58. C. K. Rowland, Donald Songer, and Robert Carp, "Presidential Effects on Criminal Justice Policy in the Lower Federal Courts: The Reagan Judges," *Law and Society Review*, 22 (1988:1): 191-200.

59. Henning, *Wit and Wisdom*, 108.

60. Joan Vennochi, "The White Knight Makes His Move," *Boston Globe*, May 24, 1988, 25.

61. Richard N. Smith, *Thomas E. Dewey and His Times* (New York: Simon & Schuster, 1982), Chs. 5–9.

62. As quoted in C. Herman - Pritchett, 1959, *The American Constitution* (New York: McGraw-Hill, 1959), 65, 215.

63. John B. Gates, "Partisan Realignment, Unconstitutional State Policies and the U.S. Supreme Court, 1837–1964," *American Journal of Political Science* 31 (May 1987): 259–280.

64. Pritchett, *American Constitution*, 134.

65. Herbert Jacob and Kenneth Vines, "Courts," in Virginia Gray, Herbert Jacob and Kenneth Vines, eds., *Politics in the American States: A Comparative Analysis*, 4th ed. (Boston: Little, Brown, 1983), 238.

66. Jacob and Vines, "Courts," 239.

67. Excerpted with ellipses deleted. Milton Rakove, *Don't Make No Waves; Don't Back No Losers*

(Bloomington: Indiana University Press, 1975), 223–25.

68. V. O. Key, *Southern Politics* (New York: Random House, 1949), 53, 171.

69. Jamie B. W. Stecher, "Democratic and Republican Justice: Judicial Decision Making in Five State Supreme Courts," *Columbia Journal of Law and Social Problems* 13 (1977): 137–181.

70. John Paul Ryan, Allen A. Ashman, Bruce D. Sales, and Sandra Shane-Dubow *American Trial Judges* (New York: Free Press, 1980): 125.

71. Henning, *Wit and Wisdom*, 187.

72. *In re Chapman* 16 U.S. 661 (1897).

73. As quoted by Austin Ranney, "Peltason Created a New Way to Look at What Judges Do," Public Affairs Report, Institute of Governmental Studies, Vol 36, No. 6, November 1995, 7.

74. Excerpted with ellipses deleted. *Federalist No. 78*, ed., with introduction by Jacob E. Cooke, (Wesleyan University Press, 1961), 522–23.

75. Pritchett, *American Constitution*, 99.

76. Robert H. Birkby, "The Supreme Court and the Bible Belt: Tennessee Reaction to the 'Shempp Decision,'" *Midwest Journal of Political Science* 10 (August 1966), as reprinted in Theodore L. Becker and Malcolm M. Feeley, eds. *The Impact of Supreme Court Decisions* (New York: Oxford University Press, 1973): 114.

77. Steven Lee Myers, "U.S. Judge Upsets Rules to Control How Jails Are Run," *New York Times* July 24, 1996: 1, B2.

78. Abram Chayes, "The Role of the Judge in Public Law Litigation," *Harvard Law Review* 89 (May 1976): 1281–1316.

79. Alexis de Toqueville, *Democracy in America*, J. P. Mayer, ed. (New York: Harper, 1988), 270.

80. R. Shep Melnick, *Between the Lines* (Washington, DC: Brookings, 1994), 149.

81. Francis T. Cullen, William J. Maakestad and Gary Cavendar, *Corporate Crime Under Attack: The Ford Pinto Case and Beyond* (Cincinnati, Ohio: Anderson, 1987): 297.

82. Amy Stevens, "The Mouthpieces: Class-Action Lawyers Brawl Over Big Fees in Milli Vanilli

Fraud," *Wall Street Journal*, October 24, 1991; "Judge Approves Settlement of Some Milli Vanilli Suits, *Wall Street Journal*, March 25, 1992.

CHAPTER 16

1. Michael Decourcy Hinds, "A Campus Case: Speech or Harassment?" *New York Times*, May 15, 1993, I, 62. Ibid., "Blacks at Penn Drop a Charge of Harassment," *New York Times*, May 25, 1993, A, 10.

2. Maria Newman, "Free Speech Lesson," *New York Times*, May 16, 1993, I, 33; Ibid., "Jury Faults CUNY Officials in Jeffries Lawsuit Decision," *New York Times*, May 18, 1993, B, 6.

3. Henry Steele Commager, ed. *Documents of American History* (New York: Appleton-Century-Crofts, 1958), 6th ed., 125–26; also see Willi Paul Adams, *The First American Constitutions: Republican Ideology and the Making of the State Constitutions in the Revolutionary Era* (Chapel Hill: University of North Carolina Press, 1980).

4. Arthur M. Schlesinger, *Prelude to Independence: The Newspaper War on Britain, 1764–1776* (New York: Alfred Knopf, 1958), 297–98.

5. Schlesinger, *Prelude to Independence*, 1958, 299.

6. *Barron v. Baltimore*, 1833, as quoted in C. Herman Pritchett, *Constitutional Civil Liberties* (Englewood Cliffs, NJ: Prentice Hall, 1984), 6.

7. *Federalist, No. 10*.

8. John Dalberg-Acton, 1907, as quoted in John Bartlett, *Familiar Quotations* 15th ed. (Boston: Little Brown, 1980), 616.

9. John Stuart Mill, as quoted in Bartlett, 508.

10. Schlesinger, *Prelude to Independence*, 64–65.

11. Robert G. McCloskey, *The American Supreme Court* (Chicago: University of Chicago Press, 1960), 224.

12. Quoted in Robert Goldstein, *Political Repression in Modern America: 1870 to the Present* (New York: Schenkman, 1978), 565.

13. *Schenck v. United States* 249 US 47 (1919).

14. *Stromberg v. California*, 283 US 359 (1931).

15. *Near v. Minnesota*, 283 US 697 (1931).

16. Goldstein, *Political Repression*, 262.

17. *Chaplinsky v. New Hampshire*, 315 US 568 (1942).

18. As quoted in C. Herman Pritchett, *The American Constitution* 3rd ed. (New York: McGraw-Hill, 1969), 375.

19. *United States v. Carolene Products Co.*, 304 US 144 (1938).

20. George Anastaplo, as quoted in Goldstein, *Political Repression*, 532.

21. *Papish v. the Board of Curators of the University of Missouri* 410 US 667 (1973).

22. Robert Goldstein, *Saving "Old Glory": The History of the Desecration Controversy* (Boulder, CO: Westview, 1995).

23. *Eichman v. United States* 496 US 310 (1990).

24. *R.A.V. v. City of St. Paul, Minnesota* 112 S. Ct. 2541 (1992).

25. Anthony Lewis, *Make No Law: The Sullivan Case and the First Amendment* (New York: Random House, 1992).

26. *Jenkins v. Georgia* 418 US 153 (1974).

27. As quoted in Charles L. Glenn, Jr., *The Myth of the Common School* (Amherst, MA: University of Massachusetts Press, 1987), 84.

28. Diane Ravitch, *The Great School Wars: New York City, 1805–1973* (New York: Basic Books, 1974); Paul E. Peterson, *The Politics of School Reform, 1870–1940* (Chicago: University of Chicago Press, 1985).

29. *Meek v. Pittenger*, 421. US 349 (1975).

30. *Engel v. Vitale*, 370 US 421 (1962); *School District of Abington Township v. Schempp*, 374 US 273 (1963); *Wallace v. Jaffree*, 472 US 38 (1985).

31. Benjamin I. Page and Robert Y. Shapiro, *The Rational Public: Fifty Years of Trends in Americans' Policy Preferences* (Chicago: University of Chicago Press, 1992), 113.

32. *Board of Education v. Mergens*, 496 US 226 (1990).

33. *Meyer v. Nebraska*, 262 US 399 (1923). See also *Pierce v. Society of Sisters*, 268 US 510 (1925).

34. Pritchett, *The American Constitution*, 477.

35. Ibid., 478.

36. *Wisconsin v. Yoder*, 406 US 205 (1972).

37. Paul E. Peterson, "The New Politics of Choice," in Diane Ravitch and Maris Vinovskis, eds., *Learning from the Past* (Baltimore: Johns Hopkins University Press, 1995).

38. *Mueller v. Allen*, 463 US 388 (1983).

39. Publius Syrus, as quoted in John Bartlett, *Familiar Quotations*, 15th ed. (Boston: Little, Brown, 1980), 111.

40. *Olmstead v. United States* 277 US 438 (1927).

41. *New York Times*, November 12, 1993, 1.

42. Senator Joe Biden, as quoted in Chuck Henning, *The Wit and Wisdom of Politics: Expanded Edition* (Golden, CO: Fulcrum Publishing, 1992), 47.

43. New York Mayor Ed Koch, as quoted in Henning, *Wit and Wisdom of Politics*, 107.

44. *Mapp v. Ohio.* 167 US 643 (1961).

45. *Washington v. Chrisman* 455 US 1 (1982), 182.

46. Pritchett, *Constitutional Civil Liberties*, 78.

47. *Sheppard v. Maxwell*, 384 US 333 (1966).

48. *Nebraska Press Association v. Stuart* 427 US 539 (1976).

49. Lisa J. McIntyre, *The Public Defender: The Practice of Law in the Shadows of Repute* (Chicago: University of Chicago Press, 1987), 162.

50. Jonathan D. Casper, *American Criminal Justice: The Defendant's Perspective* (Englewood Cliffs, NJ: Prentice-Hall, 1972); 101.

51. McIntyre, *The Public Defender*, 41.

52. *In re Chapman* 166 US 661 (1897).

53. Casper, *American Criminal Justice*; Jerome Skolnick, *Justice Without Trial* (New York: John Wiley and Sons, 1966).

54. *Santobello v. New York* (1971), as quoted in Lawrence M. Friedman, *Crime and Punishment in American History* (New York: Basic Books, 1993); 392.

55. Robert H. Bork, "Neutral Principles and Some First Amendment Problems," *Indiana Law Journal* 47 (1971); 8.

56. *Griswold v. Connecticut* 381 US 479 (1965).

57. Ibid.

58. *Bowers v. Hardwick* 106 SCt 2841 (1986).

59. *Harris v. McRae* 448 US 297 (1980).

60. *Webster v. Reproductive Health Services* 492 US 490 (1989).

61. *Planned Parenthood v. Casey* 112 SCt 291 (1992).

CHAPTER 17

1. Ruth Bader Ginsburg, "Employment of the Constitution to Advance the Equal Status of Men and Women," in Shlomo Slonim, ed., *The Constitutional Bases of Political and Social Change in the United States* (New York: Praeger, 1990), 188.

2. Philip Converse, "The Nature of Belief Systems in Mass Publics," in David E. Apter, *Ideology and Discontent* (New York: Free Press, 1964), 206–61.

3. John Agresto, *The Supreme Court and Constitutional Democracy* (Ithaca, NY: Cornell University Press, 1984): 27. Ellipses deleted.

4. John D. Hicks, *The American Nation* (Cambridge, MA: Riverside Press, 1949), 21.

5. Eric Foner, *A Short History of Reconstruction* (New York: Harper, 1990).

6. Richard M. Valelly, "National Parties and Racial Disfranchisement," in Paul E. Peterson, ed., *Classifying by Race* (Princeton: Princeton University Press, 1995), 188–216.

7. U.S. Commission on Civil Rights, *Report of the Commission on Civil Rights*, 1959 (Washington, DC: Government Printing Office, 1959), 32. Ellipses deleted.

8. V. O. Key, Jr. *Southern Politics* (New York: Random House, 1949).

9. J. Morgan Kousser, *The Shaping of Southern Politics: Suffrage Restriction and the Establishment of the One-Party South, 1880–1910* (New Haven: Yale University Press, 1974), 61.

10. *Civil Rights Cases*, 109 US 3 (1883).

11. *Plessy v. Ferguson*, 163 US 537 (1896).

12. Edward Banfield and James Q. Wilson, *City Politics* (New York: Vintage Books, 1963); James Q. Wilson, *Negro Politics* (New York: Free Press, 1960).

13. Harold Gosnell, *Negro Politicians* [1935] (Chicago: University of

Chicago Press, 1967); Thomas M. Guterbock, *Machine Politics in Transition* (Chicago: University of Chicago Press, 1980); Ira Katznelson, *Black Men, White Cities* (Chicago: University of Chicago Press, 1976).

14. *Nixon v. Herndon*, 273 US 536 (1927).

15. Gerald N. Rosenberg, *The Hollow Hope: Can Courts Bring About Social Change?* (Chicago: University of Chicago Press, 1991), 61.

16. *Smith v. Allwright*, 321 US 649 (1944).

17. *Shelley v. Kraemer*, 334 US 1 (1948).

18. *Cumming v. Richmond County Board of Education*, 357 US 528 (1899).

19. *Missouri ex rel. Gaines v. Canada*, 305 US 337 (1938).

20. *Sweatt v. Painter* 339 US 629 (1950).

21. *Brown v. Board of Education*, 347 US 483 (1954).

22. *Brown v. Board of Education*, 347 US 483 (1954), note 11. The citation of six psychological and sociological studies in this note led Herbert Garfinkel to charge that the Court was making decisions on the basis of sociology, not law. "Social Science Evidence and the School Segregation Cases," 21 *Journal of Politics* 37 (1959). Kenneth B. Clar, "Effect of Prejudice and Discrimination on Personality Development" (Midcentury White House Conference on Children and Youth 1950, as cited in note 11).

23. *San Antonio School District v. Rodriguez* 411 US 1 (1973). Similar reasoning can be found in *Cooper v. Aaron*, 358 US 1 (1958).

24. A. Leon Higgenbotham, Jr., *Shades of Freedom: Racial Politics and Presumptions of the American Legal Process* (New York: Oxford University Press, 1996).

25. A. D. Morris, *Origins of the Civil Rights Movement: Black Communities Organizing for Change* (New York: Free Press, 1984).

26. Morris, *Origins of the Civil Rights Movement*, 51–63.

27. Michael Lipsky, "Protest as a Political Resource," *American Political Science Review* LXII (December 1968), 1144–58.

28. Rosenberg, *The Hollow Hope*, 50.

29. Gerald D. Jaynes and Robin M. Williams, Jr., eds., *A Common*

Destiny: Blacks and American Society (Washington, DC: National Academy Press, 1989), 224.

30. Patricia Gurin, Shirley Hatchett, and James S. Jackson, *Hope and Independence: Blacks' Response to Electoral and Party Politics* (New York: Russell Sage, 1989), 42–49.

31. Jaynes and Williams, *A Common Destiny*, 233.

32. Joint Center for Political and Economic Studies, *Focus* (Washington, DC: Joint Center for Political and Economic Studies, 1993), 1996 data provided by Center Staff, telephone communication, May 15, 1997.

33. William J. Grimshaw, *Bitter Fruit: Black Politics and the Chicago Machine, 1931–1991* (Chicago: University of Chicago Press, 1992).

34. Gary Orfield, *The Reconstruction of Southern Education: The Schools and the 1964 Civil Rights Act* (New York: Wiley, 1969); Gary Orfield, *Must We Bus?* (Washington, DC, Brookings, 1978); Jennifer Hochschild, *The New American Dilemma* (New Haven: Yale University Press, 1984).

35. Katherine Tate, *From Protest to Politics* (Cambridge, MA: Harvard, 1993, Ch. 8.

36. *Milliken v. Bradley I*, 418 US 717 (1974); 433 US 267 (1977).

37. *Regents of the University of California v. Bakke*, 438 US 265 (1978).

38. U.S. Bureau of the Census, *Statistical Abstract of the United States*, Table 276, p. 178

39. Jaynes and Williams, *A Common Destiny*, 313.

40. U.S. Bureau of the Census, *Statistical Abstract of the United States*, 1996, Table 617, 395.

41. U.S. Bureau of the Census, *Statistical Abstract of the United States*, 1996, Table 730, 472.

42. *Lau v. Nichols*, 414 US 563 (1974).

43. Bernard Grofman, Lisa Handley, and Richard G. Niemi, *Minority Representation and the Quest for Voting Equality* (New York: Cambridge University Press, 1992), 16–25. Also, see Thomas Weyr, *Hispanic U.S.A.: Breaking the Melting Pot* (New York: Harper, 1959); Peter Skerry, *Mexican Americans: the Ambivalent Minority* (New York: Free Press, 1993).

44. Stanley Karnow and Nancy Yoshihara, *Asian Americans in*

Transition (New York: Asia Society, 1992).

45. Vine Deloria, Jr. "The Distinctive Status of Indian Rights," in Peter Iverson, ed., *The Plains Indians of the Twentieth Century* (Norman: University of Oklahoma Press, 1985), 241.

46. Deloria, "The Distinctive Status of Indian Rights," 237–48.

47. Deloria, 237.

48. Agresto, *The Supreme Court and Constitutional Democracy*, 148–49.

49. Theda Skocpol, *Protecting Soldiers and Mothers: The Political Origins of Social Policy in the United States* (Cambridge, MA: Harvard University Press, 1992); Sara Evans, *Personal Politics: The Roots of Women's Liberation in the Civil Rights Movement and the New Left* (New York: Knopf, 1979).

50. Nancy McGlen and Karen O'Conner, *Women's Rights: The Struggle for Equality in the Nineteenth and Twentieth Centuries* (New York: Praeger, 1983), Ch. 9.

51. Jane J. Mansbridge, *Why We Lost the ERA.* (Chicago: University of Chicago Press, 1986).

52. Ruth B. Mandel, "The Political Woman," in Sherri Matteo, ed., *American Women in the Nineties: Today's Critical Issues* (Boston: Northeastern University Press, 1993), 34–65.

53. *Hoyt v. Florida*, 368 US 57 (1961).

54. *Craig v. Boren*, 429 US 190 (1976).

55. Ginsburg, *Employment of the Constitution*, 191.

56. *Rostker v. Goldberg*, 453 US 65 (1981).

57. Mansbridge, *Why We Lost the ERA*, Ch. 7.

58. *Watson v. Fort Worth Bank & Trust* 487 U.S. 997–999; *New York City Transit Authority v. Beazer*, 440 US at 587, no 31; *Griggs v. Duke Power*, 401 US at 432.

59. *Wards Cove v. Antonio*, 490 US 642, (1989).

60. Ibid. 661.

61. *Meritor Savings Bank v. Vinson*, 477 US 57 (1986).

62. *Harris v. Forklift Systems*, 510 US 77 (1993).

63. Frontline: Hillary's Class (PBS television broadcast, No. 15, 1994), as cited in Karla Cooper-Boggs, "The Link Between Private and Public Single-Sex Colleges: Will Wellesley

Stand or Fall with the Citadel?" *Indiana Law Review* 29 (1995), 137.

64. Cooper-Boggs, "The Link Between Private and Public Single-Sex Colleges," 135.

65. *United States* v. *Virginia* 116 SCt 2264 (1966).

66. Stephen L. Percy, *Disability, Civil Rights, and Public Policy: The Politics of Implementation* (Tuscaloosa: University of Alabama Press, 1989), 3.

67. Authors' 1995 estimate based on 1989 estimate provided by Percy, *Disability, Civil Rights, and Public Policy*, Ch 5.

68. Robert A. Katzman, *Institutional Disability: The Saga of Transportation Policy for the Disabled* (Washington, DC: Brookings, 1986).

69. Frederick J. Weintraub, ed., *Public Policy and the Education of Exceptional Children* (Washington, DC: Council for Exceptional Children, 1976).

70. Paul E. Peterson, "Background Paper" in Twentieth Century Fund, *Making the Grade: Report of the Twentieth Century Fund Task Force on Federal Elementary and Secondary Education Policy* (New York: Twentieth Century Fund, 1983), Ch. 5.

71. *Southeastern Community College* v. *Davis*, 442 US 397 (1979).

72. Rufus Browning, Dale Rogers Marshall, and David H. Tabb. *Protest Is Not Enough: The Struggle of Blacks and Hispanics for Equality in Urban Politics* (Berkeley: University of California Press, 1984).

CHAPTER 18

1. Ed Gillespie and Bob Schellhas, eds., *Contract with America: The Bold Plan by Rep. Newt Gingrich, Rep. Dick Armey and the House Republicans to Change the Nation* (New York: Random House, 1994).

2. John Kingdon, *Agenda, Alternatives and Public Policies* (Boston: Little Brown, 1984); Paul Light, *The President's Agenda* (Baltimore: Johns Hopkins University Press, 1991).

3. Arthur Maass, *Congress and the Common Good* (New York: Basic Books, 1983).

4. Eugene Bardach, *The Implementation Game*, 4th ed. (Cambridge, MA: MIT Press, 1982); Jeffrey L. Pressman and Aaron

Wildavsky, *Implementation*, 3rd ed. (Berkeley: University of California Press, 1984).

5. Thomas R. Dye, *Politics, Economics and the Public: Policy Outcomes in the American States* (Chicago: Rand McNally, 1966).

6. Mark C. Rom, "AFDC Is Gone for Good," Paper presented before the Conference of the Association for Public Policy Analysis and Management, Pittsburgh PA, November 1996; R. Kent Weaver, Robert Y. Shapiro, and Lawrence Jacobs, "Public Opinion on 'Welfare Reform': A Mandate for What?" in R. Kent Weaver and William T. Dickens, *Looking before We Leap: Social Science and Welfare Reform* (Washington, DC.: Brookings, 1995).

7. Timothy Smeeding, Michael O'Higgins, and Lee Rainwater, eds., *Poverty, Inequality and Income Distribution in Comparative Perspective* (New York: Harvester Wheatsheaf, 1990); Lee Rainwater and Timothy M. Smeeding, "Doing Poorly: The Real Income of American Children in a Comparative Perspective," Maxwell School of Citizenship and Public Affairs, Syracuse University, Syracuse, New York, August 1995, Working Paper No. 127.

8. Neil Howe and Richard Jackson, *Entitlements and the Aging of America* (Washington, D.C.: National Taxpayers Union Foundation, 1994).

9. Howe and Jackson, *Entitlements and the Aging of America*, Chart 4-27, comment.

10. Thomas A. Bailey, *The American Pageant: A History of the Republic* (Boston: D. C. Heath, 1956): 840.

11. Martha Derthick, *Policymaking for Social Security* (Washington, DC: Brookings, 1979); Theda Skocpol, *Protecting Soldiers and Mothers: The Politics of Social Provision in the United States* (Cambridge, MA: Harvard University Press, 1993).

12. R. Kent Weaver, *Automatic Government: The Politics of Indexation* (Washington, DC: Brookings, 1988).

13. Howe and Jackson, *Entitlements and the Aging of America*, Chart 4-27.

14. *Boston Globe*, December 27, 1994, 70.

15. As quoted in Chuck Henning *Wit and Wisdom of Politics: Expanded Edition* (Golden, CO: Fulcrum, 1992): 252.

16. Donald F. Kettl, *Deficit Politics: Public Budgeting in its Institutional and Historical Context* (New York: Macmillan, 1992); Steve Langon, "Gloomy Medicare Report Causes Partisan Finger-Pointing," *Congressional Quarterly*, June 8, 1996, 1603.

17. Roper Center for Public Opinion Research, *Public Perspective: Roper Center Review of Public Opinion and Voting*, February/March 1995.

18. As quoted in Henning, *Wit and Wisdom of Politics*, 95.

19. Paul Light, *Artful Work: The Politics of Social Security Reform* (New York: Random House, 1985).

20. "The Budget," *Congressional Quarterly*, June 18, 1994, 179; Robin Toner and Robert Pear, "Medicare, Turning 30, Won't Be What It Was," *New York Times*, July 23, 1995, A1.

21. Ruy A. Teixeira, *The Disappearing American Voter* (Washington, DC: Brookings, 1992), 74, 83.

22. Susan A. MacManus, with Patricia A. Turner, *Young v. Old: Generational Combat in the 21st Century* (Boulder, CO: Westview, 1996): 60, 141.

23. Marilyn Werber Serafini, "Senior Schism," *National Journal*, No. 18, May 6, 1995, 1089–93.

24. Robert Rector, *Welfare Reform* (Washington, DC: Heritage Foundation, 1996).

25. Michael Lipsky, *Street Level Bureaucracy* (New York: Russell Sage Foundation, 1980); Theda Skocpol, "Targeting within Universalism: Politically Viable Policies to Combat Poverty in the United States," in *The Urban Underclass*, Christopher Jencks and Paul E. Peterson, eds. (Washington, DC: Brookings, 1991): 411–36.

26. Jeff Shear, "The Credit Card," *National Journal*, Vol. 27, No. 2, August 12, 1995, 2056.

27. Percentage of monies going for services to the elderly in the fiscal year 1993. Marilyn Werber Serafini, "Pinching Pennies," *National Journal*, Vol. 27, No. 37, September 16, 1995, 2273; also see Mark Rom, "Health and Welfare in the American States," *Politics in the American States*, 6th ed., Virginia Gray and Herbert Jacob, eds. (Washington, DC: Congressional Quarterly, 1995).

28. Paul E. Peterson, "An Immodest Proposal," *Daedalus* 121 (Fall 1992): 151–74.

29. Calculated from *Green Book*, Table 1, 1579. Until 1995, the *Green Book*, issued annually since 1981, was one of the most comprehensive sources of information on U.S. social policy. U.S. House of Representatives, Committee on Ways and Means, *Overview of Entitlement Programs: Background Material and Data on Programs within the Jurisdiction of the Committee on Ways and Means (otherwise known as the 1992 Green Book)* (Washington, DC: U.S. Government Printing Office, 1992), Table 1, 1579. All subsequent references to this document in this chapter will be simply to the *Green Book*. They refer to the 1992 edition.

30. *Green Book*, Table 2, 1582.

31. *Green Book*, Table 12, 643–45.

32. Paul E. Peterson and Mark Rom, *Welfare Magnets: A New Case for a National Standard* (Washington, DC: Brookings, 1990).

33. *Green Book*, Table 12, 1212.

34. Sandra Jaszczak, ed. *Encyclopedia of Associations*, 32nd ed. (Detroit: Gale Press, 1997), vol. 1, part 2, 1165.

35. Skocpol, *Protecting Soldiers and Mothers*.

36. Charles Murray, *Losing Ground: American Social Policy: 1950–1980* (New York: Basic Books, 1984).

37. Christopher Jencks, "Is the American Underclass Growing?" in *The Urban Underclass*, Christopher Jencks and Paul E. Peterson, eds. (Washington, DC: Brookings, 1991), 33, 88.

38. William J. Wilson, *The Truly Disadvantaged: The Inner City, the Underclass, and Public Policy* (Chicago: University of Chicago Press, 1987).

39. Christopher Jencks, "Is the American Underclass Growing?" in *The Urban Underclass*, Christopher Jencks and Paul E. Peterson, eds. (Washington, DC: Brookings, 1991), 56.

40. *Public Perspective*, February/March 1995, 39.

41. Eliza Newlin Carney, "Family Time," *National Journal*, No. 30, July 29, 1995, 1947–49.

42. Shear, "The Credit Card," 2056–58; Marilyn W. Serafini, "Turning Up the Heat," *National Journal*, Vol. 27, No. 32, August 12, 1995, 2051–55.

43. "Land Ordinance of 1785," in Henry S. Commager, ed. *Documents of American History* 6th ed. (New York: Appleton-Century-Crofts, 1958): 124.

44. Charles L. Glenn, Jr. *The Myth of the Common School* (Amherst, MA: University of Massachusetts Press, 1987); Diane Ravitch, *The Great School Wars: New York City, 1805–1973* (New York: Basic Books, 1974); David Tyack and Elizabeth Hansot, *Managers of Virtue: Public School Leadership in America, 1820–1980* (New York: Basic Books, 1982); Paul E. Peterson, *The Politics of School Reform, 1870–1940* (Chicago: University of Chicago Press, 1985).

45. Paul E. Peterson, "Background Paper," in Twentieth Century Fund Task Force on Federal Elementary and Secondary Education Policy, *Making the Grade* (New York: Twentieth Century Fund, 1983).

46. Helen F. Ladd, "Introduction," in Helen F. Ladd, ed. *Holding Schools Accountable: Performance-Based Reform in Education.* (Washington, DC: Brookings, 1996), 1–22.

47. National Education Association Research Division, *Salaries Paid Classroom Teachers, Principals, and Certain Others, 1960–61, Urban Districts 100,000 and Over in Population*; ibid., 1970–71; Educational Research Service, Inc., *Salaries Paid Professional Personnel in Public Schools, 1974–75*; ibid., 1979–80; ibid., 1984–85; ibid., 1989–90; National Education Association, *Estimates of School Statistics, 1960–61*, 13; ibid., 1989–90, 19; National Center for Education Statistics, *Digest of Education Statistics, 1988*, table 57, 72.

48. Eric A. Hanushek, "School Resources and Student Performance," in *Does Money Matter? The Effect of School Resources on Student Achievement and Adult Success*, Gary Burtless, ed. (Washington, DC: Brookings, 1996), 43–73.

49. *Wall Street Journal*, March 14, 1997; Roper Center for Public Opinion Research, *Public Perspective, Roper Center Review of Public Opinion and Polling* (November/December, 1993).

50. Peter W. Cookson, Jr. *School Choice: The Struggle for the Soul of American Education* (New Haven: Yale University Press, 1994); Carnegie Foundation for the Advancement of Teaching, *School Choice* (Princeton, NJ: Carnegie Foundation, 1992); Larry V. Hedges and Rob Greenwald, "Have Times Changed? The Relation between School Resources and Student Performances," in *Does Money Matter? The Effect of School Resources on Student Achievement and Adult Success*, Gary Burtless, ed. (Washington, DC: Brookings, 1996): 74–92; Amy Gutmann, *Democratic Education* (Princeton: Princeton University Press, 1987); Jeffrey Henig, *Rethinking School Choice: Limits of the Market Metaphor* (Princeton: Princeton University Press, 1994).

51. "A Headache," *Economist*, March 8, 1997, 57.

52. U.S. Department of Education, National Center for Education Statistics, *Digest of Education Statistics 1994*, 430.

53. Eric A. Hanushek, "The Economics of Schooling: Production and Efficiency in Public Schools," *Journal of Economic Literature* 24 (September 1986): 1141–77.

54. Diane Ravitch, *National Standards in American Education: A Citizen's Guide* (Washington, DC: Brookings, 1995).

55. David K. Kirkpatrick, *Choice in Schooling: A Case for Tuition Vouchers* (Chicago: Loyola University Press, 1990); Terry Moe, ed., *Private Vouchers* (Stanford, CA: Hoover Institution Press, 1995).

56. William H. Clune and John F. Witte, eds., *Choice and Control in American Education*, vols. I and II (New York: Falmer Press, 1990); Henig, *Rethinking School Choice*.

57. Robert Manor, "Firms Linked in Plane Crash Ignored Rules, Oxygen Generators Improperly Loaded," *St. Louis Post-Dispatch*, June 2, 1996, 11A.

58. Craig Petersen, *Business and Government*, 2nd ed. (New York: Harper & Row, 1985), 173.

59. *Heart of Atlanta Motel* v. *United States*, 322 US 533 (1964); *United States* v. *South-Eastern Underwriters Association* 322 US 533 (1944).

60. Gregg Easterbrook, *A Moment on the Earth: The Coming Age of Environmental Optimism* (New York:

Penguin, 1995), xv; for a more pessimistic view, see Paul R. Ehrlich and Anne H. Ehrlich, *Betrayal of Science and Reason: How Anti-Environmental Rhetoric Threatens Our Future* (Washington, DC: Island Press, 1996).

61. Murray Weidenbaum, "Government Power and Business Performance," in *The United States in the 1980s*, Peter Duignan and Alvin Rabushka, eds. (Stanford, CA: Hoover Institution Press, 1990): 197–220.

62. Michael Brown, *Laying Waste: The Poisoning of America by Toxic Chemicals* (New York: Pantheon Books, 1980).

63. Jerry Anderson, "The Environmental Revolution at Twenty-Five," *Rutgers Law Journal* 26 (Winter 1995): 406.

64. Clair Wilcox. *Public Policies Toward Business*, 4th ed. (Homewood, IL: Irwin, 1971), 589.

65. Marc K. Landy, Marc J. Roberts, and Stephen R. Thomas. *The Environmental Protection Agency: Asking the Wrong Questions from Nixon to Clinton*, expanded edition. (New York: Oxford University Press, 1994).

66. Landy, Roberts, and Thomas, *The Environmental Protection Agency.*

67. Landy, Roberts, and Thomas, *The Environmental Protection Agency*, 290.

68. Kenneth Meier, *Regulation: Politics, Bureaucracy, and Economics* (New York: St. Martin's Press, 1985).

69. Landy, Roberts, and Thomas, *The Environmental Protection Agency*, 279–89.

70. "Fiscal 1996 VA-HUD-Independent Agencies Spending," *Congressional Quarterly*, May 11, 1196, 1334.

71. Anderson, "The Environmental Revolution at Twenty-Five," 406.

72. Martha Derthick and Paul Quirk, *The Politics of Deregulation* (Washington, DC: Brookings, 1985): Mark C. Rom, *Public Spirit in the Thrift Tragedy* (Pittsburgh, PA: University of Pittsburgh Press, 1996).

73. Cited in Robert Hardaway, "Transportation Deregulation (1976–1984): Turning the Tide," *Transportation Law Journal*, 14 (1985:1), 101–52.

74. H. Craig Petersen, *Business and Government*, 2nd ed. (New York: Harper and Row, 1985), 198.

75. Hardaway, "Transportation Deregulation," 143. Another view is given by Paul Dempsey, "The State of the Airline, Airport and Aviation Industries," *Transportation Law Journal* 129 (1992:2), 130–200.

76. David Monk, "The Lessons of Airline Regulation and Deregulation: Will We Make the Same Mistakes in Space?" *Journal of Air Law and Commerce* 57:3 (Spring 1992), 715–53.

77. See, for example, Dennis Carlton and William Landes, "Benefits and Costs of Airline Mergers: A Case Study," *Bell Journal of Economics and Management Science* 65, 11 (1982), 65–83.

CHAPTER 19

1. Bush Acceptance Speech, *Congressional Quarterly Almanac* 44(1988): 43A.

2. Charles Jones, *Separate But Equal Branches* (Chatham, NJ: Chatham House Publishers, 1995): 241, 243.

3. George Hager, "Though He Shares Comrades' Elation . . . Dole Knows Hazards of Majority Rule," *Congressional Quarterly Weekly Report*, November 12, 1994: 3227.

4. Bush Acceptance Speech, *Congressional Quarterly Almanac* 48(1992): 76A.

5. Myron Levine, *Presidential Campaigns and Elections*, 2nd ed., (Itasca, IL: Peacock, 1995): 250.

6. Charles Smith and John Kessel, "The Partisan Choice: George Bush or Bill Clinton," in Herbert Weisberg, ed., *Democracy's Feast* (Chatham, NJ: Chatham House, 1995): 124–125.

7. Morris Fiorina, "Elections and Economics in the 1980s," in Alberto Alesina and Geoffrey Carliner, eds. *Politics and Economics in the 1980s* (Chicago: University of Chicago Press, 1991): 17–38.

8. John Mueller, *Wars, Presidents, and Public Opinion* (New York: Wiley, 1973). Douglas Hibbs, *The American Political Economy* (Cambridge, MA: Harvard, 1987): Ch. 5.

9. A.W. Phillips, "The Relationship Between Unemployment and the Rate of Change of Money Wage Rates in the United Kingdom 1862–1957," *Economica* 25(1958): 283–299.

10. For a summary of the relevant literature, see Fiorina, "Elections and Economics in the 1980s."

11. Morris Fiorina, *Retrospective Voting in American National Elections* (New Haven: Yale University Press, 1981): 164–167.

12. John Chubb, "Institutions, the Economy, and the Dynamics of State Elections," *American Political Science Review* 82(1988): 133–154; Dennis Simon, Charles Ostrom, and Robin Marra, "The President, Referendum Voting, and Subnational Elections in the United States," *American Political Science Review* 85(1991): 1177–92.

13. Paul Peretz, *The Political Economy of Inflation in the United States* (Chicago: University of Chicago, Press, 1983): 42.

14. Peretz, *The Political Economy of Inflation.*

15. Bruce Oppenheimer, "The Importance of Elections in a Strong Congressional Party Era: The Effect of Unified v. Divided Government," manuscript, 1995.

16. Paul Krugman, *Peddling Prosperity* (New York: Norton, 1994): Chs. 3,6.

17. For a general discussion see Steven Sheffrin, *Rational Expectations* (London: Cambridge University Press, 1983).

18. Louis Uchitelle, "Ideas and Trends: The Bondholders Are Winning: Why America Won't Boom," *The New York Times*, June 12, 1994: D4.

19. Board of Governors of the Federal Reserve System, *80th Annual Report*, (Washington, DC: 1993).

20. William Greider, *Secrets of the Temple: How the Federal Reserve Runs the Country* (New York: Simon and Schuster, 1987).

21. Schrage, Michael, "It's Time to Put a Transaction Tax on Credit Card Purchases," *Washington Post*, Oct. 17, 1990, p. F3.

22. John Wooley, *Monetary Politics: The Federal Reserve and the Politics of Monetary Policy* (New York: Cambridge University Press, 1984).

23. Alberto Alesina, "Macroeconomics and Politics," in Stanley Fischer, ed., *NBER Macroeconomics Annual, 1988* (Cambridge, MA: MIT Press, 1988): 13–52.

24. Douglas Hibbs, "The Dynamics of Political Support for

American Presidents Among Occupational and Partisan Groups," *American Journal of Political Science* 26(1982): 312–332.

25. Douglas Hibbs, "The Partisan Model of Macroeconomic Cycles: More Theory and Evidence for the United States," *Economics and Politics* 6(1994): 1–23.

26. Edward Tufte, *Political Control of the Economy* (Princeton: Princeton University Press, 1978): Ch. 2.

27. Donald Kettl, *Leadership at the Fed* (New Haven, Yale University Press, 1986).

28. Jean-Baptiste Colbert, as quoted in Henning, *The Wit and Wisdom of Politics*, 251.

29. R. Douglas Arnold, *The Logic of Congressional Action* (New Haven: Yale University Press, 1990): Ch. 4.

30. Wesley McCune, *The Farm Bloc* (Garden City, NY: Doubleday, Doran and Co., 1943); R. Kent Weaver, *Automatic Government* (Washington, DC: Brookings, 1988): Ch. 7.

31. Angus Campbell, Philip Converse, Warren Miller, and Donal Donald Stokes, *The American Voter* (New York: Wiley, 1960): 416–421.

32. This section draws heavily from Weaver, *Automatic Government*.

33. Mervin Field, "Sending a Message: Californians Strike Back," *Public Opinion*, July/August, 1978: 3–7.

34. Paul Light, *Artful Work: The Politics of Social Security Reform* (New York: Random House, 1985).

35. David Bradford, *Untangling the Income Tax* (Cambridge, MA: Harvard University Press, 1986).

36. "The Demographics of Taxes," *The Public Perspective* (Storrs, CT: The Roper Center, March/April 1992): 94.

37. Howard Schuman, *Politics and the Budget* (Englewood Cliffs, NJ: Prentice-Hall, 3rd ed., 1992): 121.

38. The specific statistic in the text is for a family of four with median income. Reductions were similar for both higher- and lower-income families. C. Eugene Stuerle, *The Tax Decade* (Washington, D.C.: Urban Institute Press, 1992), 216.

39. The intellectual basis of such proposals is usually credited to Robert Hall and Alvin Rabushka, *The Flat Tax* (Stanford, CA: Hoover Institution Press, 1985).

40. "Why Tax Reform?" *The American Enterprise*, July/August 1995: 17. Murray Weidenbaum, "The Nunn-Domenici 'USA Tax' Proposal," *The American Enterprise*, July/August 1995, 67.

41. Murray Weidenbaum, *The Savings-Exempt Income Tax* (St. Louis, MO: Center for the Study of American Business, Policy Study No. 122, July 1994).

42. "Judgment Day," *The Economist* (February 18, 1995): 49–51.

43. Study by the McKinsey Global Institute summarized in "How Regulation Kills New Jobs," *The Economist*, November 19, 1994, 78.

44. Francois Poncet, quoted in "The Hidden Costs," *The Economist*, June 22, 1996, 7.

45. For a critical survey see Krugman, *Peddling Prosperity*: Ch. 5.

CHAPTER 20

1. Aaron Wildavsky, "The Two Presidencies [1965]," in Steven A. Shull, *The Two Presidencies: A Quarter Century Assessment* (Chicago: Nelson-Hall, 1991): 11–25.

2. Alexander Hamilton, *The Federalist Papers*, No. 70, (Baltimore: Johns Hopkins University Press, 1981): 199.

3. Chuck Henning, *The Wit and Wisdom of Politics: Expanded Edition* (Golden, CO: Fulcrum, 1992): 56.

4. Wildavksy, "The Two Presidencies," 15.

5. John E. Mueller, *War, Presidents and Public Opinion* (New York: John Wiley & Sons, 1973); Gary King and Lyn Ragsdale, *The Elusive Executive: Discovering Statistical Patterns in the Presidency* (Washington, DC: CQ Press, 1988).

6. Mueller, *War, Presidents and Public Opinion*.

7. George F. Kennan, "Somalia, Through a Glass Darkly," *New York Times*, September 30, 1993, A25.

8. Jessica Mathews, "Policy vs. TV," *Washington Post*, March 8, 1994, A19.

9. Wildavksy, "The Two Presidencies," 16.

10. James Baker, III, with Thomas M. DeFrank, *The Politics of Diplomacy: Revolution, War, and Peace, 1989–1992* (New York: G. P. Putnam & Sons, 1995): 116.

11. *Statistical Abstract*, 1996, 3.

12. Middle East expert William Quandt, as quoted in Steven Erlanger, "Albright May Be Facing Unfamiliar Tests," *New York Times*, December 7, 1966, 5.

13. Wildavksy, "The Two Presidencies," 17.

14. Samuel Huntington, *The Common Defense* (New York: Columbia University Press, 1961): 127–28, 146.

15. Robert Dahl, *Congress and American Foreign Policy* (New York: W. W. Norton, 1964): 58.

16. Barry M. Blechman, *The Politics of National Security: Congress and U.S. Defense Policy* (New York: Oxford University Press, 1990); Duane M. Oldfield and Aaron Wildavsky, "Reconsidering the Two Presidencies," in Steve A. Shull, ed. *The Two Presidencies: A Quarter Century Assessment* (Chicago: Nelson-Hall, 1991): 181–90; Thomas Franck and Edward Weisband, *Foreign Policy by Congress* (New York: Oxford University Press, 1979); Thomas E. Mann, ed., *A Question of Balance: The President, the Congress and Foreign Policy* (Washington, DC: Brookings, 1990); Stephen R. Weissman, *A Culture of Deference: Congress's Failure of Leadership in Foreign Policy* (New York: Basic Books, 1955).

17. Paul E. Peterson, "The International System and Foreign Policy," in Paul E. Peterson, ed., *The President, The Congress, and the Making of Foreign Policy* (Norman, OK: Oklahoma University Press, 1994): 3–22.

18. Hamilton, *Federalist 74*. Ellipses deleted.

19. Speech before the House of Representatives, March 7, 1800, as quoted in *Marbury v. Madison* 5 US (1 Cranch) 137 (1803).

20. As quoted in Henning, *The Wit and Wisdom of Politics*, 240.

21. *U.S. v. Curtiss-Wright Export Corporation*, 299 US 304 (1936).

22. *Youngstown Sheet & Tube Co. v. Sawyer* 343 US 579 (1952).

23. Harold Hongju Koh, *The National Security Constitution: Sharing Power after the Iran-Contra Affair* (New Haven: Yale University Press, 1990); Gordon Silverstein, "Judicial Expansion of Presidential Power," in Peterson, "The International

System," 23–48; Gordon Silverstein, *The Imbalance of Powers: Constitutional Interpretation and the Making of American Foreign Policy* (New York: Oxford University Press, 1996).

24. James L. Sundquist, *The Decline and Resurgence of Congress* (Washington, DC: Brookings, 1981), 93.

25. *United States* v. *Belmont* 301 US 324 (1937).

26. Lawrence Margolis, *Executive Agreements and Presidential Power in Foreign Policy* (New York: Praeger, 1986); Richard J. Erickson, "The Making of Executive Agreements by the United States Department of Defense: An Agenda for Progress," 13 *Boston University International Law Journal* 45 (Spring 1995).

27. Address at Westminster College, Fulton, Missouri, March 5, 1946, as reprinted in John Bartlett, *Familiar Quotations* (Boston: Little, Brown, 1980): 746.

28. George F. Kennan, "The Sources of Soviet Conduct," *Foreign Affairs* 25 (July 1947): 566–82.

29. George Marshall, secretary of state under Harry Truman, as quoted in Alexander De Conde, "George C. Marshall," in Norman A. Graebner, ed., *An Uncertain Tradition: American Secretaries of State in the Twentieth Century* (New York: McGraw-Hill, 1961): 252.

30. Henning, *The Wit and Wisdom of Politics*, 69.

31. Henning, *The Wit and Wisdom of Politics*, 68.

32. Norman A. Graebner, "Dean G. Acheson," in Norman A. Graebner, ed., *An Uncertain Tradition: American Secretaries of State in the Twentieth Century* (New York: McGraw-Hill, 1961): 13.

33. Barry Rubin, *Secrets of State: The State Department and the Struggle over U.S. Foreign Policy* (New York: Oxford University Press, 1985): 64.

34. Rubin, *Secrets of State*, 239.

35. Dan Kubiske, "The Issue of Gender," *Foreign Service Journal* (November 1996): vol. 73, no. 11.

36. General Omar Bradley, Chair of Joint Chiefs, Testimony to the Committee on Armed Services, House of Representatives, October 19, 1949, as quoted in Bartlett, 1980, 824.

37. Henning, *The Wit and Wisdom of Politics*, 154.

38. John Kennedy, Press Conference, December 12, 1962, as reprinted in Bartlett, 1980, 891.

39. Loch K. Johnson, *America's Secret Power: The CIA in a Democratic Society* (New York: Oxford University Press, 1989): 12, 43.

40. Johnson, *America's Secret Power*, Ch. 2.

41. Graham Allison, *Essence of Decision* (Boston: Little, Brown, 1971).

42. Johnson, *America's Secret Power*; Rhodri Jeffreys–Johnes, *The CIA and American Democracy* (New Haven: Yale University Press, 1989).

43. Rubin, *Secrets of State*, 50.

44. Robert Pastor, "Disagreeing on Latin America," in Peterson, *The President*, 216.

45. As quoted in Pastor, "Disagreeing on Latin America," 217.

46. *New York Times*, January 23, 1993, Sec. E, 4

47. Speech at the Constitutional Convention, as quoted in Hans J. Morgenthau, *Politics Among Nations*, 4th ed. (New York: Alfred Knopf, 1966): 12.

48. Speech in Philadelphia, February 22, 1861, as quoted in Morgenthau, *Politics Among Nations*, 35.

49. Annual Message to Congress, December 2, 1823, as quoted in Bartlett, *Familiar Quotations*, 408.

50. John Louis O' Sullivan, *United States Magazine and Democratic Review* (July–August 1845), as reprinted in Bartlett, 552.

51. Address to Congress, asking for a declaration of war, April 2, 1917, as reprinted in Bartlett, 682.

52. Carl B. Swisher, *American Constitutional Development*, 2nd ed. (Cambridge, MA: Houghton Miflin, 1958): 992–93.

53. Address at Sioux Falls, September 8, 1919, as quoted in Bartlett, 682.

54. George Washington, Farewell Address, September 17, 1796, as quoted in Bartlett, 379.

55. Message to the Senate, August 19, 1914, as quoted in Bartlett, 682.

56. Campaign speech in Boston, October 30, 1940, as reprinted in Bartlett, 780.

57. Fireside Chat to the Nation, December 29, 1940, as quoted in Bartlett, 780.

58. Robert Keohane, *After Hegemony: Cooperation and Discord in the World Political Economy* (Princeton, NJ: Princeton University Press, 1984).

59. Morgenthau, *Politics Among Nations*; Kenneth N. Waltz, *Theory of International Politics* (New York: McGraw Hill, 1979); John J. Mearscheimer, "Back to the Future: Instability in Europe after the Cold War," *International Security* 15:1 (Summer 1990): 5–56; Samuel Huntington, *The Clash of Civilizations* (New York: Simon & Schuster, 1996).

60. Byron Schafer, *The Two Majorities: The Issue Context of Modern American Politics* (Baltimore: Johns Hopkins University Press, 1995); Byron Schafer, "The Election of 1988 and the Structure of American Politics: Thoughts on Interpreting an Electoral Order," *Electoral Studies* 8 (April 1989): 5–21.

names index

A

Acheson, Dean, 661
Acton, Lord, 520
Adams, Abigail, 46
Adams, John, 15, 46, 71, 76, 232, 314, 446, 489, 517
Adams, John Quincy, 169
Adams, Samuel, 42
Agnew, Spiro, 315
Agresto, John, 493
Albright, Madeleine, 661
Alexander, Lamar, 307
Anderson, John B., 249, 252
Aristotle, 13, 185
Armey, Richard, 200, 359, 387
Arnold, Benedict, 98
Arthur, Chester, 461

B

Baer, Harold, Jr., 510
Bagdikian, Ben, 283
Bagehot, Walter, 436
Bailyn, Bernard, 62
Baird, Zoe, 466
Baker, Howard, 429
Baker, James, 652
Bakke, Allen, 564-565
Baltimore, Lord, 102
Barber, Benjamin, 168
Barber, James, 444-445
Barbour, Haley, 254
Bartlett, E. L., 574
Bates, Tom, 345
Bauer, Gary L., 593, 595
Beard, Charles, 62

Begala, Paul, 154
Bennett, William, 128
Bentsen, Lloyd, 450
Berman, Michael, 214
Best, Judith A., 56
Bibby, John, 258
Biden, Joseph, 486
Black, Justice Hugo 490
Blackmun, Harry, 498-499, 543, 572
Blaine, James G., 388
Boesky, Ivan, 506
Bolivar, Simon, 71
Bonior, David E., 387, 408, 413
Bono, Cher, 238
Bono, Sonny, 238
Bork, Robert, 484, 487, 488, 504, 541
Bradlee, Ben, 284
Bradley, Bill, 134, 218, 238, 335
Bradley, Omar, 662
Brady, David, 393
Breaux, John B., 387
Brennan, William, 495
Breyer, Stephen, 487, 498, 499
Brinkley, David, 284
Brock, William, 255-257
Broder, David, 252, 296
Broderick, Anthony, 599-600
Brown, Jerry, 134
Brown, John, 220
Brown, Linda, 557
Brown, Oliver, 557
Brown, Ronald, 463, 473
Brownlow, Louis, 428, 430

Bryan, William Jennings, 183, 244, 630
Bryce, James, 88
Bryce, Lord, 239
Buchanan, Pat, 292, 306, 307, 420, 614
Bunning, Jim, 238
Burger, Warren E., 485, 496, 540
Burnham, Walter Dean, 252
Burns, James MacGregor, 253
Burr, Aaron, 76, 232
Burress, Geraldine, 609
Bush, Barbara, 438, 439
Bush, George, 21, 134-135, 154, 181, 203, 214, 272-273, 279-280, 282, 292, 293, 308, 315, 330, 419, 420, 429, 444, 463, 466, 484, 485, 508, 526, 539, 550, 565, 572, 575, 606-607, 613-614, 615, 625, 628, 632, 647, 648-649, 650, 654-656, 674-675
Butler, Nicholas, 523
Byrd, Robert, 349, 350-351, 399, 468-469

C

Calhoun, John C., 77, 381
Cannon, Joseph "Boss," 388, 389
Card, Andrew, 463
Carlisle, John, 388
Carson, Johnny, 282

Carter, Jimmy, 12, 150, 163, 214, 282, 305, 306, 310, 327, 328, 405, 420, 422, 428, 436-437, 438, 445, 467, 503, 508, 599, 603, 616, 617, 625, 628, 646-647, 648, 650, 656-657
Carville, James, 154, 623
Casey, Robert, 154
Castro, Fidel, 652
Chaplinsky, Walter, 523
Chrétien, Jean, 10
Chung, Connie, 529
Churchill, Winston, 22, 30, 658, 667
Clay, Henry, 169, 381
Cleland, Max, 575
Cleveland, Grover, 244
Clinton, Bill, 3, 4, 5, 10, 11, 16, 20, 23, 26, 27, 29, 56, 72, 88, 124, 134, 149, 155, 181, 188, 203, 225, 234, 269, 270, 272, 282, 292, 293, 294, 295, 296, 297, 301-302, 303, 306, 310, 316, 320, 322-323, 326, 329-336, 341-342, 405, 406, 408-409, 417-418, 426-427, 430, 432, 433, 435, 437-438, 440, 441, 443, 444, 445, 449, 466, 475, 487, 504, 508, 530, 536, 537, 539, 542, 550, 575, 580, 581, 587, 595, 599, 606-607, 614, 621, 625, 632, 635, 650, 656, 660, 661, 674-675
Clinton, George, 232

Nixon, Richard, 11, 54, 56, 84, 85, 163, 170, 247, 272-273, 281-282, 285, 292, 315, 319, 324, 327, 431, 436, 441, 443, 445, 527, 535-536, 559-560, 573, 595, 616, 625

Nunn, Sam, 134, 418, 575, 636

O

O'Brien, Lawrence F., III, 214

O'Connor, Sandra Day, 490, 498, 499, 507-508, 545, 572

Odegard, Peter, 215

O'Neill, Thomas P. "Tip," 363, 384

P

Page, Benjamin, 163

Pahlavi, Mohammed Reza, 646

Paine, Thomas, 45

Panetta, Leon, 476

Parks, Rosa, 558, 559

Pataki, George, 162

Patterson, Thomas, 310, 311

Patterson, William, 51

Payne, Lewis F., Jr., 409

Peltason, Jack, 508

Perot, H. Ross, 56, 212, 237, 249, 252, 270, 272, 273, 282, 288, 614, 674

Peterson, Paul E., 28-29

Pinckney, Charles, 58, 517-518

Plunkitt, George Washington, 242-243, 456

Polk, James Knox, 654, 669

Pol Pot, 13

Polsby, Nelson, 239, 380

Powell, Adam Clayton, 554

Powell, Colin, 10, 675

Powell, Lewis, 496, 564-565

Pulaski, Casimir, 98

Purdue, Linda, 431

Putnam, Robert, 126, 189

Q

Quayle, Dan, 315

R

Raines, Franklin, 476

Rakove, Milton, 507

Raleigh, Walter, 39

Randolph, John, 660

Rangel, Charles, 450

Ranney, Austin, 239

Rather, Dan, 281

Rayburn, Sam, 391, 393

Reagan, Nancy, 438

Reagan, Ronald, 4, 150, 151, 163, 194, 210, 224, 237, 269, 275, 281-282, 293, 305, 310, 315, 318, 321, 330, 362, 425, 427, 429, 433, 435, 436, 437, 440, 445, 446, 503, 504, 586, 615, 616, 617, 625, 647, 656, 665

Reed, Jack, 406-407

Reed, Thomas, 381, 388

Regan, Donald, 431

Rehnquist, William, 70, 498, 499, 572

Reid, Harry, 362

Reiner, Ira, 507

Resnick, Faye, 529

Revere, Paul, 43

Riordan, William, 242

Rivlin, Alice, 476

Roberts, Cokie, 284

Robertson, Pat, 308

Robinson, Michael, 282

Rockefeller, Nelson, 305, 439

Rogers, Will, 7, 623

Rohmer, Roy, 253

Rollins, Ed, 176

Roosevelt, Eleanor, 438

Roosevelt, Franklin D., 79, 80, 101, 114, 236-237, 269, 285, 315, 318, 425, 428, 433, 434, 444-446, 492-493, 503-504, 524, 555, 575, 583, 601, 618, 663, 777

Roosevelt, Theodore, 236, 244, 245, 246, 249, 268, 423, 424, 425, 433, 440, 446, 467, 654, 669, 670

Rosenstone, Steven, 188

Rousseau, Jean Jacques, 114

Rudman, Warren B., 632

S

Sabato, Larry, 252, 285, 288

Salisbury, Robert, 205

Sanders, Bernie, 203

Sanders, Deion, 295

Scalia, Antonin, 497, 498, 499, 526-527

Schattschneider, E. E., 225, 226. 233

Schenck, Charles, 522-523

Schlafly, Phyllis, 212

Schlesinger, Arthur, 661

Schlesinger, Joseph, 252

Schlozman, Kay, 223

Schmitt, Harrison, 238

Schroeder, Pat, 662

Schwarzkopf, Norman, 477, 648-649, 662

Scott, Dred, 491, 519

Shapiro, Robert, 163

Shays, Daniel, 48

Sheppard, Sam, 537-538

Shute, Neville, 458

Silbey, Joel, 248

Simpson, Nicole Brown, 502, 529

Simpson, O. J., 501, 502, 529

Sinclair, Barbara, 390

Sinclair, Upton, 268, 601

Skocpol, Theda, 593

Skowronek, Stephen, 445, 446

Small, Stephen, 566

Smith, Al, 108

Smith, Denny, 606

Smith, Howard, 571

Smith, Joseph, 103-104

Sojourner Truth, 570

Souljah, Sister, 4, 329

Souter, David, 487, 499

Specter, Arlen, 302, 359

Stalin, Joseph, 13, 14

Stanton, Elizabeth, 570

Stark, Pete, 296, 297

Starr, Kenneth, 432

Steffins, Lincoln, 268

Steinmo, Sven, 127

Stevens, John, 498

Stevens, John Paul, 490, 499

Stevens, Thaddeus, 654

Stevenson, Adlai, 322, 559

Stewart, Justice Potter 541

Stewart, Patsy, 609

Stimson, James, 163

Stockman, David, 476

Stone, Sharon, 282, 297

Stromberg, Yetta, 523

Sundquist, James L., 29, 422

Swan, Robert, 475

Swift, Jonathon, 494, 584

T

Taft, Robert, Sr., 114, 402

Taft, William Howard, 244, 245, 486-487

Taney, Roger, 519

Tarbell, Ida, 268

Tatel, David, 575

Taylor, Zachary, 241

Teixeira, Ruy, 194

Thatcher, Margaret, 249

Theroux, Paul, 566

Thomas, Clarence, 396, 484-485, 486, 490, 499, 572-573

Thompson, Fred, 238

Thomson, Carole, 293

Thornburgh, Richard, 154

Thurmond, Strom, 249, 391
Tierney, John, 223
Tower, John, 466
Townsend, Francis E., 543
Truman, Harry, 315, 402-403, 423, 439, 440, 486, 506, 554, 555, 556, 562, 650, 654, 655, 658-659
Tsongas, Paul, 134
Tufte, Edward, 625
Turner, Ted, 530
Twain, Mark, 379, 528

V

Van Buren, Martin, 241, 249
Vinson, Michelle, 572

Volcker, Paul, 624, 625
von Steuben, Wilhelm, 9

W

Walker, Jack, 205
Wallace, George C., 247, 249, 252
Wallace, Henry A., 249, 403
Warren, Earl, 466, 486, 496, 505, 524, 535, 536, 557-558, 570
Washington, George, 11, 20, 37, 38, 47, 48, 227, 231-232, 436, 440, 667
Weaver, James B., 249
Weber, Max, 11, 458
Webster, Daniel, 381

Wegner, Alfred, 521
Weicker, Lowell, 93
Weidenbaum, Murray, 602
Weld, William, 294, 466, 506
Wells, H. G., 101
Wellstone, Paul, 5
Whalen, Robert, 603
Whitman, Christine Todd, 176, 510
Wicker, Tom, 265
Wildavsky, Aaron, 647, 650, 652, 653
Will, George, 193, 344, 412
Williams, J. D., 214
Williams, Michael, 550
Williams, Pat, 342

Wilson, James Q., 206, 542
Wilson, Pete, 565
Wilson, William J., 542, 594-595
Wilson, Woodrow, 172, 245, 246, 390, 394, 423, 424, 656, 667-668
Wofford, Harris, 154
Wolfinger, Raymond, 188
Wood, Gordon, 62
Wotton, Henry, 660
Wu, Harry, 673

Z

Zangwill, Israel, 108
Zenger, Peter, 522, 526

subject index

Aristocracy, 13
Armed Forces Committee, 391
Arsenio Hall Show, 272, 291
Articles of Confederation, 37, 47-48
 government under, 48
 plain-meaning theory and, 490
 on presidency, 423
 provisions of, 47-48
Asia, immigration from, 110
Asian Americans
 civil rights of, 567-568
 in Congress, 365
 Voting Rights Act of 1965 and, 171
Associated Press (AP), 269, 279
Associate Justices of Supreme Court, 496
Atomic Energy Commission, 470
AT&T, action on, 406-407
Attorney General, 500
Attorneys, right to, 538-539
Australia, 181
Austria, 181
Authorization process, 404
Automobiles, search of, 536-537
Azerbaijan, 30

B

Balancing doctrine, 524-525
Baltimore, Lord, 40
Bates v. *Jones,* 345
Bay of Pigs, 664
Belgium, 181
Bell Telephone monopoly, 275
Beltway insiders, 443
Benton v. *Maryland,* 539
Berlin Wall, 419, 659
Bhopal, India disaster, 604
Biases of media, 281-290

Bicameral, 381
Bill of Rights, 63, 516.
 See also Freedom of religion; specific amendments
 Constitutional Convention and, 58
 and indigenous peoples, 568
 Madison, James and, 518
 origins of, 517-520
 pre-Civil War liberties, 518-519
 protected liberties, 59
 selective incorporation, 520
 state governments and, 519-520
 Tenth Amendment, 73
Bills or resolutions
 appropriations process, 404
 authorization process, 404
 closed rule, 401
 conference committee on, 403
 king of the mountain rules, 401-402
 law, process of becoming, 400-404
 markup of bill, 400
 multiple referrals, 400
 open rule, 401
 restrictive rule, 401
 rule, granting of, 401-402
 sponsors of, 400
 suspension of the rules, 400-401
Black Americans. *See* African Americans
Black codes, 551
Black power, 109
Blacks. *See also* African Americans
 in Great Britain, 566
Blame avoidance, 604, 605
 taxation and, 631-632

Block grants, 8-88
 benefits of, 86
 categorical grants, change to, 85
Block voting, 370
Blue-collar jobs, 594
Blue Laws, 105
Borking, 487
Bosnia, 30, 651-652, 671
 War Powers Resolution, 656
Boston Tea Party, 43
Bowers v. *Hardwick,* 543
Boycotts, 220
Bracket creep, 631
Brady Bill, 203
Branch Davidians, 450, 477
Briefs, 498
 amicus curiae briefs, 221
Britain. *See* Great Britain
British Broadcasting Channel (BBC), 279
Brownlow Committee, 428
Brown v. *Board of Education of Topeka, Kansas,* 220-221, 486, 496, 557-558
Buckley v. *Valeo,* 218
Budget and Accounting Act of 1921, 620
Budget and Impoundment Control Act of 1974, 620
Budget Committee, 396
Budget Compromise of 1990, 632
Budget Enforcement Act of 1990, 620-621
Budget Resolution, 620
Budgets. *See also* Office of Management and Budget (OMB)
 appropriations committees and, 621
 bickering over, 621
 Congressional Budget Office (CBO), 476
 earmarking, 468-469

 federal budget process, 620-621
 PAYGO rule, 620-621
Bull Moose party, 236, 245
Bully-pulpit, 425
Bureaucracy
 budgetary control and, 468-469
 caution, administrative, 478
 coercive powers of, 477-478
 compromised capacity, 478-479
 congressional jurisdiction and, 467
 defined, 451
 duplication of efforts in, 450
 expansionary tendencies of, 453
 experience with, 479
 federal regulation and discretion of, 605
 impossibility of tasks of, 452
 in-and-outers, 462-643
 independent regulatory agencies, 473-475
 iron triangles, 469-471
 issue networks, 471
 legislative detail and, 467-468
 management of, 473-476
 mugwumps and, 460-461
 oversight hearings, 469, 471
 party loyalists in, 646
 patronage in, 455
 performance measurement, 453
 political appointees, 461-465
 political nature of, 454-465
 professional experts in, 464
 red tape, 454

Elections *(continued)*
  financing campaigns,
    23-24
  first national election,
    37-39
  first presidential elec-
    tion, 38
  foreign policy affecting,
    672-675
  general elections, 7
  importance of, 6
  initiatives, 7
  list of, 8
  local elections, 7-9,
    90-91
  majorities and, 25-26
  mass communications,
    19-20
  minorities and, 22-24
  national elections, 6
  nonpartisan elections, 7
  in other democracies,
    10
  party organizations,
    17-18
  permanent campaign,
    16-17
  realigning elections,
    240
  reasons for participating
    in, 173-175
  recall elections, 7
  referenda, 7
  reforms, 26-29
  separation of, 17
  state elections, 7-9, 93
  on Tuesdays, 180
Electoral College, 54-57,
  314, 316-317
  criticisms of, 63
  in first presidential elec-
    tion, 38
  reforms of, 56
Electoral incentives, 27
Electoral participation,
  184-185
Electoral system, 248
Electoral vote, 316
Elementary and Sec-
  ondary Education Act
  of 1965, 199-200, 406

Eleventh Amendment,
  509
Eligible voting age popu-
  lation, 178
Elitist democracy, 15
Emancipation Proclama-
  tion, 20-21, 442
Embassies, 660
Emergency Banking
  Relief Act, 434
Emergency Planning and
  Community Right-to-
  Know Act, 604
Emergency School Aid, 85
Endangered Species Act,
  509
  spotted owl dispute,
    606-607
"The End of American
  Party Politics" (Burn-
  ham), 252
End-runs around Office of
  Management and
  Budget (OMB), 476
England. *See* Great
  Britain
Enterprise zones, 378
Environmental Protection
  Agency (EPA), 452,
  453, 602
  location of, 472
  zone of acceptance, 605
Environmental protection
  movement, 204, 210.
  See also Endangered
  Species Act
E Pluribus Unum, 104
Equality of condition,
  121-122
Equality of opportunity,
  121-122
Equal protection clause,
  551, 557-566
Equal Rights Amendment
  (ERA), 61, 210, 332,
  569
Equal time rule, 275
Espionage Act, 522
Establishment of religion
  clause, 529, 530-531

Ethiopia, 279
Ethno-cultural conflict,
  104-105
European University Insti-
  tute, 233
Executive agreements,
  657
Executive Office of the
  President (EOP), 428
Executive orders, 440
Executive power, 45. *See
  also* Presidency
  under Constitution, 54
Executive privilege,
  440-441
Exit polls, 139-140
Externalities, 602-603
Exxon Valdez, 604

F

Fair Employment Prac-
  tices Commission,
  555
Fairness doctrine, 275
Family Research Council,
  593, 595
Fascism, 101, 109
Federal Aviation Adminis-
  tration (FAA), 599
Federal bureaucracy. *See*
  Bureaucracy
Federal Bureau of Investigation (FBI), 450
  cooperative federalism
    and, 81
  criminal code viola-
    tions, 505
Federal Bureau of Prisons,
  477
Federal Communications
  Commission (FCC),
  275
Federal courts, 501-506
  appellate courts, 503
  checks on power of,
    508-510
  circuit court of appeals,
    503
  civil code, 501
  class actions, 511

  criminal code, 502
  defendants, 501
  district attorneys, 505
  district courts, 502-503
  double jeopardy, 508
  Eleventh Amendment,
    509
  federal regulation and,
    605-607
  nonimplementation of
    decisions, 509-510
  partisan affiliation of
    judges, 504
  plaintiffs, 501
  prosecution, decision
    for, 505-506
  state courts, relations
    with, 507-508
  statutory revision and,
    509
  strategy, litigation as,
    510-511
Federal district courts,
  502-503
Federal Elections Cam-
  paign Act (FECA),
  217, 336
Federal Elections Com-
  mission (FEC), 305
Federal Equal Employ-
  ment Opportunity
  Commission, 571
Federal grants, defined, 71
Federalism. *See also* Dual
  sovereignty
  contemporary debate
    on, 72-73
  cooperative federalism,
    81-88
  debate on, 71-74
  dual sovereignty, 75
  election of 1800 and, 76
  Gun-Free School Zones
    Act, 70
  local governments and,
    88-92
  Lopez decision, 70
  New Deal policies and,
    80
  nullification doctrine,
    75-77

Freedom of religion
(continued)
　separation of church
　　and state doctrine,
　　530-531
　tribal religious freedom,
　　568
Freedom of speech, 490
　balancing doctrine,
　　524-525
　clear and present dan-
　　ger doctrine,
　　522-523
　commercial speech,
　　527-528
　evolution of doctrine,
　　522
　fighting words doctrine,
　　516, 523-524
　fundamental freedoms
　　doctrine, 525-527
　libel, 527-529
　limits on, 527-529
　majoritarian democracy
　　and, 520-521
　obscenity, 529
　origins of, 521-522
　prior restraint doctrine,
　　521-522
　public opinion and, 152
　tyranny of the majority,
　　520-521, 522
　on university campuses,
　　521
　Watergate scandal and,
　　527
Free exercise of religion
　clause, 529, 531-532
Free rider problem, 207-
　212
Free Soil Party, 241, 249
Fundamental freedoms
　doctrine, 525–527

G

Gallup Polls, 22, 141-142
Gambling referenda, 9
Gays. See Homosexuality
Gazette of the United
　States, 267

Gender discrimination.
　See Women's rights
General Accounting
　Office (GAO), 382
General elections, 7
General Motors, 601
General revenue sharing,
　85
Genocides, 30
Geography and Congress,
　383-384
Germany
　citizenship in, 100
　evaluating political sys-
　　tem, 30
　proportional representa-
　　tion (PR) in, 248
　taxes in, 641
Gerrymandering, 346-347
Gideon v. Wainwright,
　528-529
Glen Steagall Banking
　Recovery Act, 434
Government. See also
　Federalism; Federal
　regulation
　under Articles of Con-
　　federation, 48
　defined, 71
　politics and, 10-12
　types of, 12-16
　unitary government, 71
Government opinion
　polls, 139
Government regulation.
　See Federal regulation
Governors in colonial
　America, 40-41
Gramm-Rudman-Hollings
　Act, 632
Grandfather clause, 552
Grants
　block grants, 8-88
　categorical grants, 83-84
　federal grants, defined,
　　71
　implementation of pro-
　　grams, 84-85
　intergovernmental
　　grants, 81-82

Grassroots lobbying,
　215-216
Great Britain. See also
　Colonial America
　Blacks in, 566
　Chief of State in, 437
　Civil War, 103
　Court of St. James, 660
　elections in, 10
　emigration, 102
　members of parliament
　　(MPs), 385
　police officers in, 31
　prime ministers, 421
　responsible model of
　　democracy in, 15
　single-member, simple
　　plurality (SMSP)
　　system, 248-249
　statutory interpretations,
　　495
　Whigs, 45
Great Depression, 615
　critical elections during,
　　244
　New Deal legislation,
　　247, 434
　Smoot-Hawley tariff
　　and, 226
Great presidents, 444-446
Great Society, 327, 595
　federal regulation and,
　　600, 601
　legislation, 199, 406,
　　410
Greece, 181
Green Party, 601
Greenpeace, 211
Grenada invasion, 656
Gross domestic product
　(GDP), 638
Gross national product
　(GNP)
　education, support for,
　　597
　national health insur-
　　ance plan and,
　　155-156
　recession and, 614
　social welfare spending,
　　122

tax receipts as percent-
　age of, 633
Group allegiances, 148
Guest workers, 638
Gulf War, 133-134, 419,
　675
　Congress and, 653
　foreign policy success
　　and, 648-649
　military and, 662
　priming by media and,
　　279-280
　secrecy during, 477
　war power issue,
　　655-656
Gun control, 4
Gun-Free School Zones
　Act, 69-70

H

Haiti invasion, 650, 651
Hammers, 605
Hanukkah celebrations,
　531
Harris v. Forklift Systems,
　497, 498, 572
Harris v. New York, 537
Hatch Act, 461
Head Start program, 83
Health and Human Ser-
　vices Department, 473
　location of, 472
Health care
　divided government
　　and, 237
　public opinion and,
　　154-157
　unfunded mandates, 73
　universal coverage plan,
　　4, 156-157
Health maintenance orga-
　nizations (HMOs),
　587
Health Security Act, 157
Higher education. See
　Education
Hispanic Americans
　civil rights of, 567
　in Congress, 365

Interest groups *(continued)*
  formal organizations, 205
  forming interest groups, 206-212
  free rider problem, 207-212
  group characteristics, 221
  incentives to join, 206-207
  influence of, 222-223
  international comparison of, 202
  in iron triangles, 469-471
  issue networks, 223
  leaders of, 227
  litigation by, 220-221
  lobbying by, 213-216
  membership groups, 205
  narrowly-based groups, 204
  National Rifle Association (NRA), 203
  persuasion of public by, 219-220
  pluralism, 224-226
  political action committees (PACs), 214, 216-218
  political entrepreneurs, 211-212
  political parties compared, 258-259
  proliferation of, 205
  public opinion and, 153-154
  public/private goods and, 208
  purposive incentives, 207
  ratings of Congress members, 359
  selective benefits, 210-211
  shared interest groups, 204-205
  situational characteristics, 221-222

  social movements, 209-210
  soft money and, 256-257
  solidary incentives, 206
  specialized associations, 204
  subgovernments, 222-223
  tactics of, 221-222
  variety of, 205
  wealthy patrons and, 211-212
Intergovernmental grants, 81-82
Interior Department, 473
Internal Revenue Service (IRS), 11, 477
  resentment of, 637
International comparisons
  Blacks in Great Britain, 566
  campaign finances, 336-337
  of Chief of State, 437
  crime, 534
  debt of U.S., 639
  high-level administrative positions, 463
  incarceration rates, 540
  of interest groups, 202
  mass media, 286
  out-of-wedlock births, 593, 595
  political parties, 250-251
  presidential v. parliamentary systems, 413
  statutory interpretations, 495
  student learning/school expenditures, 596
  value-added tax (VAT), 636
  of voter turnout, 177
  women legislators, 369
Internationalization of fiscal policy, 622-623
Internet, 20
  addresses, governmental, 274

  ideological bias, 283
  political use of, 274-275
Interstate commerce, 79-80
Intrastate commerce, 79-80
Iowa caucuses, 304
  media and, 310-311
  political activists and, 308
Iran-Contra scandal, 431, 665
Iranian hostage crisis, 328, 646-647
Iraq, 9. *See also* Gulf War
Irish immigration, 104
Iron curtain, 658
Iron triangles, 222-223, 469-471
  independent regulatory agencies in, 474
Island communities, 204
Isolationism, 666-669
  leadership *versus*, 671-672
Israel, 652
  proportional representation (PR) in, 248
Issue networks, 223, 471
Issue publics, 147
Italy
  compulsory voting in, 181
  taxes in, 641
Item veto, 427

J

Jacksonian democracy, 241
Jacobins, 232
Japan. *See also* Asian Americans
  Chief of State in, 437
  elections in, 10
  evaluating political system, 30
  high-level administrative positions in, 463
  immigrants from, 108
  monetarism in, 619

  out-of-wedlock births, 593, 595
  police officers in, 31
  public administrators in, 31
  taxes in, 641
Japanese-American internment, 524
Jeffersonians, 240-241
Jehovah's Witnesses, 531-532
Jews
  Israel policy and, 652
  in melting pot, 108
  party loyalty of, 318
Jim Crow laws, 105, 552
Job Corps program, 83
John Birch society, 504
Johnson v. *Texas*, 526
Joint Chiefs of Staff, 662
  in National Security Council (NSC), 664
Journalists
  honoraria to, 284
  professional bias, 287-288
Judges. *See also* Supreme Court
  federal judges, 503-505
  impeachment of, 505
  partisan affiliation of, 504
  in state trial courts, 507
Judicial activism, 498
Judicial power, 45
  compromise on, 57
Judicial review, 57, 74, 488-494
  living-Constitution theory, 490
  original intent theory, 489-490
  origins of, 489-490
  plain meaning of the text theory, 490
  practice of, 491-494
  pros and cons of, 493
  of state laws, 506
The Jungle (Sinclair), 601
Junkyard dog mentality, 285

Media (continued)
    exit polls by, 139
    fairness doctrine, 275
    framing and, 280
    government regulation
        of, 275-276
    ideological bias in,
        281-283
    international compar-
        isons, 286
    minimal effects thesis,
        278-281
    national convention
        coverage, 291-292
    negative, emphasis on,
        297
    new media, 272-275
    newspapers, 266-269
    persuasion and, 280
    presidential coverage,
        295
        debates, coverage of,
            292-293
        elections, 325-326
    primary elections and,
        310-313
    priming by, 279-280
    professional bias,
        287-288
    public opinion and, 139
    radio, 269-271
    role of, 289
    scandal, emphasis on,
        297
    selection bias, 285-287
    senators, coverage of,
        361
    spin in, 282
    Supreme Court nomi-
        nations, 487
    Vietnam War, 263-265
    White House staff and,
        432
Media consultants, 293
Medicaid, 73, 85, 87,
    590-591
Medicare, 478, 583
    broad support for, 589
    indexing and, 632
    1996 campaign and,
        331

politics of, 587
popularity of, 584
Meek v. *Pittenger*, 530
Melting pot, 107, 108
Mentally disabled persons,
    574-575
Mexican American Legal
    Defense and Educa-
    tion Fund
    (MALDEF), 567
Mexico. *See also* Hispanic
    Americans
    elections in, 10
    immigrants from, 108,
        110, 128
    manifest destiny and,
        666
    North American Free
        Trade Agreement
        (NAFTA) and, 405,
        408-409
Middle East policies, 652
Military. *See also* Defense
    Department
    gays in, 4, 417-418
    rivalries in services, 662
    unified military force,
        662
Miller v. *California*, 529
Miller v. *Johnson*, 371
Milliken v. *Bradley*,
    562-563
Minimal effects thesis,
    278-281
Minorities. *See also* Civil
    rights; specific
    minorities
    block voting, 370
    in Congress, 365,
        370-373
    elections and, 22-24
    individualistic ethic
        and, 119-120
    majority-minority dis-
        tricts, 370-372
    redistricting, 370-372
    schools and, 597
    and television, 278
    voting and, 191-192
Wards Cove v. *Antonio*,
    509

Minority leader, 390
Miranda v. *Arizona*, 537
Misery index, 617
Missouri Compromise,
    491
Mobilization to vote, 175,
    182-184
    declining mobilization,
        188
Monarchies, 13
Monetarism, 619
Monetary policy, 617,
    623. *See also* Federal
    Reserve Board
Monopolies, 78
Monroe Doctrine, 669,
    777
Moralistic politics, 123
Mormons, 103-104
Mortgage tax deduction,
    634
Motor Voter law, 179
MTV, 272, 273, 291
Muckraking, 267, 268,
    284
Mueller v. *Allen*, 532
Mugwumps, 460-461
Multiculturalism, 102-104
Multicultural societies, 100
Multilateralism, 670-671
Multiparty systems, 248
Multiple referrals, 400
Multiple use doctrine, 479
Municipal governments,
    90
Murder rates, 534

N

Nader's Raiders, 601
National Abortion and
    Reproductive Rights
    Action League
    (NARAL), 359
National Aeronautics and
    Space Agency
    (NASA), 476
National American
    Women's Rights
    Association
    (NAWRA), 172

National Association for
    the Advancement of
    Colored People
    (NAACP), 550
    Supreme Court actions,
        555-557
National conventions, 241
    media coverage, 291-292
    two-thirds rule, 247
National Credit Union
    Administration,
    474-475
National elections, 6
National forces, 363-365
National Forest, 440
National Gazette, 267
National health insurance
    plan, 154-157
National Industrial Recov-
    ery Act, 434, 493
National Opinion
    Research Center
    (NORC), 158-159
National Organization for
    Women (NOW), 569,
    571
National Park Service, 81
National Recovery Admin-
    istration, 434
National Republicans,
    244
National Rifle Association
    (NRA), 24, 25-26,
    203, 359
National Science Founda-
    tion (NSF), 476-477
National Security Act of
    1947, 661
National Security Advisor
    (NSA), 659, 665-666
National Security Council
    (NSC), 664-665
National Unity Cam-
    paign, 249
National Voter Registra-
    tion Act of 1993, 179
Native Americans, 103
    California Gold Rush
        and, 105
    civil rights of, 568

Senate *(continued)*
unanimous consent agreements, 390-391
Senate Appropriations Committee, 399
Senatorial courtesy, 466
Senior citizens
influence of, 587-588
Medicare, 583
programs for, 379-380
public assistance programs and, 591
social insurance programs, 583-589
social policy and, 582-583
voter turnout and, 23
Seniority, 397
Sensationalism, 529
Separate but equal doctrine, 553
Separation of church and state doctrine, 530-531
Separation of powers, 44-45
Sequestered jury, 537
Settlement of claims, 511
Seventeenth Amendment, 343
Sexual behavior, regulation of, 541, 543
Sexual harassment, 572-573
The Shame of the Cities, 267, 268
Shared interest groups, 204-205
Shaw v. *Hunt*, 371
Shaw v. *Reno*, 370
Shay's Rebellion, 48, 220
Shelley v. *Kraemer*, 557
Sheppard v. *Maxwell*, 537-538
Sherman Act, 601
Single-issue voters, 24
Single-member, simple plurality (SMSP) system, 248-249, 252
congressional elections and, 248-249, 252, 373

members of Congress and, 383-384
Single ruler government, 13
Sit-ins, 220
Sixth party system, 247-248
Slavery
Bill of Rights and, 519
Civil Rights Amendments, 519-520
Constitutional compromise on, 57-58
Constitution and, 66, 67
Fourteenth Amendment, 105
Missouri Compromise, 491
nullification doctrine and, 77
three-fifths compromise, 58
Slippery slope, tax preferences as, 635
Smith Act, 523, 525
Smith v. *Allwright*, 556
Smoking initiatives, 9
Smoot-Hawley tariff, 226
Social connectedness, 188-191
Social Democrats, 101
Social diversity, 102-104
Social insurance programs, 583-589. *See also* Medicare; Social security
politics of, 586
Socialism, 125
Social issues, 194
presidential elections and, 329
Socialization, 126, 136-137
Social movements, 209-210
interest groups for, 205
Social policy, 582-583.
See also Federal regulation
and education, 595-599
Social security, 583
broad support for, 589
change and, 586-587

indexing and, 632
1964 presidential election and, 585
popularity of, 584
Social Security Act, 583
Sodomy, 543
Soft money, 256-257, 356
Solicitor general, 500
Solidary, 206
Somalia, 650, 651, 671
executive agreements and, 657
media coverage, 279
South American immigrants, 110
Southern Christian Leadership Council (SCLC), 558
Southern Manifesto, 559
Southern Politics (Key), 373
South Korea, 619, 672
Soviet Union
Cold War, 658-659
collapse of, 419
Congress and, 653
Cuba, missiles in, 664
former Soviet Union, policy toward, 672
Strategic Arms Limitation Treaty II (SALT II), l656-657
Spain, 140
Spanish American War, 670
Speaker of the House, 388-389
bills introduced by, 400
strengthened position of, 391
Special districts, 90
Special interest groups.
See Interest groups
Special prosecutor, office of, 441
Spending clause, 80-81
Spin, 282
Spoils system, 455, 457-458
mugwumps and, 460-461
Sponsors of bills, 400

Spotted owl dispute, 606-607
Stagflation, 616
Stamp Act Congress, 42
Stamp tax, 42
Standard Oil Company, 600
Standing committees, 394, 395
Stare decisis
Brown v. *Board of Education of Topeka Kansas* and, 557-558
stare decisis principle, 494, 498
Star Wars system, 321
State action doctrine, 553
State courts, 502, 506-508
double jeopardy, 508
federal courts, relations with, 507-508
judicial review in, 506
nonimplementation of decisions, 510
trial courts, 506-507
State Department, 473, 659, 660-661
patronage at, 660-661
State governments, 16
Bill of Rights and, 519-520
civil rights and, 552-553
devolution, 73
Dillon's rule, 71
dual sovereignty, 75
elections, 7-9, 93
federalism and, 92-94
nullification doctrine, 75-77
public assistance programs, 592
responsibilities of, 93-94
sovereignty of states, 74
tax deductions, 634
unfunded mandates, 72-73
women in, 368
State of the Union address, 423
States' Rights Democratic Party, 249

State tax deduction, 634

Statutory interpretations, 495-496

Strategic Arms Limitation Treaty II (SALT II), 656-657

Strict scrutiny, 345

Stromberg v. *California*, 523

Student Nonviolent Coordinating Committee (SNCC), 558

Subgovernments, 222-223

Substance abuse programs, 92

Suffrage, 170. *See also* Civil rights; Women's suffrage
  youth suffrage, 170, 172

Sullivan v. *New York Times*, 528-529

Supplemental Social Insurance (SSI), 590, 595

Supply-side economics, 619

Supremacy clause, 57, 74

Supreme Court. *See also* Judicial review
  abortion issue, 543-545
  accused, rights of, 535-536
  African American justices, 483-485
  ambiguous Constitutional phrases, 64
  amicus curiae briefs, 500
  appeals, 494
  associate justice, 496
  borking, 487
  briefs, 496-497
  certiorari, writ of, 499-500
  chief justice of, 496
  civil rights issues, 551, 555-557, 562-563
  concurring opinions, 497-498

Constitutional Convention compromise on, 57
  decision-making by, 496-498
  definition of powers, 63
  dissenting opinions, 497-498
  federalism and, 74-77
  judicial activism, 498
  law clerks, 500-501
  legal distinction, 494
  New Deal and, 492-493
  nonconfirmed presidential nominees, 487
  opinions, 494
  oral arguments, 497
  plenary sessions, 496-497
  as political institution, 488
  politics of nominations, 485-488
  precedents, 494
  public opposition to decisions of, 510
  refusal to obey decision, 509-510
  remand of case, 498
  remedies, 496
  restorationists, 498
  reversal on appeal, 494
  Roosevelt's reelection and, 492
  solicitor general, role of, 500
  spending clause and, 80-81
  stare decisis principle, 494, 498
  statutory interpretations, 495-496
  voting on, 498-499
  war power, 655
  women's rights issues, 570-572

Survey research, 141

Suspension of the rules, 400-401

Sweden
  evaluating political system, 30

taxes in, 641
  welfare system in, 31

Switzerland, 173

T

Taiwan
  human rights policy and, 672
  monetarism in, 619

Talk radio, 20, 269-271
  ideological bias, 283

Tammany Hall Machine, 242-243

Tariffs
  North/South split on, 58
  nullification doctrine and, 77

Taxation, 4
  blame avoidance and, 631-632
  bracket creep, 631
  broad-based taxes, 634
  burden of, 633
  deductions, 634-635
  deficit and, 630
  Earned Income Tax Credit (EITC), 590
  flat tax, 635-637
  immigrants and, 111-112
  indexation of benefits, 632
  perspective on, 639-641
  private schools, tax breaks for, 532
  progressive tax, 119, 635
  referenda on, 9
  reforms, 635-637
  regressive taxes, 635
  representation, taxation without, 42-43
  stamp tax, 42
  tax base, 634-635
  tax preferences, 634-635
  VAT tax, 636

Tax base, 634-635

Tax preferences, 634-635

Technology, 356, 358

Telecommunications Act of 1996, 406-407

Television, 271-272
  cable television, 273-274
  CBS news coverage, 277
  CNN effect, 279
  infomercials, 288
  as information source, 276-278
  minorities and, 278
  national convention coverage, 291-292
  networks, 271
  public opinion and, 145

Temporary Assistance of Needy Families (TANF), 581, 589
  earnings and, 592

Tennessee Valley Authority Act, 434

Term limits, 60-61, 344-345
  in Congress, 411-412
  referenda, 9

Third party system, 242-244, 249

Thirteenth Amendment, 519-520

Thirty Years' War, 103

Thornburg v. *Gingles*, 371

Three-fifths compromise, 58

Three Mile Island, 471

Tiananmen Square demonstration, 672, 673

Tibet and, 673

Ticket-splitting, 247-248

Time, 269

Tolerance, education and, 137-138

Tonkin Gulf Resolution, 655

Tories, 43

Townships, 90

Transition period, 435

Transportation Department, 472

Treasury bonds, 626

reference index

T

Tabb, David H., ch. 14
n. 33; ch. 17 n. 72
Takaki, Ronald, ch. 4 n. 15
Talbert, Jeffrey, ch. 12
n. 42
Tate, Katherine, ch. 6
n. 43, ch 17 n. 35
Taylor, Andrew, ch. 11
n. 52
Teeter, Scott, ch. 10 n. 33
Teixeira, Ruy A., ch. 6
n. 18, 29, 52; ch. 18
n. 21
Theiss-Morse, Elizabeth,
ch. 7 n. 50; ch. 12
n. 3
Thomas, Norman C.,
ch. 13 n. 30
Thomas, Stephen R.,
ch. 18 n. 65-67, 69
Thurber, James, ch. 7
n. 26
Tierney, John, ch. 7 n. 4,
25, 49
Tilly, L., ch. 5 n. 13
Tingsten, Herbert, ch. 6
n. 46
Toner, Robin, ch. 18 n. 20
Traugott, Santa, ch. 5 n. 9,
28; ch. 10 n. 22
Trilling, Richard, ch. 10
n. 31
Truman, David, ch. 1
n. 42; ch. 7 n. 51
Tufte, Edward, ch. 19
n. 26
Tulis, Jeffrey, ch. 13 n. 23,
45, 46, 81
Tunney, John, ch. 11 n. 43
Turner, Frederick Jackson,
ch. 4 n. 44
Turner, Julius, ch. 8 n. 40
Turner, Patricia A., ch. 18
n. 22
Turner, Rebecca, ch. 7
n. 10
Tyack, David, ch. 18 n. 44

U

Uchitelle, Louis, ch. 19
n. 18
Uslaner, Eric, ch. 6 n. 37

V

Vallely, Richard M., ch. 6
n. 6; ch. 8 n. 25;
ch. 17 n. 6
Van Beek, Stephen, ch. 12
n. 45
Van Dyke, Vernon, ch. 5
n. 30
Vennochi, Joan, ch. 15
n. 60
Verba, Sidney, ch. 4 n.40;
ch. 6 n. 26, 27, 41, 44;
ch. 7 n. 12
Vidich, A. J., ch. 3 n. 38
Vines, Kenneth, ch. 1
n. 9; ch. 15 n. 65, 66
Vinovskis, Maris, ch. 16
n. 37

W

Wagner, Richard, ch. 7
n. 22
Wald, Kenneth, ch. 5 n. 8;
ch. 7 n. 19
Walker, Jack, ch. 7 n. 2,
23, 24
Washington, George,
ch. 20 n. 54
Watson, Mary Ann, ch. 9
n. 17
Watson, Richard A.,
ch. 13 n. 30
Wattenberg, Martin, ch. 1
n. 34; ch. 6 n. 23;
ch. 8 n. 5; ch. 9 n. 79,
80
Wayman, Frank, ch. 7
n. 35
Weaver, R. Kent, ch. 18
n. 6; ch. 18 n. 12;
ch. 19 n. 30, 32
Weber, David, ch. 11 n. 39

Weber, Max, ch. 14 n. 11
Weidenbaum, Murray,
ch. 18 n. 61; ch. 19
n. 40, 41
Weingast, Barry R., ch. 8
n. 21; ch. 9 n. 58;
ch. 12 n. 38; ch. 14
n. 67
Weingtraub, Frederick J.,
ch. 17 n. 69
Weir, Margaret, ch. 14
n. 37
Weisband, Edward, ch. 20
n. 16
Weisberg, Herbert, ch. 10
n. 45
Weiss, Thomas, ch. 9
n. 32
Weko, Thomas, ch. 8
n. 42
Welch, Susan, ch. 11
n. 60
Wells, H. G., ch. 4 n. 7
Wells, Robert, ch. 12 n. 50
West, Darrel, ch. 9 n. 76
Weyr, Thomas, ch. 17
n. 43
White, Loenard, ch. 14
n. 41
Wiebe, Robert, ch. 7 n. 5
Wilcox, Clair, ch. 18 n. 64
Wilcox, Clyde, ch. 5 n. 7,
47; ch. 10 n. 13, 52
Wildavsky, Aaron, ch. 3
n. 25, 27; ch. 10
n. 20; ch. 14 n. 16;
ch. 18
n. 4; ch. 20 n. 1, 4, 9,
13, 16
Wildenmann, R., ch. 8 n. 3
Will, George F., ch. 6
n. 49; ch. 12 n. 54
Williams, Robin M., Jr.,
ch. 17 n. 29, 31, 39
Williamson, Chilton,
ch. 6 n. 4, 5
Wilmerding, Lucius,
ch. 14 n. 22

Wilson, James Q., ch. 14
n. 12, 30, 50; ch. 17
n. 12
Wilson, Robert, ch. 7
n. 26
Wilson, William J., ch. 18
n. 38
Wilson, Woodrow, ch. 12
n. 31
Wines, Michael, ch. 1
n. 48
Winson, Chief Justice,
ch. 15 n. 49
Wissel, Peter, ch. 11 n. 6,
8
Witte, John F., ch. 18
n. 56
Wlezien, Christopher,
ch. 5 n. 54
Wolf, Patrick, ch. 14 n. 10,
75
Wolfinger, Raymond E.,
ch. 6 n. 13, 17, 20, 51;
ch. 14 n. 30
Wong, Kenneth K., ch. 3
n. 28; ch. 14 n. 74
Wood, Gordon S., ch. 2
n. 6, 8
Woodward, Robert, ch. 9
n. 49
Wooley, John, ch. 19 n. 22
Wright, Gavin, ch. 8 n. 12

Y

Yankelovich, Daniel, ch. 5
n. 46
Yoshihara, Nancy, ch. 17
n. 44
Young, James S., ch. 11
n. 7; ch. 14 n. 23; 22
Young, Oran, ch. 7 n. 22

Z

Zaller, John, ch. 5 n. 37
Zelikow, Philip D., ch. 1
n. 13
Zuckman, Jill, ch. 9 n. 42

Chapter 1: p. 2, Markel/Liaison International; p. 6, Bob Daemmrich, p. 9, AP/*Santa Cruz Sentinel*, Dan Coyro/Wide World Photos; p. 12, Christian Vioujard/The Gamma Liaison Network; p. 12, *Calvin and Hobbes* © Watterson, Distributed by Universal Press Syndicate, reprinted with permission, all rights reserved; p. 13, V.P.A./The Gamma Liaison Network; p. 17 (left), AP/Danny Johnston/Wide World Photos; p. 17 (right), Phil Matt; p. 18, Couder, Louis Charles Auguste/Giraudon/ Art Resources, NY; p. 20, AP/Wide World Photos; p. 23, Reuters/Mark Cardwell/Archive Photos; p. 25, Rhoda Sidney/Stock Boston; p. 27, *Doonesbury* © G. B. Trudeau, reprinted with permission of Universal Press Syndicate, all rights reserved.

Chapter 2: p. 34, Jon Feingersh/Stock Boston; p. 38, Photri, Inc.; p. 43, The Bostonian Society; P. 44, Stock Montage; p. 47 (top), Corbis-Bettmann; p. 47 (bottom), Photri-Microstock; p. 48, Corbis-Bettmann; p. 53, Stock Montage; p. 59, Colonial Williamsburg Foundation; p. 65, Reuters/ Radu Sigheti/Archive Photos.

Chapter 3: p. 68, Bonnie Kamin; p. 79, AP/Reed Saxon/Wide World Photos; p. 83, Brooks Kraft/Sygma; p. 83, *Rube Goldberg* ™ and © property of Rube Goldberg Inc., distributed by United Media, reprinted by permission; p. 84, Steve Leonard/ Black Star; p. 90 (top), Thomas Ames, Jr./f/STOP Pictures; p.90 (bottom), Corbis-Bettmann.

Chapter 4: p. 96, J. L. Atlan-Sygma; p. 101, Lisa Quinones/Black Star; p. 103, Corbis-Bettmann; p. 105, Fredrik D. Bodin; p. 106, Culver Pictures Inc., p. 109, Stock Montage; p. 111, Singe Wilkinson, reprinted by permission of Cartoonists & Writers Syndicate; p. 119, Bob Daemmrich/The Image Works; p. 124, AP/Ron Edmonds/Wide World Photos; p. 126, Terry Ashe/ The Gamma Liaison Network.

Chapter 5: p. 132, Bob Daemmrich/Stock Boston; p. 139, Charles Gupton/Stock Boston; p. 140, David Kennerly/The Gamma Liaison Network; p. 141, B. Markel/Liaison International; p. 143, Mark Ludac/Impact Visuals; p. 146, 1995 Tristar/NBC/Motion Picture Television Archives; p. 151, AP/Joe Marquette/Wide World Photos; p. 154, Forest McMullin/Black Star; p. 155, Rick Reinhart/Impact Visuals; p. 158, © Tribune Media Services, Inc., all rights reserved, reprinted with per-

mission; p. 160, AP/Tim Sharp/ Wide World Photos; p, 162, by permission of Jeff Shesol and Creators Syndicate..

Chapter 6: p. 168, David Young-Wolff/PhotoEdit; p. 170, Stock Montage; p. 172, AP/Wide World Photos; p. 174, The Image Works; p. 175, *Dilbert* reprinted by permission of United Features Syndicate, Inc.; p. 176, Reuters/Peter Morgan/ Archive Photos; p. 178, Piet van Lier/Impact Visuals; p. 179, Dennis Brack/Black Star; p. 181, Archive Photos; p. 185, Bob Daemmrich/ The Image Works.

Chapter 7: p. 198, Robin L. Sachs/PhotoEdit; p. 203, Paul Conklin/ PhotoEdit; p.205 Mark Richards/ PhotoEdit; p. 206, Michael Grecco/ Stock Boston; p. 208, Stephen Jaffe/ Liaison International; p. 209, Stock Montage; P. 211, D. Walker/ The Gamma Liaison Network; p. 214, Ronay/Folio; p. 216, David Young-Wolff/PhotoEdit; p. 220 © 1976 Cour tesy of the Mobil Oil Corporation.

Chapter 8: p. 230, Robert Kusel/ Tony Stone Images; p. 234, Jeffrey Markowitz/Sygma; p. 236, John Harrington/Black Star; p. 238, Jeffrey Markowitz/Sygma; p. 243, Brown Brothers; p. 245, Culver Pictures Inc.; p. 253 (left), AP/J. Scott Applewhite/Wide World Photos; p. 253 (right), AP/Karin Cooper/Wide World Photos.

Chapter 9: p. 262, Rick Friedman/ Black Star; p. 265, UPI/Corbis-Bettmann; p. 267, Culver Pictures Inc.; p. 270, Jacques M. Chenet/ The Gamma Liaison Network; p. 273, UPI/Corbis-Bettmann; p. 278, by permission of Chip Bok and Creators Syndicate; p. 279, AP/ Wide World Photos; p. 284, Mark Richards/PhotoEdit; p. 285, *Dilbert* reprinted by permission of United Features Syndicate, Inc.; p. 289, *Calvin and Hobbes* © Watterson, distributed by Universal Press Syndicate, reprinted with permission, all rights reserved; p. 294, Richard Harbus/The Gamma Liaison Network; p. 296, Rick Friedman/Black Star.

Chapter 10: p. 300, Paul Howell/ Liaison International; p. 304, Linda Kahlburg/*The Gazette*; p. 309, Jacques Chenet/Woodfin Camp & Associates; p. 313, *Toles* © *The Buffalo News*, reprinted with permission of Universal Press Syndicate, all rights reserved; p. 314, Porter Gifford/The Gamma Liaison Network; p. 315, *Doonesbury* © G. B. Trudeau, reprinted with permission of Universal Press Syndicate, all rights reserved; p. 324, UPI/

Corbis-Bettmann; p. 326, Dan Habib/Impact Visuals; p. 335, Reprinted by permission of Mike Keefe, *The Denver Post*.

Chapter 11: p. 340, Reuters/Mike Theiler/Archive Photos; p. 343, Archive Photos/American Stock; p. 349, Michael Ventura/Folio; p. 350, AP/John Duricka/Wide World Photos; p. 352, Michael Ventura/ Folio; p. 353, Ted Soqui/ Sigma. 367, Jeffrey Markowitz/ Sygma; p. 368, Kyodo News International, Inc.

Chapter 12: p. 376, AP/Charles Rex Arbogast/Wide World Photos; p. 379, Stock Montage; p. 382, Jacques M. Chenet/The Gamma Liaison Network; p. 383, © Tribune Media Services, Inc., all rights reserved, reprinted with permission; p. 384, Steve Liss/Liaison International; p. 388 FPG International; p. 389, Dennis Brack/Black Star; p. 391, AP/*Montgomery Advertiser*, Mickey Welsh/Wide World Photos; p. 396, Reuters/The Bettmann Archive; p. 397, Terry Ashe/The Gamma Liaison Network; p. 405, Reprinted with special permission of King Features Syndicate; p. 407, AP/Doug Mills/Wide World Photos.

Chapter 13: p. 416, Larry Downing/ Sygma; p. 419, AP/Dennis Cook/ Wide World Photos; p. 420, AP/Eric Draper/Wide World Photos; p. 422, Rick Friedman/Black Star; p. 424, Stock Montage; p. 425, Stock Montage; p. 430, Dirck Halstead/The Gamma Liaison Network; p. 431, Reuters/Win McNamee/Archive Photos; p. 435 (left) D. Walker/The Gamma Liaison Network; p. 435 (right) Reuters/ Win McNamee/ Archive Photos; p. 436, J. L. Atlan/ Sygma; p. 439, David A. Rodgers/ Sygma; p. 442, Stock Montage; p. 443, J. P. Laffont/Sygma.

Chapter 14: p. 448, AP/J. Scott Applewhite/Wide World Photos; p. 451, Pat Lanza/Folio, Inc.; p. 453, Richard Falco/Black Star; p. 455 (left), Jean-Baptiste Martin/ Giraudon/ Art Resource; p. 455 (right), Photri; p. 456, Corbis-Bettmann; p. 457, AP/Wide World Photos; p. 459 (top), Corbis-Bettmann; p. 459 (bottom), Courtesy of the Peabody Essex Museum, Salem, MA; p. 472, Photri; p. 476, Reuters/Win McNamee/Corbis-Bettmann; p. 477, Reuters/ Corbis-Bettmann.

Chapter 15: p. 482, Brad Markel/ The Gamma Liaison Network; p. 487, Mark Reinstein/The Image Works; p. 491, Courtesy of Missouri Historical Society; p. 499, Reuters/ Corbis-Bettmann; p. 500, David

Burnett/Contact Press Images; p. 501, Bob Riha/The Gamma Liaison Network; p. 506, Courtesy of the Boston Athenaeum; p. 510, Deborah L. Hynes/Courtesy of Elizabeth O'Neill LaStaiti.

Chapter 16: p. 514, AP/Santa Cruz Sentinel, Bill Lovejoy/Wide World Photos; p. 517, The Metropolitan Museum of Art/Bequest of Charles Allen Munn, print by J. W. Barber; P. 525, Robert Phillips/Black Star; p. 526, UPI/Corbis-Bettmann; p. 528, AP/Richard Drew/Wide World Photo; p. 529, Reuters/ Archive Photos; p. 530 (left), AP/ Wilfredo Lee/ Wide World Photos; p. 530 (right) David Young-Wolff/ PhotoEdit; p. 531, Gary A. Connor/PhotoEdit; p. 537, AP/Wide World Photos; p. 538, AP/Wide World Photos; p. 543, J. Patrick Forden/Sygma.

Chapter 17: p. 548, Walt Sanders/ Black Star; p. 553, Archive Photos; p. 557, AP/Wide World Photos; p. 559, Charles Moore/ Black Star; p. 561, Archive Photos; p. 565, AP/Wide World Photos; P. 569, AP/Wide World Photos; p. 573, Roger Cureton/*The Post and Courier*/Sygma; p. 575, Reuters/ Tami Chappell/Archive Photos.

Chapter 18: p. 578, Stephen Jaffe/The Image Works; p. 584, UPI/Corbis-Bettmann; p. 588, Stephen Crowley/*The New York Times*; p. 590, Bob Daemmrich/The Image Works; p. 593, Larry Dowing/Woodfin Camp & Associates; p. 598, *Toles* © *The Buffalo News*, reprinted with permission of Universal Press Syndicate, all rights reserves; p. 600, A. Itkoff/Sygma; p. 603, Kathleen Foster/Black Star; p. 607, Dale & Marian Zimmerman/Animals Animals.

Chapter 19: p. 612, Ken Hawking/Sygma; p. 615, UPI/ Corbis-Bettmann; p. 618, AP/Wide World Photo; p. 625, Archive Photos; p. 627, Dennis Brack/Black Star; p. 628, *Dilbert* reprinted by permission of United Features Syndicate, Inc.; p. 632, UPI/Corbis-Bettmann; p. 634, *Dilbert* reprinted by permission of United Features Syndicate, Inc.; p. 637, Steve Liss/The Gamma Liaison Network.

Chapter 20: p. 644, Alain Mingam/The Gamma Liaison Network; p. 648, Charles Crowell/Black Star; p. 650, Reuters/Rick Wilking/ Archive Photos; p. 656, UPI/Corbis-Bettmann; p. 661, Librado Romero/ *The New York Times*; p. 671, Liz Gilbert/Sygma; p. 674, AP/Wide World Photos; p. 675, UPI/Corbis-Bettmann.

The States in Proportion to Their Electoral Votes

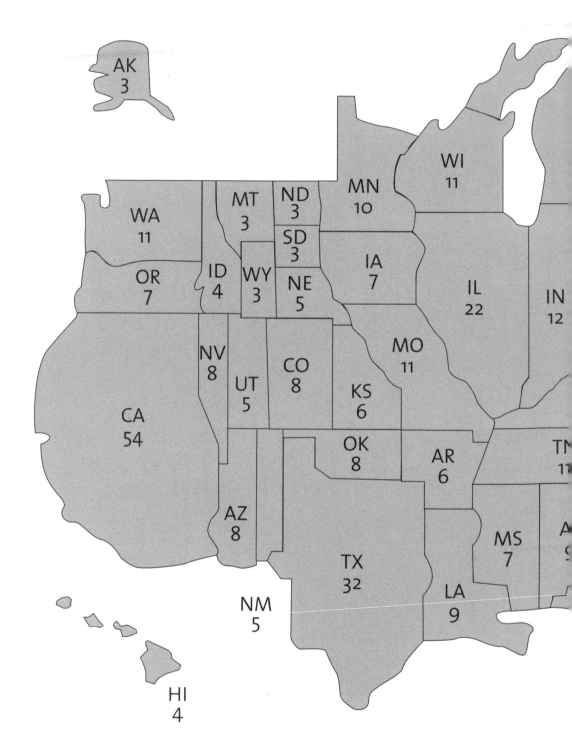